JOHN BENSON'S A to Z BASEBALL PLAYER GUIDE 1998

DIAMOND LIBRARY

Executive Editor:
Marc Bowman

Associate Editors:
James Benson and Jesse Dubow

Layout and Design:
Wade Lunsford and John Nestor

Copyright (c) 1997 by John Chapman Benson with licenses to Diamond Analytics Corporation

All rights reserved under International and Pan-American Copyright Conventions

Library of Congress Catalog Data: Benson, John, *Baseball Player Guide A to Z 1998*
1. Baseball — United States — History
2. Baseball — United States — Records
I. Title

ISBN 1-880876-67-1

No part of this book may be reproduced or transmitted in any form by any means, electronic or mechanical, including photocopying, recording, electronic imaging or scanning, or by any information storage and retrieval system or method, unless expressly permitted in writing by the author and the publisher.
For information contact Diamond Library Publishers.

Published by Diamond Library Publishers, a division of Diamond Analytics Corporation, with offices at 15 Cannon Road, Wilton, Connecticut, 06897. Telephone 203-834-1231.

PRINTED IN THE UNITED STATES OF AMERICA

Cover design by - Wade Lunsford
Production Manager - John Nestor
Editorial Consultant - James Benson

Statistics are provided by STATS, Inc. 8131 Monticello Ave. Skokie, IL 60076-3300
Telephone 847-676-3322.

This book is sold for entertainment purposes only. Neither the writers, nor the editors or publishers assume any liability beyond the purchase price for any reason.

PREFACE

Hi. My name is John Benson, and I write about baseball. That statement was true fifteen years ago, and it's still true today ... but the world has changed. It doesn't seem all that long ago that baseball writing was simpler. Baseball America, today the one and only undisputed professional journal of the baseball business community, was a fledgling publication just beginning to creep into the consciousness of players, managers, coaches, GM's and fans ("baseball junkies," as the early readers were proud to be known). Fifteen years ago, there was no such thing as USA Today Baseball Weekly, no STATS On Line, and no Scouting Notebook. Expanded box scores didn't exist except in the charts that managers used. Most major league teams had a part-time coach whose job it was to chart with a pencil and ruler where each batter hit the ball against each pitcher, with color codes to indicate how hard the ball was hit; these illuminated manuscripts were carefully stored in three-ring binders never seen outside of the clubhouse. The Sporting News Baseball Register didn't have separate columns for saves and stolen bases; they were mere footnote material in the world of consumer information.

Readers want more now, a lot more. Baseball and The Information Age are speeding along together. This book serves one purpose that no other book fulfills, and the best way to explain that purpose is to tell how this book came into existence. It was born during the winter. Like all good researchers, I have always kept a shelf of books beside my desk, to go with all the notes I had accumulated during the previous summer from interviews and all my pitch-by-pitch scoresheets. Sometimes I would become frustrated when I couldn't find anything about a player who had disappeared from all the books (and I mean all of them). Did he go to Japan? Spend the last season nursing a serious injury? And if a player was injured, how seriously? My standard method for facing these little crises was to call the front office of the team where he last played, and ask. Sometimes I got a quick and easy answer, and sometimes I found that even the player's last employer in organized baseball didn't know any more than I did.

So I wanted this book for my own use, something truly comprehensive. It was a bigger project than I thought it would be. The first effort was modest. The book has grown over the years. This year it has grown a lot. In fact, this year is the last time you will be able to buy this book for the modest price of $19.95. It's worth a lot more than that. When we are pulling the text together to send to the printer, having scoured the majors and minors and Taiwan and Mexico and independent leagues, we have a critical mass of knowledge that doesn't exist anywhere else on the planet. I don't make this claim from guesswork; I send sneak previews of this manuscript to every major league GM, and their thank-you letters tell me what I am telling you.

If you flip through the pages, the contents speak for themselves. There is just one important aspect that isn't readily visible, and that is all the help I get from all the writers who make it possible. They are friends, colleagues, professionals, and experts in their chosen fields. Most of them follow one major league baseball team, and that is what they do in life, aside from family and community service. They are the best at what they do. And without them, there wouldn't be any book like this.

My 1998 forecasts are in the back of the book, same as last year. The early editions elicited fan mail asking for all the forecasts to be in one place, so that anyone scanning for home run hitters or ace relief pitchers could spot them quickly. This method is consistent with all the leading preseason guidebooks which include forecasts. I know that some readers would prefer to have the forecasts scattered through the book, but this decision was made by the readers through democratic input.

This book is the starting point of my winter effort to construct an informed vision of the future. That vision doesn't reach full maturity until just before Opening Day. I hope you will take advantage of the various other Diamond Library publications and sources that keep you current right up until the first pitch is thrown in 1998 and throughout the coming season. The players won't change, but their situations will ... and that reality keeps me busy.

Finally, I feel overwhelmed with a sense of thanks for all the people who make this book what it is, in a way that cannot be written into acknowledgments: general managers who make time for my phone calls in the midst of their busy schedules and tell me what they think, the field managers who share their time with me so generously before and after games, the ballplayers, the coaches, the scouts who don't want to be quoted, and everyone who comes to the ballpark early. How many jobs are there in the world today, where people show up for work three of four hours before they are required? Baseball is full of such jobs, and that fact alone tells you how they feel about their chosen profession. We all owe them a debt of gratitude.

STAY CURRENT YEAR ROUND......

The Benson Baseball Monthly

25 to 40+ PAGES EVERY MONTH, YEAR ROUND

- The ultimate publication for insider tips, news before it happens, and analysis of unfolding events.

- The first, best, largest periodical for serious fans including scouts, management personnel, and Rotisserie league enthusiasts. Benson and his network of beat writers cover the major and minor leagues like no one else. Not just who's going to be traded, but who else gets affected and why and not just who's hurt or slumping or streaking, but who gets to play more, for how long, and why.

- The focus is always on the future. Benson's monthly features EXCLUSIVE QUOTES AND INTERVIEWS with players, coaches, managers, GM's and agents — everyone with the most inside information and the power to make decisions. John Benson talks to GM's, front office executives, scouts, coaches, players and managers in their homes, offices, dugouts and clubhouses, for REAL, FIRST-HAND INFORMATION AND GENUINE SCOOPS!

- The Benson Monthly is featured in the book TOTAL BASEBALL, by John Thorn and Pete Palmer, as the pace-setter for the future in baseball analysis. Much too big to be called a "newsletter" the Benson Baseball Monthly packs every issue with 26 to 40+ pages of tips, commentary, letters, and insights from fifty writers and analysts nationwide.

- The Monthly offers both preseason forecast stats and values for all players, and in-season changes in forecasts and values — always forward-looking.

Subscriptions are just $69 per year for FIRST CLASS MAIL. Or choose six months for $49, or the most popular option: two years for $129. Sample issues, $10. Also available from our website. See the last page of this book for an order form.

Visit our Website at:

www.johnbenson.com

Our Own All-Star Roster

JAMES BENSON - One of the few serious baseball analyst/historians to grow up without being a die-hard fan of any particular team, James loves pitching duels. He enjoyed the Mets of the late 1980's and the Braves of the 1990's, both because of pitching. His favorite players include Dutch Leonard, Addie Joss, Ed Walsh, Smoky Joe Wood, Walter Johnson and Greg Maddux. He has played hardball as recently as anyone involved with this book, using his deadly two-seam sinker to induce groundball double plays. James has spent at least a week at spring training every year since 1986. He is the reigning champion of the Spahn league in CompuServe Sports Forum.

JOHN BENSON - Since he began selling his player valuations through an ad in The Sporting News in 1987, Benson has expanded from writing and editing into publishing. He founded Diamond Library with one book in 1989 and will have nine 1998 titles in "Books in Print" plus two new magazines, the Baseball Preview and the Football Preview. His business plan is simple: bring together the best writers and the smartest readers. John has been a regular columnist for USA Today Baseball Weekly and currently writes for Baseball America. Benson saw his first game at Ebbets Field in 1956. He still enjoys watching tapes of games from the 1950's, when the strike zone was bigger than the catcher's mitt.

TONY BLENGINO - Blengino is a lifelong Philadelphia Phillies fan who fell in love with the baseball after attending his first game at the age of eight and getting his first simulation baseball game on Christmas Day in 1971. He is a CPA who is currently the Director of Finance for Samaritan Hospice in Moorestown, NJ. He's a prodigious contributor to various Diamond Library publications, including his own special production: "Future Stars," an annual in-depth analysis of the best minor-league prospects. Tony and his wife of eleven years, Kathy, reside in the Philadelphia area with their two children, Jessica (aged 8) and Anthony (6). Tony says baseball "is a great game because it is at once the most simple and most complex of sports; there is something for everyone. The institution of baseball may have seen better days, but the game of baseball is alive and well. Enjoy."

MARC BOWMAN - Despite never learning to play the game very well himself (decent fielder/ awful hitter), Bowman has been a fan of baseball as long as he can remember, enduring a childhood filled with the minor-league Wichita Aeros and wretched Kansas City A's, then maturing along with the Royals. Listening to Denny Matthews and Fred White's exquisite radio descriptions helped him gain appreciation for the smallest details of the game. Bowman has been reporting on baseball for Project Scoresheet, STATS, Inc., and Diamond Library for about a dozen years and has, alas, finally given up hope of ever playing second base for his beloved Royals. He is eternally grateful to his family for allowing him to pursue a small part of the major league dream through sports journalism.

JIM CALLIS - Jim Callis took his many years of experience as Managing Editor of Baseball America to join STATS Inc. after the 1997 season. In his new capacity he will be adding tremendous professionalism to an already outstanding organization.

BILL CENTER - Center is 52 years old and has been a sportswriter with the San Diego Union-Tribune for 30 years. He has covered baseball on a regular basis three different times during his tenure, for more than a dozen years - mostly recently 1994-97. Center also covers motorsports, boxing, sailing, college football, etc. He is the backup Padres beat writer in addition to his duties as the Union-Tribune's national baseball writer.

BILL CHASTAIN - One of the senior baseball writers in the Tampa area, Bill has been covering the Devil Rays since the franchise was born, and covering both the major leagues and the minor leagues in Florida for more than a decade. He writes for the Tampa Tribune.

KIMBALL CROSSLEY - Crossley grew up a Mets fan in New York City, but has lived in New England for ten years. He covered the Pawtucket Red Sox for a newspaper for nine years and now works as a scout for the Los Angeles Dodgers, covering the International League. He has always been obsessed with what makes teams win and loves his ongoing pursuit of knowledge about the game of baseball. Kimball also coaches basketball and teaches theater part-time.

JESSE DUBOW - A life-long Cubs fan, Dubow knows as much about Chicago's senior circuit franchise as anyone on the East Coast. He is a workhorse in the publications business, saving incredible amounts of research time by knowing things without having to look them up. His tips for 1998 include, "Get Kerry Wood."

MIKE EISENBATH - Eisenbath has been covering the Cardinals for more than a decade, currently with the St. Louis Post Dispatch. His beat includes both the farm system and the major league team. His work is in such demand, he was the last writer to leave the Cardinals press box after the 1997 season ended, with every story filed on time and filled with his trademark imprints of exclusive news and penetrating insight.

GREG GAJUS - Gajus has been writing about the Reds and others for the various Diamond Library projects since the first Rotisserie Baseball Annual in 1989. He recalls, "It seems like only yesterday that I was touting Kal Daniels as an MVP candidate." He grew up following the Big Red Machine and became a serious fan/analyst after being exposed to Bill James' work in the early 80's. He has won his Rotisserie league in three of the last four years and is also an addict of the STATS, Inc., historical Classic Game simulation. When he is not analyzing baseball statistics, he is analyzing television ratings for Turner Broadcasting in Atlanta, where he gets the benefit of free tickets to Braves game and wishes that a small part of the Braves payroll could be diverted to the Research department budget.

BILL GILBERT - Gilbert has been a baseball nut ever since his mother started taking him to see the Los Angeles Angels play in the Pacific Coast League during World War II. Retired after a 35-year career with Exxon, he writes about the Houston Astros and also works on the staff of Astros President Tal Smith on baseball salary arbitration cases. Still active on the field, Gilbert played on a Houston team that participated in the Senior Softball World Championships in Salt Lake City last year.

PETER GRAVES - A lawyer by training and a former university professor, Graves currently is the head of a private primary and secondary school in Central Texas, from where he follows the Texas Rangers with a pathological intensity. He became a baseball fan listening to re-created Double-A games of the Dallas-Fort Worth Spurs on the radio at night as a kid, which prepared him for decades of mediocre major league baseball later on. His wife and four children have learned to tolerate Dad's little obsession, as it keeps him out of bars and off the golf course. A well-rounded person, he has appearances on Jeopardy and Wheel of Fortune to his credit as well.

BILL GRAY - A sales and marketing executive from Columbus, Ohio, Gray is a native of the Pittsburgh area where he followed the Clemente teams with rare enthusiasm and understanding. Today he knows the all ins and outs of the Cincinnati Reds, the Cleveland Indians, and the Columbus Clippers. Bill has been a central force in the growth of Diamond Library publications since their inception, right up to and including his editing work on the 1998 edition of Rotisserie League Baseball. He publishes his own insider's vision, aptly titled "Baseball Futures."

GREGG HOFFMANN - Hoffmann has covered the Milwaukee Brewers since 1978. He serves as the Milwaukee correspondent for the Kenosha (WI.) News and covers the Milwaukee Bucks and Green Bay Packers, as well as the Brewers. He also serves as the Brewers' correspondent for USA Today and Baseball Weekly. In his "other" life, he teaches journalism and semantics-based media literacy at the University of Wisconsin-Milwaukee.

TERRY JOHNSON - Terry covers the Anaheim Angels and has covered the Dodgers. He has an extensive knowledge of the farm systems of both teams.

PETER KEISER - Keiser has more than a decade of experience as a sportswriter for various newspapers and spent "five years" in one season as the Assistant General Manager of the Waterbury Angels in the Double-A Eastern League. Keiser also opened a baseball memorabilia shop called Forever Baseball which he owned and operated for four years.

GEORGE KING - King covers the New York Yankees for the New York Post and for Baseball America. Prior to his New York beat, King covered the Philadelphia Phillies from 1989-96 for the Trenton (N.J.) Times.

MIKE KLIS - Klis grew up in Oswego, Ill. and from the time he was eight years old he wanted Jack Brickhouse's job as the announcer for the Cubs. Instead he wound up a writer which he says is pretty close. He covers the Rockies for the Colorado Springs Gazette, where he has been for 13 years. His time with the Rockies started on August 6, 1990 when the six county metropolitan voters approved a .1 percent sales tax to build a baseball stadium. The 38 year old says his seven year old daughter Kaitlyn is his life.

DANNY KNOBLER - Knobler grew up in Los Angeles, taking the bus to Dodger Stadium and trying to find a way to sneak down from the fifth deck into better seats. He graduated from UCLA, spent five and a half years working at Baseball America, and has made it through eight years of watching the Detroit Tigers lose games (and also win a few, too).

WILL LINGO - Lingo has been with Baseball America for many years and he became Managing Editor in 1997. He has long been one of the premiere writers in the baseball business.

DAVID LUCIANI - Luciani is a 29-year-old Toronto writer who has been affiliated with John Benson's publications since 1992. The author of David Luciani's Baseball Yearbook, Luciani specializes in performance forecasting with emphasis on the Toronto Blue Jays. He was a systems analyst for the Federal Government of Canada from 1990-93 and was a primary designer of budgeting and forecasting software still in use. Luciani is currently completing an honors degree in economics at York University and plans to attend law school upon completion.

STEPHEN LUNSFORD - Lunsford has been with Diamond Library in varying capacities since 1992. Stephen handles production for several companies. He uses those talents to see our books through every stage in the production process from initial typesetting through cover design and the final printed product. Stephen first began following baseball in the early 70's as a White Sox fan. He began playing Rotisserie baseball in the early 80's and that helped grow his interest in the game to include all major league clubs. He's an invaluable asset on the Diamond Library team.

JACK MAGRUDER - Jack Magruder covers the Arizona Diamondbacks for The Arizona Daily Star and Baseball America. A Kansas City native, he became an A's season ticket holder one high school summer when a friend won the sack race from center field to home plate at one of owner Charlie O. Finley's designated "Farm Nights." The two doctored the resulting prize - a general admission pass for one - to read "admit bearer and one guest to any unoccupied seats." A good time was had by all.

FRED MATOS - Long time Indians' fan Matos is a senior telecommunications policy analyst with the United States government in Washington, DC. He has a master's degree in electrical engineering, but he is very happy being a Washington policy wonk and writing on baseball as a loving diversion. His affection for baseball goes back to 1948 when he was a kid growing up in eastern Ohio and got caught up in the excitement of the Lou Boudreau-led Indians and Red Sox pennant race. His own baseball career peaked in American Legion ball when he was a deep reserve on a team that had Phil Niekro pitching and John Havlicek playing first base. Fred lives in Annapolis, Maryland.

LAWR MICHAELS - Michaels is a writer/analyst living in the San Francisco Bay Area. He has written for all the "Benson" books since 1994, covers the Athletics for the STATS, Inc., Scouting Notebook, and writes regularly for several Internet sites, including his own at www.CREATIVESPORTS.com. When not writing, Lawr works as a Project Manager in the telecommunications industry. He cannot boast a favorite team as fantasy baseball has cured him of allegiances, but he is looking forward to watching the new corps of Oakland's future stars. An inveterate rock'n'roller (he plays guitar and sings in the band "Mid Life Crisis") and movie junkie, Lawr lives with writer Catherine Hedgecock, his son Joey, and their dog Macaroni, a boxer-dalmation who once tried to eat a softball.

SCOTT MILLER - Scott Miller covers the Minnesota Twins for the St. Paul Pioneer Press. One of these days he would enjoy watching a well-pitched game. Then gain if a team he covered had pitching and wasn't in last place he's be lost. Before coming to Minnesota in 1994, he was involved in San Diego Padres and Anaheim Angels coverage for the Los Angeles Times.

JOHN NESTOR - Nestor was an early October call up by the Diamond Library brass and performed admirably in a number of roles down the stretch. Versatility, he's a writer, editor and layout man, will assure him of being a cornerstone in the Diamond lineup. A football and basketball player, Nestor is developing a deeper appreciation for baseball. He's a Philadelphia sports fan, currently suffering as the Phillies and Sixers rebuild, Eagles miss the playoffs and Flyers try to avenge an embarrassing Stanley Cup performance. Married in August, Nestor lives with his beautiful wife Nancy and dog Ally.

MARTY NOBLE - The Dean of New York Baseball Writers, Noble has been covering baseball in the city since 1974, mostly for the Mets. He began covering the Amazin's exclusively in 1989 and has been with Newsday since 1981. Once thin enough to jam a basketball backwards, Noble owns a large assortment of Do-Wop Music.

COLE PEPPER - A second-year contributor to A-Z, Cole Pepper has spent his working hours as a sports journalist for the past seven years in the radio, television and print media. His career has included radio play-by-play for the Iowa Cubs of the American Association and the Jacksonville Suns of the Southern League as well as covering the Kansas City Royals for three years. Pepper currently covers the Suns and the NFL Jaguars in Jacksonville.

JOHN PERROTTO - Perrotto has covered major-league baseball, particularly the Pittsburgh Pirates, since 1988. He also is a regular contributor to Baseball America and various other publications. He's been hooked on baseball since 1969 when his mother and father took him to a Pirates-Houston Astros game and Roberto Clemente belted a triple off the rightfield wall at Forbes Field.

JEFFREY SCHWARTZ - Jeffrey Schwartz has 20 years experience as a sports writer, covering mainly baseball and especially the New York and Philadelphia teams. Currently based in Redding Ridge, Connecticut, Schwartz manages his own media firm and teaches martial arts in his spare time.

DOUG WHITE - White graduated in 1990 with a degree in journalism from Ball State University, and is more than proud to say that he spent four years walking the same hallowed halls as David Letterman and Joyce DeWitt ("Janet" on Three's Company). Following graduation he worked as a sports reporter for several years at the Muncie Evening Press newspaper, covering everything from the storied Indiana high school basketball tournament to Division I basketball. Since leaving the newspaper business in the spring of 1996, White has been working strictly as a freelance writer, covering the Cincinnati Reds and baseball in general. He is a contributing editor of the internet Total Baseball Daily column, and provides articles and analysis to several magazine and book publications. White also is a college baseball umpire and officiates high school basketball and volleyball in Indiana.

HANK WIDMER - Widmer is a writer from Las Vegas who spends way too much time watching ballgames, and not enough time with his patient and supporting wife, Lisa.

ABAD, ANDY - OF/1B - BL - b: 8/25/72

Scouting: Abad is a nice player to have around because he is a smooth fielder at first base, and in left and right field. He doesn't provide speed or power, but he can hit a bit. Abad's problem is he is not strong or big (he's probably smaller than the 6'1" at which he's listed in media guides), and he needs a long swing to generate any pop in his bat. He somehow survives with his dive-into-the-ball approach because he has a good eye at the plate, but there are a lot of holes in his swing. Unless he shortens his swing and eliminates those holes he will always be considered a Triple-A player.

1998: Abad will almost certainly start his first full year in Triple-A, and begin what will most likely be a trying cycle for him. He will be seen as big-league insurance, and will probably only get time in the majors as a fill-in.

1997: Abad made it to Triple-A for the first time and showed he belonged at this level by playing well in the field and showing more power than was expected based on his prior minor-league seasons.

1996: Abad split time in Double-A and A-ball for the second season in a row. He hit for a decent average, but most impressive was his on-base percentage (.402 in Class A, .369 in Double-A).

ABBOTT, CHUCK - 2B - BB - b: 1/26/75

The first player the Angels selected in the June, 1996, draft, Abbott has already made adjustments to put himself on a fast track to the majors. He has shown power from both sides of the plate, although he hasn't hit for average yet. Abbott has played mostly second base, but has been given a try at shortstop as the Angels search for his most effective position.

ABBOTT, JEFF - OF - BR - b: 8/17/72

Scouting: Abbott is a natural hitter, one of the White Sox better pure hitters. He's limited defensively to left field and doesn't have a lot of power or speed, but he can certainly hit for average. Abbott needs to be more patient at the plate; he has consistently drawn few walks which diminishes his high-average hitting.

1998: Although he doesn't project as an immediate regular player for the White Sox in 1998, they think highly enough of him to protect him during the expansion draft. He'll make the big club at some point during the season, possibly on opening day.

1997: Abbott's .327 mark at Triple-A Nashville was a career low but it earned him his first big-league promotion. He continued to add little to his hitting beyond the high average and was a defensive liability in the outfield.

1996: Another year of typical high-average hitting by Abbott actually included a bit of power, too — fourteen homers and 27 doubles to drive in a career-best 60 runs.

	AB	R	HR	RBI	SB	BA
1997 Chicago AL	38	8	1	2	0	.263

ABBOTT, KURT - SS/3B - BR - b: 6/2/69

Scouting: Abbott will have a place in the majors for the foreseeable future, but has significant shortcomings which will preclude him from being an everyday player. He offers, at best, adequate defense at second base, shortstop, third base and the outfield, and has above-average extra-base pop for a utility player. However, he is a wild swinger who boasts a 395-to-91 career strikeout-to-walk ratio in 1528 career plate appearances.

1998: Abbott is likely to again serve as an all-purpose backup who could fill in as a starter for a period of weeks without harming his club. His ability to hit lefthanded pitching could earn him a platoon role on a squad where the defense of a world championship is not an issue.

1997: Abbott neatly bridged the gap between Luis Castillo and Craig Counsell at second base in 1997. Abbott's productive extra-base bat gave the club an offensive jolt near the top of the order after Castillo's failure, but Abbott's defensive deficiencies necessitated the acquisition of Counsell. Abbott was a non-factor in the post-season.

1996: Abbott began the season as the Marlins' shortstop, but quickly made way for Edgar Renteria. Balls that crept through the infield for singles for years suddenly became outs after Abbott vacated the position. Abbott then settled in as a productive all-purpose reserve and righthanded pinch-hitter.

	AB	R	HR	RBI	SB	BA
1995 Florida	420	60	17	60	4	.255
1996 Florida	320	37	8	33	3	.253
1997 Florida	252	35	6	30	3	.274

ABREU, BOB - OF - BL - b: 3/11/74

Scouting: Abreu has been a prospect throughout his seven-year career. He has adequate, but not outstanding, speed, power and defensive skills. He projects as a major league player but possibly not a regular. The upside is probably a career similar to that of Luis Gonzalez.

1998: Acquired by the Phillies after being drafted by Tampa Bay, Abreu will be a candidate for a starting position in 1998, but needs a strong spring. He may wind up as a fourth outfielder, but the change of scenery should help.

1997: Abreu began the season as the Astros' starting right fielder. He had modest success before suffering a broken wrist which put him on the disabled list in late-May. When he returned in mid-July, Derek Bell had taken over in right field. He was optioned to Triple-A New Orleans where he failed to excel (.268-2-22). He was promoted to Houston on August 31 to be eligible for the post-season but he was used sparingly.

1996: Abreu failed to improve in his second full year at the Triple-A level (.285-13-68 in 1996 compared to .304-10-75 in 1995).

	AB	R	HR	RBI	SB	BA
1997 Houston	188	22	3	26	7	.250

ADRIANA, SHARNOL - 3B/2B - BR - b: 11/13/70

Adriana took a step back in 1997 to Double-A Knoxville after spending 1996 at Triple-A Syracuse. His power numbers dropped and he still strikes out often (66 strikeouts in 314 at-bats last year). Adriana played second base at Knoxville after playing the hot corner at Syracuse. If he makes it to the big leagues it will be as a utility infielder.

AGBAYANI, BENNY - OF - BR - b: 12/28/71

Scouting: Whenever Mets manager Bobby Valentine read reports from Triple-A last year, he noted how Agbayani "always does something" — a sacrifice fly, an RBI, a stolen base, an extra-base hit... something. Agbayani's a get-it-done player, the kind managers covet. He doesn't have great skills. He is, though, an asset to his team.

1998: After a solid Triple-A season Agbayani is ready for a shot at the big leagues. There is nothing about him that suggests he couldn't be a reserve outfielder. Whether he fits is another issue. The Mets outfield doesn't have dominating speed, so Agbayani, although he is an accomplished minor-league base stealer, could lose his chance to a faster runner.

1997: Agbayani batted .310 in 468 Triple-A at-bats. He not only did "something" everyday, he did a little of everything — 90 runs, 24 doubles, two triples, 11 home runs, 51 RBI and 29 steals, wearing a blue collar all the time.

1996: Valentine saw Agbayani in '96 when each was with the Mets' International League affiliate in Norfolk. Agbayani's first look at Triple-A produced a .278 average, 29 extra-base hits, 56 RBI and 14 steals.

AGUILA, CHRIS - 3B - BR - b: 2/23/79

The Marlins selected the pitcher-turned-third baseman in the third round of the 1997 draft. Aguila has a high power upside, but has many rough spots in all facets of his game. He stuck out in nearly a third of his at-bats in Rookie ball, has few other tools besides his power, and will likely never be better than average with the glove at his new position. He has a fairly developed knowledge of the strike zone for a player of his age. If he can drive the ball in a full-season league in 1998, he's a prospect.

ALCANTARA, ISRAEL - 3B - BR - b: 5/6/73

The third time was a charm for Alcantara as he adjusted to Double-A pitching and put up some nice power numbers, including a .608 slugging average. Alcantara has a lightning quick bat and used it to improve his batting average and even cut back a bit on his strikeouts. He has the power potential you want in a third base prospect and should get a look at the Triple-A level in 1998.

ALDRETE, MIKE - 1B/OF - BL - b: 1/29/61

Aldrete was invited to spring training and was one of the final cuts by the Blue Jays at the end of March. He eventually agreed to play for Triple-A Syracuse, joining the SkyChiefs for part of May and June. Heading into the winter, Aldrete's career appeared over. He can still take a walk and would be useful to someone needing a lefthanded bat off the bench.

	AB	R	HR	RBI	SB	BA
1995 California	149	19	4	24	0	.268
1996 New York AL	108	16	6	20	0	.213

ALEXANDER, MANNY - 2B - BR - b: 3/20/71

Scouting: Alexander has fine range as a defender and is already considered one of the best defensive shortstops in the National League. His offense never has caught up with his defense, though, and cost him jobs in both Baltimore and New York. Alexander is somewhat guilty of making the mistakes that young hitters often make when trying to hit for power beyond their capabilities. Making a concerted effort to cut down on his swing would mean less homers, but would improve Alexander's batting average.

1998: Alexander enters the season as the Cubs everyday shortstop. He'll be able to keep the position solely for defense, but his offensive limitations will mean he'll hit low in the batting order. It's doubtful that he'll ever develop into an offensive weapon, but he'll give the Cubs plenty of value with the other things that he does.

1997: The late-season trade that brought him to Chicago from New York meant that Alexander was playing for his third team in less than a year, but he finally might have found a home on the north side of the Windy City. The Cubs were impressed with his fine play in the field and were optimistic that he could improve as a hitter.

1996: The Orioles were hoping that Alexander would blossom into a superior shortstop and would provide the incentive they wanted to move Cal Ripken to third base. Alexander failed miserably at the plate in a brief trial at shortstop and was relegated to backup duties, which meant little action at all playing behind Ripken.

	AB	R	HR	RBI	SB	BA
1995 Baltimore	242	35	3	23	11	.236
1996 Baltimore	68	6	0	4	3	.103
1997 Chicago NL	248	37	3	22	13	.266

ALFONZO, EDGARDO - 3B/2B - BR - b: 11/8/73

Scouting: He's not the prototypical third baseman, and he's not going to hit 25 to 30 home runs and drive in 130. Regardless, Alfonzo is a special player and, from all appearances, a winning player. Need a base runner leading off the ninth? He'll get on base. Need a sacrifice fly in the 12th? He'll lift a nasty pitch just deep enough. Need a runner advanced on the bases, he'll push a base hit to right field. And every so often, he'll go deep. Defensively he has no peer in the National League, and he's more apt to make the play that kills an opponent's rally than any other Mets defender.

1998: Alfonzo begins the season at age 24, so he should continue to improve, although not much more can be expected of him. Alfonzo performed so well last season, the Mets would be delighted with ten more years of the same performance, and as long as his back doesn't betray him as it did in 1995, Alfonzo can provide that level of play. He plays the game so naturally, it seems only injury can undermine him.

1997: By mid-May, he clearly was the Mets most valuable asset — young, productive and quite inexpensive. By season's end, with Hundley reduced to a spectator, Alfonzo stood as the Mets most valuable player as well. He led the Mets in batting average, batted .417 with runners in scoring position, and drove in 72 with merely ten home runs. All this after Bobby Valentine publicly mused about Alfonzo beginning the season at the Triple-A level and then had him playing at shortstop and second base, too.

1996: After fighting with club officials to have Alfonzo, then 22 years old, on the opening day roster in 1995, Dallas Green inexplicably reduced Alfonzo's role in '96. And Alfonzo didn't respond well to the inactivity. A career-low .261 average and uncommon strikeouts resulted. It was a lost season, but a year of learning for Alfonzo.

	AB	R	HR	RBI	SB	BA
1995 New York NL	335	26	4	41	1	.278
1996 New York NL	368	36	4	40	2	.261
1997 New York NL	518	84	10	72	11	.315

ALICEA, LUIS - 2B - BB - b: 7/29/65

Scouting: Signed as a backup infielder and insurance policy, Alicea paid big dividends when starting second baseman Randy Velarde suffered a season-ending elbow injury in spring training. Alicea is adequate with the bat and fast on the bases. He doesn't walk as much as he used to, but he generally puts the ball in play and can still come up with a clutch hit or two. Alicea's an excellent glove man. His only problem is durability, although he demonstrated the ability to play with nagging injuries last year.

1998: Alicea could be the starting second baseman again if Velarde is slow to recover. Alicea only has to show he's healthy to at least keep a job as a backup infielder.

1997: Alicea fielded well throughout the year and was a lifesaver in the Angels' infield, although he played far more than he or the

ballclub originally thought he would. Alicea's never been a big base stealer, but he continued to run well.
1996: Alicea returned to St. Louis, where he began his career, and was the same dependable middle infielder in helping the Cardinals reach the playoffs.

	AB	R	HR	RBI	SB	BA
1995 Boston	419	64	6	44	13	.270
1996 St. Louis	380	54	5	42	11	.258
1997 Anaheim	388	59	5	37	22	.253

ALLEN, CHAD - OF - BR - b: 2/6/75
Allen was a member of the 1996 U.S. Olympic team and is a singles hitter who makes consistent contact. He has speed to cover a lot of ground in the outfield and has good base stealing ability (27 at Class A Fort Myers). If Allen can produce against Triple-A pitching by the end of the 1998 season, he has a good shot at calling the Metrodome home by the end of 1999.

ALLEN, DUSTY - 1B - BR - b: 8/9/72
Allen is part of a growing log-jam at first base in the Padres' high minors. Fortunately, he can play the outfield and is actually a better defensive outfielder than first baseman. He's a big swinger with a good eye and has strong power potential; his strikeout totals have soared with his homer totals. A loss of aggressiveness has hurt his development. Allen led Double-A Mobile with 17 homers, but also fanned 116 times in 475 at-bats. He should spend most of 1998 at Triple-A Las Vegas.

ALLEN, MARLON - 1B - BR - 3/28/73
Allen had a solid season at Class A Burlington and earned a shot at the next level. He had a tougher time at the plate at Double-A Chattanooga in the Reds' system. His power numbers dropped and he struck out too much. At age 25 he needs to show rapid improvement to reach prospect status.

ALLENSWORTH, JERMAINE - OF - BR - b: 1/11/72
Scouting: Allensworth projects as a potential top-of-the-order hitter with good speed and an outstanding glove in center field. However, Allensworth faded in 1997 after a solid two-month stint as a rookie in 1996. He was never the same after sitting out almost six weeks with a broken bone in his left hand.
1998: Allensworth is no longer a lock to be the Pirates' center fielder. He will have to battle Adrian Brown for the starting job this spring. If Allensworth comes back strong after a disappointing '97 then the job is his. However, the Pirates privately question his desire of becoming a good player.
1997: Allensworth had a disappointing year, his season going downhill after sitting out from May 16th to June 23rd with a broken bone in his hand. He struggled so much that the Pirates benched him in favor of journeyman Turner Ward for ten straight games in the final two weeks of the season as they futilely tried to catch Houston in the National League Central race.
1996: Allensworth was recalled from Triple-A Calgary in late-July for his first taste of the big leagues and immediately was installed as the Pirates' starting center field. He made solid contact and showed some power while playing outstanding defense.

	AB	R	HR	RBI	SB	BA
1996 Pittsburgh	229	32	4	31	11	.262
1997 Pittsburgh	369	55	3	43	14	.255

ALMANZAR, RICHARD - 2B - BR - b: 4/3/76
Almanzar was once a big-time base stealer, but he's more quick than fast, and he also gets good jumps on pitchers so his stolen base numbers have been better in the past due to some cagey running. Almanzar stole 20 bases in 26 tries last season in Jacksonville, but he's lost some ground and also hit for a disappointing average last year (.243). He missed the last two weeks of the '97 season with a sprained knee, but is still relatively young for his level and remains among the Tigers' better prospects. He was rated the best defensive second baseman in the Double-A Southern League last year. He can regain his momentum as a prospect with a good 1998 campaign in a repeat season at Jacksonville.

ALMONTE, WADY - OF - BR - b: 4/20/75
Almonte is a talented young Oriole outfielder who began last year in Double-A, was overmatched, and was demoted to A-ball. He had never played in Class A before, and the jump to Double-A proved to be too much. The Orioles think highly of Almonte and protected him on their 40-man roster.

ALOMAR, ROBERTO - 2B - BB - b: 2/5/68
Scouting: In a "Baseball America" managers' poll, Alomar was voted as the best bunter, the third best baserunner, and the best defensive second baseman in the American League. Overall, he's one of the best second basemen in baseball, and has Hall-of-Fame potential. He's still fast, but he doesn't steal as many bases as he did early in his career. He has some pop in his bat and can hit as many 20 dingers. Alomar is a tough clutch hitter, and a savvy player in all facets of the game.
1998: Alomar should recover from his ailments and, at age 30, there should be no drop in his performance. He's capable of having a career-best year in all respects except base-stealing; he's unlikely to reach 53 steals again as he did in 1991.
1997: Injuries contributed to Alomar's "down" season in 1997. He played with a sore ankle, limiting him to hitting lefthanded all year. Then a serious groin injury put him on the disabled list for over a month.
1996: In his first year with the Orioles, he hit a career-high .328 with good power, speed and defense.

	AB	R	HR	RBI	SB	BA
1995 Toronto	517	71	13	66	30	.300
1996 Baltimore	588	132	22	94	17	.328
1997 Baltimore	412	64	14	60	9	.333

ALOMAR, SANDY - C - BR - b: 6/18/66
Scouting: Once regarded as the hotter prospect of the Alomar brothers, catcher Sandy has only been healthy enough to catch 90 or more games in three of his eight full major league seasons. He is a technically sound receiver who has the respect of his pitching staff, sound mechanics behind the plate and an average throwing arm. Though he is a wild swinger, he has always been productive offensively on a per at-bat basis, but few were prepared for the offensive onslaught he unleashed in 1997.
1998: A downturn in performance must be expected. However, the fact that Alomar has caught more than 120 games in two consecutive seasons could mean that his days as a part-timer are behind him. Figures closer to his career norms would be a reasonable expectation.
1997: Alomar had an explosive year, posting by far his best all-around season, putting the exclamation point on a grand campaign by winning the All-Star Game with a late-inning homer on

his home field. He ravaged left and righthanded pitching, and helped fill the void left by Kenny Lofton and Albert Belle in the Indians' lineup. Finally, his superb post-season play almost got the Indians their first World Championship in a half century.
1996: This season had to be considered a partial success, as Alomar largely remained healthy. However, it was his poorest offensive year per at-bat since 1992, as he was basically a free-swinging afterthought at the end of the lineup.

	AB	R	HR	RBI	SB	BA
1995 Cleveland	203	32	10	35	3	.300
1996 Cleveland	418	53	11	50	1	.263
1997 Cleveland	451	63	21	83	0	.324

ALOU, MOISES - OF - BR - b: 7/3/66

Scouting: Alou was perfectly cast for his 1997 role with the Marlins. He's an aggressive hitter who capitalizes on pitchers' mistakes on a routine basis. He can look foolish against quality righthanded pitching, especially on breaking pitches. However, he batted with men on base regularly in 1997, and was challenged more often by opposing pitchers. His easy swing does major damage against fastballs left over the plate, especially by lefthanded pitchers, against whom he has batted .333 and .340 the past two seasons. However, he is not a man around whom an offense can be built. He is just adequate defensively in left field with an average arm.
1998: Alou becomes a fixture in the Houston outfield. The ballpark won't help him, and the Astros' batting order is no better than the Marlins had in 1997, so don't expect a big surge, just more of the same in 1998.
1997: There were baserunners galore when Alou came to bat in 1997, and he cashed in a high percentage of them. His plate discipline improved significantly (his 70 walks exceeded his previous career high by 21), and he filled in admirably in center and right field due to injuries to Devon White and Sheffield. Wire to wire, he was the Marlins' most valuable offensive player.
1996: Alou's production flattened out at an unremarkable level for a starting left fielder. He hit for some average with some power and some patience, but excelled in no single area. It became clear that playing for his father with the Expos had about run its course.

	AB	R	HR	RBI	SB	BA
1995 Montreal	344	48	14	58	4	.273
1996 Montreal	540	87	21	96	9	.281
1997 Florida	538	88	23	115	9	.292

ALVAREZ, CLEMENTE - C - BR - b: 5/18/68

Alvarez took four swings in Class A ball and spent the rest of the year at Double-A Birmingham in the White Sox organization. 1997 was his tenth minor-league season and he has yet to be called up. He didn't hit in Birmingham and the White Sox have catching prospects ahead of him. At age 30, Alvarez is watching his baseball career wind down.

ALVAREZ, GABE - 3B - BR - b: 3/6/74

Scouting: Alvarez, drafted fifth by Arizona and then traded to Detroit, had been ticketed by the Padres as an eventual successor to third baseman Ken Caminiti. The second-round '95 pick from the University of Southern California has good bat control, and scouts see 30-homer potential. Errors, mostly on throws, are a problem for this former shortstop who is still learning to play third base. Alvarez is a future starter in the major leagues.

1998: Alvarez is good enough to jump to Triple-A. The hope is to see steadier play at third base and a continuing power increase.
1997: An injured wrist hampered Alvarez for first part of the season at Double-A; he was hitting .220 after 40 games. He finished at .300 with 14 homers and struck out only 64 times in 427 at-bats. However, Alvarez made 32 errors, resulting in a .884 fielding percentage.
1996: After hitting .344 at the Class A level in '95, Alvarez struggled in his first year at Double-A, hitting only .240 with eight home runs in 104 games while striking out 87 times in 368 at-bats.

AMADOR, MANNY - SS - BB - b: 11/21/75

Scouting: Amador is a switch-hitter who is capable of playing second base, shortstop and third base. He generates solid extra-base power despite a slender 6'0", 165-pound frame. He has always been one of the youngest players at his minor-league level, but the Phillies have been reluctant to entrust him with a full-time position at any level. His baserunning ability is average, and he rarely attempts to steal a base. He is a quiet individual whose struggles with the English language have gotten in the way.
1998: The Triple-A third base job should be there for the taking for Amador in 1998. He has always shown respectable extra-base power on a per at-bat basis, and could break through with a 30-double, 15-homer season if entrusted with a full-time job. At age 22, such a season would put him into contention for a mid-season promotion to the majors should the injury bug strike the big club.
1997: Amador accumulated only 239 at-bats in a season split between Double-A and Triple-A in 1997. He languished on the bench at Double-A Reading, but was impressive in a short Triple-A trial, making consistent, authoritative contact. Amador had always been an afterthought in the Phillies' plans; his Triple-A success may have finally changed that.
1996: Amador opened the season on the Double-A Reading bench, and ended it as the higher Class A third baseman. He battled injuries but showed a productive extra-base bat when healthy.

AMARAL, RICH - OF - BR - b: 4/1/62

Scouting: Amaral is the consummate utility player. He can handle every infield position but shortstop and all three outfield positions. He is a smart, aggressive contact hitter who will not hit for power but will steal bases. Defensive shortcomings at second base preclude his starting there.
1998: Amaral's playing time usually depends on other factors, such as injuries or an adequate platoon partner. He again will be in the mix for the left field platoon now that Jose Cruz Jr. is no longer around.
1997: Amaral's role diminished greatly when Joey Cora stepped up his play at second base and Cruz Jr. was recalled early in the season. Amaral did what he always does — hit for a good average and steal some bases — but had his career low in at-bats.
1996: Amaral played in a career-high 118 games because of a mid-season injury to Ken Griffey Jr. and responded with a career-high 25 stolen bases. He platooned with Cora at second base for the final three months of the season, after Griffey's return.

	AB	R	HR	RBI	SB	BA
1995 Seattle	238	45	2	19	21	.282
1996 Seattle	312	69	1	29	25	.292
1997 Seattle	190	34	1	21	12	.284

AMARO, RUBEN - OF - BB - b: 2/12/65
Scouting: Amaro is the prototypical major league journeyman. He has served as a deep major league reserve since starting the bulk of the 1992 season for the Phillies. Amaro is a solid veteran presence on a youthful team - he doesn't complain about a lack of playing time, can play all three outfield positions well, and is the mentally-sharp type of player who excels in a pinch-hitting role. He is a switch-hitter who traditionally hits much better from the right side. He once had well-above-average speed, but it has deteriorated to major league average. He has acceptable power to the gaps and a decent eye, but is rather unexciting offensively.
1998: Despite the Phillies' acquisition of younger prospects in the second half of 1997, Amaro still has a chance to stick in his usual role. However, if Lenny Dykstra can rebound from his back injury (an unlikely prospect) or the Phillies can obtain a free-agent center fielder (a more likely prospect), then Amaro may become expendable.
1997: Amaro was a stabilizing force in the locker room on a young squad, and a reliable part-time contributor on the field. However, most good teams had a much more accomplished player in the fourth outfielder role. In fact, his playing time dropped off as the Phillies improved in the second half, a bad omen for his future.
1996: Amaro was a bright spot in an otherwise bleak Phillies' season. He was their best pinch-hitter, and was particularly effective against righthanders (.323 average).

	AB	R	HR	RBI	SB	BA
1995 Cleveland	60	5	1	7	1	.200
1996 Philadelphia	117	14	2	15	0	.316
1997 Philadelphia	175	18	2	21	1	.234

ANDERSON, BRADY - OF - BL - b: 1/18/64
Scouting: Anderson's hobby is working out, and he's always in great shape. He's fast, and is an outstanding center fielder, especially running, leaping and diving after balls. He can steal bases, and could probably steal over 50 again if the team needed him to do so. He has a fast bat and good power as shown by his 50 homers in 1996.
1998: Anderson should be recovered from his ailments, and should be able to bash 30-35 home runs and hit as high as .280.
1997: Anderson played hurt all of last year with various aches and pains, resulting in a down year. The most notable drop-off was in power, although he wasn't expected to hit 50 homers again. He was still an outstanding leadoff man, with an OBP around .400 all year.
1996: Anderson had his career-best year in everything except stolen bases. His 50 homers and .637 slugging percentage were way out of proportion to anything he had done before.

	AB	R	HR	RBI	SB	BA
1995 Baltimore	554	108	16	64	26	.262
1996 Baltimore	579	117	50	110	21	.297
1997 Baltimore	590	97	18	73	18	.288

ANDERSON, CLIFF - SS - BL - b: 7/4/70
Anderson is a good organization player, but has yet to show he's ready to take the final step to reach the major leagues. He's a solid, versatile, middle-infield type, who's a good role model for younger players and can fill holes throughout the organization. He plays hard, but hasn't yet shown enough consistent offense to get beyond Triple-A.

ANDERSON, GARRET - OF - BL - b: 6/30/72
Scouting: One of the Angels' top young outfielders, Anderson continued his development as a hitter and fielder. As a hitter he is disciplined, aggressive and patient, and he has good speed on the bases and in the field; he made significant progress in developing his throwing arm last season. He has all the tools and is probably the player other clubs ask for most in trade talks with the Angels.
1998: Management would like to see continued progress in his throwing and overall defensive play, but Anderson is a solid ballplayer — one of the youngsters who have become the foundation of the franchise.
1997: Anderson came into his own last season from the standpoint of becoming a mature, disciplined ballplayer. He finished with the second-highest hit total in Angels' history. Although he didn't display as much power as he had shown in previous years, he made up for it by driving in runs regularly.
1996: Anderson showed the hot bat he displayed after being called up midway through the 1995 season was no fluke. In his first full season in the majors, he fulfilled expectations to become part of perhaps the best young outfield in baseball, along with Tim Salmon and Jim Edmonds.

	AB	R	HR	RBI	SB	BA
1995 California	374	50	16	69	6	.321
1996 California	607	79	12	72	7	.285
1997 Anaheim	624	76	8	92	10	.303

ANDERSON, MARLON - 2B - BL - b: 1/3/74
Anderson's status as a top second base prospect is under scrutiny. He has above-average speed and decent gap power for a middle infielder, but he has been slow to improve on his shortcomings. His poor baserunning, inadequate plate discipline and inconsistent footwork in the field over the last season and a half at Double-A have taken the shine off his star. Anderson will need to show some progress at Triple-A in 1998, especially improving on his overaggressiveness at the plate; he has walked only 97 times in 1533 career plate appearances.

ANDREWS, SHANE - 3B/1B - BR - b: 8/28/71
Scouting: Andrews has outstanding power potential but is prone to strikeouts and reconstructive surgery performed on his left shoulder last August could have long-term effects on his righthanded stroke. Andrews has a strong arm at third base but it is not accurate, though his range has improved with experience.
1998: Andrews' future is in doubt after having surgery last August to repair nerve damage in his left shoulder. He isn't expected to be ready to play again in the major leagues until mid-July and the Expos rarely mention him as part of their future plans.
1997: Andrews began the season as the Expos' starting third baseman but got off to a horrible start, then infuriated Expos' management by refusing an option to Triple-A Ottawa, claiming he was injured. Andrews was proved correct as he had nerve damage in his left shoulder that eventually required reconstructive surgery in mid-August.
1996: Andrews put up decent power numbers but his batting average and on-base percentage were weak. He was bothered

throughout the season by a wrist problem.

	AB	R	HR	RBI	SB	BA
1995 Montreal	220	27	8	31	1	.214
1996 Montreal	375	43	19	64	3	.227
1997 Montreal	64	10	4	9	0	.203

ANGELI, DOUG - SS - BR - b: 1/7/71
Largely due to the recent dilapidated state of the Phillies' minor-league system, Angeli has been able to craft a five-year pro career despite a lack of any singular defining ability. Angeli is a surehanded defender at shortstop and has a strong enough arm for third base, but he lacks defensive range and speed on the bases. That's just as well, because Angeli doesn't reach base often. He has no power or plate discipline, though he does consistently put the ball in play without authority. Angeli could stick in another season as a jack-of-all-trades at Double-A or Triple-A in the Phillies' system, but stands little chance to contribute in the majors.

ANTHONY, ERIC - OF/1B - BL - b: 11/8/67
The now-veteran reserve outfielder was thought to be a budding superstar when he first broke in with Houston, but his star has faded considerably because he's never shown regular power. Anthony hasn't played much the last two seasons because he hasn't produced consistently at the major league level. Anthony hits well at the Triple-A level, but needs to show again that he can hit in the big leagues. Perhaps expansion will open a spot for him on someone's bench.

	AB	R	HR	RBI	SB	BA
1995 Cincinnati	134	19	5	23	2	.269
1996 Colorado	185	32	12	22	0	.243
1997 Los Angeles	74	8	2	5	2	.243

ARDOIN, DANNY - C - BR - b: 7/8/74
Ardoin appears to have an uphill battle — there are four catchers ahead of him on the depth chart — but his 1997 season, split between A-ball (.234 with three homers and 19 RBI) and Double-A (.231 with four homers and 23 RBI) wasn't bad. His numbers, though hardly eye-popping, showed a little long ball power. Still, he must hurdle Molina, Hinch, Williams, and Morales to make a mark, and that is a tough order.

ARIAS, ALEX - SS/3B - BR - b: 11/20/67
Scouting: Arias is a competent defensive player at three infield positions who can be counted upon for patient, professional at-bats. The original Marlin has plus range and a strong arm, and has the perfect mentality for a bench player. His lack of power or speed — he has only nine homers and four steals in his six-year major league career — will prevent him from ever obtaining a more regular role.
1998: Arias is likely to stick with the Marlins or another club in a similar role. However, even an injury to an incumbent starter won't earn Arias a significant increase in playing time, as the Marlins have more talented minor leaguers upon whom they can rely.
1997: Arias' role continued to shrink as the demotion of former starter Kurt Abbott to the top infield reserve role relegated Arias to 25th-man status. He handled the bat well, drew walks and provided steady infield defense when needed.
1996: Terry Pendleton's failure at third base opened the door for Arias to play a larger role for the Marlins. He was far from an automatic out, making consistent contact and even showing surprising pop to the gaps.

	AB	R	HR	RBI	SB	BA
1995 Florida	216	22	3	26	1	.269
1996 Florida	224	27	3	26	2	.277
1997 Florida	93	13	1	11	0	.247

ARIAS, GEORGE - 3B - BR - b: 3/12/72
Scouting: The Padres acquired this third baseman from the Angels in the Rickey Henderson trade as insurance against losing Gabe Alvarez to expansion. Arias is a solid third baseman who has played the position since high school. He's a line drive hitter whose power totals have dipped only slightly along his climb up the ladder.
1998: Arias and Alvarez are a part of the high-minors log-jam at third base for the Padres. While both seem major league-ready, Arias has more experience and might get the first shot if playing time developed, at least initially; Alvarez may pass Arias this year on the Padres' depth charts. In the meantime, Arias is headed back to Triple-A, this team with the Las Vegas Stars.
1997: He hit .280 with 11 homers and 59 RBI in 103 games at Triple-A Vancouver before the trade, then .333 with a homer in ten games at Triple-A Las Vegas before finishing the season with the Padres where he went 5-for-22 in a brief September stint.
1996: After leading the Double-A Texas League in home runs (30) and RBI (104) in '95, Arias opened '96 with the Angels and hit poorly in 84 games. He was sent to Vancouver where he batted .337 with nine home runs in 59 games.

	AB	R	HR	RBI	SB	BA
1996 California	252	19	6	28	2	.238
1997 San Diego	28	3	0	3	0	.250

ASHLEY, BILLY - OF - BR - b: 7/11/70
Scouting: Ashley is a classic big swinger, tough on lefty pitchers. He can smash impressive home runs but strikes out much too frequently to play regularly. Ashley has a good throwing arm, but overall his left field defense is a liability that can't be hidden anywhere except on the bench.
1998: If the National League had a DH, Ashley would be cast in the role of platoon DH and pinch-hitter. He would be better suited to playing in the American League.
1997: Ashley continued in the off-the-bench role to which he had been relegated in 1996. His sub-.300 on-base percentage, combined with a .289 batting average against southpaws, illustrate the one-dimensional aspect of his game.
1996: Five pinch-hit home runs tell the story of Ashley's presence in the majors. He began the year as a platoon left fielder, but defensive weakness and too many strikeouts won him a place on the bench.

	AB	R	HR	RBI	SB	BA
1995 Los Angeles	215	17	8	27	0	.237
1996 Los Angeles	110	18	9	25	0	.200
1997 Los Angeles	131	12	6	19	0	.244

ASHBY, CHRIS - 1B - BR - b: 12/15/74
Defensive limitations moved Ashby from catcher to first base, and the move gave him a chance to play more and concentrate on hitting — with good results. In four minor-league seasons before 1997, Ashby never hit more than nine homers and had only 20 in total. In 138 games for Double-A Norwich, Ashby led the club with 25 homers and 83 RBI while playing 117 games at first base. But, he also made 19 errors, so defense remains an

issue for Ashby.

AUDE, RICH - 1B - BR - b: 7/13/71
Scouting: Aude has good power and an ability to make contact. He doesn't hit enough to fill a major league spot at first base and he can't play any other position with any degree of skill. Therefore, his options are limited.
1998: A Blue Jays' team with Carlos Delgado would not take a long look at Aude unless he had a breakout year at Triple-A. Another team, however, could make use of him as a backup.
1997: Signed as a free agent, Aude spent the entire season with Triple-A Syracuse, hitting .283 with 15 home runs.
1996: Although Aude posted good numbers across the board at Triple-A, the fact that it happened in the Pacific Coast League slightly tainted his performance. In a brief call-up to the Pirates, Aude struck out eight times in 16 at-bats.

AURILIA, RICH - SS - BR - b: 9/2/71
Scouting: Aurilia is a line-drive hitter with decent power for a middle infielder. He is not a particularly patient hitter, nor is his speed anything unusual. Defensively, Aurilia appeared only as a substitute for incumbent shortstop Jose Vizcaino. This fact was mostly a factor of the good and versatile bench the Giants assembled during the 1997 off-season.
1998: Chemistry is important, and unfortunately for Aurilia, the chemistry between Vizcaino and his fellow San Francisco infielders is good. So, Aurilia should enter 1998 with much the same role he had in 1997.
1997: Aurilia was pegged as the opening day shortstop for the Giants last fall, but that expectation quickly fell by the wayside when San Francisco traded for Vizcaino. However, Aurilia was just fine coming off the bench, hitting with power and playing good defense.
1996: Aurilia clobbered the ball in ten Triple-A games, then was called up to fill in for Robby Thompson, and then Shawon Dunston. Aurilia has excellent range, a good glove, and a fair bat. Though he's hardly All-Star material, he is a serviceable day-to-day shortstop who will improve with experience.

	AB	R	HR	RBI	SB	BA
1995 San Francisco	19	4	2	4	1	.474
1996 San Francisco	318	27	3	26	4	.239
1997 San Francisco	102	16	5	19	1	.275

AUSMUS, BRAD - C - BR - b: 4/14/69
Scouting: Ausmus is a strong defensive catcher in every respect. He calls an intelligent game, blocks pitches in the dirt well and has a strong arm with a quick release. He has above-average speed for a catcher and is a respectable hitter but without much power. He has proven his durability.
1998: Ausmus is a lock as the starting catcher for the Astros. He is in his prime and could put up numbers slightly better than in 1997.
1997: Ausmus was the key player for Houston in an off-season trade with Detroit. Handed the starting position, he quickly gained respect by twice throwing out Kenny Lofton trying to steal in the season's opening series. He was consistent both offensively and defensively all year.
1996: Ausmus started the season in San Diego and didn't hit well. He did somewhat better after a trade to Detroit but, overall, it was a disappointing year.

	AB	R	HR	RBI	SB	BA
1995 San Diego	328	44	5	34	16	.293
1996 San Diego	149	16	1	13	1	.181
1996 Detroit	226	30	4	22	3	.248
1997 Houston	425	45	4	44	14	.266

AVEN, BRUCE - OF - BR - b: 3/4/72
Scouting: Aven is a true underdog; a diminutive 30th-round draft pick who somehow overcame the odds to reach the majors at the end of the 1997 season. Aven is a free-swinging power hitter who has maintained his power stroke at higher minor-league levels. He also has decent speed and is good enough defensively to be able to play all three outfield positions. He's less a prospect than an overachiever.
1998: In most organizations, Aven would be good enough to have a major league role by now. Instead, Brian Giles has wedging his way into the big-league picture, leaving no room for Aven. Expansion may open up enough major league opportunities that Aven can get a fourth outfielder role elsewhere, though.
1997: Aven drove the ball to the gaps with occasional homer power and decent speed at Triple-A Buffalo. He drove a high percentage of his hits for extra bases and fielded his position well.
1996: Aven successfully made the jump to Double-A, posting his best minor-league season ever, exhibiting a fine power/speed combination, hitting 23 homers with 22 steals.

	AB	R	HR	RBI	SB	BA
1997 Cleveland	19	4	0	2	0	.211

AVERSA, JOE - SS/2B - BB - b: 5/20/68
Aversa is your classic good-field, no-hit shortstop. He entered 1997 with a .209 career average over seven minor-league seasons, and managed to lower it despite playing down at lower Class A Kane County in the Marlins' system due to an organizational void. He has mustered but one homer and a .250 slugging percentage in his career. Aversa's time has likely reached its end, as another two-level drop would dump him into an American Legion league.

AVILA, ROLO - OF - BR - b: 8/10/73
A center fielder with promise, Avila was pried away from Baltimore when the Dodgers gave up former top draft pick Ryan Luzinski for him. Avila's a leadoff type who can run and steal a base. He has struggled a bit in Double-A in the past, so 1998 will be a big test for him. Avila needs to show the Dodgers something extra and start fulfilling his promise or risk being buried in the system behind other outfield prospects.

AYRAULT, JOE - C - BR - b: 10/8/71
A big guy with limited ability in all facets of the game, Ayrault was injured most of the '97 season, getting just 56 at-bats at the Triple-A level. He's never been much of a hitter, so even if he comes back healthy his best bet at a major league career is as a backup catcher.

AZUAJE, JESUS - 2B - BR - b: 1/16/73
Azuaje picked it up last season, hitting .278 in Double-A and .306 in Triple-A. He stole eleven bases and hit seven homers. Another good season at Norfolk, or an open slot in the Mets infield could get him to the majors. Azuaje is a spray hitter with average speed and average defense for the high minors.

BADY, ED - OF - BB - b: 2/5/73
Bady, a switch-hitting outfielder, had trouble making contact at Double-A Harrisburg. He was second on the team in stolen bases but he doesn't get on base enough to take advantage of his base-stealing ability.

BAERGA, CARLOS - 2B - BB - b: 11/4/68
Scouting: You know something's missing here. Baerga is not the offensive force he was with the Indians as recently as 1995. The Mets believe the missing element is Baerga's use of his lower body, particularly when the veteran, switch-hitting second baseman bats righthanded. When he's hot, he's apt to hit pitches over first base and third base and through the middle for hits in the same game. He doesn't reach the gaps as often as he used to. His defense is deceiving; he makes plays and hangs in well at the second base bag — those thick legs help him withstand the hard and late slides.
1998: Because Baerga's 1997 season was difficult to read, figuring his 1998 season is all but impossible. The Mets believe — or is it hope? — more of the pre-1996 Baerga will resurface next season. "If he keeps getting the lower half of his body into his swing, he'll start to drive the ball again," Mets general manager Steve Phillips said. "We saw improvement in that area as the season went on." Even if Baerga produces only on the level he established last season — 53 runs and 52 RBI — he will be a positive force.
1997: The full extent of Baerga's considerable value to the Mets could be judged only by everyday observation. The season totals he produced sell him short. He often was a critical element in a critical victory; witness in his contributions — four RBI and three hits — to the Mets first ever victory against Pedro Martinez in May and his score-tying and game-winning hits against the Braves in the Mets uplifting victory June 24th. And he became as much a part of fabric of the team as any Mets player since Keith Hernandez. "No one in this clubhouse is more respected than Carlos," Matt Franco says.
1996: It was a spring and summer of fall for a player who had been among the premier offensive performers in the American League for five years. The decline, partially fueled by a pulled stomach muscle, was steep and, at times it seemed almost complete. The Indians thought he was out of shape. They put him on the market long before the Mets bit.

	AB	R	HR	RBI	SB	BA
1995 Cleveland	557	87	15	90	11	.314
1996 Cleveland	424	54	10	55	1	.267
1996 New York NL	83	5	2	11	0	.193
1997 New York NL	467	53	9	52	2	.281

BAEZ, KEVIN - SS - BR - b: 1/10/67
Baez is a 31-year-old veteran of the minor leagues; he reached the bigs with the Mets for part of three seasons. During his stay at Shea, Baez was a good-glove/no-bat shortstop. In 1997, he played at Triple-A Salt Lake in the Twins organization. He was decent at the plate but nothing that changes his prospectus.

BAGWELL, JEFF - 1B - BR - b: 5/27/68
Scouting: Bagwell is one of the premiere power hitters in the major leagues. Larry Walker had one of the best seasons in recent memory in 1996 including a slugging average of .720. Bagwell may have been even better in 1994 with a slugging average of .750, the highest in the National League since Rogers Hornsby's .756 in 1925. However, he is subject to lengthy slumps when his complex batting stance gets out of kilter. While he has only average speed, he has excellent baserunning instincts. He is a aggressive defensive player with a Gold Glove to his credit in 1994.
1998: Bagwell will play every day and should put up his typical numbers (.300-35-120-25). Still in his prime, he should continue at this level for several years.
1997: Bagwell broke his own club records for homers and RBI. However, a lengthy slump in July and August resulted in his lowest batting average since 1992. He finished second in the league to Walker in home runs and second in RBI behind Andres Galarraga. He was third in slugging (.592) and fourth in on-base average (.425). He reached a personal high in stolen bases, becoming the only first baseman to record 40 home runs and 30 stolen bases in the same year.
1996: Bagwell played in every game and recorded excellent numbers in every category.

	AB	R	HR	RBI	SB	BA
1995 Houston	448	88	21	87	12	.290
1996 Houston	568	111	31	120	21	.315
1997 Houston	566	109	43	135	31	.286

BAILEY, JEFF - C - BR - b: 11/19/78
The Marlins reached for Bailey - a catcher coming off of a rotator cuff injury - in the second round of the 1997 draft. He was limited to designated hitter duty throughout his senior year in high school and his brief stint with the Marlins. If he regains his throwing ability, Bailey projects as an above average defensive receiver who is a major question mark with the bat. All in all, a curious second round reach with Charles Johnson in place.

BAINES, HAROLD - DH - BL - b: 3/15/59
Scouting: Harold Baines could fall out of bed on Christmas morning, pick up a bat, and hit a double off the right field wall. He has a sweet swing with power. He's got baseball smarts and isn't easily overmatched or fooled. His major shortcomings are bad legs limiting him only to DH duty. Some managers platoon him, which is a waste of talent because he can hit lefties well.
1998: Baines can make big contributions to many teams needing a good lefthanded bat, and who can afford to have a player who can only DH. He's capable of a .280-20-80 season, even at age 39. The Orioles like to rotate position players through the DH slot, giving them some rest and providing for more roster flexibility, so Baines is probably not in their 1998 plans.
1997: The Orioles acquired Baines from the White Sox late last year because they felt they needed another lefthanded batter for the stretch run.
1996: The Orioles let Baines go following after the 1995 season, and he signed with the White Sox, his original team. He had a great year with the Sox.

	AB	R	HR	RBI	SB	BA
1995 Baltimore	385	60	24	63	0	.299
1996 Chicago AL	495	80	22	95	3	.311
1997 Chi. AL - Bal	452	55	16	67	0	.301

BAKO, PAUL - C - BL - b: 6/20/72
A lefthanded hitting catcher, Bako made progress in 1996 in Double-A but stalled out at Triple-A Indianapolis in 1997. He is a good defensive catcher, and he could get a chance as a third catcher, but he is too old to be considered a serious prospect.

BALFE, RYAN - 3B - BB - b: 11/11/75
Balfe's season ended early with a shoulder injury. He possesses an outstanding glove and has been a pleasant surprise with a powerful bat. He bashed 13 homers while hitting .269 in his second season at higher Class A Lakeland. He's still among the younger starters at his level and will be again when he moves up to Double-A Jacksonville in 1998. The Tigers have no prospects at third base ahead of him, so Balfe will advance quickly if he keeps producing like last year.

BALL, JEFF - 1B/3B - BR - b: 4/17/69
A good corner-infield prospect, Ball has a log jam of third basemen ahead of him in San Francisco. His 1997 season at Phoenix (hitting .321 with 18 homers and 103 RBI) mirrored that of 1996 when he batted .324 with 19 homers and 73 RBI. He is a good Triple-A hitter, but because he has had trouble finding a defensive position, he will probably be no more than a utility player in the majors, if that.

BANKS, BRIAN - OF - BB - b: 9/28/70
Scouting: Banks' versatility has kept him hanging around Triple-A and the majors. He isn't fast, is, at best, an adequate fielder and doesn't have much pop in his bat. But, he can play infield, outfield and do a little catching. Plus, he's a switch-hitter and has a good work ethic.
1998: It's doubtful Banks will have much of a role with the Brewers, but expansion could open more major league opportunities. A return trip to Triple-A is the most realistic expectation.
1997: Banks stuck around for a significant chunk of the season again because of his versatility. He struck out 17 times in 68 at-bats, too often for a hitter who doesn't have major league power.
1996: Banks spent most of his season at Triple-A New Orleans. He had his best home run year and was a late-season callup by the Brewers.

	AB	R	HR	RBI	SB	BA
1997 Milwaukee	68	9	1	8	0	.206

BARAJAS, ROD - C - BR - b: 9/5/75
Signed as a free agent out of a tryout camp in California in 1996, Barajas has been a real find. He hit .337 with ten homers at Rookie League Lethbridge in 1996 before missing the first half of 1997 following back surgery. He hit seven homers in 199 at-bats after his return.

BARKER, GLEN - OF - BR - b: 5/10/71
Barker just had not hit during the first four years of his minor-league career with the Tigers. In 1997, he changed that around a bit with successful stints at Class A Lakeland and Double-A Jacksonville, batting .280 with six homers and 29 RBI. Barker did hit .288 at Class A Fayetteville to start the 1996 season and then floundered at Triple-A and was demoted to Double-A. If he doesn't follow up with a strong 1998 season he will probably never get another chance.

BARKER, KEVIN - 1B - BL - b: 7/26/75
Barker advanced from Class A Stockton in the California League to Double-A El Paso of the Texas League in 1997 in his first full season of pro ball. He was envisioned as a power prospect when drafted but showed an all-around game, hitting for average as well as cranking the longball. An outfielder in college, Barker has adjusted nicely to his new position and looks to be about a year away from challenging for the Brewers' first base job.

BARKER, TIM - IF/OF - BR - b: 6/30/68
In his second season with Triple-A Columbus, Barker improved his batting average, on-base percentage, slugging average and had more home runs even though his at-bat total of 208 is half as many as he had in 1996. Barker has good speed, but is long past the prospect stage. His best hope for the majors would be a pinch-runner/utility role.

BARKETT, ANDY - 1B - BL - b: 9/5/74
Barkett successfully made the jump from the Florida State League to Double-A Tulsa, hitting .299 with eight homers and 65 RBI. Since he doesn't project as a power hitter, Barkett will have to continue to hit for a high average as he moves up. He should make it to Triple-A sometime next season.

BARNES, LARRY - 1B - BL - b: 7/23/74
Barnes grabbed the Angels' attention by showing some power early in his career. His power dropped a bit as he made the jump to higher Class A in 1997, but Barnes' potential is still there and he's a good RBI man. The 6'1", 195-pound first sacker has the potential to hit for average as well. His bat could carry him high in the organization.

BARRETT, MICHAEL - C - BR - b: 10/22/76
The Expos converted Barrett, their top pick in the 1995 draft, from shortstop to catcher after his first pro season. He has taken to catching well and has the skills to become above-average at that position. He doesn't project to hit for a high average when he gets to the majors but has a decent power stroke. Still new to catching, Barrett will need a full season at both the Double-A and Triple-A levels before arriving in Montreal in 2000, just about the time Chris Widger will become too expensive for the frugal Expos to keep.

BARRON, TONY - OF - BR - b: 8/17/66
Scouting: Barron has bounced around the minor leagues since 1987 but had only batted once in the majors entering 1997. Like many successful minor-league journeymen, Barron has just enough bat speed to drive the ball for serious home run power against Triple-A pitching. In the majors, Barron was not overmatched, but was incapable of hitting for better than average power. His plate discipline is poor, and his baserunning speed is below average. His defense has always had a poor reputation, but he overcame his lack of tools with raw hustle in his major league stint.
1998: Barron will likely be right back where he belongs in 1998 - at Triple-A. He is a hard-nosed bulldog of a player, but is incapable of approaching the production required of a starting major league outfielder. His lack of speed and versatility make him an unattractive bench option. Barron's best chance for a return to the majors is a repeat of the Phillies' outfield injury woes.
1997: The breakdown of Danny Tartabull and the trade of Darren Daulton paved the way for Barron's big chance. He gave a solid, blue-collar effort, diving all over the field defensively and driving the ball for occasional power at the plate. He was especially effective against lefties, but his production tailed off late in the season after pitchers realized that he would get himself out on bad pitches routinely.
1996: After over 3000 minor-league at-bats, Barron finally got a

single major league at-bat - and struck out. The wild swinger was a productive power hitter in the Expos' chain, even approaching his career high in walks (26, versus 30 in 1990).

	AB	R	HR	RBI	SB	BA
1997 Philadelphia	189	22	4	24	0	.286

BARRY, JEFF - OF/3B - BB - b: 9/22/68
Barry got 15 at-bats with the Mets in 1995 but since then was traded to the Padres and ended up in the Rockies organization in 1997. He played at both Double-A and Triple-A and hit better at the higher level. He showed some power (13 homers, 70 RBI) in 273 at-bats at Colorado Springs and could be an in-season callup as a backup outfielder. At age 29, he isn't a prospect to become an everyday player.

BARTEE, KIMERA - OF - BB - b: 7/21/72
Scouting: If he can hit, he can play, because he's one of the fastest players in the game. He's now into his second year as a switch-hitter, but the results are still inconclusive. Defensively, he could be one of the best. He'll only get the chance to show it if he proves he can get on base.
1998: The emergence of Brian Hunter and the continued solid play of Bobby Higginson have pushed Bartee back somewhat in the Tiger plans. No one questions his defense; playing time depends on how much improvement he can make at the plate, particularly from the left side.
1997: After playing in the Arizona Fall League, Bartee was sent to Triple-A Toledo for a full season of switch-hitting. He batted just .198 from the left side, and the Tigers were concerned that his progress had slowed so they sent him back to the Fall League for more work.
1996: Bartee became a true prospect, playing in 110 major-league games after being chosen in the Rule 5 draft. He became the starting center-fielder after Chad Curtis was traded, and he impressed the Tigers with his improvement at the plate and especially with his defense.

	AB	R	HR	RBI	SB	BA
1996 Detroit	217	32	1	14	20	.253
1997 Detroit	5	4	0	0	3	.200

BARTHOL, BLAKE - C - BR - b: 4/7/73
Barthol has a squatty build and is a good defensive catcher. He has an average throwing arm, but a quick release. Barthol possesses a great knowledge of the game, though he needs to work on pitch selection and sequences. He has valley-to-valley power, though he can occasionally yank a fastball. Though he's not swift, he's a smart, sneaky baserunner. He could be a backup guy in the big leagues this season. His stick (.244, six homers, 39 RBI in 110 games at Double-A New Haven in 1997) will probably prevent him from ever becoming a top catcher in the majors.

BATES, FLETCHER - OF - BB - b: 3/24/74
Bates started 1997 at high A St. Lucie and earned a mid season promotion to Double-A Binghamton. He hit a combined 23 homers and had 82 RBI. In 1998 Bates is expected to start the season at Double-A where he will have to show he can produce a similar offensive output to advance.

BATES, JASON - 2B/3B/SS - BB - b: 1/5/71
Scouting: An experienced utility player who is best at second base, Bates is just adequate at shortstop and third base. He has an accurate arm, though it is not a gun. His range has seemingly slowed as he added bulk after his impressive 1995 rookie year. A switch-hitter with decent pop from the left side for a middle infielder, Bates is average, at best, as a baserunner.
1998: Because Colorado has a shortage of middle infielders, Bates would be the leading candidate for the utility infield job in spring training — if he stays. Bates believes he can play every day at second base, so he was hoping to move to another organization, either through the expansion draft or via trade.
1997: After a disappointing sophomore season in 1996, Bates bounced back to have a productive year, though his numbers were only ordinary. After spending the previous two full seasons in the majors, he was twice demoted to Triple-A Colorado Springs as he was pushed out to make room for Neifi Perez.
1996: Once considered a promising big-league infielder, Bates lost the confidence of Rockies management by slumping badly all year.

	AB	R	HR	RBI	SB	BA
1995 Colorado	322	42	8	46	3	.267
1996 Colorado	160	19	1	9	2	.206
1997 Colorado	121	17	3	11	0	.240

BATISTA, TONY - SS - BR - b: 12/9/73
Scouting: Batista has the capability to put up big numbers on offense. He has good strength and a quick bat. At this point his hitting is undisciplined, and he needs to show more desire to learn and develop his talent further. He can field well and possesses a strong arm, but overconfidence and mental lapses have been a shortcoming.
1998: Batista came through the expansion draft as a big winner on paper, a probable starter for Arizona. In Oakland he faced plenty of stiff competition for playing time. If Batista learned from his 1997 miscues, he could well find himself on a path toward stardom.
1997: Batista cruised through spring training on the strength of his hot debut of 1996, knowing he was the everyday shortstop. His fall was hardly one from grace — he simply wasn't good enough to fall a long way. He came to spring ill-prepared both mentally and physically to be able to handle the everyday role as a major league starting shortstop, and spent most of the season on the bench or on the DL.
1996: Batista chewed up the Pacific Coast League and won Oakland's second base spot, courtesy of an injured Brent Gates and a weak hitting Rafael Bournigal.

	AB	R	HR	RBI	SB	BA
1996 Oakland	238	38	6	25	7	.298
1997 Oakland	188	22	4	18	2	.202

BATTLE, ALLEN - OF - BR - b: 11/29/68
The curse of potential looms large over the speedy Battle, who seems to turn it on in Triple-A and shrivel once he is promoted. Battle, who had the center field job handed to him not once but twice, couldn't hit enough to stay on either the Oakland or Edmonton roster; he is now with the White Sox. He is no better than a minor-league player.

	AB	R	HR	RBI	SB	BA
1995 St. Louis	118	13	0	2	3	.271
1996 Oakland	130	20	1	5	10	.192

BATTLE, HOWARD - 3B - BR - b: 3/25/72
Scouting: Battle is a defensive gem among third basemen. He doesn't hit for a high average and doesn't have much power. In

eight years of minor-league play, Battle never had more than 20 homers in a single season at any level, and he has never reached the .290 mark. His biggest offensive assets are contact hitting and speed on the bases (he has stolen as many as 26 bases in a minor-league season).
1998: Unless he moves to his fourth organization in 1998, Battle will likely remain stuck behind third basemen who can hit better. He is a nice asset in a reserve role, but won't be a starter unless he lands with a weak team.
1997: Battle hit .237 at Triple-A Albuquerque and .242 at Double-A San Antonio while waiting for the major league call which never came.
1996: Although he surfaced briefly with the Phillies, Battle was stuck behind superprospect Scott Rolen on the major league depth chart. He hit .228 at Triple-A Scranton.

BAUGHMAN, JUSTIN - SS - BR - b: 8/1/74
Scouting: Baughman is, without question, one of the fastest and quickest infielders in the Angels' organization, and maybe the fastest player in the system. He's a solid defensive shortstop; his error totals have been a little high, but that's probably because his great range lets Baughman get to a lot of balls other players can't reach. He hits for average and may wage a spirited battle with top draft pick Troy Glaus to see who has the first shot at eventually replacing shortstop Gary DiSarcina.
1998: The Angels would like to see Baughman cut down on the errors a bit, but understand that guys who reach as many balls as he does are going to commit an error once in a while.
1997: Baughman's blazing speed was evident in his 68 stolen bases for Class A Lake Elsinore. He also scored 71 runs, second-highest total on the club, and had a solid year with the glove.
1996: Baughman stole 50 bases in 127 games for Class A Cedar Rapids in his second professional season and played well defensively.

BAUTISTA, DANNY - OF - BR - b: 5/24/72
Bautista is a pretty good all-around athlete with some speed and power skills. However, he lacks discipline in most facets of the game. He's still young and has potential, but he needs to put in a full season at Triple-A to shorten his swing and improve his approach at the plate. But, after spending half the season there last year, hitting .282, he was called up to Atlanta to fill the Braves need for a righthanded hitting outfielder. It appears he may be destined to fourth outfielder status for the rest of his career.

	AB	R	HR	RBI	SB	BA
1995 Detroit	271	28	7	27	4	.203
1996 Detroit	64	12	2	8	1	.250
1997 Atlanta	103	14	3	9	2	.243

BAUTISTA, JUAN - SS - BR - b: 6/24/75
White Sox minor-leaguer Juan Bautista is another shortstop from the shortstop factory of San Pedro de Macoris in the Dominican Republic. He has struggled at the plate in A-ball and in Double-A, limiting his progress. Last season was an injury-filled year, and he didn't make any progress. He's a superb fielder with excellent range and a strong arm, but he needs to learn patience and selectivity at the plate. He's only 22 and he's still learning how to hit. Bautista was the "player to be named later" going to the White Sox in the trade bringing Harold Baines to the Orioles.

BEAMON, TREY - OF - BL - b: 2/11/74
Scouting: Beamon is a line-drive hitter who uses all fields. He doesn't yet have great power, blazing speed or a strong arm on defense. But Beamon hits well enough to be a fourth or fifth outfielder in the major leagues now, at an age when most players are just finishing Double-A. An excellent disposition and attitude boost his stock.
1998: Beamon is a candidate for a reserve outfield spot with the Tigers, with better chances than he had in San Diego. The promise that he showed as a young minor leaguer has not yet come through, but it will.
1997: Acquired from Pittsburgh during spring training, Beamon hit .328 at Triple-A Las Vegas but had only five homers in the hitting-happy Pacific Coast League, then impressed the Padres with a .277 average in 65 at-bats, mostly off the bench.
1996: Beamon finished his second straight year at Triple-A Calgary by hitting .288, which was 46 points below his '95 mark. He hit only five homers in each of his two seasons with Calgary.

	AB	R	HR	RBI	SB	BA
1996 Pittsburgh	51	7	0	6	1	.216
1997 San Diego	65	5	0	7	1	.277

BEASLEY, TONY - OF/2B - BR - b: 12/5/66
Replacement baseball in the spring of 1995 resurrected Beasley's career with the Pittsburgh Pirates. Beasley was out of baseball after being released by the Pirates in the spring of 1994 and Pittsburgh found him working for his father's logging company in northern Virginia. Beasley has spent the past two seasons as a utility infielder at the Double-A and Triple-A levels and doesn't figure to advance beyond that. Hey, it's easier work than logging.

BECKER, RICH - OF - BL - b: 2/1/72
Scouting: Becker's potential and the fact that he's only 26 will keep teams interested, but he still has not been able to put together a consistent, full season in the majors. He strikes out too much to be a number two hitter and he doesn't have enough power to be a middle-of-the-lineup hitter. He's OK defensively, although not a Gold Glove candidate in center field. Even after three seasons, he has difficulty picking up the ball in the Metrodome roof.
1998: Becker has the potential to put things together in 1998 and make himself a solid .280 hitter, but also has the potential to let struggles make the game a psychological minefield for him that will drive him out before he ever makes a mark.
1997: Becker began the year as the Twins' second-place hitter but struck out too much to be effective. He developed a maddening quality of taking third strikes and 29% of his at-bats wound up in strikeouts. He eventually was dropped to the bottom of the order.
1996: Becker put himself into the Twins' future plans by rebounding from an .070 average at the end of April to hit a solid .291. He batted .326 with runners in scoring position.

	AB	R	HR	RBI	SB	BA
1995 Minnesota	392	45	2	33	8	.237
1996 Minnesota	525	92	12	71	19	.291
1997 Minnesota	443	61	10	45	17	.264

BELK, TIM - 1B - BR - b: 4/6/70
Belk has consistently hit for a high average but only marginal power in the minors. At best he could catch on as a pinch-hitter in the majors, but he is too old to be considered a serious prospect.

BELL, DAVID - 2B/3B - BR - b: 9/14/72

Scouting: Once considered a good-fielding third baseman with developing power, Bell has turned into a player with defensive versatility but he's unable to show enough to gain a regular job. He works hard enough to catch the eye of management. His inconsistency doesn't keep the attention, though.

1998: He can be expected to get a crack at the everyday third baseman role in the spring. Without showing an ability to hit consistently and produce some runs, Bell should return to a reserve spot — and even that wouldn't be guaranteed if the Cards finally can satisfy their search for a solid backup infielder.

1997: A broken finger on his left hand kept Bell off the field most of the first half of the season. He started at least nine games each at shortstop, second base and third base, and the Cards gave him a serious look in September. But he had only two hits in his final 48 at-bats.

1996: Bell split the season between the Cardinals and Triple-A, thanks to Gary Gaetti's fine showing as the third baseman and Bell's failure to hit in the early season.

	AB	R	HR	RBI	SB	BA
1995 St. Louis	144	13	2	19	1	.250
1996 St. Louis	145	12	1	9	1	.214
1997 St. Louis	142	9	1	12	1	.211

BELL, DEREK - OF - BR - b: 12/11/68

Scouting: Bell is an enigma. In the past he has hit for average (.334 in 1995), power (21 home runs in 1993) and has produced runs (113 RBI in 1996) but he has never put it all together. He didn't do particularly well in any category in 1997 and he stole only 15 bases after stealing at least 24 in each of the previous four years. His fielding is brilliant at times but is frequently lackadaisical, a word that probably best describes his overall demeanor. He shows no signs of being willing to put in the effort to move to the next level.

1998: Bell appears to be coasting through what should be his prime years. He should be capable of putting up better numbers than he did in 1997, but there is no guarantee that he will.

1997: Bell had a disappointing season, particularly when he batted in the fourth or fifth slot. He generally hit well in the second spot between Craig Biggio and Jeff Bagwell, but this created a void in the middle of the lineup that Bell was being paid to fill.

1996: Bell's batting average dropped from .334 in 1995 to .263 in 1996. His RBI total of 113 looks impressive but he batted only .233 with runners in scoring position.

	AB	R	HR	RBI	SB	BA
1995 Houston	452	63	8	86	27	.334
1996 Houston	627	84	17	113	29	.263
1997 Houston	493	67	15	71	15	.276

BELL, JAY - SS - BR - b: 12/11/65

Scouting: Bell is a productive player in all respects. He has shown unusual power the last two seasons but has always been above-average as a hitter among middle infielders, getting on base well enough, hitting an occasional homer and stealing a few bases. He's not a flashy glove man, but is steady with just average range in the field; he might move to third base later in his career. Bell has certainly peaked; he can't duplicate his '96-'97 performance for long.

1998: Bell was among the first big names slated to play for Arizona. The Diamondbacks will feature his use-all-fields style of hitting in a good batting order. Expect another solid year.

1997: Bell was the Royals' most productive hitter over the first four months of the season, eventually being moved to the third spot in the batting order. In most years — and for most teams — Bell isn't strong enough for that position, but, after all, that's why they call them career years.

1996: Bell's previous best season in his last year with the Pirates featured unusually robust power and otherwise above-average all-around play at the plate and in the field, where he led all major league shortstops in fielding average (.986).

	AB	R	HR	RBI	SB	BA
1995 Pittsburgh	530	79	13	55	2	.262
1996 Pittsburgh	527	65	13	71	6	.250
1997 Kansas City	573	89	21	92	10	.291

BELL, MIKE - 3B - BR - b: 12/7/74

Scouting: Bell has decent power and has developed into a solid third baseman, even playing quite a bit of second base at Triple-A. He has yet to learn how to handle good breaking pitches, especially from righthanded pitchers. Since he's not fast or a 30-homer threat, he'll need to hit for a high average in order to advance. At age 23, he still has time on his side.

1998: Bell will probably begin the year in the minors. His further advancement will depend upon his ability to produce runs. He was taken by the Diamondbacks at the end of the second round of the expansion draft.

1997: After opening the season with Triple-A Oklahoma City, Bell was leapfrogged by Fernando Tatis, the Rangers' Double-A third sacker, when Dean Palmer was traded. After hitting only .235 with five homers and 38 RBI in 328 Triple-A at-bats, Bell finished up well at Tulsa, where he hit .285 with eight homers in 123 at-bats.

1996: Bell made good progress toward the majors in his first Double-A season, improving his power stats and his fielding.

BELLE, ALBERT - OF - BR - b: 8/25/66

Scouting: Belle is one of the most fearsome sluggers in the game. He hits everything hard and often for extra-bases. He has had at least 30 homers, 30 doubles and 100 RBI for six straight seasons. Belle's power stroke is quick, though, and lets him hit for a good average without a ton of strikeouts. He has been a defensive liability for most of his career and he is not fast although he has shown surprising base-stealing ability.

1998: Although he's unlikely to admit it, Belle knows he had a bad year with the Sox in '97 and has a lot of ground to make up to earn his huge contract. He's still in the prime of his career and still has a great deal of power, so another high-power season would be a realistic expectation.

1997: Only the uniform changed. Despite declarations that fans would see a new Albert Belle with the Sox, Belle's legendary attitude remained constant — and he was reported to be a clubhouse troublemaker, too. It was also a disappointing season on the field as Belle paled beside fellow slugger Frank Thomas. His power production was down and often came in unimportant situations. Belle fanned more often and had his lowest batting average in five years.

1996: Belle's last year with the Indians produced a career high in RBI and nearly 100 walks without a noticeable drop in other areas. He didn't repeat his unprecedented 50/50 (doubles and homers) season from 1995 but was still among league leaders in most power-hitting categories. And he remained as volatile as ever, earning suspensions for on-field incidents and inciting disputes with his boorish off-field behavior.

	AB	R	HR	RBI	SB	BA
1995 Cleveland	546	121	50	126	5	.317
1996 Cleveland	602	124	48	148	11	.311
1997 Chicago AL	634	90	30	116	4	.274

BELLHORN, MARK - 2B/SS - BB - b: 8/23/74

Scouting: Bellhorn is a switch-hitting third sacker who flip-flopped spots with former second baseman Scott Spiezio when both reached the majors. Bellhorn has developing power and is more inconsistent hitting lefthanded than he is as a righthander. Defensively, Bellhorn needs some work; his nine errors were a lot for a part-time player.

1998: With many of the problems of both quick promotions and a rookie season on a struggling team behind him, Bellhorn is poised to nab a starting role this year. It may be a reach for him to play third on a daily basis, but it seems more likely than most of the other alternatives, such as Spiezio being moved from second.

1997: After ripping up the Pacific Coast League over the first two months of the season, Bellhorn was promoted to the big club and showed flashes of his immense potential, both at the plate and in the field where he played both second and third upon request.

1996: Bellhorn turned in a credible second professional season at Huntsville. He struck out a lot, but his walks and power numbers both increased, as did his steals.

	AB	R	HR	RBI	SB	BA
1997 Oakland	224	33	6	19	7	.228

BELLIARD, RAFAEL - SS/2B - BR - b: 10/24/61

Scouting: What Belliard lacks in hitting ability he more than recoups with outstanding defense. He has phenomenal range at the middle-infield slots and displays a strong, accurate arm. He has been frequently used as a defensive replacement over the last five years with the Braves. Belliard couldn't hit water if he fell out of a boat, though. He has hit over .230 just twice in the last eleven years and hasn't homered since 1987. He can be overmatched by any kind of pitching.

1998: It's possible that Belliard will hang 'em up, particularly if his super-sub role in Atlanta goes to one of the many utilityman hopefuls the Braves will have in their spring camp. His is such a specialized role that only a team with outstanding offensive strength can afford the luxury of having Belliard on the bench all year, so his opportunities for major league employment are extremely limited. If he plays, Belliard will be used for defense two or three times a week.

1997: It's not a misprint on his stat line; Belliard really did drive in just one run last year. His defense was good, as always, but his role become less important with Jeff Blauser having a big year and other young infielders stepping to the fore in reserve roles.

1996: Belliard managed 33 starts at shortstop and second base replacing Blauser and Mark Lemke when they were injured frequently. Belliard hit little, as usual, but saved some offensive heroics for the playoffs, going four-for-six against the Cardinals in the National League Championship Series and driving in two runs — he had just three RBI in the entire regular season.

	AB	R	HR	RBI	SB	BA
1995 Atlanta	180	12	0	7	2	.222
1996 Atlanta	142	9	0	3	3	.169
1997 Atlanta	71	9	1	3	0	.211

BELLIARD, RONNIE - 2B - BR - b: 7/4/76

Scouting: Ronnie is the cousin of Rafael Belliard and while the defensive abilities are similar, Ronnie has a much better bat. Belliard has good strikezone judgment and can draw a walk. What is especially nice is that once he gets on base he has speed that he can put to use.

1998: Belliard should be showcasing his soft hands and excellent range at County Stadium with the big club from the start of the season. With Fernando Vina on the club, Belliard will begin as a part-timer.

1997: After a slow start, Belliard made a smooth transition to Triple-A ball at Tucson. He showed power to the gaps and that he still has a good eye, walking almost as many times as striking out.

1996: Belliard made the jump from the Midwest League to the Texas League with a bang as he was named the league's Best Defensive Second Baseman.

BELLINGER, CLAY - SS - BR - b: 11/18/68

1997 was Bellinger's first season in the Yankees' organization, spent playing for Triple-A Columbus. He had a promising 1996 season, while in Orioles' system, but 1997 was a disappointment; he hit .274 with 12 homers and 59 RBI in 416 at-bats. He has some speed (ten steals), but is way past prospect status. He once had a chance in the majors to supplement Manny Alexander at shortstop for the Orioles, but now must set his sights on a utility infield role instead.

BELTRE, ADRIAN - 3B - BR - b: 4/7/78

Scouting: At age 19, Beltre gives definition to the term "superprospect." He can do it all: hit for average, hit for power, run the bases well, win games with defense (what an arm!) and draw a walk. With normal progress, he will be one of the best third basemen in the majors for the next 15 years.

1998: Rushing to the majors isn't likely, as Beltre just played a year in A-ball, and the Dodgers are consistently cautious with their best prospects. A mid-season promotion from Double-A to Triple-A and a September callup for a couple of games in the majors would be fast year for Beltre.

1997: Beltre dominated the higher Class A Florida State League with a .317 average, 26 home runs, 104 RBI and 25 stolen bases, while playing sterling defense at third base. He swept the voting in numerous categories in Baseball America's poll of the league's managers.

1996: Beltre won a mid-season promotion from Savannah in the South Atlantic League to San Bernardino in the California League. Overall he hit 26 homers and drove in 99 runs.

BELTRE, ESTEBAN - SS - BR - b: 12/26/67

This former major leaguer (Rangers and Red Sox) was last seen with Independent St. Paul in limited action. Beltre's career is probably over.

	AB	R	HR	RBI	SB	BA
1995 Texas	92	7	0	7	0	.217
1996 Boston	62	6	0	6	1	.258

BENARD, MARVIN - OF - BL - b: 1/20/70

Scouting: Excellent off the bench, Benard handles most pitches well. He has developed a little more patience than exhibited previously in his career, but part of what seems to make him successful as a pinch-hitter is his aggressiveness.

1998: Benard has seemingly found a niche, but that is about it.

Benson's Baseball Player Guide: 1998

The Giants outfield is already solid and the anticipated arrival of Jacob Cruz and Dante Powell leave no room for Benard. If expansion doesn't give Benard a bigger chance, an unlikely proposition considering his overall talent, he'll continue his bench role.

1997: The Giants were a team whose success was really a sum of their parts, and no one exemplified this better than Benard. Coming off a disappointing season, Benard established himself as a premier pinch-hitter, connecting with clutch hits 15 times last year and contributing to the Giants championship effort.

1996: Called up during the Giants spate of injuries, Benard, a speedster, was given the center field job. He was in over his head and was later relegated strictly to a fourth outfielder role. His lack of patience hurt his performance, as did an occasional loss of concentration.

	AB	R	HR	RBI	SB	BA
1995 San Francisco	34	5	1	4	1	.382
1996 San Francisco	488	89	5	27	25	.248
1997 San Francisco	114	13	1	13	3	.228

BENBOW, LOU - 3B - BR - b: 1/12/71

Benbow is an infielder who has barely hit his weight in seven minor-league seasons — and he's not that big. He also isn't that quick. He's a minor-league utilityman, who is unlikely to have a big-league career.

BENITEZ, YAMIL - OF - BR - b: 5/10/72

Scouting: Benitez is one of the most free-swinging hitters on the planet and when he makes contact he hits the ball a long, long way. He has always had a high percentage of extra-base hits — and strikeouts. Despite eight years as a professional, Benitez is still a raw talent; it shows in the way he swings the bat, runs the bases and plays the field. He has good speed, but makes no use of it as an outfielder or baserunner. In right field he often showed off a powerful arm — by throwing the ball thirty feet over an infielder's head.

1998: Benitez will challenge for a platoon role in the Diamondbacks' outfield, but will need to show improvement for them to let him stay in the majors and regularly hit against major league pitching while he has a chance to refine his outfield and baserunning skills.

1997: Obtained by the Royals in an off-season deal, Benitez was a leading power threat at Triple-A Omaha (36 extra-base hits, 71 RBI in 329 at-bats) before getting an August recall and becoming a semi-regular for new manager Tony Muser.

1996: Benitez got another cup of coffee in the majors after his most powerful campaign yet; he hit 23 homers with 20 doubles and 81 RBI in 114 games for Triple-A Ottawa in the Expos' farm system. It was his second year in a row with Ottawa and for the third straight year Benitez fanned more than 120 times.

	AB	R	HR	RBI	SB	BA
1997 Kansas City	191	22	8	21	2	.267

BENJAMIN, MIKE - 2B/SS - BR - b: 11/22/65

Scouting: Benjamin has a solid, if unspectacular glove, at shortstop. He is a weak hitter, but can make enough contact on fastballs that he is considered a reliable big-league backup. He is in good shape and is capable of playing at this same level for a couple of more seasons. He is not an ideal bench player because he doesn't provide speed or power and he hasn't played a lot of different positions over his career.

1998: Benjamin will provide depth for some organization at shortstop, whether at the Triple-A level or coming off the big-league bench.

1997: Benjamin started the season in Triple-A Pawtucket, as insurance in case phenom Nomar Garciaparra flopped in Boston. He was called up to the Red Sox after a couple of injuries, and remained on the Boston bench for the rest of the year.

1996: Benjamin spent most of the year with Philadelphia, but got only 103 at-bats. He hit .223 to raise his career big-league average to .200.

	AB	R	HR	RBI	SB	BA
1995 San Francisco	186	19	3	12	11	.220
1996 Philadelphia	103	13	4	13	3	.223
1997 Boston	116	12	0	7	2	.233

BENNETT, GARY - C - BR - b: 4/17/72

Scouting: Bennett is a quality receiver. His arm and defensive ability are major league. However, he has an extremely slow bat and has always struggled to hit. He has a solid build, but his bat is so slow that he has trouble pulling pitches and generating any power. It is unlikely at this point that he can find a way to improve his hitting.

1998: Unless he ends up in the right situation and gets a job as a major league backup catcher, Bennett will spend another season at Triple-A as insurance.

1997: Bennett saw more time than usual as a backup to Walt McKeel at Triple-A Pawtucket, catching two of the five pitchers in the regular rotation. He got more playing time when McKeel was called up, but did not show any improvement.

1996: Bennett spent the season at Triple-A Scranton/Wilkes-Barre in the Phillies' chain and hit .248 with eight homers in 286 at-bats.

BERBLINGER, JEFF - 2B - BR - b: 11/19/70

Long appreciated by Cardinals' player development officials as an above-average batsman for a middle infielder, Berblinger returned to the organization after being taken by Detroit in the Rule 5 draft and then traded to the Dodgers last spring. He failed in an attempt to win the everyday second base job in the big leagues with Los Angeles, then started slowly at Triple-A back with the Cards. His .263 batting average was a minor-league career low and 98 strikeouts uncommonly high. Even though he spent September in the majors, he's sandwiched between regular Delino DeShields and coming prospect Placido Polanco.

BERG, DAVE - SS/2B - BR - b: 9/3/70

Scouting: The whole of Berg's abilities is clearly greater then the sum of its parts. He isn't particularly big, strong or fast, but he has developed into a credible defensive shortstop with a consistent line-drive bat and solid baserunning instincts. He is willing to draw a walk and has above-average power to the gaps for a middle infielder. He is a feisty player whose spirit on the field is infectious. He's already 27 years, so what you see is what you get.

1998: Berg has a chance to wrest away Alex Arias' major league utility spot this year. He is capable of competent defense at shortstop and third base, and swings a better bat than Arias. Otherwise, he will be a Triple-A All-Star.

1997: Berg was a key top-of-the-order presence at Triple-A Charlotte, getting on base consistently and aggressively running the bases despite only adequate speed. He stabilized the middle-infield defense, as the Marlins' constant organizational shuffling at second base provided him a steady stream of new double play partners.

1996: Berg gained the notice of Marlins' brass by ramping up his offensive performance in his first season above Class A. He showed improved physical strength and was more aggressive in all facets of the game than in previous seasons.

BERKMAN, LANCE - OF - BB - b: 2/10/76
Scouting: Berkman was the Astros' first-round draft choice in 1997 after an outstanding career at Rice. He was a first baseman in college but is being converted to left field. There has been some concern that his power would be significantly diminished in switching to a wooden bat since he hit only one home run in the Cape Cod League in 1996 even though he led the league in hitting. Berkman is a switch hitter with good power from both sides; baseball people have always liked his makeup. As evidence of this, he quickly signed after being drafted so that he could get his professional career started as soon as possible.
1998: The Astros typically move players slowly through the system. Berkman's bat will challenge them to make an exception in his case. He should get an opportunity to start the season at the Double-A level in 1998.
1997: Berkman's 1997 season at Rice (.431-41-134) ranks among the best collegiate performances ever. He began his professional career at High Class A Kissimmee in the pitcher-friendly Florida State League, batting .293 with twelve homers and 35 RBI in only 184 at-bats, leading the team in home runs despite playing less than half of the season.
1996: Berkman batted .398 with 20 home runs and 92 RBI in his sophomore season at Rice. He then batted .352 to lead the Cape Cod Amateur Summer League in hitting while stealing twelve bases.

BERNHARDT, STEVE - 3B - BR - b: 10/9/70
In his first full season in Double-A, Bernhardt struggled at the plate. He posted a career best .300 batting average at Class A Salem in 1996 but showed none of that hitting ability for the Rockies' New Haven affiliate. Bernhardt will have a tough time advancing past the Double-A level.

BERRIOS, HARRY - OF - BR - b: 12/2/71
The Orioles' 1994 minor-league player of the year, Berrios was with Sioux Falls in the Independent League in 1997, hitting .282 with 14 homers and 61 RBI. He has lost his prospect status.

BERROA, GERONIMO - OF - BR - b: 3/18/65
Scouting: Berroa is a good power hitter, and he can hit for a decent average. He has a big power swing, but makes good contact nevertheless and he has a good eye at the plate. He thrives on lefthanded pitching, owning a large platoon differential. Berroa can be an adventure in the outfield, especially on slicing line drives which may sail occasionally over his head. The Orioles used him in right field even though his arm is not all that strong, and he didn't embarrass himself. The Orioles like his team-play attitude and hustle.
1998: The Orioles prefer to rotate position players through the DH to give them rest and to provide roster flexibility. Berroa fits into their plans even though he's a below-average outfielder. He should love to hit in Camden yards; he could hit 30 homers and drive in 100 runs.
1997: The Orioles acquired Berroa last year because they needed another bat for the stretch run. He struggled at first, but then settled in and began to come through with some clutch hits — and he hustled in right field.
1996: As did many hitters in the 1996 lively-ball year, Berroa had his career best year.

	AB	R	HR	RBI	SB	BA
1995 Oakland	546	87	22	88	7	.278
1996 Oakland	586	101	36	106	0	.290
1997 Oak.-Bal.	561	88	26	90	4	.283

BERRY, MIKE - 3B - BR - b: 8/12/70
Sean's brother Mike was in the high minors of the Orioles' farm system last year. He began the season in Double-A where he struggled although he did hit three homers in one game. It was a surprise that he hit better in Triple-A. He has a little power but no speed. Berry is not a prospect, and will have a tough time getting major league playing time.

BERRY, SEAN - 3B - BR - b: 3/22/66
Scouting: Berry's career took a downturn in 1997 in an injury-plagued season. He needs a strong comeback in 1998 to prove that he is capable of holding a regular job at the major league level. He is below average defensively and is limited to third base. His offensive production is no better than average for a third baseman.
1998: Berry is at the age where improvement will be difficult. A batting average of .275 with 15 home runs and 60 RBI is a reasonable expectation if he is healthy.
1997: Berry was on the disabled list twice. He missed two weeks in April with a pulled groin muscle and two weeks later in the season with a strained calf muscle. He never claimed the third base job for himself, splitting time with Bill Spiers and Ricky Gutierrez.
1996: Berry was the regular third baseman for Houston despite a torn rotator cuff which required surgery after the season. It was the only year that he has had more than 400 at-bats.

	AB	R	HR	RBI	SB	BA
1995 Montreal	314	38	14	55	3	.318
1996 Houston	431	55	17	95	12	.281
1997 Houston	301	37	8	43	1	.256

BERRYHILL, DAMON - C - BB - b: 12/3/63
Berryhill's playing time over the past three seasons has been limited. He was certainly a presence on the Giants, adding savvy to the young pitchers and catchers, and offering a switch-hitting bat from the bench. He is a capable backup catcher for a major league squad — possibly even the Giants. His abysmal 1995 season began with a .183 batting average, two homers and eleven RBI over 34 games before he spent six weeks on the DL with bone chips in his elbow. The post-season surgery cost him the entire 1996 season.

	AB	R	HR	RBI	SB	BA
1997 San Francisco	167	17	3	23	0	.257

BESS, JOHNNY - C - BB - b: 4/6/70
Bess did his job in Double-A Shreveport in 1996. Nothing fancy, nothing to be embarrassed about either. He is stuck behind a couple of real catching prospects in the Giants organization is probably not going too much farther. In 1997 Bess ended the season in the Expos organization.

BETTEN, RANDY - 2B - BR - 7/28/71
The jury's still out on how much of a prospect Betten is, but he's

done some things the Angels definitely like while playing the outfield, third base and the middle infield. Betten's versatility (he does everything but catch) is a plus and he helps out a pitching staff with his defensive skills. Learning to hit for more consistent contact would enhance his status.

BETTS, TODD - 3B - BL - b: 6/24/73
Betts either bulked up physically or loaded up his bats with plutonium in 1997; he went from one homer in 238 Double-A at-bats in 1996 to 20 in 439 at-bats at the same level in 1997. Betts is a patient hitter with power capability about halfway between his actual 1996 and 1997 levels. His defense is average, and he is about to be trampled by much younger, more exciting prospects. Betts is a candidate for a future major league bench role at best.

BETZSOLD, JAMES - OF - BR - b: 8/7/72
Betzsold is a musclebound free-swinging power hitter whose bat speed is likely too slow for him to compete against major league pitching. The outfielder has struck out in nearly 30% of his pro at-bats, often on bad pitches. His defensive and baserunning ability are both adequate at best. He is likely to drift up a level to Triple-A in 1998, but is no threat to make more than a cameo appearance in the Indians' major league lineup.

BICHETTE, DANTE - OF - BR - b: 11/18/63
Scouting: Bichette is the team's best clutch hitter. Even with the strike shortened seasons, and a broken hand that sidelined him the last three weeks of 1993, Bichette has averaged .316 with 29 homers and 114 RBI in his five years with the Rockies. His devil-may-care attitude helps him handle pressure situations late in the game. Defensively, however, most people feel his best position is DH. He played four seasons with a non-functional anterior cruciate ligament in his left knee, then had reconstructive surgery before last season in hopes that he could become a more complete player. Even with late-season improvement, however, his defense was still below-average.
1998: The Rockies' decision to re-sign free-agent Bichette hinged upon their dilemma with another free agent: Andres Galarraga. Only one of the two can stay because the team wants to make room for highly-touted rookie Todd Helton. With the Rockies, Bichette would again play left field and bat cleanup.
1997: Slowed by his return from off-season reconstructive knee surgery, Bichette lost power in his swing and mobility in the field. After averaging 35.5 homers the previous two seasons, he had just 26, and his stolen base total fell precipitously, too. Still, he was productive at the plate even with his loss of both power and speed.
1996: After his near-MVP season of 1995, Bichette slipped a little, but he still drove in 141 runs and recorded his only 30/30 season.

	AB	R	HR	RBI	SB	BA
1995 Colorado	579	102	40	128	13	.340
1996 Colorado	633	114	31	141	31	.313
1997 Colorado	561	81	26	118	6	.308

BIEREK, KURT - OF - BL - 9/13/72
In his first season at the Double-A level, playing at Norwich, Bierek showed some promise by hitting .269 with 18 home runs and 78 RBI in 480 at-bats. He was the Yankees' sixth-round selection in the 1993 draft, but has not been moving up the minor-league ladder fast.

BIESER, STEVE - C/OF - BB - b: 8/4/67
Bieser has bounced around the minors since 1989, peaking at Triple-A Ottawa in 1996 when he hit .322 with 27 steals. Last year, he was on the Mets' farm at Triple-A Norfolk. His journey appeared over, after he hit just .164 in 41 games.

	AB	R	HR	RBI	SB	BA
1997 New York NL	69	16	0	4	2	.246

BIGGIO, CRAIG - 2B - BR - b: 12/14/65
Scouting: Biggio is the best second baseman in baseball. A solid major league performer for nine seasons, Biggio gained recognition as one of the top players in the game in 1997. He has a rare combination of speed, power, defensive skills and overall baseball instincts. He and teammate Jeff Bagwell are the two best players the Astros have ever had. Neither has missed a game in the last two years. Biggio's durability is especially noteworthy since he plays so hard and he has led the league in being hit by pitches for the each of the last three years.
1998: Biggio will have trouble matching what appears to be a career year in 1997. At age 32, he is on the back end of his peak years. However, he should remain near the top of his game for at least three more seasons.
1997: Biggio had his best season, reaching personal highs in runs, hits, RBI, on-base percentage (.415) and slugging average (.501). His 146 runs scored were the highest National League total since Chuck Klein in 1932.
1996: Biggio's production was down slightly in every category compared to 1995. He appeared to tire late in the season and had a poor September. He temporarily yielded his position as the top second baseman in the National League to Eric Young.

	AB	R	HR	RBI	SB	BA
1995 Houston	553	123	22	77	33	.302
1996 Houston	605	113	15	75	25	.288
1997 Houston	619	146	22	81	47	.309

BLAIR, BRIAN - OF - BL - b: 4/9/72
A lefty outfielder with little power or speed, Blair didn't hit much even though it was his second go-around at Double-A Tulsa in the Rangers organization. That's not a surprise though, his .262 average of this past season is a career high.

BLANCO, HENRY - C - BR - b: 8/29/71
A career minor-league catcher with a .234 lifetime average in seven seasons on the Dodger farm before 1997, Blanco hit .313 at Triple-A Albuquerque in 1997, and then went two-for-five with the Dodgers, including a home run. If he retired now, Blanco would have a career .400 batting average and 1.000 slugging average. In previous brief attempts to master Triple-A pitching, Blanco had managed only a .227 mark in 1995 and one-for-six in 1996, so it was something of a breakthrough year. Blanco had been a third baseman before he converted to catcher two years ago, so he offers some versatility, too.

BLAUSER, JEFF - SS - BR - b: 11/8/65
Scouting: Unlike most shortstops, Blauser is something of a free-swinging power hitter, striking out and walking more than most. He doesn't have much speed, and his defense is unspectacular, but at his 1997 level he is one of the most valuable shortstops in the National League.
1998: The Braves worked hard to re-sign Blauser but settled on Walt Weiss. Blauser just had his career year. Don't expect a repeat of his spectacular 1997 season, but another season of

double-digit home runs with a good on-base percentage would seem probable.

1997: Rebounding from numerous injuries in 1996, Blauser saved his job and possibly his career with a great year, posting higher slugging and on-base percentages than Chipper Jones. He hit .405 in April and was a big part of the Braves strong start.

1996: Knee problems and a broken hand hampered Blauser, who missed half the season. The injuries and low average hid a decent offensive performance when healthy; Blauser's slugging and on-base percentages were his highest since his breakout 1993 campaign.

	AB	R	HR	RBI	SB	BA
1995 Atlanta	431	60	12	31	8	.211
1996 Atlanta	265	48	10	35	6	.245
1997 Atlanta	519	90	17	70	5	.308

BLOSSER, GREG - OF - BL - b: 6/26/71

This former major leaguer accepted a trip to the low minors to sign with the Devil Rays and have a shot at the big club in its inaugural season. After tearing up the Florida State League, Blosser was loaned by the Devil Rays to Triple-A Oklahoma City, where the competition was more in line with his abilities. In less than a half a season at Oklahoma City, Blosser hit .303 with twelve home runs. Blosser is a good all-around player and will get a shot at a starting outfield position with the Devil Rays.

BLOWERS, MIKE - 3B - BR - b: 4/24/65

Scouting: Blowers parlayed a career year in Seattle in 1995 — 23 homers, 96 RBI — into a lucrative free-agent deal with the Dodgers, who opted to let him go after his season was cut short by a torn anterior cruciate ligament and torn lateral cartilage in his left knee in July of 1996. He has some power and is a career .300 hitter against lefthanders.

1998: Blowers is expected to again be a platoon player, although he could see more time if his knee continues to improve.

1997: Used almost exclusively as a first baseman while playing a few games in left field, Blowers showed he could still hit lefthanders, batting .319 with all five of his homers against lefthanders. He was seldom used at his nominal position, third base.

1996: The Dodgers' starting third baseman after being obtained in the off-season, Blowers had a career-high 19-game hitting streak before suffering his season-ending knee injury in July.

	AB	R	HR	RBI	SB	BA
1995 Seattle	439	59	23	96	2	.257
1996 Los Angeles	317	31	6	38	0	.265
1997 Seattle	150	22	5	20	0	.293

BLUM, GEOFF - 2B - BB - b: 4/26/73

Blum is a tall, awkward infielder, whose range is short at both second base and shortstop, and who doesn't swing a potent bat. For some reason, the Expos like him. He's still young enough that he could improve, and, since he seems to be liked, he could work himself into a utility role in the majors at some point. However, he's unlikely to have any great impact.

BOCACHICA, HIRAM - SS - BR - b: 3/4/76

Bocachica, the Expos' first-round draft pick in 1994, is a good hitting prospect with above-average speed. He had a solid season in 1997 at Double-A Harrisburg but can't find a position. He's washed out at second base and shortstop and may not have enough power to play the outfield in the major leagues.

BOGAR, TIM - SS - BR - b: 10/28/66

Scouting: Bogar is an outstanding defensive player and is exceptionally popular in the clubhouse. He doesn't hit for power or average but his offensive production is adequate for a middle infielder; Bogar has strong defensive skills.

1998: Bogar should build on his success in 1997 and is likely to get more playing time than in any other season. He should hit about .240 with five to ten each of home runs and stolen bases.

1997: Houston obtained Bogar in a trade with the Mets when it became evident that Pat Listach was not the answer at shortstop. Bogar took over as the starting shortstop in late June and had his best major league season. His year ended in early September when he was hit by a pitch and broke his wrist. He reached personal highs in at-bats, runs, RBI, homers and stolen bases.

1996: Bogar had a poor season as a utility infielder with the Mets.

	AB	R	HR	RBI	SB	BA
1995 New York NL	145	17	1	21	1	.290
1996 New York NL	89	17	0	6	1	.213
1997 Houston	241	30	4	30	4	.249

BOGGS, WADE - 3B - BL - b: 6/15/58

Scouting: Boggs remains a dangerous, crafty bat handler with excellent strikezone judgment, quick hands, and a prescient ability to know where the ball is going to be pitched. Age has brought on problems with his back, wrists and, in 1997, vision difficulties. All these problems come and go; he can dominate pitchers one day and then be dominated by them the next day. One problem that persists is an inability to drive in runs in critical situations. Boggs has come a long way down from his "comeback" level when he first arrived in New York — and that was a long way down from his glory days with the Red Sox.

1998: Inconsistency has made Boggs a risk as an everyday third baseman. Platooning doesn't produce steady results, either, because his problems are his own physical woes, not a question of which arm the pitcher is using. The Yankees declined to pick up the $2 million option on Boggs' contract. He will need to be open-minded about a backup role and a lower salary this year.

1997: Boggs won the everyday third base job in spring training, hit .311 in April, and then slumped to .143 in May. He was in and out of the lineup all summer. It took a .417 finish in September to bring his average up to a more acceptable level for the year. Boggs was obviously not the same player he had once been.

1996: The beginning of his decline was visible. By mid-summer Boggs had a stiff back, resulting in the lowest RBI total of his 15-year career. Concerned Yankees' General Manager Bob Watson acquired Charlie Hayes, and Boggs appeared in only 14 games during September, but he got the World Series ring that escaped him in Boston.

	AB	R	HR	RBI	SB	BA
1995 New York AL	460	76	5	63	1	.324
1996 New York AL	501	80	2	41	1	.311
1997 New York AL	353	55	4	28	0	.292

BOGLE, BRYAN - OF - BR - b: 5/18/73

Bogle was formerly in the Cubs organization, and later signed as a free agent by the Orioles in 1995. He had an unimpressive season at Double-A last year and doesn't have any outstanding tools or skills. He is not considered a prospect.

BOKEMEIER, MATT - SS - BB - b: 8/7/72

Bokemeier's first season at Double-A did little to make him a prospect at the major league level; he hit .231 with five homers and 43 RBI. Since Bokemeier is not a base stealer, he'll need to show more at the plate to advance.

BOLICK, FRANK - DH - BB - b: 6/28/66

At age 31, he's pretty old to be considered a prospect, but the career minor-leaguer hit for average and power in limited playing time at Double-A Midland last year. Bolick would help himself by cutting down the strikeouts. He's not one of the youngsters the Angels are grooming, but he has a chance to get another shot at the majors if he keeps hitting, particularly if he hits for power.

BONDS, BARRY - OF - BL - b: 7/24/64

Scouting: Bonds is a tremendous all-around hitter — the biggest failing he has is that pitchers pretty much refuse to pitch to him, as witnessed by his 34 intentional walks last year and 296 total walks over the past two seasons. Bonds has excellent plate discipline, works the count well, hits for excellent power and average, has outstanding speed and is a Gold Glove left fielder. Even more to the point, his presence makes good players around him even better.

1998: Expect more of the same from Bonds.

1997: Bonds endured a lot of nagging from fans and press for not stepping up to the task of being a leader or carrying the team for much of the year. He got off to a slow start but was consistently phenomenal over the last four months of the year and finished with his usual statistical brilliance. Bonds was truly at his best in September, when he hit seven homers, including one in each game against the Dodgers in mid-September. Those blows broke L.A.'s back and essentially sealed a pennant for San Francisco.

1996: Bonds was as consistent as always. The only things that differentiate his 1996 season from all others are: 1) He put up MVP numbers and didn't win, 2) he became the second player to join the 40/40 club, and 3) he set a National League record with 151 walks.

	AB	R	HR	RBI	SB	BA
1995 San Francisco	506	109	33	104	31	.294
1996 San Francisco	517	122	42	129	40	.308
1997 San Francisco	532	123	40	101	37	.291

BONIFAY, KEN - 3B - BL - b: 9/1/70

There is doubt that this guy would still be playing professional baseball if it wasn't for the fact his uncle, Cam Bonifay, is the Pirates' General Manager. He hit .243-6-42 in 95 games at Double-A Carolina in 1996. In 1997 Bonifay played in 22 games for Carolina posting a .176 batting average in 68 at-bats.

BONILLA, BOBBY - OF/3B - BB - b: 2/23/63

Scouting: Bonilla has become a much more cerebral hitter as he has aged, though his raw power has begun to wane. He chases bad pitches less often, and has learned to identify the most hittable pitch of an at-bat and attack it. Defensively, he gives a professional effort at third base, but has below-average range and a passable arm. He did not serve as the designated hitter in the post-season, as he conclusively proved in his American League days that he is more effective at the plate when he has to play the field. His willingness to play hurt in the post-season erased any doubts about his ability to lead a ballclub.

1998: Though the Marlins were interested in reducing their financial commitments for 1998, Bonilla's contract figured to be difficult to move. Therefore, he's likely to return to South Florida, where his career decline should begin in earnest. His on-base percentages have trended upward in recent years, but his slugging percentages have trended downward. He's on his way to becoming a barely average third baseman.

1997: The switch-hitting Bonilla was a major upgrade over Terry Pendleton at third base, and was one of the major reasons for the Marlins' evolution into a powerhouse. He benefited from opposing pitchers' unwillingness to challenge Gary Sheffield, and the abundance of runners on base made him an RBI force despite his reduced power.

1996: Bonilla navigated right field with the Orioles after flopping as a designated hitter. He overcame his slow start to post trademark Bonilla numbers, albeit in a context of similar players with the O's. The Orioles wanted him back, but the Marlins made him an offer he couldn't refuse.

	AB	R	HR	RBI	SB	BA
1995 two teams	554	96	28	99	0	.329
1996 Baltimore	595	107	28	116	1	.287
1997 Florida	562	77	17	96	6	.297

BONNICI, JAMES - 1B - BR - b: 1/21/72

After a solid 1996 season at Triple-A Tacoma (.292, 26 homers and 74 RBI), Bonnici regressed in 1997 and is unlikely ever to reach the majors.

BOONE, AARON - 3B - BR - b: 3/9/73

Scouting: Boone has developed into the Reds' best prospect, featuring good power, a high average and some speed. His only weakness offensively is a lack of patience, which could hurt him when he moves to the next level. Boone is considered a good defensive third baseman and is ready for the majors. He is a little old to be considered a great prospect, but he should be a productive everyday player. Aaron is the younger brother of teammate Bret.

1998: Boone could get a chance as a regular if he has a strong spring and the Reds decide to move Willie Greene (who has struggled defensively at third base) to another position or another team. If Greene remains, a platoon/reserve role for Boone is likely at the start of the season. Boone's defense may give him the edge in the long run over Greene.

1997: Boone followed up his solid Double-A season with a fine season at Triple-A Indianapolis, hitting .290 with 22 home runs and 11 steals. His performance earned him a late-season callup to Cincinnati.

1996: After struggling in his first shot at Double-A in 1995, Boone established himself as a significant prospect with a strong season at Chattanooga, hitting .288 with 44 doubles, 17 home runs and 21 steals.

	AB	R	HR	RBI	SB	BA
1997 Cincinnati	49	5	0	5	1	.245

BOONE, BRET - 2B - BR - b: 4/6/69

Scouting: Before having surgery on his elbow to remove bone spurs in April of 1997, Boone was one of the National League's best second basemen as he was a combination of good power and solid defense. He hasn't been the same since rushing back two weeks after the operation.

1998: If Boone can return to his former self, he can play second base for just about anybody. He has a lot to prove as he's coming off two bad seasons.

1997: Boone posted career low numbers in batting and slugging averages and his on base percentage was under .300 for the second consecutive season.

1996: Boone rushed back to the Reds lineup two weeks after having bone spurs removed from his elbow in April. He suffered for it posting numbers in batting, slugging and on base averages that were career lows at the time.

	AB	R	HR	RBI	SB	BA
1995 Cincinnati	513	63	15	68	5	.267
1996 Cincinnati	520	56	12	69	3	.233
1997 Cincinnati	443	40	7	46	5	.223

BOOTY, JOSH - 3B - BR - b: 4/29/75

Scouting: The Marlins' 1994 first-round pick has understandably had second thoughts about spurning a budding football career, as he has tallied 503 strikeouts in 1371 minor-league at-bats, versus only 108 walks. The wild swinger does have excellent raw physical ability — his offensive performance has gradually improved against better pitching, and he has a cannon arm at third base. The Marlins will be patient to a fault with a player possessing such obvious tools.

1998: Booty will continue to move upwards despite his struggles, and will play third base at Triple-A Charlotte. He will never be a high average contact hitter, but if he could just manage a .250 average with 50 walks, he could be a viable major leaguer. He has 25-30 homer potential, possibly more if he would work a deep count now and then.

1997: Booty crashed some prodigious homers at Double-A Portland, and nailed almost half of his hits for extra bases while playing solid defense. He barely kept his average above the Mendoza line, however. The season must be considered a success, as he improved all of his numbers despite a two-level jump.

1996: It was an awful season for Booty. At age 21, he could do no better than .206 with 195 strikeouts at lower Class A Kane County. He tried to hit every pitch eight miles, and was openly pining for football by season's end.

BORDERS, PAT - C - BR - b: 5/14/63

Scouting: Borders was a backup catcher for five different teams in 1995 and 1996 before finding a home with the Indians in 1997. He is a veteran who has the respect of his pitching staff, and is a sound technical receiver behind the plate, though his throwing arm is now below major league average. He is a wild swinger who will rip a mistake fastball into the gaps with occasional home run power. He is a perfect backup catcher on a playoff-caliber team because of his postseason pedigree.

1998: The Indians would love him back, as they aren't excited about prospect Einar Diaz as the major league backup. However, if Sandy Alomar were to revert to his injury-riddled ways, Borders wouldn't be an everyday answer. Another professional 150 at-bat season is likely in store.

1997: Borders' workload was the lightest of his career, and it perked up his bat. He was suddenly nearly a .300 hitter for the first time in his major league career. Opposing baserunners challenged him often, and their success rate against Borders was above league average. He was a stabilizing influence in the clubhouse on a team in transition.

1996: Borders bounced from the Cards to the Angels to the White Sox, filling in for injured incumbent catchers. His performance was satisfactory, but he was released in favor of younger backup catcher options.

	AB	R	HR	RBI	SB	BA
1995 two teams	178	15	4	13	0	.208
1996 St. Louis	69	3	0	4	0	.319
1996 Chicago AL	151	12	5	14	0	.258
1997 Cleveland	159	17	4	15	0	.296

BORDICK, MIKE - SS - BR - b: 7/21/65

Scouting: Bordick's "blue collar" playing style is a throwback to the old days. He's a strong team player, bunting, moving runners up, hustling in the field, etc. A solid contact hitter who can hit .250-.280, Bordick has enough power for a handful of homers, 15-20 doubles and 50 RBI in a good year; he can steal a dozen bases if needed. He's not expected to provide hitting, so he bats ninth for the Orioles which diminishes the pitches he gets to hit. Bordick plays for his glove; he's an excellent fielder with good range, a strong arm and good hands. He works well with other Oriole infielders to form one of the best infields in baseball.

1998: The early season pressures of a big new contract and filling Cal Ripken' shoes at shortstop are things of the past, and he should avoid the early season slump that he had in 1997.

1997: Signed to a big contract by the Orioles and supplanting legendary Cal Ripken at shortstop, Bordick began the season trying hard to show that he was worth the money and, especially, the shift of Ripken to third base. The result was overswinging and poor hitting. But Bordick came around at mid-season, contributing to a strong Orioles stretch run with some timely clutch hits and excellent defensive play.

1996: Bordick had one of his weaker hitting seasons in his last year with the Athletics.

	AB	R	HR	RBI	SB	BA
1995 Oakland	428	46	8	44	11	.264
1996 Oakland	525	46	5	54	5	.240
1997 Baltimore	509	55	7	46	0	.236

BORRERO, RITCHIE - C - BR - b: 1/5/73

Scouting: Borrero is an awkward catcher with no obvious strengths right now. His mechanics are sloppy and he doesn't throw that well. He also is not much of a hitter. He has a slow bat and poor command of the strike zone. Borrero has decent size and might be able to add needed strength to his frame.

1998: Borrero will find himself in Double-A or Triple-A, but it might be as a backup to a catcher with more promise or big-league potential.

1997: Borrero began the season in Double-A, splitting time with Joe DePastino. He got a promotion to Triple-A only because of the promotion of Walt McKeel to the majors. When the Red Sox acquired Jason Varitek from the Mariners, Borrero was returned to Double-A.

1996: Borrero, perhaps already cast as an organizational catcher, spent time with three different teams at the lower levels of the minors, getting no more than 92 at-bats at any one stop.

BOSTON, D.J. - 1B - BL - b: 9/6/71

Boston is strong and looks like he's a hitter when he's at the plate; he's 6'7", but he doesn't produce often enough. The brother of Daryl Boston, he played the 1997 season in the Rockies organization, his third in the past two years. He hit one less homer this season at the Double-A level and the chance of him following in big brother's footsteps to the majors is growing increasingly slim.

BOURNIGAL, RAFAEL - 2B/SS - BR - b: 5/12/66
Scouting: The quintessential utility player, Bournigal is a good contact hitter who can execute well with the bat, be it hit-and-run or sacrifice bunt. He has no power, though he is subject to hot streaks at the plate. He can fill in at second, third and short, and is a great player off the bench in the event of injury. That is, however, the only reason he would start on a regular basis.
1998: 1997 redux. Bournigal will cull a couple of hundred at-bats, field well, hit no homers, and generally do everything that is expected of him. He doesn't seem to have what it takes to play every day, but as a replacement he is just fine.
1997: Filling in for the oft-injured, in-over-his-head Batista, Bournigal hit well enough and handled his duties on the field well. He knows his role, and his manager knows his capabilities, and thus got the most out of him.
1996: Bournigal actually surprised everyone by flirting with the .300 mark for a few weeks, though his final numbers were much more in line with his capabilities. His glove was what kept him around in a utility role.

	AB	R	HR	RBI	SB	BA
1996 Oakland	252	33	0	18	4	.242
1997 Oakland	222	29	1	20	2	.279

BOWERS, BRENT - OF - BL - b: 5/2/71
Concerned about their lack of major league quality outfielders, the Phillies invited every journeyman flychaser they could find to 1997 spring training, leading to a Triple-A logjam of underachievers. Bowers lost out for playing time and had trouble getting off the bench. He's a hard-nosed scrapper who gets the most out of his limited natural ability. He swings at just about anything, and flares the ball to all fields while making consistent contact. He is an aggressive defender but a sub-par arm limits him to left field. Bowers is an entertaining player with a secure future at the Double-A or Triple-A level, but with no real chance of securing a big-league job.

BRADSHAW, TERRY - OF - BL - b: 2/3/69
Bradshaw was regarded among the Cardinals' top prospects just a couple of years ago, but his age and the log jam of outfielders in front of him have pushed him out of the picture. Taken off the 40-man roster before 1997, the fine defensive outfielder with generally average offensive skills returned to Triple-A for a fourth year and batted .249; 13 points below his minor-league average. He probably will need to be signed into another organization as a minor-league free agent to find a fresh chance.

BRADY, DOUG - 2B - BB - b: 11/23/69
A former replacement player, this little infielder is not in the White Sox' long-range plans. Brady is a switch-hitter with poor plate discipline, negligible power and only marginal speed; he's a career .260 hitter in seven minor-league seasons. Considering his serious shortcomings with the bat he'd need to do a lot of "little" things to earn a big-league job, but he's not an especially brilliant fielder, either. Brady has peaked at Triple-A.

BRAGG, DARREN - OF - BL - b: 9/7/69
Scouting: Bragg is not a physically gifted player. He has some strength for a small player, but can still be overpowered by a good fastball. Even though he's been cast as a leadoff type in the past, he does not have base-stealing speed. Defensively, his range is below average for a center fielder, but he plays hard and does a good job of hustling to the ball.
1998: Bragg will find himself back in a fourth outfielder role, especially with the great improvement of young center fielder Michael Coleman in '97. At best, Bragg will regain at least a platoon role in center field if Coleman struggles in the spring.
1997: Bragg proved with his play that he is not a quality regular. Pitchers found his bat a little slow and started challenging him more, leading to a drop in his previously impressive on-base percentage. Bragg held his own against righthanders, but struggled against lefties, showing again that he needs help there.
1996: Bragg responded to a mid-season trade and a chance to play every day by posting a fine .357 on-base percentage in Boston and helping to ignite a late-season surge by the Red Sox.

	AB	R	HR	RBI	SB	BA
1995 Seattle	145	20	3	12	9	.234
1996 Seattle-Boston	417	74	10	47	14	.261
1997 Boston	513	65	9	57	10	.257

BRANSON, JEFF - 3B/SS - BL - b: 1/26/71
Scouting: Branson is a versatile utilityman capable of filling in at second base, shortstop and third base. The lefthanded hitter has better offensive credentials than most of his ilk; his slugging percentage exceeded .400 in his last three full seasons with the Reds (1994-96). Branson is a viable platooner who handles the bat well against righthanders with some power to the gaps. His defensive ability and speed are adequate at best.
1998: Enrique Wilson will likely be entrusted with the Tribe's second base job in 1998; Branson should ease that transition by spelling the switch-hitter against tough righthanded hurlers.
1997: Branson began the year in Cincinnati, but didn't fit into the ongoing youth movement. The Indians needed a veteran middle-infield backup to serve as insurance against a breakdown by Tony Fernandez, so it was a natural fit. He was also a valuable lefthanded bat off the bench, as the Indians' bench listed heavily to the right before his acquisition. He was a consistent line drive hitter who made all of the plays within his limited range in the field.
1996: With Willie Greene again unable to take the third base job and run with it on a full time basis, Branson again wound up with more playing time than expected in Cincinnati. He had his worst season since 1993, as his numbers fell across the board.

	AB	R	HR	RBI	SB	BA
1995 Cincinnati	331	43	12	45	2	.260
1996 Cincinnati	311	34	9	37	2	.244
1997 Cleveland	170	14	3	12	1	.200

BRANYAN, RUSSELL - 3B - BB - b: 12/19/75
Branyan is a home run machine. After taking a little time to adjust to pitching at each successive minor-league level, Branyan then levels that pitching. His homers are hit deep to all fields; his power is for real. Branyan also strikes out often but has reduced his strikeout rate each of the last three seasons while drawing more walks. He's a limited defensive player with below-average speed, but has a good arm. Branyan led Class A Kinston with 25 homers and 70 RBI in 1997 and will likely advance to Double-A Akron. He's a candidate to reach the majors as a cleanup hitter.

BREAM, SCOTT - 2B/OF - BB - b: 11/4/70
Bream played at Double-A and Triple-A for the Tigers in 1997 without distinguishing himself at either stop. He can steal some

bases but is a utility player at best should he reach the majors.

BREDE, BRENT - OF - BL - b: 9/13/71
Scouting: Brede offers a quick bat that will allow him to hit for average. The problem is he plays right field and first base and doesn't have the power needed at those positions to establish himself. At age 25, he is still developing but, so far, has not shown power potential. Defensively he is no better than average.
1998: With Minnesota, Brede was relegated to a reserve role or to the minor leagues, but with Arizona he has a shot to be a regular outfielder or a multi-position utility player with lots of playing time.
1997: Entering the season with only 20 major-league at-bats, Brede handled big-league pitching well, batting .270 in 190 at-bats. He spent much of the season getting extra lessons on proper techniques in right field.
1996: Brede hit .348 for Triple-A Salt Lake — the highest average of his six-year professional career.

	AB	R	HR	RBI	SB	BA
1997 Minnesota	190	25	3	21	7	.274

BRIDGES, KARY - 2B - BL - b: 10/27/71
The Pittsburgh Pirates picked up the speedy second baseman from the Houston organization early last season in a minor-league deal and he split the year between Double-A and Triple-A. Bridges brings some speed to the table but his woeful defense will likely prevent him from ever reaching the major leagues.

BRIGGS, STONEY - OF - BR - b: 13/26/71
Briggs has a little power, a little speed, but nowhere to play in the Padres outfield, with Steve Finley patrolling center field. He's still young enough that his prospects for major league playing time are a little better than slim, but not much.

BRINKLEY, DARRYL - OF - BR - b: 23/23/68
An outfielder with an interesting story, Brinkley has played in Italy, Holland, Mexico and the independent Northern League. Signed by the Padres, he has played well in their farm system. Brinkley has good range but a weak arm. He hit .307 with five homers, 33 RBI and ten stolen bases. He's old and running out of time but he may end up as a reserve outfielder in the majors. It's about the only league where he hasn't yet played.

BRITO, JORGE - C - BR - b: 6/22/66
After receiving little playing time in the Colorado system in 1996, Brito signed with Toronto and received even less playing time with Triple-A Syracuse last year. Barring a miracle Brito's career is finished.

BRITO, LUIS - SS - BB - b: 4/12/71
Brito has spent nine years in the minors, first with the Phillies, lately with the Braves. He had his best season ever in a full year at Double-A Greenville, batting .289 in 97 games. But he has no power, only marginal speed and swings at too many bad pitches. He's a decent defensive player, but won't advance much more because he just can't hit enough.

BRITO, TILSON - SS - BR - b: 5/28/72
Scouting: Brito's speed and ability to make contact were once considered strengths, but neither has translated to the major league level. He strikes out too often for someone with modest power potential and although he has good range at second base, he has not looked confident as a shortstop.
1998: Brito will turn twenty-six this season so there is still time for him to achieve. Brito is the type of player that would land at least a bench job if he doesn't win a starting spot outright.
1997: The acquisition of Carlos Garcia and then Mariano Duncan made Brito redundant to the Blue Jays. He was placed on waivers and was promptly picked up by Oakland. With Toronto, he spent most of the season on the major league bench and had little chance to gain any consistent playing time, thereby hurting his performance.
1996: With Toronto conducting an open audition for a second baseman and an injury to Felipe Crespo, Brito played 26 games with the Jays but spent most of the year with Triple-A Syracuse. He had his best year there power-wise (ten home runs, 22 doubles) and when he was with the big league team, he often started.

	AB	R	HR	RBI	SB	BA
1996 Toronto	80	10	1	7	1	.238
1997 Oakland	172	17	2	14	1	.238

BROACH, DONALD - OF - BR - b: 7/18/71
Broach is an organizational player whose chance for advancement suffered when the Reds traded for Jon Nunnally and Chris Stynes. He was a middle-round draft pick out of college, and has had mediocre seasons in the minor leagues. He has little power and doesn't have good base stealing ability. That, combined with the other, much better outfield prospects in the Reds' farm system, means Broach has no future in the majors.

BROGNA, RICO - 1B - BL - b: 4/18/70
Scouting: Brogna has 20-homer power, which isn't all that impressive compared to other first basemen. He has settled in as a major league caliber hitter since the Mets allowed him to return to his opposite field-hitting ways, after the Tigers had encouraged him to pull the ball as a minor-leaguer. However, he struggles against lefthanded pitching, batting under .200 against southpaws in each of the last two seasons. He is brilliant defensively, showing solid range and saving many errors with excellent scoops of bad throws. His plate discipline is poor, and he runs the bases intelligently despite being hampered with chronic knee problems.
1998: Though Brogna will turn 27 — a peak production age — chances are high that Brogna will falter. His knee problems risk an extended disabled list stint. Also, his overaggressive approach at the plate leaves him vulnerable to extended slumps. He is so good with the glove that he would be allowed to play his way out of any bad hitting spell.
1997: Brogna added much needed home run power to the Phillies' puny offense in 1997. He benefited from batting between righthanders Scott Rolen and Mike Lieberthal, minimizing exposure to lefthanded pitching. Though his mainstream power numbers looked respectable in 1997, his on-base and slugging percentages ranked near the bottom of National League first basemen. A contending team couldn't carry Brogna at first base unless they had substantial offensive surpluses elsewhere.
1996: Brogna was limited by knee problems to 55 games with the Mets. When healthy, he showed opposite-field power but poor plate discipline. After the season, he was traded to Philadelphia for Toby Borland and Ricardo Jordan.

Benson's Baseball Player Guide: 1998

	AB	R	HR	RBI	SB	BA
1995 New York NL	495	72	22	76	0	.289
1996 New York NL	188	18	7	30	0	.255
1997 Philadelphia	543	68	20	81	12	.252

BROOKS, JERRY - OF - BR - b: 3/23/67
Brooks hit .288 with 34 homers and 107 RBI for the Marlins' Triple-A Charlotte team in 1996 but got only five at-bats in the majors that year; he had previously surfaced with the Dodgers in 1993. Brooks went to Japan to play last year, and had more trouble with Japanese Pacific League pitching than he had with the International League in 1996. The memory of what he did with Charlotte provided the best hope that he might find work in the post-expansion major leagues.

BROOKS, RAMY - C - BR - b: 4/12/70
Long-time A-ball farmhand Brooks got to Double-A in 1997 for the first time in his eight-year pro career, and also played three games at Triple-A Omaha. For Wichita he slumped to .229 with four homers and sixteen RBI. Brooks is a below-average defensive catcher whose power has dried up in the higher minors. He is a dim prospect.

BROSIUS, SCOTT - 3B/OF - BR - b: 8/15/66
Scouting: Brosius has solid long-ball power, but is inconsistent in applying his hitting skills and then adjusting to pitchers over a prolonged period. On defense, he is a revelation, as he plays a fabulous third base, can handle short just fine, as well as playing the outfield; he has a great arm. Brosius also has good speed.
1998: Because of the combination of salary, free agency, expansion, and the number of infield candidates the A's possess, Brosius' role was expendable in Oakland, and he went to New York for Kenny Rogers. The change of scenery will bring an improvement over a rugged 1997.
1997: Brosius' average dropped 100 points, and his production plummeted accordingly as he was never able to get on track offensively. Fraught with second guessing and the passivity which often accompany a slump, Brosius lost much of his aggressiveness and was thus victimized by most of the pitchers in the league. Fortunately, his glove continued to be glue no matter where on the field he played, or what he did at the plate.
1996: Given a chance to play regularly, including a shot at playing through slumps, Brosius turned in a fine year at the plate and in the field, reaching career highs in offensive categories despite missing six weeks with a broken elbow.

	AB	R	HR	RBI	SB	BA
1995 Oakland	388	69	17	46	4	.262
1996 Oakland	428	73	22	71	7	.304
1997 Oakland	479	59	11	41	9	.203

BROWN, ADRIAN - OF - BR - b: 2/7/74
Scouting: Brown is a speedy center fielder whose stock has risen in the Pirates' organization over the past two seasons. Brown plays outstanding defense and began to hit for a high batting average last season. He is a late bloomer, having been a 48th-round draft pick from a Mississippi high school in 1992.
1998: Considering the Pirates are down on Jermaine Allensworth, Brown will be given a chance to win the starting centerfielder's job this spring. He has come on strong in the minor leagues the past two years and caught the attention of Pirates' manager Gene Lamont.

1997: Brown was a surprise recall from Double-A Carolina in mid-May when Allensworth went on the disabled list with a broken hand. Though Brown's offensive numbers weren't impressive, he played good defense and showed flashes of being able to hit major-league pitching just before Allensworth got healthy.
1996: Brown emerged as a legitimate prospect, stealing an organization-high 45 bases while splitting the season between Class A Lynchburg and Carolina. He followed that up with a strong performance in the Arizona Fall League.

	AB	R	HR	RBI	SB	BA
1997 Pittsburgh	147	17	1	10	8	.190

BROWN, BRANT - 1B - BL - b: 6/22/71
Scouting: Brown is a poor-man's Mark Grace. He's a lefthanded hitter with a smooth swing, but he's not the hitter nor the fielder that Grace is. Grace was often maligned, especially early in his career, for not hitting for enough power, but Brown has even less than that.
1998: Brown's future with the Cubs, as for many of Chicago's players, is in limbo. If Grace doesn't return Brown could be the starting first baseman, although fans ultimately will be disappointed with his offense. And it's obvious from his performance in 1997 that he simply doesn't have what it takes to play the outfield. His most likely scenario for 1998 is as a reserve/pinch-hitter in the majors, or full-time play in Triple-A.
1997: Brown started the season as the Cubs opening day left fielder because of a strong showing in spring training. Brown beat out Brooks Kieschnick and Robin Jennings for the job, although both other players had equally fine spring showings. But the regular season was a disaster for Brown, who didn't hit and fielded the position poorly. He was sent down after only a few weeks and never got another chance the rest of the season, despite hitting .301 with sixteen homers for Triple-A Iowa.
1996: Brown came out of nowhere and had an awesome three-week stretch filling in for an injured Mark Grace. Brown, always a good hitter for batting average in the minors, went on a home run tear his first week in Chicago, which fooled Cub fans and management alike into thinking he was a much better player than he actually is.

	AB	R	HR	RBI	SB	BA
1996 Chicago NL	69	11	5	9	3	.304
1997 Chicago NL	137	15	5	15	2	.234

BROWN, DERMAL - OF - BL - b: 3/27/78
Brown was the Royals' top draft pick in 1996 and is considered a top power-hitting prospect. His first professional year bore out those expectations as he hit 13 homers in 298 at-bats for lower Class A Spokane last year; he was among Northwest League leaders in most hitting categories. Brown has some speed, but not enough to steal a lot of bases in the majors. He'll be pushed through the Royals' farm system quickly; they are desperate for credible power threats.

BROWN, EMIL - CF - BR - b: 12/29/74
Scouting: Brown is still raw; he jumped from Class A to the major leagues last season after being selected by Pittsburgh from Oakland in the Rule 5 Draft. Brown has power potential and good speed and is capable of playing all three outfield positions.
1998: Because Rule 5 dictates a player must stay on the major-league roster all year or be offered back to his original organization, Brown rotted on the bench with the Pirates last season.

Most likely, he will begin the season at Double-A Carolina, though Class A Lynchburg could also be his destination if he struggles in spring training. The Pirates will look at Brown in all three outfield spots to see where he fits best.
1997: The grand plan was for Brown to start about once a week. However, the grand plan also didn't include the Pirates' surprising run at a National League Central title that lasted until the season's final week. Thus, he didn't start a game in the second half until the last weekend of the year. Brown went to the Arizona Fall League at the end of the season to gain some much needed at-bats.
1996: Brown missed a majority of the season with Oakland's Class A Modesto farm club because of a broken bone in his right hand. Pirates assistant player development director Bill Bryk knew Brown from his days as a high school player in Chicago and recommended he be taken in the Rule 5 Draft.

	AB	R	HR	RBI	SB	BA
1997 Pittsburgh	95	16	2	6	5	.179

BROWN, JARVIS - OF - BR - b: 9/26/67
Brown is a speedy outfielder who doesn't hit much, can steal some bases and is stuck in Triple-A; he has been there for the past seven seasons. Brown has played some in the majors but his time is running out. At the age of 31 he is Triple-A outfield insurance for the big club.

BROWN, KEVIN - C - BR - b: 4/21/73
Scouting: Brown is a power-hitting catcher with a good arm. Like many young power hitters, Brown is a free-swinger, although he is making contact more frequently as he moves up through the minors. With the exception of throwing, his defensive skills behind the plate are adequate at best; he also has had some back problems, and thus he may need a position change at some point.
1998: Brown will turn 25 shortly after the season opens, and he needs to win at least a backup job in the majors by the end of the season. He could need both an impressive spring and a change of organization to accomplish that goal. He should start out at Triple-A once again.
1997: Brown's first season at Triple-A saw him struggle to a .241 average, but he did hit for power, clubbing 19 homers. His 111 strikeouts represented a decrease from 1996, when he struck out 150 times at Double-A. For the second straight year, he got a September cup of coffee in the majors. He languished behind both Ivan Rodriguez and Jim Leyritz on the Rangers' depth chart.
1996: Brown made great strides, particularly in hitting for power, and established himself as a major league hitting prospect, hitting .263 with 26 homers and 86 RBI at Double-A Tulsa.

BROWN, RANDY - SS - BR - b: 5/1/70
1996 was Brown's most successful season despite time spent on the DL. His .298 average and 11 homers for Double-A Trenton were easily career highs and earned Brown a promotion to Pawtucket. He's a good athlete who may be getting a little long in the tooth to be playing regularly at Double-A. In 1997 Brown played Double-A ball in Trenton for the Red Sox and Albany in the Yankees organization without putting up any significant numbers.

BROWN, RAY - 1B - BL - b: 7/30/72
Brown, Dusty Allen and Derrek Lee are causing a pileup at first base in the high minors for the Padres. Brown is considered one of the best pure hitting prospects in the organization and scouts love his bat control. He hit .352 with four homers and 30 RBI in 57 games at Double-A Mobile, then hit .257 in 41 games at Triple-A Las Vegas. Slow and stiff defensively, Brown is rough around the bag. He belongs in Triple-A, but where he plays is largely dependent upon where Lee ends up.

BROWN, RON - OF - BR - b: 1/17/70
Brown was the Marlins' 24th-round pick in 1993, but was used to fill the roster while younger prospects developed. Prior last year, his general offensive skills had been consistently below-average across the board, but 1997 was a surprising year for Brown at Double-A Norwich as he hit .286 with five homers, 50 RBI and a .350 on-base percentage.

BROWN, ROOSEVELT - OF - BL - b: 8/3/75
The Marlins obtained Brown from the Braves in the Terry Pendleton trade in late-1996. He showed a promising power/speed combination that year, but suffered through a disappointing campaign at both Class A levels last season. The lefthanded hitter swung wildly, was reluctant to use his above-average speed, and rarely drove the ball with authority. In the Marlins' deep system, it isn't wise to take a detour off of the fast track, especially if you're a 22-year-old, A-ball outfielder. Brown needs to unfurl a 20/20 season at Double-A in 1998 to get back in the hunt.

BRUMFIELD, JACOB - OF - BR - b: 5/27/65
Scouting: Brumfield has improved as a contact hitter the last few years. His 1997 totals don't show it but he has good power and at least average speed as a baserunner. He can play any of the three outfield positions with ease.
1998: Brumfield stated that he was not happy with his limited playing time in Toronto and, as the season ended last year, it appeared that he would not return. He turns thirty-three in May and although he has shown both power and speed in the past, he is running out of time.
1997: What little Brumfield did play was mostly as an emergency outfielder or as an occasional starter (about once a week). The addition of Jose Cruz, Jr., and a midseason appearance by Ruben Sierra didn't help him earn playing time.
1996: A trade from the Pirates to the Blue Jays brought Brumfield to life. He hit 12 home runs with the Blue Jays, eight of them at Sky Dome.

	AB	R	HR	RBI	SB	BA
1995 Pittsburgh	402	64	4	26	22	.271
1996 Pittsburgh	80	11	2	8	3	.250
1996 Toronto	308	52	12	52	12	.256
1997 Toronto	174	22	2	20	4	.207

BRUNO, JULIO - 2B - BR - b: 10/15/72
The third baseman showed some of the quickest reflexes in the Southern League in '97. His glove is as good as you'll find and no one in the league played the bunt better. His high number of errors are mostly a result of his terrific range. Bruno batted .265 with 31 extra-base hits in 438 at-bats at Jacksonville. He is a great clubhouse guy, but isn't much of a prospect for the majors. The Tigers are more enthralled with Ryan Balfe as a third base prospect; Bruno will be surpassed by Balfe this year.

BRYANT, PAT - OF - BR - b: 10/27/72
Scouting: Bryant is a good athlete, possessing some strength and speed. He is a bit awkward and raw as a baseball player, though. He doesn't react well to balls in left or right field. He also has a long swing at the plate and will struggle to hit at the higher levels.
1998: Bryant will probably get a chance to play a full season at Triple-A for the first time. It's likely that he'll struggle to hit for average at this level because of the serious holes in his swing.
1997: Bryant was released by the Indians in the spring, but ended up with the Boston organization. It may have helped that he is the nephew of Boston Assistant Scouting Director Erwin Bryant. Pat played well at Double-A Trenton (his fourth season in that league), and was promoted to Triple-A for the last few weeks of the season, but did not play a lot there.
1996: Apparently being phased out of Cleveland's plans, Bryant split the season between Double-A and Triple-A, but got only 173 at-bats total.

BUCCHERI, JIM - OF - BR - b: 11/12/68
Tendinitis in the elbow of his throwing arm healed last season when he played at Mexico City and Class A St. Petersburg. Throughout his minor-league career, Buccheri has been a respectable line-drive hitter with a game centered around speed, which he utilizes in the field and particularly on the basepaths; he stole 44 bases for Triple-A Ottawa in 1995. Buccheri likely will get a good look as a fourth outfielder with the Devil Rays.

BUCHANAN, BRIAN - OF - BR - b: 7/21/73
Buchanan has overcome what many believed to be a career-ending ankle injury to project himself into the big-league picture with a solid season at Double-A Norwich. Buchanan hit .312 with ten homers and 69 RBI in 117 games before being promoted to Triple-A Columbus where he hit .279 with four homers and seven RBI in 18 games. His outfield defense is adequate but not outstanding.

BUFORD, DAMON - OF - BR - b: 6/12/70
Scouting: Buford is a fleet-footed outfielder with an average arm. He hits lefthanded pitching well enough to be a platoon player, but he struggles against righthanders with decent stuff. He has occasional power, and that part of his game will likely to continue to develop. On a team loaded with offense at other positions, Buford would be an adequate center fielder, hitting toward the bottom of the lineup, but he doesn't get on base nearly enough to bat leadoff.
1998: Buford's speed and defense will guarantee him a roster spot in the majors, but he will need an impressive spring to earn more than a platoon role.
1997: After being handed the starting center field job in spring training, Buford never got going at the plate. In mid-summer, the Rangers traded for Tom Goodwin, and Buford's playing time disappeared. One bright spot was his stolen base efficiency; he was successful on 72% of his attempts, after a previous career mark of 57% coming into the season.
1996: Buford hit 70 points over his previous career average as an extra outfielder with Texas. He played errorless ball in center and right field.

	AB	R	HR	RBI	SB	BA
1995 New York NL	136	24	4	12	7	.235
1996 Texas	145	30	6	20	8	.283

BUHNER, JAY - OF - BR - b: 8/13/64
Scouting: Buhner is one of the most consistent power hitters in the game, averaging 41.3 homers and 128.7 RBI over the last three seasons while maintaining his solid defensive play in right field and a strong arm. His injury bugaboo is a thing of the past.
1998: The Mariners expect another strong, consistent season out of Buhner, a man who looks as if he could scare a ball out of the park.
1997: Buhner became only the fourth player in the American League to hit 40 homers in three consecutive seasons; Harmon Killebrew (1961-64), Frank Howard (1968-70) and Jimmie Foxx (1932-34) were the others. With the emphasis on power, Buhner's batting average slipped.
1996: Buhner settled into his power groove, setting career highs in every long-ball swinger's category — doubles, homers, RBI, runs and strikeouts.

	AB	R	HR	RBI	SB	BA
1995 Seattle	470	86	40	121	0	.262
1996 Seattle	564	107	44	138	0	.271
1997 Seattle	540	104	40	109	0	.243

BULLETT, SCOTT - OF - BL - b: 12/25/68
Ex-Cub Bullett played for the Orioles' Triple-A club last year. He didn't hit well, but stole some bases. He's a Triple-A extension of the bench awaiting a call from a major league team needing an experienced outfielder. The call won't likely come from the Orioles; they passed over Bullett last year, instead promoting David Dellucci from Double-A.

	AB	R	HR	RBI	SB	BA
1995 Chicago NL	150	19	3	22	8	.273
1996 Chicago NL	165	26	3	16	7	.212

BURKE, JAMIE - 3B - BR - b: 9/24/71
Burke is a utility type whom the Angels sent to the Arizona Fall League so he could gain some catching experience. He can play each position well defensively and has shown flashes of brilliance with the bat at a couple of levels in the organization. Learning to catch well could help move Burke ahead of other prospects in his class.

BURKS, ELLIS - OF - BR - b: 9/11/64
Scouting: A rare blend of power and speed, Burks ranks among the game's elite for his pure athleticism and overall abilities. His problem has been injuries. Once a Gold Glove center fielder, he now plays the position timidly — opposition runners automatically advance from first to third on grounders to center. He is much more comfortable in left field, where he was sensational in 1996, his career-best season. He has bulked up considerably with weights the past three seasons and the result has been considerably more power. In his first nine seasons, his career-high was 21 homers. He nearly doubled that in 1996, then still hit a high number of homers last year despite starting only 106 games. Burks can still catch up with high heat and he still runs all out on the bases.
1998: Don't expect Burks to stay healthy or to return to his base thievery of the past, but the power is for real. Plus, he's a good batsman, so he should continue to hit for a high average. Burks would be better off in left field than in center, but that's not going to happen in Colorado.
1997: Various injuries, especially a strained groin, limited Burks to just 119 games. He started slowly, hitting below .200 through mid-May. His stint on the DL through July coincided with the

team's swoon that included 15 losses in 16 games. Though his stolen base total dropped considerably, he finished strong — just like the Rockies — and had a respectable season.
1996: The key to his dream season was simple: good health. In the final season of a three-year, $9-million contract, Burks played in a career-high 156 games. After playing with enormous expectations most of his career, Burks finally reached them when he joined Henry Aaron (1963) as the only players to amass at least 200 hits, 30 stolen bases and 40 homers in the same season.

	AB	R	HR	RBI	SB	BA
1995 Colorado	278	41	14	49	7	.266
1996 Colorado	613	142	40	128	32	.344
1997 Colorado	424	91	32	82	7	.290

BURNITZ, JEROMY - OF - BL - b: 4/15/69
Scouting: A well-traveled player, Burnitz looks to have found a spot as a regular. He showed speed on the basepaths and in the field with power at the plate (a career-high homer total). He also showed he could hit lefthanders, which earned him a regular spot. He was prone to baserunning mistakes and tends to be streaky at the plate.
1998: Burnitz likely will start the season as the regular right fielder. In fact, the Brewers are interested in signing him to a contract extension.
1997: Burnitz had a breakthrough season and became the regular right fielder for the Brewers after starting the season in a platoon. He became only the third Brewer in team history to go over 20 homers and 20 steals in the same season. He led the team in homers and RBI and also showed a strong arm; he was near the top of the league in outfield assists.
1996: After playing 71 games as a fourth outfielder for the Indians, he came to Milwaukee in a deal for Kevin Seitzer. Burnitz didn't hit much in a part-time role.

	AB	R	HR	RBI	SB	BA
1996 Clev-Milwaukee	200	38	9	40	4	.265
1997 Milwaukee	494	85	27	85	20	.281

BURTON, DARREN - OF - BB - b: 9/16/72
Burton was once considered an above-average outfield prospect in the Royals' chain, but has now seemingly settled in as a Triple-A journeyman, most recently with the Phillies. He is a switch-hitter with decent power to the gaps who once possessed excellent speed. He stole 83 bases in the minors by age 20, but only 33 in the four years since. Burton was only a part-timer at Triple-A in 1997, and will likely find himself in a similar predicament in 1998. The Phillies never considered bringing up Burton last year despite giving several non-prospects a major league chance.

BURTON, ESSEX - 2B - BR - b: 5/16/69
Burton, a perennial fan pleaser and speedster, spent last year in the Independent League. He has limited range, a weak arm, and poor technique, with only his speed keeping his career alive.

BUSCH, MIKE - 1B/3B - BR - b: 7/7/68
The long-time Dodger farmhand hit a career-low .181 for the Indians with some power but still piled up the strikeouts at Triple-A Buffalo. He has had some good power years in the high minors, but it appears that he only has Triple-A bat speed and Pacific Coast League power. At best, Busch will find a Triple-A DH job. At worst, his pro career will be over in 1998.

	AB	R	HR	RBI	SB	BA
1995 Los Angeles	17	3	3	6	0	.235
1996 Los Angeles	83	8	4	17	0	.217

BUSH, HOMER - 2B - BR - b: 11/12/72
Bush broke his leg in 1996 at Triple-A Las Vegas in the Padres' organization. He came to the Yankees in 1997 as a part of the Hideki Irabu deal but it doesn't look like he is all the way back from the leg injury. He has lost his once-considerable speed which has diminished his base-stealing prowess and lessened his range in the field. Bush also swings at everything: in 2,200 minor-league plate appearances he is still yet to reach 100 walks. If he contributes to the Yanks at all it will be as a backup infielder.

BUTLER, BRETT - OF - BL - b: 6/15/57
Scouting: Although he says he's retired, we've heard that before. Butler is a speedy center fielder with good defense, a good batting eye and excellent on-base skills.
1998: Butler said he isn't going to play, but we'll see.
1997: He came all the way back from cancer and put up good numbers before hanging up the spikes.
1996: Butler came down with throat cancer, was operated upon and had to undergo six weeks of radiation treatment. All that didn't stop him from returning to the team in September. His comeback was courageous but short; after five games he suffered a broken hand that finally ended his season.

	AB	R	HR	RBI	SB	BA
1995 two teams	513	78	1	38	32	.300
1996 Los Angeles	131	22	0	8	8	.267
1997 Los Angeles	343	52	0	18	15	.283

BUTLER, RICH - OF - BL - b: 5/1/73
Scouting: Suddenly a top prospect, and taken early by the Devil Rays, Butler has the tools to be a successful major league player. He can hit for average and power, has a good eye and can steal bases. The Blue Jays' outfield was too crowded to accommodate him last year. Rich is the brother of ex-Jay Rob Butler.
1998: Although not guaranteed a roster spot, Butler will be in the major leagues this year and in the event of an injury, could sneak in as an everyday player. He is only getting better and could become an impact player soon.
1997: Butler had a fantastic Triple-A season, hitting for power (24 home runs) and average (.300). For good measure, he added 20 stolen bases and walked 60 times. He stated that he has already accomplished what he needs to in the minor leagues. Butler led the International League in runs scored and hits.
1996: Butler missed most of the season but did manage to steal four bases in ten games played with Class A Dunedin.

BUTLER, ROB - OF - BL - b: 4/10/70
Scouting: Butler is a slap hitter who got his first extended major league opportunity in 1997 with the Phillies. He has no extra-base power, and is not a viable top of the order candidate because of a lack of plate discipline. His speed was once an asset, but he has a sub-50% success rate stealing bases in five Triple-A seasons, with a seasonal high of seven steals over that period. His defensive range is average in center field, and his arm is adequate at best.
1998: Butler will likely head back to Triple-A on a full-time basis

in 1998. The Phillies consider at least three other minor-league outfielders to be ahead of him on their depth chart, and were expected to add a free agent by opening day, too. There might not even be room at Triple-A in the Phillies' organization for Butler.

1997: Truth be told, Butler did nothing to warrant a demotion during his 1997 major league trial. He hit as well or better than he had in recent memory in the minor leagues, stabilizing the center field position and the leadoff spot for a brief period prior to the acquisition of Midre Cummings.

1996: Butler suffered through his worst pro season at Triple-A Scranton, hitting for a career-low average (.255) with only three steals, not good production for a leadoff type.

	AB	R	HR	RBI	SB	BA
1997 Philadelphia	89	10	0	13	1	.292

BUXBAUM, DANNY - 1B - BR - b: 1/17/73

Strikeouts have been a bit of a problem, but Buxbaum has been impressive with his power. He was sent to the Mexican Winter League to learn how to hit breaking pitches better and perhaps cut down on the whiffs. He's limited to first base because of his range, but his power makes him a prospect well worth watching.

BYINGTON, JIMMIE - OF - BR - b: 8/22/73

In his fifth pro season, Byington made it out of A-ball, but hit just .235 in a platoon role at Double-A Wichita. He split time in the outfield, at second base and at shortstop as an all-purpose reserve. Byington is not on the Royals' hot track to the majors and will need another full year at Double-A with a better-defined role before he can be considered a true prospect.

CABRERA, JOLBERT - SS - BR - b: 12/8/72

Cabrera has a good arm, which allows him to play all over the infield, although his lack of agility makes third base his best position. He also has some speed. However, he's skinny and weak, and does not swing a powerful bat. He'll get some time in the majors because of his range of skills, but he's not likely to ever be a productive regular because of his lack of power.

CABRERA, ORLANDO - SS - BR - b: 3/2/74

Scouting: Cabrera, who began his professional career as a pitcher in 1993, has outstanding speed and a solid stroke. However, he still needs work on his strikezone judgment to become an effective leadoff hitter. He has good range and a strong arm at both middle-infield positions, though he is still inconsistent in making the routine play.

1998: Mike Lansing has become too expensive for the Expos, meaning second base will open up for Cabrera. The Expos are hoping Cabrera can handle leadoff duties, so shortstop Mark Grudzielanek can move down to a run-producing spot in the Expos' revamped batting order. However, Cabrera has just part of a year of experience at Triple-A and not too much can be expected of him too soon.

1997: Cabrera climbed three rungs of the Expos' organizational ladder, starting at Class A West Palm Beach then moving to Double-A Harrisburg and Triple-A Ottawa before landing in Montreal in September. Cabrera stole bases and hit with some pop in the lower levels but had a tougher time at Triple-A and in the majors.

1996: In his first full season of professional baseball, Cabrera had an outstanding season for the Expos' lower Class A Delmarva farm club.

CACERES, EDGAR - 2B - BB - b: 6/6/64

An older player obtained to help out at Triple-A, Caceres nonetheless hit for a high average and lent Vancouver the stability typical of six-year minor-league free agent. Caceres played mostly second base, but he's a utility type who once played several infield positions in the majors (Kansas City). His error total was up a bit last year, but he was moved around a lot in the Canadians' infield.

CAIRO, MIGUEL - 2B - BR - b: 5/4/74

Scouting: Cairo is a disciplined hitter and has been one of the hardest players to strike out in each of the professional leagues in which he has played. He has consistently hit in the .270's and .280's in the minor leagues, but has yet to learn how to take many walks despite his outstanding batting eye. Cairo also is an outstanding baserunner and has excelled in stealing bases.

1998: Cairo was one of the players expected to get a shot at the second base job opened by the retirement of Ryne Sandberg, but he was taken by the Devil Rays as their fourth pick. Cairo's outstanding defense and low strikeout total will give him a good chance at staying on the big-league roster the whole season. If he were to walk a little more he would make an outstanding leadoff hitter. He won't turn 24 until May, which is something that also will work in his favor; Cairo could improve rapidly over the next few seasons.

1997: Cairo saw a brief tour of duty with the Cubs at the end of the season, but was used primarily as a late-inning defensive replacement or pinch-hitter. He had a pretty good year at Triple-A Iowa, setting a career high with 35 doubles and stealing 40 bases in 55 attempts.

1996: His stock dropped somewhat after he had a below-average year with Toronto's Triple-A team. Cairo got in nine games with the Blue Jays early in the season, but spent the rest of the time in Syracuse, where he had only 14 doubles in 465 at-bats.

CAMERON, MIKE - OF - BR - b: 1/8/73

Scouting: Cameron has all the tools, he can hit, hit for power, run, field and throw. He doesn't have a great deal of power, but the ball just jumps off his bat. Cameron has good plate discipline that will get even better as he learns American League pitchers; he takes a lot of pitches. The White Sox are understandably high on their center fielder of the future.

1998: Cameron will have an everyday center field job and an important role in the White Sox' batting order. Expect him to add power gradually while providing all-around offensive production.

1997: Going into spring training, Cameron was not expected to have such an important role with the White Sox in 1997. But he finished the year as one of their most productive hitters and the regular center fielder. It was a solid rookie campaign.

1996: Cameron led the Double-A Southern League with 120 runs scored and 39 stolen bases. He also hit .300 with 28 homers and 71 walks to earn his second September cameo in the majors.

	AB	R	HR	RBI	SB	BA
1997 Chicago AL	379	63	14	55	23	.259

CAMERON, STANTON - OF - BR - b: 7/5/69

A career minor-leaguer signed out of the independent Big South League to protect Travis Lee in the Class A High Desert batting order in 1997, Cameron also protected his future with career highs in homers (33) and RBI (113) while adding 31 doubles. Like most power hitters, he'll strike out. Cameron's defense is adequate.

CAMERON, TROY - SS - BB - b: 8/31/78
Cameron, the first-round pick of the Braves in 1997 (29th overall), played at Rookie level Danville in the Appalachian League last year. Cameron showed above-average power for a middle infielder, but that was when he actually made contact. He struck out 80 times in 208 at-bats. Look for him to make his mark in A-ball this year.

CAMINITI, KEN - 3B - BB - b: 4/21/63
Scouting: When Caminiti had post-season surgery in the fall of '96 to repair two tears in his left rotator cuff, doctors said he wouldn't be 100 percent until the All-Star break of '97. Caminiti pushed the limits and was ready to play on opening day. But he wasn't the real Caminiti until the second half of the season. Defensively, Caminiti still made spectacular plays in '97 although he had problems with some balls hit right at him and on throws for un-Gold Glove like 24 errors.
1998: Caminiti is entering the final season of his Padre contract. If he remains injury-free and puts two '97 second halves together — it's like '96 all over again.
1997: Although they were off from his '96 career-year totals, Caminiti's final numbers were good. He was hitting .247 with six homers and 25 RBI at the break, but after the All-Star game, Caminiti hit .331 with 20 home runs and 65 RBI, replicating his MVP pace in '96.
1996: Caminiti was the unanimous National League MVP. His 40 homers and 130 RBI were both club records, and he won his second straight Gold Glove with spectacular play at third base.

	AB	R	HR	RBI	SB	BA
1995 San Diego	526	74	26	94	12	.302
1996 San Diego	546	109	40	130	11	.326
1997 San Diego	486	92	26	90	11	.290

CAMPOS, JESUS - OF - BR - b: 10/12/73
Campos hit 119 points higher at Double-A Harrisburg than at Class A West Palm Beach last season (.309, compared to .190). He is a little guy without power and speed that has kicked around the minor leagues for six years. He is not a prospect.

CANDAELE, CASEY - 2B/OF - BB - b: 1/12/61
Scouting: Candaele first appeared on the major league scene with Montreal in 1986. He has spent the better part of the last five seasons as a Triple-A vagabond, filling in at second base, shortstop and third base. Candaele has no tools, but often outperforms "tools" players; he doesn't hit for average or power, his speed is barely adequate, and his defensive range is unremarkable. However, he has a heart a mile wide, and has consistently been a solid veteran presence who has positively impacted the career of many young prospects.
1998: Candaele's ability to get the most out of limited abilities should make him a great coach in the near future.
1997: Candaele's production dropped way off at Triple-A Buffalo, though he still did yank the ball down the lines with some frequency, and drew more than his share of walks.
1996: Candaele had his best offensive minor-league season in memory, and even earned a brief, productive major league trial after an injury to Carlos Baerga. He was an unselfish professional on an Indians' team with too many immature players.

	AB	R	HR	RBI	SB	BA
1996 Cleveland	44	8	1	4	0	.250
1997 Cleveland	26	5	0	4	1	.308

CANDELARIA, BENJAMIN - OF - BL - b: 1/29/75
Scouting: A lefthanded batter with good bat control, Candelaria is starting to develop a power swing to go with what is already good selection at the plate. A small man by baseball standards, Candelaria already has six professional seasons under his belt even though he is just twenty-three years old.
1998: Candelaria is better suited for an organization other than Toronto, unless he changes positions. With the Blue Jays already having a young outfield, Candelaria would have a better shot at making another roster. Another season at Double-A would not hurt although Candelaria is ready for Triple-A pitching.
1997: Candelaria achieved career-highs in every offensive category with Double-A Knoxville. His stolen base total continued to be disappointing but he showed an ability to walk and started to hit consistently for average.
1996: Splitting time with Double-A Knoxville and Class A Dunedin, Candelaria showed good patience and little power. He struck out 65 times in 287 composite at-bats.

CANGELOSI, JOHN - OF - BB - b: 3/10/63
Scouting Cangelosi has fashioned an eleven-year major league career out of above-average speed and an ability to reach base via walks largely attributable to his diminutive 5'8" frame. His skills are on the wane, however. His speed has been in steady decline in recent seasons, and his lack of throwing ability makes him a defensive liability, even in left field. He's the type of player you'd like to have around to draw a walk leading off an inning late in a close game, but that's about the extent of his usefulness.
1998: Cangelosi may have reached the end of his major league career. Now 35 years old, he would be of limited use to most major league clubs. Formerly a potential threat as a pinch-hitter and runner, he no longer does enough to warrant a roster spot.
1997: Cangelosi played a limited role for the World Champions, despite a run of injuries to the Marlins' starting outfielders. He started in left field occasionally during Devon White's injury (with Moises Alou in center field), but was outproduced by other veteran bench players. He got a ring, however.
1996: Cangelosi played a significant role for the Astros for the second straight season, leading off on a part-time basis, getting on base at a high rate and posing a consistent stolen base threat. However, he was substantially less effective than in 1995, when he posted a remarkable .457 OBP in a similar role.

	AB	R	HR	RBI	SB	BA
1995 Houston	201	46	2	18	21	.318
1996 Houston	262	49	1	16	17	.263
1997 Florida	192	28	1	12	5	.245

CANIZARO, JAY - 2B - BR - b: 7/4/73
Canizaro's career looked so promising just two years ago, resulting in an advance to the majors for 120 at-bats in 1996. But last year he spent an unsatisfying season split between Triple-A Phoenix, where he hit .198 with two homers and 12 RBI in 81 at-bats, and Double-A Shreveport, where he hit .256 with 11 homers and 38 RBI. After seeming to handle Triple-A pitching in the past, Canizaro has seen his career go in reverse in recent years.

	AB	R	HR	RBI	SB	BA
1996 San Francisco	120	11	2	8	0	.200

CANSECO, JOSE - DH - BR - b: 7/2/73

Scouting: One of the most electrifying players in the majors, a more settled Canseco seems to have more battles with his body than with his inner self at this point of his career. Still, he is a force with the bat and can put a mistake, let alone a less-than-perfect fastball, into orbit. He has become a liability in the field, which is a shame as he was a good fielder with a good arm when he arrived on the scene in 1987.

1998: Canseco has become a DH, which means he will remain an American League player. His career with the A's, however, is probably at an end. Injuries prevented Canseco from obtaining the requisite at-bats to force a contract renewal. Canseco remains, when the opportunity presents itself, a solid 30-homer, 100-RBI player.

1997: The prospect of Canseco joining former bash brother Mark McGwire proved to be less than the sum of its parts. Injuries continued to haunt Canseco, limiting him to less than 400 at-bats for the third straight year. Despite the power and run production, his strikeouts were way up from 1996 in a similar number of plate appearances.

1996: A strained hip flexor muscle, then a bad back limited Canseco's playing time, but he still put up impressive numbers and healed enough to help the Red Sox limp to contention.

	AB	R	HR	RBI	SB	BA
1995 Boston	396	64	24	81	4	.306
1996 Boston	360	68	28	82	3	.289
1997 Oakland	388	56	23	74	8	.235

CAPPUCCIO, CARMINE - OF - BL - b: 2/1/70

Cappuccio has spent six years in the White Sox organization, with 1997 being one of his worst. He's always been impatient at the plate but able to make contact — it wasn't the case last season as he hit just .220 in 177 at-bats. There are other outfield prospects in the chain ahead of him so Cappuccio seems destined to be a journeyman minor leaguer.

CARABALLO, RAMON - 2B - BB - b: 5/23/69

The end of the line appears near for the 28-year-old Caraballo, who missed the entire 1996 season with an injury and hit poorly in the Cubs' farm system in 1997 (.211 at Triple-A Iowa). Caraballo, a former Braves farmhand who earned a brief callup with Atlanta in 1993 and got in 34 games for St. Louis in 1995, did not hit for average or power in 1997 and played himself out of a shot at an infield position with the Cubs for the upcoming season. Caraballo will turn 29 in May and it doesn't appear that he'll get another shot.

CAREY, TODD - 3B - BL - b: 8/14/71

Scouting: Carey does a lot of things, but not many well. He plays everywhere on the infield, but really is not good anywhere. His reactions and hands are poor, but sometimes he's like the Sundance Kid in that he's better when he moves. Still, his range is below average at second base and shortstop. Carey has a slow bat, but gets his share of home runs by trying to jerk every pitch out of the park. Twelve out of 400 times this approach works.

1998: Carey will hang around Triple-A this season and perhaps for a couple of more, simply because he can be a handy utilityman at this level. His weaknesses would be glaring should he reach the majors.

1997: Carey made it to Triple-A and spent the entire season with Pawtucket. His versatility and the frequent moving of bodies at this level earned him a lot of at-bats, not the quality of his play.

1996: Carey appeared to break through as a fringe prospect by hitting 20 homers for Double-A Trenton, his second season at that level.

CARNEY, BART - OF - BB - b: 12/16/73

Oriole minor-leaguer Carney filled in wherever the club needed an outfielder in 1997. He's a good organization man and is always ready to travel, but doesn't hit enough to make much progress.

CARPENTER, BUBBA - OF - BL - b: 7/23/68

After seven years in the Yankees' farm system, Carpenter has been stuck at Triple-A for three and a half seasons. He improved his batting average, on-base percentage and slugging average last year, but he is no closer to the majors than he was four years ago.

CARR, CHUCK - OF - BR - b: 8/10/68

Scouting: When the Astros signed Carr to a minor-league contract after his release by Milwaukee in May, it was considered a non-event. However, Carr went to Triple-A New Orleans, shed several pounds of jewelry, worked hard and was brought up to the Astros on June 24th. He became the regular center fielder in July when Larry Dierker decided to go with his best defensive players. The strategy worked and Carr was an integral part of the team's run in July which put them on top of the Division to stay. He was a semi-regular in August and September when he was hampered by a quadriceps injury. Carr has two assets, speed and defense. He doesn't hit for average or power. He has a reputation for being uncoachable but did not create any problems in Houston.

1998: Carr has already played for five major league teams and will have to scramble for a job every year. He will probably be a fourth outfielder on a major league club where he will be used in situations where he can take advantage of his speed.

1997: After a poor start in Milwaukee and mediocre numbers at New Orleans (.246-0-3 with five stolen bases in 65 at-bats), Carr's performance in Houston was his best since 1993 in Florida.

1996: Carr had an injury plagued season and was used sparingly in Milwaukee.

	AB	R	H	RBI	SB	BA
1995 Florida	308	54	2	20	25	.227
1996 Milwaukee	106	18	1	11	5	.274
1997 Milw.-Hou.	238	37	4	17	12	.248

CARR, JEREMY - 2B - BR - b: 3/30/71

Scouting: Speed is central to Carr's game. He's fast enough to steal 30 or 40 bases in the majors and can also use his speed to get on base by chopping grounders into the turf and beating them out. He has been able to put his speed to use on defense since a shift to the outfield; Carr is not yet a good outfielder, however. He has recently shown an improved batting eye, enough to be considered a minor prospect for major league playing time.

1998: If Carr continues to progress he can earn a fifth outfield spot as a pinch-runner and deep bench reserve in the majors. He's unlikely to get more than a platoon role in the majors in the near future. Carr should begin the year at Triple-A.

1997: After starting the year at Double-A Wichita, Carr stole everything in sight with excellent on-base ability (.408 on-base

percentage), earning a promotion to Triple-A Omaha. Carr finished the year with 51 steals and was caught just 11 times; he has now stolen 226 bases in five pro seasons.
1996: Carr's first full season above A-ball was a success as he hit .260 with 41 steals, the fourth most among all Double-A and Triple-A players. His defense at second base was so poor that he had to move to the outfield.

CARREON, MARK - 1B/OF - BR - b: 7/9/63
Carreon peaked with a .301-17-65 season for the Giants in 1995. He even found a defensive home at first base, after working for years in the outfield where he was visibly misplaced. In 1996, Carreon collected 11 more homers as a part-timer with the Giants and Indians. Then he went to Japan for the 1997 season. His hitting in Japan was no more impressive than what he did in the majors.

	AB	R	HR	RBI	SB	BA
1995 San Francisco	396	53	17	65	0	.301
1996 San Francisco	292	40	9	51	2	.260
1996 Cleveland	142	16	2	14	1	.324

CARTER, JOE - OF - BR - b: 3/7/60
Scouting: Carter is not the player he was five years ago but can still hit for power and is a run-producer year after year. He quietly stole eight bases last year although his base-stealing game is gone. His ability to make contact and his power is still above average, despite how bad he looks at times.
1998: Carter received a standing ovation on the final day of the 1997 season from Blue Jays fans who were confident he would not be back. A return to Toronto would mean a reduction in playing time as a part-time DH. As he is likely not to bat cleanup much more, expect a drop in his RBI total.
1997: Although he finished with his usual century mark in RBI, Carter's bat was absent early when the Jays needed it. His average was the lowest since he was with San Diego in 1990 and the home run total was his lowest since 1985.
1996: Carter enjoyed his typical year as the Blue Jays' usual cleanup hitter, finishing with 30 home runs and 107 RBI, the sixth time in his career he had achieved the 30/100 marks.

	AB	R	HR	RBI	SB	BA
1995 Toronto	558	70	25	76	12	.253
1996 Toronto	625	84	30	107	7	.253
1997 Toronto	612	76	21	102	8	.234

CARTER, MIKE - SS/OF - BR - b: 5/5/69
After leading the American Association in hitting with a .325 average in 1995, Carter dropped off considerably in '96. Some, not all, of his dropoff can be attributed to nagging injuries he fought most of the season. Carter has averaged 19 walks per year in his professional career. He has good speed but doesn't run the bases well. After committing 71 errors in his first two years of pro ball at shortstop, Carter has developed into an above-average outfielder, mostly due to his speed. Many of the Cubs younger outfielders vaulted past him and in 1997 Carter took his game to Double-A Midland in the Angels organization, playing in 15 games there.

CARVAJAL, JHONNY - SS/2B - BR - b: 7/24/74
Carvajal broke into professional baseball with the Cincinnati organization in 1993 and the Reds considered him an outstanding defensive shortstop. He was dealt to the Montreal organization in 1996 and the Expos made him a third baseman at Double-A Harrisburg last season. He has a grand total of five homers in five minor-league seasons, meaning he has no chance of playing in the majors as a third baseman.

CARVAJAL, JOVINO - OF - BB - b: 9/2/68
One of the fastest players in the Angels' organization, Carvajal remains a prospect primarily because of his speed. It makes him an exciting player to watch and he has above-average tools. Carvajal has turned heads with his offense and defense, but he has to hit for a higher average in order to make it to the next level.

CARVER, STEVE - 1B - BL - b: 9/27/72
Collegiate third baseman Carver has seen time at first base and in the outfield at Double-A Reading for the Phillies. He has decent bat speed and has maintained his power output when promoted to higher levels, but the rest of his skills are limited. His speed and defense are below average and he's relatively old for his level. Being injury prone has not helped Carver advance, either; his fast start in 1997 was sidetracked by a two-month DL stint. Carver's ability to play both infield and outfield positions, plus his lefthanded power potential, could get him to the major league bench. The Phillies seem to like him a lot.

CASANOVA, RAUL - C - BB - b: 8/23/72
Scouting: Casanova possesses great potential as a switch-hitting catcher with power. The questions have always been about his desire and his work ethic, and last year he made great progress with both. The progress must continue, but he'll get the chance to reward the faith shown by his biggest supporter - Tigers General Manager Randy Smith.
1998: For the first time, Casanova will go into a season as the Tigers' main catcher. They'll want him to show that off-season work has indeed improved his durability, and also that he can perform consistently. But he will get the chance.
1997: Forced into the big leagues at the end of April by an injury to Matt Walbeck, Casanova ended up winning the starting catching job and forcing Brian Johnson first to Toledo and then to San Francisco. It wasn't a consistently good season, but it was good enough to show why the Tigers wanted Casanova in the first place.
1996: The one mistake the Tigers admitted to was calling a then 23-year-old Casanova up from Triple-A Toledo too early. In early May, the team was struggling, and the young catcher struggled, also. He later broke the hamate bone in his left wrist, and ended up with an unremarkable season.

	AB	R	HR	RBI	SB	BA
1996 Detroit	85	6	4	9	0	.188
1997 Detroit	304	27	5	24	1	.243

CASEY, SEAN - 1B - BL - b: 7/2/74
Scouting: The Indians' second-round draft pick (1995), Casey could hit .300 in any league, and be a 35-homer hitter if he so desired. Instead, he's content to hit the ball hard where it's pitched, and rarely strikes out. He's basically a bigger (6'4", 215-pound) Mark Grace who has battled injuries in his brief career, most notably a broken wrist. Judging by his .380 average and 84 RBI in 313 Double-A and Triple-A at-bats in 1997, he appears to be fully recovered.
1998: Casey has likely surpassed Richie Sexson as the Indians' first baseman of the future. Unfortunately for Casey, the Indians have an entrenched first baseman of the present in Jim Thome. If the Indians can clear the DH logjam for playing time, Casey

could be an extremely productive hitter for the Indians in 1998. Given 500 at-bats, he's a .300 hitter with 15 homer/80 RBI ability right away.

1997: Casey sat for half the season, then had an explosive second half. The numbers speak for themselves: .380 average; .438 OBP, .613 slugging average, and a pro-ball best .27 RBI per at-bat — all produced with a contagious fire and zest for the game.

1996: In yet another injury-shortened campaign, Casey led the pitcher-dominated, high Class A Carolina League with a .331 average. Even more impressive were his 47 strikeouts in 344 at-bats.

CASTELLANO, PEDRO - 3B - BR - b: 3/11/70

Castellano had a stint with the Rockies in May, 1996 but was not offered a contract for 1997 and wound up in the Minnesota organization. Castellano played at Triple-A Salt Lake and hit well in a reserve role. That would likely be his role should he return to the majors.

CASTILLA, VINNY - 3B - BR - b: 7/4/67

Scouting: Though there is statistical evidence to the contrary, Castilla is not a Coors Field creation. Ask the hardest throwers in the National League and they'll tell you Castilla is, flat out, the best fastball hitter in the game. In 1997 alone, Castilla hit one homer off Mark Wohlers, two game-winning homers off Billy Wagner and a triple off Robb Nen. Castilla is becoming more disciplined against the breaking ball, though it's still the way to beat him. Though he has poor range at third base, he compensates with sure hands and arguably the truest throwing arm in the majors. His durability shows in the fact that he has missed just ten games in three years.

1998: Look for more RBI if manager Don Baylor feels he's ready to handle the fifth spot in the batting order. Though Castilla has hit 112 homers in his last three years, his RBI-to-homer ratio is only 2.8. His 22-game hitting streak last season shows he may be the next Rockie to challenge for the batting title.

1997: Castilla remained a model of consistency. His triple-crown numbers were identical to the previous season. He did go through a long spell of swinging at bad pitches when he had homers on his mind; he struck out 108 times, a career-high. His career-best 44 walks were due mostly to Kirt Manwaring hitting behind him, not greater patience.

1996: For the most part, he has been the same hitter for three seasons, but 1996 was the year that Castilla proved he was not a fluke. Until occupying Coors Field in 1995, he had never hit more than 12 homers in a professional season. When he hit 32 in 1995, people wondered if it was Castilla or the park; 1996 showed he was for real.

	AB	R	HR	RBI	SB	BA
1995 Colorado	527	82	32	90	2	.309
1996 Colorado	629	97	40	113	7	.304
1997 Colorado	612	94	40	113	2	.304

CASTILLO, ALBERTO - C - BR - b: 2/10/70

Scouting: His receiving, throwing and ability to work with pitchers keep him in the game. Managers and pitchers appreciate his low target and low-key approach. Some baseball people are not inclined to have Spanish-speaking catchers because of potential communication problems. Castillo has worked to learn English and even learned some basic Japanese to communicate with Takashi Kashiwada last spring. But his bat keeps him from playing regularly even on the Triple-A level. Castillo has batted .210 over the last two seasons in Triple-A.

1998: Even with expansion and even with Todd Hundley expected to miss the first months of the season, Castillo will be hard-pressed to find work on the major league level, especially with a team that regularly plays another primary defensive player, such as shortstop Rey Ordonez. But if a team has personnel similar to the Braves, it could carry Castillo like the Braves carry Eddie Perez.

1997: The Mets carried Castillo on their roster, playing him sparingly before Todd Hundley was betrayed by his elbow. At that point, the club demoted Castillo and summoned Todd Pratt, a strong indication of its thoughts and needs. No team can carry a catcher with a .220 slugging percentage.

1996: Castillo took a step backward, batting .208 in 341 Triple-A at-bats after hitting .267 in 217 at-bats the previous season. He didn't hit in winter ball, either.

	AB	R	HR	RBI	SB	BA
1997 New York NL	59	3	0	7	0	.203

CASTILLO, LUIS - 2B - BB - b: 9/12/75

Scouting At the age of 21, Castillo was awarded the full-time major league second base job at the beginning of 1997. He was not ready. Offensively, he relies on his speed, and needs to make consistent ground-ball contact and draw walks to succeed as a leadoff man. He has zero extra-base power. Though he has great speed, he has a great deal to learn about the art of stealing a base. He struggles reading pitchers' moves and adjusting to game situations. He has great range in the field and an adequate arm.

1998: Castillo will need to dazzle during spring training to retrieve the second base job from the reliable Craig Counsell. Castillo has a much higher upside, but is still young and will not be rushed again. If he successfully cuts his strikeout rate and improves his discipline on the bases, he will eventually star in the majors.

1997: Castillo flopped in the majors, striking out too often and hitting too many weak fly balls. He tried to steal bases in the wrong situations, and was not consistent with the glove. He excelled after being returned to Triple-A, rekindling hope for the future.

1996: Castillo was brilliant at Double-A Portland, earning a late-summer recall to the majors. A patient, prototypical leadoff man in the minors, Castillo was overaggressive in the majors, often retiring himself on bad pitches. Still, if you're 20 years old and in the majors, the odds are strong that you will eventually excel.

	AB	R	HR	RBI	SB	BA
1996 Florida	164	26	1	8	17	.262
1997 Florida	263	27	0	8	16	.240

CASTLEBERRY, KEVIN - 2B - BL - b: 4/2268

Castleberry played at Triple-A Oklahoma City in the Rangers farm system in 1997, the fifth different organization of his career. He wasn't an everyday player and he was moved to the outfield from his regular second base position where he has demonstrated good hands during his career. He's 29 years old and just a minor-league journeyman without much of a major league future.

CASTRO, JUAN - SS/2B/3B - BR - b: 6/20/72

Castro's utility role was cut back in 1997 as he appeared in 40 games compared to 70 in 1996. He can fill in at second base, third base and at shortstop but that's all you get from Castro — defense. He didn't hit in 1996 and he hit worse in 1997. His lack of at least an average bat could end up costing him his utility role.

	AB	R	HR	RBI	SB	BA
1996 Los Angeles	132	16	0	5	1	.197
1997 Los Angeles	75	3	0	4	0	.147

CASTRO, RAMON - C - BR - b: 3/1/76

Scouting: Castro is a catcher from Puerto Rico who was drafted in the first round by the Astros in 1994 because of his power potential. His progress has been slow as he works on his catching skills, but he is still young enough to be considered a prospect. He hasn't yet played a game above the Class A level.

1998: Castro should get his first opportunity at the Double-A level and needs to make the most of it to stay on track.

1997: Castro spent the entire season at High Class A Kissimmee and had a respectable year (.280-8-65). His power has been slow to develop as he has not yet reached double digits in home runs.

1996: Castro spent the entire season at Low Class A Quad Cities where he hit only .248 with seven homers.

CATALANOTTO, FRANK - 2B - BL - b: 4/27/74

Scouting: Everyone expects him to hit, even in the major leagues. The Tigers aren't sure he'll ever be able to field, which is why they left him unprotected in the Rule 5 draft a year and a half ago. They got him back, and they've taught him to play third base as well as second. He's not great at either one, and he's not a power hitter, so a utility job seems to be in his future.

1998: The Tigers will need help on the bench, and Catalanotto could get a chance. But a lot depends on how much they think he has improved defensively.

1997: He went to spring training with Oakland as a Rule 5 draftee, but Catalanotto didn't play well in spring training and was returned to the Tigers. He adjusted to Triple-A and had another big year at the plate, hitting .300 with sixteen homers. He also played 36 games at third base, as the Tigers tried to work on making him a utility player.

1996: A second year at Double-A Jacksonville proved big for Catalanotto, who batted .298 with 34 doubles and 17 home runs. The batting average ranked him eighth in the Southern League, and he was also in the top ten in hits, doubles and runs.

	AB	R	HR	RBI	SB	BA
1997 Detroit	26	2	0	3	0	.308

CEDENO, ANDUJAR - SS - BR - b: 8/21/69

Once a bright power-hitting middle-infield prospect in the Astros' system, Cedeno has been traded twice in the last two years and has finally hit bottom as a potential major league regular, and couldn't find a job at spring training in 1997.

	AB	R	HR	RBI	SB	BA
1995 San Diego	390	42	6	31	5	.210
1996 Houston	153	11	3	18	3	.231
1996 Detroit	179	19	7	20	2	.196

CEDENO, DOMINGO - SS/2B - BB - b: 11/4/68

Scouting: As his career has progressed, Cedeno's hitting has improved considerably, but his erratic play and limited range in the field have kept him from a starting role. Cedeno is a free swinger, and frequently chases balls out of the strike zone.

1998: Cedeno has shown enough versatility and can hit well enough to remain a viable candidate as a major league backup infielder. Having played for three teams in the last two seasons, he has reached that point in his career where he'll change addresses frequently.

1997: Because of injuries to Mark McLemore and Bill Ripken, and the ineffectiveness of Benji Gil, Cedeno wound up with more at-bats than any other Ranger middle infielder, despite starting the season in the minors. He hit well, but was inconsistent with the glove.

1996: Cedeno landed an everyday job early in the year but his light bat and the improving play of Tomas Perez allowed the Blue Jays to ship him off to the White Sox.

	AB	R	HR	RBI	SB	BA
1995 Toronto	161	18	4	14	0	.236
1996 Tor-Chicago AL	301	46	2	20	6	.272
1997 Texas	365	49	4	36	3	.282

CEDENO, ROGER - OF - BB - b: 8/16/74

Scouting: Cedeno appears to be the heir apparent to Butler for the Dodgers in center field. He's a switch-hitter who can spray the ball all over the park from both sides of the plate. Cedeno has been touted as an excellent fielder although he struggled during his first trial in 1996.

1998: Butler is gone but Otis Nixon, who was picked up down the stretch in 1997, stands in his way for now in center field. If Nixon is not a Dodger to start the season, Cedeno should get the chance to make the position his.

1997: Cedeno played in 80 games and improved his hitting while sharing time with Brett Butler until his retirement. Otis Nixon was then acquired by the Dodgers and Cedeno didn't play a game in September.

1996: When Butler left the team because of throat cancer, Cedeno was handed his first opportunity to take the center field job. He didn't handle it well. He proved to be a 21-year-old not yet ready for the majors, struggling at the plate and misplaying several balls in the outfield despite his reputation as a fine fielder.

	AB	R	HR	RBI	SB	BA
1995 Los Angeles	42	4	0	3	1	.238
1996 Los Angeles	211	26	2	18	5	.246
1997 Los Angeles	194	31	3	17	9	.273

CEPEDA, JOSE - 3B - BR - b: 8/1/74

Cepeda has no power and little speed; he's a singles hitter only. He hasn't hit enough singles, either, as he was demoted from higher Class A Wilmington to Lansing after only a month of hitting .282; Cepeda hit .279 with two homers and 35 RBI at Lansing. He's a smooth fielder at second base but with only average range. Cepeda needs to take a big step forward or he will be relegated to a career in the minors.

CHAMBERLAIN, WES - OF - BR - b: 4/13/66

A 32-year-old faded "all-tools" prospect who got a major league job after hitting .331 at Triple-A Scranton in 1992, Chamberlain has not been a favorite player of most managers. After a tour in Japan, Chamberlain returned to the U.S. last year and played for the Mets' Triple-A team at Norfolk. A .273-7-50 season showed he can still play, but he isn't a standout even among his minor-league peers.

CHARLES, FRANK - C/1B - BR - b: 2/23/69

Charles is a career minor-league catcher with no serious chance of appearing in the majors. He hit .230 with nine home runs at

Double-A Tulsa in 1997.

CHAVEZ, ERIC - 3B - BL - b: 12/7/77
Chavez was the tenth overall pick in the 1996 draft by the Athletics. He was considered the best pure hitter in that draft and showed signs of backing up that distinction last year. He played at Class A Visalia of the California League and used his short, compact stroke to blast a team high 17 homers and 94 RBI. 1997 was his pro debut. He should use 1998 to work his way up the organizational ladder and looks like a mid-1999 addition to the big-league club.

CHAVEZ, RAUL - C - BR - b: 3/18/73
Scouting: Chavez is the epitome of a good-field, no-hit catcher. He has no power and has struggled to hit for much of an average as he has progressed higher in the minor league levels. He is strictly a backup catcher, if that.
1998: The cost-conscious Expos allowed starting catcher Darrin Fletcher to leave as a free agent at the end of last season. That opened the top catching job for Chris Widger and gives Chavez a good shot at the backup job. Chavez will adequately spell the defensively-challenged Widger behind the plate but will provide minimal offense.
1997: Chavez spent the majority of the season as Triple-A Ottawa's starting catcher and had minimal offensive success. He had two stints with the Expos, actually hitting better at the major league level, but in a limited opportunity.
1996: Acquired from Houston in a trade prior to the season, Chavez spent most of the season as the starting catcher at Ottawa then got a September callup to Montreal.

	AB	R	HR	RBI	SB	BA
1997 Montreal	26	0	0	2	1	.269

CHOLOWSKY, DAN - OF/3B - BR - b: 10/30/70
Moving from the Cubs' system to the Rockies, Cholowsky hit .268 with six homers and 23 RBI in 150 at-bats at Triple-A Colorado Springs. In the Cubs' system, he saw limited action at Triple-A Iowa and struggled at the plate.

CHRISTENSEN, McKAY - OF - BL - b: 8/14/75
The Angels selected the speedy Christensen in the first round of the 1994 draft, even though he went on a mission for the Mormon church until 1996. In 1997 he hit .280 with 28 steals at Class A.

CHRISTIAN, EDDIE - OF - BB - 8/26/71
Christian ate up Double-A pitching at Memphis where he also showed a good eye as well as a hot contact-hitting bat by walking 12 more times than he struck out. A DH in Double-A ball, Christian played in the outfield at Triple-A Tacoma where he continued his hot hitting. If he keeps hitting he may have a chance to catch on with the Mariners' in left field or as a reserve.

CHRISTENSON, RYAN - OF - BR - b: 3/28/74
Christenson displayed speed, power, a good eye and the ability to make contact at Class A Visalia of the California League, earning a trip to Double-A Huntsville. He did more of the same in his Southern League stop and marked himself as a potential prospect for the A's.

CHRISTOPHERSON, ERIC - C - BR - b: 4/25/69
A second-round draft choice by the Giants in 1990, Christopherson played Double-A ball in the Rangers organization in 1997. It was the third different organization he has played for in the past three seasons and, after two seasons at Triple-A, 1997 was a step back. Christopherson appears to be a player who will top out in the high minors.

CIANFROCCO, ARCHI - 1B/SS - BR - b: 10/6/66
Scouting: Cianfrocco is a dream player in the National League scheme of double-switches. He can play all outfield and infield positions plus catch in an emergency; he has even started games at all four infield positions. He's not fast, but is a smart baserunner. Cianfrocco doesn't have much power for his size, but is an above-average clutch hitter and is a rare player who is able to play daily or come off the bench and deliver after long stretches of inactivity.
1998: With the talent pool thinned in an expansion year, a versatile player with Cianfrocco's skills is highly coveted. In an expansion emergency, he could start regularly.
1997: Cianfrocco spent the entire season in the majors for the second straight year. His average dipped 36 points and he struck out 80 times in only 220 at-bats.
1996: While starting at six different positions, Cianfrocco also set a career high with a .281 batting average.

	AB	R	HR	RBI	SB	BA
1995 San Diego	118	22	5	31	0	.263
1996 San Diego	192	21	2	32	1	.281
1997 San Diego	220	25	4	26	7	.245

CIRILLO, JEFF - 3B/2B - BR - b: 9/23/69
Scouting: A good contact hitter and steady fielder, Cirillo has developed into an All-Star for the Brewers. He hits to all fields, and has been near the top of the league in doubles and average with runners in scoring position. He does not have that much power and tends to get down on himself when he slumps.
1998: The Brewers have made a long range commitment to Cirillo as one of their core players.
1997: Cirillo was the Brewers' lone All-Star representative and hit over .300 in the first half of the season. He slumped a bit in the second half, but still finished among league leaders in doubles and hitting with men in scoring position.
1996: Cirillo had a breakthrough season establishing highs in all primary offensive categories. He started the season sharing time with Kevin Seitzer, but quickly became the regular third baseman.

	AB	R	HR	RBI	SB	BA
1995 Milwaukee	328	57	9	39	7	.277
1996 Milwaukee	566	101	15	83	4	.325
1997 Milwaukee	580	74	10	82	4	.288

CLAPINSKI, CHRIS - SS/3B - BB - b: 8/20/71
The switch-hitting Clapinski is a dependable middle-infielder capable of playing second base and shortstop. His range is unspectacular, but he has sure hands and an adequate arm. He makes consistent contact, handles the bat well, and has developed some power to the gaps in the past two seasons, though he will never be a high average hitter. He doesn't have great speed, but is an instinctive baserunner. He is not a future major league starter, but could fit in as a utility man because of his versatility. He was the Marlins' regular Triple-A second baseman prior to the demotion of Luis Castillo; Clapinski will likely

return to Triple-A for a third season in 1998.

CLARK, DAVE - OF - BL - b: 9/3/62
Scouting: Clark is a solid platoon outfielder with decent power and good strikezone judgment. He has frequently filled a lefty pinch-hitting role on a major league bench and has demonstrated the rather rare ability to enter a game cold and get a hit.
1998: A free agent at the end of last year, Clark will continue his travels and once again earn a major league bench role. On a good team, Clark can be a valuable asset off the bench as a fourth outfielder or lefthanded pinch-hitter.
1997: As a reserve outfielder and pinch-hitter Clark was used sparingly, but he was effective for the Cubs, particular when coming off the bench.
1996: Acquired by the Dodgers during the Pirates' fire sale, Clark again served his clubs well in a platoon outfield/pinch-hitting role.

	AB	R	HR	RBI	SB	BA
1995 Pittsburgh	196	30	4	24	3	.281
1996 Los Angeles	226	28	8	36	2	.270
1997 Chicago NL	143	19	5	32	1	.301

CLARK, HOWIE - 2B - BL - b: 2/13/74
Last year was Clark's second season in Double-A. He's consistent, hitting .272 in 1996, and .282 in 1997. He has a little power to the gaps and bangs a few homers, but runs like a duck. Clark's not a prospect, and will have an uphill battle to reach the majors.

CLARK, JERALD - OF/1B - BR - b: 8/10/63
Clark is a much traveled veteran of the majors, minors, Japan, and — most recently — the Independent League. The sun is setting on Clark's career.

CLARK, PHIL - OF/3B - BR - b: 5/6/68
A versatile player (outfielder, catcher, first or third baseman, pinch-hitter or pinch-runner — you name it) Clark was a productive off-the-bench player for the Padres in 1993 but struggled at the plate in 1994 and '95 and found himself in the minors in 1996. Last year he was in Japan and again productive, hitting .320 with 18 homers and 70 RBI for Kintetsu. Clark hit well at Triple-A in 1996 (.329 with 12 homers and 69 RBI in a pitchers' park at Pawtucket) so there's still hope remaining for a return to the majors.

CLARK, TONY - 1B - BB - b: 6/15/72
Scouting: Starting with what he can't do — he's not fast. Now, on to everything else. Clark has great power from both sides of the plate, with the potential to be a .300 hitter, too. He understands the game, and understands what he needs to do to get even better. The best evidence is his defense, which was once poor and is now above-average for major-league first basemen.
1998: There's no question that Clark will play. There's little question that Clark will hit, and hit for power. With the Tigers determined to include more "professional hitters" in their lineup, there may even be more baserunners for Clark to drive in. He's already good, and he'll likely get even better.
1997: Clark didn't keep up his early power pace after bashing 17 home runs and driving in 49 runs through May, but he didn't really tail off badly, either. It's easy to forget that this was his first full big-league season, and — as he'll reminds you — he's still learning.
1996: In his first long-term exposure in the big leagues, Clark was one of the Tigers' biggest highlights. Only six big leaguers had more home runs than Clark after he was promoted on June 7th. Clark finished third in American League rookie of the year voting.

	AB	R	HR	RBI	SB	BA
1995 Detroit	101	10	3	11	0	.238
1996 Detroit	376	56	27	72	0	.250
1997 Detroit	580	105	32	117	1	.276

CLARK, WILL - 1B - BL - b: 3/13/64
Scouting: Clark has become one of the more brittle first basemen in the American League. Five times in the last two seasons he has wound up on the disabled list, missing 99 games in all. Clark still can hit for average, but his power days are long gone, especially against lefthanded pitching. He has a good eye, and will hit the ball where it is pitched. In the field, he plays a solid first base, and seldom makes mistakes on the basepaths.
1998: After the last two seasons, there is some doubt as to whether Clark should be a full-time starter at first base, but with one year remaining on his contract at $6.65 million, Texas may have little choice in the matter.
1997: Freshly recovered from off-season surgery to remove bone chips in his elbow, Clark tripped over a bullpen mound at the end of the exhibition season and sprained his wrist. Once off the DL, he recovered to post his highest batting average since 1994, but his power and run production were inadequate. Then, Clark missed the last five weeks of the season with a heel injury. The Rangers had hoped that Clark's power would return after his elbow surgery, but his power numbers weren't much different from those of the previous season.
1996: Clark's season was nearly a duplicate of 1993, his last — and least productive — year with the Giants. Clark was struggling at the plate, especially toward the end of the year. Some observers believed that his chronic elbow problems were to blame. Never particularly durable, Clark made three trips to the disabled list in the last two months of the season.

	AB	R	HR	RBI	SB	BA
1995 Texas	454	85	16	92	0	.302
1996 Texas	436	69	13	72	2	.284
1997 Texas	393	56	12	51	0	.326

CLAYTON, ROYCE - SS - BR - b: 1/2/70
Scouting: In many respects, Clayton has begun to realize his true potential as a fine defensive shortstop, offensive force and leader in the clubhouse. He shows outstanding range afield (Clayton led the National League in fielding chances) and at the plate he can drive the ball with gap power. Clayton also has developed into a threat on the bases, but he's still too much of a free swinger and prone to concentration lapses on defense.
1998: He would like to play every game, bat second in the lineup and earn a long-term contract. The Cardinals might hold off on a long-term deal, pending the progress of their glut of talented shortstop prospects. Clayton's proclivity to striking out should keep him in the number eight spot in the batting order, where he still can thrive as a base stealer.
1997: Clayton had his most productive season since 1993 with the Giants, which happened to be the only other time he played more than 150 games. He had career highs in doubles and home runs, helping him earn his first All-Star berth. He also had a struggling second half in the field, sometimes unable to tame his strong throwing arm, and occasional trouble making contact at the plate.

1996: Clayton played a low-key role in sharing time with retiring shortstop Ozzie Smith, but earned much respect for the way he handled the difficult situation, as well as his overall play.

	AB	R	HR	RBI	SB	BA
1995 San Francisco	509	56	5	58	24	.244
1996 St. Louis	491	64	6	35	33	.277
1997 St. Louis	576	75	9	61	30	.266

CLINE, PAT - C - BR - b: 10/9/74

Scouting: Cline, a sixth-round pick by the Cubs in 1993 out of high school, has impressed the Cubs with his power on a rapid rise through the Chicago farm system. Despite missing all but three games of the 1994 season with a wrist injury that required surgery, Cline has shown remarkable progress and is considered one of the Cubs' top prospects.

1998: The Cubs view Cline as their catcher of the future, but he's still at least a year away from being ready. With the always dependable Scott Servais around the Cubs won't have to rush Cline to the bigs like they did with a few of their top-flight pitching prospects, and that's always a good thing. He'll start the season in the minors and should remain there the entire season since the Cubs won't be feeling any pressure to bring him up early.

1997: Cline made the jump to Double-A Orlando in only his third full minor-league season and even saw brief action with Triple-A Iowa. He had a decent season overall, although his power numbers weren't quite as good as they were in his first two seasons in A-ball. Cline hit .255 with seven homers in 271 at-bats at Orlando, then got 95 at-bats for Iowa.

1996: Cline enjoyed a fine year with the Cubs higher Class A team in Daytona, where he set career highs in every offensive category. He performed well enough that he was one of Chicago's selections to play in the Arizona Fall League for top prospects.

CLYBURN, DANNY - OF - BR - b: 4/8/74

Scouting: Although he hasn't made any "Top Ten Prospect" lists, Clyburn is one of the Orioles top hitting prospects. Until 1997, he was a power-only hitter looking like a minor-league version of Rob Deer. But he's making some progress as a more disciplined hitter as shown by his .300 batting average in Triple-A last year. His defense is almost non-existent; he's limited to left field and DH duties. He's been in the Pirates and Reds organizations, and acquired an "attitude problem" label before joining the Orioles.

1998: Clyburn's only 23, and he will probably spend another year or two in Triple-A, with short callups to the Orioles in 1998 and 1999. He has a shot at making the majors in a limited role where he could hit some homers and steal a base or two. If he matures to become a more selective and consistent hitter, and works on his defense, then he has a good chance of landing a starting job in the majors.

1997: Clyburn had a solid year for the Orioles Triple-A Rochester club showing much-improved plate discipline, some power, and a little base stealing speed.

1996: Clyburn hit a weak .252 in the Double-A Eastern League, a tough league for hitters.

COFFEE, GARY - 1B - BR - b: 3/13/75

A leading power threat for higher Class A Wilmington, Coffee is a big man, generously listed at 6'3", 250 pounds. He connected for eleven homers, exactly, for the third straight season, but also whiffed 157 times in 427 at-bats, one of the highest totals in professional baseball. His power carried over to the tough hitters' parks in the Carolina League, but he simply has to learn how to take a pitch if he is to succeed at higher levels. Coffee has enough speed to play the outfield, but has been a first baseman for his first four years as a pro.

COLBERT, CRAIG - C - BR - b: 2/13/65

A former major leaguer (Giants, 1992), Colbert has been mired in Triple-A ever since. In 1997, he was with Las Vegas in the Padres' system where he received little playing time.

COLBRUNN, GREG - 1B - BR - b: 7/26/69

Scouting: Poor plate discipline has plagued Colbrunn's major league career. He has a powerful swing and good contact-hitting ability but simply refuses to lay off the bad pitches. Colbrunn was trained as a catcher in the minors but is no longer capable of playing behind the plate and is only a fair first sacker.

1998: Colbrunn may have gotten a glimpse of his future in his season-ending stint with the Braves last year. Because he has been unable to produce enough runs as a regular first baseman, he may be relegated to a pinch-hitting role or, at best, a platoon job.

1997: Colbrunn got significant playing time as a semi-regular in Minnesota, primarily due to an injury to Scott Stahoviak. When Stahoviak returned, Colbrunn's opportunities waned until he was dealt to Atlanta. With the Braves he was primarily a righthanded pinch-hitter, giving the club extra sock off the bench.

1996: After a fine 1995 campaign, Colbrunn was a disappointment as a full-time first baseman in Florida. He was slowed by a wrist injury at mid-season, but generally didn't make contract well or drive in as many runs as the Marlins' had hoped he would. He was allowed to leave the club via free agency after the year.

	AB	R	HR	RBI	SB	BA
1995 Florida	528	70	23	89	11	.277
1996 Florida	511	60	16	69	4	.286
1997 Minn.-Atl.	271	27	7	35	1	.280

COLE, ALEX - OF - BL - b: 8/17/65

Cole spent 1997 playing center field for Triple-A Charlotte in the Marlins' organization. Formerly a greyhound with awesome speed and little else, Cole has seen his chances for major league success wither away due to a series of leg injuries. He has never been an adequate defensive outfielder despite his speed, due to poor judgment and throwing ability. He is a singles hitter who sometimes negated his speed on the bases with poor decisions. Without speed, Cole will have a hard time getting a job in 1998 at any level. His last major opportunity (1996 with the Red Sox) was a disaster —even expansion won't save Cole.

	AB	R	HR	RBI	SB	BA
1995 Minnesota	79	10	1	14	1	.342
1996 Boston	72	13	0	7	5	.222

COLEMAN, MICHAEL - OF - BR - b: 8/16/75

Scouting: A former football player, Coleman is a flashy standout athlete, possessing power, speed and quickness. He gets a great jump on the ball in center field, and is at his quickest out there. He has a weak arm, and struggles with his throwing motion. At the plate, he is capable of hitting for average and power. For a raw player, he has shown the ability to make adjustments and beat pitchers who try to get him out the same way a couple of times in a row.

1998: Coleman has a chance to be the everyday center fielder for Boston. Since he's still raw, and has just a month of Triple-A under his belt, he might have to start the year in the minors if he has a bad spring training. Another possibility is he'll start out in a platoon with Darren Bragg, but will eventually win the job.
1997: Coleman had a break-through year, putting his considerable skills together in his first exposure to Double-A, earning a bump up to Pawtucket, where he continued to impress, and finally being promoted to Boston. His "Prime Time" antics reportedly did not sit well with manager Jimy Williams and the veteran Red Sox.
1996: Coleman struggled in a higher Class A league after a solid season in lower Class A the year before. He said his struggles in '96, though, motivated him to work harder to get the most out of his considerable athletic talent.

COLEMAN, VINCE - OF - BB - b: 9/22/61
Scouting: Coleman likes to believe he can adapt to a part-time role, prolonging a career that has already lasted more than eleven years. He can still run well, but he no longer hits well enough to play every day. Chances are, his playing career is over.
1998: Coaching? Maybe. Coleman enjoys talking baseball, and especially baserunning. But he'll need to get over the idea that he can still play regularly in the major leagues.
1997: The Tigers led the American League in steals for the first time since 1934, the year Sparky Anderson was born; it must have been Coleman's mere presence - or, more likely, Brian's Hunter's. In the two weeks he spent with them before getting released, Coleman didn't steal any bases although Hunter credited Coleman with teaching him a lot about taking leads off first base.
1996: Coleman made the Reds out of spring training, but when he didn't get a chance to play regularly, he wasn't happy. He was sent to the minor leagues on May 29th, eventually released and then re-signed to a Triple-A contract with the Angels.

	AB	R	HR	RBI	SB	BA
1995 two teams	455	66	5	29	42	.288
1996 Cincinnati	84	10	1	4	12	.155

COLES, DARNELL - OF - BR - b: 6/2/62
Coles had his best season 12 years ago with the Tigers, hitting .273 with 20 home runs. He has been in Japan more recently, hitting .313 with 28 home runs for Chunichi in 1996. Last year he slipped to .246 and his power hitting was way down while he was playing for the Hanshin Tigers.

COLLIER, DAN - OF - BR - b: 8/13/70
After six years in the lower echelons of the Boston farm system, Collier signed with the Rangers' Double-A affiliate. After averaging ten home runs per year over those six seasons, he managed to hit 26 as a DH to lead Tulsa. He has a good personality and is a strong role model for younger players, attributes that should keep him in pro ball in one capacity or another.

COLLIER, LOUIS - SS - BR - b: 8/21/73
Scouting: Collier has good speed and a quick, line-drive bat. However, his power has not developed as the Pirates had hoped. He also has a strong arm and good range at shortstop and the Pirates have abandoned the idea of moving him to second base or the outfield.
1998: Collier seems to be getting lost in the shuffle in the Pirates' organization. Abraham Nunez, acquired as part of a nine-player trade with Toronto following the 1995 season, is now the Pirates' shortstop of the future and Collier isn't suited to playing any other position. He looks like someone in need of a change of scenery.
1997: The Pirates tried to convert Collier into a second baseman at Triple-A Calgary at the beginning of the season but it turned into a disaster. He was with the Pirates for three weeks at mid-season and again in September but major-league pitching overmatched him. He was selected to the Triple-A All-Star Game, the fourth straight year he has been selected to an All-Star team.
1996: Collier had a solid season as Double-A Carolina's shortstop and was selected to play in the Double-A All-Star Game.

	AB	R	HR	RBI	SB	BA
1997 Pittsburgh	37	3	0	3	1	.135

COLON, DENNIS - 1B - BB - b: 8/4/73
In his first year of Triple-A ball Colon hit .270-6-64. He's 25 years old and in the wrong organization to become a major league first baseman. He's never going to supplant Jeff Bagwell.

CONGER, JEFF - OF - BL - b: 8/6/71
Conger is good defensively and has speed but his lack of hitting has kept him from becoming the outfield prospect the Pirates hoped he would be. 1997 was no different as Conger hit .213 in 61 at-bats at Class A Lynchburg and .196 in 138 at-bats at Double-A Carolina. His bat will more than likely keep him out of Three Rivers Stadium.

CONINE, JEFF - 1B/OF - BR - b: 6/27/66
Scouting: Conine's bat has slowed considerably of late; he is a fastball hitter who can still hit a mistake on the inside half of the plate a long way. He has traditionally hammered lefthanded pitching, although he didn't show that platoon differential last year. Conine has a long swing which has consistently racked up high strikeout totals. An increasingly immobile outfielder, Conine was moved to first base in 1997, where he showed solid range and sure hands. He is strictly a station-to-station baserunner. His all-around game appears to be aging rapidly.
1998: Conine's option for 1998 was not picked up by the Marlins. He is clearly a below-average offensive first baseman at this stage in his career, and doesn't match up much better with leftfielders. His best bet would be a role as a platooner against lefthanded pitching; Conine could be effective on a per at-bat basis in a more limited major league role.
1997: Conine got off to a woeful start in 1997, necessitating the mid-season acquisition of Darren Daulton. Only a late-season surge made Conine's power numbers respectable; it also earned him some post-season playing time.
1996: Conine posted his third consecutive premium offensive season, reaching a career high in homers. Opposing pitchers pitched around Gary Sheffield often, and had to challenge Conine. Such a formula was good for Conine's numbers, but not for the Marlins, who had limited offensive weaponry.

	AB	R	HR	RBI	SB	BA
1995 Florida	483	72	25	105	2	.302
1996 Florida	597	84	26	95	1	.293
1997 Florida	405	46	17	61	2	.242

CONNER, DECOMBA - OF - BR - b: 7/17/72
Conner struggled at Double-A Jacksonville and was sent down to Class A Lakeland at mid-season, where he thrived with the

bat. He batted just .208 and fanned in almost a third of his 154 at-bats at Jacksonville, then hit .318 with seven homers in 201 at-bats at Lakeland. He still strikes out too much and hasn't shown outstanding skills at the plate or in the field above A-ball.

CONTI, JASON - OF - BL - b: 1/27/75
A 32nd-round find in the Diamondbacks' first draft in 1996, Conti has speed and is a good contact hitter with gap power. He has hit no lower than .310 at three stops in the organization, including .356 in a late-1997 promotion to High Desert of the Class A California League. He has stolen 61 bases in two years. Conti covers a lot of ground in the field.

COOK, HAYWARD - OF - BR - b: 6/24/72
Cook was a spare Double-A outfielder last year. He has a live line-drive bat with some power to the gaps, but is a free swinger who has been plagued by nagging injuries throughout his minor-league career. He is in the wrong organization — he is surrounded by supremely talented younger athletes who have been passing him at blinding speed. He is likely to remain a spare minor-league outfielder with no chance of reaching the major leagues.

COOK, JASON - 2B/3B - BR - b: 12/9/71
A 55th-round draft pick out of the University of Virginia, Cook played at Double-A Memphis last year, his first time above A-ball in five minor-league seasons. He is a strong defensive second baseman and has also played shortstop which will help him make it to the bigs as a utility infielder. He also has a good eye, walking 24 more times than striking out during his career.

COOLBAUGH, MIKE - 1B - BR - b: 6/5/72
Coolbaugh arrived at Double-A Huntsville in 1997 and proceeded to tear the roof off, drilling 30 homers, knocking in 132, while hitting .308. His strikeouts aren't so much a problem as are the lack of walks (105 whiffs to 52 bases on balls), but Coolbaugh will get a chance to improve upon that this year at Triple-A Edmonton. His 100 runs and eight steals indicate good speed for a corner infielder.

COOLBAUGH, SCOTT - 3B - BR - b: 6/13/66
Coolbaugh has made it to the majors in four different seasons with three different organizations. He spent 1995 in Japan, 1996 with the Expos and 1997 in the White Sox system. Once a power threat with little plate discipline, he has turned into a former power threat with a little plate discipline. He split time in Double-A in 1997 and doesn't appear to have a return ticket to the majors left.

COOMER, RON - 3B - BR - b: 11/18/66
Scouting: Coomer has a good bat and will hit anywhere he goes. He won't rack up huge home run totals but, if given the at-bats, will consistently reach double figures. Moreover, he hits well with runners in scoring position and will be a productive hitter in the middle of the lineup. Defensively, Coomer is a mediocre third baseman with limited range. He moves better to his left than to his right.
1998: Coomer enters the season with momentum coming off of the best year of his career. He will be a productive third baseman, a solid designated hitter or even a dependable pinch-hitter — or, maybe, all of the above.

1997: Given an opportunity to play third base in the majors on an everyday basis for the first time in his career, Coomer responded by posting better numbers than anybody would have expected.
1996: His first full season in the majors resulted in splitting time at third base and first base. And, more importantly, he showed could he handle major league pitching after nine and a half minor-league seasons.

	AB	R	HR	RBI	SB	BA
1995 Minnesota	101	15	5	19	0	.257
1996 Minnesota	233	34	12	41	3	.296
1997 Minnesota	523	63	13	85	4	.298

COONEY, KYLE - C - BR - 3/31/73
This catcher has made slow, but steady, progress through the organization. He has some power and some major league ability in calling a game. Cooney could make it to the major leagues as a solid backup, but he must show the Dodgers this spring he's ready to make the step to Triple-A. If he can improve significantly this season, Cooney has the chance to emerge from a pack of catching prospects the Dodgers are bringing up.

COOPER, SCOTT - 3B - BL - b: 10/13/67
Scouting: Cooper is trying to adjust to a bench role after years of being a regular third baseman and former two-time All-Star ('93 and '94 with Boston). It's been a struggle for Cooper who hit for a low average and disappointing power for the Royals last year. He is mostly a pull hitter and has a respectable platoon differential, but he has been too strikeout-prone to support his low power output over the last few years. Cooper is merely an average fielder and has no speed.
1998: Cooper will look for a corner-infield reserve role in the majors. He's a replacement level player at this point and needs to demonstrate the ability to hit for power against righthanders in a pinch-hitting role in order to keep a major league job.
1997: Cooper had a disappointing year in Kansas City, hitting for a low average and not enough power to warrant the important bench role he was given. He hit below .200 with just one RBI as a pinch-hitter.
1996: After suffering through a seriously disappointing season in his 1995 return to his childhood home (St. Louis), Cooper snuck off to Japan where he had a disappointing season for the Seibu Lions.

	AB	R	HR	RBI	SB	BA
1997 Kansas City	159	12	3	15	1	.201

COQUILLETTE, TRACE - 2B - BR - b: 6/4/74
The second baseman has been in the Expos' farm system for five years and finally had a breakthrough season last year with Double-A Harrisburg and Class A West Palm Beach. Coquillette exhibited previously unseen power and stamped himself as a player to watch. He's a California kid but the Expos would love to cash in on his French surname.

CORA, ALEX - SS - BL - b: 10/18/75
Scouting: Cora is predominately a glove man at this stage of his career. In 1997, he was voted the best defensive shortstop in the Double-A Texas League by its managers in the Baseball America mid-season tools survey. He has little power or plate discipline but he can run the bases well. He might be ready to succeed Greg Gagne in 1999.
1998: Cora is expected to have another year to work on his offense in the minor leagues, probably at the Triple-A level.

1997: Cora had a solid defensive season in the Double-A Texas League, however he still needs work with the stick. He hit just .234 in 448 at-bats at San Antonio.
1996: Cora was the Dodgers third-round pick in the June, 1996 draft out of the University of Miami and went on to play at Vero Beach, appearing in 61 games.

CORA, JOEY - 2B - BB - b: 5/14/65

Scouting: Cora, a switch-hitter once considered a platoon player because of greater effectiveness against righthanders, has brought his bat up to the level of his good glove to become one of the top table-setters in the league.
1998: Cora is ensconced at second base after spending his last season in Chicago (1994) and first in Seattle (1995) as a part-timer at second base.
1997: Improving his ability to turn on the ball, Cora had career highs in homers and RBI while also putting up career numbers in almost every offensive category. He runs less frequently, a concession to the Mariners' overall, power-based offense.
1996: Cora showed some power in spurts — three homers in his first 39 at-bats and three in his final 57 — while taking over second base full time.

	AB	R	HR	RBI	SB	BA
1995 Seattle	427	64	3	39	18	.297
1996 Seattle	530	90	6	45	5	.291
1997 Seattle	574	105	11	54	6	.300

CORDERO, WILFREDO - 2B/OF - BR - b: 10/3/71

Scouting: Cordero has grown and played himself out of the infield and is now a full-time outfielder. He's not a bad outfielder, but not a good one either. His legs appear to be getting heavy and his body is slowing down. Cordero, as he fills out, is becoming more of a power hitter, but still hits for a decent average. He has a good swing, but he is over-anxious, and lacks discipline.
1998: His well-publicized domestic problems put his career in Boston in jeopardy. However, Cordero's bat is still potent enough that he's going to be a regular somewhere. Still, because he has not blossomed into the dynamic young hitter he figured to be a few years ago, this season might be a pivotal year for Cordero.
1997: Cordero found himself battling the courts as much as the opposing pitchers because of his spousal abuse case. He was held out of the lineup briefly, but the players association forced the Red Sox to keep playing him. His level of play dropped off afterward, and he ended up having a disappointing season.
1996: After being acquired by Boston, Cordero was converted from shortstop to second base, and never made the transition. He finally suffered a broken bone in his leg when he was taken out by a slide at second, an injury which many attributed to his inexperience at the position. He came back from the injury at the end of the season, but saw most of his time as a pinch-hitter or designated hitter.

	AB	R	HR	RBI	SB	BA
1995 Montreal	514	64	10	49	9	.286
1996 Boston	198	29	3	37	2	.288
1997 Boston	570	82	18	72	1	.281

CORDOVA, MARTY - OF - BR - b: 7/10/69

Scouting: The 1995 American League Rookie of the Year was on an upward spiral until a foot injury caused him to miss two months and ruin his 1997 season. Although he didn't show it last year, Cordova is a solid contact hitter with a good dose of power. He will consistently bat .280 with 18 to 20 home runs and 90 to 100 RBI in the majors. His defense is OK, but his future depends upon his bat.
1998: Cordova is one of the hardest working Twins, which will let him bounce back this summer after a sub-par year in 1997. He will enter the season healthy, which automatically is a step forward.
1997: A sore left foot caused him to miss two weeks during spring training. It didn't heal and he went on the disabled list for two months in mid-April. When he came back, his swing was never the same and he struggled as badly as any Twin hitter has struggled in recent memory.
1996: Sophomore jinx? Cordova ignored it after his Rookie of the Year season. Although his homers were down, his RBI were way up. As a hitter who would prefer driving in runs to hitting homers, Cordova was happy.

	AB	R	HR	RBI	SB	BA
1995 Minnesota	512	81	24	84	20	.277
1996 Minnesota	569	97	16	111	11	.309
1997 Minnesota	378	44	15	51	5	.246

CORREA, MIGUEL - OF - BB - b: 9/10/71

After two failed tries at Double-A Greenville in the Atlanta organization, Correa tried a change of scenery and ended up in the Mariners system. He ripped A-ball pitching, hitting .329-15-47 in 213 at-bats at Lancaster and was promoted to Double-A Memphis where he held his own but failed to impress. Correa has power potential but strikes out too much. He's at least a couple of seasons away from having a shot at the show.

CORREIA, ROD - OF/IF - BR - b: 9/13/67

Correia surfaced in the Boston organization in 1997 playing at both the Double-A and Triple-A levels. After spending a year in the outfield in the Cardinals organization, Correia was moved back to shortstop where he has an average glove. He's been a weak hitter throughout his career. He did hit .293 at Double-A Trenton but was back to his old self at Triple-A Pawtucket, batting .195 in 128 at-bats.

COSSINS, TIM - C - BR - b: 3/31/70

Cossins shared time at Double-A Tulsa in the Texas organization in 1997. When he did play he made contact with average power. He's not near the top of the organization's catching prospects list and the Rangers have one of the game's better catchers locked up for years to come at the major league level.

COSTO, TIM - 1B/OF - BR - b: 2/16/69

Signed by the Cardinals' Triple-A club as a minor-league free agent, Costo had a strong season with Louisville. He showed decent discipline for a run-producer, a role he filled nicely with a .303 batting mark, 14 homers and 54 RBI. The first baseman is stuck well down on the list of possibilities in the Cardinals' options at that position, however. After eight seasons in pro ball, the former first-round draft pick probably needs to move to his fourth different organization to have an opportunity.

COTTON, JOHN - OF - BL - b: 10/30/70

A nine-year minor-league veteran, Cotton had his most successful Triple-A season to date in 1997, batting .269 with eleven homers and 50 RBI in 182 at-bats for Triple-A Nashville. Still, Cotton is far too old to be considered a prospect. He has never shown more than marginal power and the .269 mark last year was his best ever. He's a decent outfielder and a smart baserunner, but it's not enough for Cotton to ever get more than a handful of major league at-bats.

COUGHLIN, KEVIN - 1B - BL - b: 9/7/70
In nine minor-league seasons Coughlin has just nine home runs. He was a part-time outfielder in the Cincinnati farm system in 1997 and played at the Double-A level. The Reds are his third organization in the past three seasons and Coughlin doesn't hit for a high enough average to make up for his lack of power.

COUNSELL, CRAIG - SS - BL - b: 8/21/70
Scouting: Counsell's 1997 success was a victory for working stiffs everywhere. He has no singular outstanding ability; he is a contact hitter who will take a walk, a surehanded defensive player who positions himself well, and a limited but instinctive baserunner. After the more talented Luis Castillo fell short at second base, these were the exact traits the Marlins needed in a second baseman. The conventional wisdom is that Counsell doesn't win games, but he prevents you from losing them — but he just might have won the biggest game of all in 1997.
1998: His 1997 post-season success gives Counsell a chance to be more than a stopgap solution in South Florida. He should not be expected to hit as well as he did last year, but a .260 average with a decent walk total is quite possible. Of course, if Luis Castillo decides to play up to his potential in the spring, it's back to that familiar utility role for Counsell.
1997: After being acquired from Colorado at mid-season, Counsell, along with Darren Daulton, was the final piece in the World Championship puzzle. Counsell did all of the little things at bat and in the field, and effectively turned over the lineup by getting on base at a high rate. His run won a World Series — how many people can say that?
1996: Counsell's season was washed out by injuries, eliminating his chances for playing time in Colorado. He showed promise by posting a spectacular 7-to-24 strikeout-to-walk ratio in 99 Triple-A plate appearances.

	AB	R	HR	RBI	SB	BA
1997 Florida	164	20	1	16	1	.299

COX, DARRON - C - BR - b: 11/21/67
Cox was the starting catcher at Mexico City where he was the Mexican League's best defensive catcher. Said Mexico City manager Dan Firova: "No one steals on him, and when they do, they get a drink of water. He's really opened eyes for his defense all over this league." Cox will likely get a shot at the backup catcher's job with the Devil Rays given his defense and the fact that he seems to be coming around with the bat after hitting .287 last year; he lacks any semblance of power.

COX, STEVE - 1B - BL - b: 10/31/74
A second round pick by Tampa Bay, Cox soon found himself behind Fred McGriff and Herbert Perry in the first base depth chart. Cox has potential for the long term. He struggled some at Double-A Hunstville (.281 with 12 homers and 61 RBI) in 1996, held his own last year at Triple-A Edmonton, clubbing 15 homers, while driving in 93. More telling were his 88 walks to 90 strikeouts. Cox is just one of many hot-hitting prospects the A's have had in the wings.

CRADLE, RICKEY - OF - BR - b: 6/20/73
Once considered a top power/speed prospect, Cradle has been unable to adjust to breaking-ball pitching in the high minors. After reaching career highs in homers while splitting the 1996 season between Double-A and Triple-A, Cradle struggled so badly at Triple-A Syracuse in 1997 (.115 in 26 at-bats) he was quickly demoted to Double-A Knoxville where he continued to flounder, hitting .214 with 67 strikeouts in 84 games. Cradle has to learn to hit something other than a fastball or his baseball career could quickly be over.

CRESPO, FELIPE - 2B - BB - b: 3/5/73
Scouting: At least twice Crespo has had an opportunity to play regularly with the Blue Jays and both times he was injured. He has good range although he occasionally has mental lapses with the glove, botching what would otherwise be a routine play. He has excellent power for an infielder and walks more than he strikes out. Crespo makes better contact than his minor-league numbers imply.
1998: Crespo is easily good enough to be on a major league team and deserves to be a regular starter, although it's unlikely that anyone will take that chance. Expect dramatically more playing time and some surprising power.
1997: Crespo spent most of the season with Triple-A Syracuse and hit 12 home runs in just 290 at-bats. Called up to the Blue Jays and when Ed Sprague and Tom Evans were both unavailable, he had an opportunity to crack the lineup. A sore back kept him out of the lineup as Juan Samuel filled in for emergency duty at third.
1996: Crespo had won the second base job in spring training but a pulled hamstring put him out of action just before the season started. Domingo Cedeno got the nod instead and Crespo saw little action with the big league team.

	AB	R	HR	RBI	SB	BA
1997 Toronto	28	3	1	5	0	.286

CROMER, BRANDON - SS - BL - b: 1/25/74
Scouting: Cromer, a first-round draft pick of Toronto in 1992, has a lot of skills but most of them are average. He can hit for a decent average, show occasional pop and plays adequate defense at both middle-infield positions.
1998: The Pirates have a glut of middle infielders and Cromer will go to spring training as a long shot to win a utility job behind Kevin Polcovich. He will likely wind up as the utility man in Triple-A with prospects Chad Hermansen (second base) and Lou Collier (shortstop) manning the regular middle-infield spots.
1997: Acquired from Toronto as part of a nine-player trade the previous winter, Cromer emerged as the early favorite in spring training to become the Pirates' second baseman. However, he faded while Tony Womack claimed the job and never let go. Cromer wound up bouncing between Triple-A Calgary and Double-A Carolina and struggled with both clubs.
1996: Cromer had his best professional season with Toronto's Double-A Knoxville farm club, playing both second and third base. He also hit well in the Arizona Fall League, drawing the attention of Pirates' scouts.

CROMER, D.T. - DH - BL - b: 3/19/71
First sacker Cromer, younger brother to shortstop Tripp, came off a super year at Class A Modesto in 1996 when he was the California League MVP, to have an equally impressive year at Double-A Huntsville in 1997; Cromer hit .323, with 15 homers,

121 RBI, and 40 doubles last year. The guy can hit. His worst problems are his age and the log-jam of first sackers ahead of him in the organization.

CROMER, TRIPP - SS - BR - b: 11/21/67

Scouting: Cromer is not a particularly good hitter or fielder and was stored as Triple-A insurance for the Cardinals from 1993-96. He did make it to the bigs in St. Louis on three occasions, playing a career high 105 games in 1995.
1998: With younger Dodger prospects in line with higher upsides, Cromer's best bet is to make another club as a utility infielder. A more likely scenario is another year as a high-minors insurance policy.
1997: Cromer got back to the majors for 28 games in June and July with the Dodgers. He held his own, but was eventually returned to Albuquerque.
1996: Cromer was in Triple-A Louisville for the season and led all American Association shortstops with a .986 fielding percentage in 80 games played.

	AB	R	HR	RBI	SB	BA
1997 Los Angeles	86	8	4	20	0	.291

CRUZ, DEIVI - SS - BR - b: 6/11/75

Scouting: Cruz was the find of the year in '97, for the Tigers and maybe in all of baseball. He has great hands at shortstop, good range and a strong, accurate arm. Besides all that, he learned to hit at the big-league level, and his instincts for the game were outstanding. The only thing he lacks is speed, a result of a minor-league collision and the knee surgery that followed.
1998: There will be no surprise when Cruz starts on opening day this year. He is the Tiger shortstop, and they won't begin the year waiting for Orlando Miller or anyone else to get healthy. They won't ask any more from Cruz defensively, but they hope he continues the improvement he's shown at the plate.
1997: The Tigers will take the credit for finding Cruz in the Rule 5 draft (he was property of San Francisco), but even the Tigers didn't realize what they were getting. Cruz became the starting shortstop only because Orlando Miller suffered a spring training back injury. Then he showed what he could do, at one point going 48 games between errors.
1996: It doesn't seem like much compared to what he would do in 1997, but Cruz had a pretty good year in '96. He set a Class A Midwest League record for fielding percentage (.980), and he was in the league's top twenty in hitting at .294. League managers still ranked nine prospects better than him, which right now seems hard to believe.

	AB	R	HR	RBI	SB	BA
1997 Detroit	436	35	2	40	3	.241

CRUZ, EDGAR - C - BR - b: 8/12/78

The Indians were thrilled to find this 17-year-old catcher available to them in the second round (67th overall pick) of the 1997 draft. Though still just a kid, he's already big (6'2", 195 pounds), and has special defensive skills that could eventually place among him the best major league receivers. Cruz hit for a low average with good power in Rookie ball, and might be ready to carry a full season load in the low Class A South Atlantic League at age 18 in 1998.

CRUZ, FAUSTO - SS - BR - b: 5/1/72

Scouting: Cruz has yet to fulfill his full potential, but he can play the middle infield well and has shown surprising power for someone 5'10" and 165 pounds.
1998: Cruz must show the Angels he's ready to take the next step if he's to win a job as a backup infielder in the majors. He's still young, but this could be a pivotal year for Cruz.
1997: If Luis Alicea hadn't been signed, Cruz probably would have had his role. Acquired as a six-year, minor-league free agent, Cruz went down to the last cut in spring training, then had a solid year at Triple-A Vancouver, hitting eleven home runs. He lacked consistent defense, but he hit and did other things to help the Canadians win.
1996: Cruz split time between Detroit and Triple-A Toledo. He didn't hit as well as he had in the past, but his 18 home runs at Toledo caught the Tigers' eye.

CRUZ, IVAN - 1B - BL - b: 5/3/68

Cruz had a breakthrough year in power hitting at the Double-A level in 1995, then a good winter performance in Puerto Rico, and has made cameo appearances in the majors the last two years. The journeyman hit .300 with 24 homers and 95 RBI at Triple-A Columbus last year and has enough pop to warrant a long look in spring training by some team in an expansion year.

CRUZ, JACOB - OF - BL - b: 1/28/73

Scouting: Cruz improved in many respects over the last year, showing good plate discipline and good speed while hitting for an excellent batting average at Triple-A Phoenix last year. Cruz was considered a minor prospect before the season, but now is on the hot track to the majors.
1998: Look for Cruz to join the Giants for opening day in 1998. He could win a platoon role in the outfield, or serve as a fourth outfielder; he's ready to play regularly in the bigs.
1997: Improved patience at the plate and the hitter-friendly Pacific Coast League helped Cruz hit .361 with twelve homers, 94 RBI and 18 stolen bases at Triple-A Phoenix. Cruz walked as often as he struck out.
1996: Cruz split the year between Phoenix and the majors, hitting .234 in 33 games for the Giants. Despite hitting just seven homers in 435 at-bats, he continued to show RBI ability by driving in 75 runs at Phoenix. Cruz' good batting eye resulted in 62 bases on balls. His first major league hit was a homer.

	AB	R	HR	RBI	SB	BA
1996 San Francisco	77	10	3	10	0	.234

CRUZ, JOSE Jr. - OF - BR - b: 4/19/74

Scouting: Cruz was the top prospect in the Seattle organization — and perhaps all of baseball — before the trade that sent him to Toronto. Eventually, he will hit for average although his big swing limits his potential in that area. Consider that he hit 26 home runs in only 104 games and it provides a clear picture of his power potential. His base-stealing ability will improve and he's also improving in the outfield.
1998: Regardless of how he starts, Cruz will play every day. He may become a center fielder eventually although his immediate future is in left field. Expect the emergence of a superstar, even if he does strike out 180 times.
1997: Cruz didn't even make the Mariners out of spring training although when he was eventually recalled, he made his presence known. Seattle's bullpen difficulties forced them to deal Cruz for Mike Timlin and Paul Spoljaric, neither of whom turned out to be major factors in the Mariners' season. Cruz quickly established his presence with the Blue Jays, so much so that he saw time as the number three hitter in a weak Blue Jay lineup.

1996: Rising from Class A Lancaster at the beginning of the year to Triple-A Tacoma, Cruz made an impact in only his second professional season. He finished with 15 home runs and 89 RBI over 122 games with three different teams and by the end of the season was being called the Mariners' top prospect.

	AB	R	HR	RBI	SB	BA
1997 Sea.-Tor.	395	59	26	68	7	.248

CUDDYER, MICHAEL - SS - BR - b: 4/1/79
Minnesota's first-round pick in the 1997 draft (ninth overall) nearly bypassed the Twins' organization for Florida State University but the Twins came up with a late $1.85 million bonus to land their prized shortstop. He has good hands and a great arm but may grow his way out of the position and end up at third base. In his senior season of high school ball in Virginia, Cuddyer toyed with opposing pitchers and hit at a .500 clip.

CUMMINGS, MIDRE - OF - BL - b: 10/14/71
Scouting: Due to a questionable attitude and lack of production, Cummings' once-bright future as a potential star faded, but a mid-1997 move to Philadelphia gave him a new lease on life. He lines the ball to all fields against left and righthanded pitching, and has respectable power to the gaps. He is not a protoypical leadoff man — he does not walk enough, and doesn't know how to use his slightly above-average speed on the basepaths. He is aggressive afield, but sometimes takes indirect routes to fly balls. Cummings' arm is unspectacular.
1998: Cummings will be given a chance at the Phillies' fourth outfield role, but is unlikely to play everyday in 1998. For all the promise and progress he showed in the second half of 1997, Cummings does not have enough pluses to start every day in such an offense-oriented position.
1997: Cummings was immediately inserted as the Phillies' everyday leadoff hitter upon acquisition, and was instrumental in their second-half turnaround. He presented an extra-base threat at the top of the order, and was far from a pushover against lefthanded pitching. Still, he did not walk enough for a leadoff hitter, and lacks the requisite baserunning instincts for that role. He was adventurous at times in the outfield, but generally got the job done.
1996: Cummings continued to frustrate the Pirates, failing again to win the right field job. Though he hit .304 in Triple-A, he did so in the hitting-oriented Pacific Coast League, without power, speed or patience.

	AB	R	HR	RBI	SB	BA
1995 Pittsburgh	152	13	2	15	1	.243
1996 Pittsburgh	85	11	3	7	0	.224
1997 Pit.-Phi.	314	35	4	31	2	.264

CURTIS, CHAD - OF - BR - b: 11/6/68
Scouting: Once a terrific power/speed threat, Curtis still has a compact swing with no holes, and he runs the bases well. Age has slowed all aspects of his game except enthusiasm. He is on the borderline between everyday playing ability and inconsistency which would dictate a reserve role.
1998: On a team as strong as the Yankees, Curtis can expect no more than a fourth outfielder's job. A team with less talent or a team with injury problems could try him in an everyday role again, but he hasn't been that type of player for two years. The Yankees hoped to bring Curtis back as insurance behind rookie Ricky Ledee in left field.
1997: Curtis was a pleasant surprise for a team that had more than its fair share of outfield injuries, and he became a favorite of manager Joe Torre. A wrist problem affected Curtis at times, but overall he was a major factor in the Yankees' charge into post-season play.
1996: Curtis was traded from a full-time job with Detroit into a backup role with the Dodgers. He didn't like National League pitching, and he didn't do well as a fill-in veteran appearing between experiments with various youngsters. It was a down year for him.

	AB	R	HR	RBI	SB	BA
1995 Detroit	586	96	21	67	27	.268
1996 Det.-LA	504	85	12	46	18	.252
1997 Det.-NY AL	349	59	15	55	12	.284

CURTIS, KEVIN - OF - BR - b: 8/19/72
Curtis is a converted first baseman who covers a lot of ground in the outfield and has a strong arm. He spent four years in the Baltimore farm system before turning up at Double-A New Haven of the Rockies organization. Curtis is a good athlete and showed some pop last year, banging 18 homers with 82 RBI while batting .273. He could develop into a reserve outfielder in the big leagues.

CURTIS, RANDY - OF - BL - 1/16/71
Curtis played A-ball as a 26-year old in the Padres' organization in 1996 and ended up in the Indians' farm system in 1997. He played both Double-A and Triple-A ball for the Indians and had identical power numbers at both stops: five homers, fifteen RBI. He wasn't a regular at either stop, doesn't hit for much of an average and, at age 27, is not a prospect.

CUST, JACK - 1B - BL - b: 1/7/79
A bit of a mystifying pick for the Arizona expansion club in that scouts feel Cust, the number 30 pick in the 1997 draft, can't play anywhere but first base and that's the position the Diamondbacks spent $10 million to fill with Travis Lee. Cust got a chance to play outfield at Rookie level Peoria in the Arizona Fall League and hit over .300 there.

DALESANDRO, MARK - 3B/OF - BR - b: 5/14/68
Dalesandro always has put up good batting averages in the minor leagues, but never has hit for any power at all. In fact, his average this year — .262 at Triple-A Iowa — was the lowest average he's had in any full season in his long minor-league career. Dalesandro saw brief action with the Angels in 1994 and 1995, but got only 35 big-league at-bats combined. If he's going to get to play another year in professional baseball, he's going to have to go to spring training as a free agent and show something he hasn't yet demonstrated in eight minor-league seasons.

DALTON, DEE - 3B - BR - b: 6/17/72
In his second year at Double-A Arkansas, Dalton did not overcome his plate problems, hitting only .228 with four homers and 43 RBI in 360 at-bats. He has a high strikeout rate for his limited power and needs to improve in a number of areas to get noticed. He lacks the hitting tools necessary for a thirdbaseman and his fielding is only fair.

DALTON, JED - OF - BR - 4/3/73
The Angels might get a surprising bonus from their scouting of

Darin Erstad at the University of Nebraska, where Dalton was his teammate. Dalton can play third base and the outfield, and helped Double-A Midland last year with his versatility and smarts. He knows how to play the game and has good baseball instincts.

DAMON, JOHNNY - OF - BL - b: 11/5/73

Scouting: Damon still demonstrates some of the same weaknesses he has had since his major league debut late in 1995; he doesn't hit particularly well against lefthanded pitching, occasionally looking timid at the plate. But, he is progressing, albeit slowly. Both his average and power against lefties continues to improve. He's not there yet, but Damon is close to taking the big step forward that will make him the kind of high-average/doubles-power hitter who can fuel an offense. Damon has outstanding speed but is not a good outfielder; his arm might be the worst among major league outfielders.

1998: Damon is the center fielder and will be featured in the Royals' offense. The organization, and now the manager, are committed to developing his talent, meaning lineup, positioning and other field decisions will be made with that goal in mind. A big year is expected.

1997: The progress Damon made last year wasn't quite what the Royals had hoped for from their 23-year-old superstar-of-the-future. He improved ever-so-slightly in some areas without backsliding in any significant way. More was expected, certainly.

1996: Damon's first full season in the majors was full of sparkle and fizzle, both. Frequent lineup tinkering left Damon with an undefined role in the Royals' offense but he was still productive, especially on the basepaths where he stole 25 bases in 30 tries, running his career record to 32-for-39.

	AB	R	HR	RBI	SB	BA
1995 Kansas City	188	32	3	23	7	.282
1996 Kansas City	517	61	6	50	25	.271
1997 Kansas City	472	70	8	48	16	.275

DANDRIDGE, BRAD - OF - BR - b: 11/29/71

The former Fresno State star is a solid organizational player who can play catcher, first base and the outfield. At age 26, he's a little older than some prospects, but the Dodgers still see some promise and the potential for him to make it to the big leagues as a role player. Dandridge may not be a standout at any one position, but he does a solid job at all of them and has been a good guy to have on the club at each level where he's played so far.

DARR, MIKE - OF - BL - b: 3/21/76

Darr blossomed overnight to become the Padres' Minor League Player of the Year in 1997; he hit .344 with fifteen homers and 94 RBI at Class A Rancho Cucamonga while stealing 23 bases, scoring 104 runs and drawing 57 walks against 90 strikeouts. Acquired from Detroit for Jody Reed, the Padres believe Darr is a future starter in the major leagues. He possesses solid defensive tools in the outfield and is a player to watch at Double-A Mobile in 1998.

DASCENZO, DOUG - OF - BB - b: 6/30/64

Dascenzo falls under the category of veteran minor-league outfielder. He's not going to ever impress anyone enough to get a call from any major league team, but will certainly find a home on someone's Triple-A roster.

DAUBACH, BRIAN - 1B - BL - 2/11/72

After six undistinguished minor-league seasons in the Mets' chain, Daubach has established himself as a viable minor-league power hitter, most recently at Triple-A Charlotte in the Marlins' system. The lefthanded hitter drove nearly half of his hits for extra bases in 1997, but does not appear to possess the bat speed to post comparable success in the major leagues. He is a strikeout machine who has averaged well over 100 whiffs per season over the last four years. He is just an adequate defender at first base and is heading for a career in the minors.

DAULTON, DARREN - OF - BL - b: 1/3/62

Scouting: The magnitude of Darren Daulton's 1997 comeback has not been adequately emphasized by the mainstream media. This is a man with nine knee surgeries in his past who could barely walk in 1996. Against all odds, he gave it a go in 1997 — and wound up playing a key role in the winning of a World Championship. Despite being held together with string and baling wire, Daulton played aggressively — make that recklessly — banging out eight triples and playing a decent right field with the Phillies early in the season. At first base, he was a poor defender for the Marlins. He remains a patient hitter who can bash inside fastballs. He is a clubhouse leader without peer — a true warrior.

1998: It's probably off to the broadcast booth for Daulton. He has a keen baseball mind, and will be probably be around the game for decades.

1997: The sight of Daulton playing the game as he did last year was truly inspirational. This was no farewell tour — it was a hellbent quest for a championship that was justly rewarded. He was the Phillies' second best everyday player before the trade, and he commandeered a laid-back Marlins' clubhouse within days of his arrival, catalyzing the championship run.

1996: Daulton began the season as the Phillies' left fielder; he lasted all of five games before yet another knee surgery. He tried to come back at Class A Clearwater, and didn't make it through a single game. Daulton didn't call it quits, though.

	AB	R	HR	RBI	SB	BA
1997 Phi.-Fla.	395	68	14	63	6	.263

DAVALILLO, DAVID - 2B - BR - b: 12/27/74

A solid defensive player, Davalillo helps a team with his glove only. The diminutive glove man has advanced through the Angels' organization so far because of his work with the glove — any offense he's provided has been a plus, and often lacking.

DAVIS, BEN - C - BB - b: 3/10/77

Scouting: The Padres are breathing easier about their second pick of the '95 draft, who struggled with the bat in 1996. Although off-speed pitches still give him problems, he finally showed he could make adjustments at the plate last year. His catching skills were never in doubt. Davis has a great arm and his footwook behind plate improved considerably this season.

1998: Switch-hitting Davis will start next season on a Double-A roster, but will probably be with Padres in September. He will be 21 years old.

1997: Davis spent his second season in the Class A California League and hit .278 with 17 homers and 76 RBI. He struck out 107 times while drawing only 28 walks.

1996: Davis struggled, hitting only .201 with six home runs and 41 RBI against 89 strikeouts in 353 at-bats.

Benson's Baseball Player Guide: 1998

DAVIS, CHILI - DH - BB - b: 1/17/60
Scouting: Davis is one of the best power-hitting switch-hitters in the history of the game. His status as a top run producer is evident in the fact that he's driven in at least 70 runs in 13 of his 17 big-league seasons — including the strike years. Davis has a good batting eye and will work the count to get a pitch he can drive. Having played just four games in the field over the last five seasons, he's a serious liability with the glove; it's strictly DH work for Davis.
1998: Davis wants to win another championship before his career is over. His stated goal for the season is to play for a contender. Davis intended to make his decision on where to sign as a free agent largely upon which team was willing to go the extra mile to bring in players and be a contender. He still has a potent bat, for now, and will be a credible RBI threat in the middle of a major league batting order as he enters his 21st season as a professional.
1997: Acquired in an off-season trade for Mark Gubicza, Davis was supposed to give the Royals a professional RBI bat in the middle of their order and, for the most part, he delivered. His infrequent slumps left a bit of a hole in the lineup at times, but he also carried the offense sometimes, too. Davis was not happy with the change in management when Tony Muser replaced Bob Boone at the Royals' helm.
1996: In his last year in his second stint with the Angels, Davis showed that age had not slowed his bat; he was among club leaders in many offensive categories and reached near-career bests in many power categories while also hitting for a good average and getting on base regularly. He was one of the best DH's in the game.

	AB	R	HR	RBI	SB	BA
1995 California	424	81	20	86	3	.318
1996 California	530	73	28	95	5	.292
1997 Kansas City	477	71	30	90	6	.279

DAVIS, EDDIE - OF - BR - b: 12/22/72
Davis' career has been slowed by a dramatic position change, but he's started to get back on track and may be in a position to speed his rise through the ranks. Davis had a couple big years in the minors as an outfielder, then was tried as a righthanded pitcher in an experiment that didn't work out. Back in his better-suited position, Davis came up with some big hits for Double-A San Antonio in 1997 and showed he's a good physical outfielder.

DAVIS, ERIC - OF - BR - b: 5/29/62
Scouting: Davis is outstanding when healthy, but he's been beset with various aliments in his career. He was once mentioned as the next Willie Mays. The cancer with which he was diagnosed last year came as real shock to all baseball fans.
1998: The Orioles extended Davis' contract through 1998 indicating that there is at least one baseball team owner who is a nice person. Everybody wishes for Davis to make a complete recovery.
1997: Davis was having a great year with the Orioles when he came down with severe stomach pains that turned out to be colon cancer. He underwent surgery and chemotherapy, and recovered enough to be added to the Orioles roster in September.
1996: Out of baseball in 1995, the Reds gave him a chance and 1996 was a great comeback year for him.

	AB	R	HR	RBI	SB	BA
1996 Cincinnati	415	81	26	83	23	.287
1997 Baltimore	158	29	8	25	6	.304

DAVIS, GLENN - 1B - BB - b: 11/25/75
With Eric Karros and possibly Paul Konerko already in place at first base, Davis was a peculiar pick (first round, 1997) for a franchise in need of athletes. Davis turned up at Class A San Bernadino of the California League last year and held his own considering he's an 18 year old just out of Immaculata High School in Flemington, N.J.

DAVIS, J.J. - 1B/RHP - b: 10/25/78
Davis is a huge kid (6'6", 230 pounds) who was considered to be one of the best high school players in southern California heading into the draft. The Pirates have a history of drafting athletes and waiting to see what happens; they snapped Davis up with the eighth pick of the 1997 June Draft.

DAVIS, JAMES - C - BR - b: 4/14/73
Davis has always been known as a defensive specialist. In 1996, he was picked as the best defensive catcher in the lower Class A South Atlantic League by its managers. Last year, he produced decent offensive numbers (.292-5-46), but he is too old to still be in A-ball.

DAVIS, REGGIE - C - BR - b: 11/2/74
A shoulder injury incurred when he absorbed a collision at home plate in June kept Davis off the field the rest of 1997, although he demonstrated power — eight homers, 35 RBI in 154 at-bats at Class A High Desert — and a strong arm.

DAVIS, RUSSELL - 3B - BR - b: 9/13/69
Scouting: Injuries the past two seasons have limited Davis, the key piece on the Mariners' side of the December, 1995, trade in which they also received Sterling Hitchcock for Tino Martinez, Jeff Nelson and Jim Mecir. Since 1991, Davis has spent time on the disabled list with a bruised heel, a broken wrist, and a fractured fibula.
1998: Davis again will be the starting third baseman after posting career-high power numbers in two-thirds of a season, although the Mariners may begin to wonder about his durability.
1997: Davis showed the power the Mariners saw when they made the trade, recovering nicely from his fibula injury with a homer and a double every 21 at-bats.
1996: Finally getting a chance to play after being backed up in the Yankees' system behind Wade Boggs et al, Davis hit .306 against lefthanders before catching his spikes in the warning track chasing a foul pop June 7th and missing the rest of the year.

	AB	R	HR	RBI	SB	BA
1995 New York AL	98	14	2	12	0	.276
1996 Seattle	167	24	5	18	2	.234
1997 Seattle	420	57	20	63	6	.271

DAVIS, TOMMY - 1B/3B - BR - b: 5/21/73
Scouting: Orioles prospect Davis is a power hitter with a big swing. He strikes out about 20 percent of the time, but he improved his plate discipline last year. He has an iron glove, and was moved from third to first base where he can cause the least amount of damage in the field. He has a ways to go before he can compete for a major league job.
1998: With the solid depth on the Orioles, Davis will likely spend

most of the year in Triple-A, improving his plate discipline and glove work. Prospects for a "cup of coffee" callup in September look good.
1997: Davis had his career best year in the minors hitting over .300 for the first time. His plate discipline and defense improved.
1996: Davis hit .261-14-54 in the Double-A Eastern League, a league known to be tough on hitters. He didn't look good at third base.

DAWKINS, WALTER - OF - BR - b: 8/6/72
Dawkins slid backwards in his second Double-A season in 1997; his strikeout rate increased and his batting average plummeted as he attempted to focus on driving the ball for distance. He is a line-drive, gap hitter who needs to hit around .300 to be effective. He was drafted at age 22, so quick development was required for him to have a chance to reach the majors —his 1997 setback is a major blow to his opportunity for regular big-league play. He is a solid defensive center fielder, but does not have exceptional speed on the bases. In 1998, Dawkins' playing time could be squeezed by superior prospects.

DEAK, DARREL - 2B - BB - b: 7/5/69
Once a touted prospect in the St. Louis organization, Deak spent 1997 with Fargo of the Independent League. Barring a miracle, Deak's chances of attaining his once lofty potential are low.

DEAN, CHRIS - 2B - BB - 1/3/74
A switch-hitting second baseman, Dean advanced from Class A Lancaster to Double-A Memphis of the Southern League in 1997. He showed that he has some pop in his bat and can steal bases when he gets on. He has a good eye as he walks almost as many times as he strikes out. He'll probably start 1998 at Double-A.

DeBOER, ROB - C - BR - b: 2/4/71
A catcher converted to a DH, DeBoer certainly put up some lofty power numbers last year (18 homers in 288 at-bats) but he also struck out almost 45% of the time. At age 26, he is too old too be mucking around at Double-A.

DECKER, STEVE - C - BR - b: 10/25/65
Scouting: Decker has spent his career on the borderline between Triple-A and the majors. He was given the Giants' starting catching job in 1991 but hit only .205 in 233 at-bats and has not had a steady major league gig since. A back injury limited his 1993 season to eight games.
1998: Decker will contend for a major league backup catching position with significant Triple-A playing time a distinct possibility.
1997: Decker returned to Triple-A for a full season at Tacoma in his first year in the Mariners' organization.
1996: Decker played a lot early when Giants' starting catcher Kirt Manwaring suffered a broken bone in his left hand. His contract was purchased by Colorado after he was waived August 21st.

	AB	R	HR	RBI	SB	BA
1995 Florida	133	12	3	13	1	.226
1996 Colorado	147	24	2	20	1	.245

De La CRUZ, LORENZO - OF - BR - b: 9/5/71
A power-hitting outfielder with a huge swing and little plate discipline, DeLaCruz needs to demonstrate more patience at the plate and more selectivity on the bases. His future is cloudy at best and given his impatience at the plate, he may not have any more opportunities.

DELEON, ROBERTO - 2B/3B - BR - b: 3/29/71
A former Padre and Giant farmhand, DeLeon moved on to Independent ball in 1997 where he mostly platooned at shortstop and third base. Do not look for DeLeon to be cracking any 40-man rosters any time soon.

DELGADO, ALEX - C - BR - b: 1/11/71
Delgado has never been a major league regular, but rather a backup catcher insurance policy for when injuries occurred in Boston. Last season, Delgado saw limited action with Triple-A Charlotte, and his career will never amount to more than injury insurance.

DELGADO, CARLOS - 1B/OF - BL - b: 6/25/72
Scouting: Delgado continues to improve at hitting hard, breaking stuff although he continues to have troubles with lefties. His defensive skills have gotten better, so much so that he stole the first base job back from Joe Carter. He is an explosive power threat and has a good eye. Although he takes his share of pitches, he needs to concentrate on putting the ball in play with two strikes.
1998: Delgado will start against all types of pitching and should enjoy a career year.
1997: With the rest of the Blue Jays' offense slumping, Delgado hit 30 home runs. He established himself as the Blue Jays' first baseman of the present, prying the job away from Joe Carter.
1996: Delgado drove in 92 runs in only 138 games in his first full season in the major leagues.

	AB	R	HR	RBI	SB	BA
1995 Toronto	91	7	3	11	0	.165
1996 Toronto	488	68	25	92	0	.270
1997 Toronto	519	79	30	91	0	.262

DELGADO, WILSON - SS - BB - b: 7/15/75
Delgado made "Giant" strides with his hitting in 1997, batting .288 with nine homers and 59 RBI. For a 22-year old making his first appearance at Triple-A that is good. He is still a free-swinger (70 whiffs to 24 walks) but give him a little time. The switch-hitter should slide into the major league shortstop spot in a year or so.

DELLAERO, JASON - SS - BB - b: 12/17/76
The White Sox first-round selection (15th overall in 1997) made his pro debut at Hickory of the South Atlantic League last year. He hit .277 with six homers and 29 RBI in less than a full season. Guillen is gone and Dallaero could eventually fill that void after a few more seasons of minor-league seasoning. He's already got an above-average arm and power at the plate.

DELLUCCI, DAVID - OF - BL - b: 10/31/71
Taken by Arizona in the second round, Dellucci was a top Oriole prospect who was jumped from Double-A to the Orioles when they needed outfield help at mid-year due to Eric Davis being diagnosed with colon cancer. He didn't hit much for his month in the majors, but he made some spectacular highlight-tape catches in the outfield. He had a great year in the Double-A Eastern League which is usually tough on hitters, showing that he's developed good power to go along with his base stealing speed.

He's a multidimensional player, much like Steve Finley. Dellucci has the ability to take over the Diamondbacks starting right field job by beating out some veterans.

	AB	R	HR	RBI	SB	BA
1997 Baltimore	27	3	1	3	0	.222

DEMETRAL, CHRIS - 2B - BL - b: 12/8/69
Demetral is a career minor-leaguer who does not excel in any offensive category. In 1997, he was demoted by the Dodgers from Triple-A Albuquerque to Class A Vero Beach.

DEPASTINO, JOE - C - BR - b: 9/4/73
DePastino, a former seventh-round pick was converted to catcher during the '94 season, and has played there almost exclusively since, although he has never been a team's number one receiver. He had his best season with the bat at Double-A Trenton last year, hitting .254 with 17 homers in 276 at-bats. He's still young enough that if he keeps improving on offense and defense he has a chance to play in the majors.

DEROSSO, TONY - 3B - BR - 11/7/75
DeRosso, a tall third baseman, struggled with the bat in his first season at Double-A Trenton, hitting just .216. He has never hit higher than .257 in a season, but has been moved along fairly quickly. His size and youth mean he still has a chance to develop, but it's going to take a while.

DESHIELDS, DELINO - 2B - BL - b: 1/15/69
Scouting: Maybe wearing a Dodgers uniform was DeShields' problem after all. He has reclaimed much of the high regard he enjoyed while with the Montreal Expos. DeShields fills the Cardinals' needs for a leadoff man able to get on base and run, and even went beyond that a little with some pop in his bat. It also has to be accepted that DeShields is, at best, an average defensive second baseman, capable of mistakes on the routine plays.
1998: It's hoped that further improvement at making contact and being more patient about taking pitches will make DeShields a .300 hitter and produce his second successive season of at least 50 stolen bases. He'll be back in the leadoff spot and is a year away from being pushed for playing time, so he needs to stay healthy.
1997: DeShields set career highs with a league-leading 14 triples and also had career bests in homers and RBI. Occasional perceived valleys in work ethic didn't last long, and he played through several nagging injuries.
1996: He completed a miserable three-year stint of disappointment with Los Angeles by batting just .224 and striking out 124 times. Many Dodgers sympathizers placed considerable blame on DeShields, who came to be ranked as a has-been and borderline clubhouse cancer.

	AB	R	HR	RBI	SB	BA
1995 Los Angeles	425	66	8	37	39	.256
1996 Los Angeles	581	75	5	41	48	.224
1997 St. Louis	572	92	11	58	55	.295

DEVAREZ, CESAR - C - BR - b: 9/22/69
Devarez does not possess the skills required of a major league catcher. In 1997, he had 95 at-bats at Double-A Orlando as a backup to prospect Pat Cline.

DEVEREAUX, MIKE - OF - BR - b: 4/10/63
Scouting: Devereaux has been a versatile extra outfielder, but appears to have reached the end of the road. He has trouble catching up to the high fastballs he has made a career of hitting, and no longer has much speed.
1998: The expansion draft may allow Devereaux one final chance to stick on a major league roster, but the odds aren't in his favor.
1997: Devereaux had a chance to grab playing time from Damon Buford and the injured Juan Gonzalez early in the season and couldn't capitalize.
1996: Devereaux got over 300 at-bats because of injuries to other outfielders. Although he hit a weak .229, he came through with some clutch hits.

	AB	R	HR	RBI	SB	BA
1995 Atlanta	55	7	1	8	2	.255
1996 Baltimore	323	49	8	34	8	.229
1997 Texas	72	8	0	7	1	.208

DIAZ, ALEX - OF - BB - b: 10/5/68
Scouting: Diaz is a journeyman outfielder with just enough speed to surface now and then in the majors. He is erratic in the field, and lacks power at the plate.
1998: With expansion, Diaz might find a spot as an extra outfielder somewhere, but he should once again get more minor-league than major league at-bats.
1997: Late in the season, Diaz became the everyday right fielder for Texas by default, as numerous injuries reduced the pool of available players. He had some good games, but his chance to be a major league regular came and went a few years ago. Diaz spent most of the year at Triple-A where he hit .286 with 12 homers, 49 RBI and 26 steals.
1996: Elbow and ankle injuries ruined Diaz' chance to get significant playing time with the Mariners.

	AB	R	HR	RBI	SB	BA
1995 Seattle	270	44	3	27	18	.248
1996 Seattle	79	11	1	5	6	.241
1997 Texas	90	8	2	12	1	.222

DIAZ, ALFREDO - SS - BB - 9/10/72
A journeyman minor leaguer, Diaz may be past the prospect stage. He's been around a while, but has yet to put together a spectacular year that would catch management's eye. He's a utility type without a lot of power, who filled a role at Triple-A Vancouver last year.

DIAZ, EDDY - 3B - BR - 9/29/71
Scouting: Diaz has good fielding skills while filling in at shortstop and second base, but probably doesn't have the bat to be a regular in the big leagues. He has hit at the Triple-A level.
1998: Diaz could stick around the Brewers' organization as infield insurance, although expansion could certainly afford him a larger role with another club.
1997: Diaz was called up by the Brewers on a couple of occasions in emergencies. He played well when second baseman Fernando Vina was injured, but could not sustain his hitting and stick with the club.
1996: Diaz spent the season with Triple-A Tacoma. The Brewers signed him as a minor-league free agent after the season.

	AB	R	HR	RBI	SB	BA
1997 Milwaukee	50	4	0	7	0	.220

DIAZ, EDWIN - 2B - BR - b: 1/15/75

Scouting: Diaz is a good fastball hitter who still needs to learn to hit off-speed pitches. His strikezone judgment has never been good, and he has struck out approximately once in every four at-bats in his minor-league career. Diaz is still young enough to develop as a hitter, and as a former second-round pick, he should get every opportunity. He has worked hard on his defense, which is adequate. Diaz is not much of a stolen base threat.
1998: Diaz was taken by the Diamondbacks, and will get an opportunity for a major league role. With the Rangers he was ticketed to be at Triple-A. If he cannot learn to lay off breaking pitches out of the strike zone, it will be another long season.
1997: In his first try at Triple-A, Diaz hit .100 with 29 strikeouts in 80 at-bats. The Rangers sent him back to Tulsa, where he rebounded nicely, hitting .275 with 15 home runs.
1996: Diaz' first Double-A season was solid (.265 with 16 homers and 65 RBI). There was concern over his high strikeout total (122 in 499 at-bats).

DIAZ, EINAR - C - BR - b: 12/28/72

Scouting: Diaz is a durable, if undersized (5'10", 165 pounds) receiver who possesses solid defensive skills. In 2097 minor-league plate appearances, he has had just 88 walks and 136 strikeouts. Diaz is a scrappy hitter who puts the ball in play though he has little extra-base power. His mechanics are sound behind the plate and he has an above-average arm, but he is likely hurt by the perception that he doesn't look like a catcher because of his size.
1998: Diaz is ready to inherit the backup catcher job in Cleveland, but the Indians have been reluctant to entrust young position players with major league roles until after a year or two of experience. Unless expansion gives Diaz a larger role, he will head back to Triple-A Buffalo for another year of seasoning.
1997: Diaz was a reliable full-time catcher for the fourth consecutive season in 1997. He showed maturity behind the plate, though his offensive game did not develop as hoped. Diaz neither hurt nor helped himself with his 1997 campaign.
1996: Diaz hit a career-high .281, with career-best power to the gaps. His defensive skills withstood the difficult transition to Double-A. He was rewarded with a late-season promotion to the majors.

DIAZ, LINO - 3B - BR - b: 7/22/70

Diaz looks to have topped out as a prospect as he played the entire 1997 season at the Double-A level. Diaz made it to Triple-A in 1996, was demoted and didn't make it back last season. He has good range and is a hustler. He has a short stroke and gap power but has been passed on the third base prospect list and will have a tough time making it to the big leagues.

DIFELICE, MIKE - C - BR - b: 5/28/69

Scouting: His strength is behind the plate, where Difelice has the confidence of his pitching staff on his pitch selection and gritty effort. He has a good arm, though not remarkable. Difelice also has shown he can handle himself with a bat as a big-leaguer. Though a seven-year pro, he's still growing as a hitter, considering his 260 major league at-bats last season were more than he ever had in any minor-league season.
1998: The Cardinals left Difelice exposed to expansion, because they had plans for Eli Marrero. The Devil Rays took Difelice but then quickly obtained John Flaherty for the front line.

The amount Difelice plays will depend on the health and progress of those around him, as well as any improvement Difelice might continue to make offensively.
1997: He threw out better than a third of the runners who tried to steal off him and, particularly in the season's first half, was a defensive stalwart. Perhaps it was fatigue from catching more than any other time in his career, but Difelice had increasing trouble blocking balls in the dirt — not persistent, but more than his reputation. His bat exceeded his reputation too, particularly in the clutch.
1996: Though he had steadily climbed through the farm system, Difelice always had been a backup minor-league catcher with little offensive promise until he batted .285 and hit nine homers in 79 Triple-A games.

	AB	R	HR	RBI	SB	BA
1997 St. Louis	260	16	4	30	1	.238

DiSARCINA, GARY - SS - BR - b: 11/19/67

Scouting: DiSarcina remains one of the cornerstones of the ballclub with his solid fielding and clubhouse leadership. The level of his defensive play has hardly dropped, despite the fact he played last season with a damaged right elbow that required off-season surgery. DiSarcina has fulfilled his potential as a hitter in only one season — 1995, when he hit .307 — but he still has the ability to get some clutch hits as the Angels' ninth-place hitter.
1998: The Angels acquired a potential replacement for DiSarcina by choosing UCLA shortstop Troy Glaus in the first round of the 1997 draft, but it will be a while before he plays shortstop for the Angels. DiSarcina remains at the top of his game defensively and will again be a vital part of the team.
1997: DiSarcina's defense helped the Angels win a number of close games and his consistency with the glove was a model for young players. His continued batting average drop is a mild concern, but he was primarily in the lineup for his glove anyway.
1996: Another solid defensive year overshadowed a season-long struggle at the plate in which DiSarcina's batting average fell 49 points to .258.

	AB	R	HR	RBI	SB	BA
1995 California	362	61	5	41	7	.307
1996 California	536	62	5	48	2	.256
1997 Anaheim	549	52	4	47	7	.246

DOBROLSKY, BILL - C - BR - b: 3/16/70

Dobrolsky is not considered a high prospect in the Brewers' organization and spent the year at Double-A El Paso in the Texas League. Dobrolsky strikes out too frequently and, at age 28, looks like an organizational catcher.

DODSON, BO - 1B - BL - b: 12/7/70

He missed most of the season after shoulder surgery, but came back in the final month and appeared fine physically, although out of shape. He's a pure hitter, capable of hitting .300 in the majors with walks, although not much power. He's also an exceptional defensive first baseman. With Mo Vaughn and Reggie Jefferson in Boston, he might need to go elsewhere to play, but he has big-league ability.

DONATO, DAN - 3B - BL - b: 11/15/72

Donato is a good all-round athlete (a college hockey star), but failed to make any significant improvement last year over his 1996 season. If he wants to maintain progress up the Yankees' farm ladder, he will have to do better than his 1997 campaign in which he hit .275 with five homers and 43 RBI.

DONNELS, CHRIS - 3B/1B - BL - b: 4/21/66
A fringe major leaguer with the Red Sox, Donnels went to Japan after the 1995 season. He had a productive year in 1996, knocking 20 home runs, but he got released by Kintetsu. Last year, Donnels joined the Orix Blue Wave and hit over .300, but he is not a star in Japan.

DOSTER, DAVID - 2B - BR - b: 10/8/70
Scouting: Doster is a professional hitter who drives the ball to the alleys, hitting it where it's pitched; he makes regular contact and has good doubles power. Doster's plate discipline is below average and his inability to play positions other than second base is a roadblock to his major league goals. He's a productive player in the higher minors but is a prime example of the kind of player who is unlikely to take the next step — to the majors — in a significant role. Doster's tools are just fair: his defensive range and arm are adequate and his speed is below average.
1998: Doster will be squeezed out of the Phillies' future by better, younger prospects. He can't advance to the big-league club because Mickey Morandini is entrenched there and Doster would not make a good bench player in the majors. Expansion gives him hope of finding a major league role but he is more likely destined for Triple-A with a new organization.
1997: As usual, Doster was the linchpin of his minor-league team in 1997. In addition to his substantial on-field production, Doster has always been a fan favorite and team leader because of his fiery demeanor and consistent hustle on the field. However, his lack of a future with the Phillies was underscored by the fact that he was not called up to the majors in September, after getting a chance in 1996.
1996: A mid-season injury to Morandini gave Doster a brief shot at second base in the majors. He was so unimpressive that the Phillies' didn't ask him back in September until Scott Rolen broke his hand. Doster showed decent extra-base power for a middle infielder at Triple-A Scranton, but his lack of versatility made him an inadequate utility player.

	AB	R	HR	RBI	SB	BA
1996 Philadelphia	105	14	1	8	0	.267

DOWLER, DEMITRIUS - OF - BR - b: 7/23/71
Dowler split time between Chicago's Double-A and Triple-A farm teams last year but didn't do anything to distinguish himself; he batted a combined .244 with just 14 extra-base hits in 268 at-bats. He's a decent basestealer, but he has trouble with the strike zone and doesn't hit for a high enough average to justify his lack of power. Dowler also is old for a player with no major league experience (he'll be 27 in July). That, combined with the overflow of outfielders on the Cubs' major league and minor-league rosters means Dowler doesn't have much chance at all.

DREW, J.D. - OF - BL - b: 11/20/75
A dominant collegiate player, Drew possesses patience at the plate and a good line-drive stroke, a combination that should let him hit .300 in the majors with an on-base percentage approaching .400. Drew combines power and speed; he was the first 30/30 (homers and steals) player in the history of the NCAA in 1997. He's an above-average center fielder with a strong arm. Drew is also a client of Scott Boras and, therefore, is a prime implement with which Boras is attacking the major league draft. It caused Drew to play his first "pro" season in the independent Northern League in 1997, where he was overwhelming. Drew and Boras' contract demands — $10 million — will keep him out of the major leagues which his skills make him seem so ready to join.

DRINKWATER, SEAN - 3B - BR - b: 6/22/71
Drinkwater is a below-average fielder at third base and has a weak bat, a combination that does not bring many teams knocking at your door. In 1997, Drinkwater moved on to the Independent League where, in all likelihood, he will finish his career.

DUCEY, ROB - OF - BL - b: 5/24/65
Scouting: Another of the many outfield prospects produced by the Toronto farm system who got away, Ducey got tired of fighting the numbers game in the U.S. and instead became a Nippon Ham Fighter in 1995-96, where he displayed heretofore unseen power.
1998: Another candidate for the Mariners' left field platoon, Ducey may get his last chance; he's not getting any younger.
1997: Ducey's return from Japan was marred by injuries and a traffic jam in left field, although his 22 extra-base hits in 143 at-bats made for a good power ratio.
1996: Ducey played for a second year in Japan.

	AB	R	HR	RBI	SB	BA
1997 Seattle	143	25	5	10	3	.287

DUNCAN, MARIANO - 2B/SS - BR - b: 3/13/63
Scouting: If Duncan could take a walk, he would be a much more valuable player. As it is, he needs to have a 1996-like year to be valuable. His fielding is suspect, he swings at everything, no longer steals bases and doesn't hit for power. He is a useful player in that he is relatively comfortable at any position other than catcher, although he's a below-average fielder at all positions.
1998: Duncan's days as a starting second baseman are behind him although he is a virtual certainty to make an opening day roster as a backup. He always finds his way into the lineup and has had more than 250 at-bats every year of his eleven-season career.
1997: Duncan wanted out of New York because he wasn't starting often enough. He was traded earlier in the year to the San Diego Padres along with Kenny Rogers in the Greg Vaughn deal that fell through. Shortly after, he was shipped off to the Blue Jays for a minor-leaguer and was promptly inserted in the everyday lineup. He finished with has lowest batting average in a decade, since 1987 with the Dodgers.
1996: A .340 season offset the fact that Duncan walked only nine times. He was the Yankees' usual second baseman in their World Championship season.

	AB	R	HR	RBI	SB	BA
1995 Cincinnati	265	36	6	36	1	.287
1996 New York AL	400	62	8	56	4	.340
1997 NY AL - Tor	339	36	1	25	6	.236

DUNN, TODD - OF - BR - b: 7/29/70
Scouting: Dunn looks to have the tools. He is big, fast and hit for power in the minors. He has yet to prove he can do so in the majors, however. He needs to work on cutting down on his strikeouts.
1998: The Brewers don't want to give up on this guy because of his physical attributes, but he really is no longer a kid. This may

be Dunn's last chance to earn a major league job.

1997: Dunn flopped badly in his first callup early in the season. He looked intimidated, played awkwardly in the field and had trouble making contact at the plate. But, he improved in the field and in making contact at the plate when he was recalled later in the season.

1996: Dunn hit a powerful .340 at Double-A El Paso and was a late-season callup by the Brewers. He showed some promise in six games.

	AB	R	HR	RBI	SB	BA
1997 Milwaukee	118	17	3	9	3	.229

DUNSTON, SHAWON - SS - BR - b: 3/21/63

Scouting: After all this time in the big leagues Dunston still doesn't know how to take a walk, but he has demonstrated that he can be an effective hitter without the free passes to first. And he remains one of the better shortstops in the National League with his strong arm making up for some deficiencies in range.

1998: Dunston will be a starting shortstop for one of the thirty big-league teams, but it isn't clear where he'll play. It won't be in Chicago, where he remains a fan favorite but was traded because the Cubs decided to go with younger players. After Dunston discovered that playing on artificial turf didn't aggravate his back as much as he though it would he began discussing a return to the Pirates, although it seemed more likely they'd go with Kevin Elster instead.

1997: Dunston had a good season in his return to Wrigley Field after a one-year absence. He solidified Chicago's infield and was one of the team's best hitters until the late-season trade that sent him to Pittsburgh for the stretch drive. He had an outstanding last month for the Pirates, which only increased his value for the off-season free-agent market.

1996: Dunston spent an uncomfortable year in San Francisco, signing with the Giants only after the Cubs rejected his offers to stay in Chicago. He was having one of his best seasons when he suffered a broken bone in his eye socket in early-August that ended his season and limited him to 82 games.

	AB	R	HR	RBI	SB	BA
1995 Chicago NL	477	58	14	69	10	.296
1996 San Francisco	287	27	5	25	8	.300
1997 Chi. NL - Pitt.	490	71	14	57	32	.300

DUNWOODY, TODD - OF - BL - b: 4/11/75

Scouting: Dunwoody is multi-talented center fielder who combines power, speed and defensive ability as few minor-league prospects can. He's a strapping lefty hitter who has prodigious power to center and right field. He is overaggressive at the plate, often getting himself out on bad pitches. He has above-average speed, but sometimes takes undue chances on the bases. He has good range in center field and an above-average arm. Dunwoody is someone's center fielder of the present or not-too-distant future.

1998: Dunwoody is ready to at least platoon in the major leagues. Though most of his experience is in center field, right field could be his eventual destination. The presence of Gary Sheffield and Mark Kotsay makes Dunwoody a prime candidate for trade.

1997: Dunwoody got a brief mid-season major league trial and was quite productive batting out of the third spot in the order. One major problem —he whiffed 21 times in 50 at-bats. He has averaged 128 strikeouts versus only 45 walks in his three minor-league seasons.

1996: Dunwoody made an impressive two-level jump to the talent-laden Double-A Eastern League, where he was an All-Star. His 24-homer/24-steal season as one of his level's youngest starters cemented his status as a top prospect.

	AB	R	HR	RBI	SB	BA
1997 Florida	50	7	2	7	2	.260

DURANT, MIKE - C/DH - BR - b: 9/14/69

Durant spent time with the Twins in 1996 but was a number two catcher at Triple-A Salt Lake in 1997. He's not a good defensive receiver but he does run well. He used to be a hitter in the minors, too, but he came in at .206 in 223 at-bats in the Pacific Coast League this past season. He is a long shot to ever see the Metrodome again.

	AB	R	HR	RBI	SB	BA
1996 Minnesota	81	15	0	5	3	.210

DURHAM, RAY - 2B - BB - b: 11/30/71

Scouting: Durham is blessed with incredible talents, including top-notch speed and growing power. He is usually steady in the field, but occasionally prone to periods where he lets the ball play him instead of the other way around. He has improved his plate discipline since he first came up to the majors although he still swings at too many bad pitches. He may not become the next Joe Morgan as some overly optimistic observers predicted he would, but Durham will be one of the game's better second basemen.

1998: Expect a strong rebound by Durham; he has too much talent not to succeed. The White Sox are counting on him to grab a top-of-the-order spot and spark their offense while showing improved defense, too.

1997: Serious fielding problems effected his hitting and baserunning and turned the whole season into a big disappointment. But, Durham was still an effective hitter in a limited role and the club's leading base thief. It was a bad year, but not a trend.

1996: Durham's second full year in the majors featured improvements in nearly ever facet of the game and he was particularly successful on the bases, stealing 30 bases in 34 tries, a league-best 88.2% success rate, running his career record to 48 steals in 57 tries.

	AB	R	HR	RBI	SB	BA
1995 Chicago AL	471	68	7	51	18	.257
1996 Chicago AL	557	79	10	65	30	.275
1997 Chicago AL	634	106	11	53	33	.271

DURKAC, BO - 3B - BB - b: 12/12/72

A switch-hitting corner infielder, Durkac displayed gap power with 56 doubles and 152 RBI in his first two years in the organization after being signed as a free agent in 1996.

DURKIN, CHRIS - OF - BL - b: 8/12/70

1997 was Durkin's second year at the Double-A level, playing at San Antonio. Although he was voted the best power prospect in the Florida State League in 1996, by Baseball America, his power and his batting in general dropped in 1997; he hit only four homers in 125 at-bats. Durkins is too old for the level where he is playing.

DYE, JERMAINE - OF - BR - b: 1/28/74

Scouting: Dye has a quick, potent bat and improving plate discipline. He is also an accomplished outfielder with a strong, accurate arm. Dye will get himself out by chasing bad breaking pitches; he's just too impatient to wait for his pitch and his reputation as a free-swinger rarely lets him see a hittable pitch. Dye has only average speed, at best, and isn't a big stolen base threat.

1998: Sometimes these things take a while. Dye is healthy again; he's motivated by the criticism levelled at him based upon the perception of the Tucker trade being lopsided; he's young, improving and talented. All the ingredients are in place for Dye to have a surprising, breakout season.

1997: High expectations for Dye following his trade from Atlanta for popular Michael Tucker turned to disaster when Tucker hit lights out for a month while Dye struggled with the bat and went on the disabled list twice with a stress fracture in his foot. Once healed, Dye gradually turned his season around and won another shot at the Royals' right field job.

1996: Dye achieved fame and popularity in Atlanta by stepping in for injured superstar David Justice and assisting the Braves to yet another National League championship; he homered in his first big-league at-bat. He also swung at just about every pitch he saw, posting a strikeout-to-walk ratio of 67-to-8.

	AB	R	HR	RBI	SB	BA
1996 Atlanta	292	32	12	37	1	.281
1997 Kansas City	263	26	7	22	2	.236

DYKSTRA, LENNY - OF - BL - b: 2/10/63

Scouting: Dykstra's battles with injuries have been legion. Since his phenomenal 1993 campaign he has appeared in just 186 games and none in 1997. He's a patient hitter who works the count and fouls off pitches to get one to drive; his on-base ability is outstanding. Dykstra's defense and baserunning have waned with age and injuries and he always possessed one of the worst throwing arms in the majors. His recent battles with spinal stenosis — a narrowing of the spinal column — have likely ended his baseball playing career.

1998: Dykstra is expected to retire from playing and manage in the Phillies' minor-league system. There is a remote chance that he will take one last shot at playing during spring training.

1997: Dykstra sat out the entire 1997 season rehabilitating his injured back. His concerns centered around living a normal life, a much higher priority.

1996: Dykstra looked good for a couple of weeks at the season's outset, but was quickly rendered useless by his back problems. His inability to throw prompted the Phillies to consider moving him to left field before he was shut down permanently.

	AB	R	HR	RBI	SB	BA
1995 Philadelphia	254	37	2	18	10	.264
1996 Philadelphia	134	21	3	13	3	.261

EAGLIN, MIKE - 2B - BR - b: 4/25/73

In his sixth minor-league season, Eaglin finally advanced beyond A-ball, to become the starting second baseman at Double-A Greenville in 1997. He had a surprisingly good year, hitting .288 with five homers and 47 RBI in 126 games. Eaglin continued to show good plate discipline, and also stole 15 bases. His speed doesn't translate well to the majors, though and he doesn't have a great deal of power. If his glove were better than average he might be a good prospect. As it is, though, Eaglin has only a marginal chance to reach the majors.

EASLEY, DAMION - 3B/2B - BR - b: 11/11/69

Scouting: Everyone wondered what he could do if he stayed healthy; now we know. Easley isn't the best second baseman in baseball, but he does a lot of things well. He's consistent in the field, has good power for a middle infielder and can steal a base. He can even play shortstop if needed, although second base is his best position.

1998: The Tigers will count on him to play every day at second base, something they weren't comfortable with going into last year. Easley wants to get better at driving in runs, but the Tigers would certainly accept a complete repeat of his 1997 season.

1997: The most significant stat for Easley is that he was available to play every day of the season. Without the nagging injuries that had stopped him in the past, Easley became just the fourth player in Tiger history to hit 20 home runs and steal 20 bases in the same season.

1996: The year that the Angels finally gave up on him became the year that Easley found a home in Detroit. The Tigers sent the since-retired Greg Gohr to the Angels for Easley, who had been demoted to the minor leagues. Easley batted .343 after the trade, but he also had some of the injury problems that hurt his career in California.

	AB	R	HR	RBI	SB	BA
1995 California	357	35	4	35	5	.216
1996 Detroit	112	14	4	17	3	.268
1997 Detroit	527	97	22	72	28	.264

ECHEVARRIA, ANGEL - OF - BR - b: 5/25/71

A member of the Rockies' original draft class in 1992, Echevarria began to emerge at Double-A New Haven in 1995, when he batted .300 with 21 homers and 100 RBI. He has been given chances to come off the bench as a righthanded hitter for the Rockies the past two years and he performed well in that role. But with the big-league team's outfield already crowded and with no outstanding skill, Echevarria is not likely to ever crack the starting lineup with this team.

EDDIE, STEVE - 3B - BR - b: 1/6/71

Eddie had a decent season at Double-A Chattanooga last year, but he hasn't shown any big-league ability in his five minor-league seasons out of college, and he certainly doesn't fit into the Reds' plans for the future. The Reds are set at the infield positions, and already are wondering how they're going to fit their established veterans and emerging youngsters into the left side of their infield as it is. Eddie isn't going to reach the bigs in Cincinnati.

EDGE, TIM - C - BR - b: 10/26/68

Edge has spent eight years in the Pittsburgh farm system, hitting .221 and failing to get 200 at-bats in any season since 1992. He has hung around as a backup catcher in the minor leagues because of his defense and positive attitude. After spending last season with Triple-A Calgary, he joined the Pirates in September as insurance in the event catchers Jason Kendall or Keith Osik got hurt. The Pirates, though, never put Edge on the active roster and that's almost certainly as close as he'll ever get to the big leagues.

EDMONDS, JIM - OF - BL - b: 6/27/70

Scouting: When healthy, Edmonds hits for power and average, and makes highlight-reel plays in center field. The problem is Edmonds hasn't been healthy for two years. His excellent talent is starting to be overshadowed by the fact that he's always hurt, at least, to the point where developing a conditioning program to try to keep Edmonds healthier longer is one of Manager Terry Collins' major off-season projects.

1998: Edmonds has to show the Angels they can count on him to be in the lineup and not break down continually. Any chance to win a championship will depend, in large measure, on his being in the lineup every day.

1997: Edmonds showed major courage and tenacity that belies his laid-back appearance by just finishing the year. He played the second half with cartilage damage in both knees that required surgery. Through the year, he was also bothered by shoulder, wrist, neck and rib injuries. Even so, he hit with power and made spectacular plays in the outfield.

1996: Injuries, primarily an abdominal strain and sprained thumb, were a major problem. Even so, Edmonds hit well for average and power, and showed excellent range in the outfield.

	AB	R	HR	RBI	SB	BA
1995 California	558	120	33	107	1	.290
1996 California	431	73	27	66	4	.304
1997 Anaheim	502	82	26	80	5	.291

EENHOORN, ROBERT - SS - BR - b: 2/9/68

Scouting: Eenhoorn has good speed, quickness and range for someone who stands 6'3". He plays solid defense and possesses a good arm, and has always hit well in the minor leagues. However, he has yet to hit well enough to win a permanent job in the majors.

1998: Eenhoorn will have to show some improvement at the plate to increase his status as an infield prospect. If he can do it this spring, he'll have a solid opportunity to earn a backup job in the majors. Eenhoorn is at a crossroads — he'll have to hit soon or risk being labeled a career minor-leaguer.

1997: Eenhoorn was Vancouver's MVP, which is both good and bad for a player who's 29 years old. He stuck with the Canadians the entire season and didn't earn a promotion to Anaheim until the last few weeks. His excellent defense and a few big hits probably earned him a longer look in spring training, 1998.

1996: A hot bat at the Triple-A level again couldn't translate into decent hitting in the majors and the New York Yankees finally gave up on Eenhoorn as a prospect, putting him on waivers in September. The Angels claimed him and gave him a brief look. He did enough to convince the Angels to give him an extended trial the following season.

EISENREICH, JIM - OF - BL - b: 4/18/59

Scouting: Eisenreich is one of baseball's most fundamentally sound players, not to mention one of its nicest and most courageous individuals. He doesn't swing at bad pitches, hits the ball where it's pitched with authority, runs the bases intelligently and overcomes a lack of raw ability with expert positioning at first base and in the outfield. He doesn't have prodigious power, but clobbers fastballs thrown on the inside half of the plate at the knees. His skills are just now eroding, but that's to be expected from a 39-year-old.

1998: Eisenreich's role is likely to become more limited in 1998. His speed and arm are deteriorating, making him incapable of playing center or right field. He could roll out of bed and hit .280 — that's what should be expected of him over 200 at-bats per season for the next couple of seasons.

1997: Despite being one of the Phillies' best loved players, he was allowed to escape to Florida, with exciting results. Though he was used less than originally anticipated, he filled in expertly at first base and in left field due to the Marlins' myriad injuries. He helped lead a youthful, impressionable team by example.

1996: Eisenreich's last season in Philadelphia was a marvel, featuring a high batting average, a remarkable number of doubles and excellent success stealing bases (11 steals in 12 attempts to run his record in Philadelphia to 32 steals in 35 tries). He will go down as one of the most popular athletes in recent Philadelphia history because of his dignity and class.

	AB	R	HR	RBI	SB	BA
1995 Philadelphia	377	46	10	55	10	.316
1996 Philadelphia	338	45	3	41	11	.361
1997 Florida	293	36	2	34	0	.280

ELLIS, KEVIN - OF - BR - b: 11/21/71

Ellis was signed by the Cubs as a non-drafted free agent early in 1993 after a less-than-stellar collegiate career at Baylor. In his six seasons in the Cubs' farm system the only thing of note that he has done was lead the Class A Florida State League in RBI in 1996 as a 24-year-old. That finally earned him a promotion to Double-A Orlando for the 1997 season where he had a below-average year, batting .255 with eight homers and 41 RBI in 330 at-bats. Ellis has about as little of a chance of making it to Chicago as anybody on the Orlando roster.

ELLIS, PAUL - C - BL - b: 11/28/68

Ellis has a reputation as an adept handler of pitchers, which is his main reason for being in uniform. He's a weak contact hitter with little power and no speed. Ellis is at Double-A for one reason only; to help develop young Cards' pitchers. Perhaps he'll reach the majors as a coach.

ELSTER, KEVIN - SS - BR - b: 8/3/64

Scouting: Elster remade himself into a power hitter with Texas in 1996 after being basically a good-field, no-hit shortstop throughout his career. He continued his power surge with Pittsburgh last year but his season ended early due to a fractured left wrist.

1998: Elster became a free agent with the hopes of still having a chance to be someone's everyday shortstop. The Pirates were interested in re-signing him to a one-year contract if they couldn't re-sign Shawon Dunston. Either Elster or Dunston would keep shortstop warm in Pittsburgh until top prospect Abraham Nunez takes over in 1998. Elster will probably have to go to someone's camp as a non-roster player as he has played in at least 100 games in a major-league season just once since 1992.

1997: Elster was leading the Pirates in homers and RBI while playing a steady shortstop when the fractured left wrist ended his season in mid-May. Signed as a free agent from Texas the previous winter, Elster was on the verge of signing a two-year contract extension with the Pirates when injured.

1996: After having played just 49 major-league games in the previous four seasons because of shoulder problems and hitting just 35 homers in his nine-year career, Elster belted 24 homers in helping Texas to the American League West title.

	AB	R	HR	RBI	SB	BA
1995 New York AL	17	1	0	0	0	.118
1995 Philadelphia	53	10	1	9	0	.208
1996 Texas	515	79	24	99	4	.252
1997 Pittsburgh	138	14	7	25	0	.225

ENCARNACION, ANGELO - C - BR - b: 4/18/73

Stuck behind Jason Kendall in Pittsburgh, Encarnacion hoped for better in San Diego, but ended up moving to Anaheim in the Rickey Henderson trade. The trade was good for Encarnacion, he'll get a chance to back up Todd Greene at the major league level. Unfortunately, the same problems will plague Encarnacion with the Angels: above-average defensive skills, but below-average offensive production.

ENCARNACION, JUAN - OF - BR - b: 3/8/76

Scouting: An exciting young player, Encarnacion excels in all phases of the game. Besides the outstanding offensive numbers (.323, 26 home runs, 90 RBI, 17 steals at Double-A Jacksonville), he plays good defense and has a good arm. The Tigers see him as a potential star.

1998: He'll most likely begin the season at Triple-A Toledo, but it would be no surprise if Encarnacion ended up in Detroit by mid-season. His chances of beginning the year in the big leagues were hurt when he suffered a broken bone last September and was forced to miss the Arizona Fall League.

1997: The Tigers always liked Encarnacion's potential, but it was last year that he emerged as the best prospect in their farm system. After three and a half years spent in rookie ball and Class A, he went to Double-A Jacksonville and had a breakout year. Then he came to the Tigers in September and played well.

1996: Encarnacion's numbers at Class A Lakeland were really nothing special. He batted .240 and struck out 104 times with only 24 walks. But he hit 15 home runs in a difficult league for power hitters, and he hit for his best average in the last month of the season - .273.

	AB	R	HR	RBI	SB	BA
1997 Detroit	33	3	1	5	3	.212

ERSTAD, DARIN - OF - BL - b: 6/4/74

Scouting: The first pick overall in the 1995 draft, Erstad showed why he was a successful four-sport star in high school with his conversion from the outfield to start as the Angels' first baseman last season. He has the athletic ability to play at least five positions well and a football player's toughness — he was a punter at Nebraska. Erstad is the prototypical five-point player. He can hit for average and power, run, throw, and field.

1998: Erstad needs only to build on the progress he began last year and work on becoming a successful leadoff hitter, a process he also started at the beginning of last year. If he stays healthy, he's on a path to stardom.

1997: Erstad showed what he's made of by shrugging off the pressure of being a top draft pick in his first full season in the major leagues, learning a new position and learning to become a leadoff hitter. He held his own in the leadoff spot, but the Angels backed off on that part of his education by re-acquiring Tony Phillips in a May trade.

1996: Erstad made an immediate impact when he was called up in June to replace injured Jim Edmonds. Erstad did so well the Angels tried to keep him around after Edmonds recovered, going to a four-man outfield rotation. Garret Anderson's complaints scotched the attempt, but Erstad had already played well enough to assure himself of a job the following season.

	AB	R	HR	RBI	SB	BA
1996 California	208	34	4	20	3	.284
1997 Anaheim	539	99	16	77	23	.299

ESPINOSA, RAMON - OF - BR - b: 2/7/72

Any future this outfielder had with the Pirates was tied to his speed. However, he lost that after undergoing knee surgery in 1995 and is now nothing more than a Triple-A singles-hitting reserve outfielder. In 1997 Espinosa began the season with Double-A Carolina in the Pirates organization and ended up a Met where he played Double and Triple-A ball.

ESPINOZA, ALVARO - 3B/SS - BR - b: 2/19/62

Espinosa has hung around the fringes of the major leagues because of a superior glove at three infield positions. His role has greatly diminished in recent years; he was the Yankees' starting shortstop for three years and also in Cleveland for one year. His inability to hit consistently cost him a starting job and he struggled mightily at the plate last year; Espinosa may have trouble locating a major league roster spot in the near future.

	AB	R	HR	RBI	SB	BA
1995 Cleveland	143	15	2	17	0	.252
1996 Cleveland	112	12	4	11	1	.223
1996 New York NL	134	19	4	16	0	.306
1997 Seattle	72	3	0	7	1	.181

ESPINOSA, RAMON - BR - b: 2/7/72

Playing for three teams last year, Espinoza made his final stop with the Mets' Triple-A franchise at Norfolk, where he hit .338 in 27 games. It was a year of improvement as Espinoza collected more than a third of his career home runs, including 11 while passing through Double-A Binghamton. He is aggressive and impatient at the plate, but makes good contact. He had good speed before knee surgery in 1995. Espinoza should begin 1998 at Triple-A but won't move up without further improvement.

ESTALELLA, BOBBY - C - BR - b: 8/23/74

Scouting: Estalella is a powerfully-built catcher who has looked like Babe Ruth in his brief major league opportunities the past two seasons. Few hitters compare to Estalella when it comes to driving a mistake fastball. However, Estalella has never batted over .250 over a full minor-league season because he is easy pickings for breaking pitches away and he tries to drive everything instead of hitting singles to right field. Defensively, he is durable and owns an above-average arm with a quick release. Estalella is still learning how to handle a pitching staff.

1998: The Phillies think so highly of Estalella that he was their choice for protection in the expansion draft in spite of the presence of incumbent catcher Mike Lieberthal. He'll play every-day, at Triple-A, instead of being a major league backup.

1997: Despite a three-homer game in the majors in September, Estalella still showed major holes in his offensive game during the minor-league season. Estalella hasn't been able to adjust at the plate.

1996: Estalella bashed fastballs at Double-A and in his brief major league trial, but was easily fooled by a steady stream of outside breaking pitches. His game-calling skills were quite raw.

	AB	R	HR	RBI	SB	BA
1997 Philadelphia	29	9	4	9	0	.345

ESTRADA, OSMANI - 3B - BR - b: 1/23/69

Estrada is a Cuban defector with a good glove and a weak bat. He has gradually progressed through the Rangers chain and spent 1997 at Triple-A Oklahoma City. He's getting up there in age and is a utility infielder in the big leagues, at best.

EUSEBIO, TONY - C - BR - b: 4/27/67

Scouting: Eusebio is an adequate defensive catcher with a better-than-average bat for a backup catcher. He is built like a power hitter, but his slashing batting style makes him a singles hitter with gap power to right-center field. He played all year with a bad right knee which required post-season surgery. Already painfully slow and with a lot of weight to carry, rehabilitation could be difficult.

1998: Eusebio can hit well enough to remain in the major leagues. However, he may not get much playing time, particularly if he is limited by his knee.

1997: Eusebio was Darryl Kile's personal catcher, playing every fifth day. He rarely caught any of the other starting pitchers. Only three of his 45 hits were for extra bases.

1996: Eusebio was hampered by injuries and had only 152 at-bats, a big drop-off from 1995 when he batted .299 in 368 at-bats.

	AB	R	HR	RBI	SB	BA
1995 Houston	368	46	6	58	0	.299
1996 Houston	152	15	1	19	0	.270
1997 Houston	164	12	1	18	0	.274

EVANS, JASON - OF - BB - b: 2/11/71

After spending 1996 in A-ball, Evans played at Double-A and Triple-A in 1997 in the White Sox organization. A switch-hitter, Evans connected at both levels and showed a good eye, especially at Triple-A where he walked 49 times compared to 45 strikeouts in 194 at-bats. He's a solid defensive outfielder who could have a shot at a fourth outfield role if he can continue to hit.

EVANS, TOM - 3B - BR - b: 7/9/74

Scouting: A righthanded hitter with power and a great batting eye, Evans is the heir-apparent to Ed Sprague at third base. He is better defensively than Sprague and could develop into a 25-homer threat eventually. Even though he has a good eye, he needs better bat control. When he swings, he often misses.

1998: Evans is good enough to be at least a backup in the major leagues and he is a more patient hitter than Ed Sprague, who had the major league job last year. He's just one notch down on the depth chart at third.

1997: Evans enjoyed a fine season at Triple-A Syracuse and got the call in September when Sprague went down. Unfortunately, Evans suffered a similar injury (torn labrum) and his first opportunity in the big leagues was wiped out after only 38 at-bats.

1996: Showing incredible patience, Evans walked an amazing 115 times in just 120 games in his first season at the Double-A level. His on-base percentage was a career-high .452 and he made a mark as a potential replacement should Sprague go down with an injury.

	AB	R	HR	RBI	SB	BA
1997 Toronto	38	7	1	2	0	.289

EVERETT, CARL - OF - BB - b: 6/3/71

Scouting: Tim Allen doesn't have the tools this guys carries — he also doesn't have the baggage. Few players match up to Everett in either regard. He can steal bases, hit for power — from either side — throw out a runner from deep in the right field corner, play the heck out of center field and, believe it or not, he can carry a team for ten days or so as he did last summer. But he is no more consistent than the weather and prone to disappear for extended periods.

1998: Which Carl Everett will be prominent this season? The one who batted .404 with a .788 slugging percentage in a 27-game sequence last summer or the one who disappeared in the last six week? The one who wasted his 1996 season? Or the one who drove 50 runs after the All-Star break in 1995? The one who batted .208 against lefthanded pitching or the one who batted .260 against righthanded pitching?

1997: Everett had cooled off by August 6th, the day of an ugly incident at Shea Stadium involving his wife Linda and one of his children. A scenario, the beginning of which is unknown, led to Everett's pleading guilty to child neglect. When some circumstances became public knowledge, Everett's production dropped off precipitously. He batted .204 with 46 total bases and 37 strikeouts in his final 137 at-bats.

1996: After a stunning second-half in 1995, Everett was invisible for most of 1996. He had 59 total bases, 53 strikeouts and 16 RBI in 192 at-bats. The Mets attributed his fall off to a too laid-back approach that they believed was an outgrowth of his overreaction to an ugly incident involving fans in Venezuela the previous winter.

	AB	R	HR	RBI	SB	BA
1995 New York NL	289	48	12	54	2	.260
1996 New York NL	192	29	1	16	6	.240
1997 New York NL	443	58	14	57	17	.248

FABREGAS, JORGE - C - BL - b: 3/13/70

Scouting: Fabregas is mostly a defensive specialist despite his brief hitting surge with the White Sox at the end of last year. He has little power and a mediocre batting eye. He can't hit the better pitches of most major league pitchers; they can beat him with fastballs or breaking pitches. He's more of a contact hitter than a pulling, power hitter. Fortunately, he has good enough catching skills to stay in the majors; pitchers like to throw to him.

1998: Fabregas drove Ron Karkovice into the free agent market, and then the White Sox lost Fabregas to Arizona in the expansion draft. Fabregas will compete with Kelly Stinnett for time as the starter. The Diamondbacks were hoping that the struggles of early '97 were a fluke.

1997: After a disappointing half-season with the Angels, Fabregas came to Chicago and suddenly started hitting. With his passable defensive skill, it was enough for him to steal the catching job away from Karkovice. It was Fabregas' best season.

1996: Fabregas continued to split catching duties in Anaheim, keeping at least part of the job because of his defense; he hit for an unusually good average, but had no extras (power, speed, walks). He did little to win a full-time role.

	AB	R	HR	RBI	SB	BA
1995 California	227	24	1	22	0	.247
1996 California	254	18	2	26	0	.287
1997 Ana. - Chi. AL	360	33	7	51	1	.258

FASANO, SAL - C - BR - b: 8/10/71

Scouting: Fasano has not made the best use of his obvious talents. He's built like a catcher, has hit for power in the minors, and has decent defensive skills, but his poor conditioning and slow learning curve has doomed him to the high minors in recent years. Fasano has had multiple chances to crack the Royals roster but has muffed them all. He throws well enough for a reserve catcher role in the majors. Fasano's good power in the lower minors has been notably absent above Double-A.

1998: Fasano will be a major league reserve, or a regular at Triple-A, depending upon the current needs of his organization. He has not made the necessary advancement in his skills or dedication to conditioning that is required to be a major league regular.

1997: Fasano was manager Bob Boone's choice for reserve duty in the majors, but just did nothing to keep the job. He hit poorly in his infrequent starts and seemed ill-prepared for spot duty coming off the bench. Fasano was relegated to the minors for good when Tony Muser took over the club; he hit just .164 in 49 games for Triple-A Omaha.

1996: Fasano was a disappointment in a few brief major league stints, hitting for a low average and only sporadic good defense. He rode the bench a lot, then was demoted at mid-season before hitting poorly at Omaha, too.

	AB	R	HR	RBI	SB	BA
1996 Kansas City	143	20	6	19	1	.203
1997 Kansas City	38	4	1	1	0	.211

FEBLES, CARLOS - 2B - BR - b: 5/24/76
Febles advanced to higher Class A Wilmington in his fourth pro season and lost much of his batting average, but retained the other elements of his game. Since the Carolina League is a notoriously difficult hitters' environment; the loss of batting average is not a big concern. Febles has outstanding speed (79 steals over the last two years) and good range at second base. He will also take a walk but his 95 strikeouts last year are a concern. Febles will advance to a hitters' park at Double-A Wichita in 1998 as one of the younger members of the Texas League. It'll be a good test of his mettle as a prospect.

FELIX, LAURO - 3B - BR - b: 6/24/70
Felix came to the Brewers organization in 1995 and, at age 27, has played just 45 Triple-A games in his six-year minor-league career. He's played shortstop and third base in his career; at Double-A El Paso in 1997 he split time at third base. He doesn't have nearly enough power to be considered a prospect at that position or any other.

FERGUSON, JEFF - 2B - BR - b: 6/18/73
Ferguson lost all of 1995 to an injury and rebounded with a solid season in Double-A in 1996. He played at both the Double-A and Triple-A level of the Twins' organization in 1997 and was impressive at Salt Lake. He showed some pop for a middle infielder and could give the Twins a viable second base option should Chuck Knoblauch become unavailable.

FERNANDEZ, TONY - SS - BB - b: 6/30/62
Scouting: Once a speedy turf shortstop and an exciting all-around package, Fernandez has seemingly completed his often rocky transformation into a reliable role player. His range has deteriorated to an weak level for a shortstop, but is still above-average for a second baseman. His bat has slowed and makes him quite vulnerable to righthanded pitchers, but he can still put the hammer to southpaws with some power to the gaps. He remains a wildly overaggressive swinger.

1998: The emergence of prospect Enrique Wilson may force Fernandez to move on. He will find a job as a platoon second baseman, and hit in the .260s with a few homers in 250 at-bats.
1997: Expected to share time with Julio Franco, Fernandez won the full-time job in the first half with a solid all-around showing. A mid-season dry spell prompted the acquisition of platoonmate Jeff Branson, which kept Fernandez fresh for the stretch run. Fernandez cranked an important post-season homer to help the Indians come within a game of the World Championship.
1996: Fernandez lost his starting Yankees' shortstop job to Derek Jeter, and his season to injury.

	AB	R	HR	RBI	SB	BA
1995 New York AL	384	57	5	45	6	.245
1997 Cleveland	409	55	11	44	6	.286

FEUERSTEIN, DAVID - OF - BR - b: 7/19/73
Feuerstein played at the Class A and Double-A levels of the Rockies organization in 1997. He doesn't have power but he has some speed to cover ground in the field and it helped him swipe 20 bases for Salem in the Carolina League. He'll probably start the 1998 season at Double-A New Haven and will have to improve at the plate to move on.

FICK, CHRIS - OF - BL - b: 10/4/69
Fick has a ton of power potential, but was inconsistent at Double-A Arkansas in 1996. He showed a lot of power, with 25 doubles and 19 home runs. A classic big swinger, Fick struck out 93 times at Arkansas. In 1997 Fick played in just 21 games, 17 with Double-A Shreveport in the Giants organization and four with Diamondback affiliate High Desert in high A ball.

FIELDER, CECIL - 1B/DH - BR - b: 9/21/63
Scouting: Fielder's biggest asset is a pair of quick hands that can still surprise any pitcher who tries to throw a fastball past him. He can pull an outside pitch with surprising power. His first base defense was never great, and now it has deteriorated. He has recovered from a 1997 thumb injury and finally showed some serious attention to conditioning.
1998: The Yankees were not interested in Fielder at his 1997 salary of $7.2 million; Fielder had seen enough of New York, anyway. He doesn't like being a full-time DH, but that's what he looks like for 1998.
1997: Fielder's season was ruined by a thumb injury in mid-July, suffered while sliding into home plate; he didn't return until September. He never got a hot streak going, and his power numbers were way down, even on a per-at-bat basis.
1996: Fielder helped the Yankees to a World Series title and did well in the power-hitting department, but he really wasn't a good fit for Yankee Stadium with its big pasture in left-center field.

	AB	R	HR	RBI	SB	BA
1995 Detroit	494	70	31	82	0	.243
1996 Det-NY AL	591	85	39	117	2	.252
1997 New York AL	361	40	13	61	0	.260

FIGGA, MIKE - C - BR - b: 7/31/70
Figga has earned his reputation as a good defensive catcher who struggles a bit at the plate. He hit .244 for Triple-A Columbus and was 0-for-4 in two games with the Yankees. Figga could be somebody's backup catcher this year but a larger role is out of the question.

FINLEY, STEVE - OF - BL - b: 3/12/65
Scouting: Finley's 1997 totals dropped way off from his career-year of '96. He was troubled much of last season by a sore throwing elbow and a bunion on the big toe of his front foot. Finley again showed the power he discovered in '96, but his batting average and on-base percentage dropped way off. Finley remains of one game's top centerfielders.
1998: The Padres need him to return to 1996 form, especially in the second spot ahead of Tony Gwynn.
1997: Finley's average fell 37 points and his on-base percent was off 41 points to a minuscule .313. He still showed power and became the first Padre to score 100 runs in three straight

seasons (thanks largely to hitting ahead of Gwynn). Finley drew only 43 walks and stole only 15 bases — his lowest totals in three seasons as a Padre.

1996: Finley set club records for runs (126), total bases (348), extra-base hits (84) and doubles (45, since broken by Gwynn this year) and won his second straight Gold Glove for play in center field. His career-high homer total was 19 more than his previous best.

	AB	R	HR	RBI	SB	BA
1995 San Diego	562	104	10	44	36	.297
1996 San Diego	655	126	30	95	22	.298
1997 San Diego	560	101	28	92	15	.261

FINN, JOHN - 2B - BR - b: 10/18/67
A utility player formerly in the Brewers farm system, Finn is a 30-year-old minor-league utility player who hit .276 for Double-A Birmingham but did nothing else to distinguish himself from a myriad of other non-prospects in the high minors.

FITHIAN, GRANT - C - BR - b: 11/20/71
Fithian made dramatic improvement last year. His batting average jumped 84 points to .285 and he had a .380 on-base percentage with eight homers and 53 RBI for Double-A Norwich. 1997 was his best season at any level and he may still have time to progress to the majors if he maintains his new level of play.

FLAHERTY, JOHN - C - BR - b: 10/21/67
Scouting: Flaherty is a durable starting catcher and strong defensively behind the plate, but with only an average arm. Offensively, he doesn't have a lot of power although he has hit for better-than-expected average in San Diego. He is one of the slower players on a team not known for speed.

1998: The Padres traded their starting catcher to Tampa Bay right after the expansion derby. Working against him were his $1.6 million salary, the emergence of Carlos Hernandez, and the promise of Ben Davis. Expansion made Flaherty's playing time safer for 1998.

1997: Flaherty finished strong after hovering between .240-.255 for much of the season. His power totals in 129 games almost matched his totals of the previous season accomplished in only 72 games.

1996: Flaherty hit in 27 straight games and was credited with assisting the Padre surge to the National League West title by helping handle the pitching staff.

	AB	R	HR	RBI	SB	BA
1995 Detroit	354	39	11	40	0	.243
1996 Detroit	152	18	4	23	1	.250
1996 San Diego	264	22	9	41	2	.303
1997 San Diego	439	38	9	46	4	.273

FLETCHER, DARRIN - C - BL - b: 10/3/66
Scouting: Fletcher has good pop for a catcher and the fact that he swings from the left side is an added bonus. Considered a poor defensive catcher earlier in his career, Fletcher has worked hard at that end of the game to the point where he is now passable.

1998: Fletcher was a free agent at the end of the last season and the Expos couldn't afford to bring him back. Fletcher certainly could help any team looking for a catcher, though age and defensive deficiencies would make him more a attractive as a platoon player getting the majority of the playing time by facing righthanders.

1997: Fletcher had the best all-around season of his career, despite being limited to 96 games by injuries. Fletcher's primary ailment was a strained ligament in his left (non-throwing) elbow that is not considered a long-term problem.

1996: Fletcher was Montreal's primary catcher, getting high marks for handling a young pitching staff.

	AB	R	HR	RBI	SB	BA
1995 Montreal	350	42	11	45	0	.286
1996 Montreal	394	41	12	57	0	.266
1997 Montreal	310	39	17	55	1	.277

FLORA, KEVIN - OF - BR - b: 6/10/69
Flora was once a speedy middle-infield prospect with the Angels. After leg injuries and grief over a family loss he turned up in Philadelphia for a brief stint in 1995. After spending 1996 in the Mets' organization, Flora played for Triple-A New Orleans in the Astros' farm system in 1997. He hit .257 and stole eight bases and has become a faded prospect.

FLORES, JOSE - 2B/SS - BR - b: 6/26/73
Flores is a limited utility player who has drifted to the top of the Phillies' chain by default due to their lack of organizational infield depth. Flores makes consistent contact, will draw a walk and has decent speed, but ranks among the least powerful hitters in the high minors. He is a useful organization player who does not mind coming off of the bench or filling any role required, but he'll likely be squeezed by the convergence of the Phillies' better prospects at the Triple-A level over the next two seasons. He has a negligible professional future.

FLOREZ, TIM - 2B - BR - b: 7/23/69
Florez had solid numbers at Triple-A Phoenix last year, but his numbers should be understood with two qualifiers. First, at his age he should be beyond Triple-A anyway if he had any chance of being a regular major leaguer. Second, though his numbers are solid, they are unspectacular for the Pacific Coast League, a notorious hitter's circuit. Florez isn't going any further.

FLOYD, CLIFF - 1B - BL - b: 12/5/72
Scouting: It wasn't all that long ago that Floyd was considered the single most talented minor-league prospect. A shattered wrist in 1995 has set him back dramatically, but Floyd still shows flashes of his abilities. Few can hit a fastball as hard or far as Floyd. He owns a power/speed combination rivaled by few. His batting eye at the plate appeared much improved in his limited 1997 major league trial. His defense at first base and in the outfield will never be Gold Glove material, though he will overcome mistakes with his raw athletic ability. His throwing arm is below-average.

1998: This could be the year. The Marlins quickly dispatched Darren Daulton and Jeff Conine following their World Series victory, opening the door for Floyd at first base. The Marlins desire to cut costs also works in Floyd's favor. He is finally healthy, and could establish himself with a 20-homer, 15-steal season. Believe it or not, this guy is still only 25 years old.

1997: Floyd ripped Triple-A pitching, batting .366 and slugging .649 with speed in a 39-game trial. Though his average was low in the majors, he walked often and showed bursts of power and speed. The time and circumstances weren't right to give Floyd a full shot in 1997.

1996: The success of Henry Rodriguez and David Segui in Montreal limited Floyd to a reserve role. Though he hit for a low average, he hit some balls that defied description. His game-winning homer against Ricky Bottalico in Philadelphia nearly tore through the backdrop in right field. He was liberated by being traded to Florida following the season.

	AB	R	HR	RBI	SB	BA
1995 Montreal	69	6	1	8	3	.130
1996 Montreal	227	29	6	26	7	.242
1997 Florida	137	23	6	19	6	.234

FONVILLE, CHAD - SS - BB - b: 3/5/71
Scouting: Fonville is versatile defensively as he can play five positions and he has some speed but he is an offensive liability.
1998: The fact that he can play defensively at five positions should get Fonville a look somewhere but his offensive shortcomings will prevent him from being a regular and could keep him from sticking in the majors.
1997: Fonville appeared in nine games with the Dodgers, in April and June, then nine games with the White Sox in September. He didn't hit and spent most of the season at Triple-A Albuquerque where his offense wasn't much better.
1996: Fonville appeared in 103 games with Los Angeles and played five different positions. He struggled at the plate and was sent to Triple-A in August.

	AB	R	HR	RBI	SB	BA
1995 two teams	320	43	0	16	20	.278
1996 Los Angeles	201	34	0	13	7	.204
1997 Chicago AL	23	2	0	2	2	.130

FORBES, P. J. - 2B - BR - b: 9/22/67
Forbes is a career minor-leaguer who played for the Orioles Triple-A Rochester club last year, basically just filling a roster spot. He's not a prospect, and he doesn't have any talents that could get him a major league job as a utility infielder. Forbes is being passed over when major league teams need utility infielders.

FORDYCE, BROOK - C - BR - b: 5/7/70
Scouting: Fordyce is your basic reserve catcher, with decent defense and limited offensive ability at the major league level.
1998: At best, Fordyce will remain in the majors as a third catcher.
1997: Fordyce received his first significant major league playing time in April when Joe Oliver was injured. He did not hit much in his limited opportunity and when Oliver returned, Fordyce was relegated to the bench and eventually to Triple-A Indianapolis.
1996: At Indianapolis, Fordyce established himself as a candidate for a major league roster spot when he set career highs by hitting .275 with 16 home runs.

	AB	R	HR	RBI	SB	BA
1997 Cincinnati	96	7	1	8	2	.208

FORKERWAY, TREY - 2B - BR - b: 5/17/71
Forkerway was not even the best player at his position (second base) at Double-A Orlando of the Cubs organization. He didn't hit (.199, 30 strikeouts in 166 at-bats) and didn't do anything else that would warrant any attention.

FORKNER, TIM - 3B - BL - b: 3/28/73
Forkner possesses good range in the field and a line-drive bat at the plate. He doesn't have the power you want from a third baseman, however. 1997 marked the second straight season that Forkner spent at Double-A Jackson of the Texas League. It was expected that he would end up at the Triple-A level this past season and he may be slipping as a prospect.

FOSTER, JIM - C - BR - b: 8/18/71
Oriole farmhand Jim Foster spent three years trying to get out of A-ball, finally making it last year after he nearly won the Carolina League triple crown. Promoted to Double-A, he hit decently. At age 25/26, he's too old to be in Double-A. Foster is a borderline prospect, and he will have to continue his hard hitting to make some upward moves soon or else he won't make the majors at all.

FOX, ANDY - 3B - BL - b: 1/12/71
Scouting: A versatile, slick fielder, Fox is a spray hitter who left a trail of mid-.200 averages going up the minor-league ladder. He has fairly good speed on the bases.
1998: Fox will be in a utility role if he is in the majors. Spending time at Triple-A, waiting for an injury, is another strong possibility.
1997: After starting the year at Triple-A Columbus, Fox got called up by the Yankees on June 6th. He worked mainly as a pinch-runner and defensive replacement, making only eight starts in the majors, at three different positions. He was 7-for-31 (.226) in the majors. For Columbus he hit .274 with six home runs, 33 RBI and 28 stolen bases.
1996: Fox was on the major league roster all year. When Pat Kelly got injured during spring training, New York planned to use a platoon of Fox and Mariano Duncan at second base, but Duncan's surprising hitting reduced Fox to a utility role. Fox didn't help himself, either, by hitting just .196.

	AB	R	HR	RBI	SB	BA
1996 New York AL	189	26	3	13	11	.196
1997 New York AL	31	13	0	1	2	.226

FOX, ERIC - OF - BB - b: 8/15/63
Fox has been bouncing around the minor leagues for 12 seasons now, most recently with Triple-A Scranton in the Phillies' organization. Once a scrappy, spray hitter with above-average speed on the bases, Fox has devolved into a scrappy, spray hitter with barely average speed on the bases. He is a switch-hitter with a little pop to the gaps in the minors, but has proved to have sub-par bat speed in his four major league trials. He's a solid defensive outfielder but has just about reached the end of the line.

FRANCO, JULIO - DH - BR - b: 8/23/61
Scouting: Franco has been displaying one of the purest hitting strokes in baseball for fifteen years now, and only struggles with his eyesight caused his productivity to finally drop off in 1997. He has always kept himself in great physical shape, and has maintained a decent percentage of foot speed at his advanced age. He has never been a good defensive player at any position; despite the Indians' best intentions early in 1997, Franco is a true DH. His 1997 eye problems resulted in a career high strikeout rate, and reduced extra-base power.
1998: Franco is no better than a part-timer in the majors at this stage in his career.
1997: The Indians tried to make a second baseman out of Franco in 1997, a move that was destined to fail. When his offense waned, he was moved to the Brewers, where he generated sparks of excitement down the stretch. It appears that his decline phase began in earnest in 1997.

1996: After a one-year tour in Japan, Franco had one of his best years ever with the bat as the Indians' primary first baseman. Batting in the thick of the lineup alongside the bigger Indian bats, Franco was only a slightly lesser version of his mid-80's self.

	AB	R	HR	RBI	SB	BA
1996 Cleveland	432	72	14	76	8	.322
1997 Clev. - Mil.	430	68	7	44	15	.270

FRANCO, MATT - 1B - BL - b: 8/19/69
Scouting: It's odd that the most difficult task in athletics is hitting a baseball and that some of the most gifted hitters are not particularly skilled in other areas. Matt Franco can hit. Not only can he hit, he can pinch-hit, and that specialized skill is even more rare. Used in the proper situation — and that means against righthanded pitching — Franco makes as much solid, extra-base contact as anyone: line drives to left field, line drives to right. He's a below-average runner, and his defensive skills at first base and third base are lacking. But he can hit.
1998: In his first full season in the big leagues — he was 27 when it began — Franco developed into a force off the bench. His future is certainly in that restrictive, but demanding, role. A player with Franco's specialized skill and impressive, though brief, resume is not a luxury, not in a game with increasingly frequent pitching changes.
1997: Franco had merely 48 major league at-bats before last season. But he more than tripled that total and performed exceptionally well in 61 pinch-hit at-bats last year. He was hitless in his first seven appearances in baseball's most difficult role, but batted .345 with three home runs and 13 RBI in 55 subsequent pinch-hitting at-bats. He started 20 games at third base and three at first base, and played each well enough that he wasn't a liability. Only 22 of his at-bats came against lefthanded pitching, and he batted .227 with no extra-base hits and one RBI in those chances.
1996: Bobby Valentine gave Franco his second chance at big-league life after Franco had performed well for him on the Triple-A level with the Norfolk Tides; Franco had batted .323 with 164 hits, including a league-high 40 doubles, and 81 RBI in 508 at-bats. He split his time between first base (42 games) and third base (91) at Triple-A and had six starts at third base and one at first base with the Mets.

	AB	R	HR	RBI	SB	BA
1997 New York NL	163	21	5	21	1	.276

FRANKLIN, MICAH - OF - BB - b: 4/25/72
A long-time minor-leaguer, Franklin finally reached the majors when injuries to big-league outfielders prompted his arrival from Triple-A last year. He had displayed some power in the minors, something the Cardinals desperately needed and, though average at best defensively, helped with a good average in limited big-league duty. He was sent back to the minors after a month, sulked some at the demotion and fizzled, thus removing himself from possible consideration down the line.

	AB	R	HR	RBI	SB	BA
1997 St. Louis	34	6	2	2	0	.324

FRASER, JOE - OF - BR - b: 8/23/74
Fraser returned to Double-A New Britain in 1997; his 1996 season there was cut short because of a groin injury. Fraser has some speed and can steal bases but doesn't get on base enough right now to take advantage of that skill. The Twins 27th-round pick in the 1995 June draft, Fraser will get another crack at Double-A in 1998.

FRAZIER, LOU - OF - BB - b: 1/26/65
Speed is Frazier's only talent, and he spent some time in the Orioles minor-league system last year, waiting for a call from a major league team needing a pinch-runner. The call never came, and his career may be over.

	AB	R	HR	RBI	SB	BA
1995 Montreal	63	6	0	3	4	.190
1995 Texas	99	19	0	8	9	.212
1996 Texas	50	5	0	5	4	.260

FREEMAN, RICKY - 1B - BR - b: 2/3/72
Scouting: Freeman has spent four seasons in the minor leagues after a four-year collegiate career but still has trouble with strikezone judgment. He strikes out far too much for a player who doesn't hit any more homers than he does and he takes far too few walks. He's a marginal prospect at best.
1998: Given Freeman's age (26 on opening day) and his lack of experience above Double-A, it would be hard for Freeman to contribute to a major league team this season. He's bound for Triple-A for the bulk of the year.
1997: Freeman's success in 1996 earned him a promotion to Double-A Orlando and he responded with the best season of his career. He showed more discipline at the plate, cutting down on his strikeouts, which helped him hit better than .300 for the second straight season. He also set career highs with 16 homers and 73 RBI. He got into 31 games at Triple-A, but showed he was nowhere near to being ready for that level.
1996: Freeman put up good numbers at Class A Daytona, but at age 24 he was one of the older players in the league and should have been expected to succeed because of experience alone. He hit a career high 13 home runs and tied for the league lead with 36 doubles.

FRENCH, ANTON - OF - BB - b: 7/25/75
A fast runner with excellent defensive skills, French has to hit for more power and make more consistent contact. A switch-hitter, he batted just .222 in 78 games with Class A Dunedin. He is several years away from getting a look in the majors.

FRIAS, HANLEY - SS - BB - b: 12/5/73
The Diamondbacks came away from the expansion draft with four shortstops. In 1997 Frias got a chance to play for the Rangers late in the season after they wanted to try an alternative to Benji Gil. Despite some success offensively in the minors (.264, with five homers, 46 RBI and 35 steals at Triple-A), Frias is unlikely to hit or field well enough at the major league level to become a regular. He has a chance to eventually be a major league backup.

	AB	R	HR	RBI	SB	BA
1997 Texas	26	4	0	1	0	.192

FRYE, JEFF - 2B - BR - b: 8/31/66
Scouting: Frye keeps having to win a full-time job, and there's a reason for that: he's a handy player, but nothing special with the bat or the glove. As hard as he plays in the field, he doesn't have great range and he doesn't turn the double play well. He's a pesky hitter, but he has no power and doesn't do a great job getting on base.
1998: Because Donnie Sadler has not come along as fast as the Red Sox had hoped, and because Tim Naehring's injury has

moved John Valentin over to third base, Frye might have the second base job full-time to start the season. If he doesn't, he will certainly see plenty of action off the bench, as he provides quality infield depth, and can also play the outfield well.

1997: Frye lost his starting job when Nomar Garciaparra took over at shortstop and Valentin moved to second base. But when Tim Naehring went down with an arm injury and Valentin move to third base, Frye took over at second base full-time, and had a decent season.

1996: Frye was one of General Manager Dan Duquette's nice pick-ups during the season, when it became obvious that the Wil Cordero experiment at second base was not going to work. Frye was acquired from Texas, where he was in Triple-A, and he eventually became Boston's starting second baseman.

	AB	R	HR	RBI	SB	BA
1995 Texas	313	38	4	29	3	.278
1996 Boston	419	74	4	41	18	.286
1997 Boston	404	56	3	51	19	.312

FRYMAN, TRAVIS - 3B - BR - b: 3/25/69

Scouting: Fryman is nothing if not consistent. He hits about .270 every year, with about 20 home runs and about 100 RBI. He doesn't have the best range at third base, but he makes few errors and has a strong, accurate arm. He has average speed, but can steal a base and rarely gets thrown out. Overall, he's a steady, productive player.

1998: As Arizona and then Cleveland noted, it's easy to just fill in the same numbers for Fryman again, because at age 29, after seven consistent years in the big leagues, there's no reason to expect anything different. The moves should maintain Fryman's self-confidence, too.

1997: General manager Randy Smith said before the season that he counted on Fryman to have the .270, 20 home run, 100-RBI year that has become his trademark — and Fryman did it.

1996: Technically, 1996 was Fryman's first year with 100 RBI. Actually, he drove in 90 or more each year from 1991-93, and was headed well past 100 when the strike shortened the 1994 season. Otherwise, it was a fairly typical Fryman year.

	AB	R	HR	RBI	SB	BA
1995 Detroit	567	79	15	81	4	.275
1996 Detroit	616	90	22	100	4	.268
1997 Detroit	595	90	22	102	16	.274

FULLER, AARON - OF - BB - b: 9/7/71

Scouting: Fuller has exciting lead-off potential, although he's old for a prospect. He's small, but has excellent speed and has shown a real ability to get on base over his minor-league career. Despite his great speed, he is not a great outfielder, and he might have to be a left fielder.

1998: Fuller will probably play full-time for Triple-A Pawtucket, and will have to have a big season to earn a chance with the Red Sox, as Michael Coleman appears to be the center fielder of the future. Because he's more of the prototypical leadoff hitter, with his ability to draw walks, there's an outside shot that Fuller can temporarily pass Coleman if the latter stumbles or doesn't endear himself to management.

1997: Fuller did his thing for Double-A Trenton. He hit just .260 with six homers, but he drew 95 walks and stole 40 bases, excellent for a leadoff man.

1996: Fuller hit .300 for Class A Sarasota with 33 steals.

FULLMER, BRAD - OF - BL - b: 1/17/75

Scouting: A supplemental second-round draft pick by Montreal in 1993, he missed that season and 1994 because of reconstructive surgery on his right shoulder. Finally healthy, Fullmer is now showing why scouts felt he could blossom into a premier power hitter, who could also hit for average. Fullmer is not a great defensive player and his days at third base are long gone but he is a good enough athlete to handle first base or left field.

1998: Continuing their perpetual youth movement, the Expos will have a spot for Fullmer in their opening day lineup. He will play either first base or left field, depending on what Montreal is able to acquire in trade for Pedro Martinez and Mike Lansing. The Expos would prefer he play first base, though he went to winter ball to work on his outfield play. Fullmer will likely struggle in his first full season as a rookie but has the potential to be a star.

1997: Fullmer had a fine season at Double-A Harrisburg, continued to hit in a 24-game stint with Triple-A Ottawa, then did fine in a September trial with the Expos. Fullmer homered in his first major-league at-bat, then added a pinch-hit, inside-the-park job later in the month.

1996: Fullmer spent most of the season at Class A West Palm Beach before a late-season promotion to Double-A Harrisburg. He hit four homers in 24 games at Harrisburg after hitting only five in 102 at West Palm Beach.

	AB	R	HR	RBI	SB	BA
1997 Montreal	40	4	3	8	0	.300

GAETTI, GARY - 3B/1B - BR - b: 8/19/58

Scouting: Age is starting to catch up with Gaetti, but it hasn't knocked him onto the retirement list just yet. He still has a quick enough bat to make pitchers pay for their mistakes, but only if he has been able to rest along the way and is not worn down by being counted on for constant duty. Gaetti still has an impressively strong arm, which makes him a defensive asset, despite reduced range at third base. He's a capable enough first baseman.

1998: Gaetti, eligible for free agency after the 1997 season, has the chance to play 100 games, perhaps all at third base or a portion of them as a late-inning first baseman. That will afford him enough rest and time to provide more power and run production than the average third baseman. And, considering the Cardinals' options at that position should include nothing more than David Bell and converting first baseman-outfielder John Mabry, Gaetti is a strong Plan A.

1997: Prone to a few extended slumps with little power, Gaetti still hit 17 homers, drove in 69 runs and struck out fewer than 90 times in almost 150 games. His play at times reflected a summer in which he turned 39, but he had the attitude of a man 15 years younger.

1996: He showed he hadn't lost the knack for hitting a fastball, with a solid power-laden season. Gaetti also was one of the club's most consistent defensive players and baserunners, with much of his success attributable to knowing the game so well.

	AB	R	HR	RBI	SB	BA
1995 Kansas City	514	76	35	96	3	.261
1996 St. Louis	522	71	23	80	2	.274
1997 St. Louis	502	63	17	69	7	.251

GAGNE, GREG - SS - BR - b: 11/12/61

Scouting: Gagne is at a point in his career where any season may just be his last. He still provides steady defense for a middle infielder but is falling off offensively.

1998: This season could be Gagne's last year in baseball. The Dodgers or any team for that matter could benefit from his quiet leadership and solid glove.

1997: Gagne played in 144 games for the Dodgers, his most games played since 159 for the Royals in 1993. He showed signs of slowing at the plate, batting .161 in September, but still put up decent numbers for a middle infielder.

1996: Gagne gave the Dodgers what they wanted, solid defense and credible offensive production. After bouncing back from a mid-May ankle sprain, Gagne nearly matched career-high numbers offensively but a September swoon (.213) made him fall short.

	AB	R	HR	RBI	SB	BA
1995 Kansas City	430	58	6	49	3	.256
1996 Los Angeles	428	48	10	55	4	.255
1997 Los Angeles	514	49	9	57	2	.251

GALARRAGA, ANDRES - 1B - BR - b: 6/18/61

Scouting: A rare player who gets better as he gets older, Galarraga is perhaps the biggest star in Rockies history; the "Big Cat" still has remarkable reflexes and plays with amazing grace around the first base bag. He also has a strong throwing arm with an extremely quick release. Despite his defensive skill, Galarraga makes too many careless errors — he has averaged 14 miscues in his last three seasons. He also has holes in his swing, averaging 148 strikeouts since 1995, but pitchers pay when they make mistakes; he is one of the strongest hitters in the game. Galarraga runs surprisingly well for a man of his size (6'3", 240 pounds).

1998: Though Galarraga has put up enormous numbers in his five years in Colorado, he has been a .281 hitter on the road. Look for a dip in 1998 with Atlanta. His age (37 in June) raises doubts as to how long he could have kept playing at this level, even in Colorado.

1997: Galarraga won the National League RBI title and reached the 40-homer plateau for the second consecutive year. Normally streaky at the plate, he was more consistent last season. At times, Galarraga was dazzling on defense.

1996: Statistically, it was his best season out of his twelve years in the big leagues; Galarraga set all-time highs in homers, RBI, hits, runs scored and stolen bases.

	AB	R	HR	RBI	SB	BA
1995 Colorado	554	89	31	106	12	.280
1996 Colorado	626	119	47	150	18	.304
1997 Colorado	600	120	41	140	15	.318

GALLEGO, MIKE - SS/2B/3B - BR - b: 10/31/60

Injuries turned Gallego from a backup middle infielder with a weak bat into a rarely seen middle infielder put out of work because his hitting average couldn't meet even his 175 pounds. At the age of 37, it's likely his playing days are finished.

	AB	R	HR	RBI	SB	BA
1995 Oakland	120	11	0	8	0	.233
1996 St. Louis	143	12	0	4	0	.210
1997 St. Louis	43	6	0	1	0	.163

GAMA, RICK - 2B - BR - b: 4/27/73

Gama is a spray-hitter who makes good contact, getting more walks (51) than strikeouts (41) while batting .288 with six homers and 43 RBI at Double-A Mobile in 1997. He's a mediocre fielder with a below-average arm, but is a heady baserunner. He'll start at second base for Double-A Mobile in 1998.

GANT, RON - OF - BR - b: 3/2/65

Scouting: It's become evident that Gant isn't the kind of player who can —or wants to — carry his team's offense. He cares, perhaps too much at times, by trying to do more than he's able. He doesn't have the speed he flashed in his youth, is an average outfielder who goes hard after flies, and tries to force success at the plate by fishing after pitches down in the strike zone (his chief weakness). Though he still could be a star, at this crucial point in his career, he could go either way.

1998: He'll be the regular left fielder and won't have to worry about being the team's primary run-producer this season — with Mark McGwire in the lineup, Ray Lankford having emerged as a chief danger and Brian Jordan again healthy. That should allow Gant to relax and serve as one of the top number five hitters in the league, though only if he can make more contact and learn to hit the breaking ball better.

1997: Injuries early to other Cardinals placed increased focus on the bat of Gant, the highest-paid player in the lineup. He got into a hole and never did escape, finishing with a batting average 27 points below his career mark and setting a club record with 162 strikeouts.

1996: Despite a hamstring injury early and a shoulder injury late, Gant's 30 homers were the most for a Cardinals left fielder in 45 years. Overall, his run production was fairly common, marked by a .264 batting average with runners in scoring position.

	AB	R	HR	RBI	SB	BA
1995 Cincinnati	410	79	39	88	23	.276
1996 St. Louis	419	74	30	82	13	.246
1997 St. Louis	502	68	17	62	14	.229

GARCIA, CARLOS - 2B - BR - b: 10/15/67

Scouting: In most others season, it could be said that Garcia is a good-hitting, slick infielder who makes decent contact, runs well and has occasional pop in the bat. Considering his 1997 season, his ability to make contact is in doubt and his future as a regular player is suddenly cloudy.

1998: Garcia has the talent to play for someone although he appeared unlikely to be back with the Blue Jays. His role as a starting second baseman for any team looked precarious after last year and depends on a fast start this season.

1997: Garcia never got on track and suffered through the worst season of his major league career, hitting just .220 and he needed a second-half surge to reach that modest level. He was nursing a right calf strain for much of the year but it didn't bother him until June and he was already in the most horrendous slump of his career. Eventually, the Blue Jays traded for Mariano Duncan and Garcia was without a job.

1996: Garcia repeated his 1995 campaign with the Pirates, adding some extra stolen bases and runs scored. He played 19 games at shortstop and 14 games at third base as the Pirates tried to fit him into the lineup.

	AB	R	HR	RBI	SB	BA
1995 Pittsburgh	367	41	6	50	8	.294
1996 Pittsburgh	390	66	6	44	16	.285
1997 Toronto	350	29	3	23	11	.220

GARCIA, FREDDY - 3B - BR - b: 8/1/72

Scouting: Garcia has outstanding power, though he hasn't really shown it above Double-A despite being 25 years old. He is at an age where he needs to step forward, or lose his status as a prospect. Garcia plays adequately at both third base and first base.

1998: The expansion pick of Joe Randa lifted Garcia's prominence. There was no room for Garcia in the Pirates' lineup with Randa at third base and Kevin Young at first base. Now there is more opportunity.

1997: Garcia had a strange year. He was jumped from A-ball to Triple-A Calgary to start the season then was promoted to the Pirates for two weeks in late-May/early-June as they had no other positions left on the 40-man roster to call up when they were hit by a rash of injuries. Garcia then was demoted to Double-A Carolina, ripped apart the Southern League, and finally returned to Pittsburgh and had a two-homer game against Cincinnati on September 5th.

1996: Garcia spent the entire season at Class A Lynchburg after being forced to stay on the Pirates' major-league roster for all of 1995 because he was a Rule 5 Draft pick from Toronto. Garcia, after a season of almost total inactivity in the majors, responded by tying teammate Jose Guillen for the Carolina League home run title.

	AB	R	HR	RBI	SB	BA
1997 Pittsburgh	40	4	3	5	0	.150

GARCIA, GUILLERMO - C - BR - b: 4/4/72

Garcia saw action at both Double-A Chattanooga and Triple-A Indianapolis last year, but he isn't close to being a prospect. He is not a good hitter and has little power. He had a good year at Chattanooga in 1996, but had only 203 at-bats and his success there was only the second time he'd hit above .274 in his minor-league career. Garcia hit just .238 in 151 at-bats at Indianapolis last year. He's not much of a player and isn't likely to see any major league action.

GARCIA, JESSE - 2B - BR - b: 9/24/73

"He makes all the plays, and he's the best double-play man there is," said Joe Ferguson, Garcia's Double-A manager. "Jesse has quick hands, great instincts around the bag and a knack for diving in either direction and getting up and throwing. He has to be a little more patient at the plate and improve his pitch recognition — but one thing I like is that he is good with men in scoring position."

GARCIA, KARIM - OF - BL - b: 10/29/75

Scouting: Garcia has a natural power swing and in the outfield has adequate range with a cannon for an arm. He was recognized for having the best outfield arm in the Pacific Coast League. Garcia also needs to become more selective at the plate to help him advance.

1998: Garcia gets a fresh start and a major league shot with the Diamondbacks. He's just 21 years old and will probably get to work on his strikezone judgment in Triple-A if he doesn't click in spring training. Garcia is a major talent, and the Dodgers were hoping that his injury history might scare off the expansion teams, but the medical reports were good enough.

1997: Garcia played 15 games with the Dodgers in June, striking out 14 times in 39 at-bats. At Triple-A Albuquerque he showed his power potential by hitting .305 with 20 homers and 66 RBI in just 262 at-bats, and showed off his cannon arm.

1996: A demotion for an attitude adjustment landed Garcia in Double-A ball. He appeared in just one game with Los Angeles.

	AB	R	HR	RBI	SB	BA
1997 Los Angeles	39	5	1	8	0	.128

GARCIA, LUIS - SS - BR - b: 5/20/75

Garcia simply won't take a walk; he drew just ten in 481 plate appearances last year and has fewer than 50 walks in over 1600 professional trips to the plate. He has cut down on his strikeouts, though. Garcia is a line-drive hitter and a good fastball hitter, but he struggles with breaking pitches; his hitting style will not succeed at higher levels. Garcia has displayed a steady glove but his range at shortstop has come into question. With his numerous limitations, Garcia has only the most remote chance to play major league ball.

GARCIA, VINCENTE - 2B - BR - b: 2/14/75

Garcia had a shoulder injury two years ago, a labrum tear, and never got going in '96, then got sent back to A-ball in '97. He's a solid second baseman who makes all the plays and has a little pop. He hits the fastball extremely well, but wants to hit homers instead of playing the short game more conducive to his build. He is improving at bunting and hitting behind the runner. Garcia has average speed but does have big-league tools; he'll return to Double-A New Haven this year.

GARCIAPARRA, NOMAR - SS - BR - b: 7/23/73

Scouting: It's hard to find any negatives. Garciaparra is an excellent shortstop, hits for average and surprising power, steals some bases, is humble, and thinks of little else but how he is going to get better. Though he looks skinny, Garciaparra has a strong upper body and powerful legs. He should only get better over the next few years, which is scary. The one area he really needs to improve is selectivity at the plate. He did not draw a lot of walks last year, and he got himself out at times by swinging at bad pitches.

1998: MVP? A 50-game hitting streak? It's hard to imagine what Garciaparra will do for an encore. The most likely scenario is that his power and average will stay the same or increase a bit, but his on-base percentage will increase significantly, as pitchers work around him more and he improves his strikezone judgment.

1997: Garciaparra had one of the great rookie seasons of all time, setting several records along the way. Miscast as the leadoff hitter on a team with little speed, Garciaparra led the league in runs, and almost led the Red Sox in homers and RBI.

1996: Garciaparra tore a tendon behind his knee early in his first Triple-A season, and was thought to be out for the year. But he rehabbed the injury and came back to play like a demon for the season's final two months, performing at the level he would meet in the majors in 1997.

	AB	R	HR	RBI	SB	BA
1996 Boston	87	11	4	16	5	.241
1997 Boston	684	122	30	98	22	.306

GARRISON, WEBSTER - 1B - BR - b: 8/24/65

Good numbers in 1997 (.289 with 15 homers and 80 RBI) show Garrison can hit, but the former first baseman is just marking minor-league time as players like Miguel Tejada and Mark Bellhorn pass him by. Expansion could create some light for him, but not too many other things will.

GATES, BRENT - 2B - BB - b: 3/14/70

Scouting: For a middle infielder, Gates has some pop in his bat, mostly gap power, but does not really have a position. Oakland grew dissatisfied with his fielding at second base, and he does not have enough power to play third base in the majors. Injuries have limited him to 64 games twice since 1994.

1998: Gates will always be in contention for a reserve infield spot on an offense-conscious team because he can drive the ball to all fields.

1997: Released by the A's when Scott Spiezio continued his ascent up the organizational ladder, Gates hooked on with the Mariners as a bench guy.

1996: Gates suffered a fractured left tibia when he fouled a pitch off his leg on June 15th and missed the rest of the year, his second in three seasons marred by injury. He suffered torn ligaments in his right thumb and a sprained left knee in 1994.

	AB	R	HR	RBI	SB	BA
1995 Oakland	524	60	5	56	3	.254
1996 Oakland	247	26	2	30	1	.263
1997 Seattle	151	18	3	20	0	.238

GAZAREK, MARTY - OF - BR - 6/1/73

After a couple of off years Gazarek rebounded to have a fine season in 1997 and might have established himself as a true prospect who is a couple of years away from the majors, he batted .331 with 33 extra-base hits in 290 at-bats at Double-A Orlando. Gazarek doesn't hit for much power but is an average hitter who can find the gaps. He has an excellent eye and knowledge of the strike zone. He's going to need at least one full year at Double-A and some time at Triple-A if he's going to be ready. And like other outfielders in the Cubs' system, he's going to have to wait for several other players to get their chance or else he'll have to have such a good year in the minors that the Cubs don't have any choice but to bring him up. While Gazarek is a good hitter, he's not good enough to make people notice him that way.

GEISLER, PHIL - OF/1B - BL - b: 10/23/69

In his seventh year in the minors, Geisler had a .257-9-57 season at Triple-A Norfolk on the Mets' farm last year. He looked better four years ago when he had a good spring training with the Phillies' major league camp; even then he didn't land a major league job.

GIAMBI, JASON - 3B - BL - b: 1/8/71

Scouting: A gap-to-gap hitter with good power, Giambi is a smart and disciplined batter who is capable of using the whole field. He has excellent mechanics and a picture-perfect, line-drive swing. Giambi is not much of an outfielder, in fact his slowness doesn't make him much of a first baseman, either, but he is too young to be a full time DH. But, with the number of solid first base prospects behind him, it is probably just a matter of time before he moves to DH.

1998: Giambi is suddenly one of the elder statesmen on a team that is going whole hog on a bundle of hot prospects. Giambi should improve his power numbers — though 41 doubles (1997) can hardly be considered bad — as he establishes himself as the team's premier hitter. Expect him to log most of his playing time at first base with the occasional date at DH.

1997: After adding muscle to his frame during the 1996 off-season, emulating his friend and mentor, Mark McGwire, it took a while for Giambi to get into the kind of hitting groove that was expected. His new physique seemed to make him more prone to muscle strains, and the stress of early platooning, playing left field then first base all took a toll. By year's end, however, Giambi reversed the trend of the previous year, actually improving his average and numbers as the season wore on instead of the reverse.

1996: No one doubted that Giambi could hit, but no one dreamed that he would hit so well, and with power, so soon after reaching the majors. He wore down some as he was unused to the long season, but he is one of those hitters who gets hot and hits everything both hard and where they ain't.

	AB	R	HR	RBI	SB	BA
1995 Oakland	176	27	6	25	2	.256
1996 Oakland	536	84	20	79	0	.291
1997 Oakland	519	66	20	81	0	.293

GIAMBI, JEREMY - OF - BL - b: 9/30/74

Jason's younger brother didn't miss a beat when jumping from Class A Lansing to Double-A Wichita, hitting for average and power at both levels. One of the Royals' early-round selections in 1996, Giambi needs to refine his abilities - particularly his defense and baserunning, but the talent is obvious; his power is real. He'll work more at first base both in winter ball this year and as he advances through the Royals' farm system. He could get his first taste of the majors by the end of 1998.

GIANNELLI, RAY - 1B - BL - b: 2/5/66

Gianelli has proven he can hit minor league pitching, but appears to have Triple-A bat speed. Hitting double-digits in homers and nearly .300 over the last five years in the upper minors has earned Gianelli two trips to the big leagues, where he has gotten 35 at-bats. He's an extra bat stored at Triple-A and 1997 was the second season in a row he played for two different organizations. Giannelli played Double-A ball for St. Louis and Toronto and had just 35 hits in a combined 175 at-bats.

GIBBS, KEVIN- OF - BB - b: 4/3/74

Scouting: A switch-hitting sixth-round pick in the 1995 draft, Gibbs is one of the fastest men in professional baseball. He doesn't have a lot of power but with his speed he can make up for it on the basepaths.

1998: Gibbs could be a candidate to contribute in the majors in 1998 as a fourth or fifth outfielder. He is more likely to get a chance to prove himself at the Triple-A level, however.

1997: Gibbs had a solid season at Double-A San Antonio hitting .335 and swiping 49 bases in 68 attempts.

1996: Gibbs stole 60 bases and lashed 11 triples at Class A Vero Beach.

GIBRALTER, DAVID - OF - BR - b: 6/19/75

Gibralter has some size and power potential with the bat. He hit .274 last year at Double-A Trenton with 14 homers and 25 doubles in 478 at-bats. However, his command of the strike zone has always been a problem; he struck out 103 times and walked just 44 times last year. He has posted even worse ratios in the past, though, so maybe he's improving; he's young enough that he might be. Gibralter's bat is his only tool, though. He's played first base the last two years after starting out at third base, and does not have speed.

GIBRALTER, STEVE - OF - BR - b: 10/9/72

A solid season in 1995 earned Gibralter consideration as a decent power/speed prospect, but his strike zone judgment (114 strikeouts and only 26 walks) and overall game disappeared in 1996. He ended the season with a sore shoulder that required surgery and missed all of 1997. Until he improves his batting eye and proves he is healthy, he is a fifth outfielder at best.

GIBSON, DERRICK - OF - BR - b: 2/5/75

Scouting: Gibson is the best power-hitting prospect in the organization, though he's still raw. Growing up, he was known more as a football player; he did not play baseball his senior year in high school, but the Rockies selected him anyway, in the 13th round of 1993 draft. He punishes mistake pitches and his strength helps him overcome his long swing; he can't hit breaking pitches and inside fastballs break his bats. Gibson's an above-average runner for someone his size (6'2", 230 pounds). His best position is left field and he's only average there, though he has improved; his arm is below-average.

1998: Gibson should spend the entire season at Triple-A Colorado Springs, then break into the majors as a September callup. With the thin Colorado air and hitter-friendly ballparks of the Pacific Coast League, a big power year is expected.

1997: It was a big year for Gibson and he delivered. He was a sensational offensive star in 1995, but a disappointment the following year after jumping from lower A-ball to Double-A. He returned to Double-A in 1997, and led New Haven in every offensive category, displaying power and speed while hitting for average. He was promoted to Triple-A Colorado Springs in the final month. Overmatched for about two weeks, Gibson adjusted and hit .423 with three homers in 21 games, then added two more homers in a three-game Pacific Coast League playoff series against Phoenix.

1996: Gibson started the season overweight and it led to chronic hamstring problems. The result was a season-long struggle at the plate and only three stolen bases in 15 attempts after he stole 31 the previous year.

GIL, BENJI - SS - BR - b: 10/6/72

Scouting: Gil has made little or no progress as a hitter. He is a free swinger with a weakness for fastballs out of the strike zone, and fans once every three plate appearances. He does have occasional power when he makes contact. In the field, Gil can make the spectacular play, but boots routine grounders too frequently to play regularly. The "potential" tag is still there, as his athletic ability is evident.

1998: A change of organization may be necessary for Gil to regain his confidence. At the age of 25, he could still establish himself as a regular, but time is running out.

1997: Gil was given the starting shortstop job three separate times in 1997, but lost it each time, to such uninspiring players like Bill Ripken and Domingo Cedeno. It was not so much his failure to hit, but his failure to play acceptable defense, that landed him on the bench. The Rangers were openly considering other options at the season's end.

1996: A back injury sidelined Gil in spring training, and Kevin Elster's improbable comeback kept Gil in the minors until September. Gil didn't exactly give the Rangers much of a reason to recall him, hitting in the low .200s and striking out once in every three trips to the plate at Triple-A.

	AB	R	HR	RBI	SB	BA
1995 Texas	415	36	9	46	2	.219
1997 Texas	317	35	5	31	1	.224

GILBERT, SHAWN - 2B/SS - BR - b: 3/12/65

Gilbert continues to be a solid minor-leaguer, batting .264 in Triple-A last year. He hit eight homers and stole sixteen bases, but is obviously a career minor leaguer. His longevity is testimony to his easy personality and ability to work well with youngsters, meaning he has the stuff to be a coach.

	AB	R	HR	RBI	SB	BA
1997 New York NL	22	3	1	1	1	.136

GILES, BRIAN - OF - BL - b: 1/21/71

Scouting: Giles would instantly become a star if the Indians would let him. He's a hitting machine who rips the ball with authority to all fields. He has excellent plate discipline, having walked more than he has struck out in all but one of his eight full professional seasons. He hits lefthanders and righthanders almost equally well, has a little better than average speed with good baserunning instincts, and can play all three outfield positions. He's a chame!eon offensively; he could be a leadoff hitter one day, and a cleanup hitter the next.

1998: Giles needs to play every day, and there are simply too many bodies for around for him to carve out 500 at-bats in Cleveland. The expansion draft could remedy his situation, of course. Giles is ready for a full-time role and would be a fine everyday player.

1997: After hearing his name tossed around in every trade rumor, Giles landed a full-time job out of spring training — then, the Lofton-for-Justice-and-Grissom trade eliminated his starting spot, but Giles hit his way into a better-than-half-time role before long. He successfully handled multiple defensive positions and batting order spots, and proved himself one of the more valuable Indians.

1996: Giles posted a third consecutive impact season at Triple-A, batting .312 with a .395 OBP and slugging .594 before being recalled at midseason. He batted .355 with power in a supporting role on the Indians' offensive juggernaut.

	AB	R	HR	RBI	SB	BA
1996 Cleveland	121	26	5	27	3	.355
1997 Cleveland	377	62	17	61	13	.268

GILKEY, BERNARD - OF - BR - b: 9/24/66

Scouting: Gilkey appears to have the skills he demonstrated in 1996 — power, ample speed, above-average talent for a left fielder and a knack of throwing out baserunners. But the skills rarely were evident last summer until the middle of August.

1998: Gilkey will be the Mets left fielder and bat anywhere from second to sixth in the order. His place will be determined as much by the team's needs as it will be by what he does, although he does seem to prosper when he bats third as he did most of 1996.

1997: Aside from the physical maladies that limited Jason Isringhausen, Bill Pulsipher and Paul Wilson to a total of 29.2 innings, the failure of Gilkey to approach the levels of production he reached in 1996 was the greatest disappointment in the Mets' season. He batted merely .226 at home and .235 against righthanded pitching, and .206 through June, but .291 thereafter. But his RBI count was down by 39.

1996: Few players not on the top level of the game produced a season in this decade that compares with Gilkey's '96. His first season with the Mets was stunningly brilliant — including a club record 117 RBI, 34 go-ahead RBI, a .406 average with runners in scoring position and a league-high 18 assists. It was comparable to any Mets' seasons and better than all but a few.

	AB	R	HR	RBI	SB	BA
1995 St. Louis	480	73	17	69	12	.298
1996 New York NL	571	108	30	117	17	.317
1997 New York NL	518	85	18	78	7	.249

GIOVANOLA, ED - SS - BL - b: 3/4/69
Giovanola could easily have a utility job in the majors, but he keeps getting nudged out by other players. He's not good at any of the infield positions, but he has good hands and can hold his own at all of them. He also will give you a quality at-bat, without power, against all kinds of pitching. When the Braves acquired Keith Lockhart, a similar, but better, player in spring training, Giovanola's '97 season was shot. He'll probably hook on somewhere else this season and should see some time in the majors off the bench.

	AB	R	HR	RBI	SB	BA
1996 Atlanta	82	10	0	7	1	.232

GIPSON, CHARLES - OF - BR - b: 12/16/72
Scouting: Gipson is a very good athlete who was also a California high school football star, but the Mariners have had trouble finding a position for him, trying him in the outfield and at every position but first base. He has good speed but little pop.
1998: Gipson appears to be headed to Triple-A after three seasons in Double-A.
1997: Gipson played third base for the first time at Double-A Memphis without the corner power numbers — one homer, 28 RBI — although he did have 31 stolen bases.
1996: Gipson was used at both shortstop and in the outfield, two years after being voted the Class A California League's best defensive outfielder in a 1994 manager's poll.

GIRARDI, JOE - C - BR - b: 10/14/64
Scouting: There are few better defensive catchers in the American League. Girardi calls a great game, blocks balls well, and has a quick release. Pitchers love throwing to him. He lacks power as a hitter but runs the bases surprisingly well. For someone who doesn't hit home runs, he is a free swinger who would rather put the ball in play than take a walk.
1998: The Yankees went into the winter with Girardi already written in as their number one catcher for 1998. Joe Torre and the coaches have always liked working with him and his playing time could actually increase.
1997: A sore right shoulder caused a down year in every aspect including hitting and throwing, and then Girardi missed 15 straight games with a broken finger in September. Through it all, Girardi never complained.
1996: It didn't take New York fans long to forget Mike Stanley and take a liking to Girardi, who became a team leader. Catching Dwight Gooden's no-hitter was just one highlight on the road to a World Championship.

	AB	R	HR	RBI	SB	BA
1995 Colorado	462	63	8	55	3	.262
1996 New York AL	422	55	2	45	13	.294
1997 New York AL	398	38	1	50	2	.264

GIUDICE, JOHN - OF - BR - b: 6/19/71
A raw tools guy who plays center and right field, Giudice suffered a labrum tear in his right throwing shoulder during his 1997 season at Double-A New Haven. He's an above-average runner, has average to above-average power and can hit for average. His arm is plenty playable and he's a aggressive fielder who is not afraid to dive or run into the wall. Unfortunately, his reckless style often leaves him on the disabled list; he needs to play under control. If he can consistently stay in the lineup, he might be able to become a more consistent offensive player. He'll open the 1998 season back at New Haven.

GLANVILLE, DOUG - OF - BR - b: 8/25/70
Scouting: Glanville has a good combination of the skills baseball teams want in centerfielders. He hits for average, has decent power to the gaps, can steal a few bases and plays outstanding defense. He has long been regarded as a front-line prospect in the Cubs organization, although it took him several years to finally get promoted to the big-league team.
1998: Glanville earned a starting outfield position with his play last season, but there still is a question as to where he'll play. He was mostly in left field last year, but the Cubs would dearly love to make him a full-time center fielder. Most of the winter trade rumors involved Lance Johnson, and if the Cubs are able to move the veteran outfielder and play Glanville every day in center he'll wind up having an outstanding year.
1997: Glanville didn't start playing every day until the Cubs were well out of the pennant race, but his performance once he was inserted in the starting lineup had many people wondering what took the team so long to get him playing time. Glanville impressed with his speed and defense in the outfield and showed he was capable of hitting major league pitching.
1996: Glanville spent the bulk of the 1996 season with Triple-A Iowa, although he did see action in two different stints with Chicago. His performance at Iowa demonstrated that he had nothing left to prove in the minors, although the Cubs couldn't figure out a way to use him in Chicago.

	AB	R	HR	RBI	SB	BA
1996 Chicago NL	83	10	1	10	2	.241
1997 Chicago NL	474	79	4	35	19	.300

GLASS, CHIP - OF - BL - b: 6/24/71
Glass is a scrappy player without any particularly dazzling skill. He's a top-of-the-order hitter who forces pitchers to throw strikes and makes consistent contact though he has little power. He makes up for a lack of raw speed with keen baserunning instincts. He has never been one of the youngest regulars in the leagues in which he's played, and may need to repeat at Double-A Akron in 1998 due to a backlog of outfielders in the Indians' chain. He has little chance of ever reaching the majors.

GLAUS, TROY - 3B - BR - b: 4/1/77
Glaus played shortstop at UCLA but is a third base prospect who is expected to become an Angel in the infield quickly after they drafted him in the first round last year. With Dave Hollins' contract scheduled to run out after the 1998 season, Glaus probably has one season of minor-league ball ahead of him. He was an offensive dynamo for the Bruins as he hit .413 with 32 homers and 88 RBI to lead them to the College World Series. And while he was in Westwood he broke Marc McGuire's Pacific-10 home run record.

GODWIN, TYRELL - OF - BB - b: 4/1/80
Godwin decided to attend the University of North Carolina and by doing so became the first first-round pick that the Yankees have failed to sign in the history of the June Draft. New York selected Godwin with the 24th pick in 1997 draft but Godwin will be playing football and baseball as a Tar Heel for at least a season.

GOLIGOSKI, JASON - SS - BL - b: 10/2/71
Released by the White Sox after being their eighth-round pick in 1993, Goligoski temporarily resurrected his career by hitting

.300 with 15 stolen bases at Class A High Desert. He's an OK fielder.

GOMEZ, CHRIS - SS/2B - BR - b: 6/16/71
Scouting: Defensively, Gomez gobbles up balls hit within his range, but he doesn't have great range. He is neither particularly quick nor fast (he has eight steals over the past two seasons). Gomez also seemed to tire late last season. Offensively, he strikes out a lot for a contact hitter. The Padres past two first-round draft picks have been shortstops.
1998: Gomez is a starting shortstop in the major leagues, although there was some question whether he would be back with the Padres this year. The club has other infield options and he was not expected to be protected from the expansion draft.
1997: Gomez hit just .253, but delivered wins with four late-game hits. He also struck out 114 times in 522 at-bats and his .326 on-base percentage was below expectations.
1996: Gomez came to the Padres from Detroit with catcher John Flaherty and helped provide the spark that led San Diego to the National League West title. Two of his three homers won crucial games.

	AB	R	HR	RBI	SB	BA
1995 Detroit	431	49	11	50	4	.223
1996 Detroit	128	21	1	16	1	.242
1996 San Diego	328	32	3	29	2	.262
1997 San Diego	522	62	5	54	5	.253

GOMEZ, LEO - 3B - BR - b: 3/2/67
The ex-Oriole, ex-Cub who collected 17 home runs in 362 at-bats with the Cubs in 1996, Gomez went to Japan and found success last year. He hit .303 with 23 home runs for the Chunichi Dragons.

	AB	R	HR	RBI	SB	BA
1995 Baltimore	127	16	4	12	0	.236
1996 Chicago NL	362	44	17	56	1	.238

GOMEZ, RUDY - 2B - BR - 9/14/74
Taken in the tenth round of the 1996 draft, Gomez followed a strong debut at Class A Tampa with a .299 season for Double-A Norwich in 1997. He played 92 games at second base, nine at third base and five at shortstop and committed only eleven errors. Gomez hit five homers and drove in 52 runs; he is a patient, line-drive hitter who puts the ball in play consistently.

GONZALES, RENE - 2B - BR - b: 9/3/61
Gonzalez has used his versatility in the infield to reach the majors for parts of the past three seasons. In 1997 he turned up at Coors Field and also played for the Rockies' Triple-A affiliate. Colorado was his third different organization in the past three years and, at age 36, his time is running short. With expansion he may have another season as a utility man left in him.

	AB	R	HR	RBI	SB	BA
1995 California	18	1	1	3	0	.333
1996 Texas	92	19	2	5	0	.217

GONZALEZ, ALEX - SS - BR - b: 4/8/73
Scouting: Even though his season was shortened by injury, his status as a top prospect has fizzled. His range has improved every year and he has shown that he can run and hit for some power. Gonzalez has yet to top the .245 mark in his short major league career and he strikes out far too often given his limited power numbers, even for a shortstop. He could develop into a slugger but for his sake, it had better happen soon.
1998: It would take a dreadful start for Gonzalez to lose his regular job but depending on the commitment of his team to winning, it could happen. Because of his age, it's safe to project continued improvement.
1997: His season was somewhere between 1995 and 1996 in terms of value although his RBI total actually dropped to its lowest level since Gonzalez first broke in to the majors. A broken right finger shortened his season by about a month.
1996: Gonzalez continued to improve and established himself as the Blue Jays' everyday shortstop. He showed some ability to make contact (although his strikeout totals were still too high) and some stolen base skill.

	AB	R	HR	RBI	SB	BA
1995 Toronto	367	51	10	42	4	.243
1996 Toronto	527	64	14	64	16	.235
1997 Toronto	426	46	12	35	15	.239

GONZALEZ, ALEXANDER - SS - BR - b: 2/15/77
One of the minor's premier shortstop prospects, Gonzalez combines defensive wizardry with above-average hitting power. He hasn't controlled his wild swing and doesn't utilize his above-average speed yet. His defensive range is spectacular and he owns a cannon arm although he has made careless errors and has let his volatile emotions get the better of him. Gonzalez is a blue-chip prospect who has occasionally been favorably compared to Edgar Renteria. Gonzalez will spend significant time at Triple-A Charlotte in 1998, ironing out the rough spots in his game.

GONZALEZ, JIMMY - C - BR - b: 3/8/73
Gonzalez was one of the seven players taken by the Astros in the first two rounds of the botched 1991 draft. He is the only one who has remained in the system continuously since then and has made little progress. He had, by far, his best season in 1997 at with a .254-14-58 log at Double-A Jackson. It was the first time he has hit above .250 and the first time he reached double figures in home runs. Gonzalez has not been considered a prospect. His improvement in 1997 could revive his career if he can build on it in 1998.

GONZALEZ, JUAN - DH/OF - BR - b: 10/16/69
Scouting: One of the best power/batting average hitters in the majors, Gonzalez can still be pitched to, as he will chase low sliders out of the strike zone, especially from righthanders. But Gonzalez can crush a mistake, and his hot streaks can carry a team. The issue with Gonzalez is his health, as he cannot seem to avoid at least one extended stint on the disabled list each season. He is adequate in the outfield, and has adapted well to the DH role.
1998: Gonzalez is in the prime of his career, and if he could stay healthy for an entire season, he could hit 50 or more homers. He has made playing in 162 games his goal for 1998.
1997: Gonzalez sprained his thumb playing outfield in winter ball prior to the season. He missed the month of April, but then remained healthy for the rest of the year. In mid-season, he reverted to chasing bad pitches for a few weeks, and endured a prolonged slump. In September, Gonzalez had one of his best months, and he attributed it in part to having Lee Stevens, rather than Will Clark, hitting behind him. He became only the 15th player ever to hit 40 homers in four separate seasons; twelve are

in the Hall of Fame, and the other two are named Griffey and McGwire.

1996: In the offseason, Gonzalez discontinued the weight training that had robbed him of flexibility and left him susceptible to back problems. The result was a career year - Gonzalez was behind only Mark McGwire in slugging average and Albert Belle in RBI. Gonzalez won the American League MVP award and carried the Rangers to their first post-season play ever.

	AB	R	HR	RBI	SB	BA
1995 Texas	352	57	27	82	0	.295
1996 Texas	541	89	47	144	2	.314
1997 Texas	533	87	42	131	0	.296

GONZALEZ, LUIS - OF - BL - b: 9/3/67

Scouting: Always popular with other players and fans, Gonzalez returned to Houston in 1997 after a season and a half with the Cubs. He plays a steady left field with above-average range but a below-average arm. He is subject to lengthy streaks and slumps but his year-to-year numbers are consistent. The slight drop-off in his 1997 numbers is partially due to the differences in hitting in the Astrodome versus Wrigley Field, but it also suggests that he has probably reached his peak.

1998: Gonzalez has been essentially an everyday player for seven seasons. He should be able to stretch it out for two or three more years.

1997: Because of Houston's lack of power, Gonzalez spent much of the season as the cleanup hitter, a role for which he is not well-suited. Ideally, he is a number six or seven hitter. His 23-game hitting streak was the longest in the National League.

1996: Gonzalez' only full season in Chicago was similar to the 1995 season which was split between Houston and Chicago.

	AB	R	HR	RBI	SB	BA
1995 Chicago NL	471	69	13	69	6	.276
1996 Chicago NL	483	70	15	79	9	.271
1997 Houston	550	78	10	68	10	.258

GONZALEZ, RAUL - OF - BR - b: 12/27/73

Gonzalez recovered from a broken thumb that decimated his 1996 season to be an important RBI bat for Wichita, spending his first full season at Double-A. He's not overly impressive as a power hitter, mostly having gap power, but he's got other positives, too. He's not a free-swinger like many Double-A power threats and he's got a little speed. Gonzalez could reach the majors in a reserve, corner outfield role by late 1999. His opportunity for a big-league future depends largely upon developing more versatility both as a hitter and as an outfielder, which he planned to do in winter ball after last year.

GONZALEZ, WIKLEMAN - C - BR - b: 5/17/74

Gonzalez was a part of the Pirates' organization in 1996 and played at both Class A and Double-A in the Padres' farm system in 1997. He hit well and showed some pop in the California League and was promoted to Mobile of the Southern League. With top prospect Ben Davis ahead of him in the organization, Gonzalez has his work cut out for him. But, if he continues to develop offensively he will have a chance to advance, probably into a backup role.

GOODWIN, CURTIS - OF - BL - b: 9/30/72

Scouting: Goodwin is an extremely fast outfielder with no power, but marginal strikezone judgment, limiting his value as a leadoff hitter. His offensive skills are nearly identical to Deion Sanders, with whom he shared time in center field last year until he was sent down after a disagreement with Reds management. He is still young enough to develop into a productive leadoff hitter.

1998: Goodwin could start for a major league team willing to overlook his limitations as a leadoff hitter in exchange for his defense and stolen bases. However, he would need to produce a strong spring to win a job and overcome the perception that he is a troublemaker.

1997: After Ruben Sierra flopped, Goodwin played regularly, first in left-field and then taking over from Sanders in center field due to his superior defensive skills. Goodwin, as he has always done, started out performing extremely well before reverting to his old habits. In August, when Jack McKeon suggested he work harder, Goodwin exploded, accused the Reds' organization of being racist, and was promptly sent to Indianapolis for an attitude adjustment. He was not recalled when the rosters expanded in September.

1996: Goodwin showed improvement in his greatest weakness at Triple-A Indianapolis, setting a career high in walks. He struggled at the plate in a brief trial in Cincinnati, but ended the year with 55 steals between Triple-A and the majors.

	AB	R	HR	RBI	SB	BA
1995 Baltimore	289	40	1	24	22	.263
1996 Cincinnati	136	20	0	5	15	.228
1997 Cincinnati	265	27	1	12	22	.253

GOODWIN, TOM - OF - BL - b: 7/27/68

Scouting: For pure speed, Goodwin is without peer in baseball. His speed serves him well in center field, where he covers vast amounts of territory, and as a basestealer, with at least 50 steals in each of his three major league seasons. Unfortunately, Goodwin is not a good leadoff hitter, since he rarely walks. His game is to slap the ball on the ground or to the opposite field, and he uses the threat of a bunt to draw the infield in. Goodwin does not throw well, but compensates by getting to the ball quickly.

1998: Goodwin would be best suited to a team that did not need him to bat first or second in the lineup. An ability to draw walks would move him up to the level of Otis Nixon, but for now, he's a better-hitting version of Gary Pettis.

1997: Goodwin came to Texas in mid-season in the Dean Palmer trade. He immediately replaced Damon Buford as the everyday center fielder, but was the league's worst leadoff hitter, with a .314 on-base percentage. Goodwin is an exciting player to watch, and has the ability to manufacture runs almost single-handedly with his speed.

1996: For the second straight year, Goodwin hit better than .280 with startling speed. Only a ribcage injury in the final two weeks of the season prevented him from challenging Kenny Lofton for the American League stolen base crown.

	AB	R	HR	RBI	SB	BA
1995 Kansas City	480	72	4	28	50	.288
1996 Kansas City	524	80	1	35	66	.282
1997 K.C. - Texas	574	90	2	39	50	.260

GORDON, KEITH - OF - BR - b: 1/22/69

Formerly in the Reds farm system, Gordon played in the Orioles organization in 1996 and found his way back to the Reds for four games at Double-A in 1997. He's had some below-average years in the minors. The Reds second round draft pick in 1990, Gordon had a good year at Triple-A in 1995.

GRACE, MARK - 1B - BL - b: 6/28/70

Scouting: Grace is one of the top pure hitters in all of baseball. He has an outstanding eye and is capable of hitting the ball to the opposite field as well as turning on the inside pitch and driving it to right field. He remains one of the top defensive first baseman in all of baseball and is credited with saving Cub infielders many errors each year with his ability to scoop bad throws out of the dirt.

1998: Not much will change about his status or performance. He's hit below .296 only once since he became a full-time player and hasn't fallen below that mark since 1991. He's going to be one of the Cubs' best players again.

1997: Grace continued to be one of the best hitters in the National League. He was Chicago's only consistent hitter the entire season and manager Jim Riggleman experimented with him in the cleanup spot in the order, but moved him back to his traditional third spot after a short time.

1996: Grace had his second straight outstanding season as he recorded the highest batting average for a Cubs' player in 20 years. The only black mark was a slight back problem that forced him on the disabled list for a couple of weeks. Grace won his fourth Gold Glove award for fielding excellence.

	AB	R	HR	RBI	SB	BA
1995 Chicago NL	552	97	16	92	6	.326
1996 Chicago NL	547	88	9	75	2	.331
1997 Chicago NL	555	87	13	78	2	.319

GRAFFANINO, TONY - 2B - BR - b: 6/6/72

Graffanino has made himself into a solid, if unspectacular second baseman. He does the job defensively, despite being a tad slow and tall for the position, and provides some pop with the bat. He filled in well when Mark Lemke was injured in '97, perhaps playing a little above his head, and might have earned at least a share of the job this season, as Lemke is getting old and wearing down.

	AB	R	HR	RBI	SB	BA
1997 Atlanta	186	33	8	20	6	.258

GREBECK, BRIAN - 3B/SS - BR - b: 8/31/67

Craig's brother Brian hasn't been able to hit Triple-A pitching over the past few seasons and when he hit for average at lower levels he didn't produce any runs. At age 30, his chances of catching on with the big club are non-existent.

GREBECK, CRAIG - SS - BR - b: 12/29/64

Scouting: Grebeck is a respectable reserve at third base, shortstop and second base. He has typically not been a big hitter, but he's a capable glove man. He's probably past the stage where he can be an everyday player, but he can fill in well enough in a pinch; as someone to spell the regulars and provide some depth, he gets the job done.

1998: With Randy Velarde expected to return from elbow surgery and Luis Alicea slipping into Grebeck's role in Anaheim, the Blue Jays became Grebeck's most likely employer

1997: A shoulder injury that required surgery in the off-season slowed Grebeck the second half of the season and eventually caused him to call it a year. He did a capable job filling the role for which he was obtained.

1996: Grebeck served as a backup infielder for the Florida Marlins. Again, he didn't hit, and was slowed by an elbow injury that sidelined him for five weeks in July and August.

	AB	R	HR	RBI	SB	BA
1995 Chicago AL	154	19	1	18	0	.260
1996 Florida	95	8	1	9	0	.211
1997 Anaheim	126	12	1	6	0	.270

GREEN, CHAD - OF - BB - b: 6/28/75

Green was the eighth overall pick of the 1996 June Draft by the Milwaukee Brewers. He was the fastest player available in the draft and seems to be a perfect fit for the Brewers who are in search of a leadoff hitter and center fielder. Last year Green played for Class A Stockton of the California League. He used his speed well, stealing 37 bases, but he tried to go deep too much (138 strikeouts in 513 at-bats). Green needs to make contact more and let his speed carry him.

GREEN, SCARBOROUGH - OF - BB - 6/9/74

Scouting: With major-league quality in his glove and his legs, Green has garnered status as a top prospect. He's one of the fastest players in the organization who still has plenty to learn about how to use that gift once he gets on base. Defensively, he could handle a big-league assignment now.

1998: He should spend as much time in Triple-A as possible, since he still has so much to learn about being a contact hitter, bunting, stealing bases and all the other things he needs to do to become a leadoff hitter in the big leagues. Green has struggled to hit in the second half of each of the last two seasons after gaining a promotion from one minor-league level to the next, so a year of stability might help him.

1997: Green spent only 76 games in Double-A, where he batted .307 and stole 11 bases. He got a little more than 200 at-bats in Triple-A and struck out about once a game, then was able to get his first three big-league hits out of the way during a stint with the Cardinals. Generally a confident, occasionally flashy player, he kept quiet during that time of learning in St. Louis.

1996: He had a stunning start in the Class A Florida State League — his .293 batting average was far better than any of his three previous seasons — and moved up to Double-A. Though he struggled to hit there, he was considered one of the league's more exciting players.

GREEN, SHAWN - OF - BL - b: 11/10/72

Scouting: Green is developing into an all-around player, although he needs to make more contact. He showed last year that he can steal some bases and he has underrated power. His improvement as a defensive player has been impressive. He has gone from being a liability to a strength in the outfield with an arm that continues to get stronger.

1998: This will be the year that Green gets to play regularly through the tough times. He has better power than we have seen. A notoriously slow starter, if Green takes off from day one, he will have a breakthrough year.

1997: Green's stock fell so much that the Blue Jays went with Ruben Sierra over Green for three straight weeks. But, Green rebounded and by the end of the year, he was a regular in right field and was hitting the ball with authority.

1996: Disappointing by the standards he set a year earlier, Green improved defensively and achieved at least the possibility of a platoon job in 1997.

	AB	R	HR	RBI	SB	BA
1995 Toronto	379	52	15	54	1	.288
1996 Toronto	422	52	11	45	5	.280
1997 Toronto	429	57	16	53	14	.287

GREENE, CHARLIE - C - BR - b: 1/23/71

The Orioles acquired catcher Charlie Greene off waivers from the Mets in mid-September last year for catching insurance during their stretch run. Greene hit .206 at Triple-A, representative of his hitting abilities. His strengths are his defensive skill behind the plate and his strong throwing arm.

GREENE, TODD - C - BR - b: 5/8/71

Scouting: Power and a never-say-die attitude have brought Greene a long way in a short time. As Angels bench coach Joe Maddon has said, "The best way to get Todd to do something is to tell him he can't do it." Greene has always hit for power, but the knock on the converted outfielder had been he can't play defense well enough to catch every day. Through a tremendous amount of hard work and dedication, Greene has improved his defense dramatically and has learned to be a good handler of a pitching staff, without losing any power. If he stays healthy, which hasn't happened for two years, he could be a solid power-hitting catcher for many seasons.

1998: Greene doesn't have to change a thing to keep himself solidly in the Angels' plans. The Angels thought so much of him they traded Jim Leyritz to Texas so he could be the everyday catcher the previous year.

1997: Greene opened the season with the big club but was sent to Vancouver April 15th to make room on the roster for reliever Rick DeLucia. The plan was to let Greene stay at Triple-A to prepare for his role as catcher of the future. However, Greene wrecked that plan by hitting a franchise-record 25 home runs in 64 games, slugging .727 and playing solid defense. He enjoyed only three healthy weeks as the Angels' starting catcher, though, before a broken right wrist ended his season.

1996: A broken bone in his left wrist robbed Greene of his customary power and slowed his development. A good season in the Arizona Fall League helped him recover from wrist surgery and readied him for a run at a starting job in the majors the next season.

	AB	R	HR	RBI	SB	BA
1996 California	79	9	2	9	2	.190
1997 Anaheim	124	24	9	24	2	.290

GREENE, WILLIE - 3B - BL - b: 9/23/71

Scouting: A low-average power hitter, Greene is showing signs of finally establishing himself as a productive major leaguer after an endless array of injuries and bad luck. He possesses an extremely quick bat, and his strikezone judgment has improved considerably. His defensive play at third base has been erratic at times, and Ray Knight moved Greene to the outfield for a stretch in 1997. He has struggled against lefthanders in limited opportunities, which could reduce his potential as a full-time player.

1998: With the impatient Ray Knight absent from the scene, Greene should flourish in 1998. A 30-homer, 100-RBI season is not out of the question and although the Reds have some decent prospects at third base, none will be ready to threaten Greene in 1998.

1997: Greene struggled early in the season, but improved as the season progressed. A major key was improved strikezone judgment, as Greene cut his strikeout rate by a third and doubled his walk total. He led the Reds in home runs and RBI.

1996: Greene was on the verge of nailing down the third base job, when he pulled a hamstring in June and missed almost two months. A strong September (including six home runs in the final week) re-established his credentials as the best position prospect in the Cincinnati organization.

	AB	R	HR	RBI	SB	BA
1995 Cincinnati	19	1	0	0	0	.105
1996 Cincinnati	287	48	19	63	0	.244
1997 Cincinnati	495	62	26	91	6	.253

GREENWELL, MIKE - OF - BL - b: 7/18/63

Nine RBI in one game! Greenwell set a major-league record with his early September outburst in 1996, driving in all nine runs in a 9-8 victory over Seattle. He spent nearly all year on the disabled list or otherwise hurt; he was a non-factor for the first five months of the year. Greenwell went to Japan in 1997 and got injured again.

	AB	R	HR	RBI	SB	BA
1995 Boston	481	67	15	76	9	.297
1996 Boston	295	35	7	44	4	.295

GREER, RUSTY - OF - BL - b: 1/21/69

Scouting: Greer is one of those hard-nosed players that managers and fans love. A contact hitter with power to all fields, Greer hits lefthanders and righthanders alike. Over the last three seasons, Greer has demonstrated an ability to hit in the clutch, delivering the winning hit in the Rangers' final at-bat twelve times. He's a steady and sometimes spectacular outfielder, and has decent speed on the bases.

1998: Greer is in his prime. He should be able to continue to hit over .300 with good power. A return to the 100-RBI level depends upon the Rangers finding a capable leadoff hitter.

1997: Greer reached new heights in power without a decline in batting average. He accomplished this while playing through an assortment of minor injuries. Greer established or equaled his career high in runs, doubles, homers and steals. The only blemish on his season was an uncharacteristically high number of errors (12).

1996: Establishing himself firmly as an everyday player, Greer set career highs in almost every offensive category despite missing nearly three weeks down the stretch with bruised ribs.

	AB	R	HR	RBI	SB	BA
1995 Texas	417	58	13	61	3	.271
1996 Texas	542	96	18	100	9	.332
1997 Texas	601	112	26	87	9	.321

GREGG, TOMMY - OF - BL - b: 7/29/63

As he has for most of the past decade, Gregg feasted on Triple-A pitching and even got a few at-bats with the Braves. He's a line-drive hitter with an occasional homer in his bat but in numerous major league trials has not shown the bat speed to carry that hitting to the bigs. Gregg remains a Triple-A insurance policy.

GRESHAM, KRIS - C - BR - b: 8/30/70

Gresham is a reserve catcher in the Orioles farm system. He retired in 1996 rather than take a demotion from Double-A to Class A, and then "unretired" to return in 1997 as a reserve catcher. Gresham peaked in 1995 when he hit .250 in 64 Triple-A at-bats.

GRIEVE, BEN - OF - BL - b: 5/4/76

Scouting: Grieve, after his hot 1995 debut, has arrived in the bigs. He is the prototypical power hitter, who has a good eye and simply drives the ball in the direction in which it is going. He is a decent right fielder with a good, but not great, arm.

1998: Grieve will take his hot rookie act to the Coliseum and patrol right field for now, and a number of years to come. He is still young so he has some learning ahead, but on a hitting scale he is ahead of Pittsburgh's right field counterpart, Jose Guillen, who debuted under similar circumstances last year. He'll get the hang of it quickly and will be fun to watch in the process.

1997: Grieve started at Double-A Huntsville, and proceeded to shred Southern League pitchers, hitting .328 with 24 homers and 108 RBI despite only 372 at-bats. Life in Tacoma was similarly short-lived as he hit .426 with seven homers and 28 RBI in 108 at-bats, and Grieve proceeded to Oakland where he clubbed three doubles in his first game.

1996: After tearing up the California League while at Modesto (hitting .356 with eleven homers and 51 RBI), Grieve was promoted to Huntsville where he struggled a bit before figuring out Double-A pitching. He finished the year at Huntsville hitting .237 with eight homers and 32 RBI.

	AB	R	HR	RBI	SB	BA
1997 Oakland	93	12	3	24	0	.312

GRIFFEY, CRAIG - OF - BR - b: 6/3/71

Griffey runs well, like his brother Junior, but sure doesn't hit like the other members of the Griffey clan. He has no power, strikes out a lot and doesn't make up for it with a good average either. He spent the first six years of his minor-league career in the Mariners' organization and played at Double-A Chattanooga in the Reds' farm system in 1997. He's gotten more than a fair look and is not a prospect.

GRIFFEY, KEN JR - OF - BL - b: 11/21/69

Scouting: Griffey may not win the MVP award every year, but is there another player you would rather have on your team? He combines upper-deck power with speed, defense and savvy. He could be working on five straight 40-homer seasons except for a broken left wrist that cost him 11 weeks in 1994.

1998: Another run at an MVP award is a safe bet for Griffey.

1997: Griffey challenged Maris and Ruth up until the final week, and his homer total was the largest in the American League since Maris' record 61 in 1961. He posted career highs in hits and RBI.

1996: Consider this power: Griffey had 49 homers despite missing 20 games with a broken right hamate bone suffered June 20th. He homered and doubled in his first game back, July 14th.

	AB	R	HR	RBI	SB	BA
1995 Seattle	260	52	17	42	4	.258
1996 Seattle	545	125	49	140	16	.303
1997 Seattle	608	125	56	147	15	.304

GRIFOL, PEDRO - C - BR - b: 11/28/69

Grifol continued to supply mature defense behind the plate in Double-A last year. His offensive ability declined however, as he only managed to hit .200 with three home runs. The Mets staff their minor-league rosters with catchers in a manner similar to a major league spring training camp: plenty of good receiving talent to help pitchers develop.

GRIJAK, KEVIN - 1B - BL - b: 8/6/70

Grijak is a power-hitting, poor-fielding first baseman whom the Braves seem to be stashing at the minor-league level in case those players ever put it all together. The Braves don't seem to have a lot of faith in him because they keep giving playing time to other players and sending him to Mexico or Double-A, but he keeps hitting. Perhaps expansion will be kind to him and he'll get a chance to see if he can pop some homers in the majors.

GRISSOM, MARQUIS - OF - BR - b: 4/17/67

Scouting: For the better part of the nineties — and for no apparent reason — Grissom has been regarded as one of the best leadoff hitters in the majors. This despite a sub-.330 career on-base percentage, and just one season in which his OBP exceeded .350 (1993, at .351). Grissom often gets himself out on bad pitches and he strikes out too frequently for a table-setter. He has a little pop to the gaps, and though he still has above-average speed, it has deteriorated rapidly from its peak. He would help the Indians more if used near the bottom of the order, where he would get more RBI opportunities and could turn the lineup over for the real table-setters; he was used in that manner down the stretch in 1997. His defense is a little below Gold Glove caliber; he has great range and a so-so arm.

1998: Grissom was locked into a long-term deal in Cleveland, who traded him to Milwaukee. He's a .270 hitter with 12-homer and 20-steal ability at this stage in his career.

1997: Grissom was a near automatic out for much of the season's first half. He came on strong in the second half to make his numbers respectable, but apparently lost his leadoff job to Omar Vizquel. Grissom's baseball skills appear to be aging rapidly, and he could be a role player by the end of his contract.

1996: Grissom hit .300 for the only time thus far in his major league career as leadoff man for the Braves. That said, it was his power that was most impressive (32 doubles, 23 homers, .489 slugging average). Batting sixth, Grissom could have had a 100-RBI season. Grissom is one of those players whose skills will never be maximized because he has been miscast into a role for which he isn't suited.

	AB	R	HR	RBI	SB	BA
1995 Atlanta	551	80	12	42	29	.258
1996 Atlanta	671	106	23	74	28	.308
1997 Cleveland	558	74	12	66	22	.262

GROPPUSO, MIKE - 3B - BR - b: 3/9/70

Groppuso was a first round compensation pick in the Astros' 1991 draft. He is prone to strikeouts and, although he received some playing time at the Triple-A level in 1996. Groppuso started 1997 at Independent Leagie Rio Grande and finished it at Double-A El Paso in the Milwaukee organization.

GRUBER, KELLY - 2B - BR - b: 2/26/62

Once a power-hitting third baseman for some strong Blue Jay teams, Gruber was out of baseball for about four years. He tried a comeback last year with the Orioles, almost making it as a utility player following a strong spring showing. But he got caught up in the roster numbers, and had to accept a Triple-A job as a second baseman. He was okay but not exceptional in Triple-A before getting hurt. He couldn't get back into a groove after returning from the disabled list and was finally waived in July. Unless he gets a Japanese contract, Gruber will probably hang 'em for good.

GRUDZIELANEK, MARK - 2B/SS - BR - b: 6/30/70

Scouting: Grudzielanek is blossoming into a rarity, a shortstop who has an outstanding combination of power and speed. Grudzielanek already has exhibited outstanding gap power in his youthful major-league career and has the potential to be-

come a 20-homer man. Grudzielanek is not a good fielder, though he should become steady with more experience.
1998: Grudzielanek has been miscast as a leadoff hitter during his two full seasons in the major leagues and the Expos want to move him down in the batting order, probably to number three. He will again be the starting shortstop, though he will need to get acclimated to a new double-play partner in rookie Orlando Cabrera as veteran second baseman Mike Lansing was slated to be traded after last season ended. Lansing had served as a steadying influence on Grudzielanek.
1997: Despite a late-season slide, Grudzielanek had an outstanding year for the Expos. He hit with decent power, though his on-base percentage was low for a leadoff man. His 54 doubles tied the major league single-season record for a shortstop that was set by Seattle's Alex Rodriguez the previous season. His 32 errors were cause for concern, leading some to believe he might be better off moving to second base.
1996: Grudzielanek had a fine first full-season in the majors, hitting .300 and being selected to the All-Star game.

	AB	R	HR	RBI	SB	BA
1995 Montreal	269	27	1	20	8	.245
1996 Montreal	657	99	6	49	33	.306
1997 Montreal	649	76	4	51	25	.273

GRUNEWALD, KEITH - 3B - BB - b: 10/15/71
Grunewald can play all four infield positions, and does all the little man things — bunting, hitting behind the runner, running the bases well — but he simply hasn't hit enough for the Rockies to consider him a big-league prospect.

GUBANICH, CREIGHTON - C - BR - b: 3/27/72
After six minor-league seasons in the A's organization, Gubanich spent 1997 in the Milwaukee and then Colorado farm systems. A so-so defensive catcher with some power, Gubanich put up solid numbers at Triple-A Tucson for the Brewers, hitting .335 with twelve homers and 51 RBI. At Colorado Springs he got only 47 at-bats and struggled to a .191 average. He did hit three homers in his short time there and could hit his way to a backup receiver spot in the future.

GUERRERO, VLADIMIR - OF - BR - b: 2/9/76
Scouting: Guerrero is the prototypical five-tool talent. Scouts universally feel he will turns into an eventual 30/30 man while winning Gold Gloves. Some feel he will eventually wind up in the Hall of Fame.
1998: The Expos expect big things from Guerrero now that he has had a year to settle into the major leagues. He still has some learning to do but he will play every day, starting in right field while hitting fifth or sixth. Guerrero is still young and extremely raw, so it's not fair to expect him to become a superstar right away.
1997: Guerrero was hyped throughout spring training as a future superstar but injuries sabotaged his rookie season. Guerrero spent three separate stints on the disabled list with a broken left foot, a strained right hamstring and a broken left hand. He never had the chance to get anything going, then was sent to the Florida Instructional League at the end of the season in an effort to brush up on fundamentals and learn how to play under control.
1996: Guerrero was named MVP of the Eastern League, despite playing only 118 games at Double-A Harrisburg after starting the year at Class A West Palm Beach. He finished the season in Montreal as a September callup.

	AB	R	HR	RBI	SB	BA
1997 Montreal	325	44	11	40	3	.302

GUERRERO, WILTON - 2B/SS - BR - b: 10/24/74
Scouting: Guerrero is a slick fielder who can play both shortstop and second base. At the plate he slaps the ball — he doesn't have much power to speak of — which allows him to utilize his speed to get on base.
1998: The Dodgers were down on Guerrero at the end of the season and in some circles his name did not appear on projected protect lists for the expansion draft. He's just 23 years old with speed and is a good fielder, so he will play in someone's infield if not the Dodgers'.
1997: Guerrero played in 111 games for the Dodgers but just nine in September when he got only ten at-bats. The acquisition of Eric Young, whom the Dodgers lost in the last expansion draft, cut into Guerrero's playing time.
1996: Guerrero hit .344 at Triple-A Albuquerque and put himself in line for a regular Dodgers' infield job.

	AB	R	HR	RBI	SB	BA
1997 Los Angeles	357	39	4	32	6	.291

GUEVARA, GIOMAR - SS/2B - BB - b: 10/23/72
Scouting: Guevara is a usually slick-fielding middle infielder who was named the best defensive second baseball in the Midwest League in a poll of league managers in 1994. He has little power and has not refined his base-stealing technique.
1998: Guevara should start the season at Triple-A, but whether he plays second base or short depends upon the roster makeup.
1997: Guevara spent the first half of the season at shortstop for Double-A Memphis before being promoted to Triple-A Tacoma, where he played second base. He combined for six homers and eight stolen bases on the season, but was caught stealing 12 times.
1996: Guevara set a career-high with 21 stolen bases at Memphis, one more steal than in his three previous pro seasons, while playing both middle infield positions.

GUIEL, AARON - 3B - BL - b: 10/5/72
Guiel has shown a little power and hitting smarts in the minors, and could make the Angels as a reserve infielder. He was shifted from second to third base to increase his promotability. In 1997 Guiel had a good season for Double-A Midland in the Angels orgainzation, batting .329-22-85 in 116 games, he finished the season playing in eight games for Double-A Mobile in the Padres farm system.

GUIEL, JEFF - OF - BL - 1/12/74
His brother, Aaron, was a prospect in the Angels' organization until they traded him to San Diego for catching help in August. Jeff has many of the same skills and, like his brother, is a hard-nosed competitor with a hockey mentality. He can hit for average and power, and had a solid year at Class A Cedar Rapids last year, despite being held up by visa problems.

GUILIANO, MATT - SS - BR - b: 6/7/72
Guiliano gravitated into the Double-A Reading Phillies' shortstop job by default due to the Phillies' lack of organizational depth. He is a capable defender within his somewhat limited range, and has a good enough arm to play third base in a pinch. However, he's a career .221 hitter whose seven homers last

year are a career high. He's a useful organization player who can hold down the fort until better prospects pass him.

GUILLEN, CARLOS - SS - BB - b: 9/30/75
Scouting: Guillen has been touted as a slick fielding shortstop prospect with power. However, his career has been hampered by serious injuries. A Venezuelan, he was signed before his 17th birthday in 1992, but did not play in the United States until 1995. He missed the entire 1994 season with injuries. He was added to the 40-man roster a year ago even though he had never played above the Low Class A level.
1998: Guillen should get a shot at the Triple-A level in 1998 at the age of 21. If successful, he could reach the majors at a early age.
1997: Guillen finally played a full season without serious injury. He made a successful jump from Low Class A to Double-A where he hit .254 with ten home runs and 39 RBI. He also hit .308 in a brief appearance at Triple-A New Orleans.
1996: Guillen had only 112 at-bats at Low Class A Quad Cities due to injuries. However, he hit .330 with three homers.

GUILLEN, JOSE - OF - BR - b: 5/17/76
Scouting: Guillen has a wealth of unrefined talent. He has a quick bat with the ability to hit for average and power. He also possesses one of the strongest arms in the game, though he tries to show it off too much and makes numerous wild throws.
1998: Guillen will open the season as the Pirates' starting right fielder. He is fully expected to improve on last year's solid numbers after an up-and-down rookie year. Guillen has a great love of the game and realizes which areas of his game he needs to improve, particularly strike zone judgment and controlling his great arm.
1997: The Pirates jumped Guillen all the way from Class A to the majors at the start of last season and he held his own after a shaky start. He swung at too many bad pitches but settled down as the season went on and wound up having one of the better rookie years in the National League.
1996: Guillen was MVP of the Class A Carolina League for Lynchburg, tying for the league lead in home runs just a year after leading the short-season Class A New York-Penn League in homers while with Erie.

	AB	R	HR	RBI	SB	BA
1997 Pittsburgh	498	58	14	70	1	.267

GUILLEN, OZZIE - SS - BL - b: 1/20/64
Scouting: A steady defensive player with the White Sox for thirteen years, Guillen is one of the best-loved players in the game. He has always been a liability with the bat, hitting for a decent average but never taking a walk and exhibiting no power. Guillen is a kamikaze baserunner who has almost stopped trying to steal bases. He makes few errors, but his range has been shrinking for several years; he has lost a lot of mobility to his right, especially.
1998: It's fitting that an organization that shows so little heart will now have lost it's soul, too. Guillen's skills have deteriorated too much to help a contending club, but he should be able to fill a role with a young team that needs an example of how to play the game.
1997: Guillen had another typical year but increasingly fell into disfavor as the Sox tried to find a way to pump more offense into their lineup. He probably played his last game in a Sox uniform.
1996: Guillen placed among the league's best defensive shortstops with typically one-dimensional offense; his .263 batting average represented about 90% of his offensive production.

	AB	R	HR	RBI	SB	BA
1995 Chicago AL	415	50	1	41	6	.248
1996 Chicago AL	499	62	4	45	6	.263
1997 Chicago AL	490	59	4	52	5	.245

GULAN, MIKE - 3B - BR - b: 12/18/70
At one time, Gulan was the top power prospect in the organization and future heir to the third base job. He has fallen from favor, that humbled status hastened by his poor showing in a brief big-league chance in 1997. He struck out 121 times in Triple-A last season, his big swing having led to wild inconsistency in the past that turned horrid, at times, last year. Normally a strong defensive player, his 16 errors reflected how far he's fallen.

GUNDERSON, SHANE - OF - BR - 10/16/73
Gunderson started 1997 at the Twins' Class A affiliate Fort Wayne and then was promoted to Double-A New Britain. He has some speed but hasn't found the stroke that made him the co-Big 10 Player of the Year at Minnesota in 1995. Gunderson should start the 1998 season back at Double-A.

GUTIERREZ, RICKY - SS - BR - b: 5/23/70
Scouting: Gutierrez and Derek Bell were the only players remaining on the Houston roster in 1997 who came in the trade that sent Ken Caminiti and Steve Finley to San Diego. Gutierrez filled a valuable role as a utility infielder and as the starting shortstop down the stretch after Tim Bogar was injured. He is a steady fielder with average range and has hit above .260 in his three years in Houston. He has limited power and speed.
1998: Gutierrez will probably be a utility infielder but his versatility should result in about 250 at-bats.
1997: Gutierrez missed most of spring training and the first month of the season with a thumb injury. However, he finished the season with more playing time than in any season since his rookie year in 1993.
1996: Gutierrez was a utility infielder with most of his action at shortstop. His .284 batting average was a career high.

	AB	R	HR	RBI	SB	BA
1995 Houston	156	22	0	12	5	.276
1996 Houston	218	28	1	15	6	.284
1997 Houston	303	33	3	34	5	.261

GUZMAN, CRISTIAN - SS - BB - b: 3/21/78
Look past the 37 errors Guzman made while playing 122 games at shortstop for Class A Greensboro in 1997. This youngster has what it takes defensively to play in the big leagues — perhaps sooner than people think. His impressive range and accurate arm had scouts raving about him. At bat he is already adequate for a middle infielder, hitting .273 before a promotion to higher Class A Tampa.

GUZMAN, EDWARDS - 3B - BL - b: 9/11/76
At first sight, Guzman's youth and batting average impress. He was a starting third baseman at Double-A at age 19. Although he hit .284 for Shreveport, Guzman only banged three homers and drove in 42 over 380 at-bats. For a man his size (212 pounds) playing a power position, he'll have to do better. He didn't hit many doubles, either (15), so his power potential seems light.

GWYNN, TONY - OF - BL - b: 5/9/60
Scouting: There is no book on how to pitch Gwynn. Pitchers who work him outside give up hits to left. Last year, he turned on inside pitches and hit a career-high 17 homers and a club-record 49 doubles. Age and injuries (knees, Achilles tendon, foot) have diminished his speed. But Tony Gwynn hits with the best of the all-time greats. His eight batting titles ties Honus Wagner's National League record and ranks second in total only to Ty Cobb.
1998: He is a fixture in right field for the Padres and at the All-Star Game. Gwynn needs to match his '97 total of 220 hits to reach 3,000. A fifth straight batting title is not out of the question. Gwynn's average over past five seasons, .373, is only one point over last year's average. He shows no sign of losing his batting eye or desire.
1997: Gwynn played in his most games since 1989 and set career-highs in hits (a club-record 220), homers, RBI and doubles (49). He hit an incredible .459 (67-for-146) with runners in scoring position.
1996: Despite playing with a frayed Achilles tendon and a painful bursa sac in his left leg, Gwynn hit for a high average although he had a career-low homer count and drove in relatively few runs.

	AB	R	HR	RBI	SB	BA
1995 San Diego	535	82	9	90	17	.368
1996 San Diego	451	67	3	50	11	.353
1997 San Diego	592	97	17	119	12	.372

HAJEK, DAVE - 2B - BR - b: 10/14/67
Hajek was claimed off waivers from Houston and started 1997 in the Tigers' farm system at Triple-A Toledo. A solid defensive second baseman with a pretty good bat, Hajek struggled in Toledo and finished the season at Triple-A Las Vegas in the Padres' organization. He regained his stroke in the desert, and could be a steady contributor to a major league lineup if he's given the chance. At age 30, though, his chance may have already passed.

HALE, CHIP - 2B - BL - b: 12/2/64
Hale spent 1995-96 with the Twins and filled a role there as a valuable pinch-hitter who was not an easy out. He signed with the Dodgers as a free agent in October of 1996 and started the 1997 season with the Dodgers. He got 12 at-bats in 14 games in April and May and was sent down to Triple-A Albuquerque. He could catch on with a big-league team as a pinch-hitter in 1998.

	AB	R	HR	RBI	SB	BA
1995 Minnesota	103	10	2	18	0	.262
1996 Minnesota	87	8	1	16	0	.276

HALL, BILLY 2B - BB - b: 6/17/69
The Reds have a ton of players like Hall in the high minors — older players who have been able to hit in the low minors, but who don't have the talent and ability to succeed against the better players. Hall has failed in every attempt at Triple-A, and, at 28 years of age, he is out of time. He'll never be a major league player and it's questionable why the Reds are wasting their time on him, and other players like him.

HALL, JOE - OF - BR - b: 3/6/66
Veteran minor leaguer Joe Hall had another solid season in Triple-A in 1996, and his 95 RBI were tops for his Rochester club. Except for a total of 43 at-bats in the majors with the White Sox and Tigers in 1994 and 1995, Hall has been in the minors for nine years. In past years, in addition to the outfield, Hall has also played first, second, third and caught. Hall spent most of 1997 at Triple-A Toledo and also appeared in two games for the Tigers.

HALLORAN, MATT - SS - b: 3/3/78
Halloran was the Padres' first-round pick in the June 1996 draft (15th overall). Last year, Halloran played for the Padres Class A team at Clinton in the Midwest League. He struggled at the plate and is at least a few seasons away from appearing at the Murph.

HALTER, SHANE - SS - BR - b: 11/8/69
Scouting: Halter has no special talent that stands out, but can do a lot of things well enough to play a utility role in the majors. He's above-average at all infield spots and has recently learned to play the outfield, too. Halter is a below-average hitter in most respects — a contact hitter with little power or speed. He's unlikely to hit for a high average or show superior on-base ability.
1998: Halter can play in the majors, but there are only a few of the specialized all-purpose jobs available for which Halter is suited. Some Triple-A play is in Halter's immediate future, but he should also play some in the major leagues, too.
1997: Due to injuries to David Howard, Halter got an early callup to Kansas City, then proceeded to steal Howard's role by hitting for an unusually high average and playing every position except catcher and pitcher.
1996: A six-year organizational player, Halter was loaned to Triple-A Charlotte when injuries decimated the Marlins' Triple-A franchise. He had his usual low-power, mediocre-batting average, solid defense year; it was his second season spent in Triple-A.

	AB	R	HR	RBI	SB	BA
1997 Kansas City	123	16	2	10	4	.276

HAMELIN, BOB - 1B - BL - b: 11/29/67
Scouting: The big first baseman rescued his career after a spring training release by Kansas City last year. Hamelin played so well for the Tigers that he brought back memories of his 1994 Rookie of the Year season. He has outstanding power, hits for a good average and draws lots of walks. He doesn't run well, but that's not expected of him anyway.
1998: Hamelin settled in last year as the Tiger DH against righthanders, and he could fill that role again. He'd like to play against lefthanders, too, but he didn't have great success against them last year. He's not necessarily part of the long-term plans, but if he keeps hitting, that could change.
1997: Leaving Kansas City may have been the best thing for Hamelin, who fit well into a Tiger lineup that includes others who can hit the ball out of the park. With the focus off him, Hamelin flourished. He signed late, after being released by the Royals, and he spent a month at Triple-A Toledo, but Hamelin still hit 18 home runs in just 318 at-bats.
1996: The dropoff that began in 1995 continued in '96. Hamelin started slow, and even though he eventually raised his average to .255, he hit only nine home runs and drove in just 40 runs. Constant battles with Royals management left him riding the bench as the season wound to a close.

	AB	R	HR	RBI	SB	BA
1995 Kansas City	208	20	7	25	0	.168
1996 Kansas City	239	31	9	40	5	.255
1997 Kansas City	318	47	18	52	2	.270

HAMILTON, DARRYL - OF - BL - b: 12/3/64
Scouting: Hamilton is an excellent contact hitter with a goodly amount of patience. He doesn't have much power, but he does do what a leadoff hitter is supposed to do: get on base. He also supplies good speed for the top of the order. He does, however, have trouble staying healthy. Hamilton is an excellent defensive player.
1998: Hamilton was a key part of the Giants' surprising Cinderella year of 1997, and the odds are they would like to have him back. San Francisco, however, has several excellent prospects in the wings, so his time in a Giants' uniform may be short lived. Wherever he plays, he can be counted upon to put up numbers consistent with his career: .275 average, five homers, 15 to 20 steals, and an on-base percentage in excess of .350.
1997: Signed at the last minute by the Giants, Hamilton displaced both incumbent Stan Javier and another free-agent signee, Darrin Jackson. Though he did battle injuries and a terrible September slump, Hamilton was a solid contributor to the San Francisco success story.
1996: Released by the Brewers, then signed by the Rangers, Hamilton promptly had one of his best years. He consistently hit for average and supplied moderate speed. Hamilton played 147 games in center field without making an error.

	AB	R	HR	RBI	SB	BA
1995 Milwaukee	398	54	5	44	11	.271
1996 Texas	627	94	6	51	15	.293
1997 San Francisco	460	78	5	43	15	.270

HAMMONDS, JEFFREY - OF - BR - b: 3/5/71
Scouting: Hammonds improved his plate discipline, but he still loves high fastballs, sometimes as high as his eyes. He has some power but is not considered a major power threat. He has some base stealing speed, but he's not a big base-stealing threat, either. His defense is merely adequate. Rather than developing into an impact player as the Orioles expected when they drafted him, he's developing into a solid but not spectacular outfielder. He's been fragile in the past, spending time on the disabled list every year except last season.
1998: Hammonds will get playing time in the outfield and at DH, but it's a cloudy and competitive picture including Eric Davis, Geronimo Berroa, and talented rookie David Dellucci vying for two slots. If Dellucci breaks through and hits major league pitching, then he could take over the right-field slot, and the rest will get fewer at-bats.
1997: Hammonds was nearly traded after a disappointing 1996 season, but the deals fell through. It's fortunate for the Orioles because he rose to the occasion with a good year when Eric Davis developed cancer. He played right field, avoided his annual injury, and came through with a solid performance in his first year with more than 250 at-bats. Hammonds came through in his make-or-break year.
1996: Hammonds began the year as the starting left fielder, but after a hot start, he slumped to .200 in June and was back in Triple-A. The demotion was a real eye opener, and he worked hard in the minors, but he didn't do much better when recalled.

	AB	R	HR	RBI	SB	BA
1995 Baltimore	178	18	4	23	4	.242
1996 Baltimore	248	38	9	27	3	.226
1997 Baltimore	397	71	21	55	15	.264

HANEL, MARCUS - C - BR - b: 10/19/71
1997 was Hanel's ninth minor-league season and he has reached Triple-A once, in 1995, where he played in two games. He's a good receiver behind the plate but not much good when he's at the plate. He spent 1997 at the Double-A level and may have a future as a coach but not as a major leaguer.

HANEY, TODD - 2B - BR - b: 7/30/65
A journeyman infielder, Haney has spent parts of four seasons in the majors (including last year with the Astros) and has played for four different organizations. He makes good contact, but with limited power and speed. He's primarily a second baseman, but lacks the defensive skill to keep a major league job. Haney is likely to continue his role as a high minors regular, awaiting an occasional stint as a major league utility player.

	AB	R	HR	RBI	SB	BA
1995 Chicago NL	73	11	2	6	0	.411
1996 Chicago NL	82	11	0	3	1	.134

HANSEN, DAVE - 3B - BL - b: 11/24/68
Scouting: Hansen has fashioned himself a fine career as a fifth or sixth infielder and pinch-hitting specialist. He has shown a knack for coming off the bench cold and being able to get hits, and he's also a decent defensive player.
1998: Hansen again will be employed as a backup infielder and pinch-hitting specialist. With the development and improvement of Kevin Orie he won't get a chance to start in Chicago, but will be excellent insurance against injury. His presence gives the Cubs added depth off the bench and versatility with late-inning defensive changes and double switches. He isn't good enough to be an everyday player at this point, but will be fine if used in the proper role.
1997: Hansen had an excellent year coming off the bench for the Cubs. He didn't get many starts but was a valuable contributor, providing several clutch hits for the North Siders. He got less than two at-bats per game but managed to stay sharp, which is something that many players have had trouble doing in a reserve role.
1996: Hansen had his first sub-par season in four years and was released by Los Angeles after the year was over. His batting average plummeted 140 points over just a couple of years earlier and he didn't provide any help for the Dodgers in pinch-hitting situations.

	AB	R	HR	RBI	SB	BA
1995 Los Angeles	181	19	1	14	0	.287
1996 Los Angeles	104	7	0	6	0	.221
1997 Chicago NL	151	19	3	21	1	.311

HANSEN, JED - 2B - BR - b: 8/19/72
Scouting: Hansen is a solid talent in many respects. He's a line-drive hitter with above-average power for a middle infielder. His batting eye has been good in the minors and he makes contact well enough to hit for a good batting average, although he's not going to hit .300 often. Hansen is a steady fielder, too, and has above-average speed. Since his selection in the second round of the 1994 draft, Hansen has been among the Royals' best prospects. He has done nothing recently to take the shine off his star. Hansen is not a future All-Star, but should be a good regular in the majors.
1998: Hansen will get a crack at winning the Royals' second base job in spring training. His impressive, two-month trial with Kansas City the year before showed the club that he was major league ready. If Hansen doesn't win the job outright he'll return to Triple-A Omaha — the Royals want him to play regularly — but

he'll be among the first to be recalled if an opening occurs on the Royals' infield.

1997: In his first full year at Triple-A Omaha, Hansen was one of the steadiest players at the plate and in the field; he batted .268 with 11 homers and 44 RBI, plus eight steals in nine attempts. When Jose Offerman was disabled for the third time that season, Hansen got his major league opportunity. He made the most of the chance, hitting over .300 and flashing a solid glove at second base. It was a good enough performance to give Hansen a serious shot for a regular major league job.

1996: Hansen's play at Double-A Wichita earned him a berth in the Double-A All-Star game, plus a late-season promotion to Omaha. He hit .286 with a career-high 12 homers and 50 RBI, although his walk total dropped sharply. Hansen played in the Arizona Fall League after the season.

	AB	R	HR	RBI	SB	BA
1997 Kansas City	94	11	1	14	3	.309

HARDTKE, JASON - 2B - BB - b: 9/15/71

One of Bobby Valentine's favorite players when they were together at Triple-A Norfolk, Hardtke was called up to the majors at the end of 1996, but just didn't compare favorably with the likes of Edgardo Alfonzo and Carlos Baerga. Hardtke split time through a brief stint in Double-A and a solid season with Norfolk in 1997. His .276 average with 11 home runs and 45 RBI, along with improved defensive skills, showed promise that he will return to the major leagues some day to fill an off-the-bench role.

	AB	R	HR	RBI	SB	BA
1996 New York NL	57	3	0	6	0	.193
1997 New York NL	56	9	2	8	1	.268

HARKRIDER, TIM - SS - BB - b: 9/5/71

A broken ankle and the lingering after-effects of same have caused Harkrider problems the last two seasons and have slowed his development. He underwent a second operation on his ankle near the end of 1997, so he's not out of the woods yet. Harkrider has the potential to hit for average and play solidly in the field, but his health remains a major question mark.

HARRIS, LENNY - 3B/2B - BL - b: 10/28/64

Scouting: Harris has been a useful reserve the past few years, combining versatility, a high average, and surprising speed. However, his poor strikezone judgment and mediocre defensive value limit his overall value, and given his age and 1997 performance, he may be at the end of his career.

1998: Harris in under contract and considered a good influence in the clubhouse, so he should retain a job and accumulate a few at-bats as a pinch-hitter. He will not receive significant playing time unless the Reds are struck by mass injuries.

1997: One of Ray Knight's favorite players, Harris started games at second base, third base, left and right field but was unable to match his fine 1996 season at the plate. His playing time rightfully disappeared when Jack McKeon took over.

1996: Harris had a surprisingly good season, hitting .285 in 302 at-bats as a multi-position reserve. He was able to parlay his performance into a two-year contract with the Reds.

	AB	R	HR	RBI	SB	BA
1995 Cincinnati	197	32	2	16	10	.208
1996 Cincinnati	302	33	5	32	14	.285
1997 Cincinnati	238	32	3	28	4	.273

HARRISS, ROBIN - C - BR - b: 8/7/71

Harriss advanced to Double-A Akron in the Indians' organization in 1997 and was a part-time catcher. He doesn't possess power or hit for average. Einar Diaz seems to be in line to back up Sandy Alomar behind the plate at Jacobs Field, leaving Harriss little hope for major league advancement with the Tribe.

HARTMAN, RON - 3B - BR - b: 12/12/74

A Maryland product who led the Pioneer League in extra-base hits (39) and tied for the lead in RBI (72) in 1996, Hartman continued his climb by hitting .292 with 14 homers at Class A High Desert. Defense is a question mark for Hartman.

HASELMAN, BILL - C - BR - b: 5/25/66

Scouting: Haselman has size and strength, but lacks finesse. He's a bull of a hitter, but he can cause damage, especially against lefthanded pitchers. He works hard defensively, but he's not a great receiver, and he has trouble throwing out runners.

1998: Unless the Red Sox acquire a first-string catcher and make Scott Hatteberg the backup, Haselman should be the righthanded portion of a platoon again this year. He has some security as a big-league backup, but no chance now of claiming a full-time role.

1997: Haselman started the season as the first-string catcher, but lost the job due to a broken thumb, ineffective play, and perhaps a move to a younger player, Hatteberg, by the Red Sox.

1996: Haselman got to play nearly every day down the stretch because of an injury to starting catcher Mike Stanley. He responded by holding his own with the bat and behind the plate.

	AB	R	HR	RBI	SB	BA
1995 Boston	152	22	5	23	0	.243
1996 Boston	237	33	8	34	4	.274
1997 Boston	212	22	6	26	0	.236

HASTINGS, LIONEL - 3B - BR - b: 1/26/73

Hastings is a patient hitter with a live line-drive bat who can play adequate defense at second and third base, but is not above-average in any particular area. He handles the bat well and is a good bunter, but his lack of speed and defensive range makes even a future as a major league utility player unlikely. If Hastings can produce another .300+ season at Triple-A Charlotte in 1998, then he could enter the mix for a potential major league bench role in 1999.

HATCHER, CHRIS - OF - BR - b: 1/7/69

Hatcher has spent the last five years in the high minors without ever cracking a major league roster. He has decent power (11 homers in 222 at-bats at Triple-A Omaha last year), but strikes out a great deal (68 last year) and is a below-average outfielder. He's Triple-A roster filler right now, with only a remote chance to get a few major league at-bats off of the bench.

HATTEBERG, SCOTT - C - BL - b: 12/14/69

Scouting: Hatteberg is a handy catcher in that he swings a decent bat from the left side, which is rare for a receiver. However, his bat, while solid, is not powerful enough to overcome his defensive liabilities. Hatteberg is slow throwing to second base and has had trouble throwing out baserunners in the majors and the minors.

1998: Hatteberg would appear to have the starting job unless Boston acquires a front-line catcher. If he does play every day, he will probably hit as well or better than he did in '97, especially since he's shown a good batting eye in the past. However, Hatteberg's defensive skills will most likely not improve significantly.

1997: Hatteberg started the season playing once every five days, but he took over the front-line duties after Bill Haselman suffered a broken thumb, and Hatteberg played well enough to hold onto them the rest of the way.

1996: In his third straight season at Triple-A Pawtucket, Hatteberg continued to gradually improve. He still had trouble throwing out runners, but posted an impressive .391 on-base percentage.

	AB	R	HR	RBI	SB	BA
1997 Boston	350	46	10	44	0	.277

HAWKINS, KRAIG - OF - BR - b: 12/4/71

Hawkins produced his usual season in his second year at the Double-A level: no power but good speed and the ability to get on base. He stole 12 bases with a .347 on-base percentage in 193 at-bats. Hawkins has just two homers in his minor-league career (none in 1997).

HAWS, SCOTT - C - BL - b: 1/11/72

Haws has struggled since undergoing reconstructive elbow surgery in 1995. Before the surgery he was a prospect, but last year he received little playing time at Class A Clearwater — not progress for an injury-plagued former prospect of Haws' age.

HAYES, CHARLIE - 3B - BR - b: 5/29/65

Scouting: Hayes is a top defensive third baseman who doesn't get the recognition he deserves. Pressing to drive in runs, he has developed an uppercut swing that has diminished his strike zone coverage. Hayes has been weak at the plate in clutch situations.

1998: The Yankees had Hayes under contract for 1998, but they were actively looking for another third baseman during the winter. Hayes was trade bait for anyone who wanted him, because of friction resulting from his part-time status last year.

1997: Hayes shared third base with Wade Boggs, but that wasn't manager Joe Torre's choice until Boggs slumped with nagging injuries. Hayes was a little too outspoken about not liking the situation, and he wasn't exactly a cheerful presence in the clubhouse.

1996: Coming from Pittsburgh to New York to help the Yankees' September march toward a World Championship was a highlight of Hayes' career. He stepped right in and helped fill the void when Boggs was missing time with a sore back. It was Hayes who caught the pop fly for the final out to win the World Series.

	AB	R	HR	RBI	SB	BA
1995 Philadelphia	529	58	11	85	5	.276
1996 Pittsburgh	459	51	10	62	6	.248
1996 New York AL	67	7	2	13	0	.284
1997 New York AL	353	39	11	53	3	.258

HAZLETT, STEVE - OF - BR - b: 3/30/70

Hazlett spent six seasons in the Twins' farm system and ended up with the Pirates' organization in 1997. His batting average plummeted nearly 100 points from 1996 and he hit just .235 at Double-A Carolina. He had a better average at Triple-A Calgary (.298 in 94 at-bats), but is too old to be considered a prospect.

HELD, DAN - 1B - BR - b: 10/7/70

Held has been the Phillies' Double-A first baseman the past two seasons, and has hit for power while exhibiting solid defensive skills. He strikes out frequently, even for a power hitter, often on pitches outside the strike zone. He can drive a minor-league fastball a long way, but likely doesn't have bat speed to do it in the majors. He is surehanded though slow in the field, and is a station-to-station baserunner. Held's slow progress in the higher minors make him a remote prospect for significant big-league play. He should advance to a full-time role at Triple-A in 1998, with a chance for a major league cameo.

HELFAND, ERIC - C - BL - b: 3/25/69

Helfand had a limited chance with Oakland in 1995, but since then has toiled in the minors with little chance to make it back into the majors. It's not out of the question for him to be a third catcher on a major league roster, but his limited offensive skills make him undesirable for a larger role.

HELMS, WESLEY - 3B - BR - b: 5/12/76

Helms is big and strong, one of the Braves top prospects and the guy they hope can take over third base and allow them to move Chipper Jones to another position. The Braves rushed him to Triple-A in '97 and he struggled. But he regrouped when they sent him back to Double-A, hitting .296 with 11 homers, and his career is back on track. Expect him to earn a regular job in the majors in 1999.

HELTON, TODD - 1B - BL - b: 8/20/73

Scouting: A good athlete with a sweet lefthanded swing and a great eye, Helton is a former University of Tennessee quarterback who continues to prove he is an exceptional ballplayer, reaching the majors sooner than expected when the Rockies promoted him, mostly likely for good, on July 31st last year. He isn't slow, but not a base-stealer, either. He's expected to be a .330, 25-homer hitter. His best position is first base, but the Rockies are considering moving him to left field. He played there sparingly last season and, though he hustles and displays a fair arm, he obviously needs work there.

1998: Helton will play regularly for the Rockies next season, but where depended upon whether the club re-signed Andres Galarraga. Believing they would, the Rockies sent Helton to the fall instructional league for further practice in left field.

1997: There were a pair of firsts for Helton last season: Power and left field. Until 1997, the only knock on Helton's ability to hit was hitting with power. But after hitting nine homers at two levels combined the previous season, Helton belted 21 last year, including five in just 93 at-bats for the Rockies. He began playing left field a couple times per week for Triple-A Colorado Springs, then got 11 of his 17 big-league starts in left for the Rockies.

1996: In his first full professional season, Helton jumped all the way to Triple-A. He impressed the Rockies' brass in spring training, prompting his two-step promotion from Class A Asheville, where he batted just .254 with one homer and 15 RBI in 1995, to Double-A New Haven. After consistently hitting for average against Eastern League pitching, Helton was promoted in the final month to Colorado Springs, where he continued to rake pitchers.

	AB	R	HR	RBI	SB	BA
1997 Colorado NL	93	13	5	11	0	.280

HEMPHILL, BRET - C - BB - b: 12/17/71

Hemphill is an excellent receiver with an above-average throwing arm, and he is accomplished enough in those areas that any offense he provides is considered a bonus. Shoulder surgery has set Hemphill back, but if his arm can rebound, he could wind up in the major leagues before too long. The Angels like his size, (6'3", 200 pounds), makeup and toughness.

HENDERSON, RICKEY - OF - BR - b: 12/25/58

Scouting: As long as he can get on base (40 percent of the time the past two seasons) and find a way to score runs, there will be a place for baseball's all-time stolen base leader. And Henderson is well aware of his place in baseball history, which is what keeps him running at age 39. He keeps himself in excellent condition. Henderson has lost a couple of steps in outright speed, but remains savvy; his defensive skills are not the best.

1998: Henderson can still provide an offensive spark. San Diego's offense wasn't the same after Henderson was traded to Anaheim in mid-July of '97. If he matches his '97 totals, he'll climb to fifth on the all-time runs scored list and third on walks while extending his stolen base lead. His dream is to finish with 2,000 runs, 2,000 walks, and 3,000 hits.

1997: Despite a poor finish with the Angels (.183 over the last seven weeks), Henderson still had a .343 on-base percentage. He drew 97 walks and stole 45 more bases to push his **record** total to 1,231.

1996: Henderson hit only .241 in his first National League season, but drew 125 walks to finish with a .410 on-base percentage and scored 110 runs. He was the trigger that ignited the Padre offense.

	AB	R	HR	RBI	SB	BA
1995 Oakland	407	67	9	54	32	.300
1996 San Diego	465	110	9	29	37	.241
1997 SD - Ana.	403	84	8	34	45	.248

HENLEY, BOB - C - BR - b: 1/30/73

Henley had a fine season for the Expos' Double-A Harrisburg farm club last year. Considering the Expos let Darrin Fletcher leave as a free agent at the end of last season and have only journeymen Raul Chavez and Joe Siddall to back up Chris Widger behind the plate, Henley is a good spring training away from going north with the big-league club. He has some power and would be a productive backup catcher.

HENRY, SANTIAGO - SS/2B - BR - b: 7/27/72

In 1997, Henry bounced between Triple-A Syracuse and Double-A Knoxville, playing both second base and shortstop. Although he has played regularly, his potential as an impact player is minimal considering that he has no power and does not take a walk (just two free passes against 116 Triple-A at-bats last year). Considering that he is already twenty-five, he has little time to develop better hitting skills.

HERMANSEN, CHAD - SS - BR - b: 9/10/77

Scouting: Hermansen, the Pirates' first-round draft pick in 1995, is one of the top hitting prospects in baseball. He had already hit 53 professional home runs, including 20 at the Double-A level, before turning 20 last September. Defense is Hermansen's problem as the Pirates have already determined he will not be able to play shortstop or center field in the major leagues.

1998: The Pirates feel Hermansen needs a season in Triple-A, more to allow him to find a position than work on his hitting. Hermansen will begin the season at second base, his third position in four pro seasons, and will likely get a September promotion to Pittsburgh.

1997: Hermansen shined at Double-A Carolina despite being the youngest player in the tough Southern League. Hermansen was in transition the entire season, though. He was moved from shortstop to center field in mid-May then to second base in early-August. He went to the Arizona Fall League to continue working on his second-base skills.

1996: Hermansen split the season between the Pirates' two full-season Class A farm clubs at Augusta and Lynchburg, hitting 24 homers despite not turning 19 until a week after the season ended.

HERNANDEZ, CARLOS - C - BR - b: 5/24/67

Scouting: Hernandez is an excellent defensive catcher with a strong arm who hit much better than expected last season. Mike Piazza's former backup was the surprise of the Padres spring camp in '97 and played well enough to tempt the Padres to expose John Flaherty to the expansion draft, and then trade him to the expansion Devil Rays.

1998: Free-agent Hernandez was being pursued by the Padres. He's a good candidate for increased playing time with the expansion draft opening up new major league catching jobs. His great defensive skills will also let him stay in the lineup once he wins a regular job. Look for Hernandez' major league role to grow a lot over the next twelve months.

1997: Hernandez hit for a career-best batting average in 50 games. He saw his most major league action since 1992 and was used as a part-time starter late in the season. Hernandez drew only three walks in 137 plate appearances.

1996: After four seasons as Piazza's primary backup in Los Angeles, Hernandez shuttled between the Dodgers and Triple-A Albuquerque. He played only 13 games with the Dodgers and 66 in the Pacific Coast League where he hit .240.

	AB	R	HR	RBI	SB	BA
1997 San Diego	134	15	3	14	0	.313

HERNANDEZ, CARLOS - 2B - BR - b: 12/12/75

One of several Venezuelan youngsters signed by the Astros before age 17, Hernandez's biggest asset is speed; he has stolen 124 bases in his first three seasons in the United States. He's a strong defensive player who handles the bat well; he makes good contact but doesn't have much power. Hernandez jumped from lower Class A to a successful season at Double-A Jackson, hitting .292 with four homers, 33 RBI and 17 stolen bases. He is likely to start 1998 at Triple-A with a chance to compete for a major league job by late in the seasons or at least by 1999.

HERNANDEZ, JOSE M. - SS/2B - BR - b: 7/14/69

Scouting: Hernandez is a slick fielder who has never shown an ability to hit at any level. He has some power, but has hit at a respectable level only one time in his career, and never at the major league level. His primary position is shortstop, but he can play third base and second, which increases his value as a utility infielder.

1998: Hernandez will be one of the contenders for the second base position, but it's not likely that he'll emerge as the starter. And even if he does, it's even more unlikely that he'll hit enough to be able to keep the regular job. Being able to play multiple positions will help him keep a roster spot, but he's never going to amount to much more than a utility infielder.

1997: Hernandez recorded the highest batting average of his major league career, but he was used in a late-inning and pinch-

hitting role and didn't get many starts at all. He saw even less playing time after the Cubs traded for Manny Alexander.
1996: Hernandez had an opportunity to be the everyday shortstop because of Shawon Dunston's departure, but was miserable at the plate and couldn't hang on to the position. He also saw significant time at third base, but he was only holding that spot a year in anticipation of Kevin Orie's arrival.

	AB	R	HR	RBI	SB	BA
1995 Chicago NL	245	37	13	40	1	.245
1996 Chicago NL	331	52	10	41	4	.242
1997 Chicago NL	183	33	7	26	2	.273

HERNANDEZ, RAMON - C - BR - b: 5/20/76
Hernandez could prove to be the best catching prospect in the organization, and that is no small feat — there are at least two more solid prospects behind major leaguer George Williams. Hernandez clobbered California League pitching to the tune of a .361 batting average, with 15 homers and 85 RBI, then struggled after moving to Double-A last year. At low Class A in 1996, at the age of 19, he hit .255 with 12 homers and 68 RBI.

HERRERA, JOSE - OF - BL - b: 8/30/72
Slowly dropping off the prospect list, Herrera spent 1997 in Triple-A in an attempt to facilitate his concentration. His numbers appear consistent, but in the Pacific Coast League they are average at best; he hit .296 with four homers, 41 RBI and seven stolen bases. His power numbers actually decreased — Herrera hit two more homers in 150 fewer at-bats bats while in the majors in 1996. At age 25 he is neither a spring chicken nor an exciting new face to be anticipated.

	AB	R	HR	RBI	SB	BA
1995 Oakland	70	9	0	2	1	.243
1996 Oakland	320	44	6	30	8	.269

HERRICK, JASON - OF - BL - b: 7/29/73
Herrick has been around for a few years now and has shown an ability to hit. He has good makeup and work ethic, but it hasn't been determined yet how hot a prospect he is. A solid right fielder on defense, Herrick has shown some power, too. Cutting down a bit on the strikeouts would help him advance.

HIATT, PHIL - 3B/OF - BR - b: 5/1/69
A good power hitter whose third base defense was so shaky that he moved to the outfield, Hiatt had a big year at Triple-A Toledo on the Tigers' farm in 1996, smashing 42 homers. Last year, he played in Japan and struggled (.198 average) while getting adjusted to the pitching style which features breaking stuff. Hiatt never did like a slow curve.

HIDALGO, RICHARD - OF - BR - b: 7/2/75
Scouting: Hidalgo is the brightest prospect in the Houston organization and should provide the first major dividend on the Astros' investment in their Venezuelan Academy. While his minor league numbers have not been eye-popping, he has been among the youngest players at his level every year. He was signed by the Astros on his sixteenth birthday in 1991 and played his first season in this country in 1992. Hidalgo has all the tools and an excellent makeup. He should hit for both average and power and he has outstanding defensive instincts with an exceptional arm; he had 23 outfield assists in 1994. In his last two years in the high minors, he struck out in less than 11% of his at-bats.

1998: Hidalgo should be in the major leagues to stay and should start in either center or right field. He is not likely to achieve star status in the next couple of years, but he should be ready for a breakthrough year at age 25 when the Astros move into their new stadium in 2000.
1997: Hidalgo batted .279 with 11 home runs, 78 RBI and six stolen bases at Triple-A New Orleans. He was promoted to Houston on August 31st to be eligible for post-season play. He played in 19 games in September and was the starting center fielder in the playoffs.
1996: Hidalgo spent his second year at Double-A Jackson and showed expected improvement. He was a Double-A All-Star, batting .298 with 14 home runs and 78 RBI.

	AB	R	HR	RBI	SB	BA
1997 Houston	62	8	2	6	1	.306

HIGGINSON, BOB - OF - BL - b: 8/18/70
Scouting: When he realized that he needed to be a line-drive hitter, Higginson developed into a .300 hitter who still has good power. He can hit almost anywhere in the lineup, but has settled in as a number two or three hitter for the Tigers. In the outfield, he has decent range and a accurate arm that has allowed him to lead the league in assists in two of his three seasons.
1998: The Tigers, who have too many all-or-nothing hitters, will want Higginson to continue being the high-average, line-drive hitter he's been for the last two years. Rested sometimes against lefthanders early last season, he'll likely play nearly every day this year.
1997: Higginson finished one hit shy of becoming the first Tiger since Alan Trammell (1987-88) to bat .300 in back-to-back years. Despite sticking with the line-drive stroke that made him a good hitter, Higginson still hit for the most power he's shown in his career.
1996: In his second big-league season, Higginson proved he belongs, raising his average from .224 to .320, the biggest increase in American League history. He finished strong, hitting .352 in September, and .345 over the final 56 games.

	AB	R	HR	RBI	SB	BA
1995 Detroit	410	61	14	43	6	.224
1996 Detroit	440	75	26	81	6	.320
1997 Detroit	546	94	27	101	12	.299

HIGHTOWER, VEE - OF - BB - b: 4/26/72
The Cubs were high on Hightower a few years ago, but his performance in the last couple of seasons has taken him out of prospect status. He's had two chances now at the Double-A level, but hasn't been able to take advantage of them. His .233 average at Orlando was a significant improvement over his 1996 performance at Double-A, but it wasn't nearly enough to make the Cubs consider him for a promotion. He didn't demonstrate any ability to steal bases, either, getting caught in 11 of 27 attempts. At this point Hightower is not in the Cubs' plans for the future.

HILL, GLENALLEN - OF - BR - b: 3/22/65
Scouting: Hill is a deadly hitter against lefties, and crushes inside fastballs, but his skill against righthanded pitchers has deteriorated such that Dusty Baker has begun to use him as a platoon player. His defense seems to have disintegrated all at once. Hill, who once possessed a fine glove and great arm seems to be out of sorts when playing the field.
1998: As with several of the other Giants' outfielders, the happy

problem is several prospects, several established stars and only two open spots. San Francisco cannot keep everyone, and Hill will probably be playing elsewhere in 1998. He has become a solid, if unspectacular outfielder who, if playing full time, will hit 20 homers, drive in 80 runs and hit in the .270s.
1997: Hill has to be somewhat disappointed with his 1997 season, despite the fact that he was on a winner. Hill began the year as the starting right fielder, but as he struggled both at the plate and in the field, his playing time eroded. Though he actually managed more at-bats than he did the previous year, Hill was not injured. His production was off his previous two seasons by a large margin.
1996: Injured for a good part of the season, Hill continued to improve nearly every aspect of his game. He was on a pace to eclipse personal highs in walks, homers, RBI, runs, and slugging had he not suffered a broken wrist.

	AB	R	HR	RBI	SB	BA
1995 San Francisco	497	71	24	86	25	.264
1996 San Francisco	379	56	19	67	6	.280
1997 San Francisco	398	47	11	64	7	.261

HILLS, RICH - 3B - BR - b: 7/28/73
Hills played both corner infield positions in the Padres' organization in 1997; there are prospects ahead of him at both positions. After playing at Class A and Double-A this past season, Hills should get a chance to prove himself full-time at Double-A in 1998.

HINCH, A.J. - C - BR - b: 5/15/74
A third-round selection in the 1996 free-agent draft, and former Olympian, Hinch had eye-popping numbers during his first professional season. At Class A Modesto Hinch distributed a .309 average, 20 homers, and 73 RBI over 333 at-bats. He kept it up at Triple-A Edmonton, too. After his promotion, Hinch batted .376 with four homers and 24 RBI over 125 additional plate appearances. He is primed for a big-league job.

HINDS, ROB - 2B - BR - b: 4/26/71
The Yankees' 12th-round selection in the June, 1992 draft, Hinds is a utility infielder with little hitting talent. Last year at Double-A Norwich he hit .236 with no home runs and 12 RBI in 123 at-bats. Since 1995, his hitting production hasn't improved at the Double-A level.

HOCKING, DENNY - SS/OF - BB - b: 4/2/70
Scouting: Hocking offers a good glove, a strong arm and the versatility to be a solid utilityman for years to come. He can play any of the infield positions as well as center field. He nearly beat out Pat Meares for the shortstop job in the Twins' camp in 1994. Hocking's biggest drawback is that he's shown a tendency to get hurt, although he remained healthy in 1997.
1998: Hocking will build off of a solid 1997 campaign, gaining more playing time as he has earned the club's trust. With a more aggressive approach at the plate, he will improve his batting average and offensive production.
1997: It was a solid year in which Hocking proved he could stay healthy in the majors. After battling ankle, knee, hamstring and mouth injuries in the past, Hocking reported to camp stronger and lasted for an entire season.
1996: It was a disappointing 49-game stint for a man who nearly won the major-league shortstop job in 1994 — and for a man who hit .277 while playing every day at Triple-A Salt Lake.

	AB	R	HR	RBI	SB	BA
1995 Minnesota	25	4	0	3	1	.200
1996 Minnesota	127	16	1	10	3	.197
1997 Minnesota	253	28	2	25	3	.257

HOILES, CHRIS - C - BR - b: 3/20/65
Scouting: Hoiles is overpaid for his skills and production. He has some power, but he's a below-average hitter overall, and with the plodding speed that's typical of catchers. His throwing arm is weak, and even slow runners take advantage of him. His handling of pitchers is adequate except that Scott Erickson prefers Lenny Webster.
1998: Hoiles will be the starting catcher, and the expectation is about the same offensively. His throwing arm will probably be weaker, resulting in increasingly more opposition stolen bases. Webster is a good backup but not a long-term starter, and there are no strong catching prospects in the Oriole farm system, so Hoiles has the job by default.
1997: Hoiles usually begins a season slowly and doesn't begin to get rolling until the All-Star game. Last year was an exception as he started off strong. But an injury put him on the disabled list, and he played with minor aches and pains at other times, cutting into his production. For the stretch run, it's significant that the Orioles called up not one, but two, weak-hitting minor-league catchers with cannon arms.
1996: Hoiles had his typical slow start, but followed up with a solid second half to salvage the year. This is the year when his throwing arm really went south, even letting catchers run on him. The Orioles put him on waivers during the season, but there were no takers because they all believed that he wasn't worth his big salary.

	AB	R	HR	RBI	SB	BA
1995 Baltimore	352	53	19	58	1	.250
1996 Baltimore	407	64	25	73	0	.258
1997 Baltimore	320	45	12	49	1	.259

HOLBERT, AARON - SS - BR - b: 1/9/73
The Cardinals hoped he would inherit the shortstop job from Ozzie Smith when they drafted Holbert in the first round in 1990. Injuries, a below-average arm, generally ineffective defense at shortstop, and an inability to make a conversion to second base have turned Holbert from prospect to suspect. He's only 25 years old, so maybe a change of organizations would help.

HOLBERT, RAY - SS - BR - b: 9/25/70
Holbert spent the entire 1995 season with San Diego except for a short rehab stint at Triple-A. After a trade to Houston, he failed to make the major league team in 1996. At Triple-A Tucson, he was injured and missed most of the season, batting .247 in 97 at-bats. He has speed but his career batting average is under .250. In 1997 he didn't make any progress toward getting back to the majors as he hit just .242 at Triple-A Toledo.

HOLDREN, NATE - 1B - BR - b: 12/8/71
This former Michigan football player has good power in his bat, but faces a host of talent ahead of him in Helton and Kennedy. Cutting down on his strikeouts could help Holdren to the Triple-A level, he struck out 28 times in 25 games in 1997 at Double-A New Haven.

HOLIFIELD, RICK - OF - BL - b: 3/25/70
1997 was Holifield's tenth minor-league season and it wasn't a

good one. He hit just .216 and wasn't an everyday player. This former speed/power combo prospect has played in three different organizations in the past three seasons and his time has passed.

HOLLANDSWORTH, TODD - OF - BL - b: 4/20/73
Scouting: Hollandsworth has above-average speed but below-average power and strikezone judgment. He doesn't have a good slugging percentage for a left fielder and doesn't get on base enough to lead off like he did in 1996. He'll have to continue to develop or run the risk of getting overtaken by some of the Dodgers good outfield prospects.
1998: Hollandsworth is expected to be in the mix for a Dodger outfield job but is not a lock.
1997: Hollandsworth slumped after a strong 1996 season. His strength at the plate has been his batting average because of his lack of power and even that took a tumble during the 1997 season.
1996: Hollandsworth eventually became the every day left fielder for the Dodgers and went on to win the Rookie of the Year Award, the fifth consecutive Dodger to do so.

	AB	R	HR	RBI	SB	BA
1995 Los Angeles	103	16	5	13	2	.233
1996 Los Angeles	478	64	12	59	21	.291
1997 Los Angeles	296	39	4	31	5	.247

HOLLINS, DAMON - OF - BR - b: 6/12/74
Hollins is a raw, athletic outfielder, who does a lot wrong, but can do a lot right, too. The ball jumps off his bat (20 homers in Triple-A in '97), but he opens up and tries to pull everything, making him vulnerable to anything off-speed. Even though he has some speed, he hasn't turned it into stolen bases, partly because he doesn't play hard. He's still young, but don't be surprised if he stagnates at the Triple-A level.

HOLLINS, DAVE - 3B/1B - BB - b: 5/25/66
Scouting: It would be extremely difficult, if not impossible, to find a more intense player in all of baseball. Hollins typically puts on his game face at 9:30 a.m. — for a night game. Hollins is a solid third baseman, although his one weakness is he often double-clutches his throws, which leads to throwing errors. He runs well, is extremely aggressive on the bases, and hits for average and power. Hollins is diabetic and playing so hard often leaves him exhausted after games and in need of regular rest over the course of a full season.
1998: Hollins only has to recover from off-season arthroscopic surgery on his right knee to have an important major league job. He will again be a factor on offense and defense, and a leader in the clubhouse.
1997: Hollins' intensity and inspirational value were just what the lethargic Angels needed after a dismal 1996 season. His bat was a big help to a club that lacked a third-place hitter and his glove helped solidify the defense.
1996: Hollins split the year between Minnesota and Seattle. He couldn't help the struggling Twins win, but he did help the Mariners make a run at Texas in the American League West. He hit .351 after the late-August trade to Seattle and drove in 25 runs in 28 games.

	AB	R	HR	RBI	SB	BA
1995 Philadelphia	205	46	7	25	1	.229
1995 Boston	13	2	0	1	0	.154
1996 Seattle	516	88	16	78	6	.262
1997 Anaheim	572	101	16	85	16	.288

HORN, JEFF - C - BR - b: 8/23/70
Horn can hit for average but doesn't possess a lot of power. For his minor-league career he's thrown out just over 30 percent of would-be basestealers. He showed off his bat in limited duty at Triple-A Salt Lake, hitting .333 in 78 at-bats and could eventually make the majors as a backup.

HORN, SAM - 1B - BL - b: 4/1/65
A big, slugging first baseman who nearly became a major league success, Horn surfaced in Taiwan last year and led the league with 31 home runs, tying a league record.

HOSEY, DWAYNE - OF - BB - b: 3/11/67
Briefly tried as the Red Sox center fielder in 1996 (he hit .218 in 78 at-bats) Hosey moved on to Japan. For the Yakult Swallows, he hit .303 with 34 homers.

	AB	R	HR	RBI	SB	BA
1995 Boston	68	20	3	7	6	.338
1996 Boston	78	13	1	3	6	.218

HOUSTON, TYLER - 1B - BL - b: 1/17/71
Scouting: Houston was a catcher coming up through the Atlanta farm system, but has been flexible enough to get some starts in the infield with Chicago, at third base, second, and first. He hasn't shown any real power in the minors or in his two seasons in the major leagues, and he doesn't hit for a high average.
1998: Houston again will be a jack-of-all-trades with the Cubs. He'll get some starts as the backup catcher behind Scott Servais, and he'll see additional playing time at third base. He'll also be one of the first lefthanded pinch-hitters off the bench for manager Jim Riggleman. He'll be 27 on opening day, so time is running out for Houston; the only way he'll be an everyday player is if Servais gets hurt.
1997: Houston got into only 72 games last season. Servais was the team's primary catcher, which left Houston to get only the occasional start behind the plate.
1996: Houston started the season on Atlanta's opening day roster. He didn't see much action with the Braves and was traded to Chicago on June 26th. He hit surprisingly well with the Cubs, and the team tried to get him as many at-bats as it could, starting him at four different positions.

	AB	R	HR	RBI	SB	BA
1996 Atl.-Chi. NL	142	21	3	27	3	.317
1997 Chicago NL	196	15	2	28	1	.260

HOWARD, DAVID - SS/2B - BB - b: 2/26/67
Scouting: Howard is as spectacular with the glove as he is inadequate at the plate. He can cover a lot of ground at any infield spot, displaying a strong, accurate arm, and he has also acquitted himself well in various outfield appearances, too. However, Howard has no discernible hitting skill; he's overmatched by even average pitching, has trouble making regular contact, has no power and little speed. His versatility makes him a fine bench player, but when forced into the starting lineup, Howard leaves a lot to be desired.
1998: Howard will play a reserve role on a major league bench, filling in occasionally for an infielder, but mostly serving as a defensive replacement. It's a specialized role, and Howard is among the best at it. If used more regularly he will hurt his team.
1997: A shoulder strain limited Howard's availability over the second half of the season and he played little under new manager Tony Muser, losing his super-sub role to Shane Halter.

Howard's hitting was as weak as always, just as his glove shined liked always. His importance to the Royals was severely diminished over previous seasons due to the solid year turned in by shortstop Jay Bell.

1996: Howard was nearly a full-season regular, winning the shortstop job after Jose Offerman was shifted to first base. His batting average was among the lowest for major league regulars, but he set new highs in nearly all offensive categories. His .982 fielding average and eleven errors committed were both tops among American League shortstops.

	AB	R	HR	RBI	SB	BA
1995 Kansas City	255	23	0	19	6	.243
1996 Kansas City	420	51	4	48	5	.219
1997 Kansas City	162	24	1	13	2	.241

HOWARD, MATT - SS/2B - BR - b: 9/22/67

For his third straight season in the minors, Howard hit over .300. He had a good season for Triple-A Columbus, playing full-time. He has base-stealing potential — once stealing 50 bases — and has proven he is capable of hitting for a high average. His role in the majors would be as a pinch-runner/reserve outfielder.

	AB	R	HR	RBI	SB	BA
1996 New York AL	54	9	1	9	1	.204

HOWARD, THOMAS - OF - BB - b: 12/11/64

Scouting: Howard is a journeyman who doesn't hit for enough power or average to be a regular outfielder in the major leagues. He has had success as a pinch hitter and is a capable defensive outfielder. He has played in the major leagues in each of the last eight years for four different teams. Formerly a switch hitter, he now bats only lefthanded and struggles against lefthanded pitchers.

1998: Howard should find work as a reserve outfielder for a couple more years.

1997: Howard spent all season on the Houston active roster. He made an occasional start but was primarily a pinch hitter. His age and his numbers suggest he is on the downside of his career.

1996: Injuries to Reggie Sanders provided an opportunity for Howard to play 121 games for Cincinnati. His production was consistent with his career numbers.

	AB	R	HR	RBI	SB	BA
1995 Cincinnati	281	42	3	26	17	.302
1996 Cincinnati	360	50	6	42	6	.272
1997 Houston	255	24	3	22	1	.247

HOWELL, JACK - 3B - BL - b: 8/18/61

Scouting: Howell is one of the few veteran player who spent time in Japan and came back a better ballplayer than when he left. His career appeared to be over after the 1991 season, but he embarked on a four-year stint in Japan determined to learn to hit breaking pitches. Howell became a star in Japan hitting a steady diet of off-speed stuff, then returned to the Angels in 1996 as the mainstay of their bench. Howell hits for average and power, pinch-hits well, and can play solid defense at first and third.

1998: Howell can be a one-man reserve squad; he has excelled in a variety of roles over the last two seasons back in the States.

1997: Howell was the perfect guy to spell Dave Hollins at third base on days when the latter needed a breather because of a debilitating illness. Howell also came up with a number of clutch hits as a pinch-hitter and reserve, and did well at third base after Hollins moved to first base the last three weeks of the season.

1996: After four seasons in Japan, Howell returned to the major leagues in a reserve infield/pinch-hitter role and hit for his highest batting average in a decade. He spent a little time on the disabled list, but was generally a useful bench player in a surprising rebound year.

	AB	R	HR	RBI	SB	BA
1996 California	126	20	8	21	0	.270
1997 Anaheim	174	25	14	34	1	.259

HOWITT, DANN - OF/1B - BL - b: 2/13/64

Howitt appeared in the bigs from 1989-94 and was once Mark McGuire's main minor-league competition in the A's organization. He's now a minor-league nomad who played for the Rockies at Triple-A Colorado Springs in 1997. He showed some power and had a pretty good average in a DH role, but, at age 34, he's just about done.

HUBBARD, MIKE - C - BR - b: 2/16/71

Hubbard isn't a good hitter and he isn't an outstanding defensive player, either, so his time as a big-leaguer is running out. He has stuck with the Cubs as an inexpensive third catcher who doesn't complain about playing time. Hubbard hit poorly in 29 games for the Cubs last year. He can play a little third base, and has even played a couple of games in the outfield, but that doesn't increase his value enough for him to be worth anything to a major league team.

	AB	R	HR	RBI	SB	BA
1997 Chicago NL	64	4	1	2	0	.203

HUBBARD, TRENIDAD - OF - BR - b: 5/11/66

Hubbard has accumulated 359 stolen bases in his 12-year minor-league career, including parts of eight years in Triple-A. He hit .300 for the sixth straight Triple-A season in 1997, but his first outside of the hitting-happy Pacific Coast League. Hubbard had his best chance to earn a regular major league job in 1996, first with Colorado, where he was beaten out for a fourth outfield spot by Quinton McCracken, then in San Francisco, where he lost out to Marvin Benard. He has no future with the Indians (his 1997 organization) and was just marking time at Buffalo. He'll continue his Triple-A travels in 1998.

	AB	R	HR	RBI	SB	BA
1995 Colorado	58	13	3	9	2	.310
1996 San Francisco	89	15	2	14	2	.213
1997 Cleveland	12	3	0	0	2	.250

HUCKABY, KEN - C - BR - b: 1/27/71

A second-round pick in the June, 1991, draft, Huckaby has yet to fulfill his potential and was cut loose at the end of the 1997 season as a six-year minor-league free agent. Huckaby's been decent behind the plate and has hit well for average at times, but lacks power and has yet to justify the Dodgers' making him the 32nd player chosen overall six years ago.

HUDLER, REX - OF/IF - BR - b: 9/2/60

Scouting: Hudler has always played the game all-out. His ability to hit lefthanded pitching and his defensive versatility have made him a valuable reserve. Hudler has used his speed and aggressiveness to his advantage, but a knee injury may reduce the pace at which he plays the game. He's not a strong defensive outfielder and his bat has slowed considerably. Hudler's enthusiasm for the game is unsurpassed by any other player.

1998: Hudler is signed for $1.1 million which might make him unattractive to other franchises, including expansion teams. He'll be given every opportunity to win a utility spot in spring training. Hudler's trouble playing the infield and loss of speed due to a serious knee injury could result in a serious downturn for his career. The Wonder Dog is running out of tricks.

1997: A knee injury turned Hudler's season to disaster; he could no longer overcome increasing deficiencies in skill with all-out hustle. He struggled against all kinds of pitching and lost half his speed — and half the season — to injuries.

1996: Hudler earned his expensive free-agent contract with the Phillies by posting his career year with the Angels. He filled in at four positions, hit lefties at a .345 clip, and doubled his previous career high in homers.

	AB	R	HR	RBI	SB	BA
1995 California	223	30	6	27	13	.265
1996 California	302	60	16	40	14	.311
1997 Philadelphia	122	17	5	10	1	.221

HUFF, LARRY - 3B - BR - b: 1/24/72

Huff is a scrappy third baseman with limited tools who has overachieved during his tenure in the Phillies' organization, most recently in 1997 at Double-A Reading. He makes consistent contact, sprays the ball to all fields and generates high stolen base totals due more to his instincts than to his speed. He has limited range but good hands and mechanics at third base. He didn't reach Double-A until age 25, and Scott Rolen is in place for the long haul in Philadelphia — Huff's major league chances are nil.

HUGHES, BOBBY - C - BR - b: 3/10/71

Hughes was drafted in the second round out of USC in 1992 but has been a disappointment for the Brewers who thought he would be their everyday catcher by now. In 1997 he got another crack at Triple-A ball and fared much better than the year before, hitting .310 with seven homers and 51 RBI at Tucson. Catching is an organizational need and Hughes looks like he could be the man for the job with a strong arm and some power in his stroke. He may have a chance to gain a spot with the big-league club come spring training.

HUGHES, TROY - OF - BR - b: BR - 1/3/71

Hughes struggled at Double-A Huntsville in 1997, hitting .209 with five homers in 258 at-bats, and position player depth within the organization make it unlikely that his name will surface on a major league playing field.

HUNDLEY, TODD - C - BB - b: 5/27/69

Scouting: To throw Hundley a low fastball when he's batting lefthanded is to commit pitching suicide, but it does afford the pitcher opportunity to rest — while the Mets catcher is taking a victory lap. A guess hitter and a big swinger, Hundley occasionally reduces his swing and still drives the ball well. As a righthanded hitter, he is more apt to hit ground balls through the middle or chase high pitches than to inflict home run damage.

1998: Because of reconstructive surgery in his right elbow performed September 25th last year, Hundley was expected to miss at least one third and perhaps significantly more of the Mets schedule. The club has said it would consider moving him to first base if the need arose. But neither Hundley nor general manager Steve Phillips consider first base a viable alternative. When Hundley does return, he will be playing pain-free for the first time in his major league career.

1997: Hundley was a force and the critical factor in the Mets batting order until his elbow betrayed him in early July. Thereafter, he was a threat, but too often anchored to the bench. Given the condition of his elbow, a severely bruised toe, a cracked rib and the everyday problems of a catcher, his 30 home runs and 86 RBI in 417 at-bats were comparable to his production in 540 at-bats in 1996.

1996: What Hundley did was the definition of a breakout season. His respective career highs in home runs increased from 16 to 41 — a record for catchers, and his RBI jumped from 53 to 112. His strikeouts increased appreciably too, but so did his walks. It was in 1996 that he became feared and recognized as a legitimate run producer.

	AB	R	HR	RBI	SB	BA
1995 New York NL	275	39	15	51	1	.280
1996 New York NL	540	85	41	112	1	.259
1997 New York NL	417	78	30	86	2	.273

HUNTER, BRIAN L. - OF - BR - b: 3/5/71

Scouting: Hunter quickly developed into the exciting player the Tigers hoped they were getting in the ten-player December 1996 trade with Houston. His long strides and great speed remind you of Devon White from 1992-93 when Toronto was winning the World Series. He covers plenty of ground in center field, has learned to get on base by adding infield hits and walks, and is a true force on the basepaths.

1998: Just like last year, the Tigers plan on having Hunter lead off and play center field in every game. The only difference is that right from the start of the year, they'll know what to expect. Hunter should get even better, because he knows the pitchers' moves, and also is more confident taking pitches and drawing walks at the plate.

1997: Hunter stole bases the way only Ty Cobb and Ron LeFlore ever had for the Tigers. He became the first Tiger since Cobb to lead the majors in steals. He also learned how to be a leadoff hitter, increasing his walk total from 17 in 1996 to 66 in '97.

1996: The Astros got frustrated with Hunter, because he didn't get on base often enough, and too often took bad routes in the outfield. He also missed a month with a strained ribcage.

	AB	R	HR	RBI	SB	BA
1995 Houston	321	52	2	28	24	.302
1996 Houston	526	74	5	35	35	.276
1997 Detroit	658	112	4	45	74	.269

HUNTER, BRIAN R. - 1B - BR - b: 3/4/68

A decent power-hitting prospect when he came up 1992, Hunter is hanging on hoping for one more opportunity in the big leagues. He has always been a low-average power hitter and a defensive liability; at best he could secure a role as the righthanded half of a first base platoon.

	AB	R	HR	RBI	SB	BA
1995 Cincinnati	79	9	1	9	2	.215
1996 Seattle	198	21	7	28	0	.268

HUNTER, SCOTT - OF - BR - b: 12/17/75

Proceeds of the trade of Brett Butler to the Dodgers, Hunter is a genuine prospect. The young outfielder has good speed, and he finally showed some power with ten home runs last year for Double-A Binghamton on the Mets' farm. He is still at least a year or two away from a major league chance.

HUNTER, TORII - OF - BR - b: 7/18/75
A first-round pick by the Twins in 1993, Hunter's lack of improvement offensively is threatening to derail what once was a promising career. Hunter is a swift runner with a good glove who excels in center field. But too many holes in his swing have prevented him from climbing above the Double-A level in five minor-league seasons. Batting .231 with only eight homers and 56 RBI at Double-A New Britain last summer certainly got the attention of those in the Twins' front office — but in the wrong way. Hunter also stole only eight bases.

HURST, JIMMY - OF - BR - b: 3/1/71
Scouting: At 6'6" and 225 pounds, Hurst looks like a baseball player — or a linebacker. He ran out of chances with the White Sox, but the Tigers are interested in seeing whether he can develop his potentially good talents. Hurst has power and can run, and he plays the outfield well. The only question is whether he can hit consistently at the big-league level.
1998: Hurst is out of options, so this will be another year of decision for him. A good spring would put him on the club as an extra outfielder.
1997: It was a strange year, in which Hurst was first claimed by the Tigers on waivers, then taken off their 40-man roster, then finally brought back to spend his first September in the big leagues. His overall numbers at Triple-A Toledo were decent (.270, 18 home runs, 58 RBI), but he was especially good after being taken off the 40-man roster at midseason.
1996: Hurst played a second straight year at Double-A Birmingham, putting together a good season and being named to the Southern League All-Star team.

HUSKEY, BUTCH - 3B - BR - b: 11/10/71
Scouting: The question remains: Why does any pitcher throw him a fastball? Huskey can turn around anyone's heater and hit it into areas seldom reached by others. And this year, he showed signs of an increased ability — and willingness — to go with the pitches. He has more than enough power to hit homers to the opposite field. Most of his power is gap to gap, but when he pulls pitches he can reach the upper deck. Despite his size and the perception that he could be clumsy, Huskey can become comfortable at a position and play it pretty well. He accelerates slowly, but has pretty good speed once he gets going.
1998: Given his accomplishments last season, Huskey begins this season as a most intriguing figure. The likely extended absence of Todd Hundley will move Huskey higher in the batting order and afford him greater opportunity to produce runs. But with that opportunity will come greater responsibility. Hitting 30 home runs isn't beyond his reach — he hit 24 in merely 471 at-bats. And if he can maintain or even approach the .302 average he produced in his final 242 at-bats last season, significant run production will result.
1997: Since the early stages of his career, Huskey has been considered a second-story man; give him a year at a given level to find himself and then duck. That growth and development was particularly evident last year. When rosters expanded in early September, Huskey gave the impression he couldn't be pitched to without care. He shortened his stroke but still hit baseballs over the walls and into areas recognized sluggers had never reached. And because of expansion, too many of those September pitchers will be working regularly in the big leagues come April.
1996: It was an ample beginning. Hits and home runs came in bunches as Huskey and then-batting coach Tom McGraw worked to remove minor-league wrinkles from a young slugger's swing. He began the season as the cleanup hitter, and the responsibility dwarfed him. Huskey did most of his work at first base and started 40 games in right field.

	AB	R	HR	RBI	SB	BA
1995 New York NL	90	8	3	11	1	.189
1996 New York NL	414	43	15	60	1	.278
1997 New York NL	471	61	24	81	8	.287

HUSON, JEFF - SS/2B - BL - b: 8/15/64
Scouting: Huson has versatility. He played outfield and infield for the Brewers. He doesn't seem to have a major league bat anymore, but the Colorado air will help, and Huson will hustle and has a good attitude. He could make a great coach.
1998: Huson could help the Rockies as a utility man for a season or two, or provide Triple-A insurance for an organization, but his regular playing days are behind him.
1997: Huson was rescued from the Rockies' Triple-A team when the Brewers needed infield help. His versatility kept him with the club, but he struggled at the plate in a utility role.
1996: Huson hit .321 in 17 games for Baltimore and spent the rest of the season with four minor-league teams. He signed with Colorado in August and played at Triple-A.

	AB	R	HR	RBI	SB	BA
1997 Milwaukee	143	12	0	11	3	.203

HUTCHINS, NORMAN - OF - BL - b: 11/20/75
Regarded as one of the top long-range prospects in the organization, Hutchins is coming off a solid year at Class A Lake Elsinore. He hit for average and power, and has been compared favorably with former Angel Devon White. Still raw, Hutchins needs to polish his skills, but the Angels are excited about his prospects because of his talent and potential to be an exciting major league center fielder.

HYERS, TIM - 1B - BL - b: 10/3/71
Hyers has played in three organizations. He probably won't do more than pinch hit and spot duty in the major leagues. In 1997 he again played at Triple-A Toledo and had slightly better numbers than the year before, but he didn't make it to Tiger stadium like in 1996.

HYZDU, ADAM - OF - BR - b: 12/6/71
Don't be fooled; Hyzdu is a classic Triple-A slugger. He posts good minor-league numbers, but, as hard as he plays, he has no tools, is a shaky outfielder, and has few ways he can help a big-league team. Even though it appears that he can really hit (.276, 23 homers last year), he has a slow bat and feasts on weak Triple-A fastballs and a general inability of minor-league pitchers to locate their stuff inside.

IBANEZ, RAUL - OF - BL - b: 6/2/72
Scouting: A former catcher who has been moved to first base and the corner outfield positions during his rise through the organization, Ibanez has a quick bat that accounts for good power numbers.
1998: As deep as the Mariners are in hitting, Ibanez will have to wait his turn as either an everyday player at Tacoma or as a bat off the bench in Seattle.
1997: Confirming that his previous seasons were no fluke, Ibanez hit .304 with 15 homers and 84 RBI at Triple-A Tacoma

before being recalled by the Mariners.
1996: Ibanez played at three levels of the Seattle organization, including the majors, in his first year after being converted from catcher, where he was the Mariners' minor-league player of the year in 1995 after hitting .332 with 20 homers at Riverside.

IBARRA, JESSE - 1B - BB - b: 7/12/72
In 1997, Ibarra became the first player in the history of professional baseball to hit grand slams from both sides of the plate in the same game against Memphis on July 25th. A terrific RBI guy (a team-high 91 in 115 games last year), Ibarra has quick hands. At times, he tries to pull the ball too much from the left side. He is slow afoot and is a liability at first base; he's probably best suited to be a major league DH. Ibarra hit .283 in 441 at-bats and his 25 homers were second best for Double-A Jacksonville in 1997. He is a legitimate major league prospect.

INCAVIGLIA, PETE - OF - BR - b: 4/2/64
Scouting: Incaviglia is a slow, plodding slugger. His bat speed is also slow, much slower than in 1995 or '96, and he's now overmatched by average fastballs. He's barely adequate in left field, so he's primarily a DH. He's strictly a one-dimensional player, and even his single dimension is rapidly disappearing.
1998: Incaviglia may get a spring training tryout by some team desperate for power. He doesn't have much to offer, and it's unlikely that he will make it. He may retire for good.
1997: He couldn't produce much for the Orioles in a limited role off the bench and in occasional outfield play. He got rusty, couldn't get untracked, and was waived in July. He was signed by the Yankees to replace injured Cecil Fielder, but he didn't show much in his two weeks in pinstripes and was waived again.
1996: Taking all things into consideration, Incaviglia had a good year for the Orioles, but the decline in his playing skills became increasingly evident.

	AB	R	HR	RBI	SB	BA
1996 Philadelphia	269	33	16	42	2	.234
1996 Baltimore	33	4	2	8	0	.303
1997 Bal. - N.Y. AL	154	19	5	12	0	.247

INGRAM, GAREY - 3B - BR - b: 7/25/70
Ingram made his way back to the majors for 12 games after missing out on the big leagues in 1996. His job as emergency reserve for the Dodgers has been lost and he's now filling a roster spot at the Double-A level. He hit .299 at Double-A San Antonio last year, the first time he's hit over .270 in the minors since 1992.

ISOM, JOHNNY - OF - BR - b: 8/9/73
Isom is progressing steadily up the Orioles' ladder. He had a good season in Double-A last year, showing some power and driving in so many runs that he was called an "RBI machine." On the negative side, he struck out almost 25 percent of the time. Isom is a good prospect but the Orioles are loaded with experienced and talented outfielders. In 1998, he may get a "cup of coffee" callup in September.

JACKSON, DAMIAN - SS - BR - b: 8/16/73
Scouting: A longtime shortstop prospect in the Indians' chain, Jackson was dealt to the Reds in the midseason deal which netted the Indians John Smiley. Jackson had hit a brick wall in the Indians' organization, and was also held in lower regard than fellow prospect Enrique Wilson. His range and arm in the field are above average, and Jackson no longer fancies himself a potential power hitter, finally content to slap the ball on the ground and use his wheels. He has refined his basestealing technique, and raised his success rate in recent seasons.
1998: Should Bret Boone leave the Reds, Jackson and Pokey Reese will battle for the second base job in Cincinnati. Jackson's more understated defensive style may be better suited to that position, and he also has the upper hand with the bat. A job share, with Jackson earning 300 at-bats, could be the result.
1997: Jackson finally pieced the components of his game into a mature package, cutting his strikeouts while raising his average and walk frequency. The trade will be a long-term benefit to Jackson; he was going to be the odd man out in Cleveland.
1996: His star fell somewhat in the Indians' eyes, as he was slow to make adjustments at the plate. Jackson continued to try to drive the ball for distance, and posted a career-low .333 OBP as a result.

	AB	R	HR	RBI	SB	BA
1997 Cincinnati	36	8	1	2	2	.194

JACKSON, DARRIN - OF - BR - b: 8/22/63
Scouting: Jackson has been a true journeyman, but showed signs he might still be able to contribute. After his move to Milwaukee, he showed he can still make contact and has some pop to the gaps. He is a steady outfielder, who can play center or right field and he can go above the fence to take away homers.
1998: Milwaukee manager Phil Garner said he liked Jackson's approach to the game and some of the leadership the veteran could bring to the team. So, the Brewers were interested in re-signing him. He offers a veteran presence who is better at a supporting role than as an everyday player.
1997: Cut by San Francisco on the last day of spring training, Jackson was lost on the Twins' bench most of the year, but produced when he was acquired by the Brewers. He made contact, with occasional pop, and showed he still is an adequate fielder.
1996: Jackson played his second season with the Seibu Lions of the Japanese Pacific League and hit .266 with 19 homers and 64 RBI in 126 games. He signed with the San Francisco Giants as a free agent in December.

	AB	R	HR	RBI	SB	BA
1997 Milwaukee	211	26	5	36	4	.261

JACKSON, GAVIN - SS - BR - b: 7/19/73
A shortstop, he is a decent athlete, but it hasn't translated too well into results in the diamond. He swings a weak bat, having hit all of one homer in five minor-league seasons, and he was two-for-eight stealing bases in '97. He did show some improvement last year at Double-A Trenton, hitting .272. His strikeout-to-walk ratio of 36-to-48 is also a good sign, indicating he controls the bat and the zone well, and he should continue to improve.

JACKSON, RYAN - 1B/OF - BL - b: 11/15/71
Jackson came off an injury-shortened 1996 campaign to display above-average plate discipline and line-drive hitting at Double-A Portland. He's got a textbook lefthanded batting stroke with power and batting average potential but he may not have adequate bat speed for the major leagues. He hasn't spent a day above Double-A, marking him as too old for his level. Jackson should advance into an everyday role at Triple-A Charlotte this year.

JAHA, JOHN - 1B - BR - b: 5/27/66

Scouting: Jaha's future depends on how he can come back from major shoulder surgery. He has natural power and can hit for average when healthy. He also surprises people at first base, with steady hands and decent range. One of his problems was he hit the weights too hard, but he has since moderated his training regimen.

1998: Jaha was a free agent after 1997, but the Brewers wanted him back and might get him within their price range because of his shoulder surgery. He is one of the few legitimate power hitters in the Brewers' organization.

1997: After a fine season in '96, Jaha underwent shoulder surgery and missed most of the '97 season.

1996: Jaha had a breakthrough season with career highs in at-bats, runs, doubles (28), home runs and RBI. He was named the Brewers' MVP. He rankled the Brewers' management a bit by threatening to boycott the MVP dinner because of stalled contract negotiations, but an agreement was reached and both sides seemed content.

	AB	R	HR	RBI	SB	BA
1995 Milwaukee	316	59	20	65	2	.313
1996 Milwaukee	543	108	34	118	3	.300
1997 Milwaukee	162	25	11	26	1	.247

JARRETT, LINK - 2B - BB - b: 1/26/72

A switch-hitting, utility-type player who had a big year at Double-A New Haven in 1997, hitting .307, Jarrett primarily plays shortstop. Though he has poor range, by big-league shortstop standards, balls he gets to are outs. He has solid hands and an extremely accurate arm. He has gained some weight since his days as a star at Florida State and the Rockies feel the extra pounds may have slowed him a step. He'll return to New Haven in 1998.

JAVIER, STAN - OF - BB - b: 1/9/64

Scouting: Javier, a switch hitter, makes good contact, and has little power but fine speed. He has become more patient and, especially at the end of last season, an excellent clutch hitter. He can play all the outfield positions, plus first base. He's a solid player who has been durable, despite his 1996 injury problems.

1998: Javier became a free agent after the 1997 season and while the Giants were happy with his performance and versatility, their growing list of prospects in the outfield made him a less-attractive fit for their 1998 roster. Javier can be a major league starter, or serve as a valuable reserve in several different roles.

1997: Javier became the lefthanded hitting complement to Glenallen Hill in right field and spelled center fielder Darryl Hamilton, making him as valuable as a fourth outfielder can be. His numbers mimicked those of the past several full seasons. Javier's game-winning hits over three games against Colorado and San Diego during the last week of the season were instrumental in helping to clinch the National League West crown.

1996: Signed to play center field and bat leadoff, Javier pulled a hamstring and never really recovered. By the All-Star break, push became shove and Javier had to hang it up for a disappointing year. He did supply good speed and defense when he was in the lineup.

	AB	R	HR	RBI	SB	BA
1995 Oakland	442	81	8	56	36	.278
1996 San Francisco	274	44	2	22	14	.270
1997 San Francisco	440	69	8	50	25	.286

JEFFERIES, GREGG - 1B - BB - b: 8/1/67

Scouting: Jefferies has been hailed as one of the game's best pure hitters; he rarely strikes out. But in his tenure with the Phillies, Jefferies has overanalyzed his at-bats and has seemingly lost his zest for the game. He no longer follows his pattern of working the count, then aggressively attacking fastballs to drive them to the gaps for extra bases. Jefferies' speed has rapidly diminished and hamstring problems slowed him even further last year. He now has sub-par power and speed for a major league outfielder. Jefferies works hard on defense but is barely average, with a poor arm.

1998: Jefferies expensive contract ($5 million per year) will keep him playing left field in Philadelphia. He's a much better player than he has shown recently and should hit for a better average with marginal power and speed.

1997: Jefferies again got off to a woeful start with the Phillies in 1997, then once again rallied to make his stats respectable. He was unable to be the run producer the Phillies needed in their mediocre offense. Jefferies often let his temper get the best of him, too.

1996: Jefferies season the started on a bad note when he broke his hand on an awkward slide at third base in the season's first week. He split time between first and third base, and only a strong September prevented him from reaching career lows in most offensive categories.

	AB	R	HR	RBI	SB	BA
1995 Philadelphia	480	69	11	56	9	.306
1996 Philadelphia	404	59	7	51	20	.292
1997 Philadelphia	476	68	11	48	12	.256

JEFFERSON, REGGIE - 1B - BB - b: 9/25/68

Scouting: Jefferson has become a top-notch line-drive hitter. He has the perfect inside-out swing for Fenway Park because of the Green Monster. He has improved at hitting the inside pitch, has some power and will probably show more over the next couple of seasons. Jefferson loves to hit the cripple pitch, so he doesn't draw a lot of walks. He has played the outfield in the past, but is not an outfielder; he's not a good first baseman either, but probably better than Mo Vaughn. Still, he gets almost all of his at-bats as the designated hitter.

1998: Jefferson should duplicate his fine performance from the previous two seasons. His power should increase, and on-base percentage might as well. He might have won full-time status with his performance last year, but he doesn't hit lefties well and he will eventually end up sitting against them.

1997: Jefferson responded to being handed the DH role against righthanders by posting a batting average among the league leaders. He tailed off a bit at end of season after Mike Stanley was traded and he was awarded the DH duties full-time with a chance to get enough at-bats to qualify for the batting title.

1996: Jefferson kept hitting his way into the lineup. When an injury to DH Jose Canseco opened the door for playing time, he jumped on the opportunity and hit so well that he was worked into the lineup as an outfielder when Canseco returned.

	AB	R	HR	RBI	SB	BA
1995 Boston	121	21	5	26	0	.289
1996 Boston	386	67	19	74	0	.347
1997 Boston	489	74	13	67	1	.319

JENKINS, COREY - OF - BR - b: 8/25/76

Jenkins was the 24th player taken in the first round of the 1995 draft and spent 1997 in the Red Sox' farm system at the Class

A level. At Michigan in the Midwest League, Jenkins showed power potential but not a lot of plate discipline. He managed to belt 18 homers and had 62 RBI but he batted just .239 and struck out 129 times in 426 at-bats. If he's going to make it to Fenway it's going to probably be the year 2000 at the earliest.

JENKINS, GEOFF - BL - OF - BL - b: 7/21/74
Scouting: A first-round pick from USC in 1995, Jenkins remains a prospect despite injury problems the last two seasons. He is a good outfielder, with a strong arm, and has power potential at the plate. But, he has been limited by injuries his last couple of seasons.
1998: This would have been the target year for Jenkins to arrive in the big leagues, but the schedule is unknown now because of the injuries.
1997: Jenkins struggled with shoulder and leg problems again while hitting .236 in 93 games at Triple-A Tucson.
1996: Shoulder injuries wiped out the season for Jenkins after he had impressed the Brewers in spring training.

JENNINGS, DOUG - 1B - BL - b: 9/30/64
After missing success in opportunities with the Cubs, Athletics and Reds, Jennings went to Japan. He was something of a disappointment with the Orix Blue Wave in 1996, hitting only .220. His 15 home runs in 247 at-bats sparked enough interest to keep him around for 1997, but he didn't impress and lost playing time.

JENNINGS, ROBIN - OF - BL - b: 4/11/72
Scouting: Jennings is one of the Cubs most talked-about prospects. He never hit for any power at all until three years ago when he went from a career high eight homers to 17 while jumping from A-ball to Double-A. Jennings doesn't have much speed at all but he has decent knowledge of the strike zone and has consistently hit near .300 for his entire minor-league career.
1998: With the Cubs' crowded outfield situation it will be hard for Jennings to get substantial playing time. And if Chicago trades for a more traditional left fielder and moves Doug Glanville to center field it will be even harder for Jennings and others to crack the lineup. Jennings can hit 20 homers if he gets the chance, but it doesn't look like he will.
1997: Jennings had an outstanding spring and many observers felt he should have been the Cubs' opening day left fielder. However, Jennings didn't start the season with the team and only got 18 at-bats in Chicago when he was with the team as September callup.
1996: Jennings was on the Cubs' roster for a month early in the season, but spent most of the year at Triple-A Iowa. He had one of his best minor-league seasons and his 18 homers had many Cub fans clamoring for him to get called up permanently.

	AB	R	HR	RBI	SB	BA
1996 Chicago NL	58	7	0	4	1	.224
1997 Chicago NL	18	1	0	2	0	.167

JENSEN, MARCUS - C - BB - b: 12/14/72
Scouting: If Jensen were even a decent big-league hitter, he'd be guaranteed a big-league job. He's outstanding defensively, with a strong arm and a good presence behind the plate. The Tigers worked with him quite a bit on his hitting, and they hope he can improve.
1998: Jensen is out of options, so once again the Tigers will be faced with a decision. As a backup to Raul Casanova, he doesn't need to hit a lot, but he does need to hit some.
1997: The Giants kept Jensen, who was already out of options, until the middle of July. Finally they wanted more offense, so they traded him to the Tigers for Brian Johnson. Jensen rejected a waiver claim and agreed to go to Triple-A Toledo, and he returned to the Tigers in September.
1996: Jensen got a small taste of the big leagues, spending two weeks with the Giants when Kirt Manwaring was injured in April, then rejoining them in September. He hit .264 at Triple-A Phoenix, which may not sound like much but it was his third highest average in seven minor-league seasons.

	AB	R	HR	RBI	SB	BA
1997 Detroit	85	6	1	4	0	.153

JETER, DEREK - SS - BR - b: 6/26/74
Scouting: Jeter doesn't have the flash of Omar Vizquel or Alex Rodriguez, but if you watch him play everyday you'll see Jeter just might be the best all-around shortstop in the American League. Jeter is special. He has great range, soft hands and a strong arm that make him an outstanding defensive player. He hits the ball hard wherever it's pitched, and he runs the bases well.
1998: Jeter will be the Yankees' everyday shortstop for years to come. At his age he is already good and still improving. Look for the power numbers, in particular, to go up in 1998. When his breakthrough year comes, it will be astonishing.
1997: Jeter played in 159 games and showed no signs of wearing down. If he seemed less impressive than he was in 1996, it was just from us getting used to his all-around excellent play. Jeter insisted he was a better player last year than in 1996, whatever the stats may say.
1996: He was the AL Rookie of the Year in 1996. He did it all, at bat and in the field. Jeter had the unusual distinction of being an on-field leader for a team that won a World Series, as a rookie.

	AB	R	HR	RBI	SB	BA
1995 New York AL	48	5	0	7	0	.250
1996 New York AL	582	104	10	78	14	.314
1997 New York AL	654	116	10	70	23	.291

JIMENEZ, MANNY - SS - BR - b: 7/4/71
Jimenez is an eighth-year pro who has advanced at a snail's pace through the Atlanta farm system. He has never been much of a hitter although he did hit .291 at Double-A Greenville in 1997. However, he's 26 years old and not a strong defensive shortstop. He's a dim prospect.

JOHNS, KEITH - SS - BR - b: 7/19/71
Johns is a super defensive shortstop but has always wielded a weak bat. He did improve on his hitting in 1997 at Triple-A Tucson, batting .264 and showing some gap power. It was his highest batting average since his first year in the minors and he will have to prove its no fluke to have a big-league impact. If and when he does make it to the bigs it will probably be as a utility infielder.

JOHNSON, BRIAN D. - C - BR - b: 1/8/68
Scouting: Johnson is a good fastball hitter and though not a great defensive catcher, he handles pitchers well. Considering the short time he had to establish a rapport with the Giants staff, he did a fabulous job.
1998: Johnson clearly established himself as the number-one catcher last year, and with the release of Rick Wilkins and the

trade of Marcus Jensen (for Johnson himself), Johnson is the man pending the emergence of Doug Mirabelli. He should be more settled, therefore putting up more consistent numbers over the course of the season.

1997: A Bay Area native (Johnson was born in Oakland) and Stanford graduate, Johnson played as if possessed when he returned home as a pro for the first time. His hitting was not only magical, but homers he belted the last part of the season to win games against the Dodgers, in extra innings, and the Padres, in the ninth, will live in the memories of San Francisco sports fans.

1996: Johnson was one of the better hitting backup catchers in the majors; he could probably have been a starter on many clubs. He was traded from the Padres, where he was a backup to John Flaherty, to the Tigers in the off-season.

	AB	R	HR	RBI	SB	BA
1995 San Diego	207	20	3	29	0	.251
1996 San Diego	243	18	8	35	0	.272
1997 San Francisco	318	32	13	45	1	.261

JOHNSON, CHARLES - C - BR - b: 7/20/71

Scouting: Johnson is the state of the art defensive catcher, a latter day Johnny Bench. He combines perfect body mechanics with a cannon arm and unquestioned game-calling skills. His offense is coming along — though he digs himself a mid-season .190 hole every year, he has prodigious power against lefthanded pitching. If he can stay afloat in the first half, he could have a .275, 30-homer season in his future, though his 1997 performance will be his career norm.

1998: Expect Johnson's maturation to continue, particularly with the bat. He is learning to hit breaking pitches, and can hammer a mistake fastball a long way. His plate discipline has been gradually improving. Expect him to win another Gold Glove, and begin to become a true offensive force from wire to wire.

1997: Johnson threw out 47.5% of would-be basestealers, and allowed only .52 steals per nine innings, ranking second in both categories behind Brad Ausmus. He got off to another woeful offensive start, but was one of the clutch-hitting stars of the Marlins' second-half surge. His defensive mastery got a national stage during the post-season.

1996: Johnson was poor offensively, only emerging above the Mendoza line to stay in August, and grounding into 20 double plays. His defensive skills were even better than in 1997 (47.6% caught-stealing percentage, .40 steals per nine innings).

	AB	R	HR	RBI	SB	BA
1995 Florida	315	40	11	39	0	.251
1996 Florida	386	34	13	37	1	.218
1997 Florida	416	43	19	63	0	.250

JOHNSON, EARL - OF - BB - b: 10/3/71

After six weak-hitting years in the Tigers' chain, Johnson ended up in the Padres' organization in 1997. He has blazing speed and is an excellent defensive outfielder. He stole 42 bases in 1997 so the speed is still there but the bat is not; he hit .245 in 453 at-bats. He's 26 years old and hasn't reached Triple-A yet. If he improves at the plate his speed and defense could help him sneak into the bigs as a backup outfielder.

JOHNSON, J.J. - OF - BR - b: 8/31/73

Obtained as the player to be named later from Boston in the Rick Aguilera trade in 1995, Johnson didn't develop in 1996 as many had hoped. Last year he hit only .236 with three homers and 42 RBI at Double-A New Britain and .146 with five RBI in 26 games at Triple-A Salt Lake. Not only are those numbers disappointing, they represented a decline from 1996, when Johnson hit .273 with 16 homers and 59 RBI at New Britain.

JOHNSON, KEITH - 2B - BR - b: 4/17/71

Johnson has shown some potential as a utility type who has some offensive punch. The Dodgers had hoped Johnson would emerge as a super utility player in 1997, but he didn't quite get there. Nevertheless, the Dodgers believe he's one of those players who gets better with age. He's been tried at catcher in a move to increase his value and perhaps speed his rise to the majors.

JOHNSON, LANCE - OF - BL - b: 7/6/63

Scouting: Johnson, while approaching the end of his career, still has plenty of speed and knows how to get on base. He's a slap hitter but can hit the ball into the gaps and occasionally can pull the ball into the seats. He's also one of the most highly regarded centerfielders in the National League.

1998: It's doubtful that Johnson will have another season like he did in 1995 and 1996, but he should still be productive. He may not be with the Cubs at the start of the season, though, as the club would like to move Doug Glanville to center. But there are plenty of teams that could use a pure leadoff hitter and an outstanding defensive center fielder.

1997: Johnson suffered through injuries in the first part of the season and never quite got on track. He was traded to the Cubs in July and took over as their leadoff hitter, serving a role the Cubs had been looking to fill for a couple of seasons.

1996: Johnson followed up an outstanding 1995 campaign with another super year in his first with the New York Mets. Johnson led the National League in hits (he did the same in the American League with the White Sox in 1995) and made many Sox fans unhappy with management for letting him go.

	AB	R	HR	RBI	SB	BA
1995 Chicago AL	607	98	10	57	40	.306
1996 New York NL	682	117	9	69	50	.333
1997 N.Y. - Chi. NL	410	60	5	39	20	.307

JOHNSON, MARK - C - BL - b: 9/12/75

A patient hitter, Johnson led the Carolina League with 106 walks in 375 plate appearances. He's not an especially good hitter in other respects, but should get the most out of his meager hitting ability because of his keen batting eye. Johnson is an above-average receiver with a good arm; he'll advance because of the glove first, but will have to produce with the bat before he gets to the majors. Johnson was the White Sox first-round draft pick in 1994 and batted .253 for Class A Winston-Salem last year. He is not the Sox' best catching prospect (see Josh Paul).

JOHNSON, MARK - 1B - BL - b: 10/17/67

Scouting: The former Pirate suspect is a low-average slugger with huge holes in his swing and no defensive value. Unlike many hitters of this type, Johnson draws his share of walks, but his low average negates that strength. At age 30, he is not likely to get any better.

1998: Johnson could catch on somewhere as a pinch-hitter, but he is not likely to get a chance at any significant role in Cincinnati.

1997: Johnson started the year as the regular at first base for the Pirates, but was released after Kevin Young took over the position in mid-season. The Reds signed him and shipped him to Triple-A Indianapolis; he was not recalled in September.

1996: After starting the season well, Johnson hit only one homer in the final two months. He played well enough overall to get the first shot at the first base job in 1997.

	AB	R	HR	RBI	SB	BA
1995 Pittsburgh	221	32	13	28	5	.208
1996 Pittsburgh	343	55	13	47	6	.274
1997 Pittsburgh	219	30	4	29	1	.215

JOHNSON, NICK - 1B - BL - b: 9/14/78
The nephew of former major league star Larry Bowa, Johnson followed up an impressive professional debut in 1996 with a stellar season at Class A Greensboro where he batted .273 and led the team with 16 homers and 75 RBI. Johnson has been described by scouts as a "Mark Grace-type player."

JOHNSON, RUSS - SS - BR - b: 2/22/73
Scouting: Johnson was part of the double play combination with Todd Walker for one of LSU's National Champions. He was drafted by Houston in 1994 as a compensation pick following the first round. After playing his first two seasons at Double-A Jackson at shortstop, the Astros' decided he didn't have the defensive tools to play that position in the majors. He was moved to third base where the concern is whether he carries a big enough bat. Johnson is a hard-nosed player who is popular with the fans. With his makeup, the organization would like to see him make good but there is concern about where he might fit in.
1998: Johnson will be competing for a job at the major league level. He is not likely to be an everyday player unless he develops more pop.
1997: Johnson received some playing time at third base in Houston in April when Sean Berry was on the disabled list. When Berry came back, Johnson was optioned to Triple-A New Orleans where he started slowly, eventually compiling a batting average of .276 with four homers and seven stolen bases. The concern is that his slugging average was only .370, way below par for a third baseman. Johnson was recalled to Houston in September and hit well in limited action.
1996: Johnson showed significant improvement in his second year at Double-A Jackson. He batted .310 with 15 home runs, 74 RBI and nine stolen bases.

	AB	R	HR	RBI	SB	BA
1997 Houston	60	7	2	9	1	.300

JONES, ANDRUW - OF - BR - b: 4/23/77
Scouting: Everything you have heard is true - Jones the younger has all of the tools and it is only a matter of time before he is one of the biggest stars in the game. A second-half slump hid the fact that Jones showed good strikezone judgment (walking eight fewer times than Kenny Lofton in 100 fewer at-bats). Jones also impressed with his defensive play when Lofton was out with an injury; he was widely considered to be the team's best defensive outfielder. His season was comparable to Barry Bonds' and Ken Griffey's first years (Bonds was two years older when he broke in); as soon as he adjusts, watch out.
1998: Unless the Braves re-sign Kenny Lofton, Jones should be the regular center fielder and, while he will be a solid player, don't expect Hall-of-Fame production in 1998. Bonds and Griffey were good players while in their early 20's, but it took them a few years to develop stardom.
1997: Jones started the season platooning with Michael Tucker, and became a regular when Lofton suffered a groin pull. Jones hit well early, but struggled in the second half when pitchers starting working him away with junk. His adjustment to that pitching pattern will be the key in his continued development in 1998.
1996: Starting the season in A-ball, Jones tore through the minor leagues and was deservedly promoted to the majors by mid-August. He capped his season with two homers in his first two World Series at-bats, becoming the youngest player to homer in the Series.

	AB	R	HR	RBI	SB	BA
1996 Atlanta	106	11	5	13	3	.217
1997 Atlanta	399	60	18	70	20	.231

JONES, CHIPPER - 3B - BB - b: 4/24/72
Scouting: At age 25, the elder Jones is already considered one of the best players in the National League and there is not much he cannot do. He hits for power, a good average, has good strikezone judgment, is a high percentage base stealer, and plays a good third base. About his only weakness is a lack of power from the right side; he hit only one homer righthanded last year and has only ten home runs from the right side in his career.
1998: The best player on the best team, Jones is an MVP candidate entering the peak seasons of his career.
1997: The ability of Jones can be best characterized in that many considered his 1997 season — when he led the Braves in runs, RBI, doubles, and walks — a disappointment. Like the other Atlanta lefthanded power hitters, Jones suffered from the spacious dimensions of new Turner Field (390 feet to right-center).
1996: Jones emerged as the Braves best player, recording the first of what should be many triple milestone (.300 batting average, 30 homers, 100 RBI) seasons. He even played 38 games at shortstop, filling in for injured Jeff Blauser.

	AB	R	HR	RBI	SB	BA
1995 Atlanta	524	87	23	86	8	.265
1996 Atlanta	598	114	30	110	14	.309
1997 Atlanta	597	100	21	111	20	.295

JONES, CHRIS - OF - BR - b: 12/16/65
Scouting: Jones is an excellent spare outfielder with good power and defense. He's a good pinch-hitter and solid all-around player.
1998: Jones went to Arizona as a free agent. He was in a crowded situation in San Diego, so the move helped.
1997: Jones was regularly employed in late innings as a defensive replacement for Padre corner outfielders and hit .286 as a pinch-hitter. His fine defensive play saved several wins.
1996: Jones filled a backup role with the Mets.

	AB	R	HR	RBI	SB	BA
1995 New York NL	182	33	8	31	2	.280
1996 New York NL	149	22	4	18	1	.242
1997 San Diego	152	24	7	25	7	.243

JONES, DAX - OF - BR - b: 8/4/70
San Francisco released Jones at the end of the 1996 season. He was re-signed during the off-season and spent 1997 at Phoenix. Jones had always looked like a solid career Triple-A player, but after his dismal showing in the majors in 1996, he continued the downward trend when he returned to Phoenix last year. Since there are now several youngsters ahead of him on the depth chart, don't expect him to reappear in a major league city soon.

JONES, JAIME - OF - BL - b: 8/2/76
After an injury-shortened 1996 season, Jones drove 40% of his

hits for extra bases although he has generally been a disappointment since being the Marlins' first-round draft pick in 1995. He has a textbook lefthanded swing that appears capable of generating power and a good batting average. His results have been rather underwhelming so far in his pro career although he has usually been among the younger players at his minor-league levels so far. He'll graduate to Double-A Portland in 1998, hoping to take advantage of the hitter-friendly park there to regenerate his prospect status.

JONES, RYAN - 1B - BR - b: 11/5/74

Scouting: A decent defensive player, Jones is a durable, consistent power hitter who can take a walk.
1998: Because Jones was so badly overmatched at Triple-A Syracuse, a second trip to Triple-A is in order. A shot at the big-league club is unlikely unless he tears up Triple-A before September.
1997: Jones started the season with Syracuse but struggled so badly (.138 in 123 at-bats) that he was sent back down to Double-A to regain his stroke, after which he posted his usual minor-league numbers.
1996: Jones continued the logical progression up the Blue Jays' ladder, achieving a career high in home runs (20) and RBI (97).

JONES, TERRY - OF - BB - b: 2/15/71

He's the fastest man in the Rockies' organization. Jones' remarkable speed earned him a spot on the 40-man roster each of the past two seasons. Unfortunately for Jones, his next stolen-base attempt in the majors will be his first. A slap-hitting switch-hitter, Jones has become better at hitting the ball on the ground. He was much better at judging balls in center field at Triple-A Colorado Springs in 1996, though he still has a poor arm. Although his baserunning and defense improved in 1997, a chronic hamstring problem — he first pulled it in spring training — cost him a chance for a second straight September callup. He is likely to return to Colorado Springs in 1998.

JORDAN, BRIAN - OF - BR - b: 3/29/67

Scouting: He probably won't erase all the question marks until well into this season. Jordan could be one of the top talents in the league, as he seemed to be with a breakthrough 1996 season. Or he could be one of the most disappointing, prevented from ever showing his true abilities for an extended period of time because of a seemingly never-ending supply of injured body parts. Even when limited, though, Jordan is able to contribute because of his speed and enthusiasm. He's still a terrific athlete heading into his prime years.
1998: He'll get first crack at playing every day in right field. The only thing that possibly could hold Jordan back would be slow recovery from his injuries. Points of curiosity will be whether he takes hold in the middle of the lineup, where he was one of the league's top run producers two years ago, or whether his bat has been sapped of enough power to make him settle into the number two spot in the order, where his sound batting stroke would serve him well.
1997: His power clearly gone because of a wrist injury, Jordan at least could have helped as a singles hitter until even that became impossible, thanks to a bulging disc in his back suffered during spring training. That limited him to 145 at-bats and he ended the season rehabbing on the disabled list, during which time he underwent surgery to tighten ligaments in his wrist.
1996: He emerged as the team leader in the clubhouse and on the field. He showed tape-measure power and excelled in the clutch, with a .422 batting average with runners in scoring position.

	AB	R	HR	RBI	SB	BA
1995 St. Louis	490	83	22	81	24	.296
1996 St. Louis	513	82	17	104	22	.310
1997 St. Louis	145	17	0	10	6	.234

JORDAN, KEVIN - 2B - BR - b: 10/9/69

Scouting: Jordan is a versatile utility player who can handle all infield spots except shortstop at a respectable level. He's a wild swinger with occasional long-ball power and is known to battle pitchers through lengthy at-bats. Jordan once had decent speed as a Yankee farmhand, but that was eliminated by a 1994 broken leg. He's not a viable platoon candidate since he doesn't display normal platoon differentials; Jordan hits righthanded pitching much better than he hits lefties. He's a solid major league reserve.
1998: The Phillies would be pleased to have Jordan back in the same reserve role in 1998. Jordan may be the only righthanded power threat on their bench. He's peaked, so a bench job is his best expectation.
1997: Despite a fairly productive season in 1996, Jordan didn't break camp with the Phillies in 1997. However, injuries immediately opened a bench slot and Jordan served as a backup at the corner infield spots as well as being a reliable pinch-hitter.
1996: Jordan earned a role as part of a first base platoon, then blew out his knee, costing him the bulk of the season. It eliminated what speed he might have had after the 1994 broken leg.

	AB	R	HR	RBI	SB	BA
1995 Philadelphia	54	6	2	6	0	.185
1996 Philadelphia	131	15	3	12	2	.282
1997 Philadelphia	177	19	6	30	0	.266

JORDAN, RICKY - 1B - BR - b: 5/26/65

Remember when Ricky Jordan was supposed to be Philadelphia's first baseman of the future? That was 10 years ago. He spent the first half of last season with the Pirates' Double-A Carolina farm club before being released. Jordan turns 33 in May and, even with expansion, it's hard to imagine him resurfacing in the big leagues.

JORGENSEN, RANDY - 1B - BL - b: 4/3/72

Jorgensen has always been able to hit for a high average and 1997 was no exception. He is also an exceptional fielding first baseman but doesn't possess the power of a prototypical first sacker. He may never earn an everyday major league role but a defensive-sub/pinch-hitting platoon spot isn't out of the question.

JOSEPH, TERRY - OF - BR - b: 11/20/73

Joseph is a speedster who hits for some power but is remarkably undisciplined at the plate. He has twice reached double-figures in triples, but he also strikes out 80 or 90 times each season — too many for the leadoff hitter which Joseph projects to be in the majors. After spending two seasons in lower A-ball, he jumped to Double-A and had a pretty good year in 1997, showing improved plate patience and adding some power. He's already 25 years old, though, so he's too old to be just now mastering that level. Joseph has some talent, but too many weaknesses and is behind too many other prospects to be a factor in the bigs.

JOYNER, WALLY - 1B - BL - b: 6/16/62

Scouting: Regular rest for Joyner resulted in a career-best batting average and his best overall production since 1991. He remains one of the game's top defensive first basemen. Joyner is a line-drive hitter who is tough on righthanded pitchers. The Padres would like more power from their first baseman.

1998: The Padres exercised their option and re-signed Joyner for $3.75 million.

1997: Joyner finished fifth in the National League batting derby with his career-high batting average and his power totals of were his best since '91. He played only 135 games as the Padres regularly rested him, especially against tough lefthanders, helping to keep his strength up.

1996: Joyner led majors with .407 batting average through April and was hitting .321 on June 2nd when he broke his thumb. Joyner hit only .245 with three homers after the injury. His defense played a huge role in the Padres division title.

	AB	R	HR	RBI	SB	BA
1995 Kansas City	465	69	12	83	3	.310
1996 San Diego	433	59	8	65	5	.277
1997 San Diego	455	59	13	83	3	.327

JUSTICE, DAVID - OF - BL - b: 4/14/66

Scouting: Any doubts about Justice's health were dispelled in 1997, as Justice showed he still belongs in the top echelon of major league hitters. He is a patient hitter who works the count into his favor and then pounces. He has lightning-quick bat speed, capable of turning around most fastballs. His strikeout rate has always been acceptable for a power hitter; his career high in strikeouts is 92 as a rookie in 1990. He is quickly lapsing into DH territory with the glove. His range has deteriorated, and his arm is average.

1998: Justice cannot be expected to dominate the way he did in 1997, especially considering his extensive injury history. Justice's decline phase will be slow because he can hit lefties well.

1997: Justice was a godsend, posting better all-around offensive numbers than Albert Belle, whose job he inherited. He carried the club in the early going, keeping the club afloat until the other big bats in the Indian lineup joined the party. The ability of lefties Justice, Thome and Brian Giles to hit southpaws makes this a resilient lineup.

1996: It was a lost season. Justice logged 140 highly productive at-bats, and then missed the rest of the season. The emergence of Jermaine Dye and Andruw Jones made his presence unnecessary in Atlanta, hence the blockbuster trade with the Indians.

	AB	R	HR	RBI	SB	BA
1995 Atlanta	411	73	24	78	4	.253
1996 Atlanta	140	23	6	25	1	.321
1997 Cleveland	495	84	33	101	3	.329

KARKOVICE, RON - C - BR - b: 8/8/63

Scouting: One of the premier defensive catchers of the '90s, Karkovice's numerous (seven) knee surgeries have finally caught up with him. He can no longer position himself properly behind the plate in order to throw or get out of the box on bunts. Karkovice has some power but has always been one of the worst major league hitters for average.

1998: Karkovice will have to battle for a reserve catching job somewhere other than Comiskey Park. His criticism of White Sox management hastened his departure, but he's probably happy to go elsewhere. He won't contribute with the bat, but Karkovice can help shore up defensive liabilities behind the plate.

1997: Karkovice was supplanted by Jorge Fabregas at mid-season and had his worst season ever. His role was sharply reduced as the Sox struggled to get into the pennant race. The White Sox probably could have moved him to a playoff contender in a late-season deal but instead chose to let him rot on the bench.

1996: It was another typical season for Karkovice: great defense, moderate power at the plate and a poor batting average.

	AB	R	HR	RBI	SB	BA
1995 Chicago AL	323	44	13	51	2	.217
1996 Chicago AL	355	44	10	38	0	.220
1997 Chicago AL	138	10	6	18	0	.181

KARROS, ERIC - 1B - BR - b: 11/4/67

Scouting: Karros is a pull hitter with a short swing who likes the ball down and in. Defensively Karros doesn't have much range and is slow but he makes up for it with a good glove.

1998: Karros puts the Dodgers in a bit of a bind with his presence at first base because he's keeping Mike Piazza and his bad knees behind the plate and/or Baseball America's Minor League Player of the Year Paul Konerko out of the big-league lineup. He will be a productive part of someone's lineup in 1998, most likely the Dodgers for another season.

1997: Karros came through with big offensive numbers but effectively cooled off after the All-Star break. Twenty of his homers came before the mid-summer classic.

1996: Karros overcame a slow start and his offensive push in August (27 RBI) helped propel the Dodgers into the playoffs.

	AB	R	HR	RBI	SB	BA
1995 Los Angeles	551	83	32	105	4	.298
1996 Los Angeles	608	84	34	111	8	.260
1997 Los Angeles	628	86	31	104	15	.266

KEEFE, JAMIE - 2B - BR - b: 8/29/73

Keefe played at the Double-A and Triple-A levels of the Padres' organization in 1997. A patient hitter who slaps the ball to all fields, Keefe played outfield in Double-A and shortstop in Triple-A. He only got 100 at-bats in 1997 and appears to be a utility infield prospect, at best.

KELLNER, FRANK - SS - BB - b: 1/5/67

A 31-year-old career minor-leaguer, Kellner spent the entire 1997 season at Triple-A Tucson. He is a steady organizational player with little chance at the big leagues.

KELLY, MIKE - OF - BR - b: 6/2/70

Scouting: A classic "great tools" prospect, Kelly has all of the physical attributes (size, speed, power, throwing arm) that scouts love. He can play all three outfield positions. Inability to make contact and poor strikezone judgment had prevented him from progressing far past Triple-A, but in 1997 he posted a career high in batting average and cut down on his troublesome strikeout rate. If this improvement lasts, Kelly could develop into a useful fourth outfielder with good power and speed.

1998: Kelly should be able to grab at least a platoon role with Tampa Bay, and he could expand his role with a strong spring. Given his age, he is not a great long-term prospect, but he should be useful for a few years.

1997: Buried on the Reds bench behind several other outfielders at the start of the season, Kelly began to pick up occasional playing time when Ruben Sierra flopped, Deion Sanders was hurt, and Curtis Goodwin was sent to Triple-A. Jack McKeon platooned Kelly with Jon Nunnally in center field after he took over the team in July and Kelly responded with a much-improved performance over his dismal 1996.

1996: Kelly was acquired by the Reds in exchange for Chad Fox at the beginning of the season, and he began the year as the Reds' regular center fielder. A dismal start resulted in a return to the minors, where he turned in one of his worst years, hitting .209 with 80 strikeouts in 292 at-bats at Triple-A Indianapolis.

	AB	R	HR	RBI	SB	BA
1995 Atlanta	137	26	3	17	7	.190
1996 Cincinnati	49	5	1	7	4	.184
1997 Cincinnati	140	27	6	19	6	.293

KELLY, PAT - 2B - BR - b: 10/14/67

Scouting: Kelly is a good all-around athlete, and a fine second baseman — when he plays. He has good speed and handles a bat well. Injuries have been the undoing of his career. The Yankees tried several times to give Kelly the starting second base job. George Steinbrenner even went as far as instructing Joe Torre not to play Mariano Duncan so Kelly could be given a shot. However, every time Kelly got a chance, something happened to prevent his success at that spot.

1998: The Yankees had an option to bring Kelly back at $1.4 million and chose not to exercise it. The organization simply lost confidence in Kelly.

1997: As usual, the story was medical: a strained right Achilles tendon (15-day DL on May 12th), an inflamed nerve in his lower left leg (DL again on August 17th), a ganglion cyst and a compressed nerve in his right foot, and surgery on his lower left leg on September 24th.

1996: Kelly was pencilled in as the starting second baseman during spring training, but he was on the DL by opening day.

	AB	R	HR	RBI	SB	BA
1995 New York AL	270	32	4	29	8	.237
1996 New York AL	21	4	0	2	0	.143
1997 New York AL	120	25	2	10	8	.242

KELLY, ROBERTO - OF - BR - b: 10/1/64

Scouting: The '90s answer to Harry "Suitcase" Simpson, Kelly has been a starting major league outfielder for six organizations in the last four seasons — and none of them the Yankees, where he had his best success. His days as a premier base-stealer are long gone, but he can still take a base now and then.

1998: Kelly is another among the teeming horde of candidates for the Mariners' left field job, although it would surprise no one if he was on the move again.

1997: Kelly regained some of his pop with Minnesota before being acquired for the stretch run by Seattle; after the trade he was placed in left field and batted second, moving Alex Rodriguez down in the order.

1996: Kelly was a free-agent off-season signee by Minnesota after splitting the previous year between Montreal and Los Angeles and the year before that between Atlanta and Cincinnati.

	AB	R	HR	RBI	SB	BA
1995 two teams	504	58	7	57	19	.278
1996 Minnesota AL	322	41	6	47	10	.323
1997 Minn. - Sea.	368	58	12	59	9	.291

KENDALL, JASON - C - BR - b: 6/26/74

Scouting: Kendall is a contact hitter who sprays line drives and is beginning to develop power now that he has two major-league seasons under his belt. The only question about Kendall was his defense behind the plate. It was poor as a rookie in 1996 but he improved dramatically in 1997, quelling talk about a move to second base.

1998: All doubts lifted about his ability to play catcher in the major leagues, Kendall will be behind the plate for 135-140 games for the Pirates. It will continue that way for a long time. Manager Gene Lamont will again hit Kendall sixth in the belief he will develop into an RBI guy.

1997: Kendall's batting average dropped slightly from his rookie season of 1996 but the rest of his game improved. He began to show more gap power and the ability to turn on some pitchers. He also played outstanding defense, showing much-improved throwing mechanics.

1996: Kendall was the only rookie to appear in the All-Star Game and his .300 batting average was one of the few bright spots in the Pirates' dismal season. He made the jump from Double-A to the majors with little problem.

	AB	R	HR	RBI	SB	BA
1996 Pittsburgh	414	54	3	42	5	.300
1997 Pittsburgh	486	71	8	49	18	.294

KENNEDY, ADAM - SS - BL - b: 1/10/76

Kennedy advanced from college ball to higher Class A in the Carolina League last year. The Cardinals' first-round pick in the 1997 June Draft (20th overall) out of Cal State Northridge, Kennedy is a great athlete who shows the instincts to be a professional shortstop. He can also swing the bat pretty well as he hit .342 in 112 at-bats in the New York-Penn League and then hit at a .325 clip in the Carolina League.

KENNEDY, DARRYL - C - BR - b: 1/23/69

A good defensive catcher, Kennedy played Double-A and Triple-A ball in the Giants' farm system in 1997. He struggled at the plate in Triple-A and if he makes it to the majors it will be as a backup.

KENT, JEFF - 2B - BR - b: 3/7/68

Scouting: Kent, who looks like he finally has a home for a while — at second base in San Francisco — is a good fastball hitter with excellent power for a middle infielder. He can play first, second, or third base (he didn't play third in 1997), which fit in well with the Giants mix last year. His range is not spectacular, but he has good hands and is a smart ballplayer, which makes up for an awful lot. He is also one of those hitters who comes out of the blocks red-hot.

1998: Kent will have a tough time repeating his career year of 1997, but he has proven capable of hitting 20 homers and driving in 80 runs on a regular basis. Certainly, batting behind Barry Bonds helps, but Kent had already proven his hitting skills before the Giants acquired him. He'll be the second sacker again this year, although a return to more normal levels of production would be a reasonable expectation.

1997: It was certainly a career year, but the timeliness of his hitting and his contribution to his new team cannot be underestimated. Kent reached personal highs in homers, slugging, and RBI, and played in nearly all (155) of his team's games.

1996: Kent went from being an above-average offensive second sacker in the National League to a little-used, backup corner infielder in the American League. Kent was a free-swinger with decent power. He was traded to the Giants during the off-season that followed.

	AB	R	HR	RBI	SB	BA
1995 New York NL	472	65	20	65	3	.278
1996 New York NL	335	45	9	39	4	.290
1996 Cleveland	102	16	3	16	2	.265
1997 San Francisco	580	90	29	121	11	.250

KEY, JEFF - OF - BL - b: 11/22/74

Key has spent five pro seasons in A-ball. He has above-average power and speed, but remains a wild swinger who tends to jump at the first hittable pitch he sees. He's a passable outfielder who can play either left or right field. Key had his best season (65 extra-base hits and 15 steals) in his second try in the higher Class A Florida State League last year. But, he's not one of the younger starters in his league and his lack of plate discipline makes him only a minor prospect despite his selection as Co-Organizational Player of the Year by the Phillies last year. He'll advance to Double-A this year, but doesn't have a bright major league future.

KIESCHNICK, BROOKS - OF - BL - b: 6/6/72

Scouting: Kieschnick has been one of the most highly-touted players in the Cubs' farm system ever since the club took him in the first round of the 1993 draft after three outstanding collegiate seasons at the University of Texas. Although he led the Triple-A American Association in hits and home runs in 1995, Kieschnick never has developed into quite the power hitter the Cubs thought he would be. He has no speed and strikes out a lot. His defense has improved with experience.
1998: Kieschnick was at the top of the long list of Cubs' outfielders waiting for a chance to play, when the Devil Rays picked him in the expansion draft. Scouts who said he would be a good DH will have a chance to see.
1997: Kieschnick had a disappointing year at Triple-A Iowa, hitting just .258, but leading the club with 21 homers. He felt he should have been the opening day left fielder and he seemed to let his discouragement carry over into his play at Iowa. He had the lowest batting average of his minor-league career and didn't hit for the kind of power that the Cubs were looking for out of a Triple-A veteran.
1996: Kieschnick followed up a good year at Triple-A with another good season. He struggled a little more — he struck out more and hit fewer home runs, but hit well enough to earn a couple of trips to Chicago.

	AB	R	HR	RBI	SB	BA
1997 Chicago NL	90	9	4	12	1	.200

KILLEEN, TIM - C - BL - b: 7/26/70

He has shown some power in the past but Killeen struggled to even make contact at Double-A Mobile last year in the Padres' organization. He fanned 60 times in 168 at-bats and he has reached Triple-A once, in the A's organization for just three games. Because he's a lefthanded bat he will probably get a longer look than other catchers but he's a longshot to make the big leagues.

KING, BRETT - SS - BR - b: 7/20/72

A less than stellar second season at Double-A Shreveport leaves King at a new position — he moved from shortstop to third base — with numbers way down (.218 with six homers and 20 RBI) and playing time reduced accordingly. King is probably not going to advance much, if any, further.

KING, JEFF - 3B/1B - BR - b: 12/26/64

Scouting: King's an RBI man; he lives for hitting situations where runners are on base, waiting to be driven home. Despite sub-par batting averages over the last few years, King has driven in over 300 runs since 1995, primarily because he has hit so well with runners in scoring position. King has a keen batting eye, he works the count well and will take a walk; he is willing to open up the strike zone some when runners are on base, though. King is an accomplished glove man; he played well at third base and at second base in his eight years with the Pirates, then was a revelation at first base for the Royals, saving some of their scatter-armed infielders numerous throwing errors. King has just average speed but makes excellent use of it to steal bases in critical situations and also steal successfully at a high rate.
1998: King signed a multi-year deal near the end of the previous season. The Royals would be happy to get exactly the same kind of play from King this year — superior run production in an RBI spot in the lineup coupled with outstanding defense at first base.
1997: In his first year with the Royals, King gave his new club exactly what they asked for — an RBI bat in the middle of their lineup. He hit for power, drove in runs and got on base well despite the low batting average; he set a new career high in walks and had one of the Royals' best all-time seasons in drawing bases on balls. King's spectacular defense at first base was a pleasant surprise.
1996: King's last year with the Pirates was his best as he reached unusual power totals and set career highs in many categories while splitting time between first base and second base, where he was pressed into duty due to multiple injuries to Pirates' infielders. King also stole 15 bases in 16 tries.

	AB	R	HR	RBI	SB	BA
1995 Pittsburgh	445	61	18	87	7	.265
1996 Pittsburgh	591	91	30	111	15	.271
1997 Kansas City	543	84	28	112	16	.238

KINGSALE, GENE - OF - BB - b: 8/20/76

When healthy, Kingsale is the fastest man in the Oriole organization, if not the major leagues. He had some horrible luck last year with Double-A Bowie by spraining a knee ligament on opening day, missing three months, and, in his first game back, having his hand broken by a pitched ball. Coming back again in late-August, he was hit by another pitched ball, fracturing the same wrist. It wrecked any chance he had to being recalled by the Orioles as he had been late in 1996 when they needed a pinch-running specialist. In 1998, Kingsale will play in Double-A to recapture his batting eye.

KINKADE, MIKE - 3B - BR - b: 5/6/73

Scouting: Drafted as a catcher out of Washington State in the ninth round in 1995, Kinkade has been moved to third base because of injury problems. He has a good arm and hands but needs more experience at the hot corner. He needs no help at the plate, though. He makes contact, has power and even has speed on the basepaths.
1998: Kinkade's a prospect to take over the Brewers third base job but not this year. He will have to improve defensively and spend the year honing his game at Triple-A.
1997: Kinkade was an offensive force at Double-A El Paso in the Texas League. He hit for average and power (.385-12-109). Kinkade runs the bases well, evidenced by the fact that he was tied for second on the team in stolen bases with 17 and tied for the club lead in runs scored with 112.

1996: As a 23-year old, Kinkade had his way with Midwest League pitching at Class A Beloit, hitting .303 with fifteen homers, 100 RBI, and 23 stolen bases.

KIRBY, WAYNE - OF - BL - b: 1/22/64
Scouting: Kirby is an aging platoon outfielder who offers defense and above-average speed as his strengths. He doesn't have much power and has been known as a hacker who tries to spray the ball around the park.

1998: At age 34 and with a number of young outfield prospect waiting in the wings, Kirby could be an odd man out of the Dodgers outfield situation. If he makes a big-league club it will probably be as a fourth outfielder.

1997: Kirby started and finished the season at Chavez Ravine. He played in 46 games in April, May, August and September. For the other months he was a Triple-A injury insurance policy.

1996: Kirby returned to the Dodger organization where he started his professional career 13 years earlier. He filled in admirably for Brett Butler as he hit at a .283 clip when leading off.

	AB	R	HR	RBI	SB	BA
1995 Cleveland	188	29	1	14	10	.207
1996 Cleveland	16	3	0	1	0	.250
1996 Los Angeles	188	23	1	11	4	.271
1997 Los Angeles	65	6	0	4	0	.169

KIRGAN, CHRIS - 1B - BL - b: 6/29/73
Kirgan is a big, slow power hitter who batted .230-19-71 in the tough Double-A Eastern League last year. The low average is a weak point, and he struck almost 30 percent of the time. Kirgan isn't a prospect; he needs to be a more consistent and disciplined hitter before he gets a shot at the majors.

KIRKPATRICK, JAY - 1B - BL - b: 7/10/69
Kirkpatrick had a great 1994 season at Double-A San Antonio with much promise, but since then he has risen and fallen though Triple-A and A-ball, never again reaching the same level. His production has been decreasing since 1995 partly due to injuries in 1996. Last year at Double-A San Antonio, right back where he was in 1993, Kirkpatrick hit .260 with eight home runs and 42 RBI in 215 at-bats. However he struck out 53 times with only eight walks. He no longer is a prospect.

KLASSEN, DANNY - SS - BR - b: 9/22/75
A second-round pick by Arizona, Klassen looks like he is fully recovered from the serious knee injury he suffered in 1995. Last year he emerged as an offensive force at Double-A El Paso of the Texas League, lining the ball all over the park with above-average power for a shortstop (.331-14-81); he even stole 16 bases. The knee injury has taken away some of his range and while he has good hands his throws are inconsistent. His defensive development is the key to a starting job in the bigs, and a move to second base is not out of the question in the future. Look for him to compete for a utility job by 1999 at the least.

KLESKO, RYAN - OF - BL - b: 6/12/71
Scouting: A giant, lefty power hitter that is never cheated at the plate, Klesko has as much raw power as anyone in baseball. However, his ability as a power hitter is offset by struggles against lefthanded pitchers (hitting .198 against them in 1997) and his defensive liabilities; he is a natural first baseman playing left field. If he can improve against lefties he will be a star, but as long as he struggles Bobby Cox has several righthanded options.

1998: Klesko could have become the regular at first base, his natural position, after the trade of Fred McGriff to Tampa Bay, but the Galarraga signing raised another obstacle for Klesko who, at age 26, he should be entering his best seasons.

1997: Klesko started the season as the Braves regular left fielder, but the need to find playing time for Andruw Jones and Klesko's wrist injury cut into his at-bats. Klesko led the Braves in home runs, but his strikezone judgment worsened and, like the rest of the Braves lefty power hitters, he was hurt by the move to spacious Turner Field.

1996: Klesko developed into the one of the best power hitters in the National League, but manager Bobby Cox sat him on the bench against lefthanded pitching during the World Series.

	AB	R	HR	RBI	SB	BA
1995 Atlanta	329	48	23	70	5	.310
1996 Atlanta	528	90	34	93	6	.282
1997 Atlanta	467	67	24	84	4	.261

KMAK, JOE - C - BR - b: 5/3/63
Kmak is a veteran of 13 pro seasons, including two cups of coffee in the major leagues, and stints at the Triple-A level in five different organizations in the past eight years. He has never amassed 300 at-bats in any single season. Once a patient singles hitter who made consistent contact, Kmak now has no marketable skills. His defensive ability is average, at best, at this stage in his career. He is a steadying veteran presence on a minor-league club, but has likely reached the end of his playing career.

KNOBLAUCH, CHUCK - 2B - BR - b: 7/7/68
Scouting: Knoblauch is a perennial All-Star who improves in at least one area each season. Last year, it was in the steals department as he set a Twins' record with 62 stolen bases. Knoblauch is the consummate leadoff hitter who will hit for average, collect his share of extra-base hits and display superb base-stealing ability. Defensively, Knoblauch has some of the finest range in the game.

1998: Knoblauch is in his prime at age 28 and will continue as one of baseball's finest leadoff men. His on-base percentage will be up around .400. That combined with his defensive prowess will make him one of the most sought-after infielders in the game.

1997: Knoblauch was invited to his second consecutive All-Star game — and the fourth of his career. Despite his lowest batting average since 1993, he was among the league leaders in walks and still had an on-base percentage of just under .400.

1996: While most around the league already respected Knoblauch, he had perhaps his finest year at the plate with a career-high .341 average and a career-high 14 triples.

	AB	R	HR	RBI	SB	BA
1995 Minnesota	538	107	11	63	46	.333
1996 Minnesota	578	140	13	72	45	.341
1997 Minnesota	611	117	9	58	62	.291

KNORR, RANDY - C - BR - b: 11/12/68
A capable defensive catcher with a strong arm, Knorr lacks hitting ability to be anything more than a backup catcher; he has played in the majors in each of the last seven seasons, but never garnered more than 132 at-bats in any season. Knorr spent 1997 at Triple-A New Orleans, hitting .238 with five home runs and 27 RBI. He's unlikely to expand his Triple-A regular/ major league backup role.

	AB	R	HR	RBI	SB	BA
1995 Toronto	132	18	3	16	0	.212
1996 Houston	87	7	1	7	0	.195

KNOWLES, ERIC - SS - BR - b: 10/21/73
After six years in the Yankees' organization buried behind Derek Jeter, Knowles spent 1997 on the Mets' farm. He played both third base at Class A St. Lucie and shortstop at Double-A Binghamton. A light hitter who batted .236 with three homers in 157 at-bats at Binghamton, Knowles will have a hard time displacing Edgardo Alfonso or Rey Ordonez in the Mets' lineup.

KOELLING, BRIAN - 2B - BR - b: 6/11/69
After being obtained by the Phillies in a 1995 trade for Mariano Duncan, Koelling spent the 1996 season on the Scranton-Wilkes Barre disabled list and ended up back in the Reds' organization last year. He's average defensively and a spray hitter lacking power but he did steal 18 bases at Double-A Chattanooga last year. He doesn't have an eye-catching ability in any area that would signify him making a big-league impact.

KOEYERS, RAMSEY - C - BR - b: 8/7/74
Considering that Koeyers, a .209 career hitter with eight homers in 1037 plate appearances prior to 1997, suddenly drilled 12 homers in 309 plate appearances while batting .263 last year, you know some serious park effects were at work at the Marlins' Double-A Portland affiliate. Koeyers is a defensive specialist who could become a contender for a major league backup job should he prove that his 1997 offensive improvement was legitimate.

KONERKO, PAUL - 1B/C - BR - b: 3/5/76
Scouting: Konerko is one of the best prospects in baseball and was named Minor League Player of the Year by Baseball America. He has a quick bat and great strength which he uses to hit for average and power. Defense is his only question mark. He spent 1997 at third base to try getting to the bigs quicker. Eventually he should take over at first base.
1998: He's too good for the Dodgers to not find a place for him in the lineup. Konerko has nothing left to prove in the minors.
1997: Konerko was an offensive machine at Triple-A Albuquerque in the Pacific Coast League, batting .323 with 37 homers and 127 RBI. He also displayed good patience at the plate, walking more than he struck out. Konerko enjoyed his first big-league promotion, getting seven September at-bats for the Dodgers and his first major league hit.
1996: Konerko moved to first base in 1996 and established himself as one of the best power hitters in the minors.

KOSKIE, COREY - 3B - BL - b: 6/28/73
A surprise addition to the Twins' 40-man roster in November, 1996, Koskie responded with a strong year at Double-A New Britain, batting .286 with 23 homers and 79 RBI. He is a solid third baseman with offensive potential. Although he is 24 years old, he has only three full minor-league seasons behind him, and he played in only 95 games at Class A Fort Myers in 1996 because of hamstring injuries. Koskie's ceiling for improvement remains high.

KOSLOFSKI, KEVIN - OF - BL - b: 9/24/66
Once noted for his speed and defensive abilities in the outfield, Koslofski signed with the Cards' Triple-A club a year ago as a free agent. He played regularly at first, then saw his opportunities diminish because he couldn't hit and younger prospects received some opportunity. A pro since 1984, he's running out of chances for another big-league shot (he played for the Royals earlier this decade).

KOTSAY, MARK - OF - BR - b: 12/2/75
Scouting: The Marlins' 1996 first-round pick has rocketed through the their farm system despite just average raw tools. He is a patient lefthanded hitter who drives the ball where it's pitched with authority. He can bash low, inside fastballs, but must work on spraying base hits to the opposite field on tough breaking pitches from lefties. He has excellent defensive and baserunning instincts which make up for a lack of raw foot speed. He is a cerebral player who possesses all of the intangibles needed to play winning baseball. He made a believer out of Jim Leyland in his short major league trial in 1997.
1998: With Devon White not returning to the Marlins in 1998, it could be a wide-open battle between Kotsay and Todd Dunwoody for the starting center field job. Though Dunwoody is older and more experienced, Kotsay's skills fit the Marlins' needs perfectly — he is a top of the order hitter with superior defensive ability.
1997: Kotsay was brilliant in his first full pro season at Double-A Portland, showing excellent on-base, slugging, baserunning and defensive skills plus a fierce competitive desire. He has been proving doubters wrong his whole life, and wasn't about to stop last year.
1996: Kotsay was selected with the ninth overall pick in the draft, and promptly showed exemplary on-base skills in a short trial in lower A-ball. He dispelled any notion that he would have difficulty driving the ball with the wooden bat.

	AB	R	HR	RBI	SB	BA
1997 Florida	52	5	0	4	3	.192

KRAUSE, SCOTT - OF - BR - b: 8/16/73
Krause followed up a successful 1996 campaign by continuing to be an offensive force, this time in the Texas League at El Paso for the Brewers organization. Krause proved to be a nice combination of power and speed (.361-16-88 with 13 stolen bases) but needs to cut down on his whiffs, 108 in 474 at-bats. He is an adequate defensive outfielder and if this 10th-round pick from New Orleans continues to hit he will continue to advance.

KREUTER, CHAD - C - BB - b: 8/26/64
Scouting: He was an add-on in a May trade with the Chicago White Sox that brought Tony Phillips back to the Angels, but the veteran catcher wound up filling an important role. The original starting catcher, Jim Leyritz, was traded in July. His backup, Todd Greene, broke his wrist August 21st. After that, Kreuter played well defensively as the starter. Kreuter doesn't hit for a high average or power, but his value lies in defensive play and handling pitchers.
1998: Kreuter could be an important man again if Greene is slow to recover from his broken wrist. Kreuter is a prototypical backup. You can stick him in any situation and he won't embarrass the club.
1997: Kreuter showed his toughness in a late-August game in Detroit when he accidentally ran into a dugout overhang so hard an hour before the game he knocked himself cold and dislodged the caps on two of his front teeth — and then he played later that

day. He didn't hit much, but filled a vital role as someone to catch every day the last five weeks of the season.

1996: Kreuter's season ended after his right shoulder was broken in eight places in a home-plate collision in mid-July. He was having a typical season until the injury, then showed incredible grit in recovering from reconstructive surgery.

	AB	R	HR	RBI	SB	BA
1995 Seattle	75	12	1	8	0	.227
1996 Chicago AL	114	14	3	18	0	.219
1997 Chi. AL - Ana.	255	25	5	21	0	.231

LADELL, CLEVELAND - OF - BR - b: 9/19/70

Ladell is a five year minor league veteran of the Reds' system with one marketable tool - speed. He has poor plate discipline, little power for an outfielder, and an inconsistent uppercut swing, but has averaged 26 steals per season. In 1997 he played in only 14 games for Double-A Chattanooga.

LAKER, TIM - C - BR - b: 11/27/69

Laker was once a top prospect with the Expos, but didn't develop as expected. He missed all of 1996 following elbow surgery, and last year he attempted a comeback with the Orioles Triple-A Rochester club. He got into a few games with the Orioles last year when he was called up to back up Lenny Webster with Chris Hoiles on the disabled list. Laker is the number three catcher on the Orioles catching depth chart, but other rookies are knocking on the door.

LAMB, DAVID - 3B/SS/ 2B - BB - b: 6/6/75

Orioles farmhand Lamb had a solid season in Double-A last year. He hustles, but he doesn't have much power and no speed. He's not a prospect, and will have an uphill battle to make the majors. His best chance of major league play is as a utility infielder.

LAMPKIN, TOM - C - BL - b: 3/4/64

Scouting: Lampkin has established himself as a capable catcher defensively, a smart baserunner and a precious commodity as a lefthand-hitting receiver. He seems to do some of his best hitting in late-inning, clutch situations. That's not enough to build an entire career upon, really, but it's certainly enough to keep him working for a few more years.

1998: With so many catchers who have the potential of earning a starting spot with the Cardinals, Lampkin would seem the likely odd man out. His only hope of sticking as a reserve would be his lefthanded bat. He probably is destined to swing it for another team.

1997: He hit a career-high seven home runs, all off righthanded pitchers, and batted almost .300 in his final 60-plus games of the season. The Cards' pitching staff had a 3.60 ERA with Lampkin behind the plate, nearly a half-run below the season ERA, as he made great use of the thick book on National League hitters he developed over previous years.

1996: Though he hit just .232 in 66 games with the Giants, Lampkin earned his spot with excellent defense. He threw out 47 percent of the runners who tried to steal against him and didn't allow a passed ball.

	AB	R	HR	RBI	SB	BA
1995 San Francisco	76	8	1	9	2	.276
1996 San Francisco	177	26	6	29	1	.232
1997 St. Louis	229	28	7	22	2	.245

LANDRY, TODD - 1B - BR - b: 8/21/72

After spending 1996 at Triple-A New Orleans, Landry found himself back at the Double-A level in 1997. That's because he couldn't hit Triple-A pitching (.240 in 191 at-bats in 1996). Landry is also not a power hitter but does have above-average speed for his position. With Antone Williamson getting a shot at first base, Landry's shot at the big club appears slim unless he changes organizations.

LANE, RYAN - SS/2B - BR - b: 7/6/64

Lane has decent power for a second baseman and good speed. He is a slightly above-average fielder but his batting average slipped a bit in his first full season at Double-A for the Twins. He has moved around while in the Twins' organization from second to shortstop and back again. He's a year if not two away from having a shot to make the bigs.

LANKFORD, RAY - OF - BL - b: 6/5/67

Scouting: Lankford still isn't disciplined enough at the plate to fulfill all his vast potential. He's learned to be a smarter, more patient hitter, though, and likes the fact he's considered an important run-producer in the lineup. He has harnessed his excellent bat speed, turning him into a power threat against any kind of pitcher. A five-tool player, he's worth the strikeouts because he'll win many more games with his bat, glove and legs than he'll ever lose.

1998: He'll have a difficult time topping his 1997 season, though it's entirely possible. Another year of healing for his shoulder should get him closer to throwing as well as ever and, if healthy all year, he seems likely to repeat his All-Star berth.

1997: Even though he opened the year on the disabled list following off-season rotator cuff surgery, Lankford had the best offensive season of his career. He was the first product of the Cardinals' farm system to hit at least 30 homers since Ken Boyer and also reached career highs in batting average and RBI. The surgery limited his throwing ability. Still, Lankford was one of the top defensive centerfielders in the league. He added the wrinkle of hitting 12 homers against lefthanded pitchers after belting none against lefties the previous season.

1996: A dive that resulted in a torn rotator cuff near the end of the season put the only damper on what was one of his best summer-long performances. Despite striking out at least 100 times for the sixth consecutive year, Lankford again displayed a combination of power, speed and defense, and he led the club with 100 runs scored.

	AB	R	HR	RBI	SB	BA
1995 St. Louis	483	81	25	82	24	.277
1996 St. Louis	545	100	21	86	35	.275
1997 St. Louis	465	94	31	98	21	.295

LANSING, MIKE - 2B - BR - b: 4/3/68

Scouting: Lansing has blossomed into one of the better second baseman in the major leagues. He has uncommon power for a middle infielder and runs extremely well. He is also among the best defensive second basemen in the game.

1998: Lansing will be sparking some team as a standout second baseman but it won't be Montreal. The Expos couldn't afford what Lansing might make in salary arbitration. Many teams would love to have him and the Expos expected to get a nice cache of prospects back in a trade.

1997: Despite slumping in September, Lansing had his best season. He set career highs for home runs and did an outstanding job hitting in the second slot in the batting order. He was also the unquestioned leader of the Expos, complaining loudly when management sat by and did nothing while Montreal fell out of the National League wild card race in late-July.

1996: Lansing had a fine season for the Expos, continuing to establish himself as a rising star.

	AB	R	HR	RBI	SB	BA
1995 Montreal	467	47	10	62	27	.255
1996 Montreal	641	99	11	53	23	.285
1997 Montreal	572	86	20	70	11	.281

LaRIVIERE, JASON - OF - BR - b: 9/30/73
This 44th-round selection of the 1995 draft had the second-most RBI total for Double-A Arkansas last year but needs to work on his plate discipline as he also lead his team in strikeouts. LaRiviere hit .274 with six homers, 60 RBI and four steals last year. 1997 was his first year at the Double-A level.

LARKIN, BARRY - SS - BR - b: 4/28/64
Scouting: When healthy, Larkin is a Hall-of-Fame shortstop with no weaknesses either offensively or defensively. September surgery repaired heel and Achilles tendon problems that plagued him throughout the 1997 season. The only question about Larkin's game besides his health is whether his 1996 power surge was real or a fluke season, but even if it was a fluke he more than compensates with a high average, excellent strikezone judgment and speed.

1998: Larkin should be fully recovered by opening day from his heel/foot surgery, and a strong comeback is likely.

1997: Larkin's heel problem surfaced during spring training, but he chose to try playing through the injury. As a result, he was unable to drive the ball with any authority and was rarely able to play more than a few games in a row. He played well when able, but he went on the DL for six weeks with a strained calf muscle and finally submitted to surgery in September.

1996: Larkin posted one of the better seasons ever for a shortstop, becoming the first to record a 30/30 season. In a curious vote, the 1995 MVP did not finish in the top 10 even though he set career highs in almost every category.

	AB	R	HR	RBI	SB	BA
1995 Cincinnati	496	98	15	66	51	.319
1996 Cincinnati	517	117	33	89	36	.298
1997 Cincinnati	224	34	4	20	14	.317

LAROCCA, GREG - 2B - BR - b: 11/10/72
LaRocca has invoked visions of Tim Flannery with his rise through the Padre organization on the strength of his solid middle-infield play. He's sound defensively at second base with average speed and below-average power. LaRocca would be a utility player should he reach the majors.

LARSON, BRANDON - SS - BR - b: 5/24/76
The Reds top draft pick in 1997, Larson was the MVP of the College World Series and set an NCAA record for home runs by a shortstop with 40. After a lengthy holdout, he played only 11 games for Double-A Chattanooga before ending his season with a severe ankle sprain. Larson will start 1998 in Triple-A.

LATHAM, CHRIS - OF - BB - b: 5/26/73
A fleet center fielder with solid potential, Latham was acquired by the Twins as a player to be named later in the Kevin Tapani trade with Los Angeles in the summer of 1995. Just 24, Latham already has seven years in the minor leagues and batted .309 with 21 stolen bases last summer. He appeared in a handful of games with the Twins and hit for a poor batting average while being badly overmatched.

LAWRENCE, JOE - SS - BR - b: 2/13/77
Lawrence was selected by the Blue Jays with the 16th pick of the June 1996 draft. He was a compensation pick Toronto picked up for the loss of Roberto Alomar and last year Lawrence played at Class A Hagerstown of the South Atlantic League. He should be able to hit for average with some power for a middle infielder and could possibly end up as a third baseman if he outgrows shortstop; he was selected by the Jays out of high school.

LAWTON, MATT - OF - BL - b: 11/3/71
Scouting: A spunky hitter with a little pop, Lawton remains a hitter with major-league potential. He is questionable defensively. Still, center field is his best bet because he doesn't have the power required to play right field, unless it is for a team with a weak outfield. Lawton is an aggressive hitter who will make pitchers pay for mistakes.

1998: Lawton needs to prove that he can hit consistently in the majors instead of going through prolonged periods of ineffectiveness. He has shown signs of being more than a .250 or .260 hitter in the majors but, so far, hasn't done it.

1997: After leading the league with seven spring training home runs, Lawton poked 14 during the regular season for a team that could use more power. On a stronger team, though, Lawton's average would have relegated him to the bench.

1996: He got enough playing time and did well enough to keep the Twins interested, earning himself a stronger look for 1997. Lawton was rushed to the major leagues too soon because of the career-ending case of glaucoma suffered by Kirby Puckett. As a result, a lot was asked of Lawton — more than he was ready to produce.

	AB	R	HR	RBI	SB	BA
1995 Minnesota	60	11	1	12	1	.317
1996 Minnesota	252	34	6	42	4	.258
1997 Minnesota	460	74	14	60	7	.248

LEACH, JALAL - OF - BL - b: 3/14/69
Leach spent the 1997 season at Triple-A Tacoma in the Seattle farm system, his third organization in three years. He has some power and is a lefthanded hitter but strikes out too often. He also is not a good defensive player, has lost his speed and more than likely lost his chance of making more than a brief appearance in the majors.

LeBRON, JUAN - OF - BR - b: 6/7/77
To call this guy "free swinging" is an understatement. As a top power prospect, LeBron was the Royals' first-round draft pick on his eighteenth birthday out of a Puerto Rican high school in 1995. He struggled in his first try at Rookie ball, then had a better year in 1996. Last year he hit .212 in 113 at-bats at Class A Lansing and was demoted when he fanned 32 times — with no walks! At Spokane he hit .306 with seven homers but 74 whiffs in 288 at-bats. LeBron is still young, but will go nowhere fast if he doesn't make better contact.

LEDEE, RICKY - OF - BL - b: 11/22/73
Scouting: Ledee has a compact swing from the left side and can generate home run power to right, perfect for the short porch in

the Bronx. Offense is his main tool; he's limited on defense to playing left field and is an adequate baserunner.
1998: The Yankees refuse to include Ledee in any deals and he will contend for the starting left field job. Even if he doesn't earn the job outright he could end up in a platoon situation with Chad Curtis or whomever else the Yankees have on the roster for that position.
1997: Ledee missed three months of the season with a groin pull, limiting him to 43 games at Triple-A Columbus. He still managed to hit at a .309 clip with ten homers and 39 RBI.
1996: Ledee went from Double-A Norwich to Triple-A Columbus. He showed power at both stops as he hit a total of 29 homers combined and knocked in 101 runs.

LEDESMA, AARON - SS - BR - b: 6/3/71

Scouting: Ledesma can play all of the infield positions adequately. He's hit around .300 in the high minors, but he doesn't have home run power, only occasional gap power. He has a little stolen base speed, but hasn't run much in recent years. He hustles and is an excellent team player who sacrifices himself for the good of the team.
1998: Ledesma will compete for a utility role with the expansion Devil Rays. Starting the year in the minors would not mean he is out of the major league picture. Ledesma doesn't have anything to prove, but he might make a better reserve if he spends his waiting time playing regularly until needed.
1997: It was Ledesma's first year in the Baltimore organization, and he lucked out when he was called up to replace the injured Roberto Alomar on the roster. He played all of the infield positions, hustled, and hit well although he didn't get many at-bats.
1996: After six years in the Mets minor-league system, he signed with the Angels where he played Triple-A and had his best minor-league season, hitting .305 with 51 RBI.

	AB	R	HR	RBI	SB	BA
1995 New York NL	33	4	0	3	0	.242
1997 Baltimore	88	24	2	11	1	.352

LEE, CARLOS - 3B - BR - b: 6/20/76

A young power-hitting corner infield prospect, Lee has an undisciplined hitting approach and may not be able to hold down the hot corner. He does have a natural swing, though, that has scouts touting his potential. Lee has a little speed, too, but it's his bat that will carry him. He's still a long ways away from the majors and may have to shift positions before he gets there, but if he adds power as many expect him to do the White Sox will make room for his bat in their lineup.

LEE, DEREK - OF - BL - b: 7/28/66

Scouting: This is not the Lee who's a top prospect in the Padres organization, this Derek (one "r") Lee has been bouncing from one minor-league team to another (seven of them) since 1988, only reaching the majors once, in 1993 with Minnesota. He has proven he can hit at the Triple-A level - he's been there since 1991 - and yet he can't seem to get a break with any major league team. He's got decent speed, covers ground in the outfield, and makes contact with the ball.
1998: It looks like another year in the high minors for Lee, as his age is going to deny him a prospect label.
1997: It was another solid minor-league season from Lee, trading playing time with younger players moving past him in the organization.

1996: Lee should have gotten a chance to help the Rangers in September; he had an exceptional year in Oklahoma City.

LEE, DERREK - 1B - BR - b: 9/6/75

Scouting: The free-swinging son of former Padre Leron Lee figures to be the club's first baseman of the future; the only question is when. Lee thinks he is ready, but the Padres have signed Wally Joyner for 1998. Lee has great power potential. If not '98, Lee is sure bet in '99.
1998: If he starts the '98 season in San Diego, Lee could find his stride by late summer. But the Padres probably want him at Triple-A for one more season.
1997: Lee hit .324 with 13 homers and 64 RBI at Las Vegas, but also struck out 116 times in 472 at-bats. In a cameo appearance with the Padres Lee struck out 24 times in 54 at-bats.
1996: Lee led the Southern League with 34 homers and 104 RBI while hitting .280; he also struck out 170 times while drawing only 65 walks.

	AB	R	HR	RBI	SB	BA
1997 San Diego	54	9	1	4	0	.259

LEE, TRAVIS - 1B - BL - b: 5/26/75

Scouting: Lee is the complete package, as one could expect from the second player taken in the 1996 draft; he signed as a loophole free agent in late-1996 when selecting team Minnesota failed to offer him a written contract proposal within 15 days of the draft. Lee can hit for average and power, runs well — well for a first baseman — and already has created a stir with his glove work.
1998: Lee should begin a long and prosperous career as the Diamondbacks' first and only first baseman for the next decade or so. His patience at the plate combined with a short stroke enable him to drive the ball to all fields. He can also play the outfield.
1997: Lee hit .363 with 18 homers and 63 RBI in a half-season at Class A High Desert before being loaned to Milwaukee's Triple-A affiliate in Tucson, where he hit .300 with 14 more homers and 46 RBI. Lee made an over-the-shoulder running catch of a foul pop down the right field line that one scout said was the best play he had ever seen a first baseman make.
1996: Lee was the Golden Spikes Award winner as the nation's best amateur player when he played for San Diego State before joining the U.S. Olympic team. He hit .427 during the pre-Olympic summer tour while setting a USA Baseball season record for homers (17).

LEGREE, KEITH - OF - BL - b: 12/26/71

Legree's development has been slowed because of his time on the University of Cincinnati basketball team, where he started as a guard on the Bearcats' Final Four team. That shows his athleticism. However, he needs to channel that into baseball now. He reached Double-A New Britain last summer, where he hit only .242 with nine homers and 58 RBI. He is adequate as an outfielder.

LEIUS, SCOTT - 3B/SS - BR - b: 9/24/65

Once a challenger for an everyday job in the majors, Leius has gradually slipped to a reserve role and now to a backup job in Triple-A. He hit .240 in 104 at-bats for Triple-A Nashville but bashed seven homers in that short stint. He's a journeyman at this stage of his career with hopes to return to a major league reserve role.

LEMKE, MARK - 2B - BB - b: 8/13/65
Scouting: Lemke's value to a team is greater than his statistics, and the Braves deserve some credit for keeping him in the lineup despite mediocre (at best) offensive performance. He bunts well, hits behind the runner, and turns the double play. On a team like the Braves, he provides valuable support for the stars; on a bad team he would much less valuable.
1998: A free agent at the end of the 1997 season, Lemke could not expect a multi-year deal on the free-agent market. He is no longer up to full-time play, and the Braves have alternatives in Tony Graffanino and Keith Lockhart.
1997: The development of the Braves young outfielders moved Lemke out of the second spot in the lineup, and his offensive performance declined slightly from 1996. In late-August, he suffered a severe ankle sprain in a collision at second base that effectively ended his season.
1996: Lemke turned in a fairly decent year by his standards, batting second most of the season and having another good post season.

	AB	R	HR	RBI	SB	BA
1995 Atlanta	399	42	5	38	2	.253
1996 Atlanta	498	64	5	37	5	.255
1997 Atlanta	351	33	2	26	2	.245

LENNON, PATRICK - OF - BR - b: 4/27/68
Scouting: Lennon possesses a solid swing, has a good work ethic, is in excellent shape, is well liked by his teammates, and is unable to deliver upon his promise as a number one draft pick. He remains a free-swinger at the plate, and is at an age where something should have kicked in. "Should have," is the key, as it hasn't.
1998: A change of scenery helps most players, and it is not beyond the realm of comprehension that Lennon be helped by the expansion draft. If so, and given the right set of circumstance — 500 at-bats and the thin air of Arizona, for example — it is possible that he could become the new Dante Bichette, hitting 25-plus homers and driving in 80 runs. Unfortunately, he'll probably continue to bounce between the majors and minors, surfacing as a substitute and pinch-hitting the occasional homer.
1997: After leading the A's sluggers with eight spring training homers, Lennon began the season in the minors, and he never really had a chance to establish himself. This is a familiar scenario for the once highly touted slugger, who led the spring training Royals in homers in 1995, earned a starting spot and then couldn't hit the real thing in a 50 at-bat major league trial.
1996: Lennon had a good year at Edmonton in many ways, but he still swung at too many bad pitches.

	AB	R	HR	RBI	SB	BA
1997 Oakland	116	14	1	14	0	.293

LESHER, BRIAN - OF - BR - b: 3/5/71
Lesher has produced well in the minors, but he is going nowhere fast in the majors. He is well beyond the age where he should have settled in comfortably with major league pitchers. As we said last year, "he swings too much and makes contact too little." It's still true.

	AB	R	HR	RBI	SB	BA
1996 Oakland	82	11	5	16	0	.232
1997 Oakland	131	17	4	16	4	.229

LEVIS, JESSE - C - BL - b: 4/14/68
Scouting: Levis doesn't have power and is only an average defensive catcher, but he can hit for a decent batting average from the left side. He also has earned a reputation as a good handler of pitchers and has developed into a fairly reliable pinch-hitter.
1998: The Brewers were looking to upgrade their catching overall, so Levis' future with the club was unknown. He has enough experience, and has proven to be a decent pinch-hitter to stay in the big leagues as a backup with Milwaukee or somewhere else.
1997: Levis set a Brewer record for pinch-hit appearances and shared the catching duties with Mike Matheny.
1996: The Brewers acquired Levis in a trade with Cleveland for pitchers Scott Nate and Jared Camp. He shared catching duties with Matheny. As a pinch-hitter, he hit .306 and tied a club record for pinch-hit appearances with 36. He broke that record in 1997.

	AB	R	HR	RBI	SB	BA
1995 Cleveland	18	1	0	3	0	.333
1996 Milwaukee	233	27	1	21	0	.236
1997 Milwaukee	200	19	1	19	1	.285

LEWIS, ANTHONY - DH/OF - BL - b: 2/2/71
Lewis hit 24 homers in both 1995 and 1996 but took a step backward in 1997. He played at Double-A New Haven in the Rockies' organization and struggled to make consistent contact. He struck out nearly once every four at-bats and has made just one Triple-A appearance in nine minor-league seasons. He is a long shot for advancement to the majors.

LEWIS, DARREN - OF - BR - b: 8/28/67
Scouting: Defense is Lewis' forte and the reason the Dodgers collected him from Chicago in a trade deadline deal. He never really hit enough to warrant a full-time job, despite his stellar fielding skills. His one offensive plus, above-average speed, is diminished by his inability to get on base where he can use the speed to steal bases. Lewis is a career .226 hitter with no power or plate discipline.
1998: Even expansion might not be enough for Lewis to reclaim a starting role in the majors. Since he can't hit much, a fourth outfield job might be a stretch, too. He'll be a luxury for a strong club that can afford a outfield defensive specialist and occasional pinch-runner, or possibly share a more regular role for a weaker team.
1997: Lewis lost his starting job to the White Sox' hot new rookie, Mike Cameron, becoming a forgotten man on their bench. He played sparingly both before and after his trade to Los Angeles.
1996: Lewis made a career-high three errors and had his worst major league batting average but had his most RBI ever and was an unusually effective base stealer, swiping 21 bases in 26 attempts.

	AB	R	HR	RBI	SB	BA
1995 two teams	472	66	1	24	32	.250
1996 Chicago AL	337	55	4	53	21	.228
1997 Chi. AL - L.A.	154	22	1	15	14	.266

LEWIS, MARC - OF - BR - b: 5/20/75
Lewis came to the Braves from Boston in the 1995 Mike Stanton deal and emerged as a prospect during a fine 1996 campaign split between two A-ball venues; he was added to the Braves' 40-man roster after that season. In 1997, Lewis' power came to the forefront as he banged 17 homers at Double-A Greenville. He has above-average speed and growing power, although he is still too willing to swing at bad pitches. Lewis is young enough

to learn patience at the plate and has to be considered one of the brighter prospects in an already-strong Atlanta organization.

LEWIS, MARK - 3B - BR - b: 11/30/69
Scouting: With the ability to play both third base and second base, Lewis has versatility in the field, and he's a boost to the team at the plate. He has good power, but likes to pull the ball rather than use the field, and his all-around numbers suffer. Lewis is not a particularly patient hitter; when he uses the whole field and forces the count more often, he is more successful.
1998: Lewis was a solid contributor to San Francisco last year, but his playing time waned as the season progressed and Bill Mueller established himself as the third baseman. As a result, he will probably have reduced playing time in San Francisco. He could well find himself on another team.
1997: After starting the season with what seemed to be the upper hand at the third base spot, Lewis' numbers and playing time wilted as the season progressed. He actually proved more valuable off the bench. Lewis added some pop and speed (six triples).
1996: After a red-hot start (.302, eight homers, 33 RBI over the first half) Lewis cooled considerably (.223, three homers, 22 RBI over the second half) and even broke down under the rigors of the long season. He proved to be better in a part-time role than as a full-time player.

	AB	R	HR	RBI	SB	BA
1995 Cincinnati	171	25	3	30	0	.339
1996 Detroit	545	69	11	55	6	.270
1997 San Francisco	341	50	10	42	3	.267

LEWIS, T.R. - OF/DH - BR - b: 4/17/71
Lewis is a nice little player, but probably a career minor leaguer. He doesn't have speed or power, but is a smart hitter with a sound stroke. He also does a good job judging balls in the outfield, so he's capable of filling in anywhere out there. He's had a lot of arm problems, though, and can't throw anybody out. All of which makes him a good Triple-A fourth outfielder, a role he's filled for three different teams the last three years.

LEYRITZ, JIM - 1B/C - BR - b: 12/27/63
Scouting: Leyritz is an above-average hitter with great versatility, making him one of the most valuable bench players in baseball. Capable of starting at every position but shortstop, second base and center field, Leyritz isn't a good enough fielder to play regularly at most positions, but he is a competent substitute. A dead-pull hitter, Leyritz has decent power but can be overmatched against a power pitcher. As a catcher, Leyritz handles pitchers well, but has only an average arm. He is a surprisingly good baserunner, although he doesn't steal much.
1998: Leyritz should get 300-plus at-bats for someone, with double-digit home runs and an average in the high .200s. His knee is expected to be healthy by spring training.
1997: Traded in mid-season from the Angels to the Rangers, Leyritz had a career high in at-bats, runs and RBI. His chance to be a regular fizzled when the Ranger re-signed Ivan Rodriguez, but he was in the lineup more often than not, DHing, catching or at first base. Leyritz' season ended in September with a knee injury.
1996: A gritty competitor who became the longevity king in the Yankee clubhouse in 1996, Leyritz offers a variety of skills on offense and defense. He is good under pressure and is worth more than his stats would indicate.

	AB	R	HR	RBI	SB	BA
1995 New York AL	264	37	7	37	1	.269
1996 New York AL	265	23	7	40	2	.264
1997 Texas	379	58	11	64	2	.277

LIDLE, KEVIN - C - BR - b: 3/22/72
Lidle spent the 1997 season at Double-A Jacksonville in the Tigers' organization and didn't raise his stock any. He split time at catcher and didn't make contact often or overcome his low batting average with any signs of power. He's getting too old to be struggling at Double-A. The highlight of his baseball career may have already happened when he was a member of the 1992 U.S. Olympic team that played in Barcelona.

LIEBERTHAL, MIKE - C - BR - b: 1/18/72
Scouting: Few players improved more than Lieberthal did over the last full season. He has always been a fine defensive receiver, but made major strides which have helped him evolve into a durable power hitter with a strong arm and quick release behind the plate. Lieberthal still has sub-par plate discipline and hits too many lazy fly balls, but these are relatively minor deficiencies in the big picture.
1998: Just a season ago, it was assumed that Lieberthal was just keeping a spot warm for Bobby Estalella. Though the Phillies still love Estalella, the current catching job is Lieberthal's. There is no reason to believe that his defensive game won't continue to mature, but Lieberthal likely got a bit ahead of himself offensively in 1997. He will remain a .250 hitter, and a fairly substantial power decline wouldn't be surprising.
1997: Lieberthal exceeded the wildest expectations of Phils' brass in 1997. He emerged as a quiet team leader who was instrumental in the second half surge of the Phillies' young pitching staff, while earning the trust of veteran Curt Schilling with his game-calling.
1996: Lieberthal proved to be a functional but limited backup catcher, showing surprising extra-base power and a strong arm behind the plate. He lost the last third of the season to a knee injury.

	AB	R	HR	RBI	SB	BA
1995 Philadelphia	47	1	0	4	0	.255
1996 Philadelphia	166	21	7	23	0	.253
1997 Philadelphia	455	59	20	77	3	.246

LIEFER, JEFF - 3B - BL - b: 8/17/74
Scouting: Liefer was a first-round draft pick (1995) for his bat and has lived up to that prognosis. He has been described as a pure hitter, but hasn't shown more than potential thus far. He's a defensive liability who lacks a true position. Liefer has to make some great strides soon to keep his prospect label.
1998: Look for Liefer to advance to Triple-A for the first time. It may be a make-or-break season.
1997: Liefer had a mediocre year following a promotion to Double-A Birmingham. He hit 15 homers and drove in 71 runs, but batted just .238 and fanned 115 times in 474 at-bats in his first season above A-ball. He slumped over the second half of the year and continued to struggle in the field.
1996: Liefer's first pro season was split between two Class A venues with vastly different results. He showed power and hit for a high average for South Bend (.325-15-58) but was overmatched when playing for Prince William (.224-1-13). Liefer's 23 errors in 74 games at South Bend illustrate his poor fielding abilities.

LINIAK, COLE - 3B - BR - b: 8/23/76
The Red Sox are pushing him through the system fast, perhaps too fast. He started the year in A-ball, but earned a promotion to Double-A Trenton, where he hit .280, but with only two homers in 200 at-bats. He has a good glove and is considered Boston's third baseman of the future. He's not that big (6'1", 180 pounds), so the key will be if he develops any power. He's young enough that he has two to three years to do that.

LIRIANO, NELSON - 2B - BB - b: 6/3/64
Scouting: Liriano is in the final stages of his career and is used now as a pinch-hitter and utility infielder. He's better from the left side of the plate and defensively he's limited to second base because of diminished range effecting him at shortstop and a weak arm that won't allow him to play third base.
1998: He'll be 33 years old on opening day and this could be the end of the road for Liriano. He'll be a pinch-hitter/reserve second baseman if he's on a big-league roster.
1997: Liriano landed with the Dodgers after spending the previous season with the Pirates. He appeared in 76 games for Los Angeles throughout the year.
1996: Liriano was solid off the bench for the Bucs as he knocked 17 pinch-hits, three short of setting a new club record. He also started 34 games in the infield at second base, shortstop and third base.

	AB	R	HR	RBI	SB	BA
1995 Pittsburgh	259	29	5	38	2	.286
1996 Pittsburgh	217	23	3	30	2	.267
1997 Los Angeles	88	10	1	11	0	.227

LISTACH, PAT - SS - BB - b: 9/12/67
Scouting: Once an exciting player whose entire game revolved around his speed, Listach failed to develop complementary skills is now on the wrong side of the major league fringe since his speed has departed. The switch-hitter has toned down his once legendary wild swinging ways only slightly over the years, and has never developed an iota of extra-base power. His range at shortstop has deteriorated, and he has also tried his hand as a center fielder without much success.
1998: Listach will likely open the 1998 season on someone's Triple-A roster. He played fairly well in a brief trial at Triple-A Buffalo late in the 1997 season, so he could open there. The Indians prefer a veteran Triple-A club, and Listach can serve as injury insurance for the big club.
1997: Listach failed miserably after starting the season as the Astros' shortstop. They envisioned him as a number two hitter, but he wasn't patient or speedy enough to handle the demands of that role. He landed at Triple-A Buffalo in the Cleveland organization late in the season.
1996: It was a strange season. Listach showed flashes of his speedy youth, though he hit poorly as the Brewers' center fielder, and then was traded to the Yankees, only to be deemed damaged goods, and returned to the Brewers' chain.

	AB	R	HR	RBI	SB	BA
1995 Milwaukee	334	35	0	25	13	.219
1996 Milw-NY AL	317	51	1	33	25	.240
1997 Houston	132	13	0	6	4	.182

LITTLE, MARK - OF - BR - b: 7/11/72
Scouting: Little is a speedy outfielder with surprisingly good power for his size. He has usually been a leadoff hitter, and has generally been able to reach base often enough to justify that status. Little is a legitimate center fielder, and has an adequate arm. He's a hard worker who responds well to coaching.
1998: Little needs further development in Triple-A to work on hitting breaking pitches, and with continued development would be a useful extra outfielder in the majors.
1997: In his first season at Triple-A Oklahoma City, Little's on-base percentage declined, but in most other areas he made a successful transition, hitting .263 with 15 home runs and 21 steals.
1996: Little's first Double-A season saw him improve on his 1995 season in the Florida State League, and helped confirm his status as a major league prospect.

LIVINGSTONE, SCOTT - 3B/DH - BL - b: 7/15/65
Scouting: He's a capable lefthanded pinch hitter who hits line drives into the gaps, but rarely out of the park. Lacking power will probably keep Livingstone from finding everyday work and might keep him out of consideration from a lot of reserve jobs. As a lefty who generally hasn't struck out much, he will help someone.
1998: The Cardinals need lefthanded bats on the bench. Livingstone probably isn't their guy, considering he won't contribute much pop and can't run well. Don't look for him to play regularly, since he hasn't batted much against lefthanded pitchers for two years.
1997: He was damaged goods when the Cardinals acquired him from the Padres during the season, his arm injury limiting his work severely. With eight hits in 46 pinch at-bats, Livingstone didn't fulfill any of the club's needs.
1996: Livingstone's 19 pinch-hits led the league for the Padres and he batted .353 with runners in scoring position.

	AB	R	HR	RBI	SB	BA
1995 San Diego	196	26	5	32	2	.337
1996 San Diego	172	20	2	20	0	.297
1997 St. Louis	67	4	0	6	1	.164

LOBATON, JOSE - SS - BR - b: 3/29/74
1997 was Lobaton's first season at the Double-A level. He has some speed, but he hit only .194 with one home run and 15 RBI in 201 at-bats for Norwich last year. He also struck out 62 times, nearly on pace for 200 over the course of a full season. His 1993 Rookie League success is a faded memory now and Lobaton needs to improve dramatically in Double-A ball to have any chance of playing in the major leagues.

LOCKHART, KEITH - 2B/3B - BL - b: 11/10/64
Scouting: Lockhart's versatility bears witness to his ten years surviving as a minor-league player. He has learned to perform a myriad of useful tasks on a baseball field: he's a good contact hitter who will take a pitch, he knows how to hit behind runners, he runs the bases well even if he's only an average basestealing threat, he handles several infield positions competently and is an exceptional pinch-hitter. Lockhart is a fine reserve player but his relatively poor range afield make him a below-average regular. He lacks enough offensive muscle to overcome his defensive deficiencies, so he would be a bad choice for regular duty.
1998: Lockhart has proven his mettle as a valuable big-league reserve. It's a role that he accepts and he will again flourish in it. If forced into more regular action, Lockhart will be less helpful to his team.
1997: Statistically, Lockhart's 1997 campaign is a mirror image

for his previous two years in the majors. But, he showed remarkable ability to hit in clutch situations — note his exception RBI per at-bat rate — and he became a valuable lefty bat off the bench; Lockhart was a pinch-hitter in more than two-thirds of his appearances. The Braves' style of play kept him nailed to first base; he didn't attempt a stolen base all year after getting 20 the previous two years combined.
1996: Lockhart nearly won an All-Star berth for the Royals by hitting over .300 in the first half while being a sparkplug for the weak Kansas City offense. He fell on his face in the second half, though, eventually losing his full-time spot to Jose Offerman; Lockhart played well once returned to his accustomed bench role.

	AB	R	HR	RBI	SB	BA
1995 Kansas City	274	41	6	33	8	.321
1996 Kansas City	433	49	7	55	11	.273
1997 Atlanta	147	25	6	32	0	.279

LoDUCA, PAUL - C - BR - b: 4/12/72
LoDuca is an up-and-coming player in the eyes of the organization. He's coming off an excellent season at Double-A San Antonio, during which he distinguished himself with his ability to throw out baserunners. LoDuca hasn't shown a lot of power yet, but he's demonstrated that he's competent with the bat. He began his career as a utility player, but has stepped up as a catcher and may soon be in a position to win a job in the majors as a backup.

LOFTON, KENNY - OF - BL - b: 5/31/67
Scouting: Lofton is still fast, a good leadoff hitter and a fine defensive outfielder, but at age 31 there are concerns that he is starting to slow. At his peak, he was good for 60 extra-base hits per year and 50-70 steals with an 80% success rate. In 1997 he had 31 extra-base hits and 27 steals with only a 57% success rate. Another concern was a big increase in his strikeout rate. He can still help most teams, but he is long way from his peak in 1994.
1998: Lofton ended the 1997 season as a free agent, and his outlook depends upon where he signs. If he goes to a conservative baserunning team he's unlikely to reach 50 steals again. He could bounce back nicely on astroturf, or back in the American League, where pitchers do not hold runners as well as in the National League. At his age, he may be good for a year or two, but the last three years of the long-term deal he expected to get will be a major gamble.
1997: At the plate, Lofton easily adjusted to the National League after his spring training trade to the Braves. However, he struggled on the basepaths as his stolen base totals and success rate plummeted from his American League performance. A pulled groin in late-June sidelined him for over a month, and gave Andruw Jones an opportunity to show that he was a viable alternative to Lofton for 1998.
1996: Lofton turned in a good season for the Indians, leading the American League in steals and setting a career high in home runs. After the Albert Belle defection, the Indians chose to trade Lofton rather than risk losing him following the 1997 season.

	AB	R	HR	RBI	SB	BA
1995 Cleveland	481	93	7	53	54	.310
1996 Cleveland	662	132	14	67	75	.317
1997 Atlanta	493	90	5	48	27	.333

LOMBARD, GEORGE - OF - BL - b: 9/14/75
Lombard is a stocky, powerfully built athlete with great quickness. He also is a strong, disciplined hitter. His below-average arm makes him a left fielder. He's a lot like the Cardinals Ray Lankford, but he still has to put some time in the minors after hitting .264 with 14 homers in A-ball in '97. Look for him in the majors in a couple of years.

LONG, R.D. - SS - BB - b: 4/2/71
Long spent most of the 1997 season at Double-A Norwich, a step down from 1996 when he spent most of the year at the Triple-A level. He hit .281 with two homers, 17 RBI, five steals and a .375 OBP in 89 at-bats at Norwich last year. His 49 at-bats for Triple-A Columbus were less successful; he hit only .184 with nine times as many strikeouts as walks. Long seems comfortable at Double-A, but struggles at higher levels.

LONG, RYAN - 3B - BR - b: 2/3/73
Scouting: The Royals like Long's power potential, but he has to cut down on the strikeouts before he can be considered a true prospect; he has consistently struck out three or four times more often than drawing walks throughout his seven-year pro career. Long is only a fair outfielder who is confined to left field. His upper-cut swing will be exploited by major league pitchers.
1998: Long could challenge for a reserve outfield role in the majors, but is more likely to spend the year in Triple-A again. He needs to shorten his stroke a little to cut down on the whiffs.
1997: Long spent the whole year at Triple-A Omaha, hitting .265 with 19 homers and 56 RBI. Once again he had a poor strikeout-to-walk ratio, fanning 98 times with just 18 walks.
1996: In Long's second year at Double-A Wichita, he added fifty points to his batting average and quadrupled his homer output, but continued to strikeout frequently; his totals: .283 batting average, 20 homers, 78 RBI, 17 walks, 71 strikeouts.

LONG, TERRENCE - OF - BR - b: 2/29/76
In his first year at the higher Class A level, Long hit .251 with eight homers, 61 RBI and 24 steals for St. Lucie on the Mets' farm. He is still too aggressive at the plate. Long will advance as he learns how to put the ball in play more consistently and leg out base hits. He has earned a 1998 start at the Double-A level.

LOPEZ, JAVIER - C - BR - b: 1/5/70
Scouting: Lopez has improved every year, and he is now competing with Todd Hundley and Charles Johnson to be the league's second best catcher. He is a better hitter than Johnson and a better catcher than Hundley, and he has as much raw power as anyone on the Braves. He will chase bad pitches; his marginal strikezone judgment is his only weakness. Bobby Cox is careful to limit his playing time, so Lopez is unlikely to post a monster season to gain full recognition for his ability.
1998: Lopez will continue to be Atlanta's primary catcher, and one has to wonder why a pitcher who suffers from poor run support like Greg Maddux wouldn't want him in the lineup. Another 130 games of 20+ homers with a good average is a reasonable expectation from Lopez in 1998.
1997: Lopez essentially matched his 1996 production, but did it in 75 fewer at-bats. He missed time due to a fractured thumb, but played well most of the season. He was second on the Braves in home runs despite playing in only 123 games.
1996: Lopez set career highs in home runs,, RBI, and walks, but declined from 1995 on a per at-bat basis. His most important

improvement was on defensive, where he approached the league average in throwing out runners.

	AB	R	HR	RBI	SB	BA
1995 Atlanta	333	37	14	51	0	.315
1996 Atlanta	489	56	23	69	1	.282
1997 Atlanta	414	52	23	68	1	.295

LOPEZ, LUIS - 2B - BB - b: 9/4/70

Scouting: Watch Lopez throw and you may or may not be particularly impressed. His arm is above major league, though short of Shawon Dunston's. But understand that Lopez underwent reconstructive surgery on his right elbow in spring, 1995; given that consideration, his throwing is truly remarkable. The rest of his defensive game is solid, too, and while Lopez isn't outstanding with a bat in his hand, he is a useful offensive player, particularly in a reserve role and because he bats lefthanded. He doesn't make contact as often as he should, but playing irregularly can lead to strikeouts. His base-stealing acumen is questionable.
1998: Lopez showed enough with the Mets last summer that any club would be happy with him as their primary utility infielder. He showed no lingering effects from surgery and demonstrated he has value as a quasi-regular. A lefthanded-hitting shortstop with reliable hands and a good arm always will find work.
1997: Lopez proved to be an able understudy after the injury to Rey Ordonez prompted the Mets to promote him from Triple-A. He started 21 games at shortstop, nine at second base and one at third and played each position adequately and shortstop well enough that Ordonez' absence was less damaging. Lopez batted .235 in 51 at-bats against lefthanded pitching and .283 in 127 at-bats against righthanded pitching. He struck out too much — 42 times in the majors.
1998: Once he overcame his elbow problem, he began the season in rehab. Lopez played reliably for the Padres; he started 20 games at shortstop and 11 at second base. His season was interrupted by a left shoulder strain. His offensive production was down; Lopez batted .180 with 11 RBI in 63 games.

	AB	R	HR	RBI	SB	BA
1995 San Diego	Did Not Play - Injured					
1996 San Diego	139	10	2	11	0	.180
1997 New York NL	178	19	1	19	2	.270

LOPEZ, LUIS - OF - BR - b: 9/1/64

Former PCL batting champion Lopez never made it as a major leaguer, but he found success in Japan. As cleanup hitter for the Hiroshima Carp, Lopez hit .315 with 22 homers and 99 RBI in 1996 and .319 with 23 home runs and 92 RBI last year. He is an aggressive free-swinger, and arguably the best first baseman in Japan.

LOPEZ, MENDY - 3B - BR - b: 10/15/74

Often described as the Royals' third baseman of the future, Lopez had a disappointing season last year after switching to shortstop and playing mostly at Double-A Wichita. He doesn't have much power and has seen his high batting average in the low minors slip significantly in the higher minors. His hitting ability fits better as a shortstop, so the position switch might help him reach the majors more easily, but he'll have a hard time making the adjustment with the glove; he made 20 errors in 101 games at shortstop last year.

LOPEZ, MICKEY - 2B - BB - b: 11/17/73

Lopez continued his quick rise through the Brewers system with a solid season at Double-A El Paso in 1997. A 13th-round draft pick in 1995, Lopez displayed a line-drive stroke from both sides of the plate and rarely struck out. Lopez is solid defensively and can steal bases with his above-average speed. He looks to be a top of the order candidate for the Brew Crew around 1999.

LORETTA, MARK - SS - BR - b: 8/14/71

Scouting: Loretta could start for several major league clubs, but has been a utilityman with the Brewers. He does not have great speed, but still covers ground at shortstop or second base. He also can play third or first base, and even the outfield. Loretta has developed into a solid hitter with clutch-hitting capability.
1998: The Brewers really wanted to protect Loretta, but he seemed to be caught in a numbers game in the infield. If he returns, he likely will be a utilityman again in Milwaukee. Getting more regular play is a possibility due to expansion, but Loretta would be among the weak regulars in the majors.
1997: Loretta established himself as a valuable utility infielder who could start on several teams. He hit for a respectable average and showed some power at times. Loretta played well while starting at second base during the injury absence of Fernando Vina.
1996: Loretta started the season at Triple-A New Orleans, but was called up and hit well in 73 games. He hit .467 with two out and runners in scoring position.

	AB	R	HR	RBI	SB	BA
1995 Milwaukee	50	13	1	3	1	.260
1996 Milwaukee	154	20	1	13	2	.279
1997 Milwaukee	418	56	5	47	5	.287

LOTT, BILLY - OF - BR - b: 8/16/70

The Pirates picked up Lott for their Triple-A Calgary farm club last season after he was released by Montreal out of Triple-A Ottawa. Lott, who had spent his first eight seasons in the Los Angeles farm system, put up decent power numbers in a half-season at Calgary, no doubt aided by the thin western Alberta air. He turns 28 in August but has some power and speed. He looks like he might be a late bloomer.

LOVULLO, TOREY - 2B - BB - b: 7/25/65

Lovullo has had six brief major league trials which, when combined, are about the equivalent of a full major league season. He has never lived up to the potential which prompted Sparky Anderson to declare him a future star. Lovullo rarely swings at bad pitches, but is a low-average hitter with only moderate power. He's experienced at all positions except pitcher and catcher but isn't an outstanding defensive player anywhere. He's Triple-A roster filler at this point in his career.

LOWELL, MIKE - 3B - BR - b: 2/24/74

With Wade Boggs' option not being picked up and the Yankees willing to let go of Charlie Hayes, observers began to focus on Lowell as having an opportunity to show if his minor-league power can carry over into the big leagues and land him the third base job. Between Triple-A Columbus and Double-A Norwich last year, Lowell hit 30 homers and drove in 92 runs. He still needs further work in the field.

LOWERY, TERRELL - OF - BR - b: 10/25/70
Scouting: Lowery, a former honorable mention All-American basketball player at Loyola Marymount, has been plagued with injuries throughout his minor-league career. He missed the entire 1992 season and most of the 1995 season with injuries, which have hurt his development. Lowery stole a lot of bases in the low minors early in his career, but has given up some speed and gotten more power as he has gotten older and more experienced.
1998: If Lowery were three or four years younger, or hadn't lost those seasons because of injuries, his big-league future would be a lot brighter. However, he's 27 years old and his entire major league experience consists of the 14 at-bats he got at the end of last season with the Cubs, and that makes his situation a lot more unclear. He's too old to be a star, but he'll be a decent fourth or fifth outfielder if given the chance.
1997: Lowery easily had the best season of his career, hitting above .300 for the first time and easily surpassing his single-season mark in homers. He played so well that he earned a nine-game trial with the Cubs late in the year, his major league debut.
1996: Lowery split time between Double-A and Triple-A in the Rangers' farm system. He had a decent year — much better at Double-A — but didn't do anything to indicate that he was ready to take a big step forward. He did stay injury free, which was a victory of sorts.

LUCCA, LOU - 3B - BR - b: 10/13/70
This Marlins' minor-league lifer has progressed glacially through the ranks in his six-year pro career, displaying a consistent line-drive bat with occasional power plus excellent defensive reactions at third base. However, his plate discipline has inexplicably disappeared — he had a 248-to-224 strikeout-to-walk ratio through 1995, but a 118-to-33 ratio since. Lucca is quite slow afoot, and his bat speed is likely insufficient for him to dent major league pitching. He will likely serve as a Triple-A insurance policy for someone in 1998 — though not likely for the Marlins, who will have Josh Booty at Charlotte.

LUKACHYK, ROB - OF - BL - b: 7/24/68
Lukachyk has spent 11 seasons in professional baseball, bouncing around five different organizations. He got his only two major league at-bats with Montreal in 1996 and failed to get a hit. Those figure to be his final lifetime stats as he had a non-descript season with the Expos' Triple-A Ottawa farm club last year.

LUKE, MATT - OF - BL - b: 2/26/71
Luke's biggest strength throughout his minor-league career has been high power, but 1997 was a severe disappointment; Luke hit only .228 with a sub-.300 on-base percentage. He also seemed to have lost his power potential, hitting only eight home runs in 337 at-bats. Age is becoming a factor in his career outlook.

LUULOA, KEITH - 2B - BR - b: 12/24/74
Luuloa caught the Angels' eye two years ago with an excellent season at Double-A Midland and they've kept watch on him ever since. He's played mostly second base, but projects more as a utility type. He's learning to make more contact, which will help him advance and solidify his status as a hot prospect.

LUZINSKI, RYAN - C - BR - b: 8/22/73
Greg's son Ryan hasn't inherited his father's power-hitting genes. Hitting around the Mendoza line in Triple-A without any power won't get him promoted to the majors. His record shows that he's not much of a prospect, and he will have to show something soon. The Orioles got him from the Dodgers in a trade, and they think highly of him, too; he was added to their 40-man roster last year.

MAAS, KEVIN - DH/1B - BL - b: 1/20/65
Maas first gained notoriety in his 1990 major league debut with the Yankees when he bashed 21 homers in just 254 at-bats. After a few years in the majors, Maas' one-dimensional play relegated him to the minors. He has since become a Triple-A fixture, playing for four different organizations, most recently at New Orleans (Astros) where he batted .219 with seven home runs. Maas is a defensive liability and an all-or-nothing power swinger at the plate. Expansion in 1998 gives Maas a dim hope to return to the majors.

MABRY, JOHN - OF - BL - b: 10/17/70
Scouting: His baseball lot in life seems clear now after three big-league seasons. Mabry is likely to hit .300, though without much power and not nearly as well in the clutch. He won't run well. He'll generally swing at the first pitch and has his most trouble with breaking pitches, while he's fond of high strikes. He will work hard, take a business-like approach to hitting and playing whatever position he's asked to play — and he'll force his way into a lineup when it seems someone better is around.
1998: With his old positions of right field and first base occupied by others with more impressive talent, Mabry probably will contend for a spot on the team as a third baseman with capabilities of playing elsewhere. He worked on his new position at the instructional league following the regular season and took to it well, with the arm that made him a superb right fielder and good reflexes that served him well at first base. Mabry could end up as the team's regular at third.
1997: It was an unsettled year for Mabry, who played considerably in the outfield and first base, then ended the season on the disabled list because of a broken jaw. He finished with a .284 batting average, one of the worst in his seven-year pro career, and drove in only 36 runs, just one after mid-July.
1996: Playing first base for a full season for the first time in his life, Mabry flirted with the .300 mark and prompted projections that he some day would lead the league in batting. His 13 homers also made observers wonder if he might hit 25 in a future season.

	AB	R	HR	RBI	SB	BA
1995 St. Louis	388	35	5	41	0	.307
1996 St. Louis	543	63	13	74	3	.297
1997 St. Louis	388	40	5	36	0	.284

MACFARLANE, MIKE - C - BR - b: 4/12/64
Scouting: One of the most extreme pull hitters in the game, Macfarlane crowds the plate and tries to smack everything deep down the left field line. It results in decent extra-base power, a lot of strikeouts, a low batting average — and a lot of HBPs. Macfarlane features good plate blocking and pitch blocking skills, throws well and calls a good game; pitchers ask for him specifically and he's a clubhouse leader.
1998: Macfarlane may be relegated to a reserve role in the majors. He has the ability to play full time, but is no longer among the better hitting catchers. His defense has improved in recent years, so a second-catcher job could be a good fit.
1997: An abdominal strain and a strained right shoulder helped

Macfarlane get off to a dreadful start. When he was finally healthy again, new manager Tony Muser had given the regular catching chores to youngster Mike Sweeney. Macfarlane used a torrid finish to reach meager totals in his worst full season in the majors.

1996: Macfarlane returned to Kansas City after a one-year hiatus to Boston and posted some of his best all-around hitting totals while playing solid defense behind the plate. It was one of his best major league seasons.

	AB	R	HR	RBI	SB	BA
1995 Boston	364	45	15	51	2	.225
1996 Kansas City	379	58	19	54	3	.274
1997 Kansas City	257	34	8	35	0	.237

MACHADO, ROBERT - C - BR - b: 6/3/73

Scouting: Machado features above-average defensive skills behind the plate. Standing at the plate, though, Machado is less effective. He has only passable power and has only recently hit for a good batting average while striking out too frequently at higher minor-league levels. His skills give him a backup catcher look.

1998: Machado has an excellent chance to be in the majors as a backup catcher solely because he can catch and throw. The departure of Ron Karkovice opens an opportunity on the White Sox bench.

1997: Machado split catching duties at Triple-A Nashville and hit for an unusually good average, .269, with moderate power, but continued to have an undisciplined batting eye; he walked just 12 times against 61 strikeouts.

1996: Machado dominated Southern League baserunners, nailing 38 of 67 runners who tried to steal against him — a league best 56.7%. He hit just .239 in his first year above A-ball, a career-low mark. Machado earned his first major league recall and went 4-for-6 in two brief big-league stints.

MACK, SHANE - OF - BR - b: 12/7/63

Scouting: Mack is still a good contact hitter, capable of hitting .300 if he played every day, but without a lot of power or walks. He has a damaged throwing arm, though, and is incapable of playing every day, especially in center field, where the Red Sox hoped he would be.

1998: Mack has a year left on his Boston contract, but does not seem to be in the Red Sox plans and will almost certainly end up somewhere else. His full-time playing days appear over, but he will probably be a quality bat off some team's bench.

1997: Mack was buried in Boston after being signed out of Japan to be the Red Sox everyday center fielder. A right shoulder injury, which supposedly had healed, had not, and he was considered all but unable to play the outfield by manager Jimy Williams. When he played he hit well. In the final months, he was seldom even called on to pinch-hit.

1996: Mack hit .293 with 22 homers in Japan, his second straight strong season there.

	AB	R	HR	RBI	SB	BA
1997 Boston	130	13	3	17	2	.315

MADDOX, GARRY - OF - BL - b: 10/24/74

Maddox is the son of the legendary defensive whiz by the same name. He was sidelined in 1996 with a shoulder injury but answered all questions in 1997 by hitting .306 with 12 triples and 25 stolen bases for Class A High Desert. He has great range, and his arm is improving.

MAGADAN, DAVE - 3B/1B - BL - b: 9/30/62

Scouting: A disciplined hitter, with an excellent eye, Magadan uses the entire field to hit and brings consistent results. He is a solid .300 hitter, but has little power. He hits righthanders (.320) well, but not so lefthanders (.231). Magadan can play either corner spot, but is adequate at each, at best. But he is smart, makes few mistakes, and that makes up for a lot.

1998: Magadan adds both a good knowledge of the game and a veteran perspective, so keeping him on a team which will be even younger than the 1997 team makes him a valuable commodity. He hits well off the bench, and plays his role as a part-timer well. That role will continue.

1997: Spelling Giambi, McGwire, and Brosius at corner infield spots, Magadan did an excellent job for Oakland. His high on-base percentage made him a valuable commodity as both a pinch-hitter and periodic starter.

1996: Though generally a solid hitter against righthanders, Magadan struggled through his 169 at-bats with Chicago.

	AB	R	HR	RBI	SB	BA
1995 Houston	348	44	2	51	2	.313
1996 Chicago NL	169	23	3	17	0	.254
1997 Oakland	271	38	4	30	1	.303

MAGDALENO, RICKY - SS - BR - b: 7/6/74

Magdaleno improved impressively in 1997, which was his third season at Double-A. That might be horrible news for some, but Magdaleno is only 23 years old. He cut down on his swing a little, which decreased his home run totals, but increased his average. However, it wasn't enough of an improvement to move him up the ladder in the Reds organization. Right now, he's behind several veterans and emerging youngsters. Expansion will help him advance a little, but he's still not likely to see action in Cincinnati.

MAGEE, DANNY - 3B - BR - b: 11/25/74

Scouts love Magee's arm and his versatility as a hitter. He hits for average and power, has some speed and a good glove, too. The only concern may be his propensity for striking out, although Magee reduced his whiffs in 1996. In his second season at Durham, he hit .299-12-40 with 17 steals after moving to third base from shortstop. Magee may have a better chance back at shortstop, though, because third base is already well stocked with Chipper Jones, Bobby Smith and Wes Helms in front of him in the Braves' system. MaGee started 1997 at Double-A Greenville but played only seven games during the season.

MAGEE, WENDELL - OF - BR - b: 8/3/72

Scouting: A former high school and collegiate football star, Magee has above-average speed and physical tools, and is a powerfully built player. But his speed hasn't yet let him steal bases, just as his strength hasn't led to power hitting, yet. Magee is a wild swinger who doesn't know how to work counts, so he rarely sees a fastball over the plate. He's a hard-nosed player who plays with enthusiasm, but his late start in the game is going to limit his upside potential.

1998: The acquisition of Midre Cummings will put a dent in Magee's chance for extended major league play in Philadelphia. He'd be hard-pressed to earn a bench job out of spring training, but expansion may increase his role.

1997: Magee was handed the center field job in spring training, and was given every opportunity to hold it. He simply couldn't handle breaking pitches in the majors. His defense, excellent at

first, deteriorated near the end. He was not recalled in September, underscoring his fall in the club's eyes.
1996: Magee rifled through the upper half of the Phillies' system, combining slightly above-average power (16 homers) and speed (13 steals) with aggressive center field play. The Phillies gave him a full month and a half to lay claim to the major league job, but he was overmatched at the plate, though effective in the field.

	AB	R	HR	RBI	SB	BA
1996 Philadelphia	142	9	2	14	0	.204
1997 Philadelphia	115	7	1	9	1	.200

MAHALIK, JOHN - 2B - BR - b: 7/28/71
Mahalik played backup second base at Double-A Binghamton last year. His .219 batting average demonstrates that, without offensive improvement, he has reached his highest level. Mahalik has never hit well at any level, so that improvement isn't likely.

MAHONEY, MIKE - C - BR - b: 3/22/72
He's not a great hitter but good defensive ability may be enough to get Mahoney some time as a major league backstop in the future. A 40th-round draft pick out of Creighton University in 1995, Mahoney threw out 45 percent of the runners that tested him at Class A Durham in 1996. He has the ability to handle a pitching staff and with his arm could eventually be a second catcher in the big leagues.

MAKAREWICZ, SCOTT - C - BR - b: 3/1/67
The former Astro farmhand played with Double-A Jacksonville in 1996, then advanced to Triple-A Toledo last year. He's an outstanding defensive catcher with some pop. He also calls an excellent game, but his defense is his most redeeming quality. Makarewicz batted .235 in 100 games at Toledo. His combination of poor plate discipline, only moderate power, below-average contact hitting, and good defensive skills give Makarewicz a chance for major league play as a reserve catcher.

MALAVE, JOSE - OF - BR - b: 5/31/71
Scouting: Malave has power and has improved as a hitter in terms of going with the pitch. However, as a player who needs to be known for his bat, his bat-speed is slow and he has trouble turning on inside pitches. He has become a hard worker and made an effort to be at least a competent fielder in left field, right field, and at first base, but is not good anywhere.
1998: Malave has earned a look as a major league platoon outfielder, if not in Boston, then somewhere else. But he would probably disappoint if given a full-time job.
1997: After being waived off the 40-man roster, Malave responded by maturing. He stopped trying to pull every pitch and instead became a solid hitter to all fields at the Triple-A level. He also improved his conditioning habits, a problem in the past. After being added to the roster and called up to the majors in August, he barely played.
1996: Malave's promising career took a step back. Injuries limited his Triple-A at-bats and caused him to press at the plate in order to try to earn a quick promotion. When he was promoted to the majors, he proved an easy out, and quickly found himself on the end of the bench, which did not help his development.

MALLOY, MARTY - 2B - BL - b: 7/6/72
Malloy is a steady, hard-working second baseman. But he lacks size and strength. His best bet is to someday earn part of a platoon role in the majors, batting from the left side. He doesn't make a great utilityman off the bench because of his lack of raw tools. Don't be surprised if he spends a lot of years at the Triple-A level.

MANESS, DWIGHT - OF - BR - b: 4/3/74
In his second try at Double-A Binghamton, Maness ended up hitting only .189. He had won a promotion by hitting .296 after a step back down to higher Class A St. Lucie. He is still young enough to get another chance and advance if he can show more patience to make contact and use his speed to leg out some hits.

MANTO, JEFF - 3B/1B - BR - b: 8/23/64
Manto has been one of the most prolific minor-league hitters of his generation. He's a fairly patient hitter with enough bat speed to turn around any Triple-A fastball. However, over six separate major league trials, he has conclusively proven that he cannot consistently do the same against major league heaters. Manto has little footspeed, but is a technically sound fielder who gives an honest effort at all infield positions, catcher and left field. His versatility makes him a good bench player, in the majors or in the minors.

	AB	R	HR	RBI	SB	BA
1995 Baltimore	254	31	17	38	0	.256
1996 Boston	102	15	3	10	0	.196
1997 Cleveland	30	3	2	7	0	.267

MANWARING, KIRT - C - BR - b: 7/15/65
Scouting: The stocky Manwaring is so comfortable when it comes to receiving, blocking balls and the plate, it is almost as if he was raised around dirt. So desperate were the Rockies for a catcher with pitch-handling and defensive skills they gave him a two-year, $4.3-million contract prior to 1997. His bat does not help him earn his paychecks, though. Despite playing half his games in baseball's best hitter's park, Manwaring had just 11 extra-base hits all season. His arm got stronger as the season went along, though his throws have lot zip in recent years; he is accurate.
1998: Manwaring may have to settle for a platoon role. Because he's a righthanded hitter, that means far less playing time. He started just 95 games in 1997 — or about 30 fewer than expected when he signed. In the final six weeks of the season, lefthanded hitting catcher Jeff Reed received the bulk of the playing time.
1997: Though he upgraded the team's catching position on defense, his bat was too much of a liability and overall he was a disappointment. He threw out 23.8 percent of would-be basestealers, respectable considering the staff as a whole isn't great at holding runners. Few catchers are more adept at blocking pitches in the dirt. Even the worst major-league hitters should be able to hit at least .250 while playing home games at Coors Field, so Manwaring's mark should speak volumes about his hitting ability.
1996: It was the toughest year in his professional career. First a hand injury limited him to just 86 games. Then, after spending his entire ten-year professional career with the San Francisco Giants, he was traded to Houston. Manwaring threw well for both teams — his 45 percent success rate was second only to Florida's Charles Johnson in the National League — but Manwaring didn't hit for either team.

	AB	R	HR	RBI	SB	BA
1995 San Francisco	379	21	4	36	1	.251
1996 Houston	227	14	1	18	0	.229
1997 Colorado	337	22	1	27	1	.226

MARINE, DEL - C - BR - b: 10/18/71

Marine has decent pop in his bat, but his defense needs a lot of work. He doesn't move around behind the plate well and his high crouch sometimes loses strikes for his pitchers. He hit 12 homers with 43 RBI and drew a good number of walks for Double-A Jacksonville last year, but hit only .238 and he runs like a catcher. Marine is not a major league prospect.

MARQUEZ, JESUS - OF - BL - b: 3/12/73

Marquez's swing looks sweet but he isn't patient at the plate. He doesn't always run out grounders and has been tagged with the "lazy" moniker. He has a pretty good glove and has hit for a good average (.267 at Double-A Jacksonville last year). He has good pop when he pulls the ball (12 in 1997), but not to the opposite field. He was productive in A-ball, but was a bit old for the league.

MARRERO, ELIESER - C - BR - b: 11/17/73

Scouting: Arguably the best catching prospect produced by the Cardinals since Ted Simmons, Marrero is a full package. He hits for power, can run better than average — not just for a catcher, but for any player — and is a supremely talented defensive catcher. His free-swinging, hacking approach will need some time to be refined on the big-league level. The Cardinals can patiently wait for that, since he already frightens opponents into not running against him. His only defensive weakness seems to be calling a game, though he has improved immensely.
1998: Marrero should contend for the regular job as the Cardinals' catcher, though Tony LaRussa seems hesitant in handing it to him while wondering if a team can win it all with a rookie catcher. At worst, Marrero will share duties early because he's ready for the big leagues.
1997: The Cards' only doubts about Marrero concerned how quickly he would adjust to hitting at the Triple-A level. No problem, since he was the best batsman on his club. He had 20 homers, most of them long blasts to left field — not taking advantage of a short right field fence. He flashed his defensive abilities and occasionally powerful bat while spending September in the big leagues.
1996: After struggling briefly adapting to Double-A pitching, Marrero proved himself capable offensively with 19 homers and an RBI every other game. Though using a somewhat unorthodox throwing style, he gunned down 43 percent of the runners who tried to steal against him and the Cardinals decided not to change anything about his defensive approach.

	AB	R	HR	RBI	SB	BA
1997 St. Louis	45	4	2	7	4	.244

MARRERO, ORESTE - 1B - BL - b: 10/31/69

A good lefthanded hitter with power, Marrero still has the Dodgers remembering how he was called up and help the m win some games in the second half of 1996. He followed that with a decent year at Triple-A Albuquerque, but some club officials are wondering why he hasn't yet taken the final step, because the potential's there. At age 28, Marrero is helped by his experience and willingness to be a role player, but, on the other hand, time may soon run out on his opportunity to return to the bigs.

MARTIN, AL - OF - BL - b: 11/24/67

Scouting: Martin seemingly has the tools to be a star player in the major leagues: power, speed and hustle. However, he swings at too many bad pitches and is not consistent. Furthermore, he is a defensive liability in left field.
1998: While the Pirates were jettisoning almost everyone during the final four months of 1996, they were re-signing Martin to a two-year contract extension and then tacking on another year midway through last season. He is the guy they are rebuilding around, for better or worse, and figures to again bat third and start in left field. He is better than he showed last year but the jury is out on whether he can repeat his stellar 1996 numbers.
1997: Martin was on the disabled list for five weeks in the first half of the season with a sprained right hand and never fully regained his batting stroke until September. Though he did heat up down the stretch, a torn stomach muscle sidelined him during the last week of the season as the Pirates' remarkable run at Houston in the National League Central fell short.
1996: Martin was one of the most underrated players in the National League as he put up career-best power and speed numbers while hitting from the second spot in the batting order. If the Pirates wouldn't have finished last in the Central, he might have garnered a few points in the MVP voting.

	AB	R	HR	RBI	SB	BA
1995 Pittsburgh	439	70	13	41	20	.282
1996 Pittsburgh	630	101	18	72	38	.300
1997 Pittsburgh	423	64	13	59	23	.291

MARTIN, CHRIS - SS/2B - BR - b: 1/25/68

A veteran of eight minor-league seasons, Martin had to play at St. Petersburg in 1997 as the Devil Rays did not have any higher affiliates. But Martin played just like he had at the Triple-A level from 1994 to 1996. His nine home runs in what is regarded as a pitching-oriented league was a testament to this experience. Martin will get an invitation to spring training with a shot at being the team's starting shortstop or an infielder who frequently comes off the bench.

MARTIN, JIM - OF - BL - b: 12/10/70

A well-traveled journeyman, Martin moved from Triple-A on the Mets' farm to Double-A on the Astros' farm in 1997. Overall it was a disappointing season. Martin is no closer to the majors now than he was a year ago.

MARTIN, NORBERTO - 2B/SS - BR - b: 12/10/66

Scouting: Martin is a good fastball hitter with little power who will swing at almost anything, making contact and spraying the ball around. He has average defensive ability at second base and can also play shortstop, but is not among the best at that spot. Martin always plays the game with a great deal of enthusiasm.
1998: Ozzie Guillen is expected to go elsewhere and Martin has the inside track for the shortstop job. Some question if Martin is really ready for a regular role, though; this may be a case of a popular utility player being forced into a starting role for which he is unprepared.
1997: A personal favorite of former Sox manager Terry Bevington, Martin had a decent season as the club's primary reserve infielder. Bevington thought so highly of Martin's abilities that he occasionally used him in a DH role. His defense was passable.
1996: Despite missing two months with a fractured jaw suffered on a foul tip while trying to bunt, Martin had the best season of his career hitting for an unusually high average and reaching

double-digits in stolen bases.

	AB	R	HR	RBI	SB	BA
1995 Chicago AL	160	17	2	17	5	.269
1996 Chicago AL	140	30	1	14	10	.350
1997 Chicago AL	213	24	2	27	1	.300

MARTINEZ, DAVE - OF - BL - b: 9/26/64

Scouting: An under-appreciated, versatile ballplayer with multiple skills, Martinez is a hard worker who does all the "little" things well. An outfielder by trade, Martinez has become a superior defensive first baseman; he's still above average in right field although his once fine center field skills have diminished in recent years. Martinez is a smart baserunner who appreciates the value of plate discipline; he'll take a walk or work the count to get a good pitch to drive.

1998: Martinez has found a niche as a fourth outfielder and reserve first baseman; he works his way into the lineup more frequently than other major league reserves and should continue in that role. His hitting and fielding skills are showing no signs of decline.

1997: In his twelfth season in the big leagues, Martinez had another solid season as the White Sox fourth outfielder and occasional first baseman. He hit for moderate power, got on base and ran the bases well; his defense in right field and at first base was first rate. He was one of the best all-purpose players in the game last year.

1996: Martinez had a terrific year, hitting for a high average, adding power and stealing bases, too. He displayed above-average range afield as an extremely versatile and valuable player.

	AB	R	HR	RBI	SB	BA
1995 Chicago AL	303	49	5	37	8	.307
1996 Chicago AL	440	85	10	53	15	.318
1997 Chicago AL	504	78	12	55	12	.286

MARTINEZ, DOMINGO - 1B - BR - b: 8/4/67

Mr. International, Martinez has played in Mexico and Japan as well as with the Blue Jays, Cardinals, White Sox and Orioles' organizations. Last year, he was the hitting star of the Seibu Lions (.305 with 31 homers and 108 RBI).

MARTINEZ, EDDY - SS - BR - b: 10/23/77

Martinez is a young shortstop in the Orioles system. He's from the shortstop factory of San Pedro de Macoris in the Dominican Republic. He played in Class A, Double-A, and Triple-A last year, but he didn't hit much. It's significant that he was in Triple-A at age 19 as one of the youngest players at that level last year. He's an excellent defensive player with good range. Martinez is young and still learning how to hit. He can be in the majors quickly when he matures and his hitting comes around.

MARTINEZ, EDGAR - 1B - BR - b: 1/2/63

Scouting: The latest incarnation of Hal McRae, Martinez is a fearsome hitter with long-ball power who has become the definition of the DH. His days of playing third base or even first base regularly are long gone, but he hits everything; Martinez is the only American League righthanded hitter in 50 years to win two batting titles (1992, 1995).

1998: Expect another typical season from Martinez, including a high batting average, 40-50 doubles, 25-30 homers and more than 100 RBI. In order to stay healthy, Martinez is unlikely to play in the field more than a handful of games.

1997: Hitting cleanup in a loaded batting order, Martinez had his usual success. Even when Russ Davis went down at third base, the Mariners resisted the temptation to play Martinez in the field.

1996: Martinez suffered four fractured ribs while playing third base when he collided with catcher John Marzano on an infield pop-up, but despite missing three weeks he still had 52 doubles for the second straight year.

	AB	R	HR	RBI	SB	BA
1995 Seattle	511	121	29	113	4	.356
1996 Seattle	499	121	26	103	3	.327
1997 Seattle	542	104	28	108	2	.330

MARTINEZ, FELIX - SS - BB - b: 5/18/74

Scouting: Martinez is a slick fielder who has more trouble with the routine play than he does going deep into the hole or making a throw on the run; he has an outstanding arm. At the plate he is a low-average, high-speed hitter who often has trouble making contact, but he does have good speed and could steal some bases in the majors. Martinez has a hot temper which has frequently earned him some suspensions in the minors.

1998: Martinez has an outside shot to be the Royals' opening day shortstop. He's not ready yet, but may be forced into regular duty if no one else is available. He should spend another year in Triple-A.

1997: Martinez got his first opportunity in the majors despite making 36 errors in 112 games for Triple-A Omaha. He hit .254 with only a .313 on-base percentage, then got a trial at shortstop in the bigs as the Royals shifted Jay Bell to third base. He was the same player in Kansas City that he has been in the high minors.

1996: In a season spent entirely at Omaha, Martinez hit just .235 with 79 strikeouts in 395 at-bats and he made a ton of errors, too, while his stolen base total fell from 44 at Double-A the year before to just 18. It was a disappointing year, but Martinez remained on most prospect lists nonetheless.

MARTINEZ, GABBY - SS - BR - b: 1/7/74

Martinez gave up switch-hitting to bat righthanded, and the move paid off with the type of year that had some observers thinking Martinez could help the Yankees at second base — and soon. In 77 games at Double-A Norwich, Martinez batted .321 with six homers and 54 RBI. He was bothered by a leg injury which kept him out of the Eastern League playoffs.

MARTINEZ, GREG, OF - BB - b: 1/27/72

In his fifth professional season, Martinez spent the year at Double-A El Paso and was a terror on the basepaths, with a team-high 39 steals. He also hit ten triples but doesn't have a lot of power. That's acceptable because Martinez has the potential to be a speedy leadoff hitter in the majors; he bats for average and can swipe bases.

MARTINEZ, MANNY - OF - BR - b: 10/3/70

Martinez had a good year with the Pirates' Triple-A Calgary farm club last year and was named to the Pacific Coast League's post-season All-Star team. However, it wasn't enough to warrant a callup to Pittsburgh, a good indicator he has little future in the organization. That has been the story of Martinez' career. He puts up decent minor-league numbers but his only crack at the majors has been 22 games with Seattle and Philadelphia in 1996. Martinez is only 27 and, in the right circumstances, looks like he would be an effective bench player in the majors.

MARTINEZ, PABLO - SS - BB - b: 6/29/69
Martinez is a weak hitter who keeps getting jobs at the Triple-A level because he is a good defensive shortstop. He played all over the diamond at Triple-A Richmond in '97 because the Braves converted Robert Smith to shortstop. Martinez' best bet at a major league career is to find a team with a serious lack of depth at the shortstop position and then hope for a couple of injuries. He won't provide anything offensively, though.

MARTINEZ, RAMON - 2B - BR - b: 10/10/72
Martinez began last season in capable fashion, putting together a .317 average with five homers and 54 RBI while playing shortstop at Double-A Shreveport. He showed good discipline, drawing 40 walks while whiffing only 48 times. Martinez finished the season playing second base at Phoenix and hitting .281 in 57 at-bats. He's a prospect worth watching.

MARTINEZ, SANDY - C - BL - b: 10/3/72
Scouting: Martinez, once projected as the Blue Jays' catcher of the future, spent almost the entire season in the minor leagues. He strikes out too often and has occasional power at best. Defensively, he has the tools to succeed and could develop into a solid backup catcher.
1998: Martinez is trying to find a spot somewhere. Projecting anything more than a backup role is risky and his career to date doesn't indicate an ability to respond to fluctuating playing time. He should be playing at Double-A or Triple-A next year.
1997: Given the chance to be the Triple-A catcher, Martinez hit just .224 with four homers in 321 at-bats. Only a year after he was projected as the Blue Jays' main catcher, Martinez's career took a turn for the worse.
1996: He started the season as the Blue Jays' projected catcher but injuries and the emergence of Charlie O'Brien as a surprisingly reliable hitter forced Martinez out of the lineup. He finished with just 229 at-bats and a poor average.

	AB	R	HR	RBI	SB	BA
1995 Toronto	191	12	2	25	0	.241
1996 Toronto	229	17	3	18	0	.227

MARTINEZ, TINO - 1B - BL - b: 12/7/67
Scouting: Durable and from the old school way of thinking that ballplayers are supposed to play even when they aren't 100 percent, Martinez is a powerful line-drive hitter who can hit the ball where it's pitched. He has shown increased patience the last three years, with obvious results. For a power hitter, he doesn't strike out much. He is a slow runner.
1998: When the Yankees think of 1998, they don't even look at first base for consideration, because they know Martinez will be there and probably hit fourth most of the season. He is under contract through 2000.
1997: The ultimate professional, Martinez spent the winter prior to the 1997 season making sure his body would be strong all year long. The work paid off in a career year in which Martinez put fear into every pitcher who had to work to him, especially with men on base.
1996: Martinez accomplished the difficult feat of helping Yankee fans forget about the loss of Don Mattingly. The pressure was there, but Martinez handled it so well that it wasn't news.

	AB	R	HR	RBI	SB	BA
1995 Seattle	519	92	31	111	0	.293
1996 New York AL	595	82	25	117	2	.292
1997 New York AL	594	96	44	141	3	.296

MARTINS, ERIC - 3B - BR - b: 11/19/72
In 1997, Martins split time between Double-A Huntsville, where he hit .259 with three homers and 31 RBI, and Triple-A Edmonton where he hit .280 with a homer and eight RBI. Martins resembles Ron Cey without the power; he stands 5'9", and despite good initial showings at lower Class A Southern Oregon and higher Class A Modesto in 1996, he hasn't adjusted. There are a lot of good prospects ahead of him; his major league future doesn't look good.

MARX, TIM - C - BR - b: 11/27/67
Marx has been in the minor-leagues seven years, including the past three seasons with the Pirates' Triple-A Calgary farm club. He hits for a decent average and has the reputation of being a solid defensive catcher. However, he is also 29 years old and has never been considered for a callup by the Pirates, which tells you that his skills aren't quite good enough to make the final jump to the big leagues.

MARZANO, JOHN - C - BR - b: 2/14/63
Scouting: Marzano has good defensive fundamentals and is not afraid to block the plate, requisites for a career reserve.
1998: Marzano is the likely candidate as Dan Wilson's backup in Seattle.
1997: Marzano hit his first homer since 1989, when he was a rising young player in the Red Sox organization. His batting average in limited time last season was 54 points above his career average.
1996: Marzano made the Mariners' club as a non-roster spring training invitee after spending 1995 in the Texas chain.

	AB	R	HR	RBI	SB	BA
1996 Seattle	106	8	0	6	0	.245
1997 Seattle	87	7	1	10	0	.287

MASHORE, DAMON - OF - BB - b: 10/31/69
Scouting: Mashore is fast and has both a good eye and good discipline at the plate. He is prone to streakiness, and though he is a good opposite field hitter, he doesn't pull the ball at all. He is a good defensive outfielder with an average arm.
1998: There are so many spots up for grabs, that Mashore could well land a starting spot as much as anyone. His body broke down under the rigors of the full season in 1997, so he must prove more consistency both mentally and physically to be able to step into a full-time role.
1997: Upon his April call-up Mashore looked like everything the A's wanted in both a center fielder and a leadoff hitter. But, time became his enemy and a slump, followed by a cluster of nagging injuries, took the spotlight away and he lost his starting job.
1996: Heralded years ago by Baseball America as a future center fielder for the A's, Mashore did arrive, did play center, but didn't look like much more than a fourth outfielder.

	AB	R	HR	RBI	SB	BA
1996 Oakland	105	20	3	12	4	.267
1997 Oakland	279	55	3	18	5	.247

MASHORE, JUSTIN - OF - BR - b: 2/14/72
Damon Mashore's little brother has some power and speed but has reached Triple-A just once, playing 72 games in Toledo before being demoted in 1995. He played last season at Double-A Mobile in the Padres' organization and struggled at the plate, hitting just .238.

MATEO, RUBEN - OF - BR - b: 2/10/78
Scouting: Mateo is a raw talent, and early returns are encouraging. As a hitter, he has good power and hits for average. Mateo has excellent speed, good range and a major league rightfielder's arm. He needs further development in handling off-speed pitches, strikezone judgment and most of the baseball fundamentals. He is recovering from wrist surgery, but is expected to be ready for the 1998 season.
1998: Mateo should spend the season at Double-A. The Rangers will resist the temptation to rush this 20-year old any faster.
1997: Mateo had no problems making the jump from the South Atlantic League to Port Charlotte, hitting .314 with 12 homers and 67 RBI despite missing the last month with an injury to his left wrist. Mateo was selected to the Florida State League All-Star team and is considered the Rangers' best hitting prospect.
1996: In his first professional season, Mateo acquitted himself well at Charleston, batting .260 with eight homers, 58 RBI and 30 steals.

MATHENY, MIKE - C - BR - b: 9/22/70
Scouting: Matheny has established himself as a solid defensive catcher with a good throwing arm, but he has trouble hitting the breaking ball. He might end up a second-string catcher rather than a starter.
1998: The Brewers were looking for more offense from the catching spot, but they love Matheny's defense. Manager Phil Garner also likes his game-calling ability. He could end up back in Milwaukee and should be in the big leagues someplace.
1997: Matheny's average was up 40 points from 1996, but the Brewers would still have liked more. He struck out 68 times and walked only 17 times to account in part for a .294 on-base average.
1996: Matheny became the regular at the start of the season, but was sent to Triple-A after he struggled at the plate. He returned later in the season and finished with a poor batting average.

	AB	R	HR	RBI	SB	BA
1995 Milwaukee	166	13	0	21	2	.247
1996 Milwaukee	313	31	8	46	3	.204
1997 Milwaukee	320	29	4	32	0	.244

MATOS, FRANCISCO - 2B/SS - BR - b: 7/23/69
The Orioles are Matos's fourth organization, he was previously with the A's, Pirates and Expos. He had an outstanding, career-best year at the plate in 1997, hitting .324-4-51 at Triple-A, and it looks like he's learned how to hit. But it's significant that he didn't get the call when the Orioles needed infield help. He's a singles hitter who can steal an occasional base. Matos hasn't been regarded as a prospect, but the great year in Triple-A may warrant another look.

MAURER, RON - SS/C - BR - b: 6/10/68
Maurer loves to play the game and has established himself as a good utility player, but he's also pretty much established himself as an organizational player. Maurer still has an outside chance to make it to the major leagues, if nothing else, though his determination and desire. However, the clock's ticking and he needs to show the club he's ready to do something beyond filling holes and playing well in Triple-A.

MAXWELL, JASON - SS - BR - b: 3/21/72
Scouting: Maxwell has progressed nicely since being a 74th-round selection in the 1993 draft. He's improved every year since signing soon after the draft. He's not the most gifted athlete, but has decent speed and his power numbers have improved as he's climbed the organizational ladder. One of his strengths is a fairly good strikezone judgment.
1998: The Cubs are fairly high on Maxwell and considered him a front-runner for the open second base job during the off-season. Maxwell could start the year at Triple-A Iowa if a veteran supplants him. Expansion could help him get a regular job in the majors.
1997: Maxwell gave the impression that he might be a big leaguer one day by continuing to make progress in his second year at Double-A Orlando. He hit for a higher average (.279) and had more home runs (14) and RBI (58) than in his first year, which is a real indication that he's getting better.
1996: Maxwell spent the entire year at Double-A, his first at that level. He struck out a bit more than he did the previous year, but not enough to make anybody panic. He was good enough, in fact, to be selected to play in the prestigious Arizona Fall League.

MAY, DERRICK - OF - BL - b: 7/14/68
Scouting: In his prime, May was a classic platoon player; his lone skill was hitting the ball into the gaps against righthanded pitching. His other skills were all below average: power, speed, defensive range, and throwing arm. May has always been difficult to strike out but he also will get himself out on bad pitches. Unfortunately for May, his lone skill has now declined enough that he's no longer capable of holding down a major league bench job.
1998: Even with expansion, May's chances of earning a major league job would appear to be slight. His hitting skills have diminished to the point that he is a liability on a major league roster because of his lack of complementary skills.
1997: May had hope for playing time in April when Danny Tartabull got hurt in his first game and oft-injured Darren Daulton took over in right field. Daulton played nearly every day before being traded while May didn't perform in his brief opportunities. When May confronted manager Terry Francona with a request for more playing time after Daulton was traded, May was given an unconditional release.
1996: May showed signs of decline by hitting just .256 against righthanders in a left field platoon in Houston while hitting a career-low five homers.

	AB	R	HR	RBI	SB	BA
1995 Milwaukee	113	15	1	9	0	.248
1995 Houston	206	29	8	41	5	.301
1996 Houston	259	24	5	33	2	.251
1997 Philadelphia	149	8	1	13	4	.228

MAYES, CRAIG - C - BL - b: 5/8/70
A catching prospect with reasonable hitting skills, Mayes hit .273 with a couple of homers and 38 RBI at Shreveport, then moved to Phoenix when Doug Mirabelli was called up. He didn't hit much at Triple-A. He'll spend another year there and get his major league chance only if can move past Mirabelli, which is unlikely.

MAYNE, BRENT - C - BL - b: 4/19/68
Scouting: Mayne is an adequate lefthanded hitter who has learned to consistently hit a half-dozen homers over his appointed 250 at-bats. Surprisingly, he has also managed to hit lefties, though his ability to draw a walk is still derelict. Mayne is

a good defensive backstop.
1998: Mayne is certainly an experienced pro compared the litany of young backstops in the wings, so his tenure as the grizzled veteran is safe for now. Aside from his catching skills, Mayne can be a good lefthanded bat off the bench. Those young catchers, however, will be breathing down his neck shortly.
1997: A late addition to the Oakland roster, Mayne responded well to his new environs with some timely hitting and replaced George Williams, who endured several injuries. Mayne actually looked like he had captured the starting role in May, but his bat cooled, Williams returned, and so did platoon duty. He did a good job breaking in the gaggle of young pitchers Oakland used last year.
1996: Mayne was good enough with the bat and the glove to be a starter for most teams. Like most other years, though, Mayne was confined to a reserve role, this time behind Todd Hundley.

	AB	R	HR	RBI	SB	BA
1995 Kansas City	307	23	1	27	0	.251
1996 New York	99	9	1	6	0	.263
1997 Oakland	256	29	6	22	1	.289

McBRIDE, CHARLIE - OF - BR - b: 8/12/73
McBride's second season at Double-A Greenville was a disappointment. After hitting .268 with 50 RBI in just 291 at-bats at the same location in 1996, McBride hit a weak .244 last year. He was still aggressive at the plate, but made good contact for the first time in his career. McBride has likely peaked at Double-A.

McCALL, ROD - 1B - BL - b: 11/4/71
After spending seven seasons in the Cleveland organization, McCall turned up at Triple-A Iowa in the Cubs farm system. He isn't a good defensive player and is best suited for a DH role. Offensively he hit the ball hard or not at all; he batted .263 with 20 homers and 55 RBI, but 90 strikeouts in 255 at-bats last year. He may be able to provide bench power to a major league team in the future, if he can make better contact without losing his power.

McCARTY, DAVID - OF/1B - BR - b: 11/23/69
Not too many players have been handed a starter's job twice and blown it the way McCarty has. First he muffed a chance with a struggling Twins' squad in 1995, then couldn't cut it with a last-place Giants team in 1996. McCarty can hit — he batted .353 with 22 homers and 92 RBI last year at Triple-A Phoenix. The Giants released him at the end of 1996, then got him back as an insurance policy. Expansion may help McCarty get yet another chance at the majors.

	AB	R	HR	RBI	SB	BA
1995 Minnesota	55	10	0	4	0	.218
1995 San Francisco	20	1	0	2	1	.250
1996 San Francisco	175	16	6	24	2	.217

McCLAIN, SCOTT - 3B - BR - b: 5/19/72
After seven seasons in the Orioles' farm system McClain played the hot corner at Triple-A Norfolk in the Mets' organization. Always considered a strong fielder, he has been voted the best defensive third baseman in the International League. McClain had a solid season at the plate last year, batting .280 with 21 homers and 64 RBI, and his range and strong arm could earn him a big-league roster spot.

McCRACKEN, QUINTON - OF - BB - b: 3/16/70
Scouting: A switch-hitter with a great eye, McCracken makes contact and has good speed. There are coaches and scouts who feel he has the potential to win a batting title, though that's a push because he doesn't consistently hit the ball with authority. Considered one of the best fourth outfielders in the league the past two years, McCracken is best suited for left field, even though he has played mostly center for the Rockies. He has great range, good hands and a decent arm. His biggest problem on defense is instinct —he simply misplays too many balls, particularly those hit over his head.
1998: McCracken figured to be a prime candidate for the expansion draft, and the Devil Rays took him as their second pick. He thus became the starting center fielder and leadoff man on paper, pending further moves by Tampa Bay. At worst, he will once again be a fourth outfielder. Just don't expect numbers on the scale of Colorado-style hitting.
1997: He played in 147 games, a testament to his all-around abilities. He had a career-high in stolen bases and had a solid season at the plate. But, for the first time since his professional rookie season in 1993, McCracken's stock slid slightly. When given a chance to play everyday in place of injured Ellis Burks in center field, McCracken made several costly misplays, causing the Rockies to wonder if he can ever be a regular player.
1996: One of the team's most pleasant surprises, McCracken struggled early in a seldom-use, part-time role, batting just .188 entering June. A shoulder injury to Larry Walker, however, brought more playing time to McCracken and he took advantage, especially in July when he batted .350.

	AB	R	HR	RBI	SB	BA
1996 Colorado	283	50	3	40	17	.290
1997 Colorado	325	69	3	36	28	.292

McCLAIN, SCOTT - 3B - BR - b: 5/19/72
After seven seasons in the Orioles' farm system McClain played the hot corner at Triple-A Norfolk in the Mets' organization. Always considered a strong fielder, he has been voted the best defensive third baseman in the International League. McClain had a solid season at the plate last year, batting .280 with 21 homers and 64 RBI, and his range and strong arm could earn him a big-league roster spot.

McDONALD, DARNELL - OF - b: 4/1/70
McDonald was the best high school athlete available in the June 1997 draft but slipped a bit because of the possibility that he would be hard to sign; he already had a football scholarship to Texas locked up. The Orioles gladly used the 26th pick of the first round to pick him up. McDonald is a potential five-tool outfielder and he was also a star pitcher in high school. But the $1.9 million bonus the Orioles spent was for his speed and power game.

McDONALD, DONZELL - OF - BB - b: 2/20/75
Described by Class A Tampa manager Lee Mazzilli as "a young Tim Raines," this exciting outfielder had his 1997 season limited to 77 games due to a broken finger, the result of a head-first slide. McDonald batted .296 with 39 stolen bases in 57 attempts.

McDONALD, JASON - SS/2B - BB - b: 3/20/72
Scouting: From his breakout 1995 season at Class A Modesto (110 walks, 70 steals) he has struggled a little when moving to the next level, then finally mastered it. McDonald is both fast and patient, and is able to spray the ball around and use his speed.

That speed helps him afield as well. He is just fine in center field, which is a switch from second base where he played in the minors. McDonald's arm is fair.

1998: McDonald is probably at the head of the class to grab one of the unclaimed outfield spots in Oakland. Centerfield is a good place for him, as is the leadoff spot, though it isn't inconceivable that he play left field. He is a good player and a quick learner. Furthermore, McDonald has both the excellent speed and patient eye required of a leadoff hitter. Since the A's have a dearth of other potential leadoff candidates, he is the likely choice. Over a full season he can hit in the .280s and swipe 40 bases.

1997: Pressed into big-league service way ahead of schedule, McDonald suffered some adjustment problems, went down, then came back up, to stay. His 31 steals and 74 walks — with just 58 strikeouts — over only 276 at-bats at Triple-A Edmonton had the A's thinking they might finally have a leadoff hitter. He finished the season strong, raising his average and adjusting to big league pitching. He also did the job in center field.

1996: McDonald found the going a little tougher after jumping from Class A to Triple-A in one giant leap. All-in-all, he weathered the experience. He showed that he has what it takes to be a good leadoff or number two hitter.

	AB	R	HR	RBI	SB	BA
1997 Oakland	236	47	4	14	13	.263

McDONALD, KEITH - C - BR - b: 2/8/73

McDonald was the number one catcher for Double-A Arkansas; 1997 was his first season at the Double-A level. Even though he had almost 200 fewer at-bats last year than he did in 1996, he still managed to produce more runs and home runs, and improve his on-base percentage and slugging average. His .240 average with five homers and 30 RBI in 233 at-bats shows that there is still much room for improvement, though.

McEWING, JOE - OF - BR - b: 10/19/72

McEwing improved in 1997 at Double-A Arkansas in the Texas League over his 1996 season but still lacks power, and does not hit for high average. He possesses above-average speed but his stolen base totals have been low for the last few years partly due to his low on-base percentage.

McGEE, WILLIE - OF - BB - b: 11/2/58

Scouting: Gone are the days McGee can bat .300 playing every day, though he still will give his maximum effort if called upon to play for extended stretches. He's a professional hitter who still can rip a fastball to any field and runs better than most players ten years younger. Though always on the verge of retirement, he has been rejuvenated in St. Louis and likes his role as a pinch-hitter and number four outfielder.

1998: With the Cards' three primary outfielders healthy, McGee probably will settle happily into the role of their backup and mentor. He can be expected to continue his status as one of the top late-inning pinch-hitters in the league, particularly at Busch Stadium.

1997: He got 300 at-bats again — more than he wanted — as injuries put him in the lineup more than he had bargained for. With a .300 batting average and 16 hits in 51 pinch at-bats, McGee was up to most challenges. He batted .336 at home and hit better against lefthanded pitchers, though without much power.

1996: Re-acquired as a free agent, McGee enjoyed a resurgence as a Cardinal and batted over .300 while playing all three outfield positions.

	AB	R	HR	RBI	SB	BA
1995 Boston	200	32	2	15	5	.285
1996 St. Louis	309	52	5	41	5	.307
1997 St. Louis	300	29	3	38	8	.300

McGRIFF, FRED - 1B - BL - b: 10/31/63

Scouting: McGriff is still a decent lefthanded power hitter, and unlike most hitters of his type, he handles lefthanded pitching fairly well. In the past, he was most notable for his durability and consistency, but his performance has declined noticeably in the last two seasons. McGriff has reached the age where further decline cannot be a surprise.

1998: McGriff will undoubtedly start for the Devil Rays and provide a power bat, although he's unlikely to reach the same levels he did in the early '90s.

1997: McGriff's performance declined significantly from 1996, partly a phenomenon caused by the new Turner Field dimensions. It's 390 feet to right-center and all Braves lefthanded power hitters were impacted negatively. McGriff also played through shoulder problems that hampered his performance throughout the summer.

1996: On the surface it was a typical Fred McGriff season featuring a good average, high power, and high RBI production. However, a power decline in the second half (20 homers before the break, eight after) was of some concern.

	AB	R	HR	RBI	SB	BA
1995 Atlanta	528	85	27	93	3	.280
1996 Atlanta	617	81	28	107	7	.295
1997 Atlanta	564	77	22	97	5	.277

McGUIRE, RYAN - 1B - BL - b: 11/23/71

Scouting: McGuire was once considered a top prospect in Boston's farm system but has never developed the power expected of a first baseman. He is a solid hitter for average and a decent defensive player.

1998: The Expos will have openings at both first base and left field as they plan to cut the payroll by jettisoning most of their veterans. Rookie Brad Fullmer will man one of those spots and McGuire could win a job at the other, depending on what the Expos gets back in trade. McGuire really doesn't have the power to play either spot on a regular basis and looks more useful as a lefthanded pinch-hitter.

1997: McGuire was called up to the Expos from Triple-A Ottawa in early-June and started off extremely hot, replacing injured first baseman David Segui. However, McGuire soon cooled off and his playing time decreased sharply once Segui got healthy.

1996: McGuire was a major disappointment at Ottawa after the Expos acquired him from the Boston organization in an off-season trade. McGuire set a career high in homers but didn't do much else.

	AB	R	HR	RBI	SB	BA
1997 Montreal	199	22	3	17	1	.256

McGWIRE, MARK - 1B - BR - b: 10/1/63

Scouting: There is no more impressive power hitter in the game today, and it would be easy to get lost in the talk of how he's hit more home runs per hundred at-bats than anyone in history other than Babe Ruth, in the list of his 500-foot home runs, and in the possibility of him chasing Roger Maris. That would overlook how McGwire also is one of the finest fielding first basemen in the big leagues, how he's likely to drive in 120 runs each season because be can patiently drive the ball for a clutch single or double, and how he's one of the best team players in baseball. And he's never been better.

1998: As wonderful as his 1997 was, McGwire could take it several steps beyond. Not that he will hit more home runs — but he actually could, since he'll be a little more familiar with National League pitchers, parks and style. That could also allow him to cut down on his strikeouts, boost his batting average to normal levels and drive in more runs. With Ray Lankford batting behind him, he'll have better protection than at any time in his career.

1997: He became the first player to hit 20 home runs for teams in each of the two leagues in the same season and finished with 58, a sign of his ability to adapt to situations. He was healthy and rejuvenated by the St. Louis atmosphere — unlike anything he's known.

1996: McGwire belted 52 home runs despite missing 30 games with an injury. He homered every 8.13 at-bats and, despite striking out 112 times, still walked more than he fanned.

	AB	R	HR	RBI	SB	BA
1995 Oakland	317	75	39	90	1	.274
1996 Oakland	423	104	52	113	0	.312
1997 Oak. - Stl.	540	86	58	123	3	.274

McINTOSH, TIM - C - BR - b: 3/21/65

It only seems like McIntosh has been around since the dawn of time. He had several really good seasons in a row in the Milwaukee farm system after a good collegiate career at Minnesota, but got lost somewhere along the way and never got more than a handful of at-bats with the Brewers. Time seems to have run out for McIntosh, though. He'll be 33 at the start of the season and coming off a year where he got few at-bats (54) at Triple-A Iowa. McIntosh hangs around purely as insurance at this point. It's doubtful that he'll even be a big-league backup.

McKEEL, WALT - C - BR - b: 1/17/72

Scouting: McKeel has a dumpy body and looks like a softball player. His sloppy look carries over to his defense, where he is a lazy, slow receiver, who has trouble throwing out baserunners. McKeel has been an erratic hitter, but has found an open-stance approach which makes him a tough out and gives him good plate coverage, although with limited power.

1998: McKeel will spend the season in the minors, trying to prove he can still be a catcher, at least a backup catcher. He also needs to refine his approach at the plate and become a more potent bat, especially if his defensive skills force a move to another position.

1997: McKeel began the season in Triple-A, looking like the Red Sox' catcher of the future. But his defensive skills were not sharp. He got called up to Boston when Bill Haselman broke his thumb, but his skills were so poor manager Jimy Williams was afraid to use him. He was eventually sent back to Double-A after the Red Sox acquired Jason Varitek to play at Triple-A Pawtucket.

1996: McKeel appeared to take a huge step forward as a prospect by hitting .302 with 16 homers in Double-A, by far his best offensive season.

McKINNON, SANDY - OF - BR - b: 9/20/73

After four years in A-ball, McKinnon advanced to Double-A Birmingham for the first time in 1997. He's a diminutive outfielder (5'8", 175 pounds) who is a little too old for his level. He's a decent outfielder and can run a little. McKinnon's numbers at Birmingham are similar to those he posted the previous two years at Class A Prince William: .271 with four homers, 31 RBI and 13 steals, but his strikeout-to-walk ratio isn't getting any better and his .334 on-base percentage is too weak for a non-power hitter. Even more telling is that McKinnon is playing less frequently as he advances up the ladder.

McLEMORE, MARK - 2B - BB - b: 10/4/64

Scouting: McLemore is a contact hitter with a good batting eye. When healthy, he has been an above-average basestealer, but surgery to repair torn cartilage in both knees puts that part of his game in question. McLemore doesn't have great range at second base, but turns the double play well and is sure-handed.

1998: McLemore may not be ready for opening day, as he recovers from surgery on both knees. If and when he is healthy, he should resume his role as a starting second baseman, but his days as a serious basestealing threat are probably over.

1997: A lingering early-season hand injury resulted in McLemore getting off to a poor start. Then, just as he was reaching his stride, knee problems ended his season early.

1996: McLemore quietly went about having a career year in his second season with Texas. Underrated defensively, he makes up for limited range with steady play. Even in the power-oriented Ranger lineup, he finished seventh in steals in the American League.

	AB	R	HR	RBI	SB	BA
1995 Texas	467	73	5	41	21	.261
1996 Texas	517	84	5	46	27	.290
1997 Texas	349	47	1	25	7	.261

McMILLON, BILL - OF - BL - b: 11/17/71

Scouting: McMillon is the prototypical "professional" hitter. Though he lacks raw power or exceptional speed, he has a smooth swing capable of generating surprising extra-base pop, and he has batted .300 or better at most minor-league stops. He has traditionally hit lefthanded pitching well, and therefore could overcome his perception as a platoon player. He runs the bases well, and has generally swiped bases in double figure quantities each year despite his limited speed. A below-average throwing arm limits him to left field, where he is an adequate defender at best.

1998: In the unlikely event that the Phillies are able to unload Gregg Jefferies' big contract, McMillon could get a shot in left field this year. More likely, McMillon will share an outfield reserve job and serve as a lefty pinch-hitter, too. He can be productive in a part-time role.

1997: McMillon was traded by the Marlins to the Phillies in mid-1997 for Darren Daulton. They intended to give McMillon a full look in left field down the stretch, but his early struggles at the plate and then the death of his mother robbed McMillon of playing time and focus. He appeared too eager to impress, forsaking the more patient approach he showed in the minors for a free-swinging mentality.

1996: McMillon smashed liners to all fields at Triple-A Charlotte and even hit lefthanders at a .359 clip, but he struggled in his brief major league opportunity with Florida.

	AB	R	HR	RBI	SB	BA
1996 Florida	51	4	0	4	0	.216
1997 Fla. - Phil.	90	10	2	14	2	.256

McNABB, BUCK - OF - BL - b: 1/17/73

For the first time in his seven-year pro career McNabb made a Triple-A appearance, albeit a brief one; he spent a majority of last season at Double-A Jackson. His batting average dropped over 40 points and he remains a speedy outfielder with no power and little chance of advancement.

McRAE, BRIAN - OF - BB - b: 8/27/67

Scouting: After he joined the Mets in August, McRae said he intended to retire when his current contract expired following the 1999 season. Cynics in the Mets' clubhouse judged his performance of the three weeks that followed the trade that imported McRae and suggested retirement already had happened. It wasn't really that bad, but the skills of the switch-hitting center fielder did appear tarnished.

1998: McRae's role with the Mets was loosely defined last summer; it became no clearer as the club approached the expansion draft. At best, he would serve as the regular center fielder and, by default, leadoff man. More likely was a time-sharing arrangement with Carl Everett.

1997: His Mets' teammates were angered by the trade that moved Lance Johnson and Mark Clark to the Cubs and looked for flaws in McRae's game: some were evident. McRae provided more power (five home runs in 145 at-bats) than expected but he hit for a mediocre average and, though a gifted outfielder with skills that exceed Johnson's, McRae had several tough moments in Shea's unforgiving center field.

1996: With 32 doubles, five triples and a career-high 17 home runs, McRae scored 111 runs, also a career high, and drove in 66 runs. It was his finest season. And it probably led to somewhat unrealistic expectations for '97.

	AB	R	HR	RBI	SB	BA
1995 Chicago NL	580	92	12	48	27	.288
1996 Chicago NL	624	111	17	66	37	.276
1997 two teams	562	86	11	43	17	.242

MEARES, PAT - SS - BR - b: 9/6/68

Scouting: He isn't the natural athlete that, say, Alex Rodriguez is, but Meares has made the most of his abilities. He is a solid, .270 hitter who will make some outstanding plays at shortstop. He'll sometimes botch a routine play, but he will help you more often than he will hurt you. For some reason, he gets hit with a lot of pitches. His 16 HBP were second in the league last year.

1998: Pencil Meares in for .270-something and about ten home runs. At age 29, and with four years already in the majors, Meares isn't going to suddenly develop into a superstar. At the same time, with four years in, his track record is pretty good.

1997: Meares had a career-high batting average and had a solid year in the field despite missing several games when he was hit in the right calf with a pitch. With more experience and a better knowledge of the league's hitters, Meares did a better job of positioning himself defensively, which helped him improve that part of his game.

1996: Meares played in a career-high 152 games and proved that, over the long stretch of a full season, he had what it takes to be an everyday player. Playoff teams require a bit more offensively, but Meares does the job admirably.

	AB	R	HR	RBI	SB	BA
1995 Minnesota	390	57	12	49	10	.269
1996 Minnesota	517	66	8	67	9	.267
1997 Minnesota	439	63	10	60	7	.276

MEDRANO, TONY - SS - BR - b: 12/8/74

Medrano is being groomed as a utility infielder. He has been switching between shortstop and second base each of the last two seasons spent at Double-A Wichita and Triple-A Omaha. He has learned to hit the pitching at the lower level, but struggled in his first trip to Omaha. Medrano will advance as far as his glove takes him; he's a minor prospect only.

MEJIA, MIGUEL - OF - BR - b: 3/25/75

Acquired by the Cardinals in the Rule 5 draft before the 1996 season, Mejia spent that entire year with the big-league club even though he rarely was used. The Cards felt good about using the roster spot for him because of Mejia's talents — a strong throwing arm and uncommonly swift legs. They sent him to the Class A Carolina League to open the 1997 season, which initially proved too much for him. After recovering from an injury, he joined the organization's affiliate in the New York-Penn League and the 22-year-old starred with a .331 batting average. He needs seasoning to improve his pitch selection and to tame his free-swinging batting approach.

MEJIA, ROBERTO - 2B - BR - b: 6/15/72

Scouting: Mejia is better than average in nearly every respect, as far as potential and his minor-league history are concerned. He hits with better power than most second basemen, runs well, has good range and a strong arm. It's just that Mejia hasn't found a way to make the leap into the big leagues, having failed for several reasons in attempts to win jobs with four different organizations. Still young enough, he has time to make it with someone.

1998: His chance with the Cardinals probably will be as a backup to second baseman Delino DeShields. The Cards might not have room for a player so locked into one position and so overaggressive at the plate, thus making it possible he'll have to move elsewhere yet again.

1997: He spent nearly the entire season on the disabled list, first with a relatively minor leg injury and then with a shoulder injury suffered on his rehab assignment.

1996: Mejia began the year with Cincinnati's Triple-A affiliate before being traded to the Red Sox, then finishing the season in their farm system. He had an excellent 101 games in the Cincinnati organization, showing power and posting a .291 batting average.

MELENDEZ, DAN - 1B - BL - b: 1/4/71

A former Pepperdine University star and a second-round draft pick in 1992, Melendez doesn't look pretty, but he gets the job done. He has a big, looping swing that reminds scouts of Will Clark, but Melendez has yet to show the same kind of power. Melendez was set back by a broken elbow in 1997, so 1998 will be a big year for him to show whether he has what it takes to get to the big leagues.

MELHUSE, ADAM - C - BB - b: 3/27/72

Scouting: A power hitter who can take a walk, Melhuse needs more experience behind the plate before he can be in the major leagues. He turns twenty-six in March and although he has other hitting skills, he will never hit for average.

1998: Melhuse finished last year at Triple-A and that's where he will start 1998. As a switch-hitter, he could get noticed but he needs more playing time in the high minors before he'll have a serious shot of cracking the big club. He has an outside shot at being a September call-up.

1997: Splitting time between Double-A Knoxville and Triple-A Syracuse, Melhuse didn't crack the .240 mark at either level.

1996: Although Melhuse hit a career-high 13 home runs for Class A Dunedin, he batted just .248. He did show good patience, walking more often (69) than he struck out (68).

MELIAN, JACKSON - OF - BR - 1/7/80

In his first professional season, the 17-year-old outfielder batted .263 with three homers and 36 RBI for Rookie-ball Tampa and did nothing to give the Yankees any idea they wasted the $1.4 million they gave Melian as a 16-year-old. Melian is a tremendous worker and weight room warrior; the Yankees expect his home run output to climb each year.

MELO, JUAN - SS - BB - b: 5/11/76

Scouting: Melo is considered an outstanding defensive shortstop with strong arm, range and quickness; however, he often plays too deep because of his arm. Offensively, Padres want him to be more disciplined at the plate. Melo swings at too many bad pitches and rarely walks, but he's only 21 years old.
1998: Melo's defensive skills could get him to majors this season if an opening develops on the major league squad. If not, he'll start the year in Triple-A with a shot for a September call-up; he'll challenge for a big-league job in 1999.
1997: Melo hit .287 at Double-A Mobile with seven homers and 67 RBI despite striking out 90 times and drawing just 29 walks. He was a aggressive shortstop who made only 16 errors in 113 games.
1996: Melo hit .304 in the Class A California League with six home runs and 75 RBI in 128 games. He also struck out 20 percent of the time.

MELUSKEY, MITCH - C - BB - b: 9/18/73

Scouting: Meluskey has a good bat from both sides of the plate. He makes good contact and has some power. His catching skills need significant improvement before he can challenge for a major league job. He floundered in the Cleveland organization for his first three years, never hitting above .250 in the low minors. He has batted .289 since joining the Houston system in 1995 as he has moved from Class A up to Triple-A.
1998: Meluskey needs a full season at Triple-A to sharpen his defense and demonstrate that he can continue his hitting improvement.
1997: Meluskey started the season at Double-A Jackson and batted .340 with 14 home runs in 241 at-bats. He was promoted to Triple-A New Orleans where he hit .250 with three homers in 172 at-bats.
1996: Meluskey entered the season with a .235 batting average for his minor league career. He had a breakout year, splitting the season between Class A Kissimmee and Double-A Jackson, hitting over .300 at both stops and achieving prospect status.

MENDEZ, CARLOS - 1B/C - BR - b: 6/18/74

Mendez's newfound power may be an illusion created by Wichita's short left field porch; he banged twelve homers last year after never getting more than seven in any A-ball season. Mendez's game is to hit doubles and hit for average; his 32 doubles and .325 batting average in 1997 are much in line with his career norms. Mendez's defensive prowess around first base and versatility (he can catch and also play the outfield) can make him a useful major-league reserve, although it's unlikely he'll ever get an expanded role.

MENDEZ, SERGIO - C - BR - b: 10/12/73

The Pirates once felt this minor-league catcher could eventually get to the big leagues but he has been dogged by injuries throughout his six-year professional career. He spent last season as the backup catcher at Double-A Carolina behind non-prospect Jon Sweet which is a pretty strong indication his chances of getting to the major leagues are extremely slim.

MENDOZA, CARLOS - OF - BL - b: 11/4/74

Scouting: He can hit. He can hit. He can hit. And the Devil Rays knew it when they plucked him from the Mets farm. If not for his production as a hitter, Mendoza might be hard-pressed to play in Double-A, though; he is modestly talented in other areas. Mendoza hits everywhere he goes, though never for power. Sooner or later those skills will allow him to graduate to the big leagues.
1998: He's 23 years old and has merely 47 at-bats at levels higher than Double-A. But Mendoza bats lefthanded and he hits and hits. It's not likely he will win a major league job in spring training. But it is likely he'll be batting over .300 when he is promoted.
1997: Put aside Mendoza's brief tenure and ineffective work at Triple-A, and 1997 was a natural extension of his previous years. He entered the season with a .326 average in four minor-league seasons and 789 minor-league at-bats and then produced a .384 average in 60 games and 232 at-bats with the Double-A Binghamton Mets. His season was interrupted for two months due to a fractured left leg.
1996: Mendoza led the South Atlantic League in hitting with a .337 average and had 101 hits in 85 games. His walks outnumbered his strikeouts — 57 to 46 — and he stole 31 bases.

MENECHINO, FRANKIE - 2B - BR - b: 1/7/71

One of the White Sox's favorite organizational players, Menechino is a gutsy little player who works hard, will take a walk and always, always hustles. He doesn't have a lot of power or hit for a high average, but has remarkable on-base ability and will fight a pitcher tooth and nail in every plate appearance. His range is adequate but he is sure-handed at second base. Menechino is too old for his minor-league level, though, and is a longshot for major league playing time.

MERCED, ORLANDO - 1B/OF - BL - b: 11/2/66

Scouting: Despite Merced's 1998 performance, he is a good contact hitter with some pop who will also take a walk. Always a threat to hit .280-.300, Merced can hit to the gaps and puts the ball in play when he has to. He has an excellent arm and is always in the game. Last year, in one of the rarer plays, Merced threw out Jody Reed at first base on what looked like a single to right.
1998: His injury-shortened season will not cause teams to underrate him. Although the Blue Jays entered the off-season indicating little interest, Merced is at least a platoon player. The days of 80+ RBI may be gone but he should be a solid run-producer.
1997: Merced was one of the few ex-Pirates who was playing up to ability when he had to have arthroscopic surgery in August, ending what might have been at least an ordinary season.
1996: Despite missing time, Merced hit a career-high in home runs (17) and knocked in 80 runs in just 120 games.

	AB	R	HR	RBI	SB	BA
1995 Pittsburgh	487	75	15	83	7	.300
1996 Pittsburgh	453	69	17	80	8	.287
1997 Toronto	368	45	9	40	7	.266

MERCEDES, GUILLERMO - SS - BB - b: 1/17/74
Mercedes had trouble with Double-A pitching at Akron in the Indians' organization, his first season at that level; Mercedes hit .208 with no homers and 27 RBI. He'll have plenty of time to spend in the minors to develop an adequate bat; he's behind Omar Vizquel on the Cleveland depth chart.

MERCEDES, HENRY - C - BR - b: 7/23/69
Scouting: Mercedes is a light-hitting catcher with solid defensive skills.
1998: Mercedes has some chance of sticking as a number two or three catcher in the majors, particularly with expansion a reality, but he'll be lucky ever to reach 100 major league at-bats in any season.
1997: The latest in a long line of little-used caddies for Ivan Rodriguez, Mercedes was no more than adequate in the role. He split time between the majors and Triple-A Oklahoma City.
1996: Just as in 1995, Mercedes hit .215 in a season spent mostly in Triple-A.

MERCHANT, MARK - DH - BL - b: 1/23/69
An eleven-year minor-league veteran once rated by Baseball America as the Pirates' best prospect (1988), Merchant is now a part-time DH and outfielder at Double-A. He can still hit (.340 average and .585 slugging last year), but is a defensive liability. It's hard to believe that even another round of expansion could get Merchant to the majors.

MERLONI, LOU - 3B - BR - b: 4/6/71
Previously considered just an organizational infielder, Merloni improved his stock to a potential big-league utilityman last year. He did this by undergoing an intense work-out routine, which gave him needed athleticism and strength. He became a tough out at the plate, hitting .297 in Triple-A, and also improved his range, which had been short. He's now a solid glove at second and third base.

MEULENS, HENSLEY - OF - BR - b: 6/23/67
Once upon a time, Meulens was supposed to be the next great New York Yankees power hitter. That never happened. After appearing in 159 games with the Yankees from 1989-93, Meulens bolted for Japan. He returned to North America last year, had a good season with Montreal's Triple-A Ottawa farm club, then spent September with the Expos. Meulens played well in a limited role for the Expos but was released at the end of the season. Meulens is now looking eastward again — in the direction of Japan.

MIENTKIEWICZ, DOUG - 1B - BL - b: 6/19/74
The Twins fifth-round pick in the June 1995 draft out of Florida State, Mientkiewicz tore through Fort Myers of the Class A Florida State League in 1996 and spent the 1997 season at Double-A New Britain. An excellent defensive first baseman, Mientkiewicz saw his average drop at the Double-A level but he did show power potential with 15 homers and 61 runs batted in. He also runs well for a big man and stole 21 bases for New Britain. He will likely get a chance to prove himself at Triple-A sometime in 1998.

MIESKE, MATT - OF - BR - b: 2/13/68
Scouting: Mieske has a good throwing arm, is a steady outfielder and can hit for a decent average, but he lacks pop overall and has been tagged as a player who doesn't hit in the clutch. Part of his problem might be that he has never had a chance to play regularly for Milwaukee. He has platooned most of his time, in part because he has struggled against righthanders.
1998: It's unlikely that Mieske will be back with Milwaukee. He would like a shot at playing every day, and the Brewers are looking at other outfielders.
1997: Mieske started the season platooning in right field, but injuries and ineffectiveness at the plate buried him on the Brewers' bench. He hit only .200 with runners in scoring position.
1996: Mieske set career highs in every offensive category. He hit .352 against lefties and .231 against righthanders. He led the club with seven outfield assists.

	AB	R	HR	RBI	SB	BA
1995 Milwaukee	267	42	12	48	2	.251
1996 Milwaukee	374	46	14	64	1	.278
1997 Milwaukee	253	39	5	21	1	.249

MILLAN, ADAN - C - BR - b: 3/26/72
Millan is a journeyman who had only brief Double-A time until age 25, not a good sign for the future. He's a useful player because of his ability to hit for some power with a good eye at the plate, and because he can play catcher and first base. His bat speed is unspectacular, and his ability to produce at higher levels is questionable. Millan's catching skills are inadequate for an everyday receiver, but are acceptable for a backup. The Phillies have little or no catching help behind Triple-A prospect Bobby Estalella — this fact alone should keep Millan employed for another season, but he has little chance for a major league future.

MILLAR, KEVIN - 1B - BR - b: 9/24/71
Millar has little left to prove in the minors after being named the MVP of the Double-A Eastern League in 1997 by leading the league in batting average (.342) and RBI (131). But, he was playing in a hitters' park and was one of the league's oldest starters in his second season at that level. Expansion could open an opportunity for Millar to earn a big-league role, but his relatively slow bat, and below-average speed and defensive ability should keep him confined to a reserve role.

MILLER, DAMIAN - C - BR - b: 10/13/69
Scouting: Miller is a solid all-around catcher who does nothing great but who also has no major weaknesses. With Terry Steinbach set to catch for the Twins this season, Miller didn't figure to get a ton of playing time, and the Twins left him exposed. Arizona took him. Miller can win the backup catcher's job and will chip in with some big hits offensively.
1998: If he's a major leaguer, don't expect Miller to get much playing time, but he will succeed with spot duty.
1997: After nearly eight seasons in the minors, Miller finally took that last step to the majors on the basis of an outstanding season at Triple-A Salt Lake. Miller batted .338 with 11 homers and 82 RBI for the Buzz.
1996: As Triple-A Salt Lake's usual catcher, Miller had a 15-game hitting streak that caught the attention of those in the

Twins' organization. He also hit well in the clutch, batting .417 with the bases loaded.

	AB	R	HR	RBI	SB	BA
1997 Minnesota	66	5	2	13	0	.273

MILLER, DAVID - OF - BL - b: 12/9/73
Miller is an over-sized line-drive hitter with limited gap power who has above-average speed and baserunning instincts. He's a decent fielder at first base and in the outfield, but simply hasn't developed expected power since being drafted by the Indians in the first round in 1995. He lacks the power to reach the majors. He'll make his Triple-A debut at Buffalo in 1998.

MILLER, ORLANDO - SS - BR - b: 1/13/69
Scouting: Miller never really got a chance with the Tigers, because his spring training back injury allowed them to realize how good a shortstop Deivi Cruz is. Even when he played, Miller never played enough to get in any kind of rhythm. Given a chance to play regularly, Miller would figure to still be the player he was in Houston — an adequate defensive shortstop who provides some power.
1998: Now that Cruz is established in Detroit, the Tigers have no plans to bring Miller back. Put in the right situation, he should be able to play regularly in the major leagues.
1997: It was a lost year for Miller, and not just because of the back injury that put him on the disabled list at the end of spring training. The Tigers didn't rush Miller to return, because by mid-April they'd decided that Cruz would be their starter.
1996: Miller hit more home runs than any National League shortstop but Barry Larkin, but the Astros weren't satisfied. Miller's inconsistent play in the field didn't improve their view of him, either. By December, he was included in the ten-player trade with the Tigers.

	AB	R	HR	RBI	SB	BA
1995 Houston	324	36	5	36	3	.262
1996 Houston	468	43	15	58	3	.256
1997 Detroit	111	13	2	10	1	.234

MILLETTE, JOE - SS - BR - b: 8/12/66
Millette was a reserve infielder for Triple-A Tacoma in the Mariner farm system last year; it was Millette's third different organization in the past three seasons. Light-hitting 31-year olds rarely make it back to the majors. His brief stint in the bigs with the Phillies will be his only taste of the major leagues.

MILLIARD, RALPH - 2B - BR - b: 12/30/73
Milliard's excellent defensive skills, contact hitting, good plate discipline, and above-average speed have marked him as one of the minors' finest second base prospects. He has spent the last two years stuck behind other young prospects in the Marlins' farm system, splitting each season between Double-A Portland and Triple-A Charlotte. Should expansion give him an everyday opportunity, Milliard is a good bet to be a pleasant surprise.

MINOR, RYAN - 3B - BR - b: 1/5/74
Scouting: Oriole prospect Minor is a great athlete; he was a basketball All-American at Oklahoma. He has good power, and he's great in the field with a gun for an arm. Minor has great potential.
1998: Minor should make rapid progress in the Oriole farm system. But this year will be the true test to see if he can hit better pitching in the higher minor-leagues.

1997: Minor showed hitting skills with good power in the higher Class-A South Atlantic League last year, and was named as the top prospect in the league.
1996: Many organizations believed that Minor would be a pro basketball player, so he went undrafted until the Orioles picked him in the 33rd round in the 1996 draft.

MIRABELLI, DOUG - C - BR - b: 10/18/70
Scouting: Mirabelli has a little pop and is selective at the plate. He is not the best defensive catcher in the organization, but is good enough to play occasionally in the majors. His skills are well-suited to a reserve catching role in the bigs.
1998: Mirabelli's emergence made expendable the most recent Giants' "catcher of the future" — Marcus Jensen. Mirabelli is expected to become Brian Johnson's backup in San Francisco.
1997: Mirabelli continued his steady progress with a good performance at Triple-A Phoenix, hitting .265 with eight homers and 48 RBI, then spent a little time in San Francisco, too. He showed a good batting eye (58 walks against 69 strikeouts) and doubles power (23).
1996: At the age of 26, Mirabelli was older than most other Double-A players so it should have been no surprise that he had a solid year at Shreveport.

MITCHELL, DONOVAN - 2B - BL - b: 11/27/69
1997 was Mitchell's second consecutive season at Double-A Jackson. At the age of 28 and with this being his highest level reached, he doesn't appear to be a major league outfield prospect. He did demonstrate a good eye with 61 walks to 48 strikeouts and also stole 22 bases.

MITCHELL, KEITH - OF - BR - b: 8/6/69
A solid hitter, Mitchell has decent power, walks as much as he strikes out, and steals an occasional base. Despite those credentials the Reds refused to give him a chance even when they were desperate for outfielders in mid-1997. He is too old to be considered a prospect, but he could be a pleasant surprise for a team that gave him an opportunity as a fourth outfielder.

MITCHELL, KEVIN - OF - BR - b: 1/13/62
Mitchell's reputation precedes him and if he gets another shot with anyone, it will be a huge surprise. Although he can definitely still hit for power, a brawl with Chad Curtis that put Curtis on the disabled list early last season may have sealed Mitchell's fate. Considering his weight problem and the fact that he is thirty-six years old, it takes a truly desperate team to give Mitchell yet another chance.

	AB	R	HR	RBI	SB	BA
1996 Boston	92	9	2	13	0	.304
1996 Cincinnati	114	18	6	26	0	.325
1997 Cleveland	59	7	4	11	1	.153

MITCHELL, TONY - OF - BB - b: 10/14/70
Mitchell rode a .312-11-41 performance at Double-A Jacksonville to reach Triple-A for the first time in 1996. He continued to hit for power at Toledo. 1997 was a different story. Mitchell hit .186 at Toledo in 22 games and then found himself at Double-A Carolina in the Pirates farm system where he hit .091 in four games.

MOLINA, BEN - C - BR - b: 7/20/74
Molina made it to the major league camp last spring and enhanced his prospects with a big year at the plate for Double-A Midland last year. Molina can catch and throw, and can hit for average. He's still a raw talent, but he's shown he's solid defensively and at the plate.

MOLINA, IZZY - C - BR - b: 6/3/71
A former California League All-Star, Molina can play defense, but offense is a foreign word. He did manage to hit .262 at Triple-A, but that was in the Pacific Coast League. As means of comparison, catcher Willie Morales drove in one more run, hit one less homer, and batted 30 points higher in 39 fewer at-bats. Molina is strictly a number three catcher in most organizations.

	AB	R	HR	RBI	SB	BA
1997 Oakland	111	6	3	7	0	.198

MOLINA, JOSE- C - BR - b: 6/3/75
Molina made an appearance at all three levels in the Cub farm system in 1997. He's just 22 so he has time to develop — and he needs that time to improve his offensive game. He had trouble at the plate at both Class A and Double-A, and played in just one game in Triple-A. Because Molina is behind catching prospect Pat Cline on the Cubs' depth chart he'll get plenty of opportunity to strengthen his offensive abilities.

MOLITOR, PAUL - DH - BR - b: 8/22/56
Scouting: It seems like this future Hall-of-Famer collects another milestone with every base hit any more. Even at age 41, Molitor has a swing that remains as quick as ever. He still will hit .300. He still will steal a base here and there. He is smart, savvy and still has talent. He isn't much more than a designated hitter anymore, although he will play some first base. But he needs to be in the American League. And his one drawback as a DH is that most of his power is gone.
1998: He will hit .300 or better and, in the right situation, will drive in 70 or 80 runs. He remains an adequate first baseman, although he physically won't be able to handle more than a handful of games there. He went into the winter with the option of declaring himself a free agent but was expected to return to the Twins.
1997: Molitor was the Twins' best hitter despite his advancing age — plus, he was third on the team with 11 steals. The low point of his season was having to go onto the disabled list with pulled abdominal muscles, which was frustrating for him after playing in 161 of 162 games the year before. Still, especially given his age, Molitor remains in good enough condition to play another year or two.
1996: It was a dream season in which Molitor returned to his hometown team and collected his 3,000th hit in mid-September. He collected a career-high 225 hits. Molitor played better than the Twins ever expected him to.

	AB	R	HR	RBI	SB	BA
1995 Toronto	525	63	15	60	12	.270
1996 Minnesota	660	99	9	113	18	.341
1997 Minnesota	538	63	10	89	11	.305

MONAHAN, SHANE - BL - OF - b: 8/12/74
With the departure of Jose Cruz Jr., Monahan could be close to making his major league debut. The Mariners' second-round pick in 1996, Monahan is a solid offensive player. A line-drive hitter with home run power, he still needs to develop better selectivity at the plate, he could hit upwards of .320 if he stopped getting himself out on bad pitches. As it was he hit .302 with 12 homers and 76 RBI at Double-A Memphis in 1997, then .294 in 85 at-bats at Triple-A Tacoma.

MONDESI, RAUL - OF - BR - b: 3/12/71
Scouting: Mondesi has great power at the plate and one of the best arms in baseball that he uses to patrol right field for the Dodgers. He hits for a high average as well as for power despite not having great strikezone judgment.
1998: Mondesi is locked into right field for the Dodgers and has a chance at another 30/30 year with more than a .300 batting average.
1997: Mondesi was one of the reasons the Dodgers were in contention in the National League West right down to the wire. His steals were back up after a down year in 1996, allowing him to join the 30/30 club, reaching both milestones for the first time in his career.
1996: A solid contributor on the Dodger playoff team, Mondesi raised his batting average while slightly lowering his steal total of the previous year.

	AB	R	HR	RBI	SB	BA
1995 Los Angeles	536	91	26	88	27	.285
1996 Los Angeles	634	98	24	88	14	.297
1997 Los Angeles	616	95	30	87	32	.310

MONDS, WONDERFUL - OF - BR - b: 1/11/73
Wonderful Terrific Monds the Third is his actual name and he was wonderful enough at Double-A Greenville in 1996 to earn addition to the Braves' 40-man roster over the following winter. But, Monds didn't think it was terrific to be sent back to Greenville for 1997 and, despite playing well for a month (.315 batting average with eight homers in 89 at-bats), he didn't get promoted and asked for a release. He got it. He has decent speed but his 1997 power was an illusion. Expansion could help Monds get a shot in the high minors in 1998 and possibly a major league debut later in the year, probably in a fifth outfield role.

MONTGOMERY, RAY - OF - BR - b: 8/8/69
Scouting: Montgomery is a big, strong outfielder who spent seven years in the minor leagues perfecting his skills before getting his first chance to play in the majors in 1996. His power took several years to develop. His game doesn't have any significant weaknesses but he hasn't shown any exceptional attributes that would allow him to secure a starting job. He will need to show he can hit consistently to be more than a fifth outfielder in the majors.
1998: Montgomery faces a challenge in 1998 demonstrating that he can come back after missing most of the 1997 season with shoulder surgery. If successful, he should be a reserve outfielder in the major leagues.
1997: Montgomery started the season in Houston as the fifth outfielder but was optioned to Triple-A New Orleans in early May. He hit .288 with six home runs in 73 at-bats before being recalled in late-May when Bob Abreu went on the disabled list. Montgomery suffered a severe setback when he hurt his shoulder in June. The shoulder later required surgery and he missed the rest of the season.
1996: Montgomery spent most of the season at Triple-A Tucson where he batted .306 with 22 homers and 75 RBI in 360 at-bats. He was brought up to Houston on three separate occasions where he batted only 14 times with a .214 average, but hit a

game-winning home run.

	AB	R	HR	RBI	SB	BA
1997 Houston	68	8	0	4	0	.235

MONZON, JOSE - C - BR - b: 11/8/68
Playing at age 29 in Class-A and then Triple-A, Angels farmhand Monzon is getting passed over by younger and better prospects. His major weakness is hitting, and his role is back-up catcher in the minors.

MOORE, BRANDON - SS - BR - b: 8/23/72
A scrappy infielder with a little speed, Moore is not a good hitter. He was on his way to a career high in batting average when he struggled in the second half. His base-stealing and plate discipline fell off significantly in his first year above A-ball. His 82 walks in 1996 at Class A Prince William were an organizational high, but dropped to just 45 free passes in 414 plate appearances last year at Birmingham and his four stolen bases were a career low for Moore. Despite being a good shortstop, Moore is not considered a good prospect.

MOORE, MIKE - OF - BR - b: 3/7/71
At age 26, Moore appeared in part-time roles with the Mets' Double-A and Triple-A teams, hitting .241 at the higher level. The former first-round pick (1992) by the Dodgers now looks about out of chances.

MOORE, VINCE - OF - BL - b: 9/22/71
Moore has been above A-ball just twice in seven minor-league seasons. He has problems hitting for average and has no power. He can steal bases but that skill alone will not get him near the majors. He played the entire 1997 season at Class A Rancho Cucamonga, hitting a paltry .234.

MORA, MELVIN - OF/3B - BR - b: 2/2/72
Through 1995 Mora was known as a speedy outfielder but he has stolen just 14 bases combined over the past two seasons. At Triple-A New Orleans of the Astro organization he did nothing to distinguish himself as a prospect, hitting .257 with two homers and 38 RBI.

MORALES, WILLIE - C - BR - b: 9/7/72
Morales, who has been nurtured with slow advancement, split 1997 between Double-A Huntsville, hitting .272 with three homers and 24 RBI, and Triple-A Edmonton, hitting .291 with five homers and 35 RBI. He has a fine glove and his hitting has developed along with his experience. Morales faces more competition from A.J. Hinch and Ramon Hernandez than he does from Izzy Molina. This makes the A's lucky beneficiaries of three good-looking catching prospects.

MORANDINI, MICKEY - 2B - BL - b: 4/22/66
Scouting: Morandini has developed into one of the most consistent second-tier second basemen in either league. He consistently hits the ball where it's pitched with doubles power, especially down the lines. He has slightly above-average speed — although it's declining — and is an instinctively good baserunner. Few second basemen can match his smooth hands, but his range is below average. Morandini recently improved upon one of his shortcomings by hitting 100 points better against lefthanders last year.
1998: Morandini has likely peaked but has a number of skills that will keep him near the top of his game for awhile. His speed is declining but he will retain most of his other offensive and defensive abilities. He's a good number two hitter and is signed at a bargain rate ($1.7 million), relative to other above-average major league regulars.
1997: Along with Scott Rolen, Curt Schilling and Mike Lieberthal, Morandini was the glue of a resilient Phillies' club. He exhibited no singular outstanding trait, but did everything quite well. With a bonafide leadoff hitter in place, Morandini could have driven in 60 runs.
1996: Morandini got off to a brilliant start, but was never the same after colliding with much larger Mark Whiten in an early season game in Colorado. He led the league in steals at the time, but was much less aggressive on the bases the rest of the way.

	AB	R	HR	RBI	SB	BA
1995 Philadelphia	494	65	6	49	9	.283
1996 Philadelphia	539	64	3	32	26	.250
1997 Philadelphia	553	83	1	39	16	.295

MORDECAI, MIKE - SS/2B - BR - b: 12/13/67
Scouting: Mordecai's versatility in the field is his calling card. He can play any infield position better than average, with a strong arm and good range. He isn't spectacular at shortstop, but is steady and will make more plays than many utility/multi-positional players. Mordecai is a decent hitter who can usually put the bat on the ball and has marginal power and speed.
1998: Mordecai is the favorite for Rafael Belliard's utility infield job; he certainly hit like Belliard last year anyway. He'll compete with young utility hopefuls for the primary reserve infield spot in spring training.
1997: Mordecai is a much better hitter than he showed last year; he has not adapted well to the difficulty of coming into a game cold and being able to hit. But, since it's his glove the Braves are most interested in, his poor offensive showing was not a major concern.
1996: Mordecai's second season in the majors was a mirror image of his first. Although his batting average dropped some, he was still occasionally productive at the plate and was, as usual, helpful as a versatile utility man.

	AB	R	HR	RBI	SB	BA
1995 Atlanta	75	10	3	11	0	.280
1996 Atlanta	108	12	2	8	1	.241
1997 Atlanta	81	8	0	3	0	.173

MORGAN, KEVIN - 2B - BR - b: 3/3/70
In his seventh minor-league season, Morgan split time between Triple-A Norfolk and Double-A Binghamton in 1997. He performed better at the higher level but not good enough to warrant a look by the big club. With Gold Glover Rey Ordonez firmly entrenched as the Mets' shortstop, Morgan will continue to fill an organizational player role.

MORGAN, SCOTT - OF - BR - b: 7/19/73
Morgan is a massive (6'7", 230 pounds) power hitter whose long swing was exposed during a 1997 promotion to Double-A after power rampages at both Class A levels. Morgan is basically a one-tool prospect; his speed and defense are below average, and he will likely struggle to hit for average at higher levels. Morgan will get a full season at Double-A in the Indians' farm system in 1998; he must refine his long swing and develop better plate discipline to advance further.

MORIARTY, MIKE - SS - BR - b: 3/8/74
A two-time All-Big East performer at Seton Hall in 1994-95, Moriarty moved up to Double-A ball last year after a successful stint in the Florida State League in 1996. Moriarty can run and field but will have to improve at the plate before he can advance to the next level. He hit just .221 with six homers and 48 RBI in 421 at-bats.

MORILLO, CESAR - SS - BB - b: 7/21/73
The Royals let Morillo go after seven minor-league seasons, and he spent 1997 with the Rangers' Double-A club. He hit .264 with no speed or power, and has little chance to make it to the majors.

MORMAN, RUSS - OF - BR - b: 4/28/62
Scouting: Morman is the consummate slugging minor-league journeyman with just enough bat speed to consistently dominate Triple-A pitching, but fall short against major league hurlers. He is a wild swinger who only recently has developed a modicum of plate discipline, and has learned to level off on outside pitches and hit them to the opposite field for singles. He is a below-average defender at first base who logs quite a bit of designated hitter time. At age 36, even expansion is unlikely to produce much more than another major league cup of coffee for Morman.
1998: Morman is likely to serve another season as a Triple-A regular, though the presence of Kevin Millar might necessitate a move away from the Marlins' organization. He has shown little evidence of tailing off with the bat in a Triple-A setting, and might have another three years or so as a DH ahead of him.
1997: Morman devastated International League pitching to the tune of a .623 slugging percentage with a homer every 12 at-bats. He earned his ninth brief major league trial, and lashed his tenth homer in 470 at-bats in the bigs.
1996: Morman was limited to 289 Triple-A at-bats, but had another strong season, hitting for average with extreme power. He earned six September at-bats in the majors, managing only a double.

MORRIS, BOBBY - 1B - BL - b: 11/22/72
The younger brother of Hal, Morris has gone from a promising Cubs' prospect to a journeyman Indians' prospect on the verge of extinction in a short period of time. Morris batted .354 with patience at lower Class A for the Cubs in 1994, but exhibited few complementary skills. He's an average fielder whose chances for a major league job disappeared when he had to be moved from second base to first base, where power beyond Morris' capability is required. His plate discipline is exemplary, but he'll have a hard time scoring a full-time job for someone's Double-A squad in 1998.

MORRIS, HAL - 1B - BL - b: 4/9/65
Scouting: Morris is a fine contact hitter and a good defensive first baseman, however he has no other notable skills. His career high in walks is 50, his career high in home runs is 16, and he has been injury prone the last few seasons. He has a large platoon split and hits best on astroturf. His combination of high average and doubles power is valuable if he hits .330, but he is replaceable if he hits .280.
1998: After becoming a free agent in the off-season, Morris wasn't highly sought due to his age, injury history, and poor 1997 season. He could hold a full-time role for a team that is bargain hunting, but would be most effective in a platoon role.
1997: Bothered by shoulder problems most of the season, Morris was in the midst of the worst season of his career when he finally underwent arthroscopic surgery in August. He subsequently lost his starting job to Eduardo Perez.
1996: Morris had one of the best years of his career, setting career highs in home runs, RBI, runs scored, and walks.

	AB	R	HR	RBI	SB	BA
1995 Cincinnati	359	53	11	51	1	.279
1996 Cincinnati	528	82	16	80	7	.313
1997 Cincinnati	333	42	1	33	3	.276

MOSQUERA, JULIO - C - BR - b: 1/29/72
Scouting: Mosquera has a lightning-quick throwing arm and can hit to all fields. Although he is not blessed with power, he is improving as a hitter.
1998: With an outside shot to make the big-league club as a backup out of spring training, Mosquera should start the year at Triple-A. He will appear in the majors at some point this year.
1997: Spending most of the season at Double-A Knoxville, Mosquera improved to a .291 average over 309 at-bats, including 23 doubles.
1996: Mosquera was called upon briefly by the Blue Jays when Sandy Martinez was injured. He didn't look out of place either but his hitting left something to be desired. He established himself as the next man down on the Toronto depth chart.

MOTTOLA, CHAD - OF - BR - b: 10/15/71
A former first-round draft pick, Mottola has failed to develop offensively. He is considered a good outfielder with a strong arm. In 1997, he cut his strikeouts and raised his batting average at Triple-A Indianapolis, but at the expense of what little power he had. He is too old to be considered a good prospect, but he could compete for a fifth outfielder role in 1998.

MOUTON, JAMES - OF - BR - b: 12/29/68
Scouting: Mouton's first three seasons with Houston were nearly identical with an average of 302 at-bats, three home runs, 23 stolen bases, a batting average of .257, an on-base average of .328 and a slugging average of .341. The club was disappointed that he hadn't shown improvement. In his fourth season in 1997, he took a sharp downturn with a batting average of .211, an on-base average of .287 and a slugging average of .322 in 180 at-bats. These numbers won't keep him in the major leagues. Like Kenny Lofton before him and Brian Hunter after him, Mouton arrived in the big leagues after a big year at Triple-A Tucson. Only Mouton has failed to build on that success.
1998: Mouton is still young enough to salvage his career but he must do it in 1998. He will have to scramble for a job and will have a tough time getting significant playing time.
1997: Mouton's career hit a new low when he was bypassed for the post-season roster in favor of rookies Richard Hidalgo and Bob Abreu.
1996: Mouton failed to show improvement in his third year as a semi-regular with Houston.

	AB	R	HR	RBI	SB	BA
1995 Houston	298	42	4	27	25	.262
1997 Houston	180	24	3	23	9	.211

MOUTON, LYLE - OF - BR - b: 5/13/69
Scouting: Mouton is a multi-talented athlete who played basketball at Louisiana State University, but he doesn't make good use of his physical attributes. He has a big build (6'4", 240 pounds) but isn't a strong hitter. His inability to make consistent contact

or to drive the ball over the fence with regularity has resulted in a reserve outfield role. His defense is barely adequate as a corner outfielder.
1998: Available in the expansion draft, Mouton went unnoticed by everyone except Baseball Weekly. He is more likely to end up playing in Japan than in the outfield of Tampa Bay or Arizona. Wherever he plays, Mouton will offer some home run pop and a little speed, but nothing stellar.
1997: This time Mouton lost out to rookie sensation Mike Cameron; as the season wore on he became less frequently a part of the Sox lineup; it was a disappointing season.
1996: Mouton lost a regular job to the surging Davey Martinez, but still had a good batting average with some power.

	AB	R	HR	RBI	SB	BA
1995 Chicago AL	179	23	5	27	1	.302
1996 Chicago AL	214	25	7	39	3	.294
1997 Chicago AL	242	26	5	23	4	.269

MOYLE, MIKE - C - BR - b: 9/8/71
Moyle is a six-year minor-league veteran who finally cracked the Double-A barrier in the Indians' organization in 1997. He's a sturdy receiver who carried a career-high workload and showed significant development with the bat. He will always be a low-average hitter, but he showed an ability to drive Double-A fastballs for power while displaying good plate discipline. He's not a threat for a major league job, but he should be a credible Triple-A player in the intermediate term.

MUELLER, BILL - 3B - BB - b: 3/17/71
Scouting: A selective hitter, Mueller finally has emerged with some power and even a little speed, to claim the third base job with the Giants. He has good hands, reacts well and owns a strong arm, and he is a good and quick learner. He'll just get better.
1998: Last year was no fluke for Mueller, whose previous low batting average as a pro was .297. Mueller also had to prove himself in the eyes of Giants' management — something he did as the season wore on. Third base will be his this year, he'll get his 500 at-bats, and will be fun to watch in the process.
1997: After a hot spring training, Mueller began the season as part of a platoon with Mark Lewis. But, as the season progressed, he saw more playing time, showing a better eye and better glove than Lewis. He had often been projected as a number two hitter and those projections proved prophetic as Mueller helped set the table for the middle of the Giants' batting order.
1996: Mueller had a fine three-quarters of a season at Triple-A Phoenix, batting .302 with four homers and 46 RBI, then continued his great contact hitting and plate discipline with the Giants, subbing for injured Matt Williams.

	AB	R	HR	RBI	SB	BA
1996 San Francisco	200	31	0	19	0	.330
1997 San Francisco	390	51	7	44	4	.292

MULLIGAN, SEAN - C - BR - b: 4/25/70
Mulligan matured into a power hitter in 1996, and had a good year in Triple-A. With John Flaherty and Brad Johnson, the Padres are solid at catching, so he has an uphill battle to win a roster spot. In 1997 he turned up in the Cleveland organization at Double-A Akron but played in just two games.

MUMMAU, BOB - 2B/SS - BR - b: 8/21/70
Mummau is a decent defensive second baseman with occasional pop in his bat. He hit .255 with eight homers and 40 RBI while splitting the second base job at Triple-A Syracuse with Jeff Patzke, who is considered a better prospect. Mummau is not considered a prospect, and would need both to upgrade his performance and have the right circumstances (major league injuries, for example) to get a shot at the majors. He's a reserve, at best, in the bigs.

MURPHY, MIKE - OF - BR - b: 1/23/72
Murphy split time between Double-A Tulsa and Triple-A Oklahoma City last season, playing well for the 89ers (.329 with five homers, 25 RBI and 14 steals in 243 at-bats). Speed is his main asset and he showed an improved ability to draw walks last season. Murphy has some chance to make it to the majors, probably as a fifth outfielder/pinch-runner type.

MURRAY, CALVIN - OF - BR - b: 7/30/71
A former number one draft pick, Murray has fallen so far off the map he no longer rates as a top ten prospect. He had a decent year at Double-A Shreveport, hitting .272 with ten homers, 56 RBI and 52 steals, but he should be well past that level of play by now. Murray is showing better plate discipline; he drew 66 walks with 73 strikeouts last year.

MURRAY, EDDIE - DH - BB - b: 2/24/56
Scouting: Too slow to play first base, Murray is strictly a DH and pinch-hitter now that he's in the twilight of an illustrious career.
1998: Murray will be 42 years old on opening day and may have played the last season of his career. He could catch on with a team looking for a DH and clubhouse presence, but Murray's days as a regular position player are behind him.
1997: Murray played in 55 games during 1997 and may be best remembered for two crucial ground-ball double plays that he hit into down the stretch for the Dodgers when battling for the National League West title.
1996: Murray started with Cleveland, who believed his bat had slowed considerably and shipped him off to Baltimore. Murray was productive with the Orioles, launching career home run number 500 during the year.

	AB	R	HR	RBI	SB	BA
1995 Cleveland	436	68	21	82	5	.323
1996 Clev-Baltimore	566	69	22	79	4	.260
1997 two teams	167	13	3	18	1	.222

MURRAY, GLENN - OF - BR - b: 11/23/70
Murray platooned in the Phillies' outfield in 1996 before a wrist injury cut his season short. He is a weak defender with a below-average arm who hasn't proven he can hit big-league pitching. He spent the 1997 season in the Reds' system and was successful at the Double-A level, hitting .283 with 26 homers and 73 RBI. He got a late promotion to Triple-A but got just 12 at-bats. He may get a longer look in Triple-A this year and could hit his way a into another reserve outfield opportunity in the majors.

	AB	R	HR	RBI	SB	BA
1996 Philadelphia	97	8	2	6	1	.196

MYERS, GREG - C - BL - b: 4/14/66
Scouting: A solid receiver who hits — and hits well — lefthanded, Myers will have a job in the majors for the next few seasons. He will hit the occasional home run and will rattle several fences for

extra-base hits, and he can hit both righthanders and lefthanders. His biggest drawback is that he usually goes to the disabled list at least once each season.

1998: Because of his propensity toward nagging injuries, the best situation for Myers is as a back-up catcher who will pinch-hit often. Or, in the American League, as a designated hitter.
1997: Myers collected some important hits for the Twins before being traded to Atlanta but never saw the hot streak that he usually finds at least a couple of times per season. An August trade to Atlanta landed him in his first career post-season.
1996: Although he wasn't close to any awards, Myers had the best season of his career, establishing career-highs in batting, at-bats, runs, hits and RBI.

	AB	R	HR	RBI	SB	BA
1995 California AL	273	35	9	38	0	.260
1996 Minnesota AL	329	37	6	47	0	.286
1997 two teams	174	24	5	29	0	.259

MYERS, RODERICK - OF - BL - b: 1/14/73

Scouting: Myers is a talented player who can hit for average with a little power, excellent speed, and above-average defense in the outfield. He's a little strikeout-prone, but will also take a walk. He has not yet learned to hit good lefthanded pitching, but he has had little opportunity so far. Myers is a rising star.
1998: One of the least-known prospects, Myers is ready for an everyday role in the majors. He may start the year in a left field platoon, but his defense, all-around offensive talents and above-average baserunning ability make Myers an odds-on favorite to win a full-time job this year.
1997: Scheduled to open the season in center field for the Royals, Myers broke his wrist playing winter ball and missed half the season. When he recovered, Myers wowed the Royals with marvelous defense, good hitting and base-stealing ability. He showed he was, indeed, ready for the big leagues.
1996: Myers earned his first major league recall with a fine season at Triple-A Omaha, hitting .292 with sixteen homers, 54 RBI and 37 stolen bases. After winning back-to-back American Association Player of the Week awards as the season wound down, Myers homered in his first at-bat after returning to the majors.

	AB	R	HR	RBI	SB	BA
1996 Kansas City	63	9	1	11	3	.286
1997 Kansas City	101	14	2	9	4	.257

NAEHRING, TIM - 3B - BR - b: 2/1/67

Scouting: Naehring is a solid player all around. He's a capable hitter against all kinds of pitching, shows some power and works the count well. He's a good third baseman, and capable of filling in at other positions. However, his career is now in limbo after he suffered a major elbow injury and had reconstructive surgery. He may not be all the way back to start the season. Another thing to keep in mind: you can look at them as freak accidents, but the injuries which have hampered Naehring's career might all be linked to back problems caused by one of his legs being shorter than the other.
1998: If he's healthy he'll be a full-time player with some team. But, as an infielder with a solid, but unspectacular bat, if Naehring can't throw he's not of much use.
1997: Naehring was having a typically good season and playing nearly every day until he tore up his elbow making a throw from third base and was lost for the season.
1996: Naehring had more than 400 at-bats for the second year in a row — the only two times he's done it — and posted a career high in homers an RBI.

	AB	R	HR	RBI	SB	BA
1995 Boston	433	61	10	57	0	.307
1996 Boston	430	77	17	65	2	.288
1997 Boston	259	38	9	40	1	.286

NATAL, BOB - C - BR - b: 11/13/65

Because he's a poor hitter but a fundamentally sound catcher, Natal has shuttled between Triple-A and the majors during his five years in the Marlins' organization. His role with Florida was significantly downgraded last season due to the presence of Gregg Zaun although Natal had an unusually good season with the bat at Triple-A Charlotte. Natal has reached his level; he'll continue in a backup catcher role in his sporadic major league trials and will play more regularly in the high minors.

	AB	R	HR	RBI	SB	BA
1995 Florida	43	2	2	6	0	.233
1996 Florida	90	4	0	2	0	.133

NAVA, LIPSO - 3B - BR - b: 11/28/68

The Cubs signed Nava as a free agent after he spent a year playing in an independent league. He hit 17 home runs that year, playing against obviously weaker competition, but nothing he's done before or since indicates that he's got major league ability at all. In fact, his performance in 1997 is by far the best year he's had in the professional minor leagues; Nava hit .266 with nine homers in 109 games for Double-A Orlando last year. But despite the fact that the Cubs need middle-infield help, Nava isn't going to get much of a shot. It would be a shock to see him on anybody's big-league roster.

NEAL, MIKE - 2B - BR - b: 11/5/71

Neal is a scrappy hustler who showed much offensive improvement in his third tour of the Double-A Eastern League. His 17 homers nearly matched his previous career total of 18 and he didn't sacrifice batting average in the process. He's not a defensive whiz in the field, but is sure-handed within his limited range. His lack of upward movement through the organization makes it clear that Neal does not have a major league future, but he finally has proven himself ready to inherit the starting Triple-A second base position.

NEEL, TROY - 1B - BL - b: 9/14/65

One of the Japanese players who might actually be expected to do well if he ever returns to America, Neel has been in Japan since 1995. He hit .266 with 15 home runs as part-timer with Oakland in 1994. In Japan, Neel has been a consistently productive power hitter, but age is becoming an issue with reference to a possible return to the majors.

NEILL, MIKE - OF - BL - b: 4/27/70

At age 27, Neill barely got a chance to hit at Triple-A in 1997, and when he did the results were less than pretty (.190 batting average). He isn't a prospect and he is going nowhere, despite his gaudy numbers at Huntsville: .340 batting average with 14 homers, 80 RBI and 16 stolen bases.

NELSON, BRYANT - SS - BB - b: 1/27/74

A 44th-round pick by the Astros in 1993, Nelson turned up in the Cubs organization at Double-A Orlando and had a solid season.

He has good range and a strong arm at third base and made consistent contact, showing some power to the gaps. He led the team in doubles with 33 and walked 45 times against 43 punchouts. He has the ability to play multiple positions in the infield and outfield, giving him a shot at a utility player role in the majors someday.

NEVERS, TOM - SS - BR - b: 9/13/71

As a first-round draft pick, Nevers looks like a bust. 1997 was a disappointing season as he hit only .233 with eight homers and 27 RBI at Louisville in his first season at the Triple-A level; he had four times more strikeouts than walks. He has been in the minors for eight years but still has yet to prove he has major league potential.

NEVIN, PHIL - 3B - BR - b: 1/19/71

Scouting: A one-time top overall pick in the June draft, Nevin has never been able to win and hold a regular job in the big leagues. He's learned to play many positions besides third base, which is still his best. He even learned to catch. But he's not outstanding on defense anywhere, even at third. He has to hit, and in '97, given his biggest chance, he didn't.

1998: If Nevin had done better in his '97 opportunities, he could have become the successor to Travis Fryman, whose big contract had the Tigers thinking of trading him. Instead, a .235 batting average had the Tigers thinking of Nevin as no more than a utility player.

1997: Nevin played well at times, but his average peaked at .289 just after the All-Star break, and fell almost non-stop thereafter. He did play everywhere, from third base to left field to first base to catcher.

1996: The year began with Nevin a little disappointed at being sent to Double-A Jacksonville to become a catcher. It ended with Nevin starting 23 of the last 30 games at third base, with Fryman playing shortstop. He hit well in that short chance, batting .284 with eight home runs in September.

	AB	R	HR	RBI	SB	BA
1995 two teams	156	13	2	13	1	.179
1996 Detroit	120	15	8	19	1	.292
1997 Detroit	251	32	9	35	0	.235

NEWFIELD, MARC - OF/1B - BR - b: 10/19/72

Scouting: Newfield has power potential and was projected as a future star, but his shoulder surgery in 1997 raises some questions. He had been pencilled in as the starter in left field for Milwaukee, but had a nagging leg problem in spring training and then developed his shoulder problems. The Brewers have urged him to change his weight training because he bulked up too quickly.

1998: The Brewers don't want to give up on Newfield. He will come to spring training and, if fully recovered from his injury, will have a chance to start in left field.

1997: Newfield was dogged by injuries from the start and finally underwent surgery at mid-season.

1996: Newfield hit for a mediocre average in 84 games with San Diego and then went to Milwaukee as part of the trade that sent pitchers Bryce Florie and Ron Villone to the Brewers for Greg Vaughn. He hit 15 homers in 49 games and was projected as the starter in left field in 1997.

	AB	R	HR	RBI	SB	BA
1995 Seattle	85	7	3	14	0	.188
1995 San Diego	55	6	1	7	0	.309
1996 San Diego	191	27	5	26	1	.251
1996 Milwaukee	179	21	7	31	0	.307
1997 Milwaukee	157	14	1	18	0	.229

NEWHAN, DAVID - 2B - BL - b: 9/7/73

Newhan provides great hustle and great versatility with the glove for the A's organization. Good bat speed and strikezone judgment help Newhan overcome his lack of size. He has hit well throughout his three-year minor-league career and can play all outfield and infield spots except shortstop and catcher. His best position is the outfield but he played second base at Double-A Huntsville. His versatility with the glove could buy him a spot in the majors eventually.

NEWSON, WARREN - OF - BL - b: 7/3/64

Scouting: Newson is a capable fourth outfielder, although he has not enjoyed much recent success as a pinch-hitter. He's a fastball hitter with surprising power, but has a tendency to strike out frequently (once in every three at-bats over the past two seasons). Newson is only adequate in the field, and has little speed.

1998: Newson should be fully recovered for the start of spring training, and should be on someone's roster as a spare outfielder.

1997: Before a torn biceps tendon ended his season in August, Newson was having a typical year - good power with lots of walks and strikeouts.

1996: Newson had a good season as a part-time player, hitting a career-high ten homers but striking out at an alarming rate.

	AB	R	HR	RBI	SB	BA
1995 Chi. AL - Sea.	157	34	5	15	2	.261
1996 Texas	235	34	10	31	3	.255
1997 Texas	169	23	10	23	3	.213

NEWSTROM, DOUG - 3B - BL - b: 9/18/71

An excellent lefthanded hitter, Newstrom has a chance to make a big-league roster one day as a backup catcher, first baseman and outfielder. An offensive player who hits for average, he's especially tough in the clutch or with two strikes, but has no power. Newstrom is not going to win a job with his glove.

NICHOLAS, DARRELL - OF - BR - b: 5/26/72

Nicholas is a speedy outfielder who improved at the plate in 1997 at Double-A El Paso in the Brewers organization. Nicholas stole 17 bases and legged out 47 doubles. He can cover ground in the outfield and if he keeps improving at the plate he could become a prospect for a fourth outfielder/ pinch-runner role in the majors.

NICHOLSON, KEVIN - SS - BB - b: 3/29/76

San Diego took Nicholson with the 27th pick in the first round of the 1997 draft. That made Nicholson, who calls Surrey, British Columbia home, the highest drafted Canadian ever. Last year, he played A-ball in the Arizona League and the California League. He showed some power in a short season and should start 1998 in higher A-ball.

NIEVES, MELVIN - OF - BB - b: 12/28/71

Scouting: As a switch-hitter with outstanding power, Nieves was always a player scouts loved. Not anymore, now that two teams have decided that he simply strikes out too much to contribute. Even Tigers General Manager Randy Smith, who

twice traded for Nieves (once with the Padres, then with the Tigers), was more than ready to let him go play somewhere else.
1998: Given 500 at-bats, Nieves should hit 30 home runs. The problem is finding a chance for 500 at-bats, because it would also mean 200 or more strikeouts. The chance won't come with the Tigers.
1997: Nieves started only four games in September, an example of just how much the Tigers had given up on him. He still struck out 15 times in September, an example of why they did. Nieves did hit 20 home runs in just 359 at-bats, and his batting average of .406 when he makes contact was nothing short of sensational.
1996: Traded to the Tigers in spring training, Nieves got a chance to play regularly and at times deserved it. His 24 home runs included one that went over the Tiger Stadium roof.

	AB	R	HR	RBI	SB	BA
1995 San Diego	234	32	14	38	2	.205
1996 Detroit	431	71	24	60	1	.246
1997 Detroit	359	46	20	64	1	.228

NILSSON, DAVE - OF - BL - b: 12/14/69

Scouting: Nilsson has developed into a good line drive hitter, with some power potential. He still struggles at times against lefties. A converted catcher, Nilsson can play first base and the outfield, as well as DH. Because of a variety of physical problems, his stamina is suspect at times.
1998: The Brewers have signed Nilsson to a long-term contract and hope he is one of their core players. He likely will split time between first and DH if the Brewers stay in the American League, and play the outfield if they go to the National League with John Jaha returning to first base.
1997: Nilsson set career high in homers and drove in over 80 runs, but slumped badly in the last month. He didn't hit a homer after August fifth. A toe problem bothered him in the last couple of weeks.
1996: Nilsson earned the Brewers' Harvey Kuenn Award for hitting following his .331 average with 84 RBI. His biggest accomplishment might have been coming back from a rare case of Ross River Fever, contracted in his native Australia from a mosquito bite.

	AB	R	HR	RBI	SB	BA
1995 Milwaukee	263	41	12	53	2	.278
1996 Milwaukee	453	81	17	84	2	.331
1997 Milwaukee	554	71	20	81	2	.278

NIXON, OTIS - OF - BB - b: 1/9/59

Scouting: Nixon still has great speed at the age of 38, which makes him a base-stealing threat and a great outfielder with sure hands and super range. His one defensive drawback is a weak arm. At the plate, Nixon switch-hits with no power from either side but makes up for it with speed.
1998: Nixon has the ability to be a solid center fielder in the majors for another season, even though he'll be 39 years old on opening day.
1997: Nixon started the season in Toronto and was acquired late by the Dodgers for their unsuccessful playoff push. Nixon put together a fine season that included 59 stolen bases — his second-best career total — and good outfield play.
1996: Nixon signed with the Blue Jays as a free agent to plug the hole left by the departed Devon White. Nixon supplied the Jays with a defensive presence and a good leadoff hitter.

	AB	R	HR	RBI	SB	BA
1995 Texas	589	87	0	45	50	.295
1996 Toronto	496	87	1	29	54	.286
1997 two teams	576	84	2	44	59	.266

NIXON, TROT - OF - BL - b: 4/11/74

Scouting: After back problems, Nixon is no longer the dynamic athlete he was as a top draft pick coming out of high school, but he's got a chance to be a solid player. He's an average runner, but he gets a great jump on the ball in the outfield and works hard at that part of the game. He's a right fielder, but he can play center; he has a strong, accurate arm. Nixon's swing is a little long and he doesn't react well to off-speed pitches, but he sits on the fastball well and has a good eye, laying off anything out of the strike zone.
1998: Nixon will start the year in Triple-A. How well he does and whether or not he's promoted during the season will depend on his lowering his hands and shortening his swing.
1997: Nixon started out at Triple-A by hitting .123 over the first month. The Red Sox resisted the urge to demote him, and he showed a lot of character by improving each month of the season, finally finishing at .244 with 20 homers and 63 walks. He played well in the outfield.
1996: In his first full year at Double-A, Nixon played solidly, but not spectacularly. Of concern was his total of 26 extra-base hits in 438 at-bats, to go with a .251 batting average.

NORMAN, LES - OF - BR - b: 2/25/69

Norman is a journeyman who spent six years in the Royals' system, making two brief major league appearances, before moving to Triple-A Buffalo in the Indians' chain in 1997. He is a wild swinger with only enough bat speed to hit for mid-range home run power against Triple-A pitchers. Against major league pitching, he has been overmatched, and he isn't likely to get another chance. His defensive skills are acceptable, with decent range and a strong enough arm to play right field.

	AB	R	HR	RBI	SB	BA
1995 Kansas City	40	6	0	4	0	.225
1996 Kansas City	49	9	0	0	1	.122

NORTHEIMER, JAMIE - C - BR - b: 7/5/72

Northeimer made appearances at all three levels in the Phillies' organization in 1997 after spending 1996 at Class A Clearwater. He had problems at the plate, having his best luck in Clearwater and will probably start 1998 at Double-A.

NORTON, CHRIS - DH - BR - b: 9/21/70

Signed out of the independent Texas-Louisiana League a year ago, Norton can catch and play first base, but he's increased his value by showing he can play the outfield as well. Norton can hit with some power, too, although he is not considered one of the Angels' better prospects.

NORTON, GREG - SS - BB - b: 7/6/72

Scouting: Norton can do a little bit of just about anything, but doesn't stand out in any particular area. He's a good defensive player, if a bit awkward looking. His batting eye has not been as good in recent years, but is still a positive. He isn't a serious power threat, but has a little bit of pop, too. Focusing on, and developing, more specific skills would make Norton a slightly better prospect.
1998: Even with the volatile infield situation in Chicago and the expansion draft, it's hard to see where Norton fits into the White Sox's plans. His best position, third base, is ably manned by Robin Ventura; Norton can't play shortstop on a regular basis.

But utility infield roles are already filled with more experienced players with better-defined skills. Another season at Triple-A is probably in Norton's immediate future.

1997: In his first full year at Triple-A Nashville, Norton had a disappointing batting average, but hit for decent power (12 homers) in 253 at-bats and earned a second September cameo with the White Sox.

1996: Norton earned his major-league debut with solid play for Double-A Birmingham and Nashville. He batted .284 with 15 homers, 43 extra-base hits and 70 RBI in 451 at-bats split between the two levels. He made a notable big-league debut by getting two hits in his first two plate appearances —both in the same inning.

NUNEZ, ABRAHAM - SS - BB - b: 3/16/76

Scouting: Nunez has outstanding speed and Gold-Glove caliber defensive skills. While many have questioned whether the switch-hitter will have a high enough batting average to play in the majors, he has gone about answering that question. He is improving from both sides of the plate.

1998: The Pirates won't be forced into rushing Nunez to the starting lineup. They will try to re-sign a free agent for one year instead, or, if that fails, they will get by with Kevin Polcovich and Lou Collier while Nunez takes some time to develop at Triple-A Nashville. Nunez, though, could force his way onto the major league scene at some point in the season.

1997: Nunez played well at Class A Lynchburg and Double-A Carolina, prompting the Pirates to promote him to the major league level in time to be eligible for post-season play. Though the Pirates wound up second in the National League Central race, Nunez flashed his outstanding skills in his brief time at the major league level.

1996: After spending two seasons in the Dominican Summer League with the Blue Jays, Nunez went to short-season Class A St. Catherine's and was one of the top players in the New York-Penn League. Pirates scouts fell in love with him and Pittsburgh insisted he be part of the nine-player trade with Toronto in November.

NUNEZ, RAMON - 1B/OF - BR - b: 9/22/72

Scouting: Nunez was once a promising infield prospect in the rich Atlanta Braves' farm system. He hit 17 homers in A-ball in 1994, but failed miserably in two Double-A trials and was released by the Braves after the 1996 season. He's got decent power for a middle infielder, but pitchers at higher levels have been able to take advantage of his lack of knowledge of the strike zone. He's struck out at levels usually associated with big-time power hitters and he walks far too infrequently.

1998: Nunez had a good enough year in 1997 to get another shot at least in Double-A. But it's highly doubtful that Nunez will be a major league regular at any point in his career.

1997: Nunez had a surprisingly good year for the Cubs' Double-A team in Orlando, hitting .296 with sixteen homers and 65 RBI. He couldn't take advantage of two shots at Double-A while in the Braves' farm system, but he had his best minor-league season in 1997. He didn't show any improvement in his strikezone judgment, however.

1996: Nunez started the season in Double-A for the second straight year, but had a miserable season there and was again demoted back to A-ball. The Braves released him following the season.

NUNEZ, SERGIO - 2B - BR - b: 1/3/75

Nunez advanced to Double-A for the first time in 1997, hitting .277 in just 34 games for Wichita; his season was shortened by injury. Nunez has good speed; he led the Carolina League and the Royals farm system with 44 steals for Wilmington in 1996. He's a good fielder with above-average range. Nunez will advance to Triple-A Omaha in 1998; he may start the season there. He's behind Jed Hansen on the Royals' second base depth chart, but not far behind.

NUNNALLY JON - OF - BL - b: 11/9/71

Scouting: Nunnally is a free-swinging power hitter, and despite a high strikeout rate has shown signs of developing into a solid major league hitter. His walk rate in the minors and with the Royals was acceptable and his outfield defense was good enough for the Reds to give him an extended trial in center field in 1997.

1998: On a team desperate for power and holding open auditions for outfielders, Nunnally has an excellent opportunity to grab a full-time role with a strong spring. At worst, he will be a platoon regular.

1997: Due to a slow start and an overabundance of outfielders, the Royals gave up on Nunnally and dealt him (along with Chris Stynes) in exchange for Hector Carrasco. One of Jack McKeon's first moves after taking over the Reds was to make Nunnally a platoon regular, and he turned in a strong performance in a 200 at-bat trial, although he was overshadowed by the hot start had by Chris Stynes.

1996: Nunnally established his credentials as a prospect with a fine season at Triple-A Omaha, where he hit .281 with 25 home runs in only 345 at-bats. He struggled in a 90 at-bat trial in Kansas City, after performing well as a Rule Five draftee in 1995.

	AB	R	HR	RBI	SB	BA
1995 Kansas City	303	51	14	42	6	.244
1996 Kansas City	90	16	5	17	0	.211
1997 Cincinnati	230	46	14	39	7	.309

OBANDO, SHERMAN - OF/DH - BR - b: 1/23/70

Obando was once such a hot prospect that Baltimore selected him from the New York Yankees in the Rule 5 Draft and kept him on the major league roster throughout the 1993 season. Obando, though, has never lived up to his potential. He struggled mightily with the Expos last year, underwent reconstructive left elbow surgery in August and was released at the end of the season. The injury and continued lack of strong performances leaves Obando's major league future in serious doubt. His chances of stardom are now zero.

	AB	R	HR	RBI	SB	BA
1995 Baltimore	38	0	0	3	1	.263
1996 Montreal	178	30	8	22	2	.247

O'BRIEN, CHARLIE - C - BR - b: 5/1/61

Scouting: A catcher with a reputation for calling a good game, O'Brien has occasional power and can still throw runners out. He'll never win a batting title but is useful to a team with young pitchers.

1998: Most felt after last year that O'Brien would not be back with the Blue Jays but he is good enough defensively that he can still play. It will be surprising if he ever gets over 200 at-bats in a season again and his average is unlikely to top .230.

1997: Benito Santiago's struggles gave O'Brien an opportunity to play more, though not as much as the previous year. He was outspoken about the Blue Jays' dismal performance and apparent lack of effort.

1996: Sandy Martinez started 1996 as the regular catcher but a subpar performance mixed with O'Brien's surprising power numbers enabled O'Brien to achieve career highs in at-bats (324) and home runs (13).

	AB	R	HR	RBI	SB	BA
1995 Atlanta	198	18	9	23	0	.227
1996 Toronto	324	33	13	44	0	.238
1997 Toronto	225	22	4	27	0	.218

OCHOA, ALEX - OF - BR - b: 3/29/72

Scouting: Ochoa's arm is immediately noticeable. Unfortunately, it's the only component of his game that is above major league average. At least that's how it looked last season when a young player who always had hit, didn't hit a lick. His outfielding improved dramatically when he improved his ability to read fly balls.

1998: Ochoa was likely to be excluded from the Mets protected list. The club would be delighted if the heavy coat of tarnish on Ochoa's hitting skills disappeared. But it was concerned by all he endured last season.

1997: No aspect of the Mets' season other than Bernard Gilkey's production and the injuries to pitchers was more disappointing than Ochoa's offensive production. Having batted .295 in 319 major league at-bats before last season, Ochoa came to spring training looking much stronger and then improved his outfield work. But his poor hitting denied him regular work. He batted .224 with a .290 slugging percentage in 107 at-bats against lefthanded pitching and .260 with a .397 slugging percentage in 131 at-bats against righthanded pitching.

1996: Ochoa was battering Triple-A pitching when summoned to the big leagues. And while his production tailed off, he did hit for a good average and, one glorious July night in Philadelphia, he hit for the cycle. It seemed that his career had taken off.

	AB	R	HR	RBI	SB	BA
1995 New York NL	37	7	0	0	1	.297
1996 New York NL	282	37	4	33	4	.294
1997 New York NL	238	31	3	22	3	.244

OFFERMAN, JOSE - 2B/SS - BB - b: 11/8/68

Scouting: Offerman's move to second base has been a success. He no longer shows his customary throwing problems and has decent range and a steady glove. He has also been one of the better major league regulars at getting on-base. Offerman is extremely streaky, often hitting over .500 for a week or more, before reverting to a month of less spectacular hitting. He has gap power, a good batting eye and above-average speed, but is among the worst baserunners in the majors; Offerman runs into outs so frequently on the bases that it negates his high on-base percentage.

1998: Jed Hansen's steady play is in contrast to Offerman's streakiness and unsteady baserunning; if Offerman loses the battle for the second base job, expect him to move on to another organization, he'd be a poor reserve player. As a major league regular, Offerman will hit for a high average, steal some bases, and get caught off base frequently.

1997: Offerman went to the disabled list three times with a strained groin, the chicken pox, and an ankle sprain. The last DL stint resulted in Jed Hansen's recall and a new challenge for his second base job. Offerman was again among team leaders in batting average, on-base percentage, and triples.

1996: Offerman first failed as a shortstop, making a ton of errors and hitting for a low average. Shifted to first base, he displaced popular Bob Hamelin, but was reborn as a player. His hitting return to normal levels, he stole bases once again and his throwing problems disappeared. Offerman eventually shifted to second base and remained a successful and productive player.

	AB	R	HR	RBI	SB	BA
1995 Los Angeles	429	69	4	33	2	.287
1996 Kansas City	561	85	5	47	24	.303
1997 Kansas City	424	59	2	39	9	.297

OGDEN, JAMIE - 1B/OF - BL - b: 1/19/72

A hometown favorite because he's from the suburban Twin Cities, Ogden appears to have peaked at Triple-A Salt Lake, where he batted .286 with 14 homers and 53 RBI last season. He's yet to make his major-league debut after eight seasons in the minors.

OJEDA, AUGIE - SS - BB - b: 12/20/74

Last year was Ojeda's first professional season. Previously, he played two years on Team USA, winning a Bronze Medal in the Atlanta Olympics. Although he played at three different minor-league levels last year, he spent most of his time in Double-A where he had a solid season. Ojeda is a singles hitter who can steal a few bases.

O'LEARY, TROY - OF - BL - b: 8/4/69

Scouting: O'Leary is a solid line-drive hitter, who is a little short on power and on-base percentage. He's an average fielder with an average arm, but plays right field for the Red Sox by default. He made some improvements at the plate last year, in terms of not pulling off the ball and hanging in better against lefthanded pitching. However, he's still best cast as a platoon outfielder.

1998: O'Leary may have convinced Boston manager Jimy Williams to give him a full-time job to start the season, but, as an average hitter at best against lefthanders, it's likely he will end up being a platoon starter.

1997: O'Leary had his best season, and probably finally won some job security, after starting the campaign as a fourth outfielder.

1996: A year after he was one of Boston's most pleasant surprises, O'Leary had a disappointing season, as pitchers caught on to some of his weaknesses at the plate.

	AB	R	HR	RBI	SB	BA
1995 Boston	399	60	10	49	5	.308
1996 Boston	497	68	15	81	3	.260
1997 Boston	499	65	15	80	0	.309

OLERUD, JOHN - 1B - BL - b: 8/5/68

Scouting: Dismissed Blue Jays' manager Cito Gaston badly misjudged Olerud's talent when publicly burying him last spring. Olerud still can damage an opponent. Lefthanded pitching can undermine him, but only to degree. He has extra-base power to all fields against all kinds of pitching. He remains a patient hitter with the ability to cover the plate. Defensively, he is sound: clearly above-average but rarely spectacular.

1998: Olerud and Mets general manager Steve Phillips met on the final weekend of last season to discuss the first baseman's free agency, and while neither side expressed overwhelming desire to extend the marriage, they essentially agreed that each has interest in Olerud's returning. Without Olerud and with Todd Hundley down for at least half the season, the Mets will play too

many games without players who produced 49 home runs and 174 RBI from lefthanded hitting.
1997: The season was nothing less than a renaissance for the player who produced a stunning season in 1993 and then three seasons of decline. With 22 home runs and 102 RBI, Olerud nearly matched what he accomplished in 1993 (24 and 107). But he still was well behind in batting (.294 compared with .363 in '93) and 34 doubles (compared with 54 in '93). But the Mets were pleased with his work. They hadn't anticipated the run production — or Olerud's first triple since '94.
1996: Gaston benched Olerud against lefthanded hitters, and Olerud batted .274 overall in '96 with only 33 extra-base hits in 398 at-bats, his fewest since his rookie season in 1990.

	AB	R	HR	RBI	SB	BA
1995 Toronto	492	72	8	54	0	.291
1996 Toronto	398	59	18	61	1	.274
1997 New York NL	524	90	22	102	0	.294

OLIVA, JOSE - 3B - BR - b: 3/3/71
A former Braves and Cardinals prospect who led the St. Louis franchise in home runs and RBI (while playing at Triple-A) in 1996, Oliva played in Taiwan last year. He joined the league after the season was underway and still made a run at the Taiwan home run title. His accomplishments included hitting homers in five consecutive games and collecting eleven RBI in one game.

OLIVER, JOE - C - BR - b: 7/24/65
Scouting: Oliver is an useful veteran catcher with a well-earned reputation as a good handler of pitchers and a decent throwing arm. Offensively, he makes a small contribution, featuring decent power for a catcher without many other peripheral skills.
1998: Oliver became a free agent following the 1997 season, but the Reds hoped to re-sign him. He is a solid backstop, and the role of primary catcher with around a 100 starts a year appears ideal for him.
1997: Signed to a minor-league contract by the Reds, Oliver missed most of April with torn ligaments in his left thumb. Reds pitching struggled in early April, but improved when Oliver returned. Oliver became the regular catcher and posted one of his better seasons, thanks in part to improved performance against righthanded pitching, against which he struggled in the past.
1996: Returning to the Reds after spending a year in Milwaukee, Oliver was adequate as a platoon catcher, splitting time with Eddie Taubensee.

	AB	R	HR	RBI	SB	BA
1995 Milwaukee	337	43	12	51	2	.273
1996 Cincinnati	289	31	11	46	2	.242
1997 Cincinnati	349	28	14	43	1	.258

OLIVER, JOHN - OF - BR - b: 5/14/78
Oliver was the Reds first-round pick in the 1996 draft (25th overall). Last year he had eleven at-bats at Rookie level Billings in the Pioneer League.

OLMEDA, JOSE - 2B - BB - b: 6/20/68
Olmeda is a switch-hitting utilityman who has logged nine years of minor-league time — the last two seasons at Triple-A Charlotte in the Marlins' organization. He is capable of playing second base, shortstop, third base and the outfield, but his offensive skills are quickly eroding. He has little power or plate discipline and his once impressive speed has withered. Olmeda's versatility has extended his career significantly, but even that will likely be insufficient to keep him around much longer.

O'NEAL, TROY - C - BR - b: 4/24/72
O'Neal was a reserve catcher at Double-A El Paso in the Texas League for the Brewers organization. When he did play, he didn't hit with any power — just one homer and 11 RBI in 122 at-bats. At his age, he doesn't appear to be a major league prospect.

O'NEILL, DOUG - OF - BR - b: 6/29/70
O'Neill is a minor-league journeyman who jump-started his career in the independent Northern League in 1995. He had his best season last year for Double-A Tulsa (.277 with 20 homers and 64 RBI), then struggled against Triple-A pitching in a late-season callup. O'Neill is unlikely to make it to the major leagues.

O'NEILL, PAUL - OF - BL - b: 2/25/63
Scouting: A former American League batting champion, O'Neill uses the entire field to his advantage, and he has the muscle to hit home runs while also hitting for average. He is murder in clutch situations, as a .428 average with runners in scoring position bears out. A lefty with a good curve is the only pitcher who can face O'Neill with any kind of confidence.
1998: O'Neill has given hints that 1998 will be his final season because he has already missed too much of life with his children. The Yankees feel fortunate to have O'Neill around for 1998. Unless plans change, he will hit third.
1997: O'Neill started spring training concerned that a lingering hamstring injury would hamper his ability to hit, play outfield and run. Despite feeling it from time to time, the problem never developed into anything serious.
1996: Playing on one leg from the All-Star break on, O'Neill nonetheless provided good offense and managed to hold his own in the field. He had a career-high 14-game hitting streak and a .400 average for the month of April.

	AB	R	HR	RBI	SB	BA
1995 New York AL	460	82	22	96	1	.300
1996 New York AL	546	89	19	91	0	.302
1997 New York AL	553	89	21	117	10	.324

ORDAZ, LUIS - SS - BR - b: 8/12/75
A candidate to take over at shortstop in the big leagues some day, Ordaz was the only player promoted from Double-A to the majors during the 1997 September roster expansion by the Cardinals. Always a flashy fielder, he broke through somewhat offensively in 1996 in A-ball and took another huge step with a .287 average last year in Double-A. He makes excellent contact for a young player, striking out once every ten at-bats last year. And Ordaz truly impressed the Cardinals' management and coaches with the way he conducted himself during the end of the season. He'll probably benefit from an entire 1998 season spent at Triple-A Louisville.

ORDONEZ, MAGGLIO - OF - BR - b: 1/28/74
Scouting: A natural hitter for average, Ordonez has really stepped his game up a notch with each successive rise through the White Sox's farm system. He's an aggressive hitter who needs to learn a little more patience when he gets to the majors. Ordonez has the kind of line-drive stroke and gap power that could produce a big year in doubles in the majors. He is an average fielder with a good arm and a little speed.

1998: Ordonez has forced the White Sox to pay attention and may win the starting right field job out of spring training. His arm is good enough already and he can hit. He has proven all he needs to in the minors.

1997: Ordonez led the American Association with a .329 average at Nashville with moderate power (14 homers and a club-high 90 RBI) and decent speed (14 steals, but caught ten times).

1996: Ordonez made his first step above A-ball memorable by adding batting average and power (18 homers and 41 doubles - sixth most in the minors); he also ran off a long errorless streak.

	AB	R	HR	RBI	SB	BA
1997 Chicago AL	69	12	4	11	1	.319

ORDONEZ, REY - SS - BB - b: 11/11/72

Scouting: Often, words fail to describe Ordonez as a shortstop. He regularly does stuff no one has done — not Ozzie Smith or anyone else. All of which is not to say Ordonez is the best of them. But he's right there with any of them. And within 15 feet of second base — be it on a double play, a pickoff, a stolen base attempt or a ball up the middle — Ordonez has no equal. He has quick feet, quick hands and a release on double play relays that is a blur; "getting" him at second is nearly impossible for baserunners. There are, however, two parts to the game. And Ordonez hits like the prototypical "good-glove, no-bat" shortstop. He lacks patience, pop and a plan.

1998: Defensively, Ordonez can't improve as much this season as he did last year; there isn't enough room. He increased his concentration and, as a result, decreased the number of silly errors. The only place left for improvement would be in offensive production. He's going to bat eighth unless a better-hitting pitcher displaces him, and he's going to lose at-bats to pinch-hitters. That could change if he exercises more patience and goes back to hitting the ball the other way. Then again, if the hits he takes away are factored into the calculations that produce his batting average, he'll be challenging Tony Gwynn come September.

1997: After batting .257 as a rookie, Ordonez produced a sorry .216 average last season. A 37-at-bat hitless streak in September was a primary reason; overzealous swings were to blame, too. His RBI production was up from 30 to 33 despite his six-week absence in early summer because of a broken left pinky, and his extra-base production was down appropriately for the time missed. But playing shortstop is where he earns his salary. Ordonez reduced his errors from 27 in 705 chances to nine in 535. That increased his fielding percentage 21 points to .983.

1996: Ordonez exceeded expectations on offense and fell short on defense. But he committed 19 of his 27 errors before the All-Star break and before Dallas Green and Bobby Wine suggested he take his defense a tad more seriously. He took his offense quite seriously at the behest of hitting coach Tom McGraw who paid Ordonez for each ball hit to the right side of second base.

	AB	R	HR	RBI	SB	BA
1996 New York NL	502	51	1	30	1	.257
1997 New York NL	356	35	1	33	11	.216

ORIE, KEVIN - 3B - BR - b: 9/1/72

Scouting: Orie already is a good defensive player which will only help his development as a hitter. Because he can help the Cubs in the field he's more likely to ride out hitting slumps. He has a quick bat and a good knowledge of the strike zone, which should help him take advantage of the short power alleys in Wrigley Field.

1998: Orie will be the starting third baseman for the Cubs come rain or come shine, and shouldn't have a problem staying there for several years to come. The Cubs avoided rushing Orie to the big leagues, which could have destroyed the youngster's confidence. There's no reason to think that he won't get better each year.

1997: Orie was one of the few bright spots for the Cubs in 1997. He started slowly, but the Cubs showed their faith in him by keeping him in the lineup most every day and he responded by having a solid rookie season. His power numbers were exactly along the lines that he put up in the minors.

1996: Orie began the season in Double-A even though many Cub fans felt that he belonged in the majors. He had a good year at Orlando and earned a promotion to Triple-A Iowa. He played in only 12 games at Iowa before a separated shoulder knocked him out for a month, but he came back in time to play in the Arizona Fall League and was named it's co-MVP after leading the league in batting average and slugging percentage.

	AB	R	HR	RBI	SB	BA
1997 Chicago NL	364	40	8	44	2	.275

ORSULAK, JOE - OF - BL - b: 5/31/62

Without fanfare and ever so steadily, Orsulak fashioned a fine major league career despite being struck by personal tragedy. However, his career could be coming to a close now. He rarely played with Florida in 1996 and his playing time was also scarce last year in Montreal. His lefthanded bat has slowed and his release by the Expos at the end of last season could well have signaled the end for Orsulak.

	AB	R	HR	RBI	SB	BA
1995 New York NL	290	41	1	37	1	.283
1996 Florida	217	23	2	19	1	.221
1997 Montreal	150	13	1	7	0	.227

ORTIZ, BO - OF - BR - b: 4/4/70

This outfielder hit all of .219 for the Expos' Double-A Harrisburg farm club last season. It's not a real good sign that Ortiz will ever get any higher on Montreal's organizational ladder.

ORTIZ, DAVID - DH - BL - b: 11/18/75

Scouting: Acquired from Seattle in a trade for Dave Hollins in August of 1996, Ortiz is taking the momentum of a spectacular 1997 campaign into next season with him. He is big (6'4", 230 pounds), has a powerful swing and is aggressive at the plate. His aggressiveness produces results, but it also gets him into trouble at times by causing too many strikeouts. But an organization desperate for power will give Ortiz a long look.

1998: Ortiz will get a chance to win a spot on the major league roster although he is too raw and almost certainly will open the season at Triple-A Salt Lake. Still, Ortiz will continue to develop his superior potential and make some impact with the Twins.

1997: There was some confusion at the start of the year regarding his name. He came to the Twins from Seattle as David Arias but changed his last name to Ortiz during the spring of 1997 for family reasons. That change confused several scouts attempting to identify him last season. They will get to know his name, though, because Ortiz banged 13 homers for Double-A New Britain and Class A Fort Myers and led the Twins organization with 114 RBI last season. He made the jump from Fort Myers to the majors in one year and hit enough to keep the Twins intrigued.

1996: A member of the Midwest League All-Star team, Ortiz hit

.322 with 18 home runs and 93 RBI for Class A Wisconsin. He was second in the league in extra base hits (54).

	AB	R	HR	RBI	SB	BA
1997 Minnesota	49	10	0	7	0	.327

ORTIZ, HECTOR - C - BR - b: 10/14/69
Ortiz has a good arm but in ten minor-league seasons he has hit three home runs. He didn't do anything in 1997 to raise his stock and, at age 28, he's not a major league catching prospect.

ORTIZ, LUIS - 1B/DH - BR - b: 5/25/70
Ortiz has nothing left to prove in the minors, but still awaits the chance to play regularly in the majors. If he ever gets the chance, he'll probably be a high average hitter with occasional power. He can't play third base, so he spent the year successfully learning to play first base. Unfortunately, there aren't many teams for whom a high-average first baseman with moderate power would be a marked improvement, so there are legitimate questions as to Ortiz' major league future. In 1997 Ortiz appeared in only 22 games for Triple-A Oklahoma City.

ORTIZ, NICK - 2B - BR - b: 7/9/73
Ortiz has played all over the infield throughout his minor-league career. He doesn't have power or speed, but has hit for average for the most part. He hit .281 in first full year in Double-A, with eight homers. He appears to be a utility candidate at best, and that's a couple of years away.

OSBORNE, MARK - C - BL - b: 2/1/78
A third-round pick in the 1996 draft, Osborne had eight homers and 51 RBI at Class A South Bend before being selected to play in the 1997 Arizona Fall League, which identified him as a true prospect. Osborne is a plus defensively.

OSIK, KEITH - C/3B - BR - b: 10/22/68
Scouting: Osik is a solid backup catcher who does an adequate job behind the plate and hits for average but no power. He also has added value in the fact he can play first, second and third base, left and right field and played in two college World Series as a shortstop for Louisiana State.
1998: The Pirates went into the winter with only two catchers on their 40-man roster, Osik and starter Jason Kendall; Osik will again back up Kendall. Kendall is an iron man, though, so Osik figures to only get 25-30 starts.
1997: Osik's playing time was limited and he struggled from a lack of at-bats. Twice, Osik went two weeks without getting a start and his bat became rusty.
1996: A year after serving as a replacement player for the Pirates, Osik was one of the biggest surprises of spring training as he won the second catching job. Osik had a good year for a rookie reserve.

	AB	R	HR	RBI	SB	BA
1996 Pittsburgh	140	18	1	14	1	.293
1997 Pittsburgh	105	10	0	7	0	.257

OTANEZ, WILLIS - 3B - BR - b: 4/19/73
Otanez was promoted to Triple-A last year, but he struggled with a batting average near the Mendoza line. He developed bone chips in his elbow requiring surgery, and lost a big chunk of the season. He has shown some power in the tough Eastern League, but needs to be a more consistent hitter.

OTERO, RICKY - OF - BB - b: 4/15/72
Scouting: At 5'5" and 150 pounds Otero is one of the more diminuitive major leaguers in recent memory. At that size, he must show excellent table-setting skills to be a viable major leaguer. Though he has above-average speed, he sometimes appears to be afraid to use it. Otero's offensive game is also hampered by his overaggressiveness at the plate, especially early in the count. He overcomes a multitude of mistakes in center field with his speed, but has a penchant for diving for balls unnecessarily. His throwing arm is also quite weak. There are few center field prospects in Philadelphia but that fact alone doesn't make Otero a great prospect.
1998: The Phillies no longer view Otero as part of their major league plans. However, he could be a useful Triple-A insurance policy; he was actually younger than most of their 1997 Triple-A outfielders. The presence of Wendell Magee could force Otero to left field.
1997: Otero returned to the minors for most of the year, managing just 50 games in the majors after being almost a regular the previous year. He took his turn in center field in 1997 for the Phillies but frustrated management with indisciplined play and lack of aggressiveness on the bases. He was not recalled in September.
1996: The Phillies' overall futility was underscored by their liberal use of Otero in 1996. His poor baserunning instincts and defensive shortcomings in center field more than offset his respectable batting success against righthanders.

	AB	R	HR	RBI	SB	BA
1995 New York NL	51	5	0	1	2	.137
1996 Philadelphia	411	54	2	32	16	.273
1997 Philadelphia	151	20	0	3	0	.252

OWENS, ERIC - SS - BR - b: 2/3/71
Scouting: An infielder with speed, decent strikezone judgment, and doubles power, Owens has done everything except get a fair trial in the major leagues, having been sent down a total of seven times in two seasons with the Reds. He has been moved between second base, third base and the outfield, suggesting he is not a strong defensive player. Owens' performance in Triple-A indicates he would be decent major league hitter if given a chance, and at worst he should catch on as a utility infielder.
1998: It's a key season for Owens, who must take advantage of any opportunity generated by expansion. He is not likely to get a real chance with the Reds, who acquired Damian Jackson and Chris Stynes, who along with Pokey Reese and Aaron Boone are ahead of Owens on the Reds depth chart.
1997: It was another frustrating year for Owens, who made the Reds out of spring training but was sent down in mid-April. Following that he was shuttled on and off the roster, but it did not affect his play at Indianapolis, where he hit .286 with eleven homers and 23 steals in 391 at-bats.
1996: Shuttled between Cincinnati and Indianapolis at every opportunity, Owens missed his best chance to secure a roster spot by hitting only .200 in 205 at-bats. Learning a new position (left field) at the major league level contributed to his struggles in the majors. At Triple-A, Owens continued to play well, hitting .320.

	AB	R	HR	RBI	SB	BA
1996 Cincinnati	205	26	0	9	16	.200
1997 Cincinnati	57	8	0	3	3	.263

OWENS, JAYHAWK - C - BR - b: 2/10/69
Once considered the team's catcher of the future and projected to be the Rockies' everyday catcher in 1996, Owens now must fight the label "Triple-A player" after spending the entire 1997 season in Colorado Springs, where he batted .260 with ten homers, 34 RBI and four stolen bases. Though he runs well for a catcher, hits with power and has a strong arm, Owens has struggled to pull his game together since suffering torn ligaments in his left thumb late in spring training of 1996, an injury that crippled his career.

	AB	R	HR	RBI	SB	BA
1995 Colorado	45	7	4	12	0	.244
1996 Colorado	180	31	4	17	4	.239

PACHOT, JOHN - C - BR - b: 11/11/74
After four seasons as a light-hitting catcher in the Expos' system, Pachot had a fine 1997 season backing up Bob Henley at Double-A Harrisburg. He'll go to Triple-A this season, particularly if Henley wins the backup job at the major league level behind Chris Widger. Considering the Expos lack of catching depth in their organization, Pachot is worth keeping an eye on.

PAGANO, SCOTT - OF - BB - b: 4/26/71
Pagano is a battler who puts the ball in play consistently, draws walks, runs the bases with reckless abandon, and fields his position aggressively. However, he is limited in all respects. He has little extra-base power, is too old for his level and has not reached Triple-A yet. He's more likely to become a minor-league journeyman than to reach the majors with the Phillies. Pagano may seem like a prospect on the surface, but he isn't.

PAGNOZZI, TOM - C - BR - b: 7/30/62
Scouting: When healthy, Pagnozzi is able to deliver a hit in clutch situations and serve as the stabilizer for the pitching staff because of his leadership, defensive skills and experience behind the plate. His days as a Gold Glove catcher might be in the past, but not because he has lost his strong arm or pitch-calling knack. He's been on the disabled list each of the last five seasons and, at the age of 35, probably can't be counted on to work 120-130 games anymore.
1998: Even though the Cards' top prospect is catcher Eli Marrero, the club might not want to hand so much responsibility to him yet. A trimmed-down Pagnozzi probably would be a more productive player overall, at least early, as he's learned to pull the ball consistently and has a better knowledge of how to pitch National League hitters than any other catcher.
1997: His season was a bust as he spent nearly all of it hobbled by a torn hip flexor. He got only 50 big-league at-bats, many of them coming when he was out of tip-top shape thanks to an injury that hadn't allowed him to stay conditioned. Pagnozzi got more action on minor-league rehab, with a .317 average and five homers in Double-A.
1996: Though he tapered off some following an excellent — albeit injury-riddled — first half, Pagnozzi showed more power than at any time in his career. He threw out nearly a third of the runners who tried to steal against him, something the Cardinals had come to expect.

	AB	R	HR	RBI	SB	BA
1995 St. Louis	219	17	2	15	0	.215
1996 St. Louis	407	48	13	55	4	.270
1997 St. Louis	50	4	1	8	0	.220

PALMEIRO, ORLANDO - OF - BL - b: 1/19/69
Scouting: Next to Darin Erstad, Palmeiro is the fastest man on the 25-man roster. He's speedy on the bases and in the outfield, with good defensive instincts and the ability to cover a lot of ground. He can play all three outfield positions, but excels in center field because of his speed. He's faster than Jim Edmonds and has a better throwing arm, but can't begin to match Edmonds' power. Power is the only thing missing from Palmeiro's game. He would be a solid backup outfielder on any club and a capable starter on a lot of clubs as well.
1998: Palmeiro has gone from prospect to major leaguer. He probably won't start because of who's in front of him in Anaheim, but he'll fill an important fourth-outfielder role nonetheless.
1997: Palmeiro established himself as a major leaguer after finally being given a chance to do so by new manager Terry Collins. Palmeiro played outstanding defense and hit well, and made some things happen on the bases with his speed.
1996: Again the cast ahead of him held him back, but Palmeiro hit near .300 and showed himself to be a budding major leaguer in 50 games with the Angels.

	AB	R	HR	RBI	SB	BA
1995 California	20	3	0	1	0	.350
1996 California	87	6	0	6	0	.287
1997 California	134	19	0	8	2	.216

PALMEIRO, RAFAEL - 1B - BL - b: 9/24/64
Scouting: Palmeiro has become one of the best hitters in baseball, but as publicity goes, he's overshadowed as a first baseman by Frank Thomas, Tino Martinez, and others. Palmeiro has a good compact swing with excellent power. His defense is outstanding, and Palmeiro has some base-stealing speed although he doesn't use it much.
1998: The early-season overswinging of 1997 will disappear, and his consistency should return; his batting average should return to nearly .300, along with comparable increases in other hitting categories. A great, breakthrough year is still possible.
1997: Palmeiro was overswinging during the first part of 1997, trying to make up for the power loss created when Bobby Bonilla and other power hitters left the Orioles. Although he had some hot streaks, the overall result was a poor season, shown by his lower batting average. But it's a "poor" season only when compared to his strong and consistent seasons in the recent past.
1996: Palmeiro set a club record for RBI, with consistent offensive production in other categories. He remained an underrated, but highly productive hitter.

	AB	R	HR	RBI	SB	BA
1995 Baltimore	554	89	39	104	3	.310
1996 Baltimore	626	110	39	142	8	.289
1997 Baltimore	614	95	38	110	5	.254

PALMER, DEAN - 3B - BR - b: 12/27/68
Scouting: Palmer is among the better power-hitting third basemen in baseball. He's a classic power hitter, too, a free-swinger who hits for a low batting average and strikes out in bunches. Palmer is a below-average fielder, but his ability to hit the ball out of the park makes him a much sought after player.
1998: Palmer's status as the best power-hitting third basemen available as a free agent after the previous season brought him a big contract. As always, he'll hit a bunch of balls over the outfield fence while providing little else of use.
1997: In an odd waiver-wire deal, Palmer was traded from the

Rangers to the last-place Royals — usually high-priced, free-agents-to-be go to contenders instead of also-rans. But the Royals had a big hole at third base and new manager Tony Muser wanted to give Palmer a test drive. It gave the Royals a more respectable lineup and actually improved the defense, too. Palmer had his usual high power, high strikeout season.

1996: It was Palmer's best season as he set career highs in most offensive categories while hitting for a good average and helping the Rangers to their first-ever post-season. His post-season play was a microcosm of his overall abilities; he helped win Game One with a two-run homer, but made a twelfth-inning error to help lose Game Two and he struck out five times in 19 at-bats.

	AB	R	HR	RBI	SB	BA
1995 Texas	119	30	9	24	1	.336
1996 Texas	582	98	38	107	2	.280
1997 two teams	542	70	23	86	2	.256

PAQUETTE, CRAIG - 3B - BR - b: 3/28/69

Scouting: Paquette's lone skill is above-average power. In every other respect he is far below average; he has been clearly the worst hitting and worst fielding regular third baseman in many, many years. He is a pull hitter with little ability to adjust to count or situation. Paquette is strikeout prone, barely an average baserunner, and simply weak in the field with poor range, an erratic glove, and a wild arm.

1998: Paquette has not demonstrated any skills which would warrant a return to the majors. Still, in an expansion year, Paquette could get back to the bigs, particularly if Bob Boone is managing in the majors. Paquette can't be expected to succeed, though.

1997: When Boone was fired, his pet player, Paquette, wasn't long for the majors; it took just two weeks before he was designated for assignment. Paquette accepted a demotion to the minors where he did exactly the same for Triple-A Omaha as he had in Kansas City — occasional power with lots of strikeouts and porous defense.

1996: Paquette was released by the Athletics in spring training, but found a home in Kansas City. Despite spending a month at Omaha, Paquette led the Royals in homers and RBI. He also made a ton of errors and struck out a quarter of the time.

	AB	R	HR	RBI	SB	BA
1995 Oakland	283	42	13	49	5	.226
1996 Kansas City	429	61	22	67	5	.259
1997 Kansas City	252	26	8	33	2	.230

PARENT, MARK - C - BR - b: 9/16/61

Scouting: Parent has functioned as a passable backup catcher for the better part of the last decade, combining an above-average throwing arm with occasional bursts of home run power. However, he is a .213 career hitter who strikes out every fourth at-bat, while never walking. At age 36, Parent is beginning to break down physically, and his bat speed is beginning to slow. His arm remains strong, but his release is slow, and baserunners look to run against him often.

1998: Parent is signed for 1998, but might not stay long in Philadelphia. He's a valued veteran presence in the clubhouse, and is a candidate to be a coach or manager down the road. Even if Bobby Estalella returns to full-time duty in Triple-A, the Phillies may still not have a place for Parent on their major league bench.

1997: Parent looked like he had reached the end of the line. His usual ability to put on short bursts of power as a backup catcher was absent last year. He also broke down physically, despite limited use. Parent was a good man to have on the bench and in the clubhouse, but it didn't make up for his consistent lack of production on the field.

1996: Parent had a typical season as a backup catcher for the Tigers and Orioles. He had more extra-base hits than singles (16 to 15), and over seven times as many strikeouts as walks (37 to five) while improving his career average to .220.

	AB	R	HR	RBI	SB	BA
1995 two teams	265	30	18	38	0	.234
1996 Baltimore	137	17	9	23	0	.226
1997 Philadelphia	113	4	0	8	0	.150

PARKER, RICK - OF - BR - b: 3/20/63

Parker is the consummate utility man. He can run, but has yet to do anything else well enough to earn him more than a temporary spot on a major league roster. He bounced around through several organizations because he's a solid player and is an excellent role model for the younger players coming up. At this point in his career, he's a father figure for the kids more than a prospect.

PATZKE, JEFF - 2B - BB - b: 11/19/73

Scouting: Patzke is a contact hitter with a solid glove, albeit limited range. He has little power and no base-stealing ability but is patient and makes the routine plays.

1998: Patzke is close to a major league reserve job but he needs an opportunity such as an injury or trade. In the majors, he would not be likely to play much until 1999 but he could develop into a solid .280 hitter.

1997: Patzke shared time with Rob Mummau at Triple-A Syracuse, hitting .285 with 51 walks in 96 games.

1996: At Double-A Knoxville, Patzke had 80 walks and cleared the .300 mark (.303) for the first time.

PAUL, JOSH - OF/C - BR - b: 5/19/75

Scouting: A good hitter who throws well, too, Paul is the White Sox' catcher of the future. He's a local (Chicago) product who has hit well in every league in which he has played. Paul is a good enough hitter that he has been used frequently in the outfield. His future is behind the plate, though, and although his defensive skills are rough, he throws well and will advance quickly through the minors.

1998: Paul is on the hot track to the majors. He has surpassed other catcher prospects in the White Sox farm system and just needs some polish before he's ready to step in at Comiskey Park.

1997: Paul reached Double-A Birmingham for a brief time in 1997 and lost some playing time due to injury.

1996: Paul won a batting crown at Class A Hickory in his first pro season after skipping Rookie ball entirely; he hit .327 with eight homers and 37 RBI.

PAYTON, JAY - OF - BR - b: 11/22/72

Scouting: One of the most determined players the Mets ever have signed, Payton also is among the least fortunate. If only his right elbow had the strength of his heart. If Payton is able to swing a bat as he did before the elbow betrayed him, he will hit his way into a lineup with line drives into the gaps. His game is more than adequate, although his throwing must be suspect at this point.

1998: If his elbow allows, Payton will begin the season in Triple-A, or maybe Double-A because he has gone so long without playing. Too many uncertainties exist in Payton's case to predict much more than that.

1997: The season was lost, and in some ways more than lost. Payton underwent reconstructive surgery on the elbow — for the second time in 18 months — in March. And six months later, at a point when he had hoped to begin rehabilitation, he still experienced significant pain.

1996: Payton played at four minor-league levels in his first season following the first surgery, but his at-bat total was merely 202. Of course he batted .307 which dropped his career average to .319. There were no signs then that he wasn't the Mets' primary hitting prospect.

PEARSON, EDDIE - 1B - BL - b: 1/31/74

A fractured hamate (hand) bone wrecked Pearson's 1995 campaign and he has needed two years to recover his batting stroke. His 1997 season was the first in which he had shown any hitting ability above A-ball. Pearson is limited defensively to first base. He still can hit the ball to the gaps, but has not recovered his home run stroke since his injury. Pearson is no longer a good prospect and is not going to make much progress with the White Sox.

PECORILLI, ALDO - 1B - BR - b: 9/12/70

Always a good hitter, Pecorilli has been frustrated trying to find a position. Although he hit .360 in 31 games at Double-A Arkansas in 1997 (a demotion from Triple-A on the Braves' farm in 1996) he was thinking about retirement.

PEGUES, STEVE - OF - BR - b: 5/21/68

The one-time first-round draft pick of Detroit has been out of the major leagues since he was a reserve outfielder with Pittsburgh in 1994. Pegues was released by Montreal's Triple-A Ottawa farm club, spent a week with Winnipeg in the independent Northern League then finished up with the Chicago Cubs' Triple-A Iowa affiliate. He's a nice guy, but he never lived up to his potential and time has run out.

PELLOW, KIT - 3B - BR - b: 8/28/73

Erstwhile catcher/first-baseman/outfielder Pellow was pressed into service at third base for Double-A Wichita last year and the results showed — 24 errors in 65 games. His struggles in the field contributed to an off season at the plate, too. But, Pellow is a better player than he showed in 1997 and can get to the major leagues in a utility role.

PEMBERTON, RUDY - OF - BR - b: 12/17/69

Pemberton is a very good raw athlete, whose poor fundamentals in all areas did not impress manager Jimy Williams in the season's first couple of months. Rather than accept assignment to the minors, for his tenth season there, Pemberton took an offer to play in Japan. He makes mistakes at the plate, on the bases and in the field, but given a chance to play he would be a poor man's Sammy Sosa, hitting for a better average, but with less power.

	AB	R	HR	RBI	SB	BA
1995 Detroit	30	3	0	3	0	.300
1996 Boston	41	11	1	10	3	.512
1997 Boston	63	8	2	10	0	.238

PENA, TONY - C - BR - b: 6/4/57

Scouting: Pena is valued for his steady defense behind the plate and steady demeanor in the clubhouse; he's a "veteran presence" in his eighteenth major league season. A four-time Gold Glove winner, he still throws well enough although he can no longer hit major league pitching. Pena is fourth on the all-time list of games caught; it's unlikely he'll be playing much longer.

1998: Players like Pena can become good coaches. He has the patience and steadiness to teach young catchers the finer points of the game. If Pena plays another year, it'll be as a deep backup catcher.

1997: Pena served as the backup catcher for the White Sox until Jorge Fabregas was acquired, making Ron Karkovice the backup and Pena redundant. He was rescued by the Astros who wanted a veteran catcher for their pennant drive.

1996: Pena was a second catcher for the Indians, hitting little but giving the Indians pitching staff a boost with his game-calling and overall good defense.

	AB	R	HR	RBI	SB	BA
1995 Cleveland	263	25	5	28	1	.262
1996 Cleveland	174	14	1	27	0	.195
1997 two teams	86	6	0	10	0	.174

PENDLETON, TERRY - 3B - BB - b: 7/16/60

After the 1996 season, the Reds ignored the overwhelming evidence that Pendleton was finished and brought him in to provide veteran leadership and insurance at third base. He took a few at-bats away from Willie Greene early in the year, but was released in late-July when the Reds started their youth movement.

	AB	R	HR	RBI	SB	BA
1995 Florida	513	70	14	78	1	.290
1996 Florida-Atlanta	568	51	11	75	2	.238
1997 Cincinnati	113	11	1	17	2	.248

PENNYFEATHER, WILLIAM - OF - BR - b: 5/25/68

At one time, Pennyfeather was considered to be an outstanding prospect in Pittsburgh's organization, but he never fulfilled his promise as a hitter for average or for power. Pennyfeather has hit well in spurts, but has established himself pretty much as a middling power guy stuck in Triple-A. He's big and strong, but has yet to put it together, which is why he's been through three organizations now.

PEOPLES, DANNY - 1B/3B - BR - b: 1/20/75

Peoples has prodigious power, but is a low-average hitter whose lack of speed and throwing ability limit him to left field. He strikes out too much on pitches out of the strike zone and must shorten his swing as he spends 1998 at Double-A Akron. He hit for a low average with good power but a lot of strikeouts at Class A Kinston in 1997 after losing almost the entire 1996 season to a shoulder injury. He still has time to develop into a power-hitting major league outfielder.

PEREZ, EDDIE - C - BR - b: 5/4/68

Scouting: Perez' skills make him well-suited to a backup backstop job. He hits an occasional homer or double and calls a good game behind the plate while playing exceptional defense. He doesn't run well, make good contact at the plate or get on base well. But, in his limited role, Perez can be a valuable reserve player.

1998: Because he has earned Greg Maddux' trust with his catching and game-calling skills, Perez will start behind the plate every fifth day wherever Maddux is working. He won't hit much, probably not much better than Maddux, actually, but will pop a few doubles and homers.

1997: Perez hit for a poor average, but decent power; he had eleven extra-base hits and 18 RBI in limited play. He was again the personal catcher for Maddux.

1996: Perez' first full season in the majors was a big success. He showed unusual power, slugging over .400, and became Maddux' personal catcher due to above-average defense and calling a great game; Maddux had a 1.89 ERA in the sixteen starts that Perez caught.

	AB	R	HR	RBI	SB	BA
1995 Atlanta	13	1	1	4	0	.308
1996 Atlanta	156	19	4	17	0	.256
1997 Atlanta	191	20	6	18	0	.215

PEREZ, EDUARDO - 3B/1B - BR - b: 9/11/69

Scouting: Perez has developed into a replica of his father, although obviously not quite as good. He has good power, okay strikezone judgment, a knack for driving in runs, and can play first and third base. If he were 23 years old (the age at which Tony had a similar year in 1965) Eduardo would be a decent prospect, but at age 29 he is not likely to get much better.

1998: Perez starts the season as the regular first baseman, but will need to continue to hit well to hold the entire job. The Reds have several lefthanded hitters that could be part of a platoon if Perez falters.

1997: Perez started the season as a little-used pinch-hitter, but picked up a few starts in left field and third base during Ray Knight experiments and hit well enough to continue to get chances. After Hal Morris was hurt Perez became a regular at first base, and he was one of the few offensive threats on the team when Reggie Sanders and Barry Larkin were out with injuries.

1996: The Reds acquired Perez from the Angels, and his strong season at Triple-A Indianapolis (.293-21-84 in 122 games) made him a candidate for the majors as a reserve.

	AB	R	HR	RBI	SB	BA
1995 California	71	9	1	7	0	.169
1996 Cincinnati	36	8	3	5	0	.222
1997 Cincinnati	297	44	16	52	5	.253

PEREZ, JHONNY - SS - BR - b: 10/23/76

One of several young shortstops in the Astro farm system with major league potential, Perez is young but hasn't been overmatched during his steady movement in the minors, reaching Double-A for the first time in 1997 at the age of 20. He has some speed and power to augment his defensive skills. Perez could move to another position before reaching the majors; he'll be brought along slowly.

PEREZ, NEIFI - SS - BB - b: 2/2/75

Scouting: The Rockies think he's already an All-Star caliber shortstop. Though he's just 21 years of age, they hope Perez will be their starting shortstop for the next ten years. An acrobatic fielder whose biggest asset is his bazooka arm, he doesn't have terrific range but he has remarkable hands and plays the game with unbridled enthusiasm. His offense has improved every year. A switch-hitter with pop from both sides, he only has average speed and though he runs well from first to third — he needed just 83 games to set a team record with ten triples in 1997 — he has yet to acquire the knack for basestealing.

1998: Though he played mostly second base the previous year, Perez has been promised the starting shortstop position. He hates to bat leadoff, loves to bat second, but will probably spend most of the season batting either seventh or eighth.

1997: Upset that he was returned to Triple-A Colorado Springs, Perez nevertheless was outstanding in the season's first half, forcing the Rockies to promote him for good June 19th. He initially started three times per week, rotating at second base, shortstop and third bat, but a hamstring injury to shortstop Walt Weiss moved Perez into the starting lineup permanently. When Eric Young was traded away, Perez inherited his second base position. Outstanding on defense, Perez contributed several key hits on offense.

1996: After a sensational season at Colorado Springs, where he was named the starting shortstop on the Triple-A All-Star team, Perez struggled through his big-league debut, swinging wildly at bad pitches and committing two errors in 17 games.

	AB	R	HR	RBI	SB	BA
1997 Colorado	313	46	5	31	4	.291

PEREZ, ROBERT - OF - BR - b: 6/4/69

Scouting: Although he was originally projected as a potential .300 hitter, Perez will turn twenty-nine this summer and the amount of time he spent on the bench in 1997 could not have furthered his development as a hitter. He is a contact hitter who swings at everything. Defensively, he is adequate at best.

1998: A change of scenery would benefit Perez but his playing opportunities appear limited. He is obviously better than a .192 hitter, but will not hit for power nor steal bases. He is a one-category player.

1997: Instead of a trip to the minor leagues, Perez spent the entire year as the forgotten man on the Blue Jays' bench. He appeared in a game just better than once per week and started just 16 games in the outfield. It was a disappointing year all around.

1996: Perez responded to the playing time he received, hitting .327 in just over 200 at-bats.

	AB	R	HR	RBI	SB	BA
1996 Toronto	202	30	2	21	3	.327
1997 Toronto	78	4	2	6	0	.192

PEREZ, TOMAS - SS - BB - b: 12/29/73

Scouting: An infielder capable of playing any position, Perez will never win a batting title and doesn't hit for power. He's a reliable utility player who doesn't complain and has occasional moments of brilliance in the field.

1998: Perez didn't help his chances with his performance last year. Add to that his .224 average at Triple-A and you have a certain recipe for disaster if he plays. He is bench material only.

1997: Perez got a chance to play with the Blue Jays after spending most of the season at Triple-A Syracuse. Alex Gonzalez's broken finger opened up a spot for Perez and he filled in adequately as far as his defense was concerned. Offensively, things got so bad that he suffered through an 0-for-21 streak in September, finishing with a sub-par average for his brief major league season.

1996: An injury to Felipe Crespo and then the eventual trade of Domingo Cedeno created an opportunity for Perez at second base. He responded by hitting .251 in almost 300 at-bats, not bad considering it was his second exposure to the major leagues.

	AB	R	HR	RBI	SB	BA
1995 Toronto	98	12	1	8	0	.245
1996 Toronto	295	24	1	19	1	.251

1997 Toronto   123   9   0   9   1   .195

PERRY, CHAN - DH - BR - b: 9/13/72
Chan is the younger brother of Herbert, the oft-injured fellow Indians' prospect. The younger Perry is a late-round draft pick (1994) who surprised scouts with a 96 RBI showing at Double-A Akron in 1997. He's actually a similar player to his brother; a consistent line-drive hitter with gap power, relatively poor plate discipline and a solid glove at first base. However, at age 25, Perry is way too old to have never faced Triple-A pitching, and is blocked by Sean Casey and Richie Sexson, younger first base prospects with much greater potential. Perry will likely be a long-term Double-A and Triple-A standout, but nothing more.

PERRY, HERBERT - 1B/3B - BR - b: 9/15/69
Scouting: Perry's future appeared bright when he was a defensive standout at first base in the 1995 World Series against the Braves. However, knee injuries derailed his once-promising career, and left him with much to prove at age 28. Before missing nearly all of the last two seasons, Perry was a high-average hitter with power to the gaps and excellent quickness around the bag at first. He struck out infrequently, and had enough of a throwing arm to play third base. Now, all bets are off until he proves himself healthy.
1998: A move to the Tampa Bay Devil Rays via expansion offered a fresh start for Perry to prove his health. If his quickness returns, he could still be a viable backup first baseman in the majors.
1997: Perry lost the entire season when he had knee surgery to repair torn cartilage.
1996: Perry surprisingly didn't make the Indians' club out of spring training despite his 1995 postseason heroics and was off to a brilliant start at Triple-A Buffalo — hitting .338 in 151 at-bats — when he suffered his first major knee injury.

PETAGINE, ROBERTO - 1B - BL - b: 6/2/71
Scouting: Give him Triple-A pitching, preferably fastballs, and duck. Petagine has developed into a productive Triple-A hitter. Some might call him a 4-A player, able to batter pitchers at the highest level of the minor leagues, but unable to handle big-league stuff. Lefthanded pitching — particularly off-speed lefthanded pitching — confuses him and defuses his power. He has soft and fairly sure hands, but he doesn't play first base aggressively and he isn't fast enough in the outfield to do an adequate job.
1998: Expansion will bring another two dozen Triple-A pitchers to the big leagues. If Petagine can get most of his at-bats against them, he may find regular or semi-regular work. Without that unlikely scenario, he will be hard-pressed to gain or retain major league status.
1997: Petagine's fourth season in Triple-A was the most productive season of his professional career. He hit as a slugger for the first time. Having never hit more than 16 home runs in a season (12 in Triple-A and four in the big leagues in 1996), he hit 31 with Norfolk. He also produced a career-high 100 RBI, 64 extra-base hits and a .317 batting average. That production was enough to warrant election as the Most Valuable Player in the International League. But he hardly distinguished himself in his brief tour with the Mets — six strikeouts, two runs and a .067 average in 15 at-bats.
1996 Former Mets General Manager Joe McIlvayne had sought to acquire Petagine in a trade for several years. He finally succeeded in late March and filled a Triple-A void. Petagine had two separate tours with the Mets, but neither was a glowing success. Still, he showed signs. His major league production extrapolated over just 400 at-bats-- and given the percentages of lefthanded and righthanded pitchers, he probably wouldn't get more than that--would have yielded 16 home runs and 68 RBI.

	AB	R	HR	RBI	SB	BA
1995 San Diego	124	15	3	17	0	.234
1996 New York AL	99	10	4	17	0	.232

PETERSEN, CHRIS - 2B - BR - b: 11/6/70
Petersen is a light-hitting middle infielder who hasn't done much of anything to show that he's a prospect at all. Only a surprise 1996 season where he hit .296 in a third of a season at Double-A has kept him in the Cubs' system. He spent all of 1997 at Triple-A Iowa and hit a weak .240, and that was his best average for a full season at any one level by more than 20 points. He's not a major league player.

PETERSON, CHARLES - OF - BR - b: 5/8/74
The Pirates have about given up on Peterson, their top draft pick in 1993. He has not hit for the kind of power they envisioned and has been stuck at Double-A Carolina for three straight seasons. The Pirates tried to give Peterson away last year at the end of the spring training as they tried to clear spots on the 40-man roster but nobody wanted him. Peterson started wearing contact lenses midway through last season but they didn't help.

PETERSON, NATE - OF - BL - b: 7/12/71
An outfielder from Australia, Peterson spent time in both the Houston and Montreal organizations in 1997. He continued to hit for average with little power at Double-A Jackson for the Astros but found the going tougher at Double-A Harrisburg for the Expos. He moved up slightly each of the past four seasons in the Astro farm system but hitting about .280 with three homers per year will not get him a quick ticket to the big leagues.

PETRICK, BEN - C - BR - b: 4/7/77
Simply, Petrick is the Rockies' best prospect: a catcher with all the tools, including intelligence, speed and power. He won't turn 21 until April, and by then, he should be at Double-A New Haven. An all-state football player as both a safety and running back out of Hillsboro, Ore., Petrick signed with the Rockies following the 1995 season. The Rockies have placed him in leagues where he has been among the youngest in each of his two seasons and his stats — .235 at Class A Asheville in 1996 and .248 at Class A Salem in 1997 — have yet to catch up to his promise. More telling, perhaps, is Petrick has 29 homers and 49 stolen bases in his two seasons. Because he plays the position where the Rockies are the weakest, there is an outside chance he could be a September callup this year.

PHILLIPS, J.R. - 1B - BL - b: 4/29/70
A power-hitter with a long swing, Phillips fans frequently. He has had vastly different levels of success from Triple-A to the majors. Phillips' 1997 marks at Triple-A New Orleans (Astros) were typical of his Triple-A success: .290, 21 homers, 71 RBI. But, his major league performance has been different; he has balanced his 19 major league homers with 145 strikeouts in 404 at-bats and a career .183 batting average. Phillips is no prospect, but has hope of landing a major league job created by expansion in 1998.

	AB	R	HR	RBI	SB	BA
1995 San Francisco	231	27	9	28	1	.195
1996 Philadelphia	104	12	7	15	0	.163

PHILLIPS, TONY - 3B/OF - BB - b: 4/25/59
Scouting: Even after 16 seasons, the veteran hasn't lost any of his ability to fire a team up in the clubhouse or as a leadoff hitter. Phillips was the shot in the arm the Angels needed when they re-acquired him from the White Sox. Unfortunately, he also dealt the Angels a crippling blow when he was arrested on felony cocaine charges August 10th last year. His clouded future caused the Angels to give up three good prospects to San Diego for Rickey Henderson, who was a bust offensively.
1998: Phillips must clear his name before returning to the Angels, a club run by the image-conscious Walt Disney Co. He still has the ability to play major league ball, but his off-field problems now raise questions about his future.
1997: It was a typical Tony Phillips season, until his arrest. Phillips was the catalyst of the offense the same way he had been in 1995 when the Angels came within a game of winning the division title. He played a variety of positions and filled a lot of holes when a rash of injuries struck the club. Disney tried — and failed — to force Phillips into a drug rehabilitation center. An arbitrator overturned his suspension, and once Phillips was returned to the active roster, he played with the same fervor and zeal.
1996: Phillips' play in the outfield helped the White Sox make a run at Cleveland in the American League Central. After a brief spring-training flirtation with retirement, he led the league in walks (125) and finished in the top ten in runs scored (119), and further enhanced his reputation as one of the top leadoff men in baseball.

	AB	R	HR	RBI	SB	BA
1995 California	525	119	27	61	13	.261
1996 Chicago AL	581	119	12	63	13	.277
1997 California	534	96	8	57	13	.275

PIAZZA, MIKE - C - BR - b: 9/4/68
Scouting: Piazza is a terror at the plate, he gets on base and hits for average and power. His lightning-quick bat allows him to look at pitches just a split-second longer and crush them. His strikezone judgment is also improving each year. Defensively he's improved at blocking balls in the dirt but is not going to ever be a stellar defensive catcher. With his offensive production it's not a problem. Piazza's future could include a position shift. He has bad knees and catchers who catch as often as he does are about as injury prone as a starting pitcher.
1998: Piazza should be among the leaders in just about every major offensive category barring injury.
1997: It was an outstanding season by anyone's standards. And Piazza was a workhorse, too, playing 140 games at the most grueling position.
1996: Despite an injured right knee, Piazza caught 147 games and was the backbone of the Dodgers' offense.

	AB	R	HR	RBI	SB	BA
1995 Los Angeles	434	82	32	93	1	.346
1996 Los Angeles	547	87	36	105	0	.336
1997 Los Angeles	556	104	40	124	5	.362

PIERZYNSKI, A.J. - C - BL - b: 12/30/76
Pierzynski has a quick release and a strong arm, two definite plusses for a young catcher. He played the 1997 season at Class A Fort Myers in the Florida State League. He has gap power and hits for average but is a bit overaggressive at the plate at this stage of his career. He has a chance to pass Javier Valentin as the Twins' catcher of the future. Pierzynski has a better batting stroke than Valentin and with his strong arm all he needs is some work on his mechanics.

PINTO, RENE - C - BR - b: 7/17/77
After batting .284 for Rookie-League Tampa in 1994, this catcher didn't do much in the following two seasons. But he showed signs of progress last year by hitting .289 in 52 games for Class A Oneonta and .286 in 35 games for higher Class A Greensboro. Pinto's main asset is youth. He hasn't shown any remarkable speed, power or ability to draw a walk, but he's still improving. His defense is above average for this stage of his career.

PIRKL, GREG - 1B - BR - b: 8/7/70
Given a chance to platoon with Paul Sorrento at first base with Seattle in 1996, Pirkl hit just .190. He drifted back to the minors, surfaced briefly with the Red Sox later in '96, and was in Japan last year, again failing to impress.

PLANTIER, PHIL - OF - BL - b: 1/27/69
Scouting: Though he probably isn't really the power hitter who produced 34 homers in 1993 with the Padres, Plantier can drive the ball as well as many lefthand hitters. He also has a relatively small hitting zone and will pile up strikeouts in bunches. Only 29 years old, and serviceable defensively in the outfield, Plantier can help a team if he just can manage to stay healthy for a full season, a goal that seems to elude him almost every year.
1998: He probably can fit into the Cardinals' plans as a reserve outfielder and much-needed power source on the bench if he just can stay free of injuries during the early part of the season. He was eligible for free agency after the 1997 season.
1997: Plantier thought he could show someone he still could play every day if given the chance. The Cards didn't give him much of a chance until the latter stages because he was injured when acquired from San Diego and seemed too prone to striking out on a team that led the league in that category. He had a strong September and, overall, batted .259 with four homers in 108 at-bats against righthanders.
1996: Another injury-filled season had Plantier stuttering through a horrid start as the starting left fielder in Oakland. Considering his early slump, his final totals don't look so bad.

	AB	R	HR	RBI	SB	BA
1995 San Diego	216	33	9	34	1	.255
1996 Oakland	231	29	7	31	2	.212
1997 St. Louis	121	13	5	18	0	.248

PLEDGER, KINNIS - OF - BL - b: 7/17/68
He's a good defensive player with speed and some power but he's also pushing 30 and has spent 11 years in the minor leagues. Pledger turned up at Double-A New Haven in the Rockies' organization in 1997 and is near the end of his baseball career.

PODSEDNIK, SCOTT - OF - BL - b: 3/18/76
Podsednik reversed field in 1997, sliding back a level to lower Class A Kane County in the Marlins' organization. He still was unable to dominate. He is a spray-hitting lefty with slightly above-average speed, a good eye and little extra-base power. Anything

less than a two-level jump to Double-A in 1998 will result in Podsednik being overrun by younger, more exciting prospects like Jaime Jones and Julio Ramirez. He is not likely to dent the major leagues.

POE, CHARLES - OF - BR - b: 11/9/71
A sixth-year minor-league free agent, Poe showed signs of hitting in his first year with the Padres, batting .311 in 53 games at Mobile before earning a promotion to Triple-A Las Vegas. Most notably he cut down on his strikeouts after fanning 99 times in 416 at-bats at Double-A Huntsville in 1996. Poe is a steady defensive player and ready to play a full year at Triple-A.

POLANCO, ENOHEL - SS - BR - b: 8/11/75
Polanco was promoted from high A ball to Double-A in the Mets organization and it helped his offense. He hit .300 at the higher level and both his on base and slugging percentages also rose. Polanco should get a shot at full time Double-A duty to start 1998.

POLANCO, PLACIDO - 2B - BR - b: 10/10/75
Polanco doesn't run with blazing speed. He's not an acrobatic second baseman who will dazzle anyone with his defense. He won't hit a lot of home runs. But ever since the second half of the 1996 season in the Class A Florida State League, Polanco has done everything well enough to draw notice. He showed a steady-to-excellent glove in Double-A last year and batted .291 with 51 RBI: the second successive season he finished with those exact totals. His strikeouts were up so he will need to focus on better pitch selection through at least one full season in Triple-A.

POLCOVICH, KEVIN - SS - BR - b: 6/28/70
Scouting: From a scouting standpoint, Polcovich is ordinary in all phases of the game. However, no one works harder or gets more from his limited ability. Polcovich is primarily a shortstop but also plays an adequate second base and third base.
1998: Polcovich's chances of starting depend on what the Pirates do at shortstop. They have three other options: re-sign Shawon Dunston as a free agent, re-sign Kevin Elster as a free agent, or give the job to prospect Abraham Nunez. At season's end it appeared the Pirates would re-sign one of the veterans and make Polcovich their utility infielder.
1997: In a season filled with surprise for the Pirates, Polcovich might have been the biggest. The journeyman minor-league, who began the season at Double-A Carolina, was called up from Triple-A Calgary on May 17th, a day after Elster fractured his left wrist, and he gave the Pirates three months of solid play at shortstop. Polcovich suffered a sprained left ankle in late-August that ended his season.
1996: Polcovich spent the year splitting time between shortstop and second base at Triple-A Calgary after having off-season surgery for an inner ear problem that nearly ended his career.

	AB	R	HR	RBI	SB	BA
1997 Pittsburgh	245	37	4	21	2	.273

POLIDOR, WILFREDO - 2B - BB - b: 9/23/73
A Native of Caracas, Venezuala, Polidor was signed as a free agent by the White Sox in 1990 at the age of 17. 1997 was his seventh season in the Sox organization and he saw action at all three levels. He's struggled at the plate the past three seasons and in 1997 his best average came in 93 at-bats at Double-A Birmingham where he hit .269. He was overmatched against Triple-A pitchers but got only 31 at-bats. He's only 24 years old but hasn't made anything happen in seven seasons. Right now he doesn't look like a prospect.

POLONIA, LUIS - OF - BL - b: 12/10/64
Polonia is a career .292 hitter over ten big-league seasons with five different teams. He's considered an above-average spray hitter with base-stealing ability. Polonia played at Mexico City in 1997 where he was considered the league's best hitter and gained star status as a fan favorite. Polonia wants to be an everyday play, which is why he signed with the Devil Rays rather than accepting a limited role with another major league team. Polonia has his sights set on the starting left field job in 1998.

	AB	R	HR	RBI	SB	BA
1995 NY AL - Atlanta	291	43	2	17	13	.261
1996 Baltimore	175	25	2	14	8	.240
1996 Atlanta	31	3	0	2	1	.419

POSADA, JORGE - C - BB - b: 8/17/71
Scouting: This switch-hitting catcher is an interesting study. Some people, including Yankee management, believe Posada has the ability to be a number one catcher in the big leagues. Others see nothing more than a career backup. A compact line-drive swing indicates Posada will be able to hit no matter what his role eventually becomes. An above-average throwing arm masks some slowness in his release.
1998: The Yankees had their fingers crossed they didn't lose Posada in the expansion draft. Posada himself was hoping not to be included in a deal for Montreal's Pedro Martinez. The 1998 plan was for Posada to back up Joe Girardi, if Girardi remained, and then take over the starting spot in 1999.
1997: Posada hit just .208 (10-for-48) when asked to fill in for a 15-game stretch when Girardi was shelved in September. The 1997 season was Posada's first full year in the big leagues. He was impressive enough to raise expectations, not lower them.
1996: Posada appeared in eight games in 1996 and played in one post-season game. He hit .271 with 11 homers and 62 RBI for Triple-A Columbus.

	AB	R	HR	RBI	SB	BA
1997 New York AL	188	29	6	25	1	.250

POSE, SCOTT - OF - BL - b: 2/11/67
Pose remains a good defensive outfielder with no power. For pure running speed, he is one of the fastest runners in the Yankees' organization. Pose had a successful 1997 season at Triple-A Columbus, hitting over .303 and posting a .404 on-base percentage, but with limited power.

	AB	R	HR	RBI	SB	BA
1997 New York AL	87	19	0	5	3	.218

POST, DAVE - 2B - BR - b: 9/3/73
Post is a light-hitting second baseman who finally reached Double-A last season for the first time in his six-year professional career. He had a non-descript season with the Expos' Harrisburg affiliate and has almost zero chance of getting to the big leagues.

POUGH, PORK CHOP - 3B/1B - BR - b: 12/25/69
Pough has spent the majority of the last four years as a power-hitter stuck in Triple-A with no major league opportunity. Last

year he was one of Omaha's leading power hitters, bashing 22 homers with 59 RBI while hitting .252. Pough is a below-average third baseman and outfielder who doesn't make contact well enough to hit for a useful average in the majors. If he gets to the big leagues he'll be a righthanded pinch-hitter.

POWELL, ALONZO - OF - BR - b: 12/12/64
Powell has been among the most successful Americans playing in Japan, winning three batting titles with the Chunichi Dragons, including a .349 season in 1996. 1997 wasn't his year, however. Powell didn't like hitting in the new Nagoya Dome, slipped to .253, and got released.

POWELL, DANTE - OF - BR - b: 8/25/73
Scouting: Powell is the total package. He's an outstanding athlete who hits for power with excellent speed and decent plate discipline. Powell is considered a top-flight center fielder with a strong arm. He was a first-round draft choice by the Giants in 1994 out of Fullerton State after being a supplemental first-round draft pick by the Blue Jays in 1991 out of high school (but he didn't sign). Powell is on many top prospect lists.
1998: Powell will challenge for a role in the Giants' outfield right from the outset. He's considered one of the brighter prospects — among several bright outfield prospects. The difficult task for the Giants is finding him sufficient playing time if they bring back all three outfielders from their NL West championship squad. Powell may return to Triple-A just to play regularly.
1997: Against the better and more experienced Triple-A pitchers, Powell lost a little patience at the plate, but still turned in a fine year, batting .241 with 11 homers, 42 RBI and 34 stolen bases. He also spent some time with the Giants, showing a little bit of all his skills, mostly in a pinch-hitting role.
1996: Powell burst upon the scene as an outstanding prospect with a breakout year for Double-A Shreveport, hitting .280 with 21 homers, 78 RBI and 43 steals. He also drew 72 walks, an indication of his willingness to take a pitch.

POZO, ARQUIMEDEZ - 2B - BR - b: 8/24/73
Scouting: Tiny, but powerful, Pozo has a big-man's approach at the plate. He tries to pull just about every pitch he sees out of the park. He's successful more than you would think, but his long swing and tendency to pull off breaking pitches makes him a poor big-league candidate. Pozo lacks range at second base, but has become a good third baseman. He has only average speed.
1998: Pozo will likely find himself back in Triple-A, and will remain there until he refines his approach at the plate. With his strength and hand-quickness, if he would just protect the plate and hit to all fields he would be a tough out, and a big-leaguer.
1997: Pozo spent nearly the entire season in Triple-A. He had a brief trial with Boston when Tim Naehring was hurt, but did not impress Manager Jimy Williams and soon found himself back in the minors. He hit 22 homers in 377 at-bats and played a good third base.
1996: Pozo, once a top prospect in the Seattle system, was basically given to the Red Sox for aging journeyman Jeff Manto at mid-season. After a hot start with Boston, his offensive and defensive flaws showed up and he was sent back to Triple-A.

PRATT, TODD - C - BR - b: 2/9/67
Scouting: Even the scouts didn't see this coming. Even before he took a year off from the game — he worked at Bucky Dent's baseball camp in 1996 after quitting the game — Pratt wasn't much of an offensive player. But he shortened his stroke during his Triple-A tour last season and the results were immediate and dramatically different. Most guys can't make a living on hitting fastballs alone, but Pratt made a nice contribution with that limited diet. Meanwhile, his throwing and receiving blossomed, exceeding anything the Phillies and Cubs, his previous teams, had envisioned.
1998: Pratt was an element in the most confounding issue the Mets faced entering the next season — what to do for a catcher while Todd Hundley rehabbed his elbow. Pratt was regarded as an ideal understudy last season; give him 40 starts and maybe 200 at-bats, and he would benefit the team. But the club wasn't convinced increased exposure wouldn't bring Pratt to the point of diminishing return. The Mets were looking for another catcher.
1997: As Yogi once said, "He exceeded expectations... and more." The Mets summoned Pratt from the minor leagues when it realized Hundley's availability would be compromised, and Pratt performed exceptionally well until his own physical problem, torn knee cartilage, undermined his performance; the knee required arthroscopic surgery. He batted .447 with both home runs and 12 RBI in 38 at-bats against lefthanded pitching. Righthanded pitchers had their way with him: he had 12 singles and a double, a .191 average and 24 strikeouts in 68 at-bats.
1996: Pratt signed with the Mariners as a six-year minor-league free agent in January and appeared with them in eight exhibition games, batting .364 in eleven at-bats. But he was released March 26th and didn't catch on elsewhere. He worked in Bucky Dent's baseball camp instead of playing ball.

	AB	R	HR	RBI	SB	BA
1997 New York NL	106	12	2	19	0	.283

PRIDE, CURTIS - OF - BL - b: 12/17/68
Scouting: Pride is a great human interest story, because he made it to the big leagues despite being deaf, but he isn't a great player. He's not a bad hitter, especially when he's thrown fastballs, and he has decent speed. But he's not fast enough to steal bases, not good enough in the outfield to play there regularly and not a good enough hitter to be a full-time DH.
1998: The Tigers decided they didn't want Pride; he declined an assignment to the minors, became a free agent and signed with Boston. He spent last September with the Red Sox, but played sparingly. Even with expansion, Pride isn't guaranteed a big-league job.
1997: Pride got a few chances to play for the Tigers early in the season, but his average quickly tailed off and so did his playing time. He started only six games after the All-Star break, and was finally taken off the roster in mid-August.
1996: In his first full year in the big leagues, Pride batted .300. He played a lot, became a part-time leadoff hitter in the second half of the year, and finished strong, with a .314 average in his last 84 games.

	AB	R	HR	RBI	SB	BA
1995 Montreal	63	10	0	2	3	.175
1996 Detroit	267	52	10	31	11	.300
1997 Boston	164	22	3	20	6	.213

PRIETO, ALEJANDRO - SS - BB - b: 6/19/76
Signed as a sixteen-year-old from a Venezuelan high school, Prieto spent his fifth pro season in a repeat at higher Class A Wilmington with much worse results than in 1996. He lost 70 points off his batting average and made 37 errors in 129 games

at shortstop. Prieto has decent speed but little power and only marginal plate discipline. He's still young enough to advance, but he must make major improvements in the accuracy of his throws and in making contact at the plate to be considered a prospect.

PRIETO, CHRIS - OF - BL - b: 8/24/72

Prieto is a good contact hitter with above-average speed and is an excellent defensive outfielder. In 1997, he hit .320 with 26 steals and more walks than strikeouts at Double-A Mobile in his first full season above A-ball. A heady player, Prieto has a chance to become a fourth outfielder in the major leagues.

PRINCE, TOM - C - BR - b: 8/13/64

Scouting: Prince is a strong defensive catcher who has even turned up his offensive production as Mike Piazza's backup.
1998: Prince hits well enough and has the defensive skills to warrant another season as a backup receiver in the majors.
1997: Prince played in 47 games and was productive at the plate when he did play, which wasn't often with Piazza having such a stellar offensive season.
1996: Prince wrested the Dodger backup catching duties from Carlos Hernandez and hit well in 64 at-bats, earning himself an invite back for the 1997 season.

	AB	R	HR	RBI	SB	BA
1996 Los Angeles	64	6	1	11	0	.297
1997 Los Angeles	100	17	3	14	0	.220

PRITCHETT, CHRIS - 1B - BL - b: 1/31/70

Scouting: Pritchett has done everything he's been asked to do in order to become a major league player. Asked to learn to hit for power two years ago, Pritchett spent a winter in Mexico and responded with a good power year in Vancouver. If the Angels hadn't reloaded with a bunch of veterans, he might be in the major leagues by now. He's a tireless worker, who's pleased the Angels with his attitude and patience.
1998: Pritchett may face a watershed year in which he could become a major leaguer, but the time is coming soon when he'll have to take that final step up to the majors.
1997: Pritchett's power numbers were down with Vancouver, but he drove in a lot of runs for the Canadians. He played well defensively and kept his name fairly high on the Angels' list of prospects.
1996: Pritchett's lesson in power in Mexico the previous off-season paid good dividends as he hit 16 home runs and drove in 73 runs, without sacrificing batting average. He showed the Angels that he had major league potential.

PULLIAM, HARVEY - OF - BR - b: 10/20/67

Scouting: A 30-year-old veteran who has put up big Triple-A numbers for years, Pulliam finally received the chance to become a dependable, big-league bench player last year. He's a quality, righthanded hitter with punch and is a corner outfielder who throws and runs adequately. He had seven pinch-hits, including two homers, in '97.
1998: As has been the case the past several years, Pulliam will go to spring training with a fair shot at the 25-man roster. His chances with Arizona will be better than they were with Colorado.
1997: Pulliam started the season on the Triple-A Colorado Springs bench. But after 40 games, he was batting .401 with 12 homers and 43 RBI and he was called up to the Rockies in mid-May. He stayed through the season.
1996: Pulliam was perhaps a favorite to win the righthanded pinch-hitting job out of spring training but his bothersome right knee never came around. He underwent arthroscopic surgery right after spring training and missed the first eleven weeks of the season. He finally came on in the last month with Colorado Springs and was called up in September.

PYE, EDDIE - 2B - BR - b: 2/13/67

Pye had cups of coffee with the Dodgers in 1994 and 1995 and averaged over .320 in the Pacific Coast League from 1991 through 1995. Pye batted .257 for Triple-A Tucson in 1996 before becoming disenchanted with his playing time and leaving the team in midseason. In 1997 he played just three games for Triple-A Norfolk in the Mets organization.

QUINLAN, TOM - 3B - BR - b: 3/27/68

A perennial, six-year free agent who continues to put up impressive numbers at Triple-A, Quinlan just doesn't get a chance to perform in the majors. Playing mostly third base for Triple-A Colorado Springs, Quinlan had his best season in 1997, hitting .285 and leading the club with 23 homers and 113 RBI. He's a steady fielder with a sweet, effortless, righthanded swing.

QUINN, MARK - OF - BR - b: 5/21/74

Off-season weight training helped Quinn improve his power in 1997; he combined for 18 homers, 89 RBI, 56 extra-base hits, and a .565 slugging average between Class A Wilmington and Double-A Wichita. Better control and more fastballs from Double-A pitchers improved his batting eye. Playing center field as he did in 1997 is not a long-range goal; he'll shift to a corner outfield position or possibly to third base where he has played in the past. Quinn's two years away from the majors.

RAABE, BRIAN - 2B - BR - b: 11/5/67

Scouting: After advancing through the Minnesota farm system, Raabe was signed by Seattle as a six-year minor-league free agent prior to the 1997 season before going to Colorado. He has a great batting eye and good batting stroke with a good glove, too. Raabe has limited speed for a middle infielder but with more pop than most.
1998: Based strictly upon his numbers, Raabe deserves a major league chance. He could stick with a team in search of proven, veteran backup help. Expansion will help him get his shot at a utility role in the bigs.
1997: Raabe had another big hitting season in Triple-A, his second in a row. He hit .352 with 14 homers and 80 RBI and struck out only 20 times in 543 at-bats.
1996: Raabe had an explosive year at Triple-A Salt Lake City, hitting .351 with 18 homers and 69 RBI while striking out only 19 times in 482 at-bats.

RADMANOVICH, RYAN - OF - BL - b: 8/9/71

Radmanovich has overcome a torn anterior cruciate ligament that cost him his entire 1995 season. After leading the Twins' Double-A team in homers in 1996 with 25, he spent the 1997 season at Triple-A Salt Lake, belting 28 homers, good for second on the team. He still strikes out a lot but still has good range in the outfield, despite the knee injury, and he has a strong arm. He is a candidate to become a fourth or fifth outfielder for the Twins.

RAINES, TIM - OF - BB - b: 9/16/59
Scouting: When he is available, the aging left fielder can still produce. The problem is that he misses huge chunks of the season due to cranky hamstrings. Still, when the switch-hitter gets on the field, he hits for a good average and runs well, too. Years ago he was in the top tier of high-speed, high batting average outfielders.

1998: With the Yankees planning to turn left field over to rookie Ricky Ledee and hoping to have Chad Curtis around as a safety net, the club decided not to pick up Raines' option. There was brief talk of asking him back at a reduced rate but he was expected to sign elsewhere as a free agent.

1997: Raines started the season on the DL with a strained left hamstring. He returned in mid-April only to go back on the shelf again July 3rd. He didn't surface again until mid-August. Leg woes robbed him of the confidence needed to be the base stealer he was in his youth. He was caught in five of thirteen steal attempts; it was his first season without double-digit steals since he played 15 games for Montreal in 1980.

1996: His playing time dropped with the first appearance of serious leg problems, but Raines was part of the Yankees' late-season surge into post-season play.

	AB	R	HR	RBI	SB	BA
1995 Chicago AL	502	81	12	67	13	.285
1996 New York AL	201	45	9	33	10	.284
1997 New York AL	271	56	4	38	8	.321

RALEIGH, MATT - 1B/3B - BR - b: 7/18/70
In his first full season of Double-A ball, Raleigh was a hit or miss swinger. He hit 37 homers but missed to the tune of 173 strikeouts in 406 at-bats. No doubt the Mets like his power potential but Raleigh will have to cut down on his strikeouts considerably to advance.

RAMIREZ, ALEX - OF - BR - b: 10/3/74
An under-sized outfielder with surprising extra-base power, Ramirez is a wild swinger with slightly above-average speed and has always been among the younger players at his minor-league level. He's an average defensive outfielder with a plus throwing arm. He hit .286 with eleven homers in 416 at-bats at Triple-A Buffalo in 1997, but fanned 95 times against just 24 walks. Ramirez has to improve his plate discipline significantly.

RAMIREZ, ANGEL - OF - BR - b: 1/24/73
Other than a week with Triple-A Syracuse in April, he spent most of the year with Double-A Knoxville. Ramirez was traded to the New York Yankees for Mariano Duncan. A fast runner who may develop into a contact hitter eventually, he has great range in the outfield. He needs to be more selective at the plate.

RAMIREZ, ARAMIS - 3B - BR - b: 6/25/78
Ramirez was the Most Valuable Player of the higher Class A Carolina League last season with the Pirates' Lynchburg farm club despite not turning 19 until late-June. The third baseman is a special talent, though a bit a immature. The Pirates feel he isn't the type of guy who should be rushed, so he likely won't see Pittsburgh until late in the 1999 season. Once he gets to the Pirates, he will be a superstar in the making.

RAMIREZ, HIRAM - C - BR - b: 9/10/72
For the second straight season Ramirez saw action at both Class A and Double-A. He showed some pop in the California League but struggled to make contact at Double-A Shreveport. The Giants have a couple of catching prospects ahead of Ramirez and he will have a hard time making the big-league roster with San Francisco.

RAMIREZ, JULIO - OF - BR - b: 8/10/77
Ramirez is a five-tool prospect with power, speed and defensive ability in large doses. Despite a small frame, he can drive the ball with authority but needs to put the ball into play more consistently. He's a greyhound in center field, combining great range with a plus throwing arm. He spent 1997 at lower Class A Kane County with his season being cut short by torn thumb ligaments. He'll advance quickly if he can improve his strikezone judgment, possibly reaching Double-A Portland this year.

RAMIREZ, MANNY - OF - BR - b: 5/30/72
Scouting: Ramirez is one of the purest offensive talents in major league baseball, and one of the most credentialed 25-year-olds of recent times. Once a hacker who strictly went for the fences and vulnerable to good righthanded pitching, Ramirez is now an equal opportunity power threat who takes what the pitcher gives him — and sometimes more. He is capable of prodigious power to all fields, and is now content to sling singles to right on breaking pitches from tough righthanders. His foot speed is just adequate, but he is an improving defensive right fielder with an above-average arm.

1998: Ramirez is ready for a simultaneous onslaught on all three Triple Crown categories. Not many players can claim career highs of a .328 batting average, 33 homers and 112 RBI at his young age. Ramirez is a good bet to improve upon all three and possibly win an MVP award in the not-too-distant future.

1997: A casual observation of Ramirez' power numbers as a disappointment would be a mistake because Ramirez posted a .415 on-base percentage, .538 slugging average and hit well over .300 against righthanded pitching — a marked improvement over a few seasons ago.

1996: Ramirez unfurled a carbon copy of his 1995 season, reaching the .300-30-100 Triple Crown milestones while adding a career-high 45 doubles. His overall dominance made it easier for the Indians to let Albert Belle escape.

	AB	R	HR	RBI	SB	BA
1995 Cleveland	484	85	31	107	6	.308
1996 Cleveland	550	94	33	112	8	.309
1997 Cleveland	561	99	26	88	2	.328

RAMOS, KEN - OF - BL - b: 6/8/67
A nine-year minor-league veteran who finally got his major league cup of coffee in 1997 (12 at-bats spread out over a month), Ramos has lasted this long primarily because he can make contact at the plate; he has never struck out more often than he has walked. He led two different minor leagues in hitting early in his career and owns a career .302 batting average, but has only average speed and little power (19 career homers). Ramos is hopeful that expansion will give him another shot in the bigs.

RANDA, JOE - 3B - BR - b: 12/18/69
Scouting: Randa is a line-drive hitter with marginal power but the Tigers feel he can develop power as he matures. He had trouble defensively at third base last season, struggling on the artificial surface, after establishing himself as an above-average

fielder in the American League with Kansas City.
1998: Randa will be the Tigers' starting third baseman, though it remains to be seen if he will be their number five hitter. Detroit feels he can improve on his decent numbers of 1997.
1997: After a slow start in his adjustment to the National League, Randa caught fire until a broken little finger on his left hand put him on the disabled list for a month at mid-season. It took Randa a long time to regain his batting stroke and he rarely showed any power after the injury.
1996: Randa hit over .300 for Kansas City in his first full season in the majors. However, former Royals manager Bob Boone preferred Craig Paquette as his third baseman and Randa was part of a six-player trade with the Pirates during the following winter.

	AB	R	HR	RBI	SB	BA
1995 Kansas City	70	6	1	5	0	.171
1996 Kansas City	337	36	6	47	13	.303
1997 Pittsburgh	443	58	7	60	4	.302

RAVEN, LUIS - 3B - BR - b: 11/19/68
Briefly a hot prospect with the Angels after hitting .305 with 31 homers and 116 RBI in a season split between Double-A Midland and Triple-A Vancouver in 1994, Raven has been unable to sustain his success and never reached the majors. Part of the problem has been defense: once a first basemen, then an outfielder, and now a third baseman, Raven has no real position. He has spent the last two years stuck in Double-A and, last year, led Birmingham with 30 homers. Raven can get to the majors as an extra bat off the bench but will never be a regular.

RAYNOR, MARK - SS - BR - b: 4/1/73
Raynor is a limited minor-league shortstop who will advance to regular duty at Double-A Reading in 1998. He hustles in all phases of the game, but he's too old for that level and lacks the raw tools to advance. Raynor is a disciplined hitter but has no extra-base power. He's surehanded within his limited range afield and is an instinctively good baserunner despite possessing just marginal speed. He is admired for his hustling playing style, but Raynor simply doesn't have the goods to advance much farther.

REBOULET, JEFF - SS/3B - BR - b: 4/30/64
Scouting: Reboulet is an all-around utility player, making him valuable to a team that carries 12 or more pitchers and fewer position-playing reserves. He can play all of the infield positions, and can move to the outfield when needed. Although he's hit as high as .292, he doesn't often hit for a high average, and he pops an occasional home run; Reboulet has good plate discipline. He's not slow, but neither does he have any base stealing speed. His defense is above average, and he's not overly strong at any one position. As a hustling team player with a good attitude, Reboulet is a valuable asset to a major league team.
1998: The Orioles like Reboulet and his playing style, and he has a job for 1998. They have strong regulars at all positions, so his playing time may decrease if the regulars remain healthy. But Manager Davey Johnson likes to play his reserves occasionally to keep them sharp, so he won't languish on the bench all year.
1997: Signed as a free agent by the Orioles, Reboulet did a good job filling in at second base for over a month when Roberto Alomar went down with a groin injury. While he didn't hit for a high average, he came through with a few unexpected clutch hits to win some games. He also played third, short and right field.

1996: Reboulet hit a weak .222 for the Twins in 234 at-bats with no homers and only nine extra base hits. It looked like he was washed up.

	AB	R	HR	RBI	SB	BA
1995 Minnesota	216	39	4	23	1	.292
1996 Minnesota	234	20	0	23	4	.222
1997 Baltimore	228	26	4	27	3	.237

REDMOND, MIKE - C - BR - b: 5/5/71
Redmond has adequate defensive skills, and was much improved in his second tour of the Double-A Eastern League IN 1996. Most impressive was his durability. In 1997 he played 43 games for the Marlins at the Triple-A, Rookie League and Class-A levels.

REED, JEFF - C - BL - b: 11/12/62
Scouting: The veteran catcher of twelve major league seasons was reborn when he signed two years ago with the Rockies. A career backup backstop, Reed had hit just 16 homers in his first ten-plus big-league seasons. He hit a career-high eight in 1996, his first season with the Rockies, then 17 in just 90 games last year. He has a natural uppercut swing that is well-suited for Coors Field's most reachable home run target in right-center. He has a strong arm but the reason why he doesn't play more is that he is considered a below-average receiver. He does not block balls well and his pitch-selection is sometimes questioned.
1998: After the 1997 season, Reed was expected to enter free agency, where he could command a $1 million salary for the first time in his lengthy career. The Rockies would have liked to re-sign him but probably not for the money Reed's big season figured to command. Returning to the Rockies might let him start three or four times per week, not two to three times as he did last year.
1997: His best season came in his twelfth big-league season. His 17 homers were one more than he had in his first ten years in the majors. Reed threw out seven of his first ten would-be basestealers and finished with an impressive 32.4 percent caught-stealing rate. He started about twice per week until the final six weeks, when his bat wrestled additional playing time away from Kirt Manwaring.
1996: When Jayhawk Owens suffered a thumb injury in spring training, Reed became a starting catcher for the first time in his career. He responded with career highs in nearly every category and the Rockies decided to pick up the second-year option on his contract.

	AB	R	HR	RBI	SB	BA
1995 San Francisco	113	12	0	9	0	.265
1996 Colorado	341	34	8	37	2	.284
1997 Colorado	256	43	17	47	2	.297

REED, JODY - 2B - BR - b: 7/26/62
Scouting: Even at age 35, Reed remains a good defensive second baseman. However, his offensive production has declined each of the last three seasons. He's obviously not the 40-double, 50-60 RBI threat he once was in Boston. A smart player and a good clubhouse influence, Reed will have a chance to stay in baseball as a coach, and the time for that might be coming fast.
1998: Reed won't be back with the Tigers, the team that traded for him in spring training 1997 and released him in early September. If he can find a chance to play, he'll need to prove he can still hit.
1997: The Tigers acquired Reed as a hedge, in case Damion

Easley got hurt. He didn't, so Reed spent most of the year on the bench. He had only 112 at-bats, by far the fewest of his career.
1996: Reed was the regular second baseman in San Diego, helping the Padres to the playoffs. He didn't commit an error in 45 games after July 31st. The Padres decided they wanted more, and they acquired Quilvio Veras to play second base in '97.

	AB	R	HR	RBI	SB	BA
1995 San Diego	445	58	4	40	6	.256
1996 San Diego	495	45	2	49	2	.244
1997 Detroit	112	6	0	8	3	.196

REESE, POKEY - SS - BR - b: 6/10/73
Scouting: "Pokey" is a spectacular defensive shortstop, runs well, but has yet to develop into a marginal major league hitter. Reese can drive a mistake, but his poor strikezone judgment and low average make him a poor offensive player.
1998: Reese may stick with the Reds in a utility role, but the return of Barry Larkin will cut into his playing time. There is some talk of moving Larkin to another position to play Reese, but that would take playing time from a better-hitting prospect for a slight gain (at best) in defense at shortstop.
1997: Larkin's season-long injury problems gave Reese an opportunity to play most of the season, and he impressed the Reds with his defensive ability. After Deion Sanders was injured, Jack McKeon made Reese his leadoff hitter, a curious choice given his offensive deficiencies.
1996: Reese regressed in his second year in Triple-A, hitting only .232 with one homer in an injury-plagued season at Indianapolis.

	AB	R	HR	RBI	SB	BA
1997 Cincinnati	397	48	4	26	25	.219

REEVES, GLENN - OF - BR - 1/19/74
The outfielder from Australia finally cracked the Double-A barrier in his fifth professional season in the Marlins' organization. He dazzled offensively, forcing pitchers to throw strikes and lining balls to all fields. However, he has shown little home run power or speed on the bases throughout his career, a no-no for an outfielder trying to draw attention to himself. He is a fundamentally sound defensive player capable of playing both outfield corners. Reeves could earn a brief major league trial or two, but will never play a significant role.

REIMER, KEVIN - OF/DH - BL - b: 6/28/64
Reimer is a poor outfielder, who's old to boot. He's made it to the bigs on several occasions, where he compiled a .258 batting average with a lot of strikeouts. He hit well as a DH at Triple-A Tacoma in the Mariners system last year but the only chance he has left to make it back to the show is as a lefty bat off the bench.

RELAFORD, DESI - SS - BB - b: 9/16/73
Scouting: Relaford is an athletic player who combines solid on-base skills, above-average speed and defensive range, and an exceptionally strong throwing arm. Though only 5'8" and 155 pounds, he's quite strong and has above-average power to the gaps for a middle infielder. However, he often falls in love with his power potential and extends his swing. His plate discipline is average, but needs to be better for him to bat near the top of a major league order. He would be an above-average major league shortstop with the glove with no further improvement; with a little more consistency he could be special.
1998: The departure of Kevin Stocker created an opportunity for Relaford, who had been relegated to a major league bench or might have ended up back in Triple-A. Now, if he doesn't become a starter, Relaford's portfolio of skills and second base experience make him an attractive utility candidate and he's athletic enough to learn other positions. His ability to steal bases is sorely needed in the Phillies' slow lineup.
1997: After enduring two subpar Triple-A seasons with the bat, Relaford put it together at Scranton in 1997. He was above average in all areas except power hitting, and was at times a spectacular turf shortstop. In a Triple-A lineup that was basically a revolving door, Relaford was constantly productive. He's ready for the majors.
1996: Relaford was shifted to second base at Triple-A by the Mariners. Unhappy with the move, Relaford sulked and let his offense suffer, enabling the Phillies to acquire him in a trade deadline deal for Terry Mulholland. They moved him back to shortstop, where his strong arm was fully utilized.

	AB	R	HR	RBI	SB	BA
1996 Philadelphia	40	2	0	1	1	.175

RENNHACK, MIKE - OF - BB - b: 8/25/74
Rennhack was drafted out of high school by the Astros in 1992 and proceeded to flop in the Houston organization and was released in 1995. The Brewers picked him up and he had a great year in the California League in 1996. At Double-A El Paso in 1997, Rennhack showed some power and is still young enough to have a chance to recover his prospect status.

RENTERIA, EDGAR - SS - BR - b: 8/7/75
Scouting: Renteria's coming-out party was on an international stage in the 1997 post-season. He dazzled all with his athleticism in the field and his remarkable calm and clutch-hitting ability at the plate — all at the age of 22. Offensively, Renteria still has some work to do. He swings a live line-drive bat and occasionally turns on an inside pitch to drive it for power, but he remains a relatively wild swinger who does not get on base enough for a top of the order hitter. He has excellent speed, but is refining his basestealing technique. He is a fluid fielder who could graduate to Gold Glove status as he improves his handling of routine chances. Renteria is a money player with the tools and desire to be a star.
1998: The Marlins will again use Renteria in the second spot in the order in 1998. He must cut down his strikeouts and increase his walks to be an adequate table setter. With mega-prospect Alex Gonzalez just behind him, Renteria will constantly face a challenge, and should respond. Expect significant offensive improvement.
1997: What can you say about a season that ends with a game-winning hit in Game Seven of the World Series? And he did it as the major leagues' youngest regular. The image of Renteria playing shortstop in a ski mask in the snow in Cleveland will not soon be forgotten.
1996: Renteria arrived in the majors to stay after only 35 Triple-A games. He batted .326 against righthanders, hit the ball with authority and took charge of the infield defense. He had one of the more underrated rookie seasons of anyone in recent memory.

	AB	R	HR	RBI	SB	BA
1996 Florida	431	68	5	31	16	.309
1997 Florida	617	90	4	52	32	.277

RHODES, KARL - OF - BL - b: 8/21/68
A/k/a Tuffy, a/k/a "Mr. Three Home Runs on Opening Day," Rhodes faded rapidly after his hot start in 1995 and went to Japan in 1996. He still has good tools, is still young enough to get another major league opportunity, and his .318-20-88 production for the Kintetsu Buffaloes last year was encouraging.

RICHARD, CHRIS - 1B - BL - b: 6/7/74
A contact hitter with some gap power, Richard should get to play first base on a steady basis in Triple-A this year. He's reached double figures in home runs each of the last two seasons and, though he still strikes out too much, looks like a solid run-producer. A good athlete who can run perhaps better than average, Richard could benefit from playing more in the outfield and enhancing his future as a big-league reserve. His defensive work at first base and sub-.280 minor-league career batting average certainly doesn't project him as being able to unseat Mark McGwire anytime soon.

RICHARDSON, BRIAN - 3B - BR - b: 8/31/75
Signed as a high school senior at the age of 16, Richardson has needed more time to develop than some players, but he's shown promise as a third baseman. A move from Triple-A Albuquerque to Double-A San Antonio in 1997 helped Richardson, not because he regressed, but because he needed to show what he can do at the lower level first. His defense and hitting improved at San Antonio. Richardson still lacks some experience, but he's shown steady progress.

RICHARDSON, SCOTT - OF - BR - b: 2/19/71
Richardson, acquired by the Dodgers from Milwaukee in the Rule V draft in 1995, has shown some potential as a center fielder. The Dodgers like his speed, both on the bases and in the outfield. He hit well at Double-A San Antonio last year and may have put himself in position to rise through the organization fairly rapidly.

RIGGS, ADAM - 2B - BR - b: 10/4/72
Scouting: Riggs is not a great glove man but he has decent range and may be able to survive as a second baseman. He has above-average power for a second baseman and has proven he can hit at every minor-league level.
1998: Riggs could work his way into at least a utility position with the Dodgers. If he doesn't, another year at Triple-A Albuquerque will be in the plans.
1997: 1997 was Riggs' first year at the Triple-A level and he had a strong season, hitting .304 with 13 homers and 28 RBI. He also showed good speed with 12 stolen bases and improved plate discipline as he walked 29 times against 39 strikeouts.
1996: Riggs spent 1996 at the Double-A level for the first time, showing his offensive production in the California League the year before was not a fluke and that his defense was not as bad as advertised.

RIGGS, KEVIN - 2B - BL - b: 2/3/69
Riggs played the 1997 season at Double-A Akron in the Cleveland organization. A lifetime .302 hitter in seven previous seasons, Riggs struggled at the plate in Akron and has little more than a Double-A future in front of him.

RILEY, MARQUIS - OF - BR - b: 12/27/70
Scouting: A switch-hitting outfielder with speed, Riley made some strides after returning to the Angels' organization in late-March. The Angels had lost him on waivers, but re-signed him after he was released by Florida's Triple-A club. He can run the bases and play solid defense, but needs to work on his hitting.
1998: Riley has to show the Angels he can hit if he wants to rise above his present "organizational-depth" level. His speed's an asset, but he has to learn to make better contact to make the final jump to the big leagues.
1997: Riley was Vancouver's second-leading base stealer with 27 and played all three outfield positions well, committing only one error in 65 games. He scored only 33 runs, which isn't impressive for a player with his speed, but his .267 average and a series of injuries limited his opportunities.
1996: A poor season at the plate convinced the Angels to put Riley on waivers and he was claimed by the Marlins.

RIOS, ARMANDO - OF - BL - b: 9/13/71
Rios had solid numbers at Shreveport in 1997, hitting .289 with 14 homers, 79 RBI and 17 steals, but he's getting to be rather old for a Double-A player. The Giants are not particularly high on Rios, having never advanced him to Triple-A. Rios may reach that level in 1998 and could eventually get to the majors although his upper limit is probably as a fourth outfielder or bench player.

RIPKEN, BILLY - 2B - BR - b: 12/16/64
Scouting: Ripken is a contact hitter with little power and no speed. Although he has occasionally hit for average, he's sub-.250 for his career. He can play all four infield positions capably and doesn't make many mistakes, which will probably keep him in the majors for a while longer. He has had back problems, but they seemed to be under control by the end of last season.
1998: Especially in an expansion year, Ripken should find work as a decent-field, no-hit utility player.
1997: Ripken actually was anointed the starting shortstop in June, but went on the DL with back problems five days later. The Rangers like his surehandedness, and it was one of his better seasons at the plate. In what is surely a statistical anomaly, the Rangers were 30-15 when Ripken started at a middle infield spot.
1996: Ripken never got to play much behind his brother and Roberto Alomar. His .230 average was in line with his career norms.

	AB	R	HR	RBI	SB	BA
1995 Cleveland	17	4	2	3	0	.412
1996 Baltimore	135	19	2	12	0	.230
1997 Texas	203	18	3	24	0	.276

RIPKEN, CAL - SS - BR - b: 8/24/60
Scouting: Ripken is a streaky hitter who goes into slumps, and tinkers with his batting stance to work his way out them. He has enough power to pop 20 homers for another few years, and his bat speed and reactions are still strong. It took Ripken about 100 games to get adjusted to playing third base, and now he's a Gold Glove candidate. He was rated the second best defensive third baseman in the American League in the Baseball America managers' poll. Ripken is one of baseball's best assets.
1998: Ripken should be fully adjusted to third base, and another year of good hitting is expected. Of course, he'll play every game, too.
1997: Ripken had some slumps caused, in part, by back

spasms. He's a streaky hitter as shown by his .242 average in July followed with a .357 mark in August.
1996: Ripken hit well in a lively-ball year reaching 26 homers and hitting triple-digits in RBI for the first time since 1991.

	AB	R	HR	RBI	SB	BA
1995 Baltimore	550	71	17	88	0	.262
1996 Baltimore	640	94	26	102	1	.278
1997 Baltimore	615	79	17	84	1	.270

RIVERA, LUIS - 2B/SS - BR - b: 1/3/64
A veteran utility infielder who has played in the majors in ten of his sixteen seasons (for five different teams, most recently for the Astros in 1997), Rivera spent most of last year at Triple-A New Orleans. He's a career .230 hitter in both the majors and the minors with limited power and speed. His strong suit is his dependable defensive play, despite limited range.

RIVERA, RUBEN - OF - BR - b: 11/14/73
Scouting: Acquired in the Hideki Irabu deal, Rivera is ticketed as the Padre left fielder of the future. Rivera has excellent tools, including power and speed, but his work habits are a concern.
1998: Rivera could be the opening day left fielder for the Padres, who were hoping to move Greg Vaughn to create an opening.
1997: He lost most of the season due to spring training biceps tendon surgery and played 29 games total, mostly as a pinch-hitter or pinch-runner. Rivera had only 68 at-bats all season.
1996: Rivera divided time between the Yankees Triple-A Columbus club and the major leagues. He hit only .235 at Triple-A with ten homers in 101 games and his effort was questioned. Rivera hit much better in 88 at-bats with the Yankees.

ROBERGE, J.P. - 3B - BR - b: 9/12/72
Although Roberge had a good season at Double-A San Antonio, hitting .322 with 17 homers and 105 RBI in 516 at-bats and also stealing 18 bases, he is old for his level and is only a distant prospect. He consistently hits for a high average but needs to once again prove himself at Triple-A.

ROBERSON, KEVIN - OF - BB - b: 1/29/68
Roberson is a former Met and a former Cub — and a former prospect. He had a decent year for Triple-A Phoenix last year, hitting .287 with 14 homers and 67 RBI. His hitting has not translated well to the majors and at this stage of his career he's no more than injury insurance stored in the high minors. Even with expansion, Roberson has only a dim hope for significant major league play.

ROBERTS, BIP - 2B - BB - b: 10/27/63
Scouting: Roberts has quietly fashioned a long, productive major league career as one of baseball's most underrated leadoff men. The tiny outfielder and erstwhile second baseman doesn't have the raw speed of his younger days, but is a savvy baserunner who knows when to take the extra base. The switch-hitter slaps the ball where it's pitched, with quite limited extra-base power. However, his walk rate has dropped off during the last three seasons, making his on-base percentages below average for a leadoff man. He is no longer adequate with the glove at second base; he's capable of playing only left field over the long haul.
1998: Roberts has begun his decline phase, and is no longer a viable candidate to lead off every day. There is a major logjam for playing time in Cleveland, and Roberts could be a casualty.

1997: Roberts lost his second base job in Kansas City to Jose Offerman, shared a left field job, then was dispatched to Cleveland late in the season. He was a catalyst in the Indians' late hot streak, inheriting the leadoff spot from Marquis Grissom and setting the table more effectively for Cleveland's loaded middle of the order.
1996: Roberts made his American League debut after spending the better part of a decade in the National League. He was hampered by multiple injuries, and limited to 339 at-bats — and no homers. The latter fact wouldn't be notable except that he occasionally batted cleanup for the Royals.

	AB	R	HR	RBI	SB	BA
1995 San Diego	296	40	2	25	20	.304
1996 Kansas City	339	39	0	52	12	.283
1997 two teams	431	63	4	44	18	.302

ROBERTS, DAVE - DH - BL - b: 5/31/72
Roberts is a great hustler who is a good contact hitter and possesses above-average speed — he led the minor leagues with 65 steals in '96. He's a strong man, but it doesn't translate to his swing, and therefore he hits to the opposite field more often than not. He has a good glove with a below-average arm. He's an older minor-leaguer, but is great in the clubhouse and may get a promotion just for his good work with some of the Tigers' younger prospects at Double-A Jacksonville. Roberts hit .296 in 105 games last year.

ROBERTS, LONELL - OF - BB - b: 6/7/71
The emergence of Shannon Stewart made Roberts' presence in the Toronto farm system redundant. Although Roberts is a fast runner, he struggled at Triple-A last year to a .156 clip over 173 at-bats. Once a top prospect, he is quickly disappearing in favor of other prospects.

ROBERTSON, MIKE - 1B - BL - b: 10/9/70
Scouting: Robertson is a seven-year minor-league veteran who has had brief major league trials the past two seasons, most recently with the Phillies. For the bulk of his career, he has been a low-average hitter with respectable power, though below par for a first baseman. Robertson's plate discipline has improved, reaching a career-best 67-to-58 strikeout-to-walk ratio at Triple-A Scranton last year. He is an above-average defensive first baseman, but the Phillies moved him to the outfield anyway.
1998: Robertson is on the major league fringe. Shoring up the outfield situation was rated as a top off-season priority of the Phillies' brass, and Robertson will not likely be part of the answer. Look for Robertson to play first base in Triple-A for someone — probably not the Phillies — and again serve as injury insurance.
1997: Robertson had his best minor-league season to date, drawing walks, putting the ball in play and showing occasional long-ball power at Scranton. He got a late-season major league trial, but got himself out on a regular basis. He rarely hit balls with authority, and appeared to have Triple-A bat speed.
1996: Robertson spent his second straight season as the White Sox' Triple-A first baseman. He was impressive with the glove, but his offensive numbers were held down by his poor plate discipline and his struggles against southpaws (.232 average).

ROBINSON, KERRY - OF - BL - b: 10/3/73
Scouting: If he could play the outfield like a major leaguer, Robinson probably would have gotten more serious consider-

ation for a job at that level before now. His arm is below average, and he doesn't get a good jump on fly balls. He has two assets that most players only can imagine: remarkable speed and an uncanny ability to produce base hits. Robinson started to hone his base-stealing skills near the end of the 1997 season, so he's a legitimate threat to cause trouble every time he reaches base.
1998: Drafted by Tampa Bay, Robinson will get a long look but will probably will spend time in Triple-A, where he will patrol left field and work further on his leadoff abilities. Though he's not ready for the defensive demands of the outfield on a higher level yet, he could possibly handle some of the requirements at the plate if the Rays need a speedy reserve.
1997: Robinson spent nearly all season at Double-A Arkansas, where his .321 batting average actually lowered his minor-league career mark to .330. After getting some tutoring shortly after the All-Star break, he stole 18 bases in his final 19 attempts to finish with 40 overall.
1996: A former 34th-round pick out of Southeast Missouri State University, Robinson turned into a must-watch prospect with a .359 average and 90 stolen bases in the Class A Midwest League. Cardinals player development personnel guessed that Robinson's speed accounted for at least 40 points of that batting average.

RODARTE, RAUL - OF - BR - b: 4/9/70
Rodarte is a big, strong, slow hitter with no position whatsoever. The Braves have kept him around the last couple of years because he's hit the ball, but they've been unsuccessfully trying to find a place for him to play. His bat isn't so good that you'll just throw him out there and live with him, though, as he hit .221 for part of the '97 season in Double-A.

RODRIGUEZ, ALEX - SS - BR - b: 7/27/75
Scouting: What's not to like? Rodriguez is poised to be the American League All-Star shortstop forever. A line-drive hitter with power, fastballs go out faster than they come in. At age 22, he's still learning the game's nuances.
1998: The cornerstone of the Mariners' franchise, Rodriguez may get even more RBI if he remains in the fifth spot in the potent Seattle lineup.
1997: Rodriguez' successful sophomore season included 66 more extra-base hits, although his fielding slipped a tad to 24 errors. He doubled his stolen base total.
1996: In his first full season with the Mariners after being the first player taken overall in the 1993 draft, Rodriguez was second in MVP voting while getting 91 extra-base hits and leading the league in five hitting categories, including doubles (54) and batting average (.358).

	AB	R	HR	RBI	SB	BA
1995 Seattle	142	15	5	19	4	.232
1996 Seattle	601	141	36	123	15	.358
1997 Seattle	587	100	23	84	29	.300

RODRIGUEZ, BOI - 3B - b: 4/14/66
A long-time Braves' farmhand who was at Double-A in the Royals' system in 1996, Rodriguez became the home run champion of Taiwan last year, with 27 dingers. The most he ever had in the U.S. was 16 for Richmond in 1992.

RODRIGUEZ, HENRY - OF - BL - b: 11/8/67
Season: Rodriguez has changed dramatically as a hitter during the last two seasons. He has gone from a guy who makes contract and hits for average to a power hitter that strikes out constantly. Rodriguez's defense is below average both in left field and at first base.
1998: Rodriguez was eligible for salary arbitration and a big boost in income. That meant the Expos were actively looking to dump his salary and get some young players in return. Rodriguez has power, though he is not a premier slugger and has serious contact problems. He could be intriguing to a team in search of power but the buyer should be aware that he has steadily gone downhill since two strong months to start 1996.
1997: Rodriguez didn't match his surprising power numbers of 1996 while striking out seemingly every other time he stepped to the plate. His high strikeout rate so annoyed usually-patient Expos manager Felipe Alou that he found reasons to put Rodriguez on the bench.
1996: Rodriguez was the talk of baseball as he became the first player in National League history to hit 20 homers by the end of May. However, Rodriguez slowly, but steadily declined from there.

	AB	R	HR	RBI	SB	BA
1995 Montreal	138	13	2	15	0	.239
1996 Montreal	532	81	36	103	2	.276
1997 Montreal	476	55	26	83	3	.244

RODRIGUEZ, IVAN - C - BR - b: 11/30/71
Scouting: Rodriguez has now established himself firmly as a .300 hitter with power. It's difficult to know how to pitch him, since he can make contact on almost any kind of pitch. Rodriguez is a good opposite-field hitter and is an above-average baserunner for a catcher. Defensively, he's the toughest catcher in the American League to steal against, and few runners will challenge him. He has become the iron man of major league catchers, leading the majors in starts and innings for each of the last two seasons. Rodriguez' one weakness is in calling games; Ranger pitchers have consistently had better ERA's when pitching to his backups.
1998: If the Rangers can find a better-hitting backup catcher, Rodriguez will get more rest. Regardless, look for him to continue as the American League's premier catcher. He is likely to move down in the order, hitting fifth or sixth.
1997: It's becoming harder to remember that Rodriguez used to be prone to nagging injuries earlier in his career. For the second straight year, Rodriguez played nearly all the time. He was in the league's top ten in hitting with men on base, but hitting second in the order kept his RBI total down. As good as Rodriguez has been, he seems to still be improving, as he set or equalled his personal bests in batting average, home runs, on-base percentage and walks.
1996: Rodriguez established career highs in runs, hits, homers, RBI and walks while displaying a new level of durability. He also threw out 50% of opposing basestealers.

	AB	R	HR	RBI	SB	BA
1995 Texas	492	56	12	67	0	.303
1996 Texas	639	116	19	86	5	.300
1997 Texas	597	98	20	77	7	.313

RODRIGUEZ, STEVE - SS - BR - b: 11/29/70
A three-time All-American at Pepperdine University and a key member of the Waves' 1992 National Championship squad, Rodriguez was claimed by the Tigers off waivers in September of 1995. It looked like he might have played his way into a reserve infield role with a strong 1996 season at Triple-A Toledo but last year was a backslide season for him. He was second on

the Toledo squad in doubles with 30 but hit just .233 in 425 at-bats. At age 27 he's starting to run out of time.

RODRIGUEZ, TONY - SS - BR - b: 8/15/70
Rodriguez has a solid glove at shortstop, second and third base, but is a weak, undisciplined hitter. He is kept around simply because he can catch the ball with some reliability. He has no speed and does not help a team in any way other than with his glove. He might have to find another Triple-A team for which to provide insurance, as the Red Sox now prefer other players for his role.

RODRIGUEZ, VICTOR - SS - BR - b: 10/25/76
Rodriguez is yet another top second base prospect in the Marlins' farm system. A converted shortstop with above-average range and a slick-fielding glove, he has begun to drive the ball with authority at the plate. He has above-average speed and should gradually increase his power-hitting as he fills out his 6'2" frame. Rodriguez was among the youngest Double-A regulars at the age of 20, but his path to the majors is blocked by established regulars and other prospects in Florida. Expansion could improve his immediate prospects.

ROHRMEIER, DAN - OF/DH - BR - b: 9/27/65
A slow developing, career minor-leaguer, Rohrmeier has learned to turn on pitches he can drive and has increased his power numbers dramatically over the last two seasons spent in the Seattle chain. He hit .344 (seventh best in all of the minor leagues) for Double-A Memphis with 28 homers and 95 RBI in 1996, then reached career highs in doubles (43), homers (33) and RBI (120) in his second full season at Triple-A. Still, Rohrmeier is an unlikely candidate for playing time in Seattle although expansion could help him win a major league platoon job at first base or in left field.

ROLEN, SCOTT - 3B - BR - b: 4/4/75
Scouting: Rolen is an aggressive hitter who drives the ball where it's pitched, with occasionally prodigious power. He could be a 40-homer guy if he so desired, but he's more productive hitting .300 with 25-30 homers per year. His eye at the plate is above average, and defensively he is spectacular. Despite a high number of errors (mostly on throws), Rolen has Gold Glove ability. He has the range of a shortstop and amazing reactions on balls hit to either side, and he has a cannon arm. More than anything else, it is his baseball instinct that truly impresses. He was the team leader from day one: he hustles constantly, is one of the best baserunners in baseball, and has earned the respect of his peers in record time.
1998: The sharp, upward progression should continue as Rolen asserts himself as a .300 hitter with 25-homer power. His on-base ability will increase just as his error count decreases. Expectations are high.
1997: Rolen entered the 1997 season drawing comparisons to Mike Schmidt; not many players draw such parallels. Rolen is a unique player who won't join the 500-homer club, but he showed that he can help a team win a game in as many ways as any other major leaguer. His impact can be summed in one incident: after being beaned by Hideo Nomo, Rolen summoned him to the Phillies' clubhouse. Many expected a fight, but Rolen simply administered a finger-wagging lecture — and Nomo listened.
1996: Rolen blitzed through Double-A and Triple-A, and earned the Phillies' third base job early in August. His defensive range and arm were noteworthy from the start, and he had just locked into a power groove when his hand was broken by a pitch, ending his season.

	AB	R	HR	RBI	SB	BA
1996 Philadelphia	130	10	4	18	0	.254
1997 Philadelphia	561	93	21	92	16	.283

ROLISON, NATE - 1B - BL - b: 3/27/77
Rolison is an all-or-nothing hitter, equally capable of striking out in bunches or hitting fastballs a mile. He's a slow-footed first sacker who was the Marlins' second-round draft pick in 1995. Rolison is a raw power hitter who struck out in 30% of his at-bats in the Florida State League last year; he has great tools including power and bat speed, but needs to make mental adjustments to help him advance. His progress in the Double-A Eastern League will determine how much his star will shine.

ROLLINS, JIMMY - SS - BB - b: 11/27/78
Rollins is a sparkplug player with natural leadoff-hitter abilities who is arguably the best prospect in the Phillies' system. He lines the ball to all fields with occasional gap power and has respectable plate discipline. Although Rollins doesn't have dominating speed, he's an instinctively good baserunner with a knack for scoring runs. His range is good enough for a shortstop, but his sub-par arm may necessitate a shift to second base. The Phillies are in no hurry to rush Rollins; he was the second youngest everyday player in a full-season minor league last year where he got on base regularly and stole at will while anchoring the lower Class A Piedmont infield defense. He will start 1998 in higher Class A with an advance to Double-A later in the year a possibility. Rollins is a future big-league starter with star potential.

ROMERO, MANDY - C - BB - b: 10/19/67
Scouting: Injuries twice kept Romero from advancing when he was a top Pirates prospect. The Padres signed him as a free agent before the '96 season. Romero is a good catcher with an adequate arm. He has some power.
1998: If the Padres lose either John Flaherty or Carlos Hernandez, look for Romero to be a front-runner for the second catcher job until Ben Davis is promoted.
1997: After nearly a decade in the minors, Romero finally made it to majors in midseason as an injury replacement for Hernandez. He hit only .208 but had two key homers. Romero had hit .320 with 13 homers and 52 RBI in 61 games at Double-A Mobile before joining Padres. He later hit .308 in 33 games at Triple-A Las Vegas.
1996: Romero hit .269 for Double-A Memphis with ten home runs and 46 RBI.

ROMERO, WILLIE - OF - BR - b: 8/5/74
Romero has shown plenty of potential as a solid defensive center fielder in the major leagues. The trick for him will be improving his skills in other facets of the game well enough to allow him to make that jump. Romero's offense has improved slowly, but he's started to come around at the plate the last two seasons. If he can continue to improve, he may have a shot at playing in Los Angeles.

RONAN, MARC - C - BL - b: 9/19/69
His last two seasons have seen a dramatic improvement in his hitting. Prior to 1996, his career average in the minors was .230

with a career slugging average just barely over .300. Ronan had a fine performance in 1996, then stepped it up a notch again last year. He's a fine defensive catcher, and now seems to have reached a new offensive level, too.

ROSARIO, MEL - C - BB - b: 5/25/73
"He can really throw," said Bowie BaySox Double-A manager Joe Ferguson of Melvin Rosario. A former major league catcher, Ferguson continued: "his defense has been outstanding. He blocks well, receives well, and seems to throw everybody out." His defense earned him a September promotion to the Orioles. His hitting is inconsistent, but he showed a little power last year in the tough Double-A Eastern League. His defense brought him to the majors, but Rosario could help his chances of earning a steady major league roster spot with better hitting.

ROSE, BOBBY - IF/OF - BR - b: 3/15/67
A fringe major leaguer with the Angels for several years, Rose went to Japan and found success. Rose hit .304 with 16 homers and 86 RBI in 1996 to lead the Yokohama BayStars, and got even better last year, when his .329 average was second highest in the Central League.

ROSE, PETE Jr. - 3B - BL - b: 11/16/69
After eight years of undistinguished play mostly in A-ball, the 27-year-old Rose posted a good year at Double-A Chattanooga, hitting nearly as many home runs in one season as he had in the previous eight. His performance earned him a callup to the majors and one of the better moments of the Reds season when he singled in his first major league game. He obviously is not a prospect — his major league callup was purely a public relations ploy —and he plays the one position (third base) in which the Reds are deep in young talent.

ROSKOS, JOHN - 1B - BR - b: 11/19/74
Returning to catching after a one-year trial at first base, Roskos has great home run power and above-average plate discipline. His defensive skill is adequate, but he's behind Charles Johnson on the Marlins' depth chart. Roskos spent his second year in the Double-A Eastern League last year, hitting for average with prodigious power. He should reach the majors in 1998, especially as a second catcher, although he might play more regularly for a weaker team.

ROSSY, RICO - SS - BR - b: 2/16/64
The journeyman infielder hasn't been in the major leagues since 1993, will be 34 when the season starts, is coming off a .252 season with San Diego's Triple-A Las Vegas farm club in 1996, and a .251 season with Montreal's Triple-A Ottawa farm club in 1997. Even expansion won't open enough jobs for Rossy to get back to the big leagues.

ROWLAND, RICH - C - BR - b: 2/25/64
Rowland, a former Red Sox prospect, toiled at Triple-A Phoenix last year. He hit .237 with two homers and 13 RBI in just 59 at-bats while playing backup to real prospect Doug Mirabelli. When the Giants went looking for a new backup major league catcher after they waived Rick Wilkins, they added Damon Berryhill to their roster instead of Rowland. This after Berryhill sat out the entire 1996 season; it was not exactly a vote of confidence in Rowland's abilities. He is merely a minor-league reserve just a few short years after almost winning the regular catching chores in Boston.

ROYSTER, AARON - OF - BR - b: 11/30/72
Royster has been a serviceable starting outfielder at Double-A Reading in the Phillies' chain for the past season and a half. He has a long swing capable of generating respectable home run power, but his bat speed doesn't appear sufficient to allow him to compete at the major league level. His age, build and skills are similar to fellow Phillies' prospect Wendell Magee. They both run well but haven't shown ability to steal bases. Royster is decent on defense, but not enough to offset his shortcomings. He can be a passable high-minors player without much chance to reach the majors.

RUMFIELD, TOBY - 1B - BR - b: 9/4/72
Rumfield opened a lot of eyes four years ago when he hit 29 home runs at Class A Winston-Salem, but had done nothing like that before and hasn't done anything like it since, either. In 1994, Rumfield was in his second full year in A-ball after spending two full seasons in Rookie ball. When he moved up to Double-A Chattanooga the following season his home run total dropped back to the high single digits, where it was before. He had a decent season last year at Chattanooga, where he hit a fair number of doubles and struck out only 32 times in 331 at-bats. But he's now 25 years old and has to be regarded as a long shot to make the majors.

RUPP, BRIAN - 1B - BR - b: 9/20/71
Versatility and a steady, if less than remarkable, bat could someday earn Rupp a shot at a major-league job. A native of the St. Louis area and former 43rd-round draft pick, he split his 1997 season between Double-A Arkansas and Triple-A Louisville. His .276 overall batting average actually was 27 points below his career mark, and he counted only 19 extra-base hits and 31 RBI. He probably needs to develop some bigger run-producing numbers this year in Triple-A, since there's not much call for a first baseman or third baseman who hits singles. He's played some in the outfield and at shortstop, though, so a utility spot could be possible if he posts another .300 minor-league season.

RUPP, CHAD - 1B - BR - b: 9/30/71
Rupp played at the Triple-A level for the first time in his five-year minor-league career and had success. After hitting 18 homers in 278 at-bats in 1996 at Double-A New Britain, Rupp blasted 32 round trippers to lead Triple-A Salt Lake. He even raised his batting average, hitting nearly 20 points higher than his career average. He'll probably begin this year at Triple-A, but he's not a hot prospect because of his relatively advanced age. Rupp has to break through soon or won't ever reach the majors.

RUSSO, PAUL - 3B - BR - b: 8/26/69
Russo was formerly in the Twins organization where he had some good years in Triple-A, but he was never called up even though the Twins had big holes at third, and he was never considered to be a prospect. He played for the Padres Triple-A club in 1996, his fourth year in Triple-A, and unfortunately, his worst. In 1997 he played for yet another Triple-A team, Columbus for the Yankees, but for only nine games.

RYAN, ROB - OF - BL - b: 6/24/73
A smart gap-hitter with a good knowledge of the strike zone, Ryan led Class A South Bend in batting average (.314), doubles

(35), RBI (73) and walks (89).

SADLER, DONNIE - SS - BR - b: 6/17/75
Scouting: Sadler is a very good all-around athlete despite being just 5'6" tall. He has strength and quickness, he is as fast as anyone in the game, and capable of stealing 50 or 60 bases if he can get on base enough. The problem is his hitting. Sadler takes too big of a swing and tries to pull the ball too much. He has strength, but not enough to hit with that approach. His fielding is top-notch at both second base and shortstop.
1998: Sadler will spend his second year in Triple-A, trying to learn how to hit line drives and get on base, so that he can better use his great speed. He is young enough that he can still improve into a good hitter. However, he has gone backwards the last two years, and will have to overcome his stubbornness at the plate.
1997: Sadler proved himself as a good second baseman and shortstop, playing both in Triple-A. But he took a big step back as a hitter, and was lost at the plate when the season ended.
1996: Sadler was rushed to Double-A, and held his own at the plate, hitting .267. The Red Sox were so excited about his athleticism that they converted him into a center fielder at mid-season, thinking he might solve their problems there. The experiment lasted only a couple of weeks, as Sadler's bat struggled and didn't justify the move, and he didn't take to the outfield as well as the Red Sox expected.

SAFFER, JON - OF - BL - b: 7/6/73
Saffer is an awkward player, who doesn't move gracefully and has trouble in the outfield. What he does best is hit, although he does that in an awkward fashion as well. His swing is long with a lot wasted hand action, but somehow he hits the ball. He also knows how to draw a walk. It won't be easy for him to win a big-league job, but he'll probably stick around long enough and hit the ball well enough to earn some time as a pinch-hitter or role player.

SAGMOEN, MARC - OF - BL - b: 4/6/71
Sagmoen's promotion to the majors was due less to the Rangers' belief in his readiness than to an acute lack of outfield talent in the high minors. At his age, hitting .263 with five homers and 44 RBI at Triple-A Oklahoma City didn't impress anyone, and major league pitchers had their way with him when he was called up. Sagmoen needs to hit in the high .200s at Triple-A next season to reclaim his former status as a prospect. He projects as a line-drive hitter with below-average power for an outfielder.

SALMON, TIM - OF - BR - b: 8/24/68
Scouting: Salmon is the cornerstone of the franchise as a player who can hit for average and power, runs and throws well. He's become a star player due to a combination of talent and an incredible work ethic. He does everything well, but traditionally starts the season slowly. Salmon leads by example with consistent effort and dedication to duty.
1998: Salmon may be only a hot April away from reaching superstar status. He more than makes up for his slow starts with hot months from June through September, but he leaves the Angels wondering what might happen if he ever got out of the blocks fast.
1997: A cold April and May only slowed Salmon down. He still finished among league leaders in batting average, home runs and RBI. His solid play in the outfield was typical of what he's done year in and year out. Like other seasons, he carried the offense on his back at times, particularly in July when he hit nearly .400 and was named American League Player of the month.
1996: It was a typical Salmon season in that he finished as one of the top offensive producers in the league. His consistently solid play was one of the few bright spots in a season where just about everything went wrong for the Angels.

	AB	R	HR	RBI	SB	BA
1995 California	537	111	34	105	5	.330
1996 California	581	90	30	98	4	.286
1997 Anaheim	582	95	33	129	9	.296

SAMUEL, JUAN - 1B/OF - BR - b: 12/9/60
Scouting: Samuel still possesses some of the great speed that was once his main offensive weapon and he has good power. He's an above-average bat off the bench.
1998: Someone will notice that he did not get a chance to play much last year. Samuel spoke openly of his desire for more playing time. If he makes an opening day roster, he will play more this year and could post surprising power numbers.
1997: Samuel spent nearly all of the season on the bench, eventually landing in the starting lineup at third base for the final week of the season. He openly expressed frustration at not playing and implied that he would not return to the Blue Jays in 1998.
1996: Samuel continued to show good power in limited work, clubbing eight home runs in just 188 at-bats.

	AB	R	HR	RBI	SB	BA
1995 Kansas City	205	31	12	39	6	.263
1996 Toronto	188	34	8	26	9	.255
1997 Toronto	95	13	3	15	5	.284

SAMUELS, SCOTT - OF - BL - b: 5/19/71
Samuels had a decent year for the Expos in 1997, spending the time with Triple-A Ottawa and Double-A Harrisburg. That said, he is not considered a prospect. Samuels hit .296 and stole 13 bases in 64 games at Harrisburg, then hit well in a short stint at Ottawa, batting .345 in 20 games.

SANCHEZ, REY - SS - BR - b: 10/5/67
Scouting: An erstwhile starter for the Cubs, Sanchez has above-average range, hands and arm in the field. When the opportunity has arisen for him to grab a full-time job, he has usually been injured. At other times, he has split duty between shortstop and second base. Sanchez is a capable hitter who can get on base some, but has limited power and speed.
1998: Depending on what the Yankees did to fill other holes at third base and in the starting rotation, Sanchez had a chance to fit into their plans. Even if they upgraded at second base, the club wanted to bring Sanchez back as a utility infielder due to his ability to play shortstop as well as second base.
1997: Acquired from the Cubs for minor-league pitcher Frisco Parotte in mid-August, Sanchez filled a season-long void at second base. In his 38 games with the Yankees, he hit .312 and added life to the bottom of the order. He developed a reputation as a tough out, coming back from a wrist problem that had bothered him for two years.
1996: Sanchez' wrist problem was finally diagnosed: a broken hamate bone. Overall, he had a lost season.

	AB	R	HR	RBI	SB	BA
1995 Chicago NL	428	57	3	27	6	.278
1996 Chicago NL	289	28	1	12	7	.211
1997 two teams	343	35	2	27	4	.274

SANCHEZ, VICTOR - 1B - BR - b: 12/20/71
In his second season of Double-A ball for the Astros, Sanchez continued to struggle with the bat. He has some power, but doesn't make enough contact. It looks like Sanchez will have trouble advancing past the Double-A level.

SANDBERG, RYNE - 2B - BR - b: 9/18/58
Sandberg retired for the second time in his career after the season, but this time should be for good. While Sandberg didn't embarrass himself in his two seasons of "un-retirement," it was fairly obvious that his skills had eroded substantially. His bat was extremely slow and it was hard for him to hit off-speed pitches, and he had lost most of his range defensively. While Cub fans might miss Sandberg's presence at second base, the team will be far better off with a young prospect.

	AB	R	HR	RBI	SB	BA
1995			Did Not Play			
1996 Chicago NL	554	85	25	92	12	.244
1997 Chicago NL	447	54	12	64	7	.264

SANDERS, ANTHONY - OF - BR - b: 3/2/74
Scouting: A great power/speed combination with a good glove makes Sanders one to watch. His arm is weak but his range is above-average and he is an all-out hustler.
1998: Sanders could benefit with another season in the minor leagues and could make his presence felt by September, if not sooner. As a major leaguer, he is not ready, although the potential skills are there.
1997: Sanders had his best season to date with a career-high in home runs (26).
1996: Splitting time between Class A Dunedin and Double-A Knoxville, Sanders posted what then was a career high in homers (18).

SANDERS, DEION - OF - BL - b: 8/9/67
Scouting: Sanders is a good baserunner and hits for decent average, but that sums up his positives as a baseball player. His weaknesses include poor strikezone judgment, lack of power, mediocre outfield defense, a weak arm, and football commitments that mean you never know if he is going to be around in September. He doesn't get on base enough to hit at the top of the order, doesn't have enough power to hit lower in the lineup, and doesn't play good enough defense to carry his limited offensive contribution.
1998: It is unclear whether Sanders will come back for another year of baseball, and he and the Reds must both agree to exercise a $2.5-million option for him to return with Cincinnati. Sanders is a Jim Bowden favorite, but Jon Nunnally is a better baseball player, and Curtis Goodwin offers the same skills as Sanders for considerably less money.
1997: After a year off, Sanders started the season in a hot streak and showed some improvement in patience at the plate, a major weakness. Old habits returned, and by the All-Star game his performance was back to normal levels. A bulging disc in his back took him out of the lineup in late-July, and he never returned to the lineup, leaving for the Cowboys full-time in mid-September.
1996: Sanders did not play baseball, instead playing only football for the Dallas Cowboys.

	AB	R	HR	RBI	SB	BA
1997 Cincinnati	465	53	5	23	56	.273

SANDERS, REGGIE - OF - BR - b: 12/1/67
Scouting: When healthy (a rare occurrence the last two seasons), Sanders is one of the better rightfielders in the National League, providing power, speed, good defense and a strong arm. His biggest weakness is strikezone judgment, where an inability to lay off high fastballs has led to weak strikeout totals.
1998: Sanders offers All-Star potential if he can improve his strikezone judgment and stay healthy, however he hasn't done either since 1995.
1997: Two trips to the DL (bulging disc and severe ankle sprain) limited Sanders in 1997, but his generally fine play after he returned to action in late-July was a factor in the Reds improved play after Ray Knight was fired.
1996: After an MVP candidate season in 1995, Sanders disappeared in 1996 as injuries and poor strikezone judgment wrecked his season.

	AB	R	HR	RBI	SB	BA
1995 Cincinnati	484	91	28	99	36	.306
1996 Cincinnati	287	49	14	33	24	.251
1997 Cincinnati	312	52	19	56	13	.253

SANDERS, TRACY - 1B - BL - b: 7/26/69
Sanders was once considered a premier outfield prospect in the Cleveland organization. Since then, he has bounced from one organization to another, making minor-league stops with San Diego, the New York Mets and Texas before winding up as the regular first baseman with the Pirates' Double-A Carolina farm club last season. Sanders had a fine year and played in the Double-A All-Star game. However, Sanders also turns 29 midway through this season and his window for ever reaching the major leagues has closed.

SANDOVAL, JHENSY - OF - BR - b: 9/11/78
In the tradition of Frank White in Kansas City, Sandoval is the first touted prospect to emerge from the Diamondbacks' baseball academy run by Junior Noboa in the Dominican Republic.

SANFORD, CHANCE - 2B - BL - b: 6/2/72
Sanford has recovered fully from a knee injury he suffered in 1995. After a setback season in 1996, Sanford played at both the Double-A and Triple-A levels of the Pirates' organization this past season. He doesn't have great glove skills and his range is average but he may have a chance to hit his way into a utility infield role with the Bucs. Sanford hit .292 with six homers and 60 RBI at Triple-A Calgary last year.

SANTANGELO, F.P. - 3B/OF - BB - b: 10/24/67
Scouting: Santangelo is a scrappy little player who can get on base and hit with surprising authority. He is an invaluable player, a switch-hitter with the ability to play all four infield positions along with each of the three outfield spots. He is also an above-average runner and is a defensive plus at any position.
1998: Santangelo will again getting plenty of at-bats and play plenty of positions. Whatever position he plays and wherever he hits in the batting order, Santangelo will provide solid offense. He could wind up seeing a lot of action in left field, and second base is also a possibility if rookie Orlando Cabrera isn't ready.
1997: Santangelo's offensive statistics suffered a drop off. However, he was plagued by hand injuries throughout the year, then had season-ending arthroscopic surgery on his right knee in mid-September. He was expected to be ready for the start of spring training.

1996: Santangelo finished fourth in National League Rookie of the Year voting as he filled in capably at a multitude of positions for the Expos. Santangelo spent seven seasons in the Montreal farm system before finally breaking through.

	AB	R	HR	RBI	SB	BA
1995 Montreal	98	11	1	9	1	.296
1996 Montreal	393	54	7	56	5	.277
1997 Montreal	350	56	5	31	8	.249

SANTIAGO, BENITO - C - BR - b: 3/9/65

Scouting: Santiago is not the 30-home run threat he was in Philadelphia but he still has some power and a great glove. He was rumored to be a negative influence in the clubhouse.

1998: It appeared at the end of last season that he would not be back with the Blue Jays. Santiago is still a starting catcher and his performance slowly climbed to normal levels by the end of last season. This is his comeback year.

1997: A disastrous start left Santiago under the .200 mark for much of the season, starting with four strikeouts on opening day. By July, he had requested a trade from the Blue Jays, one that GM Gord Ash could not grant because of Santiago's contract and performance.

1996: What will be recorded as Santiago's career year saw him hit 30 home runs for an otherwise-weak Philadelphia Phillies team. His previous high was 18 with the Padres in 1987.

	AB	R	HR	RBI	SB	BA
1995 Cincinnati	266	40	11	44	2	.286
1996 Philadelphia	481	71	30	85	2	.264
1997 Toronto	341	31	13	42	1	.243

SASSER, ROB - 3B - BR - b: 3/6/75

Scouting: A big guy with potentially a big future is the way the Angels look at Sasser. The Angels feel they stole him in the Rule 5 draft in 1996 when the Atlanta Braves had more players than they could protect. Sasser has shown power when he needs to. He plays solid infield defense, but has to cut down on strikeouts and errors — typical of young players. The Angels feel it's just a matter of a young talent putting things together before he can make a rapid ascent to the majors.

1998: Sasser can help his rise through the ranks by continuing the progress he made last season. Another year of experience will help him mature as a ballplayer and enhance his status as a solid prospect. He can become a hot prospect with a good season at Double-A Midland.

1997: Sasser hit 17 home runs and drove in 77 runs as the third baseman for Class A Cedar Rapids. He needed to step up his power production to speed his advance in the system and responded well.

1996: Sasser had a decent year for Atlanta's Class A Macon farm club, but hadn't shown he could hit for power yet, a major reason why he was left unprotected in the winter draft.

SAUNDERS, CHRIS - 3B - BR - b: 7/19/70

Coming off a career year at Double-A Binghamton in 1996, Saunders again continued to dominate pitchers at that level. He hit .324 in 111 at-bats before getting the call to Triple-A Norfolk where he found it tougher to get base knocks. He's already 27 years old and not the Mets' best prospect at his position.

SAUNDERS, DOUG - 3B - BR - b: 12/13/69

Saunders reached the majors with the Mets for 23 games back in 1993 and that will likely be the pinnacle of his career. He spent 1997 at Double-A Memphis in the Mariners organization and will spend the rest of his career as minor-league roster filler.

SBROCCO, JON - 2B - BL - b: 1/5/71

Sbrocco's first season at Double-A — at the age of 27 — was not a big success; he hit .263 with two homers and 27 RBI in part-time play for Shreveport. He doesn't have much power although he does have a decent batting eye and makes fine contact. Still, his age and lack of any one outstanding skill makes Sbrocco a dim prospect.

SCARSONE, STEVE - 3B/1B - BR - b: 4/11/66

Picked up by the Padres just before the season started, Scarsone had a undistinguished year in the minors, not even warranting a late-season callup. His prospects for future major league employment are dim, but he could become a utility infielder on a major league roster; it'll be a move to add defense because Scarsone is a weak hitter.

	AB	R	HR	RBI	SB	BA
1995 San Francisco	233	33	11	29	3	.266
1996 San Francisco	283	28	5	23	2	.219

SCHALL, GENE - OF/1B - BR - b: 6/5/70

After changing organizations in a minor-league trade from Philadelphia, Schall was unable to make it back to the majors last year. He had his worst professional season, hitting just .196 in a limited DH role for Triple-A Nashville. Schall has a little power but is not a good hitter overall and is limited to first base. He's your basic Triple-A extension of the bench.

	AB	R	HR	RBI	SB	BA
1995 Philadelphia	65	2	0	5	0	.231
1996 Philadelphia	66	7	2	10	0	.273

SCHMIDT, TOM - 3B - BR - b: 2/12/73

Schmidt possesses good physical tools, especially for a utility player. His glove and bat improved in '97 and he was productive at Double-A Jacksonville, collecting 27 extra-base hits in 291 at-bats and driving in 44 runs. He's a former prospect who lost his prospect status, but has bounced back to give himself a slim chance at the majors.

SCHU, RICK - 3B - BR - b: 1/26/62

Old failed phenoms never die. Schu returned from the baseball dead to play in one game for the Expos last season. 1997 looks like it will be his last, he played in only eight games for Triple-A Ottawa.

SCHWAB, CHRIS - OF - BR - b: 7/25/74

It has been a long and painfully slow learning process in professional baseball for Schwab, Montreal's first-round draft pick in 1993. Last season wasn't great but represented somewhat of a breakthrough year for the big first baseman who had never hit higher than .227 or more than nine homers in his first four pro seasons. He hit .268 with 11 homers in 209 at-bats with lower Class A Cape Fear then only .188 but with nine homers in 207 at-bats with higher Class A West Palm Beach. The homer figure at West Palm was encouraging because hitting homers is nearly impossible in the Florida State League. He's got a long way to go and isn't going to be a star in the big leagues but at least Schwab is starting to figure some things out.

SCUTARO, MARCO - 2B - BR - b: 10/30/75

Scutaro possesses a lively, line-drive bat with decent power potential for a middle infielder, plus above-average speed. He has solid range afield and a good enough arm to play third base on occasion. Scutaro must shorten his swing and improve his plate discipline. He showed a good combination of power and speed with ten homers and 23 steals for Class A Kinston in 1997. Scutaro is expected to advance to Double-A Akron to become their full-time second baseman, one of the Indians' least fortified positions; a good showing in 1998 would put Scutaro on the prospect list.

SEALY, SCOT - C - BR - b: 2/10/71

Sealy spent time at both the Double-A and Triple-A affiliates in the Mariners organization in 1997. He doesn't hit for average or power but with Jason Varitek gone to the Red Sox, Sealy may have another year or two to develop into a prospect.

SECRIST, REED - 3B - BL - b: 5/7/70

After hitting 36 homers over the past two seasons, Secrist couldn't maintain his power hitting ability when he advanced to Triple-A Calgary in 1997, hitting just five round-trippers in 122 at-bats. He is average with the glove and if he ever advances to the majors it will be as a reserve infielder.

SEEFRIED, TATE - 1B - BL - b: 4/22/72

After toiling for seven seasons in the Yankees' organization, Seefried found a change of scenery to his liking and had one of his best seasons ever at Double-A Binghamton, hitting .318 with 30 homers and 81 RBI. Promoted to Triple-A Norfolk, Seefried reverted back to his old form, striking out once every three at-bats.

SEFCIK, KEVIN - SS/2B - BR - b: 2/10/71

Scouting: Sefcik is a versatile utilityman with limited tools who has been a reserve at three positions for the Phillies during the past two seasons. He's an overaggressive contact hitter who consistently, but weakly, puts the ball in play. He is a surehanded defender with limited range and a barely adequate throwing arm. He is major league quality at second base, but third base and shortstop are a stretch for Sefcik. It is unlikely that Sefcik would have survived the past two seasons in the majors as a member of just about any other team.
1998: The Phillies have solid starters at Sefcik's positions and he will get a challenge from Desi Relaford for a reserve role. Sefcik is unlikely to start the season on a major league roster.
1997: The Phillies' infield stayed healthy, allowing Sefcik to be used sparingly. He wasn't a highly-regarded prospect in any case and would have been moved aside by better prospects if regular playing time had appeared. Sefcik gave the club some professional at-bats off the bench, and gobbled up all of the grounders within his limited range. He met all of the requirements of his limited role.
1996: Sefcik was a competent shortstop and third base backup, surprisingly hitting for a solid average despite rarely making authoritative contact. He competently filled in for injured Scott Rolen down the homestretch.

	AB	R	HR	RBI	SB	BA
1996 Philadelphia	116	10	0	9	3	.284
1997 Philadelphia	119	11	2	6	1	.269

SEGUI, DAVID - 1B - BB - b: 7/19/66

Scouting: Segui has a solid line-drive stroke from both sides of the plate, and has started developing some power lately. Segui is an above-average defensive first baseman, who would be a star if he hit more homers.
1998: Segui filed for free agency at the end of last season. Though Segui wanted to stay, the penny-pinching Expos felt they had no room in their budget to retain him. Segui may find the pickings somewhat slim on the free-agent market as he doesn't provide the power most teams looks for in a first baseman.
1997: Segui had the best season of his career heading into the free-agent market as he set career highs in homers and RBI while leading the Expos in hitting. Segui had surgery on his left knee in early-June but missed only three weeks. After struggling initially upon his return from the disabled list, he finished up strong.
1996: Segui started off well but faded after being hampered by tendinitis in his left wrist and a broken right hand.

	AB	R	HR	RBI	SB	BA
1995 NY NL - Mon.	456	68	12	68	2	.309
1996 Montreal	416	69	11	58	4	.286
1997 Montreal	459	75	21	68	1	.307

SEITZER, BRAD - 3B - BR - b: 2/2/70

Kevin's brother Brad played in the Milwaukee and Montreal organizations in 1997. He's a hitter but too old to be considered a prospect. He was a third baseman in the Brewers farm system but when he arrived in Montreal they gave him a look at first base. He doesn't have a major league future at either position.

SEITZER, KEVIN - 1B/3B - BR - b: 3/26/62

Scouting: Seitzer has consistently exhibited all of the traits desired in a leadoff hitter over the years except for the most obvious one - speed. Seitzer is a fiery sparkplug who sprays line drives to all fields, draws walks, and runs the bases intelligently, if not swiftly. His skills are diminishing with age, but his core abilities age well, which should make him a viable major leaguer hitter for as he long as he wishes. Defensively, he's little more than a designated hitter at this point.
1998: Seitzer is being squeezed out of the picture in Cleveland. Players like Sean Casey and Richie Sexson are ready, and at least one must be on the major league roster in 1998, likely in Seitzer's stead. Seitzer can handle more than the Indians asked of him in 1997; in the right situation, Seitzer can hit .280 with a high on-base percentage in 1998.
1997: Seitzer was a man without a role in Cleveland. He served mainly as insurance for Jim Thome and Matt Williams, and as a pinch-hitter with solid table-setting skills. He's capable of more.
1996: It seems like so long ago, but Seitzer was downright dominant as a Brewer for most of 1996. He posted career highs in batting average and doubles, and his second-best season in hits, homers, RBI and walks, before being acquired by the Indians for the stretch run.

	AB	R	HR	RBI	SB	BA
1995 Milwaukee	492	56	5	69	2	.311
1996 Milw-Cleveland	573	85	13	78	6	.326
1997 Cleveland	198	27	2	24	0	.268

SELBY, BILL - 2B - BL - b: 6/11/70

A versatile infielder who got 76 at-bats with the Red Sox in 1996, Selby was playing in Japan last year. He was unimpressive, hitting .236 with five homers.

	AB	R	HR	RBI	SB	BA
1996 Boston	95	12	3	6	1	.270

SERVAIS, SCOTT - C - BR - b: 6/4/67
Scouting: The main thing Servais has to offer is his ability to call a game. He's not a good hitter, he's extremely slow, and his other defensive abilities aren't that great. But Servais knows his pitching staff and the opposing hitters well. He's been a durable player, which has definitely worked in his favor.
1998: The Cubs would love for a better alternative to Servais until a prospect like Pat Cline is ready, but it doesn't appear that they're going to get it. The team thought Tyler Houston might have been the answer, but he's weaker than Servais. Servais will get the majority of playing time again and should hit about equal to what he's done in the past three seasons.
1997: Servais had another average season for the Cubs, putting up numbers that are in line with his abilities. He was better in the first half of the season, but wore down a little in the second half.
1996: Servais had a decent year in his first full season in Chicago. He hit twelve home runs in half a season with the Cubs in 1995 after being traded from Houston, which probably raised everybody's expectations too much for 1996.

	AB	R	HR	RBI	SB	BA
1995 Hou. - Chi NL	264	38	13	47	2	.265
1996 Chicago NL	445	42	11	63	0	.265
1997 Chicago NL	385	36	6	45	0	.260

SEXSON, RICHIE - 1B - BR - b: 12/29/74
Scouting: Sexson is a lean power-hitter and a wild swinger who expands an already large strike zone by often swinging at bad pitches. He has exceptional power to all fields and is quite nimble around the bag at first base for a big man (6'6"). Sexson faces intense organizational competition from Jim Thome and Sean Casey, and doesn't stand a chance unless he dramatically improves his plate discipline.
1998: The Indians faced a tough decision regarding Sexson when preparing their expansion-draft protection list. If Sexson returns in 1998, he will likely battle Casey for a major league role; as the underdog, he's likely headed back to Triple-A.
1997: As usual, Sexson was among the younger players at his level (Triple-A), and the most powerful. However, his poor .307 on-base percentage underscores his primary weakness. He got a late-season major league recall, along with Casey.
1996: Sexson followed up a dominant 1995 high Class A campaign with a rather disappointing Double-A season. Holes in his swing abounded, as evidenced by his 118-to-39 strikeout-to-walk ratio and then career-low .331 on-base percentage.

SEXTON, CHRIS - SS - BR - b: 8/3/71
Sexton is a rare player who can play six positions. His best position is shortstop, where he has average hands and an arm that is plenty playable. His second-best position is center field. He can play three infield positions and all three outfield positions. Sexton could become a legitimate big-league utility player, though he needs to improve his hitting. He's not a basestealer (nine steals in 26 combined attempts for Double-A New Haven and Triple-A Colorado Springs in 1997) but a good baserunner. He can bunt and has good bat control, but has little pop.

SHAVE, JON - 2B - BR - b: 11/4/67
Shave was signed by the Twins as a free agent in November of 1996. He was a non-roster invitee to spring training who spent the 1997 season in Triple-A where he hit .329. He showed a bit of power for a shortstop and he has some speed as well. At age 30 he's running out of chances to hang on with a big club as a utility infielder.

SHEAFFER, DANNY - C - BR - b: 8/2/61
Scouting: Sheaffer won't let a team ignore him. Though not good enough to be a regular anywhere, he can play a variety of positions with enough ability to make him useful in double switches. He lacks power, doesn't run well, won't walk often, and he hasn't dazzled anyone as a pinch-hitter since he swings so aggressively.
1998: Sheaffer probably won't find a spot on the Cardinals' roster unless the team runs into enough early injuries so as to compromise its depth at several positions. His experience and versatility should keep him working somewhere, though.
1997: Twice the Cardinals tried to send him to Triple-A. Each time, they quickly bumped into an emergency that caused them to bring Sheaffer back before he'd ever joined the Triple-A club. He batted only .250 overall, but .324 with runners in scoring position. Even though he rarely played his regular position as a catcher — because of a large organizational stockpile at that position — Sheaffer proved valuable because of his ability to play all three outfield positions, second base and third base.
1996: Sheaffer handled the fundamentals and his occasional opportunities well, though he hit poorly in the second half and only .189 with runners in scoring position.

	AB	R	HR	RBI	SB	BA
1995 St. Louis	208	24	5	30	0	.231
1996 St. Louis	198	10	2	20	3	.227
1997 St. Louis	132	10	0	11	1	.250

SHEETS, ANDY - SS/2B - BR - b: 11/19/71
Scouting: Sheets is a down-and-dirty kind of player who can fill a utility role, which he has been asked to do because of injuries to Alex Rodriguez and Russ Davis in Seattle the last two years. He lacks power and strikes out a lot for a contact hitter.
1998: Traded to San Diego in the deal for John Flaherty after the expansion draft, Sheets will compete for a major league roster spot as a backup infielder.
1997: Among the fill-ins used at third base when Davis went down, Sheets made errors twice as often as he homered.
1996: Sheets made his major league debut April 22nd after a hamstring injury to Rodriguez but did not adjust to big-league pitching, although he hit .358 after returning to Triple-A Tacoma.

	AB	R	HR	RBI	SB	BA
1996 Seattle	110	18	0	9	2	.191
1997 Seattle	89	18	4	9	2	.247

SHEFF, CHRIS - OF - BR - b: 2/4/71
An original Marlins' farmhand, Sheff has crept gradually through the ranks in his six-year minor-league career. he has gap power with good speed and is a solid defensive outfielder at all three spots. Since his bat speed is too slow for regular duty in the majors, Sheff appears ticketed for a fifth outfield role should he get to the majors. In the meantime, he'll bide his time in the high minors, waiting for injuries to present a major league chance.

SHEFFIELD, GARY - OF - BR - b: 11/18/68
Scouting: While Sheffield is not deserving of the richest contract in major league baseball, he has an exciting package of

offensive skills. His bat speed is truly scary, he has the best plate discipline of any power hitter this side of Frank Thomas, and is an aggressive baserunner with decent speed. He has only 440 strikeouts in 3659 career at-bats, an amazing ratio for a power hitter. He was a dead pull hitter in 1997 — he must get back to hitting the ball where it's pitched to revisit his peak. Defensively, he's recklessly aggressive, causing him to both make spectacular plays and injure himself frequently. Look for explosive offensive performances in the intermediate future.

1998: If Sheffield sheds his pure pull-hitting ways, he'll contend for the MVP Award. Expect him to add at least 40 points to his batting average, with significantly improved power numbers.

1997: True superstars can be an offensive force in an off year as Sheffield was in 1997. He hit for a mediocre average, but he walked 121 times, giving him a .424 on-base percentage. He was limited by a poor .233 average against righthanders. He exploded in the playoffs, creating a series of RBI opportunities for Bobby Bonilla and Moises Alou. The Marlins couldn't have done it without him.

1996: Sheffield's .465 on-base percentage, .624 slugging average, and 66-to-142 strikeout-to-walk ratio are straight out of Ted Williams' book. Most importantly, he was healthy from wire to wire for the first time in his career.

	AB	R	HR	RBI	SB	BA
1995 Florida	213	46	16	46	19	.324
1996 Florida	519	118	42	120	16	.314
1997 Florida	444	86	21	71	11	.250

SHELDON, SCOTT - SS - BR - b: 11/28/68
At one time the A's could have filled their infield with Scotts (Brosius, Spiezio, and Sheldon) and Jasons (Giambi and McDonald). Sheldon was the first of a group who tried out at shortstop when Tony Batista failed to deliver last year. Sheldon has some power, and put up good numbers at Edmonton: .315 average with 19 homers and 77 RBI. He is also old for a rookie and has far too many better and younger prospects ahead of him now to challenge for any major league role.

SHIPLEY, CRAIG - 3B/SS - BR - b: 1/7/63
Scouting: When healthy, Shipley is one of the best utility men in the game. But hamstring problems have plagued him the last two seasons. He's capable of hitting .300 with above-average power for a middle infielder. Shipley has started games at shortstop and second base and is a backup in center field.

1998: If he's healthy and the Padres lose Gomez, Shipley could start at shortstop if Jorge Velandia and Juan Melo wash out.

1997: Shipley hit for a decent average, but was only 2-for-24 as a pinch-hitter. Most of his action came in the second half following the latest round of strained hamstrings.

1996: He was unavailable for more than 100 games due to a series of hamstring injuries and played in only 33 games.

	AB	R	HR	RBI	SB	BA
1995 Houston	232	23	3	24	6	.263
1996 San Diego	92	13	1	7	7	.315
1997 San Diego	139	22	5	19	1	.273

SHIRLEY, AL - OF - BR - b: 10/18/73
A former top draft pick by the Mets (1991), Shirley struggled through six A-ball seasons before landing at Double-A Wichita where he had his best pro season. Shirley was aided by the small ballpark at Wichita, hitting for one of his best averages ever, .271, in a part-time role. But, strikeout-prone Shirley hasn't changed that much from the player who once whiffed 208 times in 437 at-bats (1994, at Columbia); he fanned more than a third of the time last year. Shirley is minor-league roster filler and one of the all-time biggest busts as a first-round draft pick.

SHOCKEY, GREG - OF - BL - b: 4/11/70
A good hitter who didn't find a groove until last year, Shockey is entering his seventh minor-league season. He had a good year in 1997 (.339-14-78 at Rancho Cucamonga) but is too old for A-ball; he needs to have success quickly in the higher minors.

SHORT, RICK - 3B/2B/SS - BR - b: 12/6/72
Orioles farmhand Short had a good year in high Class-A last year, but it was his second year in the league. He's too old for A-ball, and needs to make rapid progress. His best shot is as a utility man.

SHUMPERT, DEREK - OF - BR - b: 9/30/75
In his third year at Class A Greensboro this former second baseman was expected to improve as he shifted to the outfield — and he did, batting .301 in 86 games. Promoted to higher Class A Tampa, Shumpert hit .260 in 40 games. Shumpert's defense is already above average. He has good speed but still has a few things to learn about running the bases.

SHUMPERT, TERRY - 2B - BR - b: 8/16/66
Shumpert is an extremely weak singles-hitting utility infielder, and even with expansion there's no guarantee he'll make anybody's major league roster. He may have trouble finding regular work in the high minors, too.

	AB	R	HR	RBI	SB	BA
1995 Boston	47	6	0	3	3	.234
1996 Chicago NL	31	5	2	6	0	.226

SIDDALL, JOE - C - BL - b: 10/25/67
Siddall is a good-field, no-hit journeyman catcher who has had cups of major-league coffee with Montreal (1993-95) and Florida (1996). He has raised his batting average the past two years in Triple-A but still has no power. Though he is 30 years old, he could stick with the Expos as the backup catcher behind Chris Widger this season.

	AB	R	HR	RBI	SB	BA
1995 Montreal	10	4	0	1	0	.300
1996 Florida	47	0	0	3	0	.149

SIERRA, RUBEN - OF/DH - BB - b: 10/6/65
When the Blue Jays gave up on him, everyone knew that he was through. The weakest-hitting team in the league felt he couldn't help and after a brief stint with his sixth team in three years, Sierra's career appeared officially over. He has a little power left but the fact that so many teams have given up on him recently is significant.

	AB	R	HR	RBI	SB	BA
1995 Oak. - NY AL	479	73	19	86	5	.263
1996 NY AL - Det.	518	61	12	72	4	.247
1997 Toronto	138	10	3	12	0	.232

SILVESTRI, DAVE - 2B - BR - b: 9/29/67
Silvestri is now a minor-league journeyman whose slim chance of significant playing time in the majors are only slightly enhanced by expansion. His 1997 season at Triple-A Oklahoma

City (.240, 17 homers, 68 RBI) would translate into an average at or below .200 should he return to the big leagues.

	AB	R	HR	RBI	SB	BA
1995 NY AL - Mon.	93	16	3	11	2	.226
1996 Montreal	162	16	1	17	2	.204

SIMMONS, BRIAN - OF - BB - b: 9/4/73
Scouting: A collegiate star for Michigan from 1993 to 1995, Simmons is an excellent athlete. He's a switch-hitter with good power and a quick bat. Simmons is fast enough and with quick enough reflexes to play center field well. His speed won't translate into high major league stolen base totals, though. Simmons is still a raw talent who will be brought through the White Sox farm system steadily.
1998: Triple-A Nashville is a likely next stop for Simmons. He could earn a September callup if he makes normal progress.
1997: Simmons was one of Double-A Birmingham's more consistent hitters and displayed a good batting eye although hitting for a disappointing batting average (.262). Simmons' good speed was shown in his club-high nine triples.
1996: Simmons split the season between two Class A venues, hitting 100 points higher at South Bend than at Prince William, but his power was constant; Simmons collected 63 extra-base hits in 487 at-bats.

SIMMS, MIKE - 1B - BR - b: 1/12/67
Scouting: Simms has a big swing, and can hit with power if he makes contact. Unfortunately, that hasn't happened often enough in his major league career. Defensively, he is adequate at best in the outfield or at first base.
1998: Simms was slated to work at catcher in the off-season, in an attempt to prolong his career as a utility player. He will probably wind up on a major league bench to start the season.
1997: One of the Rangers' better pinch-hitters, Simms batted .300 with two homers and ten RBI in that role. A knee injury ended his season in September, but he was expected to be ready for spring training.
1996: Simms finally showed that he could hit major league pitching in his fifth trial with the Astros, providing power in a reserve role.

	AB	R	HR	RBI	SB	BA
1995 Houston	121	14	9	24	1	.256
1996 Houston	68	6	1	8	1	.176
1997 Texas	111	13	5	22	0	.252

SIMON, RANDELL - 1B - BL - b: 5/26/75
Simon had a huge season for Triple-A Richmond in '97, hitting .308 with 45 doubles and knocking in 102 runs, but don't get too excited. He's got a long swing and offers at everything, two weaknesses that should be exploited in the majors. He's also overweight and not a good first baseman. He appears to be a top-flight prospect because of his age and numbers, but his weaknesses could hold him back for a while.

SIMONS, MITCH - 2B - BR - b: 12/13/68
Simons joined the Twins' organization in April 1994 as a free agent and was a non-roster invitee to spring training last year. He hit .325 at Triple-A Salt Lake in 1995, took a step back in 1996 (.264) but rebounded last year with a .299-5-59 season that included 47 walks against 48 strikeouts. He has good speed (26 stolen bases in 1997). He may be better off in another organization as his path at second base is blocked for the foreseeable future.

SIMONTON, BENJI - 1B - BR - b: 5/12/72
Simonton showed good power during his first full season at Double-A Shreveport. The first sacker banged 20 homers and drove in 79 while hitting .256. He did whiff a third of the time (120 strikeouts in 387 at-bats) but he also drew 81 walks. His combination of power and on-base ability will help him against the more refined pitching in Triple-A where he will play in 1998.

SINGLETON, CHRIS - OF - BL - b: 8/15/72
Singleton is an aggressive hitter with good speed and flashes of power. He is not considered an especially good outfielder despite good range afield. He makes good contact but is too impatient at the plate. Singleton's second Double-A season was a repeat of his first at Shreveport. After hitting .295 with five homers, 72 RBI and 27 steals in 1996, he batted .317 last year with nine homers, 61 RBI and, again, 27 stolen bases. He made little improvement in any area; he'll need to be more productive in Double-A — or at least hold this level of production at Triple-A — in order to get noticed among the better Giants' outfield prospects.

SINGLETON, DUANE - OF - BL - b: 8/6/72
After being released by the Chicago Cubs last spring, he was picked up by the Angels to help out at Triple-A Vancouver. Singleton has the ability to hit with power, but didn't show it that much with the Canadians. He can hold his own as an outfielder, but didn't help his status by hitting only .206 in the Pacific Coast League in 1997.

SISCO, STEVE - OF/2B - BR - b: 12/2/69
An elderly high-minors infielder, Sisco split 1997 between Double-A Wichita and Triple-A Omaha, hitting a combined .273 with six homers and 36 RBI in 370 at-bats. It was the third straight year that Sisco has spent mostly in Double-A as he is gradually shifting from strictly second base duty to more of a utility role; he played all infield positions except shortstop, plus some outfield, too. Sisco is Triple-A roster filler at this point with little hope of advancing.

SLAUGHT, DON - C - BR - b: 9/11/58
Slaught put together a long and solid career by hitting for a good average and knowing how to handle pitchers. He never made an All-Star game but managed to hang around for 16 major-league seasons before being released by San Diego last May. Slaught is an intelligent and thoughtful man who would someday make a fine big-league manager if he so desired.

	AB	R	HR	RBI	SB	BA
1995 Pittsburgh	112	13	0	13	0	.304
1996 Cal-Chi. AL	243	25	6	36	0	.313

SMITH, BOBBY - 3B - BR - b: 4/10/74
Smith has a decent collection of skills, and the Braves hoped he could make the transition to shortstop and perhaps eventually replace Jeff Blauser, but the Devil Rays grabbed him. His bat has some potential, especially for a shortstop, but is not complete enough to make him a good-hitting regular third baseman yet (he hit .246 with 12 homers in Triple-A in '97). Tampa Bay planned to give him a long look in spring training as a candidate to start.

SMITH, BUBBA - 1B - BR - b: 12/18/69
Fan favorite Smith is a perennial minor-league All-Star who hit

.255 with 27 homers and 94 RBI for Triple-A Oklahoma City. He had off-season surgery to repair torn cartilage in his right knee. He probably won't make it to the majors, but it would be fun to see it happen.

SMITH, DEMOND - OF - BB - b: 11/6/72
If there is a sleeper to crack the Oakland outfield in 1998, it would be switch-hitting Smith. He started the year at Double-A Huntsville, hitting .279 with eight homers, 39 RBI and 31 steals, before being promoted to Triple-A Edmonton where he batted .219 with five homers, 22 RBI and ten stolen bases. His steals and 88 walks indicate Smith is a potential leadoff hitter, so his occasional power is that much more of a bonus.

SMITH, IRA - OF - BR - b: 8/4/67
Smith started '97 at Double-A Jacksonville and finished at Triple-A Toledo. A good line-drive hitter who is smart at the plate, Smith overmatched most of the Double-A pitchers while hitting .308 in 53 games before the promotion; he had more difficulty at Toledo, hitting .243 in 39 games. He's not a bad outfielder, but he DH'ed a lot. The former replacement player with the Padres was voted off the team by the San Diego players and wound up in the Tigers' system. He was another veteran who helped out some of Detroit's young prospects in the minor leagues.

SMITH, MARK - OF - BR - b: 5/7/70
Scouting: Smith, a former top draft pick of Baltimore after an All-American career at the University of Southern California, was considered a bust by the Orioles as he never reached his power potential. However, the outfielder developed his power with the Pirates last year. He also learned to play first base last fall at the Pirates' Florida Instructional League camp, which should only boost his chances of receiving more playing time.
1998: The Pirates love Smith's bat but have nowhere to play him. Leftfielder Al Martin and right fielder Jose Guillen man the outfield corners while Kevin Young is back to play first base with top prospect Ron Wright on the horizon. The Pirates, though, will try to work Smith's righthanded bat into the lineup as often as possible.
1997: San Diego, which acquired Smith from Baltimore the previous off-season, dealt him to the Pirates in a four-player trade on the final day of spring training. Smith tore up the Triple-A Pacific Coast League at Calgary then was summoned to Pittsburgh in late-May. Smith showed outstanding power in limited opportunities, hitting three game-winning homers, including a dramatic three-run pinch-hit shot July 12th against Houston that sealed the combined no-hitter of Francisco Cordova and Ricardo Rincon.
1996: Smith shuttled between Baltimore and Triple-A Rochester for a third consecutive season, seeing only occasional action with the Orioles as a corner outfielder or designated hitter.

	AB	R	HR	RBI	SB	BA
1995 Baltimore	104	11	3	15	3	.231
1996 Baltimore	78	9	4	10	0	.244
1997 Pittsburgh	193	29	9	35	3	.285

SMITH, MATT - 1B - BL - b: 6/2/76
It's been a slow climb for the Royals' top draft pick of 1994; he finally reached Double-A in his fourth pro season after hitting .278 for Class A Lansing - easily a career high. Smith still doesn't show much power and still fans too much, but he's still young for his level, so hope lingers that he'll eventually blossom.

SMITH, SCOTT - OF - BR - b: 10/14/71
After a strong offensive season in A-ball in 1996, Smith found the going a lot tougher at Double-A Memphis in the Mariner organization last year. Smith displayed some power, hitting 14 homers with 67 RBI, but he struck out too much and hit just .249. At his age, not being dominant at Double-A will mark him as a career minor-leaguer.

SNOPEK, CHRIS - 3B - BR - b: 9/20/70
Scouting: Snopek was a career .285 hitter with moderate power as a major league hitter before last year and had frequently hit for both average and power in the minors, so his inability to hit much at all last year was inexplicable. He's clearly a better hitter than he showed in 1997. He's also a good fielder at third base who can fill in at shortstop, too.
1998: With the White Sox, Snopek will be a regular at Triple-A. He is probably better off in another organization where he could get a fresh start after such a poor season last year; with a weaker team he might even get another chance at a starting job this year.
1997: It was a major disappointment for the White Sox that Snopek could not step in to fill the big hole left by the injury to Robin Ventura. Snopek hit so poorly that he had to be sent back to the minors.
1996: Snopek returned to the majors for a longer stint in 1996 after making a splash in his 1995 major league debut (.322). This time he hit for less of an average but far more power and established himself as major league ready.

	AB	R	HR	RBI	SB	BA
1995 Chicago AL	68	12	1	7	1	.324
1996 Chicago AL	104	18	6	18	0	.260
1997 Chicago AL	298	27	5	35	3	.218

SNOW, J.T. - 1B - BL - b: 2/26/68
Scouting: Snow is a switch-hitter with good power who hits righthanders better than lefties. He is a good fastball hitter which is one of the reasons he excelled after being traded to the National League. The Giants were sending him to switch-hitting school over the winter to improve his stroke against southpaws. On defense he is spectacular — Snow is among the best defensive first basemen in the game.
1998: On the heels of his great 1997 season, Snow will patrol first base for the Giants again. It would not be unreasonable to expect a drop in his offensive numbers. After a big season in 1995, he struggled when pitchers adjusted to his fastball-hitting ability. His success in 1998 will depend upon his ability to adjust as he sees fewer fastballs in his second tour of the senior circuit.
1997: Snow made an amazing comeback, both in terms of on-field performance and in terms of rebounding to play at all. He was beaned over the left eye by Randy Johnson in spring training and missed most of the rest of the spring season. He came back in time for opening day, however; it set the tone for a scrappy Giants' team. He also improved his overall performance in a number of ways, especially on-base ability, raising his on-base percentage 60 points.
1996: Snow suffered through a forgettable year. The fastballs he feasted upon in 1995 were nowhere to be seen as the league's pitchers wisened to his hitting tendencies.

	AB	R	HR	RBI	SB	BA
1995 California	544	80	24	102	2	.289

	AB	R	HR	RBI	SB	BA
1996 California	575	69	17	67	1	.257
1997 San Francisco	531	81	28	104	6	.281

SOJO, LUIS - 2B/SS - BR - b: 1/3/66
Scouting: With smooth-as-silk hands and the ability to offer backup versatility to the infield, Sojo is the type of player who can help any team. Although he lacks power and doesn't run well, he can handle a bat well, knows what to do in every situation, and is tough in the clutch.
1998: Although eligible for free agency, Sojo was expected to return as a utility infielder who can give Derek Jeter a break at shortstop and play as much as needed at second base. If he doesn't fill this role for New York he can do the same for just about any team.
1997: Sojo was on his way to a career year when he broke his left arm in mid-August. He had taken the second base job away from the 1996 surprise, Mariano Duncan.
1996: After starting the year with Seattle by hitting .211, Sojo was claimed off waivers by the Yankees and added defensive stability during their march to the World Series title.

	AB	R	HR	RBI	SB	BA
1995 Seattle	339	50	7	39	4	.289
1996 Sea. - NY AL	287	23	1	21	2	.220
1997 New York AL	215	27	2	25	3	.307

SOLANO, FAUSTO - SS - BR - b: 6/19/74
Solano showed above-average power for a shortstop in his first season at Double-A Knoxville. He has a good eye at the plate as well. With more-highly regarded shortstop prospects ahead of him in the Blue Jays' organization, Solano will get time to improve his hitting even further.

SOLIZ, STEVE - C - BR - b: 1/27/71
Soliz had been unable to secure a regular spot throughout his minor-league career and 1997 was no exception. In limited duty he struggled at the plate, hitting .192 with a homer and 13 RBI at Cleveland's Triple-A affiliate in Buffalo. He is a solid defensive catcher but that won't help him overcome his offensive shortcomings as his career seems to be winding down.

SORRENTO, PAUL - 1B - BL - b: 11/17/65
Scouting: Sorrento continues to excel against lefthanders in platoon situations, and has a power stroke many envy. He was the first player in major league history with at least 50 RBI to have more RBI than hits in 1995 — 76 hits, 79 RBI.
1998: Solidly entrenched against righthanders, Sorrento may even play against some lefthanders, too.
1997: Sorrento had a career high in homers despite hitting lower in the Seattle order than he would have for almost any other team.
1996: Sorrento posted a career-high in RBI in his first season with the Mariners after he was signed as a free agent to compensate for the loss of Tino Martinez in a trade with the Yankees.

	AB	R	HR	RBI	SB	BA
1995 Cleveland	323	50	25	79	1	.235
1996 Seattle	471	67	23	93	0	.289
1997 Seattle	457	68	31	80	0	.269

SOSA, SAMMY - OF - BR - b: 11/12/68
Scouting: The Cubs bill Sosa as one of the top players in all of baseball, but he has far too many holes to be considered in the same vein as players like Ken Griffey, Jr., Barry Bonds and Frank Thomas. He hit a lot of home runs, but strikes out way, way too much, doesn't hit as many doubles as he probably should, and, although he has improved, he's still not an above-average defender. He has a strong throwing arm, but sometimes even he doesn't know where the ball is going.
1998: The Cubs signed Sosa to a long-term contract before he could become a free agent, which means Sosa will be under a lot of pressure to have an MVP season. He's capable of putting up big numbers, but he's also capable of going into prolonged slumps. He'll get his share of home runs, but he's not likely to have the really big season Cubs fans and management will expect.
1997: Sosa had a disappointing season despite putting up decent home run and RBI totals. His batting average dipped considerably over the previous couple of seasons and he struck out a whopping 174 times. Sosa, like most home run hitters, has always struck out a lot, but he had 42 more strikeouts last season than he'd had in any previous year.
1996: Sosa had his best year in terms of home runs, but began to show some of his offensive weaknesses. He struck out more and walked less as pitchers began to take advantage of his free-swinging style. He had 15 outfield assists, but teams continued to run on him to exploit his less-than-accurate arm.

	AB	R	HR	RBI	SB	BA
1995 Chicago NL	564	89	36	119	34	.268
1996 Chicago NL	498	84	40	100	18	.273
1997 Chicago NL	642	90	36	119	22	.251

SPEARMAN, VERN - OF - BL - b: 12/17/69
Spearman is too old to be playing at Double-A, where he hit .279 with a homer and seven RBI in 136 at-bats last year. He also got 92 at-bats at Triple-A Albuquerque, but hit just .217. Over his eight-year minor-league career, he has been passed over by many other prospects in the Dodgers' farm system.

SPEHR, TIM - C - BR - b: 7/2/66
Scouting: Once prized for his defensive ability, Spehr has slipped into the gray area where his defense isn't enough for a reserve catcher and his hitting isn't enough to play more regularly. He has bounced around from one organization to another over the last few years and is barely on the fringe of the majors at this point. Spehr makes poor contact at the plate and his abilities behind the plate have deteriorated rapidly since he lost most of the 1995 season to a broken wrist and he also had to overcome cancer three years ago.
1998: Spehr has a 50-50 chance to open the season in the majors as a reserve, or more likely, third-string catcher. If he goes to Triple-A he'll still be a good bet for a reserve role.
1997: Spehr started the season with the Royals and finished with the Braves but hit poorly and struck out a third of the time with only marginal skills behind the plate.
1996: With the Expos he was a third-string catcher who rarely batted; he played in 63 games but only got 44 at-bats. Obviously the limited use effected his hitting as he managed just four hits all year.

	AB	R	HR	RBI	SB	BA
1995 Montreal	35	4	1	3	0	.257
1996 Montreal	44	4	1	3	1	.091

SPENCER, SHANE - OF - BR - b: 2/20/72
Because of his more advanced age, Spencer doesn't receive

the publicity of fellow prospects Ricky Ledee or Mike Lowell, and his name is rarely mentioned as a possible major leaguer, but Spencer's Triple-A production numbers are strong enough to get him a look by somebody. He led Columbus with 30 homers and drove in 86 runs. He needs to cut down on strikeouts (105) to lift his .241 average.

SPIERS, BILL - 2B - BL - b: 6/5/66
Scouting: Spiers was a first round draft choice by Milwaukee out of Clemson in 1987. Two years later, he was a regular with the Brewers, but his career was derailed by injuries. He drifted to the Mets and then the Astros. After a modest comeback with Houston in 1996, he broke out with a career year in 1997. Expected to be a utility infielder, he was a semi-regular at third base. Spiers has recurring back problems which prevent him from playing every day. He is an excellent pinch-hitter and hit well in the clutch last year.

1998: Spiers rejuvenated his career in the last two years and should have a job as a utility infielder and occasional starter. He is not likely to match his 1997 production.

1997: Spiers set career highs in batting average, on-base average (.438) and slugging average (.481). These numbers are out of context with anything he has achieved in the past.

1996: Spiers was a valuable utility man, playing every infield position as well as center and right field.

	AB	R	HR	RBI	SB	BA
1995 New York NL	72	5	0	11	0	.208
1996 Houston	218	27	6	26	7	.252
1997 Houston	291	51	4	48	10	.320

SPIEZIO, SCOTT - 3B - BB - b: 9/21/72
Scouting: Spiezio possesses good power and is capable of both gap and long ball hits, however, he is more of a "guess" hitter than one who uses intelligence and experience to dictate the count and pitch. At age 24, he has come far, fast, so now that he is established it is time for him to grow into an all-around player. The skills and the attitude are there for Spiezio to succeed.

1998: Spiezio will once again be manning his second base spot, and providing good power from the middle infield position. If he can learn to master more of the mental aspects of hitting, he can make another huge leap in his progress. In the mean time, considering his age, and what has been asked of him, he is doing just fine.

1997: During spring training, Spiezio was thought to be no more than the Triple-A starting third baseman, but he forced the departure of under-achieving Brent Gates, and in the process led the league in fielding percentage in his new spot. Plus, he added power and a little speed.

1996: Spiezio used a good eye, excellent power, and a good glove to advance despite the number of quality corner infielders ahead of him.

	AB	R	HR	RBI	SB	BA
1997 Oakland	538	58	14	65	9	.243

SPIVEY, JUNIOR - 2B - BR - b: 1/28/75
A productive middle infielder — 53 RBI, 14 stolen bases — Spivey needs a better knowledge of the strike zone after striking out 115 times at Class A High Desert in 1997.

SPRAGUE, ED - 3B - BR - b: 7/25/67
Scouting: A power hitter with average defensive skills, Sprague strikes out more than he should and does not run exceptionally well.

1998: A comeback season is almost guaranteed, provided Sprague recovers from surgery on his right shoulder. Sprague will play often and other than his injury last year, he has proven to be durable.

1997: Sprague's streak of consecutive games played came to end thanks to surgery on his right shoulder which ended his season at the beginning of September. Regardless, he was suffering an off year and finished with the lowest average of his career.

1996: This will be remembered as his career year. Sprague clubbed 36 home runs and knocked in 101 runs. For this year, Sprague became the offensive center of the Blue Jays.

	AB	R	HR	RBI	SB	BA
1995 Toronto	521	77	18	74	0	.244
1996 Toronto	591	88	36	101	0	.247
1997 Toronto	504	63	14	48	0	.228

STAHOVIAK, SCOTT - 3B/1B - BL - b: 3/6/70
Scouting: Stahoviak is a project player with the Twins who appears to have gone as far as he could go. Stahoviak is too passive at the plate, resulting in far too many called third strikes. He is mediocre defensively and doesn't hit enough home runs to play first base regularly in the major leagues. He is an exemplary worker who has made the most out of his limited ability.

1998: Stahoviak will play first base for a second-division team. He is almost guaranteed to hit better than the .229 with which he finished last season but he won't hit more than 14 or 15 home runs.

1997: Stahoviak fractured his left little finger on opening day and it ruined his season. He never found his swing and looked lost all season. For a project who needed to take several steps forward to guarantee himself a job, he didn't.

1996: Stahoviak showed enough promise to keep the Twins interested but not enough to say he had arrived. He compiled a solid batting average but not enough home runs to please the denizens of the Metrodome who expect lefthanded batters to reach the short right field fence.

	AB	R	HR	RBI	SB	BA
1995 Minnesota	263	28	3	23	5	.266
1996 Minnesota	405	72	13	61	3	.284
1997 Minnesota	275	33	10	33	5	.229

STAIRS, MATT - OF - BL - b: 2/27/68
Scouting: Stairs is an aggressive hitter who drives the ball to all fields when he is hot, and to left-center when he's not. He is a fabulous pinch-hitter who generates good power, can turn on a pitch and send it out accordingly. His pitch selection is his biggest enemy — impatience sometimes costs him. He's a decent fielder possessing a strong arm from right field.

1998: Based upon his 1997 performance, Stairs would probably retain his right field/DH role with the A's, logging 400 at-bats and clubbing another 20 homers. Expansion could bring a new team and/or role for Stairs in 1998. A duplication of his 1997 numbers is a reasonable expectation.

1997: Stairs' emergence, with both power and clutch-hitting numbers, made the loss of Mark McGwire a little more palatable. When finally getting a chance to play on a daily basis, Stairs delivered career highs in all offensive categories. He also played the field well enough, collecting nine assists from right field.

1996: Stairs played well in a limited role with Oakland through the stretch. His offense can be scary, but so can his defense. He wasn't a bad guy to have coming off the bench, however.

	AB	R	HR	RBI	SB	BA
1995 Boston	88	8	1	17	0	.261
1996 Oakland	137	21	10	23	1	.277
1997 Oakland	352	62	27	73	3	.298

STANKIEWICZ, ANDY - 2B - BR - b: 8/10/64

Scouting: Stankiewicz has survived in the major leagues because of his ability to play well defensively at second base, shortstop and third base. He doesn't have much of a bat but throws in his share of clutch hits.

1998: Stankiewicz will retain his utility infield role with the Expos as long as he is willing to play at a low salary. His batting average slipped last season but his value lies in his glove rather than his bat. He'll never get 400 at-bats as he did with the Yankees as a rookie in 1992, but he is still a good guy to have on the bench.

1997: Stankiewicz had a tough year at the plate but his chances were extremely limited as second baseman Mike Lansing and shortstop Mark Grudzielanek rarely got a day off. He played solid defense, making just three errors.

1996: Stankiewicz had a fine year in a utility role with the Expos, only the second full season he has spent in the majors in a career that started in 1986.

	AB	R	HR	RBI	SB	BA
1995 Houston	52	6	0	7	4	.115
1996 Montreal	77	12	0	9	1	.286
1997 Montreal	107	11	1	5	1	.224

STANLEY, MIKE - C - BR - b: 6/25/63

Scouting: Stanley has a good righthanded bat; the Red Sox decided his defense was below the level they required. There are worse catchers in the major leagues (pitchers enjoy throwing to Stanley, whatever faults he may have with throwing and fielding) but his catching days appear to be over. The main point is: he is good enough with the bat to be a DH. Stanley lends a lineup righthanded pop, but he has to play regularly to stay sharp. His swing was well-suited to Yankee Stadium's gap in right-center field.

1998: Stanley told the Yankees he wasn't interested in coming back if there wasn't going to be full-time work as a DH. The Yankees couldn't give him that guarantee so he was expected to land with his third team in two years, as a free agent.

1997: When the Yankees needed another righthanded bat down the stretch due to the unavailability of Cecil Fielder, they traded pitcher Tony Armas to Boston for Stanley. He hit well enough for New York in 28 games (.287), then became a free agent.

1996: Stanley missed the last three weeks of the season with a herniated disk in his lower back but still managed one of his more productive seasons with the bat in his first season with the Red Sox. His weakening defense and below-average arm continued to raise doubts about his ability to be an everyday catcher in the majors.

	AB	R	HR	RBI	SB	BA
1995 New York AL	399	63	18	83	1	.268
1996 Boston	397	73	24	69	2	.270
1997 two teams	347	61	16	65	0	.297

STATON, T.J. - OF - BL - b: 2/17/75

Going into last season, the Pirates felt Staton was one of their top prospects. However, he failed miserably at Triple-A Calgary to begin the year, then didn't play all that great at Double-A Carolina, either. Staton was only 22 years old and the Pirates obviously rushed him. However, scouts question his bat speed and work ethic. He's too young to give up on but it's obvious that some people have overrated him.

STEFANSKI, MIKE - C - BR - b: 9/12/69

Stefanski was installed as a backup catcher at Triple-A Louisville two years ago. He's got a good strong arm and managed a .305 average in 197 at-bats in 1997. The Cardinals are deep at catcher, so he'll have to go elsewhere to have a reasonable shot at the majors.

STEINBACH, TERRY - C - BR - b: 3/2/62

Scouting: a solid catching package, Steinbach is a terrific receiver who will help improve any pitching staff, a capable hitter and a good guy in the clubhouse. Pitchers like working with him because he is a good communicator who works with them. He is 34 years old and is just beginning to show signs of advancing age, but he keeps himself in good shape.

1998: Realistically, Steinbach's 1998 season will fall somewhere between the past two years. He won't hit the 35 home runs he smacked two years ago, but he shouldn't strike out in 25% of his at-bats as he did in 1997. Now that he's used to his new surroundings in Minnesota, and now that he's become accustomed to the pressures of playing at home, Steinbach will improve in many areas this season.

1997: After taking a bit less money so he could play at home in the Twin Cities, Steinbach never really got untracked. He didn't have a poor year, just mediocre. The Twins certainly didn't expect 35 home runs, but more than a .248 average would have been nice. The club's pitching staff still finished 13th in the league even with Steinbach's acumen.

1996: It was a career season that isn't expected to be duplicated anytime soon. Of Steinbach's 35 home runs, 34 came as a catcher — an American League record.

	AB	R	HR	RBI	SB	BA
1995 Oakland	406	43	15	65	1	.278
1996 Oakland	514	79	35	100	0	.272
1997 Minnesota	447	60	12	54	6	.248

STEVENS, LEE - OF - BL - b: 7/10/67

Scouting: Stevens is a much more disciplined hitter than he was prior to his stint in Japan. He has shortened his swing while maintaining his power, and hits well with men on base. Although Stevens occasionally looks bad against lefthanders with good breaking stuff, he is improving against them. Defensively, Stevens is average at first base and can play a passable right field. For a big guy, he runs the bases well.

1998: For the first time in several years, Stevens has a chance to win a starting job out of spring training, either at first base or as a DH.

1997: Stevens took advantage of injuries to Will Clark and Juan Gonzalez to prove that he not only belongs in the big leagues, but that he can be a productive everyday player as well. Only Gonzalez, Ivan Rodriguez and Rusty Greer had more extra-base hits for Texas in 1997.

1996: The American Association MVP, Stevens capped a successful return from Japan by playing well down the stretch in a late-season callup by Texas.

	AB	R	HR	RBI	SB	BA
1996 Texas	78	6	3	12	0	.231
1997 Texas	426	58	21	74	1	.300

STEWART, ANDY - 1B/C - BR - b: 12/5/70

Scouting: Stewart is an over-achiever. He's not blessed with especially good talents either at the plate or in the field, but he has learned to play first base, catcher and the outfield sufficiently well enough while also hitting well enough to stay in the high minors and get regular playing time. Stewart has little power and would be a below-average contact hitter in the majors; his best skill is his throwing arm from behind the plate. He is, at best, a deep bench reserve in the majors.

1998: Despite his perseverance, Stewart will return to the high minors again and await injuries to major leaguers which may open a bench role for him with a big-league club.

1997: Stewart finally spent a whole minor-league season at Triple-A and even got a September callup that was only intended as a non-playing role (as bullpen catcher) but later improved and he got his first big-league playing time. Stewart had a good year as a reserve catcher and first baseman for Omaha, hitting .274 with six homers and 24 RBI in 288 at-bats.

1996: Stewart split the year between Triple-A Omaha and Double-A Wichita for the second year, this time hitting much better for Wichita than at Omaha; he batted .302 in the Texas League and was added to the Royals' 40-man roster.

STEWART, SHANNON - OF - BR - b: 2/25/74

Scouting: A speedy runner who can occasionally hit the long ball, Stewart has all the tools to be a successful major leaguer for years to come.

1998: Stewart, in the absence of anyone better, starts his first full major league season. Expect big numbers all around including stolen bases, walks and extra-base hits. He doesn't hit for much power but that will develop quickly.

1997: The trade of Otis Nixon in August automatically made Stewart the center fielder and he responded, hitting seven triples in just 44 games.

1996: Stewart continued his rise up the Blue Jays' ladder with a solid .298 season in his first year at Triple-A Syracuse. He stole 35 bases and scored 77 runs in 112 games.

	AB	R	HR	RBI	SB	BA
1997 Toronto	168	25	0	22	10	.286

STINNETT, KELLY - C - BR - b: 2/14/70

Scouting: Stinnett tattoos minor-league pitching, but has trouble with the breaking stuff at the major league level. He is an average defensive catcher, at best, with an adequate throwing arm.

1998: Stinnett looked like a backup catcher in the Milwaukee system, and he looked like a backup for the Diamondbacks after the expansion draft. He is not too old to improve, however.

1997: Stinnett had a couple spot stays with the Brewers, but saw limited action. He ended the season as one of three catchers on the roster.

1996: The Brewers acquired Stinnett from the New York Mets for pitcher Cory Lidle. He made the club out of spring training, but spent most of the season at Triple-A New Orleans.

STOCKER, KEVIN - SS - BB - b: 2/13/70

Scouting: Stocker is a consistent if unexciting performer who gives the Phillies consistent defensive play and acceptable bottom of the order offensive production. He knows his offensive limitations, hits the ball where it's pitched and is willing to draw a walk to turn over the lineup. He has a touch of doubles power, and tends to cluster most or all of his handful of a season's homers during the same week. His range at shortstop is below average, but he consistently makes the routine play. He has an average arm, and is a smart baserunner with enough speed to reach double figures in steals.

1998: Stocker is just coming into his prime. Joining the expansion Devil Rays will give him an opportunity to play in front of enthusiastic fans. Look for another good year like he had in 1997.

1997: Stocker was effective for the Phillies in 1997, anchoring a solid double-play combination along with Mickey Morandini and a strong left side of the infield with Scott Rolen. He avoided extended slumps and lapses of confidence at the plate that had plagued him in previous seasons. His physical conditioning was improved over prior years and he didn't run out of gas late in the summer like he did in previous years.

1996: Stocker showed up mentally unprepared to play, and got a wake-up call with a mid-season demotion to Triple-A Scranton. He was a new man after his return, showing improved physical conditioning and better range afield, and a more controlled stroke at the plate. He likely saved his major league career.

	AB	R	HR	RBI	SB	BA
1995 Philadelphia	412	42	1	32	6	.218
1996 Philadelphia	394	46	5	41	6	.254
1997 Philadelphia	504	51	4	40	11	.266

STONER, MIKE - OF - BR - b: 5/23/73

Scouting: Stoner made Baseball America's minor-league All-Star team last season when he was the first minor leaguer since 1987 to record 200 hits, getting 203 at Class A High Desert. A disciplined hitter with good power to all fields, Stoner was signed as a free agent out of North Carolina hours after the 1996 ACC tournament. He's a left fielder all the way.

1998: Stoner will start the year at Triple-A Tucson, another hitter's paradise, not only because the ball carries so well but because the sun bakes the infield to the consistency of asphalt.

1997: Stoner produced arguably the best minor-league numbers extant — a .358 batting average with California League highs in doubles (44), homers (33) and RBI (142 - the most in the minors). He missed the triple crown by .003 batting average points, to a player who spent the final six weeks of the season in Double-A.

1996: Available to all because he was a college senior, Stoner signed a week short of his 23rd birthday.

STOVALL, DAROND - OF - BB - b: 1/3/73

Stovall was the key player the Expos got back in the spring 1995 trade that sent pitcher Ken Hill to St. Louis. Hill washed out with the Cardinals and Stovall is doing the same in the Montreal organization. Stovall is a good little athlete, but not a baseball player. He has good speed and covers a lot of ground in center field, but he won't ever hit enough to be an effective big-leaguer. He's weak and easily overpowered at the plate. Stovall got to Triple-A Ottawa last season but didn't do much of anything but strike out a lot.

STRANGE, DOUG - 3B - BB - b: 4/13/64

Scouting: The book on Strange has always been that he is nothing more than a switch-hitting utilityman who can only play against lefthanders. However, Strange shattered those myths last season. He still is better suited to a reserve role but showed

he is capable of filling in and playing a good third base.
1998: Strange was headed to spring training to try out for the void created by Joe Randa's departure. There will be stiff competition, and Strange will turn 34 in April. Even if he loses the starting job, Strange still has value as a bench player.
1997: It was indeed a strange year for Strange. His wife gave birth to quadruplets just before the start of spring training and then he wound up being the Expos' primary third baseman after Shane Andrews was lost for the season in the May with a nerve problem in his left shoulder that eventually led to reconstructive surgery. It was only the second time Strange has been a regular in his career — he was Texas' third baseman in 1993 — and he acquitted himself well.
1996: Strange had a sub-par season as a utilityman with Seattle and was released at the end of the season.

	AB	R	HR	RBI	SB	BA
1995 Seattle	155	19	2	21	0	.271
1996 Seattle	183	19	3	23	1	.235
1997 Montreal	327	40	12	47	0	.257

STRAWBERRY, DARRYL - OF - BL - b: 3/12/62
Scouting: The big questions are: How much does Strawberry have left? What effect will missing nearly an entire season have on him? Can he sill produce those majestic homers? And what about his knee — can it hold up? If it does, Strawberry will remain a potent power threat, and he might even be able to show some speed on the bases; long ago, he was fast.
1998: If the knee is OK, it's not out of the question Strawberry could receive 400 at-bats and be a productive player again. The body is still chiseled, and he insists the left knee will allow him to contribute in 1998. If he's right, he has ability to hit home runs. Since he's a favorite of George Steinbrenner, there was a good chance Strawberry would return to the Yankees even after he filed for free agency. Steinbrenner brought Strawberry to the minor-league complex in November to make sure his knee was healthy.
1997: Strawberry arrived at spring training in great shape and Joe Torre said the veteran lefty slugger was his starting left fielder. Knee woes that required surgery ended that idea, and he appeared in only 11 games — his least major league time ever in fifteen big-league seasons.
1996: Playing his way back to the major leagues, via the Independent Northern League, made Strawberry one of the bigger comeback stories of the 1990's.

	AB	R	HR	RBI	SB	BA
1995 New York AL	87	15	3	13	0	.276
1996 New York AL	202	35	11	36	6	.262

STRICKLIN, SCOTT - C - BL - b: 2/17/72
Stricklin is a good defensive receiver who improved slightly at the plate in 1997. He still displays little or no power but since he's in the Tampa Bay organization he may get a chance to break into the big leagues in the next season or two.

STRITTMATTER, MARK - C - BR - b: 4/4/69
A solid backup catcher, Strittmatter is prototypical catch-and-throw guy. There are no better catchers at calling a game; pitchers love throwing to him. His offense is improving, though he'll never hit enough to become a regular, big-league catcher.

STURDIVANT, MARCUS - OF - BL - b: 10/29/73
Scouting: A poor man's Mickey Rivers, Sturdivant slaps the ball and can use all fields. He uses his speed on the bases and is learning the strike zone. He is a good defensive player.
1998: Sturdivant may compete for a fifth outfielder's job, although probably will make a stop at Triple-A first.
1997: Sturdivant did what he always does — hit for a good average with little power while stealing 20 bases; but he was caught stealing 17 times.
1996: Sturdivant made the Class A California League mid-season All-Star team before earning a promotion to Double-A Port City. He had a career-high 36 stolen bases at the two levels, combined.

STYNES, CHRIS - 2B/3B - BR - b: 1/19/73
Scouting: Stynes is a high-average hitter, who doesn't walk or strikeout much, and is capable of double-digit home runs and steals. His hustle and aggressiveness made him an instant crowd favorite in Cincinnati, reminiscent of Chris Sabo. Defense is his biggest weakness, as he has been shifted between second base, third base, and the outfield.
1998: The Reds talked openly of using Stynes as a multi-position regular like Bip Roberts, and there is no reason to think he won't hold that role. He isn't going to improve on his strong 1997 performance but his minor-league and 1997 performances suggest he will be a solid regular for the Reds.
1997: Stynes was a throw-in in the Carrasco/Nunnally trade and promptly paid major dividends when he was called up from the minors on August 7th. He recorded hits in his first seven at-bats and went 20 for his first 40. After Deion Sanders stopped playing, Stynes became the regular left fielder and number three hitter for the Reds.
1996: A strong season at Triple-A Omaha (.356-10-40 in 284 at-bats) resulted in a callup to Kansas City, where he hit .293 in a utility role.

	AB	R	HR	RBI	SB	BA
1995 Kansas City	35	7	0	2	0	.171
1996 Kansas City	92	8	0	6	5	.293
1997 Cincinnati	198	31	6	28	11	.348

SURHOFF, B.J. - 3B/OF - BL - b: 8/4/64
Scouting: Surhoff is a strong hitter who quietly does his job playing left field for the Orioles. He's a talented, "blue-collar" hustler, just the type of good team player with great character that the Orioles prefer. He hits righties and lefties equally well, both around .285, and he plays solid defense in left field. If needed, Surhoff can play first or third base, or even catch. He's a good clutch hitter, and the Orioles frequently bat him third in the order.
1998: Another solid year is expected. He's got a lock on left field, with the others fighting over right field and DH.
1997: Surhoff played left field and had his typical solid year.
1996: Surhoff's first year as an Oriole was a smooth adjustment. He was one of new GM Pat Gillick's first major signings with the Orioles, as the club began to stress teamwork, defense and pitching rather than home run power.

	AB	R	HR	RBI	SB	BA
1995 Milwaukee	415	72	13	73	7	.320
1996 Baltimore	537	74	21	82	0	.292
1997 Baltimore	528	80	18	88	1	.284

SUTTON, LARRY - 1B - BL - b: 5/14/70
Scouting: Sutton is a polished player. He's a fine defensive first baseman with a refined batting eye and some power. He has hit

for a high average in the high minors and would likely retain most of that batting average in the majors. Because he's unlikely to hit 30 homers or bat .330 in the big leagues, though, Sutton isn't going to be a regular. His ability to adjust to various offensive roles will let Sutton become a good major league pinch-hitter.
1998: Sutton will hope to spend all of 1998 the way he ended 1997 — as a pinch-hitting reserve first baseman on the major league bench. He doesn't have much left to learn or to prove in the minors, but may be relegated there nonetheless. Expansion could give him a much larger role, however.
1997: Sutton's first season in Triple-A was a big success as he hit .300 with 19 homers and a club-high 72 RBI for Omaha, with more walks than strikeouts. It earned him his first taste of the big leagues where he continued a fine season by quickly grabbing the Royals' primary righthanded pinch-hitter role and led the club in pinch-hit RBI.
1996: In his second year with Double-A Wichita, Sutton was among league leaders in most hitting categories, including a high on-base percentage (.401) and, as usual, more walks than strikeouts. He batted .296 with 22 homers, 22 doubles and 84 RBI in 463 at-bats.

	AB	R	HR	RBI	SB	BA
1997 Kansas City	69	9	2	8	0	.290

SVEUM, DALE - 1B - BB - b: 11/23/63
Scouting: Sveum has some pop in his bat, particularly from the left side, and is versatile with his ability to start at all four infield positions. Sveum is one of the game's true professionals, working hard to stay on the fringes of the big leagues after a broken leg suffered while playing for Milwaukee in 1988 ended his hopes for stardom.
1998: Sveum was a free agent at the end of last season but the Pirates figured to re-sign him. He will again be a valuable reserve, a dangerous switch-hitter off the bench with the ability to make spot starts all around the infield.
1997: Sveum spent his first full season in the major leagues since 1992 and proved to be the Pirates' most valuable bench player. His on-field contributions were more than anyone could have hoped and he provided a steadying influence in a young clubhouse.
1996: Sveum led Triple-A Calgary in home runs and RBI then got a chance to prove he could still play at the major league level with a September callup to Pittsburgh.

	AB	R	HR	RBI	SB	BA
1997 Pittsburgh	306	30	12	47	0	.261

SWANN, PEDRO - OF - BL - b: 10/27/70
Swann, a 6'0" outfielder, has some power potential at the plate, but does not provide much in any other way. The Braves sent him back to Double-A in '97 after he struggled in Triple-A in '96. He hit .286 with 24 homers in '97, but his season wasn't that impressive considering he was a 26-year old playing in Double-A for the fifth time. His potential is limited.

SWEENEY, KEVIN - DH - BL - b: 3/30/74
Baseball's Cinderella story after hitting .424 in rookie ball as a 29th-round draft pick in 1996, Sweeney suffered a quadriceps injury in spring training that limited him to a half-season in 1997, where he hit .263 at Class A South Bend.

SWEENEY, MARK - 1B - BL - b: 10/26/69
Scouting: Sweeney is an excellent pinch-hitter and lefthanded bat off the bench. He's a good spare outfielder who also plays first base, but doesn't have the power most teams seek in a regular.
1998: The Padres wanted to retain Sweeney, who was one of few pleasant surprises for them in '97. Deciding whether or not to protect him from the expansion draft was one of the club's most difficult decisions after the season. He can serve as a productive fourth outfield and part-time first baseman for a strong major league team, or perhaps start at first or in a corner outfield spot on a weaker team.
1997: A throw-in to balance the Fernando Valenzuela and Scott Livingstone for Danny Jackson deal with the Cardinals, Sweeney finished the year as the only part of the trade who produced. As a pinch-hitter, he hit .366 with two homers and 14 RBI.
1996: Sweeney served as a part-time outfielder but more often as a pinch-hitter for the Cardinals.

	AB	R	HR	RBI	SB	BA
1995 St. Louis	77	5	2	13	1	.273
1996 St. Louis	170	32	3	22	3	.265
1997 San Diego	164	16	2	23	2	.280

SWEENEY, MIKE - C - BR - b: 7/22/73
Scouting: Sweeney is an unpolished player with loads of raw talent; he has a sweet, line-drive swing that generates moderate power and has an above-average arm behind the plate. However, he has been prone to swinging at bad pitches and his inability to block pitches in the dirt has been a cause for concern among Royals' pitchers. These are deficiencies that will be rectified with more regular major league play, though, and his hitting will make Sweeney one of the better catchers in the American League soon.
1998: Sweeney is the favorite for regular play behind the plate. New manager Tony Muser is committed to developing young Royals' position players and Sweeney is at the forefront of that movement. Continued growth is expected for Sweeney in 1998; he'll improve in nearly every aspect but will be prone to streaky play.
1997: In order to get regular playing time, Sweeney spent the season on a shuttle between Triple-A Omaha and Kansas City. He finally won the starting job outright when Tony Muser took over the reigns of the club. His final season totals were a bit disappointing, but Sweeney made significant strides toward becoming a regular catcher in the major leagues.
1996: Sweeney split time between Kansas City, Omaha and Double-A Wichita, displaying above-average power, a good batting average and improving defensive skills. Sweeney was named to Baseball America's minor-league All-Star team and Howe SportsData's All-Star team, too. He finished his best pro season by playing in the Arizona Fall League.

	AB	R	HR	RBI	SB	BA
1996 Kansas City	165	23	4	24	1	.279
1997 Kansas City	240	30	7	31	3	.242

SWEET, JOHN - C - BL - b: 11/10/71
Sweet is a good-field, no-hit catcher who was the primary starter with the Pirates' Double-A Carolina farm club last season. He has hit just two home runs in four professional seasons and his only hope at getting to the major leagues is as a defensive specialist. Don't count on it.

TACKETT, JEFF - C - BR - b: 12/1/65
It has now been three full seasons since Tackett was in the

majors. He's a serviceable journeyman receiver, but that's about it. Tackett batted .273 with five homers and 19 RBI in Triple-A last year.

TARASCO, TONY - OF - BL - b: 12/9/70

Scouting: Once considered a potential major league impact player, Tarasco has not realized his potential — and maybe he never will. He has hit well at times but not often. He's still capable of a home run or extra base hit every time he bats. He has base-stealing speed, having swiped 24 for the Expos in 1995. His defense is excellent, and he's been used as a late-inning defensive replacement. Tarasco now has a poor career batting line of .243-27-96 in over 850 at-bats, but he's only 27 and, if given another chance, could still break out to live up to his potential.

1998: The Orioles outfield and DH situation is cluttered with veterans and talented rookies all vying for playing time. Tarasco is the lowest on the depth chart, and may get a better shot with another team.

1997: Tarasco spent some time in Triple-A, and got into some games with the Orioles, hitting poorly. He was frequently used as a late-inning defensive replacement in the outfield.

1996: Tarasco's year is memorable only because of the Jeffrey Maier flyball incident in the Yankees/Orioles playoff game.

	AB	R	HR	RBI	SB	BA
1995 Montreal	438	64	14	40	24	.249
1996 Baltimore	84	14	1	9	5	.238
1997 Baltimore	166	26	7	26	2	.205

TARTABULL, DANNY - OF/DH - BR - b: 10/30/62

Scouting: Tartabull has one skill: he hits homers. He can't run, field or hit for average. He is far beyond his prime, is injury-prone and has a reputation as a clubhouse troublemaker. Tartabull is no longer a regular in the major leagues and will have to make serious adjustments to be a success in a reserve role.

1998: Tartabull will have to convince someone that he's healthy enough to warrant a contract for 1998. The Phillies aren't buying, of course, so he'll shop his wares elsewhere. Tartabull might not be a bad gamble on a make-good minimum salary contract, but that won't happen in Philadelphia.

1997: A serious lack of hitting in the middle of their lineup led the Phillies to sign Tartabull to a big contract. He proceeded to foul a ball off his foot in April and missed the rest of the season. It made his $2.5 million contract one of the worst free-agent signings ever. Missing Tartabull, the Phillies helped Darren Daulton resurrect his career as an everyday outfielder.

1996: Tartabull made it through an entire season without a significant injury, posting power numbers consistent with his career norms as the White Sox' primary right fielder. It was the last year of his contract and he once again excelled in his free-agent year. Tartabull's fielding was among the worst for major league rightfielders.

	AB	R	HR	RBI	SB	BA
1995 NY AL - Oak.	280	34	8	35	0	.236
1996 Chicago AL	472	58	27	101	1	.254

TATIS, FERNANDO - 3B - BB - b: 1/1/75

Scouting: Tatis offers surprising power for his size (6'1", 175 pounds), and should continue to develop as a power hitter. He has trouble catching up to some of the better fastball pitchers, but showed a good batting eye and patience at the plate. Tatis is also hard-working and coachable. Defensively, he is steady at third base, with good range and a good arm. Although not really fast, Tatis is capable of stealing 10 or 15 bases in a full season.

1998: Tatis could be sent to Triple-A for a few months of additional seasoning, or he could be given a starting third base job in the majors. He may struggle initially as American League pitchers get another look at him, but he has the talent and work ethic to succeed.

1997: After Dean Palmer was traded to Kansas City, Tatis jumped to the majors from Double-A Tulsa, where he had hit .314 with 24 homers, 61 RBI and 17 steals; he led the club in batting average, homers, extra base hits (51) and stolen bases despite playing only 102 games. His first time through the American League, Tatis was seldom overmatched, and hopes are high for his future. He played nearly every game after his callup, and established himself as a serious contender for a starting job in 1998.

1996: After missing nearly half of the season at high Class A Charlotte with a broken hamate bone in his wrist, Tatis came back to hit .286 with 12 homers and 53 RBI, establishing himself as the Rangers' best offensive prospect.

	AB	R	HR	RBI	SB	BA
1997 Texas	223	29	8	29	3	.256

TATUM, JIM - 1B/3B/C - BR - b: 10/9/67

Tatum continued to whack Triple-A pitching in 1997 while with Las Vegas in the Padres' organization. He tried hard to get a shot at the bigs, learning to play catcher and first base as well as third but it didn't work out. After posting a .317-9-25 start at Vegas in 161 at-bats, Tatum left the States to play in Japan.

TAUBENSEE, EDDIE - C - BL - b: 10/31/68

Scouting: Taubensee is a fine platoon catcher, hitting for power and a good average against righthanders. He has never gotten the chance to show what he could do as a full-time player due to a reputation as a poor handler of pitchers, and while he isn't as good at that as Joe Oliver, he is not as bad as his reputation.

1998: It is unclear what role Taubensee will assume next year. He could become a regular catcher if Joe Oliver leaves, or remain a twice-a-week catcher and pinch-hitter/reserve first baseman.

1997: Taubensee started the season as the regular catcher (Joe Oliver was hurt) but reverted to a less-than-platoon role when Oliver returned. Ray Knight experimented with Taubensee in the outfield to get more pop in the lineup, but those experiments ended when Knight was fired. Taubensee's offensive output was the lowest of his career.

1996: Taubensee turned in a good performance at the plate, but evenly split playing time with Joe Oliver, despite outhitting him by 50 points.

	AB	R	HR	RBI	SB	BA
1995 Cincinnati	218	32	9	44	2	.284
1996 Cincinnati	327	46	12	48	3	.291
1997 Cincinnati	254	26	10	34	0	.268

TAVAREZ, JESUS - OF - BB - b: 3/26/71

Scouting: Tavarez has a lot of tools. He runs extremely well and throws well. Despite some miscues in the majors, Tavarez is a good center fielder. His biggest problem is with the bat. Though he will never have power, he has enough strength to be a decent line-drive hitter and a tough out. However, he has some bad habits at the plate, the biggest being that he pulls his front shoulder off the ball. He's had a lot of time to fix that, so maybe he never will. But if he can, he's an okay regular. If not, he's a backup outfielder.

1998: Tavarez, an expansion pick by the Marlins, again must hope that expansion grants him a job somewhere. He's probably blown any chance of being a regular, but his tools will give him a good shot at making some team's roster.

1997: Tavarez had an outside shot at being the center fielder that Boston sorely needed, but didn't impress in spring training. He was playing well in the field and hitting poorly when the Red Sox called him up to provide defense off the bench in the majors. Once called up, he seldom was called on to hit.

1996: Tavarez spent the season as a backup outfielder for the Marlins after failing in a couple of brief full-time trials the previous year.

	AB	R	HR	RBI	SB	BA
1995 Florida	190	31	2	13	7	.289
1996 Florida	114	14	0	6	5	.219
1997 Boston	69	12	0	9	0	.174

TAYLOR, JAMIE - 3B - BL - b: 10/10/70

An outstanding defensive third baseman, Taylor had a nice year in 1997 at Double-A New Haven, hitting .321 with eight homers and 41 RBI in 105 games. His lateral range is questionable but he has an accurate throwing arm and a great work-ethic. The Rockies might try giving him time at catcher in 1998 to increase his versatility. Taylor is a good hitter who will hit for average, but he had shown no power until the final month of the 1997 season, when he made an adjustment and hit five homers. He's not a good baserunner. Taylor could see time at Triple-A Colorado Springs in 1997.

TAYLOR, REGGIE - OF - BL - b: 1/12/77

Taylor is a blend of intriguing abilities and noticeable flaws. He has blazing speed and occasional long-ball power, but is also a wild swinger who doesn't use his speed by hitting the ball on the ground. The Phillies envision Taylor as a leadoff hitter but he hasn't developed the requisite skills, especially plate discipline. He'll swing at a borderline pitch early in the count when down a run late in the game, then wonder what he has done wrong. Taylor would be better served if developed as a lower-order defensive wizard; he has great range and an above-average throwing arm. He has been one of the younger starters at his level in his minor-league career, but hasn't developed good habits at the plate yet. Taylor will move to Double-A Reading in 1998 and play center field; he needs at least a full year each at Double-A and Triple-A before he'll contend for a major league role.

TEJADA, MIGUEL - SS - BR - b: 5/25/76

Scouting: The ranks of fabulous young shortstops has swollen a lot in recent years, but will have to welcome one more member soon: Miguel Tejada. A five-tool player, 21-year-old Tejada has consecutive 20-homer seasons in each of his first two professional seasons. He hits with power, has excellent speed, a strong arm, and just about everything else you could ask from a budding star. Tejada's biggest drawback is that he is still a bit raw. That will change as he gets more experience.

1998: Tejada has to be the front runner in the race for the starting shortstop job in Oakland. His 1997 spring alone was nearly enough to merit the promotion, but management felt that since Tejada had had only one professional season, they would be forcing the issue. Thus, he spent the majority of the season at Double-A Huntsville last year. 1998 will be different.

1997: At Huntsville, Tejada started slow, but wound up with similar numbers to those of his first year at Modesto; he hit .275 for Huntsville with 22 homers, 97 RBI and 15 steals. Tejada's arrival in September was a result of the many injuries Oakland infielders suffered during the season.

1996: In a great pro ball debut, Tejada hit .279 with 20 homers, 79 RBI and 27 steals and immediately vaulted into the light as the Oakland shortstop of the future. He showed inexperience and bad selectivity at the plate, but he was young.

TEJERO, FAUSTO - C - BR - b: 140/26/68

Tejero is a journeyman catcher with good defensive skills, but an extremely weak bat. He gets Triple-A jobs because organizations need depth at the catcher position, but he's unlikely to ever have any kind of an impact at the big-league level.

TETTLETON, MICKEY - C/1B/OF - BB - b: 9/16/60

After sustaining a badly bruised knee early in the season, Tettleton went on the disabled list. He came back briefly, only to retire shortly thereafter when the Rangers needed his roster spot. It was a typically classy move by a well-respected ballplayer.

	AB	R	HR	RBI	SB	BA
1995 Texas	429	76	32	78	0	.238
1996 Texas	491	78	24	83	2	.246

THOBE, STEVE - 3B - BR - b: 5/26/72

Thobe started the 1997 season at Double-A Carolina, putting up solid numbers and getting a shot at Triple-A Calgary in the Pittsburgh organization. He likely will start this season at Double-A and has an uphill climb to the majors in the Pirates' system with at least two third base prospects ahead of him.

THOMAS, FRANK - 1B - BR - b: 5/27/68

Scouting: Arguably the game's best hitter, Thomas is an unusual combination of power, outstanding batting average and a great batting eye. He is the only player in major league history to hit at least .300 with 20 homers, 100 RBI, 100 walks and 100 runs scored in seven consecutive seasons — no one else has ever had four straight years like that. He's a defensive liability around the bag at first and is not a good baserunner, but those are only minor negatives. Thomas is a future Hall-of-Famer.

1998: Thomas is a perennial MVP and triple crown champion threat. His defense has gotten bad enough that the White Sox will try to ease him into a regular DH role although Thomas really prefers to play first base.

1997: It's hard to believe but Thomas got off to a bad start last year before cruising easily to his first batting crown, becoming one of the largest men to ever win a batting title. His power numbers were down only slightly, but he was every bit as productive as he has been since he became a major league offensive force in 1990.

1996: Thomas set a career high in RBI and finished among American League leaders in nearly all hitting categories, actually outperforming his own MVP seasons of 1993-4. He was the offensive force behind a pennant-contending White Sox club.

	AB	R	HR	RBI	SB	BA
1995 Chicago AL	493	102	40	111	3	.308
1996 Chicago AL	527	110	40	134	1	.349
1997 Chicago AL	530	110	35	125	1	.347

THOMAS, GREG - OF - BL - b: 7/19/72
Thomas is a primarily a first baseman, but has been chased from that position to the outfield by superior Indians' prospects Richie Sexson and Sean Casey. Thomas has some extra-base power, but his bat is too slow for him to excel against higher-level pitching. His plate discipline is poor, and his defense and speed are unremarkable. He is likely nearing the end of his professional career.

THOMAS, JUAN - 1B - BR - b: 4/17/72
Thomas spent five years in A-ball before reaching Double-A for the first time at the age of 25. He has decent power, having led his league in homers a couple of times. But, he has also led his league in strikeouts a couple of times, too. Thomas is a slow-footed first sacker who is below average with the glove. While the White Sox are probably pleased with his good batting average (.302) last year, his drop in power was a disappointment. After hitting 46 homers over the previous two years at Class A Prince William, he managed just 28 extra-base hits in 311 at-bats for Birmingham, while still fanning 92 times. Thomas is a one-dimensional player whose one dimension is fading. There's little chance he'll join that other Thomas in Chicago.

THOME, JIM - 3B - BL - b: 8/27/70
Scouting: Thome is one of the best all-around offensive players in the major leagues today. He combines superior plate discipline with a textbook swing capable of prodigious power. A previous weak link, his ability to hit lefthanded pitching, has seemingly been overcome. Problems with wild throws chased him across the diamond from third to first base in 1997. He is an intense player who leads by example.
1998: Thome has flirted with leading the league in all of the Triple Crown categories, and might finally break through in 1998. Over the past three seasons Thome's lowest OBP has been .423 and his lowest slugging average has been .558. That stamps him as the most productive offensive player not named Frank Thomas.
1997: The Indians became Thome's and Manny Ramirez's team after the disappearance of Albert Belle and Kenny Lofton. Thome led the club in nearly every offensive category, and had his first 40-homer season.
1996: Thome proved his 1995 breakout season was no fluke, hitting over .300 and exceeding all power hitting expectations. However, his struggles at third base intensified, leading the Indians to acquire Matt Williams during the off-season.

	AB	R	HR	RBI	SB	BA
1995 Cleveland	452	92	25	73	4	.314
1996 Cleveland	505	122	38	116	2	.311
1997 Cleveland	496	104	40	102	1	.286

THOMPSON, JASON - 1B - BL - b: 6/12/71
Squeezed out of the Padres' depth chart by the emergence of Derrek Lee as the heir apparent to succeed Wally Joyner at first base, Thompson went to Japan to play last year. Thompson passed the 20-homer mark twice in the high minors in the U.S. He hasn't added anything impressive to his credentials in Japan, except that we know he has now seen every type of breaking pitch.

THOMPSON, KARL - C - BR - b: 12/30/73
Thompson spent 1996 in the Midwest League and, after a start in A-ball in the California League, he spent most of 1997 at Double-A Memphis in the Mariners organization. At the plate, Thompson found the going tougher in Double-A and will get another crack at it in 1998.

THOMPSON, ROBBY - 2B - BR - b: 5/10/62
Despite not exceeding 336 at-bats or a .223 average since 1993, Thompson entered spring training in 1997 with a shot at the Indians' second base job. He was easily beaten out by Tony Fernandez, and sat out the 1997 season. His body has been broken down by a multitude of injuries, and his career has likely reached its end. Thompson might surface in someone's camp in 1998, but rates as the longest of longshots.

	AB	R	HR	RBI	SB	BA
1995 San Francisco	336	51	8	23	1	.223
1996 San Francisco	227	35	5	21	2	.211

THOMPSON, RYAN - OF - BR - b: 11/4/67
Scouting: Thompson is familiar to most Mets fans as a power-hitting outfield prospect who was once traded by the Blue Jays for David Cone (Jeff Kent also went to the Mets in that deal). He runs decently but strikes out too much to be any good. His skills have not improved much in the last five years and he is not projected as a long-term major leaguer.
1998: Thompson is trying to hang on. He has good power but has never made himself valuable enough for a team to give him a regular spot in the lineup. Because of expansion, he has a remote chance of landing in the big leagues this year. Anything more than a .240 average with occasional power would be surprising.
1997: He started the year with the Cleveland Indians organization before being picked up by the Blue Jays in June. Assigned to Triple-A Syracuse, Thompson responded with 16 home runs in 330 at-bats and a .288 average, at least enough to make expansion teams take notice.
1996: Thompson put up solid numbers at Triple-A Buffalo (including 21 home runs) and earned a brief appearance with the Indians, going 7-for-22 with Cleveland.

	AB	R	HR	RBI	SB	BA
1995 New York NL	267	39	7	31	3	.251
1996 Cleveland	22	2	1	5	0	.318

THURMAN, GARY - OF - BR - b: 11/12/64
A backup outfielder always on the fringe of the big leagues but never getting more than 200 at-bats in all or parts of nine major-league seasons, Thurman received just six at-bats in an eleven-game trial with the New York Mets earlier last season then was released out of Triple-A Norfolk. Montreal signed him as a free agent and he finished the year with Ottawa, playing poorly. Thurman is 34 years old and it appears all the sand has run through his hourglass.

THURSTON, JERRY - C - BR - b: 4/17/72
Thurston split time at catcher for Triple-A Vancouver of the Angels' organization in 1997. When he did play he showed no power and didn't make much contact, striking out 59 times in 195 at-bats. He may get another look in Triple-A to start the year but he hasn't hit better than .244 at any stop in his eight-year minor-league career.

TIMMONS, OZZIE - OF - BR - b: 9/18/70
A righthanded power hitter, Timmons doesn't do much else to help a team. The Reds gave him a nine at-bat trial after acquiring

him from the Cubs, then sent him to Triple-A where he struggled most of the year. At age 27, he is running out of time, but he could catch on as a fifth outfielder if he has a good spring.

	AB	R	HR	RBI	SB	BA
1995 Chicago NL	171	30	8	28	3	.263
1996 Chicago NL	140	18	7	16	1	.200

TINSLEY, LEE - OF - BB - b: 3/4/69
Scouting: Tinsley has some speed and a little pop, but he has never been able to hang onto a starting position despite repeated attempts in Boston, Philadelphia, and Seattle. His time has come ... and gone.
1998: Tinsley is a fifth outfielder, at best, in the majors and will probably have a hard time winning a full-time role in Triple-A.
1997: Brought into spring training to compete for a left field platoon, Tinsley suffered an early injury was never a factor. He did not get over the Mendoza line in more than 100 at-bats at either Seattle or Triple-A Tacoma.
1996: Sent to Philadelphia as part of the Heathcliff Slocumb deal, Tinsley was back in Beantown by mid-season when the Phillies gave up on him.

	AB	R	HR	RBI	SB	BA
1995 Boston	341	61	7	41	18	.284
1996 Philadelphia	52	1	0	2	2	.135
1996 Boston	192	28	3	14	6	.245
1997 Seattle	122	12	0	6	2	.197

TOLENTINO, JOSE - 1B - BL - b: 6/3/71
Tolentino, one of the top sluggers in the University of Texas' storied history, keeps rolling along. He tears up minor-league pitching but never gets a chance to prove he can hit in the majors. Tolentino finished last season as a first baseman and designated hitter with the Pirates' Triple-A Calgary farm club after being released by Baltimore out of Triple-A Rochester. Tolentino's lone major-league experience consists of a long-ago cup of coffee with Houston. It's a shame; he could have been a productive power hitter if someone would have just given him the chance.

TOMBERLIN, ANDY - OF - BL - b: 11/7/66
Noted for his unusual 1995 move from minor-league regular season play into the A's major league spring training camp (which started late because of the strike) when Tomberlin was in top physical condition and most major leaguers weren't, he has accumulated a career batting average of .237 with nine homers and 26 RBI in 236 major league at-bats. Tomberlin spent 1997 on the 60-day DL with a herniated disc in his neck; he didn't appear except for some brief rehab work in the low minors.

	AB	R	HR	RBI	SB	BA
1995 Oakland	85	15	4	10	4	.212
1996 New York NL	66	12	3	10	0	.258

TORRES, JAIME - C - BR - b: 3/12/73
A journeyman minor-league catcher with strong defensive skills and a fair bat, Torres took a step down last year because the Yankees wanted his pitcher-handling skill at Class A Tampa. After playing 100 games at Double-A in 1996, Torres hit .294 with ten homers and 56 RBI in 1997. But, he was in A-ball because of his ability to work with pitchers, not because he needed refinement of his batting skills.

TORRES, PAUL - OF/1B - BR - b: 10/19/70
Torres ripped Double-A pitching to a tune of a .344 average with six homers and 55 RBI, earning a promotion to Triple-A Tacoma in the Seattle organization in 1997. Torres has been in the minors since 1989 and last year was his first significant time at Triple-A. He has a little pop in his bat but little speed to go with it. He's a longshot to see the big leagues since he far too old to be a prospect, despite his torrid hitting.

TORRES, TONY - 2B/3B - BR - b: 6/1/70
Torres has been a deep reserve on the Marlins' upper minor-league clubs for the past three seasons. He is primarily a second baseman, but can fill in at the other infield spots as well. He is a steadying presence for the Marlins' parade of much younger, more talented middle-infield prospects. He keeps himself ready to play, usually provides a professional at-bat, runs the bases well, and is surehanded in the field. He's now 28 years old, and has little chance to play in the major leagues, but the original Marlin minor-leaguer has made a positive impression on most of the players and managers he has encountered.

TOTH, DAVE - C - BR - b: 12/8/69
At age 28 and having spent all of his playing days in the Braves' farm system, Toth appears to be heading toward a coaching career. He spent most of 1997 at Double-A Greenville and also took a few swings in Triple-A Richmond.

TOWLE, JUSTIN - C - BR - b: 2/21/74
Towle had his best minor-league season last year in his first season at Double-A. He had his highest batting average (.309) and hit for the most power (37 doubles in 418 at-bats). The Reds drafted Towle out of high school, so he's spent considerable time in their farm system, but it looks like he might finally be putting it all together. Towle is the Reds' only real catching prospect in the minor leagues, so he'll get plenty of chances to make the big leagues. He made good progress last season, but he's getting old for a real prospect (he'll be 24 on opening day) and he could find himself lost in the shuffle if he takes a step back this year.

TRAMMELL, BUBBA - OF - BR - b: 11/6/71
Scouting: Trammell's first chance at the big leagues didn't show his potential. If he emphasizes a line-drive stroke and doesn't try too hard to hit home runs, the power should come and Trammell could become a good big-league player. He needs to hit, because he has only average speed and isn't a good outfielder.
1998: Trammell went from a reserve with the Tigers to a probable starting role, when the Devil Rays drafted him. With a spring training anything like he had a year ago, Trammell will be in the opening day lineup again.
1997: The high point of Trammell's season might have come in spring training, when he hit his way onto the Tigers' opening day roster. He started struggling as soon as he made the team, and he only made it to May 11th before he was sent back to Triple-A. Once he got there, the Tigers were disappointed that he seemed to think too much about home runs.
1996: Trammell established himself as a prospect with a great first half at Double-A Jacksonville (.328, 27 home runs, 75 RBI in 83 games), then kept it going with a good second half at Triple-A Toledo. And he was named the co-MVP of the Arizona Fall League later that year.

	AB	R	HR	RBI	SB	BA
1997 Detroit	123	14	4	13	3	.228

TRAMMELL, GARY - OF - BL - b: 10/16/72
Trammell played at Double-A Jackson, his first year at that level, for the Houston organization in 1997. He didn't hit for any type of power and after four minor-league seasons in double figures in stolen bases, Trammell failed even to get one in 1997.

TREANOR, MATT - C - BR - b: 3/3/76
Treanor was acquired by the Marlins from the Royals for lefthanded pitcher Matt Whisenant late in 1997. He is a solid defensive receiver who has been slow to develop offensively. He has acceptable plate discipline, but has a slow bat and has not generated extra-base power. He's still relatively young, and continued refinement of his defensive skills could eventually land him in the majors as a backup assuming he experiences some offensive development.

TREDAWAY, CHAD - 2B - BB - b: 6/18/72
Scouting: Tredaway hits like a second baseman he was: lots of singles with occasional doubles power. He's got good hands and a good arm, but his future will be limited if he doesn't develop some power. Time is running out for Tredaway.
1998: Tredaway will return to Triple-A for another try at hitting Pacific Coast League pitching.
1997: Tredaway was a full-time third baseman at Triple-A Las Vegas, shifting over from second base to make room for Homer Bush. Tredaway was well below average among Pacific Coast League hitters. Most troubling was his increase in strikeouts, suggesting that Triple-A is as high as he'll go.
1996: Due to injuries in the Padres farm system, Tredaway advanced from A-ball to Triple-A ball and struggled both offensively and defensively.

TREMIE, CHRIS - C - BR - b: 10/17/69
After five years in the White Sox organization, including a brief stop at Comiskey in 1995, Tremie played last season at Double-A Reading in the Phillies' farm system. He has never been a hitter and 1997 was no different as Tremie batted .203 in 295 at-bats. At his age a return to the majors appears unlikely.

TUCKER, MICHAEL - OF - BL - b: 6/25/71
Scouting: Few lefthanded hitters have a quicker bat than Tucker; it was the reason the Braves wanted to acquire him in the first place. He generates surprising power and is able to pull almost any pitch. He is occasionally too aggressive at the plate, but he needs that style of hitting to succeed. Tucker is a below-average outfielder, possessing a weak arm and he hasn't made good use of his above-average speed on defense although he can steal some bases.
1998: The Braves want to get super-prospect Andruw Jones into their outfield mix and may have to put him into Tucker's right field spot occasionally if he isn't playing regularly in center field. Tucker will again hit for moderate power and speed, with a decent batting average; his aggressive hitting style is a good fit for the fastball-oriented pitching in the National League.
1997: Tucker appeared determined to show the Royals they had made a mistake when they traded him. He got off to a blazing start, hitting for average and power; he was flirting with .400 entering May. He came back to earth, of course, and finished the year splitting the right field job with Jones.
1996: Tucker again started slowly for the Royals. He regained his stroke at Triple-A Omaha when he stopped listening to then-batting coach Greg Luzinski and went back to his natural upper-cut swing. He returned to the Royals' lineup a more aggressive, determined hitter and was immediately successful, but a broken wrist ended his season late in August.

	AB	R	HR	RBI	SB	BA
1995 Kansas City	177	23	4	17	2	.260
1996 Kansas City	339	55	12	53	10	.260
1997 Atlanta	499	80	14	56	12	.283

TURNER, CHRIS - C - BR - b: 3/23/69
Scouting: Turner has increased his value because he can now play all infield and outfield corner positions, in addition to his accustomed catching duties, but he has yet to put everything together long enough to earn a serious look in the majors. He has hit well for average in spots, although he has never hit for power or played well defensively. Turner's versatility has kept him from slipping into career minor-leaguer status.
1998: Turner needs a solid spring in order to convince management he's worthy of an extended shot as a bench player in the major leagues. He's made good strides in handling pitchers and on defense, but he'll only go as far as his bat takes him.
1997: A severely sprained wrist limited Turner to only 37 games, although he did hit .370 in a limited opportunity. He earned a callup after Todd Greene went out with a broken wrist and did some good things defensively as he improved his ability to play at several different positions.
1996: Turner proved his value at Vancouver with his versatility, but had a mediocre year at the plate. He was designated for assignment and cleared waivers in April, then returned to the Canadians and played five different positions. A sprained ankle kept him from being called up early in September and he wound up playing just four games for the Angels.

TYLER, BRAD - 2B - BL - b: 3/3/69
Tyler could earn a job as a backup infielder in the majors, but falls short in a couple of categories. His range is short at second base, and he is too pull-conscious as a hitter. If he finds a manager who appreciates his lefthanded power potential off the bench, he could finally get the backup job he's been trying to earn for the last four years.

UNROE, TIM - 3B - BR - b: 10/7/70
Scouting: Unroe is versatile as a first baseman, third baseman and outfielder. He has shown some pop in the minors and has hit for average. But, he has not gotten enough of a chance at the major league level to show what he can do.
1998: The Brewers have told Unroe to look elsewhere if he can hook on with another team. But, he also was told that in 1997 and stayed with the organization.
1997: Unroe was told by the Brewers in the spring he was no longer in their plans, but then he spent a substantial stretch of the season with them. His versatility helped him stick with the club.
1996: Unroe hit for a good average and showed some power at Triple-A. That earned him three callups by the Brewers, but he saw only limited action and didn't produce.

VALDES, PEDRO - OF - BL - b: 6/29/73
Scouting: Valdes is a good hitter, but lacks enough power to hit in the heart of the order and doesn't have enough speed to hit at the top of the lineup. He is a good outfielder, although he lacks a particularly strong throwing arm.
1998: Valdes likely will wind up on someone's opening day

roster. If it's in Chicago, he won't be a starter, at least not at the beginning. The Cubs have several outfielders waiting in line for a chance to start and Valdes is third or fourth in line, at best. He would have value as a fifth outfielder and pinch-hitter, though.
1997: Valdes spent the entire season at Triple-A Iowa and had another good year, hitting .284 with 45 extra-base hits in 464 at-bats. If nothing else he showed that he doesn't have much left to prove in the minors and that he deserves a big-league roster spot.
1996: Valdes spent most of the year at Iowa, but did get brief experience with the Cubs. His 15 home runs nearly doubled his previous high total and he led Iowa in hits and runs scored.

VALDEZ, MARIO - 1B - BL - b: 11/19/74

Scouting: Valdez has gotten a lot of attention recently but may be in over his head in the majors. He advanced quickly through the White Sox farm system and some question if he has enough bat speed to hit major league fastballs. He does have good plate discipline although his power is merely line-drive, gap power; it won't translate well to the majors. Valdez was impressive around the first base bag in his short major league trial last year.
1998: Despite the hype, Valdez may not be ready to take over the first base job for Chicago just yet. More time at Triple-A could help him handle hard stuff better. Valdez will get a long look early next year as the White Sox regular first sacker.
1997: Valdez batted .280 with 15 homers and 61 RBI in his first trip to Triple-A Nashville. He showed the Sox enough all-around hitting and good first base defense to earn his first big-league promotion, but he was used sparingly.
1996: Valdez earned an aggressive in-season promotion from lower Class A South Bend to Double-A Birmingham based upon a .376 average with good power and patience at the plate. He was less impressive in 51 games at Birmingham but still finished with one of the best minor-league seasons in the White Sox' organization.

	AB	R	HR	RBI	SB	BA
1997 Chicago AL	115	11	1	13	1	.243

VALENTIN, JAVIER - C - BB - b: 9/19/75

The future of the Twins behind the plate, Valentin is the younger brother of Milwaukee shortstop Jose Valentin and has all of the tools to catch in the big leagues one day. He is stronger defensively than offensively. His bat was disappointing at Double-A New Britain in 1997, where he hit just .243 with eight homers and 50 RBI. He already has played on a couple of minor-league All-Star teams.

VALENTIN, JOHN - SS - BR - b: 2/18/67

Scouting: Valentin loves to hit and finds a way to be successful at it every season. He is less pull-conscious than he was, and he doesn't cream the fastball as he did a couple of years ago, but he is a dangerous hitter and a tough out. He can be lazy in the field, failing to get in front of grounders, and probably could be in better shape, but he has a good arm and usually has excellent hands. His speed is all but gone.
1998: Though he would love a long-term deal, Valentin will most likely be playing his last season for the Red Sox. There's no reason he shouldn't post another strong season with the bat. However, his body seems to be aging quickly and his fielding will probably drop off over the next couple of years.
1997: Though he resisted the shift from shortstop, it helped Valentin, who probably has aged and grown out of the position. He didn't take well to second, though, as he has lost some quickness over the years. However, when moved to third after a season-ending injury to Tim Naehring, Valentin found his new home.
1996: Valentin, bothered by a shoulder injury, had trouble duplicating the power he showed the season before, but he plugged away and had his third straight strong season with the bat.

	AB	R	HR	RBI	SB	BA
1995 Boston	520	108	27	102	20	.298
1996 Boston	527	84	13	59	9	.296
1997 Boston	575	95	18	77	7	.306

VALENTIN, JOSE - SS - BB - b: 10/12/69

Scouting: Valentin has decent power from the left side and has improved his average from the right side. He still can be inconsistent at the plate and at shortstop. He makes some outstanding plays in the field, but can lack concentration on routine plays. Milwaukee manager Phil Garner likes Valentin's instincts for the game.
1998: The Brewers have signed Valentin to a long-term contract and hope he develops into one of the team's stars. Some think he would be better in the outfield, where he has played in winter ball, but he likely will remain at shortstop.
1997: Valentin missed part of the early season with a hand injury and did not put up the power stats he showed in '96. He had a bad strikeout-to-walk ratio of 109-to-39. He did reduce his errors from 37 to 20.
1996: Valentin set career highs in all offensive categories and surprised a lot of people with his power. While he impressed people on offense, he committed 37 errors.

	AB	R	HR	RBI	SB	BA
1995 Milwaukee	338	62	11	49	16	.219
1996 Milwaukee	552	90	24	95	17	.259
1997 Milwaukee	494	58	17	58	19	.253

VALLE, DAVE - C - BR - b: 10/30/60

The Braves brought Valle to Triple-A in '97 as insurance at the catcher position. But his heart and body weren't into it and he retired a month into the season, just before Eddie Perez was injured and his services may have been called upon. Valle's age and declining physical abilities make a comeback unlikely.

	AB	R	HR	RBI	SB	BA
1995 two teams	75	7	0	5	1	.240
1996 Texas	86	14	3	17	0	.302

VALRIE, KERRY - OF - BR - b: 10/31/68

Valrie has spent each of his eight pro seasons in the minors. After seven seasons in the White Sox chain he spent 1997 at Triple-A Ottawa in the Expos organization. He was used in a reserve role and hit just .221. Valrie doesn't have a major league future.

VANDER WAL, JOHN - 1B/OF - BL - b: 4/29/66

Scouting: A pure lefthanded hitter whose success off the bench may have been a curse in 1997, VanderWal set a major-league record in 1995 with 28 pinch-hits in a 144-game season. So good was VanderWal that manager Don Baylor rarely gave him a chance to play, opting instead to save him for a possible key moment late in the game. His stroke became rusty and VanderWal finished 1997 with a poor average. If he played everyday, he could probably hit .300 with 20 homers. He does not run well. He

is an adequate outfielder and first baseman, though again, inactivity has made it difficult for him to maintain his defensive skills.
1998: VanderWal is in the final year of his contract, and will once again be used as the team's top lefthanded pinch-hitter.
1997: He never got it going. VanderWal was going so bad, he did not refuse a July 31st assignment to Triple-A Colorado Springs, as would have been his contractual right. Instead, VanderWal relished the opportunity to play everyday and hit .408 with 16 extra-base hits in 25 games for the Sky Sox. He returned a month later and helped the Rockies win a game at Atlanta with a three-run, pinch-hit homer off John Smoltz.
1996: After his sensational 1995 season, VanderWal discovered that opposing managers would not let him beat them. VanderWal's announced appearance often prompted a change to a lefthanded pitcher. He still delivered three pinch-hit homers, including a dramatic, game-ending three-run homer off Dennis Eckersley.

	AB	R	HR	RBI	SB	BA
1995 Colorado	101	15	5	21	1	.347
1996 Colorado	151	20	5	31	2	.252
1997 Colorado	92	7	1	11	1	.174

VARITEK, JASON - C - BB - b: 4/11/72
Scouting: Varitek, Baseball America's 1993 Collegiate Player of the Year and a member of that publication's all-time college All-Star team, has been slow to develop after wrangling over a signing bonus that cost him the 1994 season. He has good power and receiving skills but is still learning the strike zone.
1998: Varitek was expected to move into the mix for Boston's starting catching position after being acquired in the waiver-wire deadline trade that sent Heathcliff Slocumb to the Mariners.
1997: Varitek hit a career-high 15 homers but still struck out about once every four at-bats at Triple-A Tacoma before the trade, after which he struggled.
1996: Varitek had good power numbers — 34 doubles, 12 homers, 67 RBI —in his second year in Double-A.

VAUGHN, GREG - OF/DH - BR - b: 7/3/65
Scouting: The Padres would love to move Vaughn, but at $11 million over the next two years there are few takers — even in an expansion year. He played left field and ran better than expected, but has been a major disappointment at the plate for the Padres. Vaughn is a bust in the National League thus far.
1998: Either Vaughn or Ruben Rivera figure to be the Padres every day left fielder.
1997: Vaughn made a late-season rush after adding contact lenses. Still, he only hit just with .215 with runners in scoring position. His 110 strikeouts in 361 at-bats counter-balanced his home run production.
1996: Vaughn's season totals were good. But he had most of his production for Milwaukee before coming to Padres in trade for Marc Newfield, Bryce Florie and Ron Villone. As a Padre, Vaughn hit .206 with ten homers and 22 RBI, and hit only .125 with runners in scoring position.

	AB	R	HR	RBI	SB	BA
1995 Milwaukee	392	67	17	59	10	.224
1996 Milwaukee	375	78	31	95	5	.280
1996 San Diego	141	20	10	22	4	.206
1997 San Diego	361	60	18	57	7	.216

VAUGHN, MO - 1B - BL - b: 12/25/67
Scouting: Vaughn is one of the top hitters in the game, with few weaknesses, and has shown no signs of slowing down in that regard. However, he does carry too much weight and he suffered a knee injury last year which cost him 20 games. His defense, never great, is also hurt by his poor conditioning.
1998: There's no reason Vaughn shouldn't post another great offensive season. The only concern is a possible trade. Vaughn is in the last season of his contract and there is some concern that he might not re-sign with the Red Sox because of a growing rift with General Manager Dan Duquette, and therefore that Boston may deal him before the season is over.
1997: Vaughn's final totals were not as impressive as his previous two seasons because of the missed games due to injury. But he was just as effective as a hitter as he had been the last few years.
1996: Vaughn responded to his MVP season of '95 with perhaps an even better season statistically.

	AB	R	HR	RBI	SB	BA
1995 Boston	550	98	39	126	11	.300
1996 Boston	635	118	44	143	2	.326
1997 Boston	527	91	35	96	2	.315

VELANDIA, JORGE - SS - BR - b: 1/12/75
Scouting: The book on Velandia is that he's a slick-fielding shortstop who could have trouble at the plate in the major leagues. But he also struggled in the field in two cameo appearances with the Padres in '97, looking timid at times. Velandia is a fringe major leaguer.
1998: Velandia was given a long look at the end of last season at shortstop as the Padres tinkered with idea of leaving Chris Gomez unprotected for the expansion draft. Velandia's audition did not go well, but he could still be the Padres shortstop in '98.
1997: He didn't impress at the plate with the Padres or that much in field, either. Velandia hit .272 at Triple-A Las Vegas with little pop.
1996: Velandia showed some signs of offensive spark at Double-A Memphis with a .240 average and nine homers for 48 RBI.

VELARDE, RANDY - OF/SS - BR - b: 11/24/62
Scouting: This veteran infielder is solid, offensively and defensively. After excelling in Yankee Stadium as a utility player, Velarde proved he could produce as an everyday player when the Angels signed him as a free agent in 1996 and gave him the job at second base. Velarde's the kind of veteran player every organization needs to round out the club. He may not be a star — or even a starter — but he's the kind of solid all-around player no club can win without.
1998: Although he missed the entire 1997 season (except for one pinch-running appearance) because of an elbow injury, the second base job is his — if he's healthy. The Angels expect Velarde to pick up where he left off in 1996.
1997: An ill-fated stint in the outfield in an exhibition game against Milwaukee resulted in a torn medial collateral ligament in his right elbow when Velarde made a strong throw to home plate. Surgery at the end of spring ended his season before it began.
1996: Velarde set career bests in all offensive categories as he played in a career-high 136 games as an everyday player for the first time in his career. Velarde showed surprising power and played the same solid defense that characterized his eight previous seasons in New York.

	AB	R	HR	RBI	SB	BA
1995 New York AL	367	60	7	46	5	.278
1996 California	530	82	14	54	7	.285
1997 Anaheim	Did Not Play - Injured					

VELAZQUEZ, EDGARD - OF - BR - b: 12/15/75

Scouting: The nephew of the late, great Roberto Clemente, Velazquez figures to one day make his family proud. He plays right field but does not have his uncle's arm or reckless abandon. Then again, who does? At age 22, Velazquez already has a full Triple-A season behind him. At present, he's a three-plus-tool player. He can hit, field, and throw, and may develop 25-homer power. Like most young players, he struggles with off-speed pitches. Though he has good speed, he has never picked up more than nine stolen bases in any of his five minor-league seasons. At 5'11" and 190 pounds, he is thicker than Clemente, but management is concerned about his commitment. It seems he doesn't come ready to play every day, perhaps one reason why he was not among the September callups.

1998: He'll return to Triple-A Colorado Springs for a second straight season. If he gets off to a fast start and there's an injury to a starting Rockies' outfielder, Velazquez will be considered for a promotion.

1997: Velazquez continued his steady climb up the organizational ladder by reaching Triple-A at age 21. He held his own, batting .281 with 17 homers and 73 RBI. He moved from center field, where he had played most of his life, to right field.

1996: He got off to a torrid start at Double-A New Haven, hitting seven homers during one ten-game stretch in April. It was the first time Velazquez showed he could develop into a legitimate power hitter.

VENTURA, ROBIN - 3B - BL - b: 7/14/67

Scouting: Ventura is one of the game's steadiest players. He always hits for a decent average and above-average power, displays a sharp batting eye and rarely goes through prolonged slumps. He's a Gold Glove fielder at the hot corner with an accurate arm.

1998: Ventura should return to full strength and have another year as one of the better all-around third basemen in baseball. He'll have an important role for the White Sox. Ventura is the emotional center of the club and in the prime of his career; expect a big rebound season.

1997: Ventura's spring training ankle fracture sent the whole team into a nose-dive and set the tone for a dismal season for the White Sox. The injury cost him 350 at-bats and by the time Ventura returned after the All-Star break the White Sox were already spiraling out of the pennant race. When he returned he was the same as he has always been, hitting for average with some power and fine defense.

1996: It was another solid season for Ventura as he again hit for a good average and set career highs in homers and RBI. He won his fourth Gold Glove with outstanding defensive work and was a steadying influence on and off the field.

	AB	R	HR	RBI	SB	BA
1995 Chicago AL	492	79	26	93	4	.295
1996 Chicago AL	586	96	34	105	1	.287
1997 Chicago AL	183	27	6	26	0	.262

VERAS, QUILVIO - 2B - BB - b: 4/3/71

Scouting: It may be surprising, but Veras is not overly fast, despite his stolen base crown in 1995. He's still a better-than-average baserunner. The Padres got him from Florida as leadoff successor to Rickey Henderson. Veras needs to find ways to reach base more to master the leadoff job. At times, Veras displays excellent bat control, but he is erratic. As a second baseman, he gets to a lot of tough balls, but makes costly mental errors around the bag.

1998: The Padres are counting on him to trigger their offense. He'll be their regular second baseman again and leadoff hitter; they hope he'll improve his on-base ability to provide more RBI opportunities for Steve Finley, Tony Gwynn and Ken Caminiti.

1997: Veras blew hot and cold all year. He hit only .194 from his more natural righthand side. Veras' on-base percentage of .357 was low for a leadoff man as were his steals and runs scored.

1996: The Padres gave up former first-round draft choice Dustin Hermanson to aquire Veras from Marlins — who had all but given up on the injury-plagued (hamstring) Veras. After a marginal start with Marlins, Veras hit .327 at Triple-A.

	AB	R	HR	RBI	SB	BA
1995 Florida	440	86	5	32	56	.261
1996 Florida	253	40	4	14	8	.253
1997 San Diego	539	74	3	45	33	.265

VESSEL, ANDREW - OF - BR - b: 3/11/75

A couple of years ago, Vessel was considered the Rangers' best hitting prospect. Two rather ordinary years later, Vessel still has a chance to reclaim the prospect label, but it will take better results than he has produced to date. Vessel has good raw skills, but hasn't shown the inclination to do much with them. He hit .261 in his first Double-A season last year with 12 home runs, and was second on the team with 75 RBI.

VIDRO, JOSE - 3B - BB - b: 8/27/74

Scouting: Vidro has shown power throughout his time in the Expos' organization but has yet to settle on a position. He started off as a shortstop, then moved to second base, where he has yet to settle as Montreal has also tried him at third base and in the outfield.

1998: The Expos are going with a low payroll and Vidro fits right in. With Shane Andrews out until at least mid-season because of reconstructive shoulder surgery, Vidro figures to battle Doug Strange for the starting third baseman's job. The Expos will likely lean to Vidro because of his youth and power potential.

1997: Vidro got off to a hot start at Triple-A Ottawa and then spent the final four months in Montreal. He got sporadic playing time and was inconsistent. He did drive in some big runs as a pinch-hitter in September, including one that severely damaged Pittsburgh's hopes of a National League Central title.

1996: Vidro showed good power at Double-A Harrisburg but was not placed on the Expos' 40-man roster. Somewhat surprisingly, he was not taken in the Rule 5 Draft despite interest from a handful of teams.

	AB	R	HR	RBI	SB	BA
1997 Montreal	169	19	2	17	1	.249

VINA, FERNANDO - 2B - BL - b: 4/16/69

Scouting: Seen as a utilityman only a couple seasons ago, Vina has developed into a good second baseman in Milwaukee. He is one of the quickest at turning the double play. At the plate, he sprays the ball to all fields and can turn on a pitch for an occasional homer. He has a tendency to go after the first pitch and not be selective.

1998: Vina has signed a long-term contract and is seen as the regular second baseman in 1998.

1997: Vina broke his ankle early in the season and missed three months. When he was healthy, he provided a spark in the leadoff spot. His .312 on-base percentage was one of the lowest among leadoff hitters in the league, however, and manager Phil Garner wants him to work on his selectivity at the plate.

1996: He appeared in a career-high 140 games and set career-highs in every offensive category. He also set a club record by being hit by a pitch 13 times.

	AB	R	HR	RBI	SB	BA
1995 Milwaukee	288	46	3	29	6	.257
1996 Milwaukee	554	94	7	46	16	.283
1997 Milwaukee	324	37	4	28	8	.275

VINAS, JULIO - C - BR - b: 2/14/73

Vinas is far down the White Sox' depth chart at catcher. He has never hit much and has only marginal power. He's not a spectacular defensive backstop, either. In 1997, Vinas spent his second full year at Triple-A Nashville and enjoyed a decent season with the bat while splitting the catching duties with Robert Machado and Rick Wrona. Vinas hit eleven homers and drove in 41 runs but batted just .232 and struck out a fifth of the time with rather poor on-base ability. Vinas is not a prospect.

VITIELLO, JOE - 1B/OF - BR - b: 4/11/70

Scouting: Despite his size (6'3", 230 pounds), Vitiello is a line-drive hitter who has frequently posted a high batting average; he won the American Association batting crown by hitting .344 for Omaha in 1994. His professional career has been beset by serious knee injuries. Vitiello was once able to play in the outfield, but is now relegated to a first base or designated hitter role; he just can't run any more. He has worked hard to improve his power in recent years, in anticipation of a pinch-hitting, reserve first-baseman role in the majors.

1998: Vitiello will battle for a major league bench role. A return to full health would be a necessary part of winning the job, but he also has to show occasional power to stay in the majors. It's been an uphill battle for Vitiello and will likely remain so. Just staying healthy all year would be a victory for Vitiello in 1998.

1997: Vitiello was a disaster in a brief right field stint in Kansas City. He put on occasional power displays but was mostly relegated to a bench job before losing the rest of the season to July arthroscopic surgery on his knee.

1996: As a part-time DH for Kansas City, Vitiello displayed some RBI ability. He was struggling at mid-season, got demoted to Triple-A Omaha, then returned to the majors in August with a much improved bat. It was his longest major league stint and put him in line for a more important role the next season.

	AB	R	HR	RBI	SB	BA
1995 Kansas City	130	13	7	21	0	.254
1996 Kansas City	257	29	8	40	2	.241
1997 Kansas City	130	11	5	18	0	.238

VIZCAINO, JOSE - SS/3B/2B - BB - b: 3/26/68

Scouting: Vizcaino, who never really gets his legs into his swing, is not much of a power hitter nor is he particularly patient. He is a switch hitter, who hits righthanders (.273 in 1997) better than lefties (.240), and though he can handle a fastball, he can't do much with off-speed stuff. He is a solid, if unspectacular middle infielder, and he has good speed, though he isn't a great baserunner.

1998: The shortstop job in Los Angeles belongs to Vizcaino, a player who manned that spot for the Mets at one time. Vizcaino is really a steady player, so it's reasonable to expect production similar to his 1997 totals, which are pretty much in line with his career numbers.

1997: Acquired as part of the blockbuster Matt Williams trade, the arrival of Vizcaino signaled some real stability up the middle for the Giants last year. He is a hard worker who fit in well with the re-vamped Giants.

1996: Vizcaino earned a starting job with the Mets in 1996, on the strength of his surprising 1995 campaign, but with Rey Ordonez ready for the majors, Vizcaino had to slide over to second base. With the arrival of Edgardo Alfonzo, he slid over to Cleveland, where he made solid contributions to their pennant drive.

	AB	R	HR	RBI	SB	BA
1995 New York NL	509	66	3	56	8	.287
1996 New York NL	363	47	1	32	9	.303
1996 Cleveland	179	23	0	13	6	.285
1997 San Francisco	568	77	5	50	8	.266

VIZQUEL, OMAR - SS - BB - b: 4/24/67

Scouting: Once a slick fielder who was a near automatic out at the plate, Vizquel has evolved into one of the best all-around shortstops in the game. Though his once remarkable range may have slipped a notch, Vizquel is the most sure-handed of baseball's many acrobatic shortstops, and also has a strong arm. The switch-hitter has learned to spray the ball to all fields from both sides of the plate with little power. His solid plate discipline makes him a viable number two hitter who wouldn't embarrass himself as a leadoff man. He has above-average speed and has developed impeccable basestealing form.

1998: Vizquel is locked in for the long haul in Cleveland. While the juggernaut assembled around him has been dissembled, Vizquel has been a constant.

1997: Vizquel became even more valuable to the Indians as they changed their style of offensive play in 1997, relying on "little ball" more often. Vizquel's bunting, stealing and bat control skills put him squarely in the middle of many rallies, while his glove again anchored the infield defense.

1996: Vizquel posted what will likely be seen as his best year, recording career highs in runs, hits, batting average, doubles, homers, RBI and steals. The Indians realized his value and inked him to a long-term deal.

	AB	R	HR	RBI	SB	BA
1995 Cleveland	542	87	6	56	29	.266
1996 Cleveland	542	98	9	64	35	.297
1997 Cleveland	565	89	5	49	43	.280

VOIGT, JACK - OF - BR - b: 5/17/66

Scouting: This journeyman might have revived his career in 1997. Voigt showed some pop at the plate and played both infield and outfield in Milwaukee. He is an adequate defensive player at several positions.

1998: Voigt played well enough in spot roles that the Brewers would be interested in bringing him back again for a spot on their bench. His ability to hit for power as a pinch-hitter and play several different defensive positions is a useful commodity on a major league bench.

1997: Voigt was called up from the minors when the Brewers had injury problems and might have saved his career. Nineteen of his 37 hits were for extra bases and many came at important points in ballgames.

1996: Voigt spent most of the season at two Triple-A venues: Charlotte and Oklahoma City; he hit 21 homers with 80 RBI for Oklahoma City. Voigt appeared in only five major league games for the Rangers and signed with the Brewers as a minor-league free agent after the season.

	AB	R	HR	RBI	SB	BA
1997 Milwaukee	151	20	8	22	1	.245

WACHTER, DEREK - OF - BR - b: 8/28/70
Wachter advanced from Double-A to Triple-A in 1997 in the Milwaukee farm system. He put the ball in play at both minor-league stops but didn't show any power potential. After missing 1996 it was a nice bounce-back season for Wachter but he doesn't seem to be a big-league outfield prospect.

WALBECK, MATT - C - BB - b: 10/2/69
Scouting: A good backup catcher, Walbeck has never produced enough offensively to be a top starter. Even last year, when he hit a career-high .277, Walbeck drove in just ten runs in 137 at-bats. He's a good, but not dominating, defensive player.
1998: Walbeck always figures to have a job, because catchers who have proven they can play in the big leagues aren't easy to find. He may have to move around, because teams often think they can do better.
1997: The Tigers acquired Walbeck as part of their two-headed attempt (with Brian Johnson) to give Raul Casanova another year to develop in the minors. Walbeck broke a bone in his wrist in mid-April, giving Casanova a chance to become the regular. Then the Tigers decided on Walbeck over Johnson as the backup, and eventually traded Johnson to San Francisco, where he become a late-season savior.
1996: In his second and final year with the Twins, Walbeck played regularly. He missed the first couple of months because of a stress fracture of the right hamate bone, but eventually came back and took over as the starter. The Twins traded him to the Tigers after the season, once they had signed Terry Steinbach as a free agent.

	AB	R	HR	RBI	SB	BA
1995 Minnesota	393	40	1	44	3	.257
1996 Minnesota	215	25	2	24	3	.223
1997 Detroit	137	18	3	10	3	.277

WALKER, DANE - 2B - BL - b: 11/16/69
Not great, not bad: Walker did his job at Double-A Huntsville last year. He has a good eye (68 walks), but not a lot of power, or much of anything else to grab one's attention. And there are so many better middle infielders ahead of him that he stands little chance of playing in an Oakland uniform.

WALKER, LARRY - OF - BL - b: 12/1/66
Scouting: Walker was simply the best player in baseball the past season. A legitimate five-tool player, Walker has enormous power to all fields. He hit for a high average in 1997 mainly because he demonstrated more patience at the plate (78 walks) and utilized the opposite field. He may be the most instinctive player in the game. Walker has great speed, belying his 6'3", 225-pound frame. He is a daring runner but is rarely caught. He's also a Gold Glove right fielder. Though he still has a strong, accurate arm, shoulder injuries in recent years have robbed of some velocity. Walker can fall into funks of impatience when he chases breaking balls out of the strike zone.
1998: Coming off his career-best season, Walker will return to right field at Coors Field and bat third.
1997: Walker was a leading candidate to become the Rockies' first National League Most Valuable Player. After being plagued by injuries most of his career, Walker played in a career-best 153 games last season. As late as July 17th, the 96th game of the season, Walker's average was above .400 (at .402); he finished at second to Tony Gwynn in the batting crown race, led the league in homers and was third in RBI. Walker led the senior circuit in slugging percentage and on-base percentage.
1996: Moved to center field for the first time in his career, Walker was out of position. The experiment failed as he was never comfortable in center and it seemed to affect his hitting, too. Though he was leading the National League in homers through most of the first two months, he struggled to hit for average. His season was nearly finished on June ninth, when he ran into the center field wall and fractured his left collarbone.

	AB	R	HR	RBI	SB	BA
1995 Colorado	494	96	36	101	16	.306
1996 Colorado	272	58	18	58	18	.276
1997 Colorado	568	143	49	130	33	.366

WALKER, SHON - OF - BL - b: 6/9/74
Scouting: Ward is a solid reserve outfield. He is a switch-hitter with decent power and speed, and adequately mans all three outfield spots.
1998: Ward was eligible for arbitration after last year. If his salary demands weren't outrageous, the Pirates were ready to welcome him back with open arms. He would again serve as a reserve outfielder and pinch-hitter.
1997: The Pirates rescued Ward off the scrap heap and he became a key player for them in their unlikely and unsuccessful bid to beat out Houston in the National League Central. Ward went to minor-league spring training with the Chicago White Sox, hopeful of catching the eyes of scouts from Japan. However, Ward wasn't able to cut a deal overseas and was released on the last day of spring training. The Pirates signed him as a free agent for Triple-A Calgary in late-April and he was promoted to the majors July 4th. He had an outstanding season as a role player, even starting ten straight games in center field in late-September as struggling Jermaine Allensworth was benched.
1996: Ward served as a reserve outfielder for Milwaukee, though his season was curtailed by chronic shoulder problems that led to reconstructive surgery.

WALKER, TODD - 3B/2B - BL - b: 5/25/73
Scouting: One of the best pure hitters to come out of the college game in quite some time, Walker struggled upon reaching the major leagues early in 1997. His bat is good enough, though, that it is just a matter of time until he starts racking up impressive numbers. He won't be a 30-home run hitter, but he will hit for average and display gap power with the ability to go deep on occasion. Defensively, Walker has split time between second and third base. He's more comfortable at second although he needs work at both.
1998: Expect this to be Walker's breakout year after he got his feet wet in 1997. He won't have the concerns about his defense that he did last year, which will allow him to concentrate fully on what will earn him fame and money in the future: Swinging the bat.
1997: He entered the year as an American League Rookie of the Year candidate but fell so low he was dispatched to Triple-A Salt

Lake by the end of May. By then, he was batting only .194 — and only .107 with runners in scoring position. He is smooth and polished, but his poor start even had Walker doubting himself.
1996: Walker prepared for his major-league coming out party by batting .339 with 28 homers and 111 RBI at Salt Lake. He was called up to Minnesota at the end of the season after the Twins traded Dave Hollins to make room for him.

	AB	R	HR	RBI	SB	BA
1996 Minnesota	82	8	0	6	2	.256
1997 Minnesota	156	15	3	16	7	.237

WALTON, JEROME - OF - BR - b: 7/8/65
Scouting: Walton's best asset is his base-stealing speed, although he doesn't have a high success rate. His hitting peaked in 1989 when he was rookie-of-the-year, declining to a weak .219 in 1991, and back up to the .290 area in 1995 and '96. He doesn't have much power, but still pops an occasional homer. He's a good fielder, but doesn't have a strong arm. He's been fragile physically in recent years, spending a lot time on the disabled list. Walton's best role is as a reserve outfielder, late-inning defensive replacement, pinch-runner and pinch-hitter.
1998: Walton has some talents that some major league teams can use. The Orioles outfield and DH slots are congested with veterans and talented rookies, so Walton's best opportunity may be with another team.
1997: Signed by the Orioles, Walton was a reserve outfielder. He had some serious injuries which put him on the disabled list nearly all year.
1996: Walton was with Atlanta in an injury-filled year getting only 47 at-bats.

	AB	R	HR	RBI	SB	BA
1995 Cincinnati	162	32	8	22	10	.290
1996 Atlanta	47	9	1	4	0	.340
1997 Baltimore	68	8	3	9	0	.294

WARD, DARYLE - 1B - BR - b: 6/27/75
Scouting: Ward is a left-handed power-hitting first baseman in the style of Mo Vaughn. The son of former major leaguer Gary Ward was obtained from Detroit with Brad Ausmus in the trade involving Todd Jones and Brian Hunter. He immediately became one of the top hitting prospects in the Astro organization. In his three years in the Tiger system, his power was not commensurate with his 6' 2", 240-pound frame but it showed strong development in 1997. He makes good contact for a power hitter, striking out in less than 20% of his at-bats while hitting .297 for his minor-league career.
1998: Ward will probably spend a full season at Triple-A New Orleans. He should be ready for the major leagues in 1999 but he would appear to be blocked by Jeff Bagwell.
1997: Ward was an All-Star at Double-A Jackson, hitting .329 with 19 home runs and 90 RBI in 422 at-bats. His .524 slugging average and a .398 on-base average were also impressive. His success continued when he moved up to Triple-A New Orleans, batting .378 with two home runs in 45 at-bats.
1996: Ward spent most of the season at High Class A Lakeland where he hit .291 with ten homers and 68 RBI in 464 at-bats.

WARD, TURNER - OF - BB - b: 4/11/65
Scouting: Ward is a solid reserve outfielder. He is a switch-hitter with decent power and speed, and adequately mans all three outfield spots.
1998: Ward was eligible for arbitration after last year. If his salary demands weren't outrageous, the Pirates were ready to welcome him back with open arms. He would again serve as a reserve outfielder and pinch-hitter.
1997: The Pirates rescued Ward off the scrap heap and he became a key player for them in their unlikely and unsuccessful bid to beat out Houston in the National League Central. Ward went to minor-league spring training with the Chicago White Sox, hopeful of catching the eyes of scouts from Japan. However, Ward wasn't able to cut a deal overseas and was released on the last day of spring training. The Pirates signed him as a free agent for Triple-A Calgary in late-April and he was promoted to the majors July 4th. He had an outstanding season as a role player, even starting ten straight games in center field in late-September as struggling Jermaine Allensworth was benched.
1996: Ward served as a reserve outfielder for Milwaukee, though his season was curtailed by chronic shoulder problems that led to reconstructive surgery.

	AB	R	HR	RBI	SB	BA
1995 Milwaukee	129	19	4	16	6	.264
1996 Milwaukee	67	7	2	10	3	.179
1997 Pittsburgh	167	33	7	33	4	.353

WARNER, MIKE - OF - BL - b: 5/9/71
Warner has good on-base skills, but his physical skills are short for a big-league center fielder. He's not strong or quick enough. It's possible someone might look at his ability to get on base (he hit .320 with 61 walks in 303 Double-A at-bats for a .432 on-base percentage in 1997), and give him a chance at Triple-A or higher, but his chances of having a substantial major league career are small.

WARNER, RON - 1B/3B/SS - BR - b: 12/2/68
After spending three years at Double-A, Warner finally made it to Triple-A on the Cardinals' farm in 1997. For Louisville he hit .232 with seven home runs and 30 RBI in 276 at-bats. Warner is a good defensive player, versatile around the infield, but he can't hit well enough to play at the major league level — except perhaps as a defensive reserve.

WASZGIS, BJ - C - BR - b: 8/24/70
Waszgis was the Orioles Triple-A catcher last year. He was passed over when they needed help in Baltimore. He has a decent bat with some power, and he's improving his defense. Waszgis isn't a prospect.

WATHAN, DUSTY - C - BB - b: 8/22/73
John's son Dusty hit A-ball pitching well and advanced to Double-A Memphis in the Seattle organization. Wathan's hitting fell off at the next level, but his defense and strong arm remain first rate. He'll start the 1998 season back at Double-A and is considered a good catching prospect.

WATKINS, PAT - OF - BR - b: 9/2/72
Watkins made some progress in 1997, with a decent season at Triple-A Indianapolis. He is too old to be considered a great prospect, and his strikezone judgment is a major weakness. In the past he has shown flashes of power and speed, but did not show much of either last season. Thanks to Reds cost cutting, he could catch on as a fifth outfielder if he has a good spring.

WAWRUCK, JIM - OF - BL - b: 4/23/70

Wawruck has good speed in the outfield but a weak arm which hinders his shot at the majors because he can't play all of the outfield positions. He has been in the Orioles' organization for all of his seven minor-league seasons, spending 1997 at Triple-A Rochester. A singles hitter who has always hit for a decent average, Wawruck may have a shot at a reserve outfield role.

WEBSTER, LENNY - C - BR - b: 2/10/65

Scouting: Webster's best role is as a backup catcher. He's a better hitter than the statistics show, especially in the clutch. His defensive is above average, and he hustles, diving for foul balls all over the place. He has the plodding speed typical of many catchers.

1998: With his solid play and hustle in 1997, Webster earned a permanent job as the Orioles backup catcher. The Orioles rookie catching prospects are thin, so he's not under much competitive pressure. He is Scott Erickson's preferred catcher, so he gets a starting assignment every five days. Starting catcher Chris Hoiles has a poor arm, giving Webster more playing time as an occasional defensive replacement.

1997: Webster took over the starting job when Hoiles was injured, and he's also Erickson's personal catcher providing additional starts. It was the first year that he got more than 200 at-bats. He hustled, played hurt, and did a good job all around, coming through with some clutch hits, especially against Randy Johnson.

1996: Webster had a poor year in 78 games with the Expos.

	AB	R	HR	RBI	SB	BA
1995 Philadelphia	150	18	4	14	0	.267
1996 Montreal	174	18	2	17	0	.230
1997 Baltimore	259	29	7	37	0	.255

WEDGE, ERIC - 1B/C - BR - b: 1/27/68

Wedge is a nine-year minor-league veteran who has been a Triple-A fixture for the last six years, most recently in the Phillies' chain. The former top Red Sox draft pick is a lumbering backup catcher and designated hitter who tends to hit for low averages with above-average power. He has a long swing which would be exposed at the major league level. His defensive skills are too limited for him to serve as a reserve catcher in the majors, and he doesn't bring enough offense to the table to contribute in any other role. His minor-league career is winding down, as his at-bat total has declined over the past three seasons.

WEHNER, JOHN - 3B - BR - b: 6/29/67

Wehner is the consummate 25th man on a major league roster. He can play everywhere except shortstop, pitcher and catcher, is a scrappy pinch-hitter and aggressive baserunner who keeps himself ready to play at all times. He is content with his role as a deep reserve, and is a positive presence in the clubhouse. Wehner spent six years with the Pirates in a utility role before assisting the Marlins' championship drive last year. It was no accident that Wehner followed Manager Jim Leyland to South Florida; his style of play is well-appreciated by Leyland. It's unlikely he can expand his reserve role but Wehner should again be a valuable spare part on a major league roster in 1998.

	AB	R	HR	RBI	SB	BA
1995 Pittsburgh	107	13	0	5	3	.308
1996 Pittsburgh	139	19	2	13	1	.259

WEISS, WALT - SS - BB - b: 11/28/63

Scouting: The American League Rookie of the Year in 1988, Weiss was still playing a solid shortstop in his tenth big-league season. When he started hearing reports that his arm strength was deteriorating, he simply started throwing the ball across the diamond with plenty of zip. At age 34, he will be one of the oldest middle infielders in the game but he compensates by getting a remarkable read of the ball off the bat. A switch-hitter who is much more productive from the left side, Weiss doesn't have much power and doesn't have base-stealing speed, but he has developed a keen eye at the plate and his on-base percentage has approached .400 each of the past two seasons.

1998: Weiss was expected to decline his option on the 1998 season and enter free agency. The Rockies wanted to re-sign him, but also wanted him to shift to second base for the first time in his career, making room at shortstop for rookie Neifi Perez. Weiss went to Atlanta, where his hitting will decline.

1997: Trade rumors, the promotion of Perez and a chronic hamstring problem left Weiss frustrated through most of the season. He was outstanding in the final six weeks, however, convincing management to try bringing him back.

1996: It was by far the best offensive season of his career, but it was also his worst defensively. Weiss set career highs in batting average, homers, RBI, runs scored — and errors (30); his previous career-high in errors was 19.

	AB	R	HR	RBI	SB	BA
1995 Colorado	427	65	1	25	15	.260
1996 Colorado	517	89	8	48	10	.282
1997 Colorado	393	52	4	38	5	.270

WELLS, FORRY - OF - BL - b: 3/21/71

Wells platooned in the Double-A New Haven outfield in 1996, getting occasional clutch hits but hitting for a disappointing average. He started 1997 in New Haven, continued his disappointing hitting, and was demoted to high A Salem. He's too old to be at that level and not a prospect.

WELLS, VERNON - OF - BR - b: 12/8/78

The fifth pick of the 1997 draft went to the Blue Jays and they used it on this schoolboy from Texas. Wells was preferred by the Jays over Baltimore first rounder Darnell McDonald because they believe Wells is the better hitter. They could be right. He signed right away and had a strong season in the New York-Penn League where he hit .307 with ten homers and 31 RBI in 264 at-bats.

WERTH, JAYSON - C - BR - b: 5/20/79

Werth's certainly built to be a catcher, at 6'5" and 200 pounds. The Orioles thought so, too, and made him their first-round pick in the 1997 draft (22nd overall). He hit .295 in the Gulf Coast League but will almost certainly develop more power (just one homer). If bloodlines have anything to do with major league success, Werth will definitely make it to the bigs. He's the grandson of Ducky Schofield, nephew of Dick Schofield and stepson of Dennis Werth, all of whom played in the majors.

WHATLEY, GABE - OF - BL - b: 12/29/71

Whatley's first year above A-ball was a big success. He followed up a half-season of fine hitting at Class A Durham in 1996 by batting .303 with 37 extra-base hits in 310 at-bats for Double-A

Greenville. More important, he maintained his outstanding plate discipline, collecting more walks than strikeouts while posting a .403 on-base percentage. The biggest drawback for Whatley is his age; he's already 26 years old and was older than most of his Double-A peers last year. With similar progress next year, Whatley can get to the majors in a reserve outfield role by the end of 1998.

WHITAKER, CHAD - OF - BL - b: 9/16/76

An over-aggressive nature at the plate has hindered Whitaker and his powerful batting stroke. He gets behind in the count, then has to swing at bad pitches out of the strike zone. Whitaker has spent the last two years at lower Class A venues; he hit .275 with ten homers and 51 RBI for Columbus last year. He's a decent defensive outfielder, but it's offensive development that will make or break his career.

WHITE, DERRICK - OF - BR - b: 10/12/69

Signed as a six-year minor-league free agent, White is an outfielder/first baseman who can provide some offense. He moved himself up on the Angels' depth chart by hitting .324 at Triple-A Vancouver and showing a little power, too. He was sent to Mexico over the winter to fine tune his offensive abilities.

WHITE, DEVON - OF - BB - b: 12/29/62

Scouting: White has been one of the best defensive centerfielders of his generation, but is slowing down physically. Despite being used as a leadoff man throughout his career, he has never been proficient in that role; he has struck out nearly three times as often as he has walked and has a career on-base percentage below .320. His single-season high in OBP is only .342. His bat and foot speed have both slowed and he now rarely drives the ball for distance, except in clutch post-season situations. At age 35, it appears that his days as a full-timer are dwindling.
1998: The Marlins were thinking of turning their starting center field job over to one of their youngsters, and let White go in trade for pitching prospect Jesus Martinez. White retained his full-time status on paper with Arizona, but a slump could change him into a platoon or fourth outfielder role.
1997: White was limited to 265 at-bats by a steady stream of aches and pains. When he was healthy, his speed was less of a factor than ever, and he showed an inability to drive the ball, especially from the right side of the plate, where he has traditionally excelled.
1996: White posted one of his best seasons, nailing 60 extra-base hits and tying a career high with a .455 slugging percentage. His ability to adjust to a new population of pitchers after spending his career in the American League was quite impressive.

	AB	R	HR	RBI	SB	BA
1995 Toronto	427	61	10	53	11	.283
1996 Florida	552	77	17	84	22	.274
1997 Florida	265	37	6	34	13	.245

WHITE, RONDELL - OF - BR - b: 2/23/72

Scouting: White has the ability to become one of the top all-around players in the game with developing power and outstanding speed. A 30/30 season isn't out of the question in the near future and he is also a good defensive center fielder.
1998: White is clearly the player around whom the Expos will rebuild. While they put Pedro Martinez, Mike Lansing and Henry Rodriguez on the trading block at the end of last season, the Expos have committed to keeping White around as he is signed through the year 2000. White took a step closer to superstar status last season and seems poised for a breakthrough this year, although he will be surrounded by a weaker lineup.
1997: White had an outstanding season, largely unnoticed because Montreal fell out of contention in late-July. White increased his power, hitting a career-high 28 home runs. Ironically, a chip fracture of the right hand suffered in early-August helped spark White. The injury caused White to hold the bat less tightly and freed up his swing.
1996: White signed the longest contract in Montreal history during spring training, then struggled through a frustrating season. He sat out from late-April to mid-July with a bruised spleen and left kidney suffered when he ran into the center field fence at Denver's Coors Field. White was then hampered by a strained rib cage muscle following his return.

	AB	R	HR	RBI	SB	BA
1995 Montreal	474	87	13	57	25	.295
1996 Montreal	334	35	6	41	14	.293
1997 Montreal	592	84	28	82	16	.270

WHITEN, MARK - OF - BB - b: 11/25/66

Scouting: Without a doubt Whiten has strength and he can hit mistakes a long way. But for having so much power his home run totals aren't as high as you'd expect. He takes a lot of pitches which results in a number of walks and strikeouts. And, at other times, he shows his lack of baseball savvy by swinging at pitches early in the count with his team trailing in the late innings. Defensively his arm is a cannon. However, his lack of accuracy and his penchant for throwing to the wrong base offset the strength.
1998: Whiten will likely get at least 250 at-bats as a part of someone's outfield, more if he ends up on a weak team.
1997: Whiten signed with the Yankees in the off-season, his fifth team in three years. An incident in Milwaukee put him in the doghouse and he was eventually released in August.
1996: Whiten went from worst to first and east to west in a weird season. Released by the Phillies, one of the worst teams in the NL, Whiten was picked up by the Braves and then traded to the Mariners on August 14th. In 40 games with Seattle he hit .300 and smacked 12 home runs, helping to key a September surge that nearly resulted in a playoff berth.

	AB	R	HR	RBI	SB	BA
1995 two teams	320	51	12	47	8	.241
1996 Atlanta	272	45	10	38	15	.243
1996 Seattle	140	31	12	33	2	.300
1997 New York AL	215	34	5	24	4	.265

WHITMORE, DARRELL - OF - BL - b: 11/18/68

Last seen in the Pirates organization, Whitmore was trying to hang on to a precarious professional career. He hit .256 playing the outfield for Triple-A Syracuse but his minor-league season of 1994 (with Edmonton) was likely his peak year. It's unlikely we'll see him in the majors again unless he gets an invite to spring training. Whitmore doesn't hit enough to be a major league outfielder.

WIDGER, CHRIS - C - BR - b: 5/21/71

Scouting: Widger has the tools to become an above-average offensive catcher with the ability to hit for average and power. He had the reputation of being a fine defensive catcher while coming up through the Seattle farm system, though he struggled mightily last season in Montreal.

1998: Widger will become the Expos' first-string catcher as Darrin Fletcher filed for free agency at the end of last season and won't return. Widger has a chance to develop into a power hitter with the ability to hit .300. However, he needs to improve his defense or risk losing playing time to backups Raul Chavez or Joe Siddall.

1997: Widger served as Fletcher's backup and flashed some power in part-time duty. Widger's defense was horrendous, though, as 11 errors in 85 games just doesn't cut it as a major league catcher.

1996: Widger spent most of the season with Seattle's Triple-A Tacoma farm club, also appearing in seven major league games in three different stints with the Mariners.

	AB	R	HR	RBI	SB	BA
1995 Seattle	45	2	1	2	0	.200
1997 Montreal	278	30	7	37	2	.234

WILCOX, LUKE - OF - BL - b: 11/15/73

In his first Double-A season at Norwich last year, Wilcox hit .280 but with little power and many strikeouts. He has some speed (13 steals in 1997) but needs to work on his plate discipline. He needs to demonstrate that he can handle Double-A pitching before he proceeds to the higher levels. The Devil Rays picked him near the end of the expansion draft.

WILKINS, RICK - C - BL - b: 6/4/67

The fact is that while Wilkins hasn't hit with power for two consecutive seasons, he has suffered a precipitous dropoff the next two seasons after a big power year. Although Wilkins is still a capable catcher, his offense may be in the process of unchecked decline.

	AB	R	HR	RBI	SB	BA
1995 Houston	202	30	7	19	0	.203
1996 San Francisco	411	53	14	59	0	.243
1997 Seattle	202	20	7	27	0	.198

WILLIAMS, BERNIE - OF - BB - b: 9/13/68

Scouting: The Yankees center fielder and number three hitter is on the verge of superstardom. The switch-hitter hits with power, runs, drives in runs and can track a fly ball down with anybody in the game. And Williams still has some untapped potential in getting more stolen bases out of his good speed.

1998: The pace of negotiation for a long-term contract was slower than some in the Yankee organization wanted, so there was mumbling about the possibility of trading Williams. But if they are serious about getting back to the World Series, they need Williams.

1997: Williams was on the DL twice with left hamstring trouble but wasn't bothered when he returned the second time. Consistently solid from both sides of the plate, he hit .322 righthanded and .331 lefthanded. Williams won his first Gold Glove in 1997.

1996: Williams took a big step into the upper echelon of outfielders. He is not quite Ken Griffey Jr. or Barry Bonds, but beginning in 1996, Williams showed he can be compared to them.

	AB	R	HR	RBI	SB	BA
1995 New York AL	563	93	18	82	8	.307
1996 New York AL	551	108	29	102	17	.305
1997 New York AL	509	107	21	100	15	.328

WILLIAMS, DREW - 1B - BL - b: 3/27/72

After some solid seasons in A-ball, where he showed a lefthanded power bat, Williams was slowed at Double-A El Paso in the Brewers organization. He doesn't field well and he's not a threat on the basepaths either. If he doesn't regain his hitting prowess, at his age he will disappear from major league prospect status.

WILLIAMS, EDDIE - 1B - BR - b: 11/1/64

Williams' future is hazy after he was released by the Pirates at end of last season. He is coming off back-to-back sub-par seasons with Detroit and Pittsburgh and is not getting any younger. He'll have to go to someone's camp as a non-roster player and try to make a club that way. He still has some pop in his bat as evidenced by the way he tore up the Pacific Coast League with Triple-A Albuquerque last season before Los Angeles traded him to the Pirates.

	AB	R	HR	RBI	SB	BA
1995 San Diego	296	35	12	47	0	.260
1996 Detroit	215	22	6	26	0	.200
1997 Pittsburgh	96	12	3	12	1	.240

WILLIAMS, GEORGE - C - BB - b: 4/22/69

Scouting: Williams is one of the good looking catching prospects the Athletics have stocked in recent years: a spray hitter who will take a pitch, and will garner a walk accordingly. He hits to all fields, but has little power. He is a good defensive catcher with an average arm. The edge Williams held over the other prospects was a familiarity with the pitchers — an edge that may be lost as the youngsters catch up.

1998: Williams has the upper hand on the backstop spot, but not without a little competition from Brent Mayne as well as the great collection of catching prospects. At best he can hope to platoon in 1998.

1997: After grabbing the starting catcher role, as much by default as anything else, Williams suffered a rash of minor injuries and the results were a platoon with Mayne. Furthermore, having advanced through the ranks with the likes of hurlers Adams, Wengert, et al, it was thought Williams would have an easier time communicating with the young hurlers. As it was, Williams' contribution wasn't nearly as significant as was hoped.

1996: It was an ugly season for Williams. Considering that he was a former Pacific Coast League All-Star, and bearing in mind his .291 average in 1995 over 79 at-bats, 1996 has to be considered an aberration.

	AB	R	HR	RBI	SB	BA
1995 Oakland	79	13	3	14	0	.291
1996 Oakland	132	17	3	10	0	.152
1997 Oakland	201	30	3	22	0	.289

WILLIAMS, GERALD - OF - BR - b: 8/10/66

Scouting: A fourth outfielder for most of his career, Williams played regularly in center field in 1997. He has speed defensively and a good throwing arm. At the plate, he is aggressive, but tends to swing at bad pitches. He also is an aggressive baserunner who can make foolish decisions on the basepaths.

1998: Williams played well enough to have a shot at starting again in center field for Milwaukee. He will have to fight off some challengers in spring training again.

1997: Williams won the starting center field position when Chuckie Carr was injured in the spring. He kept it with hustle in the field and at the plate, but he slumped badly lately in the season.

1996: Williams came to the Brewers with pitcher Bob Wickman in an August 23rd trade that sent reliever Graeme Lloyd and infielder Pat Listach to the Yankees. He didn't hit much in 26 games for the Brewers. Before the trade, he had played steady ball in the field and at the plate in a reserve outfield role for New York.

	AB	R	HR	RBI	SB	BA
1995 New York AL	182	33	6	28	4	.247
1996 NY-Milwaukee	325	43	5	34	10	.252
1997 Milwaukee	566	73	10	41	23	.253

WILLIAMS, JASON - 2B - BR - b: 12/18/73
Williams had a productive first season with the Reds in his first taste of pro ball. He was a 16th-round pick by Cincinnati in the 1996 draft out of Louisiana State but he didn't play pro ball that year as he was a member of the U.S. Olympic team. He played second base at Class A Burlington of the Midwest League and was a hit, batting .324 with seven homers and 41 RBI. At Double-A Chattanooga, Williams hit at a .310 clip, adding five homers, 21 doubles and 28 RBI. He obviously has good power for a middle infielder.

WILLIAMS, JUAN - OF - BL - b: 10/9/72
Williams appeared to be in a good spot when the Red Sox brought him in as a six-year, minor-league free agent. But he bombed out in Pawtucket and was demoted to Double-A early in the season. He hit .203 there, but with 12 homers in 192 at-bats. Williams does little to help you, and is remarkably stubborn at the plate, trying to yank every pitch he sees out of the ballpark. He can't hit anything off-speed or away from him, and appears to be a career minor-leaguer.

WILLIAMS, KEITH - OF - BR - b: 4/21/72
Following his solid, if unspectacular 1996 season at Shreveport, where he hit .274 with 13 homers and 63 RBI, a jump to Triple-A Phoenix would seem in order. Instead, Williams returned to Double-A where he had fine numbers — .320 batting average, 22 homers, 106 RBI — but nothing that disproved what was already known: that Williams can hit Double-A pitching. It is time for Williams to try his hand at Triple-A if he is to ever have a chance at the majors.

WILLIAMS, MATT - 3B - BR - b: 11/28/65
Scouting: Williams' .307 on-base percentage contributed to the diminished offense of the Indians' powerful lineup in 1997. He's a wild swinger who has never walked 40 times in a season despite the respect accorded him as a long-time power threat. He has quick reflexes and a decent arm at third base, though his range is beginning to deteriorate.
1998: The Diamondbacks looked at Williams at age 32 and decided that he had plenty of gas left in the tank. One ability that Williams possesses in more abundance than Travis Fryman is the power to go deep -- very deep -- against lefty pitching. There is a clue about how Arizona views its ballpark effects.
1997: On the surface it was a nice year. However, a deeper look reveals Williams as a rally killer — with the years posted by Manny Ramirez, Jim Thome and David Justice ahead of him, he could have knocked in 150 runs. Williams had the lowest on-base percentage in the lineup.
1996: Williams missed a chunk of his last season with the Giants with a shoulder injury, and batted over .300 despite hitting a career low .223 against lefties. Giants' GM Brian Sabean's fears that Williams' days as a third baseman and impact hitter were over led him to overhaul his last-place club and deal Williams to Cleveland.

	AB	R	HR	RBI	SB	BA
1995 San Francisco	283	53	23	65	2	.336
1996 San Francisco	404	69	22	85	1	.302
1997 Cleveland	596	86	32	105	12	.263

WILLIAMS, REGGIE - OF - BB - b: 5/5/66
The Angels originally picked the veteran outfielder up from the Mexican league and traded him to the Dodgers for reliever Mike James, then re-signed him as a free agent. Williams has some major league experience, which makes him valuable at Triple-A and he has some speed. He's good insurance and may be only an injury away from returning to the major leagues.

WILLIAMS, RICKY - OF - BR - b: 5/21/77
The Texas Longhorn halfback just completed his junior football season, and his second full pro baseball season. He struck out nearly every third at bat, and his flawed mechanics wouldn't allow his solid 6'0", 215 pound, body to generate consistent longball power, but he showed excellent basestealing ability, and would occasionally induce gasps with feats which can be performed only by world-class athletes. He can excel at whichever sport he chooses.

WILLIAMSON, ANTONE - 3B - BL - b: 7/18/73
Scouting: After being a first-round draft selection in 1994, Williamson is seeing his time is run out. He has hit for average in the minors, but has not shown much power. He also has struggled in the field and was switched from third base to first base because of those difficulties. Williamson's progress has been hampered by shoulder problems.
1998: The Brewers would like Williamson to become a major leaguer, but are suspect of his fielding and lack of power. He could end up elsewhere.
1997: Williamson got his first shot at the major league level and did not produce well enough to remain there. He hit .286 at Triple-A Tucson.
1996: A shoulder injury put Williamson on the DL at the start of the season. He hit .261 in 55 games after coming back from the injury.

	AB	R	HR	RBI	SB	BA
1997 Milwaukee	54	2	0	6	0	.204

WILSON, BRANDON - SS - BR - b: 2/26/69
Wilson was at Triple-A Iowa in the Cubs' farm system last year, his third organization in three seasons. He's a steady defensive player who has fallen off at the plate over the past two years. Unless he improves his hitting, Wilson will be relegated to the high minors for the foreseeable future.

WILSON, CRAIG - SS - BR - b: 9/3/70
A few years ago Wilson was considered an above-average prospect, particularly after 1994 when he led the Carolina League with 36 doubles while setting a league record for shortstop fielding percentage. The following year at Double-A Birmingham he retained most of his hitting ability but committed errors in bunches. When advanced to Triple-A Nashville in 1996, his hitting ability disappeared and he was demoted to Birmingham. 1997 was a better year, but he is no longer any kind of a prospect. Wilson is a hard-nosed player, a scrapper, but is not

going to have much of a career in the majors.

WILSON, DAN - C - BR - b: 3/25/69
Scouting: A good defensive catcher and staff-handler, Wilson has blossomed as a hitter the last two seasons, developing a solid stroke while learning to turn on pitches he can handle.
1998: There is no reason to expect anything different out of Wilson, a solid member of the Mariners' inner core.
1997: Wilson proved his breakthrough 1996 season was built on a solid foundation by increasing his extra-base hits and even flashing some speed, too.
1996: Wilson stepped into the full-time starting role with a flourish, more than doubling his previous major league home run total while driving in a career high 83 runs.

	AB	R	HR	RBI	SB	BA
1995 Seattle	399	40	9	51	2	.278
1996 Seattle	491	51	18	83	1	.285
1997 Seattle	508	66	15	74	7	.270

WILSON, DESI - OF - BL - b: 5/9/69
Wilson is big (6'7") so one would think he could supply some power. Not so. His seven homers last year matched the career high he set in 1996. He had a chance to win the first base job outright late in 1996, but couldn't hold it — just like Dan Peltier and David McCarty before him. Wilson has proven he can hit at Triple-A — he hit .344 at Phoenix with 53 RBI last year after a .339 mark with 59 RBI in 1996. But with J. T. Snow entrenched at first base in San Francisco, his best bet for time in the show is the expansion draft.

	AB	R	HR	RBI	SB	BA
1996 San Francisco	118	10	2	12	0	.271

WILSON, ENRIQUE - SS - BB - b: 7/27/75
Scouting: Wilson is one of the best all-around middle infield prospects in baseball, combining slick defensive skills with contact hitting and above-average speed. This "shortstop of the future" will now become the "second baseman of the present." He has the range and arm to play shortstop, and his footwork is solid at second. His extra-base power potential is above-average for a player of his small stature, but he hasn't quite figured out how to incorporate his speed into his offensive game.
1998: Barring unforeseen off-season developments, Wilson should be the Indians' regular second baseman in 1998. Defense will be his main priority; there won't be any offensive pressure on him as he'll likely bat eighth or ninth.
1997: As one of Triple-A's youngest starters, Wilson hit for average with excellent plate discipline and some extra-base pop, all while learning a new position. The Indians had considered rushing Wilson to the majors in spring training, but the infusion of maturity into his game made the additional seasoning worthwhile.
1996: Wilson batted .300 for the first time in his pro career as a 20-year-old at Double-A Canton-Akron. He continued to run the bases aggressively —some might say recklessly — as he was successful in only 23 of 39 steal attempts.

WILSON, NIGEL - OF - BL - b: 1/12/70
Wilson's biggest fame resulted from his being the first pick overall in the 1993 expansion draft, by the Marlins. He made a brief appearance with Florida in 1996 after an undistinguished tenure in their farm system, and he went to Japan to play last year. Wilson was among the top home run hitters in the Japanese Pacific League, but he looked much better as a prospect four years ago.

WILSON, POOKIE - OF - BL - b: 10/24/70
Once a spray hitting lefthanded outfielder with good speed and decent plate discipline, Wilson has devolved into a slower, more impatient version of his former self. The Marlins' outfield prospect has stagnated at the upper end of their system over the past three seasons, but is about to be overrun by the next wave of Marlins' flycatchers, featuring Jaime Jones and Julio Ramirez. There isn't much of a market for 27-year-old outfielders without a single above average skill.

WILSON, PRESTON - OF - BR - b: 7/19/74
The Mets number one draft pick in 1992, Wilson earned a mid season jump to Double-A ball thanks to some impressive power hitting. He hit a total of 30 homers in 1997 and had 95 RBI. He has unquestioned athletic ability, a combination of speed and awesome power. He could earn a trip north with the big club with an impressive spring.

WILSON, TOM - C - BR - b: 12/19/70
A veteran minor-league catcher helping young pitchers develop, Wilson finally started to hit well during his sixth year in the minors: 1996. With his age and experience, the hitting is not impressive. For the record he batted .293 in 126 games, clubbed 21 homers and drove in 80 runs. His path to big leagues is blocked with the Yankees, but Wilson could help out at Triple-A Columbus.

WILSON, VANCE - C - BR - b: 3/17/73
After three seasons of A ball, Wilson spent 1997 at the Double-A level in the Mets organization. He showed some signs of power, a third of his hits were for extra bases. Because of the organizations unsettled catching situation, Wilson could benefit and advance in 1998.

WIMMER, CHRIS - OF - BR - b: 9/25/70
Wimmer didn't improve much from 1996, he hit the same two homers and drove in just 28 runs in 372 at-bats at Double-A Orlando. He has some speed to cover the outfield and did steal 23 bases but this former Wichita State star and one-time Giants' prospect doesn't look like he'll make it out of the minors.

WINN, RANDY - OF - BR - b: 6/9/74
Winn fails to make full use of his game-breaking speed because of relatively poor plate discipline. He draws enough walks after fouling off several pitches, but he swings too much and strikes out too frequently. Winn has above-average range in center field but just an average arm. The spray-hitting Winn will advance only if he shortens his swing and puts the ball in play more consistently. He'll likely begin the year in the minors again, after graduating from Class A to Double-A during the 1997 season. Tampa Bay took him in the third round of expansion.

WITT, KEVIN - 3B/SS - BL - b: 1/5/76
Scouting: A first-round draft pick, Witt has moved around in search of a defensive position. Drafted as a shortstop, he has tried third base and now first base. The best power-hitting prospect in the Blue Jays organization last year, he does not steal bases and is only adequate with the glove.

1998: It's possible but unlikely that Witt could land a spot with the big-league team as a backup infielder. More likely, he's going to Triple-A for more seasoning.
1997: Witt led the Jays' farm system in home runs (30) and completed his transition to becoming a first baseman — all in his first season above Class A.
1996: Witt showed some power with 13 home runs and 70 RBI in just 124 games at Class A Dunedin.

WOLFF, MIKE - OF - BR - b: 12/19/70
Scouting: Wolff has hit well at almost every level he's played and came close to making the Angels' opening day roster in spring training last year with a red-hot spring. Wolff needs to work on his defense, but power is his forte.
1998: Wolff can help himself by showing the Angels some improvement defensively this spring, but he may be limited in that regard because an ankle injury suffered at the end of the 1997 season took him out of a scheduled trip to Mexico over the winter to work on his defense.
1997: Wolff rebounded from a mediocre year in Vancouver the year before to hit .279 with a career-high 21 home runs and 64 RBI for the Canadians, and also showed some defensive improvement.
1996: Wolff struggled a bit as he made the jump from Double-A ball. His power numbers were down and he took a big step backwards, even playing for Class A Lake Elsinore for a spell.

WOMACK, TONY - SS - BL - b: 9/25/69
Scouting: Womack has exceptional speed and has learned how to use it as he has gotten older. He is content to chop the ball on the ground and he has also developed an outstanding feel for pitcher's moves and the optimal situations for running. Womack strikes out a lot, though, for a speedster and his defense at second base is barely acceptable.
1998: Womack will go into the season as the Pirates' starting second baseman and leadoff hitter. Despite the great strides he made in 1997, Womack will have to repeat that success in '98 because mega-prospect Chad Hermansen is now playing second base and breathing down his neck.
1997: Womack entered spring training in a three-way battle with rookies Lou Collier and Brandon Cromer for the Pirates' second-base job. He wound up not only starting but playing in the All-Star game and leading the National League in stolen bases during his first full season in the majors.
1996: Womack spent the majority of the season in Triple-A, playing both second base and shortstop after being dropped from the Pirates' roster the previous winter. He received a September callup to Pittsburgh and the Pirates spent most of that time trying to turn him into a center fielder.

	AB	R	HR	RBI	SB	BA
1997 Pittsburgh	641	85	6	50	60	.278

WOOD, JASON - 3B - BL - b: 12/16/69
Wood had an excellent season at Edmonton in 1997, clubbing 19 homers, driving in 87, while hitting .321. He should get a long look in the spring, but will most likely become the victim of numbers. Wood might get a major league opportunity due to expansion.

WOOD, TED - OF - BL - b: 1/4/67
Once a promising outfield prospect in the Giants' system, Wood found big success in Taiwan last year. He hit .373, drove in 94 runs, and set a Taiwan record with 139 hits in a season.

WOODS, KEN - OF/3B - BR - b: 8/2/70
Woods' numbers at Shreveport look okay — he hit .300 with two homers and 32 RBI in 293 at-bats — but he is too old to have spent another season at Double-A. Woods is rapidly losing playing time to better prospects; he is gradually shifting into a platoon/fourth outfield role. Woods has the look of a career minor leaguer.

WOODS, TYRONE - OF - BR - b: 8/19/69
A good line-drive power stroke kept Woods going as a career minor-leaguer for nine years. His best season came in 1996 when he hit .312 with 25 homers and 71 RBI for Double-A Trenton. Unfortunately for Woods, enough scouts had already seen him struggle against Triple-A pitching, so his best opportunity for 1997 was in Mexico. He hit well enough, .342 with 18 home runs for Minatitian.

WRIGHT, RON - 1B - BR - b: 1/21/76
Scouting: Wright has shown exceptional power while playing in the minor leagues with Atlanta and now Pittsburgh. He began to hit for average last season but still needs to cut his strikeout rate. Wright is below average at first base but his power potential offsets any weakness with the mitt.
1998: Wright will likely begin the season with the Pirates' Triple-A farm club as Kevin Young will begin the season at first base in Pittsburgh. The Pirates feel Wright needs a little more time to develop in the minors but won't hesitate to promote him to Pittsburgh if Young falters.
1997: Wright hit over .300 for the first time in his career and showed better strikezone judgment at Triple-A Calgary, despite being one of the youngest players in the Pacific Coast League at age 21. A broken bone in his left wrist ended his season and cost him his first chance to play in the majors. The Pirates could have used him at first base after Young tore a ligament in his right thumb August 2nd and missed six weeks.
1996: Wright hit a combined 36 homers for Atlanta's Class A Durham and Double-A Greenville farm clubs before being one of three players packaged in a trade with Pittsburgh for lefthander Denny Neagle in late-August.

WRONA, RICK - C - BR - b: 12/10/63
Wrona is the definition of journeyman catcher, having spent parts of six seasons in the majors — parts of the seasons, only, never a full year — for four different organizations. He has become the kind of player who shares a catching job in the high minors with an organization's better prospect, then goes on his way after the season. In 1997, he was with the White Sox at Triple-A Nashville where he helped Robert Machado learn the finer points of catching. It was his thirteenth professional season.

YARD, BRUCE - SS - BL - b: 10/17/71
After spending two seasons at Double-A San Antonio, Yard spent 1997 at Class A Vero Beach. He hits for average but without much power and is average defensively.

YOUNG, DMITRI - 3B - BB - b: 10/11/73
Scouting: The ceiling of possibility for Young remains quite high, particularly as a hitter, and his rookie season proved to him

again that nothing comes easily. A switch-hitter with a hint of possible power in the future, Young fared better against lefthanders but seems to drive the ball better from the left side. He's barely adequate as a first baseman and, though better than some might think in the outfield, won't be a terrific asset there, either.

1998: With Mark McGwire at first base and the outfield loaded, the Cardinals traded Young to the Reds, who lost him to expansion and then reacquired him in trade. Being a switch-hitter will help him find a spot as a reserve, if he doesn't rise to the level of starter.

1997: Young gained an early opportunity to play regularly as the first baseman because of injuries elsewhere, a chance which could have led to him contending for Rookie of the Year status. Instead, he played himself out of the lineup by squandering too many RBI opportunities (a .256 average with runners in scoring position) and too many errors in the field. After a demotion to Triple-A, Young returned in late-August with an improved outlook and seemed to have regained his hitting stroke down the stretch.

1996: He proved he was ready for the big leagues as a hitter by leading the American Association with a .333 batting average, with an added boost from his fifteen home runs.

	AB	R	HR	RBI	SB	BA
1997 St. Louis	333	38	5	34	6	.258

YOUNG, ERIC - 2B - BR - b: 5/18/67

Scouting: Young is a good fastball hitter and has become one of the most disciplined hitters in the league and also one of the hardest to strikeout. Defensively, Young has worked hard and improved his range and in turning the double play. He has excellent speed and is a threat to swipe a base just about any time he gets on base.

1998: Young finished the 1997 season with the Dodgers who were disappointed with rookie Wilton Guerrero. If the Dodgers don't want Young as their second sacker, plenty of teams will inquire about having him bring his speed, improved defense and hitting ability to their club.

1997: Young had a strong season with the Rockies and was then traded to the Dodgers for the stretch run. He stole plenty of bases and played good defense.

1996: Young missed nearly the entire first month of the season with a broken hand but rebounded to make the All-Star team and contend for the batting title for most of the season. Young also put his improved defense on display.

	AB	R	HR	RBI	SB	BA
1995 Colorado	366	68	6	36	35	.317
1996 Colorado	568	113	8	74	53	.324
1997 two teams	622	106	8	61	45	.280

YOUNG, ERNIE - OF - BR - b: 7/8/69

Scouting: Young hits with power, especially to right-center. He is a hard worker, who had improved — until 1997 — in each successive year at the same level. He can be impatient, so he can be pitched to. Though he spent the early part of the season playing center field, Young is much better suited to left field. His arm is fair, as is his speed.

1998: As deep as the A's are with infielders, the number of quality outfielders ready to take a major league job and run with it is not the same. Thus, Young could find himself back in the outfield with a full-time job. After all, Oakland wouldn't deal Young to Boston in exchange for Canseco prior to the '97 season, so they must value him to some degree.

1997: If he could have a mulligan, Young would certainly ask for a replay of last year. Young lost his job early, and was sent down after only 34 at-bats. He did return to the team, but never really to form. He hit .323 with nine homers over 195 at-bats in the Pacific Coast League, but it wasn't Triple-A that he needed to master.

1996: Young finally got a full season worth of at-bats, and he responded, showing his capabilities. He has always fared better during his second season at a given level; it raised expectations for a fine 1997 season.

	AB	R	HR	RBI	SB	BA
1995 Oakland	50	9	2	5	0	.200
1996 Oakland	462	72	19	64	7	.242
1997 Oakland	175	22	5	15	1	.223

YOUNG, KEVIN - 1B - BR - b: 6/16/69

Scouting: Young has become the classic late bloomer. Expected to become a star when he broke in with the Pirates in 1993, he finally began to realize his potential last season in Pittsburgh. He has learned to turn on balls, giving hope that his home run total can continue to rise. Young also is a Gold Glove-caliber first baseman.

1998: Young will go into the season as the Pirates' starting first baseman and cleanup hitter. He is not a prototypical number four hitter but is the most reasonable facsimile the Pirates have at this time. The Pirates, though, are still slightly wary that Young's fine '97 season was a fluke.

1997: Young returned to the Pirates as a minor-league free agent and made the club in spring training as a backup corner infielder. Young moved into the starting lineup in late-June after first baseman Mark Johnson struggled and Young became the Pirates' most consistent power hitter until being felled by a torn ligament in his right thumb on August 2nd. Young returned in mid-September but failed to regain his batting stroke before the season ended.

1996: Young was released by the Pirates late in spring training and signed with his hometown Kansas City Royals. He split the season between the Royals and Triple-A Omaha, showing new-found power but getting infrequent starts at the major-league level as former manager Bob Boone couldn't find anywhere to play him.

	AB	R	HR	RBI	SB	BA
1995 Pittsburgh	181	13	6	22	1	.232
1996 Kansas City	132	20	8	23	3	.242
1997 Pittsburgh	333	59	18	74	11	.300

YOUNG, KEVIN - OF - BR - b: 1/22/72

Young has been a utility type, and was tried at second base at Double-A Midland in 1997 and did well, thereby boosting his stock. He's a steady, consistent player who can hit for average.

ZAPP, A.J. - 1B - BL - b: 4/24/78

Zapp was selected by the Braves 27th overall in the first round of the 1996 June Draft. He had the best raw power of any player in that draft and Atlanta said he was the best power hitter they drafted since they selected Bob Horner number one overall in 1978. Last year, Zapp played at Rookie level Danville and had solid numbers at the plate: .338 with seven homers and 56 RBI.

ZAUN, GREGG - C - BB - b: 4/14/71

Scouting: Zaun is an ideal major league backup catcher. He is a scrappy offensive player who switch-hits, handles the bat well, draws walks, and has above-average speed for a receiver. He is fundamentally sound behind the plate, making up for an average throwing arm with a quick release. His chief drawbacks are a lack of size and home run power at the plate. As long as he is not pressed into service for much more than 200 at-bats, Zaun should be one of baseball's best part-time catchers on a per at-bat basis.

1998: The Marlins hoped that neither expansion team was enamored of Zaun's skills, as they loved him in his 1997 role. His role should be minimal, however, unless Charles Johnson is injured.

1997: Zaun was one of the Marlins' many low-wage contributors on their high-wage ballclub. He didn't control opposing baserunners particularly well, but was a subtle offensive force, getting on base consistently and driving the ball to the gaps.

1996: Zaun escaped Baltimore late in the season in a deal for reliever Terry Mathews. He immediately was an obvious upgrade over previous Marlin backups because of his unique skill set for a catcher.

	AB	R	HR	RBI	SB	BA
1995 Baltimore	104	18	3	14	1	.260
1996 Baltimore	108	16	1	13	0	.231
1996 Florida	31	4	1	2	1	.290
1997 Florida	143	21	2	20	1	.301

ZEILE, TODD - 3B - BR - b: 9/9/65

Scouting: Zeile is a line-drive hitter who has improved in the home run department in recent seasons. After being converted from catcher a few seasons ago, Zeile has turned into a decent defensive third baseman and he has enough power for the position.

1998: Zeile is a productive player who is one of two Dodger players holding back phenom Paul Konerko. If the Dodgers make Konerko an everyday member of the club for the 1998 season, Zeile or former UCLA teammate Eric Karros could get moved.

1997: Zeile improved his home run output to a career high-level and was steady if unspectacular at third base for the Dodgers.

1996: Zeile made it to the playoffs thanks to a late-season trade from the Phillies to the Orioles. He came through with some clutch hits for the Birds but with the move of Cal Ripken Jr. to third base, Zeile's days with Baltimore came to an end; they didn't make a serious attempt to re-sign him when he became a free agent.

	AB	R	HR	RBI	SB	BA
1995 Chicago NL	426	50	14	52	1	.246
1996 Philadelphia	500	61	20	80	1	.268
1996 Baltimore	117	17	5	19	0	.239
1997 Los Angeles	575	89	31	90	8	.268

ZINTER, ALAN - C/1B - BB - b: 5/19/68

Scouting: A career minor-league power hitter with slider bat speed and no true position, Zinter is a former first-round Mets' draft pick as a switch-hitting catcher who was traded straight up for first baseman Rico Brogna in 1994.

1998: Expansion may help Zinter's chances of landing his first major league job.

1997: Zinter was remarkably consistent, hitting 20 homers — exactly his average over the last six seasons — in his first season in the Seattle organization at Triple-A Tacoma, where he played mostly first base.

1996: Zinter had a minor-league career-high 26 homers at Triple-A Pawtucket in his lone season in the Boston organization, where he was a catcher/first baseman/DH.

ZOSKY, EDDIE - SS - BR - b: 2/10/68

In 1991 and '92 the Blue Jays gave Zosky their starting shortstop job and he lost it. He also did some time on the major league bench for the Marlins and the Orioles. Last year he was exclusively a Triple-A player, hitting .278 with nine homers and 45 RBI in 241 at-bats for Phoenix. At age 30, Zosky has still not learned how to take a pitch; he drew just 16 walks last year. Zosky's fifteen minutes of fame have passed.

ZUBER, JON - 1B/OF - BL - b: 12/10/69

Zuber is a line drive hitter who can be counted upon to slash singles and doubles while walking regularly at the Triple-A level. He rarely strikes out, but has no home run power or speed - a severe detriment for a first baseman and outfielder. He got a brief major league trial in 1996, and showed Triple-A bat speed; Zuber didn't hit many balls with authority in his 91 at-bats. Despite an impressive 1997 Triple-A season, he remained anchored at Scranton while non-prospects advanced to the majors. Zuber is an above-average defensive first baseman, but his range in the outfield is extremely poor. In the right situation, Zuber could be a deep reserve in the majors, but that's unlikely to happen in Philadelphia.

ABBOTT, JIM - TL - b: 9/1/67
Abbott, whose loss of velocity turned him into a batting practice pitcher, could have pitched in 1997, or at least he could have been paid big bucks for pitching in the minors while on a long-term major league contract. Typically, he took the high-class approach and decided to call it quits.

ABBOTT, PAUL - TR - b: 9/15/67
Abbott has appeared in 33 major league games during his 13-year pro career but none since 1993 with Cleveland. He's been with five different organizations over the past five seasons, pitching for Triple-A Tacoma in the Mariners' farm system last year. He made 14 starts in 1997, displayed good control and struck out better than a batter per inning. At age 30, his time is running out but he could make another major league appearance before he hangs up the spikes.

ACEVEDO, JUAN - TR - b: 5/5/70
Scouting: Not many pitchers can throw such a variety of pitches. But that ability has been a curse for Acevedo, the pitcher so highly regarded when the Mets obtained him (for Bret Saberhagen) in 1995. The problem is that Acevedo has mastered none of those pitches and injuries have interfered regularly with his progress. He needs to be more consistent with his fastball, decide on one breaking ball — preferably his slider — and polish his straight changeup.
1998: The Mets say they saw improvement in 1997. It wasn't evident to the naked eye. Acevedo, 28 years old in May, needs to assert himself this season or risk evolving into a "never was." He is more willing to pitch in relief, but retains reservations about the role.
1997: Had Acevedo warmed to and performed well in the relief role, the Mets might not have made the deal for Mel Rojas, and Acevedo might have assured himself of major league duty. But he hardly distinguished himself when the Mets tried to make him a set-up man, allowing 57 baserunners, five of whom were in their home run trot, in 38.1 innings. He won his two starts, allowing three earned runs in 12 innings. His work in the minor-leagues was unremarkable — a 6-6 record, 3.86 ERA and 145 baserunners over 116.2 innings and 18 starts.
1996: Acevedo would have begun the season in the rotation, but a hamstring pull suffered in the final days of spring training undermined him. His poor pitching and a stress fracture in his right leg denied him any chance of pitching in the major leagues.

	W	SV	ERA	IP	H	BB	SO	B/I
1997 New York NL	3	0	3.58	48	52	22	33	1.55

ACRE, MARK - TR - b: 9/16/68
Scouting: At one time Acre was the Eck's heir apparent, hopelessly labeled a "can't miss" prospect. When Acre is aggressive, and uses his forkball to set up his fastball, he is deadly. When he is tentative, which has been the case in the majors, he fails.
1998: That "can't miss" designation is a tough albatross to wear. For the most part, throughout his minor-league career, Acre has been dominating, but since his last failure in the majors, that is no longer the case. It isn't unusual for closers to get the hang of their job in the majors at a later age, so Acre could still get it together. It seems, however, that if he is a major leaguer this year, it will be in a set-up role, at best. Both T. J. Mathews and Gary Haught have passed Acre on the A's depth chart.
1997: Seeing a little daylight in Oakland, but more of it at Triple-A Edmonton last year, Acre pitched mop-up while at the show. His numbers tumbled (4.15 ERA, 11 saves) in comparison to those of previous years in Triple-A.
1996: Given every shot to grab the closer job in spring training, Acre, who at one point was asked to throw his forkball exclusively, couldn't (or wouldn't) do it, and was demoted. He pitched well at Edmonton (2.09, eight saves) but success at Triple-A hasn't been his problem.

	W	SV	ERA	IP	H	BB	SO	B/I
1995 Oakland	1	0	5.71	52	52	28	47	1.54
1996 Oakland	1	2	6.12	25	38	9	18	1.88
1997 Oakland	2	0	5.73	16	21	8	12	1.85

ADAMS, TERRY - TR - b: 3/6/73
Scouting: Adams has been groomed to be the Cubs' closer since he was shifted to the bullpen in the 1994 season, and he's got all the tools to be successful. He's a hard thrower who has a decent slider. Adams still has some control problems and he really needs to walk fewer than one every other inning to be a top-flight closer.
1998: Adams will be the Cubs closer this season. He struggled at times last year, but never seemed to have more than a couple of bad games in a row before he was able to rebound. That was to be expected for a pitcher of his age and experience who is asked to close games at the big-league level for the first time. He'll be effective in his role, although he won't be among the league leaders because the Cubs won't be a good enough team.
1997: Adams started the season as the set-up man for Mel Rojas, but he got several save opportunities early in the season when Rojas was ineffective. Adams pitched well enough that the Cubs were comfortable with trading Rojas to the Mets and giving Adams the job. He pitched especially well at the end of the season after the Rojas trade.
1996: Adams was effective for the Cubs despite having minimal experience above A-ball. He came up as a green 23-year-old, but showed he had what it took to get major league hitters out.

	W	SV	ERA	IP	H	BB	SO	B/I
1995 Chicago NL	1	1	6.50	18	22	10	15	1.78
1996 Chicago NL	3	4	2.94	101	84	49	78	1.32
1997 Chicago NL	2	18	4.62	74	91	40	64	1.77

ADAMS, WILLIE - TR - b: 10/8/72
Scouting: Adams, when on, possesses a devastating sinker to complement his fastball, which he brings in the low 90s, and a changeup. However, inconsistency and shoulder problems have limited his effectiveness. Still, he is a hard thrower. He is struggling, but it's not uncommon for pitchers of his type to take awhile to reach the top of their game. Adams may not be a Cy Young type, but he does have the stuff.
1998: There are so many questions concerning the A's rotation, that Adams could just as likely be the staff ace as he could spend the year in Edmonton. The latter scenario is less likely, but Adams must prove himself both healthy and consistent. It is much too early to write him off, however.
1997: Adams started the season as the most likely to grab the ace role. It didn't happen as he struggled, spent time on the DL, and was ultimately relegated to the obscurity of Triple-A. His control was evident (58 whiffs, 19 walks) but so was everything else (6.45 ERA, 105 hits over 75.1 innings).

1996: A former number one pick, Adams arrived on the scene and pitched well over 12 starts. He has a good fastball, a killer sinker, and excellent control.

	W	SV	ERA	IP	H	BB	SO	B/I
1996 Oakland	3	0	4.01	76	76	23	68	1.30
1997 Oakland	3	0	8.18	58	73	32	37	1.80

ADAMSON, JOEL - TL - b: 7/2/71
Scouting: Adamson has good control and can pitch in middle or long relief, as well as start. He lacks velocity, but has decent breaking stuff and has learned to spot his pitches. A quick worker, Adamson can keep hitters off guard.
1998: Adamson was on the bubble among those players the Brewers considered protecting in the expansion draft. When he was left open, Arizona took him in the first round. He has already proved himself to be a valuable lefthander in '97. His versatility should help him stay in the big leagues as a swingman.
1997: Adamson started the season with the Brewers as a long reliever and worked his way into the rotation to make six starts.
1996: Adamson began the season with Triple-A Charlotte and ranked third on the club in games (44) and strikeouts (84). He was called up by Florida and appeared in nine games, with a lofty 7.36 ERA.

	W	SV	ERA	IP	H	BB	SO	B/I
1997 Milwaukee	5	0	3.54	76	78	19	56	1.27

AGOSTO, JUAN - TL - b: 2/23/58
After a strong performance in Puerto Rican winter ball, Agosto got an invitation to spring training with the Royals. The opportunity led to nothing for 1997, but with expansion there will be more spring successes in 1998 than in a normal year.

AGOSTO, STEVENSON- TL - b: 9/2/75
Agosto has spent four years in A-ball, finishing 1997 with Lake Elsinore after being traded from Anaheim to San Diego in the Rickey Henderson deal. He throws a low-90s fastball from a low arm angle, reminiscent of Sid Fernandez, but his breaking balls roll. He's just 21 years old but needs to move to Double-A soon to remain a prospect.

AGUILERA, RICK - TR - b: 12/31/61
Scouting: Few players have a pitch as nasty as Aguilera's forkball, which continues to make him one of the game's better and more effective closers. His fastball is good as well and combined with his forkball makes for a superb one-two punch. Aguilera usually comes up with at least one injury per year, though, that sidelines him for a brief time.
1998: Another 20 to 25 saves should be in Aguilera's future — more if he were on a better team, and possibly less because he remained with the Twins. After a one-year flirtation with the starting rotation, Aguilera is back where he belongs — in the bullpen.
1997: After missing much of spring training with a knee injury, Aguilera's return to starting officially ended when he was returned to the bullpen. He was rusty when the season opened due to a lack of work but improved as the season went along.
1996: In his first full season as a starter since 1987, Aguilera didn't get as much work as expected because of tendinitis in his right wrist. He started 19 games but, especially because of advanced age, simply wasn't the workhorse the Twins needed.

	W	SV	ERA	IP	H	BB	SO	B/I
1995 Min - Boston	3	32	2.60	55	46	13	52	1.08
1996 Minnesota	8	0	5.42	111	124	27	83	1.36
1997 Minnesota	5	26	3.82	68	65	22	68	1.27

AHEARNE, PAT - TR - b: 12/10/69
Ahearne did nothing to dispel the belief that he is heading towards a career spent in the minor leagues. In 1997 he spent time with two Dodger farm teams and was hit hard at both stops. He's not a strikeout pitcher and won't make an impact at Chavez Ravine.

AKIN, AARON- TR - b: 6/13/77
A first-round draft pick in 1997, Akin's main challenge will be the development of a breaking-pitch repertoire; early indications from Rookie ball suggest that Akin won't be a strikeout pitcher until that happens. He has above-average command of his heater, and could be a short reliever if he needs to rely solely on the gas. If he can lay claim to a full-season rotation spot and dominate in 1998, then he will stamp himself as a budding prospect.

ALBERRO, JOSE - TR - b: 6/29/69
Scouting: Alberro has a live, low-90s, sinking fastball and a slider. In the minors, he has demonstrated good control, but in his brief major league stints, he has been reluctant to go at the hitters, preferring to nibble around the plate, and the results have been poor. Alberro is looking more and more like a pitcher who may not be able to make the jump to the majors.
1998: Alberro's age will begin to work against him as he tries to establish himself as a major league pitcher. He needs an impressive spring to avoid being passed by younger prospects.
1997: Alberro failed in another brief trial with Texas, and was dealt to the Yankees late in the season. He had another good season at Triple-A, and has nothing left to prove at that level.
1996: Alberro continued to make good progress in the minors. A reliever for most of his career, Alberro was used as a starter, with good results.

	W	SV	ERA	IP	H	BB	SO	B/I
1997 Texas	0	0	7.95	28	37	17	11	1.91

ALDRED, SCOTT - TL - b: 6/12/68
Scouting: The Twins claimed him off of waivers from Detroit in 1996 because they thought he could come back from surgery but, so far, he hasn't rewarded their faith in him. Aldred is at his best when his sharp curve is working. But it isn't working often enough and, as a result, he doesn't have the confidence in it that he needs.
1998: Aldred is no more than a fifth starter on a decent staff, a fourth starter on a mediocre staff. He will hurt you as often as he will help you — even if he is lefthanded.
1997: The Twins kept running him out there and Aldred kept disappointing. He finally was shipped back to Triple-A Salt Lake in June after failing in several chances.
1996: Aldred posted better numbers than probably could have been expected with Minnesota after washing out in a second trial with Detroit. The numbers, though, were just enough to keep teams interested but not enough to warrant serious consideration for a permanent job.

	W	SV	ERA	IP	H	BB	SO	B/I
1996 Minnesota	6	0	6.21	165	194	68	111	1.59
1997 Minnesota	2	0	7.68	77	102	28	33	1.68

ALFONSECA, ANTONIO - TR - b: 4/16/72

Scouting: Alfonseca is a hard thrower with a limited repertoire who was finally switched to the bullpen in 1997. His fastball is hard but straight — he has never been a strikeout pitcher, and he doesn't navigate the corners of the strike zone particularly well, either. His conditioning was a question in 1997 — he needs to shape up and refine his mechanics to gain more movement on his fastball.

1998: The departure of Robb Nen created the opportunity for a whole new fresh look at Alfonseca. He needs to show the Marlins he can get ahead of hitters and throw quality strikes on the corners to rise to the occasion.

1997: Alfonseca displayed a live arm and solid peak velocity at Triple-A Charlotte, and was in the right place at the right time when the other pitchers were traded. He struggled with strike one and grooved too many pitches, with predictably poor results.

1996: Alfonseca's last year as a starting pitcher was an exercise in frustration. He threw hard, straight strikes down the middle of the plate at Triple-A Charlotte and was hit hard. The subsequent move to the pen clearly kept Alfonseca's career alive.

	W	SV	ERA	IP	H	BB	SO	B/I
1997 Florida	1	0	4.90	26	36	10	19	1.79

ALMANZAR, CARLOS - TR - b: 11/16/73

Scouting: A strikeout pitcher, Almanzar is a converted starter with a tiny frame and good control. Earlier in his career, he kept the ball down more and must regain that ability to be effective.

1998: Although he got a look with the Blue Jays, he's headed back to Triple-A for further development.

1997: Almanzar started the year with Double-A Knoxville and was promoted to Syracuse in June. He was called up in September by the Blue Jays and struck out four of the twelve batters he faced.

1996: Completing the transition from starter to reliever, Almanzar picked up nine saves in 54 games at Double-A Knoxville. He struck out 105 batters in just 94.2 innings.

	W	SV	ERA	IP	H	BB	SO	B/I
1997 Toronto	0	0	2.73	3	1	1	4	0.61

ALSTON, GARVIN - TR - b: 12/8/71

Alston saw limited duty with the Rockies in 1996 but right arm troubles cost him the 1997 season. He has a 90-plus fastball but needed to work on his control before the injury. He was projected as a future closer or set-up man. That will now depend upon how well he can bounce back from missing all of last year.

ALVAREZ, TAVO - TR - b: 12/25/71

Seemingly forever a prospect, Alvarez struggled as a swingman with the Expos' Triple-A Ottawa farm club last year and Montreal has just given up. His strikeout-to-walk ratio and weight have always been a problem. He spent parts of 1995-96 in the majors with Montreal.

	W	SV	ERA	IP	H	BB	SO	B/I
1995 Montreal	1	0	6.75	37	46	14	17	1.62
1996 Montreal	2	0	3.00	21	19	12	9	1.48

ALVAREZ, WILSON - TL - b: 3/24/70

Scouting: Alvarez throws fastballs in the 90-MPH range and has a good curve to go with it, plus the requisite slider and changeup. He does seem to go deep into the count frequently, so he is generally only good for six or seven innings. He is also prone to giving up the long ball. Alvarez is a tough competitor, however, which makes him a go-to guy in important games.

1998: Because he was a free agent at the end of the 1997 season, Alvarez was expected to command a good deal of money, despite his late-season struggles after going to San Francisco. The Giants wanted him back but his contract demands made it a doubtful situation. He'll be a top starting pitcher in a major league rotation.

1997: Despite his 4-3 record, Alvarez didn't deliver in the manner the Giants were hoping when they traded for him. Though the team did win a title, and he did pitch a big game to clinch the last Saturday of the season, Alvarez often struggled with his control in San Francisco. Apparently it was tough for Alvarez to adjust to the National League.

1996: Alvarez rebounded well from his 8-11 season in 1995 to go 15-10. He pitched well in Venezuela over the winter, but tired towards the end of the season.

	W	SV	ERA	IP	H	BB	SO	B/I
1995 Chicago AL	8	0	4.32	175	171	93	118	1.51
1996 Chicago AL	15	0	4.22	217	216	97	181	1.44
1997 Two teams	13	0	3.48	212	180	91	179	1.28

ANDERSON, BRIAN - TL - b: 4/26/72

Scouting: Anderson is a first-round draft pick and a first pick overall in expansion. He has yet to assert himself as a full-time member of a major league rotation. The lefthander has a diverse repertoire, but has been limited by his lack of a true out pitch. His pinpoint control and ability to vary speed and location have made him a Triple-A standout, usually good for seven plus innings. However, he can't blow the ball past major leaguers. He has averaged four strikeouts per nine innings in his five major league trials.

1998: Expansion should finally net Anderson a spot in a major league rotation, with the Diamondbacks. Anderson would likely keep his team in the ballgame, and maybe even excel once around the league before the hitters get adjusted.

1997: Anderson was spectacular at Triple-A Buffalo, then hitters tuned him up at a .301 clip in eight major league starts, but his refusal to walk hitters and his ability to pitch out of jams kept the damage to a minimum.

1996: After being acquired from the Angels during the offseason, Anderson anchored the rotation of the Indians' veteran-laden Triple-A juggernaut, averaging nearly seven innings per start, before barely averaging five innings and four strikeouts per start in the majors.

	W	SV	ERA	IP	H	BB	SO	B/I
1995 California	6	0	5.87	99	110	30	45	1.40
1996 Cleveland	3	0	4.91	51	58	14	21	1.41

ANDERSON, JIMMY - TL - b: 1/22/76

Scouting: Anderson's forte is outstanding control of a rather ordinary arsenal of pitches that includes a sinking fastball in the high 80s, a curveball, slider and changeup. Anderson, though, lost his command last season at Triple-A Calgary. If he can't throw strikes, he is in trouble because he doesn't have the ability to dominate hitters.

1998: Anderson is no longer on the fast track in the Pirates'

organization. After stumbling last season at Calgary, he is headed back to Triple-A for the start of this season. The Pirates are still high on him, though, and he will be promoted to Pittsburgh as soon as he gets straightened out and there's a need at the major league level.
1997: Anderson started well with four strong outings at Double-A Carolina then struggled mightily at Calgary. The most alarming part of Anderson's first taste of Triple-A was walking 64 in 106 innings after averaging less than two walks per nine innings during his first three pro seasons. He couldn't get his breaking pitches over for strikes, causing him to rely on an ordinary fastball.
1996: Anderson split the season between Class A Lynchburg and Carolina and did well at both spots. Particularly impressive was the way he dominated Southern League hitters at the tender age of 20.

ANDERSON, MATT - TR - b: 4/1/78
Anderson remains unsigned even though he and the Tigers, who made him the number one pick in the 1997 draft, are just $90,000 apart. If he had signed he probably would have already pitched for the Tigers. Anderson throws a 98-MPH heater and has said that he may return to Rice for the spring semester and play his senior season.

ANDERSON, MIKE - TR - b: 7/30/66
Former Cub farmhand Anderson was hittable in a brief trial with Oklahoma City; he's a longshot to make it to the majors. In 1997 Anderson pitched at three levels on the Dodgers farm. He was unimpressive.

ANDERSON, RYAN - TL - b: 4/1/80
Too bad the Mariners don't play in the NBA because with Anderson and Randy Johnson they would have a formidable front line. Instead they will have a formidable pitching staff when Anderson reaches the Kingdome. The 6'10" high schooler from Michigan was the Mariners' first-round pick in the June 1997 draft (19th overall). He throws in the high 90's and is ahead of the Big Unit at this stage; Anderson is just 17 years old.

ANDUJAR, LUIS - TR - b: 11/22/72
Scouting: Although blessed with an overpowering fastball, Andujar has trouble keeping the ball down in the strike zone. His control remains erratic at best and he should strike out more batters considering how hard he throws.
1998: Andujar has a shot to be a starting pitcher with the Blue Jays and, if not, will likely go back to Triple-A.
1997: His season was shortened because he had bone chips removed from his elbow in September. He split time as a starter/reliever with the Blue Jays and also pitched for Syracuse for much of the season. Overall, his performance was disappointing.
1996: Beginning the season in the White Sox organization, Andujar started five games for Chicago before being traded to the Blue Jays for Domingo Cedeno and Tony Castillo.

	W	SV	ERA	IP	H	BB	SO	B/I
1995 Chicago AL	2	0	3.26	30	26	14	9	1.33
1996 Chicago-Tor.	1	0	6.99	37	46	16	11	1.67
1997 Toronto	0	0	6.48	50	76	21	28	1.94

APANA, MATT - TR - b: 1/16/71
1997 was Apana's fifth season in the Mariners' organization and he made stops at both the Class A and Double-A sites. Apana was the California League Pitcher of the Year in 1994 when he sported a 14-4 record. He hasn't made much progress since then and has control problems. He pitched a majority of last season at Double-A Memphis where he gave up less than a hit per inning but runners reached via base on balls (47 walks, 45 strikeouts). He's only got so long to improve his control, at his age he should be able to handle Double-A hitters better if he were truly a prospect.

APPIER, KEVIN - TR - b: 12/6/67
Scouting: Appier undoubtedly has some of the best stuff in the majors. He throws everything hard, a mid-90s fastball, a nasty slider and an explosive, low-90s split-fingered fastball. The splitter is his out pitch but it's hard to tell sometimes if he's throwing it or it's throwing him. Appier's delivery causes him to fall off the mound towards the first base line which induces sideways movement to his pitches; he often walks a fine line between unhittable and uncontrollable.
1998: Appier has ace starter stuff but has to learn to pitch "smarter." New manager Tony Muser wants Appier to get hitters to put the ball in play more instead of trying to strikeout the world. While his peripheral numbers will remain among the best in the game, his all-important bottom line — his win/loss record — depends heavily upon Appier's ability to adjust and become a smarter pitcher.
1997: Appier's first full-season losing record can be attributed at least partially to pitching in bad luck; as usual he got little run support. But Appier beat himself too often, also, by letting his unruly splitter get away at the most inopportune times. It was a disappointing season.
1996: Shoulder problems for a third straight season slowed Appier but he still finished among league leaders in most pitching categories and received an expensive two-year contract extension late in the season.

	W	SV	ERA	IP	H	BB	SO	B/I
1995 Kansas City	15	0	3.89	201	163	80	185	1.21
1996 Kansas City	14	0	3.62	211	192	75	207	1.26
1997 Kansas City	9	0	3.40	236	215	74	196	1.23

ARNOLD, JAMIE - TR - b: 3/24/74
The Braves' first-round pick in 1992 has not developed as expected. In his first full-season above A-ball, Arnold went 7-7 with a 4.92 ERA in 23 starts. In four-plus seasons, he has yet to post a record over .500, his strikeout rate is getting weaker every year and he continues to allow homers at a frightening pace. Arnold is beginning to look like a first-round bust.

AROCHA, RENE - TR - b: 2/24/66
Scouting: Arocha, who had his best success as a closer for St. Louis during the 1994 season, has never been the same after losing his spot. Arocha has a wide assortment of slow stuff, but he doesn't seem to be able to put it together at the major league level.
1998: If Arocha is ever going to do anything as a major leaguer, it will likely be for a new team. It is not unreasonable, as fellow Cubans Luis Tiant and Mike Cueller didn't blossom until they were older and with new teams.
1997: Arocha went 7-3, with a 4.76 ERA for Triple-A Phoenix last year. However, when the Giants were looking for pitching

help at mid-season, they never looked to Arocha. He was released by San Francisco and made his way to Columbus, where he pitched well enough over four games, but with his experience in the majors and international ball, Arocha should be successful in the minors.
1996: Arocha did not play due to injuries.

	W	SV	ERA	IP	H	BB	SO	B/I
1997 San Francisco	0	0	11.36	10	17	5	7	2.14

ARRANDALE, MATT - TR - b: 12/14/70

As they look to fill their bullpen, the Cardinals might give Arrandale consideration. He'll have to show plenty more than he did the last two seasons in Triple-A where, overall, he's compiled a 4.21 ERA with 238 baserunners allowed in 162 innings — all in relief. The 27-year-old righthander is durable and was considered a prospect as a starting pitcher as recently as 1994. Without a top fastball or above-average breaking pitch, he hasn't become a key prospect as a reliever yet.

ARROJO, ROLANDO - TR - b: 7/18/68

This Cuban phenom was too inconsistent at St. Petersburg to be considered anything more than a longshot for the Devil Rays' rotation in 1998. However, one major-league scout said Arrojo had good enough stuff to be included in his team's rotation in 1997. Club officials believe he got bored during the 1997 season; in addition he had to make the transition to living in a new country. Both were factors that could have affected his performance.

ARROYO, BRONSON - TR - b: 2/24/77

The Pirates' third-round draft pick in 1995 is on the fast track to the majors after being one of the top pitchers in the Class A Carolina League last season at Lynchburg. Arroyo throws hard and throws strikes. However, he needs to pack a little more than 165 pounds on his 6'5" frame before he gets to the majors, probably sometime in the 1999 season.

ASHBY, ANDY - TR - b: 7/11/67

Scouting: Ashby hasn't lived up to ace starter projections. He has a good fastball/slider/changeup combination and at times has no-hit stuff (he took a no-hitter into the ninth against the Braves last year). But he has also been inconsistent. The Padres believed Ashby to be on the verge of stardom after his 12-10, 2.94 ERA campaign in '95. But his results have slipped each of the past two seasons, partially due to injuries.
1998: Ashby and Joey Hamilton are again projected as co-staff aces.
1997: Ashby led the Padres with 30 starts, but averaged less than seven innings per outing and had only two complete games. His 4.13 ERA represented a 1.3 run increase over the last two years. Ashby missed five starts at midseason due to tendinitis. His opposition batting average of .266 was the best among Padre starters.
1996: Ashby was on the disabled list three times with right shoulder problems including a frayed labrum, but still finished with a winning record and respectable ERA.

	W	SV	ERA	IP	H	BB	SO	B/I
1995 San Diego	12	0	2.94	192	180	62	150	1.26
1996 San Diego	9	0	3.23	150	147	34	85	1.21
1997 San Diego	9	0	4.13	201	207	49	144	1.28

ASSENMACHER, PAUL - TL - b: 12/10/60

Scouting: Assenmacher has been one of the most underrated specialty relievers of this or any generation. He has been at it for 12 years now, and is creeping up the all-time games pitched list (760). His approach is simple; throw quality strikes, early and often. His overhand curves, changeups and other assorted junk give lefties problems and are no picnic for righthanders, either. He is asked to retired a batter or two per outing; he has pitched only 776 innings in his 760 outings, and only 291 innings over his last 371 games.
1998: Assenmacher is happy in Cleveland, and there is no comparable replacement in sight. His control — the key to his success — hasn't deteriorated a bit, so there is no reason to expect any change from Assenmacher in the near future.
1997: The Indians reaffirmed their faith in Assenmacher by trading young lefty flamethrower Alan Embree to the Braves. Assenmacher was allowed to face more righthanders than in most past seasons, and he held them to a .231 average. He was a quiet constant while co-closers Jose Mesa and Mike Jackson both had down periods.
1996: It was another typical Assenmacher season: a hit allowed per inning, three-to-one strikeout-to-walk ratio — and a winning record. There hasn't been a more consistent lefty set-up man over the past decade.

	W	SV	ERA	IP	H	BB	SO	B/I
1995 Cleveland	6	0	2.82	38	32	12	40	1.15
1996 Cleveland	4	1	3.09	46	46	14	44	1.30
1997 Cleveland	5	4	2.94	49	43	15	53	1.18

ASTACIO, PEDRO - TR - b: 11/28/69

Scouting: Astacio has an outstanding changeup that he started throwing more often after he was traded from Los Angeles to the Rockies in August. He's a tenacious competitor who refuses to give in when he's in trouble. When he loses it, though, he can become combative and really lose it. He had lost up to five MPH on his fastball three years ago, but he was throwing around 90 MPH with the Rockies. Astacio has good control and is not afraid to pitch inside.
1998: Astacio went into the off-season as the Rockies' staff ace.
1997: Extremely streaky, Astacio started the season 3-0 with the Dodgers; he then lost seven straight. He won four straight to even his record at 7-7. He lost his next two and was about to get demoted from the rotation to the bullpen when he was traded to the Rockies. He immediately became their best pitcher, pitching well in his first six starts, all Rockies victories. He was finally blasted in his last start, when he was pounded by his ex-teammates at Coors Field.
1996: Astacio rebounded from two consecutive disappointing seasons to regain his spot in the Dodgers' rotation.

	W	SV	ERA	IP	H	BB	SO	B/I
1995 Los Angeles	7	0	4.24	104	103	29	80	1.27
1996 Los Angeles	9	0	3.44	211	207	67	130	1.30
1997 two teams	12	0	4.14	202	200	61	166	1.29

ATCHLEY, JUSTIN - TL - b: 9/5/75

Atchley is not in the Reds' long-term plans, at least not now. He's old for a player in his position (he turned 24 in September) and he's been unspectacular in the low minors (4.70 ERA in 13 starts at Double-A Chattanooga last year). And the three pitchers the Reds acquired from Cleveland for John Smiley have pushed Atchley even further down the ladder. The Reds need pitching, but Atchley will have to do better to earn a shot in Cincinnati.

AUCOIN, DEREK - TR - b: 3/27/70
About the only thing the Expos can possibly see in Aucoin is his size (6'7") and the fact that he is French-Canadian. He had no control at both Triple-A Ottawa and Class A West Palm Beach, walking 21 batters in 6.1 innings at Ottawa; that's more than a walk for every hitter he retired. At his age he's not a prospect.

AVERY, STEVE - TL - b: 4/14/70
Scouting: Avery's fastball, which used to come in at more than 90 MPH, now lives in the mid-80s and he has become one of the most hittable pitchers in baseball. His curve has also lost it's bite, and he has been unable to make the transition from power pitcher to finesse pitcher.
1998: A bounceback is unlikely since Avery has been struggling, in a declining fashion, for the last three years. Of course, there is the possibility that he can suddenly learn how to win with his now below-average stuff, as some lefthanders do.
1997: Avery battled a couple of minor injuries, and used them as excuses at times for his poor performance. But even when healthy he was awful. Facing possible pressure from the Players Association, the Red Sox allowed Avery to reach an incentive-based contract option based on starts so he will get a chance to pitch somewhere for big bucks this season.
1996: Avery fell out of favor with Atlanta by having his second straight sub-par season, and was relegated to the bullpen, where he pitched poorly, in the off-season.

	W	SV	ERA	IP	H	BB	SO	B/I
1995 Atlanta	7	0	4.67	173	165	52	141	1.25
1996 Atlanta	7	0	4.47	131	146	40	86	1.42
1997 Boston	6	0	6.42	97	127	49	51	1.82

AYALA, BOBBY - TR - b: 7/8/69
Scouting: Ayala's unorthodox delivery — his leg kick carries him toward the left side of the mound — helps his 90-plus fastball but often hinders his location, causing performance swings from unhittable to being so bad the Mariners traded prospect Jose Cruz, Jr. for relief help.
1998: Ayala will start the season as a set-up man after the Mariners' flurry of last-second deals for relievers last year, but he can be a capable closer when he is on, as his 48 saves the last four years attest.
1997: There were times in the season when he closed for Randy Johnson. Ayala tied for the American League lead in relief wins with Arthur Rhodes. Ayala's hits per inning and strikeouts per inning rates were good but he allowed 14 homers in 96.2 innings.
1996: Ayala was to have split time with Norm Charlton as the closer, but he suffered a lacerated right hand and wrist in late April. By the time he returned two months later, he was strictly a set-up man after getting 37 saves the previous two years.

	W	SV	ERA	IP	H	BB	SO	B/I
1995 Seattle	6	19	4.44	71	73	30	77	1.45
1996 Seattle	6	3	5.88	67	65	25	61	1.34
1997 Seattle	10	8	3.82	97	91	41	92	1.37

AYBAR, MANUEL - TR - b: 10/5/74
Scouting: A former shortstop, Aybar has a live arm and still is learning much about pitching. He actually was regarded as further along than Matt Morris at the end of the 1996 season. A delayed beginning to his spring of 1997 because of visa problems perhaps set him back, then he quickly caught up and established himself as a key part of the Cardinals' immediate plans. With an excellent fastball and slider, he could be important in the bullpen — perhaps even as a closer. He had expected to work on his changeup in the Dominican winter league, though, and could nudge into the starting rotation because of assorted skills that include excellent control.
1998: So much depends upon his opportunities as a starter. Aybar probably will be given serious consideration to crack the rotation and would be sent to the major league bullpen if there's no room for him to start. He would benefit from being broken in slowly that way.
1997: Aybar started slowly in Triple-A but had a 1.88 ERA in the eight starts before his promotion to the big leagues and at the time led the American Association in strikeouts. After some inconsistency early on, he had flashes of excellence in late-August and early-September with the Cardinals before beginning to show some wear. His 205 innings pitched overall were by far the most of his career.
1996: In only the fourth season of pitching in his life, Aybar ranked sixth in the Cardinals organization with a 3.05 ERA in Double-A ball.

	W	SV	ERA	IP	H	BB	SO	B/I
1997 St. Louis	2	0	4.24	68	66	29	41	1.40

BAILES, SCOTT - TL - b: 12/18/62
Scouting: As a lefty bullpen specialist, Bailes can get lefthanded hitters out with a good curveball. He has to rely on good location otherwise, because his stuff isn't anything special.
1998: There isn't any reason that Bailes shouldn't be able to pitch for another year or two as a situational lefty out of someone's bullpen.
1997: Bailes' story is still remarkable, but underlines the scarcity of lefthanded pitching talent in professional baseball. Out of baseball for three full years, Bailes signed to play winter ball and pitched well enough to catch on with the Rangers as a non-roster invitee. After more than half a season with Oklahoma City (2-3, 3.98, four saves), Bailes was promoted to Texas and became their top bullpen lefty.
1996: Bailes was out of baseball for the third consecutive season.

	W	SV	ERA	IP	H	BB	SO	B/I
1997 Texas	1	0	2.86	22	18	10	14	1.27

BAILEY, CORY - TR - b: 1/24/71
Scouting: Bailey's out pitch is a sinker, and he has had some success when he keeps the ball down. When he is on, he induces mostly ground balls. Bailey's stuff has not been impressive enough to keep him in the big leagues, so he has split each of the past five seasons between the majors and minors. Bailey is strictly a reliever.
1998: Bailey once again finds himself in the position of having to compete for a middle-relief spot on someone's roster. Whatever the initial result, he will likely split time between the majors and minors once again.
1997: After a good spring, Bailey was nonetheless assigned to begin the season at Triple-A, where he was the closer for Oklahoma City (3.40 ERA, 15 saves). Late in the season, he was traded to the Giants and didn't impress anyone in his brief stint in the majors.

1996: Bailey had the most effective stretch of his career as a middle reliever for the Cardinals. In 57 innings, he yielded only one home run and was adept at working out of trouble.

	W	SV	ERA	IP	H	BB	SO	B/I
1995 St. Louis	0	0	7.36	3	2	2	5	1.09
1996 St. Louis	5	0	3.00	57	57	30	38	1.53
1997 San Francisco	0	0	8.35	10	15	4	5	1.96

BAILEY, ROGER - TR - b: 10/3/70

Scouting: When he's on, as he was through the first two months of the season, Bailey conjures comparisons to Greg Maddux; his outstanding changeup allows him to mix speeds well. His fastball is average, but it has great sink when he's on. Consistency has been the problem; he can have outstanding control one month, and be erratic the next. Bailey is a bulldog of a competitor who showed great stamina earlier in 1997, but then faded the final two months as his innings piled up.
1998: For the first time in his career, he will report to spring training as a lock for the rotation. If he takes another step up to become more consistent, Bailey could win fifteen games.
1997: Bailey was one of the Rockies' most pleasant surprises. It took him just seven starts to set a team record for complete games (five); he also had two shutouts. He was having an All Star-type season until June 19th, when he suffered a torn hamstring while trying to score from second base on a base hit. At the time, Bailey was 8-5 with a 3.27 ERA. Sidelined for nearly a month, he lost his groove and was never the same pitcher.
1996: Bailey struggled while being used periodically in the rotation and in a long-relief job; he fared better when his role was limited strictly to middle relief.

	W	SV	ERA	IP	H	BB	SO	B/I
1995 Colorado	7	0	4.98	81	88	39	33	1.57
1996 Colorado	2	1	6.24	83.2	94	52	45	1.75
1997 Colorado	9	0	4.29	191	210	70	84	1.47

BALDWIN, JAMES - TR - b: 7/15/71

Scouting: Baldwin has good stuff with a low-90s fastball, an above-average curve and he's now throwing a split-fingered fastball. He has lost a few MPH off the fastball, now hitting 90 MPH on the radar gun; some scouts blame his newly-found splitter which they believe is damaging his arm. Another cause for the velocity drop might be the increasing number of innings he has thrown the last two years. Baldwin sometimes exhibits poor control due to release point problems.
1998: Baldwin is ticketed for an important role in the White Sox rotation.
1997: Losing Alex Fernandez and Wilson Alvarez thrust Baldwin into an ace starter position, a role for which he is not yet suited. All his peripheral numbers were worse than the previous year and his record suffered, too.
1996: Baldwin was the Sporting News' Rookie Pitcher of the Year as he placed among league leaders in opponent batting average (eighth best - .257) and fewest baserunners per nine innings (ninth - 12.2). Baldwin's much-ballyhooed potential came to fruition.

	W	SV	ERA	IP	H	BB	SO	B/I
1995 Chicago AL	0	0	12.89	14	32	9	10	2.80
1996 Chicago AL	11	0	4.42	169	168	57	127	1.33
1997 Chicago AL	12	0	5.27	200	205	83	140	1.44

BANKS, WILLIE - TR - b: 2/27/69

Scouting: Banks made a remarkable comeback after missing the entire 1996 season with a circulation problem in his right shoulder. The former top draft pick of the Twins no longer blows hitters away with a high-octane fastball but has finally learned location is more important that pushing the speed guns into the mid-90s. His best pitch is still the heater but he has a good changeup and can throw strikes with his breaking stuff.
1996: After nurturing Banks back from oblivion and giving him a chance to pitch again, the Yankees feared losing him in the expansion draft. The Yankees' plans call for him to work in long relief.
1997: Banks stayed away from injury to re-establish himself as a pitcher with a future at Triple-A Columbus and increased his value by pitching well after being converted from a starter to a reliever. He went 14-5 with a 4.27 ERA in 33 games (24 starts) for Columbus and pitched five times for the Yankees, making one start.
1996: Banks was out of baseball in 1996 after being released by the Phillies in spring training. He spent the summer working out with one goal in mind — pitching for the Yankees.

	W	SV	ERA	IP	H	BB	SO	B/I
1997 New York AL	3	0	1.93	14	9	6	8	1.07

BAPTIST, TRAVIS - TL - b: 12/30/71

After leading his league in hits allowed in 1996, Baptist was used more as a relief pitcher in 1997 and with better results. Pitching at Double-A New Britain, and Triple-A Salt Lake, he posted ERA's of 3.41 and 2.08, respectively. His struggles in 1995 and 1996 are attributable to a sore arm — his prospect status has healed along with his arm.

BARBAO, JOE - TR - b: 4/18/72

Barbao has been the last resort, the guy who pitches a couple of innings in a blowout, during his last two seasons in the Phillies' chain, most recently at Double-A Reading. His velocity and command were barely adequate in A-ball, and he was in over his head in 1997. He allowed 15 baserunners and struck out fewer than four batters per nine innings while debuting in Double-A at age 25.

BARBER, BRIAN - TR - b: 3/4/73

His chances of pitching for the Cardinals keep getting slimmer and slimmer, despite all their investment in this former first-round draft pick. After several frustrating minor-league seasons and a couple of failed attempts in the big leagues, he spent most of the 1997 season trying to come back from off-season arm surgery. He never fully regained his former velocity and, though experience has made him a better-rounded pitcher, Barber struggled with his control all summer at Triple-A. Still only 25 years old, he could make it if his fastball regains its old 90+ MPH zip.

BARCELO, MARC - TR - b: 1/10/72

After four years in the Twins' system Barcelo turned up in the Cubs' organization last year. A first-round draft pick by the Twins in 1993, Barcelo has experienced shoulder troubles and inconsistency of late. He was an A-ball pitcher in 1997 and he didn't do anything to improve his stock. He was hittable and didn't have good control. He's in jeopardy of having his baseball career come to an abrupt end.

BARK, BRIAN - TL - b: 3/4/73

A crafty lefty who wasn't good enough to make it with the

Braves, Bark got a second chance with the Red Sox and then a third chance with Mets, who weren't impressed and released him.

BARKLEY, BRIAN - TL - b: 12/8/75
Barkley was in the class of young pitchers who made the jump to Double-A in 1996, along with Carl Pavano and Brian Rose. But Barkley did not share their success and remained in Double-A in '97. His performance was a tad better, but just a tad. He's still young and he is lefthanded, so he'll get a lot more chances, but he's unlikely to help a major league team this season.

BARNES, BRIAN - TL - b: 3/25/67
A former major leaguer, Barnes spent another season at Triple-A Toledo on the Tigers farm in 1997. His performance was weaker in '97 than it had been in 1996, but he was good enough to work 115 innings and win seven games.

BARRIOS, MANUEL - TR - b: 9/21/74
Scouting: Barrios is a hard-throwing righthander from Panama who has been used exclusively in relief in his four-year career. He led the entire Astro organization in saves in both 1995 and 1996 with 23 each season. For his minor-league career, he has averaged 8.4 strikeouts and only 3.3 walks per nine innings.
1998: Barrios will be competing for a middle relief job at the major league level. He will probably spend another year at Triple-A.
1997: Barrios pitched at the Triple-A level for the first time where he was 4-8 with a 3.27 ERA in 57 games. He was used in a set-up role for Oscar Henriquez and didn't have any saves. He was called up to Houston in September.
1996: Barrios gained notice when he successfully jumped from Low Class A Quad Cities to Double-A Jackson. He was 6-4 with 23 saves and an ERA of 2.37 and 69 strikeouts in 68 innings.

	W	SV	ERA	IP	H	BB	SO	B/I
1997 Houston	0	0	12.00	3	6	3	3	3.00

BATCHELOR, RICHARD - TR - b: 4/8/67
Once a closer prospect, Batchelor has been bouncing from the bigs to Triple-A and back the past few seasons. He pitched at Triple-A Las Vegas in the Padres' organization last year. He had a good strikeout-to-walk ratio but only pitched 21 innings and gave up 23 hits. He's never going to get that major league closer job, but he could turn up in a big-league bullpen in long relief to eat up garbage-time innings.

	W	SV	ERA	IP	H	BB	SO	B/I
1997 San Diego	3	0	5.96	29	40	14	18	1.88

BATISTA, MIGUEL - TR - b: 2/19/71
It wasn't that long ago that Batista was a pretty good prospect in the Montreal system. He was so highly thought of that the Pirates claimed him in the Rule 5 draft before the 1992 season, but returned him to Montreal before the end of April. But Batista suffered a shoulder injury that sidelined him for most of the 1994 season and he never really recovered. He's only been a mediocre pitcher since then, both in Florida's farm system and in Chicago's. He got his first significant big-league playing time last year, but got beat around pretty good pitching for the Cubs. Batista never will be a productive starter, but he could wind up being an average middle reliever.

	W	SV	ERA	IP	H	BB	SO	B/I
1997 Chicago NL	0	0	5.70	36	36	24	27	1.65

BAUTISTA, JOSE - TR - b: 7/26/64
Bautista was released by the Giants at the end of the '96 season. He got a look from the Tigers and Cardinals in 1997. His past success depended on sharp control of his forkball, and he's lost that command. Bautista can still throw a variety of pitches, a fastball, curve and change, but his velocity is down. Unless he suddenly regains command of the forkball, he won't be a factor in the majors in 1998.

	W	SV	ERA	IP	H	BB	SO	B/I
1995 San Francisco	3	0	6.44	100	120	26	45	1.46
1996 San Francisco	3	0	3.36	69	66	15	28	1.17
1997 Det. - St. Louis	2	0	6.66	53	70	14	23	1.59

BEATTY, BLAINE - TL - b: 4/25/64
Beatty is pitching now solely for the love of the game. He hasn't pitched in the major leagues since 1991, though he has developed a pretty good knuckleball since he was last in the bigs. His claim to fame was finishing last season with more minor-league wins than any active pitcher. He will likely stay in the Pirates' organization if he decides to pitch in 1998. He lives in Wendell, N.C., close to the Pirates' Double-A Carolina farm club.

BECK, ROD - TR - b: 8/3/68
Scouting: No one really represents the heart and soul of the Giants like Beck. Unlikely looking, yet effective, Beck gets by with a fastball in the low 90s, a curve and a split-fingered pitch. His velocity isn't what it was earlier in his career, and Beck performs better when he kept to pitching one inning per outing.
1998: With Beck and fellow major league closer Roberto Hernandez both eligible for free agency, the Giants had an off-season dilemma. Getting Robb Nen made the question even more complicated. Beck is obviously a closer wherever he pitches. He'll go through some shaky periods, but will likely collect 30 saves.
1997: Beck was on the mound, facing the Padres, when the Giants got their final out to clinch their 1997 title. It wasn't a save situation, but manager Dusty Baker wanted Beck on the hill when the time came. Beck did convert 37 saves, but he also blew eight. He was much more effective during the first half.
1996: Though he was still the "man" for the Giants, his velocity faded — a bad sign for a closer. He got off to a hot streak, allowing nothing over his first 15 appearances. From then on, he was often ineffective. Beck had not yet learned how to pitch when he didn't have Grade A stuff.

	W	SV	ERA	IP	H	BB	SO	B/I
1995 San Francisco	5	33	4.45	58	60	21	42	1.39
1996 San Francisco	0	35	3.34	62	56	10	48	1.06
1997 San Francisco	7	37	3.47	70	67	8	53	1.07

BECKETT, ROBBIE - TL - b: 7/16/72
A power pitcher, Beckett is a former top draft choice who has never thrown enough strikes to complement a fastball that is clocked at 95 MPH when he lets it go. A great teaser, who will always get a chance to make a club out of spring training, Beckett usually spends most of the season at Triple-A. In 54.1 innings at Colorado Springs last year, he struck out 67, but walked 47 and had a 6.79 ERA.

	W	SV	ERA	IP	H	BB	SO	B/I
1997 Colorado	0	0	5.29	2	1	1	2	1.18

BEECH, MATT - TL - b: 1/20/72

Scouting: Beech is a promising lefthander with a diverse repertoire and above-average power and control which were masked by his poor mainstream numbers in 1997. Beech reaches the upper-80's with a darting fastball, that he complements with a changeup and a curveball which locks up lefthanded hitters. Southpaws have been unable to touch him at any level during his pro career. Beech's control is sometimes too impeccable; he catches too much of the plate and gives up more than his share of home runs. Like many promising youngsters, Beech is susceptible to the big inning, and allows an alarmingly high percentage of baserunners to score. He does not hold baserunners well.

1998: Beech is a prime breakout prospect. His confidence grew late last year as he began to get ahead of hitters regularly. He has the diversity to keep hitters off stride, and a multitude of pitches to put hitters away.

1997: Beech lost an opportunity to begin 1997 in the major league rotation by hurting his arm in spring training. When he finally earned a promotion, he pitched four dominant innings against the Cardinals - only to sprain an ankle running out a double. He was hammered in his first few starts after a stint on the disabled list, but played a part in the Phillies' second-half surge, though his win total was limited by poor run support.

1996: Beech owned lefties at Double-A Reading, and posted a 146-to-33 minor-league strikeout-to-walk ratio before a late-summer recall. Beech won his first start over Greg Maddux, then struggled with his confidence and the gopher ball (eight homers in 41 innings) the rest of the way.

	W	SV	ERA	IP	H	BB	SO	B/I
1996 Philadelphia	1	0	6.97	41	49	11	33	1.46
1997 Philadelphia	4	0	5.07	137	147	57	120	1.49

BEIRNE, KEVIN - TR - b: 1/1/74

Beirne is a good athlete. He was picked by the White Sox in the 11th round of the 1995 June draft out of Texas A&M. While he was an Aggie, Bierne played outfield as well as pitched for the baseball team and was a wide receiver on the football squad. In 1997, he made his first appearance at the Double-A level. He pitched well in A-ball, giving up less than a hit per inning while striking out 75 in 82.2 innings. Beirne found it tougher going at Double-A, allowing a hit per inning, and having some control problems. Starting out in Double-A in 1998 is likely for Beirne.

BELCHER, TIM - TR - b: 10/19/61

Scouting: Belcher throws four different fastballs and a curveball. His two-seam and four-seam fastballs reach the upper 80s but his sinker and cut fastballs are often more effective pitches. He's got a good enough repertoire and usually enough command to find at least one pitch that is working on any particular day. Belcher is most effective when he gets hitters to beat his sinker into the ground; his best starts are often low strikeout affairs. He gets pounded — and allows too many homers — when he gets his pitches up too much in the strike zone.

1998: Belcher has another year left on his contract and, after two years of leading the Royals in victories, should be back in a number two starter role. He's obviously on the downhill side of his career, but Belcher is a wily veteran, capable of getting the most out of the least.

1997: His ERA increased more than a run from his successful 1996 campaign, mostly due to too many high fastballs that were ridden out of the park; Belcher led the Royals in homers allowed. But, he was still the club's winningest pitcher and was, for the first half of the season, a effective starter.

1996: Belcher's best season in five years featured the most innings of his career and his most victories and starts. It was a surprising rebound for Belcher after several sub-par seasons for four different organizations from 1992-5 and it earned him a new two-year contract.

	W	SV	ERA	IP	H	BB	SO	B/I
1995 Seattle	10	0	4.52	179	188	88	96	1.55
1996 Kansas City	15	0	3.92	238	262	68	113	1.39
1997 Kansas City	13	0	5.02	213	242	70	113	1.46

BELINDA, STAN - TR - b: 8/6/66

Scouting: Belinda features a decent fastball that tops out in the low 90's, a changeup, and a good slider. The slider, combined with his sidearm delivery, made him particularly effective against righthanded hitters, whom he held to a .203 average in 1997. He is one of the few gambles that paid off for Jim Bowden last year.

1998: Belinda is likely to remain in a set-up role behind Jeff Shaw and Jeff Brantley. If the Reds lose Brantley, Belinda would become the most likely alternative to Jeff Shaw as closer.

1997: Belinda was a pleasant surprise for the Reds after an injury plagued 1996, setting career highs in games, innings, holds and strikeouts. The Reds were shopping him before the trade deadline, then signed him to a two-year deal in August.

1996: Belinda suffered through 28 injury-filled innings in Boston, was released after the season and signed by the Reds.

	W	SV	ERA	IP	H	BB	SO	B/I
1995 Boston	8	10	3.10	69	51	28	57	1.13
1996 Boston	2	2	6.59	28	31	20	18	1.81
1997 Cincinnati	1	1	3.72	99	84	33	114	1.18

BELL, JASON - TR - b: 9/30/74

A control pitcher with a good curve, Bell has impressed in his first few stops in the Twins' system. He went 11-9 with a 3.39 ERA in 28 games for Double-A New Britain last summer. Most noticeable were his 142 strikeouts as compared to only 64 walks in 164.2 innings. Bell will move on to Triple-A Salt Lake's rotation this season but is another year away from the majors.

BELTRAN, RIGO - TL - b: 11/13/69

Scouting: A relatively soft-throwing lefthander, Beltran didn't seem to have a chance to ever get out of Triple-A with the Cardinals. Injuries made his promotion a necessity in 1997, and he baffled batters who clearly haven't seen screwballs often. He balances the pitch well with his fastball and uses excellent control. Though he's not likely to gain a spot in anyone's starting rotation, he's proven himself able to work in any situation and is actually most effective against righthanded batters.

1998: Though not assured of roster spot, the fact that he throws from the left side and proved himself a big-leaguer probably will gain him a role as a workhorse out of the bullpen.

1997: Beltran was excellent through eight Triple-A starts at the beginning of the season, giving him 71 career starts at that level. Beltran joined the Cardinals and became one of the

steadiest members of their bullpen.
1996: Splitting time as a starter and reliever for the first time since turning pro in 1991, Beltran had no trouble moving back and forth. His 4.35 ERA was among the lowest in the American Association and he struck out 132 batters with only 24 walks.

	W	SV	ERA	IP	H	BB	SO	B/I
1997 St. Louis	1	1	3.48	54	47	17	50	1.18

BENE, BILL - TR - b: 11/21/67
Bene pitched at Double-A and Triple-A for the Angels last year. He gave up a hit and a walk per inning. There's no way a pitcher with that kind of stuff is getting anywhere near a major league bullpen any time soon. Bene will have to make significant strides just to stay in pro ball.

BENES, ALAN - TR - b: 1/21/72
Scouting: Benes started to fulfill his great promise in just his second big-league season. Clearly much more comfortable in the majors, he combines an often-overpowering fastball with an excellent curveball and cut fastball. His calm demeanor on the mound gives him a veteran's presence, he likes to work deep into the game, and his pitch control showed improvement. That could be the only piece missing in making Benes a Cy Young candidate. He needs to throw more strikes when behind in the count.
1998: He might not be in top form from the outset, considering he was coming off shoulder surgery and didn't even start throwing again until January. When Benes returns to full health, he's likely to stake a claim to the top spot in the team's rotation.
1997: Benes was as good as any pitcher in the league through his first 20 starts, as he ranked among the leaders in opponent's batting average and struck out more than a batter per inning. He showed marginally improved control as well but seemed to pitch just well enough to lose. His shoulder trouble — eventually diagnosed as a slight problem in the rotator cuff —led to three sub-standard starts before he was placed on the DL.
1996: He either was outstanding or frustrating, either working into the late innings with a chance to win or being knocked out after just a few innings. Such was Benes' inconsistent, albeit promising, rookie season.

	W	SV	ERA	IP	H	BB	SO	B/I
1995 St. Louis	1	0	8.44	16	24	4	20	1.75
1996 St. Louis	13	0	4.90	191	192	87	131	1.46
1997 St. Louis	9	0	2.89	162	128	68	160	1.21

BENES, ANDY - TR - b: 8/20/67
Scouting: An often overpowering pitcher with a wide variety of pitches, Benes has developed into an ace largely because he can rely on an extensive experience. He uses two different fastballs, each of which zooms into the mid-90s and has excellent movement within the strike zone. Usually prone to giving up a lot of home runs, Benes has learned to work the ball down more. That and his improved changeup and slider have put him on the verge of being a big winner.
1998: He went into the winter as a free agent, though he should be a number one starter capable of 20 victories and Cy Young consideration wherever he pitches.
1997: After getting off to a slow start because of a strained muscle in his side, Benes turned in a steady string of excellent but frustrating outings. He suffered from lack of offensive support and occasional lapses after falling behind late in several close games. Benes was particularly effective at home, where he went 7-2.
1996: He lost seven of his first eight decisions, then won 17 of his final 20 to silence critics who always held that Benes never would develop his great potential into being a big winner.

	W	SV	ERA	IP	H	BB	SO	B/I
1995 San Diego	4	0	4.17	118	121	45	126	1.40
1995 Seattle	7	0	5.86	63	72	33	45	1.67
1996 St. Louis	18	1	3.83	230	215	77	160	1.27
1997 St. Louis	10	0	3.10	177	149	61	175	1.19

BENITEZ, ARMANDO - TR - b: 11/3/72
Scouting: Benitez is one of the hardest throwers in baseball, occasionally hitting 100-MPH on the radar gun. He gets a lot of strikeouts with the fastball, but he also throws a good slider and an occasional changeup. His weakness is immaturity, but he's coming around. Although he's been closing occasionally, some doubt if he has the mental makeup to be a first-rate closer over the course of long, pressure-packed season.
1998: Benitez' 1998 role depends on closer Randy Myers's contract situation. If Myers signs elsewhere, Benitez has a good chance to become a closer, or at least share the job with Arthur Rhodes.
1997: He was nearly unhittable last year, holding both right and lefthanded batters to less than .200 batting averages.
1996: Benitez used to get rattled when he gave up a key hit, but he came through late in the season in some tough playoff-pressure situations. He displayed a slight tendency to being home run prone.

	W	SV	ERA	IP	H	BB	SO	B/I
1995 Baltimore	1	2	5.66	47	37	37	56	1.55
1996 Baltimore	1	4	3.77	14	7	6	20	0.92
1997 Baltimore	4	9	2.46	73	49	43	106	1.26

BENNETT, BOB - TR - b: 12/30/70
Bennett has good control. The upside means he gives up few walks (15 over 42.2 innings at Double-A Huntsville last year). The bad news is he gives up a lot of hits (64) and homers (seven). He is not overpowering, so he must learn to let hitters get themselves out by changing speeds and hitting the corners.

BENNETT, ERIK - TR - b: 9/13/68
After seeing limited duty in Minnesota in 1996, Bennett spent 1997 in the Indians organization at Double-A Akron. For a middle reliever Bennett was much too hittable, resulting in a high ERA. He's pushing 30 will get only spot duty if he makes it back to the show.

BENNETT, JOEL - TR - b: 1/31/70
The Orioles drafted Bennett out of the Red Sox organization as a sixth-year minor-league free agent. He spent parts of 1995 and 1996 in Triple-A as a starter and reliever with poor results. He's been at Double-A for the past two years, posting solid records as a middle reliever and set-up man. If Bennett doesn't make the majors soon, he won't make it at all.

BENNETT, SHAYNE - TR - b: 4/10/72
Scouting: Bennett has an average fastball and a decent curveball but his out pitch is a nasty split-finger fastball. He doesn't have the stuff to be a closer but could become an effective set-up reliever in the majors. If nothing else, the

Australian has a good sense of humor as evidenced by his funny Internet columns on the Major League Baseball web site last summer.

1998: The Expos like cheap talent and Bennett makes the minimum. Therefore, he has a good chance of being a middle reliever in their bullpen.

1997: Bennett started slowly at Double-A Harrisburg but pitched extremely well upon his promotion to Triple-A Ottawa at mid-season. He held his own after being promoted to Montreal in mid-August, though his control was shaky.

1996: After being acquired from the Boston organization in an off-season trade, Bennett had a fine year in short relief with the Expos' Double-A Harrisburg farm club.

	W	SV	ERA	IP	H	BB	SO	B/I
1997 Montreal	0	0	3.17	23	21	9	8	1.32

BENSON, KRIS - TR - b: 11/7/74

Scouting: The Pirates made Benson the first overall pick in the 1996 draft and gave him a then-draft-record bonus of $2 million after a standout career at Clemson University. Many scouts said Benson was the finest college pitching prospect ever with his 94-MPH fastball, drop-off-the-table curveball, sharp slider and developing changeup. However, his changeup needs improvement before he can effectively pitch as a starter in the big leagues.

1998: Benson will start the season at either Triple-A Calgary or Double-A Carolina, depending on how well he performs in spring training. The Pirates have a pretty solid group of young starting pitchers and there's no need to rush Benson. However, as soon as he shows he is ready to pitch in the majors, the Pirates will make room for him.

1997: Benson began his professional career with Class A Lynchburg and was dominating in ten starts. He strained a hamstring upon his late-May promotion to Double-A Carolina. That injury, combined with facing more experienced hitters, led Benson to having some rough times in the Southern League.

1996: Benson was named College Player of the Year by Baseball America and Collegiate Baseball after going 14-2 with a 2.02 ERA in 19 starts with 204 strikeouts and 35 walks over 156 innings for Clemson. He also pitched for the bronze-medal winning U.S. Olympic team, pushing his professional debut back to 1997.

BENZ, JAKE - TL - b: 2/27/72

Benz has had four straight fine seasons as a reliever in the Expos' farm system, pitching well as a set-up man in 1997 at Double-A Harrisburg and Class A West Palm Beach. The most encouraging part for Benz is that he is also starting to throw strikes consistently. He could be in the majors by 1999. Though he projects as only a set-up man, Benz could be a good one in the big leagues.

BERE, JASON - TR - b: 5/26/71

Scouting: Extensive elbow surgeries and other elbow trouble have kept Bere out of action for most of the last two years. He had a high-90s fastball before the surgery, but has lost some velocity, dropping to the low-90s now. Bere is still working his way back into shape, throwing a lot of breaking pitches to strengthen his elbow.

1998: Bere is aiming for a rotation job out of spring training, assuming his elbow is ready again. If not, he could start the year in rehab with a quick re-introduction into the White Sox rotation when he's ready.

1997: The White Sox were happy to see Bere back to pitching again and he actually had some good results, too.

1996: Two trips to the 60-day disabled list, two surgeries and tendinitis wrecked his 1996 campaign. He made just eleven starts, six of them in rehab. assignments.

	W	SV	ERA	IP	H	BB	SO	B/I
1995 Chicago AL	8	0	7.19	137	151	106	110	1.88
1996 Chicago AL	0	0	10.26	16	26	18	19	2.72
1997 Chicago AL	4	0	4.70	29	20	17	21	1.29

BERGMAN, SEAN - TR - b: 4/11/70

Scouting: The Padres don't know what to make of Bergman. When he is throwing on the side or warming up, Bergman has some of the best stuff on the staff. But he can't throw his "A" stuff consistently during games. He's been a major disappointment and a bigger puzzle; his results are miserable. Bergman has lost his spot in the starting rotation in two straight years.

1998: Bergman will pitch somewhere in '98, but probably not for the Padres. There are ample opportunities for anyone with a mid-90s fastball and a sharp slider. But he's got to solve his "great one pitch, terrible the next" syndrome.

1997: Bergman's ERA ballooned in '97 and he allowed 11 homers in 99 innings. He was ineffective as a starter and as a reliever; opponents hit .316 against him.

1996: Bergman was acquired from Detroit late in the spring and made 14 starts, going 3-7 with a 5.12 ERA, before being sent to the bullpen. He fared somewhat better in relief, going 3-1 with a 2.75 ERA in 27 appearances. It resulted in a career-best 4.37 ERA for Bergman who had been primarily a starter for the Tigers.

	W	SV	ERA	IP	H	BB	SO	B/I
1995 Detroit	7	0	5.12	135	169	67	86	1.75
1996 San Diego	6	0	4.37	113	119	33	85	1.34
1997 San Diego	2	0	6.09	99	126	38	74	1.66

BERTOTTI, MIKE - TL - b: 1/18/70

Scouting: Bertotti has good velocity with a running, sinking fastball that often moves out of the strike zone, but he loses his velocity after just a few hitters.

1998: Bertotti may be better suited for situational relief than the swingman role to which he is accustomed. He will challenge for a major league bullpen job.

1997: Bertotti didn't get as much time in the majors in 1997 as he had the previous two seasons and was a non-factor in the White Sox' season.

1996: In another season split between the high minors and the majors, Bertotti was unimpressive in fifteen big-league appearances (two starts), walking more batters than he struck out with a high ERA.

	W	SV	ERA	IP	H	BB	SO	B/I
1995 Chicago AL	1	0	12.56	14	23	11	15	2.37
1996 Chicago AL	2	0	5.14	28	28	20	19	1.71
1997 Chicago AL	0	0	7.30	4	9	2	4	2.97

BERUMEN, ANDRES - TR - b: 4/5/71

Hard-throwing Berumen never turned out to be the pitcher the Padres hoped for and was sent to the Mariners for a pitcher who didn't live up to Seattle's expectations (Paul Menhart). Berumen, however, is unlike a lot of Seattle's righthanders in that he's a strikeout pitcher. Unfortunately, he's too much like many of their righthanders in that he walks more than he should. He has a slim chance to make the Mariners, and will spend the year moving between Tacoma and Seattle.

BETTI, RICK - TL - b: 9/16/73
After being released by the Braves and sitting out a season in '94, Betti signed with his hometown Red Sox after attending an open tryout. A lefthanded reliever, he enjoyed great success with the Red Sox until he reached Double-A in '96. He had a 6.35 ERA in 40 innings for Double-A Trenton in '97 and is unlikely to make the majors or have a great impact if he does.

BEVERLIN, JAY- TR - b: 11/27/73
Beverlin was acquired by the Yankees in the Ruben Sierra/ Danny Tartabull trade in 1995. Since then, he has been mostly a bust for the Yankees, even struggling in A-ball where he had once been dominant in 1995 and 1994. His 1997 season was split evenly between Double-A Norwich and Class A Tampa. He posted a 7.78 ERA in Double-A, also giving up 50 hits in 41.2 innings. With Tampa, he had a 4.79 ERA but did not give up more than a hit per inning.

BEVIL, BRIAN - TR - b: 9/5/71
Scouting: Bevil is a fastball/slider pitcher who hits the radar gun in the low 90s; he also throws an occasional splitter. Bevil is a good, but not great prospect for the Royals. They believe he throws hard enough to pitch short relief but he has to improve the command of his off-speed pitches since his fastball isn't enough by itself, although he may be able to add a few more MPH to it.
1998: The Royals are counting on Bevil as a set-up man in the bullpen. He started 1997 in that role and was a failure before being demoted to the minors. It could be a good learning environment, provided the bullpen as a whole isn't the disaster area it was the first half of last year.
1997: Injuries to Jeff Montgomery and Jaime Bluma opened an opportunity for Bevil to start the year with Kansas City. He was hit hard in too many of his early-season outings and fell as far as Double-A Wichita. Bevil was more consistent once recalled late in the year.
1996: As a starter, Bevil climbed from Double-A Wichita, through Triple-A Omaha, to pitch three games in Kansas City (one start). He won 17 games overall in his most successful season as a pro. Despite just 13 starts at Wichita, his nine wins were second on the staff for the entire season.

	W	SV	ERA	IP	H	BB	SO	B/I
1997 Kansas City	1	1	6.63	16	16	9	13	1.53

BIELECKI, MIKE - TR - b: 7/31/59
Scouting: Bielecki works off of a low-90s fastball, tossing an occasional slider but his out pitch is an above-average forkball. He has resurrected his career after nearly fading into obscurity three years ago. Regaining velocity on his fastball has been the key, but he doesn't throw hard enough to blow the ball past hitters. Bielecki has to work the corners and make hitters beat the ball into the ground with his forkball.
1998: It's hard to say when the 38-year-old Bielecki will finally hang up his spikes. The end can always come quickly for elderly pitchers and will for Bielecki when his velocity fades again. If he remains effective, he'll retain his bullpen role for Atlanta.
1997: Back in the Braves' pen, Bielecki did his job as a set-up man although the results weren't as spectacular as in the previous year. When the pen struggled at mid-season, Bielecki struggled along with the other relievers; his usually good command of fastball and forkball was sometimes lacking.
1996: After shoulder problems nearly ended his career the previous year, Bielecki won a job at Triple-A Richmond out of spring training, got a quick recall to Atlanta, then went on to one of his finest seasons ever. He moved from a mop-up man to a middle-innings guy to eventually become the club's most effective set-up man and even helped the Braves win four of his five spot starts. It was an amazing rebound in his eighteenth professional season.

	W	SV	ERA	IP	H	BB	SO	B/I
1995 California	4	0	5.97	75	80	31	45	1.48
1996 Atlanta	4	2	2.63	75	63	33	71	1.28
1997 Atlanta	3	2	4.08	57	56	21	60	1.34

BIERBRODT, NICK - TL - b: 5/16/78
Scouting: A first-round pick in the 1996 draft, Bierbrodt was ignored by the established franchises because of a high school basketball injury. He has a 90-MPH fastball, a good breaking ball and good composure on the mound.
1998: Bierbrodt is expected to open the season at higher Class A in High Desert as the Diamondbacks exercise their favorite word, patience, with their young pitchers.
1997: Bierbrodt missed the first month of the season with arm tenderness but had a reliable season at Class A South Bend, going 2-4 with a 4.04 ERA in 15 starts for a team that had trouble hitting; he recorded 64 strikeouts in 75.2 innings.
1996: Bierbrodt signed early so he could join the Diamondbacks' Rookie League team. He overpowered the competition with a 1.66 ERA in 38 innings, fanning 46 and allowing just 25 hits. After a late-season promotion to the Pioneer League he was 2-0 with a 1.50 ERA and 23 strikeouts in 18 innings.

BLAIR, WILLIE - TR - b: 12/18/65
Scouting: At his best, he gets compared to Greg Maddux, because of perfect command and great movement that makes games go by quickly. Obviously, he's tough as proven by the way he recovered from a broken jaw. The only negative is his track record. Since he was 11-25 as a big-league starter before 1997, he'll need to prove that he wasn't a one-year wonder.
1998: Everyone will be watching to see if Blair's 1997 season was a fluke, or just a career year in an otherwise fairly undistinguished career. On the other hand, the reason Blair gave for his sudden success was getting a chance to stay in a starting rotation right from opening day. His '97 success will guarantee that he gets that chance again.
1997: For the first time in his career, Blair got a chance at the starting rotation in spring training. He won a job, started off all right and then had his jaw fractured by Julio Franco's line drive. Then he started winning big. Blair won seven games in a row, and 15 of his last 21 decisions.
1996: Left in the bullpen all season by the Padres, Blair pitched a lot and sometimes pitched well, but didn't have a great year. He had a 2.93 ERA in his last 17 appearances, though, as the Padres battled the Dodgers in the pennant race.

	W	L	ERA	IP	H	BB	SO	B/I
1995 San Diego	7	0	4.34	114	112	45	83	1.38
1996 San Diego	2	1	4.60	88	80	29	67	1.24
1997 Detroit	16	0	4.17	175	186	46	90	1.33

BLAIS, MIKE - TR - b: 10/2/71
Blais would have to be considered an organizational pitcher. He has slightly below-average stuff across the board, but some idea of how to pitch. He did well in the lower minors, but his lack of stuff caught up with him the last couple of years at the higher minor-league levels. He did get a brief call-up to Triple-A in '97, where he struggled to an 8.31 ERA over 13 innings, but that was more because he was a needed body than anything else. It will take a similar manpower shortage for him to ever reach the majors.

BLANCO, ALBERTO - TL - b: 6/27/76
Scouting: A promising, hard-throwing lefthander signed at age 16, Blanco took a giant stride forward in 1997 with his 7-4, 2.83 ERA season at High Class A Kissimmee, advancing to Double-A Jackson at season's end; he set personal bests in starts, innings pitched, wins and ERA. It was enough to put the youngster back in "prospect" status after an injury-shortened 1996 campaign (strained elbow ligament).

BLAZIER, RON - TR - b: 7/30/71
SCOUTING: Blazier has spent eight seasons bouncing through the Phillies' organization, with extended major league trials in 1996 and 1997. A starter until 1995, Blazier struggled at high levels because of the similarity between the velocity of his fastball and slider. He was shifted to the bullpen, and in 1997 began to experiment with a split-fingered fastball under the tutelage of Bruce Sutter.
1998: The Phillies' bullpen situation is wide open for 1998. Not much is expected of Blazier, but his ceiling is higher than most of his competition should he suddenly successfully integrate the splitter into his repertoire. The best guess is that Blazier will remain in a similar role in 1998; a top Triple-A set-up man or the mop-up man on the big club.
1997: Blazier racked up the frequent flyer miles, starting at Triple-A, going to the majors, then down to Class A Clearwater to work with Sutter, than back to Triple-A and finally back to the Phillies again. His performance at each respective level summed up his status — his fastball dominated lower-level hitters, but his repertoire isn't diverse enough, nor his command sharp enough to consistently retire more refined hitters.
1996: Blazier dominated as the Triple-A closer, and then got his first major league chance in his seventh pro season. His fastball was placed poorly and hit hard, and he had no useful off-speed pitch.

	W	SV	ERA	IP	H	BB	SO	B/I
1996 Philadelphia	3	0	5.87	38	49	10	25	1.55
1997 Philadelphia	1	0	5.03	54	62	21	42	1.55

BLOMDAHL, BEN - TR - b: 12/30/71
After six seasons as a Tiger farmhand, with one disappointing major league trial, Blomdahl moved on to the Indians' chain in 1997, where he served as a swingman. He is a battler with average stuff who has good control and a mature approach on the mound. However, he has been eminently hittable over the past two seasons, and might be about out of time. He certainly has no chance of playing a major league role for the Indians.

BLOOD, DARIN - TR - b: 8/31/74
Blood found the going at Double-A Shreveport a bit tougher than it had been at Class A San Jose. He was 8-10 with a 4.33 ERA in 1997 after going 17-5 with a 2.76 ERA the previous year. The control he displayed in 1996 was missing last year, as he walked 83 in 156 innings with only 90 strikeouts. The jump to Double-A often separates the true power pitching prospects from the pretenders, but pitchers sometimes need an extra year to adjust at that level. Blood will get that extra year in 1998.

BLUMA, JAIME - TR - b: 5/18/72
Scouting: His fastball isn't overpowering (low-90s), but he spots it well and will cut a fastball to give hitters a different look. Bluma has been groomed as a future closer since being selected in the third round of the 1994 draft out of regional collegiate powerhouse Wichita State University.
1998: The Royals are hopeful that Bluma can fully recover after losing the entire 1997 season to shoulder problems. If he comes back, he'll get the primary set-up job in front of closer Jeff Montgomery and will also get to finish a few games, too. He's likely to begin the season in Omaha as a tune up.
1997: Bluma had shoulder surgery in the spring, then was slow to recover, eventually losing the entire year.
1996: When Jeff Montgomery was sidelined with a shoulder injury, Bluma jumped straight from his Triple-A closer job (25 saves at Omaha) to save five games in as many tries for the big-league club. It was a brief, but impressive major league debut, particularly considering how Bluma was suddenly thrust into an important bullpen job on short notice.

	W	SV	ERA	IP	H	BB	SO	B/I
1996 Kansas City	0	5	3.60	20	18	4	14	1.10

BOCHTLER, DOUG - TR - b: 7/5/70
Scouting: When his pitches are working, Bochtler has a nasty fastball/slider/changeup combination. But the mechanics of his unstructured delivery fell apart in '97 and the Padres lost their reliable '96 bridge from the starters to closer Trevor Hoffman.
1998: Bochtler will still have to pitch his way back into the Padre bullpen after his miserable '97 campaign.
1997: Bochtler failed as a set-up man for Hoffman, issuing 50 walks in 60.1 innings. He was still hard to hit (.229), but opponents took the walk instead. He could not find the plate, and usually at critical times; his strikeout rate also dropped.
1996: Bochtler was an excellent set-up man, limiting rival hitters to a .195 average while he posted more than a strikeout per inning.

	W	SV	ERA	IP	H	BB	SO	B/I
1995 San Diego	4	1	3.57	45	38	19	45	1.26
1996 San Diego	2	3	3.02	65	45	39	68	1.29
1997 San Diego	3	2	4.78	60	51	50	46	1.68

BOEHRINGER, BRIAN - TR - b: 1/8/70
Scouting: Boehringer has a decent fastball/slider repertoire and can throw 90 MPH. He appeared in only 34 games last year and worked 48 innings due to an operation on his right elbow that removed boned chips early in June. However, when the reliever returned there was added velocity to his fastball and the slider had more bite.
1998: The Padres traded for Boehringer after Tampa Bay drafted him. San Diego planned to use his talents in their bullpen and were looking for him to work middle relief or even be a spot starter.
1997: Bone chips were causing control problems for Boehringer.

When they were removed, has fastball — which is his best pitch — showed a lot more life. He also has a good slider, and both pitches were located better after the surgery.

1996: Boehringer appeared in 15 games for the Yankees, including three starts, but split time at Triple-A Columbus, too. His results were unremarkable as he had a good strikeout rate, but walked too many hitters.

	W	SV	ERA	IP	H	BB	SO	B/I
1996 New York AL	2	0	5.44	46	46	21	37	1.45
1997 New York AL	3	0	2.63	48	39	32	53	1.48

BOEVER, JOE - TR - b: 10/4/60

Boever is no longer capable of closing as he did with Atlanta back in the last part of the 1980's. He can still occasionally fool hitters with his palmball but his professional career is hanging by a thread at age 37. Boever was released by the Pirates out of Triple-A Calgary then hooked on with Oakland's Triple-A Edmonton farm club. He didn't pitch well at either stop and even expansion won't get him back to the big leagues.

	W	SV	ERA	IP	H	BB	SO	BP
1995 Detroit	5	3	6.39	98	128	44	71	1.74
1996 Pittsburgh	0	2	5.40	15	17	6	6	1.53

BOGOTT, KURTISS - TL - b: 9/30/72

Bogott is unlikely to surface in the major leagues unless he dramatically improves his control. Although he is a lefthanded strikeout pitcher, he has yet to show the command required to be an effective major league pitcher.

BOHANON, BRIAN - TL - b: 8/1/68

Scouting: Pitching coach Bob Apodaca elicited surprisingly solid work from Bohanon, but at age 29, Bohanon is much more a journeyman than the prospect he once was (19th player chosen overall in the 1987 draft). He pitches "backwards," getting ahead with his breaking ball, then using his two-seam fastball and cut fastball. He needs to work to increase his stamina and find a way to be more effective against lefthanded batters. But he comes equipped with heart. He's better with runners on base and better yet with runners in scoring position.

1998: Even with two new teams in the game, chances are Bohanon will find himself in circumstances identical to those he experienced last season — looking for work as a spot starter in the big leagues or in a Triple-A rotation. Then again, if he's afforded an opportunity and pitches as he did last summer, he will be an asset to most teams outside Atlanta and Los Angeles. Still, the Mets couldn't enter spring training with Bohanon as a member of the rotation and consider their pitching to be improved.

1997: Bohanon's work as a major league starter — 6-3 record and a 3.27 ERA in 14 games and 88 innings — was an extension of what he did in Triple-A to earn a mid-season promotion. He won nine of 12 Triple-A decisions, producing a 2.63 ERA and striking out 84 in 96 innings.

1996: He pitched exclusively in relief for the Blue Jays and their Triple-A Syracuse affiliate and without great success. Bohanon was quite effective against lefthanded hitters, allowing 12 hits in 62 at-bats.

	W	SV	ERA	IP	H	BB	SO	B/I
1995 Detroit	1	1	5.54	105	121	41	63	1.54
1996 Toronto	0	1	7.77	22	27	19	17	2.09
1997 New York NL	6	0	3.82	94	95	34	66	1.37

BOLTON, RODNEY - TR - b: 9/23/68

Bolton spent the entire season in the minor leagues after playing the 1996 season in Japan. He got 19 starts for Cincinnati's Triple-A Indianapolis team and had limited success (9 wins, 1 shutout) but never did anything to show he deserved to get called up. Bolton doesn't throw hard and gave up way too many home runs for a control pitcher (21 in 169.2 innings) and given his age (he turned 29 in September) he seems destined to play more games in the minors than in the majors at this point in his career.

BOLTON, TOM - TL - b: 5/6/62

Bolton has spent part of eight seasons in the bigs during his 15-year professional career but hasn't been in the majors since 1994 and, based on his 1997 performance, he probably won't ever make it back. He pitched at Triple-A Tucson in the Milwaukee organization last year and was extremely hittable (142 hits in 95 innings). The only thing going for Bolton is that he's a lefty but at age 35 it probably won't be enough for a return trip to the majors.

BONES, RICKY - TR - b: 4/7/69

Scouting: Erstwhile-Brewer Bones has the standard four-pitch repertoire, but none are outstanding. His fastball reaches only the mid-80s and his off-speed pitches (slider, curve, changeup) are nothing special. He's durable, but is not fooling hitters any longer.

1998: Bones has fallen a long way from being the Milwaukee staff ace just a few years ago. His immediate future will include a lot of middle-relief work and an occasional spot start.

1997: Bones bounced through three organizations, including the Brewers, of course, to finish as a swingman with Kansas City. Despite one outstanding start for the Royals, Bones had his best success in a long-relief role. He was generally hit hard all year, allowing an opposition batting average of .325 and ten homers in just 78.1 innings.

1996: Bones' ERA soared as he lost his starting job with Milwaukee and was part of the late-season Yankees-Brewers stretch drive trade. He pitched in the Yankee bullpen with only occasional success.

	W	SV	ERA	IP	H	BB	SO	B/I
1995 Milwaukee	10	0	4.63	200	218	83	77	1.51
1996 Milw-N Y AL	7	0	6.22	152	184	68	63	1.66
1997 Kansas City	4	0	6.75	96	133	36	44	1.76

BONANNO, ROB - TR - b: 1/5/71

Bonnano is kind of restarting his career after being set back by an elbow injury, but he still has plenty of talent, he's a tough competitor and his recovery has gone well. His numbers at Double-A Midland weren't that impressive because of the injury, but he has a good repertoire — fastball, curveball, slider and changeup — and has a chance to make something happen.

BORBON, PEDRO - TL - b: 11/15/67

In late-August of 1996, Borbon tore the elbow ligament in his pitching arm and was lost for the season. In surgery, he had a tendon taken from a leg to replace the damaged elbow ligament; it cost Borbon the entire 1997 season and there is some question about his ability to come back at all. When healthy, Borbon has a good riding fastball and hard slider; he throws hard for a lefthander although he occasionally lacks sharp control. Being able to pitch at all will be Borbon's goal in 1998.

	W	SV	ERA	IP	H	BB	SO	B/I
1995 Atlanta	2	2	3.09	32	29	17	33	1.44
1996 Atlanta	3	1	2.75	36	26	7	31	0.92

BORLAND, TOBY - TR - b: 5/29/67

Scouting: Borland has more velocity on his slider and fastball than most submariners, but still is pretty typical of those style of pitchers. He has success against righthanders and struggles against lefties.

1998: Borland has a chance to be a helpful pitcher out of the bullpen, but needs to be spotted carefully against righthanders. He also needs to pitch somewhere where the pressure is not too great.

1997: Borland did not respond well to an off-season trade to New York, struggling with his control, and was quickly dealt to Boston. He didn't handle the pressure well there either, and soon found himself pitching in Triple-A. He struggled there too, although not as badly. A possible factor for Borland's quick decline was sickness. He lost 20 pounds due to pleurisy following the '96 season.

1996: Borland enjoyed his second straight solid season out of the bullpen for the Phillies.

	W	SV	ERA	IP	H	BB	SO	B/I
1995 Philadelphia	1	6	3.77	74	81	37	59	1.59
1996 Philadelphia	7	0	4.07	90	83	43	76	1.40
1997 Boston	0	1	7.54	17	17	21	8	2.28

BOROWSKI, JOE - TR - b: 5/4/71

Borowski has a solid fastball but it's not good enough to keep hitters honest without something else. He's got good size and some toughness, and he should stick around long enough to find the right pitch to complement his fastball and give him a chance of being a useful reliever. He struggled with his control in the majors in '97, but he corrected the problem when sent to Triple-A.

	W	SV	ERA	IP	H	BB	SO	B/I
1995 Baltimore	0	0	1.23	7	5	4	3	1.23
1996 Atlanta	2	0	4.85	26	33	13	15	1.77
1997 New York AL	2	0	4.15	26	29	20	8	1.88

BOSIO, CHRIS - TR - b: 4/3/63

Bosio signed with the Red Sox near the end of the '97 season because his ailing knees, which forced his retirement in '96, began to feel better with some time off. He saw limited action, pitching in just a couple of low-level minor-league games, but he and the Red Sox are hopeful that he can bounce back and help the major league team in '98 now that he is healthy again.

	W	SV	ERA	IP	H	BB	SO	B/I
1995 Seattle	10	0	4.92	170	211	69	85	1.65
1996 Seattle	4	0	5.93	60	72	24	39	1.59

BOSKIE, SHAWN - TR - b: 3/28/67

Scouting: Boskie has below-average stuff and, as a flyball pitcher, he is gopher-ball prone. His best role is as a middle reliever, mop-up man and spot starter.

1998: The Orioles were disappointed with Boskie and are unlikely to retain him for 1998. With another team, he could win 5-10 games with an ERA over 5.00.

1997: The Orioles were counting on Boskie as their fifth starter, but he struggled as a starter and was demoted to the bullpen where he was also erratic. He had a minor arm ailment and spent some time on the disabled list. Pitching hurt most of the year may have been a contributing factor to his off season.

1996: Boskie won 12 games for the Angels in 1996, his career-best year. He's a flyball pitcher and homers are a major weakness: he gave up 40 home runs, tying for first in the league.

	W	SV	ERA	IP	H	BB	SO	B/I
1995 California	7	0	5.64	111	127	25	51	1.36
1996 California	12	0	5.32	189	226	67	133	1.55
1997 Baltimore	6	1	6.43	77	95	26	50	1.57

BOST, HEATH - TR - b: 10/13/74

A young pitcher who had an impressive 1997 season at Double-A New Haven, Bost posted 20 saves and a 3.56 ERA in 38 games, though he is projected as set-up reliever in the bigs. He's not overpowering (85-88 MPH fastball), but throws a heavy sinker. Bost also has a good slider and, for lefthanded hitters, a better-than-average changeup. He has good control and pitches aggressively. He may start 1998 back at New Haven, though he figures to wind up at Triple-A Colorado Springs some time during this year.

BOTTALICO, RICKY - TR - b: 8/26/69

SCOUTING: Bottalico is a young but established closer who relies primarily on a mid-90s fastball for success. He runs into trouble when he lacks confidence in his fastball, as he did in the middle third of the 1997 season, instead relying on a breaking-ball repertoire which he controls rather poorly. Bottalico has the gunslinger mentality that one desires in a closer, but sometimes loses focus when he is brought into the game in a non-save situation, which happened quite often in early 1997, when the Phillies seemingly went entire weeks without leading a game.

1998: Look for more consistency from Bottalico. The Phillies will actively pursue better set-up support for Bottalico, in anticipation of having more leads to protect this year.

1997: Bottalico was a lonely man early in 1997, as the Phillies' stumbled until mid-summer. He then went through a dead-arm phase which cut a few MPH from his fastball for a few weeks. Bottalico tried to work through it with breaking pitches and walked a lot of hitters. After being dangled in front of the Mariners in a trade-deadline deal, Bottalico regained his arm strength and finished well.

1996: Bottalico was one of the Phillies' few bright spots in his first season as their closer. He dominated righthanders at a .185 clip, and showed the best control of his professional career.

	W	SV	ERA	IP	H	BB	SO	B/I
1995 Philadelphia	5	1	2.46	87	50	42	87	1.05
1996 Philadelphia	4	34	3.19	67	47	23	74	1.04
1997 Philadelphia	2	34	3.65	74	68	42	89	1.49

BOTTENFIELD, KENT - TR - b: 11/14/68

Scouting: Bottenfield doesn't have much to offer. His fastball is only average and he doesn't have a particularly good breaking ball that would keep hitters off balance. Bottenfield isn't good and manager Jim Riggleman knows it, using him as a long reliever and in games where the Cubs are several runs behind. He's not a strikeout pitcher, and never has been, which makes it even more difficult for him to be used in clutch situations.

1998: Bottenfield has some experience and probably will be able to get a job based upon his good 1996 season and his so-so 1997 season. He's not a bad guy to have as a long reliever, primarily because he comes cheaply and he can give a team innings, but it would be a mistake for anybody to put him into a more important role.

1997: Bottenfield had little hope of duplicating his 1996 season. He started the year in middle relief, but by mid-season he was being used only when the Cubs were behind and had little chance of catching up. He was all right in that role, but he would have been replaced on the roster if the Cubs had other options.

1996: Bottenfield put up surprisingly good numbers for the Cubs after several years of being pounded in Montreal, Colorado and San Francisco. He started the season at Triple-A Iowa and was brought up in early June. While he had a good ERA for the Cubs, his relatively few strikeouts should have been a warning signal that he really didn't deserve the praise he was getting.

	W	SV	ERA	IP	H	BB	SO	B/I
1996 Chicago NL	3	1	2.63	61	59	19	33	1.27
1997 Chicago NL	2	2	3.86	84	82	35	74	1.39

BOUGHTON, MICHAEL - TR - b: 11/8/74
After being selected as having the best infield arm in the Diamondback's organization in a 1996 Baseball America survey, Boughton took his 90-plus fastball to the mound.

BOURGEOIS, STEVE - TR - b: 8/4/74
Once a highly regarded prospect in San Francisco's farm system, Bourgeois was far too inconsistent in 1997 at Triple-A Colorado Springs to impress the Rockies. His best pitch is his slider, which he throws with deception. He also has an average fastball and changeup. He shows great stuff at times, then not so great. He tends to hang his pitches, which is not the formula for successful pitching in Colorado.

	W	SV	ERA	IP	H	BB	SO	B/I
1996 San Francisco	1	0	6.30	40	60	21	17	2.02

BOVEE, MIKE - TR - b: 8/21/73
Scouting: The Angels are extremely excited about Bovee, who came to them in the winter of 1996 from Kansas City in the Mark Gubicza/Chili Davis deal. Bovee is mentally tough and an intense competitor, which has helped him progress through the ranks probably a little faster than the Angels expected. He has an above-average fastball, plus a developing curveball, slider and changeup to go with it.

1998: Bovee needs to show that a good season of work in winter ball has prepared him to make another jump in his career. He'll have the opportunity in spring training to win a starting job or a job in middle relief. Even if Bovee starts the season in Triple-A, he doesn't appear to be far away from pitching in the majors full time.

1997: Not sure how fast Bovee would progress, the Angels started him at Double-A Midland, but he had earned a promotion to Triple-A Vancouver by June and pitched for the Angels at the end of September. He was solid as a starter at both levels and impressed the organization with his tenacity, particularly when he pitched ten innings in a 3-2 victory for Vancouver on July 31st.

1996: Although his ERA went up, Bovee rebounded from a tough season at Double-A Wichita the year before, finishing in double figures in wins, with three complete games and two shutouts.

	W	SV	ERA	IP	H	BB	SO	B/I
1997 Anaheim	0	0	5.45	3	3	1	5	1.21

BOWEN, RYAN - TR - b: 2/10/68
The charter member of the expansion Marlins got a trial at Triple-A New Orleans in the Brewers' farm system in 1996. Last year he moved on to the Yankees' farm system, pitching ten innings at Triple-A Columbus, but gave up ten earned runs. He pitched 15 innings at Class A Tampa with a 4.02 ERA but gave up 17 hits. He has good stuff, especially his heater, but he has poor command and is prone to injury.

BOWERS, SHANE - TR - b: 7/27/71
As a control specialist, Bowers succeeded as a starter at Double-A New Britain where he went 7-2 with a 3.41 ERA last year. But a lack of depth in his pitching repertoire accounted for his struggles at Triple-A Salt Lake in the Minnesota farm system.

	W	SV	ERA	IP	H	BB	SO	B/I
1997 Minnesota	0	0	8.05	19	27	8	7	1.84

BOYD, JASON - TR - b: 2/23/73
Scouting: Boyd's fastball is slightly above average, but most of his pitches have similar velocity. Such a repertoire was sufficient for him to show above-average power and control in his Class A seasons, and the Phillies moved him to a set-up relief role at Double-A Reading in 1997, where hitters would get only one look at him per game. The key for Boyd is to throw strike one; he has a tendency to fall behind and start nibbling around the edges of the plate. Development of better command is the key to his success at higher levels.

1998: Boyd was taken by Arizona. He could be a top right-handed set-up man in the minors, or an adequate reliever in the majors. He has the arsenal to achieve, but he is at the age where he needs to produce results now. If he can cut his walk rate to three or fewer per nine innings, he could have a good major league future.

1997: Boyd started the season in the Reading rotation, but was clobbered in the early going. The move from higher Class A to Double-A often weeds out hurlers like Boyd with limited repertoires and fastballs that don't reach 90 MPH regularly. However, he showed a bounce-back arm capable of pitching consecutive days or for multiple innings, and was an above-average set-up man by season's end.

1996: Boyd was the Phillies' best higher Class A starting pitcher, combining decent power with excellent control. However, he averaged barely six innings per start, and wasn't one of his level's younger hurlers.

BOZE, MARSHALL - TR - b: 5/23/71
A change of organizations did Boze no good. He was winless in 14 outings at Triple-A Las Vegas and was hittable. He doesn't throw the ball by anybody and he doesn't make up for it with any pitching savvy.

	W	SV	ERA	IP	H	BB	SO	B/I
1996 Milwaukee	0	1	7.79	32	47	25	19	2.24

BRANDENBURG, MARK - TR - b: 7/14/70
Scouting: Brandenburg is a submariner with a well-below-average fastball. But he's also got an assortment of slow, Frisbee-like off-speed pitches and manages to fool lefties at times with a funky, rushed-delivery changeup.

1998: Brandenburg, who has always fought perception problems because of his style and below-average stuff, appears to have found an organization which believes in him, returning to Texas. He should stick around as a middle reliever for Boston and pitch capably, but he has no chance at starting or closing.
1997: Brandenburg had arm problems coming out of spring training, spent some time in Triple-A to get his game back, and bounced back to pitch well in the majors at the end of the season.
1996: Brandenburg spent the entire season in the majors for the first time in his career, and pitched well. He was traded from Texas to Boston on July 31st in a deal involving Mike Stanton.

	W	SV	ERA	IP	H	BB	SO	B/I
1995 Texas	0	0	5.93	27	36	7	21	1.57
1996 Boston	5	0	3.43	76	76	33	66	1.43
1997 Boston	0	0	5.49	41	49	16	34	1.59

BRANDOW, DEREK - TR - b: 1/25/70
Scouting: A sinker/slider spot starter, Brandow needs to achieve control of his pitches before he will become an effective major league pitcher.
1998: A return to Triple-A is Brandow's best hope for now. At age twenty-eight, he's unlikely to achieve the potential some saw four or five years ago.
1997: Brandow was wild, tying Mike Drumright for the International League lead in walks allowed (91).
1996: He struck out 103 batters in 124 innings but allowed 57 walks and 14 home runs with Triple-A Syracuse.

BRANNAN, RYAN - TR - b: 4/27/75
Scouting: Brannan didn't play pro ball until 1997. He's a power closer who primarily relies on low to mid-90s fastball. Brannan is working on his breaking-ball repertoire but currently throws few for strikes. He is able to keep his fastball low in the strike zone, but it doesn't move much so he'll need a breaking pitch to succeed in the majors. Brannan has the prototypical closer's mentality and already looks like a one-inning pitcher.
1998: The Phillies have a dire need for a righthanded top set-up man, and a strong spring training would tempt the club to bring him north in April. Barring major off-season development, Brannan isn't yet ready. He must develop a consistent off-speed pitch with different velocity from his fastball. A dominant half-season as the Triple-A closer could prompt a major league recall. Look for Brannan to apprentice in the majors in the top set-up role — as Ricky Bottalico did early in his career — and possibly follow Bottalico's path to becoming a major league closer.
1997: Brannan dominated at higher Class A Clearwater, earning a quick promotion. He continued to notch saves at Double-A, but in a different manner. Double-A hitters put the ball in play against him more consistently, but without authority. Brannan did tire late in the season, but had a fine pro debut nonetheless.
1996: Brannan was drafted by the Phillies in the fourth round, but signed too late to play in 1996. He was the premier closer in the Big West Conference, notching 14 saves and leading the conference in ERA at 1.81.

BRANTLEY, JEFF - TR - b: 9/5/63
Scouting: Known as a great competitor, Brantley features a fastball, slider and excellent splitter, which is his best pitch. He is occasionally prone to gopher balls when he is hanging the splitter, but he allows few hits and has decent control for a pitcher with such good stuff.
1998: Since he's coming off rotator cuff surgery, it is unknown if the 34-year-old Brantley can return to his form of 1995 and '96. Jeff Shaw turned in an excellent year filling in for Brantley, and the Reds traded Brantley to St. Louis.
1997: It was a wasted year for Brantley, who tried to pitch through shoulder problems in early-April but was finally shut down for good in May. Surgery repaired his torn labrum and cleaned up a frayed rotator cuff.
1996: One of the few Reds to have a good year, Brantley led the league with 44 saves, and held opponents to a .215 batting average.

	W	SV	ERA	IP	H	BB	SO	B/I
1995 Cincinnati	3	28	2.82	70	53	20	62	1.04
1996 Cincinnati	1	44	2.41	71	54	28	76	1.15
1997 Cincinnati	1	1	3.85	12	9	7	16	1.37

BREWER, BILLY - TL - b: 4/15/68
Scouting: Brewer is the stereotypical "crafty lefty", who barely dents the mid-80s with his fastball and throws a high percentage of changeups. He is a nibbler who has regularly walked a batter every other inning, far above average for a situational reliever. He is rarely allowed to face righthanded hitters, but is adept at keeping lefthanded hitters off balance. His major league career is tenuous.
1998: The strained elbow that caused Brewer to go on the 60-day disabled list last year makes him a major question mark for 1998. If healthy, he'll compete for a situational relief job; he may begin the season in Triple-A.
1997: The Phillies' weak middle-relief corps provided Brewer with an opportunity to return to the majors; he helped stabilized the bullpen after his recall. Most of the damage done against Brewer occurred in a few bad outings.
1996: Brewer was a Triple-A disaster in the Dodgers' and Yankees' systems, walking 41 hitters in 57 innings. He got a brief trial in the majors with New York, and allowed 15 baserunners in six innings.

	W	SV	ERA	IP	H	BB	SO	B/I
1997 Philadelphia	1	0	4.13	24	19	13	17	1.33

BREWINGTON, JAMIE - TR - b: 9/28/71
Brewington started 13 games for the Giants in 1995 and was 6-4 but then fell apart in 1996. He turned up in the Royals' organization last year, pitching at both the Double-A and Triple-A levels. He wasn't effective at either stop, making it look more and more like 1995 was a fluke. He's not a candidate to return to the majors.

BRIDGES, DONNIE - TR - b: 12/10/78
Montreal selected Bridges with the 23rd pick in the 1997 draft. A 6'3" high schooler out of Mississippi, Bridges pitched at Rookie Level West Palm Beach last year. He got his feet wet with two starts in five appearances for the Expos' club.

BRIGGS, ANTHONY - TR - b: 9/14/73
In two straight years as a swingman, Briggs has advanced a level each year — and has gotten hit harder at each higher level. He doesn't throw especially hard, and also doesn't have particularly good control either to throw strikes or within the strike zone. He has walked a batter every other inning the last two years, a weak rate for a non-strikeout pitcher. Briggs was 6-3 for Double-A Greenville last year with a 5.44 ERA in 19

games (nine starts). Most telling were the eleven homers he allowed in just 94.1 innings. Briggs is not a good prospect and has done nothing to earn further advance in the Braves' farm system.

BRISCOE, JOHN - TR - b: 9/22/67
Once again, Briscoe piqued the curiosity of his organization (this time the Indians, by virtue of his Double-A performance) by actually throwing his heavy fastball for strikes in the minor leagues. He's done this before, earning six separate major league trials with the A's, in which he walked a cumulative 129 batters in 140 innings. He's likely through.

	W	SV	ERA	IP	H	BB	SO	B/I
1995 Oakland	0	0	8.35	18	25	21	19	2.51
1996 Oakland	0	1	3.76	26	18	24	14	1.61

BROCAIL, DOUG - TR - b: 5/16/67
Scouting: Midway through 1997, Brocail found a knuckle curve that made him one of the most effective set-up men in baseball. He throws hard enough, and has good enough command, but it was the curve that turned his season around. Now, if he can just overcome a history of injuries, Brocail should find new life at age 30.
1998: The way he's throwing now, Brocail can close games. As long as he's with the Tigers, though, the save opportunities will go to elsewhere — to Todd Jones. So, Brocail remains a set-up man as long as he's effective.
1997: First, he was the opening day starter. Then, Brocail became the Tiger closer. Finally, he settled into the set-up role, found the knuckle curve and ran off a string of successes as good as any he'd ever had in his career.
1996: Three months on the disabled list with a frayed right biceps tendon kept Brocail from ever doing much for the Astros. He split time between the bullpen and the rotation, then was traded to the Tigers in the ten-player December deal.

	W	SV	ERA	IP	H	BB	SO	B/I
1995 Houston	6	1	4.19	77	87	22	39	1.41
1996 Houston	1	0	4.58	53	58	23	34	1.53
1997 Detroit	3	2	3.23	78	74	36	60	1.41

BROCK, CHRIS - TR - b: 2/5/70
Scouting: A career minor-leaguer, Brock features a good curve (his best pitch), fastball, and changeup. He is not overpowering, and is basically Triple-A insurance for the Braves rotation.
1998: A strong spring could put Brock back on the major league roster, but he is more likely to start the season in Richmond.
1997: Brock started the season pitching well in Triple-A Richmond (season totals: 10-6, 3.34 ERA) and replaced Terrell Wade in June as the Braves fifth starter. Brock was not effective and was sent down back down in late-July. Recalled in September, he pitched in mop up roles the rest of the season.
1996: A strong winter performance in Puerto Rico earned Brock a second shot at Triple-A after he posted a 5.40 ERA in 1995. His 10-11 record was enough to retain a job in the Atlanta organization.

	W	SV	ERA	IP	H	BB	SO	B/I
1997 Atlanta	0	0	5.57	31	34	19	16	1.73

BROHAWN, TROY - TL - b: 1/14/73
After a rocky introduction to Double-A in 1996, Brohawn turned it around; He led Shreveport with a 13-5 record and a 2.56 ERA. Brohawn also limited opponents to just 148 hits over 169 innings, walking 64 with 98 strikeouts. Brohawn has proven mastery of the Double-A level, earning advancement to Triple-A Phoenix in 1998.

BROSNAN, JASON - TL - b: 1/26/68
1997 was Brosnan's second season in the Mariners' system and the first season since 1993 that he didn't pitch at the Triple-A level. In nine seasons he has yet to make a major league appearance. He was a non-roster invitee to spring training but ended up pitching the season at Double-A Memphis. He pitched well in 40 appearances out of the pen, showing good control while striking out 62 in 53.1 innings. However, he was a 30-year old pitching against Double-A hitters and his marginal offerings will keep him a career minor-leaguer.

BROW, SCOTT - TR - b: 3/17/69
After a couple of years as a Triple-A starter, Brow was converted to relief full-time for Triple-A Richmond in '97. He had some success, showing a 90-plus fastball, and a good slider, but struggled at times with the pressure of closing out a game. He has a chance to be all right as a big-league reliever, though, because the stuff is there. He's unlikely to have success in any role of significance.

	W	SV	ERA	IP	H	BB	SO	B/I
1996 Toronto	1	0	5.59	38	45	25	23	1.83

BROWER, JIM - TR - b: 12/29/72
Scouting: Brower's best pitch is his slider. He has a decent fastball, but needs to develop a reliable third pitch. Brower has consistently been used as a starter.
1998: Brower needs another year at Double-A to work on changing speed and developing an off-speed pitch that he can throw for strikes.
1997: Brower split time between Triple-A and Double-A with poor results. His control was adequate, but he couldn't keep the hitters off-balance enough and consistently got hit hard (7-13, 5.44 ERA).
1996: Brower was average in the Florida State League and pitched well in a brief stint at Tulsa.

BROWN, CHAD - TL - b: 12/9/71
After starting the 1997 season with Triple-A Syracuse, he walked as many batters as he struck out and was sent down to Double-A. He was more effective at Knoxville but has a long way to climb before we see him in the majors.

BROWN, J. KEVIN - TR - b: 3/14/65
Scouting: Brown is a sinker/slider pitcher extraordinaire. His fastball reaches about 90 MPH and breaks sharply down and away from righthanded hitters. However, his release point was inconsistent in 1997 — as brilliantly illustrated by Joe Morgan in post-season broadcasts — causing his pitches to flatten out much more often than they did in his career year in 1996. He pays little regard to opposing baserunners, allowing them to steal frequently, thereby limiting the number of double plays he induces. He is a sturdy workhorse who can be relied upon for seven quality innings on most occasions, but has likely begun a gradual career downturn.
1998: Brown's stuff is as good as ever, and there is no reason to believe he won't again anchor the Marlins' staff in 1998. He

must pay strict attention to his mechanics — the poor results are predictable when he delivers the ball at three-quarters as he did in the 1997 post-season.

1997: Brown was not as dominant as he was in 1996, but was still downright brilliant when in synch. He pitched a no-hitter against the Giants in which he didn't allow any ball to be hit particularly hard. He averaged over seven innings per start and allowed a meager ten home runs.

1996: Brown's incredible season was lost behind a veil of poor run support. He posted a minuscule ERA, walked 33 batters, allowed only eight homers —and somehow went only 17-11. Average run support would have netted Brown a Cy Young Award.

	W	SV	ERA	IP	H	BB	SO	B/I
1995 Baltimore	10	0	3.60	172	155	48	117	1.18
1996 Florida	17	0	1.89	233	187	33	159	0.94
1997 Florida	16	0	2.69	237	214	66	205	1.18

BROWNSON, MARK - TR - b: 6/17/75

With a great arm, Brownson can throw four pitches — fastball, slider, curve and changeup — for strikes. His fastball ranges from 91 to 94 MPH. His curve is slow but effective. After rising steadily through the system, he was inconsistent in his second straight season at Double-A New Haven in 1997, when he was 10-9 with a 4.19 ERA in 31 games. Impeccable control is his forte — he only walked 55 against 170 strikeouts in 184.2 innings last season. He will likely start the 1998 season in the Triple-A Colorado Springs rotation. His resilient arm has the Rockies' front-office convinced he may be better suited for a long/middle-relief role in the majors.

BRUNSON, WILLIAM - TL - b: 3/20/70

A rail-thin, 6'8" lefthander, Brunson bears some physical resemblance to Seattle ace Randy Johnson, but he has yet to show the same kind of pitching ability. After a successful year at Double-A San Antonio, Brunson struggled a bit at Triple-A Albuquerque and is converting to a sidearm delivery in the hope that will be what it takes to allow him to make the final jump to the majors. Brunson's not a power pitcher, but the success he's enjoyed with deception and finesse may be enough to earn him a shot at making the majors.

BRUSKE, JIM - TR - b: 10/7/64

Scouting: A converted outfielder, Bruske's best pitch is an excellent curve that tends to put stress on his right shoulder and elbow. His pitching career has been interrupted by stints on the disabled list, including last year.

1998: In an expansion year, there will be ample opportunities for middle relievers. Bruske should find a role in the majors.

1997: Bruske started the year at Triple-A Las Vegas, going 5-4 with a 4.90 ERA in 19 games (including nine starts). He was promoted to the Padres when their bullpen began to unravel and was one of their more effective middle relievers. At times, his curve was unhittable; opponents batted only .228 against Bruske.

1996: Bruske split the season between Los Angeles (11 appearances) and Triple-A Albuquerque (5-2, 4.06 ERA).

	W	SV	ERA	IP	H	BB	SO	B/I
1997 San Diego	4	0	3.62	45	37	25	32	1.39

BUCKLES, BUCKY - TR - b: 6/19/73

Buckles was drafted by the Rangers in the seventh round of the June 1994 draft out of the University of Oklahoma where he was the stopper for the Sooners' 1994 College World Series championship squad. Buckles had 34 saves in his first two pro seasons but missed two months in 1996 with a shoulder injury. Last year he pitched mainly at Double-A Tulsa, struggled with his control and was hittable, too. He has a lot more work to do to become a credible closer prospect.

BUCKLEY, TRAVIS - TR - b: 6/15/70

The jury's still out on the big (6'4") righthander, who needs to fulfill his potential soon or run the risk of being labeled a career minor-leaguer. Buckley has an average fastball, but also throws a curveball, slider and changeup — the changeup is probably the best of his four pitches. Buckley needs to improve a little more, but still has a chance to be a prospect.

BUDDIE, MIKE - TR - b: 12/12/70

In his first season at the Triple-A level in 1997, Buddie managed a 2.64 ERA, and had a good strikeout-to-walk ratio, counterbalanced by the high number of hits he gave up — 85. He was 6-6, pitching 75 innings in 53 games. Buddie struggled in the past as a starter in his previous seasons in the minors, but seemed to have some success as a reliever.

BULLARD, JASON - TR - b: 10/23/68

The Orioles acquired Bullard as a sixth-year minor-league free agent. Previously, he pitched in the Pirates, Rockies and Mets organizations and even made a stop with St. Paul in the independent Northern League. Last year he was a middle reliever and set-up man in Double-A, and at age 29, if he doesn't make it to majors soon, he won't make it at all.

BULLINGER, JIM - TR - b: 8/21/65

The Expos signed Bullinger as a free agent after the Cubs released him following the 1996 season. Montreal put Bullinger into its rotation and he was surprisingly effective during the first half of the season. Then, he hit the skids, was demoted to the bullpen in mid-August and was released at the end of the season. The Cubs never knew how to use him and the Expos found out he isn't particularly effective in either the rotation or the bullpen. His only plus pitch is a sinking fastball that all too often loses its sink.

	W	SV	ERA	IP	H	BB	SO	B/I
1995 Chicago NL	12	0	4.14	150	152	65	93	1.45
1996 Chicago NL	6	1	6.54	129	144	68	90	1.64
1997 Montreal	7	0	5.56	155	165	74	87	1.54

BULLINGER, KIRK - TR - b: 10/28/69

Bullinger is not big or strong and has a below-average fastball, but somehow succeeds by throwing a good variety of off-speed pitches. He's been successful at the lower levels of the minors because of his ability to throw strikes with all of his pitches. None of his pitches are outstanding, though, so it's unlikely that his success will continue in the majors, even in a long relief role.

BUNCH, MELVIN - TR - b: 11/4/71

The book on Bunch never changes: Good arm, no control. Bunch, who appeared in 13 games with Kansas City in 1995, split last season between the Expos' Triple-A Ottawa and Double-A Harrisburg farm clubs with little success. He is only

26 but he'd better learn to throw strikes if he ever wants to get back to the big leagues.

BURBA, DAVE - TR - b: 7/7/66
Scouting: Burba features a good, moving fastball and slider, but has struggled to come up with an effective third pitch. He strikes out and walks more hitters than most pitchers, leading to high pitch counts and an inability to pitch deep into a game. He has the stuff to be a dominant pitcher, but he won't be until he improves his control and consistency —and develops a useful third pitch.
1998: Burba enters the season as the Reds de facto ace starter, and is likely to be the most experienced member of a young starting staff. He will be overmatched against most of the top pitchers in the league, and will need to pitch deeper into games if he is to be the rotation anchor.
1997: Burba did not pitch well early in the season and was prone to control problems and the gopher ball. Back spasms sent him to the DL in early-August, but he was effective upon his return in September, going 5-0 after he was reactivated.
1996: Burba got off to a slow start due to control problems, and poor run support hurt his record in the first half. He finished strong, going 8-4 in the second half.

	W	SV	ERA	IP	H	BB	SO	B/I
1995 two teams	10	0	3.97	106	90	51	96	1.32
1996 Cincinnati	11	0	3.83	195	179	97	148	1.42
1997 Cincinnati	11	0	4.73	160	157	73	131	1.44

BURGER, ROB - TR - b: 3/25/76
Burger can hit 90 on the radar gun and all his pitches possess above-average movement. However, he has below-average command and always throws a lot of pitches which limit his stamina within a game. He has struck out a hitter per inning in A-ball, but won't likely have that kind of success as he moves to the Double-A Reading rotation this year. He held hitters in the higher Class A Florida State League to less than a hit per inning but struggled with his control and posted a high walk rate. Burger can be difficult to hit when he's on, but he'll need to improve his control to excel. A shift to a relief role may be in his future.

BURKE, JOHN - TR - b: 2/9/70
Burke's only distinction is that he was the Rockies first ever draft pick. In three starts at Triple-A Colorado Springs he walked nearly as many batters as he fanned and posted a high ERA (5.82) as hitters found him an easy mark. If he does make it back to the big club he won't help much.

	W	SV	ERA	IP	H	BB	SO	B/I
1997 Colorado	2	0	6.56	59	83	26	39	1.85

BURKETT, JOHN - TR - b: 11/28/64
Scouting: Burkett has always been a pitcher rather than a thrower, and his role is to pile up innings for his team. When he's pitching well, he keeps the ball down in the strike zone, relying on his infield to make the plays behind him. He has a fastball, curve, slider and split-finger pitch and needs to mix them well to keep the hitter off-balance. He was placed on the DL last August with "shoulder fatigue," the first time in his career that he had been disabled. No physical damage was found, and he returned to finish the season.
1998: Burkett will again be expected to soak up innings and provide the quality starts that largely eluded him last season. With no serious physical problems, he could easily return to his previous form.
1997: The league had its way with Burkett last year, as he had one of the highest opponent batting average in the league at .307. One factor was the deterioration of the Rangers' infield defense, particularly up the middle, but most of the problem was that Burkett pitched too much over the middle of the plate. Statistically, he was Bob Tewksbury with more strikeouts.
1996: Burkett was traded from Florida to Texas late in the summer and played a significant role in the Rangers' pennant drive, going 5-2 down the stretch and hurling an average of seven innings per start.

	W	SV	ERA	IP	H	BB	SO	B/I
1995 Florida	14	0	4.30	188	208	57	126	1.41
1996 Florida	6	0	4.32	154	154	42	108	1.27
1996 Texas	5	0	4.06	68	75	16	47	1.33
1997 Texas	9	0	4.56	189	240	30	139	1.43

BURROWS, TERRY - TL - b: 11/28/68
Because he's lefthanded, Burrows can always find gainful major league employment. That doesn't mean that he's a good pitcher, because he isn't. Since 1994, his earned run average in the majors is 6.42.

	W	SV	ERA	IP	H	BB	SO	B/I
1997 San Diego	0	0	10.49	10	12	8	8	1.94

BUSBY, MIKE - TR - b: 12/27/72
Scouting: Once mentioned in the same breath by Cardinals player development officials as Alan Benes and Matt Morris, Busby still has the above-average fastball, good breaking ball and fine control capable of making him a big-league success. He's got to scramble after two seasons filled with injuries and surgery, and he probably has to battle through creeping self-doubt, too.
1998: Busby likely will open the season at Triple-A, where he's made 34 starts the last three years. He could use a full year of uninterrupted work at one place to find some stability and work back into form. The Cards never have used him as a reliever since drafting him in 1991, though he could get a shot in long-relief this season.
1997: Busby spent most of the season trying to round back into shape after undergoing off-season shoulder surgery to tighten some ligaments in his pitching shoulder. He didn't make a start at Triple-A until June 10th. Two months later, he began a stretch of five starts in which he posted a 3.21 ERA and struck out 23 batters while walking nine. He didn't initially get a promotion to the big leagues until the Cardinals needed him because of injuries, then made three largely unsuccessful starts after not pitching for nearly three weeks.
1996: Busby impressed the Cardinals enough in spring camp to earn an April berth as the fifth starter. The Braves battered him in that outing, he returned to Triple-A, struggled through 14 mostly miserable starts and finally was shut down with shoulder trouble.

	W	SV	ERA	IP	H	BB	SO	B/I
1997 St. Louis	0	0	8.81	14	24	4	6	1.96

BUTEAUX, SHANE - TR - b: 12/28/71
A mid-level prospect, trained as a reliever, Buteaux is a classic sinker/slider pitcher. His results at Double-A Birmingham were merely average and he walked as many hitters as he struck out.

BUTLER, ADAM - TL - b: 8/17/73
Butler doesn't have outstanding stuff, but his fastball is good for a lefthander (upper-80s) and he has sharp control of all his pitches. He's been Double-A Greenville's ace reliever the last two seasons and was good last year, going 5-1 with 22 saves and a 2.57 ERA. Late in the year he also was pressed into rotation duty for three starts — his first time as a starter in his pro career. Butler's control problems from 1996 disappeared; he's ready for a move to Triple-A and possibly to the Atlanta bullpen although he would not be a closer at the major league level.

BYRD, MATT - TR - b: 5/17/71
Not to be confused with the other Byrd (Paul) pitching in the Braves organization, Matt is an elderly Double-A junkballer who was 3-2 with a 6.00 ERA in 28 games (six starts) for Greenville in 1997. He spent three years in A-ball, now two at Double-A and is far too old for that level; Byrd will be 27 in May. His ERA over 6.50 for his two years above A-ball and lack of any outstanding pitch will keep Byrd in the minors.

BYRD, PAUL - TR - b: 12/3/70
Scouting: Byrd features a good fastball, but his curve, slider and changeup are mediocre at best. He needs pinpoint location to be effective, but has not shown command for any extended period at the major league level.
1998: Byrd will compete for a set-up role with the Braves, but he will have to beat out several others who are younger and have better stuff for a chance.
1997: After being acquired before the season in exchange for Greg McMichael, Byrd was a major disappointment. He struggled with his control before being sent to Richmond in July during the Braves bullpen purge. He was recalled July 30th but pitched mostly in mop up roles the rest of the season; he was not on the Braves post-season roster.
1996: After beginning the season on the DL due to a herniated disc, Byrd struggled with control problems most of the year. He was unable to match a fine performance in a limited opportunity in 1995.

	W	SV	ERA	IP	H	BB	SO	B/I
1995 New York NL	2	0	2.05	22	18	7	26	1.14
1996 New York NL	1	0	4.24	46.2	48	21	31	1.49
1997 Atlanta	4	0	5.26	53	47	28	37	1.42

BYRDAK, TIM - TL - b: 10/31/73
Originally thought to be out for the entire 1997 season following off-season elbow surgery, curveball specialist Byrdak made 22 appearances (two starts) for Class A Wilmington with pleasant results: 4-3, 3.51 ERA, four-to-one strikeout-to-walk ratio. Byrdak will advance to Double-A Wichita where he was pitching in 1996 when his elbow problem erupted.

BYRNE, EARL - TL - b: 7/2/72
Scouting: Byrne is an average lefthander whose most distinguishing feature is that he's from Australia, and somehow found himself a pitcher in the United States instead of a left forward pocket in Aussie Rules Football. Other than that he's of average height and has average pitches.
1998: Byrne is lefthanded and strikes out a hitter per inning, so it's likely that he'll be considered for a major league roster spot in Chicago, especially if Bob Patterson isn't around. But he'll have to prove that his 1997 season wasn't a fluke before the Cubs take a chance and bring him up.
1997: Byrne had a good season in his second year at Double-A Orlando. Most of his success can be traced to a fine hits-to-innings pitched ratio. Byrne had given up about a hit per inning in his first four seasons in the minors, but cut that way down in 1997. He did cut down on his walks a little, although one every two innings is still too many.
1996: Byrne made the jump to Double-A and struggled mightily with his control. His other numbers weren't too bad, but he seemed to be intimidated by Double-A hitters.

CABRERA, JOSE - TR - b: 3/24/72
Scouting: Cabrera is a hard-throwing righthander whose best pitch is a four-seam fastball that he throws in the low 90s. He also throws a good changeup but does not have a reliable breaking ball. Miscast as a starter during his five years in the Cleveland organization, his repertoire seems more suited for relief work.
1998: Cabrera will be competing for a relief role at the major league level in 1998. Based on his success after being called up in September, he will get a long look and should make it in a set-up role. He has never recorded a save in his career.
1997: Cabrera was obtained by the Astros from Cleveland for Alvin Morman in May. He pitched exclusively in relief at Triple-A New Orleans where he was 5-2 with an ERA of 2.21. He allowed only 39 hits in 61 innings while striking out 59 and walking 20. He was called up to Houston in September and impressed by allowing only six hits and two runs in 15.1 innings while striking out 18 batters.
1996: Cabrera pitched for three different teams in the Cleveland organization with a record of 7-6 and an ERA of 4.38. He was in 26 games, 19 as a starter.

	W	SV	ERA	IP	H	BB	SO	B/I
1997 Houston	0	0	1.18	15	6	6	18	0.78

CADARET, GREG - TL - b: 2/27/62
A veteran lefthander, Cadaret has the experience and the savvy necessary to help him fill a hole on a major league roster. He filled a role in the Angels' bullpen in 1997 after being picked up in mid-season. He has a decent fastball and control, and has elevated himself significantly above fringe-major league status, but still has trouble putting things together for long periods of time.

	W	SV	ERA	IP	H	BB	SO	B/I
1997 Anaheim	0	0	3.28	14	11	8	11	1.39

CAIN, TIM - TR - b: 10/9/69
Cain left Triple-A Pawtucket in the middle of the 1996 season and retired. Last year he decided he wanted to pitch again and turned up in the Blue Jays' farm system at Triple-A Syracuse. His comeback was not a great success and it won't end with a trip to the majors.

CALERO, ENRIQUE - TR - b: 1/9/75
Double-A Wichita's winningest pitcher in 1997 was also one of their youngest starters. Calero's low-90s fastball lost a little steam down the stretch as he tired; it was his first full season as a pro. He works off the two-seam fastball but is adding a changeup and working to improve his slider and cut fastball. Calero needs something to use when his fastball isn't working; when he finds it he'll be ready for the big leagues.

CAMP, JARED - TR - b: 10/7/79
Camp had a wild ride in his first full pro season, passing an aggressive test at high Class A Kinston before struggling at Double-A Akron. Camp has a slightly above-average fastball, good control, and is capable of pitching deep into ballgames when he consistently gets ahead of hitters. That formula fell apart in Double-A, where Camp pitched timidly. It's too early to give up on Camp, who will get a full season at that level in 1998.

CANDIOTTI, TOM - TR - b: 8/31/57
Scouting: Candiotti is emphatic about the point: "I am a pitcher who can use a knuckleball; I am not a knuckleballer." The implication is that Candiotti has other good pitches and uses them: a fastball and a slider. His velocity is not what it used to be, so he is gradually becoming a knuckleballer, whatever he may say.
1998: Candiotti filed for free agency, and his strong rebound in a starting role for the Dodgers last year will enhance his value. The Dodgers found out how valuable Candiotti can be in the starting rotation of a contending team, and now the world knows. He has come a long way since being untradeable during the winter of 1996-97, even with the Dodgers willing to throw in some cash.
1997: After a subpar 1996, Candiotti lost his spot in the rotation. He pitched well out of the pen and continued to perform surprisingly well when pressed into the rotation again. He made 18 starts when Ramon Martinez and Ismael Valdes were disabled and then ended the season back in the bullpen. Overall, the veteran had his strongest performance since 1992.
1996: Management and media were nearly unanimous in their belief that Candiotti was near the end of his career when the '96 season ended. He had his worst ERA since 1987. He was just plain too hittable, and his self-confidence was down.

	W	SV	ERA	IP	H	BB	SO	B/I
1995 Los Angeles	7	0	3.50	190	187	58	141	1.29
1996 Los Angeles	9	0	4.49	152	172	43	79	1.41
1997 Los Angeles	10	0	3.60	135	128	40	89	1.24

CARLSON, DAN - TR - b: 1/26/70
Scouting: Except for a stay at short-season ball, in 1990, Carlson has never had a losing season. He doesn't overpower, has good control, but has been unable to make the leap from Triple-A to the bigs. Carlson is a hard worker and a good guy, but that magical extra that is required to succeed at the major league level seems to be missing in him.
1998: With the expansion Devil Rays, Carlson should get a shot at being a starter. He is not a top prospect, but neither is he aged, and he carries a good resume, at least in the minors. He is the kind of guy that you root for because of his dedication and workmanlike efforts.
1997: Despite thirteen wins at Triple-A Phoenix, and an ERA under four (3.88, actually), the Giants did not look to Carlson when they needed pitching help during the stretch. He did appear in six major league games, but would probably prefer to forget them.
1996: Carlson completed his third year at Triple-A with a solid ERA (3.44) and thirteen wins. He really has mastered this level, so one must wonder why the injury-laden Giants did not bring him up.

	W	SV	ERA	IP	H	BB	SO	B/I
1997 San Francisco	0	0	7.65	15	20	8	14	1.83

CARLYLE, KENNY - TR - b: 9/16/69
Carlyle has a below-average fastball, which, because he's a righthander, makes it unlikely that he'll be able to have an impact at the major league level. He's made some strides as a pitcher the last couple of seasons in the minors, learning to sink the ball more and use his changeup, his best pitch, but the odds are against him. He did post a 2.84 ERA for Triple-A Richmond in '97.

CARMONA, RAFAEL - TR - b: 10/2/72
Scouting: Carmona began his career in the Mariners' minor-league system as a closer and had 21 saves at Riverside in 1994 before jumping to the major leagues for three starts in 1995; he has been a middle reliever since. Control of his average fastball wanders.
1998: Carmona is a middle reliever who may fall victim to the numbers game, inasmuch as the Mariners sunk a lot of their young talent into last-season trades for relief help last season.
1997: Carmona spent most of the season in Triple-A because Bobby Ayala was healthy throughout the season and the Mariners traded for five major leaguers when their staff came up short. He collected four saves with a 2-5 record and a 3.79 ERA in 59.1 innings spread over 32 appearances (five starts) for Triple-A Tacoma. He fanned nearly one batter per inning, but as has often been the case, control was a problem as he walked more than five per nine innings. Carmona made just four appearances with the Mariners.
1996: Carmona finished second in the American League in relief victories (eight) behind Arthur Rhodes when an injury to Bobby Ayala created a roster opening in middle relief. Carmona held righthanded hitters to a .221 average.

	W	SV	ERA	IP	H	BB	SO	B/I
1995 Seattle	2	1	5.66	47	55	34	28	1.87
1996 Seattle	8	1	4.28	90	95	55	62	1.66
1997 Seattle	0	0	3.16	6	3	2	6	0.88

CARPENTER, BRIAN - TR - b: 3/3/71
Carpenter didn't have a great year at Double-A Binghamton in 1997. He throws strikes, but all you need to know is he allowed 37 hits in 23 innings of middle relief, posting a 9.00 ERA. Carpenter was a minor-league journeyman a year ago, with a mediocre fastball that didn't improve in 1997.

CARPENTER, CHRIS - TR - b: 4/27/75
Scouting: One of the Blue Jays top pitching prospects, Carpenter has a mid-90s fastball and a slow curve. The top draft pick for the Blue Jays in 1994, Carpenter is excellent at keeping the ball down in the strike zone.
1998: There were signs that he is ready for the major leagues now and he will get a long look in spring training as a fifth starter. He may need a year to develop before his performance becomes acceptable but he will get the innings.
1997: Carpenter spent most of the year at Triple-A Syracuse and joined the Blue Jays in July. Although the 3-7 record wasn't pretty, he did throw a complete game shutout and finished up strong.
1996: His 7-9 record was misleading as he struck out 150 batters in 171.1 innings at Double-A Knoxville.

	W	SV	ERA	IP	H	BB	SO	B/I
1997 Toronto	3	0	5.09	81	108	37	55	1.78

CARRARA, GIOVANNI - TR - b: 3/4/68
Scouting: Carrara throws fairly hard, but has trouble throwing to locations and leaves plenty of pitches in the hitting zone. Many times he does alright his first time through a batting order, but falters in the fourth or fifth innings when he has to face hitters a second time.
1998: With two new teams in the majors, Carrara will undoubtedly be invited to someone's spring training camp, but he's done nothing to indicate that he can get big-league hitters out. There's a chance he could get a few starts with a major league team, but if he does there's an even better chance that he won't get more than a few.
1997: Carrara spent most of the time at Triple-A Indianapolis and posted good numbers for the Reds' top farm team. However, he was pounded at the major league level in his two brief stints with the Reds (both coming in emergency situations when the Reds were desperate for somebody to fill in).
1996: Carrara was claimed off waivers by the Reds in the middle of the season and was great in Triple-A (4-0, 0.76 ERA) but pretty bad in Cincinnati (1-0, 5.87 ERA).

	W	SV	ERA	IP	H	BB	SO	B/I
1997 Cincinnati	0	0	7.86	10	14	6	5	1.94

CARRASCO, HECTOR - TR - b: 10/22/69
Scouting: Carrasco can really bring it, but has erratic control. His fastball reaches the mid-90s and his slider is also thrown hard; Carrasco uses a splitter as a changeup, but his off-speed stuff is only useful when he can throw his fastball over the plate, which is to say, not all the time. Once thought of as a potential closer, Carrasco's wildness has him ticketed only for a set-up role in the near future.
1998: Despite his control difficulties, Carrasco is expected to serve as a set-up man in the Diamondbacks' bullpen. It's hard to believe he'll be a success unless he can locate the plate more often.
1997: Carrasco came to the Royals along with Scott Service for Jon Nunnally and Chris Stynes as they tried to shore up a bullpen that was so bad it contributed to the firing of manager Bob Boone. His numbers seem to be alright, but behind the pitching line is an uneasy feeling because it was impossible to count on Carrasco; his manager never knew what he'd get when he brought Carrasco into the game.
1996: Control problems contributed to a poor start and Carrasco was demoted to Triple-A Indianapolis. He pitched much better after his return but his control problems lingered.

	W	SV	ERA	IP	H	BB	SO	B/I
1995 Cincinnati	2	5	4.12	87	86	46	64	1.51
1996 Cincinnati	4	0	3.75	74	58	45	59	1.39
1997 Kansas City	2	0	4.40	86	80	41	76	1.41

CARRASCO, TROY - TL - b: 1/27/75
Carrasco has struggled the last two years. Pitching at Class A Fort Meyers and Double-A New Britain, he posted 5.37 and 4.96 ERA's, respectively. He has given up more than a hit per inning since his promotion to Double-A in 1996 and has control problems. He is still young, and has more chances to prove himself.

CARTER, JOHN - TR - b: 2/16/72
Carter's career came full circle in 1997 as he was acquired by the Pirates' organization in a minor-league trade with the New York Mets early in the season. Carter was drafted by the Pirates in 1991, then dealt with minor-league outfielder Tony Mitchell a year later to Cleveland for outfielder Alex Cole. Like Carter, Mitchell also returned to the Pirates' organization last season. Neither lasted long, Carter being released after a handful of horrible outings at Triple-A Calgary and Double-A Carolina. Carter has been plagued by arm problems throughout his career, robbing him of any chance of making the majors.

CASIAN, LARRY - TL - b: 10/28/65
Scouting: Casian lives and dies with a usually good curveball; his fastball barely reaches the mid-80s and he uses it only for show. The curve, when it is working, has been good enough for Casian to serve a specialized situational bullpen role.
1998: If he gets the curveball back on track he can reclaim a situational relief role in a major league bullpen. Otherwise, he's Triple-A bound.
1997: Casian lost the feel for his curve and was given his walking papers by the Cubs. With the Royals searching for any lefthander with a pulse, Casian got another opportunity. He still didn't have a workable pitch, though, and ended up being released for a second time.
1996: For the second year in a row, Casian put up a sparkling ERA, but this time he earned it by retiring the toughest lefthanders in the National League as the Cubs' lefty situational reliever.

	W	SV	ERA	IP	H	BB	SO	B/I
1995 Chicago NL	1	0	1.93	23	23	15	11	1.63
1996 Chicago NL	1	0	1.88	24	14	11	15	1.04
1997 Kansas City	0	0	5.70	36	48	8	23	1.54

CASTILLO, CARLOS - TR - b: 4/21/75
Scouting: Castillo throws a low-90s fastball, slider and a curve. He was used in several different roles by the White Sox after making a jump from A-ball to the majors last year.
1998: Castillo's role will certainly increase; he had fallen into since-fired manager Terry Bevington's doghouse. Castillo could need a full season in the high minors to consolidate his skills and aim at a specific role but he should be a good pitcher in the long run.
1997: Castillo wore several hats for the White Sox, pitching in long relief, making a few starts and also being used as a situational reliever. It was an impressive year in his first season above A-ball.
1996: Castillo showed remarkable control for two Class A teams, fanning 158 in 176.2 innings while walking just 33. He tied for the league led in complete games for both the Midwest League (while pitching for South Bend), and the Carolina League (while pitching for Prince William; four complete games in just six starts).

	W	SV	ERA	IP	H	BB	SO	B/I
1997 Chicago AL	2	1	4.48	66	68	33	43	1.52

CASTILLO, FRANK - TR - b: 4/1/69
Scouting: His best pitch is a changeup; Castillo has the ability to keep hitters off-balance by mixing speeds and moving the ball in and out. He knows how to pitch, but he tends to pitch up in the strike zone. His fastball and breaking ball are average, though he can throw them for strikes when he's not nibbling.
1998: He was headed for free agency after the 1997 season and it was not a high priority for the Rockies to re-sign him. With Colorado, Castillo would be a third or fourth starter in their rotation.

1997: After spending his entire professional career with the Chicago Cubs, Castillo was traded in July to the Rockies for a minor-leaguer. He brought stability to a tattered Rockies' rotation by posting a 6-3 record while recording a little better than six innings per start over his 14 outings, though he did have a high ERA. Before the trade he was having a tough year as the fifth starter for the Cubs.
1996: Though he made 33 starts and pitched 182.1 innings for the Cubs, Castillo had a bad year, suffering a National League-high 16 losses.

	W	SV	ERA	IP	H	BB	SO	B/I
1995 Chicago NL	11	0	3.21	188	179	52	135	1.23
1996 Chicago NL	7	0	5.28	182	209	46	139	1.40
1997 Colorado	12	0	5.42	184	220	69	126	1.57

CASTILLO, MARINO - TR - b: 3/17/71
Scouting: He has been used in relief in the minors but does not have the stuff to be a closer. He's more a set-up man or possible starter. Castillo doesn't overpower hitters but has good control and nearly a three-to-one strikeout-to-walk ratio for his career. Because he isn't a strikeout pitcher he's not a good candidate for short relief, but he lacks sufficient durability and repertoire to succeed as a starter.
1998: With the right team Castillo's control could land him in a major league bullpen. If not, he'll return to a part-time starter/reliever role in Triple-A.
1997: After seven minor-league seasons with the Giants, Castillo was signed by the Padres as a minor-league free agent in November of 1996 and pitched at Double-A and Triple-A. He appeared in 31 games at Triple-A Las Vegas, 18 as a starter, and exhibited good control but also gave up well more than a hit per inning.
1996: Castillo split the season between Double-A Shreveport and Class A San Jose. He fanned 72 and walked only 14 combined over 61.2 innings.

CASTILLO, TONY - TL - b: 3/1/63
Scouting: Castillo isn't overpowering but has enough stuff to be successful in his accustomed situational relief role. He has briefly been a closer (for Toronto in 1995) but is ill-suited to the job; he quickly loses effectiveness after only a few hitters.
1998: Despite being signed through 1998, Castillo may not be back with the White Sox. The lack of quality lefty relievers in professional baseball assures Castillo a major league bullpen job somewhere.
1997: Castillo had a truly awful year; he was highly ineffectual while being used in his usual situational relief role. He had a career-high ERA while permitting an unusually high number of hits.
1996: Acquired by the White Sox for their pennant chase, Castillo was marvelous in short relief, earning a two-year contract with the Sox.

	W	SV	ERA	IP	H	BB	SO	B/I
1995 Toronto	1	13	3.22	72	64	24	38	1.21
1996 Tor.-Chi. AL	5	2	3.60	95	95	24	57	1.25
1997 Chicago AL	4	4	4.91	62	74	23	42	1.56

CATHER, MIKE - TR - b: 12/17/70
Scouting: A sidearming righthander, Cather relies on a sinker, slider and changeup. He is not overpowering, but his deceptive motion and ability to keep the ball down make him a moderately effective set-up man. Improved control is the key to his cementing a role at the major league level.
1998: Cather will compete for a set-up role in the Braves bullpen.
1997: Starting the season at Double-A Greenville, Cather was promoted to Triple-A Richmond, where he posted three saves and a 1.73 ERA in 13 games. He was promoted to the Braves in July during their bullpen purge, and was effective initially for the Braves, surrendering only one unearned run in his first eight appearances. Cather was named to the Braves post-season roster.
1996: Signed by the Braves as a minor-league free agent out of the Ranger organization, Cather was moderately effective at Double-A Greenville, going 3-4 with a 3.70 ERA in 53 relief appearances.

	W	SV	ERA	IP	H	BB	SO	B/I
1997 Atlanta	2	0	2.39	28	23	19	29	1.11

CENSALE, SILVIO - TL - b: 11/21/71
Censale is a late bloomer who struggled with injuries early in his pro career, and didn't make his Double-A debut until 1997. He has mid-to-upper 80s velocity on his fastball, and actually improved his strikeout rate after jumping from higher Class A to Double-A — a good sign. He has good movement on his pitches, though he needs to make further refinements in his command. Censale should advance to Triple-A Scranton in 1998; he doesn't have a great deal of potential, but he's the most advanced lefthanded starter on the Phillies' farm, so he'll be given a chance to succeed.

CHARLTON, NORM - TL - b: 1/6/63
Scouting: Charlton has made a remarkable comeback from 1993 "Tommy John" surgery following a tear of his ulnar collateral ligament in his left elbow, an injury that caused him to miss the 1994 season. His fastball remains around 90 MPH, but poor location led to eleven blown saves last season.
1998: Charlton lost his portion of the closer role when he blew up last season, and he was expected to use free agency to find a new organization.
1997: Charlton opened the season as the top closer but struggled so badly that the Mariners traded for Mike Timlin, Paul Spoljaric and Heathcliff Slocumb in a vain attempt to find some help. Few relievers have lost as many games over the last two years as Charlton. Opponents hit .312 against him and he walked nearly as many as he struck out.
1996: Charlton completed his return from debilitating left elbow problems by earning 20 saves as the relief ace after supplanting Bobby Ayala in that role in the latter stages of 1995. Charlton's 70 appearances were a career best and he held lefties to a .187 batting average.

	W	SV	ERA	IP	H	BB	SO	B/I
1995 Philadelphia	2	0	7.36	22	23	15	12	1.73
1995 Seattle	2	14	1.51	47	23	16	58	0.83
1996 Seattle	4	20	4.04	75	68	38	73	1.41
1997 Seattle	3	14	7.27	69	89	47	55	1.96

CHAVARRIA, DAVID - TR - b: 5/19/73
Chavaria worked 90 innings for Double-A Arkansas, half of his games as a reliever. His 4.50 ERA was his highest since 1992 and he gave up too many walks. 1997 was his first season at the Double-A level.

CHAVEZ, CARLOS - TR - b: 8/25/72
Chavez started the season in the Brewers organization before ending up at Double-A Portland in the Marlins' farm system. He now has a good slider to go along with a big-league heater. His control has come around and with a breaking pitch complementing his heater he is a candidate to appear in the Marlins' bullpen in the next few seasons.

CHAVEZ, TONY - TR - b: 10/22/70
Scouting: Chavez made a big career change for the better in 1997, turning some heads with a big year at Triple-A Vancouver. A rugged competitor, Chavez developed a stopper's mentality and took over the closer's role, a move that may have put him on the fast track to the major leagues. He relies on a good fastball, but also has effective control. Chavez keeps the ball at the knees and throws strikes, which is what caught the Angels' eye and earned him a promotion to the big leagues during the stretch drive.
1998: Chavez will have a good chance to win a relief job in the spring and perhaps could even become a backup to hard-throwing closer Troy Percival. The key for him will be to continue the turnaround he began in 1997.
1997: Six quick saves at Double-A Midland earned Chavez a promotion to Triple-A Vancouver June 20th. His determination and competitiveness did the rest. He quickly became the Canadians' closer. His biggest asset is he does not beat himself by walking or hitting a lot of batters, or by allowing the leadoff man to get on base.
1996: Chavez may have stacked the odds against him a bit by struggling after making the jump from A-ball to Double-A, but he didn't allow himself to get down. It was a "hang-in-there" season for the righthander, but his desire carried him through.

	W	SV	ERA	IP	H	BB	SO	B/I
1997 Anaheim	0	0	0.93	10	7	5	10	1.24

CHECO, ROBINSON - TR - b: 5/4/75
Checo, who was under a lot of scrutiny after Dan Duquette spent millions to bring him over from Japan, displayed great potential in '97, but did not help the major league team much. An arm injury forced the Red Sox to bring him along slowly to start the season, but by the end of the year he was pitching extremely well in Triple-A, displaying a 93-MPH fastball, a slider, splitter and a changeup. He then had a couple of good outings for Boston in September. He has the potential to pitch effectively as a starter or out of the bullpen this season.

	W	SV	ERA	IP	H	BB	SO	B/I
1997 Boston	1	0	3.38	13	12	3	14	1.13

CHERGEY, DAN - TR - b: 1/29/71
Chergey has bounced up and down through the Marlins' system for five years. He was a revelation in a set-up/closer role at Double-A and Triple-A last year, posting an 84-to-16 strikeout-to-walk ratio in 82 innings. His velocity is unspectacular, but his pitches move sharply and he consistently throws strike one on the corners. He is a versatile hurler who can handle a variety of bullpen roles, but he is likely to obtain a major league opportunity only due to the misfortune of others.

CHOUINARD, BOB - TR - b: 5/1/72
The A's once hoped Chouinard would be an anchor of the rotation, but at this point is probably not even ballast. Hitting is easy to come by in the Pacific Coast League, but Chouinard's 6.03 ERA and 129 hits allowed over 100 innings at Triple-A Edmonton last year are indicative of more than just a bunch of good hitters. Chouinard has a long way to go to become a good major league pitcher.

	W	SV	ERA	IP	H	BB	SO	B/I
1996 Oakland	4	0	6.10	59	75	32	32	1.81

CHRISTIANSEN, JASON - TL - b: 9/21/69
Scouting: Christiansen is a rarity for a lefthander, a hard thrower. His fastball routinely reaches 90-plus MPH but the big key for him is his command of a big-breaking curveball. When he throws the curve for strikes, he's nearly impossible for lefthanded batters to hit and also is tough on righthanders.
1998: Christiansen will be one of the Pirates' primary set-up relievers along with Ricardo Rincon. Pirates manager Gene Lamont, like his predecessor Jim Leyland, is a big believer in carrying three lefthanded relievers, which ensures Christiansen will pitch often.
1997: Christiansen was bombed in spring training as he wasn't fully recovered from arthroscopic elbow surgery the previous season. He stayed behind in extended spring training, slowed by a bulging disc in his neck, then was hit hard during an injury rehabilitation assignment with Double-A Carolina. However, he began to get better after his promotion to the Pirates and was extremely sharp down the stretch.
1996: Christiansen had a lost season. The Pirates tried to convert the career-long reliever into a starter in spring training then pulled the plug midway through the exhibition season. Christiansen was ineffective out of the bullpen in Pittsburgh, was shipped to Triple-A Calgary to try starting again, then wound up needing elbow surgery after only two starts in the minors.

	W	SV	ERA	IP	H	BB	SO	B/I
1995 Pittsburgh	1	0	4.15	56	49	34	53	1.48
1996 Pittsburgh	3	0	6.70	44	56	19	38	1.70
1997 Pittsburgh	3	0	2.94	34	37	17	37	1.60

CHRISTMAN, SCOTT - TL - b: 12/3/71
A first-round pick in 1993, Christman has simply never panned out. He was routinely pounded in a half-season at Double-A Birmingham, posting a 9.05 ERA in sixteen games while allowing an amazing 100 hits in just 64 innings. Christman's fastball has not developed one bit since he was drafted.

CLARK, MARK - TR - b: 5/12/68
Scouting: Clark has an above-average fastball and a good curve, and is just now learning how to pitch. He hasn't had a lot of experience yet, but being in the starting rotation all year, first with the Mets and then the Cubs, helped him to develop and grow last season.
1998: Clark once was a rising star in the Cleveland farm system, but he had a bad year at Triple-A a few years ago and the Indians gave up on him, then traded him to the New York Mets for nothing. The Mets traded him to the Cubs last year because they needed bullpen help, but he's finally found a home in Chicago. Clark will be the number two starter behind Kevin Tapani and there's a good chance he'll have his best year in the majors.
1997: Clark was effective for the Cubs after coming over in the mid-season trade with the New York Mets; he wound up equalling his 1996 win total and again threw more than 200

innings. He was a workhorse for both clubs and proved that he should be considered one of the top pitchers on a big-league staff. He gave up a lot of home runs, but not too many considering he pitched a third of the season in one of the worst pitcher's parks in all of baseball.
1996: Clark came out of nowhere to become one of the best pitchers on the Mets' staff. Once their young phenom pitchers got hurt or were ineffective, Clark took over and became the winningest pitcher on the staff.

	W	SV	ERA	IP	H	BB	SO	B/I
1995 Cleveland	9	0	5.27	124	143	42	68	1.48
1996 New York NL	14	0	3.43	212	217	48	142	1.25
1997 two teams	14	0	3.82	205	213	59	123	1.33

CLARK, TERRY - TR - b: 10/10/60
Having pitched for four major league teams in two years, with poor results, Clark is on the major league fringe. His development of a knuckleball hasn't seemed to help.

	W	SV	ERA	IP	H	BB	SO	B/I
1997 Texas	1	0	6.00	57	70	23	24	1.63

CLEMENS, ROGER - TR - b: 8/4/62
Scouting: Clemens still gets his fastball up in the mid-90s and mixes it with a devastating forkball. He still has good control and his endurance is as strong as ever. A motivated Clemens is dangerous and one cannot help but think Clemens tried to make a point about how the Red Sox let him get away.
1998: Clemens begins the season as the ace of the staff and one of the best pitchers in the league. It would be difficult to expect him to be as good as he was last year but an ordinary Clemens' season would still be better than many other pitchers could accomplish.
1997: Clemens won the triple crown of pitching, leading the American League in wins, strikeouts and ERA. His strikeout total was the highest of his career and the 21 wins were the his most since 1990.
1996: Although he led the American League with 257 strikeouts, Clemens finished at 10-13 with a 3.63 ERA. His finest moment came when he struck out 20 Detroit Tigers in one game.

	W	SV	ERA	IP	H	BB	SO	B/I
1995 Boston	10	0	4.18	140	141	60	132	1.44
1996 Boston	10	0	3.63	242	216	106	257	1.33
1997 Toronto	21	0	2.05	264	204	68	292	1.03

CLEMENT, MATT - TR - b: 8/12/74
Scouting: All that's missing from Clement's repetoire is a changeup. He has an above-average, low-90s fastball and the best slider in the organization. The Padres, who are loaded with laid-back pitchers, love Clement's "hand me the ball" attitude.
1998: Clement could be in the San Diego rotation by the end of the season, or maybe immediately if he impresses in spring training. Clement figures to open the season at Triple-A Las Vegas.
1997: Clement was the Padres' Minor League Pitcher of the Year. He started at Class A Rancho Cucamonga (6-3, 1.60 ERA, 109 strikeouts in 101 innings) and finished at Double-A Mobile (6-5, 2.56 ERA, 92 strikeouts in 88 innings). Clement allowed 157 hits in 189 total innings and finished among minor-league leaders in ERA, innings and strikeouts.
1996: Clement pitched at two Class A levels, going 8-3 with a 2.80 ERA and 10.19 strikeouts per nine innings in the Midwest League and 4-5 with a 5.89 ERA at Rancho Cucamonga.

CLEMONS, CHRIS - TR - b: 10/31/72
Scouting: A fastball/slider pitcher, Clemons doesn't have great velocity but he knows how to pitch and moves the ball around. He is subject to occasional bouts of wildness.
1998: The White Sox were high on Clemons; he was one of their better righthanded starter prospects. When he was still unprotected after one round, Arizona took him in the second. He has an inside track to a rotation spot, the main question being: when. He's a "finished" product who needs little refinement.
1997: As the top starter for Triple-A Nashville (5-2, 3.96 ERA), Clemons earned a late-season callup to the White Sox following the team's stretch-drive salary (and pennant) dump. He made a couple of decent starts, enough to put him on the short list for a future major league role.
1996: Clemons made a quick jump from Class A Prince William after just six starts and had a successful campaign for Double-A Birmingham, going 5-2 with a 3.15 ERA in nineteen appearances (sixteen starts), including a 1.78 ERA over his final twelve outings.

	W	SV	ERA	IP	H	BB	SO	B/I
1997 Chicago AL	0	0	8.50	13	19	11	8	2.36

CLONTZ, BRAD - TR - b: 4/25/71
Scouting: Clontz' sidearm delivery puts unusual movement on his high-80s fastball and slider; it's particularly effective against righthanders, but Clontz gets lit up by lefties. He has become a one-out righthanded situational specialist whose durability is obvious: Clontz has pitched in 148 games over the last two years.
1998: Clontz has earned another chance at a short relief role in Atlanta. He'll have to be more consistent to keep the job, though.
1997: Frustration with inconsistent middle relief led Braves' management to conduct a wholesale demotion of Clontz and others to Triple-A Richmond. Clontz took the move seriously and was unhittable at Richmond. He collected six saves in 16 appearances (including two starts) while allowing just one run (unearned) in 22 innings. Clontz returned to Atlanta with much better, more consistent stuff.
1996: Clontz began the year with an important set-up role in the Atlanta bullpen, but gradually wore down as the season wore on. It's no wonder; he pitched in 81 games to lead the National League in appearances. While he had good results early, his final numbers look bad. Clontz was a better pitcher than the stat line shows.

	W	SV	ERA	IP	H	BB	SO	B/I
1995 Atlanta	8	4	3.65	69	71	22	55	1.35
1996 Atlanta	6	1	5.69	80	78	33	49	1.38
1997 Atlanta	5	1	3.75	48	52	18	42	1.46

CLOUDE, KEN - TR - b: 1/9/75
Scouting: Cloude has progressed rapidly through the organization by combining a 90-MPH fastball and strong location with a work ethic similar to that of his idol, fellow Baltimorean Cal Ripken Jr.
1998: Cloude is expected to contend for the final spot in a starting rotation that is top-heavy with lefthanders. He may be the lone righthanded starter for Seattle.

1997: Promoted to the parent Mariners in August, Cloude had a no-hitter for five innings in his first start. He won 11 games in 22 starts with a 3.87 ERA at Double-A Memphis before the promotion, then won four of nine starts with the Mariners. Big-league opponents hit just .218 against Cloude but his eight homers allowed in 51 innings led to a bloated ERA.

1996: Cloude led the Mariners' minor-league organization with 15 victories, including a nine-game winning streak for Class A Lancaster, where he made the mid-season and post-season California League All-Star teams. He was named the best fielding pitcher in a vote of league managers. Cloude fanned a batter per inning with a 4.22 ERA over 28 starts.

COBB, TREVOR - TL - b: 7/13/73

Drafted in 1992, Cobb has had continued success in Rookie ball and A-ball leagues. 1997 was his first year at Double-A New Britain in the Minnesota farm system, where he posted a 3.44 ERA in 94.1 innings. He had some control difficulty but compiled a composite 13-4 record between New Britain and Class A Fort Meyers last year.

COGGIN, DAVE - TR - b: 10/30/76

Coggin is a good athlete; he was a highly recruited high school quarterback. He has an awesome array of natural skills, including a low-90s fastball, a curve and a changeup, but hasn't collected them together into a useful repertoire yet. His mechanics have been inconsistent, causing his command to waver. He struggled early in 1997 at Class A Clearwater, but improved considerably as the season wore on. He should return to Clearwater in 1998 with the hope of advancing to Double-A Reading. Coggin has the arsenal to be a top prospect as a starter, but needs to show better consistency soon.

COLE, JASON- TR - b: 9/9/72

A 34th-round selection by the Expos in the 1994 June draft, Cole reached Double-A ball for the first time last year. Cole will get another crack at Double-A this year — he needs to develop better control.

COLON, BARTOLO - TR - b: 5/24/75

SCOUTING: Colon has been considered one of the best pitching prospects in baseball for about three years now. He features a mid-90's fastball and a superb slider, and combines power with pinpoint control when he is on. He has been susceptible to myriad nagging injuries throughout his career, and is not an imposing physical specimen for a pitcher at 6'0", 185-pounds. He pays little mind to opposing baserunners; he got away with that in the minors, but won't in the majors.

1998: Colon must iron out the mechanical flaws which made him quite hittable in his rookie season. He also needs to work on his changeup; there isn't enough difference in speed between his best pitches. Expect his talent to emerge in 1998.

1997: Colon dominated at Triple-A, where he pitched a no-hitter, but wasn't nearly as impressive as fellow rookie Jaret Wright in the major leagues. He didn't throw strike one enough, and left his fastball out over the plate. His confidence waned, and team-low run support didn't help. Still, it wasn't a bad debut for the youngster.

1996: Though he missed part of the season with minor elbow problems, Colon certified his blue chip prospect status with 12 dominant Double-A starts. His slider was particularly impressive; he had relied primarily on his fastball at lower levels.

	W	SV	ERA	IP	H	BB	SO	B/I
1997 Cleveland	4	0	5.65	94	107	45	66	1.62

CONE, DAVID - TR - b: 1/2/63

Scouting: Cone has a 90+ MPH fastball which he can throw with precision. He has a curveball, split-fingered fastball and is refining his cut fastball. His slider is yet another good pitch. He's adept at changing speeds with his fastball and curve. Cone's leadership and experience are qualities which augment his value to the Yankees. October, 1997 surgery may impact the power of both his fastball and slider — his best weapons.

1998: If he's healthy, Cone will be the Yankees number two starter. He's a tough competitor and will work hard to return to full health.

1997: Cone was on his way to a 250-inning and 275-strikeout season when he was forced to leave a game on August 17th with what was then diagnosed as shoulder tendinitis. He spent two months on the shelf, then came back to make two starts at the end of the regular season, but his velocity and command were lacking; Cone was shut down again after making one post-season start. He eventually underwent surgery in October to clean out frayed tissue.

1996: Cone underwent aneurysm surgery in 1996 and returned to make eleven starts and pitch the Yankees into the postseason.

	W	SV	ERA	IP	H	BB	SO	B/I
1995 Tor. - NY AL	18	0	3.57	229	195	88	191	1.24
1996 New York AL	7	0	2.88	72	50	34	71	1.17
1997 New York AL	12	0	2.82	195	155	86	222	1.24

CONNELLY, STEVE - TR - b: 4/27/74

Connelly made the difficult jump to Double-A and weathered it well enough. He was penciled in to close at Class A Modesto so the fact that he survived with reasonable numbers (3-3 with a 3.75 ERA and seven saves with Huntsville last year) shows some skill. He does, however, look more like a middle reliever than a closer.

CONVERSE, JIM - TR - b: 8/17/71

Converse missed all of the 1996 season due to shoulder surgery. Arthroscopic surgery to repair a partial tear of the rotator cuff and torn labral cartilage effectively ended his year on June 12th. Last year he made a comeback with the Royals' Triple-A club in Omaha, appearing in six games, making three starts and he also appeared in three games with the big club. He is pitching again, and that's encouraging, despite his relatively poor results in 1997.

	W	SV	ERA	IP	H	BB	SO	B/I
1997 Kansas City	0	0	3.60	5	4	5	3	1.80

COOK, DENNIS - TL - b: 10/4/62

Scouting: Cook is a typical crafty lefty who has fashioned a long career out of an ability to outsmart lefthanded hitters. His fastball peaks in the upper 80's, but it appears faster because of his liberal use of off-speed pitches, particularly his changeup. He is a dogged competitor who wants the ball daily, and who often finds himself in the middle of on-field disputes. Cook will have a major league job — though possibly a less important one — for as long he wants it.

1998: Cook is expected to again serve the Marlins in a similar capacity. However, the Marlins expect Felix Heredia to inherit the top southpaw bullpen role in short order because of his superior stuff. Cook's value to the club will again exceed the benefit suggested by his statistics.

1997: Cook stranded 17 of 22 inherited baserunners in an average regular season performance, and easily handled an increased workload in the post-season. While you could see trepidation in the eyes of youngsters in October, Cook's confident smirk was in place throughout.

1996: Cook was the Ranger's top lefthanded reliever, posting career highs in most categories and holding lefthanded hitters to a .206 average. Unlike most southpaw specialists, Cook showed the moxie and stamina to pitch against righthanders as well, often in two-inning stints.

	W	SV	ERA	IP	H	BB	SO	B/I
1995 two teams	0	2	4.53	57	63	26	53	1.54
1996 Texas	5	0	4.09	70	53	35	64	1.26
1997 Florida	1	0	3.90	62	64	28	63	1.48

COOKE, STEVE - TL - b: 1/14/70

Scouting: Cooke is a finesse pitcher, even more now than when he was throwing 210 innings as a rookie back in 1993. Nerve damage in his shoulder caused him to miss most of the 1995-96 seasons and took away what was already average velocity. Cooke relies on sinking his fastball while mixing in a big-bending curveball, an improving slider and a mediocre changeup.

1998: Cooke will go to spring training as one of the Pirates' five incumbent starters but he is not assured of leaving Florida with a starter job after fading last season. Cooke's big advantage, though, is he was the Pirates' only lefthanded starter last season.

1997: Cooke spent nearly three months at the Pirates' extended spring training camp in Bradenton, Fla., trying to regain strength in his shoulder, weakened by nerve damage. He made three horrible relief outings with the Pirates after being recalled then spent the final two months of the season in Double-A Carolina's rotation trying to come back.

1996: Cooke came down with a weak shoulder in spring training, the result of nerve damage, and spent the whole season on the disabled list as the Pirates unsuccessfully tried to come up with a rehabilitation program that would get him back on the mound.

	W	SV	ERA	IP	H	BB	SO	B/I
1997 Pittsburgh	9	0	4.30	167	184	77	109	1.56

COOPER, BRIAN - TR - b: 8/19/74

Bad luck with injuries has kept the former University of Southern California star from realizing his potential — the latest an arm injury. Cooper will find 1998 is a good test for him; a bounce-back year. A good slider and a good strikeout-to-walk ratio give him the opportunity to move up through the organization quickly — if he can put together an injury-free season.

COPPINGER, ROCKY - TR - b: 3/19/74

Scouting: Coppinger is a young power pitcher with an excellent fastball, a power slider, and an occasional changeup. An improved changeup would make his other pitches more effective. He resembles Roger Clemens a little, at least in physique, and he can be viewed as a junior version of Clemens, but he will never approach that level of effectiveness. Coppinger displayed a bit of an attitude problem early in the 1997 season, openly disagreeing with Manager Davey Johnson on his pitching time and removal from games.

1998: To regain his starting job, Coppinger needs to work hard to come back from the surgeries. He's lost a year of experience, but he has a bright future. He could win 12-15 games with an ERA around 5.00, but will be a little erratic.

1997: Following a good but somewhat erratic rookie season in 1996, the Orioles were counting on Coppinger to be their fourth starter last season. But it was a lost season for him as he came down with an elbow injury and eventually required surgery on both his elbow and shoulder.

1996: Coppinger was called up from Triple-A in mid-year and went 10-6, showing great potential, despite inconsistency.

	W	SV	ERA	IP	H	BB	SO	B/I
1996 Baltimore	10	0	5.18	125	126	60	104	1.49
1997 Baltimore	1	0	6.30	20	21	16	22	1.85

CORBIN, ARCHIE - TR - b: 12/30/67

Scouting: Veteran Archie Corbin has a good 95-MPH fastball, but is prone to occasional wildness, limiting his usefulness as a reliever. In only a brief time in the International League in 1996, the "Baseball America" poll of managers rated his fastball as best in the league.

1998: Corbin could win a major league job as a middle reliever and mop-up man, if not with the Orioles then with another club. He proved in 1996 that he can be a valuable reliever, and he could do it again.

1997: The Orioles had the best bullpen in the majors, and Corbin spent the whole year in Triple-A. It's significant that the Orioles didn't call him up for their September stretch run.

1996: Orioles player development guru Syd Thrift signed Corbin after he was waived by a Mexican League team. It was a great addition as Corbin became a valuable part of the Orioles bullpen.

CORDOVA, FRANCISCO - TR - b: 4/26/72

Scouting: Cordova has some of the best stuff in the majors, a four-pitch arsenal that includes a hard, sinking fastball, quick-biting slider, curveball and changeup. Making him even tougher is that he'll throw any pitch from any angle — overhand, three-quarters or sidearm. Cordova's best pitch is the fastball, which has outstanding movement. Cordova's stamina is in question, though, as he frequently complains of a weary arm. He has the potential to be a big winner but it doesn't look like he can hold up through a season of 220-230 innings.

1998: Cordova has the best stuff in the Pirates' young rotation but he won't go into the season as the top starter. While he can dominate on any given day, he is a slightly built pitcher who tends to wear down at various points of the season.

1997: Cordova began the season in the Pirates' rotation and was one of the National League's best starters early, going 6-5 with a 2.41 ERA in his first 15 starts. However, Cordova was 5-3 with a 5.21 ERA in his last 14 starts, bothered by a weary arm and spending two weeks on the disabled list with an inflamed elbow. Cordova, though, showed how dominant he can be July 12th, throwing nine hitless innings against Houston before Ricardo Rincon worked the 10th to finish off the first combined extra-inning no-hitter in major league history.

1996: After spending four seasons in the Mexican League, Cordova made the Pirates as a non-roster player in spring training and went on to set a club rookie record with 12 saves. He moved to the rotation late in the season and was 2-0 with a 3.86 ERA in six starts.

	W	SV	ERA	IP	H	BB	SO	B/I
1996 Pittsburgh	4	12	4.09	99	103	20	95	1.24
1997 Pittsburgh	11	0	3.63	179	175	49	121	1.25

COREY, BRYAN - TR - b: 10/21/73
One of the last players taken in the expansion draft (Arizona, third round) Corey is still developing. He has a good, live arm and has been successful in the low minors. In 1996 he blew away the opposition at Class A Fayetteville on the Tigers farm, fanning 101 in 82 innings and collecting 34 saves with a 1.21 ERA. At Double-A in 1997, he learned that more advanced hitters will look for the fastball when a pitcher doesn't have much breaking stuff, and Corey is one of those who doesn't yet have much to go with his fastball.

CORMIER, RHEAL - TL - b: 4/23/67
Scouting: Cormier relies on changing speeds and keeping hitters off balance. His fastball and slider are only average but he complements it with an excellent changeup. Cormier's problem is he can never stay healthy. His career is in doubt after having reconstructive surgery on his left elbow last April.
1998: The Expos have been waiting for a French-Canadian star since their inception and was hoping Cormier, a New Brunswick native, would be their guy. However, he enters this season as a big question mark after reconstructive elbow surgery. If he is healthy, he will have a spot in the Expos' rotation, though no one is counting on that.
1997: Cormier made one start for the Expos then was shut down for the season after having the "Tommy John" operation on his elbow.
1996: Cormier began the season in Montreal's rotation but became a lefthanded specialist out of the bullpen in late-August after he began having elbow problems.

	W	SV	ERA	IP	H	BB	SO	B/I
1995 Boston	7	0	4.07	115	131	31	69	1.41
1996 Montreal	7	0	4.17	159	165	41	100	1.29

CORNELIUS, REID - TR - b: 6/2/70
Cornelius' gaudy 17-5 mark recorded at Double-A and Triple-A last year in the Marlins' chain should be taken with a grain of salt. Now 28 years old, this 1988 Olympian has endured a battery of arm injuries throughout his career, and is now a finesse pitcher who nibbles around the edges of the plate. Pay attention to these more vital facts — he has completed a total of five games in nine years, had a 24-to-17 strikeout-to-walk ratio in six Double-A starts in 1997, and posted a 5.10 ERA while allowing better than a hit per inning at Triple-A in 1997. It's Triple-A or bust for Cornelius in 1998.

CORPS, EDWIN - TR - b: 11/3/72
Corps filled pretty much the same role in 1997 for Double-A Shreveport that he did the previous year. He managed six saves for the Captains, but at age 25, he's just a set-up man mired in the minors. Corps has little chance to reach the majors and would be a middle-innings reliever if he does get that far.

CORREA, RAMSER - TR - b: 11/13/70
After spending 1996 at both Triple-A and Double-A as a closer, Correa spent 1997 in Vero Beach, and was a starter in all nine of his appearances. Correa still has a good fastball and was effective (1.77 ERA). He also showed better control, something that he has lacked in the past.

CORSI, JIM - TR - b: 9/9/61
Scouting: Corsi's a savvy veteran, who throws strikes, keeps the ball in the ballpark and knows how to keep hitters off-balance with a moving fastball and slider.
1998: Corsi should serve as Tom Gordon's primary set-up man for the Red Sox. It's possible he'll get some save opportunities if Gordon falters, but his stuff is not closer quality, so it's unlikely he can take over such a role.
1997: Corsi, hindered by an injury in the spring, didn't make the major league team to start the season. But he soon found himself serving a valuable set-up role. He was a steadying influence in a mess of a bullpen.
1996: Corsi had a solid season for Oakland, proving that his stellar performance in '95 was not a fluke.

	W	SV	ERA	IP	H	BB	SO	B/I
1995 Oakland	2	2	2.20	45	31	26	26	1.27
1996 Oakland	6	3	4.03	73	71	34	43	1.43
1997 Boston	5	2	3.42	58	56	21	40	1.33

COSTA, TONY - TR - b: 12/19/70
Costa returned to Double-A Reading for a second season last year and it was generally assumed that one of the better pitchers from higher Class A Clearwater would replace him by mid-season. It didn't happen, and Costa went on to rank among Eastern League leaders in a variety of dubious categories. Costa doesn't have good stuff or command. His fastball is straight and average in terms of velocity, and he has poor command of his breaking pitches. He has now accumulated a career 33-57 record.

COURTRIGHT, JOHN - TL - b: 5/30/70
Courtright was once a highly-touted prospect after a career at Duke University, and he even got a one-game stint with the Reds in 1995, but he has bounced around in the last couple of seasons. He went from the Reds to Minnesota to Baltimore and back to the Reds in a year's time (1996), but he managed to stay in the Cincinnati organization for all of the 1997 season. He didn't show any progress, though, going 5-7 with a 6.82 ERA for Double-A Chattanooga and giving up far more than a hit per inning (137 hits in 92.1 innings).

CRABTREE, TIM - TR - b: 10/13/69
Scouting: Crabtree missed most of last year but still possesses a low-90s sinking fastball and a hard slider. He needs to demonstrate that he is fully recovered from surgery. When healthy, he has good control.
1998: Crabtree, once projected as the closer of the future for Toronto, now is simply trying to win a spot in the bullpen. If he is fully recovered from having bone chips removed from his elbow each of the previous two years, he should land a spot as a middle reliever or set-up man.
1997: Crabtree missed most of the season after undergoing elbow surgery. When he returned, he was ineffective, including seven home runs allowed.
1996: The Blue Jays' most effective reliever, Crabtree went 5-3 with a 2.54 ERA over 53 games. Although he never gained the closer's role from Mike Timlin, he was the most reliable set-up man and finished 21 games.

	W	SV	ERA	IP	H	BB	SO	B/I
1995 Toronto	0	0	3.09	32	30	13	21	1.34
1996 Toronto	5	1	2.54	67	59	22	57	1.21
1997 Toronto	3	2	7.08	41	65	17	26	2.01

CRAWFORD, CARLOS - TR - b: 10/4/71
Crawford started last season as a reliever with the Pirates' Double-A Carolina farm club and was so-so. Inexplicably, he was promoted to Triple-A Calgary, turned into a starter and was bad. He was once considered a top prospect in Cleveland's organization but struggled and was claimed on waivers by Philadelphia following the 1995 season. Crawford made one major league appearance with the Phillies in 1996, allowing 10 runs in 3.2 innings — and that's likely to be it for him in the big leagues.

CRAWFORD, JOE - TL - b: 5/2/70
Scouting: Crawford is another of the projects taken on last season by Mets' pitching coach Bob Apodaca, and another who benefited from Apodaca's input. A pitcher with journeyman stuff, Crawford sometimes falls in love with his changeup, his most effective pitch. He used it so often in Triple-A last season that when he was promoted to the big leagues, opponents with affiliates in the International League were quite aware of it and were right on it. "His reputation preceded him," Apodaca said, "so he had to use his fastball more. He had to trust it more."
1998: Even with expansion, Crawford probably will be on the major league bubble. But he proved last season he can pitch adequately and eat up innings when the need arises. He was the last player cut in spring training last year; his major league fortunes may be that tight again.
1997: Crawford did a lot of mop-up work, but also provided adequate performance in his two starts. He is markedly more effective in those roles than he is short relief. He was the losing pitcher in the Mets' two 15-inning games last season. He produced an 8-2 record and 3.52 ERA in 16 starts and 99.2 innings in Triple-A. Home runs were a problem at the major league level; he allowed seven in 46.1 innings. But opponents batted merely .216 against him, and his walks-per-nine-innings ratio wasn't bad — 2.53.
1996: The Red Sox selected Crawford off the Mets' roster in the December, 1995 Rule V draft, but returned him to the Mets in March. He began the season with the Triple-A Norfolk team, returned to Double-A to get more regular work in a rotation and pitched a no-hitter. For the year, he had an 11-6 record and 2.77 ERA in 27 appearances — 23 starts — and 146.1 innings.

	W	SV	ERA	IP	H	BB	SO	B/I
1997 New York NL	4	0	3.30	46	36	13	25	1.06

CREEK, DOUG - TL - b: 3/1/69
Southpaw Creek toiled most of the 1997 at Triple-A Phoenix, where he went 8-6 with a 4.93 ERA. He has been toiling in the minors since 1991 — three years in A-ball, three at Double-A, and four (including last season) at Triple-A — he's a .500 pitcher. 1996 was Creek's one extended stay in the majors, and he got into a lot of games for the Giants but didn't perform well in most of them. '96 was so bad for San Francisco, that by the time Creek got into the game it didn't really matter. He isn't going back to the majors any time soon.

	W	SV	ERA	IP	H	BB	SO	B/I
1996 San Francisco	0	0	6.52	48	45	32	38	1.60
1997 San Francisco	1	0	6.77	13	12	14	14	1.95

CREEK, RYAN - TR - b: 9/24/72
Creek rebounded from a poor campaign at Double-A Jackson in 1996 (7-15, 5.26 ERA, more walks than strikeouts), to have a good year in his third Double-A season, going 10-5 with a 4.11 ERA. Creek throws hard and has good stuff — when he finds the strike zone. Despite the successful season in 1997, Creek's control has been poor; last year he walked 74 in 105 innings, an improvement over 1996. He's a marginal prospect who must succeed at Triple-A to have a major league future.

CROGHAN, ANDY - TR - b: 10/26/69
Croghan's surgery in 1995 made him rusty through the 1996 season but last year he did not seem to possess the same dominance that he had at Double-A Albany in 1994 where he got 16 saves in 36 innings with a 1.72 ERA. He was back in Double-A in 1997, but gave up more than a hit per inning and had a 5.72 ERA.

CROUSHORE, RICH - TR - b: 8/7/70
Originally signed as a non-drafted player from James Madison University, Croushore is a big hard-throwing prospect who has climbed through the system by piling up strikeouts. He could figure into the Cardinals' bullpen plans depending on the club's pre-season needs thanks to his second-half success last year at Triple-A Louisville. He worked nine games in relief there and five as a starter after gaining a promotion from Double-A, and overall he struck out more than 100 batters while walking half as many. The 27-year old has spent most of his minor-league career working out of the bullpen.

CROW, DEAN - TR - b: 8/21/72
Scouting: Crow has been groomed for a closer's role since being Seattle's tenth-round draft choice in 1993. Location and command are his pluses rather than a radar gun-popping fastball.
1998: Crow is expected to compete for a position in long relief for the Tigers after being acquired from Seattle in a mid-summer, 1997 trade that sent starters Felipe Lira and Omar Olivares to the Mariners.
1997: Crow regressed somewhat while pitching at Triple-A in both Tacoma and Toledo, combining for only nine saves in 51 appearances after losing the closer role in Tacoma to Mark Holzemer; Crow was rocked in Toledo after the trade. After a 4.78 ERA in 33 games at Tacoma, he stumbled to a 7.86 mark in 18 games with Toledo.
1996: Crow posted a career-high 26 saves at Double-A Port City as he continued to steadily climb up the organizational ladder after recovering from a right shoulder strain that cost him most of the 1994 season. Crow was 2-3 with a 3.04 ERA in 60 appearances, earning a berth on the Double-A All-Star team. He followed the stellar season by going 1-1 with a 1.44 ERA with Peoria in the Arizona Fall League and had the lowest opposition batting average in the league - .196.

CROWELL, JIM -TL - b: 5/14/74
Crowell pitched for Double-A and Triple-A last year — and briefly with the Reds — after spending most of the season in the Indians' organization. He gave up five walks and two long balls in 6.1 innings of work for Cincinnati. His minor-league numbers were adequate in the Reds' chain; he gave up less than a hit per inning in 38.2 innings. While with the Indians' Class A team in Kinston, Crowell made 17 starts and was impressive with a low ERA and a good strikeout-to-walk ratio. Crowell's performance at Kinston earned him a promotion to Cleveland's Double-A Akron team where he made three starts

before moving on to the Reds' farm system.

CRUZ, NELSON - TR - b: 9/13/72
Scouting: Cruz has a deceptive delivery that improves his fair-to-good stuff. He has been trained as a starter in the high minors over recent years, but was used in relief for the White Sox. Cruz was out of baseball in the United States for three years (1992-4) as he pitched in the Dominican Republic after one year with the Expos' Rookie-ball club in 1991.
1998: Cruz doesn't need much more training; he's ready to pitch in the big leagues now. He'll compete for a major league job, although it's hard to guess in what role. A favorite of deposed manager Terry Bevington, Cruz may have to win a major league role all over again.
1997: Cruz was Triple-A Nashville's winningest pitcher (8-5, 4.68 ERA) and showed good control in earning his promotion to the White Sox. He was occasionally hit hard in the majors, but still maintained his good control, walking just four against seventeen strikeouts.
1996: In his first year above A-ball, Cruz was 6-6 with a 3.32 ERA as a swingman for Double-A Birmingham, fanning 142 in 149 innings with just 41 walks; his was the tenth best ERA among all Double-A pitchers in 1996.

	W	SV	ERA	IP	H	BB	SO	B/I
1997 Chicago AL	0	0	6.50	26	29	9	23	1.44

CUMBERLAND, CHRIS - TL - b: 1/15/73
Cumberland was a top prospect, posting an ERA below 2.00 in two minor-league levels, before elbow trouble sidelined him in 1995. Since then he has struggled, not being able to lower his ERA below 4.00. He has been plagued with control difficulties and also gave up more than a hit per inning pitched. After his trade from the Yankee organization, Cumberland appeared in one game at Double-A New Britain last year.

CUMMINGS, JOHN - TL - b: 5/10/69
Cummings is one of those pitchers who's been able to hang around the majors just because he's a lefty who throws strikes. Throwing strikes became more of a problem in 1997, however, and now it is evident that Cummings lacks the stuff to have another successful season like he did working out of the bullpen for the Dodgers in 1995.

	W	SV	ERA	IP	H	BB	SO	B/I
1996 Los Angeles	0	0	6.75	5	12	2	5	2.75
1996 Detroit	3	0	5.12	31	36	20	24	1.79
1997 Detroit	2	0	5.47	25	32	14	8	1.86

CUNNANE, WILL - TR - b: 4/24/74
Scouting: A rule 5 draftee, Cunnane blew hot and cold in a premature first major league season in '97. The Padres like his potential, so they kept him on the roster all year. Cunnane has a good fastball and slider, but needs to locate his pitches better.
1998: Still only 23 at the season's start, Cunnane will be given a shot to make the Padre staff but will likely be in the starting rotation at Triple-A Las Vegas. The Padres are looking to build his confidence.
1997: Forced to spend the entire season with Padres, who pressed him into their troubled rotation for eight starts, Cunnane made 54 total appearances with opponents hitting him at a .305 clip. He was in over his head although his fastball velocity returned.
1996: Cunnane spent his second straight year with the Marlins' Double-A Portland club. His fastball lost some velocity by the end of the season and he wasn't protected. The Padres believed the change in his fastball was due to Cunnane pitching year-round for three straight seasons.

	W	SV	ERA	IP	H	BB	SO	B/I
1997 San Diego	6	0	5.82	91	114	49	79	1.79

CURTICE, JOHN - TL - b: 11/1/79
A hardthrowing southpaw from Virginia, Curtice was selected with the 17th pick of the 1997 draft by the Red Sox. A high school teammate of Twins' first-rounder Michael Cuddyer, Curtice went 2-0 in four appearances at Rookie level Fort Myers in the Gulf Coast League. He made three starts, had an ERA of 0.79 and struck out a batter per inning.

CURTIS, CHRIS - TR - b: 5/8/71
After six years in the Texas organization, 1997 was a change of scenery season for Curtis who pitched at Double-A Bowie in the Orioles' farm system. He doesn't have big-league stuff, despite posting a winning record for the first time since Rookie ball. He gave up more than a hit per inning and wasn't a strikeout pitcher in a long-relief/starter role.

CZAJKOWSKI, JIM - TR - b: 12/18/63
Czajkowski is a veteran minor-league pitcher with one brief stint in the majors with the Rockies in 1994. He walked one more batter than he struck out at Triple-A Syracuse in the Toronto organization last year and that's not going to be good enough to get him a set-up role in the majors.

DAAL, OMAR - TL - b: 3/1/72
Scouting: Daal has a good sinking fastball that reaches 90 MPH, and it sets up a nasty curveball that has a hard, late break, almost like a slider. Daal's problems come when his mechanics get fouled up. He has a tendency to become herky jerky, pulling his pitches out of the strike zone.
1998: The Diamondbacks planned to give Daal a chance at starting, something he has done with much distinction in Venezuelan winter ball year after year. Daal can also serve as a lefthanded specialist out of the bullpen but prefers starting.
1997: Daal had an up-and-down season. Twice, he was demoted by Montreal to Triple-A Ottawa, then finally lost on waivers to Toronto in late-July. The Blue Jays also sent him to Triple-A for awhile but he came back to Toronto and pitched well in September as a starter.
1996: Daal was primarily a reliever with the Expos, though he also got six starts. His results were mixed but he following that by going 9-1 in winter ball in his native Venezuela.

	W	SV	ERA	IP	H	BB	SO	B/I
1995 Los Angeles	4	0	7.20	20	29	15	11	2.20
1996 Montreal	4	0	4.02	87	74	37	82	1.27
1997 Toronto	2	1	7.07	57	82	21	44	1.80

DACE, DEREK - TL - b: 4/9/75
Dace converted from starting to relieving in 1997. He had fair results while pitching at three levels on the Tigers farm, finishing with 10 encouraging innings at Triple-A. His fastball is just lukewarm, but if can continue to hit spots and keep the batters off balance, he has potential as a lefty-lefty matchup specialist.

DALE, CARL - TR - b: 12/7/72
Dale spent last summer in the rotation at Double-A Huntsville where he posted less-than-average numbers (6-4. 5.38 ERA). It was his first tour at that level, and bearing in mind his age (24), he may have some improvement ahead. 1998 would be the make-or-break year.

D'AMICO, JEFF - TR - b: 12/27/75
Scouting: D'Amico has good velocity, with a fastball that can approach the upper 80s, and good control of his breaking stuff. He has a tendency to groove the ball at times and is susceptible to giving up home runs. He had elbow surgery early in his career and suffered some shoulder problems last season. But, if his arm holds up, he could be a star for several years.
1998: D'Amico is projected as a regular member of the Brewers' rotation, perhaps as their top starter.
1997: D'Amico missed several weeks with shoulder tendinitis, but continued to show the promise of becoming a top-notch starter. He needs to stop giving up so many home runs.
1996: He made the big jump from Double-A El Paso to the big leagues on June 28th. When D'Amico made his major league debut against Toronto on that night, he was the youngest player to start for the Brewers since Gary Sheffield made his debut at age 19 in 1988. He earned Brewers' Rookie of the Year Award.

	W	SV	ERA	IP	H	BB	SO	B/I
1996 Milwaukee	6	0	5.44	86	88	31	53	1.38
1997 Milwaukee	9	0	4.71	136	139	43	94	1.34

DANIELS, JOHN - TR - b: 2/7/74
Daniels was the closer for St. Petersburg and was a big part of the team's success as he recorded 29 saves. Daniels can be overpowering, as witnessed by his 100 strikeouts in 95 innings in 1996. Daniels likely will be the closer at Triple-A Durham in 1998. But given his 1997 season, he'll get at least a cursory look for making the big club in 1998.

DARENSBOURG, VIC - TL - b: 11/13/70
Once considered a prime Marlins' short-relief prospect, Darensbourg hasn't been the same since losing all of 1995 to elbow surgery. He has always been effective against lefthanded hitters, but has never honed his control to an acceptable level for a pitcher who normally enters the game with runners on base. As a lefthander, he will continue to receive countless opportunities to impress the major league brass, but at age 27, the window of opportunity for obtaining a significant major league role has likely closed.

DARWIN, DANNY - TR - b: 10/25/55
Scouting: At age 42, with more guile and savvy than heat, Darwin got the job done. He doesn't have much of a fastball, but he does have a pretty good combination of forkball and slider, and uses his experience to take advantage of young hitters — and to Darwin they are all young hitters. He also uses good control to reduce the number of baserunners and subsequently stay out of trouble.
1998: It doesn't seem reasonable that Darwin should be able to keep it going for another year. But, he doesn't seem to get hurt, and he certainly knows his limits, so with this in mind, it's likely Darwin will probably surface again this year, starting ten games and helping out with middle relief in 20 or 30 more. Or, he could retire at any time.

1997: Traded from the White Sox with Wilson Alvarez and Roberto Hernandez, Darwin made solid contributions to the Giants during their stretch run. He pitched well during his stint with Chicago, primarily as a starter.
1996: After two unproductive years in the American League, Darwin returned to the National League with Pittsburgh, and returned to his old form, though he did wear down as the season progressed. Darwin is still a fierce competitor, though he has lost velocity.

	W	SV	ERA	IP	H	BB	SO	B/I
1995 two teams	3	0	7.45	99	131	31	58	1.64
1996 Houston	10	0	3.77	164	160	27	96	1.14
1997 two teams	5	0	4.35	157	181	45	92	1.44

DARWIN, JEFF - TR - b: 7/6/69
Scouting: A hard-thrower with a fastball, curve and changeup, Darwin is tall and skinny (6'3", 180 pounds). He'll occasionally bounce his breaking balls in the dirt. Jeff is Danny's younger brother.
1998: Darwin has good enough stuff for a major league short relief or middle-innings job and should win such a role in the expansion year. He belongs in the majors.
1997: Darwin was the Triple-A Nashville closer, saving seventeen games in his 35 appearances while posting an unusually high ERA of 4.50.
1996: In his first year with the White Sox, Darwin split time between Nashville and Chicago, succeeding at both levels. His peripheral numbers were average or better and he saved three games in addition to making six starts for Nashville; he pitched strictly in relief for the White Sox.

	W	SV	ERA	IP	H	BB	SO	B/I
1996 Chicago AL	0	0	2.93	30	26	9	15	1.16
1997 Chicago AL	0	0	5.26	14	17	7	9	1.75

DASPIT, JAMIE - TR - b: 8/10/69
Daspit is a marginal starter who didn't perform well during an abbreviated stay at Triple-A Edmonton last year. His 0-2 record and 6.83 ERA speak volumes for a franchise that is desperate for a competent starter. Daspit surrendered six homers in his 27.2 innings at Edmonton; he'll have to improve his performance dramatically to get a chance at a major league job.

DAVEY, TOM - TR - b: 9/11/73
Destroyed at the Double-A level, he's probably two or more years away from being a Triple-A pitcher let alone a major leaguer. He has no control.

DAVIS, CLINT - TR - b: 9/26/69
Davis is a minor-league veteran reliever with mediocre stuff, but generally decent results (6-1, 3.20 ERA at Triple-A Oklahoma City last year). He has some chance of filling a middle-relief role in the majors at some point in the future.

DAVIS, JEFF - TR - b: 9/20/72
Scouting: Davis is a control pitcher with an average fastball and changeup. He is not a strikeout pitcher, and so needs reliable fielders behind him. Davis' eventual major league role would probably be as a reliever, but he needs innings and so is being used as a starter in the minors.
1998: Davis should get a promotion to Triple-A, joining Okla-

homa City's starting rotation, or possibly being used in middle relief in anticipation of advancing to the majors.
1997: Davis pitched well for Double-A Tulsa, going 4-6 with a 3.65 ERA and only 17 walks in 69 innings.
1996: In his first Double-A season, Davis was 7-2 but had a career-worst 4.59 ERA, missing half the season with an injury.

DAVIS, MARK - TL - b: 10/14/60
Scouting: The former Cy Young winner is hanging on primarily because he is lefthanded and has experience. Davis can still be effective in spots against lefthanded batters, but struggles in any appearances that are longer than a batter or two. His breaking stuff still has some snap, when he can spot it. His velocity is nothing like it once was.
1998: Davis could end up back with Arizona or another team looking for a lefty. Hitters tattooed him at a .323 clip in 1997, so his future is questionable.
1997: Davis was a late-season acquisition from the Diamondbacks' Triple-A roster. He appeared in 16 games at High Desert, mostly in situations calling for a lefty.
1996: After spending the end of the '95 season with the Marlins, Davis underwent arm surgery and did not pitch the entire '96 season. His career looked to be over until he was signed to a minor-league contract by Arizona.

	W	SV	ERA	IP	H	BB	SO	B/I
1997 Milwaukee	0	0	5.52	16	21	5	14	1.60

DAVIS, TIM - TL - b: 7/14/70
Scouting: The definitive "crafty lefty", Davis gets outs with a wide assortment of breaking pitches and changeups; his fastball tops out in the mid-80s. After making the jump from A-ball to the majors in 1994, Davis missed most of 1995 following arthroscopic surgery on his left shoulder.
1998: The Mariners' plethora of middle-relief types keeps Davis in a perpetual numbers game, although he has proven to be effective when healthy.
1997: Injuries continued to be a problem for Davis, who made only two appearances with Seattle (in relief) and one at Triple-A Tacoma (a start) after undergoing "Tommy John" surgery on his left elbow. Davis struck out 15 batters in 11.2 combined innings.
1996: Davis missed six weeks with a fractured left fibula, but still made 40 appearances for Seattle and eight at Tacoma; righthanders hit only .238 against him. He was particularly effective over the last part of the year. It was his third straight season split between the majors and Triple-A.

	W	SV	ERA	IP	H	BB	SO	B/I
1995 Seattle	2	0	6.38	24	30	18	19	2.00
1996 Seattle	2	0	4.01	42	43	17	34	1.42

DeHART, RICK - TL - b: 3/21/70
After spending five seasons in the Expos' organization and never getting above Double-A, DeHart broke through last season and had two stints in Montreal while spending the majority of the season at Triple-A Ottawa. DeHart doesn't throw hard but struck out nearly a batter per inning in the majors. However, his control was spotty which is not a long-term formula for success for a lefty relying on deception.

	W	SV	ERA	IP	H	BB	SO	B/I
1997 Montreal	2	0	5.53	29	33	14	29	1.60

DeJEAN, MIKE - TR - b: 9/28/79
Scouting: With his 93-MPH sinker and hard split-fingered pitch, DeJean is ideally suited for combating the thin-air environment at Coors Field, if there is such a thing as being ideally suited to pitch at Coors Field. He doesn't have any off-speed pitches for hitters to worry about so he's beatable if he doesn't have good location down in the strike zone. His control is usually pretty good, though, and he's extremely competitive.
1998: DeJean is expected to begin the season pitching a little closer to the middle of the game — the sixth and seventh innings — than he did near the end of 1997, when he was primarily responsible for the eighth inning.
1997: DeJean broke into the majors for the first time and was a pleasant surprise. Though he wasn't called up until May, and he spent three weeks on the disabled list with an inflamed elbow, he appeared in 55 games and posted the lowest ERA on the staff. DeJean even got a few shots at closing games, but he was primarily the set-up man.
1996: Acquired prior to the season from the New York Yankees in a trade that involved catcher Joe Girardi, DeJean had a disappointing season. Extremely nervous in spring training, he squeezed the ball and was ineffective. DeJean started the year at Triple-A Colorado Springs, was demoted to Double-A New Haven, then worked his way back to Colorado Springs before the end of the season.

	W	SV	ERA	IP	H	BB	SO	B/I
1997 Colorado	5	2	3.99	68	74	24	38	1.45

De La CRUZ, FERNANDO - TR - b: 1/25/71
De La Cruz had trouble at Double-A Midland in the Texas League for the Angels' organization last year. Control problems plagued him (more walks than strikeouts) and when he did get the ball near the plate it was hit. He also pitched in A-ball and the same problems held true. He's not a prospect for the near future.

De La MAZA, ROLAND - TR - b: 11/11/71
Scouting: Good control, not overpowering stuff, have allowed De La Maza to ring up an outstanding minor-league won/loss record. He has been a starter in the minors but merely average velocity on his fastball and a tendency to get hit hard the second time through a batting order would seem to lead De La Maza to a middle-relief role in a major league bullpen.
1998: The Royals would like De La Maza to step forward to claim a bullpen job. Otherwise, he's headed for Triple-A Omaha.
1997: De La Maza wasn't as successful in the won/loss column as in past years but still showed enough to get to the majors with the Royals following a trade from Cleveland for Bip Roberts. His major league stint was too brief for the Royals to form an opinion about his abilities.
1996: De La Maza continued his minor-league mastery, running his career record to 40-13.

De La ROSA, MAXIMO - TR - b: 7/12/71
DeLaRosa started and relieved at Double-A Akron in the Indians' system in 1997. He improved his control significantly, and completed five of his 13 starts. When his location was the slightest bit off, he paid dearly. He is eminently hittable when he leaves his fastball out over the plate, and he did so often in 1997. He is undersized at 5'11", 170 pounds, and is too old to have not yet reached Triple-A.

DE LOS SANTOS, LUIS - TR - b: 11/1/77
Next to Tony Armas, who was dealt to Boston for Mike Stanley, De Los Santos was the young pitcher other teams wanted most when the Yankees went looking for a bat in July and August. The 6'2", 187-pound 19-year old started at Class A Greensboro, moved to higher Class A Tampa and finished at Double-A Norwich in 1997. He has exceptional command for a youngster. De Los Santos was 1-1 with a 2.52 ERA in four games at Norwich and also started an Eastern League playoff game after going 5-0 with a 2.34 ERA at Tampa and 5-6 with a 3.05 ERA for Greensboro. He is on the fast track to big leagues as a mid-rotation major league starter in the year 2000.

De Los SANTOS, VALERIO - TL - b: 10/6/75
Scouting: Despite a 6-10 record at Double-A El Paso, the Brewers are high on this young pitcher. De Los Santos has good velocity, a sharp slider and has shown stamina in the minors.
1998: De Los Santos will get a good look in spring training, but likely will start the season in Triple-A.
1997: De Los Santos posted a 6-10 record, with a 5.75 ERA, in 26 games at El Paso; sixteen of his appearances were as a starter. He had a decent strikeout-to-walk ratio of 61-to-38.
1996: He spent the season at Class A Beloit and went 10-8 in 33 games, 23 as a starter; he also earned four saves. De Los Santos was selected to the Midwest League All-Star team.

DeLUCIA, RICH - TR - b: 10/7/64
Scouting: DeLucia made a career turnaround in a bullpen role after having enjoyed only moderate success with San Francisco before the Angels acquired him in an April, 1997 trade. DeLucia has good off-speed stuff to go with an above-average fastball and isn't afraid to throw any of his pitches in any situation.
1998: DeLucia will have to show he's recovered from surgery and may need a strong spring to beat out some of the Angels' young prospects for a job in the bullpen. Nonetheless, the Angels haven't forgotten what he did the first three months of 1997 when healthy and he'll have an excellent chance of winning a job.
1997: DeLucia grew more accustomed to a reliever's role after opening his career as a starter and showed amazing progress in his ability to be effective, making the most of a second chance to be successful in the majors. He became, perhaps, the Angels' most dependable set-up man through much of the season before an aneurysm in his right shoulder forced him to undergo surgery. DeLucia recovered from the surgery far quicker than expected and was back in the bullpen in September, although he wasn't the same pitcher.
1996: Two stints on the disabled list held DeLucia back. Six losses in nine decisions and a 5.84 ERA made him expendable the following April.

	W	SV	ERA	IP	H	BB	SO	B/I
1995 St. Louis	8	0	3.39	82	63	36	76	1.21
1996 San Francisco	3	0	5.84	61	62	31	55	1.52
1997 Anaheim	6	3	3.89	44	35	27	44	1.41

DEMPSTER, RYAN - TR - b: 5/3/77
Scouting: Dempster is a former top Rangers' prospect acquired in the 1996 John Burkett deal. He has slightly above-average velocity and a well-developed breaking-pitch repertoire, but is still learning to pitch after facing a low level of competition growing up in British Columbia. He is a durable hurler who could develop into a 200-inning workhorse. He needs to develop a take-charge psychological approach — he nibbled around the edges of the plate and walked too many hitters after the 1996 trade, and then overcompensated and threw room service strikes last year. He's still youthful, and Double-A success in 1998 would likely stamp him as a future member of the Marlins' rotation.
1998: Dempster needs to impress in spring training and earn a Double-A berth. He has the stuff to succeed, but must develop the mental toughness.
1997: Dempster was extremely hittable in the pitching-oriented higher Class A Florida State League due to poor pitch location. To his credit, he generally hung in there and pitched deep into ballgames despite his struggles.
1996: Dempster pitched extremely well despite a poor won-lost record in the Rangers' chain prior to the trade, but then inexplicably walked over six batters per nine innings in four starts with the Marlins' lower Class A affiliate.

DESSENS, ELMER - TR - b: 1/13/72
Scouting: Dessens' success is predicated on his command. He has the standard fastball/curveball/slider/changeup arsenal but none of the pitches are above average. He must use deception to win, changing speeds and throwing strikes.
1998: The Pirates are hoping Dessens can follow the footsteps of Francisco Cordova and Ricardo Rincon, going from Mexican League star to productive major league pitcher. Dessens' best hope is to make the Pirates as a reliever but his style makes him better suited for starting. It looks like Dessens will return to the Mexico City Reds and wait his turn for a rotation opening. And it's doubtful if he can match the success of Cordova and Rincon because he doesn't have the arm those two possess.
1997: Dessens was one of the Pirates' last cut in spring training then went 16-5 for the Mexico City Reds, raising his lifetime Mexican League record to a sparkling 37-10. The Pirates recalled him in September but used him just three times, all in meaningless relief roles.
1996: Dessens was all over the map, pitching in Pittsburgh, Mexico City, Triple-A Calgary and Double-A Carolina. He made three mid-season starts with the Pirates and was hopelessly overmatched, then didn't pitch much better in 12 relief appearances.

DETMERS, KRIS - TL - b: 6/22/74
Regarded two years ago as one of the organization's most promising lefthanded prospects, he still is considered highly — even though he took a step backwards last year. Detmers opened the season in Triple-A after three consecutive successful years of striking out scads of minor-leaguers. Blessed with a terrific curveball and generally above-average control, he struggled to get his only-average fastball past hitters at the higher level. He was demoted to Double-A and his problems continued. He's only 23 years old and one of the few lefthanded starting pitchers high in the Cardinals' organization, so he'll get plenty of chances to bounce back.

DICKEY, R.A. - TR - b: 10/29/74
Dickey was selected by the Rangers with the 18th pick of the 1996 draft. Last year, he pitched at Class A Charlotte of the Florida State League. Dickey struck out nearly a batter per inning but will have to work on his command to advance.

DICKSON, JASON - TR - b: 3/30/73
Scouting: Dickson showed a ton of promise with a brief flash of brilliance during the 1996 season, then fulfilled that promise in 1997 with grit, unusual poise for a youngster and a blazing fastball. The Angels like his mental toughness, his competitiveness and his willingness to face any situation.

1998: Dickson will again be counted on as one of the mainstays of the Angels' starting rotation. A year's experience in the major leagues, particularly a pennant race, will give the youngster a better idea of how to pitch to certain hitters and better handle the pressures of a title chase.

1997: Dickson established himself right away with a hot start, and became one of the club's pitching leaders while starter Chuck Finley and closer Troy Percival were recovering from injuries. Dickson faltered down the stretch because of an on-again, off-again sore elbow, but had the most solid year of any Angels starter. He wasn't projected to be in the rotation in spring training, but won a job with the steadiest performance by a starter in the spring, then finished the year as the club's co-leader in victories. Until Nomar Garciaparra's bat got hot, Dickson was the leading candidate for the American League Rookie of the Year award.

1996: Dickson was one of many youngsters the Angels tried when they went through a major league-record 29 pitchers. Called up from Triple-A Vancouver in July, he impressed the Angels with his tenacity and aggressiveness. Dickson showed he was a star in the making in his major league debut, giving up a home run to the first batter he faced — Derek Jeter — then going on to beat the Yankees in New York, 7-1.

	W	SV	ERA	IP	H	BB	SO	B/I
1996 California	1	0	4.57	43	52	18	20	1.62
1997 Anaheim	13	0	4.29	204	236	56	115	1.43

DILLINGER, JOHN - TR - b: 8/28/73
First things first: this Pirates' farmhand was not named after the notorious mobster but a late uncle, instead. The Pirates have always loved Dillinger's live right arm but have never figured out whether to use him as a starter or reliever. Conversely, Dillinger has never learned how to throw strikes. He is still only 24 years old and time is on his side, though the fact the Pirates dropped him from the 40-man roster last August doesn't bode well.

DIPOTO, JERRY - TR - b: 5/24/68
Scouting: The past few years, DiPoto was known for his hard sinker and slider. Midway through the 1997 season, he all but chucked his sinker and replaced it with a four-seam fastball that was consistently clocked around 94 MPH. Voila! The Rockies found themselves a closer. His greatest asset is his rubber arm — and willingness to take the ball every day. He's probably better suited for the set-up role, but he can close.

1998: DiPoto will get the first chance to establish himself as the Rockies' closer. At worst, he will fill the set-up role.

1997: After he was acquired from the New York Mets in a straight-up deal for Armando Reynoso, Dipoto got off to a horrific start. After getting bombed by St. Louis on June 3rd, his ERA was 9.12. At that point, Dipoto dropped what had been his best pitch — the two-seam sinker — and started throwing a four-seam fastball for the first time in two years. In his 50 games since the St. Louis shellacking, he was 4-2 with 15 saves and a 3.06 ERA. He set a club record with 18 consecutive scoreless innings and went 65 consecutive innings without surrendering a home run, impressive indeed in the thin air at Coors Field.

1996: DiPoto was a durable middle man for the Mets, winning a career-best seven games. He was also accused of performing better in games not in doubt than when the score was close, which would seem to be at odds with his seven victories out of the bullpen.

	W	SV	ERA	IP	H	BB	SO	B/I
1995 New York NL	4	2	3.78	78	77	29	49	1.36
1996 New York NL	7	0	4.19	77	91	45	52	1.76
1997 Colorado	5	16	4.70	96	108	33	74	1.47

DISHMAN, GLENN - TL - b: 11/5/70
Dishman spent most of 1997 at Triple-A Toledo and was one of the better starters on the Tigers farm. He has a good enough fastball and keeps trying to find the right mix of breaking stuff to advance to major league success. He's not far away at this point.

	W	SV	ERA	IP	H	BB	SO	B/I
1997 Detroit	1	0	5.28	29	30	8	20	1.31

DIXON, BUBBA - TL - b: 1/7/72
Scouting: His fastball has been clocked only in the low 80s, but his 77-MPH curve is considered the best in the Padre organization; his curve looks like a fastball, but has a late break. Dixon could have a major league future as a situational reliever.

1998: Dixon is ticketed for the bullpen at Triple-A Las Vegas.

1997: Dixon was 7-2 with a 3.45 ERA in 56 appearances, mostly relief, at Double-A Mobile, including 88 strikeouts in 75.2 innings.

1996: Dixon advanced from Class A Rancho Cucamonga to Double-A Memphis where he was 2-3 with a 4.12 ERA and 77 strikeouts in 63.1 innings.

DIXON, TIM - TL - b: 2/26/72
Dixon struggled early last season at Triple-A Ottawa as he tried to make the jump from Class A in the Montreal organization. However, he pitched extremely well in relief for Double-A Harrisburg and has a big-league future as bullpen specialist.

DODD, ROBERT - TL - b: 3/14/73
Dodd has thrived since being moved to the bullpen during the 1996 season. He throws four quality pitches, including a fastball which lacks spectacular velocity, but possesses exceptional movement. It looks fast compared to the tantalizing changeup which he will throw on any count. He's tough against lefthanded hitters, and has a durable arm which allows him to throw two innings or more every couple of days. He has greatly improved his command, and his confidence has soared since his move to the pen. Dodd became the go-to guy for Double-A Reading down the stretch last year and has a remote chance to make a major league impact this year, particularly in light of the lack of quality lefty set-up men in Philadelphia.

DOMAN, ROGER - TR - b: 1/26/73
Doman spent three weeks at Triple-A in June and was clearly not ready. Expect him to start at Triple-A this year and figure that he's at least two or three years from success at that level.

DONNELLY, BRENDAN - TR - b: 7/4/71
Three years ago Donnelly was pitching in the independent

Frontier League, but he had surprising success at Double-A Chattanooga in 1997, going 6-4 with a 3.27 ERA. However, it was his second year at that level and being 27 years old he was much older than the players he was playing against. His stats also reflected shoddy defense as he gave up 43 runs, but only 30 were earned. He turned 28 in the off-season and has only pitched 2.2 innings above Double-A in his career, so he doesn't have much of a chance of getting to the majors.

DOUGHERTY, JIM - TR - b: 3/8/68
A sidearming sinker/slider pitcher, Dougherty did a stint as a starter back in Port St. Lucie, and was successful enough (6-1, 1.93 ERA) for another shot at Triple-A Norfolk last year. He kept up the pace as a reliever, posting a 10-1 record with a 1.45 ERA and four saves.

DOUGHERTY, TONY- TR - b: 4/12/73
Dougherty is a hard thrower with average control who has evolved into a part-time closer over the past two seasons. He graduated to Triple-A Buffalo by the end of 1997, where his lack of command finally undermined his performance. He has a durable two-inning arm which will likely make him a productive member of a Triple-A set-up crew, but little more.

DOYLE, TOM - TL - b: 1/20/70
Doyle was another older Reds farmhand (and former independent league player) who enjoyed success at Double-A pitching against much younger and inexperienced players. Doyle signed out of high school with the Phillies and spent most of his first six seasons in the minors as a first baseman in the Philadelphia and San Diego organizations. He's only been pitching since 1994 so he might have a little more left in his arm than a comparable pitcher at his age. However, the Reds keep talking about going with younger players in Cincinnati and younger prospects in the minors. Plus, it's not likely that he'll be able to duplicate his 1997 numbers, even with another shot at Double-A.

DRABEK, DOUG - TR - b: 7/25/62
Scouting: Drabek has never really thrown hard to begin with and has even lost more velocity in recent years. He has also lost the bite on his curveball; it's now a roller or floater.
1998: Considered a "veteran presence" on a young White Sox staff, Drabek may return to Chicago, probably with a job in the starting rotation.
1997: It was clearly his worst season in the majors with an ERA more than a run higher than any other season, a diminishing strikeout rate and rising opposition batting average.
1996: In his last year in his native state, Drabek had an off-and-on season for the Astros. In half of his starts he went at least six innings and allowed an ERA of 2.10 while going 7-1. In his other fifteen starts he was 0-9 with an 8.43 ERA.

	W	SV	ERA	IP	H	BB	SO	B/I
1995 Houston	10	0	4.77	185	205	54	143	1.40
1996 Houston	7	0	4.57	175	208	60	137	1.53
1997 Chicago AL	12	0	5.74	169	170	69	85	1.41

DRAHMAN, BRIAN - TR - b: 11/7/66
Drahman appears to be nearing the end of the line. He's lost the stuff that got him to the majors at four different times during his 12-year professional career. He pitched only 42.2 innings at Triple-A Las Vegas in the Padres' organization last year and had control problems as well as yielding more than a hit per inning.

DREIFORT, DARREN - TR - b: 5/18/72
Scouting: Dreifort has passed all his tests and should enter the 1998 season as a strong candidate to be the closer. His mid-90's fastball is his best pitch. He also uses a good hard slider, giving him two tough out pitches. He is still a little wild, not a serious problem for anyone so overpowering.
1998: On a Dodger team without Todd Worrell, Dreifort will compete with Antonio Osuna for the ace relief job. On many teams, Dreifort would have been promoted to ace already.
1997: Dreifort was often sensational. When he got ahead in the count, he held the opposition to a .108 batting average, and he allowed just three home runs in his 63 innings.
1996: Dreifort's comeback from reconstructive elbow surgery was pronounced complete. He lost nothing off his fastball, and worked as a starter at Triple-A Albuquerque as the Dodgers wanted him seasoned for their playoff roster.

	W	SV	ERA	IP	H	BB	SO	B/I
1996 Los Angeles	1	0	4.94	23	23	12	24	1.51
1997 Los Angeles	5	4	2.86	63	45	34	63	1.25

DRESSENDORFER, KIRK - TR - b: 4/8/69
Dressendorfer is a former top draft choice of the Oakland A's, but his development has been slowed dramatically by chronic arm problems. He threw well last spring for the Dodgers, but then old shoulder problems came back to haunt him. He has good stuff, but, so far, a right shoulder that has required two operations hasn't remained sound long enough to allow him to put it together.

DREW, TIM - TR - b: 8/31/78
As expected, J.D.'s brother Tim was selected in the first round of the 1997 draft and immediately established himself as a major league prospect. The Indians' top pick throws a mid-90's fastball and a potentially lethal slider. Many considered him a first-round gamble based upon a back injury which limited him to 32 innings as a high school senior in 1997, and an often petulant attitude. The Indians feel that Drew can be a second or third starter or a top reliever in the majors in four years.

DREWS, MATT - TR - b: 8/29/74
Scouting: At 6'8", he's imposing on the mound, he throws hard (mid-90s) and he has a good breaking ball. But since his big 15-win season in 1995 in Class A, Drews hasn't had anything near the consistency he needs to get to and succeed in the big leagues.
1998: Although he gets a fresh start with Arizona, Drews will likely begin the year at Triple-A, where he began 1996 and ended 1997. With a good year, he'll get to the big leagues. With a bad year, other prospects will pass him.
1997: His numbers in Double-A weren't stunning (8-11, 5.49 ERA), but the Tigers saw enough improvement to promote Drews to Triple-A Toledo by the end of the year. He made only three Triple-A starts and didn't win any of them, with control and consistency again proving to be problems.
1996: In a mixed-up year, Drews pitched for four teams in two different organizations. The Yankees tried to jump him all the way from Class A to Triple-A, and he obviously wasn't ready for it. He began the year as the 12th-rated prospect in all of

baseball, and by July the Yankees were willing to include him in the Cecil Fielder trade with the Tigers.

DREYER, STEVE - TR - b: 11/19/69
Despite his three-to-one strikeout-to-walk ratio, Dreyer is a finesse pitcher; he worked exclusively as a starter until 1996, then posted two saves as a bullpen pitcher in 1997. He permitted 65 hits in his 44 innings last year, leading to a 7.36 ERA at the Triple-A level. It was a disappointing season for Dreyer, who was coming off a good 1996 campaign and hoping to return to the majors again after reaching the bigs briefly in 1993-4.

DRISKILL, TRAVIS - TR - b: 8/1/71
Driskill is a converted reliever with limited power and decent control who needs to keep the ball low in the strike zone to have success. He did so relatively infrequently in 1997, allowing well over a hit per inning, and rarely offered his team more than six competent innings. Driskill will likely ferment at the Triple-A level for the foreseeable future, in a steadily diminishing role.

DRUMRIGHT, MIKE - TR - b: 4/19/74
Scouting: Of the Tigers' pitching prospects, and there are many, Drumright is probably the closest to contributing in the major leagues. His consistency needs the most work, which is why he went 5-10 in Triple-A. He'll get his chance in Detroit; the only question is how soon.
1998: A good spring training could accelerate the process, just as a poor spring in 1997 pushed Drumright's timetable back. The expectation, though, is that Drumright begins the year in Toledo, and comes to the Tigers when he proves he's ready.
1997: In the spring, he wasn't throwing as hard as usual, and the Tigers weren't happy. Drumright began the year at Double-A, made five impressive starts (1.57 ERA) and was promoted to Toledo. Velocity wasn't a problem there, but consistency was.
1996: In his first full pro year, the former top draft pick out of Wichita State was named the best pitching prospect in the Double-A Southern League.

DUBOSE, ERIC - TL - b: 5/15/76
DuBose was selected by the A's with the 21st pick in the first round of the 1997 draft. He was known for having the best breaking ball in the college game while at Mississippi State. Last year he pitched at Class A stops in the Northwest League and California League. He overwhelmed batters in the Northwest League but found it a bit tougher going at Visalia although he still fanned a batter per inning.

DUNBAR, MATT - TL - b: 10/15/68
Dunbar spent seven years in the Yankees' farm system without ever reaching the Bronx. Last year he pitched for the Angels at Triple-A Vancouver. He wasn't particularly impressive but a lefty who throws strikes could have a chance to turn up in someone's bullpen.

DURAN, ROBERTO - TL - b: 3/6/73
Scouting: As a lefthander who throws in the mid-90s, Duran will get many chances. He has yet to prove that he has good enough control to stay out of trouble in the late innings, but the Tigers expect that he'll eventually do that.
1998: Duran will likely make the Tiger staff, but it could be as a middle reliever. They'd like to have another lefty to pitch in one- or two-batter situations later in the game.
1997: Picked up from Toronto for Anton French (who had been acquired from Atlanta for Danny Bautista), Duran almost immediately impressed the Tigers with his velocity. He spent most of the year at Double-A Jacksonville, where he had 16 saves, but he also made two trips to the big leagues.
1996: Toronto claimed Duran off waivers in spring training, then used him as a starter in Class A and then in Double-A. He had some success, but also had problems with his control, walking 61 in 80.2 innings at Double-A Knoxville.

	W	SV	ERA	IP	H	BB	SO	B/I
1997 Detroit	0	0	7.57	11	7	15	11	2.06

DUROCHER, JAYSON - TR - b: 8/18/74
The White Sox thought enough of Durocher that they selected him from the Montreal organization in the Rule 5 Draft after he had a fine year at Class A West Palm Beach in 1996. Durocher didn't make the White Sox, though, and had to be offered back to Montreal at the end of spring training. He pitched well again at West Palm, though he was bothered by shoulder stiffness. And, yes, he is a distant relative of Leo The Lip.

DUVALL, MIKE - TL - b: 10/11/74
Tampa Bay was delighted to find so much southpaw talent in the expansion draft. Duvall had developed into one of the Marlins' best lefthanded relief prospects after Felix Heredia became established in the majors. Duvall is not a power pitcher, but has excellent control, keeps the ball down, and is durable enough to pitch two innings per appearance. He also fares well against righthanded hitters. He doesn't have the raw stuff to close in the majors, but he could eventually become one of the Rays' lefty bullpen specialists.

DYER, MIKE - TR - b: 9/8/66
Dyer is a journeyman middle reliever with some big-league time, who may be at the end of the line. He had mediocre results at Triple-A Richmond in '97, posting a 4.87 ERA and ended the season on the DL with an arm problem. His fastball is not much any more, but he has a good slider, especially against righthanders.

	W	SV	ERA	IP	H	BB	SO	B/I
1995 Pittsburgh	4	0	4.34	74	81	30	53	1.49
1996 Montreal	5	2	4.40	75	79	34	51	1.50

EATON, ADAM - TR - b: 11/23/77
Prior to signing a pro contract, Eaton suffered a minor shoulder injury while playing second base in an American Legion game. His health was a concern since he wasn't throwing the mid-90s fastball that was the cause for the Phillies to select him in the first round of the 1996 draft. Eaton must improve his mechanics and make major strides with his breaking-ball repertoire. He's still among the younger starting pitchers at his level —lower Class A Piedmont in 1997, where he'll likely begin the 1998 season.

EBERT, DERRIN - TL - b: 8/21/76
Ebert was the Braves 18th-round pick in the 1994 draft. He pitched at Double-A Greenville in 1997 and showed excellent control with 101 strikeouts to 48 walks in 176 innings of work. He changes speeds well and consistently hurls deep into the

game. He needs to continue to improve his precision as he still allows batters more than a hit per inning. He has a chance to be a prospect in a couple more seasons.

ECKERSLEY, DENNIS - TR - b: 10/3/54
Scouting: Eckersley still is better than any 43-year-old pitcher has a right to be, thanks to control most big-leaguers envy and a stunning slider that he uses more and more as a complement to his generally lively fastball. He's not the automatic closer that he was in building a Hall-of-Fame career when Tony LaRussa sent him to the bullpen in the mid-1980s. He remains effective, though, and is at his best when he's been used regularly.
1998: A free agent heading into the winter, Eckersley can be counted on as a closer because of his experience and stamina enhanced by some of the best conditioning work of any pitcher in the big leagues. He probably will need a capable second-in-line closer on hand, though, since his fastball continues to lose speed and could move down into dangerous range.
1997: Better than any other option the Cardinals had, Eckersley also was better than most other closers in the league. His breakdown came in rare control lapses — eight walks in 53 innings was high by his standards —and when he hung some sliders that contributed to nine home runs allowed — also high by his standards.
1996: He had some trouble in the first half, marked by some poor May appearance and a June stint on the disabled list. Eckersley regained his old form through much of the second half and during the post-season. Batters did hit .274 against him.

	W	SV	ERA	IP	H	BB	SO	B/I
1995 Oakland	4	29	4.83	50	53	11	40	1.27
1996 St. Louis	0	30	3.30	60	65	6	49	1.18
1997 St. Louis	1	36	3.91	53	49	8	45	1.08

EDDY, CHRIS - TL - b: 11/27/69
Now with his third organization in two years, Eddy has become a minor-league journeyman. Eddy had a solid year at Double-A Tulsa (four wins, five saves, 3.18 ERA), but has never pitched well above that level. He is not likely to make it back to the majors.

EDMONDSON, BRIAN - TR - b: 1/29/73
Edmondson had a good season as a reliever in Double-A last year (2-0, 1.23 ERA) and ended up at Triple-A Norfolk with a 4-3 record and a 2.90 ERA. He has good control, and another season like last year could give him a shot at filling the Mets' bullpen in middle relief. He lacks velocity but changes speeds well and moves the ball around with precision.

EDSELL, GEOFF - TR - b: 12/12/71
Scouting: Inconsistency has been the main thing that has held Edsell back so far. He has a varied repertoire with a fastball clocked the 88-92 MPH range, a good slider and a good changeup. Scouts either love Edsell or hate him, depending on which day they see him pitch — because of his inconsistency.
1998: Edsell has to show the Angels more consistency if he wants the chance to make the staff in the spring, but the club remains impressed with his talent. If he's "on" for any length of time, Edsell could easily be a surprise player this season.
1997: Edsell had his ups and down at Vancouver, but put together a solid season with a staff-leading 14 victories as a starter and 183.1 innings pitched. Walks hurt Edsell at times, but he balanced that by finishing second on the staff in strikeouts (95).
1996: Edsell made a successful jump from Double-A to Triple-A in mid-season and had a solid half-season for Vancouver with four victories and a 3.43 ERA.

EILAND, DAVE - TR - b: 7/5/66
Getting chances as a major league starter every year from 1988 through 1995, Eiland never had any real success except for five good starts in 1990. He has been able to hang on around the fringe of the major leagues, mainly because he can throw strikes.

EISCHEN, JOEY - TL - b: 5/25/70
Eischen only pitched in one game for Cincinnati last season after coming down with arm problems in spring training. He pitched the second half of the season for the Reds Triple-A farm team and had a decent season there. The Reds will keep him around as lefthanded insurance for their bullpen. He could see a lot of action if Cincinnati makes Mike Remlinger a full-time starter, but if Remlinger goes back to the bullpen Eischen won't get many innings in Cincinnati.

	W	SV	ERA	IP	H	BB	SO	B/I
1995 Los Angeles	0	0	3.10	20	19	11	15	1.48
1996 Los Angeles	0	0	4.78	43	48	20	36	1.58
1996 Detroit	1	0	3.24	25	27	14	15	1.64

ELARTON, SCOTT - TR - b: 2/23/76
Scouting: Elarton is the top pitching prospect in the Houston system. As a first-round draft choice out of high school in 1994 he has made steady progress, finishing the 1997 season at the Triple-A level. Elarton is 6'7", 240-pounds with a dominating fastball and a nasty slider. He has not had the control problems frequently associated with a pitcher his size. Elarton appears to have the tools and the makeup for a successful major league career. In his four years in the minors, he has a 44-22 won-loss record.
1998: Elarton will probably start the season in Triple-A but is likely to be first in line if an opening develops at the major league level.
1997: Elarton was an All-Star at Double-A Jackson with a 7-4 record and an ERA of 3.24. He allowed 103 hits in 133.1 innings while striking out 141 and walking just 47. He moved up to Triple-A New Orleans where he started strong before struggling in his last few starts. He was 4-4 with a 5.33 ERA in nine games (six starts). He had 50 strikeouts while allowing only 17 walks in 54 innings. He ranked fourth among all minor-league pitchers with 191 strikeouts.
1996: Elarton was one of the top pitchers in the High Class A Florida State League with a 12-7 record and an ERA of 2.92.

ELDRED, CAL - TR - b: 11/24/67
Scouting: Eldred has changed from a power pitcher to a guy who mixes his pitches and nibbles at the corners. Reconstructive surgery on his right elbow in 1995 cost him much of his velocity. He remains a horse, able to pitch many innings when healthy. His work ethic was a major factor in his rehab from the surgery. He will give up home runs.
1998: Depending on what happens to Ben McDonald, Eldred could start the season as the ace starter for the Brewers. He's signed through 1999 and is seen as one of the core members

of the club.
1997: Eldred made it through his first full season after his 1995 surgery. He struggled somewhat with his control and also was near the top of the league in homers allowed. Some of these difficulties might be attributed to rustiness from his injury.
1996: Eldred made his return June 14th against Toronto after 14 months of inactivity because of Tommy John surgery. He was used on a strict pitch limit and ended up pitching .500 ball in 15 appearances.

	W	SV	ERA	IP	H	BB	SO	B/I
1995 Milwaukee	1	0	3.42	23	24	10	18	1.44
1996 Milwaukee	4	0	4.46	84	82	38	50	1.43
1997 Milwaukee	13	0	4.99	202	207	89	122	1.47

ELLIS, ROBERT - TR - b: 12/15/70
Once he develops consistent control, the 6'5" righthander could elevate his status quickly. Ellis' fastball has topped out at 91 MPH on the radar gun and he hits 89 MPH consistently. Obtained in trade from the Chicago White Sox in July of 1996, Ellis needs to work on his control this winter and probably needs a good 1998 season to keep from being bypassed by other prospects.

EMBREE, ALAN - TL - b: 1/23/70
Scouting: Few lefthanders throw as hard as Embree, but most have better control. His history has been to throw mid-90s fastballs all over the place, getting enough close to the strike zone to get a few batters to swing at them. Too often he gets too much of the plate and gets clobbered. But, that tendency was dormant last year as he suddenly found the plate regularly for the first time in the majors.
1998: Embree will continue as a top lefty situational pitcher in the majors. His ability to throw hard to a handful of batters is perfect for a set-up role.
1997: Embree was a key addition to the Braves bullpen — a hard-throwing lefthander to set-up the hard-throwing right-hander Mark Wohlers. Embree was one of the few bullpen denizens who didn't get into manager Bobby Cox' doghouse. The only disappointment for Embree was less success against lefthanders; he held them to a .247 batting average, but was stellar against righthanders, limiting them to a .200 average and just four extra-base hits.
1996: Continued control difficulties resulted in Embree being used sparingly in the Indians' bullpen. He rarely got ahead of hitters, but often threw a fastball down the middle of the plate; the result was ten homers to go with 21 walks in just 31 innings. When he had good command, though, Embree was over-powering, especially against the lefthanders whom he limited to a .186 average.

	W	SV	ERA	IP	H	BB	SO	B/I
1995 Cleveland	3	1	5.11	24	23	16	23	1.58
1996 Cleveland	1	0	6.39	31	30	21	33	1.65
1997 Atlanta	3	0	2.54	46	36	20	45	1.22

ENOCKS, CHRIS- TR - b: 10/11/75
Enochs was the first of two pitchers selected in the first round by the A's last year (11th pick overall). He pitched in the Northwest and California Class A leagues last year. At Modesto he made ten appearances (nine starts) with a 3-0 mark and a strikeout per inning.

ERDOS, TODD - TR - b: 11/21/73
Scouting: Erdos is a battler who missed all of the 1994 season due to a pituitary gland problem that robbed him of his strength. He throws his all into every pitch. There are concerns about his mechanics and the stress on his arm. He has good movement on his 92 to 94-MPH fastball and a solid changeup and slider. Some scouts consider Erdos closer material.
1998: Erdos was one of the bigger questions facing the Padres as they agonized over their expansion draft protection list. When he was left available, Arizona took him. He could return to the majors in middle relief.
1997: Erdos had a 3.36 ERA and 27 saves at Double-A Mobile when called up to the majors.
1996: Erdos had his first full season after the pituitary problem and was 3-3 at Rancho Cucamonga with 17 saves and a 3.74 ERA in 55 appearances; he fanned 82 in 67.1 innings.

	W	SV	ERA	IP	H	BB	SO	B/I
1997 San Diego	2	0	5.26	14	17	4	13	1.53

ERICKS, JOHN - TR - b: 9/16/71
Ericks is a hard thrower with a 95-MPH fastball and slider, who was moved to the bullpen midway through the 1996 season and began to flourish. He began last season as the Pirates' closer and converted six of seven save opportunities before going on the disabled list April 29th with a herniated disc in his neck. He had surgery May 23rd and never returned, despite pitching at Rookie-level Bradenton and Triple-A Calgary on an injury rehabilitation assignment as his fastball rarely topped 87 MPH. Ericks was dropped from the roster at the end of the season but will likely make the club as a set-up man if he is healthy.

	W	SV	ERA	IP	H	BB	SO	B/I
1995 Pittsburgh	3	0	4.58	106	108	50	80	1.49
1996 Pittsburgh	4	8	5.79	46	56	19	46	1.62

ERICKSON, SCOTT - TR - b: 2/2/68
Scouting: Erickson's most effective pitch is a sinking fastball, making him a groundball pitcher. He also throws a slider and an occasional changeup. He's competitive, and has been known to get upset when teammates commit errors, but that aspect was invisible last year. Erickson can have off days when his fastball isn't sinking, making him hittable; he can sometimes lose the sink when he's had a lot of time between starts.
1998: The highly competitive and energetic Erickson can have another great year in 1998.
1997: Erickson kept his sinking fastball low for most of last season, resulting in his best year since his 20-win season in 1991. He's a ground ball pitcher, and it helped that the Orioles had great infield defense. It wasn't a new pitch or better stuff that improved Erickson's results; instead, upgraded circumstances led to a fine season after five marginal years.
1996: Erickson had another mediocre year, and it began to look like he was always going to be a .500 pitcher. The Orioles had some defensive weaknesses which didn't help Erickson.

	W	SV	ERA	IP	H	BB	SO	B/I
1995 two teams	13	0	4.81	196	213	67	106	1.43
1996 Baltimore	13	0	5.02	222	262	66	100	1.48
1997 Baltimore	16	0	3.69	222	218	61	131	1.26

ESCOBAR, KELVIM - TR - b: 4/11/76
Scouting: Escobar has all the tools to be an effective closer,

including the ability to not get frustrated when things don't go his way. He has a fastball consistently in the low-90s and improving. His curve and a split-finger changeup make him intimidating as he is confident with any of his pitches at any time. His control is better than most, particular in light of his inexperience. A starting pitcher until he became the closer, he is durable.

1998: A Toronto bullpen that did not sign an established closer would go with Escobar as the closer, depending on the new manager. He has all the tools and an improved Blue Jays' offense would make Escobar a 35-40 save threat.

1997: Escobar appeared from nowhere to steal the closer's role from Mike Timlin. In May, he was in Dunedin and by June he was in Knoxville. By July he had appeared in Toronto and by August he was getting all the saves. He is intimidating and showed that he is well-equipped to be a closer, converting his first ten save opportunities.

1996: Escobar split time between Class A Dunedin and Double-A Knoxville, performing well at the lower level. He was a starting pitcher for the entire year.

	W	SV	ERA	IP	H	BB	SO	B/I
1997 Toronto	3	14	2.90	31	28	19	36	1.52

ESHELMAN, VAUGHN - TL - b: 5/22/69

Scouting: Eshelman has a fastball which touches 90 MPH, and also throws a curve, slider and changeup that are big-league pitches at times. However, he is inconsistent, both with the quality of his pitches and his command of them.

1998: Eshelman will most likely be pitching in the majors this season, although the Devil Rays were not sure about a role when they drafted him. His success will depend on how much patience his team has with him. He's capable of pitching well, as a starter or reliever, if given a steady role, and as long as his coaching staff has faith in him and lives with his inevitable inconsistency.

1997: Eshelman bounced up and down between Boston and Triple-A Pawtucket. He had success as a starter in Triple-A once he was allowed to settle into a groove, showing rediscovered arm strength. He was horribly unreliable as a starter and reliever for the Red Sox, who have apparently lost patience with him.

1996: A spring injury which left him with burns on his pitching hand forced Eshelman to start the season in Triple-A. He also experienced some arm soreness. He didn't pitch well, but was promoted to Boston out of desperation. He pitched awfully for the Red Sox, both as a starter and as a reliever.

	W	SV	ERA	IP	H	BB	SO	B/I
1995 Boston	6	0	4.85	81	86	36	41	1.49
1996 Boston	6	0	7.08	87	112	58	59	1.95
1997 Boston	3	0	6.32	43	58	17	18	1.76

ESTAVIL, MAURICIO - TL - b: 6/27/72

Estavil was pigeon-holed as a lefty situational specialist from the beginning of his career. He has been fairly tough on lefthanded hitters throughout his career, but his command has been weak. He has averaged over six walks per nine innings during his career, and allowed 36 baserunners in 20.2 higher Class A innings last year in Clearwater. Estavil would not have made it this far if he were righthanded and may not make it much further in any case.

ESTES, SHAWN - TL - b: 2/18/73

Scouting: Estes features a fastball in the mid-90s, a slider and a changeup, but it is his great overhand curve that is the key to his success. When he can spot it, hitters are helpless. Craig Biggio and Jeff Bagwell would certainly attest to it's effect after Estes' two-hitter early in 1997. Estes must deliver 30-plus starts before the stigma of "injury prone," goes away, and he similarly needs to reinforce his durability. Regardless, he is a number one starter right now.

1998: It might be optimistic to expect Estes to repeat his stellar 1997 performance, but he certainly has the talent to do it. Estes' success, however, was largely a factor of the chemistry of his team. His numbers could rise and fall accordingly, but, overall, he should again be in the top rung of National League pitchers.

1997: Estes' season was just glorious. He nearly won 20 games, pitched in the All-Star game, and even got a post-season appearance. His numbers speak for themselves. The real key to his success, aside from being injury-free, were a great team mix and his focus. Estes matured in every way as he established himself as one of the best starters in the league. He did tire a little in the second half.

1996: As a reclamation project from Seattle, Estes pitched well for both Phoenix and San Francisco.

	W	SV	ERA	IP	H	BB	SO	B/I
1995 San Francisco	0	0	6.75	17	16	5	14	1.21
1996 San Francisco	3	0	3.60	70	63	39	60	1.46
1997 San Francisco	19	0	3.18	201	162	100	181	1.30

ESTRADA, HORACIO - TL - b: 10/19/75

Estrada was signed by the Brewers at the age of 16 and 1997 marked the first season that he was not used out of the bullpen. He has above-average velocity and good movement on his pitches. He was one of the Texas League's youngest starters at age 21 last year and if he can improve on locating his pitches around the corners he could be a threat to become a fourth or fifth starter for the Brewers in 1999.

EVANS, BART - TR - b: 12/30/70

Just two years after Baseball America anointed Evans as the Carolina League's best pitching prospect (1994), he lost most of the season to elbow surgery. Considering that he entered the 1997 season with a career ERA of 11.19 above A-ball, Evans' moderate success last year has to be considered one of the best rebound stories in the minors. Now pitching exclusively in relief, Evans has retained his sparkling control and could develop into an effective short reliever. He has regained the attention of Royals' brass and could be a surprise quickly in the majors.

EVERSGERD, BRYAN - TL - b: 2/11/69

Eversgerd is an adequate Triple-A lefty who can't get major league hitters out with any consistency. Last season, he was 1-3 with a 4.25 ERA at Oklahoma City, but took the loss in two of his three appearances with Texas. In parts of three major league seasons, he has two wins, no saves and a 4.90 ERA.

EYRE, SCOTT - TL - b: 5/20/72

Scouting: Eyre throws hard, particularly for a lefthander, and owns a sharp breaking ball; all his pitches have good movement. He needs more polish but he's considered the White Sox top lefty starter prospect.

1998: Eyre has an inside track for a starter job in the majors.
1997: Far and away the best starter for Double-A Birmingham (11-4, 3.84 ERA in 18 starts), Eyre earned a late-season callup to Chicago and made the most of the opportunity. He was as effective as any other White Sox starter in September.
1996: Eyre had a successful season for Birmingham after missing most of 1995 with an arm injury and losing parts of '93 and '94 to injuries, also. He was 12-7 with a 4.38 ERA in 27 starts.

	W	SV	ERA	IP	H	BB	SO	B/I
1997 Chicago AL	4	0	5.04	61	62	31	36	1.53

FALTEISEK, STEVE - TR - b: 1/28/72
Scouting: Faltiesek throws the basic four-pitch arsenal (fastball, curveball, slider and changeup) and none of his pitches are outstanding. All but three of his appearances in six minor-league seasons have been as a starter, though the Expos looked at him in middle relief in the majors.
1998: Faltiesek has a shot to grab an opening in the Expos' rotation, though his chances appear much better of making it in long or middle relief. The Expos may also send him back to Triple-A Ottawa, so he can get more innings in as a starter.
1997: Faltiesek had a decent season at Ottawa, though his 56-to-54 strikeout-to-walk ratio was alarming for a guy who relies more on finesse than power. He was adequate in a brief trial with the Expos but showed nothing spectacular.
1996: Faltiesek was horrible at Ottawa at the start of the season but settled down after a demotion to Double-A Harrisburg.

FARMER, MIKE - TL - b: 7/3/68
The year after undergoing shoulder surgery, Farmer struggled to regain his arm strength. He started to come on near the end of the season for Triple-A Colorado Springs. Farmer is still in the Rockies' plans for 1998, when he could end up back with the big-league club. He has an average fastball (90 MPH) and a below-average breaking ball, but an outstanding changeup. He became a six-year free agent after 1997, but the Rockies worked to re-sign him.

FARRELL, JIM - TR - b: 11/1/73
Farrell has a well-below-average fastball, making everything he does difficult. He has a good feel for pitching and a decent curveball. He made it to Triple-A for one start this season, but it was only to fill a need. He struggled to a 4.37 ERA in Double-A, and, because of his poor stuff, it is unlikely he'll ever be able to do much better than that.

FARSON, BRYAN - TL - b: 7/22/72
The lefty reliever in the Pirates' farm system missed a good chunk of the 1996 and 1997 seasons because of shoulder surgery. He was considered a marginal prospect before the injury and his chances of ever reaching the big leagues are slim. He is lefthanded, though, so there's always a ray of hope.

FASSERO, JEFF - TL - b: 1/5/63
Scouting: Fassero is a quite a pitcher. He combines a hard fastball with a nasty breaking pitch and good location, causing the great Tony Gwynn to lament in spring training, 1997: "He will never give you a pitch you want."
1998: Fassero would be the top starter in any major league rotation, although he is still overshadowed in Seattle because of the presence of Randy Johnson.
1997: Fassero had 20-win stuff and a 20-win ERA, but the Mariners' bullpen proved hazardous to Fassero's record, blowing a half-dozen save chances in his games alone to negate his successful first foray into the American League. Fassero led the Mariners in starts (35) and innings and held opponents to a .249 batting average; he set a new career high in victories. Fassero was among league leaders in ERA, wins, innings and strikeouts.
1996: Pitching so well for the Expos priced Fassero out of their small-market budget and he was traded to the Mariners for catcher Chris Widger and pitchers Trey Moore and Bob Wagner. He set personal bests in wins, starts (34), innings pitched and strikeouts and finished among National League leaders in wins, innings pitched, strikeouts and ERA.

	W	SV	ERA	IP	H	BB	SO	B/I
1995 Montreal	13	0	4.33	189	207	74	164	1.49
1996 Montreal	15	0	3.30	231	217	55	222	1.18
1997 Seattle	16	0	3.61	234	226	84	189	1.32

FERMIN, RAMON - TR - b: 11/25/72
It took Fermin four years to get out of A-ball, but he quickly made the jump to the majors with Oakland in 1995. With the Tigers, Fermin was being used in a swingman role, with disappointing results. His fastball isn't enough for him to succeed in the majors.

FERNANDEZ, ALEX - TR - b: 8/13/69
Scouting: Fernandez had a 90-MPH fastball, a diverse breaking-pitch repertoire and the ability to throw all of his pitches for quality strikes on any count. Then he ripped his rotator cuff trying to gut his way through the Marlins' post-season, keeping quiet about the pain in his shoulder for weeks. It's quite possible that his deteriorating physical condition throughout 1997 and the mechanical stress it caused contributed to the injury. He'll be back, but it will take a good long while.
1998: It'll be a season of rehab for Fernandez. Watch for velocity reports late in the season to mark his progress.
1997: Fernandez held righthanders to a .192 average and brazenly challenging hitters on all counts, causing high pitch counts, and lots of strikeouts and solo homers. Even after his injury, his veteran presence was vital to the Marlins' championship run — Livan Hernandez particularly benefited from his presence.
1996: Fernandez entrenched himself as one of the game's youngest — and soon to be richest — pitchers with a stellar swansong for the White Sox. He averaged over seven innings per start and reached 200 whiffs for the first time in his career.

	W	SV	ERA	IP	H	BB	SO	B/I
1995 Chicago AL	12	0	3.80	203	200	65	159	1.30
1996 Chicago AL	16	0	3.45	258	248	72	200	1.24
1997 Florida	17	0	3.59	221	193	69	183	1.19

FERNANDEZ, JARED - TR - b: 2/2/72
Fernandez is a knuckleballer who is still learning the trade. He throws the flutter pitch about 90-percent of the time, blending in an 80-MPH fastball when he has to. He spent most of the last three seasons in Double-A, never posting an ERA better than 3.90. The Red Sox will probably keep trotting him out there because they like his attitude and his potential as a knuckleballer, but he doesn't seem close to putting it together.

FERNANDEZ, OSVALDO - TR - b: 4/15/70

Scouting: Fernandez moves his upper-80s fastball in and out, mixing in a curve and slider to keep hitters off-balance. It has worked some, but he has not been nearly as successful in the majors as he was in international play. His family immigrating to the United States last year helped him focus better, but he remains injury prone.

1998: Fernandez will certainly be in the mix of hurlers in 1998 for San Francisco. After all, they have a large investment in him. But, they were able to win without him, so that should work as incentive. Protecting him from the expansion draft was not a high priority for the Giants.

1997: Fernandez was down and out with arm problems in May; his injury became an impetus for the acquisition of the hurlers down the stretch, as the Giants needed bodies who could throw. All things considered, Fernandez' season was a disappointment for him and the Giants.

1996: The Cuban refugee suffered a lot from culture shock in 1996. When he was reunited with his family, he performed a lot better. Fernandez still had trouble with his durability, and with the quality of hitting in the majors.

	W	SV	ERA	IP	H	BB	SO	B/I
1996 San Francisco	7	0	4.61	171	193	57	106	1.46
1997 San Francisco	3	0	4.96	56	74	15	31	1.58

FERNANDEZ, SID - TL - b: 10/12/62

Fernandez signed with the Astros as a free agent in 1997. He had elbow problems in spring training but recovered enough to start and win one game during the first week of the season. It turned out to be his last major league appearance. He spent most of the season on the disabled list with recurring arm problems. He made two starts on a rehabilitation assignment at Triple-A New Orleans before announcing his retirement on August 1st. He won't be back.

	W	SV	ERA	IP	H	BB	SO	B/I
1995 Baltimore	0	0	7.39	28	36	17	31	1.89
1995 Philadelphia	6	0	3.34	64	48	21	79	1.07
1996 Philadelphia	3	0	3.43	63	50	26	77	1.21

FESH, SEAN - TL - b: 11/3/72

After recovering from elbow surgery in 1996, Fesh turned in a moderately successful year in relief. He had a 3-1 record with a 3.20 ERA, and notched four saves. Fesh has a good changeup and decent control, but he can't blow anyone away.

FETTERS, MIKE - TR - b: 12/19/64

Scouting: Fetters has a good sinker when he is on. He also is a fierce competitor with a good work ethic. The key is his control. If he comes out of the pen throwing strikes, he can be effective. But, he has a tendency to walk the first hitter he faces and then get into trouble. He can be used as a set-up man or closer.

1998: Fetters could return to a closer role with the Oakland, but more likely will work into their pen as a setup man or committee member. Fetters was viewed by the Brewers as a marketable commodity who could be traded for a hitter with some pop, and in a roundabout way, Marquis Grissom became that hitter.

1997: A spring training hamstring injury made him lose his closer job to Doug Jones, but Fetters did a respectable job as a set-up man and still closed at times. When he has control, he can still be nasty with his sinker.

1996: Fetters was named the Brewers Most Valuable Pitcher. He set a career high and a club record for saves by a righthander (since broken by Jones).

	W	SV	ERA	IP	H	BB	SO	B/I
1995 Milwaukee	0	22	3.38	34	40	20	33	1.73
1996 Milwaukee	3	32	3.38	61	65	26	53	1.49
1997 Milwaukee	1	6	3.46	70	62	33	62	1.35

FIGUEROA, NELSON - TR - b: 5/18/74

The pitcher who led all minor leaguers in strikeouts (200) in 1996 when he worked in the South Atlantic League, Figueroa found the patient hitters at Double-A to be tougher outs in 1997. He was 5-11 with a 4.34 ERA. Figueroa has just an average fastball, plus an assortment including a curveball, changeup, and splitter. He is still improving.

FINLEY, CHUCK - TL - b: 11/26/62

Scouting: Finley still has the dominating fastball and sneaky curve, and the competitiveness to be one of the most dominant pitchers in the league. Finley is the Angels' club leader in career victories at 142.

1998: Finley only has to show up in spring training to retain his job as one of the starters. Despite his 11 seasons in the majors, the lefthander shows no sign of slowing down or any drop in velocity in his intimidating fastball.

1997: Poor health was the only thing that kept the ring-wise, veteran lefty from again being the staff workhorse. He suffered a broken orbital (eye socket) bone in a freak spring-training accident when he was hit by a flying bat. In mid-August he broke his left wrist, slipping and falling while trying to backup home plate against the Yankees; it ended his season. In between injuries, Finley was the ace of the staff and helped keep the Angels in the division race with his ten straight wins. He struggled early while keeping his arm in shape, but made a mechanical adjustment in his delivery that helped him return to form.

1996: Finley's performance was one of the few things that went right for the Angels in a season where they went from almost first to worst in the American League West race. He single-handedly kept the Angels from dropping out of the race even earlier than they did with a hot April and May, and finished as the staff leader in victories.

	W	SV	ERA	IP	H	BB	SO	B/I
1995 California	15	0	4.21	203	192	93	195	1.40
1996 California	15	0	4.16	238	241	94	215	1.41
1997 Anaheim	13	0	4.23	164	152	65	155	1.32

FIORE, TONY - TR - b: 10/12/71

Fiore's junkball repertoire belies his large size; he must have extreme precision to be effective. Prior to 1997, his command had been below average, but he was in complete control at both Double-A Reading and Triple-A Scranton last year. He throws strike one, changes, speeds, and keeps the ball low. It's hard to believe his below-average stuff will let him succeed in the majors; Fiore will be a Triple-A fixture for most of his career.

FLEETHAM, BEN - TR - b: 8/3/72

Don't be fooled by his remarkable stats (69 strikeouts, 29 hits, 3.40 ERA in 50.1 Double-A innings in '97); he's not overpowering. In fact, his fastball is below average. What Fleetham has is a great slider, which he throws almost exclusively. He'll be a good reliever against righthanders in the majors because of this pitch, but won't be able to close or start because he doesn't have a good pitch against lefthanded hitters.

FLENER, HUCK - TL- b: 2/25/69
Scouting: A finesse pitcher who relies on a mid-80s fastball and slow curve, Flener may have a future as a situational reliever. He rarely strikes anyone out and although he has been a starting pitcher, he does not appear to have a long-term future in the major leagues in that role.
1998: Flener's best bet is to crack a major league team as a situational reliever. Even then, he does not possess any unusual skill that would make him valuable and his control is ordinary.
1997: Flener spent the entire season at Triple-A Syracuse, going 6-6 with a 4.14 ERA as a starting pitcher. He walked nearly as many batters (43) as he struck out (58).
1996: During the Blue Jays' rebuilding year, Flener got a look as a lefthanded starter. Although he was relatively effective, he showed no special skill or pitch to make him stand out.

	W	SV	ERA	IP	H	BB	SO	B/I
1996 Toronto	3	0	4.58	70	68	33	44	1.44
1997 Toronto	0	0	9.88	17	40	6	9	2.66

FLETCHER, PAUL - TR - b: 1/14/67
Fletcher spent 1997 in the Cubs' organization, his third different team in the past three years. He has a history of pitching well in the minors, but in a six day call-up to the A's in 1996 he was shelled and sent back to Edmonton where he pitched well. He pitched out of the bullpen last year, appearing in 54 games. He doesn't walk a lot of batters but is not overpowering. At age 30, his chances are running out and if he makes it to the bigs he'll be a long-reliever or situational specialist.

FLORES, IGNACIO - TR - b: 5/8/75
Flores has caught the eye of the organization with his command, ability to throw strikes and his durability. He's coming off a good year at Double-A San Antonio, during which he demonstrated a good deal of pitching savvy. He didn't miss a turn and threw consistently well as a sinker/slider pitcher. He's rated as a middle prospect.

FLORIE, BRYCE - TR - b: 5/21/70
Scouting: Florie has the best stuff on the Brewers staff. His problem as a reliever was control. As a starter, Florie still struggled with his command at times, but he was more effective overall. He had some late-season arm stiffness, primarily due to his transition from the bullpen to the rotation.
1998: Florie was being projected as a potential member of the Brewers' rotation in '98, but had plenty of competition.
1997: Florie started the '97 season in a relief role. But, he was put into the rotation in the second half of the season and showed promise. He was able to overcome rather long periods of not working.
1996: Florie went through a streak of six straight appearances for San Diego without allowing a run and pitched well in relief. He was traded to the Brewers with Ron Villone and Marc Newfeld for Greg Vaughn on July 31st.

	W	SV	ERA	IP	H	BB	SO	B/I
1995 San Diego	2	1	3.01	68	49	38	68	1.28
1996 San Diego	2	0	4.01	49	45	27	51	1.47
1996 Milwaukee	0	0	6.63	19	20	13	12	1.74
1997 Milwaukee	4	0	4.32	75	74	42	53	1.55

FLURY, PAT - TR - b: 3/14/73
A strikeout pitcher lacking an overpowering fastball, Flury made a double jump to Double-A Wichita, then Triple-A Omaha in 1997. He was the Wranglers most effective righthanded reliever, going 8-3 with five saves and a 3.56 ERA in 42 appearances at Wichita, then found the going tougher at Omaha: a 6.07 ERA in eighteen games. Flury should get another shot at Triple-A at some point in 1998.

FLYNT, WILL - TL - b: 11/23/67
The Orioles signed Flynt out of the Mexican League to a Triple-A contract in July, 1996. He's a tall lefty who has pitched nearly everywhere except in the majors, making stops in Mexico, Canada, the Netherlands and Taiwan.

FONTENOT, JOE - TR - b: 3/20/77
At just 20 years of age, Fontenot weathered his second professional season and made the jump to Double-A Shreveport, where he started 19 games (out of 26 appearances), going 10-11 with a 5.53 ERA. As with his 1996 season at San Jose (9-4, 4.44 ERA), Fontenot's numbers don't necessarily reflect the skill or the poise of being one of the youngest starters of his respective league. Fontenot was a key prospect in the trade to get Robb Nen from the Marlins.

FORD, BEN - TR - b: 8/15/75
The Yankees have been high on this 6'7" reliever who reminds them of Jeff Nelson, only with a better fastball. Ford throws in the mid-90s and the Yankees were crossing their fingers he wasn't taken in the expansion draft, but Arizona got him. He was 4-0 with a 1.32 ERA and 18 saves for Class A Tampa where he fanned 37 in 37.1 innings. Promoted to Double-A Norwich, Ford went 4-3 with a 4.22 ERA in 28 games working as set-up man.

FORDHAM, TOM - TL - b: 2/20/74
Scouting: Fordham is a control pitcher who doesn't throw especially hard. He's a sinker/slider pitcher with a decent changeup. He's considered a good prospect, but there are other, better lefties in the White Sox organization. A shift to a relief role is probably in his future.
1998: Fordham should reprise his major league role in 1998, primarily pitching out of the bullpen, but he could also make some spot starts. If he starts out poorly he may go back to Triple-A Nashville for a third straight season.
1997: Fordham earned his first major league promotion by going 6-6 with a 4.69 ERA for Nashville. He was somewhat overmatched in his brief time in the bigs.
1996: Fordham fashioned yet another winning record, this time pitching mostly at Triple-A for the first time. Overall between Nashville and six starts for Double-A Birmingham, Fordham was 12-9 with a 3.29 ERA; his three complete games tied for third in the American Association.

	W	SV	ERA	IP	H	BB	SO	B/I
1997 Chicago AL	0	0	6.24	17	17	10	10	1.56

FORSTER, SCOTT - TL - b: 10/27/71
Forster had a second consecutive fine season as a starter with Harrisburg's Double-A farm club last season, though he was slowed by arm problems. He doesn't light up the radar gun but has an idea how to pitch and should wind up in Montreal's

rotation in 1999 or 2000.

FORTUGNO, TIMOTHY - TL - b: 4/11/62
A journeyman minor leaguer, Fortugno has some major league experience, which makes him valuable to the club as insurance in case of injury. Being a veteran, Fortugno lends leadership and rounds out a Triple-A staff.

FOSSAS, TONY - TL - b: 9/23/57
Scouting: He still benefits from specialized use in a bullpen when the only way he's used is to face a tough lefthanded batter, though even in that way he's not as effective at the age of 40 as he was as a late-bloomer in his mid-30s. Fossas never adjusts the way he pitches based on the opposing hitter. He approaches everyone the same, generally getting lefthanded batters to fish for his slider and making the most of his below-average fastball by throwing it inside. Without much zip, he's never been particularly effective against righthanders.

1998: A free agent following the 1997 season, Fossas probably isn't guaranteed a spot in anyone's bullpen thanks in part to his age (40) and question about whether he can still do the job consistently. If he finds a spot, it probably will have to be in a role working exclusively against lefthanders and for extremely short outings.

1997: His assumed task was changed because of injuries to other lefthanders in the Cardinals' bullpen, and Fossas' performance suffered. He worked considerably more than planned — the 51.2 innings were the most he'd pitched since 1991 — and actually faced more righthanders than lefties. Righthanders batted .325 with seven homers against him. Fossas did lead the league in allowing just ten percent of inherited runners to score.

1996: Thriving while facing the best lefthanded hitters of the National League, Fossas held lefthanders to a .233 average and posted the lowest ERA in the Cardinals' bullpen.

	W	SV	ERA	IP	H	BB	SO	B/I
1995 St. Louis	3	0	1.47	36	28	10	40	1.05
1996 St. Louis	0	2	2.68	47	43	21	36	1.36
1997 St. Louis	2	0	3.83	52	62	26	41	1.70

FOSTER, KEVIN - TR - b: 1/13/69
Scouting: Foster throws hard but he has all kinds of trouble keeping the ball down in the strike zone. He always has given up a lot of home runs, but it's not because he pitches home games in Wrigley Field. He began his minor-league career in the Philadelphia organization as a third baseman, but was converted to the mound within a year.

1998: This will be a critical year for Foster. The last couple of starting spots (behind Mark Clark, Kevin Tapani and Jeremi Gonzalez) will be up for grabs, so he'll get a few starts. But to stay in the rotation Foster will have to show that he can keep the ball in the park, and so far in his career he's done nothing to indicate that will happen. If he has another poor year the Cubs are likely to cut their losses and get rid of him.

1997: Foster spent the entire season with the Cubs, but still didn't look like he was really ready. He struggled with his command and again was bitten by the constant barrage of home run balls. He stayed in the starting rotation because the Cubs simply did not have any other options.

1996: Foster started the season with the Cubs, but was sent down before the end of May because he simply could not keep the ball in the park. He wound up going 14-12 combined for Iowa and Chicago, but he was not an effective pitcher at either place.

	W	SV	ERA	IP	H	BB	SO	B/I
1995 Chicago NL	12	0	4.51	167	149	65	146	1.28
1996 Chicago NL	7	0	6.21	87	98	35	53	1.53
1997 Chicago NL	10	0	4.61	146	141	66	118	1.41

FOULKE, KEITH - TR - b: 10/19/72
Scouting: No "closer" in the majors has less stuff. He was only used to close games because he was a favorite of deposed manager Terry Bevington. His fastball is just average and he lacks a sharp breaking ball.

1998: Foulke should earn a middle-innings job in a major league bullpen.

1997: Acquired from San Francisco in the Wilson Alvarez deal, Foulke was sharp in his brief time with the White Sox, earning an occasional shot at closing games. He had been less successful with the Giants.

1996: A successful season at Shreveport earned him rave reviews by Giants' scouts. He had excellent control while dominating most hitters. The good season in Double-A boosted him to a major league role later the following year.

	W	SV	ERA	IP	H	BB	SO	B/I
1997 two teams	4	3	6.38	73	88	23	54	1.51

FOX, CHAD - TR - b: 9/3/70
Scouting: Fox features a 90+ fastball, slider, and a sharp curveball that is his best pitch. A starter throughout his minor-league career, he was converted by the Braves to relief work after missing part of 1996 due to reconstructive elbow surgery.

1998: Fox will compete for a set-up role with the Braves; he has the stuff to expand his role if he can improve his control.

1997: Fox started the year in extended spring training recovering from his elbow surgery. He was effective at Triple-A Richmond before being promoted to the Braves during their bullpen purge in July. He was effective in a limited role in the Braves bullpen but was dropped from the post-season roster due to a late-season slump.

1996: Fox was traded from the Reds organization to the Braves in exchange for Mike Kelly. He struggled in his first season in the Atlanta organization, going 3-10 with a 4.73 ERA before succumbing to elbow problems.

	W	SV	ERA	IP	H	BB	SO	B/I
1997 Atlanta	0	0	3.30	27	24	16	28	1.47

FRANCO, JOHN - TL - b: 9/17/60
Scouting: Franco hasn't been a dominant reliever for a long time, but he still can undermine a rally and embarrass the impatient hitter. His improved mechanics and physical condition allowed him to retain command of his fastball. His changeup still is enticing. The Mets want him to use a breaking ball more often, particularly a slider to righthanded hitters. He needs to trust his curveball more.

1998: Franco will spend his eighth season with the Mets as he did the first seven, as the closer. And he'll probably tutor Bill Pulsipher, Derek Wallace and/or Mel Rojas in the art of closing. He will add to his career save total, 359, which stands as the fourth highest in history and the most ever by a lefthanded pitcher.

1997: Franco didn't pitch after September 13th because of a strained muscle in his back that was not considered a serious, long-term malady. To that point he produced, arguably, his finest season with the Mets, saving or gaining the victory in nearly half the Mets' wins. At the suggestion of pitching coach Bob Apodaca, Franco shifted to the third base end of the rubber, and the change made him less susceptible to lefthanded hitters. It didn't work well. Still, he converted 36 of 42 save opportunities. His first-batters-faced hit .327, but managed merely three RBI in 55 at-bats. Three of the 18 runners he inherited scored.

1996: He converted 28 of 36 save opportunities while dealing with a system he didn't appreciate for most of the season. Dallas Green would summon Franco in save situations and because the team was less successful, there were fewer save opportunities. Franco's average rest in 1996 was 2.6 days with nine periods of five or more days without work. Under Bobby Valentine last year, it was 1.8 with five periods of five or more days rest.

	W	SV	ERA	IP	H	BB	SO	B/I
1995 New York NL	5	29	2.44	51	48	17	41	1.27
1996 New York NL	4	28	1.83	54	54	21	48	1.39
1997 New York NL	5	36	2.55	60	49	20	53	1.15

FRANKLIN, RYAN - TR - b: 3/5/73

Franklin was a workhorse for Double-A Port City in 1996 and earned a shot at Triple-A for part of the 1997 season. He has always shown good control and did so again last year, with 108 strikeouts to 38 walks in 149.2 innings of work combined. He proved to be more hittable at the Triple-A level and will probably start the 1998 season in Tacoma. He has a shot to join the tail end of the Mariners' rotation in the future.

FRASCATORE, JOHN - TR - b: 2/4/70

Scouting: Bounced between starting and relieving the two previous seasons, Frascatore had shaped up as a bust despite his live arm and apparent bulldog demeanor. The Cardinals once considered him a candidate to be their closer, then a horrid 1996 season messed with his confidence and put him on last-chance alert. He has found his niche as a set-up man, though, with a hard fastball and a nice-breaking ball. Frascatore feels like he should have been in the bullpen all along, that his personality is best suited at giving all he has and not trying to pace himself. He still could be developed into a closer.

1998: As the Cardinals search for the eventual heir to Dennis Eckersley, Frascatore will get serious consideration. With his sense of ability better than any time in his career, he could win that status. At the least, he probably could become one of the more successful set-up men in the league.

1997: Assuming the role as top righthanded set-up man after T.J. Mathews was traded, Frascatore was one of the more pleasant surprises of the Cardinals' season in logging a workman-like 80 innings out of the pen. He led the team's relievers in ERA and strikeouts, though control rarely has been one of his problems. His control was markedly better against righthanded batters, but he actually punished lefthanders, who managed just a .214 batting mark.

1996: He had a wildly inconsistent year, his third in Triple-A. April included a one-hit, eight-inning victory in which he faced only 24 batters, which began an eight-outing stretch in which he compiled a 2.48 ERA. A 2-8 span pushed him to the bullpen, and he finished the season with a 5.18 ERA and 180 hits allowed in 156.1 innings.

	W	SV	ERA	IP	H	BB	SO	B/I
1997 St. Louis	5	0	2.48	80	74	33	58	1.34

FRASER, WILLIE - TR - b: 5/26/64

Fraser has had his moments in the major leagues, including two double-digit winning seasons as a starter for the Angels in 1987-88. The last two years he has been in Japan, pitching well in 1996 but looking more mediocre last year.

FREEHILL, MIKE - TR - b: 6/2/71

Freehill has an above-average fastball and a developing forkball, and has had some success as a closer type in Double-A. He had an up-and-down year in 1997, but came on strong at the end to boost his stock as a prospect. He has good stuff and the ability to get to the major leagues. For Freehill, it's a matter of putting everything together and getting over the hump.

FREEMAN, CHRIS - TR - b: 8/27/72

Scouting: A strikeout pitcher with good control, Freeman emerged as a closer candidate at Double-A Knoxville.

1998: The logical step on the ladder would be Triple-A although Freeman might benefit from an entire year as a Double-A closer before advancing. He is anywhere from a year to four years away from making an impact in the majors.

1997: Freeman struck out 86 batters in 83.1 innings at Double-A and allowed only 71 hits. His eight saves were tied for the team lead and his ERA was the best on the team among pitchers with at least 30 innings. This was his third straight season playing for Knoxville.

1996: Freeman struck out 54 batters in 45.2 innings, allowing only three home runs in 26 games.

FREEMAN, MARVIN - TR - b: 4/10/63

A ten-year major league veteran, Freeman failed to make the Blue Jays out of spring training. He pitched one game for Triple-A Syracuse in May and then called it a career.

	W	SV	ERA	IP	H	BB	SO	B/I
1995 Colorado	3	0	5.89	94	122	41	61	1.73
1996 Colorado	7	0	6.04	129	151	57	71	1.61
1996 Chicago AL	0	0	13.50	2	4	1	1	2.50

FREY, STEVE - TL - b: 7/29/63

Frey's extensive experience in the majors gives the Vancouver staff leadership. He's there to help the Triple-A staff, but is looked upon as someone who could be called up in an emergency and he even got a look last spring. Frey is a typical "crafty" lefthander. He doesn't have overpowering stuff, but he knows how to get people out.

	W	SV	ERA	IP	H	BB	SO	B/I
1995 Seattle	0	0	4.76	11	16	6	7	2.34
1995 two teams	0	1	2.12	17	10	4	7	0.82
1996 Philadelphia	0	0	4.72	34	38	18	12	1.64

FRONTERA, CHAD -TR- b: 11/22/72

Frontera was injured and did not pitch during the 1996 season after undergoing shoulder surgery. He was chosen by the Giants in the eighth-round of the June 1994 draft and was on the 40-man roster at the beginning of spring training last year. Frontera made 16 starts between Double-A and Triple-A for the Giants in 1997. He had a winning record but a high ERA at both stops, was hittable as he gave up more than a hit per inning and had control problems. He'll start 1998 in the high minors, trying to prove he can make it back after shoulder surgery.

FULTZ, AARON - TL - b: 9/4/73
A reliever, Fultz had a great season at Double-A Shreveport, notching a 6-3 mark with a 2.83 ERA. More to the point, Fultz whiffed 60 while walking only 19, and allowed only 65 hits over his 70 innings pitched. He should start 1998 at Triple-A Phoenix as he has nothing left to prove at the Double-A level.

FUSSELL, CHRIS - TR - b: 5/19/76
Scouting: Fussell has three above-average pitches, and gets a lot of strikeouts with a low number of walks, encouraging signs in a young pitcher. He just needs more time to develop.
1998: Fussell will likely begin the season in Double-A, and if he's effective, he can get a quick promotion to Triple-A, and even the majors. If he makes the Orioles at some point in the season, it will likely be as a reliever.
1997: Fussell began last year with Double-A Bowie where he went 1-8, resulting in a demotion to A-ball where his results were again good.
1996: Fussell struck out 94 in 86 Class A innings.

FYHRIE, MIKE - TR - b: 12/9/69
This long-time Royals farmhand came to the Mets organization in March 1996. Featuring good control and the ability to change speeds, Fyhrie went on to lead the International League in wins and was named the IL Most Valuable Pitcher.

GAILLARD, EDDY - TR - b: 8/13/70
Scouting: Gaillard finally opened some eyes last year with a fastball clocked in the mid-90s. The Tigers still aren't sure that he can be part of their future bullpen, but he's earned a chance to prove himself.
1998: Once again, Gaillard should get some opportunities to pitch in the major leagues. But he'll likely spend part of the year in the minors, too. He's not counted on as a key member of the big-league bullpen.
1997: A 28-save year at Triple-A Toledo earned Gaillard his first big-league shot a week before his 27th birthday. He spent most of the final two months in the big leagues, earning his first win and first save.
1996: Gaillard pitched in middle relief at Double-A Jacksonville, posting decent but not stunning numbers. He won nine games, but had only one save.

	W	SV	ERA	IP	H	BB	SO	B/I
1997 Detroit	1	1	5.32	20	16	10	12	1.28

GAJKOWSKI, STEVE - TR - b: 12/30/69
Gajkowski joined the Mariners' system last year after seven seasons in the Indians' and White Sox' farm systems. He doesn't throw hard, relying on a sinker and a slider to get batters out. He had a two-to-one strikeout-to-walk ratio in 1997, the first time he's done that well since 1993. He could reach the majors but in a limited middle-relief role at best.

GALLAHER, KEVIN - TR - b: 8/1/68
Gallaher reached the Triple-A level in both the Astro and Tiger farm systems before pitching for Double-A Bowie last year. The Orioles gave him a special workout in Camden Yards in September and sent him to winter ball, indications that they have bigger plans for him. Gallaher could latch on with the Orioles as a middle reliever in 1998.

GAMBOA, JAVIER - TR - b: 3/17/74
Off-season rotator cuff surgery limited Gamboa to just six starts for Double-A Wichita in 1997. He had little of his former command and was hit hard (49 hits in 29 innings, 8.69 ERA). It was a washout season for Gamboa, who will try again in 1998.

GAMEZ, ROBERT - TL - b: 11/18/68
The Angels traded Gamez to San Diego, then re-signed him as a free agent because of his potential. He isn't overpowering, but has an average fastball and good control. He boosted his stock with a solid year out of the bullpen at Double-A Midland and may get a look in spring training this year because he finished last season strong.

GANDARILLAS, GUS - TR - b: 7/19/71
After missing nearly all of the 1996 season with a broken arm, Gandarillas struggled at Double-A New Britain in 1997 with a 4.70 ERA and gave up more than a hit per inning. He fared better in 22.2 innings at Triple-A Salt Lake, where he posted a 3.18 ERA. Gandarillas has only marginal big-league potential, especially since he is old compared to other prospects.

GARCES, RICH - TR - b: 5/18/71
Garces overpowered hitters in Triple-A Pawtucket, posting a 1.45 ERA and 42 strikeouts in 31 innings. He has a 92-MPH fastball, a good curve and split-fingered pitch. But he has had trouble winning the Red Sox over the last two seasons because he has had control problems and battled minor injuries when in the majors. The problem is Garces is overweight and tends to break down and wear down when overused, as he has been in the majors. If Garces can hook up with a team which can afford to limit his appearances, he is capable of pitching well in the majors.

	W	SV	ERA	IP	H	BB	SO	B/I
1995 two teams	0	0	4.44	24	25	11	22	1.48
1996 Boston AL	3	0	4.91	44	42	33	55	1.70
1997 Boston	0	0	4.60	14	14	9	12	1.68

GARCIA, AL - TR - b: 6/11/74
Garcia is not a pitching prospect, despite some pretty good Double-A stats. He doesn't throw hard, but he has outstanding control and keeps the ball down, which is a prerequisite for any Cubs pitcher. But he also strikes out, few hitters (only 27 in 72 innings in 1997) and that's simply not going to be close to good enough to make it.

GARCIA, JOSE - TR - b: 6/12/72
Garcia reached Triple-A quickly, but has since leveled off and is looking for a way to jump start his career again. He has a low three-quarter delivery, which gives him deceptiveness and he has a shot at the major leagues if he can find a way to regain momentum.

GARCIA, RAMON - TR - b: 12/9/69
Scouting: Garcia began his career in the White Sox organization and pitched for seven years before he was sidelined by an elbow injury which required "Tommy John" surgery. He missed the entire 1994 and 1995 seasons, then spent 1996 in the Brewer organization before being selected by the Astros in the Rule 5 draft. He started the season in middle relief but filled

the fifth starter role for Houston after Sid Fernandez was hurt and Donne Wall was sent to the minors. His assortment of pitches make him more effective as a starter. His velocity is not impressive but he has a sinking fastball, a good slider, a changeup and a cut fastball which he can ride inside to lefthanded hitters.
1998: Garcia should retain a spot in a major league starting rotation based on his success in 1997.
1997: Garcia was consistent as a starter failing to go five innings in only four of his twenty starts.
1996: Garcia was used primarily as a relief pitcher as he split the season between Milwaukee and Triple-A New Orleans. At New Orleans, he was 2-1 with a 1.88 ERA in 38 innings.

	W	SV	ERA	IP	H	BB	SO	B/I
1996 Milwaukee	4	4	6.66	75	84	21	40	1.40
1997 Houston	9	1	3.69	159	155	52	120	1.30

GARDINER, MIKE - TR - b: 10/19/65
Gardiner pitched for both Triple-A New Orleans and Columbus in 1997. With New Orleans in 31 innings, Gardiner posted an 8.13 ERA and gave up more than a hit per inning, but he had more success in Columbus with a 3.92 ERA and a good strikeout-to-walk ratio. Gardiner has a full repertoire: fastball, slider, curveball and changeup. He was the Eastern League Pitcher of the Year in 1990, but those days are long gone and despite his strong 1996 performance, it looks like he will remain a career minor-leaguer whose brief flirtation with the major leagues will not be repeated.

GARDNER, MARK - TR - b: 3/1/62
Scouting: Gardner throws a good curve and fastball, but his main attributes as a pitcher are his experience and savvy. Gardner is one of those hurlers who is more effective over the first half of any given season.
1998: Re-signing Gardner over the off-season was not a priority with the Giants. He can still throw, though, so Gardner will start the season in a major league rotation, and will produce numbers in line with those of '96 and '97.
1997: If nothing else, Gardner has proven himself consistent. He didn't anchor the rotation so much in the first half — that was Shawn Estes' job all season — but he delivered quality starts all season at times when the Giants needed them most.
1996: A last minute addition to the pitching staff, Gardner started 28 games for the Giants and pitched especially well before the All-Star break and his appendectomy. He was given a one-year extension on his contract as a result of his contribution.

	W	SV	ERA	IP	H	BB	SO	B/I
1995 Florida	5	1	4.49	102	109	43	87	1.49
1996 San Francisco	12	0	4.42	179	200	57	145	1.43
1997 San Francisco	12	0	4.29	180	188	57	136	1.36

GARDNER, SCOTT - TR - b: 1/18/72
Gardner reached Double-A for the first time in his career at age 26 and showed why he hadn't been to that level previously. He gave up well more than a hit per inning and didn't have good control, walking 56 batters with 89 strikeouts in 139.1 innings. He made one Triple-A start and it looks like that may be the highest level he will reach.

GARLAND, JON - TR - b: 9/27/79
Garland was selected with the tenth pick of the 1997 draft by the Cubs. He had an impressive showing for a 17-year-old in the Arizona League last year. Garland had an ERA of 2.70, gave up less than a hit per inning and struck out 39 with just ten walks in 40 innings of work. He is expected to develop into the perfect bullpen companion for Kerry Wood and join the Cubs' staff in a few seasons.

GARRETT, JOSH - TR - b: 1/12/78
Boston's first-round draft pick of 1996 (26th overall) pitched at Class A Michigan in the Midwest League last year. He made 22 starts but needs to work on better command of his stuff. He yielded 164 hits in 138.2 innings.

GENTILE, SCOTT - TR - b: 12/21/70
Thought to be on the fast track prior to 1996, Gentile lost a decent chunk of the 1996 season to injury, and was no better than the number three righty in the Expos' Double-A bullpen upon his return. The stocky Gentile throws a heavy fastball and usually records about a strikeout per inning, but no longer appears to be in the hunt for a major league bullpen role.

GLAUBER, KEITH - TR - b: 1/18/72
Even though he managed five saves in 15.2 innings and had a three-to-one strikeout-to-walk ratio last year, Glauber had a 5.17 ERA and gave up more than a hit per inning at Triple-A Louisville.

GLAVINE, TOM - TL - b: 3/25/66
Scouting: As one of the most consistent and winningest pitchers of the decade, Glavine has achieved success by consistently hitting the outside corner with low-90s fastballs, sliders and changeups, getting opponents to hit one grounder after another to his infielders. He always works deep into the ballgame, never misses his turn in the rotation, holds baserunners well, wields a marvelous glove — and is a good hitter, too. It's no wonder that Glavine is sporting a 120-58 record over the last seven years.
1998: There's no reason to believe that Glavine won't be one of baseball's best and most consistent pitchers yet again.
1997: Glavine's stat line was a mirror image for his career averages. He won two out of three decisions, posted a below-3.00 ERA for the second straight year, held opponents to a low batting average (.226, lower than teammate Greg Maddux), and was among league leaders in starts and innings pitched. Although he gave up the most homers he had surrendered since 1989 (20, but still not a bad rate on a per-nine-innings basis) it was another wonderfully consistent season from Glavine; he could have won at least four more games had the bullpen not faltered behind him.
1996: Glavine led the National League in starts and finished among league leaders in innings pitched, ERA, wins, lowest home run rate — and most other categories. Occasionally throwing fastballs inside to some hitters helped him reach a higher-than-usual strikeout total.

	W	SV	ERA	IP	H	BB	SO	B/I
1995 Atlanta	16	0	3.08	198	182	66	127	1.25
1996 Atlanta	15	0	2.98	235	222	85	181	1.31
1997 Atlanta	14	0	2.96	240	197	79	152	1.15

GOETZ, GEOFF - TL - b: 4/1/79
The sixth pick of the 1997 draft out of Jesuit High School in Tampa by the Mets, Goetz pitched at Rookie level Port St.

Lucie in the Gulf Coast League. He struck out more than a batter per inning while yielding less than a hit per inning. He still needs to polish his control after allowing 18 walks in 26 innings.

GOHR, GREG - TR - b: 10/29/67
Once a Tiger prospect who never developed into the starter they had imagined he'd be, Gohr pitched for the Angels' organization again last year. He has below-average stuff and command, and was not effective as a starter or reliever in 1996. In 1997, he was merely average at Triple-A Vancouver; he gave up just over a hit per inning.

	W	SV	ERA	IP	H	BB	SO	B/I
1995 Detroit	1	0	0.87	10	9	3	12	1.16
1996 California	5	1	7.24	115	163	44	75	1.80

GOMES, WAYNE - TR - b: 1/15/73
Scouting: Gomes was the Phillies' first-round draft pick in 1993 and was expected to graduate into the major league closer role in fairly short order since he had been a closer throughout college and possessed a fastball/power-curve one-two punch. However, his conditioning has always been sub-par, and he has never acquired a true closer's mentality as a pro. Control has always been a major problem, and he was so concerned about it at the major league level in 1997 that he became overly cautious and forgot to go after hitters. For him to excel in the majors, he needs to throw his curve — his out pitch — for a strike on any count.
1998: The Phillies will need to see a different Gomes in spring training for him to make the 1998 roster. The club has a desperate need for a set-up man, but Gomes has shown nothing to indicate he can handle the role. It would be a good sign were Gomes to report to camp in top shape.
1997: Gomes started as the Triple-A closer and performed as expected, striking out a batter per inning despite control struggles. However, he pitched as if he didn't belong in the majors following his mid-season recall. His mechanics were uneven, he relied too much on his fastball, and didn't show consistently strong velocity. The Phillies aren't ready to give up on him, but he's certainly behind schedule.
1996: Gomes was used as a full-time closer for the first time in his professional career at Double-A Reading. He overmatched hitters when he threw his fastball and nasty curve for strikes, but often struggled with his control.

	W	SV	ERA	IP	H	BB	SO	B/I
1997 Philadelphia	5	0	5.27	43	45	24	24	1.62

GONZALEZ, JEREMI - TR - b: 1/8/75
Scouting: The Cubs signed Gonzalez as a 16-year-old and put up with some pretty bad numbers in the low minors while he learned how to pitch. But as he got older and matured physically he showed why the Cubs stayed with him. Gonzalez is a sinkerball pitcher who doesn't strike out a lot of hitters, but instead relies on control and his defense.
1998: The Cubs will be counting on Gonzalez to improve and be their number three starter this season. Gonzalez is only 23 years old and he hasn't had that much experience above A-ball, so he'll struggle at times. But he is a good enough pitcher to fight through the bad times and win 12-15 games.
1997: Gonzalez started the season at Triple-A Iowa, but it didn't take long for the Cubs to bring him up. He made only nine starts for Iowa and showed he was over his elbow troubles of the year before, Gonzalez went on to start 23 games for the Cubs and become one of the winningest rookie pitchers in the National League. He didn't seem intimidated by NL hitters and showed remarkable poise for such a young pitcher.
1996: Gonzalez had an outstanding first half of the season for Double-A Orlando and was selected to the Southern League's mid-season All-Star team. However, an elbow injury put him on the disabled list for much of the second half and held back his progress.

	W	SV	ERA	IP	H	BB	SO	B/I
1997 Chicago NL	11	0	4.25	144	126	69	93	1.35

LARIEL GONZALEZ - TR - 5/25/76
Scouting: An outstanding closer prospect, though he may break into the majors as a set-up guy, Gonzalez has an above-average fastball (93 MPH), a good slider, and an almost unhittable split-finger pitch. He's a big (6'4", 220 pounds), strong, power pitcher. Gonzalez took off in 1997, when he started consistently throwing all three pitches for strikes.
1998: Gonzalez was expected to be placed on the 40-man roster and receive his first taste of big-league training camp. He'll likely start the season as the closer at Double-A New Haven, though don't be surprised if the Rockies rush him to Triple-A Colorado Springs and maybe even the big leagues by season's end.
1997: It was his breakout season. Signed as a non-drafted free agent in 1993, one week prior to his 17th birthday, Gonzalez was brought along slowly until 1997, when he went 5-0 with a 2.53 ERA and eight saves in 44 games for Class A Salem. He struck out 79 while allowing just 42 hits and 23 walks in 57 innings; he recorded nearly half of his outs on whiffs.
1996: Though he pitched in just 35 games for Class A Asheville, Gonzalez showed for the first time that he was a strikeout pitcher, fanning 53 in 45 innings.

GOOCH, ARNOLD - TR - b: 11/12/76
Gooch opened eyes with a 2.58 ERA at Class A St. Lucie in 1996, but he found the hitters much tougher after moving up to Double-A Binghamton in 1997. He's still impressive for his age, however, and there is plenty of time for improvement. Gooch has a good curveball and a mid-80's sinking fastball. He is still working on his changeup. He was 10-12 with a 5.14 ERA last year.

GOODEN, DWIGHT - TR - b: 11/16/64
Scouting: Gooden's fastball isn't what it once was, but he has compensated with a split-fingered fastball and he changes speeds well. When spotted, the fastball still has enough juice in it. His strong finish last year suggests that Gooden still has something left in that talented right arm.
1998: Since the Yankees didn't pick up a $3 million option on his contract, Gooden was searching for a job in early November. While the club hadn't ruled out a return at a lesser salary, Gooden said that door had closed and he moved onto another venue. He'll be a good starting pitcher again, but is unlikely to be an ace starter.
1997: Gooden missed two months due to hernia surgery and struggled with command upon his return. He made 19 starts and did not accept or adjust well to being bounced around the rotation to make room for Hideki Irabu. Gooden made strong showings in seven of his final eight outings and had an impressive performance in an American League Division Series start against the Indians.

1996: Injuries again dominated the season for Gooden. His arm gave way to wear and tear and he missed the post-season. Subsequent hernia surgery ended up costing him two months of the next season, also. Despite a high ERA, he posted a winning record and got his most major league work in three years.

	W	SV	ERA	IP	H	BB	SO	B/I
1995			Did Not Play					
1996 New York AL	11	0	5.01	170	169	88	126	1.51
1997 New York AL	9	0	4.91	106	116	53	66	1.59

GORDON, MIKE - TR - b: 11/30/72
Scouting: A hard thrower, he has been plagued with control problems and lacks endurance, especially given the fact that he has been a starting pitcher.
1998: Gordon will complete his transition to being a reliever, likely at the Double-A level. If he does not show signs of developing control, he will not be around by the end of the year.
1997: Gordon was let go by the Blue Jays and the Cleveland Indians took a chance on him. After failing to perform the first month with Akron, the Jays reclaimed him on waivers and assigned him to Knoxville, where he went 2-3 with a 5.33 ERA over 72.2 innings.
1996: Although he struck out 102 batters in 133.1 innings with Class A Dunedin, Gordon walked 64 and went 3-12.

GORDON, TOM - TR - b: 11/18/67
Scouting: Gordon has a 95-MPH fastball and one of the best curveballs in the majors. He has always struggled with his command and has had trouble finding a third pitch.
1998: Gordon appeared ready to step into the closer's role and have a bust-out season. With Dennis Eckersley on board, Gordon's role became an open question. He has made great strides with his control and his aggressiveness over the last couple of years as a starter. Since Gordon is relatively new to short relief, the arrival of The Eck could be a benefit for the long term as Gordon makes his transition.
1997: Gordon was having his best season as a starter, limiting his poor outings and throwing more strikes consistently, when the Red Sox, having traded Heathcliff Slocumb, made him their closer. He responded to the switch, overpowering hitters in most of his save opportunities down the stretch.
1996: Gordon got lots of run support, which helped his won/loss record, but pitched poorly overall, struggling with his control.

	W	SV	ERA	IP	H	BB	SO	B/I
1995 Kansas City	12	0	4.43	189	204	89	119	1.55
1996 Boston	12	0	5.59	215	249	105	171	1.64
1997 Boston	6	11	3.74	183	155	78	159	1.28

GORECKI, RICK - TR - b: 8/27/73
After missing the entire 1996 season due to arthroscopic shoulder surgery, Gorecki advanced through the Dodgers system in 1997 and made four appearances with the big club, including one start. His best work came at Double-A San Antonio where he posted a 1.39 ERA over seven starts and gave up only 26 hits in 45 1/3 innings of work. The Devil Rays believed that Gorecki had healed; if so, they made a good pick.

GOURDIN, TOM - TR - b: 5/24/73
Gourdin struggled at the Rookie and A-ball levels since 1992 and a season-ending injury in 1994 has hampered his progress; 1997 was his first season at the Double-A level. Gourdin collected 15 saves in 61 innings for New Britain last year. He has control problems and is also susceptible to the long ball.

GRACE, MIKE - TR - b: 6/20/70
Scouting: Injuries have plagued Grace's seven-year pro career; elbow surgeries have cost him two full seasons worth of games, and he has also lost time to shoulder problems and, more recently, to muscle problems in his pitching arm. The physical ailments haven't prevented him from learning how to pitch, though. Despite a fastball that reaches only the mid-80s, Grace has been effective because he can get sharp movement on the pitch, plus he changes speeds well, gets hitters to put the ball in play, and keeps the ball low in the strike zone to limit long balls. Grace has allowed just 37 homers in 485 professional innings; he's a solid starter if healthy.
1998: The Phillies will hope Grace can stay healthy and near the top of their rotation, but it's only a hope since he has started more than 18 games in a season just once in his career. Despite his hard work to remain in top physical condition, he's always one pitch away from the end of his career. If he can make the requisite number of starts, Grace will be a good starter.
1997: Grace's command wasn't as good as usual in his Triple-A starts in 1997, but he rounded into form by the time he reached the majors. The highlight of his season was an inter-league start against the Yankees when he threw a complete game, facing the minimum 27 batters and throwing only 79 pitches. He gave up six runs in two innings against the Marlins, accounting for most of the damage done to him his six big-league starts.
1996: Grace appeared to be on his way to contention for the National League Rookie of the Year Award after 12 excellent early season starts. He averaged nearly seven innings per start, conserving pitches along the way. Then he suffered yet another elbow injury, and was shut down for the season.

	W	SV	ERA	IP	H	BB	SO	B/I
1995 Philadelphia	1	0	3.18	11	10	4	7	1.26
1996 Philadelphia	7	0	3.49	80	72	16	49	1.10
1997 Philadelphia	3	0	3.46	39	32	10	26	1.08

GRANGER, JEFF - TL - b: 12/16/71
Scouting: Granger, Kansas City's first-round draft pick in 1993 from Texas A&M, seemingly has the tools to be a good major league pitcher, a lefty with a 90-plus fastball and slider. However, he has never put it all together either as a starter or reliever. Granger's problem has always been command as he tends to overthrow and his pitches either become flat or sail out of the strike zone.
1998: Granger was taken off the 40-man roster by the Pirates last season and he didn't appear to have much of a future in the organization. The Pirates have other lefthanded relievers they like better; even some marginal lefties are ahead of Granger on the Pirates' depth chart. If Granger is still in the organization when the season begins, he will be playing at the Triple-A level. The high potential is still there.
1997: The Pirates hoped Granger would become their top lefthanded set-up reliever after acquiring him from Kansas City in a six-player trade the previous December. Granger, though, was hit hard and shipped to Triple-A Calgary at the end of April. He split time between the bullpen and rotation at Calgary and didn't pitch much better there than he did in Pittsburgh.

1996: Granger had the best of his four seasons in Kansas City's farm system, putting up solid numbers as a reliever at Omaha. However, when called up to the majors, he was bombed.

GRAVES, DANNY - TR - b: 8/7/73

Scouting: A solid prospect as a relief pitcher, Graves relies on a sinking fastball, a slider and good control to get hitters out. He has struggled in brief trials in the majors, but has pitched well at every level of the minors.

1998: Graves will compete for a middle-relief role with the Reds.

1997: Graves struggled with the Indians in a brief trial and was dealt to the Reds in the John Smiley trade. The Reds looked at him as a starter in Triple-A but used him out of the bullpen after his recall in late-August.

1996: In his second professional season, Graves dominated at Triple-A Buffalo, posting 19 saves and a 1.48 ERA; he was named the Indians top minor-league pitcher.

	W	SV	ERA	IP	H	BB	SO	B/I
1997 Cincinnati	0	0	5.54	26	41	20	11	2.35

GREEN, TYLER - TR - b: 2/18/70

Scouting: Green came out of Wichita State as a first-round pick with a deadly knuckle curve which made his high-80s fastball quite lethal. However, he is quite a different pitcher after losing the bulk of two seasons to shoulder surgery. His knuckler is gone; he now throws the fastball and a variety of much slower off-speed pitches. Green's slider and curve are just for show, but his changeup can be quite effective. His command on all pitches has been spotty. Because he has been effective against righthanders, Green could be a good situational reliever, but he doesn't have the durability to pitch on consecutive days.

1998: Green will be in the hunt for the fifth starter role in Philadelphia. His inability to pitch out of the pen could force him back to Triple-A to start the season, but he is likely to make another dozen or so major league starts. However, Green is no longer a power pitcher and has never had the command to succeed as a finesse pitcher.

1997: Green was actually much more effective in the majors than he was at Triple-A. He took a regular turn without apparent strain on his shoulder, a major breakthrough although he no longer could get by on power alone.

1996: Green missed the entire season after undergoing surgery on his pitching shoulder.

GREENE, RICK - TR - b: 1/2/71

A member of Team USA in 1992, Greene was the Tigers' first-round draft pick in 1992. Except for two spot starts in A-ball in 1994, he has been used exclusively in relief. Greene led Double-A Jacksonville with 30 saves in 1996, but his other numbers were not indicative of a closer: 4.98 ERA, 39 walks and 42 strikeouts in 56 innings. In 1997 he had a 2.83 ERA in 70 innings of Triple-A relief work.

GREENE, TOMMY - TR - b: 4/6/67

Greene was a successful major league pitcher, posting two strong seasons with Philadelphia in 1991 and 1993. However, he has suffered an assortment of arm problems. After missing the 1996 season, he attempted a comeback with Houston in 1997. Greene made 11 starts at New Orleans with a 5-3 record and a 3.38 ERA before being recalled by Houston. He made two starts before breaking down again. He had surgery to repair a torn rotator cuff in his pitching shoulder and is not likely to be back.

GREER, KEN - TR - b: 5/12/67

Greer has been in pro ball for ten years, making it to the majors for one appearance with the Mets in 1993, and eight games with the Giants in 1996. He got into a few games in the Baltimore farm system last year, but at age 30, he's now a career minor-leaguer.

GREISINGER, SETH - TR - b: 7/29/75

Scouting: The Tigers' first-round draft pick in 1996, Greisinger thrilled the team in spring training by exhibiting outstanding command and mound presence. He's not the hardest thrower in the organization (low 90s fastball), but has good command of all his pitches, and seems to know how to work batters.

1998: A spring training like last year's (eight scoreless innings) could land Greisinger in the big leagues. Much more likely, he'll move to Double-A, with a chance to move up by the end of the year.

1997: He pitched so well in spring training that there were those who wanted to keep him in the big leagues. He pitched so poorly in the first month at Double-A Jacksonville that the Tigers considered sending him to Class A. In the end, he had a 10-6 season, with a high ERA (5.20) that the Tigers attribute partly to Jacksonville's small ballpark.

1996: Not all that well known before '96, Greisinger became a University of Virginia All-America and the key starter on the U.S. Olympic team in Atlanta. Had the U.S. won its semifinal game, Greisinger would have pitched the gold medal game.

GRILLI, JASON - TR - b: 4/1/74

Grilli was the second pitcher taken in the 1997 draft — the fourth pick overall — selected by the Giants out of Seton Hall. He's a presence on the mound at 6'5" and can blow batters away; he had 125 strikeouts in 74 innings of work at the Hall.

GRIMSLEY, JASON - TR - b: 8/7/67

Scouting: Grimsley doesn't have enough stuff to consistently retire big-league hitters. His fastball is average as far as velocity and movement. Hitters now wait out the breaking stuff that Grimsley throws outside the zone and pound him when he comes over the plate. Control has also been a problem for Grimsley which isn't helped by the fact that he doesn't hold runners well and is a below-average fielder.

1998: Grimsley has shown flashes of potential in the past and may benefit from expansion. He's a fifth starter or relief candidate who will have to battle for a spot by pitching well in spring training.

1997: Pitching in the Milwaukee organization at Triple-A Tucson, Grimsley did nothing to help his chances of returning to the majors. He appeared in 36 games, including nine starts, yielding more than a hit per inning and sporting a 5.70 ERA.

1996: A complete game shutout of the Yankees was the high point of a season where Grimsley shuttled between the starting rotation and the bullpen without standing out in either role.

	W	SV	ERA	IP	H	BB	SO	B/I
1995 Cleveland	0	1	6.09	34	37	32	25	2.03
1996 California	5	0	6.84	130	150	74	82	1.72

GROOM, BUDDY - TL - b: 7/10/65
Scouting: Groom has a typical repertoire. When his slider is consistent he can be tough on hitters. His changeup has improved over the past year, and he has adjusted well to his relief role. Groom brings it in the low 90's.
1998: Middle relief and facing lefties, as the situation dictates, has become Groom's forte. He has gotten good at it, and there is no reason to assume that will change this year.
1997: Groom completed his second consecutive season in which he appeared in more than 70 games (78). Like nearly every other Oakland hurler, he was hittable and gave up the long ball (nine over 64.2 innings). But, he was dependable, and that alone helped him standout among Athletics' pitchers.
1996: Appearing in 72 games, Groom was more effective than not, especially over the first part of the season. He could no longer cut it as a spot starter, and he lost steam over the last couple of months.

	W	SV	ERA	IP	H	BB	SO	B/I
1995 Detroit	1	1	7.52	40	55	26	23	1.99
1995 Florida	1	0	7.20	15	26	6	12	2.13
1996 Oakland	5	2	3.84	77	85	34	57	1.54
1997 Oakland	2	3	5.15	65	75	24	45	1.53

GROSS, KEVIN - TR - b: 6/8/61
Gross pitched for the Angels last year after spending 1996 with the Rangers. He nearly retired during the '96 season, then wound up finishing the year on the DL. Gross pitched in 12 games for Anaheim and was not effective. He gave up 30 hits — including four homers — in 25.1 innings with 20 walks. It looks like it is time for Gross to hang up the spikes after all.

	W	SV	ERA	IP	H	BB	SO	B/I
1995 Texas	9	0	5.54	183	200	89	106	1.57
1996 Texas	11	0	5.22	129	151	50	78	1.56
1997 Anaheim	2	0	6.76	25	30	20	20	1.98

GROTT, MATT - TL - b: 12/5/67
Grott appeared in two games with the Reds in 1995, his only major league action in nine seasons. He was a starter and reliever for the Orioles' Triple-A club in 1996 but didn't get a callup even though they were desperate for bullpen help. Last year he pitched for Triple-A Tucson in the Brewers' organization and didn't distinguish himself. At age 30 he looks to be a career minor-leaguer.

GRUNDT, KEN - TL - b: 8/26/69
Grundt has below-average stuff, even for a lefty. His best pitch is a looping curveball, which he throws for strikes more often than not. He had always pitched well in the minors because of his good control, and even earned a couple of glimpses in the majors. But he lost some bite on his breaking pitches last season in Triple-A, and got hammered by both lefthanders and righthanders. Unless his arm bounces back in a big way, it's unlikely he'll get to pitch in the majors again. Even if he does it will be as a one-batter situational lefty.

GRUNDY, PHIL - TR - b: 9/8/72
Grundy's fifth season in the Royals' organization was his first spent full-time at the Double-A level. A fourth-round pick in the 1993 June draft, Grundy was not as effective as he had been in A-ball where he racked up 15 wins in 1994. His control was good last year and so was his strikeout-to-walk ratio but he was hittable and will have to work on locating his pitches better in the strike zone.

GRZANICH, MIKE - TR - b: 8/24/72
Twice converted to a starting role, but now back in the bullpen, Grzanich throws a 94-MPH fastball and an explosive curveball. He has spent the last three years at Double-A Jackson, with an increasing ERA each season. Last year he was 7-6 with a 4.96 ERA and twelve saves. Grzanich has to establish himself at Triple-A soon to have a major league future, most likely as a long reliever.

GUARDADO, EDDIE - TL - b: 10/2/70
Scouting: His fastball tops out in the low 90s, he can come out of the bullpen nearly every day and, most important of all, Guardado is lefthanded. He excels against lefthanded batters, which is why manager Tom Kelly has used him one, two or maybe three batters at a time in the past. Use him longer than that and Guardado's odds of effectiveness decrease. But in the right spots, he is useful.
1998: There's no reason not to believe that Guardado will continue to be an effective bullpen weapon late in games against lefthanded hitters. He can pitch four or five times a week without repercussion. Guardado has developed a routine over the past couple of years that keeps him at the top of his game mentally, too.
1997: His work decreased some in 1997, but not because Guardado wasn't effective. He was 0-4 based on a couple of last-swing losses. More telling: 54 strikeouts against only 17 walks in 46 innings.
1996: In his breakthrough bullpen year, Guardado tied for the major-league lead with 83 appearances. He never tired and never had any physical problems.

	W	SV	ERA	IP	H	BB	SO	B/I
1995 Minnesota	4	2	5.12	91	99	45	71	1.58
1996 Minnesota	6	4	5.25	73	61	33	74	1.28
1997 Minnesota	0	1	3.91	46	45	17	54	1.35

GUBICZA, MARK - TR - b: 8/14/62
Scouting: Even after 14 seasons, Gubicza still has plenty to contribute to a staff. Whatever has been lost from his fastball has been more than regained in experience and guile. Gubicza knows how to work hitters and set them up with his breaking pitches, and still has the ability to blow his fastball by someone when necessary.
1998: The veteran righthander must show he's recovered from surgery to shave the clavicle and clean out the shoulder joint — sort of a 40,000-mile servicing. Gubicza still has enough ability for the Angels to give him a chance as a fifth starter. However, after two injury-filled seasons, this is a make-or-break year for him.
1997: Gubicza injured his shoulder in a freak fall in spring training, slipping on a wet tarp while running in the outfield. He was obtained in trade from Kansas City to become the fourth starter, but the injury limited him to two unsuccessful starts in April before he was forced to shut it down. He underwent season-ending arthroscopic surgery in late-June.
1996: Gubicza's 5.13 ERA wasn't too bad for the American League in it's heaviest hitting year, but he suffered from the lowest run support among Kansas City starters and finished the season with a career-low four victories. His season ended

July 5th when a line drive off the bat of Minnesota's Paul Molitor broke the tibia bone in his left leg.

	W	SV	ERA	IP	H	BB	SO	B/I
1995 Kansas City	12	0	3.75	213	222	62	81	1.33
1996 Kansas City	4	0	5.13	119	132	34	55	1.39

GUERRA, MARK - TR - b: 11/4/71
Guerra worked more as a reliever in 1997. He has a full four-pitch repertoire with good control and posted a 4-8 season with a 3.23 ERA and seven saves. He is improving, but still tends to give up too many hits.

GUNDERSON, ERIC - TL - b: 3/29/66
Scouting: Gunderson has a below-average fastball and an assortment of breaking stuff. With good location, he can be effective as an extra lefty out of the bullpen.
1998: Gunderson pitched well enough last season that he should have a spot in somebody's major league bullpen.
1997: A longshot to make the team out of spring training, Gunderson outpitched an undistinguished trio of lefties to make the Texas roster. For about two-thirds of the season, he was outstanding in situational roles, but he faltered badly toward the end of the season.
1996: Gunderson pitched well at Triple-A but got hammered in a brief stint with Boston.

	W	SV	ERA	IP	H	BB	SO	B/I
1997 Texas	2	1	3.26	50	45	15	31	1.21

GUTHRIE, MARK - TL - b: 9/22/65
Scouting: A finesse pitcher, Guthrie has a mediocre fastball that he sneaks in with a curveball and changeup, with his out pitch being a splitter. With a big leg kick and average move to first Guthrie isn't good at holding runners for a lefty. He's a decent fielder.
1998: Guthrie has appeared in 128 games the past two years for the Dodgers and is expected to be a part of the Los Angeles bullpen again in 1998. Willingness to take the ball is not a question, though durability might be.
1997: Guthrie got worse as the year wore on, an exaggerated repeat of his second-half slippage the year before. He was especially weak when pitching a second consecutive day (8.53 ERA) suggesting he needs more rest at this stage of his career.
1996: Guthrie pitched well for the Dodgers and was nearly unhittable before the All-Star break. His 73 innings pitched were his most since 1992 and after he bounced back from neck spasms he was effective down the stretch for a playoff team.

	W	SV	ERA	IP	H	BB	SO	B/I
1995 Minnesota	5	0	4.46	42	47	16	48	1.49
1995 Los Angeles	0	0	3.66	19	19	9	19	1.42
1996 Los Angeles	2	1	2.22	73	65	22	56	1.19
1997 Los Angeles	1	1	5.32	69	71	30	42	1.46

GUTIERREZ, JIM - TR - b: 11/28/70
A nine-year minor-league veteran, Gutierrez finally reached Triple-A for the first time last year (for seven games) after a 4-4, 3.03 ERA season with Double-A Jackson. He has bounced through three organizations, beginning his career as a starter, but pitching primarily in relief the last three seasons. Despite his success last season, Gutierrez does not have major league stuff and is a non-prospect.

GUZMAN, JUAN - TR - b: 10/28/66
Scouting: When healthy, Guzman possesses a mid-90s fastball and sharp breaking slider, consistently clocked in the high-80s. Although not one to go the distance, Guzman can be dominating at times and has yet to achieve his single-season potential.
1998: If he is healthy, Guzman is good enough to be a number two or three starter in most rotations. Expect a return to form. Guzman has never achieved his career season in that his most effective years never last. Only once in his career has he started more than 28 games.
1997: April started with shoulder discomfort and thanks to a broken thumb and the recurring problems with his shoulder, Guzman's season was cut short to just 13 starts.
1996: A late-season appendectomy shortened his season but he still won the ERA title with a 2.93 mark over 187.2 innings.

	W	SV	ERA	IP	H	BB	SO	B/I
1995 Toronto	4	0	6.32	135	151	73	94	1.66
1996 Toronto	11	0	2.93	187	158	53	165	1.13
1997 Toronto	3	0	4.95	60	48	31	52	1.32

HALAMA, JOHN - TL - b: 2/22/72
Scouting: Halama was the biggest surprise in the Astro system in 1997. He was the most dominant pitcher in the Triple-A American Association even though he is not a hard thrower. Halama changes speeds effectively and has excellent control, but he needs to improve his curveball. Since signing as a 23rd-round draft choice in 1994 he has been highly regarded but not considered a top prospect.
1998: Based on his successful season at Triple-A in 1997, Halama has to be given a chance to make the major league rotation in 1998.
1997: Halama had an outstanding season at Triple-A New Orleans in 1997. He was 13-3 with an ERA of 2.58, allowing 150 hits in 171 innings while striking out 126 and walking only 32. He led the league in both wins and ERA and was second to teammate C.J. Nitkowski in strikeouts.
1996: Halama made the transition from a middle reliever at Low Class A Quad Cities to become a starter at Double-A Jackson. He led the club in innings pitched and had a 9-10 won-loss record. His 3.21 ERA ranked third in the Texas League.

HALL, DARREN - TR - b: 7/14/64
Scouting: Hall was already advanced in years when he finally reached the majors in 1994 with the Blue Jays and has his best season as a big leaguer, then he experienced elbow problems in 1995 and '96. He's a direct, come-at-you pitcher but is really not overpowering with his fastball and uses breaking stuff, a curveball and slider, to get by.
1998: On a team without Todd Worrell, Hall would be even more important to the Dodgers. He threw well enough in 1997 to pitch out of a major league bullpen somewhere in a set-up role even if he's not at Chavez Ravine this year.
1997: After a lot of missed time the previous two seasons, Hall recovered from elbow troubles and appeared in 63 games for the Dodgers, more than twice as many games as he'd ever had in a big-league season and more than he'd accumulated in three previous seasons in the majors. He had 15 holds and by far the lowest ERA of his major league career.
1996: Hall was wild and wasn't throwing hard in 1996 after being the Jays' surprise closer in 1994. He was off and on the disabled list and ended up pitching just 12 innings.

	W	SV	ERA	IP	H	BB	SO	B/I
1997 Los Angeles	3	2	2.30	55	58	26	39	1.54

HALLADAY, ROY - TR - b: 5/14/77

Scouting: Blessed with an overpowering fastball and an unusual knuckle-curve, Halladay's long-term future looks promising. His velocity reaches the mid-90s and, although he is wild, he is expected to eventually gain command of his pitches with more experience.

1998: Halladay finished the year at Triple-A and that's the logical level for him to resume his learning process. For a pitcher who throws as hard as he does, his strikeouts should increase. He could be in Skydome by September.

1997: Splitting time between Double-A and Triple-A, Halladay was ineffective at the lower level.

1996: Halladay dominated at Class A Dunedin, going 15-7 in 27 starts, with a 2.73 ERA and two shutouts.

HALPERIN, MIKE - TL - b: 9/8/73

The lefty was one of six prospects the Pirates acquired from Toronto in the November, 1996 trade for Orlando Merced, Carlos Garcia and Dan Plesac. He looks like the only one of the six who has little chance of making an impact at the major league level. Halperin doesn't throw hard and his stuff just isn't quite good enough for him to ever be an effective major league pitcher. He did pitch better as a starter at Double-A Carolina in the second half of last season after bombing as a swingman at Triple-A Calgary.

HAMILTON, JOEY - TR - b: 9/9/70

Scouting: By this time, the Padres had hoped that Hamilton would develop into a "staff ace" kind of pitcher. He has the physical qualities and the pitches. But his results haven't matched his potential and hints about wanting out of San Diego have raised questions about his desire. Hamilton often gets in trouble early and is susceptible to homers. When he gets on a roll, Hamilton is the best the Padres have.

1998: The Padres would love to see Hamilton and Andy Ashby step forward as a powerful 1-2 punch with 15 to 18 wins apiece.

1997: Hamilton led the Padres in victories, but his ERA climbed for the third straight season while his strikeout rate fell. He surrendered 22 homers and opposing batters hit .271 against him. His problems were usually encountered early in games.

1996: In his second full season, Hamilton led the Padres with 211.2 innings and 184 strikeouts — an average of 7.8 per nine innings. He also surrendered a staff-high 19 homers.

	W	SV	ERA	IP	H	BB	SO	B/I
1995 San Diego	6	0	3.08	204	189	56	123	1.20
1996 San Diego	15	0	4.17	211	206	83	184	1.37
1997 San Diego	12	0	4.25	193	199	69	124	1.39

HAMMACK, BRANDON - TR - b: 3/5/73

Hammack was a low-round draft choice of the Cubs out of college and has been used almost strictly in relief in his three seasons in the minors. He posted good stats as a reliever in 1996 (saving a combined 29 games for Chicago's Class A teams in Rockford and Daytona) but was obviously overmatched in 1997 at Double-A Orlando. He gave up far more hits and had far fewer strikeouts at the higher level, which proves that his earlier success was simply due to overpowering more inexperienced hitters in A-ball. He's simply not going to make it in the majors.

HAMMOND, CHRIS - TL - b: 1/21/66

Scouting: Hammond has below-average stuff, and relies on getting groundballs and keeping batters off-balance with a changeup and slider. Because his fastball is below average and his slider is hardly nasty, he has no better success against lefthanders than righthanders, and does not make a good reliever. But, because he tends to break down easily, he has not made much of a starter either.

1998: Hammond's career is in jeopardy once again as he had arm surgery prior to this year. Even if he comes back healthy, Hammond's performance the past couple of seasons was barely keeping him in the majors.

1997: Hammond pitched a couple of good games for the pitching-thin Red Sox, but soon reverted back to his '96 form, and later found himself back on the DL with arm problems.

1996: Hammond started the season in the Florida rotation, but pitched poorly and, in between stints on the DL, pitched in middle relief the rest of the season, without great success.

	W	SV	ERA	IP	H	BB	SO	B/I
1995 Florida	9	0	3.80	161	157	47	126	1.27
1996 Florida	5	0	6.56	81	104	27	50	1.62
1997 Boston	3	1	5.93	65	81	27	48	1.65

HAMPTON, MIKE - TL - b: 9/9/72

Scouting: Hampton is an excellent athlete who made it to the major leagues to stay at the age of 21. He has established himself as a solid major league starting pitcher. He is not overpowering but his fastball reaches 90 MPH and sets up his slider, sinker and changeup which have good movement. He likes to work inside which is consistent with his competitive nature. After a disappointing start in 1997, he turned his season around when he began to effectively use both sides of the plate.

1998: Hampton should be a strong number two or three starter in the major leagues for many years. He can be a consistent 15-game winner.

1997: After recovering from a slow start, Hampton had his best year. He suffered some shoulder problems in 1996, but he was injury free in 1997.

1996: His second year as a starter was similar to his first one and established him as a .500 pitcher.

	W	SV	ERA	IP	H	BB	SO	B/I
1995 Houston	9	0	3.35	150	141	49	115	1.26
1996 Houston	10	0	3.59	160	175	49	101	1.40
1997 Houston	15	0	3.83	223	217	77	139	1.32

HANCOCK, RYAN - TR - b: 11/11/71

Scouting: A former BYU quarterback, Hancock had arm problems and slipped after a quick rise through the Angels' system. He came to the Padres in the Rickey Henderson trade and is a classic fastball/slider pitcher.

1998: The Padres plan to start Hancock at Triple-A Las Vegas.

1997: Hancock was 3-3 with a 3.69 ERA at Triple-A Vancouver before the trade, then finished with four relief outings in Las Vegas.

1996: After a strong Double-A showing in '95 (12-9, 4.56 ERA), Hancock opened the season at Vancouver and was 4-6 with a 3.70 ERA. He was hit hard after advancing to the majors.

HANEY, CHRIS - TL - b: 11/16/68

Scouting: Haney will throw his upper-80s fastball inside then try to work hitters away with a cut fastball, curveball and

changeup. His success is tied directly to his ability to throw strikes. In his last full season, 1996, Haney was 8-0 in nine starts when he walked no one, but 2-14 in his other 26 starts.
1998: Haney's injuries were not expected to effect his pitching; he will be fully ready for the start of the 1998 season. Should he re-sign with the Royals, Haney would be the club's fourth starter. Haney needs to pitch in a starting rotation somewhere; his repertoire does not lend itself well to a relief role.
1997: Three stints on the disabled list with a broken foot (suffered shagging flies before a game in Toronto) made Haney almost non-existent for the Royals; he finished with the fewest starts and innings of his major league career. The season was a total washout.
1996: Haney's first full season in the majors was a qualified success. The qualification was his control. When he had the necessary pinpoint control, he won; without it he was pounded mercilessly. Haney led the American League in fewest walks per nine innings (2.0), but also allowed the most hits in the league (267).

	W	SV	ERA	IP	H	BB	SO	B/I
1995 Kansas City	3	0	3.65	81	78	33	31	1.37
1996 Kansas City	10	0	4.70	228	267	51	115	1.39
1997 Kansas City	1	0	4.37	25	29	5	16	1.38

HANSELL, GREG - TR - b: 3/12/71
Hansell has done nothing to indicate much progress in 1997. He spent most of the year at Triple-A Tucson with unimpressive results and fanned five in 4.2 innings with the Brewers but had a bloated ERA. Hansell spent more time in the Brewers' pen in 1996, so last year has to be considered a step backwards. Hansell is still considered a decent prospect, but may be heading for a "project" tag soon.

	W	SV	ERA	IP	H	BB	SO	B/I
1995 Los Angeles	0	0	7.45	19	29	6	13	1.81
1996 Minnesota	3	3	5.69	74	83	31	46	1.54

HANSON, ERIK - TR - b: 5/18/65
Scouting: Hanson has one of the best curveballs in the game to go with a decent slider and mediocre fastball. Although once a durable pitcher, his 1997 season changed the outlook and there's no guarantee that he will retain his curveball after nearly a whole season off.
1998: Hanson will be a starting pitcher but considering that he missed most of last year and with his poor performance the year before, he is a risky proposition for any team.
1997: Hanson underwent arthroscopic rotator cuff surgery in May and returned in September to pitch with the Blue Jays. He looked every bit the pitcher he once was in his brief return.
1996: Hanson's first year with the Blue Jays didn't go as planned as he went 13-17 with a 5.41 ERA over 35 starts. He allowed an uncharacteristically high number of walks (102) as well as a career-high 26 home runs.

	W	SV	ERA	IP	H	BB	SO	B/I
1995 Boston	15	0	4.24	186	187	59	139	1.32
1996 Toronto	13	0	5.41	214	243	102	156	1.61
1997 Toronto	0	0	7.80	15	15	6	18	1.40

HARIKKALA, TIM - TR - b: 7/15/71
Scouting: Harikkala's star seems to be fading after a third consecutive mediocre season at Seattle's Triple-A affiliate in Tacoma. He does not throw hard and his location is just OK.
1998: Harikkala will probably benefit from a change in organi-

zations; he is going nowhere with the Mariners.
1997: Harikkala allowed 210 baserunners — 160 hits, 50 walks — at Tacoma in 113.1 innings, a horrible ratio. He went 6-8 while leading Tacoma in starts (21), but had the starting rotation's highest ERA - 6.43. He did not get back to the majors after that performance.
1996: For the second year in a row, Harikkala made one spot start in Seattle and got roughed up for six earned runs; it improved his major league ERA to 14.09. He gave up 204 hits in 158.1 innings at Tacoma while leading the club with 27 starts. Harikkala had a 4.83 ERA and, for the second consecutive season, lost 12 games in the Pacific Coast League.

HARKEY, MIKE - TR - b: 10/25/66
Harkey was once a Cubs starter but is now in the journeyman stage of his career. In 1996 he didn't pitch in the bigs, splitting his time at Triple-A Albuquerque between starting and relieving. He still has a fairly good fastball and last year he pitched both at Triple-A and in ten games for the Dodgers, working exclusively in relief. Harkey has been with five different organizations in the past five years and if he's in the majors in 1998 it will likely be with his sixth in six years.

	W	SV	ERA	IP	H	BB	SO	B/I
1997 Los Angeles	1	0	4.29	15	12	5	6	1.16

HARNISCH, PETE - TR - b: 9/23/66
Scouting: Harnisch still has decent velocity and sharp breaking pitches when he's on. He has struggled with his control and in making the transition from a power pitcher. His battle with clinical depression makes him a question mark.
1998: Harnisch will need to regain his command and composure if he is to rejuvenate his career. The Brewers were interested in bringing him back, but were debating about making him one of their protected players.
1997: Harnisch battled clinical depression for much of the season and found himself with the Brewers after an acrimonious departure from the Mets. He lost his first two games with Milwaukee, but won his final start. He benefited from manager Phil Garner's and pitching coach Don Rowe's confidence and approach to management.
1996: Harnisch started the season on the DL, recovering from shoulder surgery in 1995, but rebounded to make 31 starts for the Mets.

	W	SV	ERA	IP	H	BB	SO	B/I
1995 New York NL	2	0	3.68	110	111	24	82	1.23
1996 New York NL	8	0	4.21	194	195	61	114	1.32
1997 two teams	1	0	7.03	40	48	23	22	1.79

HARRIGER, DENNY - TR - b: 7/21/69
Up with the Padres briefly in 1996, Harriger was at Triple-A Toledo on the Tigers farm in 1997. He lacks a major league fastball, but his control is good, and he's been durable over the years. Harriger was 11-8 with a 3.99 ERA for Toledo in 97.

HARRIS, PEP - TR - b: 9/23/72
Scouting: Harris has yet to realize his full potential, but may be on the verge of doing so after a solid season in the Angels' bullpen. The Angels feel he made a lot of progress in the mental phase of pitching this season — forming a game plan and working the hitters. Harris has an above-average fastball and a sharp slider, and plenty of courage, all of which make him an attractive prospect.

1998: Harris wants the opportunity to start and may get it this spring if he can prove to Manager Terry Collins he can formulate a game plan and make the necessary adjustments a starter must make each time through the batting order. He took some solid steps in that direction with some long relief performances the second half of 1997. Harris has to step forward this spring or risk being passed by some of the Angels' other top pitching prospects.

1997: Harris got lost in the shuffle in a mediocre spring and found himself in the bullpen, but had a solid season nonetheless. He performed well in the long relief role, particularly down the stretch, and showed some flashes of brilliance as a set-up man as well.

1996: Obtained from Cleveland before spring training, Harris opened the year at Double-A Midland, but earned a quick promotion to Triple-A Vancouver. He became one of the Canadians' top starters because of an intimidating fastball. Promoted to the big club in August when Jim Abbott was sent down for the first time in his career, Harris won two big games for the Angels as a starter and posted a respectable 3.90 ERA.

	W	SV	ERA	IP	H	BB	SO	B/I
1996 California	2	0	3.90	32	31	17	20	1.50
1997 Anaheim	5	0	3.61	80	82	38	56	1.51

HARRIS, REGGIE - TR - b: 8/12/68

Scouting: Harris is a journeyman who has the stuff to dominate minor-league hitters, but lacks the command to even compete against major league hitters. His out pitch is a split-fingered fastball which drops off the table, but which is rarely near the strike zone. When he frequently falls behind in the count he's forced to rely on his other pitches, which are below average. His fastball reaches the high-80s, but is a non-factor unless he's throwing the splitter for strikes.

1998: Among the Phillies' goals for the season are to have better set-up relievers, which means Harris will go elsewhere. He's destined for a Triple-A bullpen.

1997: Harris walked more than a batter per inning for much of the first half of the year, and was only marginally better down the stretch. He was effective against righthanded hitters when he threw strike one, which wasn't often. He was reduced to mop up duty by season's end.

1996: Harris discovered a forkball at Double-A Trenton, and was a lethal closer. He allowed about four hits per nine innings, earning a late season recall to Boston where he permitted 12 baserunners in four innings.

	W	SV	ERA	IP	H	BB	SO	B/I
1997 Philadelphia	1	0	5.30	54	55	43	45	1.80

HARRISON, BRIAN - TR - b: 12/18/68

A control pitcher who has spent the last three years in the high minors for the Royals, Harrison enjoyed his most successful Triple-A campaign in 1997, leading Omaha with ten victories and 178.1 innings. However, the strikeout dimension he added in 1996 was again lacking last year he posted a mediocre 5.05 ERA. Harrison is an organizational pitcher whom the Royals don't prize highly; he'll be a six-year minor-league free agent who will likely fill a high-minors rotation job elsewhere in 1998.

HARRISON, TOMMY - TR - b: 9/30/71

Harrison's fastball is below average and his other pitches are nothing special, although not bad. He needs to be perfect to pitch effectively with his stuff, and he hasn't been so far. He does have some guts and he likes to challenge hitters. He went 9-7 with a 4.21 ERA at Triple-A Richmond in '97. Harrison will likely stick around Triple-A for a few years and get some spot starts, but he's unlikely to be effective over the long term.

HARTGRAVES, DEAN - TL - b: 8/12/66

Hartgraves is a lefthanded reliever with four decent pitches, although none are big-league. Because he's lefthanded and teams are always looking for lefties, especially in the bullpen, he'll be around for a while and should return to the majors at some point. However, as he showed in Triple-A in '97, posting a 4.48 ERA, he's unlikely to dominate hitters.

	W	SV	ERA	IP	H	BB	SO	B/I
1995 Houston	2	0	3.22	36	30	16	24	1.27
1996 Atlanta	1	0	4.78	37	34	23	30	1.53

HARTVIGSON, CHAD - TL - b: 12/15/70

Scouting: Hartvigson throws hard — he has averaged nearly a strikeout per inning over his minor-league career; he has good stuff and is around the plate. He has been jockeyed between the rotation and the bullpen over his four-year minor-league career. He does seem to have trouble moving up the ladder, however.

1998: Despite being lefthanded and having some minor-league success, Hartvigson is not likely to get to the majors right away. A full season at Triple-A is probably in order for him this year.

1997: A minor-league ping-pong ball, Hartvigson started the season at Class A Bakersfield, going 1-1 with a 3.00 ERA, then moved to Double-A Shreveport where he was 1-0 with a 3.55 ERA. After a trip to Triple-A Phoenix, going 2-2 with a 5.37 ERA he wound up at Oklahoma City and went 2-2 with a 6.66 ERA. The promotions were a good sign, given his relatively advanced age. He showed good control, getting 52 strikeouts against 17 walks at Phoenix.

1996: Hartvigson's second year at higher Class A saw him taking on the role of starter (ten games) with acceptable results. He whiffed 114 over 94 innings and posted an ERA of 3.23. It wasn't a bad year, but the Giants have a lot of good young arms, and Hartvigson never got a chance at Double-A, despite the performance and experience.

HARVEY, BRYAN - TR - b: 6/2/63

Since his outstanding 1991 season for the Angels, Harvey has constantly battled elbow problems, eventually undergoing "Tommy John" surgery in the middle of the 1995 season when a tendon from his ankle was transplanted into his pitching elbow. He didn't pitch at all from then until 21 games for Double-A Greenville last year. The results (1-1, 5.32 ERA) weren't as important as Harvey being able to pitch again. When healthy he throws hard, but that hasn't happened in many, many years. If he has full arm strength, Harvey has a chance to get back to the majors.

HASEGAWA, SHIGETOSHI - TR - 8/1/68

Scouting: Free from the rigorous training methods in his native Japan, which wear down a pitcher's arm, Hasegawa has developed a major league fastball that turned him into one of the most dependable members of the Angels' bullpen in 1997. He also learned a great deal about the science of pitching in his first full season in the major leagues, and spent the winter working on arm strength and a curveball to go along with a

fastball that now hits 91 MPH consistently. Hasegawa impressed the Angels with his tenacity and willingness to pitch in any situation, both of which make him a valuable commodity.
1998: Hasegawa wants to start, which was his job for six previous seasons in Japan. To do that, he has to convince Manager Terry Collins he can make the adjustments a starter must make after he's been through the lineup twice. Hasegawa will have to develop the curve and sharpen his changeup.
1997: Once he become accustomed to the role, Hasegawa became a solid middle reliever, particularly after Rich DeLucia and Mike James went out with arm injuries in mid-season. He struggled as a starter early, but made several solid starts for the Angels at the end of the season.
1996: Hasegawa helped pitch the Orix Blue Waves to the Japan Series championship, but had mixed results, pitching in a career-low 18 games and recording a career-low four victories, while his ERA ballooned to a career-high 5.34. The move to America came at just the right time.

HAUGHT, GARY - TR - 9/29/70

Scouting: Haught, who looked like a career minor-leaguer, made great advances last year, improving his stature over previous seasons. Haught is not overpowering, but does throw strikes. Like most control pitchers, he is stingy with the walks, but susceptible to the long ball (49 over 474 minor-league innings). He is a battler.
1998: The righthanded Haught could stick somewhere, landing a job in middle relief, and maybe even as a set-up guy. Oakland is pretty well stocked with pitchers fitting this profile, so Haught may move along with expansion. Or, he could fill a spot vacated by an A's hurler lost to a new team.
1997: Haught climbed the Oakland ladder, starting the season at Double-A Huntsville, where he had a 5.59 ERA in six games, moving up to Triple-A Edmonton, where he picked up eleven saves with a 3.59 ERA in 30 games, ultimately appearing six times for the A's. He has good control; he walked 21 while fanning 52 in 63.2 combined innings. He could find a spot in the Oakland pen in 1998.
1996: At Double-A Huntsville, Haught showed an ability to advance a level. His numbers (3-2, 3.90 ERA, four saves) during a first full season at Double-A were fine after his 1995 campaign at Class A Lancaster when he was 9-5 with a 2.60 ERA.

HAWBLITZEL, RYAN - TR - b: 4/30/71

A Rockies' expansion draft pick who languished for four uninspiring years at Triple-A Colorado Springs, Hawblitzel joined the Phillies' farm system as a minor-league free agent before 1997. He's a nibbling junkballer with good enough control to throw strikes, but he gets hit hard. He's a savvy veteran willing to take the ball in any role and is destined for a middle-innings role in a major league bullpen or a trip back to the high minors.

HAWKINS, LaTROY - TR - b: 12/21/72

Scouting: In terms of pure stuff, Hawkins appears to have what it takes to pitch in the major leagues. His fastball travels to the plate at 92/93 MPH and his breaking stuff is passable. However, in three major league trials, Hawkins has yet to keep the ball low enough in the strike zone to win consistently.
1998: Hawkins will open the season in the Twins' rotation unless he collapses during spring training. Although he has been inconsistent to date, he has the potential to become a consistent double-digit winner.
1997: In his third big-league trial, Hawkins hit better spots in the strike zone than he did earlier in his career but still threw too many high strikes that got creamed. Both his changeup and curveball were inconsistent as well.
1996: Hawkins's career in the majors was derailed when he started the season with the Twins but couldn't hold onto the spot in the starting rotation that he had won by default. He was immature emotionally as well as on the field, which at times manifested itself at Triple-A Salt Lake.

	W	SV	ERA	IP	H	BB	SO	B/I
1995 Minnesota	2	0	8.67	27	39	12	9	1.89
1996 Minnesota	1	0	8.20	26	42	9	24	1.95
1997 Minnesota	6	0	5.84	103	134	47	58	1.75

HAYNES, JIMMY - TR - b: 9/5/72

Scouting: Haynes, a lefty, is a hard thrower who brings his fastball at 93 MPH. He also throws a slider, changeup, has an outstanding curveball and excellent control. Haynes has been far more successful in the higher minors than in the majors.
1998: Haynes is a leading candidate to make the Oakland rotation this season. He has good stuff and has established himself as a capable minor-league pitcher. It is now time for him to take the next step, and since the Oakland rotation is wide open, and bearing in mind Haynes' credentials, it is a likely fit.
1997: Acquired mid-season in exchange for outfielder/DH Geronimo Berroa, Haynes put together a 5-4 record with a 3.44 ERA at Triple-A Rochester prior to the trade. At Edmonton Haynes had some adjustment difficulties (0-2, 4.85 ERA) prior to an Oakland call-up where, all-in-all, he exceeded expectations.
1996: Expected to become a junior Mike Mussina, Haynes began the season as the fifth starter. He was a disappointment, lost his confidence, went to Triple-A Rochester, and ultimately home in lieu of being recalled in September.

	W	SV	ERA	IP	H	BB	SO	B/I
1995 Baltimore	2	0	2.25	24	11	12	22	0.96
1996 Baltimore	3	1	8.29	89	122	58	65	2.02
1997 Oakland	3	0	4.42	73	74	40	65	1.56

HEATHCOTT, MIKE - TR - b: 5/16/69

A local (Chicago) product, Heathcott spent five years in A-ball (1991-5) before advancing to Double-A Birmingham in 1996, going 11-8 with a 4.02 ERA. Shifted to a relief role in 1997, Heathcott got to Triple-A Nashville but was hit hard and returned to Birmingham. He has marginal stuff and is not considered a prospect.

HECKER, DOUG - TR - b: 1/21/71

Hecker was converted into pitching during the '95 season, but has not progressed as quickly as lefty Ron Mahay, who made a similar conversion. Hecker was injured for most of the '97 season, pitching just sparingly. He's big, strong and throws hard, but time is working against him at this point, as he's pitched just 27 innings above A-ball so far.

HEFLIN, BRONSON - TR - b: 8/29/71

An over-achieving, late-round draft pick, Heflin got to the majors quickly only because of the dearth of quality middle-relief help in the Phillies' organization. He doesn't throw hard, but works the edges of the plate and keeps the ball down in the strike zone. Heflin has walked too many batters in the high minors and his lack of good stuff would produce disastrous results in the majors. An upgrade to the quality of relief pitching in the Philadelphia bullpen in 1998 would return Heflin to the minor leagues for the bulk of the season.

HEISERMAN, RICK - TR - b: 2/22/73
After a promising season in 1996, last year was a disappointment. At Double-A Arkansas, Heiserman gave up 151 hits in only 131.2 innings, with a 4.17 ERA. He maintained a good strikeout-to-walk ratio but has yet to prove himself at the Double-A level.

HELLING, RICH - TR - b: 12/15/70
Scouting: Helling has a sinker and a cut fastball, but too often relies on trying to throw high fastballs past hitters. When he doesn't have good velocity on his fastball, he gets hit hard. As a result, Helling's starts are usually either good or awful — nothing in between.
1998: Helling showed enough to be a strong candidate for the rotation next season. If he can maintain his velocity and keep the ball down consistently, he can be successful as a starting pitcher.
1997: Helling was traded back to the Rangers late in the summer after a solid partial season with Florida as a swingman. He started out strong for Texas, but tired late in the season.
1996: After starting the season in the minors, Helling was called up by Texas, only to be traded to Florida shortly afterward. In four September starts with the Marlins, Helling pitched brilliantly.

	W	SV	ERA	IP	H	BB	SO	B/I
1995 Texas	0	0	6.57	12	17	8	5	2.03
1996 Texas	1	0	7.52	20	23	9	16	1.59
1996 Florida	2	0	1.95	27	14	7	26	0.77
1997 Texas	5	0	4.47	131	108	69	99	1.35

HENDERSON, ROD - TR - b: 3/11/71
Henderson was an early-season callup to Montreal in 1994, just two years after being the Expos' second-round draft pick from the University of Kentucky. He got hammered in three games, was sent back to the minors and has done nothing since. It's obviously not going to happen for him with the Expos and, after three straight bad seasons, it's doubtful it will happen for him anywhere else, either.

HENDERSON, RYAN - TR - b: 9/30/69
Henderson spent the first five years of his minor-league career in the Dodger organization and pitched at Double-A and Triple-A for the Rockies last year. He had some success at Double-A San Antonio in '96 but at 27 years old it was nothing to get excited about. He proved that he was no prospect in 1997 as he struggled at both levels, giving up more than a hit per inning at both stops and walking way too many batters.

HENRIQUEZ, OSCAR - TR - b: 1/28/74
Scouting: Henriquez is a big (6'6", 220 pounds) flamethrower from Venezuela. After a promising 1993 season as a starter, he was stricken with a rare muscle disease, myasthenia gravis, which sidelined him for all of the 1994 season. He returned in 1995 as a relief pitcher and spent two years at High Class A Kissimmee, the second as a closer. He has now improved his control and gained command of a changeup which should allow him to compete at the major league level.
1998: Henriquez will be given a chance to pitch in relief in the major leagues. His success will depend upon his control. With his dominating fastball, he could eventually become a major league closer.
1997: Henriquez made a double jump to Triple-A New Orleans and had a successful season as a closer. He was 4-5 with 12 saves and an ERA of 2.80. He allowed 65 hits and only 27 walks in 74 innings while striking out 80. He made his major league debut in Houston after a September callup.
1996: Henriquez became the closer in his second year with Class A Kissimmee. He had moderate success with an 0-4 record, 15 saves and a 3.97 ERA. In 34 innings, he allowed 28 hits and 29 walks while striking out 40.

HENRY, BUTCH - TL - b: 10/7/68
Scouting: Henry is one of the best control pitchers in baseball, when healthy. He almost never walks a batter. Despite a below-average fastball he gets by because of his great changeup and ability to locate the ball exactly where he wants to.
1998: Henry will start the season in the Red Sox rotation after being their best starter down the stretch of the '97 season. He's more likely to be derailed by injury than ineffectiveness, as he has never thrown more than 165 innings in a season in his major league career.
1997: Henry was brought back slowly after major arm surgery, pitching out of the bullpen. Because he could not pitch on consecutive days, he was used for longer stints and earned some three-inning saves. He did spend some time on the DL with soreness, but rebounded and showed some durability late in the season as a starter.
1996: Henry missed the entire season after having tendon transplant surgery in August of '95.

	W	SV	ERA	IP	H	BB	SO	B/I
1997 Boston	7	6	3.52	84	89	19	51	1.28

HENRY, DOUG - TR - b: 12/10/63
Scouting: The former Met added a forkball and slider to his fastball, so he now has an actual repertoire. Henry was effective coming out of the pen for the Giants, but his closer days are long gone. He's a good middle man who could hang around the majors for a few more years if he can show some consistency.
1998: Like nearly half of his San Francisco teammates, Henry was a free agent at the end of 1997. He throws strikes and is both durable and dependable, so he'll be on a major league roster this year performing his requisite middle-relief duties and plucking an occasional save.
1997: Henry was effective coming out of the Giants pen, especially during the first half of the season. He logged the most relief innings after Julian Tavarez. Henry was more effective against lefthanders than righthanders in 1997.
1996: Despite getting a handful of saves and spending most of the season as the Mets top righthanded reliever, Henry ended the year with mixed results.

	W	SV	ERA	IP	H	BB	SO	B/I
1995 New York NL	3	4	2.96	67	48	25	62	1.09
1996 New York NL	2	9	4.68	75	82	36	58	1.57
1997 San Francisco	4	3	4.71	71	70	41	69	1.57

HENTGEN, PAT - TR - b: 11/13/68
Scouting: Hentgen is a workhorse and a fierce competitor, similar to teammate Roger Clemens. Although a power pitcher with a fastball in the mid-90s, Hentgen also possesses a hard cutter to go with an occasional changeup and ordinary curve.
1998: Hentgen is the number two starter and is a safe bet to stay healthy and pitch 250+ innings. His performance the past two years projects Hentgen as a big winner with a good ERA, especially if he had some added offense in support.
1997: Although not as dominating as the previous season, he tied for the league lead in innings pitched and quietly won 15 games on a weak-hitting team.
1996: Hentgen won the American League Cy Young Award, leading the league in complete games and innings pitched while becoming a 20-game winner for the first time.

	W	SV	ERA	IP	H	BB	SO	B/I
1995 Toronto	10	0	5.11	200	236	90	135	1.62
1996 Toronto	20	0	3.22	265	238	94	177	1.25
1997 Toronto	15	0	3.68	264	253	71	160	1.23

HENTHORNE, KEVIN - TR - b: 12/9/69
Henthorne is one of the many mature pitchers in the Yankees' farm system. He had another good season at Double-A Norwich as a reliever and spot starter posting a 3.13 ERA and having a five-to-one strikeout-to-walk ratio. He is old to be at this level in the minors.

HERBERT, RUSS - TR - b: 4/21/72
Herbert is a strikeout pitcher who enjoyed a good deal of success at Double-A Birmingham in 1997, going 9-2 with a 3.92 ERA in 17 starts. He's a mid-level prospect who gets by on sharp breaking balls and lacks a good fastball. Herbert's name isn't used much when the White Sox talk about their best and brightest.

HEREDIA, FELIX - TL - b: 6/18/76
Scouting: Heredia is a slightly built reliever who has established himself as one of the most promising young pitchers in the National League. His high-80's velocity is above-average for a lefthander, and he has developed a more than passable slider. His pitches break down and away from lefthanded hitters, though he must pitch on the black more consistently. Heredia is not intimidated by entering games with men on base, and has a durable two-inning arm. He held lefties to .154 and .188 averages in 1996 and 1997, respectively. He is ready to move into the top lefty spot in the Marlins' bullpen, and is more than qualified to snatch a handful of saves.
1998: Heredia should shove Dennis Cook down a notch in the Marlins' bullpen pecking order. If Heredia enhances his control, he could become the premier lefthanded set-up man in the National League. He's a breakout prospect for 1998.
1997: Heredia was quite effective as the Marlins' number two bullpen lefty, often entering games with men on base and retiring lefties in key spots. He was used little in the post-season, but showed enough promise to secure himself an important future role.
1996: Heredia dazzled as a 20-year-old top set-up man at Double-A Portland before being recalled to the Marlins. He pitched timidly, falling behind hitters and relying too much on his fastball. He didn't get bombed, however, which put him ahead of the game for a pitcher of his age.

	W	SV	ERA	IP	H	BB	SO	B/I
1997 Florida	5	0	4.29	57	53	30	54	1.46

HEREDIA, GIL - TR - b: 10/26/65
Heredia did not pitch in the major leagues for the first time in six seasons, spending the entire season with the Cubs' Triple-A franchise in Iowa. There he was used mostly in relief, getting in only four starts the entire season. It's not a good sign for Heredia that he didn't get a chance to pitch for the Cubs, and now he must be considered a fringe player who isn't likely to make any real impact in the major leagues.

	W	SV	ERA	IP	H	BB	SO	B/I
1995 Montreal	5	1	4.31	119	137	21	74	1.33
1996 Texas	2	1	5.89	73	91	14	43	1.44

HEREDIA, WILSON - TR - b: 3/30/72
Scouting: Heredia is healthy again after missing the entire 1996 season. He throws hard, but has little movement on his pitches and is prone to wildness. Although most recently use as a starter in the minors, Heredia's future would probably be in the bullpen because of the lack of diversity in his repertoire.
1998: Although Heredia could make a major league roster with a strong spring, he needs more innings and further refinement in the minors. Top priorities are the development of a reliable off-speed pitch and work on his control.
1997: Heredia completed a full season at Triple-A, starting 27 games with a 7-12 record and a 4.97 ERA. In a late-season recall by Texas, he was hard to hit (.194 opponent batting average) but his control was non-existent.
1996: Heredia spent the entire season on the Marlins' disabled list.

	W	SV	ERA	IP	H	BB	SO	B/I
1997 Texas	1	0	3.20	20	14	16	8	1.52

HERGES, MATT - TR - b: 4/1/70
Herges took a confidence hit in 1997 with some struggles in Triple-A. He was sent back to Double-A San Antonio to regain confidence and re-establish himself as one of the better pitching prospects in the organization. He appears to be on the upswing again and may have a future in the majors as a set-up man if he can continue to progress.

HERMANSON, DUSTIN - TR - b: 12/21/72
Scouting: Hermanson was always considered a potential star closer with his outstanding fastball but Montreal converted him into a starter last season and he now has a new lease on life. Hermanson has redefined his slider with more work and his changeup has improved dramatically since he has had a chance to use it more.
1998: Hermanson will be one of the mainstays in the Expos' young rotation. Now that he has a full year of starting under his belt and expanded his array of pitches, his career is ready to take off. Playing on what figures to be a bad team might hurt his win total but it would be no surprise if he winds up among the ERA and strikeout leaders in the National League.
1997: Hermanson was traded by Florida to Montreal late in spring training after the Marlins had acquired him from San Diego in the off-season. Hermanson had been touted as the second coming of Goose Gossage since he was San Diego's first-round draft pick in 1994 but the Expos surprised everyone and made Hermanson a starter. It turned out to be a stroke of genius as Hermanson pitched great. He tired down the stretch

but that is no cause for alarm as he wasn't used to pitching so many innings.

1996: Hermanson spent the majority of the season closing for the Padres' Triple-A Las Vegas farm club and was ripped in a handful of appearances in San Diego. The Padres gave up on him at the end of the season, trading him to Florida for second baseman Quilvio Veras.

	W	SV	ERA	IP	H	BB	SO	B/I
1995 San Diego	3	0	6.82	31	35	22	19	1.80
1996 San Diego	1	0	8.56	13	18	4	11	1.67
1997 Montreal	8	0	3.70	158	134	66	136	1.26

HERNANDEZ, ELVIN - TR - b: 8/20/77

Hernandez was the Pirates' top minor-league pitcher in 1996, posting more wins (17) than walks (16) with lower Class A Augusta. The Pirates jumped him to Double-A Carolina last season and that proved to be mistake. Hernandez, whose pitching arsenal is below average, couldn't survive just by changing speeds at a higher level. Worse yet, the 19-year old's confidence was shaken. Hernandez still has a chance but one wonders if he can overcome the psychological ramifications of a horrible year.

HERNANDEZ, FERNANDO - TR - b: 6/16/71

In his first year with the Tigers organization, Hernandez worked at Triple-A Toledo and pitched in two games in the majors for Detroit. He struck out 98 in 76 2/3 innings at Toledo but in his big league performances he faced 13 batters allowing nine to get on and posting a 40.50 ERA.

HERNANDEZ, LIVAN - TR - b: 2/20/75

Scouting: This has to be one the most poignant storybook dramas in modern baseball history. The kid leaves Cuba, eats lots of burgers, then gets in shape, anchors a rotation, and becomes a World Series MVP in front of his mother on her first day on American soil. The guy's got substance, to boot. He throws a mid-90's fastball, and has uncanny precision with his curveball and changeup. He's a horse at 6'2", 220 pounds, and has the intent and ability to finish what he starts. He needs to tone down his temper and throw strike one more consistently. He might take baby steps backwards in the short term, but he's a star for the long-term.

1998: Hernandez will own a rotation spot from day one, and should hold it. The expectations will be much higher, and it will be interesting to see how Hernandez deals with the inevitable struggles he will encounter as the league adjusts to him. Before long, he will be the Marlins' number one starter, and could be truly special.

1997: Hernandez was unremarkable in an early season Triple-A stint, and then dominated in the majors, winning his first nine decisions. His September struggles have seemingly been forgotten. He only started in the post-season that he ruled because of Alex Fernandez' injury.

1996: After his much ballyhooed signing, he ate himself out of shape, and struggled with his control and mechanics at Double-A Portland. By season's end, however, he began to show flashes of brilliance at Triple-A Charlotte.

	W	SV	ERA	IP	H	BB	SO	B/I
1997 Florida	9	0	3.18	96	81	38	72	1.24

HERNANDEZ, ROBERTO - TR - b: 11/11/64

Scouting: After Hernandez clocks in near 100 MPH with his fastball, his splitter is even more deadly, and he also boasts a fine slider. He obviously throws hard, and has good command of his pitches, so he is hard to hit. He has really learned to pitch, rather than try to get a strikeout against every batter.

1998: Hernandez and Rod Beck were both free agents after the 1997 season, but there was only room for one of them (or neither, after Robb Nen's arrival) in the Giants' bullpen — and their budget. Hernandez went to the expansion Devil Rays as a key free-agent signing. He is a top-flight reliever in his prime, capable of being an ace closer for years.

1997: Joining the Giants for the stretch, Hernandez gave some necessary relief to a bullpen that needed a boost for the last couple of months. Hernandez was the right tonic, setting up Beck and nailing an occasional save. He shared the closer job over the last week of the season, and his command was deadly, as the Giants clinched.

1996: Hernandez led American League relievers in ERA and games finished (61) as he rebounded from a couple of down years as the White Sox' closer. He got off to a red-hot start by converting his first fifteen save chances and also not allowing a run in April. Hernandez tired down the stretch and permitted 10 of his 18 earned runs for the season in the last month. His 122 saves since 1993 were second best in the American League over that four-year span.

	W	SV	ERA	IP	H	BB	SO	B/I
1995 Chicago AL	3	32	3.92	59	63	28	84	1.54
1996 Chicago AL	6	38	1.91	84	65	38	85	1.22
1997 two teams	10	31	2.45	81	67	38	82	1.30

HERNANDEZ, SANTOS - TR - b: 11/3/72

Plucked from the Giants' system by Tampa Bay with the final pick of the second round of the expansion draft, Hernandez has a good split-finger pitch that helped him get a midseason promotion in 1997. His fastball is nothing special, but the Devil Rays believe he has enough to get batters out, if he can throw the splitter for strike one. Hernandez had a 2.30 ERA in 11 games for Double-A Shreveport after moving up from Class A San Jose last year.

HERNANDEZ, XAVIER - TR - b: 8/16/65

Scouting: Hernandez' best pitch is a split-fingered fastball, and when healthy he can hit 90 on the radar gun. Maybe it's coincidence, but Hernandez has generally pitched well for the Astros and poorly for every other team.

1998: With his health in doubt, it's wait and see for Hernandez in 1998; he may not be ready for opening day. If healthy, he could contribute as a middle reliever.

1997: Hernandez never got into a groove, at least partly because of worsening pain in his right shoulder. His velocity was down, and he lost command of his pitches. Hernandez began the season as the primary set-up man for John Wetteland, but found himself in middle relief for most of the year. Hernandez' season ended early with rotator cuff surgery.

1996: After being traded back to the Astros in May, Hernandez won five and saved six as a set-up man for Houston.

	W	SV	ERA	IP	H	BB	SO	B/I
1995 Cincinnati	7	3	4.60	90	95	31	84	1.40
1996 Houston	5	6	4.62	78	77	28	81	1.35
1997 Texas	0	0	4.56	49	51	22	36	1.48

HERSHISER, OREL - TR - b: 9/16/58

Scouting: Hershiser once retired hitters with stuff; now he does it with change of speed and location, plus a healthy dose of mental dexterity. He is a sinker/slider pitcher with only average velocity at this stage in his career, but he consistently throws quality strikes, keeps hitters off balance, and excels at the little things, like holding runners on base. The Indians have thrived behind him; he has a 45-21 record in three seasons despite a cumulative ERA over 4.00.

1998: Hershiser is now basically a six-inning pitcher, having completed only one game in each of the last four seasons. His performance is about to hit a steep decline, and 1998 could be the year. The Indians dynasty that never was appears to be petering out, and Hershiser simply will not pitch well without the chance for a post-season payoff.

1997: Hershiser was a more aggressive hurler than in 1996, and allowed a career-high 26 homers as a result. However, most of them were solo shots, as Hershiser generally fared well with men on base. He had a stabilizing effect on the young Indian hurlers that surrounded him in the rotation.

1996: Hershiser allowed 238 hits in 206 innings, but his excellent control and intestinal fortitude allowed him to emerge with an ERA below league average. However, that mark was artificially low, as he allowed an unusually high 18 unearned runs.

	W	SV	ERA	IP	H	BB	SO	B/I
1995 Cleveland	16	0	3.87	167	151	51	111	1.21
1996 Cleveland	15	0	4.24	206	238	58	125	1.44
1997 Cleveland	14	0	4.47	195	199	69	107	1.37

HIBBARD, GREG - TL - b: 9/13/64

Hibbard had shoulder surgery back in April of 1995; it acted up and put him on the shelf in March last year. He was released by the Mariners in October.

HILL, JASON - TL - b: 4/14/72

Scouting: At 5'11" and 175 pounds, Hill isn't big, but he may well have a big future in the Angels' organization. He's a couple years away from making it to the major leagues, but the Angels already have their eye on him and are excited about his future. Hill has an average fastball, but an above-average slider that makes up for any lack of velocity. He's also learned a great deal about the science of pitching and has been compared favorably with Mike Holtz, another little lefthander who gets big results in the majors.

1998: Hill needs to show the Angels brass he's ready to make the jump from Class A Lake Elsinore to Triple-A ball, at which point, he could be only a few injuries away from the major leagues. It's more likely he'll be sent to Double-A Midland because the Angels don't want to rush him, but the club also isn't afraid to dip into the Double-A ranks for pitching help when the need arises. Hill could get to the majors this year.

1997: Hill was Lake Elsinore's closer with a staff-leading 15 saves and showed his slider is good enough to get him out of tough situations.

1996: Hill pitched mostly in middle relief as he made the jump from lower Class A to Lake Elsinore. His 2.50 ERA in 32 games turned some heads and elevated his status as a prospect.

HILL, KEN - TR - b: 12/14/65

Scouting: He struggled for much of the year with Texas, but the veteran righthander regained the form that made him one of the National League's most consistent pitchers after being traded to the Angels in late July. Hill made some mechanical adjustments with the help of pitching coach Marcel Lachemann that restored his fastball and curveball to their earlier effectiveness.

1998: Hill just has to show up in spring training to become, at the minimum, the Angels' number two starter. Their rotation will be built around Hill, Chuck Finley and Jason Dickson.

1997: Hill was hampered early when he was struck in the side with a line drive and never regained his former effectiveness with the Rangers. When Texas dropped out of the division race in early July, he became expendable, especially considering the fact he had the opportunity to become a free agent after the World Series. He also struggled early with the Angels, but Lachemann changed his arm angle and Hill become the Angels' most consistent starter the last four weeks of the season.

1996: As the Rangers won a division championship, Hill was their most consistent starter, tying for the staff lead in victories, and leading the staff in starts, (35), shutouts (three) and innings pitched. He continued the tradition of solid seasons he had established in St. Louis and Montreal.

	W	SV	ERA	IP	H	BB	SO	B/I
1995 St. Louis	6	0	5.06	110	125	45	50	1.54
1995 Cleveland	4	0	3.98	74	77	32	48	1.46
1996 Texas	16	0	3.63	250	250	95	170	1.38
1997 Anaheim	9	0	4.55	190	194	95	106	1.52

HINCHCLIFFE, BRETT - TR - b: 7/21/74

Hinchcliffe advanced to Double-A Memphis in the Mariners' organization in 1997, the first time in his six-year career he has reached that level. He doesn't have an overpowering fastball and gave up more than a hit per inning. He was second on the staff in innings and starts, and led the club with five complete games. He is expected to advance to Triple-A sometime this year and has a good chance to make the majors in the next few seasons.

HINES, RICH - TL - b: 5/20/69

Hines spent seven years in the Yankees' organization and wound up in the Braves' farm system at Double-A Greenville in 1997. He was 4-0 in 41 appearances out of the bullpen but he was not as effective as his record indicates. He had a high ERA and allowed over a hit per inning. Hines will more than likely spend the rest of his career as a minor-league journeyman reliever.

HITCHCOCK, STERLING - TL - b: 4/29/71

Scouting: Hitchcock has an excellent cut fastball, but the Padres don't like him using it and believe his stint on the disabled list last summer with elbow tendinitis was caused by throwing the cutter. He's tough when he has location and change of speeds working for him. Hitchcock usually has excellent control.

1998: On many staffs, he'd be the fourth or fifth starter, but is number three in San Diego.

1997: Acquired from Seattle in an off-season trade for pitcher Scott Sanders, Hitchcock averaged only five innings per outing with a high ERA. He allowed a staff-high 24 homers and opponents hit .276 against him.

1996: Hitchcock led the Mariners and established career-highs in wins, starts (35), innings pitched and strikeouts.

	W	SV	ERA	IP	H	BB	SO	B/I
1995 New York AL	11	0	4.70	168	155	68	121	1.33
1996 Seattle	13	0	5.35	196	245	73	132	1.62
1997 San Diego	10	0	5.20	161	172	55	106	1.41

HOFFMAN, TREVOR - TR - b: 10/13/67

Scouting: Hoffman is one of the National League's premier closers. His fastball/changeup combination is usually enough, but he has a four-pitch repertoire. The Padres actually believe he could be a great starter, but he loves the stopper role. Unlike most closers, he has the durability to go as long as three innings when rested.
1998: Hoffman is entrenched in his role as one of the Padres' franchise players.
1997: Opponents hit .200 against Hoffman last year and he averaged 12.3 strikeouts per nine innings.
1996: Hoffman established career-bests in wins, ERA, strikeouts, and appearances (70). Opponents hit a league-low .161 against him and he averaged 11.4 strikeouts per nine innings.

	W	SV	ERA	IP	H	BB	SO	B/I
1995 San Diego	7	31	3.88	53	48	14	52	1.17
1996 San Diego	9	42	2.25	88	50	31	111	0.92
1997 San Diego	6	37	2.66	81	59	24	111	1.02

HOLDRIDGE, DAVID - TR - b: 2/5/69

Holdridge had bounced around the Philadelphia and Anaheim farm systems for nine seasons before appearing at both Double-A Memphis and Triple-A Tacoma in the Mariners' organization last year. He throws hard but is erratic. He's running out of chances at his age to earn a relief spot in the majors.

HOLLINS, STACY - TR - b: 7/31/72

Hollins worked the bulk of the year at Double-A Hunstville, starting 17 games and pitching another 15 from the bullpen. He then went to Edmonton and appeared in one more game, as a starter. His biggest enemy is poor control. Hollins walked 72 against 68 strikeouts over his 114 innings at Hunstville. If he doesn't get a handle on it, he'll never advance.

HOLMAN, CRAIG - TR - b: 3/13/69

For the last four years, Holman has served as a bullpen denizen and spot starter in the high minors for the Phillies. He has just an average fastball which is often too much over the plate. Because he has a durable arm, Holman can pitch a lot and on consecutive days. It makes him a useful bullpen pitcher, but not a good prospect for major league advancement.

HOLMES, DARREN - TR - b: 4/25/66

Scouting: Holmes has three quality, big-league pitches — fastball, slider/curve and changeup. He is known for his big breaking ball. He has pitched in a variety of roles for the Rockies, though he is clearly most effective in the middle innings — where he least likes to be. If he had a little better command, he'd be a dominant reliever, but he tends to fall behind hitters, particularly to the first two or three he faces.
1998: After spending five consecutive years with the expansion Rockies, Holmes was allowed free agency and was not expected to be re-signed in Colorado.
1997: Holmes entered spring training trying to win a spot in the rotation for the first time in his seven big-league seasons. Though he didn't make the rotation, the stamina he built up helped him get off to a quick start out of the bullpen. He did have a memorable big-league starting debut, outdueling defending Cy Young Award winner John Smoltz in a 6-1 win against the Braves. Holmes didn't pitch well in the final three months.
1996: Holmes struggled in save situations early; he was moved to the set-up role and was outstanding in the second-half, posting a 3-1 record and 2.29 ERA after the All-Star break.

	W	SV	ERA	IP	H	BB	SO	B/I
1995 Colorado	6	14	3.24	66	59	28	61	1.31
1996 Colorado	5	1	3.97	77	78	28	73	1.38
1997 Colorado	9	3	5.34	89	113	36	70	1.67

HOLT, CHRIS - TR - b: 9/18/71

Scouting: Holt was one of the top rookie pitchers in 1997 in a year of many successful rookie pitchers. He was in Houston's rotation all season and pitched much better than indicated by his won-loss record. His best pitch is a sinking fastball and he also has good command of a four-seam fastball, a slider and a curve. He is not overpowering but has always had good control. In his five years in the minor leagues, he allowed more than a hit per inning but he struck out 7.0 batters per nine innings while walking only 2.0.
1998: Holt has established himself as a major league starting pitcher and should be able to improve on his 1997 record. He is not likely to be a staff ace in his career.
1997: Holt pitched well enough to have won at least nine more games with reasonable run support.
1996: Holt's second year at Triple-A Tucson was a good one with a 9-6 record and an ERA of 3.62, sixth best in the Pacific Coast League. He led the league in innings pitched and was second in strikeouts. He made his major league debut in September with four relief appearances for Houston.

	W	SV	ERA	IP	H	BB	SO	B/I
1997 Houston	8	0	3.52	210	211	61	95	1.30

HOLTZ, MIKE - TL - b: 10/10/72

Scouting: Holtz originally thought someone was playing a joke on him when he was told he was being called up from Double-A Midland at the All-Star break in 1996. Since then, the joke has largely been on the opposition. The 5'9", 175-pounder has an above-average fastball and slider, and excellent command, which makes him perfect for the role as lefthanded stopper. He's pitched well against some of the top lefty hitters in the league, but has also done well against righthanded hitters in key situations. He's cool under fire to a degree that's unusual for a youngster, and he's fearless.
1998: It's doubtful the Angels will want to change Holtz' role because he's been so effective as a lefthanded specialist. Manager Terry Collins will be reluctant to tamper with such a valuable commodity.
1997: Holtz rarely pitched more than an inning at a time and was extremely effective in giving the opposition only brief looks at him. Holtz established himself as a top prospect the season before and, if anything, only enhanced that status.
1996: Holtz' numbers were largely unimpressive at Midland (1-2, 4.17 ERA in 33 games), but he earned a sudden callup with his ability to throw hard and with his mental makeup. Once he made it to the major leagues, his career took off.

	W	SV	ERA	IP	H	BB	SO	B/I
1996 California	3	0	2.45	29	21	19	31	1.37
1997 Anaheim	3	2	3.33	43	38	15	40	1.22

HOLZEMER, MARK - TL - b: 8/20/69

Scouting: Holzemer has shown good control and didn't give up a lot of hits in the minors but he's had trouble carrying over that success when he has faced big-league hitters. He's not

overpowering and has had shoulder problems in the past.
1998: Being a lefty with good control, Holzemer will get a chance to fill a spot in somebody's bullpen with a good showing in spring training.
1997: Holzemer pitched nine innings for the Mariners but spent most of the season at Triple-A Tacoma in the Pacific Coast League where he was effective. He racked up 13 saves in 37 appearances and struck out nearly four hitters for each walk.
1996: Holzemer started the season on the Angels' major league roster for the first time in his career. He went on the disabled list with shoulder problems and was released late in the season.

HONEYCUTT, RICK - TL - b: 6/19/54
The veteran started last season as the oldest player in the big leagues, but quickly passed that distinction on to teammate Dennis Eckersley. Honeycutt pitched only two innings all year, never even making it to a full rehab assignment thanks to an arm injury that eventually required surgery and led to the announcement of his retirement at the end of the season.

	W	SV	ERA	IP	H	BB	SO	B/I
1995 two teams	5	2	2.96	45	39	10	21	1.08
1996 St. Louis	2	4	2.85	47	42	7	30	1.04

HOOK, CHRIS - TR - b: 8/4/68
Hook pitched in the majors with the Giants in 1995 and '96. During that stint he showed he was a situational lefty, at best, who held lefthanders to a .210 average but was clubbed by righthanders. Last year he pitched Triple-A ball in the Padres' organization and then Double-A for the Angels. He gave no indication at either stop of being ready to return to the bigs.

HOPE, JOHN - TR - b: 12/21/70
Hope has been to the majors three different times, his last trial was as a starter with the Pirates in 1996 and it was not a success. He pitched with the Rockies' organization last year at Triple-A Colorado Springs. He started ten games, made 48 total appearances and did nothing to show he deserves another crack at the big leagues. 115 hits surrendered and 65 walks in 99.2 innings are not numbers put up by a pitcher returning to the show.

HOSTETLER, MIKE - TR - b: 6/5/70
Overcoming elbow ligament replacement in his right arm, Hostetler has made steady progress, reaching Triple-A Richmond in 1996, where he went 11-9 with a 4.38 ERA and a 2-to-1 strikeout-to-walk ratio. Hostetler pitched only five games in 1997.

HOWRY, BOBBY - TR - b: 8/4/73
Howry moved into the closer job at Double-A Shreveport last year, with moderate success. He did save 22 games, but his 6-3 record and 4.91 ERA didn't spell relief. More telling, 58 hits allowed over 55 innings doesn't point toward a strikeout when needed. The question Howry and the Giants must answer is whether he is a reliever or a starter.

HUBBS, DAN - TR - b: 1/23/71
The former University of Southern California star has done a solid job everywhere he's been. Hubbs may be poised to make a run at the major leagues on the basis of his good overall command. Hubbs doesn't have a dominating fastball, but he's a strikeout pitcher nonetheless. The Dodgers like his durability and desire.

HUBER, JEFF - TL - b: 12/17/70
Huber spent the 1996 season in A-ball and pitched at the Double-A and Triple-A levels of the Brewers' organization last year. In his seventh minor-league season in '97, Huber's Triple-A appearance was his first at that level and he struggled, giving up more than a hit per inning and having problems with control. Huber may have a tough time staying at Triple-A let alone advancing to the majors.

HUDEK, JOHN - TR - b: 8/8/66
Scouting: Hudek is the only pitcher to appear in an All-Star game before recording his first major league win. That was in 1994 when he came up to Houston early in the season and dominated as a closer. He has not had any significant major league success since then. He is basically a one-pitch pitcher and his one pitch, a 96-mph fastball, has not been the same since surgery in 1995. He has lost a little off the pitch, which doesn't have much movement, and he has struggled with his control. He has become a marginal major league pitcher.
1998: Hudek needs to reestablish himself as a major league pitcher in 1998. It will probably be his last chance.
1997: Hudek opened the season as a co-closer with Billy Wagner. He didn't perform well and spent the season on a shuttle between Houston and Triple-A New Orleans. He was dominating at New Orleans with an ERA of 0.44 and seven saves; he allowed only three hits and three walks in 20.2 innings while striking out 26. However, at Houston he had 33 walks and 36 strikeouts in 40.2 innings and was not on the post-season roster.
1996: Hudek had difficulty recovering from his 1995 surgery and suffered neck and rib injuries which kept him out of action for the first half of the season. He spent part of the season at Triple-A Tucson where he was 1-0, with a 3.10 ERA and four saves before coming up to Houston in late-August and finishing strong.

	W	SV	ERA	IP	H	BB	SO	B/I
1995 Houston	2	7	5.40	20	19	5	29	1.20
1996 Houston	2	2	2.81	16	12	5	14	1.06
1997 Houston	1	4	5.97	41	38	33	36	1.74

HUDSON, JOE - TR - b: 9/29/70
Scouting: Hudson has just an average fastball and below-average slider, so he lives and dies with how much sink he gets out of his fastball and how much he throws strikes. He's been erratic in both regards so far; Hudson doesn't have the stuff to close or start games.
1998: Hudson should find a home in a big-league bullpen somewhere, although it appears the Red Sox have seen him fail too many times to make it their pen.
1997: Hudson bounced between the majors and minors again, although this time he finally enjoyed some success at the big-league level. Still, the Red Sox hesitated to use him often or in tight situations.
1996: Hudson struggled with his control both in the majors and in Triple-A, but got away with it more in Pawtucket.

	W	SV	ERA	IP	H	BB	SO	B/I
1995 Boston	0	1	4.11	46	53	23	29	1.65
1996 Boston	3	1	5.40	45	57	32	19	1.98
1997 Boston	3	0	3.53	36	39	14	14	1.48

HUISMAN, RICK - TR - b: 5/17/69
Huisman throws a low-90s fastball with little movement and lacks command of any other pitch. He had a good year for Triple-A Omaha in 1997 (3.62 ERA, 57 strikeouts in 59.2 innings) but walked too many hitters and was notably ignored when the Royals were desperately holding open tryouts for their major league bullpen. He's not high on the Royals' list of relief prospects.

	W	SV	ERA	IP	H	BB	SO	B/I
1996 Kansas City	2	1	4.60	29	25	18	23	1.48

HUNTER, RICH - TR - b: 9/25/74
Scouting: Hunter has a mid-80s fastball and a sneaky group of breaking pitches featuring a changeup that is devastating when it's working. When Hunter is on, he will throw strike one on the black with any of his pitches, keeping the hitter off balance before finally putting him away on a weak grounder. That pitching style helped him go 19-2 at three minor-league stops in 1995. It pushed him through the Phillies' farm system too quickly, however, and he has struggled for much of the last two years.
1998: Hunter's success at the end of last year gives him a chance to be in the majors again this year. He should be a regular Triple-A starter for the Phillies, and will be near the top of a short list of recall possibilities as the season unwinds. Hunter will never blow anyone away, but when he is making his pitches, he is a bonafide major league starter.
1997: Early in the season, Hunter fell behind hitters and had to come into the strike zone with just an average fastball; he was hit hard and gave up some long homers. Beginning in August, though, he found his command again and was brilliant the rest of the way.
1996: Hunter's spring training brilliance allowed him to break camp with the Phillies. He pitched well early, but lost his confidence in April and began to nibble at the corners. He settled down at Double-A Reading, and pitched well in some September major league starts.

	W	SV	ERA	IP	H	BB	SO	B/I
1996 Philadelphia	3	0	6.49	69	84	33	32	1.69

HUNTSMAN, SCOTT - TR - b: 10/28/72
Huntsman was used strictly out of the pen in his first season of Double-A ball at El Paso in the Milwaukee organization. He found it much tougher going than at Class A Stockton where he had 12 saves in 1996. Huntsman was hit with regularity in 42 appearances and his strikeout-to-walk ratio suffered as well. He will have to improve in both areas to advance.

HURST, BILL - TR - b: 4/28/70
Observers overlooked Hurst's obvious control deficiencies in 1996 as he notched 30 saves at Double-A Portland in the Marlins' chain. It should not have come as a surprise when he allowed 61 baserunners in 29 Triple-A innings last year, 22 on walks. He has now walked over six batters per nine innings in his career. The big (6'7") righthander throws hard, and his deceptive motion is tough on righthanded hitters, but his command problems will likely never be rectified. If he were a lefty, he'd get more chances; instead, he may have reached the end.

HURTADO, EDWIN - TR - b: 2/1/70
Scouting: Hurtado was acquired in Seattle's 1995 trade with Toronto that also brought Paul Menhart for Bill Risley and Miguel Cairo — a deal that has benefitted no one because of serious injuries to most of the players involved. Hurtado, not an overpowering thrower, had bone chips removed from his right elbow in 1996.
1998: Hurtado is another contender for the major league rotation in Seattle, although there are precious few openings available and better candidates ahead of him.
1997: Hurtado returned from 1996 elbow surgery to win a career-high ten games at Triple-A Tacoma, where he had five complete games and three shutouts. Hurtado showed good command; he struck out 100 in 132.1 innings, with just 37 walks.
1996: Hurtado memorized the I-5 route from Tacoma to Seattle, winning with the Mariners in relief on opening night. He stopped in each place twice before season-ending elbow surgery late in July. Hurtado was 1-2 with a 3.73 ERA at Tacoma in five games (four starts), but was hit hard in the majors, going 2-5 with a 7.74 ERA in 16 games (four starts). After his recovery from elbow surgery, Hurtado pitched well in the Venezuelan winter league.

	W	SV	ERA	IP	H	BB	SO	B/I
1995 Toronto	5	0	5.45	77	81	40	33	1.56
1996 Seattle	2	2	7.74	47	61	30	36	1.93
1997 Seattle	1	0	9.00	19	25	15	10	2.11

HURTADO, VICTOR - TL - b: 6/14/77
Hurtado had established himself as a promising starting pitching prospect as a teenager at lower Class A Kane County in 1996, but suffered through an injury-shortened season last year. He only reaches the mid-80's with his fastball, and requires pinpoint precision on the corners of the plate to be effective. His pitches caught too much of the plate at higher Class A Brevard County in 1997, where he was an easy mark. He will likely need to return there this year, and must refine his mechanics to add movement so that he can get the ball past hitters at that classification before progressing upward.

HUTTON, MARK - TR - b: 2/6/70
Scouting: Hutton sure looks the part of a power pitcher, with his 6'6", 240-pound build and 90-MPH fastball. However, the lack of movement on his pitches has limited him to only 108 strikeouts in 172.2 career major league innings. To make matters worse, he doesn't have the stamina to start in the majors, or the control to be an effective reliever. His ability to keep the ball low in the strike zone gives him a fighting chance to survive in a middle-relief role in Colorado.
1998: You can never have enough hard-throwing middle relievers when you play your home games at Coors Field. At this point, most people have finally given up on the illusion that Hutton could develop into a frontline major leaguer - in fact, he must become much more precise to maintain a lesser major league role.
1997: Hutton began the season as a middle reliever with the Marlins before being traded to the Rockies. The most disappointing aspect of his season was his inability to retire righthanded hitters; they hit .353 against him.
1996: Hutton raised the Marlins' hopes with a series of successful late-season starts after being acquired from the Yankees for David Weathers. Even then, he showed a maddening inability to get his plus fastball past hitters. He held righthanders to a .223 batting average.

	W	SV	ERA	IP	H	BB	SO	B/I
1996 New York AL	0	0	5.04	30	32	18	25	1.66
1996 Florida	5	0	3.67	56	47	18	31	1.16
1997 Colorado	3	0	4.48	60	72	26	39	1.63

IGLESIAS, MIKE - TR - b: 11/9/72

The fifth player the Dodgers chose in 1991, Iglesias has made slow progress, but he's regularly shown flashes of being able to compete in the major leagues. Iglesias' progress has been slower than some, but the Dodgers haven't given up on him because of his superior arm. In 1998, Iglesias needs to show signs of putting everything together to remain on the prospect list.

IRABU, HIDEKI - TR - b: 5/5/69

Scouting: If the Yankees can get Irabu's head on straight and his body in shape, there is enough raw talent to work with him. While his fastball isn't as high powered as advertised, it has enough life to be effective. His split-fingered fastball is above average but his changeup isn't effective. Irabu is poor in fielding his position and holding base-runners. His mental makeup has been frequently questioned when he has often displayed boorish behavior on the mound during games.
1998: Despite a disastrous pitching line for Irabu in his first year in the majors, the Yankees remain hopeful that their $12.8 million investment pans out. Some are convinced that Irabu — with the benefit of a full spring training — can move as high as third in the starting rotation.
1997: Injuries were the only roadblock Irabu didn't run into in his first year out of Japan. Hitters sat on a straight fastball and made him throw his splitter for strikes. His first year in America started in Class A Tampa, then he moved to Double-A Norwich and also had two stints at Triple-A Columbus. He proved he could get minor-league hitters out but failed to dominate anybody except the Tigers in the big leagues.
1996: Irabu's record in Japan was amazingly similar to that produced by Mets' castoff Eric Hillman.

ISRINGHAUSEN, JASON - TR - b: 9/7/72

Scouting: Memories of his 1995 performance — 9-2 record and 2.81 ERA —linger. Whether or not Isringhausen still has the same high ceiling is a point of conjecture. In the two seasons since then, he has been regularly unable to spot his fastball or throw his killer curveball for strikes. That is a lethal combination working against him. In '95, he was so locked in he performed with the confidence of a five-time 20-game winner. His confidence is lagging now.
1998: Isringhausen will have every opportunity to pitch in the rotation at the outset of the season and to become the starter the club envisioned in 1995. But he will begin the season at the back of the rotation. If he fails, it would be a damaging blow to the organization.
1997: The season was all but a waste for Isringhausen. He began the season in Triple-A after undergoing two surgeries (elbow and shoulder) in September, 1996. Then he broke bones in his right wrist in a fit of anger following a poor start. Tuberculosis was diagnosed in early May. He made three starts with two Class A teams after he recovered and before he was promoted to the major leagues for an August 27th start. He hardly was a phenom upon his return to the big leagues in his six starts. Righthanded hitters batted .300 against him; lefthanders batted .362. His ERA was more indicative of his work than was his won/lost record.
1996: With unrealistic expectations facing him at every turn, Isringhausen fell to the occasion and was clobbered unrelentingly. Injuries repaired in two September surgeries played a part, as did the absence of confidence. He waited for bad things to happen — and they did.

	W	SV	ERA	IP	H	BB	SO	B/I
1995 New York NL	9	0	2.81	93	88	31	55	1.28
1996 New York NL	6	0	4.77	171	190	73	114	1.54
1997 New York NL	2	0	7.58	30	40	22	25	2.09

JACKSON, DANNY - TL - b: 1/5/62

Bouts with thyroid cancer coupled with ankle and arm injuries diminished the edge on Jackson's fastball and slider. He was hit hard after his trade from St. Louis to San Diego and retired midway through the 1997 season. Jackson was a veteran of several playoff teams for different organizations over his 14-year major league career.

	W	SV	ERA	IP	H	BB	SO	B/I
1995 St. Louis	2	0	5.90	100	120	48	52	1.68
1996 St. Louis	1	0	4.46	36	33	16	27	1.36
1997 San Diego	2	0	7.58	68	98	28	32	1.86

JACKSON, MIKE - TR - b: 12/22/64

Scouting: Jackson has closer's stuff, but has been unable to claim a closer's role for any length of time during his career. He dominates righthanded hitters (.153 average in 1997) with a 90-MPH fastball and a biting slider, both of which he throws to the corners of the plate consistently. The hits he does allow usually come in bunches. He seems to relax and pitch his best baseball in a set-up role.
1998: Jackson will likely return to his set-up role on a full-time basis. His velocity has held up well as he has aged, and he clearly remains the number one righthanded option out of the Tribe's pen.
1997: Jackson started the season as the Indians' closer due to Jose Mesa's off-field problems, and fared well during the first half. Jackson's second-half fade coincided with a Mesa surge, and the Indians played their best baseball once Jackson regrouped in his set-up role. Breakdowns by Eric Plunk and Paul Shuey made Jackson an invaluable mid-to-late-inning resource.
1996: The Mariners can blame quite a bit of their 1997 bullpen failures on their inability to retain Jackson's services. Jackson was a dominating set-up man for them in 1996, striking out a batter per inning, though his overall numbers were undermined by the 11 homers he allowed in 72 innings.

	W	SV	ERA	IP	H	BB	SO	B/I
1995 Cincinnati	6	2	2.39	49	38	19	41	1.16
1996 Seattle	1	6	3.63	72	61	24	70	1.18
1997 Cleveland	2	15	3.24	75	59	29	74	1.17

JACOBS, RYAN - TL - b: 2/3/74

Jacobs has a four-pitch repertoire — fastball, change, slider and curve —but has not shown the ability to throw any one of them effectively over the past two seasons. He followed up a 3-9, 6.68 season in 1996 with a 1-8, 7.21 showing at Double-A Greenville in the Braves' organization. He made nine starts last year after making 46 in the previous two seasons. He's only 23 years old and the Braves are not starved for immediate pitching help which may buy Jacobs some time to develop. But a repeat of the last two seasons this year could end his chances of becoming a prospect for Atlanta.

JACOBSEN, JOE - TR - b: 1/2/6/71
Jacobsen's stock soared after a 34-save season at higher Class A Vero Beach in the Dodgers' chain in 1995, which caused him to be selected in the Rule 5 draft despite the fact that he was a 23-year-old who had not yet reached Double-A ball. Now in the Marlins' system, he has backslid into a deep Double-A bullpen role. He has only an average fastball, and places the ball poorly within the strike zone. He has no upward mobility, and is likely approaching the end of his pro career.

JACOME, JASON - TL - b: 11/24/70
Scouting: Jacome arguably has the slowest fastball of any current major league pitcher, usually clocking in at below 85 MPH. He has endured as a major leaguer because he is lefthanded, and possesses above-average control, usually placing a variety of pitches low in the strike zone. He has a resilient arm which allows him to be used interchangeably as a starter and reliever, with little advance notice of a role change required.
1998: The Indians need a second lefty reliever in the bullpen, and Jacome has an outside chance to win that job. Even if he doesn't, there are other clubs with an even more pronounced need in that area. Jacome can be a useful eleventh man on a pitching staff when he's locating his pitches well, but has no chance of ever playing a front-line role in the majors.
1997: Jacome was used as a starter at Triple-A Buffalo, but exhibited just a five-inning arm. A rash of major league injuries briefly forced him into the Indians' rotation, and then into a situational bullpen role. His location was poor again in 1997, and resulted in a weak ratio of ten homers allowed in 49.1 major league innings.
1996: Jacome blew what will likely go down as his best shot to win a material major league role, allowing 89 baserunners in 48 innings as a Royals' situational lefty. He left too many batting practice fastballs up in the strike zone.

	W	SV	ERA	IP	H	BB	SO	B/I
1995 New York NL	0	0	10.29	21	33	15	11	2.29
1995 Kansas City	4	0	5.36	84	101	21	39	1.45
1996 Kansas City	0	1	4.72	47	67	22	32	1.89
1997 Cleveland	2	0	5.84	49	58	20	27	1.58

JAMES, MIKE - TR - b: 8/15/67
Scouting: James has a good fastball and has developed good command of same the last couple of years, which has taken him from career prospect to an important bullpen role in the major leagues. His status as a key set-up man has been tarnished recently due to recurring elbow problems.
1998: James will have to show he's fully recovered from the elbow problems. Making the staff won't be a big problem, but James will likely need a good spring to win back his former job as the primary table setter for Troy Percival.
1997: James had a strong start and even performed well in the closer's role when Percival was out with shoulder problems at the start of the season. After recurring elbow soreness forced him off the roster for four weeks at the All-Star break, he wasn't the same pitcher. By the time he returned, opportunities to get back in top form were few because the Angels were embroiled in a pennant race and manager Terry Collins was reluctant to tinker with a bullpen that was performing well.

prospect to set-up man. He was able to seize the opportunity when Percival supplanted Lee Smith as the closer and the Angels were searching for another set-up man.

	W	SV	ERA	IP	H	BB	SO	B/I
1995 California	3	1	3.88	55	49	26	36	1.36
1996 California	5	1	2.67	81	62	42	65	1.28
1997 Anaheim	5	7	4.31	63	69	28	57	1.55

JANICKI, PETE - TR - b: 1/26//71
Scouting: So far, injuries have derailed the career of the Angels' top choice in the 1992 June draft. Major elbow problems have kept the former UCLA star and promising righthander from fulfilling his potential, despite the tremendous courage he's shown and his battles to recover. Recurring health problems have kept Janicki on a one-step-forward, one-step-back pattern through his five seasons in the Angels' system. The Angels have been patient with Janicki, as he's hung in there himself, because of his potential and the flashes of brilliance he's shown. The time is probably coming when both the club and the pitcher will have to decide if his health is going to allow him to get to the major leagues after all.
1998: Janicki will have to show he's healthy enough to pitch a full season before any determination can be made about what level he is ready to conquer.
1997: Janicki had a tough year at Triple-A Vancouver with a 1-4 record and 7.80 ERA in 42 games, but was able to get the job done in spurts.
1996: Janicki shuttled between Double-A Midland and Vancouver, and had mixed success, but finished the season strong in Triple-A with one save and a 2.08 ERA in 17 appearances.

JANZEN, MARTY - TR - b: 5/31/73
Scouting: The main pitcher acquired in Toronto's David Cone trade with the Yankees, Janzen has a decent fastball to go with an overhand curve and a slider; his velocity peaks in the high-80s. Not overpowering, he needs to refine his breaking stuff.
1998: Even though it may be too soon for him, he'll probably work in the major league bullpen for the Diamondbacks, who drafted him with their final expansion pick. He has the stuff to be a starter when he gets more experience and better command.
1997: Janzen spent much of the year at Syracuse and was called to the majors at the end of July. He responded with an effective stint out of the bullpen, the best he has looked in his brief big-league career.
1996: Janzen was given plenty of major league innings as the Blue Jays searched for a fifth starter. He was knocked around to the tune of 95 hits and 16 home runs in 73.2 innings.

	W	SV	ERA	IP	H	BB	SO	B/I
1996 Toronto	4	0	7.33	73	95	38	47	1.82
1997 Toronto	2	0	3.60	25	23	13	17	1.44

JARVIS, KEVIN - TR - b: 8/1/69
Scouting: A hard thrower with a good breaking ball but inconsistent command, Jarvis always has pitching coaches thinking he can do better than he has done. The Tigers liked him enough that they first talked about trading for him, and later claimed him twice on waivers. But Jarvis still hasn't proven he can be a pitcher who can help the Tigers win.
1998: Some day, Jarvis may fulfill the potential scouts and pitching coaches have seen in him and become a dominant

pitcher. But while the Tigers hope for it, they're not counting on it.
1997: Jarvis began the year with Cincinnati, was claimed by the Tigers but not activated, was claimed by the Twins and then later claimed back by the Tigers. So it was an active year for a pitcher who went just 0-4.
1996: For the third straight year, Jarvis split time between the Reds and Triple-A Indianapolis. He started a career-high 20 games for the Reds, going 8-8 with a 6.15 ERA.

	W	SV	ERA	IP	H	BB	SO	B/I
1995 Cincinnati	3	0	5.70	79	91	32	33	1.56
1996 Cincinnati	8	0	5.98	120	152	43	63	1.62
1997 Detroit	0	1	7.68	68	99	29	48	1.88

JARVIS, MATT - TL - b: 2/22/72
After a 1996 season in which he did not get much of a chance in the Orioles' minor-league system, Jarvis was the premier relief pitcher for Double-A Arkansas in the Cardinals' farm system. He posted a 1.91 ERA in 80 innings pitched. However, he allowed a high number of baserunners due to too many walks.

JEAN, DOMINGO - TR - b: 1/9/69
This former Yankee phenom was converted to a closer by the Reds, and he led the Southern League in saves with 33 in 1996.

JERZEMBECK, MIKE - TR - b: 5/18/72
Jerzembeck made two stops on the Yankee's minor-league ladder in 1997 and was impressive at both levels. He has a major league fastball but needs to show better command in the strike zone to move up to the majors. He was 7-5 with a 3.59 ERA in 20 starts for Triple-A Columbus after going 2-1 with a 1.64 ERA in nine starts for Double-A Norwich.

JIMINEZ, MIGUEL - TR - b: 8/19/69
Highly touted a few years ago, Jiminez just doesn't seem to be able to develop. At age 28 he is far to old to not be dominant at Double-A. Since he was 7-6 with a 5.86 ERA at Huntsville in 1997, he's obviously not dominating. He's not likely to realize his potential.

JOHNS, DOUG - TL - b: 12/19/67
Scouting: Johns has below-average stuff, and he doesn't throw hard. He's a soft-tossing location pitcher, and judging from his record, he must frequently miss the preferred location.
1998: Given the shortage of pitchers, Johns could hook onto a rebuilding major league team to give them some innings until their rookies develop. With an ERA well over 5.00, he won't be effective.
1997: Johns was released by Oakland in mid-season last year, and signed by the Orioles to a Triple-A contract. It was a move to fill out the Triple-A roster because the Orioles farm system talent wasn't ready for promotions.
1996: In 1996, Johns won six games but gave up 187 hits in 158 innings; his major league record ran to 11-15 with a 5.63 ERA.

	W	SV	ERA	IP	H	BB	SO	B/I
1995 Oakland	5	0	4.61	54	44	26	25	1.29
1996 Oakland	6	1	5.98	158	187	69	71	1.62

JOHNSON, BARRY - TR - b: 8/21/69
This veteran has bounced around the minor leagues for seven seasons without getting a crack at the majors. The Pirates acquired Johnson from the White Sox in a minor-league trade midway through last season and sent him to Triple-A Calgary. It was more a case of the Pirates being short on pitching at their top farm club than them thinking he could ever help the major league club.

JOHNSON, DANE - TR - b: 2/10/63
Scouting: Johnson, who was the American Association pitcher of the year in 1994, has had a fine minor-league career as a closer. He saved 61 games over a three-year period (1994-96) at Nashville and Syracuse. He throws hard and has good control, but you have to wonder about pitchers who don't make a debut until they are 31 years old (he debuted for the White Sox in 1994).
1998: It is unlikely the A's, who are purging just about anyone over the age of 27, will retain the tenacious pitcher. Johnson isn't a major league closer, but he could be a serviceable set-up man on a pitching staff somewhere.
1997: Johnson filled the set-up role well enough, and even saved a couple of games. As the season wore on, his arm grew tired and Johnson spent time on the DL, and then in Triple-A Edmonton, where he saved six games.
1996: Johnson was plucked from the Blue Jays after a fine 1996 season primarily spent at Triple-A Syracuse (22 saves, 2.45). He is much like another Athletics pitcher in makeup - Billy Taylor in makeup. The Jays decided he was expendable at the end of 1996.

	W	SV	ERA	IP	H	BB	SO	B/I
1997 Oakland	4	2	4.53	46	49	31	43	1.75

JOHNSON, JASON - TR - b: 10/27/73
Scouting: Johnson was just a nondescript pitcher who had bounced around the Pirates' farm system for five seasons until he befriended Kris Benson last spring. Benson, the first overall pick in the 1996 draft, taught Johnson a curveball and it turned the Johnson's career around as he now has something to complement a 93-MPH fastball.
1998: An early expansion pick by Tampa Bay, Johnson will have a chance to make the staff as a long reliever, but they are more apt to use him as a starter in the minors to begin the year. His stock improved dramatically last season and a good performance in the minors will earn him time in the majors at some point this season.
1997: Johnson started the season at Class A Lynchburg, moved up to Double-A Carolina in June and then spent the final six weeks of the season in the Pirates' bullpen. It was quite a rapid rise for a pitcher who was not considered much of a prospect when last season began. He made only three relief appearances for the Pirates, who were engaged with Houston in a pennant race in the National League Central.
1996: Johnson split the season between the Pirates' two full-season Class A farm clubs, Lynchburg and Augusta, and also split time between the rotation and the bullpen. It was his fifth pro season without getting out of A-ball.

JOHNSON, JONATHAN - TR - b: 7/16/74
The Rangers' number-one pick in 1995 took a giant step backward last season, starting out at Triple-A Oklahoma City (1-8, 7.29 ERA) and then finishing at Double-A Tulsa (5-4,

3.52). The Rangers are hoping that a change in minor-league pitching coaches will help Johnson to get back on track as a top pitching prospect. He has a good fastball, and an above-average curve, but hasn't yet figured out how to handle Triple-A hitters.

JOHNSON, MIKE - TR - b: 10/3/75
Scouting: Johnson is a four-pitch guy with a sinking fastball, curveball, slider and changeup. He grew up in the cold climate of Edmonton, Alberta, Canada and still lacks the experience of most professional pitchers his age. However, Johnson showed pretty good control of his stuff in the minors and has earned rave reviews for his poise.
1998: Johnson jumped from low Class A to the major leagues last season and clearly wasn't ready for such a large leap. The Expos, though, feel Johnson is fairly close to being ready and plan to start him off at Triple-A Ottawa this season. He needs a full season in the minors, so he won't be seen again in Montreal until September or possibly until 1999.
1997: Johnson made Baltimore's opening day roster after being taken from Toronto in the Rule 5 Draft. The Orioles carried 12 pitches in an attempt to hide Johnson. However, coming to the conclusion they could no longer keep him on the major league roster in the middle of a pennant race and knowing the Blue Jays would take him back due to Rule 5 specifications, Baltimore traded him to Montreal in late-July. The Expos kept him around, despite ineffectiveness, looking for a larger payoff down the road.
1996: Johnson had a fine season with Toronto's low Class A Hagerstown farm club. Orioles General Manager Pat Gillick knew Johnson from his days with the Blue Jays and selected him in the Rule 5 draft despite his lack of experience.

JOHNSON, RANDY - TL - b: 9/10/63
Scouting: The Big Unit keeps posting strikeouts with a fastball that has been known to touch 100 and a slider that buckles the knees of the best lefthanded hitters in the game. No wonder All-Star jokester Larry Walker, like most lefties, is held out of Johnson's starts. Since 1993, Johnson is 75-20; he has lost just six games in the last three regular seasons and leads the majors in strikeouts by a wide margin during the 1990s.
1998: Johnson can be the top starter in the majors because he has the best stuff, but nagging injuries are a concern.
1997: Johnson posted his first 20-win season the final week of the season by pitching two innings of middle relief, but would have had it sooner if not for tendinitis in the middle finger of his pitching hand that caused him to miss four starts. He had 291 strikeouts — one behind league leader Roger Clemens — averaging 12.3 strikeouts every nine innings; Johnson was also second in the American League in ERA, behind Clemens.
1996: Season-long back discomfort was relieved when Johnson underwent surgery to repair a herniated disc September 12th. He was forced to leave an April start with back pain and was not himself all year; he gave up his first homer to a lefthanded hitter since 1992. Johnson was unbeaten in five decisions, running his consecutive win streak to twelve.

	W	SV	ERA	IP	H	BB	SO	B/I
1995 Seattle	18	0	2.48	214	159	65	294	1.05
1996 Seattle	5	1	3.67	61	48	25	85	1.19
1997 Seattle	20	0	2.28	213	147	77	291	1.05

JOHNSTONE, JOHN - TR - b: 11/25/68
Johnstone obviously knows his way around the Bay Area. He started the season in San Francisco, was waived and went to the A's, was then waived again and returned to the Giants. He throws hard and has a live arm, but at age 29, he has never been able to realize his skills. If he harnesses his control, he is the type of hurler who emerges as a closer later in his career. If he can put it all together in '98, Johnstone could really surprise, especially with expansion looming.

	W	SV	ERA	IP	H	BB	SO	B/I
1997 Oakland	0	0	3.24	25	22	14	19	1.44

JONES, BOBBY M. - TL - b: 4/11/72
An enigma with a great arm, Jones throws 90 MPH and has an above-average slider; he was initially a pleasant surprise in 1997, but was once again a disappointment by season's end. When he's on, his slider is abusive to lefthanded hitters. He sometimes has to sacrifice velocity and movement to get the ball over the plate, though. Moved to the rotation in 1997, Jones started off strong at Triple-A Colorado Springs and was promoted to the Rockies in May. But after four poor starts, Jones was sent back to Colorado Springs, where he finished the season pitching poorly. His makeup needs to mature, but he has a resilient arm. He will probably have to accept a middle-relief role if he is to stick in the majors.

	W	SV	ERA	IP	H	BB	SO	B/I
1997 Colorado	1	0	8.39	19	30	12	5	2.18

JONES, BOBBY - TR - b: 2/10/70
Scouting: Jones lacks a high-powered fastball (mid-80s) so he must be precise to succeed. He throws a sinking fastball and a cut fastball, plus a big curveball, but mostly tries to get outs with his changeup. He's even-tempered on the mound and has been consistent over the course of his career, even if his fortunes have fluctuated somewhat during each of his five big-league seasons. Jones fields his position well and has a decent pickoff move. He does all the "little" things well; he needs to in order to be successful since he can't blow batters away.
1998: Jones will be in the Mets' rotation. The club hoped it would be as a third or fourth starter, as had been predicted when Jones was in the minor leagues, not as the ace which he was for the first half of last season.
1997: Jones was en route to a signature season, winning 11 of his first 13 decisions (13 starts). But after he reached 12-3 (equalling his career high in victories), he went nine starts with no victories and five defeats. It made for an overall record that was mostly unrewarding. A muscle strain in his back, poor work in the second half and finally a strained muscle in his forearm undermined what once seemed like a 20-victory season. He missed 200 innings by fewer than seven innings for the third successive season. But, for the first time in three years, his innings exceeded his hits. Batters leading off innings batted .189 against him.
1996: His work produced his second winning record in what then was three-plus seasons. It wasn't easy. A two-start assignment to the extended spring training program was part of what he endured as were two more dreadful starts in Coors Field.

	W	SV	ERA	IP	H	BB	SO	B/I
1995 New York NL	10	0	4.19	195	209	53	127	1.33
1996 New York NL	12	0	4.42	195	219	46	116	1.36
1997 New York NL	15	0	3.63	193	177	63	125	1.24

JONES, DOUG - TR - b: 6/24/57

Scouting: Slow, slower and slowest are the speeds of this veteran's pitches, but the hitters can't time him. Jones looked to be washed up only a couple of seasons ago, but rebounded in 1997 and now looks like he could pitch forever. His command of slow breaking stuff was pinpoint. His change is his out pitch.

1998: Free-agent Jones was expected to return to the Brewers — where he began his major league career 16 years ago — and the closer role.

1997: Jones set a Brewers' save record in 1997. A highlight of his season came on September 15th when he struck out the side against the White Sox on nine pitches. He was considered a cinch for the club's Most Valuable Pitcher award. His control of his slow stuff was exceptional all season.

1996: Jones was signed by the Brewers after the Cubs released him. He made 13 appearances at Triple-A New Orleans and was then called up by the Brewers where he made 24 highly effective appearances, mostly as a set-up man.

	W	SV	ERA	IP	H	BB	SO	B/I
1995 Baltimore	0	22	5.01	46	55	16	42	1.52
1996 Chicago NL	2	2	5.01	32	41	7	26	1.50
1996 Milwaukee	5	1	3.41	31	31	13	34	1.41
1997 Milwaukee	6	36	2.02	80	62	9	82	0.88

JONES, TODD - TR - b: 4/24/68

Scouting: He may look awkward in his delivery, but Jones throws an explosive, 95-MPH fastball with a nasty curve. He has always lacked confidence, but 22 straight saves in the middle of last year did a lot to change that. He saved more games than any Tiger but John Hiller and Willie Hernandez, and they rewarded him with a new contract.

1998: Now that the Tigers are paying Jones $5.7 million for the next two years, there's no question about what he'll be doing. He's the closer.

1997: Jones came over in the ten-player trade with Houston, and was named the closer. He lost the job, got it back, and then pitched so well that he got a big contract. And, after the Tigers re-signed him, he started throwing even better than before.

1996: For the second straight year, the Astros ended up unsatisfied with Jones as their closer. He saved 17 games for Houston, but Astros management was determined to find someone else to do the job.

	W	SV	ERA	IP	H	BB	SO	B/I
1995 Houston	6	15	3.07	99	89	52	96	1.41
1996 Houston	6	17	4.40	57	61	32	44	1.63
1997 Detroit	5	31	3.09	70	60	35	70	1.36

JORDAN, RICARDO - TL - b: 6/27/70

Scouting: If only he trusted his stuff. It's as nasty as any you'll see from a lefthanded pitcher. But Jordan often picks at the corners and seldom challenges hitters — not even lefthanded hitters — until the count is decidedly against him. Then he grooves the ball and gets hammered.

1998: In the best of all plausible worlds, Jordan would have been the Mets' primary lefthanded set-up reliever. But his work last season prompted his removal from the 40-man roster and, as a twice-outrighted player, he opted for free agency. But he is lefthanded, so he'll always find work. And if he gets it all working, watch out.

1997: The Mets had hoped for far more than Jordan provided. He spent his season travelling between the major leagues and Triple-A. The Mets needed a reliever to deal with lefthanded hitters; Jordan wasn't the guy. Lefthanded hitters batted .366 in 41 at-bats against him. He struck out 12 righthanded hitters and walked 14.

1996: Jordan showed signs during his 26-appearance tenure with the Phillies that he had what it takes to deal with lefthanded hitters. Used mostly against them, he struck out 17 in 25 innings, but he also walked 12 and allowed 18 hits. The Mets took a chance, dealing Rico Brogna — whom they worried would break down — for Jordan and Toby Borland. Borland was gone before the season was eight weeks old.

	W	SV	ERA	IP	H	BB	SO	B/I
1995 Toronto	1	1	6.60	15	18	13	10	2.02
1996 Philadelphia	2	0	1.80	25	18	12	17	1.20
1997 New York NL	1	0	5.33	27	31	15	19	1.70

JUDD MICHAEL - TR - b: 6/30/75

Acquired in a trade with the Yankees in June of 1996, Judd pitched his way to a one game stop in the majors in 1997. He averaged more than a strikeout per inning combined in stops at Vero Beach and San Antonio. In his one relief appearance with the Dodgers, Judd worked 2 2/3 innings without allowing a run and striking out four.

JUDEN, JEFF - TR - b: 1/19/71

Scouting: A big (6'8", 265-pound) top draft pick, Juden has amazing stuff. He has serious, low-90's heat but his mechanics and conditioning have sometimes wavered, reducing his effectiveness. He is known for being a moody hurler who can run off a number of good — or bad — starts in a row.

1998: The Indians' need for pitching will likely give Juden another chance to make a major league impact. A relief role could be the best fit, as he is extremely tough on righthanders when he's on, and he could utilize his uneven temperament as a benefit.

1997: Juden ranked among the best starting pitchers in baseball during the first half, showing better control and changing speeds unlike ever before. It then took about a month for the Expos to pay his way out of town. Despite injuries galore, he never laid a claim to a starting role in Cleveland.

1996: Juden split the season between the Giants and Expos, blossoming under the patient style of Felipe Alou. He was generally used in a middle-relief role, and thrived because of the best physical conditioning of his career.

	W	SV	ERA	IP	H	BB	SO	B/I
1995 Philadelphia	2	0	4.02	62	53	31	47	1.34
1996 Montreal	5	0	3.27	74	61	34	61	1.28
1997 Cleveland	11	0	4.46	161	157	72	136	1.42

JUELSGAARD, JAROD - TR - b: 6/27/68

Juelsgaard's career ERA is above 5.00, he has walked nearly as many batters as he has struck out, and hasn't played an important role on any staff since 1993. About his only redeeming point is his avoidance of the home run ball. There's not much of a market for wild breaking-ball pitchers, so Juelsgaard is unlikely to be pitching professionally much longer.

KAMIENIECKI, SCOTT - TR - b: 4/19/64

Scouting: Kamieniecki has a standard four-pitch repertoire without any one outstanding pitch, but he gets guys out. He depends on location and mixing his pitches, the best of which is a curveball. He's prone to sudden bouts of wildness when his mechanics get muddled. Oriole pitching coach Ray Miller enjoys working with the coachable Kamieniecki; the club likes his competitive spirit and bulldog demeanor.

1998: With his strong 1997 performance, Kamieniecki earned a rotation spot for 1998, even with the return of Rocky Coppinger.

1997: The Orioles signed Kamieniecki following a strong performance in Venezuelan winter ball, and after beginning the season in the bullpen, he emerged as their fourth starter. Kamieniecki could have had a better record, but he didn't get much run support in some of his starts, and an otherwise strong bullpen blew some of his games.

1996: With the Yankees, Kamieniecki had an injury plagued year following off-season surgery to remove bone chips from his elbow. The Yankees eventually gave up on him.

	W	SV	ERA	IP	H	BB	SO	B/I
1995 New York AL	7	0	4.01	89	83	49	43	1.48
1996 New York AL	1	0	11.12	22	36	19	15	2.48
1997 Baltimore	10	0	4.02	179	179	67	109	1.37

KARCHNER, MATT - TR - b: 6/28/67

Scouting: A sinker/slider pitcher who has been reasonably successful, Karchner doesn't have outstanding velocity and lacks great control, too. He is not a prototypical closer, but does get a lot of ground balls. Keeping his pitches down is a key to his success, primarily because he can't blow the ball past big-league hitters. Karchner is a useful pitcher for a major league bullpen, no matter what his role.

1998: The White Sox closer job is wide open and Karchner has at least one foot already through the door. He'll get a shot at the role in the spring, but don't expect him to hold it, he may not throw hard enough to be a true closer. In any case he'll have an important bullpen job in 1998.

1997: Karchner inherited the stopper role when Roberto Hernandez was dealt to the Giants. He had unexpected success, saving 13 games with a minuscule ERA. His elbow problems (loose bodies in elbow) did not require surgery and he should be able to heal with rest and rehab. only.

1996: Karchner's first full season in the majors was a mixed bag. He was the leading winner out of the bullpen, but had an unhealthy ERA and was particularly bad over the last half of the year before having knee surgery in September.

	W	SV	ERA	IP	H	BB	SO	B/I
1995 Chicago AL	4	0	1.69	32	33	12	24	1.41
1996 Chicago AL	7	1	5.76	59	61	41	46	1.73
1997 Chicago AL	3	15	2.90	53	50	26	30	1.44

KARL, SCOTT - TL - b: 8/9/71

Scouting: A control pitcher, Karl has only average velocity, but can be effective if he keeps his breaking stuff down. Karl throws a heavy palmball that can be tough if kept low. He is a good fielder and has a tricky pickoff move.

1998: Karl is being counted on as a regular member of the Brewers' rotation. If he starts the season the way he finished 1997, he could have a good year.

1997: Karl showed good resilience in bouncing back from a 2-10 start. He won eight straight after the All-Star break despite a sore thumb. Karl was hampered early in the season by a toe that had required surgery during the off-season. Control is the key for this lefty. He didn't have it in the first half of the season, and regained it in the second half.

1996: Karl spent his first full season in the big leagues and led the Brewers in wins, complete games (three) and shutouts (one).

	W	SV	ERA	IP	H	BB	SO	B/I
1995 Milwaukee	6	0	4.14	124	141	50	59	1.54
1996 Milwaukee	13	0	4.86	207	220	72	121	1.41
1997 Milwaukee	10	0	4.47	193	212	67	119	1.44

KARP, RYAN - TL - b: 4/5/70

Scouting: After five years in a starting rotation, Karp shifted to the bullpen. His fastball is barely average and he relies on curveballs, sinkers, sliders and a deceptive delivery to keep hitters off balance. He could succeed in a situational bullpen role, but is likely to struggle against righthanders. Karp's combination of just average velocity and below-average command is not a recipe for success.

1998: Karp will compete for one of the situational lefty spots available in Tampa Bay's bullpen. He's well suited to a one-batter role, but Karp will have to beat out a horde of southpaws including some with better raw stuff.

1997: Karp's command as a reliever in 1997 was less sharp than it had ever been previously as a starter. To be a viable major league reliever he will need to consistently throw strike one, and he did not do so in 1997.

1996: Arm trouble limited Karp to just seven starts. He showed an ability to keep hitters off-balance and get key strikeouts, despite unimpressive velocity, by setting up his fastball with first strike breaking balls.

	W	SV	ERA	IP	H	BB	SO	B/I
1997 Philadelphia	1	0	5.40	15	12	9	18	1.40

KARSAY, STEVE - TR - b: 3/24/72

Scouting: Karsay can still throw hard (94 MPH) despite the "Tommy John" surgery he had in 1995. He also throws a slider but, his curve is the key to his success. When he has it, he uses it effectively and is difficult to hit, spotting his changeup, fastball and slider accordingly. When he doesn't have it, which is more often than not, he gets hammered.

1998: With a fresh start in Cleveland, Karsay will be given every opportunity to fulfill his promise, to show that he is healthy and can put up seven innings every five days. But, he must prove that he can deliver consistently both to management and to himself.

1997: All things considered, the A's were happy enough that Karsay could pitch as well as he did at the major league level. His work was spotty, to say the least, but he did show flashes of hard stuff and the sharp curve that made him so sought after as a Toronto prospect.

1996: After sitting out the 1995 season following elbow surgery, Karsay returned to Class A Modesto in an attempt to resurrect his career. He went 0-1 over 14 starts with a 2.65 ERA. His control was fabulous: 35 K's in 34 innings — with just one walk.

	W	SV	ERA	IP	H	BB	SO	B/I
1997 Oakland	3	0	5.76	133	166	47	92	1.61

KASHIWADA, TAKASHI - TL - b: 5/14/71

Scouting: When he throws strikes as he did in spring training and immediately after his May 1st promotion to the big leagues, he can be an adequate in-between reliever. When he doesn't, as became the case by summer, he serves little purpose. Lefthanded or not, he doesn't throw hard enough or have enough stuff to be an effective pitcher on the major league level.

1998: It's doubtful Kashiwada will have a role in the big

leagues. But he is lefthanded, so... A return to Japan and pitching there is more likely; lefthandedness can carry a pitcher only so far. He's now a journeyman in two countries.
1997: The Mets' purchase of a Japanese import was not a success. Gradually, Kashiwada stopped throwing strikes, and his performance suffered accordingly. His won/lost record is a tad misleading. His ERA was more to the point. He faced more righthanded hitters than lefthanders. No matter, both sides batted exactly .289 against him. He walked nine lefthanded hitters and struck out seven and was significantly more effective at night (1.69 ERA in 21.1 innings) than during the day (9.90 ERA in ten innings).
1996: Bobby Valentine, who orchestrated Kashiwada's move to the major leagues, never saw him pitch in Japan. Kashiwada pitched for the Yomiuri Giants' major league team in three successive seasons, producing an 0-1 record and 3.27 ERA in 1996. He pitched merely 33 innings in 26 appearances — all in relief — in the three years, splitting two decisions and producing a 3.82 ERA.

KAUFMAN, BRAD - TR - b: 4/26/72
Scouting: Kaufman has a 90-plus fastball and a good breaking pitch. But he has had problems with location, and that has also caused a lack of confidence. He had post-season surgery to remove bone spurs from his right elbow.
1998: With a great spring, Kaufman could make the Padres staff, but will probably be a starter at Triple-A Las Vegas or Double-A Mobile.
1997: He did not have a good season. At Las Vegas, Kaufman was 0-5 with an 8.07 ERA, although he raised hopes by throwing well in his last start. He was also 5-13 with 6.18 ERA in 22 games (19 starts) at Mobile.
1996: Two straight years at Double-A produced almost identical won/loss marks for Kaufman — 11-10 and 12-10. But along with one more win, his ERA fell from 5.76 to 3.63 in '96 as he led the Southern League with 29 starts. He struck out 163 in 178 innings.

KAUFMAN, JOHN - TL - b: 10/23/74
Kaufman is a power pitcher who excelled at St. Petersburg in 1997 after having a full recovery from off-season arm surgery. Kaufman can get the strikeout with his fastball or a nice repertoire. He has a good makeup as witnessed by the way he struck out Yankees outfielder Darryl Strawberry three times during his rehab stint in a '97 Florida State League game. Kaufman was a big winner at the University of Florida, where he is sixth on their all-time strikeout list. He's lefthanded, so he'll get a good look in the spring, but he'll be a longshot and likely will begin the season at Triple-A Durham.

KEAGLE, GREG - TR - b: 6/28/71
Scouting: Every now and then, Keagle will pitch a game that reminds you why scouts like him. He has an outstanding changeup, good enough that he can make the best hitters look bad. But when his command is poor and he needs to go to the changeup too often too early, Keagle ends up with a miserable start.
1998: Even though Keagle was the Tigers' most successful Triple-A starter in '97, he's far from guaranteed a chance to start in the big leagues in '98. He's already disappointed the Tigers too many times.
1997: Keagle finished fast at Toledo, going 5-0 with a 2.40 ERA in six starts before the Tigers called him up in early August. He didn't do well in the big leagues, with three good starts and seven bad ones. Four times in ten starts, he didn't make it out of the fourth inning.
1996: As a Rule 5 draft pick, Keagle had to be kept in the majors, even though he obviously wasn't ready. He went on the disabled list in July, which allowed the Tigers to send him to Toledo on a six-start rehabilitation assignment.

	W	SV	ERA	IP	H	BB	SO	B/I
1996 Detroit	3	0	7.39	87	104	68	70	1.97
1997 Detroit	3	0	6.56	45	58	18	33	1.68

KELLY, JEFF - TL - b: 1/11/75
Kelly was placed on the Pirates' 40-man roster prior to the 1997 season then took a big step backward at Double-A Carolina as he led the Southern League in walks. Lefties with good arms sometimes develop late, so Kelly still has a chance. He was sent to the Hawaiian Winter Baseball League to try to find his control. His status as a prospect is extremely shaky unless he finds the plate.

KERSHNER, JASON - TL - b: 12/19/76
Kershner was the lone lefthander in a highly-touted, but disappointing starting rotation for higher Class A Clearwater in 1997. His control was the best of the bunch, but he lost a lot of power from his previous season and he left too many hittable pitches out over the plate. Kershner has only enough stamina for about six innings. His good control may lead to a job in the bullpen as he advances.

KESTER, TIM - TR - b: 12/1/71
Kester has displayed great control over his five-year minor-league career but does not have enough in his arsenal to get big-league batters out. He spent 1997 at Double-A Jackson in the Astro farm system and was unimpressive in a mostly middle-relief role. He gave up well over a hit per inning and while he doesn't walk many batters, being hittable is not a trait for a quality major league reliever.

KEY, JIMMY - TL - b: 4/22/61
Scouting: Forget the radar guns when Key pitches; his fastball may only hit 88 MPH on a good day. He's a master craftsman of changing speeds, pitching to spots, and keeping hitters off balance in the style of Yankee-great Whitey Ford. Key is the ultimate "soft tosser."
1998: Key is signed by the Orioles through 1998. Barring an injury, he will continue to baffle hitters, making them shake their heads and wonder why they didn't drive the ball as they walk back to the dugout.
1997: Key had an excellent year and would have won over 20 games with adequate run support in the second half. He lost some tough games when his hitters deserted him.
1996: It was supposed to be written off as a rehab year following shoulder problems, but he had a good second half for the Yankees, then signed a two-year deal with the Orioles in the off-season.

	W	SV	ERA	IP	H	BB	SO	B/I
1995 New York AL	1	0	5.64	30	40	6	14	1.53
1996 New York AL	12	0	4.68	169	171	58	116	1.35
1997 Baltimore	16	0	3.43	212	210	82	141	1.38

KEYSER, BRIAN - TR - b: 10/31/66

A college teammate of Jack McDowell, Keyser has fallen out of the White Sox plans. He doesn't throw hard and has pitched behind in the count too much of the time. He's a bulldog who should get back to the majors again at least briefly. Keyser was 5-2 with a 2.15 ERA in 28 appearances at Triple-A Nashville in 1997, completing two of his four starts.

	W	SV	ERA	IP	H	BB	SO	B/I
1995 Chicago AL	5	0	4.97	92	114	27	48	1.53
1996 Chicago AL	1	1	4.98	59	78	28	19	1.79

KILE, DARRYL - TR - b: 12/2/68

Scouting: Kile moved his career to another level in 1997 when he became one of the game's top starting pitchers. Kile's curveball is regarded as the best in baseball. He also has a mid-nineties fastball and has developed an effective split-finger pitch as a changeup. Kile has overcome periodic control problems and now has the confidence to use all of his pitches in any situation. He is durable and should remain in the top echelon of pitchers for several years.
1998: Kile should continue the success he enjoyed in 1997.
1997: Kile was an All-Star in 1993 but failed to sustain that level of performance the next three years. He had another All-Star season in 1997 achieving the status of staff ace for the first time.
1996: Kile improved over 1994 and 1995. He was essentially an average major league starting pitcher.

	W	SV	ERA	IP	H	BB	SO	B/I
1995 Houston	4	0	4.96	127	114	73	113	1.47
1996 Houston	12	0	4.19	219	233	97	219	1.51
1997 Houston	19	0	2.57	256	208	94	205	1.18

KING, BILL - TR - b: 2/18/73

This is obviously a popular name in Oakland (the A's play-by-play announcer has the same name). King toiled at Double-A Huntsville in 1997, going 9-7 with a 4.19 ERA. He is always around the plate, as witnessed by his 103 strikeouts and 28 walks. He can also be hit as witnessed by the 216 hits he allowed over only 176 innings. King has got to refine his control within the strike zone to remain a prospect, particularly when he goes to the hitting-haven Pacific Coast League.

KING, CURTIS - TR - b: 10/25/70

Scouting: King has stormed into prominence in the Cardinals' bullpen and could be a frontrunner to handle the closing duties during the buffer time between Dennis Eckersley and Braden Looper — if not longer. Quietly intense, the athletic King didn't start working as a closer until 1996 and found it a natural role. He's not overpowering and will walk more than his share of batters. His sinking fastball nets him more than enough groundball outs, though.
1998: The Cardinals might find themselves auditioning several pitchers for the closer's job and King probably will have to pitch himself out of contention. His experience at the end of the 1997 season in the big leagues probably shook out enough of the apprehension that King could handle the role unless his control leaves him.
1997: King wore uniforms in Double-A and in the big leagues and showed the wear by season's end. He pitched a total of 78 games, actually getting better with each promotion. Righthanders weren't fooled by him that often, as they hit .372.
1996: He accumulated an organization-high 31 saves in his first season as a closer, most of them coming in the Class A Florida State League.

KING, RAY - TL - b: 1/15/74

King showed up at Atlanta's Double-A affiliate in Greenville last year and made no inroads as a starting prospect in his debut season at that level. "Not overpowering" and "hittable" are the words that best describe King at this point. He'll start 1998 at Double-A.

KIRKREIT, DARON - TR - b: 8/7/72

A top draft pick from 1993, Kirkreit has been sidetracked by a series of arm troubles that have left his fastball lacking much of it's original power. Unable to refine his breaking-ball repertoire or control, Kirkreit has become an easy mark for Double-A hitters. A relief role may best suit him at this point, but it's unlikely that his fragile arm could withstand the strain of pitching that often. His days as a professional pitcher may be numbered.

KLINE, STEVE - TL - b: 8/22/72

Scouting: Kline throws an average fastball, a sharp slider and a decent changeup. He was primarily a starter until last season but his slider makes him a candidate to have a long career as a lefthanded specialist out of the bullpen.
1998: Kline's status with Montreal depends on how the Expos decide to use him. If they look at him as a starter, he will begin the season in Triple-A Ottawa's rotation. If they want him to relieve, then he has a good chance at making the big club out of spring training. Kline was a top prospect in Cleveland's farm system until coming down with a sore arm in 1995. He hasn't been quite the same since and his future appears to be in the bullpen.
1997: Kline surprisingly made the Indians out of spring training as a reliever after two straight years as a starter in Double-A and he got the win on opening night. The Indians eventually sent him down to Triple-A Buffalo so he could start again then dealt him to Montreal on July 31st for pitcher Jeff Juden. Kline worked strictly in relief for the Expos and the results weren't good.
1996: Kline was cuffed around as a starter with Cleveland's Double-A Canton-Akron farm team, still feeling the effects of arm problems that shortened his 1995 season.

	W	SV	ERA	IP	H	BB	SO	B/I
1997 two teams	4	0	5.98	53	73	23	37	1.82

KLINGENBECK, SCOTT - TR - b: 2/3/71

The Reds claimed Klingenbeck off waivers early in the season after he was released by Minnesota. He made 21 starts for Triple-A Indianapolis and had good stats (12-8, 3.96 ERA) despite giving up 23 home runs. He never got the call to Cincinnati, though; he asked for, and was granted, his release before the end of the season. Klingenbeck will be one of the many pitchers who will benefit from having two new major league teams around. Although he was cut by two teams in less than six months, he'll get a look in somebody's spring training camp.

	W	SV	ERA	IP	H	BB	SO	B/I
1995 Baltimore	2	0	7.12	79	101	42	42	1.79
1996 Minnesota	1	0	7.85	28	42	10	15	1.84

KLINK, JOE - TL - b: 2/3/62
Klink made a cameo appearance with Seattle in 1996. He can still be tough on lefty batters.

KNIGHT, BRANDON - TR - b: 10/1/75
Knight was a positive surprise for the Rangers' organization last year and has put himself into contention for a rotation spot in 1999. He had a tough year in 1996, going 4-10 at Class A Charlotte in the Florida State League. In 1997, he returned to Charlotte to start the year and was a different pitcher thanks to improved mechanics and better movement on his stuff. He was 7-4 with a 2.23 ERA, 91 strikeouts and 82 hits in 93 innings of work. He made the jump to Double-A and handled it well, striking out nearly a batter per inning, giving up less than a hit per inning and showing good control.

KNOLL, RANDY - TR - b: 3/21/77
After emerging as one of the Phillies' better pitching prospects in A-ball in 1996, Knoll made just five starts last year before requiring arm surgery. Despite good strikeout totals, he's not a power pitcher, having just an average fastball, but relies instead upon great control and an ability to get ahead of hitters; Knoll's stamina within games is a plus. If healthy, Knoll will return to Class A Clearwater, then advance to Double-A Reading in 1998.

KNUDSEN, KURT - TR - b: 2/20/67
Knudsen filled a hole at Double-A Midland and needs to make some improvement to elevate his stock as a prospect. Knudsen has struggled to make the jump from A-ball, which has slowed his development. He has decent control and an average fastball.

KOJIMA, KEIICHI - TL - b: 7/1/68
Kojima's first American pro season was a tale of two leagues: a 1.73 ERA and four saves in 11 games in the Florida State League and a 1-8 record with an 8.83 ERA in 13 games in the Texas League. Kojima's control was good in both places, but Double-A hitters used him for batting practice. Kojima does not have overpowering stuff, and must learn how to change speeds more effectively.

KOLB, DANNY - TR - b: 3/29/75
Kolb is a raw prospect with a 95-MPH fastball. Last season was a disappointment for him, as he failed to handle the jump from the South Atlantic League to the Florida State League, going 4-10 with a 4.87 ERA and control problems. Kolb needs further work on his off-speed pitches and will probably return for a second season with Port Charlotte.

KOPPE, CLINT - TR - b: 8/14/73
Koppe is big but doesn't throw particularly hard, rather he relies on good control. He pitched at the Double-A and A-ball levels of the Reds' farm system last year; his control deserted him at Double-A Chattanooga (44 walks, 33 strikeouts in 68.1 innings). He had better control at the Class A level but allowed over a hit per inning. He doesn't appear to be a strong prospect.

KRAMER, TOM - TR - b: 1/9/68
Once a hard-throwing short reliever, Kramer has seen his fastball lose velocity; it's now just average (upper 80s), but he's still a bulldog and can fill any roll — spot starter, middle reliever, set-up man, or closer. Once a top prospect for Cleveland, Kramer hasn't pitched in the big leagues since 1993. He made 51 relief appearances for the Sky Sox in 1997, posting 11 saves with a 5.23 ERA. Kramer mixes his pitches well.

KRIVDA, RICK - TL - b: 1/19/70
Scouting: Krivda's mechanics were tightened last year resulting in a few more MPH on his fastball and a sharper slider. He still doesn't throw hard and needs to keep the ball low and hit locations to be effective. In a "Baseball America" poll of managers, he was voted as having the best control in the International League. But on his off days, his fastball will come in high, a pitch that's hittable. He's a finesse pitcher who needs to pitch regularly to stay sharp and, as the fifth starter he sometimes wasn't needed for a week or ten days, knocking Krivda out of his rhythm. Pitching regularly, Krivda could be more successful although he'll never be a staff ace.
1998: With Rocky Coppinger coming back, Krivda may be relegated to the bullpen, but the Orioles already have a strong pen, so Krivda may be back in Triple-A or with another club. His best role is as a fourth starter, a job that's likely to be unavailable to him with the Orioles. Krivda can also pitch middle relief. He's out of minor-league options, so he can't be sent back to the minors unless he clears waivers.
1997: Krivda pitched some great ball in Triple-A earning another shot with the Orioles. He was promoted late in the season to become the fifth starter and won some key games.
1996: Krivda's most memorable moment was winning a pressure-packed late season game, a crucial victory in the Orioles playoff drive.

	W	SV	ERA	IP	H	BB	SO	B/I
1995 Baltimore	2	0	4.54	75	76	25	53	1.34
1996 Baltimore	3	0	4.96	81	89	39	54	1.58
1997 Baltimore	4	0	6.30	50	67	18	29	1.70

KROON, MARC - TR - b: 4/2/73
Scouting: Kroon has a live arm. He was the only Padre to register 99 MPH on the radar gun in '97. But throwing hard is different from pitching. A great fastball is the only pitch he can routinely count on. And Kroon can be wild. Still, he is viewed as a potential closer.
1998: The Padres love his velocity and his approach. Other clubs also covet his arm.
1997: Kroon had a high ERA in 12 relief appearances with the Padres. But his worst outings were his earliest and he raised some eyebrows with twelve strikeouts in 11.1 innings. At Triple-A Las Vegas, Kroon was 1-3 with a 4.54 ERA and 15 saves in 46 outings, including 53 strikeouts in 41.2 innings.
1996: Kroon worked at the Double-A level in his steady progression through the Padre system and was 2-4 with a 2.89 ERA and 22 saves in 44 outings. Kroon struck out 56 in 46.2 innings.

	W	SV	ERA	IP	H	BB	SO	B/I
1997 San Diego	0	0	7.17	11	14	5	12	1.68

KUBINSKI, TIM - TL - b: 1/20/72
After toiling at Double-A Huntsville in 1996, where he went 8-7 with a 2.38 ERA, Kubinski spent most of 1997 at Triple-A Edmonton, where he went 4-4 with a 4.50 ERA over 47 games. His strikeout totals were down from 1995, but his overall performance was adequate. He made a couple of late-season

appearances in an Oakland uniform.

	W	SV	ERA	IP	H	BB	SO	B/I
1997 Oakland	0	0	5.67	13	12	6	10	1.42

KUSIEWICZ, MIKE - TL - b: 11/1/76
A control pitcher who didn't turn 21 until after the 1997 season, Kusiewicz still has yet to prove he can pitch in Double-A. He started last season at New Haven, but after going 2-4 with a 6.67 ERA, he was sent back to Class A Salem. He regrouped, posting an 8-6 mark with a 2.52 ERA in 19 games, 18 as a starter. His fastball has average velocity but outstanding movement —his pitch is never straight. He also has a decent curve and forkball. He gets in trouble because he tends to nibble; Kusiewicz has yet to develop supreme confidence in his stuff.

LACY, KERRY - TR - b: 8/7/72
Lacy's 90-MPH sinking fastball is big-league, but he lacks the off-speed stuff to go with it. This showed when he had a chance to take the closer role in Boston in '97, but couldn't do it. Lacy spent a lot of his time during the season in Triple-A trying to find a put-away pitch, but with little success. Lacy also was overweight in '97. If he can get in shape and find a better second pitch he has a chance to be an effective major league pitcher, but not an overpowering one.

	W	SV	ERA	IP	H	BB	SO	B/I
1997 Boston	1	3	6.11	46	60	22	18	1.79

LaGARDE, JOE - TR - b: 1/17/75
LaGarde has advanced to Double-A quick enough, primarily on the basis of his guts and pitching savvy. He did well in the closer role for Midland last year. He doesn't have a dominating fastball, but gets by with good command and a good breaking ball. He spent the winter in Australia polishing his pitching skills to put himself in a better position to turn some heads at Triple-A Albuquerque in 1998.

LANGSTON, MARK - TL - b: 8/20/60
Scouting: Once a mainstay of the Angels' starting rotation, Langston has missed most of the last two seasons with injuries. Recurring problems with his right knee limited Langston to 18 starts in 1996, while arthroscopic elbow surgery limited him to nine starts in 1997. Langston is fanatical about keeping himself in top condition, so his fastball hasn't lost any velocity and his curveball is still sharp. His problems have been breaking down the last two seasons, which, combined with his age, has created an alarming pattern.
1998: Langston wants to finish his career in Anaheim. To do that, he must convince the Angels his run of bad luck with injuries is over. Otherwise, he may have to accept a bullpen job until he shows he's physically sound or may go elsewhere to pitch.
1997: Langston's season ended in mid-May when recurring elbow stiffness forced him to the sidelines. Soon after, he underwent surgery to clean out an arthritic elbow joint. Langston tried a two-inning comeback late in August, but was shelled by the Yankees and had to call it a year when the elbow stiffness returned.
1996: Langston felt something pop in his right knee while running in the outfield before a May 1st start and soon after had surgery to repair torn cartilage. He tried twice to come back, but was forced to return to the disabled list both times and finally shut it down for the year in August.

	W	SV	ERA	IP	H	BB	SO	B/I
1995 California	15	0	4.63	200	212	64	142	1.38
1996 California	6	0	4.82	123	116	45	83	1.31
1997 Anaheim	2	0	5.85	48	61	29	30	1.89

LANKFORD, FRANK - TR - b: 3/26/71
Lankford had a successful first season at the Triple-A level, pitching for Columbus. He was 7-4 with a 2.69 ERA in 93.2 innings last year. He has been dominant the past few years despite his rapid progress up the Yankees' farm ladder.

LARKIN, ANDY - TR - b: 6/27/74
Scouting: It appears that persistent elbow troubles have dimmed hopes for Larkin, formerly one of baseball's best pitching prospects. He once featured a 90-MPH fastball, a diverse breaking-ball repertoire and excellent control. His stuff has made it most of the way back, but Larkin's command is not nearly as precise. He can still look like his former self in brief spurts. He's in a tough spot, as he can't pitch out of the bullpen due to his elbow troubles, and must improve his performance dramatically to make a major league rotation.
1998: Larkin will get another full season at Triple-A. Good health alone won't be enough this time around — Larkin needs to dominate and show the control of his early years to re-establish himself as a prospect.
1997: The Marlins were relieved to see him take a regular turn for the full season without getting hurt. Larkin's 6.05 ERA really wasn't that important in the big picture.
1996: Larkin was limited to 14 starts, but looked great and was rewarded with a late-September major league start. At this point, many believed that he could beat Livan Hernandez and Tony Saunders to the majors.

LAWRENCE, SEAN - TL - b: 9/2/70
This lefty is never mentioned among the Pirates' top prospects but has quietly gotten the job done the past two seasons, at Double-A Carolina in 1996 and at Triple-A Calgary in 1997. Lawrence is a little old at age 27 but the Pirates have had success over the years in getting mileage out of second-tier prospects.

LEBLANC, ERIC - TR - b: 7/6/73
A 34th-round pick in the 1996 June draft, LeBlanc pitched at Class A and Double-A for the Reds' organization in his second minor-league season. He gave up less than a hit per inning and had nearly a three-to-one strikeout-to-walk ratio at Class A Charleston. In Double-A ball he made six starts and allowed slightly over a hit per inning and struggled with his control. He should get another crack at Double-A to start 1998.

LEE, JEREMY - TR - b: 10/20/74
Lee got a chance to start for the Class A Dunedin Blue Jays last year and went 8-9 with a 4.64 ERA. He tends to pitch low and inside, making him relatively immune to the long ball. He is a few years away, at least.

LEE, MARK - TL - b: 7/20/64
It was thought that Lee would have a shot at becoming a situational lefty in the Braves' bullpen last year but instead he turned up in the Colorado organization. He has reached the

majors four different times in his 12-year pro career but not in the last two seasons. Lee appeared in 48 games but gave up a lot of hits, well more than one per inning. At age 33, he may have seen the big leagues for the last time with Baltimore in 1995.

LEGAULT, KEVIN - TR - b: 3/5/71
In his first year at Triple-A, Legault led Salt Lake City with fifty appearances out of the bullpen. Batters ripped him for 100 hits in 81 innings and he was prone to the home run, contributing to his 5.36 ERA. In 1997 he went back to Double-A.

LEITER, AL - TL - b: 10/12/65
Scouting: Leiter is a pure power pitcher, featuring a 90-MPH fastball, hard slider and sweeping curveball. Everything he throws moves sharply — so sharply that he has little or no command of his pitches. He routinely runs deep counts, and records more strikeouts and walks than league average on a per inning basis. Catcher Charles Johnson is a lifesaver for Leiter — 28 baserunners tried to steal on Leiter in 151.1 innings in 1997, but only 12 were successful. Leiter is a fine mid-rotation option — he can be counted upon to keep his team in the game, but also to leave before it is decided. He'll have a lengthy decline phase if he remains healthy.
1998: With the Marlins, Leiter should fit in as the number three or four starter, and contribute an eventful 170 innings, with high pitch counts, strikeout and walk totals. His power has yet to recede, so he's in little danger of blowing up.
1997: Leiter was not as reliable as in the previous year, averaging less than six innings per start and showing a vulnerability to the big inning.
1996: Leiter posted his career year, holding hitters to a puny .202 batting average and throwing a career-high 6.5 innings per start. He led the league in walks for the second straight season, but pitched out of trouble with key strikeouts.

	W	SV	ERA	IP	H	BB	SO	B/I
1995 Toronto	11	0	3.64	183	162	108	153	1.48
1996 Florida	16	0	2.93	215	153	119	200	1.26
1997 Florida	11	0	4.34	151	133	91	132	1.48

LEITER, MARK - TR - b: 4/13/63
Scouting: Leiter is unpredictable; he's as likely to pitch a gem as he is to get hammered. His stuff is above average; Leiter throws a high-80s fastball, with a curveball, slider and changeup. He's especially effective if he gets ahead of hitters. But when he loses confidence and nibbles at the corners of the plate he gets behind in the count and has to groove a fastball. He has consistently ranked among league-leaders in extra-base hits allowed and in hit batsmen.
1998: Leiter is signed for 1998, and will likely fit in at the bottom of the Phillies' rotation. He has managed a sub-4.00 ERA in only one of his seven major league seasons, and he's not about to start churning them out now. His decline will likely be a slow one; he is capable of getting the key strikeout, and his control is respectable.
1997: Leiter's fortunes ran counter to his club. While the Phillies floundered in the season's early days, Leiter was excellent at times. As the Phillies rallied down the stretch, Leiter ceded center stage to younger pitchers. He went through a un-veteranlike crisis of confidence in mid-season. The Phillies needed more consistency from Leiter.
1996: Leiter split the season between the Giants and the Expos, and led the National League in both homers allowed (37) and hit batters (16). Amazingly, it was third straight year leading the latter category.

	W	SV	ERA	IP	H	BB	SO	B/I
1995 San Francisco	10	0	3.82	195	185	55	129	1.23
1996 SF-Montreal	8	0	4.92	205	219	69	164	1.40
1997 Philadelphia	10	0	5.67	183	216	64	148	1.53

LeROY, JOHN - TR - b: 4/19/75
In his first full season at Double-A Greenville, LeRoy saw little of the success he had in eight starts there after a mid-season promotion in 1996. He kept getting his lower-90s fastball up in the strike zone, permitting 20 homers in 98.1 innings; they accounted for the majority of the runs he allowed on his way to a 5.03 ERA. LeRoy started the season in the bullpen, then seemed to get stronger over the second half when he returned to the starting rotation. He has to have better control within the strike zone to advance. The Devil Rays believe he can improve with experience.

LESKANIC, CURT - TR - b: 4/2/68
Scouting: Every report on this righthander begins with these two words: great arm. He throws his fastball in the mid-90s and his 87 MPH slider is unhittable when he throws it on a downward plane. An abusive workload in 1995 left him hurting in 1996 and he was ineffective through most of 1997, but he seemed to regain his form in the final month. Leskanic is a former starter who found his niche in short relief. The key for him is command in the strike zone — if he doesn't have it, he is hit hard.
1998: The Rockies are confident he will regain his 1995 form and then some. Leskanic will probably begin the season in the set-up role, but if he gets off to a quick start, he will likely be shifted to closing games.
1997: Leskanic started the season on the disabled list as he recovered from off-season surgeries on his shoulder and elbow. He was hit hard most of the season, as he left too many pitches up in the strike zone, but finished the year with 14 consecutive scoreless appearances, covering 11.1 innings, and striking out 12.
1996: Leskanic started the season as the closer and picked up six consecutive saves in April. His shoulder started throbbing, however, and he began pitching poorly in save situations. Moved back to set-up, Leskanic never got it going, posting a 6.23 ERA in 70 appearances.

	W	SV	ERA	IP	H	BB	SO	B/I
1995 Colorado	6	10	3.40	98	83	33	107	1.18
1996 Colorado	7	6	6.23	73	82	38	76	1.64
1997 Colorado	4	2	5.56	58	59	24	53	1.42

LEVINE, ALAN - TR - b: 5/22/68
A sinker/slider pitcher who doesn't throw hard and doesn't really have great stuff, Levine split 1997 between the White Sox and Triple-A Nashville; he had a 9.31 ERA in 12 appearances for Nashville, but fared much better in Chicago. A middle-round draft pick in 1991, Levine uses his curveball as an out pitch. He's not in the White Sox long-range plans.

	W	SV	ERA	IP	H	BB	SO	B/I
1997 Chicago AL	2	0	6.92	27	35	16	22	1.87

LEWIS, RICHIE - TR - b: 1/25/66
Scouting: Lewis, a former All-American collegiate pitcher from

Florida State, still throws in the upper 80s despite having elbow problems shortly after signing professionally with the Expos. He was a strikeout pitcher in college, but has had to rely on his defense as a professional.

1998: Lewis has been a better-than-average relief pitcher over the last few years and his struggles last season shouldn't prevent him from being on a big-league roster again. He's not closer material, but will be a competent middle-relief pitcher if he can keep the ball in the park.

1997: Lewis began the season with Oakland, but was released after several poor performances. He was claimed by the Reds, who sent him to Triple-A Indianapolis and made him a closer. He responded to that role, picking up nine saves and posting an ERA of less than 1.00. However, he wasn't any help to the big-league club and was sent back down after a couple of weeks after giving up far too many home runs.

1996: Lewis had a fine year with Detroit and arguably was one of the Tigers best pitchers. The Tigers let him go at the end of the season, in part because they didn't feel he would be worth the pay increase he would have gotten.

	W	SV	ERA	IP	H	BB	SO	B/I
1995 Florida	0	0	3.75	36	30	15	32	1.25
1996 Detroit	4	2	4.18	90	78	65	78	1.59
1997 Cincinnati	2	0	8.89	24	28	18	16	1.89

LIDLE, CORY - TR - b: 3/22/72

Scouting: Give him a strikezone and watch him hit it. Put him in a game and watch his own team score. It's a nice combination. Lidle brought out the best in the Mets' offense and threw strikes. No wonder he became a favorite of manager Bobby Valentine and coach Bob Apodaca. He was also the kind of pitcher difficult to hide from expansion draft raiders. He doesn't have a high ceiling, but he sure gets outs.

1998: Lidle fits nicely into the long-relief/spot-starter role. If the Diamondbacks had their druthers, they'd keep him in that role. He might get a chance to close out a game with a three-inning save, but his greatest value is as a staff saver.

1997: Aside from Rick Reed, Lidle was the Mets' most pleasant pitching surprise. His won/lost record is explained — at least partially — by his uncanny ability to prod the Mets' offense. Opposing hitters, particularly the righthanded ones, were not that fond of him (.237 opposition batting average). He averaged merely 2.2 walks per nine innings, an average that would have placed him among the league leaders had he maintained it in more innings. He allowed too many home runs — seven in 81.2 innings. But that's a function of his pitches being around the plate.

1996: When former General Manager Joe McIlvaine recognized a need for a catcher in the Brewers' organization in January, 1996, he called and happily took Lidle in exchange for Kelly Stinnett even though his only first-hand knowledge of Lidle had come in one inning of the Arizona Fall League in 1995. Lidle won 14 of 24 decisions (in 27 starts) with the Double-A Binghamton Mets.

	W	SV	ERA	IP	H	BB	SO	B/I
1997 New York NL	7	2	3.53	82	86	20	54	1.30

LIEBER, JON - TR - b: 4/2/70

Scouting: Dr. Jekyll meet Mr. Hyde; Lieber is as confounding as they come. He can be dominating in one start with a sinking fastball in the low 90s, a late-breaking slider that can be devastating and a decent changeup. The next time out, his sinker won't sink, his slider won't slide and he's knocked out of the box by the third inning.

1998: Lieber will go in as one of the Pirates' five starters, saving his job late last season with two strong starts in the heat of the National League Central pennant race. However, the Pirates' patience is growing thin. If he does not show signs of maturing into a consistent starter, he will be out of the rotation by the All-Star break and one of the young guys will be in.

1997: Lieber was the Pirates' Opening Day starter but that was somewhat by default as he was the closest thing to a veteran in an extremely young rotation. Lieber alternated good and bad months throughout the season. When he was good, he did things like striking out Albert Belle four times in one game. When he was bad, he had a hard time striking out Rafael Belliard.

1996: Lieber spent the first half of the season in the bullpen and the second half back in the starting rotation. He went 7-3 with a 3.88 ERA in 17 second-half games, re-establishing the spot he lost in the rotation midway through the 1995 season.

	W	SV	ERA	IP	H	BB	SO	B/I
1995 Pittsburgh	4	0	6.32	72	103	14	45	1.62
1996 Pittsburgh	9	1	3.99	142	156	28	94	1.30
1997 Pittsburgh	11	0	4.49	188	193	51	160	1.30

LIGTENBERG, KERRY - TR - b: 5/11/71

Scouting: Signed by the Braves out of the Prairie League, Ligtenberg used a fastball that tops out at 93 MPH, a slider, and a splitter to dominate hitters. His control is surprisingly good for a power pitcher with his limited experience as a professional.

1998: Ligtenberg will be a candidate for a set-up role in the Atlanta bullpen, and might have an outside chance at a few saves if Mark Wohlers were unavailable.

1997: Ligtenberg started the year at Double-A Greenville, where he recorded 16 saves with a 2.04 ERA. Promoted to Richmond, he struck out 35 and walked two before being promoted to the Braves in mid-August. He recorded his first major league save, made the Braves post-season roster, and ended the season with 97 strikeouts and only 20 walks in 75.1 innings spread over three levels.

1996: Ligtenberg displayed some promise at Class A Durham, posting 52 strikeouts in 54 innings with a 3.31 ERA working in relief.

	W	SV	ERA	IP	H	BB	SO	B/I
1997 Atlanta	1	1	3.00	15	12	4	19	1,07

LIMA, JOSE - TR - b: 9/30/72

Scouting: Lima is a workhorse reliever whose biggest asset is his bounceback arm. His best pitch is a changeup which he sometimes overuses. He doesn't walk many but his control within the strike zone is not always good; his fastball is average and he has a sharp breaking curve. He has trouble pitching with men on base which limits his usefulness.

1998: Lima will face stiff competition in the bullpen from hard throwing younger pitchers. He is not a strong candidate to be a closer or a set-up man.

1997: Lima was obtained from Detroit prior to the season in a multi-player trade. He spent the entire season in the Houston bullpen, primarily in a mop-up role.

1996: For the third straight year, Lima split the season between Detroit and the minor leagues. He was a starter in the minors but was used primarily in relief with Detroit. As a member of one of the worst major league pitching staffs ever, his ERA of 5.70

was significantly better than the staff ERA of 6.38.

	W	SV	ERA	IP	H	BB	SO	B/I
1995 Detroit	3	0	6.11	73	85	18	37	1.41
1996 Detroit	5	3	5.70	72	87	22	59	1.51
1997 Houston	1	2	5.28	75	79	16	63	1.27

LINEBARGER, KEITH - TR - b: 5/11/71
Linebarger had a successful first year in Double-A in 1996 but met with severe difficulty when advanced to the Triple-A level in 1997. He gave up 135 hits in 97.2 innings with a 6.64 ERA at Salt Lake. He was used mostly in long relief and made a few spot starts, too. He lacks an outstanding pitch but prior to 1997 he was considered a good prospect. Linebarger will now have to prove himself at the Triple-A level.

LIRA, FELIPE - TR - b: 4/26/72
Scouting: Acquired from Detroit in the first of Seattle's many 1997 prospects-for-pitching trades, Lira has average stuff but has seemingly regressed in his three seasons in the majors from a rotation guy to a mopup guy. He throws a 90-MPH fastball, a good cut fastball, a slider and a changeup. Getting the ball up in the strike zone leads to too many deep fly balls.
1998: Lira would be best served by pitching elsewhere in 1998 after his awful performance for the Mariners in 1997.
1997: Lira was ripped in four starts with the Mariners, who gave up righthanded pitcher Scott Sanders and two minor-league prospects for Lira and Omar Olivares in June. Overall, opponents hit .295 against him and he allowed 18 homers in 110.2 innings while exhibiting poor control, too.
1996: In his second season in the majors, Lira had the most innings and the most strikeouts on perhaps the worst staff in baseball in Detroit, but only managed six victories. Lira couldn't blame Tiger Stadium for his high ERA, though, he posted a road ERA of 7.11 compared to a home ERA of 3.85. A broken hand finished his season late in September.

	W	SV	ERA	IP	H	BB	SO	B/I
1995 Detroit	9	1	4.31	146	151	56	89	1.42
1996 Detroit	6	0	5.22	194	204	66	113	1.39
1997 Seattle	5	0	6.34	111	132	55	73	1.69

LLOYD, GRAEME - TL - b: 4/9/67
Scouting: Lloyd is a big (6'7") Aussie set-up man who relies primarily on a big curveball, a sharp slider and a sinking fastball. He is adept at getting hitters to hit grounders, making him an ideal pitcher to use in double-play situations. His control isn't especially sharp, though, so he can be prone to occasional bad outings.
1998: Expect more of the same from Lloyd. He's not the best lefty set-up man in the game but he's better than most. If used every other day for an inning, Lloyd can be extremely effective. If pressed into service more regularly or in more pressure-packed situations, his results may suffer.
1997: Lloyd had an even better year pitching exclusively for the Yankees, posting his best ERA in four years and mostly avoiding his occasional bouts with wildness. The success of Mike Stanton in a similar lefty set-up role gave Lloyd an opportunity to be used more effectively.
1996: After leading Milwaukee with 15 holds, Lloyd was originally thought to be damaged goods when acquired from the Brewers late in August. But he overcame an initially bad start for the Yankees to have a fine September and October as a set-up man for the World Champs.

	W	SV	ERA	IP	H	BB	SO	B/I
1995 Milwaukee	0	4	4.50	32	28	8	13	1.13
1996 Milw-NY AL	2	0	4.29	56	61	22	30	1.48
1997 New York AL	1	1	3.31	49	55	20	26	1.53

LOAIZA, ESTEBAN - TR - b: 12/31/71
Scouting: Loaiza is a bit of an enigma. He has four potentially above-average major league pitches: fastball, slider, curveball, changeup. He throws them all with good movement and a seemingly effortless motion. Yet, few pitchers in the majors are more inconsistent. It is not uncommon for him to breeze through four innings, giving up four runs in the fifth then retire the side in order in the sixth. His concentration lapses are perplexing.
1998: This is a pivotal year in Loaiza's career. He has been good at times and bad at others. Everyone universally agrees he has the stuff to be a consistent winner and, at worst, a solid third starter in the Pirates' rotation. He seemed to take the game a little more seriously last year and looks like a candidate for a breakthrough season.
1997: Loaiza came to spring training seemingly on a mission after a rocky 1996 and quickly reclaimed a spot in the Pirates' rotation. Loaiza had his ups and downs but came on strong late in the season and led the staff in innings pitched.
1996: After Loaiza lead the National League in starts in 1995, he wasn't pitching well and was taking things for granted; the Pirates delivered a rude wakeup call in the final week of spring training by demoting him to Triple-A Calgary. He was recalled for two June starts, got hammered both times, and got an even ruder awakening when he was dispatched to the Mexican League. He came back to Pittsburgh in late-August and pitched much better.

	W	SV	ERA	IP	H	BB	SO	B/I
1995 Pittsburgh	8	0	5.16	172	205	55	85	1.51
1996 Pittsburgh	2	0	4.96	52	65	19	32	1.61
1997 Pittsburgh	11	0	4.13	196	214	56	122	1.38

LOEWER, CARLTON - TR - b: 9/24/73
Scouting: Loewer is a perplexing pitcher; he has great stuff: a 90-MPH fastball, curveball and changeup, and good control with the ability to pitch deep into games. But his command within the strike zone is shaky and he overuses his breaking pitches instead of just reaching back and blowing hitters away. Loewer has the tools to be a high-quality major league pitcher, but first must improve his mental approach to the game.
1998: Loewer is likely to return to Triple-A Scranton to open the season. If he can navigate the corners of the strike zone better and pitch more low-hit games, there is no reason to believe he can't make the major league staff by mid-season. However, he has made only halting strides in those areas thus far in his pro career. 1998 will be a pivotal year in his development; without major performance enhancements he could go down as a wasted top draft pick.
1997: Loewer took a regular Triple-A turn, dazzled with his stuff, but somehow went 5-13; the Phillies elected not to recall him to the majors in September. Too often, he allowed hitters who couldn't handle his fastball take advantage of his lesser pitches. The whole has been much less than the sum of the parts up to this point.
1996: It was vintage Loewer, combining great stuff with poor location in the strike zone, resulting in poor mainstream numbers. His penchant for allowing hitters to wriggle off the hook

after being down in the count was particularly maddening.

LOGAN, MARCUS - TR - b: 5/8/72
Logan has a fastball good enough for the majors, but needs further work on his command and off-speed stuff to set up the heater. He has done well in the low minors (7-7 with a 2.91 ERA and two-to-one strikeout-to-walk ratio) in higher Class A, and Logan won 11 games for Arkansas in 1997. He was slated to begin 1998 at Triple-A and has the potential to advance.

LOISELLE, RICH - TR - b: 1/12/72
Scouting: After making only four relief appearances in his first six professional seasons, Loiselle turned into one of the game's top closers last season. Loiselle's problem as a starter was his inability to come up with an off-speed pitch. That is no longer a problem in the bullpen as he can strictly use a 97-MPH fastball and hard slider. Loiselle's velocity increased after he moved to the bullpen; he no longer worried about pacing himself.
1998: Loiselle will go into the season as the Pirates' closer. He has the makeup for the job as he throws hard, usually throws strikes and doesn't seem to let failure bother him. Loiselle came into the job by accident last season and it will be interesting to see how he does now that there are expectations placed on him.
1997: Loiselle went to spring training hoping to become the fifth starter, but he became as the long man out of the bullpen, moved into a set-up role early in the season then became the Pirates' closer when John Ericks went out for the season April 29th. Loiselle's success was stunning as he converted 29 of 33 save opportunities and posted the second-highest save total ever by a rookie behind Todd Worrell's 36 for St. Louis in 1986.
1996: Loiselle was acquired by the Pirates from Houston in a trade for Danny Darwin in late-July and then got his first taste of the major leagues with a September callup. Loiselle started three games and pitched rather effectively.

	W	SV	ERA	IP	H	BB	SO	B/I
1996 Pittsburgh	1	0	3.05	20	22	8	9	1.49
1997 Pittsburgh	1	29	3.09	73	76	24	66	1.38

LOMON, KEVIN - TR - b: 11/20/71
In 1995 and 1996, Lomon used a decent year in Triple-A to get six appearances in the majors. Last year, Lomon struggled at Triple-A Columbus, but performed well at Double-A Norwich. Expansion provided a big chance for him to advance from being a fringe player to have a more regular role in the major leagues.

LONG, JOEY - TL - b: 7/15/70
Because he's lefthanded, Long is getting more of a chance to succeed (and fail) than most pitchers. He'll get sporadic callups to the majors in the next couple of years, but he's strictly a minor-league quality pitcher at this point.

	W	SV	ERA	IP	H	BB	SO	B/I
1997 San Diego	0	0	8.18	11	17	8	8	2.27

LOONEY, BRIAN - TL - b: 9/25/69
Looney was considered to be an underachiever after his unsuccessful 1996 season at Triple-A Pawtucket, but pitched a good 24.2 innings for Triple-A Salt Lake in 1997, posting a 2.19 ERA and allowing less than a hit per inning. He has an assortment of breaking pitches and he actually reached the majors in 1995 for Boston and Montreal. Even though he's too old to be considered a prospect, Looney's wide, lefthanded repertoire will help his chances of returning to the majors.

LOOPER, BRADEN - TR - b: 8/19/74
Scouting: He's the Cardinals' closer of the future, with the only questions involving when he's ready to take the job and if the team can wait that long. Looper throws hard, with terrific movement on his fastball, complements it with a good breaking ball and has spent much time working on a changeup. Looper has spent most of the last several years excelling as a closer, so he's developed the approach and attitude necessary for the role.
1998: The Cards probably will start him in Triple-A and, ideally, would like for him to stay there all season to accumulate more professional innings. Looper could gain a spot in the big leagues with a strong spring, considering his talent and the team's needs in the bullpen.
1997: He opened his first professional season in the Class A Carolina League, where he worked as a starting pitcher to gain innings and actually experiment as to whether that might be his calling. After struggling initially, Looper began to lower his ERA significantly with help of an improving off-speed pitch and fanned about one batter per inning. He was promoted into the bullpen at Double-A and soon began to gain chances to save games. Just as he was starting to thrive in that role, the Cardinals shut Looper down for the season because of some arm discomfort. They weren't concerned — merely taking precautions.
1996: Looper had an All-American season as the closer for Wichita State and was drafted number three overall by the Cardinals. He didn't pitch professionally that summer, instead working 18 games with Team USA and getting a Bronze Medal in the Olympics. The Cards sent him to the Arizona Fall League, where he had a 2.65 ERA in 21 games.

LOPEZ, ALBIE - TR - b: 8/18/71
Scouting: The Indians have given Lopez every chance to secure a major league role over the past five seasons, and it just doesn't seem to be in the cards. He has always thrown four pitches for strikes in the minors, particularly an above-average fastball and sharp curve, but has struggled with his command at the major league level. Off-field problems and conditioning have also been concerns. He has allowed 39 homers in 288 major league innings over five seasons.
1998: It's time for a change of scenery, and the Devil Rays provided it. Lopez still has above-average stuff. He might be best suited to a middle-relief role, as he was dominant once around the order as a reliever in Triple-A in 1997.
1997: Lopez spent most of the year as a mopup man in Cleveland, where his control and confidence were both weak. Among his many problems was his indifference to opposing baserunners; 11 successfully stole against him in only 77 innings.
1996: Lopez was a dominant Triple-A starter, especially against righthanders, whom he held to a .203 average. He was again pulverized in the majors, allowing righthanders to hit .322 against him. He showed a major league fastball, but not a major league head.

	W	SV	ERA	IP	H	BB	SO	B/I
1995 Cleveland	0	0	3.13	23	17	7	22	1.04
1996 Cleveland	5	0	6.39	62	80	22	45	1.65
1997 Cleveland	3	0	6.92	77	101	40	63	1.84

LOPEZ, JOHAN - TR - b: 4/4/75

Slow, steady progress got Lopez to Double-A for the first time in 1997; he was 6-8 with a 4.38 ERA at Jackson, splitting time between the rotation and the bullpen. Lopez can hit 92-MPH with his fastball, but has occasional problems with his mechanics which causes his pitches to straighten out and ride up in the strike zone. The youngster still has time to develop and has the stuff to pitch in the majors but needs a breakout season to be considered a true prospect.

LORRAINE, ANDREW - TL - b: 8/11/72

Scouting: A former early-round pick by the Angels, Lorraine seemed to have a lot more promise early in his minor-league career than he now holds. His out pitch is a slider and he possesses a great changeup as well, but he's not overpowering, reaching the upper-80s with his fastball.
1998: As with most of the A's starters, anything is possible, so every pitcher has a shot at making the rotation. Lorraine, however, has his work cut out for him. The probable scenario has him making the club as a middle reliever, culling the occasional spot start.
1997: With big holes blown into the starting five in Oakland, Lorraine was called up from Edmonton after going 8-7 with a 5.50 ERA over 21 starts. Over his six Oakland starts he was, at best, erratic.
1996: Lorraine's performance has fallen off a lot since his 12-4 season at Vancouver in 1994. He has great stuff when he is on, but that isn't often enough.

	W	SV	ERA	IP	H	BB	SO	B/I
1997 Oakland	3	0	6.36	30	45	15	18	2.02

LOTT, BRIAN - TR - b: 5/15/72

Lott had some success in the low minors, but hasn't been able to translate that into success further up the line. After good years in rookie ball and lower Class A, Lott has had two straight bad years, including an awful one at Double-A Chattanooga in 1997 where he was overmatched. Lott doesn't throw hard, and while he doesn't walk many hitters, he hasn't shown any ability to get out more experienced hitters. He's at the end of the line with the Reds and won't get many more chances. He's got to have a good year in 1998 or he'll be out of pro ball in a hurry.

LOVINGIER, KEVIN - TR - b: 8/29/71

The lefthander has been groomed for a spot in the bullpen throughout his four-year minor-league career. He throws hard enough, with a good breaking ball. Lovingier has spent the last two years in Double-A and worked 59 games there this year, as his strikeout total continued to rise (82 in 74.1 innings). His control has helped turn him into one of the organization's more promising lefthanders. Lovingier probably needs to spend at least one full season in Triple-A.

LOWE, DEREK - TR - b: 6/1/73

Lowe is a big (6'6") righthander with good stuff. He doesn't have a dominant fastball, but has pretty good stuff, nonetheless. Lowe used ten good starts at Double-A Port City (5-3, 3.05 ERA) to reach Triple-A for the first time in 1996. He doesn't look like the kind of pitcher who will be overpowering right from the start, but he should eventually develop into a guy who can take a regular turn in the majors.

	W	SV	ERA	IP	H	BB	SO	B/I
1997 Boston	2	0	6.13	69	74	23	52	1.41

LOWE, SEAN - TR - b: 3/29/71

Scouting: Lowe has a 90-MPH, plus, sinking fastball, which he throws for strikes, a decent changeup and an improving curveball. He has a good pitcher's build and should be a quality big-league starter once he gets his feet set in the majors and is allowed to develop some confidence.
1998: Lowe has a chance to earn a spot in the Boston starting rotation, but is probably behind too many more high profile pitchers to get the nod out of spring training. He's got ability, though, and he should crack the rotation before the season is out.
1997: After pitching well in Triple-A for the Mariners, Lowe struggled in a couple of big-league appearances. He was then included in the trade to Boston for Heathcliff Slocumb. He pitched well for the Red Sox in Triple-A, and got a couple of chances to pitch for Boston, but did not fare particularly well.
1996: Lowe pitched well in Double-A and earned a promotion to Triple-A Tacoma, where he pitched decently by Pacific Coast League standards.

LOWE, SEAN - TR - b: 10/25/70

Scouting: Injuries that devastated the Cardinals' starting rotation were the only impetus for taking the disappointing Lowe into the big leagues. Without an overpowering fastball, an above-average breaking pitch or precise control, the former first-round draft pick doesn't seem likely to find himself back in the majors anytime soon.
1998: A vastly improved Lowe could make a case for a spot in the big-league bullpen, though he likely will need to prove he can maintain improvement for most of a full season on the Triple-A level.
1997: Sent to the bullpen briefly in the middle of the Triple-A season, Lowe reassessed his career and took advantage of his next chance when injuries returned him to starter's duty. Though he finished with a 4.37 ERA and more hits than innings pitched, he did pitch considerably better in the second half with noticeably better control and more strikeouts. That earned him a few big-league starts in September, which didn't go so well.
1996: Lowe split the season between two minor-league levels, including 18 starts in his first time at Triple-A. He wasn't effective at either spot, as he walked about one batter every two innings.

	W	SV	ERA	IP	H	BB	SO	B/I
1997 St. Louis	0	0	9.36	17	27	10	8	2.14

LUCE, ROBERT -TR- b: 7/19/74

Luce was the Mariners' ninth-round selection in the 1996 draft and advanced from Class A to Double-A last year. Luce made 27 starts combined and was 15-3 including a 10-1 mark at Class A Lancaster in the California League. He had good control and a better than two-to-one strikeout-to-walk ratio. He did yield slightly over one hit per inning in 1997 and will need to work on his location to improve in that area. He should start 1998 at Double-A and has a shot at the bigs if he keeps improving over the next few seasons.

LUDWICK, ERIC - TR - b: 12/14/71

Obtained mid-season as compensation for Mark McGwire, it is really make-or-break time for the righthander. Ludwick throws hard (low-90s) and has a good slider to complement the fastball. He could factor as a starter or reliever, but because of his age (27) and how slowly he has developed, he is probably closer to the end of the line than he knows.

	W	SV	ERA	IP	H	BB	SO	B/I
1997 Oakland	1	0	8.50	31	44	22	21	2.15

LUEBBERS, LARRY - TR - b: 10/11/69
Luebbers had gotten a couple of chances because he's a big, tall righthander. However, his fastball dropped below average in '97, and he struggled to a 3-14 mark and 5.38 ERA in Triple-A. He's a sinker/slider pitcher who relies on control, so it's possible he can come back and get in a better groove, but he's unlikely to ever pitch effectively in the majors.

LUKASIEWICZ, MARK - TL - b: 3/8/73
After starting the season with Double-A Knoxville, Lukasiewicz got the call to Triple-A in mid-June. At Syracuse, he struck out a batter per inning but didn't show that he could be effective at the tougher level. He is two or three years away from getting a look.

LYONS, CURT - TR - b: 10/17/74
Scouting: Lyons has excellent control and a great changeup to go with an average fastball. He baffles hitters with the change and isn't afraid to throw it at any point in the count. He succeeds despite only average velocity because he is able to keep the ball down and get hitters to hit the ball on the ground. He does get more strikeouts than might be expected, however.
1998: Lyons is back with the Cincinnati Reds, who drafted him in 1992 out of high school. The Reds got rid of most of their starting rotation shortly after the end of the season so he'll have a shot at making the rotation in spring training. If he's recovered from the arm problems that plagued him in 1997 there's a good chance he'll make the team. If he does, he'll have a pretty good rookie season.
1997: The Cubs thought they got a real bargain when they got Lyons from Cincinnati for Ozzie Timmons and a low-level minor-league pitcher. But arm problems limited his effectiveness and scared off the Cubs, who released him after the season. He was supposed to be in the Reds plans, but angered management by reporting to spring training overweight, prompting his trade.
1996: Lyons was so dominant in his first season at Double-A that the Reds called him up to Cincinnati for the last month of the season.

MACCA, CHRIS - TR - b: 11/14/74
Macca is coming off a bad year in 1997, when he was 0-4 with a 7.77 ERA in 46 relief appearances at Double-A New Haven. He pitches with a three-quarters delivery and has an average fastball with good movement on his slider, but he pitched without confidence for New Haven.

MacDONALD, BOB - TL - b: 4/27/65
One of those lefties with decent control being able to hang on forever, MacDonald was at Triple-A on the Mets' farm in 1996 after working 19 innings for the big club, and he went to Japan last year. His work for the Hanshin Tigers did nothing to raise hopes for a return to the majors.

MACEY, FAUSTO - TR - b: 10/9/75
Scouting: Macey is still a diamond in the rough that needs a good amount of polish before he will make it in the major leagues. The word on Macey is he has great stuff, but the youngster is still learning how to harness it. Macey, acquired in a winter, 1996, trade that brought lefthander Allen Watson from San Francisco, has an average fastball, plus a changeup, slider and curve. As with most young pitchers, he needs more experience in order to learn how to make his pitches work for him.
1998: Macey has made improvement, but he has to show the Angels he's got better command to warrant a shot at making the major leagues this season.
1997: Macey opened the season with Triple-A Vancouver, then was sent to Double-A Midland in late-May for more seasoning. The overall numbers don't look that good, but his biggest problem was inconsistency. At times, his great stuff was able to overcome lack of experience.
1996: Macey was one of the most dependable starters for the Giants' Double-A Shreveport farm club, particularly during a May hot streak that saw him win five of six decisions.

MADDUX, GREG - TR - b: 4/14/66
Scouting: Maddux is one of the most precise pitchers the game has ever seen. Some guys are throwers; Maddux is a pitcher. He only reaches the high-80s with his fastball, but he throws a variety of curves, sliders, circle changeups and cut fastballs to exact locations and always, always changing speeds enough to never give a hitter an good swing. His pitches have movement and he can throw them exactly where he wants every time. Because he is so precise, Maddux will often get hitters to hit the first or second pitch at which they swing, beating it into the ground for an out; this lets him pitch deep into every game with a remarkably low pitch count.
1998: No one is a better bet for the Cy Young award; Maddux will again be one of the best pitchers in the game.
1997: Maddux got reasonable run support and posted a won-lost record that was representative of his abilities. He struck out nine batters for every one that he walked, limited homers to a trickle, threw deep into every game and finished among league leaders in every conceivable category. It was a Cy Young year yet again for baseball's best pitcher.
1996: Although it was sometimes described as an "off" year for Maddux he was still among league leaders in numerous categories and was, in fact, a better pitcher than his Cy Young-winning teammate, John Smoltz. Only poor run support made Maddux' record pale beside Smoltz' 24-8 mark.

	W	SV	ERA	IP	H	BB	SO	B/I
1995 Atlanta	19	0	1.63	209	147	23	181	0.81
1996 Atlanta	15	0	2.72	245	225	28	172	1.03
1997 Atlanta	19	0	2.20	233	200	20	177	0.95

MADDUX, MIKE - TR - b: 8/27/61
After a mid-season release from the Mariners, Maddux took a few weeks off to decide his future in baseball. He signed with the Padres with the hope of working through Las Vegas to return to the majors with San Diego. Maddux was ineffective at Triple-A and never made it to the Padres. His opportunity for future major league employment is dim. Mike is Greg's older brother.

	W	SV	ERA	IP	H	BB	SO	B/I
1995 Pittsburgh	1	0	9.00	9	14	3	4	1.89
1995 Boston	4	1	3.61	89	86	15	65	1.13
1996 Boston	3	0	4.48	64	76	27	32	1.61
1997 Seattle	1	0	10.09	11	20	8	7	2.62

MADURO, CALVIN - TR - b: 9/5/74
Scouting: Finesse pitcher Maduro features a mid-80s fastball and a diverse array of breaking pitches. He underwent a major mechanical overhaul in 1997 that had negative short-term effects but should make him a better pitcher in the long run. Maduro used to have excellent control, but limited ability to get the ball past higher level hitters. His pitches now have sharper movement, but he's still learning to control them.
1998: Maduro needs to begin the year at Triple-A, but he will be in the majors as soon as he exhibits that he can control his new and improved stuff. He ranks ahead of other Triple-A pitchers on the Phillies' depth chart and projects as a major league starter, possibly by the end of 1998.
1997: At age 22, Maduro was one of the younger members of an Opening Day big-league rotation. It got ugly quickly, however. Maduro requires pinpoint precision to be effective, and he appeared scared in some of his early starts. After a demotion to Triple-A, he made major mechanical refinements that will increase his power over the long haul.
1996: Maduro excelled at Double-A Bowie but then struggled at Triple-A Rochester in the Orioles' chain. This continued his pattern of needing a second year at each level to achieve success. Maduro was dealt to the Phillies in exchange for Todd Zeile at the trading deadline.

	W	SV	ERA	IP	H	BB	SO	B/I
1997 Philadelphia	3	0	7.23	71	83	41	31	1.75

MAEDA, KATSUHIRO - TR - b: 6/23/71
Not exactly Hideo Nomo, Maeda spent 1996 mostly at Double-A Norwich with an ERA of 4.02. 1997 was his second year at Double-A, but he had a losing record and a 4.70 ERA. He needs to work on his control (66 walks and 82 strikeouts) to move up.

MAGNANTE, MIKE - TL - b: 6/17/65
Scouting: Magnante spent parts of six seasons with Kansas City primarily as a lefthanded relief specialist before signing with Houston in 1997. His best pitch is a screwball which makes him equally effective against righthanded and lefthanded batters. He has a slider and a sweeping curveball that he uses effectively against lefthanded batters. His fastball is in the high eighties.
1998: Magnante should have a job as a lefthander in a major league bullpen.
1997: Magnante did not make the major league roster out of spring training. He started the season at Triple-A New Orleans where he was 2-3, with a 4.50 ERA and one save. He was recalled on May 31st and pitched effectively in the Houston bullpen for the rest of the season. He had his best year in the major leagues which he attributed to the improvement in his curveball.
1996: Magnante had a subpar 2-2, 5.67 season in Kansas City and was released. Because of his relative ineffectiveness against lefthanded hitters, he fell into severe disuse by Royals' Manager Bob Boone.

	W	SV	ERA	IP	H	BB	SO	B/I
1995 Kansas City	1	0	4.23	44	45	16	28	1.38
1996 Kansas City	2	0	5.67	54	58	24	32	1.52
1997 Houston	3	1	2.26	48	39	11	43	1.05

MAGNUM, MARK - TR - b: 4/1/97
A Texas schoolboy, Magnum was selected by the Rockies with the 18th pick of the 1997 draft. Magnum pitched at Rookie League Mesa last year, showing strikeout ability; he fanned 72 in 61 innings.

MAHAY, RON - TR - b: 6/28/71
Scouting: Mahay, who played in the majors for Boston as an outfielder in 1995, throws his fastball at better than 90 MPH and has a good changeup to go with it. His slider, which he needs to be effective against lefthanded hitters, needs work. He's only been a pitcher for two years so he's certain to keep improving.
1998: Mahay should be the top lefthander in the Boston bullpen. He's better than most against righthanded hitters because of his good fastball and changeup, and should be even tougher against lefties when he improves his slider. His chance to save games will depend on Tom Gordon's success as the Red Sox closer.
1997: In only his second full season as a pitcher, Mahay jumped quickly from Double-A to Triple-A and then the majors, where he pitched well.
1996: Mahay had an impressive first season as a pitcher in A-ball after being converted from the outfield.

	W	SV	ERA	IP	H	BB	SO	B/I
1997 Boston	3	0	2.52	25	19	11	22	1.20

MAHOMES, PAT - TR - b: 8/9/70
Mahomes has a 93-MPH fastball and an excellent curveball. He began the '97 season in the Boston bullpen, but control problems again sent him to the minors. He was pitching well for Triple-A Pawtucket, and was probably coming into his own as a reliever, when he accepted an offer to go to Japan. Should he come back he has a chance to be a top-notch big-league reliever because of his great stuff.

	W	SV	ERA	IP	H	BB	SO	B/I
1995 Minnesota	4	3	6.37	94	100	47	67	1.56
1996 Boston	3	2	6.91	57	72	33	36	1.84
1997 Boston	1	0	8.10	10	15	10	5	2.50

MALONEY, SEAN - TR - b: 5/25/71
A minor-league closer, Maloney earned a brief debut in the majors (three games), then suffered an attack of appendicitis when returned to the minors. He appeared in just 15 games for Triple-A Tucson. He has demonstrated good poise in the high minors; Maloney is considered a prospect.

MANIAS, JIM - TL - b: 10/21/74
Manias pitched at St. Petersburg in 1997 and was quite impressive; he has good control with three different pitches. Devil Rays officials weren't sure if he could go the entire season without injury or experiencing a tired arm, but he persevered on the Florida State League champion team. Manias likely will be at the big-league spring training camp, but he's a longshot to make the squad.

MANNING, DAVID - TR - b: 8/14/72
Manning was selected by the Rangers in the third round of the 1992 June draft and split last season between the Double-A and Triple-A levels. Manning was not overpowering at either stop and looks like he'll be on the minor-league shuttle again in 1998, a season where he has to make something happen to have a serious major league future.

MANNING, DEREK - TL - b: 7/21/70
In 1995, Manning was 11-1 at Class A Modesto. At the time, however, he was 25 years old — quite old for a pitcher toiling at that level. Since then he has struggled at Double-A. He is unlikely to advance much if any further.

MANNING, LEN - TL - b: 10/7/72
Manning was the tenth man on Double-A Reading's staff in 1997. He didn't make his Double-A debut until last year at age 25, making him too old to be a prospect. His velocity is below-average and his control is sub-par. He tries to keep hitters off-balance with a variety of off-speed stuff, but generally gets behind in the count too often. Despite being lefthanded, Manning has little chance for success at higher levels.

MANTEI, MATT - TR - b: 7/7/73
The Marlins envisioned Mantei as a future closer candidate because of his fastball and bulldog mentality, but he went down in mid-1996 with a torn rotator cuff. Prior to the injury he featured a low-90's fastball, but had struggled with his location at the major league level.

MANUEL, BARRY - TR - b: 8/12/65
After a comeback with Montreal in 1996, Manuel found himself back in the minors last year as a starter and middle reliever at Triple-A Norfolk. Despite the good 1996 season as a set-up man with Montreal, he had a less than brilliant year last season with a 2-5 record and 4.87 ERA. Although his velocity is down from what it was five years ago, he still throws strikes, and he gave up less than a hit per inning in 1997.

	W	SV	ERA	IP	H	BB	SO	B/I
1996 Montreal	4	0	3.24	86	70	26	62	1.12
1997 New York NL	0	0	5.25	26	35	13	21	1.87

MANZANILLO, JOSIAS - TR - b: 10/16/67
Manzanillo missed all of 1996 while recovering from right elbow inflammation but made it back to pitch 48.2 innings with the Mariners last year; he wasn't effective with the big club. He has appeared in the bigs with the Red Sox, Brewers, Mets and Yankees as well as Seattle during his 14-year baseball career. It was a nice comeback for him but he's going to have to battle for a job in baseball this spring.

MARSONEK, SAM - TR - b: 7/10/78
Marsonek was the first-round pick by the Rangers in the 1996 draft (24th overall). Last year he pitched at Rookie League Pulaski and Charlotte of the Class A Florida State League. He struck out nearly a batter per inning at both stops but gave up just over a hit per inning as well.

MARTIN, JEFF - TR - b: 3/29/73
Martin started his fifth straight season in A-ball, then moved up to Double-A Shreveport for the first time in his career. The results were neither thrilling nor disappointing (0-2 with a 4.99 ERA). Martin held his own, but he is getting to be too old for his level and there are better pitchers in the Giants' organization.

MARTIN, TOM - TL - b: 5/21/70
Scouting: Martin entered the 1997 season as a journeyman lefthander in his fourth organization with an undistinguished minor-league record. He was a surprise in 1997 making the jump from Double-A to the major leagues and pitching effectively in the Houston bullpen. He throws harder than most lefthanded relievers and has a sharp, biting slider. He has occasional lapses in control.
1998: Martin should get a chance to prove that his major league success in 1997 was not a fluke. Arizona took him with an intention of giving plenty of work out of their pen.
1997: Martin spent the entire season in the Astro bullpen. He spent two weeks on the disabled list in June with a strained elbow which didn't give him any trouble the rest of the season.
1996: Martin spent his first year in the Houston system at Double-A Jackson where he was 6-2 with a 3.24 ERA and three saves. He also recorded five scoreless appearances with Triple-A Tucson.

	W	SV	ERA	IP	H	BB	SO	B/I
1997 Houston	5	2	2.09	56	52	23	36	1.34

MARTINEZ, DENNIS - TR - b: 5/14/55
"El Presidente" bid farewell after a final comeback attempt with Seattle, who turned to Martinez in spring training in a desperate attempt to fill the final spot in its starting rotation last season. Martinez was released by Cleveland because of elbow problems and managed just one victory in nine starts before his release from the Mariners. The well-respected veteran finished with 241 career victories.

	W	SV	ERA	IP	H	BB	SO	B/I
1995 Cleveland	12	0	3.08	187	174	46	99	1.18
1996 Cleveland	9	0	4.50	112	122	37	48	1.42
1997 Seattle	1	0	7.71	49	65	29	17	1.92

MARTINEZ, JESUS - TL - b: 3/13/74
Scouting: Like his brothers Ramon and Pedro, Jesus has some giddy-up on the fastball. Unlike his two major league siblings, he doesn't know where the ball is going to end up once he lets go of it. He's of slight build (6'2", 145-pounds) and has had trouble working deep into games as a starter. Martinez may be better suited for bullpen duty if he makes it to the majors.
1998: Drafted by Arizona and then traded to Detroit, Martinez is expected to begin the year in Triple-A as a full-time bullpen pitcher. Concentrating on better control of the fastball with less attention to maintaining the full repertoire of a starter will make him a good set-up man, it is hoped. Being a hard-throwing lefty will make him valuable to any major league team, if his control improves.
1997: Because he has had trouble lasting deep into games, Martinez was shifted to the bullpen during the 1997 season at Triple-A Albuquerque. He struck out nearly a batter per inning on the season.
1996: Martinez was the leading starter at Double-A San Antonio where he was 10-13 with a 4.40 ERA in 27 starts.

MARTINEZ, JOHNNY - TR - b: 11/25/72
Martinez is a lean righthander (6'3", 168 pounds) who was able to get by with a confusing motion, mediocre velocity and average command at high Class A in previous seasons, but not at Double-A in 1997. He was basically reduced to mopup duty at Akron, and since he's not lefthanded that likely exempts him from a potential major league future. His only positive trait is his ability to eat up two or three innings out of the pen on a semi-regular basis. He is unlikely to advance any higher.

MARTINEZ, PEDRO A. - TL - b: 9/29/68

Scouting: Martinez doesn't have the velocity or control of the "other" Pedro Martinez, but he has a decent selection of pitches. He's not overpowering, but he throws a breaking ball that is wicked to lefthanded hitters and good enough to keep righthanded hitters from teeing off.

1998: Martinez has got good enough stuff to be a serviceable major league relief pitcher and being lefthanded sure won't hurt his chances of landing a full-time big-league roster spot. If he can throw more strikes he'll have a good year coming out of the bullpen, even if it's only to retire a couple of lefthanded hitters.

1997: Martinez had a good year at Triple-A Indianapolis, going 4-3 while splitting time between the bullpen and the starting rotation. He earned a trial with the Reds, but got pounded and quickly shipped back down Interstate 74.

1996: Martinez started the season with the Mets' Triple-A team and was successful coming out of the bullpen. He earned a mid-season callup, but was ineffective in a five-game stint with the Mets and was sent back down to Norfolk to finish out the minor-league season. The Reds acquired him in September and brought him up to give him a brief tryout.

MARTINEZ, PEDRO J. - TR - b: 10/25/71

Scouting: Martinez is as tough to face as any pitcher in the game today. He throws a 95-MPH fastball with great movement and isn't afraid to throw it inside. His slider is often unhittable, and few throw a better changeup. Martinez breaks more bats than any pitcher in the game and leaves hitters shaking their heads at how a guy charitably listed at 5'11", 170 pounds can throw so hard. He also has amazing durability for a guy his size and is still young enough to get better, which is scary.

1998: Knowing he could command upwards of $8 million in salary arbitration, the Expos put Martinez on the trading block at the end of last season and Boston won the bidding. Martinez will be one of the game's premier pitchers for years..

1997: Hitters universally agreed Martinez was the nastiest pitcher in the National League. He struck out over 300 batters, had an ERA nearly 2.5 runs better than the league and would have won 20 games if he had gotten any offensive support. The only downside was a strained tendon in his pitching thumb that hampered him late in the season. The injury is not expected to have any lingering effects.

1996: Martinez established himself as the Expos' ace and began being recognized as one of the top righthanded pitchers in the game following an outstanding season.

	W	SV	ERA	IP	H	BB	SO	B/I
1995 Montreal	14	0	3.51	194	158	66	174	1.15
1996 Montreal	13	0	3.70	216	189	70	222	1.20
1997 Montreal	17	0	1.90	241	158	67	305	0.93

MARTINEZ, RAMIRO - TL - b: 1/28/72

Martinez has put together two fine seasons in middle relief in the Expos' farm system since being released by Texas early in 1996. The lefthander will start off this season at Triple-A Ottawa, his first season at that level, and could move quickly to the majors if he pitches well.

MARTINEZ, RAMON - TR - b: 3/22/68

Scouting: Martinez' ability to come back from major injuries with all his velocity and skill intact is remarkable. His bread and butter pitches are a tailing fastball, and a two-seamer which gives him a hard sinker. He's got a deceptive changeup which hitters rarely adjust to. He has a good curveball, but doesn't use it much. Now if he just doesn't strain his rotator cuff again...

1998: When healthy, he's one of the best in the game. In the past two years Martinez is 25-11 in 302.1 innings. He's a legitimate number one starter.

1997: Martinez went on the DL June 24th to rest with a small tear in his rotator cuff and didn't win again until late-August. He made a remarkably fast comeback. Minor surgery and major surgery had both been discussed as possibilities.

1996: Martinez went down early with a badly pulled groin suffered on a cold day in Chicago. A bad case of the flu followed. Overall he missed eight starts. By the middle of the season, he was back and on his typical roll. He closed the year by going 4-0 in September, leading the Dodgers to the playoffs.

	W	SV	ERA	IP	H	BB	SO	B/I
1995 Los Angeles	17	0	3.66	206	176	81	138	1.25
1996 Los Angeles	15	0	3.42	168	153	86	133	1.42
1997 Los Angeles	10	0	3.64	134	123	68	120	1.43

MARTINEZ, WILLIE - TR - b: 4/14/73

Scouting: Martinez is a highly-refined pitcher for his age. He throws a 90-MPH fastball plus a curve and changeup for quality strikes consistently, and gains velocity late in games. He has a flawless motion that puts little stress on his arm. The Indians kept him on a pitch count in 1997, his first full pro season, so he is capable of much more. He's apparently oblivious to pressure, and responds in game situations.

1998: Martinez has the type of arsenal which should allow for immediate Double-A success. The Indians will likely allow him to pitch deeper into games more consistently in 1998. He is on track for a 1999 major league debut at age 21. He'll be an excellent complement to Jaret Wright and possibly Bartolo Colon in the future Indians' rotation.

1997: Martinez dominated the high Class A Carolina League as its youngest pitcher. Most impressive was his ability to pitch better as games progressed, and as the season progressed. Despite his frail build, Martinez is a potential future major league workhorse.

1996: Martinez was clearly superior to the Rookie-ball hitters he faced in his first pro season. He was considered the best pitching prospect in the New York-Penn League as an 18-year-old.

MATHEWS, T.J. - TR - b: 1/19/70

Scouting: The real dividend earned in the Mark McGwire trade, Mathews throws a hard fastball in the mid-90s along with a slider and splitter. He is aggressive — even earning a suspension for throwing at a hitter in spring training — and is thus well suited to be a closer.

1998: Mathews has the upper hand on the closer job for the A's this year. He has the stuff and the make-up, and Billy Taylor is no longer consistently effective. One way or another, he'll be on the Oakland roster, pitching in an important relief role.

1997: After being traded, Mathews finished off 14 games, earning saves only towards the end of the season. Mathews was one of a group who set up Dennis Eckersly in St. Louis prior to his trade to Oakland.

1996: Mathews was the closer-in-waiting for the Cardinals, ready to move into the role whenever Dennis Eckersly retired. Converted to short relief in 1995, Mathews was outstanding in

'96, his first full season in the majors.

	W	SV	ERA	IP	H	BB	SO	B/I
1995 St. Louis	1	2	1.52	29	21	11	28	1.08
1996 St. Louis	2	6	3.01	83	62	32	80	1.13
1997 Oakland	10	3	3.01	75	75	30	70	1.41

MATHEWS, TERRY - TR - b: 10/5/64
Scouting: Mathews is basically a fastball/slider pitcher, and is a valuable part of the Orioles bullpen. His fastball is slightly above average, but his mechanics get out of kilter every so often, and he may unexpectedly lose the plate. Occasionally erratic pitching prevents Mathews from becoming a top reliever.
1998: Mathews should continue in his middle relief and set-up roles.
1997: As a middle reliever and set-up man, Mathews was a valuable part of the Orioles bullpen last year. The Orioles had enough bullpen depth to absorb his occasional loss of control.
1996: The Orioles obtained Mathews in a trade with the Marlins. He was a middle reliever and set-up man with the Marlins, appearing in 57 games.

	W	SV	ERA	IP	H	BB	SO	B/I
1995 Florida	4	3	3.38	82	70	27	72	1.17
1996 Florida	2	4	4.91	55	59	27	49	1.56
1997 Baltimore	4	1	4.41	63	63	36	39	1.56

MATRANGA, JEFF - TR - b: 12/14/70
After a good season in 1996 with Double-A Arkansas, Matranga struggled at Triple-A Louisville last year. He had a 5.57 ERA, and gave up 75 hits in only 53.1 innings. He did have a good strikeout-to-walk ratio, however.

MATTHEWS, MIKE - TL - b: 10/24/73
The Indians' 1993 second-round pick has had an injury-riddled career, missing over a full season due to 1993 rotator cuff surgery which permanently robbed him of much of his strikeout potential. The southpaw has learned how to pitch over the last three seasons, all spent at Double-A. However, he cannot get the ball past hitters in key spots, and is no more than a six-inning pitcher. Credit his effort, but Matthews is unlikely to make a major league impression.

MAUER, MIKE - TR - b: 7/4/72
Mauer pitched fairly well during his second season at Double-A Huntsville. His 8-7 record and 3.83 ERA were fine for the 84.2 innings he toiled. He appeared in 52 games, the same as 1996, but threw 20 more innings. He is no more than a middle-reliever or set-up man, but he could be fine in that role in the majors. It is time for him to move to the Triple-A proving grounds.

MAURER, MIKE - TR - b: 7/4/72
Maurer lacks a major league fastball, but he changes speeds and moves the ball around effectively. In his second year at Double-A Huntsville on the Athletics farm, he tried five starts in addition to his usual bullpen work. Maurer was 8-7 with a 3.83 ERA and two saves.

MAXCY, BRIAN - TR - b: 5/4/71
In his second season with Triple-A Louisville, Maxcy posted a 3.76 ERA which is deceiving since he also had more walks than strikeouts (24 to 22). He has pitched in the majors before with Detroit in 1995 and 1996, but with limited success.

MAY, DARRELL - TL - b: 6/13/72
Scouting: May is one of several top pitching prospects who may secure jobs on the Angels' staff in the next couple years. The Angels' like his fastball and his makeup, which earned him a promotion from Vancouver the second half of last season.
1998: May will be given every opportunity to win a job on the Angels' staff for a full season and has a good chance of making it. He likely won't crack the starting rotation, but could be a good insurance policy in the event of injury, while serving the club in a long relief role in the meantime.
1997: May served notice he was ready to make an impression on the Angels by throwing a no-hitter at Vancouver just before his promotion. He struggled at times after his promotion, but also got some key outs in relief to help keep the Angels in the division race, despite a rash of injuries.
1996: May was an effective starter at Pittsburgh's Triple-A Calgary farm club before the Angels claimed him on waivers from Pittsburgh in September. His career has been on a steady upswing since he joined the Angels' organization.

	W	SV	ERA	IP	H	BB	SO	B/I
1997 Anaheim	2	0	5.22	52	56	25	42	1.57

McANDREW, JAMIE - TR - b: 9/2/67
McAndrew opened the season in the Brewers' rotation and managed to post their first victory of the year, then fell apart and was shipped back to the minors in May. He also struggled in a brief recall in July. At this point the Brewers don't seem to have a place for McAndrew; his immediate future is in the high minors.

	W	SV	ERA	IP	H	BB	SO	B/I
1997 Milwaukee	1	0	8.39	19	24	23	8	2.44

McBRIDE, CHRIS - TR - b: 10/13/73
McBride split the 1997 season between Class A and Double-A ball. He gave up more than a hit per inning combined and was not overpowering at either level. He had a better ERA at Double-A and may get a chance to prove himself at that level to start 1998.

McCARTHY, GREG - TL - b: 10/30/68
Scouting: McCarthy is a strong lefty reliever who can strike people out. On the down side he has control problems and has less than 40 innings pitched in the majors in 11 seasons of pro ball.
1998: He has spent parts of the past two seasons with the Mariners and could get another look to be a part of their pen. If he can cut down on his wildness and throw strikes, he could still be of some value being that he's a lefty.
1997: McCarthy pitched part of the season in the Kingdome for the second straight year. He also pitched at Triple-A Tacoma where he continued to strike out batters at a better than one per inning rate.
1996: There was the good McCarthy and the bad McCarthy at Triple-A Tacoma. The good McCarthy fanned 90 hitters in just 68.1 innings of work. The bad McCarthy unleashed a team-high 11 wild pitches. Despite the wildness, McCarthy made his major league debut after ten seasons in the minors and was effective in ten appearances with the Mariners.

	W	SV	ERA	IP	H	BB	SO	B/I
1997 Seattle	1	0	5.45	30	26	16	34	1.41

McCOMMOM, JASON - TR - b: 8/9/71
McCommon is a four-pitch pitcher, but all four pitches are average or just below average. He needs to be perfect to be effective, but so far has not been. He might see some time in the majors the next couple of years as a fill-in due to injuries, but he's unlikely to ever be a big winner there.

McCURRY, JEFF - TR - b: 1/21/70
Scouting: One of the Rockies' surprises in 1997, McCurry spent most of the season with the big-league club. He's a reliever who goes right after hitters, even though he has average stuff. His splitter is his best pitch and he will run the fastball in. McCurry possesses a resilient arm and is willing to accept any role, so long as it's in the big leagues. He was taken off the 40-man roster at the end of the 1997 season.
1998: Entering the off-season, the Rockies were hopeful of re-signing McCurry and inviting him to their big-league camp, where he will have a chance to make the club in middle relief.
1997: Selected away from Detroit in the Rule V draft, McCurry made the Rockies' season-opening roster, even though he did not participate in the big-league camp. McCurry pitched well for Triple-A Colorado Springs in spring training so he got the call when the Rockies had to make a late-spring callup.
1996: McCurry spent the entire season at Triple-A Toledo in the Tigers' farm system. He went 1-4 with a 4.76 ERA in 39 relief appearances.

	W	SV	ERA	IP	H	BB	SO	B/I
1997 Colorado	1	0	4.42	41	43	20	9	1.55

McCUTCHEON, MIKE - TL - b: 7/5/77
McCutcheon made a successful transition from playing the outfield as a collegian to pitching in A-ball for the Diamondbacks. He has just average velocity but his stuff and his location are both pretty good.

McDERMOTT, RYAN - TR - b: 6/28/78
While many other clubs shied away from the 6'10", 230 pound McDermott because of their belief that he would opt to play basketball at Arizona State, the Indians invested a second round pick. McDermott is just a baby and has the poor mechanics often found in a prospect his size, but has a low-90's fastball with the potential for much more.

McDILL, ALLEN - TL - b: 8/23/71
Desperation for competent lefthanded relievers gave McDill his first shot in the majors in 1997. He was a bust and returned to Triple-A Omaha. He went 5-2 with a 5.88 ERA in 23 appearances (six starts) at Omaha and was demoted to Double-A Wichita where he had a 3.12 ERA in sixteen relief appearances. McDill doesn't throw especially hard, but usually has good enough command of his off-speed stuff to throw at the corners and keep hitters off-stride. He's too old to be at Double-A. Expansion might help him get to the majors again in 1998, but he needs a full year — and a good one — at Triple-A to be considered a prospect again.

McDONALD, BEN - TR - b: 11/24/67
Scouting: The Brewers' top starter until he injured his shoulder, McDonald sees his career at a crossroads after shoulder surgery in August. When he is healthy, McDonald can still get his fastball up around 90 MPH and has a slider that can keep hitters pounding the ball on the ground. His 6'7" frame has always helped him intimidate hitters, but it can be a limitation in fielding; he led American League pitchers in errors in 1996 with six.
1998: McDonald has an option with Milwaukee and is expected to exercise it, but the Brewers might still look to trade him.
1997: Before undergoing shoulder surgery, McDonald made just enough starts to qualify for a $2 million incentive in his '98 contract. The Brewers were looking to trade him before the July 31st deadline, but his shoulder acted up.
1996: McDonald signed as a free agent with the Brewers and pitched well despite frequent lack of run support (2.5 runs per game during one 11-game stretch).

	W	SV	ERA	IP	H	BB	SO	B/I
1995 Baltimore	3	0	4.16	80	67	38	62	1.31
1996 Milwaukee	12	0	3.90	221	228	67	146	1.33
1997 Milwaukee	8	0	4.06	133	120	36	110	1.17

McDOWELL, JACK - TR - b: 1/16/66
Scouting: McDowell provides further proof that most pitchers who get by with finesse in their twenties run into big trouble in their thirties. A battler who relied on the location rather than the speed of his fastball in his younger days, McDowell has been rendered useless by elbow injuries for much of the past two seasons. He threw an awful lot of pitches in his twenties, many of them the off-speed variety. The workload has apparently caught up with him.
1998: McDowell's $4.8 million option for 1998 wasn't exercised, but he still could contend for a role in the rotation at a lower price. The Indians or anyone else would be foolish to count on McDowell as an anchor, but he could fit in as a decent mid-rotation starter,
1997: McDowell was clearly not himself in his few 1997 starts. His command was poor, and he seemed to be trying to strike out hitters too often, unwilling to set them up with breaking stuff. He was shut down in mid-May, paving the way for the recalls of Jaret Wright and Bartolo Colon.
1996: McDowell was not the stalwart starter the Indians thought they were getting, as he allowed well over a hit per inning while averaging a career low 6.4 innings per start. His five complete games were his lowest total in six years, including the strike seasons.

	W	SV	ERA	IP	H	BB	SO	B/I
1995 New York AL	15	0	3.93	217	211	78	157	1.33
1996 Cleveland	13	0	5.11	192	214	67	141	1.46
1997 Cleveland	3	0	5.09	41	44	18	38	1.52

McELROY, CHUCK - TL - b: 10/1/67
Scouting: McElroy doesn't have the hard curveball anymore, but his bender does have a good break; he'll throw it inside to righthanded batters and doesn't give in to anyone. He lacks closer stuff, but pitched well in a season split between Anaheim and Chicago. McElroy is a good athlete and a good hitter, too.
1998: Drafted by Arizona and then traded to Colorado, McElroy should have a primary lefty set-up role in the Rockies' bullpen.
1997: McElroy did his job well by shutting down the opponent's tougher lefthanded bats late in the game.
1996: In McElroy's first year with the Angels he held opponents to a .239 batting average and, despite some inconsistencies, McElroy had a fine season.

	W	SV	ERA	IP	H	BB	SO	B/I
1996 Cincinnati	2	0	6.57	12	13	10	13	1.90
1996 California	5	0	2.95	36	32	13	32	1.24
1997 Chicago AL	1	1	3.84	75	73	22	62	1.27

McENTIRE, ETHAN - TL - b: 7/19/75
After a promising year in 1996 (9-6, 2.22 ERA), arm trouble limited McEntire to three games at Class A St. Lucie in 1997. His 0-1 record and 6.17 ERA belie the talent he has when he's healthy.

McGRAW, TOM - TL - b: 12/8/67
Signed as a minor-league free agent last year, McGraw didn't figure into the Cardinals' plans until he got off to a good start in Triple-A and their big-league bullpen couldn't find enough healthy lefthanders. He struggled with his control in spotty work with the Cards, then turned dreadful when demoted to the Triple-A bullpen. An eight-year pro who had spent the three previous seasons in the Eastern League, McGraw doesn't seem likely to pitch again for the Cardinals.

McKENZIE, SCOTT - TR - b: 9/30/70
McKenzie fell apart in 1997 after having good years in each of his first three seasons in pro ball. In his first three years, he jumped quickly from the rookie leagues all the way to Double-A. Last year, though, McKenzie became extremely hittable. He didn't give up a lot of home runs or walks, but was victimized for 74 hits in 53 innings at Chattanooga. McKenzie turned 27 at the end of last season so it's highly unlikely that he'll ever become a productive big-league pitcher. He's going to have to stay with the Reds or hook up with another pitching-poor system to get another chance. If he does get it he better take advantage of it or he'll be out of baseball quickly.

McKNIGHT, TONY - TR - b: 6/29/77
McKnight was selected by the Astros with the 22nd pick in the first round of the 1995 draft. He made 20 starts for Quad City of the Midwest League last year. McKnight gave up just over a hit per inning and struggled with his control while posting a 4-9 mark with a 4.68 ERA.

McMICHAEL, GREG - TR - b: 12/1/66
Scouting: On a Mets team that too often played Russian Roulette Relief —with too few empty chambers, McMichael pitched frequently, sometimes to his own detriment. He often was called upon to do the heavy lifting. On a Mets team that had too few strikeout pitchers, he also accomplished the most swings-and-misses, much to the appreciation of his manager and pitching coach who knew his slider and assortment of changeups made him effective against lefthanded hitters. "It's like having a lefty in the pen" pitching coach Bob Apodaca says. Chronically injured knees reduce McMichael's ability to cover his position.
1998: By early summer last year, the Mets recognized that frequent reliance on McMichael too often brought on a point of diminishing return. They believed the August acquisition of Mel Rojas and Turk Wendell would enhance McMichael's performance. They were right. And based on that performance, they expected more quality set-up relief from the veteran pitcher.
1997: McMichael allowed seven runs in 4.2 innings in the four appearances that directly preceded the August 8th trade for Rojas and Wendell. But, thereafter, he allowed just seven runs in his final 27.2 innings (21 appearances). His ERA in the last 21 appearances was 2.28, compared with 3.30 before the deal. He led the league in blown saves (11) and relief losses (10), and was tied for third in relief wins (seven). Set-up relievers shouldn't be measured by victories.
1996: In his last of four seasons with the Braves, McMichael did his usual job — many innings in many opportunities. The Braves, who were troubled by their bullpen in 1997, traded him partially because he became eligible for salary arbitration. McMichael played a role in Mets' history before he joined the team, throwing the pitch Todd Hundley hit for his 41st home run, the one that established a record for home runs in one season by a catcher.

	W	SV	ERA	IP	H	BB	SO	B/I
1995 Atlanta	7	2	2.79	80	64	32	74	1.19
1996 Atlanta	5	2	3.22	86	84	27	78	1.29
1997 New York NL	7	7	2.98	88	73	27	81	1.14

McNICHOL, BRIAN - TL - b: 5/20/74
McNichol, the Cubs' second-round draft choice in 1995, struggled in his first season at Double-A. He's a tall lefthander and the Cubs envision him as being similar to Randy Johnson, but he's not nearly that dominating. McNichol doesn't have the outstanding fastball that Johnson has and was overpowered at Orlando, giving up way too many hits. He'll have to spend at least one more season in the minors before he can even think about making it to Chicago.

MEACHAM, RUSTY - TR - b: 1/27/68
Meacham's career is winding down. His fastball is not what it was, which is bad news for a pitcher who relies on a fastball/splitter combination. He did not pitch particularly well for Triple-A Pawtucket in '97, posting a 4.78 ERA, and his season was cut short due to a knee injury, which required surgery.

	W	SV	ERA	IP	H	BB	SO	B/I
1995 Kansas City	4	2	4.98	59	72	19	30	1.54
1996 Seattle	1	1	5.74	42	57	13	25	1.66

MEADOWS, BRIAN - TR - b: 11/21/75
Scouting: Meadows features above-average control and slightly better than average velocity on his fastball, but has been hampered by poor location in the strike zone and a lack of sharp movement on his pitches. He has walked just over two batters per nine innings in his pro career, but has allowed over a hit per inning. When he's painting the corners he's darn near unhittable, and has the stamina to finish ballgames. He's always been one of the younger hurlers at each minor-league stop, so he still could put it all together and become a mid-rotation starter in the majors — 1998 is a pivotal year for him.
1998: Meadows will likely open the season at Triple-A Charlotte. The Marlins would be happy if he walked a few more hitters in return for better location of his strikes. An average of about 6.5 innings per start with an improved strikeout rate would put him on track for a September big-league debut.
1997: Meadows was hittable in his first full Double-A season, catching too much of the plate with straight fastballs on a regular basis. However, he ranked among Eastern League innings pitched leaders as one of the circuit's youngest hurlers.
1996: Meadows' inability to strike out higher Class A batters (69 whiffs in 146 innings) was particularly worrisome for a pitcher with such good stuff and control. It was clear that mechanical adjustments were necessary to produce sharper movement on his pitches.

MECHE, GIL - TR - b: 9/8/78
Meche went to Seattle with the 22nd overall pick in the 1996

draft. He was in A-ball last year at Everett and Wisconsin. He showed good stuff, averaging nearly a strikeout per inning and coming in at about a hit per inning.

MECIR, JIM - TR - b: 5/16/70
Mecir has been a highly effective reliever at Triple-A Columbus (1.00 ERA in 24 games in 1997) and has even made some contributions to the Yankees championship drives, including a gutsy long outing in a pivotal game against the Orioles when he first came up. Overall, Mecir has struggled in the majors. His fastball is good for Triple-A but not so good for the majors. The Devil Rays hope he can refine his breaking stuff and succeed at the major league level.

	W	SV	ERA	IP	H	BB	SO	B/I
1996 New York AL	1	0	5.13	40	42	23	38	1.62
1997 New York AL	0	0	5.88	34	36	10	25	1.36

MEDINA, RAFAEL - TR - b: 2/15/75
Scouting: The Padres project Medina as a top starter. Other scouts are not that high on the righthander acquired from Yankees in the Hideki Irabu deal. Medina is a power fastball/slider pitcher.
1998: Medina will be given every chance to make the Padre rotation this spring. If his tools are as good as projected, it won't be that hard.
1997: Medina missed most of the season recuperating from a shoulder injury suffered in a fall. After going 2-0 with a 2.00 ERA in three rehab starts at Class A Rancho Cucamonga, he finished the season with a 4-5 record and a 7.56 ERA at Triple-A Las Vegas; he struck out 50 but walked 39 in 66.2 innings.
1996: Medina wowed the scouts while pitching with the Yankees Double-A Norwich franchise, going 5-8 with a 3.06 ERA and 112 strikeouts in 103 innings.

MEINERS, DOUG - TR - b: 5/16/74
Meiners was knocked around at Double-A Knoxville last year with 161 hits allowed in 122.2 innings. His 9-5 record was misleading and his 5.43 ERA was third-worst on the team among pitchers with at least 35 innings. There's no reason to view him as much of a prospect yet, especially considering how little he's pitched at the higher levels of the professional ladder.

MENDOZA, RAMIRO - TR - b: 6/15/72
Scouting: This sinkerballer spent the second half of the season with his name involved in multiple trade rumors last year. The Yankees thought so much of him that they refused to part with him in any deal. With great command, he is effective when he keeps the ball down. He needs to add another pitch in order to be an effective starter; his sinker is just about as good a pitch as there is when he locates it well.
1998: With Dwight Gooden gone, Mendoza could move into a permanent spot in the rotation. However, Joe Torre feels Mendoza better serves the Yankees by working in long relief. One way or another, he will play a big part in the club's pitching plans.
1997: Outside of a minor neck problem, Mendoza stayed healthy. He turned some heads and jumped back to the majors after just one start at Triple-A Columbus. He made fifteen starts out of his 39 appearances with the Yankees and also recorded a pair of saves while fanning three batters for every one he walked.
1996: Mendoza did not do much to distinguish himself in 12 major league games in 1996, his first season in the big leagues. He was effective at Triple-A Columbus, going 6-2 with a 2.51 ERA in 15 starts.

	W	SV	ERA	IP	H	BB	SO	B/I
1996 New York AL	4	0	6.79	53	80	10	34	1.70
1997 New York AL	8	2	4.24	134	157	28	82	1.38

MENDOZA, REYNOL - TR - b: 10/27/70
Scouting: Mendoza was used as a starting pitcher throughout his minor-league career prior to 1997, when he was shifted to the bullpen and even served as a part-time closer. He has only average velocity and his command has waned as he has progressed through the minors. At Triple-A, he has not pitched aggressively, has fallen behind hitters and been forced to deliver room-service fastballs. If Mendoza were a lefty, he'd have a chance to sneak into the majors. He'll remain stuck at Triple-A for the foreseeable future.
1998: Mendoza is likely to fill a relatively unimportant role on a Triple-A staff. He does have a rubber arm and can be used interchangeably as a starter and reliever. He's 27 now, so what you see is what you get; Mendoza is not going to suddenly improve at that age.
1997: Mendoza started, closed and was used as a set-up man at Triple-A Charlotte. His fastballs caught too much of the plate, making him less than stellar in all three roles.
1996: Mendoza was excellent at Double-A Portland in ten early-season starts, but then pitched tentatively in his Triple-A debut, striking out only four batters per nine innings.

MENHART, PAUL - TR - b: 3/25/69
Scouting: Menhart has good control and attacks hitters with location. His fastball is below average and his breaking pitches are average. But after he joined the Padres, Menhart won praise for going after hitters. By the end of the season, he was one of the Padres most consistent starters until an ankle sprain slowed him. The Padres love his heart.
1998: Menhart's status as a fringe major leaguer could improve with expansion.
1997: Menhart came to the Padres in a swap of struggling Triple-A pitchers and struggled at Las Vegas with an 0-7 record and 5.97 ERA. With the Padres, however, Menhart was much better.
1996: Menhart started the season in Seattle and was 2-2 with a high ERA in 11 games. At Triple-A Tacoma, he struggled to an 0-3 mark and 11.08 ERA in six starts.

	W	SV	ERA	IP	H	BB	SO	B/I
1995 Toronto	1	0	4.92	78	72	47	50	1.51
1996 Seattle	2	0	7.29	42	55	25	18	1.90
1997 San Diego	2	0	4.70	44	42	13	22	1.25

MERCADO, HECTOR - TL - b: 4/29/74
After being unable to crack the Double-A barrier in the Astros' chain, Mercado became a Marlin in 1997 and earned a promotion to Triple-A with a powerful performance at Portland in the Eastern League. He primarily relies on a slightly above-average fastball with good movement, but does not feature particularly good control. It is unlikely that Mercado has a diverse enough repertoire to start in the majors, and he must still make control improvements to be a viable relief candidate. 1997 must be considered a major step forward, as he is now an injury away from a major league role.

MERCEDES, JOSE - TR - b: 3/5/71

Scouting: Mercedes emerged as a starter after spending most of his time in the Milwaukee organization as a reliever. He has good velocity (around 90 MPH when he's on) and has a sharp-breaking slider. Control is a key for him. He also seems a bit fragile; he missed most of the '95 season with elbow problems and had the '97 season cut short by a tendon problem in his hand.

1998: The Brewers were expected to protect Mercedes in hopes of making him a regular starter in 1998.

1997: Mercedes lost out in a spring training competition for the fifth starter spot, but earned it later in the season. His ERA led the Brewers' starting rotation. Mercedes' stuff is considered among the best on the Milwaukee staff.

1996: He split time between Triple-A and Milwaukee. Mercedes made 15 starts in 25 Triple-A appearances, but was used primarily as a reliever in Milwaukee.

	W	SV	ERA	IP	H	BB	SO	B/I
1997 Milwaukee	7	0	3.79	159	146	53	80	1.25

MERCKER, KENT - TL - b: 2/1/68

Scouting: Mercker appeared to be most of the way back after a disastrous season in the American League. He features a good fastball, along with a curve, slider, and changeup. Although Mercker nearly cut his ERA in half from 1996, his low strikeout rate is of some concern.

1998: Mercker was a free agent at the end of the 1997 season, and lefthanded starters with a pulse have more market value than the Reds were likely to pay. He should find a role as a fourth or fifth starter with a major league team.

1997: Signing with the Reds as a free agent, he started poorly, but was effective most of the summer. He missed time in August with a sore back, but made a couple of starts in September to prove he could still pitch.

1996: Mercker was the biggest free agent bust of the 1996 season when he fouled up his pitching mechanics in Baltimore. His good fastball dropped into the low 80's and he was hammered for a 6.98 ERA, then eventually shipped to Cleveland.

	W	SV	ERA	IP	H	BB	SO	B/I
1995 Atlanta	7	0	4.15	143	140	61	102	1.41
1996 Balt-Cleveland	4	0	6.98	69	83	38	29	1.75
1997 Cincinnati	8	0	3.92	145	135	62	75	1.36

MESA, JOSE - TR - b: 5/22/66

Scouting: Mesa relies heavily on his fastball, which is down about five MPH from its 97-MPH peak from a couple of seasons ago. Mesa is a no-nonsense hardballer who only occasionally shows hitters his breaking stuff. Conditioning is a concern, and the offseason personal problems which landed him in court instead of in the bullpen on opening day in 1997 were an unnecessary diversion.

1998: Mesa reclaimed his closer job late in the 1997 season, and will enter 1998 as the man. His stuff is slowly deteriorating, and any material decline in his strikeout rate would be an indicator of an impending blowup. He's not an elite closer any more.

1997: Mesa missed the better part of April, and struggled as a set-up man during the early going. When Mike Jackson faltered in the second half, Mesa regained the closer job — and thrived. Though Jackson has better stuff, Mesa obviously enjoys the pressure more. Warning signs: his strikeout rate declined, and lefties clubbed his heater at a .309 clip.

1996: Mesa came down off of his 1.13 ERA cloud of 1995, struggling down the stretch in September and October, during the Indians' playoff loss to the Orioles, his former team. In actuality, it was 1995, not 1996, that was out of step with the rest of his career.

	W	SV	ERA	IP	H	BB	SO	B/I
1995 Cleveland	3	46	1.13	64	49	17	58	1.03
1996 Cleveland	2	39	3.73	72	69	28	64	1.35
1997 Cleveland	4	16	2.41	82	83	28	69	1.35

MICELI, DANNY - TR - b: 9/9/70

Scouting: Watch him at his best and Miceli looks dominant. The Tigers saw that in spring training '97, when Miceli's fastball exploded and his breaking ball dropped off the table. But once the season started, Miceli showed an alarming tendency to allow home runs at the worst of times. He still showed enough to contribute in a major-league bullpen.

1998: There were those within the Tiger organization who believed that Miceli gave them a Plan B alternative to Todd Jones. After being traded to San Diego, for Trey Beamon, Miceli became an alternative to Trevor Hoffman in 1998. Displacing Hoffman won't be so easy.

1997: A great spring had the Tigers even thinking of using Miceli as a part-time closer. Big home runs allowed in the first two games of the year changed that, but Miceli still became a useful middle reliever in a bullpen that was good the second half of the season.

1996: A year after saving 21 games for the Pirates, Miceli fell into disfavor. He didn't get a save opportunity after opening day, eventually being sent to the minors and later tried as a starter. After the season, he was traded to the Tigers for Clint Sodowsky.

	W	SV	ERA	IP	H	BB	SO	B/I
1995 Pittsburgh	4	21	4.66	58	61	28	56	1.53
1996 Pittsburgh	2	1	5.78	85	99	45	66	1.69
1997 Detroit	3	3	5.01	83	77	38	79	1.39

MILACKI, BOB - TR - b: 7/28/64

Milacki peaked in 1989 with Baltimore, leading the American League in games started and producing 14 wins. The Orioles finally gave up on this soft-tossing finesse pitcher after the 1992 season. Later trials with the Indians, Royals and Mariners proved that he doesn't have any major league stuff left, although Milacki has had some spectacular fun with Triple-A batters while trying to make a comeback. He worked in Japan last year, but failed to impress.

	W	SV	ERA	IP	H	BB	SO	B/I
1996 Seattle	1	0	6.86	21	30	15	13	2.14

MILLER, KURT - TR - b: 8/24/72

Scouting: Once upon a time, Miller was about as close as you could get to a sure thing among minor-league pitching prospects. The Pirates' first-round draft pick has endured arm troubles and mechanical difficulties that have stolen some juice from his fastball, which once clocked around 95 MPH. It has been several years since he has been able to control any of his breaking pitches, so hitters know the fastball is coming. That is simply not a recipe for success at the major league level. He's still only 25 years old, so the Marlins were reluctant to give up on him, but they shipped him to the Cubs.

1998: The Marlins had decided that Miller should be a reliever.

That is probably wise, as he has the power to dominate hitters if he can only develop a credible second pitch. The Cubs will make their own evaluation.

1997: Miller was used as a reliever for the first time in his minor-league career. His velocity was fine, but his control troubles persisted though his mechanics were somewhat improved. He labored in a September trial in the majors, pitching quite tentatively.

1996: Miller's mechanics were in disarray, and he struck out just over five batters per nine innings, far below his career norm. He got an extended major league trial, and allowed about two baserunners per inning. All in all, the year was a big step backwards.

	W	SV	ERA	IP	H	BB	SO	B/I
1996 Florida	1	0	6.80	46	57	33	30	1.95

MILLER, TRAVIS - TL - b: 11/2/72

Scouting: Miller needs to get by on guile as well as stuff simply because he doesn't have dominant stuff. His fastball is average and his curve is OK. He needs to refine his location in order to contribute to a major-league starting rotation. He doesn't have the best athleticism. That combined with his so-so stuff qualifies him as more of a project than as a prospect.

1998: At best, Miller can contribute by filling the fifth-spot in somebody's rotation, but don't expect that team to be headed to the playoffs. Four years after being the Twins' first-round sandwich pick in the 1994 draft, Miller doesn't appear as close to being a solid major-leaguer as some would have hoped.

1997: Miller earned every ounce of his 7.63 ERA. He was recalled after the All-Star break mainly because the Twins had nobody else, and Miller did what he had done at Triple-A Salt Lake. He was inconsistent and showed he needed work.

1996: Other than collecting his first major-league win against Kansas City, 1996 mostly was forgettable for Miller. Before he even arrived in the majors, he was 8-10 with a 4.83 ERA at Triple-A Salt Lake.

	W	SV	ERA	IP	H	BB	SO	B/I
1997 Minnesota	1	0	7.64	48	64	23	26	1.80

MILLER, TREVER - TL - b: 5/29/73

Scouting: Miller was obtained by Houston from Detroit in a multi-player trade prior to the 1997 season. The top high school player in Kentucky in 1991, he was drafted by Detroit as a supplemental pick after the first round. He is a finesse pitcher who relies on location and changing speeds.

1998: Miller is on Houston's 40-man roster and will be a candidate for the starting rotation. The odds are against him.

1997: Miller spent the entire season at Triple-A New Orleans. He was 6-7 in 21 starts with an ERA of 3.30 which ranked sixth in the American Association.

1996: Miller compiled a 13-6 record with a 4.90 ERA for Toledo in his first year at the Triple-A level. He was promoted to Detroit in September and was hit hard in four starts with a 0-4 record and a 9.18 ERA.

MILLS, ALAN - TR - b: 10/18/66

Scouting: Orioles middle reliever and set-up man Alan Mills is fastball/slider pitcher with above-average stuff.

1998: Mills should continue in his relief roles with the Orioles. He could rebound from a poor 1997 season with a good year in 1998. There isn't much chance that he will become the closer.

1997: Mills experienced some injuries last year, resulting in a poor season. He also was plagued by occasional wildness, and he had trouble with lefthanded hitters.

1996: Mills had a good comeback year following an injury-filled 1995 season.

	W	SV	ERA	IP	H	BB	SO	B/I
1995 Baltimore	3	0	7.43	23	30	18	16	2.09
1996 Baltimore	3	3	4.28	54	40	35	50	1.38
1997 Baltimore	2	0	4.88	39	41	33	32	1.91

MILLWOOD, KEVIN - TR - b: 12/24/74

Scouting: A 6'4" righthander, Millwood features a good 90+ fastball, curve, slider and changeup. After struggling three years at Class A, he developed some command of his pitches and, as a result, made a rapid ascent to the majors in 1997.

1998: With the Braves starting four set, Millwood will compete for the fifth starter/swingman role on the Atlanta staff. His excellent strikeout rate makes him a leading candidate for the job. His role could improve if he were with another team this year.

1997: Starting the season at Double-A Greenville, Millwood moved up to Triple-A Richmond, where he dominated the International League (7-0, 1.93 ERA in eight starts). After Terrell Wade was hurt, and Chris Brock failed, Millwood became the Braves fifth starter, a role he held the rest of the season.

1996: After struggling with his control in his first two professional seasons, Millwood began to develop with Class A Durham. By the end of the season, he was the team's ace, finishing third in the Carolina League with 139 strikeouts.

	W	SV	ERA	IP	H	BB	SO	B/I
1997 Atlanta	5	0	4.04	51	55	21	42	1.48

MILTON, ERIC - TL - b: 8/4/75

The Yankees top pick in the 1996 draft didn't pitch that year due to a contract hassle but he made up for lost time in 1997, moving from Class A all the way to Triple-A. The big (6'3", 200-pound) lefty has a chance to be in the big leagues sometime during the 1998 season. He has an excellent feel for pitching, throwing a fastball, changeup, and a curve for quality strikes. Milton appeared in two International League playoff games for Columbus after making 14 regular season starts each at Norwich and Tampa. He went 6-3 with a 3.13 ERA at Norwich and 8-3 at Tampa.

MIMBS, MARK - TL - b: 2/13/69

After five years at Triple-A Albuquerque, Mimbs spent 1997 at New Orleans, going 1-2 with a 4.36 ERA in 22 appearances (four starts). Mimbs throws harder than his twin brother Mike, but he has never been impressive enough to even get a look at the major league level. An eight-year pro, Mimbs will likely be back in a Triple-A bullpen someplace in 1998.

MIMBS, MIKE - TL - b: 2/13/69

Scouting: Mimbs is a breaking-ball specialist who spent a large part of the 1995 and '96 seasons in the Phillies' rotation. He was especially effective against lefthanded hitters, even winning an endorsement from Tony Gwynn as one of the toughest pitchers he has faced. But Mimbs can't put hitters away with his mediocre fastball and has struggled with his control; he hasn't had as much success against hitters other than Gwynn. Mimbs' versatility is a plus.

1998: Mimbs has been passed by other pitchers in the Phillies' farm system. He will end up pitching in Triple-A, serving as injury insurance; being lefthanded could get him back to the majors.
1997: The Phillies used a variety of lefthanded bullpen specialists but did not recall Mimbs, which says a lot about their regard for his abilities. He was a swingman at Triple-A Scranton, posting a good strikeout rate, but was hit hard — especially by righthanded hitters.
1996: Mimbs spent much of the season in the Phillies' rotation, despite generally poor results; the club had few alternatives. Mimbs couldn't even handle lefty hitters, they batted .363 against him.

	W	SV	ERA	IP	H	BB	SO	B/I
1995 Philadelphia	9	1	4.15	136	127	75	93	1.48
1996 Philadelphia	3	0	5.53	99	116	41	56	1.58
1997 Philadelphia	0	0	7.53	29	31	27	29	2.02

MINCHEY, NATE - TR - b: 8/31/69
A minor-league veteran who knows how to pitch, Minchey has underwhelming stuff that scares the big-league brass from giving him a legitimate chance. His 87-MPH fastball is below-average. He throws a cut fastball and has an outstanding curveball and changeup. He has great makeup and outstanding command; Minchey will never start out a hitter with the same pitch twice. He was a six-year free agent after the season, though the Rockies were hoping to re-sign him.

MINOR, BLAS - TR - b: 3/20/66
The ex-Pirate, ex-Met pitched well enough at Triple-A on the Astros farm (2.27 ERA in 23 games) to get another shot at the majors. He still has the fastball, slider, curve and change, and in eleven games with Houston he showed that he has gained a little savvy, if he's lost a little velocity.

	W	SV	ERA	IP	H	BB	SO	B/I
1995 New York NL	4	1	3.66	46	44	13	43	1.22
1996 New York NL	0	0	3.51	25	23	6	20	1.15
1996 Seattle	0	0	4.97	25	27	11	14	1.51
1997 Houston	1	1	4.50	12	13	5	6	1.50

MINTZ, STEVE - TR - b: 11/28/68
Mintz is an older journeyman minor-leaguer who spent a short time in the majors with the Giants (1995). He's a below-average reliever who throws fastballs in the mid-80s and hangs curveballs. Mintz had some success as a closer for Triple-A Phoenix in 1996, but not enough to earn a major league recall, then had a really bad year in 1997, even by Pacific Coast League pitching standards. He'll have to work to get a Triple-A job.

MIRANDA, ANGEL - TL - b: 11/9/69
Scouting: Miranda is a situational lefty who has never really fared well against lefties. His fastball is adequate, but command of all his pitches is weak. He is a durable hurler who can be used in a variety of roles, but would be long out of baseball if he threw with his right hand.
1998: Miranda will show up in someone's camp, but will be an extreme longshot to stick.
1997: Miranda started his fifth consecutive season as a Brewers' swingman, with typically mediocre results. He was released at mid-season and signed a Triple-A deal with the Indians, where he lasted all of nine innings before going on the disabled list.
1996: Miranda was actually quite useful in 1996, hurling 109 credible innings as a spot starter and middle reliever in Milwaukee. However, he was done in by his inability to retire lefthanded hitters, his core responsibility. Lefties cuffed him at a .325 clip.

	W	SV	ERA	IP	H	BB	SO	B/I
1995 Milwaukee	4	1	5.23	74	83	49	45	1.78
1996 Milwaukee	7	1	4.94	109	116	69	78	1.70
1997 Milwaukee	0	0	3.86	14	17	9	8	1.86

MISURACA, MIKE - TR - b: 8/21/68
Misuraca is a career minor-leaguer with more than 1,000 minor-league innings under his belt, but he finally made it to the show on July 27th last year. It was a less-than-memorable major league debut, however, as Misuraca gave up five homers in his 10.1 innings with a double-digit ERA. He's probably headed back to the minors for the foreseeable future.

	W	SV	ERA	IP	H	BB	SO	B/I
1997 Milwaukee	0	0	11.36	10	15	7	10	2.14

MITCHELL, LARRY - TR - b: 10/16/71
The Phillies' 1992 fifth-round draft pick has always possessed above-average stuff, including a good fastball and a hard curve delivered from a deceptive, straight overhand motion. However his concentration has always wavered, from batter to batter, and from pitch to pitch. He can blow away the meat of the order, and then walk the bottom. The higher he rose through the ranks in 1996, the better he pitched. In 1997, Mitchell pitched exclusively at Double-A Norwich posting a 3.71 ERA with a good strikeout-to-walk ratio.

MIX, GREG - TR - b: 8/21/71
Mix has been a good soldier in his five seasons in the Marlins' chain, but has never held onto a rotation spot for a full season or served as a closer or primary set-up man out of the pen. He is a junkballer with a mediocre fastball who has good control but no out pitch. He has basically stood still for the better part of the last three seasons, and appears to have little chance of achieving Triple-A success, let alone earn a major league job.

MLICKI, DAVE - TR - b: 6/8/68
Scouting: Mlicki may have the best stuff of any Mets' starter since Bret Saberhagen, but he has relatively little to show for it. His control sometimes deserts him, especially when he tries to do too much in difficult circumstances. But he seemed aware of the problem and took steps to solve it in the late-season last year. He also lacks stamina, but he's getting stronger. If he harnesses all he has, the Mets will have a special pitcher.
1998: For three years now, the Mets have said no player prompts more injuries from other clubs than Mlicki. He's relatively inexpensive —$610,000 last year, and there's all that potential. He pitched himself onto the protected list in the last eight weeks last year. He was a member of the rotation whenever the club looked forward to this season.
1997: Mlicki made a career-high 32 starts and worked a career-high 193.2 innings before back spasms knocked him out of his last start after two scoreless innings. And his last eight starts — 3-3 record and 2.39 ERA —gave the Mets reasons to be encouraged. His shutout of the Yankees in the Bronx in June was one of the highpoints of the Mets' season. Mlicki was far more effective against lefthanded hitters (.246 average, seven

home runs in 362 at-bats).
1996: He began the season with two starts (both losses) and then made 49 relief appearances with uneven results — a 6-5 record, 3.13 ERA with 110 baserunners and 74 strikeouts in 77.2 innings. His lack of resilience in his pitching arm was a primary factor in his move to the rotation.

	W	SV	ERA	IP	H	BB	SO	B/I
1995 New York NL	9	0	4.26	160	160	54	123	1.33
1996 New York NL	6	1	3.30	90	95	33	83	1.42
1997 New York NL	8	0	4.00	194	194	76	157	1.39

MLICKI, DOUG - TR - b: 4/23/71
Dave's younger brother Doug has stalled in the high minors; he was unable to take the next step to the majors as Chris Holt did, despite similar progress through the Astros' chain. Mlicki has average stuff and lacks an outstanding pitch that would enable him to succeed at a higher level. He split 1997 between Triple-A New Orleans and Double-A Jackson, shifting to the bullpen for the first time at New Orleans and enjoying some success; he was 4-3 with a 3.60 ERA.

MOEHLER, BRIAN - TR - b: 12/31/71
Scouting: A cut fastball developed in Double-A got Moehler to the big leagues. Good command and some toughness on the mound made him an effective rookie starter. He gets in trouble when he tries to throw too hard, rather than moving the ball around and keeping hitters off balance.
1998: Moehler should be even better in his second year, because he has a better idea of what he needs to do to win in the big leagues. He's not guaranteed a starting spot all year no matter what, but the Tigers certainly expect him to be in their rotation.
1997: He started throwing in January, because he knew he'd need a good spring to win a big-league job. He did it, and he ended up winning in double figures and pitching the second most innings on the staff. It was a good rookie year, despite a few weeks after the All-Star break when he lost focus on how he needs to pitch.
1996: Moehler emerged as a prospect, thanks to that cut fastball. He won 15 regular-season games at Double-A Jacksonville, and won two more in the Southern League playoffs. When the Tigers needed someone to start two games in the final week of the big-league season, they called on Moehler.
When the Tigers needed someone to start two games in the final week of the big-league season, they called on Moehler.

	W	SV	ERA	IP	H	BB	SO	B/I
1997 Detroit	11	0	4.67	175	198	61	97	1.48

MOHLER, MIKE - TL - b: 7/26/68
Scouting: Considered to be the best athlete on the Oakland pitching staff, Mohler spots a 90-MPH fastball, a changeup and an excellent cut fastball. He is more effective both earlier in the season, and as a middle-man, or even as a set-up pitcher than as a spot starter or closer. He has filled all these roles.
1998: Mohler, who functions best as a situational lefty and middle reliever, should continue that role this season. His stuff is good but he is prone to giving up the long ball in pressure situations. Bearing this in mind, he should be kept out of most pressure situations.
1997: After getting a chance to fill just about every type of role a pitcher can have, Mohler settled in to the relief role. He began the season as the lone lefty in the rotation, then moved to the pen. He did have some bad luck, but he also pitched poorly, so his 1-10 record was as much indicative of odd circumstances as it was poor performance.
1996: Mohler was effective over the first portion of the season as a set-up man, and then as a closer. Then he suddenly couldn't get anyone out. He is a good pitcher, but he is not a stopper and his performance suffers when he is overused.

	W	SV	ERA	IP	H	BB	SO	B/I
1995 Oakland	1	1	3.04	23	16	18	15	1.44
1996 Oakland	6	7	3.67	81	79	41	64	1.48
1997 Oakland	1	1	5.13	102	116	54	66	1.67

MONTANE, IVAN - TR - b: 6/3/73
Montane displayed improved control at Class A Lancaster but was back to his old self at Double-A Memphis in the Southern League for the Mariners' organization. He yielded more than a hit per inning and walked 51 in 71.2 innings. The Mariners like his stuff — he was a non-roster invitee to spring training last year — but he must develop some control to advance.

MONTGOMERY, JEFF - TR - b: 1/7/62
Scouting: Shoulder surgery slowed Montgomery's return to a closer role, but he appears to have regained full use of his repertoire: upper-80s fastball, slider, curve, changeup. He's a much more complete pitcher than when he first won the stopper job in Kansas City, but he lacks the overpowering heater he once had. Montgomery now needs all his pitches to succeed.
1998: Montgomery is the closer entering the season; all indications are that his shoulder problems are behind him so he should keep the job. His best days as a closer are also behind him, though, so it may be a short-lived role; Montgomery will be 36 on opening day.
1997: Shoulder surgery the previous September left Montgomery in a weakened condition for the start of the season and he wound up on the disabled list twice in the first two months. He gradually regained command of his pitches and was nearly unhittable the last two months of the season. Montgomery retired 31 straight batters at one point late in the year and allowed no earned runs in his final 19 appearances as he regained the stopper job with a vengeance.
1996: After a typically strong start, Montgomery was hit hard over the last few months of the season before going under the knife for shoulder surgery in September; it was his worst big-league season.

	W	SV	ERA	IP	H	BB	SO	B/I
1995 Kansas City	2	31	3.43	65	60	25	49	1.29
1996 Kansas City	4	24	4.26	63	59	19	45	1.24
1997 Kansas City	1	14	3.49	59	53	18	48	1.20

MONTGOMERY, STEVE - TR - b: 12/25/70
Scouting: Montgomery has below-average stuff and is not regarded as a top prospect. But he's been more effective in the minors than could be expected based upon his radar gun readings.
1998: Labeled as a marginal prospect, Montgomery will have an uphill battle to make the Orioles. He will likely begin in Triple-A, and may get called up if he pitches well and the Orioles have an opening, probably in the bullpen. The Orioles rotation would be a real longshot for Montgomery.
1997: Montgomery was a starter in Double-A where he had a good record and made the post-season Eastern League All-

Star team. He was promoted to Triple-A Rochester and made good progress.
1996: Montgomery had a good record, striking out 79 in 72 innings.

MONTOYA, NORM - TL - b: 9/24/70
Montoya reached Triple-A for the second time in his eight-year minor-league career but gave no indication he will advance past it. He did show good control (38 walks in 131 innings) but was roped all over the yard and had an ERA over six in 28 appearances, including 22 starts.

MONTOYA, WILMER - TR - b: 3/15/74
Montoya is a diminutive (5'10", 165-pound) reliever who has had some success as a closer due to an above-average curveball. He established himself as a viable future major league middle-relief prospect in 1996 with a smooth transition to Double-A, but took a major step backward by missing the majority of the 1997 season. The Indians are likely to obtain their next generation of major league relievers from the overflow of their deep pool of starting pitcher prospects, not from limited career relievers like Montoya.

MOODY, ERIC - TR - b: 1/6/71
Scouting: Moody has a high-80s fastball and a slider, and has had modest success at each level of the Texas farm system. He has always had good control and a better than 3-to-1 strikeout-to-walk ratio over his minor-league career. Moody has been both a starter and a reliever. The biggest question will be if he can maintain his breaking ball repertoire after elbow problems the previous season.
1998: Moody has an outside shot to land a spot on a major league pitching staff next season, and will split time between Triple-A and the majors. If healthy, he could be an effective middle reliever.
1997: Moody had another good minor-league season (5-6, 3.46 ERA, 10.8 baserunners per nine innings at Triple-A Oklahoma City), and showed poise and confidence in two short major league stints. His callup was due more to injuries to other pitchers than a reward for his minor-league season, but Moody showed enough to warrant attention next spring. His season ended early with a strained ligament in his right elbow, derailing plans to send him to winter ball.
1996: After a successful season as a Double-A closer, Moody pitched in the Arizona Fall League.

	W	SV	ERA	IP	H	BB	SO	B/I
1997 Texas	0	0	4.26	19	26	2	12	1.47

MOORE, BOBBY - TR - b: 3/27/73
Moore spent last season with Tulsa, going 4-6 with a 5.35 ERA in relief in his first Double-A season. He is not considered a prospect.

MOORE, JOEL - TR - b: 8/13/72
Moore was a third-round draft pick in 1993 and was on the fast track to the majors until undergoing reconstructive elbow surgery following his superb 1995 season, when he went 14-6 with a 3.20 ERA at Double-A New Haven. He struggled in 1996 and began to regain his effectiveness in 1997, when he went 6-4 with a 3.84 ERA back at New Haven. He still has a good sinker and changeup, but his fastball, which was in the low-90s before surgery, is now four MPH slower.

MOORE, MARCUS - TR - b: 11/2/70
Scouting: Moore rears back and fires. He throws a mid-90's heater without much regard for its location. It has been enough for him to succeed against Triple-A hitters, but his lack of an effective breaking pitch has been a major problem during his major league trials. Also, he has been used exclusively as a reliever in the majors — he has been much more successful in the minors as a starter, most recently in the Indians' organization. Arms like Moore's will always get spring training invitations.
1998: Expansion will improve Moore's chances of getting another major league opportunity. However, major league hitters can hit any fastball when they know it's coming. Moore must develop another credible — not necessarily above-average - pitch to stand a chance.
1997: Moore toiled at Double-A and Triple-A in the Indians' chain, pitching the best baseball of his pro career at Buffalo in the American Association. He consistently got ahead of hitters, averaged over seven innings per start, and showed career-best command. The Indians — and others —noticed.
1996: Moore perked up Reds' brass with a couple of impressive saves in April, but lost all contact with the strike zone before finding the range as a Triple-A starter.

	W	SV	ERA	IP	H	BB	SO	B/I
1996 Cincinnati	3	2	5.81	26	26	22	27	1.84

MOORE, TREY - TL - b: 10/2/72
The lefty starter was a throw-in with Chris Widger and Matt Wagner as part of the package the Expos received from Seattle in the Jeff Fassero trade at the end of the 1996 season. Moore pitched well with the Expos' Double-A Harrisburg farm club last year and is in line to be in Montreal's starting rotation in 1999.

MORAGA, DAVID - TL - b: 7/8/75
He is a control pitcher who will not likely develop above average velocity. Moraga has the savvy to go as far as his abilities will carry him.

MOREL, RAMON - TR - b: 8/15/74
Scouting: Morel's greatest strength is control and changing speeds. He has been used in relief at the major league level, a role for which he is ill-suited. Morel is in a Catch-22. He won't get a chance to start in the majors until he proves himself out of the bullpen.
1998: Morel seemingly has no chance to make the Cubs' rotation as starting pitching is one of the club's few strengths. Morel could stick as a long reliever but most likely will spend the season in Triple-A Iowa's starting rotation. He could use the experience as his last three seasons have been interrupted by recalls to the majors, where he has been used infrequently as a reliever.
1997: Morel pitched poorly as a swingman with the Pirates' Triple-A Calgary farm club and didn't dazzle during a brief early-season stint in Pittsburgh's bullpen. The Pirates dropped Morel off the 40-man roster August 31st when they acquired shortstop Shawon Dunston from Chicago in a trade. Ironically, the Cubs claimed Morel off waivers and he did little to impress his new club in September.
1996: Morel began the season in Double-A Carolina's bullpen

and struggled. He wasn't any better after being promoted to Pittsburgh's bullpen in June.

	W	SV	ERA	IP	H	BB	SO	B/I
1996 Pittsburgh	2	0	5.36	42	57	19	22	1.81
1997 Chicago NL	0	0	4.78	11	14	7	7	1.86

MORENO, JULIO - TR - b: 10/23/75

Scouting: Moreno is young and has a slight build at 6'1" and 155 pounds. Nevertheless, he throws hard, has a good curve, and is improving his changeup. He should gain speed on his fastball as he matures and fills out.

1998: Moreno should begin the year in Triple-A, with a chance of making the Orioles sometime during the year or in September.

1997: Moreno progressed nicely, posting a solid record a starting pitcher in Double-A.

1996: Moreno pitched in the high Class A Carolina League, posting a solid record.

MORGAN, MIKE - TR - b: 10/8/58

Scouting: A typical crafty veteran, Morgan gets by on guile and a large assortment of pitches. He is the type of pitcher that can get by for a few innings if he has good control, but if he is missing his spots he gets hammered. His age and injury history make him a risk.

1998: Despite a mediocre (at best) season in 1997, expansion means there is a job as a fifth starter waiting for Mike Morgan, as long as he is willing to work cheap.

1997: Morgan got off to a horrible start, and hit the DL for two weeks with a pulled rib cage muscle. In July, he did Reds fans everywhere a great service by having the guts to go public with the numerous managerial shortcomings of Ray Knight. Morgan pitched much better after Knight was fired and Jack McKeon took over as manager.

1996: Morgan began the year as the fifth starter for the Cardinals, but was released in September after 18 poor starts. Signed by the Reds, he was given a September tryout and pitched well enough to secure a one-year deal.

	W	SV	ERA	IP	H	BB	SO	B/I
1995 St. Louis	7	0	3.56	131	133	34	61	1.27
1996 Cincinnati	6	0	4.63	130	146	47	74	1.48
1997 Cincinnati	9	0	4.78	162	165	49	103	1.32

MORMAN, ALVIN - TL - b: 1/6/69

Scouting: Morman's repertoire consists primarily of a mid-80's fastball and a changeup. The lefty was able to consistently throw quality strikes with his limited repertoire in the minors, but has been a nibbler in his two years as a major leaguer. He's an easy mark when he doesn't have confidence in his off-speed stuff early in the count — you can't sneak 85 MPH fastballs past major league hitters.

1998: Morman will likely have a second chance to earn the secondary lefthanded set-up role in the Indians' pen. The Indians' hope that his 1997 performance was a fluke and that the .239 average he allowed lefties in 1996 is more indicative of his true abilities.

1997: Morman moved from the Astros to the Indians, and was dominant in 11 Triple-A opportunities, leading the Indians to believe he would be an important addition to their bullpen. Instead, Morman was hit hard as he pitched timidly, consistently falling behind hitters. He also neglected opposing baserunners, allowing seven steals in 18.1 innings.

1996: Morman was an integral component of the Astros' bullpen, consistently shutting down lefties. However, after showing pinpoint control throughout his minor-league career, Morman walked more than five batters per nine innings.

	W	SV	ERA	IP	H	BB	SO	B/I
1996 Houston	4	0	4.93	42	43	24	31	1.60
1997 Cleveland	0	2	5.90	18	19	14	13	1.80

MORRIS, MATT - TR - b: 8/9/74

Scouting: Morris throws a 90+ fastball which has excellent movement. He changed his basic grip from two-seam to four-seam in mid-1996 and got a wonderful increase in movement with no loss of velocity. He has a major league quality curveball and the ability to change speeds and hit spots with all his pitches. Stated briefly: he is extremely talented and mentally tough.

1998: Don't expect a sophomore slump. Morris should be a big winner if he gets just average run support. He will go to spring training as the number two or three starter on a strong staff.

1997: Morris pitched eight games in which he gave up fewer than two runs and didn't get a win. With mediocre luck, he could have been the biggest-winning rookie starter to come along in years. He stepped up to the challenge when Andy Benes was injured in spring training and cruised through his rookie season with remarkable consistency.

1996: In the middle of his second summer as a pro, pitching for Double-A Arkansas, Morris made a simple shift in the way he grips the ball, and jumped immediately from being tough to being dominant. He had already shown the ability, in spring training, to throw his fastball past major league hitters. He finished '96 with a 12-12 record and a 3.88 ERA.

	W	SV	ERA	IP	H	BB	SO	B/I
1997 St. Louis	12	0	3.19	217	208	69	149	1.28

MORSE, PAUL - TR - b: 2/27/73

Morse is a hard thrower, but had a disappointing first season at the Double-A level in 1996. It was obvious that he would need to work another year at Double-A, but he fared even worse in 1997 with a 5.98 ERA, well over a hit per inning, and a poor strikeout-to-walk ratio. Morse can fan Double-A hitters but must work on his control before he can succeed at the higher minor-league levels.

MOSS, DAMIAN - TL - b: 11/24/76

Scouting: Moss complements a fine sinking fastball with an excellent curveball and an improving changeup. Durability may be a problem for this Australian product; he has never thrown 150 innings in any season and has visibly worn down near the end of each of the last two seasons. Moss is young, with above-average stuff and remarkable control. The Braves will give him time to percolate through their farm system. If he can build his strength a little more he can stay in the starting rotation; if not he may shift to a bullpen role.

1998: A third year at Greenville is in order with the focus on stamina and keeping the ball down. If he can make a few small refinements, Moss should advance to Triple-A Richmond before the season is out.

1997: Moss' return to Double-A Greenville was a disappointment. He couldn't keep the ball down in the strikezone and gave up too many extra-base hits. He still fanned a hitter per inning, but his ERA grew to 5.35.

1996: As the fifth-youngest player in the league at age 19,

Moss dominated the Carolina League, going 9-1 with a 2.25 ERA and more than a strikeout per inning over fourteen starts, earning an advance to Double-A Greenville. He kept his poise as one of that league's youngest pitchers, too, going 2-5 with a 4.97 ERA, although he tired near the end of the year.

MOUNCE, TONY - TL - b: 2/8/75

Lefty Mounce relies on finesse instead of power. He has yet to succeed above A-ball; his ERA more than doubled to 5.03 when he advanced to Double-A Jackson for the first time in 1997. Mounce has good control, but there is concern that his stuff might not be good enough for him to succeed at higher levels.

MOYER, JAMIE - TL - b: 11/18/62

Scouting: His stuff is slow, slower, slowest, but Moyer is the consummate pitcher. He sets up hitters well and works both halves of the plate. His mid-80s fastball even looks fast when he mixes it with his off-speed stuff and he has historically been more of a problem for righthanded hitters. He doesn't impress you; he just gets you out.
1998: Placed between hard throwers Randy Johnson and Jeff Fassero, Moyer is the perfect complement in the Mariners' rotation.
1997: Moyer had the best season in his career for the second straight year, seemingly finding a home in a hitter's park. He ran his two-year record to 30-8 and allowed fewer than a hit per inning for the first time in his career. Moyer combined with fellow lefty teammates Randy Johnson and Jeff Fassero to go 53-18.
1996: Acquired from Boston for Darren Bragg in late July, Moyer was immediately inserted into the starting rotation and won six of his eleven starts. He set a career high in victories and led the American League in winning percentage. Moyer walked more than two batters in just one of his 21 starts.

	W	SV	ERA	IP	H	BB	SO	B/I
1995 Baltimore	8	0	5.21	115	117	30	65	1.27
1996 Boston-Seattle	13	0	3.98	160	177	46	79	1.39
1997 Seattle	17	0	3.86	189	187	43	113	1.22

MULHOLLAND, TERRY - TL - b: 3/9/63

Scouting: Mulholland doesn't really have a money pitch. He doesn't throw as hard as he used to, so for his merely adequate fastball to be effective his slider, splitter, and occasional changeup have to be solid; it doesn't happen often enough. He's not a strikeout pitcher and is barely hanging on to his major league career at this point.
1998: Mulholland will continue his travels in 1998, moving on to yet another team in dire need of a lefthanded pitcher. Because he can throw strikes he'll be in the majors, but he will not be an especially effective pitcher.
1997: Mulholland's return to the Giants in 1997 was his sixth team change in the past four years and was more of a chess maneuver than anything else. Giants GM Brian Sabean claimed Mulholland after he was put on waivers by the Phillies in order to block any Dodgers' claims. Mulholland's contributions to the Giants' pennant drive were slight.
1996: Mulholland arrived in Seattle around the same time as Jamie Moyer and he failed to impress.

	W	SV	ERA	IP	H	BB	SO	B/I
1995 San Francisco	5	0	5.80	149	190	38	65	1.53
1996 Philadelphia	8	0	4.66	133	157	21	52	1.34
1996 Seattle	5	0	4.67	69	75	28	34	1.49
1997 San Francisco	6	0	4.24	187	190	51	99	1.29

MULL, BLAINE - TR - b: 8/14/76

Following an outstanding campaign at Class A Lansing in 1996 (15-8, 3.25 ERA), Mull picked up where he left off at higher Class A Wilmington. He was 8-6 with a 3.56 ERA in 19 starts when he got a promotion to Double-A Wichita. He stumbled through eight starts showing a weak fastball and was imminently hittable, too. Mull is still young (just 21 years old), so some difficulties were expected. But, the Royals have to be concerned that one of their top prospects couldn't throw the ball past Double-A hitters. Mull will get another shot at them in 1998.

MUNOZ, BOBBY - TR - b: 3/3/68

Munoz underwent the dreaded "Tommy John" surgery in August of 1995 and hasn't made it all the way back. He pitched in eight games for the Phillies last year, making seven starts. He gave up a lot of hits and only pitched for the Phillies in April and May. He cleared waivers and went to the minors but was eventually released outright to become a free agent.

	W	SV	ERA	IP	H	BB	SO	B/I
1995 Philadelphia	0	0	5.74	15	15	9	6	1.53
1996 Philadelphia	0	0	7.82	25	42	7	8	1.95
1997 Philadelphia	1	0	8.92	33	47	15	20	1.86

MUNOZ, MIKE - TL - b: 7/12/65

Scouting: A prototypical lefthanded relief specialist, Munoz will throw a 90-MPH fastball that has some tail on it and an above-average curveball. But the problem is he's often asked to pitch four times per week, and sometimes more. The overwork usually leads to a month-long slump each year that destroys his ERA, but Munoz is otherwise dependable. He's frequently asked to retire opponents' top lefthanded hitters in pressure situations.
1998: Munoz lives on one-year contracts and the Rockies were hoping to bring him back for a sixth year.
1997: After a slow start, Munoz became an effective situational specialist. Only 11 of his 52 inherited runners scored and he allowed runs in just three of his last 24 games.
1996: Categorically inconsistent, Munoz would go long stretches where he didn't give up anything, only to endure others where he couldn't get anybody out. His ERA soared past 6.60 for the second straight season. He was briefly demoted to Triple-A Colorado Springs, his first stint in the minors in three years.

	W	SV	ERA	IP	H	BB	SO	B/I
1995 Colorado	2	2	7.42	43	54	27	37	1.85
1996 Colorado	2	0	6.65	44	55	16	45	1.61
1997 Colorado	3	2	4.53	46	52	13	26	1.42

MUNRO, PETER - TR - b: 6/14/75

Munro is another in Boston's line of "Young Guns," as the Red Sox attempt to duplicate Atlanta's success with power pitchers. However, he has not progressed as quickly as Carl Pavano and Brian Rose did. He got to Double-A quick - last season - but struggled to a 4.95 ERA, and had some arm problems during the year. He's been pushed along quickly, so it's possible the Red Sox will promote him to Triple-A to start this season, but he doesn't appear to be ready for the majors.

MURRAY, HEATH - TL - b: 4/19/73

Scouting: Murray's running fastball and cutter are good weapons. But the Padres would like to see some fire from the 1994 third-round pick. Some scouts believe he lacks the mental makeup to thrive at the major league level. Murray showed great promise in 1996 at Memphis.
1998: The lefthander will be making a run at the Padre starting rotation in the spring.
1997: Murray spent the bulk of the season in the starting rotation of Triple-A Las Vegas where he was 6-8 with a 5.45 ERA. With the Padres, he had a high ERA in 17 outings, including three ineffective starts.
1996: Murray was 13-9 with a 3.21 ERA in his only full Double-A season. He had 156 strikeouts in 174 innings at the age of 22.

	W	SV	ERA	IP	H	BB	SO	B/I
1997 San Diego	1	0	6.76	33	50	21	16	2.13

MUSSINA, MIKE - TR - b: 12/8/68

Scouting: In the "Baseball America" poll of managers, Mussina was rated as having the second best curveball, second best changeup, the best control, and as the overall third best pitcher in the American League. But every July, he goes into a slight funk and looks awful for a few games until he rights himself. He's learned how to pitch in Camden Yards, a favorite site for power hitters. His defense is good.
1998: There's a great Cy Young year somewhere in his future. In the meantime, he's still among the best starting pitchers in the game.
1997: Mussina pitched well enough for Cy Young consideration.
1996: Mussina had a good year, but his ERA jumped to 4.81, partly a result of a lively ball that year. He also had conflicts with the pitching coach, as did other Oriole pitchers.

	W	SV	ERA	IP	H	BB	SO	B/I
1995 Baltimore	19	0	3.29	221	187	50	158	1.07
1996 Baltimore	19	0	4.81	243	264	69	204	1.37
1997 Baltimore	15	0	3.20	225	197	54	218	1.12

MYERS, JASON - TL - b: 9/19/73

Myers remains a prospect for the Giants but is still a few seasons away from having an impact with the big club. Myers has good control; after a promotion to Double-A Shreveport last year he fanned 12 batters in 12 innings without yielding a walk.

MYERS, JIMMY - TR - b: 4/28/69

Myers came to Triple-A Norfolk from the Orioles' organization, where he got into 11 games for Baltimore in 1996. The Mets never recalled him, but he had a pretty good year in relief last year with a 2-4 record, 1.82 ERA and two saves. He is a finesse pitcher without a lot of velocity. With expansion looming he will get another look from somebody.

MYERS, MIKE - TL - b: 6/26/69

Scouting: Myers' career turned around when he took a suggestion from Al Kaline and learned to throw sidearm. In his first year as one of baseball's only sidearming lefties, Myers was effective. In his second year, he was much more inconsistent. He's still uncomfortable for most lefthanded hitters to face, and with the shortage of lefties, he'll always have a job. Besides, he can pitch nearly every day of the season, without getting hurt.

1998: The Tigers may be tiring of Myers, but there's no doubt that there's room for him in the big leagues. He's most effective facing one or two lefthanded hitters at a time and he can do it four or even five days in a row without any arm trouble.
1997: Myers' record against lefthanders didn't change all that much (.250 opponent average compared to a .229 mark in '96), but he allowed too many key hits, and especially too many home runs (five - three of them game-winners). He also broke his own club record by appearing in 88 games.
1996: In a year where almost no Tiger pitched well, Myers did. Most importantly, lefthanders hit just .229 against him, and he retired 33 of the last 41 lefties he faced.

	W	SV	ERA	IP	H	BB	SO	B/I
1995 two teams	1	0	9.95	8	11	7	4	2.25
1996 Detroit	1	6	5.01	64	70	34	69	1.62
1997 Detroit	0	2	5.70	54	58	25	50	1.55

MYERS, RANDY - TL - b: 9/19/62

Scouting: Randy Myers relies on a good fastball and slider, and locating his pitches. For the most part, he keeps the ball low, and this frequently sets up the hitter who then goes after a pitch that's high and away.
1998: The Orioles worked hard to re-sign him, but Myers moved on to Toronto. He wasn't overworked in 1997, so he should be just effective again this year.
1997: Myers bounced back from a so-so and somewhat erratic 1996 season to become the top closer in the majors last season. Needless to say, Myers was tough on everybody last year.
1996: It was a down year for Myers. Righthanded hitters clipped him for a .281 average, a poor figure for a closer. He blew seven saves and almost lost his closer's job.

	W	SV	ERA	IP	H	BB	SO	B/I
1995 Chicago NL	1	38	3.88	55	49	28	59	1.39
1996 Baltimore	4	31	3.53	58	60	29	74	1.53
1997 Baltimore	2	45	1.51	60	47	22	56	1.16

MYERS, ROD - TR - b: 1/14/73

Scouting: Myers is a hard thrower, but lacks an above-average pitch that would help him be a good strikeout pitcher. He made slow progress to the major leagues for somebody who spent three years pitching Division I baseball at Wisconsin.
1998: Myers' season likely will depend on how he pitches in spring training. A good spring will mean that Myers would start the season with the Cubs, but a bad spring will send him back to Triple-A and might signal the end of his time with the Cubs. He doesn't have that much big-league experience, so it's doubtful that he'll make much of an impact if he is in Chicago.
1997: Myers spent the entire season at Triple-A where the Cubs returned him to the starting rotation. Myers was converted to a relief work in 1994 while still in the Kansas City organization, but with Mel Rojas and Terry Adams both around at the start of the season, the Cubs felt he had more to offer as a starter.
1996: Myers spent all year with the Cubs after being selected in the Rule V draft and showed promise. He was inconsistent at times, which was to be expected from someone with minimal experience above Double-A.

	W	SV	ERA	IP	H	BB	SO	B/I
1996 Chicago NL	2	0	4.68	67	61	38	50	1.48

NAGY, CHARLES - TR - b: 5/5/67

Scouting: Nagy is a sinker/slider pitcher who must consistently paint the corners and keep the ball low in the strike zone to be effective. When he's struggling, it's usually due to poor command within the strike zone, resulting in long extra-base hits. Nagy is well-conditioned and usually around for seven innings per start. He needs to be more cautious with runners on first base; he usually ranks among league leaders in stolen bases allowed.

1998: Finesse pitchers usually top out before age 30, and their decline phase is heralded by a decline in power and a loss of consistency in pitch placement. Nagy appears to be on the cusp of those negative developments.

1997: Nagy faded down the stretch to fall to the third spot in the rotation, behind rookie Jaret Wright, by playoff time. Nagy left the ball up in the strike zone too often, giving up 78 extra-base hits and he let opposing baserunners take advantage of him, allowing 24 steals. All signs are pointing to a steady decline over the next three to four seasons.

1996: Nagy posted what will likely go down as his career year, going 17-5, with a 3.41 ERA. He averaged nearly seven innings per start, and was clearly considered the staff ace by season's end. His location was impeccable, as he allowed less than a hit per inning and held righthanders to a .249 average.

	W	SV	ERA	IP	H	BB	SO	B/I
1995 Cleveland	16	0	4.55	178	194	61	139	1.43
1996 Cleveland	17	0	3.41	222	217	61	167	1.25
1997 Cleveland	15	0	4.28	227	253	77	149	1.45

NAJERA, NOE - TL - b: 12/9/70

"Who needs scouts? — all they do is watch baseball games." That philosophy of Reds' owner Marge Schott allowed her understaffed player development operation to select Najera in the Rule 5 draft following the 1996 season after he dominated the high Class A Carolina League — as a 25-year-old. He was the first Rule 5 pick to be returned to his previous club, after the Reds realized he had just an average fastball, a mediocre breaking-pitch repertoire and poor command within the strike zone. Double-A hitters exposed Najera in 1997, reducing him to mopup duty by season's end. He is lefthanded, so is in no danger of imminent unemployment.

NARCISSE, TYRONE - TR - b: 2/4/72

Narcisse bounced back from an injured shoulder suffered at the end of the 1996 season and pitched well out of the bullpen at Class A Rancho Cucamonga in the Padres' organization. A hard thrower who struck out more than a batter per inning last year, Narcisse had 125 starts in seven previous minor-league seasons but may have found a home coming out of the bullpen.

NAULTY, DAN - TR - b: 1/6/70

Scouting: Naulty has the gas it takes to throw in the majors. The question is, does he have the physical gusto it takes to get through a 162-game season? He has missed much of the past two seasons with injuries, causing many to wonder if he has bad luck or if he simply will break down each year. None of the injuries were to his arm, though, which remains sound.

1998: Despite past success, Naulty must prove himself all over again. He has the stuff to be a late-inning set-up man or a closer. With Rick Aguilera in place, he will be a set-up man.

1997: Naulty started out well but pulled a muscle near his rib cage in May and didn't return until late-August. When he did, he was inconsistent and appeared sluggish.

1996: On the verge of a breakthrough rookie season, Naulty's summer ended in bizarre manner: His hand began to go numb, he was discovered to have circulatory problems and he underwent surgery to remove part of a rib in mid-August. He held opponents to a .207 batting average.

	W	SV	ERA	IP	H	BB	SO	B/I
1996 Minnesota	3	4	3.79	57	43	35	56	1.37
1997 Minnesota	1	1	5.86	31	29	10	23	1.27

NAVARRO, JAIME - TR - b: 3/27/68

Scouting: Navarro throws a split-fingered fastball, slider and curveball, all thrown hard. Not changing speeds has helped contribute to his poor performance some years and he doesn't get the kind of strikeout totals expected from a power pitcher.

1998: Navarro got a big, four-year deal before 1997 and the White Sox would like to unload it — if they can only find a taker. He'll be a starter in the majors, but his success is not guaranteed.

1997: If he wasn't the worst free agent signing of the year he was close. Navarro led the club in innings, but also had the highest ERA among starters while allowing almost sixty hits more than innings pitched. His hard-headed approach to pitching contributed to his "bad attitude" label.

1996: Despite leading the Cubs in victories and other pitching categories, Navarro was allowed to leave via free agency; he was considered a bad influence in the clubhouse.

	W	SV	ERA	IP	H	BB	SO	B/I
1995 Chicago NL	14	0	3.28	200	194	56	128	1.25
1996 Chicago NL	15	0	3.92	236	244	72	158	1.34
1997 Chicago AL	9	0	5.79	210	267	73	142	1.62

NEAGLE, DENNY - TL - b: 9/13/68

Scouting: Neagle throws an 86-MPH fastball from a near sidearm delivery. It seems to impart a slight upwards movement to the pitch and just when the batter has it timed Neagle throws what appears to be the same pitch in the same spot, only it's a changeup delivered 10 MPH slower and the hitter can't adjust. Neagle also throws a slider but uses it for show; he's a master at changing speeds. He has fine control and the rest of his game is above average, too.

1998: Neagle may have to move up in the rotation if the Braves can't re-sign some of their other top pitchers. He should still place among the league's best pitchers, but won't be able to count on such excellent run support if he's the second starter instead of the fourth.

1997: Life ain't fair. Neagle could be a staff ace anywhere else, but with Atlanta he was a fourth starter. As a result he always matched up against lesser opposing pitchers and got fine run support which helped him lead the league in victories. Neagle was among the league's best in other areas, too, so his record wasn't undeserved; he led the Braves in shutouts (four).

1996: The costs of running a small-market franchise led the Pirates to deal Neagle to the Braves in a deadline deal. He was one of the league's top lefthanders and, although he struggled at first in an Atlanta uniform, Neagle looked good in the postseason and earned a four-year, $17.5 million contract after the season.

	W	SV	ERA	IP	H	BB	SO	B/I
1995 Pittsburgh	13	0	3.43	209	221	45	150	1.27
1996 Pitt-Atlanta	16	0	3.50	221	226	48	149	1.24
1997 Atlanta	20	0	2.97	233	204	49	172	1.08

NELSON, CHRIS - TR - b: 1/26/73

Nelson, who split 1997 between Class A Modesto and Double-A Huntsville, pitched well. At Modesto he went 3-3 with a 3.83 ERA over 47 innings. He did allow 55 hits, but he also struck out 53 while walking only seven. At Hunstville, Nelson started 15 games and logged a mark of 9-3 with a 4.97 ERA. He kept up his good control numbers, this time allowing 116 hits over 99.2 innings, striking out 71 and walking 25. He'll advance to Edmonton this year.

NELSON, JEFF - TR - b: 11/17/66

Scouting: Nelson is a large (6'7") side-armer with a good fastball, sinker and slider. He is effective in his role as a righthanded set-up-man. His slider is particularly strong in a platoon advantage.

1998: Nelson was expected to return with Mike Stanton to give the Yankees two of the best set-up men in the game. Joe Torre would like to see Nelson throw more fastballs.

1997: Nelson was asked to team with Stanton to replace Mariano Rivera in the set-up role. He got off to a rocky start but rebounded to post a sensational year despite a losing record. He fanned more than a batter per inning with his nasty slider and rebounded well from off-season elbow surgery. Righthanded hitters batted just .168 against Nelson.

1996: Despite the highest ERA of his career, Nelson's first year in pinstripes was better than anyone could have expected after Seattle Manager Lou Pinella ran him out of the Mariners' bullpen. Nelson then had off-season elbow surgery.

	W	SV	ERA	IP	H	BB	SO	B/I
1995 Seattle	7	2	2.17	78	58	27	96	1.08
1996 New York AL	4	2	4.36	74	75	36	91	1.50
1997 New York AL	3	2	2.86	79	53	37	81	1.14

NEN, ROBB - TR - b: 11/28/69

Scouting: Though Nen was a high profile closer on the World Champs in 1997, he showed areas of vulnerability that must be addressed if he is to remain among baseball's best in upcoming seasons. No one has ever doubted Nen's gas — he possesses a mid-to-upper 90's fastball with explosive late movement. However, he did not control his curve and slider as well in 1997 compared to 1996. Last year Nen also showed vulnerability to righthanded hitters (.278 average) and opposing baserunners (nine steals in nine attempts). 1998 is a key season which could determine the length of Nen's career as a dominant closer.

1998: Acquired by San Francisco for prospects, Nen remains the unquestioned closer on a championship club, Nen should have a bright prognosis. However, Manager Jim Leyland's letting rookie Livan Hernandez throw over 140 pitches in a single post-season start had as much to do with concerns about Nen as it did with confidence in Hernandez. Nen's a pro, and has a better than even chance of bouncing back with authority.

1997: Nen's control of his breaking pitches wavered, his dominance of righthanders waned, and his indifference to opposing baserunners hurt him. He allowed half of the runners he inherited to score, and parlayed seven blown saves into a misleading win total. Big save totals can mask underlying ineffectiveness.

1996: Nen was an overpowering ace reliever. He dominated righthanders (.210 average), threw his breaking stuff for strikes, and walked barely over two batters per nine innings. All in all, he was arguably baseball's best closer.

	W	SV	ERA	IP	H	BB	SO	B/I
1995 Florida	0	23	3.29	65	62	23	68	1.29
1996 Florida	5	35	1.95	83	67	21	92	1.06
1997 Florida	9	35	3.89	74	72	40	81	1.51

NEWELL, BRETT - TR - b: 10/25/72

Newell spent three seasons in the Braves' organization as a light-hitting shortstop prospect with a good glove. He must have had a good arm as well as he took to the mound in 1997 at the Braves Class A affiliate in Eugene and had good results. He appeared in 19 games, throwing 34 innings. He allowed only 17 hits while striking out 46. He will probably start the 1998 season at high Class A or Double-A and bears watching.

NEWMAN, ALAN - TL - b: 10/2/69

Former Twins' farmhand Newman returned from three years in independent ball to pitch 26 games for the White Sox' Double-A club at Birmingham in 1997. Newman has a poor fastball and not much else to go with it. Nevertheless he was 5-1 with a 2.96 ERA and limited opponents to just 35 hits in 49 innings. He is no prospect.

NICHOLS, ROD - TR - b: 12/29/64

A veteran of 400+ major league innings, and an ace reliever at Triple-A Richmond on the Braves' farm in 1995-1996, Nichols could easily have been pitching in the majors if he had been with a weaker organization. Nichols appeared briefly in Japan last year, but did nothing to brighten his future.

NICHTING, CHRIS - TR - b: 5/13/66

A former Dodger and Ranger farmhand, Nichting's future doesn't look bright. At best he is a workmanlike number four Triple-A starter. At worst he is major league cannon fodder. His nine-year career boasts only 13 big-league appearances. Last year at Edmonton he went 8-13 with a 7.44 ERA. At age 32, Nichting is nearing the end of his professional ballplaying days.

NITKOWSKI, C.J. - TL - b: 3/3/73

Scouting: Nitkowski is one of the pitchers obtained by Houston in the multi-player trade with Detroit prior to the 1997 season. He was a first round draft choice by Cincinnati in 1994 and is in his third organization. He doesn't have the overpowering arm that might be expected of a first round draft choice but he changes speeds effectively and has good control. He has had trouble being consistent in his career, having had three major league trials in 1995 and 1996 and getting hit hard each time.

1998: Nitkowski is on Houston's 40-man roster and will be a candidate for the starting rotation. There appear to be stronger candidates ahead of him.

1997: Nitkowski spent the entire season at Triple-A New Orleans. He was 8-10 in 23 starts with an ERA of 3.98. He led the American Association in strikeouts with 141 in 174.1 innings.

1996: Nitkowski split the season between Detroit and Triple-A Toledo. In Toledo he was 4-6 with a 4.46 ERA and 103 strikeouts in 111 innings.

	W	SV	ERA	IP	H	BB	SO	B/I
1995 Cincinnati	1	0	6.12	32	41	15	18	1.74
1995 Detroit	1	0	7.09	39	53	20	13	1.87
1996 Detroit	2	0	8.08	45	62	38	36	2.21

NIX, JAMES - TR - b: 9/6/70
Nix continues to be a solid Double-A reliever (at Chattanooga last year) but has yet to prove himself at a higher level. Nix does not come out of the pen with a blazing fastball and it was evident at Triple-A Indianapolis (8.82 ERA in 12 games). He does throw three other pitches, a curveball, slider and changeup, all of which will need refinement if he hopes to advance to the Cincinnati bullpen.

NOEL, TODD - TR - b: 9/28/78
Selected by the Cubs with the 17th pick in the 1996 draft, Noel spent 1997 posting an impressive season at Rookie League Mesa. He fanned 63 in 59 innings of work while surrendering just 39 base knocks. He should start 1998 at least in higher A-ball.

NOMO, HIDEO - TR - b: 8/31/68
Scouting: The main question is whether Nomo will bounce back. Following the 1997 season, he required surgery to remove calcium deposits in his right elbow. The doctors were optimistic. When healthy, Nomo's deceptive motion hides the ball well and makes his low-90's fastball look more like 96 MPH. When he's ahead in the count, he punches batters out with a tough forkball.
1998: Nomo's recovery from surgery is a concern. We do not know if his elbow was a large part of his inconsistency last year. He well could be in overall decline. The radar guns in spring training will give the answer.
1997: Nomo was hittable. Batters began to lay off the low stuff and work him deeper into the count. This approach caused Nomo to walk a career high 92. It was a dramatic downturn from 1995-96 when he held both righthanded and lefthanded batters to nearly a .200 batting average. The opposition slugged .400 against him — and .449 in the second half. Nomo's ratio of baserunners per nine innings ascended for the third straight year, from 9.50 in 1995 to 10.45 in 1996 and finally to 12.37 last year.
1996: Nomo proved to be more than a one-year wonder as he was fourth in the league in wins, seventh in ERA, third in opposition batting average, and second in strikeouts and strikeout rate.

	W	SV	ERA	IP	H	BB	SO	B/I
1995 Los Angeles	13	0	2.54	191	124	78	236	1.06
1996 Los Angeles	16	0	3.19	228	180	85	234	1.16
1997 Los Angeles	14	0	4.25	207	193	92	233	1.37

NORMAN, SCOTT - TR - b: 9/1/72
Picked up in the Rule V draft from Detroit, Norman is a sinker/slider pitcher who throws strikes but his stuff is considered short. He was 1-5 with a 6.75 ERA in 29 relief appearances at Double-A New Haven in 1997, but he will have to fight to win a spot on New Haven's roster this year.

NORRIS, JOE - TR - b: 11/29/70
Norris is a big righthander with a slightly above-average fastball who has been held back by below-average command and an inability to develop an effective breaking-ball repertoire. Norris has a durable arm and can be used in a variety of roles, but has shown a maddening tendency to be done in by a single bad inning per outing. He has been hit hard in both of his Triple-A trials, for the Twins in 1996 and for the Marlins in 1997. At age 27, he has little chance of erasing his reputation as a minor-league journeyman.

NUNEZ, VLADIMIR - TR - b: 3/15/75
Scouting: Among the second wave of emigrating Cuban pitchers, Nunez signed with the Diamondbacks through agent Joe Cubas' pipeline for a $1.7 million bonus. Nunez' repertoire includes a fastball that touches 96 MPH and a breaking ball he can locate for strikes.
1998: Nunez is expected to make the double jump to Triple-A Tucson after spending his first two years in A-ball.
1997: Nunez struggled early after a series of personal highs — his parents left Cuba to move to the Dominican Republic, and his wife had their first child. He rebounded to win seven of his final eight decisions, going 8-5 with 142 strikeouts in 158.1 innings at Class A High Desert.
1996: Dropped from the California League to the Pioneer League, Nunez was devastating; he went 10-0 with a 2.22 ERA while striking out 93 in 85 innings with just ten walks. He had been roughed up while pitching for a co-op team at Visalia.

NYE, RYAN - TR - b: 6/24/73
Scouting: Nye has pitched exceedingly well at levels below Triple-A, but has stagnated at the highest minor-league level over the past two seasons. He has an 87-MPH fastball and an array of breaking pitches which he throws well for strikes, but perhaps too well. He has been hittable over the last two years. Nye's success will be tied to his ability to more consistently work the edges of the plate instead of just throwing the ball down the middle.
1998: Nye will again start the season in the Triple-A Scranton rotation. He has the tools to be a passable major league starter, but must show short-term location enhancements to have a chance for a 1998. Nye is behind better prospects in the Phillies' high minors.
1997: Nye had a solid strikeout-to-walk ratio at Triple-A Scranton, but was prone to the big inning. He has now posted 5.00+ ERA's in his two Triple-A campaigns.
1996: Nye split the season between Double-A and Triple-A, posting a 13-4 record which brought his career mark to an impressive 32-13. However, his lack of raw stuff was exposed at the higher level, where his strikeout rate dropped precipitously while he allowed 11 hits per nine innings.

OGEA, CHAD - TR - b: 11/970
Scouting: Ogea is a finesse pitcher whose fastball only reaches 87 MPH. He needs to set up his heater by throwing his breaking pitches for strikes early in the count. When he is hitting his spots, Ogea can be downright nasty against right-handed hitters. He won't likely become a number one or two starter in a major league rotation because of his lack of arm strength, which makes him an unlikely complete game candidate. His health must be watched; he was plagued by a strained elbow in 1997.
1998: Ogea appeared to be healthy at the end of 1997, but had not regained his arm strength. His spring training performance in 1998 will be key; if he's breezing through five or six innings per start by the end of March, he's back and is ready to throw 200 innings out of the third starter's slot.
1997: The Indians needed Ogea to step up and assert himself due an injury to Jack McDowell. Unfortunately, Ogea soon joined McDowell on the disabled list with an elbow strain. He did not require surgery, and was eased back into action late in

September to prepare for the playoffs. He was sharp in his last two starts, but was held to a strict, low pitch count.
1996: The Indians inexplicably relegated Ogea to a bullpen role early in 1996, allowing Dennis Martinez to endure a painful public flogging. Ogea has always been able to swing between the rotation and bullpen with ease, and settled in as a productive starter by the end of the season after a shaky start.

	W	SV	ERA	IP	H	BB	SO	B/I
1995 Cleveland	8	0	3.05	106	95	29	57	1.17
1996 Cleveland	10	0	4.79	146	151	42	101	1.32
1997 Cleveland	8	0	4.99	126	139	47	80	1.47

OHME, KEVIN - TL - b: 4/13/71
Ohme is a finesse pitcher who was a non-roster invitee to spring training last year by the Twins. He ended up at Triple-A Salt Lake coming out of the bullpen. He yielded nearly a hit per inning and didn't have good control. He doesn't look like a major league reliever.

OJALA, KIRT - TL - b: 12/24/68
Scouting: Ojala is a typical crafty lefty, of the Triple-A journeyman variety. He has a mid-80's fastball, and liberally mixes in a variety of off-speed pitches, including a changeup. He has been a durable inning-eater at the Triple-A level for the past five seasons, keeping his clubs in ballgames while consistently posting low walk totals. Recent mechanical refinements have made him more of a strikeout threat and finally earned him a major league shot.
1998: Ojala will likely return to Triple-A in 1998. The Marlins are well fortified in lefthanded relievers, and Ojala simply doesn't have the stuff to take a regular turn over a full big-league season. He will be a decent injury insurance policy stored at Triple-A.
1997: Ojala was one of the low-budget heroes whose contributions were overlooked by those who chose to focus on the Marlins' big-money free agent signings as the reason for their championship run. He kept the Marlins in the ballgame in each of five September starts, despite pitching tentatively and walking too many hitters over the course of the season.
1996: Ojala's only season in the Reds' chain was in line with career norms. He averaged better than six innings per start, walked two hitters per nine innings, but didn't overpower anyone.

	W	SV	ERA	IP	H	BB	SO	B/I
1997 Florida	1	0	3.14	29	28	18	19	1.60

OLIVARES, OMAR - TR - b: 7/6/67
Scouting: Olivares has stuff best suited for a spot starter/long reliever role, although he has been in rotations in St. Louis, Detroit and, briefly, Colorado and Seattle. He must hit spots to succeed because he doesn't blow the ball past hitters. Olivares has a good sinking fastball but often doesn't use it enough.
1998: A likely candidate for a long relief job, Olivares' days as a regular rotation member appear through.
1997: Olivares failed to deliver after being acquired from Detroit in a mid-season deal, among several reasons the Mariners were forced to hurry prospect Ken Cloude into the rotation.
1996: Olivares found a niche in Detroit, where he threw four complete games and led the beleaguered Tigers' staff in victories with seven. He made just 25 starts due to losing eight weeks to a hamstring pull. His sinker helped him get a number of groundball double plays, an essential skill when pitching in Tiger Stadium.

	W	SV	ERA	IP	H	BB	SO	B/I
1996 Detroit	7	0	4.89	160	169	75	81	1.52
1997 Seattle	6	0	4.97	177	191	81	103	1.53

OLIVER, DARREN - TL - b: 10/6/70
Scouting: The primary question with Oliver has always been durability rather than talent. He has a fastball in the high 80s, a wicked curve and an effective changeup. Oliver's control has been suspect, but has improved in each season. He is a dogged competitor, and is not afraid to pitch inside. In the last two seasons, Oliver has not missed a turn in the rotation, and has not experienced a recurrence of the elbow and shoulder woes that dogged his first few years as a professional. He has a fine pickoff move.
1998: Oliver has established himself as a solid major league starter, and with more consistency he would become one of the better lefties in the American League.
1997: The Rangers were able to persuade Oliver to work on conditioning in the off-season, and it appears to have succeeded. Oliver established career highs in starts and innings, and in the last half of the season was Texas' most effective starting pitcher. He tends to allow lots of baserunners, but thrives on pitching his way out of trouble.
1996: This talented lefthander managed to stay healthy for the entire season, and proved that he could be a major league starter, winning 14 games. Oliver was used carefully, frequently pitching on five days' rest or more.

	W	SV	ERA	IP	H	BB	SO	B/I
1995 Texas	4	0	4.22	49	47	32	39	1.61
1996 Texas	14	0	4.66	173	190	76	112	1.54
1997 Texas	13	0	4.20	201	213	82	104	1.47

OLSEN, JASON - TR - b: 3/16/75
Olsen doesn't have a lot of velocity but he does have great, natural movement on his fastball. A late draft pick in 1994, Olsen has only recently been put on the fast track to the majors. He made 17 starts for Double-A Birmingham in 1997, going 5-9 with a 4.68 ERA.

OLSEN, STEVE - TR - b: 11/2/69
Olsen has a good fastball, but it has little movement and he has nothing much to go with it. He has frequently been on the fringe of the majors, but has never quite taken that last step. His 1997 performance (5.76 ERA at Triple-A Omaha) has to be considered a step in the wrong direction.

OLSON, GREGG - TR - b: 10/11/66
Scouting: Once possessed of a dangerous curveball, Olson will now mix his pitches more, throwing an upper-80s fastball, curve and a newly-developed changeup. It was an effective combination as long as he kept his pitches down in the strike zone. Olson can still pitch, but is no longer closer material.
1998: A one-inning set-up relief role is well-suited to Olson's abilities at this point. The dearth of good pitching in the majors assures Olson an opportunity to fill a major league bullpen job in 1998.
1997: A horrific start for the Twins made Olson available as a free agent to the Royals. After allowing a run in his first outing for Kansas City, Olson settled down to throw ten consecutive scoreless games and become one of the few reliable relievers

in their weak bullpen. He struggled with his command later in the year.

1996: Olson was ineffective in a handful of games for the Astros before earning eight saves for Detroit despite a high ERA and opposition batting average.

	W	SV	ERA	IP	H	BB	SO	B/I
1995 Clev. - K.C.	3	3	4.09	33	28	19	21	1.42
1996 Houston	1	0	4.82	9	12	7	8	2.09
1996 Detroit	3	8	5.02	43	43	28	29	1.65
1997 Kansas City	4	1	5.58	50	58	28	34	1.72

ONTIVEROS, STEVE - TR - b: 3/5/61

Ontiveros missed last season because of elbow surgery he underwent at the end of March. He missed the 1996 season when he was a member of the A's because of arthritis in his elbow. Ontiveros has come back before but it may be too much to ask of the 37-year-old to be ready for 1998.

	W	SV	ERA	IP	H	BB	SO	B/I
1995 Oakland	9	0	4.37	129	144	38	77	1.40
1996 Oakland			Did Not Play - Injured					

OQUIST, MIKE - TR - b: 5/30/68

Scouting: Signed as a free-agent in the fall of 1996, the former Padre and Oriole is a fine athlete with an 88-MPH fastball and the requisite curve, slider, changeup arsenal. Oquist has below-average stuff, so he must rely on finesse to succeed. Over his eight-year career, he never had a chance to start in the majors until last year.

1998: The A's liked what they saw in 1997, so Oquist goes into the season with a lock on a starter's job. He is really not much better than a number four man in a major league rotation, but he can be serviceable in such a role. Were the A's not so deficient in pitching to begin with, he probably wouldn't even get that chance.

1997: Obviously too good to be stuck at Triple-A, Oquist went 6-1 with a 3.25 ERA over nine starts at Edmonton. He wound his way into the A's rotation where he pitched as well as anyone else over 17 starts.

1996: Oquist pitched well in the tough Triple-A Pacific Coast League, posting the second-best ERA in the league.

	W	SV	ERA	IP	H	BB	SO	B/I
1997 Oakland	4	0	5.01	108	111	43	72	1.43

ORELLANO, RAFAEL - TL - b: 4/28/73

Orellano, a rail-thin lefthander, has hit a wall in Triple-A the last two years after moving quickly up the minor-league ladder. After going 4-11 with a 7.88 ERA in '96, Orellano came back determined to right himself in '97. He started out well, but soon started posting similar numbers (3-5, 7.14) to what he had done the year before, and was demoted to Double-A, where he experienced arm problems. Simply put, Orellano's fastball and breaking ball are below average. His only quality pitch is his changeup. He's a longshot getting longer.

OROPESA, EDDIE - TL - b: 11/23/71

Oropesa had a good showing at Double-A Shreveport (7-7, 3.92 ERA) in 1997. He is not overpowering (65 strikeouts, 64 walks), but he does limit opposition hits (124 innings, 122 hits). Oropesa is a former Dodger farmhand, who has been bouncing up and down between A-ball and Double-A over the past four years. His last two seasons have shown improvement, but he must prove success at a higher level to make the majors. Look for Oropesa in Triple-A in 1998, and mark his progress accordingly.

OROSCO, JESSE - TL - b: 4/21/57

Scouting: They say Orosco is as old as dirt, but he can still get his slider in there. Orosco's a wiley old lefty whose best pitch is a sharp slider. He has a decent fastball, and the two pitches together with good location make him a effective set-up man and situational pitcher. He's always been tough on lefties.

1998: It looks like Orosco may pitch forever. He showed no signs of losing anything in 1997, and he should continue in 1998.

1997: Orosco had another outstanding year. He had an awkward outing in Florida, due in part to an overly-high pitchers mound to which he couldn't adjust.

1996: Orosco had another outstanding year, tarnished only by a bad two days in Texas in April when he gave up twelve runs in a couple of innings, thereby deceptively ballooning his seasonal ERA.

	W	SV	ERA	IP	H	BB	SO	B/I
1995 Baltimore	2	3	3.26	49	28	27	58	1.11
1996 Baltimore	3	0	3.40	55	42	28	52	1.27
1997 Baltimore	6	0	2.33	50	29	30	46	1.17

ORTIZ, RUSS - TR - b: 6/5/74

Following a fabulous 1996 season at Class A San Jose (23 saves over 37 innings, including 63 whiffs), Ortiz found the going a little tougher last year. He started at Double-A Shreveport, going 2-3 with a 4.13 ERA, then moved to Triple-A Phoenix, where he compiled a 4-3 mark and a 5.51 ERA. Ortiz continued to log nearly a strikeout per inning, fanning 120 in 141.2 innings as the Giants let him try his hand as a starter. He needs more time to develop and may need a full year at Double-A to do so.

OSBORNE, DONOVAN - TL - b: 6/21/69

Scouting: One of the league's best lefthanders when healthy, Osborne has had more trouble with injuries than opposing hitters. He's made more than 20 big-league starts only once during the last four seasons thanks to injuries. There are whispers that Osborne, with a brilliant fastball that tails away, a good slider and an often ferocious competitiveness, won't achieve all that he can because of fragile body and psyche. Bottom line —all the intelligence and tenacity does no good on the disabled list.

1998: Osborne has seemed like the kind of pitcher who takes pride in comebacks. If his legs and left arm allow, he probably will be able to turn in a solid if not spectacular season. Frankly, the Cardinals need a strong showing from him since he's one of their few lefthanded options throughout the organization.

1997: Injuries struck early and late, the latter one a hernia requiring surgery that resulted from a persistent deep groin problem. It all limited him to 14 starts and 80.1 mostly inconsistent innings.

1996: Healthy enough to make a career-high 30 starts and work a career-high 198.2 innings, Osborne posted the best earned-run average among Cardinal starters.

	W	SV	ERA	IP	H	BB	SO	B/I
1995 St. Louis	4	0	3.81	113	112	34	82	1.29
1996 St. Louis	13	0	3.53	198	191	57	134	1.25
1997 St. Louis	3	0	4.93	80	84	23	51	1.33

OSTEEN, GALVIN - TL - b: 11/27/69
Galvin is the son of former Senator and Dodger pitcher Claude Osteen. He was in the Oakland organization from 1989-95, but was injured most of 1995 and didn't pitch at all in 1996. In 1997, he was pitching without any pain in a semi-pro league near Harrisburg, PA. He was signed by the Orioles and relieved and spot started in nineteen games for the Orioles Double-A club. Osteen doesn't throw hard; his best pitch is a circle changeup. He also has a good curve. Southpaws are always in demand, so Osteen may make it to the majors as a situational reliever.

OSUNA, AL - TL - b: 8/10/65
A veteran of 189 relief innings with the Dodgers and Astros, Osuna slipped into the minors in 1996 and went to Japan last year. He has an assortment of off-speed stuff that can be effective, especially in lefty-lefty matchup situations. Osuna was one of the hardest-working and most productive relievers in Japan in 1997, crafting a 2.58 ERA.

OSUNA, ANTONIO - TR - b: 4/12/73
Scouting: Osuna throws hard. He throws his fastball in the same range as Mark Wohlers, Armando Benitez and Robb Nen. When he has it going, he simply blows the high, hard four-seamer past hitters. If they try to time him, he usually gets a pop-up or fly out. He has a fair curve, and a changeup.
1998: On a Dodger team without Todd Worrell, Osuna will be a prime candidate for closer. The plan has been to begin the year with Osuna as the set-up man for Darren Dreifort. If Dreifort falters, Osuna will get a shot at closing, and will finish some games in which he blows away the opponents in the eighth inning.
1997: Osuna was sent to Triple-A Albuquerque after spring training to work out some mechanical flaws. He was recalled and resumed his middle-inning and set-up work.
1996: Osuna had a brilliant season. He was obviously a closer in waiting.

	W	SV	ERA	IP	H	BB	SO	B/I
1996 Los Angeles	9	4	3.00	84	65	32	85	1.15
1997 Los Angeles	3	0	2.19	62	46	19	68	1.05

PACE, SCOTTY - TL - b: 9/16/71
Pace pitched in the Brewers' organization last year, mostly at Double-A, and had a hard time of it. He didn't improve his control and his lack of velocity made him hittable despite good movement on his stuff. Pace was used almost exclusively in relief and will have to prove he can get people out consistently without the walks to advance any further.

PACHECO, ALEX - TR - b: 7/19/73
Scouting: A hard thrower obtained from Montreal as part of the Jeff Fassero deal, Pacheco showed little last season before being shut down with right shoulder tenderness. The Expos toyed with him as a closer, but his command and location are too inexact.
1998: Pacheco will have to start over in his second year with the Mariners. A full return of velocity will be required before he can compete for a big-league job.
1997: Pacheco was dreadful at Triple-A Tacoma, giving up 60 baserunners — 45 hits, 15 walks — in only 27.2 innings. In his fifteen appearances (two starts), Pacheco was 0-2 with an 8.78 ERA. He fared better at Double-A Memphis, going 1-1 with a 3.75 ERA over nine games, but still had control difficulties, walking nine in twelve innings.
1996: Despite a 6.48 ERA, Pacheco recorded six saves at Triple-A Ottawa, earning three short promotions to Montreal in April and May. It was his first trip to the majors after six seasons spent in the Expos' minor-league system.

PADUA, GERALDO - TR - b: 2/9/77
The Yankees may have found a budding star at Rookie League Tampa where Padua was 8-0 with a 2.92 ERA in 11 games (eight starts); in 61.2 innings, he allowed just 46 hits. His fastball is better than his slender 6'2", 165-pound frame might suggest.

PAINTER, LANCE - TL - b: 7/21/67
Overlooked by most observers (but not by Tony LaRussa) was an impressive relief outing by Painter in the Cardinals' final game of 1997, when Mark McGwire's 58th home run got all the attention. Painter missed most of the year following surgery, but he entered the winter looking fine and healthy. He has good velocity on his fastball and fine command.

	W	SV	ERA	IP	H	BB	SO	B/I
1995 Colorado	3	1	4.37	45	55	10	36	1.44
1996 Colorado	4	0	5.86	50	56	25	48	1.61
1997 St. Louis	1	0	4.76	17	13	8	11	1.24

PALL, DONN - TR - b: 1/11/62
Scouting: It might come as a shock that Pall has received major league time in nine of the last ten seasons. He has below-average velocity, clocking in the low-to-mid 80's with his fastball. He gets by on a steady diet of slow curves and changeups, thrown consistently for quality strikes on the fringes of the plate. He has a durable arm capable of pitching two to three innings at a clip, or on several consecutive days in smaller doses. He's a solid Triple-A insurance policy who could still be an effective middle reliever in the majors.
1998: Expansion could improve Pall's opportunity to get back to the majors. He is capable of eating up some innings and minimizing stress on the more talented relievers in a bullpen.
1997: Pall split time between the primary set-up and closer roles at Triple-A Charlotte in the Marlins' system. He posted a spectacular 70-to-11 strikeout-to-walk ratio and routinely pitched two innings per appearance.
1996: Pall was the primary closer at Triple-A Charlotte, and actually struck out better than a batter per inning. All young pitchers with high octane fastballs should be forced to watch tapes of Pall's outings to observe his skill at setting up hitters and keeping them off balance.

	W	SV	ERA	IP	H	BB	SO	B/I
1996 Florida	1	0	5.79	18	16	9	9	1.37

PANIAGUA, JOSE - TR - b: 8/20/73
Scouting: The Expos long ago fell in love with Paniagua's 95-MPH fastball and biting slider. However, Paniagua has struggled to add an off-speed pitch and often fails to find the strike zone on a consistent basis.
1998: Paniagua has good enough stuff to begin 1998 in the Tampa Bay rotation. He has made 22 appearances with the Expos over the past two seasons and struggled at times. However, he has the arm to be a standout pitcher. He'll experience some growing pains this year but watch for him to get better as the season goes along and he gains confidence.
1997: Paniagua, bothered off and on by shoulder pain, struggled

both at Triple-A Ottawa and with the Expos. He began the season on the disabled list and never found a groove.
1996: Paniagua was dominant at both Ottawa and Double-A Harrisburg, then pitched extremely well for Montreal over the final two months of the season.

	W	SV	ERA	IP	H	BB	SO	B/I
1996 Montreal	2	0	3.53	51	55	23	27	1.53
1997 Montreal	1	0	12.00	18	29	16	8	2.50

PARK, CHAN-HO - TR - b: 6/30/73
Scouting: Park has three excellent pitches. His fastball is regularly in the mid 90'S, with a wicked, late movement. He has a good tight curve, and last year consistently threw his hard slider for strikes. Park in the past has lacked command, but last year he gained control of his high-octane arsenal, especially the slider, which led to his breakthrough season.
1998: Park is now a permanent fixture in the Dodgers rotation. If the rotation stays the same, he'll be in the three spot, matching up strongly with other teams' number three starter.
1997: In a breakthrough year, Park entered the rotation for good in May and was brilliant through August, making 22 starts and going 12-5 in that span. By September, he'd pitched 170 innings. Playoff pressure and fatigue combined to slow him as he went 1-2 with a 5.11 ERA in the final month.
1996: Park struggled at times with control, but fanned ten batters per nine innings while winning five games. He started ten games and relieved in 38 more.

	W	SV	ERA	IP	H	BB	SO	B/I
1996 Los Angeles	5	0	3.64	108	82	71	119	1.41
1997 Los Angeles	14	0	3.38	192	149	70	166	1.14

PARRA, JOSE - TR - b: 11/28/72
Parra spent time with the Twins in 1995 and '96, showing he needed more minor-league seasoning to learn how to hit the corners. He got one of those seasons in 1997 as he pitched at Triple-A Salt Lake — but he didn't pitch like he'd learned anything. He gave up well more than a hit per inning and had an ERA over six. He may never see the Metrodome again as a player.

	W	SV	ERA	IP	H	BB	SO	B/I
1995 Los Angeles	0	0	4.35	10	10	6	7	1.55
1995 Minnesota	1	0	7.59	61	83	22	29	1.70
1996 Minnesota	5	0	6.04	70	88	27	50	1.64

PARRIS, STEVE - TR - b: 12/17/67
Parris is a former Pittsburgh Pirate who pitched badly for the Bucs in 1995 and 1996 and ran out of chances with that franchise. He was picked up quickly by the Reds and had an average season for Double-A Chattanooga and Triple-A Indianapolis. The Reds are looking for cheap players and Parris certainly will fit that description. Despite being 30 years old and having little major league experience, he could be a decent middle reliever, but he won't be effective at all as a starter.

	W	SV	ERA	IP	H	BB	SO	B/I
1995 Pittsburgh	6	0	5.38	82	89	33	61	1.49
1996 Pittsburgh	0	0	7.18	26	35	11	27	1.76

PATRICK, BRONSWELL - TR - b: 9/16/70
Patrick has spent eleven years in the minors, eight in the Oakland farm system; the closest he came to the majors was as a replacement player in 1995. He throws hard but lacks any outstanding pitch that would target him for major league success. Patrick's versatility has helped him stay at Triple-A for the last three years; he went 6-5 with a 3.22 ERA, making 14 starts among his thirty appearances last year. Major league expansion provides Patrick with a last, best hope for a major league opportunity.

PATTERSON, BOB - TL - b: 5/16/59
Scouting: Patterson is a soft-throwing lefthander who throws mostly off-speed pitches and breaking balls. He's good against lefthanded hitters, but has more problems with righthanders and is used mostly as a situational pitcher.
1998: Patterson has been effective the past couple of seasons with the Cubs because the team doesn't ask him to do too much. They know his weaknesses and limitations, and will continue to use him primarily against lefthanded hitters. He'll be 39 in May, so he's obviously nearing the end of the road, but his arm appears to be sound.
1997: Patterson had essentially the same kind of season that he had in his first year with the Cubs. His record wasn't good, but it was an indication that he was pitching in critical parts of the game and was a victim of bad luck as much as anything.
1996: Patterson had a good first season for the Cubs after spending two years with the Angels. He appeared in 79 games but threw far fewer innings than that because the Cubs selected his spots to pitch. He got eight saves, not because the Cubs signed him to be a closer, but because the team had no one else to trust with the ball late in the game.

	W	SV	ERA	IP	H	BB	SO	B/I
1995 California	5	0	3.04	53	48	13	41	1.14
1996 Chicago NL	3	8	3.13	54	46	22	53	1.25
1997 Chicago NL	1	0	3.34	59	47	10	58	0.96

PATTERSON, DANNY - TR - b: 2/17/71
Scouting: Patterson calls his best pitch a "Vulcan splitter", a split-finger pitch held between the middle and ring fingers. He also throws, and has good control of, an above-average fastball and slider. Patterson displays the kind of toughness on the mound that one generally associates with the best closers, although he has yet to reach that level.
1998: Patterson is the leading contender to be the main set-up man for John Wetteland, and would be in line for save opportunities should Wetteland be injured.
1997: Patterson's fine season would have been even better if he hadn't struggled toward the end when he was pitching with pain in his right shoulder. Twice during the season he experienced pain, and had surgery to clean out the area at the end of the season. He was much better against lefthanded hitters (.236 versus .282). Patterson's main negative was seven blown saves in eight opportunities.
1996: Good control helped Patterson get promoted in mid-season during 1994, 1995 and 1996. He led Oklahoma City with ten saves in '96 and pitched well in a brief September trial with Texas.

	W	SV	ERA	IP	H	BB	SO	B/I
1997 Texas	10	1	3.42	71	70	23	69	1.31

PATTERSON, JOHN - TR - b: 1/30/70
Scouting: A "loophole free-agent" available when Montreal failed to make a contract offer within 15 days of the 1996 draft, Patterson was stolen by the Diamondbacks. He has the tools one would expect from the fifth player taken overall in the draft. His fastball touches 95 MPH with good location, and he has

command of a breaking ball. Patterson has terrific mound presence and composure.
1998: Based strictly upon talent, Patterson is ready for the jump to Triple-A Tucson, but the team may want to make a slower progression by shifting him up to Class A High Desert instead.
1997: Patterson posted a 3.23 ERA at Class A South Bend, but managed only a 1-9 record due to lack of run support. He fanned 95 in 78 innings and surrendered just 63 hits while losing four games by a 1-0 score. Because it was his first professional season, Patterson spent much of the summer with a strict pitch limit.
1996: After piling up 142 strikeouts in 72.1 innings for West Orange/Stark High School in Orange, Texas, Patterson sat out the professional season while his draft status was clarified.

PAVANO, CARL - TR - b: 1/8/76
Scouting: Pavano has a 93-MPH fastball, an improving, but inconsistent, slider, and a decent changeup. He's a power pitcher who believes in throwing strikes, likes to pitch inside, and is not afraid of contact. The only concern is health. He's had elbow and shoulder tendinitis the last couple of seasons.
1998: Pavano is in line to take a regular spot in the Montreal rotation. He might struggle at first because he needs to be more consistent with his off-speed pitches and the location of his fastball, but he has the stuff and the makeup to be a top-level pitcher in the majors. Health, of course, is another concern.
1997: Pavano got a late start to his Triple-A season because of elbow tendinitis, but soon was pitching nearly as well in his first year at this level as he had the previous year in Double-A. His velocity was down slightly from the year before: 92/93 MPH as opposed to 94/95. Also, he found the hitters did a better job sitting on and hitting his fastball. Still, he went 11-6 with a 3.12 ERA, walking just 34 in 162 innings, while striking out 147.
1996: In just his second full season out of high school, Pavano blew away the competition in Double-A, going 16-5 with a 2.63 ERA. He went 8-0 with a 1.05 ERA in his last 11 starts.

PAVLAS, DAVE - TR - b: 8/12/62
Pavlas looked better a year ago. He was up with the Yankees briefly in 1995 and 1996 while spending most of his time at Triple-A Columbus. He pitched 25 effective innings up with the Yankees in '96. In 1997 Pavlas spent the whole year at Columbus and was less effective (1.99 ERA in 1996, compared to 4.62 mark in 1997). Pavlas has lost some velocity and hasn't added enough movement and command to compensate.

	W	SV	ERA	IP	H	BB	SO	B/I
1995 New York AL	0	0	3.18	5	8	0	3	1.41
1996 New York AL	0	1	2.35	23	23	7	18	1.30

PAVLIK, ROGER - TR - b: 10/4/64
Scouting: Pavlik is a fastball/sinker pitcher who is successful when he can get good downward movement on his pitches. He has an unorthodox cross-body pitching motion, and pitching coaches have given up on trying to get him to change his delivery. Even when he is pitching well, Pavlik has tenuous control and tends to work his way into and out of jams. He has had a variety of injury problems over the years, but was healthy at the end of last season.
1998: Barring injury, Pavlik will be a rotation starter somewhere in the majors. He is capable of pitching well for weeks at a time, but has never been able to maintain that level over a whole season.
1997: Pavlik's season was marred by an elbow injury that cost him four months on the disabled list, his sixth trip to the DL in seven seasons. His last three starts in September were strong outings, providing a basis for optimism about 1998.
1996: Pavlik won 12 games in the first half and was named to the All-Star team despite an ERA that hovered around 5.00. His run support declined in the second half, and Pavlik ended the season as the fifth man in the rotation.

	W	SV	ERA	IP	H	BB	SO	B/I
1995 Texas	10	0	4.37	191	174	90	149	1.38
1996 Texas	15	0	5.19	201	216	81	127	1.48
1997 texas	3	0	4.37	58	59	31	35	1.56

PEEVER, LLOYD - TR - b: 9/15/71
After going 14-0 with a 1.98 ERA at LSU in 1992, Peever was selected in the fourth round by the Rockies that summer. He didn't have much stuff to begin with, but injuries robbed him of having any chance to reach the big leagues. If he doesn't make a Double-A club in spring training, he would have a future as a pitching coach if he so desires.

PENA, JUAN - TR - b: 6/27/77
Pena, a native of the Dominican Republic who will turn 21 this season, moved quickly through the Red Sox system, before finally finding a league he couldn't overpower in Double-A last season. After posting a 2.96 ERA in A-ball and allowing just 67 hits in 91 innings, he was promoted to Double-A, where he went 5-6 with a 4.73 ERA over 97 innings. He's 6'5", young, and extremely promising. He should continue to come along quickly.

PENNINGTON, BRAD - TL - b: 4/14/69
Pennington still has a 90-plus fastball, but little to go with it. He has become a journeyman Triple-A reliever with little chance to ever reach the major league closer status to which he seemed destined earlier in his career.

	W	SV	ERA	IP	H	BB	SO	B/I
1996 California	0	0	6.20	20	11	31	20	2.09

PENNY, BRAD - TR - b: 5/24/78
Scouting: Penny grew up within shouting distance of Hall-of-Fame lefthander Warren Spahn in rural Oklahoma. He spots a 90-plus fastball and a sneaky curve in good locations while displaying superior mound presence.
1998: Penny will continue his ascent up the Diamondbacks' minor-league ladder with an initial stop at Class A High Desert, but could make it to Triple-A Tucson by the second half. He's a comer.
1997: Penny won 10 games at Class A South Bend while continuing his strikeout-per-inning pace with 116 in 118.2 innings; he gave up only 91 hits.
1996: Scouts told the Diamondbacks that fifth-round pick Penny could have been a first-rounder after watching him strike out 52 in 49 innings in the Arizona Rookie League.

PERCIBAL, WILLIAM - TR - b: 2/2/74
Oriole prospect Percibal lost most of last year rehabbing from elbow surgery; he made three A-ball starts in 1997. He was once a top prospect, but lost 1996 and much of 1997 because of an elbow problem that eventually required surgery, followed

by a lengthy rehab. He had a major league fastball before the injury, with a good breaking ball. If healthy, Percibal could be pitching in Camden Yards sometime before the year 2000.

PERCIVAL, TROY - TR - b: 8/9/69

Scouting: With a fastball that approaches 100 MPH, Percival has become one of the most intimidating closers in baseball. He started using his curveball and changeup more in 1997, but the heater is still his bread-and-butter pitch and has established him as one of the league's most dependable stoppers. His save total was down last season, but, once an early-season injury was overcome, he was the same pitcher the Angels envisioned as their closer of the future as far back as 1994.

1998: All the Angels want is for Percival to stay healthy. They thought enough of his ability that they traded Lee Smith, baseball's all-time saves leader, to Cincinnati in May of 1996 in order to make him their closer. So far, he hasn't disappointed.

1997: Percival missed half of spring training and the first five weeks of the season with a swollen nerve in his right shoulder, which he believes was a lingering result of an off-season auto accident. Once Percival returned to full health, he quickly rebuilt his arm strength and was a key factor in the Angels' drive for a pennant.

1996: Percival's chance to close came when Lee Smith had to open the season on the disabled list following knee surgery. He rapidly showed he was ready to assume the role for which the Angels — and Smith — had carefully groomed him.

	W	SV	ERA	IP	H	BB	SO	B/I
1995 California	3	3	1.95	74	37	26	94	0.85
1996 California	0	36	2.31	74	38	31	100	0.93
1997 Anaheim	5	27	3.46	52	40	22	72	1.19

PEREZ, CARLOS - TL - b: 1/14/71

Scouting: Perez has an outstanding hard/soft combination in a slider that lefthanded hitters can't touch and a split-fingered fastball that suddenly tails away from righthanders as it drops in the strike zone. His fastball and changeup are also decent pitches.

1998: Perez will become the ace of the Expos' young starting rotation with the departure of Pedro Martinez. Considering how much he enjoys attention and being in the spotlight, Perez should thrive in the ace starter role and have a fine season.

1997: Perez came back after missing all of the previous season because of shoulder surgery. He showed no ill effects from the layoff, pitching eight complete games and 200-plus innings. Perez could be good as evidenced by his five shutouts but also bad. On the whole, though, it was an encouraging season.

1996: Perez came down with a sore shoulder in spring training, underwent surgery and missed the whole season just a year after pitching in the All-Star Game as a rookie.

	W	SV	ERA	IP	H	BB	SO	B/I
1995 Montreal	10	0	3.69	141	142	28	106	1.20
1996 Montreal			Did Not Play - Injured					
1997 Montreal	12	0	3.88	207	206	48	110	1.23

PEREZ, MIKE - TR - b: 10/19/64

Scouting: Perez once had a hot fastball and a closer role; both are now long gone. Perez had a shoulder injury several years ago that diminished his fastball and his off-speed stuff has never been more than average. He never really wanted to close games in the first place, saying he preferred a set-up role. Without his fastball, he can't even do that anymore.

1998: Perez is a long shot to have a regular bullpen role in the major leagues. If he doesn't retire, he'll probably be injury insurance stored at the Triple-A level.

1997: Perez couldn't cut it in the Cubs' bullpen and was released. He wound up saving games for Triple-A Omaha before getting a call to help shore up the Royals' awful bullpen. Perez was inconsistent and eventually was released.

1996: Perez's ERA climbed a full run as he split time between Wrigley Field and Iowa. It was a significant downturn year for Perez.

	W	SV	ERA	IP	H	BB	SO	B/I
1995 Chicago NL	2	2	3.66	71	72	27	49	1.39
1996 Chicago NL	1	0	4.67	27	29	13	22	1.56
1997 Kansas City	2	0	3.55	20	15	8	17	1.13

PEREZ, YORKIS - TL - b: 9/30/67

Scouting: Perez is lefthanded so he gets opportunities not afforded righthanded pitchers with better stuff. But he doesn't get enough outs to take advantage of the opportunities. He tends to overthrow in difficult situation, reducing the movement of his fastball.

1998: The Mets outrighted Perez in October. It's hard to believe he will have a place on the 40-man roster of any club — expansion or not — before Opening Day. And the chance of him finding major league work thereafter is slim. His work last season projects him to be a Triple-A pitcher.

1997: Perez was yet another lefthanded set-up man the Mets hoped would benefit them. He didn't. Lefthanded hitters had no problems with him — six hits in 15 at-bats, and neither did righthanded hitters — nine hits, including two home runs in 25 at-bats. He wasn't all that wonderful in Triple-A either — 29 baserunners and a 3.48 ERA in 17 games and 20.2 innings.

1996: Perez pitched for the Marlins for the third successive season. The Braves acquired him from the Marlins in December for righthanded pitcher Martin Sanchez after Perez had a mostly unsuccessful season pitching against lefthanded hitters. The Mets claimed him in waivers late in spring training. Until '96, he had been extremely effectively against lefties — a .173 average in 156 at-bats against over three seasons. But in 1996, they batted .299 in 87 at-bats against Perez.

	W	SV	ERA	IP	H	BB	SO	B/I
1995 Florida	2	1	5.21	46	35	28	47	1.35
1996 Florida	3	0	5.29	47	51	31	47	1.74

PERISHO, MATT - TL - b: 6/8/75

Scouting: Good fastball, good curveball, outstanding makeup; it adds up to an outstanding future. Perisho was the man the Angels turned to in May after Mark Langston went out with elbow problems and they needed a starter. Perisho showed some flashes of brilliance after being promoted from Double-A, although he was probably overmatched at first. What the Angels like most of all is his courage and fearless approach he took to the job at hand. He has a big future in the major leagues.

1998: Perisho has an outside shot at winning a starting job in spring training, but would need to emerge the way Jason Dickson did last spring. He'll be a regular starter somewhere; the majors or, most likely, Triple-A Vancouver; it's doubtful the Angels would keep him sitting around in the bullpen because he's projected as one of their starters of the future. That future could arrive soon.

1997: Perisho may not have had enough experience to prepare him for the challenge of starting against major league hitters, but he didn't let that bother him. The way the youngster battled caught the club's eye. He may not have performed quite the way Dickson did when he first came up, but he showed the same ability to progress rapidly.
1996: Perisho was effective as a starter at both Lake Elsinore and Midland. A good season of winter ball in Mexico helped prepare him to make big strides in 1997.

	W	SV	ERA	IP	H	BB	SO	B/I
1997 Anaheim	0	0	6.00	45	59	28	35	1.93

PERKINS, DAN - TR - b: 3/15/75
A high school teammate of Seattle shortstop Alex Rodriguez, Perkins tied for first in the Twins' organization in 1996 with 13 wins. He went 7-10 with a 4.92 ERA for Double-A New Britain last summer but remains a solid prospect.

PERSON, ROBERT - TR - b: 10/6/69
Scouting: Person's low-90s fastball and hard slider make him tough. He also has a straight changeup that he goes to on occasion, although perhaps not often enough. He needs to improve his control.
1998: Although he was a starter for nearly all of last year, he might make a move to the bullpen, where his skills would be better-suited. He's almost certainly on the major league roster but beyond that, it's unlikely that he'll stick in the rotation for long unless he starts strong.
1997: Person finished the season with a sore right shoulder but did get an opportunity to start on a regular basis. He walked too many batters.
1996: Splitting time between Triple-A, the Mets' bullpen and the Mets' rotation, Person made his mark as a prospect for the future with a 4-5 record and a 4.52 ERA in 89.2 innings.

	W	SV	ERA	IP	H	BB	SO	B/I
1995 New York NL	1	0	0.75	12	5	2	10	0.58
1996 New York NL	4	0	4.52	89	86	35	76	1.36
1997 Toronto	5	0	5.61	128	125	60	99	1.44

PETERS, CHRIS - TL - b: 1/28/72
Scouting: Peters is the epitome of a soft-tossing lefty. His fastball barely reaches the mid-80s and he gets by with a good knuckle-curve and the ability to change speeds and hit spots. Peters, though, needs to establish his fastball at least a little bit if he is going to have success in the major leagues.
1998: Peters went to Puerto Rico for winter ball in an effort to win a spot in the Pirates' rotation this year. He has an outside chance at starting as Pirates manager Gene Lamont likes him. However, Peters' stuff is a little short for a big-league starter and his style of pitching isn't conducive to the bullpen. His best chance is to become a situational reliever, a guy who can come in and get one or two lefthanded hitters out with his knuckle-curve.
1997: Peters had an up-and-down year, bouncing between Pittsburgh and Triple-A Calgary three times. He was so-so at Calgary and shaky out of the Pirates' bullpen. However, he did turn in a strong start against Los Angeles in the second game of an August 27th doubleheader, seemingly boosting his shaken confidence.
1996: Peters breezed through Double-A Carolina and Calgary right on to Pittsburgh in late-July. However, he struggled as a starter and was demoted to the bullpen in September.

	W	SV	ERA	IP	H	BB	SO	B/I
1996 Pittsburgh	2	0	5.63	64	72	25	28	1.52
1997 Pittsburgh	2	0	4.58	37	38	21	17	1.58

PETERS, DON - TR - b: 10/7/69
Peters was one of the quartet of pitching prospects taken by Oakland in the first round/sandwich round of the 1990 draft — the others were Todd Van Poppel, Kirk Dressendorfer and David Zancanaro. Peters had retired after battling arm problems for years, then reclaimed his 90-plus fastball while pitching at Class A High Desert last year.

PETERSON, DEAN - TR - b: 8/3/72
Peterson is an organizational pitcher with the basic four pitches, all just below average. He filled in at Triple-A briefly last season, but did not exactly overpower the league at Double-A Trenton, going 1-3 with a 4.60 ERA, pitching nearly entirely out of the bullpen. He's likely to continue to struggle at the higher levels.

PETERSON, JAYSON - TR - b: 11/2/75
Peterson's reward for an undefeated season at Denver's East High School was being drafted in the first round by the Cubs in 1995. He's had a lot of trouble throwing strikes as a pro, never getting out of A-ball in 1996 or 1997.

PETERSON, KYLE - TR - b: 4/9/76
Scouting: Peterson was the Brewers' top draft choice out of Stanford in '97 and got a late start in the minors. He is looked upon as a top prospect, with good velocity and breaking stuff and decent control for a young pitcher.
1998: Peterson is seen as a pitcher who can rise quickly within the Milwaukee organization, but it's unlikely he will go past Double-A in 1998.
1997: Peterson posted an 0.87 ERA in three games at Ogden after completing his college career at Stanford.
1996: Peterson was a standout college pitcher for the Stanford Cardinal.

PETKOVSEK, MARK - TR - b: 11/18/65
Scouting: Conscientious, if less than outstanding, Petkovsek is an ideal team player to have as part of pitching staff — if he's able to be effective. Willing to do whatever his manager asks, he has swung from spot starting to working in long relief to turning in short shots from the bullpen. He can work long and often, with a durable arm and attitude. Petkovsek walks a thin line between success and failure, though, with an often unimpressive fastball-slider-changeup assortment that relies heavily on a sinker and his control.
1998: Despite making many friends with his approach and presence with the Cardinals the last three years, Petkovsek is guaranteed nothing. He'll need to keep his sinker down consistently to return to the club.
1997: That sinker spent too much time up in the strike zone, and Petkovsek struggled most of the season because of it (high ERA, 14 homers allowed in 96 innings). He particularly had trouble against righthanders.
1996: He worked 42 of his 48 games out of the bullpen, which he paced with an 11-2 record. Petkovsek was particularly effective in the season's second half.

	W	SV	ERA	IP	H	BB	SO	B/I
1995 St. Louis	6	0	4.00	137	136	35	71	1.25
1996 St. Louis	11	0	3.55	88	83	35	45	1.34
1997 St. Louis	4	2	5.06	96	109	31	51	1.46

PETT, JOSE - TR - b: 1/8/76
Pett has been in the spotlight since Toronto gave him a then-record signing bonus of $700,000 to sign as a 16-year-old from Brazil, which has never produced a major league player. Pett was acquired from the Blue Jays by Pittsburgh as part of a nine-player trade following the 1996 season and spent an injury-filled '97 with Double-A Carolina. Pett's injuries were all hitting related as he suffered a broken left (non-throwing) hand in spring training when trying bunt then hyperextended his right elbow three times while swinging at pitches during the season. The Pirates do not feel Pett will become the star pitcher Toronto had hoped but think he can eventually develop into a good third or fourth starter after another year or two of minor-league seasoning.

PETTITTE, ANDY - TL - b: 6/15/72
Scouting: Pettitte added a slider and changeup to a nasty cut fastball and arrived among the American League's pitching elite. His slider and changeup give hitters something to look for other than his high-velocity cutter, although Pettitte goes to the cut fastball when he needs an out. He has the top pickoff move in the game, picking off fourteen runners last year. For three years, he has avoided injury thanks to near-perfect mechanics. His singular flaw sometimes asks too much from himself; Pettitte demands perfection at all times.
1998: Pettitte is the unquestioned ace of the Yankee staff.
1997: Pettitte replaced David Cone as staff ace before Cone's shoulder difficulties appeared. He worked a staff-high 240.1 innings while posting a fantastic record and ERA. Despite a shaky post-season, Pettitte was again among the elite pitchers in baseball.
1996: A major success in 1996 at a young age, Pettitte became the true ace of the Yankee staff when injuries affected all their veteran starters throughout the year.

	W	SV	ERA	IP	H	BB	SO	B/I
1995 New York AL	12	0	4.17	175	183	63	114	1.41
1996 New York AL	21	0	3.87	221	229	72	162	1.36
1997 New York AL	18	0	2.88	240	233	65	166	1.24

PHELPS, TOM - TL - b: 3/4/74
The Expos thought enough of Phelps after he won ten games in 18 starts at Double-A Harrisburg in 1996 that he was a late addition to the 40-man roster. Slowed by arm problems, Phelps didn't pitch as well last year but still won ten games in 18 appearances for Harrisburg last season. The sinkerballer will pitch at Triple-A Ottawa this year and should be ready to challenge for a spot in Montreal's rotation in 1999.

PHILLIPS, RANDY - TR - b: 3/18/71
Phillips started the season at Double-A Shreveport, going 2-0 with a 2.66 ERA, then moved to Phoenix where he was 5-4 with a 3.04 ERA — good results for the Pacific Coast League. Although he doesn't fan many hitters, he has good control and is hard for batters to hit; he surrendered 61 hits in 68 innings last year.

PHILLIPS, TONY - TR - b: 6/9/69
The name and the team are familiar, but this Tony Phillips is a pitcher who toiled, rather unobtrusively, at Edmonton. Phillips compiled a 4-2 record with a 5.44 ERA over 81 innings of work which included two starts. His star has fallen since he was a top prospect in the Mariners' farm system a few years ago.

PHOENIX, STEVE - TR - b: 1/31/68
After eight seasons in the minors for the A's, Phoenix should make it nine this year. He made a brief rise to the majors for two games in 1994 and one game in 1995. Last year he was only good enough to pitch at Double-A Huntsville. He collected nine saves, but his 0-3 record and 5.80 ERA are not encouraging for a 29-year-old pitcher at that level.

PICHARDO, HIPOLITO - TR - b: 8/22/69
Scouting: Pichardo's fastball has good movement and is strong enough (low-90s) to be make him an effective closer. He doesn't have command of the pitch often enough to become a dominant bullpen ace, though, and his other pitches (slider, splitter) are below average. Pichardo was an unexpected success in his brief stint as closer when other Royals' relievers were injured or ineffective. Pichardo still suffers concentration lapses that hurt him at critical times in the game.
1998: Pichardo will have a primary set-up job in the Royals' bullpen.
1997: When all other relievers were throwing gasoline on the fire, Pichardo was the one guy who could be counted on for a quality outing. His success waned later in the year, but by then other pitchers had stepped forward to assist. The Royals' disastrous first-half bullpen could have been even worse without Pichardo.
1996: Despite leading the club with fifteen holds, Pichardo had a poor year as the primary set-up man in the bullpen. He lost the confidence of Manager Bob Boone by mid-season and his ERA ballooned more than a run over his 1995 mark.

	W	SV	ERA	IP	H	BB	SO	B/I
1995 Kansas City	8	1	4.36	64	66	30	43	1.50
1996 Kansas City	3	3	5.43	68	74	26	43	1.47
1997 Kansas City	3	11	4.22	49	51	24	34	1.53

PICKETT, RICKEY - TL - b: 1/19/70
Pickett, who had a good year at Double-A Shreveport in 1996, moved up a notch to Triple-A Phoenix where he saved 12 games while posting a 3-3 record and a 3.11 ERA. He is still wild, but he throws hard, and he can be a dominant reliever — Pickett struck out 83 hitters in 66.2 innings. He needs a little refinement, but the Giants' need for bullpen help may get Pickett to the big leagues at some point this year, even if Pickett hasn't gotten his needed refinement.

PISCIOTTA, MARC - TR - b: 8/7/70
Scouting: Pisciotta is 27 years old and doesn't throw particularly hard, but he has the control problems of a young fireballer. He has consistently walked about five or six batters per nine innings in addition to giving up about a hit per inning. He's been playing professional ball since 1991 and it doesn't say much for his future that he hasn't been able to develop any kind of control.
1998: It's not likely that Pisciotta will be able to duplicate his second half performance from last year over a full season. He simply doesn't have the control that is required to be a

successful major league pitcher and it's only a matter of time before hitters catch up.

1997: Pisciotta had 22 saves for Triple-A Iowa in the first half, then had a good second half of the year with Chicago. He hadn't appeared in a major league game prior to 1997, but was the team's best relief pitcher in the second half of the season despite his continued control problems. Manager Jim Riggleman used him often as a set-up man for Mel Rojas and Terry Adams.

1996: Pisciotta had a decent season for Pittsburgh's Triple-A Calgary farm team, but his age and control problems caused the Pirates to give up on him after he finished playing in the Arizona Fall League. The Cubs claimed him off waivers in November.

	W	SV	ERA	IP	H	BB	SO	B/I
1997 Chicago NL	3	0	3.18	28	20	16	21	1.27

PISCIOTTA, SCOTT - TR - b: 6/8/73

The Expos' 1991 second round pick has been a disappointment, not even making it to Double-A until 1996. The 6'7", 225, righty has lost velocity, and has struggled with his mechanics. His control has been poor and he has not been entrusted with an important staff role in years.

PITTSLEY, JIM - TR - b: 4/3/74

Scouting: Pittsley hasn't been the same since undergoing elbow surgery early in 1995. His low-90s fastball has lost about five MPH and is far too straight to be a quality big-league pitch. He also throws a curveball and changeup and is struggling to add a cut fastball, too. Despite his size (6'7", 215 pounds), Pittsley is a nibbler; he has to improve his fastball and challenge hitters in order to succeed. Pittsley has a lot of work to do before he can claim a regular major league rotation job.

1998: Pittsley is an underdog to earn a starting job with the Royals. Since his stuff doesn't lend itself well to a relief role, he's likely headed back to Triple-A Omaha for more refinement and to try to expand his fastball.

1997: His few good outings stand out in great contrast to an overwhelming number of poor starts. Pittsley simply couldn't throw the ball past anyone.

1996: Rated the Royals' top prospect by Baseball America and named the Comeback Player of the Year by Howe Sports Data, Pittsley was dominant in 18 minor-league starts after his 1995 season was cut short due to elbow surgery.

	W	SV	ERA	IP	H	BB	SO	B/I
1997 Kansas City	5	0	5.46	112	120	54	52	1.55

PLANTENBERG, ERIK - TL - b: 10/30/68

Scouting: Plantenberg's sinker/slider repertoire is effective only when he is ahead in the count. Judging by his career strikeout-to-walk ratio of 16-to-29, he is rarely pitching from strength. Once behind in the count, he then has to throw a batting-practice fastball down the middle of the plate.

1998: Plantenberg will find employment as a lefty reliever in a bullpen somewhere, but not in Philadelphia. His best bet is to start at Triple-A with a chance to return to the majors in a situational role later in the year.

1997: Plantenberg had a disastrous year as the Phillies' lefthanded bullpen specialist in the season's first half. His control was weak , and he was unable to retire lefties, the essence of his job. He was little better at Triple-A Scranton, where he allowed 31 baserunners in 14.1 innings.

1996: Plantenberg toiled at the two upper levels of the Indians' minor-league organization, where he was used as a situational middle reliever. He averaged a strikeout per inning, and fared particularly well against lefthanded hitters.

	W	SV	ERA	IP	H	BB	SO	B/I
1997 Philadelphia	0	0	4.90	26	25	12	12	1.44

PLESAC, DAN - TL - b: 2/4/62

Scouting: Plesac surprisingly retains much of the fastball that once made him a top closer. His heat still comes in the low- to mid-90s to go with an above-average slider. His control is as good as it was ten years ago, if not better.

1998: Plesac is one of the most coveted commodities in baseball, a lefthanded pitcher who can actually get batters out and work frequently. Although his days as a closer are through, he does pick up a save here or there and will pitch often.

1997: In his first season with the Blue Jays, Plesac appeared in 73 games for the second straight year. He struck out better than a batter per inning and was a favorite reliever of manager Cito Gaston.

1996: Plesac emerged as a fill-in closer for the struggling Pittsburgh Pirates, posting 11 saves — his highest mark since 1990 when he was the Brewers' primary closer.

	W	SV	ERA	IP	H	BB	SO	B/I
1995 Pittsburgh	4	3	3.58	60	53	27	57	1.33
1996 Pittsburgh	6	11	4.09	70	67	24	76	1.30
1997 Toronto	2	1	3.58	50	47	19	61	1.31

PLUNK, ERIC - TR - b: 9/3/63

Scouting: Plunk has been the prototypical two-inning set-up man for the Indians for the better part of the last six seasons, shutting down righthanded hitters with heavy, high fastballs; his breaking pitches are mostly for show. However, his power is showing some signs of fading. He rarely pitches two innings in an appearance anymore, and he has lost just enough velocity on his heater to make him vulnerable to the gopher ball for the first time in his career.

1998: Plunk remains a major league caliber reliever, but his days as a primary set-up man might be at an end. His fastball is drifting back towards 90 MPH; what used to be medium-deep fly outs are increasingly becoming homers. His role is likely to become more specialized in 1998; he should will see fewer lefties than ever before and be limited to an inning per appearance.

1997: Warning flags went up as a result of Plunk's 1997 performance. His walk rate and hits allowed per inning ratio reached seven-year highs, and righthanders hit for their highest average against him in four seasons, although it was still an impressively low .226. The presence of Mike Jackson and Jose Mesa knocked Plunk down a notch in the pen, probably for good.

1996: Plunk had arguably his finest season, posting a career-low ERA and a career high in relief innings pitched and relief strikeouts, while holding righthanders to a .170 average. He made closer Jose Mesa's life easy.

	W	SV	ERA	IP	H	BB	SO	B/I
1995 Cleveland	6	2	2.67	64	48	27	71	1.17
1996 Cleveland	3	2	2.43	77	56	34	85	1.17
1997 Cleveland	4	0	4.66	66	62	36	66	1.49

POLLEY, DALE - TL - b: 8/9/64

A non-roster invitee to spring training with the Yankees in 1996, Polley became the next-best alternative to a struggling

Steve Howe for lefty set-up work. Not fully satisfied, the Yankees obtained Graeme Lloyd from the Brewers in August, thereby reducing Polley's role substantially. Last year, with Triple-A Columbus, Polley posted a 3.75 ERA and two saves in 48 innings.

	W	SV	ERA	IP	H	BB	SO	B/I
1996 New York AL	1	0	7.89	21	23	11	14	1.60

PONSON, SIDNEY - TR - b: 11/2/76

Scouting: Oriole scouts found Ponson in Aruba. He's a powerful starting pitcher with a good fastball and curve, and a quality changeup, unusual for such a young pitcher. He also has excellent control. He gets a lot of strikeouts and is one of the Orioles top pitching prospects. Taken all together, Ponson has the talents to be an effective major league pitcher.

1998: Ponson will likely begin the season in Double-A, but he could move up quickly, even as far as Baltimore. At the least, he could be called up late in the season.

1997: Ponson was ticketed to begin the 1997 season with the Orioles Double-A club, and was expected to move up quickly. But that plan was set back by elbow problems early in the season and Ponson had surgery.

1996: Ponson pitched in the high Class A Carolina League where he went 7-6 with a 3.45 ERA, but, most significantly, he struck out 110 in 107 innings while giving up only 98 hits.

POOLE, JIM - TL - b: 4/28/66

Scouting: Poole delivers a fastball in the high 80s and has a solid changeup, but a great curveball is his bread-and-butter pitch. It ties lefthanded hitters in knots, making Poole an ideal situational reliever.

1998: As good as Poole had been over the past couple of years, it is hard to imagine him worse than he was last year. Poole is not an inning gobbler, nor is he a middle man. The former Dodger prospect was once thought to be a closer, but that has changed. Poole should return to his usual situational bullpen role, and probably with better results.

1997: Somewhere last year Poole's control went out the window. He was tagged for a .353 opposition batting average, and his walks were also up. Poole still made a high number of appearances, but they became less frequent and he was used in increasingly less important situations as his effectiveness waned during the heated pennant race.

1996: Poole did a great job after his acquisition from Cleveland, holding lefthanders to a .154 average and righthanders to .211 mark. He served his limited role well.

	W	SV	ERA	IP	H	BB	SO	B/I
1995 Cleveland	3	0	3.75	50	40	17	41	1.13
1996 Cleveland	4	0	3.04	26	29	14	19	1.64
1996 San Francisco	2	0	2.66	23	15	13	19	1.21
1997 San Francisco	3	0	7.12	49	73	25	26	1.99

PORTUGAL, MARK - TR - b: 10/30/62

Scouting: Portugal has been serviceable sinker/slider pitcher over the past decade, usually ranking about major league average in most categories. His control has always been solid, and he has been known to consistently keep his teams in ballgames for six or seven innings. His conditioning has always been sub-par, but until 1997 he had avoided debilitating injuries. He missed all but a month of last season with elbow and knee surgery, but is expected to return to a major league rotation in full health.

1998: Portugal is under contract to the Phillies, and is part of their plans. The emergence of several young pitchers over the second half of the previous year should force Portugal into a righthanded set-up job in the bullpen. He has not been a regular reliever for nearly a decade but he has the mental toughness to do the job. The question is whether his arm can stand up to the strain of pitching on short rest.

1997: Portugal threw just 13.2 innings before he required elbow and knee surgery. He had already asserted himself as a clubhouse leader and was missed from the Phillies' struggling rotation, especially early in the year.

1996: Portugal gave the Reds six competitive innings in most of his 26 starts, keeping them in ballgames. His control was exceptional, and he was particularly impressive against lefthanded hitters, holding them to a .239 average.

	W	SV	ERA	IP	H	BB	SO	B/I
1995 two teams	11	0	4.01	181	185	56	96	1.33
1996 Cincinnati	8	0	3.98	156	146	42	93	1.21
1997 Philadelphia	0	0	4.60	14	17	5	2	1.61

POWELL, JAY - TR - b: 1/19/72

Scouting: Powell is a former Orioles' first-round draft pick who was stolen by the Marlins in a 1995 exchange for Bret Barberie. He is a durable hurler capable of pitching an inning or two, three or four times a week. He has a low 90's fastball which he keeps down in the strike zone, though it doesn't break that sharply. His control was much improved in 1997, but he needs to be more aggressive early in the count. He remains an easy mark for opposing basestealers.

1998: Powell became the best candidate to succeed Robb Nen after Nen was traded. Powell is already one of the game's more reliable set-up men. Developing a good off-speed pitch would make him more effective against lefthanded hitters, a sore point in 1997. He also must develop more of a take-charge attitude on the mound.

1997: Powell was the master of the eighth inning for the Marlins in 1997. His control was much improved, and his sinking fastball handcuffed righthanded hitters (.219 average). He was not a major factor in the post-season, however.

1996: Powell had an average rookie season, struggling with his mechanics and command as the Marlins' primary set-up man. His ability to pitch on consecutive days greatly impressed Marlins' brass, however.

	W	SV	ERA	IP	H	BB	SO	B/I
1996 Florida	4	2	4.54	71	71	36	52	1.50
1997 Florida	7	2	3.27	80	71	30	65	1.27

POWELL, JEREMY - TR - b: 6/18/76

Hard-throwing Powell has pitched well in the Expos' farm system since being their fourth-round pick in 1994. He was at Class A West Palm Beach last season but should be ready to challenge for a spot in the Expos' rotation by the year 2000 as part of a big wave of fine pitchers being developed by Montreal.

POWELL, JOHN -TR - b: 4/7/71

A ninth-round pick in the 1994 June draft, Powell spent most of 1997 at Double-A Tulsa in the Rangers' organization. He appeared in 43 games at Tulsa, all out of the pen, and was effective. He gave up less than a hit per inning and struck out nearly a batter per inning. Powell may have to prove himself at Double-A again before advancing to the next level. If he can advance he could be a major league bullpen addition in a few seasons.

PRATT, RICH - TL - b: 5/7/71
A five-year minor-leaguer, Pratt is an organizational pitcher who is temporarily filling a Triple-A starter role in lieu of brighter prospects. He went 6-4 with a 4.76 ERA in eighteen games (thirteen starts) at Nashville in 1997. Pratt does not have major league stuff.

PRESS, GREGG - TR - b: 9/21/71
Press has made plodding progress in his four years in the Marlins' system, finally cracking the Double-A barrier at age 25 in 1997. He's a sinker/ slider pitcher with an average fastball and above-average control. However, Double-A batters hit him hard when his pitches were anything short of perfect. Press would be best served by a move to the bullpen, where he would have an outside chance to experience success in the high minor leagues in a specialized role. His chances for a major league breakthrough are slim to none, however.

PRICE, JAMEY - TL - b: 2/11/72
Selected in the fifth round of the 1995 free agent draft, Price spent the majority of 1997 at Double-A Huntsville, going 9-3 with a 5.30 over 20 starts, then earned a late-season promotion to Edmonton, where he was 2-0 with a 1.64 ERA. His Pacific Coast League totals included ten strikeouts and only one walk in eleven innings; good numbers for that league. The real test will come in 1998 when he has to throw 150 innings in that hitters haven.

PRICE, TOM - TL - b: 5/7/71
Price spent the first three years of his minor-league career with the Dodger organization before hurling for the Rockies at the Double-A level in 1997. Price pitched well enough, less than a hit per inning, to at least remain a prospect for a future bullpen role.

PRIEST, EDDIE - TL - b: 4/8/74
Priest, a ninth-round selection in the June 1994 draft, advanced past A-ball for the first time last year. At Class A Charleston he fanned 70 in 77 innings with just 10 walks allowed. He earned a trip to Double-A and made 13 starts. He found it tougher going but competed well enough to start this year at that level. He gave up slightly more than a hit per inning but continued to have good control (63 strikeouts, 17 walks). He still has a chance to earn a major league role in a few seasons.

PRIETO, ARIEL - TR - b: 10/22/69
Scouting: Prieto is a hard thrower (mid-90s fastball) who also throws a four-seam fastball, a curve, changeup and an excellent slider. He is good defensively, and holds runners. He also gets hurt a lot.
1998: Prieto will be given another shot at proving his worth in the Oakland rotation. He has the stuff and is a good athlete. His biggest problems have been injuries and adjusting to life in the United States. He appears to be over his shoulder problems, and seems settled, so more success is expected.
1997: Preito started the season as the number-two hurler, hot on the heels of his fine finish to 1996. He never really got going in the right direction, however. Prieto did have some good games, but his shoulder gave way, leading to erratic pitching and ultimately a long spell on the DL.
1996: Prieto was ineffective at the beginning of the season, then injured his elbow. That might have been the best thing for him, as the A's sent him to Edmonton for three starts after his rehab stint in Modesto. Prieto responded by pitching well for both the Trappers and the Athletics during the stretch.

	W	SV	ERA	IP	H	BB	SO	B/I
1995 Oakland	2	0	4.97	58	57	32	37	1.53
1996 Oakland	6	0	4.15	125	130	54	75	1.47
1997 Oakland	6	0	5.04	125	155	70	90	1.80

PRIHODA, STEVE - TL - b: 12/7/72
Seventy appearances in one season by a minor-league pitcher is a fairly rare event, but Prihoda did it for Double-A Wichita in 1997. This coming on the heels of a 1996 campaign in which he was among league leaders in appearances and games finished gives Prihoda the look of a long man in the bullpen. It's a good fit because his best pitches are off-speed stuff, particularly a deceptive changeup that makes his fastball appear quicker. The Royals believe he has a rubber arm — "he's resilient and energetic" —and are trying to build his stamina. Prihoda will never be closer material but can get to the bigs in a middle-innings role or possibly as a one-out lefty set-up man.

PUGH, TIM - TR - b: 1/26/67
Pugh pitched for his third big league team in two seasons when he made a pair of starts for the Tigers in 1997. He spent most of the season at Triple-A Toledo where he appeared in 19 games including 17 starts. He relies on a sinker and his experience to get by.

PULIDO, CARLOS - TL - b: 8/5/71
Pulido got rocked as a long reliever and spot starter with Montreal's Triple-A Ottawa farm club last season. The lefthander once was a pitcher of some promise, making 14 starts with Minnesota in 1994. That, however, seems like an awfully long time ago.

PULSIPHER, BILL - TL - b: 10/9/73
Scouting: It's hard to tell if Pulsipher is the pitcher he was in 1995 when he was the first of the "Young Gun" pitchers the Mets promoted to the big leagues, a pitcher trying to fight back from reconstructive surgery on his elbow, or the troubled pitcher he was last year when attacks of anxiety undermined his comeback and all but shattered his control. Choose the description and understand in every sense this is a dedicated man who loves the game and all that is around it.
1998: The Mets have talked about him as a short reliever, but Pulsipher and the Mets would be delighted if he forced his way into the rotation. Aside from Brian Bohanon (14 starts last season), the Mets have had no lefthanded pitcher start a game since September 11th, 1995 when Pulsipher made his last major league appearance. When Opening Day comes, Pulsipher will be two and a half years removed from that appearance and, the Mets hope, close to being the pitcher he was so sure he was going to be.
1997: His season was stolen from him first by the need to restrengthen his arm in the wake of April, 1996 surgery and then by attacks of anxiety that severely undermined his control and prompted prescriptions for Prozac. Pulsipher pitched a

total of 82 innings at four minor-league levels, walking 81 and producing a composite 5.60 ERA and 1-9 record. But his latest work produced a 1.42 ERA in 12.2 innings at Double-A.

1996: The unraveling of the Mets began March 18th when Pulsipher walked from the mound with an unusual and abnormal pain in his left elbow. A month later tendons from his wrist were used to reinforce the torn medial collateral ligament in the elbow. He didn't pitch all season.

	W	SV	ERA	IP	H	BB	SO	B/I
1995 New York NL	5	0	3.98	126	122	45	81	1.32
1996 New York NL			Did Not Play - Injured					

PURDY, SHAWN - TR - b: 7/30/68
Purdy didn't pitch as well has his won/lost record at Triple-A Phoenix might indicate. He went 10-3 despite permitting 103 hits in just 82.2 innings. He is primarily a mop-up man on any pitching staff.

PYC, DAVE - TL - b: 2/11/71
A crafty lefty who gets people out consistently, Pyc took the ball every five days at Triple-A Albuquerque and did a solid job. Pyc wasn't a standout, but he got the job done. The 1998 season will be big for him to prove he's more than an ordinary Triple-A pitcher. He needs to do something to raise himself out of a pack of pitching prospects.

QUANTRILL, PAUL - TR - b: 11/3/68
Scouting: Quantrill has an underrated fastball (low-90s) that moves. He mixes that with a hard slider and changeup. A control pitcher, he is ready to take the ball as often as called upon although he is more effective in short relief. An ex-starting pitcher, he has found new life as a reliever.

1998: Quantrill will be in a major league bullpen and will get a lot of work. Expect a dramatic drop-off in performance as his ERA was misleading. He will not have five saves this year.

1997: Although he allowed plenty of hits, Quantrill posted a fine season in relief, working often and posting the lowest ERA of his career in a career-high 77 games. He briefly took a turn as the closer for Toronto.

1996: Quantrill flipped between the rotation and the bullpen and allowed too many home runs to be effective (27). His 5-14 record was the worst of his career and he walked a career-high 51 batters.

	W	SV	ERA	IP	H	BB	SO	B/I
1995 Philadelphia	11	0	4.67	179	212	44	103	1.43
1996 Toronto	5	0	5.43	134	172	51	86	1.66
1997 Toronto	6	5	1.94	88	103	17	56	1.36

QUIRICO, RAFAEL - TL - b: 9/7/69
Quirico started the 1997 season at Class A Lake Elsinore in the Angels' organization and pitched well. He gave up a hit per inning and the lefty displayed good control. He found the going tougher at Double-A; he was hittable and his control deserted him. He should start 1998 at Double-A with a chance to prove himself again.

RADINSKY, SCOTT - TL - b: 3/3/68
Scouting: Radinsky throws a good fastball and sweeping slider with a sidearm motion which locks up most lefthanded batters. He is a classic lefty-lefty matchup ace, one of the best in the game. In the last five years he has held lefties under a .300 on-base percentage and under a .400 slugging average.

1998: As long as he can get hitters out, like he's done for two years, Radinsky will continue to get the call in situational matchups, especially in tight games.

1997: Radinsky was effective in short relief for the second straight year. He held lefty batters to a .221 average and righthanders to .245.

1996: Radinsky was surprisingly effective in situational lefty matchups. He was signed by the Dodgers after an undistinguished year with the White Sox. He appeared to be recovered from a bout with Hodgkins disease which forced him to miss the entire 1994 season.

	W	SV	ERA	IP	H	BB	SO	B/I
1995 Chicago AL	2	1	5.45	38	46	17	14	1.66
1996 Los Angeles	5	1	2.41	52	52	17	48	1.32
1997 Los Angeles	5	3	2.89	62	54	21	44	1.20

RADKE, BRAD - TR - b: 10/27/72
Scouting: Radke has four pitches that he can throw for strikes and a cool, calm demeanor that allows him to remain poised no matter what the situation. His fastball tops out at about 93 miles per hour, but his location allows him to be one of the best, most consistent pitchers in the league.

1998: Radke enters the season as the Twins' top starter — and one of the best starters in the league. His command last season began to evoke comparisons to Atlanta's Greg Maddux. Radke has improved in each of his three seasons, and there is no reason why that trend will stop now.

1997: A 12-game mid-season winning streak highlighted Radke's breakthrough season. He became the first Twin to win 20 games since Scott Erickson in 1991, and Radke did it on a team that lost 94 games.

1996: For the second season in a row, Radke led the majors in home runs allowed at 40. Too many pitches arrived too high in the zone, and batters made Radke pay. On the other hand, he tied for third in the league in fewest walks per nine innings at 2.2.

	W	SV	ERA	IP	H	BB	SO	B/I
1995 Minnesota	11	0	5.32	181	195	47	75	1.34
1996 Minnesota	11	0	4.46	232	231	57	148	1.24
1997 Minnesota	20	0	3.87	240	238	48	174	1.19

RAGGIO, BRADY - TR - b: 9/17/72
When Andy Benes was sidelined during spring training, Raggio was one of two pitchers who got a long look as a contender to begin the year in the major league starting rotation. The other candidate, Matt Morris, was clearly better, but Raggio remains a contender to start for someone, if not the Cardinals. He changes speeds well and moves the ball around. At Triple-A Louisville he was 8-11 with a 4.17 ERA.

	W	SV	ERA	IP	H	BB	SO	B/I
1997 St. Louis	1	0	6.90	31	44	16	21	1.92

RAIN, STEVE - TR - b: 6/2/75
Scouting: Rain is a hard thrower, who, like many other young fireballers, has his share of control problems. The Cubs decided early in his career that they were going to make Rain a closer and he has responded to the role. He certainly has the stuff to be a closer, but needs to come up with another pitch before he'll succeed at the higher levels.

1998: Rain is headed for another year in the minors. His lack of experience in the high minors combined with the emergence of Terry Adams means the Cubs won't bring him up to the majors unless they positively have to. They'll give him one full season in Triple-A before they bring him up, unless he blows through hitters there.

1997: Rain split time between Double-A Orlando and Triple-A Iowa, but was overmatched against the more experienced hitters at the higher level. He still struck out more than a hitter per inning, but the Triple-A hitters were able to get many more hits against him than they did the year before.

1996: Rain saved 20 games total in 1996, getting 10 saves each for Orlando and Iowa. He was outstanding at Iowa until giving up four runs in a third of an inning in his final outing, which boosted his ERA from 1.75 to 3.12.

RAJOTTE, JASON - TL - b: 12/15/72

Rajotte moved from Class A Modesto, where he went 3-6 with a 2.52 ERA and seven saves in 1996, to Double-A Huntsville, where he went 2-6 with a 4.40 ERA with three saves in 1997. He is not overpowering so he is not going to be a closer; he could do middle relief work, however. An advance to Triple-A Edmonton is in order for 1998.

RAMIREZ, HECTOR - TR - b: 12/15/71

Ramirez spent eight years in the Mets system, six of which were at the Rookie level or in Class A. Last year, the Orioles used him as a reliever and erstwhile starter at Triple-A Rochester where he posted a so-so record. There isn't much in his record to show upside potential.

RAMOS, EDGAR - TR - b: 3/6/75

Following a breakout 1996 season (9-0, 1.51 ERA, plus a no-hitter), Ramos developed arm trouble after being taken by Philadelphia in the Rule 5 draft. He was returned to the Astros and pitched a total of eight times all year in 1997. Ramos is lanky (6'5", 190 pounds) and doesn't throw especially hard. He will need to prove he's healthy again in 1998 and show that his 1996 success was no fluke.

	W	SV	ERA	IP	H	BB	SO	B/I
1997 Philadelphia	0	0	5.14	14	15	6	4	1.50

RAPP, PAT - TR - b: 7/13/67

Scouting: Rapp is frustrating: he is effective just enough to tantalize, but not often enough to breed confidence. He is not overpowering, as both his fastball and cutter reach the mid-80s. He does have a good curve but is erratic at controlling it. Getting a handle on it and his mechanics would spell an end to the confusion.

1998: Rapp will be on a major league roster somewhere, but not in San Francisco. He has a lot of upside potential, but he has never put it all together for a season, and that is obviously lacking. Unless he has a breakthrough, expect a repeat of seasons past.

1997: After his usual hot start with the Marlins, Rapp became less effective and was replaced in the rotation by Livan Hernandez. Later Rapp was dealt to the Giants, where he began his career. He was expected to thrive in the extreme conditions at 3Com Stadium, but didn't and was eventually banished to the minors.

1996: Rapp had been one of baseball's more fortunate hurlers in 1995, flirting with a high number of baserunners while getting good run support. Not so in 1996 when he struggled with control and failed to get the big out when he needed it.

	W	SV	ERA	IP	H	BB	SO	B/I
1995 Florida	14	0	3.44	167	158	76	102	1.40
1996 Florida	8	0	5.10	162	184	91	86	1.70
1997 San Francisco	5	0	4.83	142	158	72	92	1.62

RATH, FRED - TR - b: 1/5/73

A Midwest League All-Star in 1996, Rath started the 1997 season at Class A Fort Myers in the Twins' organization and ended up pitching at Double-A and Triple-A as well. He gave up less than a hit per inning at Class A and Double-A and notched 12 saves in New Britain. He looks like he has a shot to contribute in a major league bullpen after another season or two in the minors.

RATH, GARY - TL - b: 1/10/73

Rath was the Dodgers' 1994 second-round draft pick and started his first full season at Triple-A Albuquerque the next spring. He hasn't developed and is still there three years later. Rath is not a hard thrower, he's a finesse lefty who gets too much of the plate with his average stuff. With 1998 being an expansion year, Rath could get a chance to make a big-league staff but it is doubtful he'll be a major contributor.

RATLIFF, JON - TR - b: 12/22/71

Ratliff continues to show average minor-league stuff. He pitched at both Double-A and Triple-A for the Cubs last year. Expect more of the same in 1998. He is a long shot for any advancement to the majors in the coming years.

RAWITZER, KEVIN - TL - b: 2/1/8/71

In his third season at Double-A Wichita, Rawitzer had another dismal year in a long-relief/spot-starter role. He went 5-1 but had a 5.75 ERA, the highest of his career. Rawitzer appears to have topped out at Double-A.

RAY, KEN - TR - b: 11/27/74

Regarded as the hardest thrower in the Royals' farm system, his fastball hits 97 MPH on the radar gun. But he has no control of it and often pitches from behind in the count. Hitters merely wait him out, then pounce on less effective off-speed stuff. Ray advanced to Triple-A Omaha in 1997, but had his second straight poor season, going 5-12 with a 6.37 ERA and 63 walks in 113 innings. Over the last two years, Ray is 9-24 with an ERA of 6.24.

REDMAN, MARK - TL - b: 1/5/74

The Twins' top pick in the 1995 draft out of the University of Oklahoma, Redman has not advanced as quickly as the team had hoped. He is a curveball pitcher whose fastball does not get out of the 80s, but his curve has inexplicably been inconsistent since he has become a professional. He went 8-15 with a 6.31 ERA at Triple-A Salt Lake last year.

REED, BRANDON - TR - b: 12/18/74

Reed was named the Tigers' minor league player of the year after leading Fayetteville with 41 saves and a 0.97 ERA in 1995, then lost nearly all of 1996 to arm trouble. He threw hard, and with good control, before the injury and did o.k. at Double-A in 1997.

REED, CHRIS - TR - b: 8/25/74
Reed was one of the few younger pitchers the Reds had in their farm system and is one of even fewer who have a legitimate chance at being with Cincinnati in the near future. However, Reed took a giant step backwards in 1997 when he became all too hittable. Reed is a hard thrower who always had given up a lot of walks, but suddenly was giving up a bunch of hits, too. He had a sub-par year at Double-A Chattanooga, but still managed to get in three games at Triple-A Indianapolis where he continued to give up plenty of hits. He's only 24 years old, so he's not out of the picture in Cincinnati by any means.

REED, RICK - TR - b: 8/16/65
Scouting: Jim Leyland said it best: "There are 10,000 guys in the minor leagues with stuff, but Rick Reed did something most of them will never do. He learned how to pitch and what it takes to win in the big leagues."
1998: Reed began last season in the bullpen. Not this year. He is a definite part of the Mets' rotation. When last season ended, he projected as the most critical part of the '98 rotation.
1997: Reed turned out to be the irreplaceable player, emerging as the Mets' most consistent starting pitcher, their second-leading winner, and the pitcher with the sixth lowest ERA, second lowest ratio of walks per nine innings (1.30) and fourth fewest baserunners per nine (9.6) in the National League. He allowed merely 47 of the 215 batters leading off innings to reach base; the .219 on-base percentage was the lowest in the league. Reed also led the team in innings and worked at least six innings in all but three of his 31 starts.
1996: It was the first season in nine in which Reed didn't pitch in the major leagues. He spent the season pitching for Bobby Valentine and Bob Apodaca in Triple-A, winning eight of 18 decisions but also the respect of his manager and pitching coach.

	W	SV	ERA	IP	H	BB	SO	B/I
1997 New York NL	13	0	2.89	208	186	31	113	1.04

REED, STEVE - TR - b: 3/11/65
Scouting: A side-arming righthander who is traditionally tough on righthanded hitters and vulnerable to lefties, Reed has simply been the Rockies' best reliever the past five years. He's both durable and consistently effective. His fastball is below average and his slider is decent, but the keys are his deceptive delivery, ability to throw strikes and his aggressiveness. There is concern his incredible workload from 1993-96 has pilfered some of his effectiveness.
1998: In the off-season it was uncertain if he would return to the Rockies. Reed was eligible for salary arbitration but the Rockies were hesitant about raising his $1.2 million salary from 1997.
1997: Reed had a difficult year as he dealt with the health problems of his one-year-old son Logan, who suffered from complications of dwarfism. He still appeared in 63 games and posted the second-lowest ERA on the staff. He was briefly given a chance to close games but only converted six of thirteen chances.
1996: Reed reached the 70-appearance milestone for the second straight season. He had an odd season where he held the opposition scoreless in 52 of 70 games, but surrendered multiple runs in 10 games — an ERA killer for short relievers.

	W	SV	ERA	IP	H	BB	SO	B/I
1995 Colorado	5	3	2.14	84	61	21	79	0.98
1996 Colorado	4	0	3.96	75	66	19	51	1.13
1997 Colorado	4	6	4.04	62	49	27	43	1.22

REICHERT, DAN - TR - b: 7/12/76
The Royals made Reichert the seventh selection of the 1997 draft with their first-round pick. He has a nasty slider that produced 169 strikeouts in 133 innings at University of the Pacific, 22 coming in one game. Reichert made nine starts for the Royals' Class A team Spokane last year where he struck out a batter per inning.

REKAR, BRYAN - TR - b: 6/3/72
Scouting: When he pitches with confidence, Rekar can mix a 90-MPH fastball with a great slider and decent changeup. Once the Rockies' top pitching prospect, he clearly has been affected by pitching in altitude. He continuously tinkers with his wind-up. His biggest problem is he throws too many pitches up in the strike zone. He records a fair amount of strikeouts but also surrenders too many hits. The Rockies' coaching staff questioned whether he has the proper make-up, especially for Coors Field, and the team left him exposed to the expansion draft.
1998: If he hadn't been drafted by Tampa Bay, Rekar probably would have returned to Triple-A Colorado Springs for more seasoning. If he pitches well in spring training, the Rays will not hesitate in calling him up, though he may have to begin getting adjusted to the bullpen.
1997: Rekar entered spring training with a chance to win the fifth spot in the rotation, but pitched poorly and spent most of the season at Triple-A Colorado Springs. He was called up for two starts, pitched well in winning one but was demoted after he was knocked around in the second game.
1996: Rekar began the season in the Rockies' rotation but struggled, particularly at Coors Field, where he posted a 12.62 ERA in eight games. He wound up spending better than half his season at Triple-A Colorado Springs, where he was 8-8 with a 4.46 ERA in 19 starts.

	W	SV	ERA	IP	H	BB	SO	B/I
1995 Colorado	4	0	4.98	85	95	24	60	1.40
1996 Colorado	2	0	8.95	58	87	26	25	1.94

REMLINGER, MIKE - TL - b: 3/23/66
Scouting: The journeyman swing man features a good moving, but hard to control fastball, slurve and changeup. Like many pitchers, he could be a solid starter if he refines his control and develops his off-speed pitches, and as a lefty he will get plenty of opportunities to do so.
1998: Remlinger is a candidate for the Cincinnati rotation in 1998, but is not guaranteed a spot. He pitched well as a set-up man in 1997, and his limited repertoire may make him more effective as a reliever. Expanding his repertoire and improving his control will be the keys to expanding his role.
1997: Remlinger pitched well in a set-up role before moving to the rotation and was generally effective, going 6-4 as a starter the last two months of the season.
1996: A solid season at Triple-A Indianapolis that included 97 strikeouts in 89 innings earned Remlinger a limited trial in the majors as a situational specialist.

	W	SV	ERA	IP	H	BB	SO	B/I
1995 two teams	0	0	6.75	6	9	5	7	2.10
1996 Cincinnati	0	0	5.60	27	24	19	19	1.59
1997 Cincinnati	8	2	4.14	124	100	60	145	1.29

RESZ, GREG - TR - b: 12/25/71
A save artist in the low minors, Resz had a successful debut in

Double-A in 1996. Last year, his second season at Double-A Norwich, he struggled, posting a 4.70 ERA and giving up a hit per inning. His strikeout-to-walk ratio was also weak. The depth in Yankees' minor-league pitching has been a factor minimizing Resz' opportunity for advancement.

REYES, AL - TR - b: 4/10/71
Scouting: Elbow surgery has cost Reyes some of his velocity, but he still can fill a few innings in middle relief. He was a valuable member of the Brewers' bullpen in 1995 because of his ability to strike out hitters.
1998: Reyes should return to the Brewers' staff although his role is indeterminate. His strikeout ability has always interested the Brewers, who do not have many strikeout pitchers.
1997: Reyes bounced back and forth between Triple-A Tucson and Milwaukee. He struck out 98 in 87 innings of relief work combined between the two levels.
1996: Reyes started the season at Class A Beloit on rehab after undergoing Tommy John surgery on his elbow in August of 1995. He ended up pitching in only five games for Milwaukee.

	W	SV	ERA	IP	H	BB	SO	B/I
1997 Milwaukee	1	1	5.45	30	32	9	28	1.38

REYES, CARLOS - TR - b: 4/4/69
Scouting: Reyes' formula is simple: he's a sinkerballer who succeeds when he keeps the ball down and fails when he doesn't. His fastball only reaches the low 80s, however he does mix his slider and other pitches well. Since he has been most effective during the first time through a batting order, he is better suited to a middle-relief role.
1998: Reyes is likely at the end of the line with the A's. He obviously isn't a starter, and Oakland has so many candidates for the starter/middle-relief roles — and Reyes has been so inconsistent over the years — that he may be bound for another organization and/or role. With the A's Reyes would likely end up on a taxi squad, splitting time between Edmonton and Oakland.
1997: Reyes' line tells as much about his effectiveness as it does the state of Oakland's pitching last year. He was called upon much more as a last resort than anything else. All things considered, Reyes delivered pretty much what was expected.
1996: Reyes, who was routinely hammered as a starter, proved he was well-suited to middle relief work. He confused hitters the first time through the order, but give them a second look and got into trouble. He gave up lots of homers.

	W	SV	ERA	IP	H	BB	SO	B/I
1995 Oakland	4	0	5.09	69	71	28	48	1.43
1996 Oakland	7	0	4.78	122	134	61	78	1.60
1997 Oakland	3	0	5.82	77	101	25	43	1.63

REYES, DENNIS - TL - b: 4/19/77
Scouting: The next Fernando Valenzuela — or so the Dodgers hope — Reyes is a strikeout pitcher who needs seasoning. He threw a lot of innings in the minors in the last two years at age 18-19, which often increases the risk of arm trouble. He has a 94-MPH fastball, but his off-speed and breaking pitches are not yet refined.
1998: Reyes will get a shot to make the rotation, and if he starts the year at Triple-A he will be the first considered for a callup. He could give the Dodgers their first effective lefty starter since Valenzuela's heyday.
1997: General Manager Fred Claire did not believe Reyes was ready for the majors, but the loss of two starters to injury got Reyes his callup. His performance was more than satisfactory under the circumstances, for such a young pitcher.
1996: At age 19 Reyes fanned 176 batters in 166 innings in the California League, normally considered a hitters' haven.

REYNOLDS, SHANE - TR - b: 3/26/68
Scouting: Reynolds opened the season as the ace of the Houston staff but he yielded that position to Darryl Kile. He began the year with eight strong starts before a meniscus tear in his right knee reduced his effectiveness and eventually sidelined him for surgery. He was out for a month and had difficulty regaining effectiveness after his return. Reynolds' best pitch is a split-fingered fastball, the best the Astros have seen since Mike Scott. His fastball is no better than average, rarely hitting 90-MPH but he spots it well and he has a cut fastball which is effective if he keeps it down. His curveball is below average and he rarely uses it. Reynolds has always had good control with a strikeout-to-walk ratio over four for his career.
1998: Reynolds is a hard worker who can be expected to recover his former effectiveness. He should be fully recovered from his knee injury and a season similar to 1996 is a reasonable expectation.
1997: Reynolds' 1997 season was his worst since he joined the Astros' starting rotation in 1994. His stamina was not up to par because his knee problem prevented him from maintaining his running regimen.
1996: Reynolds had his best season in 1996. He was third in the National League in innings pitched and tied for fifth in wins. Only Greg Maddux, John Smoltz and Kevin Brown had better strikeout-to-walk ratios.

	W	SV	ERA	IP	H	BB	SO	B/I
1995 Houston	10	0	3.47	189	196	37	175	1.23
1996 Houston	16	0	3.65	239	227	44	204	1.13
1997 Houston	9	0	4.23	181	189	47	152	1.30

REYNOSO, ARMANDO - TR - b: 5/1/66
Scouting: "He's got such an assortment of pitches," Mets' pitching coach Bob Apodaca said in May. "I thought he might be using his off-speed pitches more than necessary. We've stressed the fastball. I wanted his fastball to be a little more dangerous. It's not a swing-and-miss fastball. But I thought it could be respected more." The advice worked wonders until Reynoso's arm betrayed him. Chances are he never will be a big winner — he hasn't approached his 1993 victory total of 12 in four subsequent seasons — but he usually keeps his team in the game.
1998: Reynoso is likely to enter spring training at the forgotten man, the eighth member of a five-man rotation. Whether he finds work as a starter will be more a function of how others perform. Chances are he'll be in long relief or pitching for another club.
1997: Before surgery ended his season prematurely, Reynoso was performing well. His first major league shutout and sixth complete game were among his six victories.
1996: Reynoso made 30 starts for the Rockies and actually pitched more effectively at Coors Field, posting a 6-4 home record with a 4.81 ERA over 15 starts; he was 2-5 with a 5.13 road ERA.

	W	SV	ERA	IP	H	BB	SO	B/I
1995 Colorado	7	0	5.32	93	116	36	40	1.63
1996 Colorado	8	0	4.96	168	195	49	88	1.45
1997 New York NL	6	0	4.53	91	95	29	47	1.36

RHODES, ARTHUR - TL - b: 10/24/69

Scouting: Arthur Rhodes has outstanding stuff, with a blazing fastball, a sharp breaking ball and good command. He can throw hard for an inning or two, and the bullpen is the ideal place for him. He has done well in pressure relief situations and appears suited for a closer role.

1998: If closer Randy Myers isn't signed for 1998, then Rhodes has a good chance of taking over the job. He has the outstanding stuff and the mental makeup to be a top closer.

1997: In 1997, Rhodes was brought into pressure-packed game situations. He came through well, demonstrating that he can indeed be a closer. Otherwise, he was effective in various relief roles including long and middle relief.

1996: Rhodes excelled in his first big year as a reliever, but shoulder inflammation slowed him later in the year.

	W	SV	ERA	IP	H	BB	SO	B/I
1995 Baltimore	2	0	6.21	75	68	48	77	1.54
1996 Baltimore	9	1	4.08	53	48	23	62	1.34
1997 Baltimore	10	1	3.02	95	75	26	102	1.06

RICCI, CHUCK - TR - b: 11/20/68

After leading Triple-A Pawtucket with 13 saves in 1996 — his second straight year leading a Triple-A staff in saves — Ricci ended up in the Expos system at Triple-A Ottawa in 1997. A sinker/slider pitcher, he struck out a batter per inning but had serious control problems that will need to be overcome if he is to advance further.

RICKEN, RAYMOND - TR - b: 8/11/73

In his first full season at the Triple-A level, Ricken posted a 5.54 ERA and gave up 172 hits in 152.2 innings, and his strikeout-to-walk ratio was poor. The Yankees need to bring him along patiently.

RIGBY, BRAD - TR - b: 5/14/73

Scouting: Rigby throws deceptively hard: his fastball actually reaches the low-90s. He also features a curveball and changeup to complement an excellent slider as part of a solid repertoire. He is not dominating, though he is usually around the plate. Rigby has a tendency to try to be too fine.

1998: After establishing himself as a solid, if unspectacular hurler in 1997, Rigby has zeroed in on a spot in this year's starting rotation in Oakland. Since the staff will be rather dynamic things could change from one week to the next. But, Rigby should get the ball regularly at the beginning of the year.

1997: After notching an 8-4 mark with a 4.37 ERA at Triple-A Edmonton for the first part of the year, Rigby was called up and pitched a lot better than his 1-7 mark indicates. He got poor run support and spotty help from the bullpen.

1996: Rigby adjusted well enough to life at Huntsville. He is durable, and though his control suffered some after his promotion, he did okay.

	W	SV	ERA	IP	H	BB	SO	B/I
1997 Oakland	1	0	4.86	78	92	22	34	1.47

RIJO, JOSE - TR - b: 5/13/65

Rijo missed the entire 1996 season because he required additional surgery on his elbow. Last year he had problems with the elbow in February and missed the season for the second straight year. In an interview after the 1996 season, Reds' General Manager Jim Bowden was not optimistic that Rijo would ever take the mound again. It looks like he is right about Rijo, who declared himself a free agent at the end of October.

	W	SV	ERA	IP	H	BB	SO	B/I
1995 Cincinnati	5	0	4.17	69	76	22	62	1.42
1996	Did Not Play - Injured							

RINCON, RICARDO - TL - b: 4/13/70

Scouting: The little lefty can run his fastball up to 90 MPH but his strength is his deceptiveness. Rincon will throw his fastball, slider, curve and changeup from various angles. His best pitch a darting slider which is nearly impossible for lefthanded batters to touch.

1998: Rincon will again be one of the Pirates' top set-up relievers. He does not rattle in tough spots and will be used to get an occasional save when a lefthander is needed to close out a game.

1997: After spending seven seasons in the Mexican League, Rincon made the Pirates as a non-roster player last season and shared closing duties with righthander Rich Loiselle for awhile after stopper John Ericks went out for the season at the end of April. Loiselle eventually took over the closer's role on a full-time basis but Rincon pitched well as a set-up guy.

1996: Rincon had a good season as a middle reliever with the Mexico City Reds of the Mexican League then really caught the Pirates' eye with a strong performance in the Caribbean World Series.

RIOS, DANNY - TR - b: 11/11/72

Rios was introduced to the big leagues in a harsh way — nine hits in 2.1 innings over two relief appearances. Rios' future is still positive following a productive year in relief at Triple-A Columbus where he was 7-4 with a 3.08 ERA in 58 games. He has a 95-MPH fastball and is ready for a major league bullpen role.

RISLEY, BILL - TR - b: 5/29/67

Scouting: A torn rotator cuff put him on the shelf for most of last year but when he returned, he looked like the pitcher that he was before surgery. When healthy, he has a fastball around 96 MPH and a slider that settles around 88 MPH. His curve is an occasional pitch but when he's at his best, he can go to it with confidence. Risley has had control problems in the past and his inactivity over the past couple of seasons will force him to pitch often before he regains what command he once had.

1998: Although he could use a season at Triple-A to get back into form, he may show the stuff in spring training to warrant a spot in the major league bullpen.

1997: Risley missed most of the season although he came back late to pitch a few games for the Blue Jays.

1996: Risley's injury problems forced him to miss much of the season although he was effective in 25 games with Toronto.

	W	SV	ERA	IP	H	BB	SO	B/I
1995 Seattle	2	1	3.13	60	55	18	65	1.21
1996 Toronto	0	0	3.89	41	33	25	29	1.41

RITCHIE, TODD - TR - b: 11/7/71

Scouting: Since he has a live fastball, it's a surprise that

Ritchie didn't arrive in the majors sooner than 1997. It's also a surprise that he hasn't had more success in the minors. He has a history of arm problems, which has caused some of his frustration, but the arm appears to be in good shape now and gave him no problems in 1997.

1998: Ritchie needs to take the improvement he exhibited in 1997 and build on it in 1998. If he does that, Ritchie can become a dependable middle reliever. He remains too raw to handle the responsibilities of a closer.

1997: After pitching only in blowouts early in the season, Ritchie improved enough that manager Tom Kelly began using him in game situations. Kelly, in fact, called Ritchie his most improved pitcher.

1996: Ritchie was mediocre in the minors where he went a combined 3-11 at Double-A New Britain and Triple-A Salt Lake, before excelling in the Arizona Fall League. That, in fact, is where the Twins took notice of him and began expecting better things from him.

	W	SV	ERA	IP	H	BB	SO	B/I
1997 Minnesota	2	0	4.58	75	87	28	44	1.54

RITZ, KEVIN - TR - b: 6/8/65

Scouting: Ritz has four pitches that he has, at times, mastered, but never in the same month. His changeup will be dominant, but then he will forget how to throw it. His most consistent pitch is his 90-MPH fastball. He will alternate between a slider or curve, depending on what's working for him. He's a workhorse who never missed a start due to physical reasons for nearly three years until he suffered a torn labrum that ended his season in July last year.

1998: Following surgery to repair his torn labrum, Ritz is questionable for Opening Day. He may begin the season pitching out of the bullpen, but because of his $3 million salary, if he has any success he will likely be back in the rotation quickly.

1997: After signing a three-year, $9 million contract, Ritz was named the Rockies' Opening Day starter for a second straight season. He finished as a disappointment, allowing 142 hits in 107.1 innings, before suffering a torn labrum in early-July that required surgery and ended his season.

1996: Ritz became the Rockies' ace, winning a team-record 17 games despite a 5.28 ERA — the highest ERA for a pitcher with at least 17 wins in major league history. He made all of his scheduled 35 starts and recorded a career-high 213 innings.

	W	SV	ERA	IP	H	BB	SO	B/I
1995 Colorado	11	2	4.21	173	171	65	120	1.36
1996 Colorado	17	0	5.28	213	236	105	105	1.60
1997 Colorado	6	0	5.87	107	142	46	56	1.75

RIVERA, MARIANO - TR - b: 11/29/69

Scouting: Early season struggles in 1997 led Rivera to believe he needed another pitch besides his 95+ MPH fastball. He later learned it was not necessary and his rising heater was adequate. He will continue to work on another pitch — he has a good slider and has tinkered with a splitter — but Rivera lives with the fastball.

1998: The Yankees enter the 1998 season knowing that they are set with Rivera as their closer. He's one of the top stoppers in the game and has developed the ability to quickly forget a bad outing — a fundamental mind-set for closers.

1997: The biggest question in the Yankees' universe going into the 1997 season was how Rivera would respond to moving from the set-up role to replacing closer John Wetteland. He answered that question with a minuscules ERA and the second most saves in the league. Rivera suffered from a tired shoulder the last two weeks of the season, but said it felt fine in the post-season, claiming that was not the reason Sandy Alomar hit a game-tying homer against him in the American League Division Series.

1996: Rivera emerged as the best set-up man in baseball with the talent to be a closer for any team. He led the American League in holds (27) and filled the closer role whenever Wetteland was unavailable.

	W	SV	ERA	IP	H	BB	SO	B/I
1995 New York AL	5	0	5.51	67	71	30	51	1.51
1996 New York AL	8	5	2.09	107	73	34	130	1.00
1997 New York AL	6	43	1.88	72	65	20	68	1.19

RIZZO, TODD - TL - b: 5/24/71

Rizzo spent a year in independent ball before joining the White Sox organization in 1995. He made an unexpected two-level jump to Triple-A Nashville in 1997, but retained every scrap of success from the lower-level minors. He doesn't have great control or an over-powering fastball; Rizzo may walk too many batters for a pitcher who can't pile up the strikeouts. It's a surprise that he got this far, but he could actually make it to the majors as a middle-innings lefty.

ROA, JOE - TR - b: 10/11/71

Scouting: Since he's only 26 years old, it's hard to believe that Roa has been at his craft for nine years, but he made his debut in the Atlanta chain in 1989. Since then he has never had a losing record, and 1997 was his first with an ERA over four. He isn't overpowering, but he knows how to get an out, at least at the minor-league level. He's a battler.

1998: Only 39 of Roa's 200 minor-league appearances have been in relief, so it is hard to imagine him in that role. He would probably do whatever it takes to get and keep a major league job, but another season in the minors is a more likely course for this year.

1997: After an off-season acquisition from the Indians, Roa got a couple of chances to start games in San Francisco (three, actually) and was not effective. Neither was he in command in relief, and when demoted to minors, where he had been unusually successful and consistent in the past, he got knocked around there as well, posting a 4.75 ERA while allowing 54 baserunners over 36 innings at Triple-A Phoenix, including four homers.

1996: Roa's 37 walks in 1996 were the highest figure of his eight-year, minor-league career — a testament to his exceptional control. Roa could actually be a clone of Dan Carlson. Both have everything a pitcher could ask for except the ability to get hitters out in the majors.

	W	SV	ERA	IP	H	BB	SO	B/I
1997 San Francisco	2	0	5.21	66	86	20	34	1.61

ROACH, PETIE - TL - b: 9/19/70

Roach's development has been slowed by a radical position change, but he still has a shot at making the major leagues, despite his age and the improvement he has to make; he has little mileage on his pitching arm. Roach was drafted by San Francisco as a first baseman, but was signed as a free agent by the Dodgers as a pitcher. He needs to sharpen his breaking stuff and command of his pitches, but the Dodgers feel that will come with time and more experience.

ROBERSON, SID - TL - b: 9/7/71
Although he got a brief trial with the Brewers in 1995, Roberson's mixture of offspeed and breaking junk hasn't retired many batters since then.

ROBERTS, BRETT - TR - b: 3/24/70
Roberts dabbled with a pro basketball career and may wish he stuck with hoops. He started 1997 at the Twins' Triple-A affiliate in Salt Lake and ended the year with Fargo of the Independent League. He's not a major league prospect.

ROBERTS, CHRIS - TL - b: 6/25/71
After a 1996 season rehabbing from labrum surgery, Roberts had a good comeback season last year. He posted a 5-8 record with a 4.86 ERA at Double-A Binghamton, and got stronger as the season went on, finishing 0-4 with a 2.89 ERA at Triple-A Norfolk. He will need to show more stamina to advance as a starter.

ROBERTSON, RICH - TL - b: 9/15/68
Scouting: He's lefthanded, so he's useful. But given consistent control problems, he's become less useful. When Robertson's mechanics are in line, he can be a winning, complete-game type of pitcher. However, he has a herky jerky delivery that uses poor body control and often gets him out of whack. Then, the walks start piling up.
1998: Robertson needs to show that he can throw strikes consistently. If he doesn't, he will lose a golden opportunity to win a starting job in the majors. He has earned less patience than he was given in the past.
1997: He was removed from an already weak rotation by season's end, a clear vote of no-confidence. His most revealing statistics are these: 70 walks and 69 strikeouts in 147 innings. Time after time, he put himself in position to lose simply by issuing too many free passes.
1996: Robertson threw too many balls but kept the Twins interested by throwing three shutouts and five complete games. He threw really well for stretches and then suddenly went through spells where he couldn't find the plate.

	W	SV	ERA	IP	H	BB	SO	B/I
1995 Minnesota	2	0	3.83	51	48	31	38	1.53
1996 Minnesota	7	0	5.12	186	197	116	114	1.68
1997 Minnesota	8	0	5.69	147	169	70	69	1.63

ROBINSON, KEN - TR - b: 11/3/69
Scouting: Robinson has an excellent fastball considering his relatively small stature. He gets his pitches into the low- to mid-90s with movement and he has a complementary change as well as an occasional curve. It's easy for opponents to underrate him when they see his 5'9" frame. He is a confident pitcher no matter what trouble he encounters.
1998: If someone takes a chance, Robinson has the stuff to be a closer at the major league level. Chances are, no one will notice but he will be in a major league bullpen as a middle reliever.
1997: Robinson dominated Triple-A batters as Syracuse's closer. He got the call to the Blue Jays on September first and struck out four of the eleven batters he faced with Toronto.
1996: Initially let go by the Blue Jays, he landed with Kansas City only to end up back with the Blue Jays by way of waivers. He struck out 78 batters in 64 innings after joining Triple-A Syracuse.

ROCKER, JOHN - TL - b: 11/3/69
Rocker was promoted to Greenville in 1997 and, like most of their pitchers, split time between the bullpen and the rotation. He was more effective than most, going 5-6 with a 4.86 ERA in 22 games (13 starts). Rocker is a strikeout pitcher who often doesn't know where his fastball is going; he led the Greenville staff with 17 wild pitches in 113 innings. His progress has been steady and he has a chance to reach the majors if he can get more consistent control of his fastball.

RODRIGUEZ, FELIX - TR - b: 12/5/72
Scouting: An extremely raw talent, Rodriguez features a moving fastball that tops out at 97 MPH — and not much else. He started out as a catcher in the Dodger system and converted to pitching in 1993. He can develop into a dominating pitcher if he adds and off-speed pitch to go with his overpowering fastball.
1998: The Diamondbacks have loaded their franchise with live arms. Primarily a starter in the Dodger system, Rodriguez was converted to the bullpen by the Reds. He will compete for a set-up role in Arizona this year.
1997: Signed by the Reds as a minor-league free agent, Rodriguez dominated early at Indianapolis (1.01 ERA and a strikeout per inning) and was called up in June. With Cincinnati, he started strong, but faded as the season progressed.
1996: Rodriguez struggled at Albuquerque (3-9, 5.53 ERA) and was released by the Dodgers.

	W	SV	ERA	IP	H	BB	SO	B/I
1997 Cincinnati	0	0	4.30	46	48	28	34	1.65

RODRIGUEZ, FRANK - TR - b: 12/11/72
Scouting: Rodriguez has a terrific fastball in the low 90s that moves, a sharp curve and a nasty changeup. He also is too flaky, as evidenced by episodes last spring in which he forgot to bring his spikes to one start and forgot to bring his glove to another. If he can put everything together, he can be a dominant pitcher. If not, he could be out of baseball in the next year or two.
1998: Rodriguez needs to re-gain the trust of those who expect him to start and pitch well. His star already is sinking, and he needs to turn that around this year.
1997: After leading the team with 13 wins a year earlier, Rodriguez became the Twins' biggest disappointment of the year in 1997. He didn't pitch winter ball for the first time in his career. Not only that, he didn't even bother throwing over the winter. It showed, from the first day of spring training to the end of the season. The Twins gave him four different chances to keep his job in the rotation and he blew every one of them.
1996: One year after arriving from Boston in a deal for Rick Aguilera, Rodriguez led the Twins with 13 wins and made the deal look like a steal. A converted shortstop, Rodriguez began fulfilling some of the promise predicted for him.

	W	SV	ERA	IP	H	BB	SO	B/I
1995 Bos. - Minn.	5	0	6.13	105	114	57	59	1.62
1996 Minnesota	13	2	5.05	206	218	78	110	1.44
1997 Minnesota	3	0	4.62	142	147	60	65	1.45

RODRIGUEZ, JOSEPH FRANK - TR - b: 1/6/73
This "Frankie Rodriguez" is a Brewers' career minor-leaguer who has toiled in the Milwaukee system for six seasons. He gets it up there velocity-wise and showed decent control in 1997 at both the Double-A and Triple-A levels. If he stays healthy he could contend for a bullpen role in the near future.

RODRIGUEZ, LARRY - TR - b: 9/9/74
Scouting: Shut down for the last month of the 1996 season because of a sore right shoulder, Rodriguez did nothing over the winter but continued to show the tools — 90-plus fastball and curve — that got him a $1.3 million bonus when he defected from Cuba to sign with the Diamondbacks in February of 1996.
1998: Rodriguez is expected to open the season at higher Class A High Desert as the Diamondbacks continue a cautious approach with their top pitching prospects. But Rodriguez could jump to Triple-A Tucson by season's end.
1997: Victimized by limited support at Class A South Bend, Rodriguez went 4-11 despite a 3.62 ERA and allowing only 102 hits in 104 innings. He began the year a month late due to shoulder rehab.
1996: Rodriguez struggled at co-op Visalia before winning seven of eight decisions for the Diamondbacks' first minor-league affiliate, Pioneer League Lethbridge.

RODRIGUEZ, NERIO - TR - b: 3/22/73
Scouting: Rodriguez is a slim (6'0", 165-pound) righthander who throws hard with a smooth, easy delivery. Until mid-1995, he was a poor-hitting catcher, whereupon his rifle arm convinced Oriole scouts to convert him to pitching. He has surprisingly good mechanics considering his short pitching career and has a good fastball, but an inconsistent breaking ball. The breaking ball could be improved.
1998: Rodriguez has a chance at the Orioles staff, either as a starter or reliever, but it'll be tough because the Orioles have both a strong bullpen and rotation.
1997: Rodriguez just needed more experience, and he got it in Triple-A and in a September callup to the Orioles. Although his record was 11-10 with a 3.90 ERA, he gave up only 124 hits in 168. innings while striking out 160 and walking 62. The combination of a high strikeout-to-walk ratio and low opponent batting average are strong indications of future success.
1996: Rodriguez began the year in the low minors and rose all the way to the Orioles where he started the last game of the year.

	W	SV	ERA	IP	H	BB	SO	B/I
1997 Baltimore	2	0	4.91	22	21	8	11	1.32

RODRIGUEZ, RICH - TL - b: 3/1/63
Scouting: Rodriguez has a number of pitches in his repertoire, including a fastball, slider, curveball and changeup. He holds runners well and is an adequate fielder.
1998: Rodriguez will have a serious, full-time role as a lefty reliever in a major league bullpen. He can earn a set-up role, but more likely will be used as a situational reliever.
1997: A non-roster invitee by the Giants to spring training, Rodriguez made the team and appeared in 71 games for the National League West champs. He registered 14 holds.
1996: A nice comeback from serious arm and shoulder trouble at the Triple-A level put Rodriguez in contention for a major league spot in 1997. He pitched at Triple-A Omaha where he was the most reliable lefty reliever on the club.

	W	SV	ERA	IP	H	BB	SO	B/I
1997 San Francisco	4	1	3.17	65	65	21	32	1.32

ROGERS, BRYAN - TR - b: 10/30/67
Rogers is a smallish righthanded reliever with a below-average fastball who had some success as a slider pitcher in Triple-A for the Mets a couple of years ago. But he hurt his arm and was not especially effective in his comeback with the Braves in '97 in Double-A or Triple-A; he posted a 5.17 ERA at Richmond. He's capable of pitching better, but he has little major league potential.

ROGERS, KENNY - TL - b: 11/10/64
Scouting: This competitive lefty has a good fastball and an outstanding curve. He is bothered by inconsistency and occasionally has failed to believe in his above-average arsenal, often working long counts and giving the impression that he's afraid to let the batter hit the ball. He throws mostly fastballs when pitching out of the bullpen and has enjoyed some success in that role.
1998: His high salary ($5 million per year for 1998 and 1999) limited the Yankees' chances of trading him; they were happy to get Scott Brosius for him. In Oakland Rogers will contend for the fourth or fifth starter spot or work in long relief. The change of scenery should help.
1997: Rogers was all over the map in 1997. He started the year in the rotation then moved to the bullpen and was traded to San Diego; the trade was eventually rescinded. He pitched effectively as a starter and reliever at times, but was far too inconsistent to remain in the rotation; he made 22 starts in his 31 appearances. Rogers was left off the post-season roster.
1996: After seven years with the Rangers in which he established himself as a premier lefthanded starter, Rogers had a nightmarish season in his first year in New York. Despite a winning record his ERA rose to it's highest mark in five years.

	W	SV	ERA	IP	H	BB	SO	B/I
1995 Texas	17	0	3.38	208	192	76	140	1.29
1996 New York AL	12	0	4.68	179	179	83	92	1.46
1997 New York AL	6	0	5.65	145	161	62	78	1.54

ROGERS, KEVIN - TL - b: 8/20/68
Rogers, the former major leaguer, came back from major arm problems in '97, but did not have his old velocity and did not pitch well for Triple-A Richmond, and was eventually released. Rogers has poor mechanics, pitching across his body, and will probably continue to break down even if he does regain his arm strength for a period.

ROJAS, MEL - TR - b: 12/10/66
Scouting: His split-fingered pitch resembles his fastball to such a degree that they almost can't be distinguished from each other. But he spent most of last season throwing each of them too high in the zone. That made for a lot of souvenirs outside Wrigley Field and too many long faces at Shea Stadium. Rojas would look unhittable for one inning and infinitely beatable the next.
1998: If the Mets are to look at their August, 1997 trade with the Cubs as anything but a failure, Rojas must regain the form he had before last season. If he does, no one will care what Lance Johnson and Mark Clark are doing. He is the key to the bullpen.
1997: Rojas was dreadful with the Cubs last season and not a

whole lot better with the Mets. Somehow, he allowed 15 home runs in 85.1 innings. They helped produce his awful won/lost record and high ERA. But his strikeout total suggested he still was throwing nasty stuff. Once he moved to the Mets, his work against lefthanded hitters improved to .196 with 18 strikeouts in 51 at-bats.

1996: Rojas posted a fine won/lost record and saved 36 games in 40 opportunities while fanning more than a hitter per inning with more strikeouts than hits allowed. It was his best year as a closer.

	W	SV	ERA	IP	H	BB	SO	B/I
1995 Montreal	1	30	4.12	67	69	29	61	1.45
1996 Montreal	7	36	3.22	81	56	28	92	1.04
1997 two teams	0	15	4.64	86	78	36	93	1.34

ROMANO, MICHAEL - TR - b: 3/3/72
Converted from being a starting pitcher to a reliever last year, Romano has no control and will not even get a look until he cuts his walks in half.

ROPER, CHAD - TR - b: 3/29/74
A second-round pick by the Twins in the 1992 June free-agent draft, Roper was rated as having the best infield arm in the Eastern League by Baseball America in 1995. Last year, he put that good arm to use by switching to the pitching mound. He went back to A-ball, and posted a 2.72 ERA in 27 games for Fort Myers in the Twins' farm system.

ROQUE, RAFAEL - TL - b: 1/1/72
Roque looked ready for Double-A competition in 1996, but the Dominican native had some bad starts (too often in cold weather) in the Eastern League, and the Mets sent him back to Class A St. Lucie, where Roque had a 2.12 ERA. He started 1997 at Double-A, hoping for warm weather. The last name rhymes with OK.

ROSADO, JOSE - TL - b: 11/9/74
Scouting: Scouts love his savvy more than his stuff. Rosado's upper-80s fastball, cut fastball, curve and changeup are good pitches, but nothing spectacular. He is effective against righthanders by throwing his changeup down and away against them, but it only works if he can spot his fastball earlier in the count. When he tired late last season, his fastball lost it's edge and Rosado became hittable.
1998: The Royals have asked Rosado to skip winter ball this year in an effort to keep his strength up for the entire season. With complete rest he should return to being one of the better young lefthanders in the American League and serve as the Royals' third starter.
1997: Pitching year-round can take it's toll. Despite Rosado's statements to the contrary, he was obviously a tired pitcher in the second half. His victory in the All-Star game was nearly his last win of the year. He was not the same pitcher in September that he was in April.
1996: Rosado fairly leaped from Double-A Wichita into the Royals rotation at mid-season, to finish fourth in American League Rookie of the Year voting as one of the youngest Royals' pitchers ever. His record could have been much better had he gotten slightly better run support.

	W	SV	ERA	IP	H	BB	SO	B/I
1996 Kansas City	8	0	3.21	106	101	26	64	1.20
1997 Kansas City	9	0	4.69	203	208	73	129	1.38

ROSE, BRIAN - TR - b: 2/1/3/76
Scouting: Rose is not an overpowering ace, but, rather, a polished pitcher. He throws his fastball 88 to 90 MPH, with impressive location, and he uses his three other pitches, all of which are solid, although unspectacular, at just the right times. He throws both a four-seam and a two-seam fastball. To succeed in the majors he will have to do a better job of locating his sinking two-seamer, because his four-seamer often ends up out of the park.
1998: Rose has earned a chance to start for Boston, but he might struggle, as many young pitchers do, until he learns the hitters (his greatest asset is his ability to pitch to hitters' weaknesses), settles down, and finds out what adjustments he needs to make with his stuff. He has the aptitude to do it with his stuff, and he should get the hang of it eventually.
1997: Everything seemed to go right at Triple-A Pawtucket for Rose, who was pitching a half-hour from his Dartmouth, Mass. home. He went 17-5 with a 3.02 ERA and seemed to put every pitch in the right place. He started one mid-season game for Boston, a double-header call-up, but got hit hard. He was not activated in September because the Red Sox did not want him to top 200 innings for the season.
1996: Rose struggled with his breaking pitches and had some arm soreness, but challenged hitters on the way to a 12-7, 4.01 ERA season for Double-A Trenton.

ROSE, SCOTT - TR - b: 5/12/70
Rose produced well in his first year with the Yankees' organization. He went 2-2 with a 3.70 ERA and 11 saves in 28 games for Triple-A Columbus and was 0-2 with a 2.67 ERA and four saves in 22 games for Double-A Norwich. He is not overpowering but is sneaky fast and can be surprising at times.

ROSENGREN, JOHN - TL - b: 8/10/72
Lefty Rosengren has a good fastball, but poor location. He'll have to find the plate to find his way farther up the Tigers' farm system.

RUEBEL, MATT - TL - b: 10/16/69
Incredibly, Ruebel spent all of 1997 in the Pirates' bullpen despite continually being hit hard. He was dropped from the roster at the end of last season. Though he will be invited to spring training with the Pirates, it's hard to imagine him winning a major league job as he is clearly behind several other lefty relievers. His best pitch is a changeup and he is better suited to starting but there is no room in the Pirates' rotation.

	W	SV	ERA	IP	H	BB	SO	B/I
1996 Pittsburgh	1	1	4.60	58	64	25	22	1.53
1997 Pittsburgh	3	0	6.32	63	77	27	50	1.66

RUETER, KIRK - TL - b: 12/1/70
Scouting: Rueter is hardly overpowering. He brings his fastball in the mid-80s and relies on an excellent change and good curve to get the job done. He also benefits from the weather and thick grass at 3Com park. He is a gritty and dependable performer who likes to keep the ball once he has it.
1998: Rueter will be relied upon by the Giants to do just what he did in 1997. Last year was a good experience, and it was also a good confidence builder for the southpaw. Rueter, who arrived in the majors at the tender age of 22, has used his seasons as building blocks. A slight improvement over his performance of last year is a reasonable expectation.

1997: Despite the obvious success of Shawn Estes, in many ways Rueter was the Giants most dependable starter. He overcame questions about his durability, turning in tough performances when it counted, and really contributing to his team. Rueter showed fine control and exceeded most expectations.
1996: Rueter gave the Giants three good starts after the deadline deal which sent him west. Since his amazing debut when he won eight straight decisions in 1994, he has struggled.

	W	SV	ERA	IP	H	BB	SO	B/I
1995 Montreal	5	0	3.23	47	38	9	28	0.99
1996 San Francisco	6	0	3.97	102	109	27	46	1.33
1997 San Francisco	13	0	3.45	191	194	51	115	1.28

RUFFCORN, SCOTT - TR - b: 12/29/69
Scouting: Ruffcorn has always thrown the heck out of the ball in spring training and in the minor leagues. At times, he has a low-90s fastball, curve and changeup, throwing all with confidence and solid command. But once he reaches the majors and pitches in tight ballgames, he gets hit hard. Ruffcorn has said he prefers to pitch in less pressurized situations; the results bear out his mental outlook. An aneurysm discovered in Ruffcorn's pitching arm late last year threatens his career.
1998: Assuming he can comeback from the aneurysm, Ruffcorn will dazzle someone with his stuff in spring training and win a Triple-A or major league bullpen job. If a pitching coach can find the key to Ruffcorn's problems pitching under pressure, they could discover a useful asset.
1997: Ruffcorn excited Phillies' manager Terry Francona with his spring training dominance, but he appeared to lose 10 MPH on his fastball once the season started. He then lost his control in a couple of mid-summer starts. Ruffcorn pitched brilliantly in five Triple-A starts before the aneurysm was discovered.
1996: It was a typical performance from Ruffcorn: he dominated the Triple-A American Association, raising his career minor league record to 54-23, and then allowed 16 baserunners in six major league innings with the White Sox. This brought his career mark to 78 baserunners — including 34 walks — in 31 career major league innings.

	W	SV	ERA	IP	H	BB	SO	B/I
1997 Philadelphia	0	0	7.71	40	42	36	33	1.96

RUFFIN, BRUCE - TL - b: 10/4/63
Scouting: When he's healthy, he throws one of the best lefthanded sliders in the game. When he's on, he can spot a 90-MPH fastball, setting up his sharp-breaking slider that is tougher on righthanded batters than lefties. He has battled control problems throughout his career. Ruffin was superb for the Rockies in 1993, '94 and '95, but he wasn't quite as sharp in '96 and, for a while in '97, he forgot how to throw strikes.
1998: Considering that he is 34 years old and underwent elbow surgery in July that finished his season last year, Ruffin entered free agency as a huge question mark. The Rockies were interested in re-signing him to an incentive-laden contract with a low, non-guaranteed base salary.
1997: Ruffin had a good first month, posting six quick saves, but his season unraveled on May 18th, when he walked three consecutive Met batters on 14 pitches at Shea Stadium. Several pitches flew high to the backstop and the humiliating outing left Ruffin shell-shocked. He spent a month on the disabled list because he was unable to throw strikes in the bullpen. He finally snapped out of it and was pitching better when bone spurs developed in his elbow. He underwent season-ending surgery in July.
1996: Ruffin became an established closer, recording personal bests with 24 saves and 71 appearances. With Curtis Leskanic opening the season as the closer, and the Rockies providing few save opportunities in May and June, Ruffin had just two saves at the season's midway point, but had 22 in the second half.

	W	SV	ERA	IP	H	BB	SO	B/I
1995 Colorado	0	11	2.12	34	26	19	23	1.32
1996 Colorado	7	24	4.00	69	55	29	74	1.21
1997 Colorado	0	7	5.32	22	18	18	31	1.64

RUFFIN, JOHNNY - TR - b: 7/29/71
Blessed with a live arm and a good fastball, Ruffin never turned these assets into major league success. His last real chance was with the Reds in 1996, and Ruffin got on the wrong side of Ray Knight's conceptual line for defining what makes a major league pitcher. Ruffin worked briefly in Japan last year; he was unimpressive there.

	W	SV	ERA	IP	H	BB	SO	B/I
1995 Cincinnati	0	0	1.35	13	4	11	11	1.13
1996 Cincinnati	1	0	5.49	62	71	37	69	1.74

RUMER, TIM - TL - b: 8/8/69
This veteran minor-leaguer moved from the rotation to the bullpen in 1996 and had good results, producing a 2.25 ERA in Double-A and a 2.72 ERA in Triple-A. Even though he was successful in the role of lefty set-up man, last year he was again used as a starter with some relief work. He struggled at Triple-A Columbus, posting a 6.16 ERA; he fared a little better in Double-A. Rumer seems to do much better in a full-time relief role.

RUNYAN, SEAN - TL - b: 6/21/74
Runyan's fastball only reaches the high 80s but has a unique sink to it due to his sidearm delivery; he also throws a slider. Padre scouts believe Runyan can jump from Double-A to become a situational reliever in their major league bullpen next year after his season at Mobile when he went 5-2 with a 2.34 ERA in 40 appearances.

RUSCH, GLENDON - TL - b: 11/7/74
Scouting: Rusch has nearly the same repertoire as fellow lefty teammate Jose Rosado: an upper-80s fastball, cut fastball, curveball and changeup. He has uncanny control of his fastball and will throw his changeup down and away to righthanded hitters, just like Rosado. Like Rosado, scouts love Rusch's savvy; he succeeds by changing speeds and location.
1998: Rusch has the inside track to a fourth or fifth starter spot in the Royals' rotation. He seemed to learn a lot about pitching as 1997 wound to a close and could be a quick surprise if he can apply that knowledge early in 1998.
1997: Rusch's first big-league season was far more successful than his pitching line would suggest. He was awful at times, but more often was at least competitive. Rusch showed he belonged in the majors.
1996: Rusch made a double jump from high Class A Wilmington to Triple-A Omaha and continued his successful minor-league career with an 11-9 record and a 3.98 ERA in 28 starts; he walked just 40 in 169.2 innings.

	W	SV	ERA	IP	H	BB	SO	B/I
1997 Kansas City	6	0	5.50	170	206	52	116	1.51

RUSSELL, JEFF - TR - b: 9/2/61
Russell, formerly a top closer with the Rangers and then the Red Sox, slipped into a set-up role back at Texas in 1996 and then retired after the season. His retirement announcements have been less than 100% reliable in the past, and there are worse pitchers in the majors right now. Russell still had some velocity left, last time we saw him.

	W	SV	ERA	IP	H	BB	SO	B/I
1995 Texas	1	20	3.03	32	36	9	21	1.38
1996 Texas	3	3	3.38	56	58	22	23	1.43
1997				Did Not Play				

RUSSELL, LaGRANDE - TR - b: 8/20/70
Russell was hittable with both the Double-A and Triple-A affiliates of the Cubs' organization. He's been on the decline over the past few seasons and just doesn't have major league stuff.

RYAN, JAY - TR - b: 1/23/76
The Cubs love high school pitchers and they drafted Ryan out of high school in 1994. He was making good progress until the Cubs decided to rush the youngster and have him start the 1996 season in Double-A. He pitched badly at Orlando and couldn't turn things around when he was sent back to Class A Daytona. He also struggled at Daytona this year and might have fallen out of favor with management. He's only 22 years old so there's plenty of time left for him to be a major league pitcher, but he's going to have to make some improvement soon.

RYAN, KEN - TR - b: 10/24/68
Scouting: Ryan missed the bulk of the 1997 season after suffering elbow ligament damage in his pitching arm. Before the injury, Ryan featured a slightly above-average fastball and a sharp curve that made him quite effective against right-handed hitters. His command has always been shaky, but he has always kept the ball low in the strike zone and has avoided the long ball. Ryan is a fierce competitor who insisted on rehabbing quickly enough to get in some action in September games rather than waiting until 1998 spring training. It is uncertain whether Ryan can regain the form that made him so effective two years ago.
1998: The Phillies want Ryan to reclaim his top bullpen set-up role in 1998. They aren't worried about his struggles after his late-1997 return; they were happy to see him throwing free and easy down the stretch. They'll worry about actual results in March.
1997: The elbow injury suffered by Ryan had a debilitating effect on the Phillies' bullpen, forcing other pitchers into roles for which they weren't prepared. Ryan returned, but got clobbered down the stretch. He left pitches up in the strike zone and got hammered by righthanders against whom he usually has the upper hand.
1996: Ryan's debut in Philadelphia was highly successful; he was a reliable two-inning set-up man who mowed down right-handed hitters, holding them to a .210 average. However, his control wavered at times, as he walked nearly five hitters per nine innings.

	W	SV	ERA	IP	H	BB	SO	B/I
1995 Boston	0	7	4.96	32	34	24	34	1.78
1996 Philadelphia	3	8	2.43	89	71	45	71	1.30
1997 Philadelphia	1	0	9.57	21	31	13	10	2.13

RYAN, MATT - TR - b: 3/20/72
Ryan was considered a decent prospect by the Pirates until he was hit hard during his first major league spring training in 1996. Ryan's confidence was shaken by his Grapefruit League beatings and he went on to get drilled at Triple-A Calgary. He put things back together at Double-A Carolina last season but the Pirates no longer consider him a prospect.

SABERHAGEN, BRET - TR - b: 4/11/64
Scouting: Saberhagen has always relied on a 90+ MPH fastball, which he locates as well as anybody, a good curve and changeup. However, coming off major arm surgery at the end of last season, Saberhagen could not reach 90 MPH with his fastball and was throwing a looping curve. It's not uncommon for a post-surgery pitcher to show improved arm-strength the next year, and that will be the key for Saberhagen.
1998: If his arm continues to bounce back from surgery, Saberhagen will get a regular nod in the Boston rotation. When healthy, and throwing at least 90 MPH, he's never had a problem retiring batters. He has said that if he can't approach his former self he would rather retire than try to get by with below-average stuff.
1997: Saberhagen missed most of the season coming back from shoulder surgery, but finally made an appearance for the Red Sox in September. Results were mixed because he threw without pain, but not at his former level.
1996: Saberhagen missed the entire season due to arm surgery.

	W	SV	ERA	IP	H	BB	SO	B/I
1995 two teams	7	0	4.18	153	165	33	100	1.29
1996			Did Not Play - Injured					
1997 Boston	0	0	6.58	26	30	10	14	1.54

SACKINSKY, BRIAN - TR - b: 6/22/71
Sackinsky was the Orioles second-round draft choice in 1992 out of Stanford where he was a teammate of Mike Mussina and Jeffrey Hammonds. He was a top prospect, and made the Orioles in 1996, pitching in three games. He has a history of chronic arm problems, serious enough that he retired during the off-season before last year, only to unretire and try again in 1997. He came down with elbow problems again, and now the Tommy-John type of ligament transplant surgery is recommended. Sackinsky may retire for good.

SADLER, ALDREN - TR - b: 2/10/72
Sadler spent nearly all of the 1997 season at Double-A El Paso in the Brewers' organization. He improved on his control and cut down on the walks but gave up well over a hit per inning, coming closer to two. He throws hard but hasn't demonstrated the ability to get outs in mostly a relief role.

SAGER, A.J. - TR - b: 3/3/65
Scouting: Sager doesn't stun you by how hard he throws or by how sharply his pitches breaks. But he throws strikes, can pitch with too little or too much rest, and can start or relieve. Basically, he's just a useful guy to have on the staff.
1998: The Tigers would like to keep Sager pitching in middle

to long relief, where they think he can be most useful to them. But he's also there if they need a spot starter, and even can close out a game when the usual short men aren't available.
1997: At age 32, Sager finally spent a whole year in the major leagues. The Tigers were more than satisfied with what they got. There were a few notable bad games — he allowed an amazing eight runs on 28 pitches one night — but there were more games where Sager gave the Tigers a chance to win.
1996: Sager came to the Tigers as a minor-league free agent, and he hardly got noticed. But they needed pitchers, any pitchers, and they called him up on June 18th. He stayed the rest of the year, and ended up as the only Tiger with a winning record as a starter (3-2).

	W	SV	ERA	IP	H	BB	SO	B/I
1995 Colorado	0	0	7.36	14	19	7	10	1.77
1996 Detroit	4	0	5.01	79	91	29	52	1.52
1997 Detroit	3	3	4.18	84	81	24	53	1.25

SAIER, MATT - TR - b: 1/29/73
Despite impressive strikeout totals in A-ball, Saier is not a strikeout pitcher. His fastball is merely average but he throws it with some inside/outside movement which, when coupled with a decent curveball and an under-utilized changeup, makes him a more effective pitcher overall. A middle-round 1995 draft pick, Saier is not on the fast track to the majors, but may get there soon just the same if he can continue to improve his fastball. Saier can be a major league starter by the end of 1999.

SAIPE, MIKE - TR - b: 9/10/73
A true finesse pitcher who understands how to mix speeds and hit spots, Saipe has an average fastball with below-average movement, which explains why he gave up 28 homers in 197 innings combined at Double-A New Haven and Triple-A Colorado Springs. He also combined for a 12-8 record, but he has to hit spots to be effective. He challenges people and has good control. Saipe could be called up in a pinch in 1998 if the Rockies need someone to help soak up some innings in middle relief.

SALAZAR, MIKE - TL - b: 7/7/70
Salazar doesn't have major league stuff. He has to have good control to succeed since he can't throw the ball past hitters. Salazar is a marginal prospect.

SALKELD, ROGER - TR - b: 3/6/71
Scouting: Salkeld doesn't throw nearly as hard as he did before he developed shoulder problems which caused him to miss the entire 1992 season. He claims he can throw a strike on any pitch he wants to, but his results never seem to back up that claim. He frequently gets behind in the count which causes him to have to throw fastballs for strikes.
1998: It will be a "make or break" season for Salkeld. He hasn't been effective in the last three seasons and he will have to prove quickly that he still has what the Mariners saw when they made him their top draft choice in 1989. But Salkeld simply doesn't have what it takes to get hitters out without the blazing fastball he had early in his career.
1997: Salkeld started the season at Triple-A Indianapolis, hoping that it wouldn't be long before the Reds called him up. But a season-long bout with wildness cost him any chance at cracking the big-league rotation.
1996: Salkeld spent much of the year in the Reds' rotation. He had some modest success but his failure to pitch into the late innings cost him, and the Reds, some wins. He was good in the first half of the season, but extremely bad after the All-Star break.

	W	SV	ERA	IP	H	BB	SO	B/I
1996 Cincinnati	8	0	5.20	116	114	54	82	1.45

SAMPSON, BENJI - TL - b: 4/27/75
Sampson pitched for New Britain in the Minnesota organization in 1997. He made an appearance there in 1996 and improved this past season. He won ten games, made 20 starts and gave up less than a hit per inning. He also struck out 92 in 118 innings and could get a shot at Triple-A to begin this season.

SANCHEZ, JESUS - TL - 10/11/74
Sanchez recorded a strong season as a starter with Double-A Binghamton in 1997. A powerful thrower, he finished 13-10 with a 4.30 ERA and notched 176 strikeouts in 165.1 innings. He shows the potential for success at a higher level but already has had elbow trouble.

SANDERS, SCOTT - TR - b: 3/25/69
Scouting: At his best, Sanders can be dominating. He throws hard, and the ball moves. But innings tend to fall apart for him, and pitching coaches are always scared that his mechanics are inconsistent. He can have success, and he has had success, but there are no guarantees.
1998: Tigers GM Randy Smith is a believer, so Sanders will get a chance. Manager Buddy Bell still has to be convinced, so Sanders must also prove himself. Chances are, he'll be in the rotation at the start of the year, but will need to pitch better than last year to stay there.
1997: A change in leagues didn't agree with Sanders. Traded from San Diego to Seattle over the winter, he quickly fell out of favor with Mariners manager Lou Pinella. Traded again in July, to the Tigers, Sanders was put in the rotation for the rest of the year. He finished 3-8 as a Tiger, but one of the wins was a September one-hitter against Texas.
1996: The potential started to show for Sanders, who went 8-3 in 16 second-half starts to help the Padres to the National League West title. He held opposing batters to a .221 average, and had an outstanding 157-48 strikeout-to-walk ratio.

	W	SV	ERA	IP	H	BB	SO	B/I
1995 San Diego	5	0	4.30	90	79	31	88	1.22
1996 San Diego	9	0	3.38	144	117	48	157	1.15
1997 two teams	6	2	5.86	140	152	62	120	1.53

SANTANA, JULIO - TR - b: 1/20/73
Scouting: A stocky converted shortstop, Santana throws a fastball, slider and changeup. Although Santana can hit 90 on the radar gun, he cannot throw that hard with any consistency, and there's not much movement on the pitch. With his limited repertoire and a tendency to tire quickly, he is better suited for the bullpen than the rotation. Santana still is raw in terms of development of his pitching skills, and with no minor-league options remaining, he may need to continue his development at the major league level. Santana has decent stuff and a tenacious attitude that he leaves on the mound; his lackadaisical approach to conditioning has been a negative factor in his progress.
1998: Santana will compete for a bullpen spot in the majors, but

would benefit from logging more innings at Triple-A.
1997: Due to injuries in the rotation and bullpen, Santana was pressed into service in more meaningful games than the Rangers would have wanted, and the results were predictably bad. There were a few fine outings that created a glimmer of hope for Santana's future.
1996: Santana arrived in spring training 20 pounds overweight and never challenged for a spot on the Rangers' staff. He did have a solid year at Triple-A Oklahoma City.

	W	SV	ERA	IP	H	BB	SO	B/I
1997 Texas	4	0	6.75	104	141	49	64	1.83

SANTIAGO, JOSE - TR - b: 11/5/74
Santiago's hot temperament got him into hot water in the Carolina League due to a suspension for fighting with a fan at a game while in uniform; his promotion to the majors for a mid-season game was at least partly a method to re-assign him to Double-A Wichita where he became an effective set-up man. His two-seam fastball is good enough for the majors, but Santiago has to improve his mechanics and his slider to get back to the bigs, most likely in his present role as a set-up reliever.

SAUERBECK, SCOTT - TL - b: 11/9/71
This curveballer spent most of the season as a starter with Double-A Binghamton. A mediocre season there (9-9, 4.78 ERA) was offset by Sauerbeck's one good start at Triple-A Norfolk, a three-hit, five-inning win.

SAUNDERS, TONY - TL - b: 4/29/74
Scouting: Saunders has a high-80's fastball which features sharp movement away from righthanded hitters, plus an above-average curveball and changeup. Command is the difference between being dominant and being dominated for Saunders, however. When he's painting the corners, he is capable of pitching complete games; when he's not, he's liable to be gone in two innings.
1998: Saunders was the player the Marlins expected to lose in the first round of expansion, and they lost him fast. The fresh start with the Devil Rays won't hurt his self-confidence, and he should benefit by learning from his late-1997 struggles; he discovered the value of throwing strike one, and he worked for a manager who entrusts major roles to young players. Look for a double-digit win total as Saunders takes a major step forward.
1997: Saunders gained a reputation as a Braves killer in 1997, posting three of his four victories against Atlanta. He was used to neutralize their lefthanded hitters, and held lefties to a .176 mark overall. However, walks were his undoing. He walked over five hitters per nine innings despite a history of good control in the minors. Manager Jim Leyland, to his credit, kept running him out there, though.
1996: Saunders proved he was fully recovered from elbow surgery which cost him parts of 1994 and 1995, striking out a batter per inning in the Double-A Eastern League. He set up hitters expertly, and his fastball appeared to be much faster than it was because of the liberal use of his changeup.

	W	SV	ERA	IP	H	BB	SO	B/I
1997 Florida	4	0	4.61	111	99	64	102	1.46

SAUVER, RICH - TL - b: 11/23/63
Sauveur has hung around for quite a while now, getting in a few big-league games every couple of years while bouncing around from organization to organization. But he's about run out of time. Sauveur has been in a grand total of 24 major league games, all but three of them coming in relief, since first getting a shot at the show with Pittsburgh in 1986. That alone should say quite enough about his ability and future as a pitcher, and his status as a fringe major leaguer.

SCANLAN, BOB - TR - b: 8/9/66
Scouting: Scanlan has one great pitch, a low 90s fastball that has excellent sink; his slider is pretty basic. But scouts believe the sinking fastball could get him back to the major leagues.
1998: At the end of the '97 season, the Padres debated whether or not to re-sign Scanlan, who was a sixth-year minor-league free agent. They believe he has a shot at making their post-expansion bullpen as a middle and situational reliever.
1997: Scanlan was 3-1 with a 3.53 ERA in 36 appearances at Triple-A Las Vegas.
1996: Scanlan struggled at Triple-A Omaha, but somehow won another chance in the majors with Kansas City, where he was pounded with regularity.

	W	SV	ERA	IP	H	BB	SO	B/I
1995 Milwaukee	4	0	6.59	83	101	44	29	1.74
1996 Kansas City	0	0	6.85	22	29	12	6	1.86

SCHILLING, CURT - TR - b: 11/14/66
Scouting: Schilling is one of the most fearsome power pitchers in baseball. He throws a 95-MPH fastball that actually increases in velocity as the game progresses, and complements it with a nasty slider and a split-fingered fastball which he used more frequently and effectively in 1997. He goes right after hitters, gets ahead in the count and puts them away with authority. He expects to finish his games; Schilling exudes confidence and it showed in the Phillies' different look when he took the mound last year. Schilling's elbow problems are now two years distant; he's one of the most dominant pitchers in the game.
1998: There is no reason to believe that Schilling won't similarly dominate this year. He might not whiff 300 hitters again, but the Phillies should be a stronger team, possibly enabling him to notch his first 20-win season.
1997: Schilling dominated from day one. He had only two poor starts all season, and was the only bright spot in a dreary first half in Philadelphia. In addition to his obvious pitching contributions, his leadership helped younger Phillies' players mature into more complete ballplayers. Schilling was constantly rumored to be on the trading block, but remained with the Phillies as they decided to build around him instead of trading for prospects.
1996: Schilling rebounded from shoulder and elbow problems which robbed him of most of the previous two seasons. He dominated National League hitters, despite his 9-10 record; Schilling led the league in complete games despite not pitching until May. He was outstanding in all aspects, even holding lefthanders to a .215 average.

	W	SV	ERA	IP	H	BB	SO	B/I
1995 Philadelphia	7	0	3.57	116	96	26	114	1.05
1996 Philadelphia	9	0	3.19	183	149	50	182	1.09
1997 Philadelphia	17	0	2.97	254	208	58	319	1.05

SCHMIDT, CURT - TR - b: 3/16/70
Schmidt finished last season with the Pirates' Triple-A Calgary

farm club after being acquired from Montreal in a minor-league trade. Schmidt was Calgary's closer and did OK, though not well enough to really open anyone's eyes. He pitched in 11 games with Montreal in 1995 but his career has gone backwards since. He turns 28 in March, giving little hope that he'll resurface in the big leagues.

SCHMIDT, JASON - TR - b: 1/29/73

Scouting: Schmidt has all the makings of an outstanding power pitcher with a 95-MPH fastball and 88-MPH slider that has good bite. Schmidt's basic problem stems from the fact that he outthinks himself on the mound and worries too much about hitting spots with his changeup. Though he needs a decent change to have long-term success in the majors, his power arsenal shouldn't be ignored.

1998: Schmidt will be in the Pirates' rotation again. The Pirates have the makings of a good pitching staff but are desperately looking for someone to emerge as their ace starter. Schmidt has the physical ability to be that ace but many wonder how badly he wants to be a star.

1997: Schmidt had an up-and-down season. His spring training was slowed when he was found to have an irregular heartbeat. Though he checked out fine, Schmidt never seemed to quite recover from the time lost. He was brilliant in some outings and out by the fourth inning in others.

1996: Schmidt began the season as the fifth starter in Atlanta's vaunted rotation but didn't handle the pressure well. A pulled ribcage muscle further slowed him and the Braves then shipped him and two other players to the Pirates in a late-August trade for Denny Neagle. Schmidt was impressive in September with the Pirates, giving them hope they had a future ace on their hands.

	W	SV	ERA	IP	H	BB	SO	B/I
1995 Atlanta	2	0	5.76	25	27	18	19	1.80
1996 Pittsburgh	5	0	5.70	96	108	53	74	1.68
1997 Pittsburgh	10	0	4.60	188	193	76	136	1.43

SCHMIDT, JEFF - TR - b: 2/21/71

Schmidt has great stuff and throws hard, and could be a great prospect once he develops a little more competitiveness. He has started games, but was tried as a closer at Triple-A Vancouver last year and had some success. His stuff is impressive, particularly an above-average fastball and a split-fingered pitch that could be devastating with a little more work. Schmidt needs to pitch with a little more fire to become a top prospect.

SCHMITT, TODD - TR - b: 2/12/70

Schmitt is a wild, strikeout pitcher who has been passed by others in the Padres organization. He's getting too old to still be a prospect and would have to have a great spring to make the Padres.

SCHOENEWEIS, SCOTT - TR - b: 10/2/73

Scouting: Along with Matt Perisho and Darrell May, Schoeneweis is one of the top lefthanded prospects in the organization. The Angels figure they stole him after other clubs passed because of his bout with cancer. Schoeneweis proved his toughness both in making a recovery from the disease and in his determination to keep his career on track. The Angels' third-round choice in 1996, Schoeneweis is projected as not being that far away from the majors because of his above-average fastball and good mix of pitches — and his outstanding competitiveness.

1998: Schoeneweis probably won't make the big club, unless the Angels suffer another long string of injuries to pitchers the way they did in 1996. He needs further development in the minor leagues, but he's likely placed himself on a fast track. Despite his minor injuries last year the Angels remain excited about his prospects.

1997: A stint on the disabled list with a rib problem at Double-A Midland and blisters on his pitching hand at the end of the season slowed Schoeneweis' development, but not by a lot.

1996: In his first season of professional ball, Schoeneweis was a solid starter for Class A Lake Elsinore. Particularly impressive was his strikeout-to-walk ratio (83-to-27).

SCHOUREK, PETE - TL - b: 5/10/69

Scouting: For the second straight season, Schourek attempted to pitch through arm miseries with little success. When healthy, he features a fastball (which was more effective before his injuries) and a big breaking curveball, supplemented by a straight change and cutter. His fall from Cy Young runner-up to injury rehab gamble is a salient reminder of the fragile nature of starting pitchers.

1998: A free agent at the end of the 1997 season, Schourek was expected to leave the budget-cutting Reds. His health is a concern, of course. If he's back to full health and able to throw his breaking stuff without pain, he'll become a top starter in the majors. But that's a big "If."

1997: Schourek's inability to come back from elbow surgery in 1996 was a major cause of the Reds slow start. Schourek went on the DL in June with a strained left triceps muscle and returned to the DL in August with an inflamed left elbow; he was ineffective when he was able to pitch.

1996: Coming off a superb season, Schourek was subjected to a 137-pitch outing by Ray Knight in a mid-April start. He was never the same after that start, and was finally shut down in July for elbow surgery.

	W	SV	ERA	IP	H	BB	SO	B/I
1995 Cincinnati	18	0	3.22	190	158	45	160	1.07
1996 Cincinnati	4	0	6.01	67	79	24	54	1.54
1997 Cincinnati	5	0	5.42	85	78	38	59	1.37

SCHRENK, STEVE - TR - b: 11/20/68

Schrenk spent ten undistinguished years in the White Sox organization, rising to Triple-A where he spent three years as a starter. Last year, he was with the Orioles Triple-A Club. It looks like Triple-A is his peak level.

SCHUTZ, CARL - TL - b: 8/22/71

Schutz is a small lefty with a below-average fastball. He doesn't have a good out-pitch versus lefties either, making his job as a lefty specialist quite difficult. He struggled in all phases of the game in '97, walking 51 and posting a 5.33 ERA in 79.1 Triple-A innings. He'll probably get more chances, because he's a lefty, but he's unlikely to help a big-league team.

SCOTT, DARRYL - TR - b: 8/6/68

Scott has been a fairly effective Triple-A closer since 1992, most recently in the Indians' organization. He doesn't throw hard, but has above-average control and a rubber arm which allows him to be used for more than an inning, multiple times per week. He used to be able to bring some heat, but his power dropped precipitously in 1997, likely signifying an imminent career downturn. If he was a lefty, he'd have a lot more than 16 games of major league experience under his belt. He'll settle into a relatively insignificant middle-relief role in 1998.

SCOTT, TIM - TR - b: 11/16/66
Scott throws hard and has pitched well during parts of his career. In 1996 he struggled with injuries and was eventually released by the Giants. Last year he pitched in 14 games with the Padres and appeared in three games with the Rockies. He wasn't effective at either stop. He also pitched at Triple-A Colorado Springs in the Rockies' organization where he had success. He struck out 18 and gave up seven hits in 14.2 innings. He could get a shot at joining a major league bullpen in the spring.

	W	SV	ERA	IP	H	BB	SO	B/I
1995 Montreal	2	2	3.98	63	52	23	57	1.18
1996 San Francisco	5	1	4.64	66	65	30	47	1.44
1997 Colorado	1	0	8.14	21	30	7	16	1.76

SEANEZ, RUDY - TR - b: 10/20/68
Seanez has fallen from a prospective closer candidate with the Dodgers to a journeyman minor-leaguer searching for a role. In 1997, he and his blazing fastball worked primarily in relief — with three starts, too — at Triple-A Omaha with poor results: 6.51 ERA and 13 homers in 47 innings. His problem is the same as it has always been; no command of the great heater.

SEAVER, MARK - TR - b: 4/6/75
Mark Seaver (no relation) is a big (6'8", 240-pound) hurler who was traded by Baltimore to Oakland for Geronimo Berroa. He has two above-average fastballs, but his breaking ball needs work. He also needs better overall command.

SEAY, BOBBY - TL - b: 6/20/78
Seay was considered the top lefthander in the 1996 draft but slipped to the White Sox at number twelve in the first round because of concerns about his bonus demands. He was declared a free agent and inked with the Devil Rays for $3 million. He followed Doug Million and Matt Drews as first rounders from Sarasota High in Florida, all since 1993. Seay has an above-average curveball and gets into the low 90's with his fastball. Last year he pitched at Class A Charleston in the South Atlantic League. He struggled with his control but gave up less than a hit per inning and posted 64 strikeouts in 61 innings.

SEELBACH, CHRIS - TR - b: 12/18/72
Once a highly-touted prospect in the Braves' system, Seelbach has displayed a glaring inability to retire Triple-A hitters in his four opportunities at that level. He has always possessed an above-average fastball with good movement, but he has been unable to consistently throw it for strikes early in the count at the Triple-A level. He has walked over five hitters per nine innings at that level. He was used as a reliever for a substantial portion of 1997 — he has an outside chance of earning a middle-relief role in the majors should he uncover and correct a mechanical flaw, improving his command.

SELE, AARON - TR - b: 6/25/70
Scouting: After experiencing some arm problems in '95, Sele has not been the pitcher he was when he first reached the big leagues. His fastball is just average, and his trademark curveball does not have the bite it once did. He's had trouble finding other pitches to blend in, so when he gets behind with his fastball he's in bad shape.
1998: Boston had other candidates with higher ceilings ready to step in, so Sele was the odd man out in their rotation and went to Texas. Because pitching is so thin and because he throws a good game every once in a while, Sele should end up in the rotation. However, there's no reason to expect him to perform at a higher level than he has the last couple of seasons.
1997: Sele kept getting the ball and posted a lot of wins, mostly because of good run support, but his final numbers were among the ugliest for starters in the majors.
1996: After sitting out most of the '95 season with arm problems, Sele proved he was healthy in '96, but his results on the mound were not pretty. Sele also battled with manager Kevin Kennedy, who said he didn't think Sele was as tough on the mound as he needs to be.

	W	SV	ERA	IP	H	BB	SO	B/I
1995 Boston	3	0	3.06	32	32	14	21	1.42
1996 Boston	7	2	5.32	157	195	67	137	1.65
1997 Boston	13	0	5.38	177	196	80	122	1.56

SERAFINI, DAN - TL - b: 1/25/74
Scouting: Serafini is a lefthander who throws hard and is still only 24 years old. The Twins' top draft pick in 1992 out of Serra High School in San Bruno, Calif., Serafini has all of the tools needed to succeed at the major league level. The only problem is, the Twins expected him to arrive by 1997. Nagging injuries at the minor-league level have slowed him.
1998: This could be the coming-out year for Serafini, who finally appears to have all of his pitches together and working. He needs to make a strong statement for a major league starting job in 1998.
1997: Finally recalled by the Twins in September, Serafini was impressive in three starts, even collecting a complete game. He needed to fine-tune his curve at times and improve his confidence — going with his best stuff rather than allow the batter to dictate what he throws.
1996: With impressive minor-league outings, Serafini could have forced himself to the Twins' clubhouse sooner than expected. He went 7-7 with a 5.58 ERA at Triple-A Salt Lake, however, killing any chances for significant time in the majors.

	W	SV	ERA	IP	H	BB	SO	B/I
1997 Minnesota	2	0	3.42	26	27	11	15	1.44

SERVICE, SCOTT - TR - b: 2/26/67
Scouting: A fastball/slider pitcher who throws everything hard (low-90s fastball), Service also throws a split-fingered fastball, but lacks good command of it. He's unlikely to win a closer job, but he has the tools to pitch short relief in the majors.
1998: The Royals are impressed with Service's velocity; his strikeout ability could be a useful asset in their much-maligned bullpen. He'll get a long look in spring training.
1997: Service was traded from Cincinnati's Triple-A club to the Royals along with Hector Carrasco for Jon Nunnally and Chris Stynes. He was sent to Triple-A Omaha where he was untouched for runs in sixteen appearances before a recall to Kansas City.
1996: In another season split between Triple-A and the majors,

Service was again effective at both levels, eventually earning a set-up relief role in the Reds' bullpen by season's end.

	W	SV	ERA	IP	H	BB	SO	B/I
1995 San Francisco	3	0	3.19	31	18	20	30	1.23
1996 Cincinnati	1	0	3.94	48	51	18	46	1.44
1997 Kansas City	0	0	6.46	22	28	6	22	1.52

SEXTON, JEFF - TR - b: 10/4/71
Anyone who questions the magnitude of the difference between Class A hitters and their Double-A counterparts should ask Sexton. In 1995, he posted a 153-to-30 strikeout-to-walk ratio in a season split between the Indians' two Class A affiliates, and then posted a 34-to-23 mark in Double-A in 1996. His fastball is just major league average; he has not gotten ahead of hitters in Double-A, and has had to groove his fastball in hitters' counts, with predictable results. He has backslid into the no-man's land of middle relief, and has no material upside.

SHAW, CURTIS - TL - b: 8/16/69
Remember Oakland's Four Aces? Kirk Dressendorfer, Don Peters, Todd Van Poppel and David Zancanaro were first-round picks that were supposed to yield the Athletics their rotation of the future. Shaw was the A's second-round pick that year; none of the Four Aces panned out and neither has Shaw. He spent last season as a reliever in the Pirates' farm system, pitching horribly at Triple-A Calgary and well at Double-A Carolina. The Pirates thought enough of him to send him to the Arizona Fall League at the end of last season. Part of the reason was injuries to better prospects but the other part is Shaw is lefthanded, and lefties always have a chance.

SHAW, JEFF - TR - b: 7/7/66
Scouting: Shaw features a sinking fastball, forkball and slider, has excellent control, and is not afraid to work hitters inside. He had no problems making the conversion from a set-up role to become a closer.
1998: Despite his fine work in 1997, Shaw is not a lock for the closer role in 1998. The Reds have a large commitment (by their standards) to Jeff Brantley, and it is possible that they could share the closer role. A more likely scenario is for Brantley to be traded and Shaw to be giving the ace relief role outright.
1997: It was a breakthrough year for Shaw, who assumed the closer role when Brantley went on the DL in May. He led the league in saves and posted a six-to-one strikeout-to-walk ratio.
1996: A low-level free agent signing by the Reds, Shaw worked up from mop-up man to the number two man in the Reds bullpen, leading the league with 22 holds.

	W	SV	ERA	IP	H	BB	SO	B/I
1995 Montreal	1	3	4.62	62	58	26	45	1.35
1995 Chicago AL	0	0	6.52	9	12	1	6	1.34
1996 Cincinnati	8	4	2.49	104	99	29	69	1.23
1997 Cincinnati	4	42	2.38	95	79	12	74	0.96

SHEPHERD, ALVIE - TR - b: 5/12/74
Scouting: Shepherd is a big (6'7", 230-pound) hard thrower out of the University of Nebraska where he was primarily a first baseman and DH, and an occasional relief pitcher. He was the Orioles first-round draft pick in 1995 and has an outstanding fastball and a slider that needs some refinement.
1998: Shepherd will probably begin in Triple-A, or in Double-A with a quick promotion if he does well. He just needs more experience.
1997: Shepherd was used as a starter in the minors to get more innings, but his future may be as a closer. He had a good first half last year, but came down with some aches and pains which reduced his effectiveness in the second half and eventually landed him on the disabled list. He was probably just tired because of never having pitched many innings before.
1996: Shepherd pitched in the high Class A Carolina League, primarily as a reliever, and he struck out 104 in 97 innings while going 6-5 with a 5.59 ERA.

SHEPHERD, KEITH - TR - b: 1/21/68
After working 20 ineffective innings for the Orioles in 1996, Shepherd moved on to his eighth organization in 1997, pitching on the Mets' farm at Triple-A Norfolk. He put in a solid 8-8, 4.37 ERA season but, at age 30, needs to come up with a new pitch to get back to the big show.

	W	SV	ERA	IP	H	BB	SO	B/I
1996 Baltimore	0	0	8.71	20	31	18	17	2.43

SHOEMAKER, STEVE -TR- b: 2/24/70
Shoemaker blew batters away at the Class A and Double-A levels and even earned a shot at Triple-A in the Rockies' organization last year. A hard-throwing righthander, Shoemaker fanned 76 in 52 innings at Class A Salem of the Carolina League and struck out 111 in 95.1 innings at Double-A New Haven. He even struck out more than a batter per inning in a short stint at Colorado Springs. With all of the strikeouts though came a number of walks. He'll have to cut down on the free passes to get a shot at the majors.

SHOUSE, BRIAN - TL - b: 9/26/68
Shouse spent six years in the Pirates organization before Baltimore acquired him in 1996; he has since pitched at Triple-A Rochester. Shouse has had some good years as a Triple-A reliever, but never got the call to the show.

SHUEY, PAUL - TR - b: 9/16/70
Scouting: Shuey has substantial talent, but has been prevented from reaching his potential by subpar conditioning and the mechanical inconsistencies it has caused. He throws a 90-MPH fastball which sets up his true strikeout pitch, a nasty forkball. This combination should make him good against righthanders, but that certainly was not the case in 1997, at least. His command has been inconsistent at the major league level; he has been unable to consistently get ahead of hitters. He also has a slow delivery which puts him at a disadvantage against would-be basestealers.
1998: Shuey was expected to be left unprotected in the expansion draft, where he would have been considered an attractive talent. Barring sheer spring training dominance, Shuey is unlikely to be either the closer or primary set-up man for the Indians in 1997. They have given him countless chances and are tired of waiting. Major mechanical adjustments must be made.
1997: Shuey took several steps backward in 1997. First and foremost, he was dogged by hamstring injuries. He allowed righthanders to bat .330 against him. He again had trouble getting ahead in the count and holding baserunners. There is still room for hope; his stuff remains intact, as indicated by the success he had against lefties (.235 average).
1996: Shuey was devastating at Triple-A Buffalo, posting a 57-

to-9 strikeout-to-walk ratio in 33 innings, and was a productive member of the Indians' pen after his recall. He held righthanders to a .225 mark, and along with Jose Mesa and Eric Plunk, gave the Indians arguably the best righthanded bullpen staff around.

	W	SV	ERA	IP	H	BB	SO	B/I
1996 Cleveland	5	4	2.85	53	45	26	44	1.33
1997 Cleveland	4	2	6.20	45	52	28	46	1.78

SHUMATE, JACOB - TR - b: 5/14/73
Shumate was Atlanta's number one draft choice in 1994 and hasn't made it out of A-ball. At Eugene of the Northwest League last year Shumate exhibited no control at all with 43 walks in 21 innings. Until he locates the plate he will never advance.

SIEVERT, MARK - TR - b: 2/16/73
Scouting: Sievert has three major league pitches although his fastball is a bit short on the radar gun. A high-80s heater is enhanced with a decent curve and a laser-straight changeup. When he focuses, he has pinpoint control and is confident enough with all his pitches to use whichever is needed in a particular situation.
1998: Sievert could get a look in spring training but is likely headed for Triple-A to refine his mechanics. In a perfect situation, he could sneak in as a sixth reliever. Don't expect much immediately, even if he pitches.
1997: Sievert appeared in just one game at Triple-A Syracuse in April before going on the shelf. He returned in mid-August to Class A Dunedin.
1996: Effective at Double-A, Sievert struggled after getting the call to Triple-A. His usual control abandoned him much of the season although all his pitches were apparently working for him.

SIKORSKI, BRIAN - TR - b: 7/27/74
Scouting: Sikorski was a fourth-round draft choice out of Western Michigan University in 1995. He is an excellent competitor with a fastball that reaches 90 MPH and reasonable command of his curve and slider. He has been successful in each of his three minor-league seasons, one as a closer and two as a starter, as he has moved up the ladder.
1998: Sikorski may start at Double-A in 1998 but he needs to get to Triple-A before the season is over to continue his progress.
1997: Sikorski made eleven starts at higher Class A Kissimmee before being promoted to Double-A Jackson where he made 17 starts. He was 8-2 with a 3.06 ERA at Kissimmee and 5-5 with a 4.63 ERA at Jackson. His 13 wins tied for second in the Astro minor-league system.
1996: Sikorski was 11-8 at Low Class A Quad Cities with an ERA of 3.13. His 150 strikeouts were tops in the Astro minor-league system.

SILVA, JOSE - TR - b: 12/19/73
Scouting: Silva has a live arm; his fastball routinely reaches 95 MPH along with a sharp slider. He still needs to develop a changeup and he has had occasional arm problems since undergoing elbow surgery in 1995. Some scouts feel Silva is better suited for the bullpen because of his hard stuff, others feel he could become a first-rate starter.
1998: The Pirates will go to spring training with the same rotation that served them well in 1997. However, Silva will push all five for a spot as a starter. If he doesn't crack the rotation, he certainly will make the Pirates' roster as a reliever.
1997: Silva began the season at Triple-A Calgary and Pacific Coast League managers rated his fastball the best in the league. Silva had three different stints with the Pirates and was shaky at times both as a starter and reliever. However, he also showed enough flashes of brilliance to allow the Pirates to think he could develop into a star.
1996: Silva spent the majority of the season at Double-A Knoxville, trying to recover from off-season shoulder surgery. Toronto gave Silva his first taste of the major leagues in September but then included him with five other prospects as part of a nine-player trade with Pittsburgh at the end of the season.

	W	SV	ERA	IP	H	BB	SO	B/I
1997 Pittsburgh	2	0	5.95	36	52	16	30	1.87

SILVA, TED - TR - b: 8/4/74
Scouting: Silva has four decent pitches: an average fastball, changeup, curve and slider. His stuff isn't impressive but he has good control, doesn't beat himself and knows how to pitch.
1998: Silva has earned a promotion to Triple-A, and needs at least a full season at that level.
1997: In his first full season at Double-A, Silva did not post a stunning won-loss record, but made good progress. He went 13-10 with a 4.09 ERA and a three-to-one strikeout-to-walk ratio. Silva led the Drillers in wins, strikeouts and innings pitched.
1996: A 17-4 record and an ERA under 3.00 with a mid-season promotion will generally get a pitcher noticed, and Silva was no exception. His strikeout rate fell noticeably with his promotion to Double-A.

SIMAS, BILL - TR - b: 11/28/71
Scouting: Simas is a fastball/slider pitcher who throws everything hard; he doesn't have anything else to go with the hard stuff, though, and is often wild. The White Sox have had a lot of expectations of Simas since they acquired him from the Angels in July, 1995, but the expectations may be beyond Simas' ability.
1998: Simas has never had extended major league success; he has to rebound 100 percent from shoulder surgery to retain his major league bullpen job.
1997: Simas enjoyed moderate success in a non-critical bullpen role for the White Sox. His ERA was deceptively low; he continued to walk too many batters and couldn't be trusted in tight games.
1996: In his first full year in the majors, Simas led the White Sox with 15 holds but also had a high ERA and poor won/loss record. It was a slightly disappointing year and cost him a primary set-up role.

	W	SV	ERA	IP	H	BB	SO	B/I
1995 Chicago AL	1	0	2.57	14	15	10	16	1.79
1996 Chicago AL	2	2	4.58	72	75	39	65	1.58
1997 Chicago AL	3	1	4.14	41	46	24	38	1.69

SIMMONS, SCOTT - TL - b: 8/15/69
Simmons gets by on guile and breaking stuff, he doesn't blow anyone away. He had a solid season at Double-A Memphis in the Mariners' organization. He gave up less than a hit per inning and had a slightly better than two-to-one ratio of strikeouts to walks. If he continues this kind of performance somebody may give him a chance as a situational lefty in a major

league bullpen.

SIROTKA, MIKE - TL - b: 5/13/71
Scouting: Some scouts think Sirotka lacks the velocity necessary to succeed in the majors, but he really has enough movement on the fastball and a fine repertoire (curveball, slide, changeup) to be a third or fourth starter in the major leagues.
1998: Sirotka belongs in a big-league rotation and may get that chance in an expansion year.
1997: Sirotka spent most of the summer at Triple-A Nashville, going 3-3 with a 3.19 ERA in eleven starts; he pitched much better than his record would indicate, posting better than a four-to-one strikeout-to-walk ratio. He made some appearances in Chicago, the last few being particularly impressive.
1996: Sirotka earned a second shot at the majors with his 7-5, 3.60 ERA performance at Nashville, but it was a disaster.

	W	SV	ERA	IP	H	BB	SO	B/I
1995 Chicago AL	1	0	4.19	34	39	17	19	1.63
1996 Chicago AL	1	0	7.18	26	34	12	11	1.76
1997 Chicago AL	3	0	2.25	32	36	5	24	1.28

SKUSE, NICK - TR - b: 1/9/72
Skuse came on strong in the closer role at Double-A Midland in 1997. In doing so, he turned a corner in his career and impressed some people in the Angels' front office. Skuse has a good fastball and showed a good strikeout-to-walk ratio, and he has become a youngster the Angels will keep a close eye on this season.

SLOCUMB, HEATHCLIFF - TR - b: 6/7/66
Scouting: Slocumb throws hard but has location problems and is probably only a fringe closer, all other things being equal. He will get his share of saves when he is locating his mid-90s fastball; he also throws a slider and a forkball. Slocumb is occasionally plagued by self-doubt leading to streaks of unreliability.
1998: Slocumb is the leading contender to again close games for Seattle, although there are several other candidates and it's likely that manager Lou Pinella will spread the work around, too.
1997: Acquired from the Red Sox for catching prospect Jason Varitek in a deadline trade, Slocumb was streaky with the Mariners, good enough at times to record ten saves, but also lost all four decisions with a 4.13 ERA; he was 0-5 with Boston and opponents batted .286 against him for the season.
1996: Given Boston's closer job after an off-season trade with the Phillies, Slocumb started poorly but contributed greatly in the Red Sox' wild-card drive. He battled manager Kevin Kennedy for much of the season but saved 15 of his last 16 games with an ERA below 1.00 over the last two months and held opponents to a .207 batting average.

	W	SV	ERA	IP	H	BB	SO	B/I
1995 Philadelphia	5	32	2.89	65	64	35	63	1.52
1996 Boston	5	31	3.02	83	68	55	88	1.48
1997 two teams	0	27	5.16	75	84	49	64	1.77

SMALL, AARON - TR - b: 11/23/71
Scouting: With an excellent fastball which hits the low 90s, Small also uses a cutter, slider and changeup as part of his arsenal. He was extremely effective in middle relief, a role for which he is well suited.
1998: Small should continue his excellent role as a middle reliever for Oakland this year. He handles the difficult job well, and the A's are happy to be able to depend upon him in tough situations.
1997: From the day Small arrived during the fifth inning of a game against Boston in early April, was handed the ball with his team tied in the ninth, and grabbed the win in the 10th, Small proved to be among the most consistent pitchers on the A's staff.
1996: A former Jay and Marlin, Small showed good stuff at Edmonton, but was lit up when he hit the majors. He might need a little more work in the minors before making the jump to the big time.

	W	SV	ERA	IP	H	BB	SO	B/I
1995 Florida	1	0	1.42	6	7	6	5	2.05
1996 Oakland	1	0	8.16	28	37	22	17	2.09
1997 Oakland	9	4	4.28	97	109	40	57	1.54

SMALL, MARK - TR - b: 11/12/67
A career minor-leaguer, Small got a small taste of the majors for the first time in 1996 (16 relief appearances). He has an average fastball and slider, but his stuff isn't good enough for him to be successful in the majors. His 1997 season was split between the disabled list, Triple-A New Orleans (1-1, 5.79 ERA) and Double-A Jackson (3-4, 3.35 ERA, nine saves).

	W	SV	ERA	IP	H	BB	SO	B/I
1996 Houston	0	0	5.92	24	33	13	16	1.91

SMART, J.D. - TR - b: 11/12/73
Smart doesn't have overpowering stuff but he doesn't hurt himself with walks and gives up about a hit per inning on average. At Class A and Double-A stops in the Expos' farm system last year, the former Texas Longhorn and fourth-round pick in the 1995 draft made 26 starts and had an 11-7 record; it was his first shot at Double-A ball. If he can make a Triple-A appearance sometime in 1998 he could become a starting prospect in the future for the Expos.

SMILEY, JOHN - TL - b: 3/17/65
Scouting: Smiley's career may have been ended by the bad-looking left arm fracture he suffered while warming up for a late-September start last year. He has always possessed good velocity for a lefthander (87-89 MPH) and has featured a diverse repertoire which he has placed on the corners throughout his career. However, he recently faced the late-career difficulties confronted by other career-long finesse pitchers. The two-strike fastballs which used to produce strikeouts are now being struck with authority. One or two MPH of lost velocity and an inch or two of location is the difference between 15 wins and being out of baseball.
1998: Smiley faces a long rehabilitation. Any type of 1998 contribution is nearly out of the question.
1997: Smiley began the season with the Reds, and was traded to the Indians' for the stretch run of the pennant race. He battled elbow and shoulder problems throughout the season, and took a cortisone shot before making a late-season start for the Indians. Smiley threw too many average heaters down the middle of the strike zone to expect continued success.
1996: Smiley's likely last hurrah was a vintage season. He averaged seven innings per start for the Reds, consistently keeping them in ballgames though he was done in by a lack of run support. He showed no signs of an imminent career downturn.

	W	SV	ERA	IP	H	BB	SO	B/I
1995 Cincinnati	12	0	3.46	176	173	39	124	1.20
1996 Cincinnati	13	0	3.64	217	207	54	171	1.20
1997 Cleveland	11	0	5.31	154	184	41	120	1.46

SMITH, BRIAN - TR - b: 7/19/72

He's nothing special yet; Smith allowed 169 hits in 137.1 innings at Triple-A Syracuse and his 7-11 record doesn't represent how bad he actually was last year.

SMITH, CAM - TR - b: 9/20/73

Scouting: Smith has a tremendous fastball. He regularly hits the mid-90s on the radar gun. But he's is a source of frustration for the Padres. He has struggled with his location and off-speed pitches and he has suffered with arm and back problems. Smith finished the '97 season with tendinitis.
1998: He will be in the bullpen at either Triple-A Las Vegas or Double-A Mobile.
1997: Acquired from Detroit last winter, Smith switched from the starting rotation to the bullpen during the season. He finished with a 3-5 record and a 7.03 ERA, striking out 88 in 79.1 innings; he also walked 73 and threw 14 wild pitches.
1996: Smith went 5-8 with a 4.59 ERA in 21 starts for the Tigers' Class A team at Lakeland, averaging a strikeout per inning.

SMITH, CHUCK - TR - b: 1/14/74

In his seventh pro season, Smith split the year between Double-A Birmingham and Triple-A Nashville with vastly different results at the two levels. In Birmingham he showed the same strikeout ability that helped him lead the Midwest League in strikeouts in 1995, while posting a 3.16 ERA over 62.2 innings. But, his Triple-A trial was a bust as he allowed a run per inning with far too many hits and walks each inning. Smith throws hard but has no control; he had 16 wild pitches combined between the two levels — in just 94.1 innings — and has unleashed 50 wild pitches the last three years. He's too old for Double-A (he'll be 27 in May) and he was demoted at mid-season instead of moving in a forward direction. Neither are positive signs to a big-league future for Smith even if he gets his stuff under control.

SMITH, DAN - TR - b: 9/15/75

This 29-year-old lefty went 3-14 for Oklahoma City last season. Multiple injuries have taken their toll, and Smith now has no chance of making it back to the major leagues.

SMITH, HUT - TR - b: 6/8/73

Smith's progress was set back by elbow problems that required Tommy John-type surgery in 1995. He pitched in ten A-ball games in 1996, and started 19 games in Class A and Double-A in 1997, making good progress.

SMITH, LEE - TR - b: 12/4/57

Smith's career ended with a whimper last July as he retired from the Expos after primarily serving as a set-up man for closer Ugueth Urbina. Smith retired as baseball's all-time saves leader, thriving for so many years in a position that often has a short shelf life. But did Smith really retire? He broadly hinted he could be coaxed out of retirement. If Smith does come back, it would be a mistake. He doesn't have it anymore and should get ready for induction day in Cooperstown while he still has his dignity.

	W	SV	ERA	IP	H	BB	SO	B/I
1995 California	0	37	3.47	49	42	25	43	1.36
1996 California	0	0	2.45	11	8	3	6	1.00
1996 Cincinnati	3	2	4.06	44	49	23	35	1.63
1997 Montreal	0	5	5.81	22	28	8	15	1.66

SMITH, PETE - TR - b: 2/27/66

Scouting: Smith is a tough competitor. Although his fastball has been diminished by surgery and his breaking pitches are not the best around, he battled his way back to the major leagues. Smith had most heart on the Padre staff. He doesn't back down from anyone or any situation.
1998: He will start somewhere in the expansion season. The Padres are hoping he returns.
1997: Smith was the only Padre who had an ERA under 4.00 (3.83) as a starter. He was the Padres last cut of the spring and started the season at Triple-A Las Vegas (3-2, 4.28 ERA in six games). He was called up to San Diego to patch holes in Padre bullpen and made his first 22 appearances in relief. He finished with 118 innings, the fourth-most on the staff. Opponents batted .267 against Smith.
1996: After signing as a free agent with the Padres, Smith spent the entire year at Las Vegas and finished with an 11-9 record and a 4.95 ERA in 26 starts.

	W	SV	ERA	IP	H	BB	SO	B/I
1997 San Diego	7	1	4.81	118	120	52	68	1.46

SMITH, RYAN - TR - b: 11/11/71

Smith spent most of the year with Seattle's Double-A team in Memphis and proved to have ordinary stuff. He was used primarily in relief and yielded more than a hit per inning. He has little chance of making a contribution to a major league bullpen.

SMITH, TOBY - TR - b: 11/16/71

Smith was a disappointment in Triple-A Omaha's bullpen before returning to Double-A Wichita and a starting role. Despite a hard fastball, his stuff isn't overly impressive; he has been eminently hittable above A-ball. The bloom is clearly off this former Wichita State U. star; expansion may be his only hope for big league play.

SMITH, TRAVIS - TR - b: 11/7/72

Smith had another productive year for the Brewers' Double-A El Paso club in the Texas League. He was 16-3 but that record is a bit deceiving. He doesn't have over powering pitches, he gave up 210 hits in 184.1 innings, but he does have good control of his arsenal. He'll probably get a look at Triple-A to start 1998 because he's proven he can win at Double-A (45 starts and a 23-7 record with eight complete games in part of 1996 and the 1997 season).

SMITH, ZANE - TL - b: 12/28/60

Smith got off to a good start in his return to the Pirates in 1996 but was released just before the All-Star break after four poor starts. No one picked him up.

	W	SV	ERA	IP	H	BB	SO	B/I
1995 Boston	8	0	5.61	110	144	23	47	1.51
1996 Pittsburgh	4	0	5.08	83	104	21	47	1.50

SMOLTZ, JOHN - TR - b: 5/15/67
Scouting: Smoltz is the hardest thrower among the Braves' fab four starters. His fastball hits 95 MPH and he also has a good splitter, a fine hard slider and a sharp curveball. He has always had great stuff, but has occasionally let poor self-confidence bring him down. In recent years, though, Smoltz has kept an even keel and thrown deep into every game, always giving his team a chance to win. For as hard as Smoltz throws, he has remarkable control; he regularly strikes out four or five times more hitters than he walks.
1998: Smoltz has the stuff to be a staff ace and might have to take over that role should the Braves be unable to re-sign their top pitchers. In any case, Smoltz will again be one of the best pitchers in baseball.
1997: Coming back to earth after his outrageous 1996 campaign, Smoltz still delivered one of the best overall pitching performances in the National League. He was fourth on the staff in ERA, but tenth in the league; he also led the league in innings pitched and was third in strikeouts and complete games.
1996: Excellent health, excellent self-confidence and excellent run support let Smoltz breakout with a Cy Young season. He pitched only a little bit better than he had in some previous seasons but with spectacular results, winning 24 of his 35 starts. Everything came together for him as he finally realized his great potential.

	W	SV	ERA	IP	H	BB	SO	B/I
1995 Atlanta	12	0	3.18	192	166	72	193	1.24
1996 Atlanta	24	0	2.94	253	199	55	276	1.00
1997 Atlanta	15	0	3.02	256	234	63	241	1.16

SNYDER, JOHN - TR - b: 8/16/74
A mid-round, 1992 draft pick, Snyder came to the White Sox as part of their Jim Abbott/Bill Simas trade in 1995. He doesn't throw hard, but the White Sox still like him in spite of disappointing results above A-ball (combined 7-10, 5.25 ERA in 23 Double-A appearances since 1995.) He spent part of the '95 season on the disabled list and should be at Triple-A in 1998.

SNYDER, MATT - TR - b: 7/7/74
Snyder posted a good record last year as the closer with the Orioles Double-A club. He has a good strikeout rate with good control. Oriole player development director Syd Thrift says "This kid has the right makeup for a closer. He's a real bulldog who takes it personally if somebody gets a hit off him." Triple-A will be a good test of Snyder's skills and, if he pitches well, he will have a shot at making the Orioles.

SOBKOVIAK, JEFF - TR - b: 8/22/71
Acquired in a spring-training trade with Colorado, Sobkoviak set a Class A High Desert franchise record for victories with 14 last year. His good location helps offset average stuff.

SODERSTROM, STEVE - TR - b: 4/3/72
A former early-round draft pick, Soderstrom spent the year at Triple-A Phoenix where he started 14 games out of 31 total appearances. He really took a "Giant" step backwards following solid, if unspectacular advances through the San Francisco chain between '94 and '96. Last year, his second season in Triple-A, he allowed a less-than-stellar 143 hits over 106.1 innings with an ERA of 6.52. Soderstrom must get it together in 1998 if he wants to have a shot at cracking a major league rotation.

SODOWSKY, CLINT - TR - b: 7/13/72
Scouting: Sodowsky failed as a starter in Detroit but showed a live arm last season as a reliever with Pittsburgh. Sodowsky's fastball reaches 93 MPH and his changeup is superb, tailing away from righthanded hitters. Sodowsky is still working on his slider, a pitch he needs to combat lefthanders.
1998: Sodowsky was taken by the Diamondbacks with plans to use him as a middle reliever. The Pirates thought they would eventually like to convert Sodowsky back into a starter once he gains command of a breaking pitch. That likely won't happen this season.
1997: Sodowsky began last season with the Pirates' Triple-A Calgary farm club after a rocky spring, including walking home the winning run in an exhibition game against Kansas City when he was called for going to his mouth with a 3-0 count on the batter. Sodowsky was racked at Calgary but pitched rather effectively after being promoted to Pittsburgh in late-April. However, he was shaky in tight situations.
1996: Sodowsky began the year in Detroit's starting rotation, one of the worst groups in baseball history. He eventually shuttled back and forth between the Tigers and Triple-A Toledo before being traded to Pittsburgh at the end of the season.

	W	SV	ERA	IP	H	BB	SO	B/I
1995 Detroit	2	0	5.01	23	24	18	14	1.80
1996 Detroit	1	0	11.84	24	40	20	9	2.49
1997 Pittsburgh	2	0	3.63	52	49	34	51	1.60

SPARKS, STEVE - TR - b: 7/2/65
Scouting: Sparks was a member of the Milwaukee rotation only a couple of seasons ago after developing an effective knuckler. But, an elbow problem in spring training last season puts his career in jeopardy. If he can regain the knuckler, and control it, Sparks can pitch in the big leagues.
1998: It's up in the air for Sparks, depending on how he recovers from his surgery. The Brewers liked him before the injury.
1997: Sparks injured his elbow in a spring training game and never threw a pitch the rest of the season.
1996: Sparks began the season in the starting rotation, but was demoted to Triple-A after struggling with his control. He spent the off-season as a pitching coach in Australia.

	W	SV	ERA	IP	H	BB	SO	B/I
1995 Milwaukee	9	0	4.63	202	210	86	96	1.47
1996 Milwaukee	4	0	6.60	88	103	52	21	1.76

SPEIER, JUSTIN - TR - b: 11/6/73
Speier has been used as a closer in the low minors during his first few professional seasons, but he doesn't have the ability to be a closer against more experienced hitters. He had some success in the low minors, but he was coming out of college and could overmatch the younger batters he was facing. The Cubs put him at Double-A Orlando for the 1997 season and he was overmatched by the better hitters he faced in the Southern League. He's nothing more than an organizational player at this point.

SPOLJARIC, PAUL - TL - b: 9/24/70
Scouting: As Spoljaric's mid-90s fastball and location con-

tinue to improve, so do his prospects for an important role. He signed with Toronto as an undrafted free agent in 1989 after playing college ball in Canada, his native land. Spoljaric also has a slider and a big curveball.

1998: Early speculation was that Spoljaric would be added to a Mariners' rotation that already includes three established lefty starters. If he doesn't make the starting rotation, though, Spoljaric would make an ideal lefty set-up man in the bullpen, particularly if he displays slightly better control.

1997: Spoljaric grabbed a share of the Blue Jays' closer job before being traded to Seattle with Mike Timlin in the Jose Cruz, Jr. deal. Spoljaric continued to fan batters at an accelerated pace with the Mariners. He held opponents to a .236 batting average and permitted just four homers in 70.2 innings.

1996: Spoljaric broke into the majors for good with Toronto, which made him a starter early in his career but converted him to short relief as he rose in their chain. He had trouble early in the season, then spent a few weeks on the disabled list, only to return and pitch better over the last month of the season.

	W	SV	ERA	IP	H	BB	SO	B/I
1996 Toronto	2	1	3.08	38	30	19	38	1.29
1997 two teams	0	3	3.69	71	61	36	70	1.37

SPRADLIN, JERRY - TR - b: 6/14/67

Scouting: Longtime minor-leaguer Spradlin has a hard, but straight, fastball, a mediocre breaking-ball repertoire and solid control. He also has durability to pitch several days in a row. However, despite his 90-MPH fastball, he leaves too many pitches up in the strike zone. When forced into a primary set-up relief role last year his inability to get a strikeout and too many high fastballs resulted in several big innings. A mechanical adjustment adding movement to his fastball would enhance Spradlin's effectiveness.

1998: Spradlin proved capable of handling a major league job last year, but should have a lesser role in 1998. Other veteran relievers are healthy again and will push Spradlin back into middle-relief, a role far more suited to his abilities. He'll pitch less frequently but for longer outings and should be more successful.

1997: Every time you looked into the Phillies' bullpen, Spradlin was warming up. He ranked among league leaders in appearances, and often served as a reliable bridge from the starters to Ricky Bottalico. Though he was generally used for one inning per appearance, he was capable of stretching to two innings.

1996: Spradlin closed games and also served as a spot starter at Triple-A Indianapolis in the Reds' chain. His control was exceptional, and he held righthanders to a .206 batting average.

	W	SV	ERA	IP	H	BB	SO	B/I
1997 Philadelphia	4	1	4.74	82	86	27	67	1.38

SPRINGER, DENNIS - TR - b: 2/12/65

Scouting: The knuckleballer has turned a corner in his career, shedding the career-minor leaguer tag and establishing himself as a major league pitcher. He's a typical knuckleballer — much of the time, Springer has no idea where the pitch is going — but he's showed the ability to fill a variety of key roles for the Angels. Manager Terry Collins gave Springer the opportunity to become a starter and he seized it.

1998: Springer was not a lock to return to the starting rotation with the Angels, but he looked like a starter on paper after the Devil Rays drafted him. If he doesn't make the rotation at first, he'll be near the head of the line if there's an injury. However, he has to show that he's less vulnerable to giving up the home run ball.

1997: Springer struggled early in a relief role, but had become a vital member of the starting staff the second half. He bailed the Angels out of some tough scrapes when other pitchers were injured, once pitching on two day's rest.

1996: Springer showed for the first time he could produce in the majors consistently as he was given the opportunity to do so in the middle of the season.

	W	SV	ERA	IP	H	BB	SO	B/I
1995 Philadelphia	0	0	4.84	22	21	9	15	1.34
1996 California	5	0	5.51	94	91	43	64	1.42
1997 Anaheim	9	0	5.18	195	199	73	75	1.40

SPRINGER, RUSS - TR - b: 11/7/68

Scouting: Springer is a hard thrower who has been used interchangeably as a starter and reliever in his six-year career with four different organizations. He has been more effective in relief and he was used exclusively in that role by Houston in 1997. He has a fastball that consistently reaches 94 MPH but his other pitches are not good enough for him to be successful as a starter.

1998: Springer has shown that he can pitch effectively in a set-up role. He should fill that role again in 1998, this time for the expansion Devil Rays. Springer has the stuff to be a highly-effective set-up man.

1997: Springer had his best major league season in 1997 despite a three-week stint on the disabled list with a lower back strain. He struck out 74 batters in 55.1 innings, one of the best ratios in the major leagues.

1996: Springer had a disappointing 3-10 season in Philadelphia as a swingman between the bullpen and the starting rotation.

	W	SV	ERA	IP	H	BB	SO	B/I
1996 Philadelphia	3	0	4.66	96	106	38	94	1.50
1997 Houston	3	3	4.23	55	48	27	74	1.36

STANDRIDGE, JASON - TR - b: 11/9/78

The Devil Rays took a gamble with the final selection of the first round of the 1997 draft by taking Standridge; he was set to go to Auburn as a quarterback on a football scholarship. Instead he signed for $700,000 and spent last year at Rookie League St. Petersburg. His ERA was 3.59 and he struck out nearly a batter per inning while surrendering less than a hit per inning.

STANIFER, ROBBY - TR - b: 3/10/72

Scouting: Stanifer is a finesse pitcher with an average major league fastball and an assortment of breaking pitches. He has risen steadily through the minor-league ranks because of his ability to consistently throw strikes — he has walked two batters per nine innings during his pro career. However, he must throw the ball consistently on the black to achieve against higher level hitters, something he did not do at Triple-A and in the majors with the Marlins last year. He is a fringe major leaguer who is unlikely to ever log as much big-league time as he did in 1997.

1998: Despite pitching 36 games for the Marlins last year, Stanifer is a longshot to make the club in 1998. The righthander doesn't have the stuff to pitch the late innings, nor the stamina to be a long man. He'll be a Triple-A insurance policy in the

intermediate term.
1997: Stanifer started 1997 at Triple-A Charlotte, and graduated into a major league middle-relief role due to the struggles and eventual trades of Rick Helling and Mark Hutton. Stanifer's control wasn't nearly as good in the majors as it had been in the minors; he often fell behind hitters, had to deliver room-service fastballs, and gave up nine homers in 45 innings.
1996: Stanifer was used as a reliever for the first time, and fashioned a 65-to-18 strikeout-to-walk ratio in 83 innings as a set-up man splitting the season between Class A and Double-A.

STANTON, MIKE -TL - b: 6/2/67
Scouting: Stanton's biting slider is difficult on lefthanded hitters and his fastball is better than average — it's an effective weapon against righthanded hitters. He's a former closer (Atlanta - 1993), used to pitching in tight situations. He's durable (145 appearances the last two years) and has recorded 48 holds in the last two seasons, among the best in the game.
1998: Stanton is signed through 1999. He will continue as a top set-up man in the Yankee bullpen.
1997: Stanton began the 1997 season with a low profile in the Yankee bullpen, but by the All-Star break had teamed with Jeff Nelson to give New York a dependable set-up combination. He was exceptional against both lefthanders and righthanders, and held lefties to a .159 batting average.
1996: Stanton was again traded into a pennant race, this time going from Boston to the Rangers. He was his usually effective self for both clubs, serving as a top lefty set-up man in both bullpens.

	W	SV	ERA	IP	H	BB	SO	B/I
1995 Atlanta	1	1	5.59	19	31	6	13	1.91
1995 Boston	1	0	3.00	21	17	8	10	1.19
1996 Boston	4	1	3.66	78	78	27	60	1.34
1997 New York AL	6	3	2.56	67	50	34	70	1.26

STEENSTRA, KENNIE - TR - b: 10/13/70
Steenstra is on the fast road to nowhere in the Cubs organization. He spent his third straight year at Triple-A Iowa in 1997, but he hasn't received the first nibble at the big leagues, which is a good indication of what the Cubs think of his ability. He's 27 years old and, despite an outstanding amateur career at Wichita State and a short stint with the U.S. national team, he's not a prospect at all, primarily because he doesn't throw hard.

STEIN, BLAKE - TR - b: 8/3/73
The Athletics acquired Stein from the Cardinals' farm and shipped him to Double-A Huntsville in late-1997. Stein has a decent fastball but not enough reliable off-speed stuff to set it up. He will start 1998 at Double-A again. His ERA in seven starts for Huntsville was 5.71.

STEPH, ROD - TR - b: 8/27/69
Steph has been in the minors for seven years, and the Orioles are his fourth organization. Last year, he was the closer in Triple-A, posting a good record and averaging more than one strikeout per inning. The Orioles have a solid bullpen, so Steph's best chance of making the majors is with another organization.

STEPHENSON, GARRET - TR - b: 1/2/72
Scouting: Stephenson is a sinker/slider pitcher with above-average control who has significantly matured during the past two seasons. He has always posted solid strikeout-to-walk ratios, but it wasn't until recently that he managed to consistently get ahead of hitters. Stephenson's quick delivery gives baserunners difficulty.
1998: Stephenson has earned a major league rotation job. With the Phillies he will be a third or fourth starter and should give them six or seven useful innings each start.
1997: Stephenson got off to a slow start at Triple-A Scranton, but injuries necessitated an early-season recall to Philadelphia. He surprised many with 12 strikeouts in his first start and had few bad starts along the way. It was assumed he would struggle in his second time around the league, but he ably adjusted to remain effective. Poor run support prevented him from having a better won-lost record.
1996: Stephenson was unimpressive at Triple-A Rochester in the Orioles' system, catching too much of the plate with his average fastball and serving up eight homers to lefthanded batters in only 179 at-bats. He was included in the trade-deadline deal that brought Calvin Maduro to the Phillies in exchange for Todd Zeile.

	W	SV	ERA	IP	H	BB	SO	B/I
1997 Philadelphia	8	0	3.15	117	104	38	81	1.21

STEVENS, DAVE - TR - b: 3/4/70
Scouting: Stevens can get his fastball into the low 90's but at times it can be too straight and hittable. He's given up on throwing his average slider and is now working with a split-fingered fastball instead. Stevens is a good athlete and holds runners pretty well for a righthander.
1998: If he develops some control at the major league level, Stevens has a chance to be a versatile part of a major league bullpen. He is now a long relief/set-up pitcher but he could also handle closer duty for brief stints when a team is in a bind.
1997: Stevens pitched with the Cubs, the team that originally drafted him in 1989, and also made a brief appearance at Triple-A Iowa; he was used sparingly by the Cubs, but he still managed to surrender an enormous amount of hits and walks in that brief time.
1996: Stevens opened the season as the Twins' closer and converted his first five opportunities. But that was his high point as a stopper and he was relieved of his closer duties in mid-July. Two days later he punched a locker after another tough relief outing and when he came back off of the DL he was a set-up man only.

	W	SV	ERA	IP	H	BB	SO	B/I
1995 Minnesota	5	10	5.07	65	74	32	47	1.61
1996 Minnesota	3	11	4.66	58	58	25	29	1.43
1997 Chicago NL	1	0	9.20	32	54	26	29	2.48

STEVENS, KRIS - TL - b: 9/19/77
Scouting: Stevens is a curveball specialist whose average fastball seems much harder when it is set up by his off-speed stuff. He has excellent mound savvy for such a youngster, but requires extreme precision to be effective. His confidence waned after a promotion to higher Class A Clearwater in 1997; he was less aggressive early in the count. He'll start 1998 back at Clearwater after being one of the league's youngest pitchers last year. Refining his precision is the key for Stevens; since he'll never be a power pitcher he has to hit spots, change

speeds and get ahead of hitters by throwing strikes low in the zone.

STEVENSON, JASON - TR - b: 8/11/74
Although he allows too many hits, he could develop into a reliable starter down the road. He is at least two or three years away from making an impact in the majors. Stevenson allows too many hits.

STEWART, RACHAAD - TL - b: 10/8/74
Acquired two years ago in the deal that sent Kent Mercker to Baltimore, Stewart has been beset by arm and shoulder miseries, limiting him to just 13 starts in 1996 and just six appearances last year. Stewart has above-average velocity for a lefty, but his off-speed stuff hasn't been sharp. At one time he may have been destined for a major league bullpen but all bets are off until Stewart can fully regain his health.

STIDHAM, PHIL - TR - b: 11/18/68
Stidham's career has taken a turn for the worse ever since a big-league appearance with the Tigers in 1994. Last year he pitched for the Rockies at Triple-A Colorado Springs. He had a 5-2 record which is almost inexplicable considering he allowed 55 hits and 26 walks in 36.1 innings of work. He's not prepared to help a major league club right now.

STONE, RICKY - TR - b: 2/28/75
Stone had shown signs of being able to blossom right out of high school, but his development has been a little slower than anticipated, perhaps largely because he hasn't developed much physically since he left high school in 1994. Nevertheless, Stone has shown flashes of brilliance with good command and an average fastball that he consistently throws for strikes. Stone will always be a finesse type, but he has a chance to make it in the majors as a middle reliever.

STOTTLEMYRE, TODD - TR - b: 5/20/65
Scouting: He's getting better as he gets older. Though Stottlemyre may never be an 18-game winner, he's a veteran who loves to battle and still can reach into a pretty fair arsenal for a low-90s fastball and strikeout-collecting split-finger pitch to go with a deceptively strong curveball and changeup. Consistency and uncommon competitive fire might be his key weapons now.
1998: He probably will be one of baseball's most effective fourth starters and could be a 15-game winner if only because of the matchups he'll see. History says he'll work from 170 to 220 innings and rank among the league's top ten in strikeouts, though at age 32 he has to maintain his physical condition better than he's ever had to before.
1997: For the middle third of the season, Stottlemyre was one of the better pitchers in the league though he frequently suffered from inadequate run support. His control was marvelous and he ran off a string of low-hit games. A chance at a third consecutive 14-victory season disappeared when he went on the shelf with arm fatigue that he thinks was solved with a new conditioning program.
1996: Still benefiting from the tutelage of pitching coach Dave Duncan, who turned his career around with Oakland, Stottlemyre worked a career-high 223.1 innings and led the Cardinals in complete games and strikeouts.

	W	SV	ERA	IP	H	BB	SO	B/I
1995 Oakland	14	0	4.55	209	228	80	205	1.47
1996 St. Louis	14	0	3.87	223	191	93	194	1.27
1997 St. Louis	12	0	3.88	181	155	65	160	1.22

STULL, EVERETT - TR - b: 8/24/71
Scouting: Stull is one of those guys that looks great on the mound. He has the perfect pitcher's body, throws his fastball as high as 97 MPH and also has a curveball, slider and changeup. Then he throws the ball and it's a different story. Stull has no idea where his pitches are going and shows no signs of gaining command of them.
1998: The Expos, frugal to begin with, plan to really be on the cheap this season. That means Stull will be given a chance to make the rotation in spring training. Considering he hasn't proven capable of getting Triple-A hitters out, it should be quite an adventure if he starts the season with the Expos.
1997: Stull made a few early-season appearances with the Expos and was overmatched. He didn't do any better in his second go-around at Triple-A Ottawa, despite being highly touted by the Montreal organization.
1996: Stull started off well at Double-A Harrisburg then was promoted to Ottawa, where International League hitters treated him like a batting practice pitcher.

STURTZE, TANYON - TR - b: 10/12/70
Sturtze is a decent Triple-A pitcher whose stuff just isn't good enough to get major league hitters out. Last season, he didn't have much luck with Triple-A hitters either, going 8-6 with a 5.10 ERA.

	W	SV	ERA	IP	H	BB	SO	B/I
1997 Texas	1	0	8.26	33	45	18	18	1.93

SULLIVAN, SCOTT - TR - b: 3/13/71
Scouting: A younger version of Stan Belinda, Sullivan features a sinking fastball and slider. His sidearm delivery is tough on righthanded hitters, and his strikeout rate and control make him an ideal set-up man.
1998: Sullivan will continue to hold a set-up role for the Reds in 1998, although he is not likely to expand his role.
1997: Called up in May, Sullivan pitched surprisingly well for the Reds, posting a strikeout per inning with decent control. The only negative was a vulnerability to the long ball.
1996: Despite a desperate need for pitching help at the major league level, the Reds kept Sullivan at Triple-A Indianapolis for most of the season where he was groomed for a set-up role and pitched well.

	W	SV	ERA	IP	H	BB	SO	B/I
1997 Cincinnati	5	1	3.24	97	79	30	96	1.12

SUPPAN, JEFF - TR - b: 1/2/75
Scouting: Suppan has just an average fastball, and tends to get it up in the zone, which can make his job difficult. He has a good feel for pitching and throws his three other solid, but not spectacular, pitches for strikes. He has been compared to Greg Maddux, but he does not get groundballs like Maddux does, and that is a huge difference. Suppan has a good head for pitching and needs to find a way to keep the ball down and in the ballpark.
1998: With his youth a big positive, Suppan has a chance to do better than any of the pitchers taken in the 1992 expansion draft. But he has not pitched well so far in the majors, and if he

continues to struggle, he could eventually be passed over by some other young pitchers with good arms.

1997: Suppan, who came into the season with some concerns about his elbow, proved he was healthy, but did not pitch well. The Red Sox babied him, limiting his innings — even in games in which he was pitching well — and his starts.

1996: Suppan had a standout season for Triple-A Pawtucket, going 10-6 with a 3.22 ERA, but struggled in Boston and eventually hurt his elbow in a late-season appearance.

	W	SV	ERA	IP	H	BB	SO	B/I
1995 Boston	1	0	5.96	22	29	5	19	1.50
1996 Boston	1	0	7.54	22	29	13	13	1.89
1997 Boston	7	0	5.69	112	140	36	67	1.57

SUTHERLAND, JOHN - TR - b: 10/11/68

This veteran minor leaguer and alumnus of the Hawaiian Winter League got into 26 games for the Yankees Triple-A Columbus team in 1996, producing a 2.74 ERA from the bullpen. In an organization with less pitching depth, he could have been given a better shot at a major league trial.

SUZUKI, MAKATO - TR - b: 5/31/75

Scouting: Suzuki has seldom delivered on the promise he showed scouts when throwing a 98-MPH fastball during free-agent workouts in 1993. He missed most of the 1994 and 1995 seasons with right shoulder and elbow tendinitis.

1998: Suzuki appears to need another year of seasoning, although considering the shape of the Mariners' relief corps, he could break through for a longer major league stint.

1997: Location and command troubles plagued Suzuki in his first extended time at Triple-A. He had more walks (64) than strikeouts (63) in 83.1 innings at Tacoma, splitting time between the rotation and the bullpen; he was 4-9 with a 5.94 ERA in 32 games.

1996: Suzuki harnessed his fastball in Double-A Port City after missing most of the previous two years with arm injuries. He earned his first major league appearance, although he allowed three runs in his 1.1 innings of work. Suzuki was unimpressive in 13 appearances (two starts) at Tacoma, going 0-3 with a 7.25 ERA.

SWARTZBAUGH, DAVE - TR - b: 2/11/68

Scouting: Swartzbaugh doesn't have an above-average pitch and it shows in his performance. He gets by in the minors with good location, but doesn't have enough velocity or movement to fool big-league hitters.

1998: Swartzbaugh doesn't figure in the Cubs plans for the future. He might crack their bullpen as a long reliever and spot starter, but if he's a regular member of their starting rotation it will be because they absolutely, positively couldn't find anyone else.

1997: Swartzbaugh spent most of the year in the minor leagues. He had a decent year for Triple-A Iowa, but bombed in his two starts with the Cubs. He was used as a long reliever at Iowa, and that seems to be his limit.

1996: Swartzbaugh split time between Iowa and Chicago. The Cubs decided to give him another shot as a starter after he was exclusively a reliever for three seasons, and he pitched well enough at Iowa to earn a few starts in Chicago; but he was horrible with the Cubs.

	W	SV	ERA	IP	H	BB	SO	B/I
1996 Chicago NL	0	0	6.38	24	26	14	13	1.67

SWIFT, BILL - TR - b: 10/27/61

Scouting: When healthy, Swift is a tough sinker/slider pitcher who gets a lot of ground balls; Swift throws a "heavy" ball. He won 21 games for the 1993 Giants; he was a good pitcher before his shoulder problems developed.

1998: There is a shortage of pitching, and Swift claims he's healthy, so he will likely get a try out in spring training; if he looks good, he'll get a contract.

1997: The Orioles signed Swift to a minor-league contract in late-August following his release by the Rockies. After pitching a couple of times in Triple-A, Swift was released; the Orioles concluding that he had not fully recovered following two years of shoulder problems.

1996: Following two shoulder surgeries in eight months, Swift tried a comeback with the Rockies, but pitched in just six games.

1995: Swift pitched 105 innings as his shoulder injures began.

	W	SV	ERA	IP	H	BB	SO	B/I
1995 Colorado	9	0	4.94	105	122	43	68	1.56
1996 Colorado	1	2	5.40	18	23	5	5	1.55
1997 Colorado	4	0	6.34	65	85	26	29	1.70

SWINDELL, GREG - TL - b: 1/2/65

Scouting: Since adding a two-seam fastball to his four-seam fastball last season, Swindell has turned his career around. Adding some still-solid stuff to a veteran's savvy has kept Swindell in the game after he nearly came to the end of his career when Cleveland released him in 1996.

1998: Swindell enters the season in the Twins' bullpen, a spot to which he became accustomed — and comfortable — in 1997. Swindell's biggest request is that he doesn't have to keep shifting from the rotation to the bullpen depending on what is needed on a given day.

1997: Invited to spring training as a non-roster player, Swindell survived the final cuts at the end of camp and then became one of the surprises of the season. He came out of the pen and went after hitters, throwing strikes and having his best success in the past couple of years.

1996: Perhaps the low point of Swindell's career, he watched September's games from his home in Houston after being released by Cleveland. It was his second pink slip of the season — Houston released him in June.

	W	SV	ERA	IP	H	BB	SO	B/I
1995 Houston	10	0	4.47	153	180	39	96	1.43
1996 Houston	0	0	7.83	23	35	11	15	2.00
1996 Cleveland	1	0	6.59	28	31	8	21	1.38
1997 Minnesota	7	1	3.58	116	102	25	75	1.10

TABAKA, JEFF - TL - b: 1/17/64

Tabaka has bounced around from organization to organization in the past few seasons because he's smart enough to be able to get minor-league hitters out, but not good enough to get big-league hitters out. He spent most of the year with Cincinnati's Triple-A farm team and stayed there despite the Reds' need for lefthanded help out of the bullpen. He posted good numbers in the minors, but that's something that he's done frequently in the past, only to fail in the majors. He'll be 34 years old on opening day and at this point it's hard to see a team keeping him around except as insurance against losing a relief pitcher to injury.

	W	SV	ERA	IP	H	BB	SO	B/I
1995 two teams	1	0	3.23	30	27	17	25	1.43
1996 Houston	0	1	6.64	20	28	14	18	2.09

TAM, JEFF - TR - b: 8/19/70
Still coming back from 1995 knee surgery, Tam worked as a set-up reliever and also made 13 starts at Triple-A Norfolk in 1997. His record (7-5, 4.68 ERA) was fair, because his control is good (14 walks in 111.2 innings) but he lacks velocity and doesn't fool anybody, giving up much more than a hit per inning.

TAPANI, KEVIN - TR - b: 2/18/64
Scouting: Tapani is one of the top pitchers in the game when he's healthy. He's got a great sinker and good control and keeps hitters off balance with a great mix of pitches. He gave up throwing the split-finger fastball after his finger injury, but added a changeup to accomplish the same results.
1998: The Cubs intend for Tapani to anchor their starting rotation and see him as a potential 20-game winner. That's not likely to happen, given the team's anemic offense, but he will win more than his share of games. His finger didn't give him any problems when he returned late in the season, so that shouldn't be of any concern.
1997: Tapani missed all of the first half of the season after having surgery on his right index finger near the end of spring training. But Tapani bounced back strong when he did return and provided the Cubs a bright spot in a season otherwise filled with darkness. He had only a couple of bad outings in his 13 starts and was close to being the type of pitcher the Cubs thought he would be when they signed him as a free agent.
1996: Tapani was a work horse for the Chicago White Sox, logging plenty of innings despite pitching in pain for much of the season. His right index finger bothered him throughout the season and limited his effectiveness because he wasn't able to use his split-finger pitch.

	W	SV	ERA	IP	H	BB	SO	B/I
1995 Minnesota	6	0	4.92	133	155	34	88	1.41
1995 Los Angeles	4	0	5.05	57	72	14	43	1.51
1996 Chicago AL	13	0	4.59	225	236	76	150	1.39
1997 Chicago NL	9	0	3.39	86	77	23	55	1.18

TATIS, RAMON - TL - b: 1/5/73
Scouting: Tatis has good stuff, but he's inexperienced. He throws pretty hard and has a decent breaking ball, but he hadn't pitched above Class A before 1997. He still needs to learn how to pitch before he'll be effective against experienced hitters.
1998: Tampa Bay grabbed five lefty pitchers among their 14 second round picks in the expansion draft. It's obvious that Tatis needs more minor-league experience, so he's probably headed for the minors to start the season, and he's likely to spend the entire season on the farm. What the Rays do with him there will signal what kind of career he might have. If they make him a starter he might have a bright future. But if they make him a reliever they'll essentially be saying they made a mistake by drafting him.
1997: There was no doubt that Tatis was overmatched against major league hitters, but the Cubs had to keep him on their roster the entire season after taking him off the Mets roster in the annual Rule V draft. He showed some promise, but he also showed he needed at least another year or two in the minors before he returns to the majors.
1996: Tatis spent his third season in A-ball after spending four seasons in rookie ball. He had decent stats, but he was used as a reliever the entire season, which isn't a good sign. The Cubs took him after the season in the Rule V draft.

TAULBEE, ANDY - TR - b: 10/5/72
Although he looks like a power pitcher (6'4" and 215 pounds) Taulbee really doesn't have much velocity. His control is fair, but when he throws his mediocre fastball for strikes, it gets hit hard, and he doesn't have command of any reliable off-speed or breaking pitch, which he will need if he hopes to advance. Taulbee pitched at Double-A and Triple-A in 1997, giving up much more than a hit per inning (5.17 ERA at Shreveport and 7.53 at Phoenix).

TAVAREZ, JULIAN - TR - b: 5/22/73
Scouting: After bouncing between starter and reliever roles for three years, Tavarez and his 95-MPH sinking fastball settled into the Giants bullpen where he established himself as the set-up man. Tavarez also throws a slider and a splitter, but it is that heavy fastball that does the trick.
1998: With all the speculation concerning which relief ace would be retained by the Giants, it was a remote possibility that Tavarez himself would move into the closer role. He has the stuff and confidence for the job. In a set-up role Tavarez will give his team an effective performance.
1997: Tavarez struggled at first as he grew accustomed to his new team and a clearer role, but for a stretch from June to August he was unhittable, logging 26 innings over which he allowed just two runs. He not only led Giants pitchers in appearances, he set a new record for San Francisco hurlers at 89 games.
1996: Tavarez hadn't been the same pitcher since struggling in the 1995 post season. He seemed to have lost confidence in his fastball and was reluctant to pitch inside during the season. By the end of the year he was reduced to a mop-up job.

	W	SV	ERA	IP	H	BB	SO	B/I
1995 Cleveland	10	0	2.44	85	76	21	68	1.14
1996 Cleveland	4	0	5.36	80	101	22	46	1.53
1997 San Francisco	6	0	3.87	88	91	34	38	1.42

TAYLOR, BILL - TR - b: 10/16/61
Scouting: Taylor has now been in the majors long enough to have outlived the human interest story of his being a 32-year-old rookie in his 1994 debut. He can be deceptive with his delivery, making his sneaky 90-MPH fastball more effective. Taylor also throws a good sinker, slider and changeup.
1998: Taylor's job as the A's closer is threatened by both the existence and skill of T.J. Mathews. He has been less than effective in the closer role, blowing 30% of his save opportunities last year. Taylor can succeed in a set-up role.
1997: After earning the closer job more by default than by skill, Taylor suffered last year. He got clobbered in spring training and the trend continued through the season, where it was painful to anticipate his arrival in a close game. The arrival of Mathews ended most of that anxiety.
1996: The long-time Braves farmhand finally got a chance for a significant major league role and fit nicely into the Oakland pen. Although he found himself in the minors to start the season, Taylor worked hard to get back to Oakland where he ultimately regained his closer job.

	W	SV	ERA	IP	H	BB	SO	B/I
1996 Oakland	6	17	4.33	60	52	25	67	1.28
1997 Oakland	3	23	3.82	73	70	36	66	1.45

TAYLOR, BRIEN - TL - b: 12/26/71
The former overall number one draft pick never recovered from

reconstructive surgery on his pitching shoulder before the 1994 season, following an off-season scuffle. He tried seven starts at Class A last year, with bad results (14.33 ERA).

TAYLOR, KERRY - TR - b: 1/25/71
Taylor's fastball is nothing special, but he can move the ball around and change speeds. He has shown slight but noticeable improvement in three years at Triple-A Las Vegas on the Padres farm. His stamina is improving as he uses fewer pitches per batter. In 1997 he threw a complete game three times, a feat that had been rare in his previous six seasons.

TAYLOR, RODNEY SCOTT - TL - b: 10/3/66
Taylor has kicked around professional baseball for nine years with his lone major league experience consisting of three poor starts for Texas in 1995. He had a good year as a middle reliever at Triple-A Calgary. However, he was also 30; not many 30-year-old middle relievers in Triple-A ever get a crack at the majors. He is an extremely bright guy, holding a chemistry degree from the University of Kansas, and figures to be one of the few who could make more money outside of baseball than in it.

TELEMACO, AMAURY - TR - b: 1/19/74
Scouting: Telemaco has a live fastball that moves. He also is composed for a pitcher of his age. He learned how to pitch in the Cubs farm system after being signed by Chicago as a 16-year-old.
1998: The Cubs still hold out high hopes for Telemaco, although injuries have set him way back from where he was a couple of years ago. He's going to have to prove once again that he belongs in the bigs before the Cubs will bring him back up. A strong spring training might be enough to convince them to put him in the rotation, but if he goes back to Triple-A he's going to have to pitch well there before he'll get another shot.
1997: Telemaco was a big disappointment for the Cubs, who were hoping he could step in and fill a spot in their rotation. Telemaco, who was rushed to the majors, again had arm problems which hindered his development, but he didn't pitch effectively when he was healthy.
1996: The Cubs brought Telemaco up in mid-season and he made quite an impression in his first few starts. However, he developed shoulder problems and wasn't the same pitcher after that. He came off the disabled list late in the season, but was used in relief to protect his shoulder.

	W	SV	ERA	IP	H	BB	SO	B/I
1996 Chicago NL	5	0	5.46	97	108	31	64	1.43
1997 Chicago NL	0	0	6.16	38	47	11	29	1.53

TELFORD, ANTHONY - TR - b: 3/6/66
Scouting: The 11-year veteran of pro ball gets by more on guile than style. His fastball and changeup are decent but he survives by changing speeds and making full use of his sharp-breaking slider.
1998: Telford figures to be a key reliever for the Expos, helping set up closer Ugueth Urbina. Telford won't impress anyone but he knows how to pitch and get out of tight spots. He is capable of the odd save on days Urbina needs a break.
1997: Telford finally spent a whole season in the majors after being the last man to make the Expos out of spring training. He had a surprisingly solid season for a journeyman, becoming Montreal's primary set-up man as Dave Veres battled inconsistency and injury problems.
1996: Telford split time between starting and relieving with Montreal's Triple-A Ottawa farm club and was relatively effective in both roles.

	W	SV	ERA	IP	H	BB	SO	B/I
1997 Montreal	4	1	3.24	89	77	33	61	1.24

TELGHEDER, DAVE - TR - b: 11/11/66
Scouting: Telgheder throws a fastball in the mid-80s, a splitter and the nominal assortment of off-speed stuff. He has to have fine location to be successful. When it works, which isn't all that often, he is tough.
1998: Telgheder will most likely get an invitation to the Oakland camp, but he is exactly the type of pitcher whom they are trying to replace. He has a reasonable arm, and is a good competitor, but he doesn't dominate major league hitters. He could be an acceptable number five starter, but going into the season all Oakland has are number five starters. They will be better served to use a younger one than Telgheder.
1997: Telgheder was no worse or better than the rest of the Oakland staff. They all struggled, on the hill, in the minors, and on the DL. In many ways, Telgheder is the poster boy for this struggle. His numbers (major and minor league) and time on the disabled list are representative of the Oakland staff over recent years.
1996: The former Mets prospect was highly effective when he got his split-finger pitch over the plate, but Telgheder has never done it consistently enough to stick around the major leagues for long.

	W	SV	ERA	IP	H	BB	SO	B/I
1995 New York NL	1	0	5.61	25	34	7	16	1.60
1996 Oakland	4	0	4.65	79	92	26	43	1.49
1997 Oakland	4	0	6.06	101	134	35	55	1.67

TESSMER, JAY - TR - b: 12/26/72
After pitching in the College World Series for the University of Miami, Tessmer began his pro career in 1995 with an 0.95 ERA while being groomed as a closer. His progress in 1996 warranted him a promotion to Double-A last year. But at Norwich in 1997, Tessmer struggled, giving up 78 hits in 62.2 innings, and posted a 5.31 ERA.

TEWKSBURY, BOB - TR - b: 11/30/60
Scouting: You know exactly what you're going to get with Tewksbury: a solid veteran who will throw strikes and keep his team in the game. Tewksbury isn't the hardest thrower, but he makes up for that with his command and location. At age 37, Tewksbury remains a valuable pitcher.
1998: The Twins picked up his option for 1998 and expect him to remain a consistent part of their rotation. While he won't be a staff ace, Tewksbury will play a valuable supporting role.
1997: The most unusual aspect of the season for Tewksbury is that he spent two stints on the disabled list. Normally the picture of health, Tewksbury hadn't had arm trouble in nearly a decade. His shoulder stiffened in July, although he got over that. Most likely, it related to a May turn on the DL when he cut his finger by slamming it in the bathroom door on the team bus.
1996: Tewksbury was in the best position for success: as the fourth starter on a San Diego staff that was good enough to win the National League West. He won five of his first six decisions.

	W	SV	ERA	IP	H	BB	SO	B/I
1995 Texas	8	0	4.58	129	169	20	53	1.46

1996 San Diego	10	0	4.31	206	224	43	126	1.29
1997 Minnesota	8	0	4.21	169	200	31	92	1.37

THEODILE, ROBERT - TR - b: 9/16/72
In his sixth season in the White Sox' organization, Theodile finally advanced to the Double-A level last year. He started the season at Class A Winston-Salem and had success, yielding less than a hit per inning. He wasn't as successful at Double-A — he was hittable and lacked control. He's running out of time to show he can advance.

THOBE, TOM - TL - b: 9/3/69
Thobe is a lanky, 6'6" lefthanded reliever with below-average stuff. He does a good job of throwing strikes and changing speeds, but he's not tough on lefties and will have a difficult time finding a major league role. Thobe had a 4.14 ERA in Triple-A in '97, but walked just 22 in 72 innings.

THOMAS, EVAN - TR - b: 6/14/74
Scouting: Thomas has only a slightly above-average fastball but has piled up the strikeouts, fanning 247 hitters in 249 professional innings — with just 78 walks. His success has come through changing speeds, good location and throwing strikes to get ahead of hitters. It has helped Thomas advance to Double-A just a year after being drafted. He started 1997 at Class A Clearwater and dominated Florida State League hitters, earning a promotion to Reading, where he'll start the 1998 season. Thomas had less success at Reading, allowing more than a hit per inning and leaving the ball too much over the plate. However, he maintained his high strikeout rate and showed excellent mound savvy. Since he doesn't throw particularly hard, Thomas does not rate as a top prospect despite his success and quick advancement. He could get to Philadelphia late in 1999 as a fifth starter or middle reliever.

THOMAS, LARRY - TL - b: 10/25/69
Scouting: Thomas is a average pitcher and borderline major leaguer. At his best he's a situational reliever; at worst he's batting practice. He lacks velocity and doesn't have outstanding stuff in any regard.
1998: Look for Thomas in a Triple-A bullpen; he could return to the majors, albeit briefly, in an expansion year.
1997: Thomas spent the season in situational relief at Triple-A Nashville, going 2-1 with a 2.81 ERA in 27 appearances.
1996: Thomas didn't get the ball over the plate enough to enjoy a great deal of success in his one-out lefty role and first full season in the majors.

	W	SV	ERA	IP	H	BB	SO	B/I
1995 Chicago AL	0	0	1.32	13	8	6	12	1.02
1996 Chicago AL	2	0	3.23	30	32	14	20	1.52

THOMPSON, JOHN - TR - 1/18/73
Thompson was a shortstop that converted to pitching in college and was drafted by the Mariners in the 45th round of the 1991 June Draft. He got his first taste of Double-A ball last year at the Mariners' Southern League affiliate in Memphis. He throws hard but had obvious control problems in Memphis. He'll probably get another shot at Double-A relief duty in 1998 and will have to harness his stuff to advance.

THOMPSON, JUSTIN - TL - b: 3/8/73
Scouting: More often than not, Thompson gets described as the best young lefthander in the American League. He can dominate games, with a good fastball and a great curve. Fingers have always been crossed, however, because at age 25, Thompson has already had a career's worth of injury trouble. The Tigers designed off-season workouts to try to keep him healthy, and in 1997 it worked.
1998: The Tigers can't ask Thompson to pitch any better than he did in 1997, when his ERA was fifth best in the American League behind some notable veteran pitchers. Really, they only ask him to stay healthy, figuring the rest will take care of itself.
1997: If the Tigers had scored a few more runs, Thompson would have been a 20-game winner in his first full year. Instead, they scored just eleven in his eleven losses, so he "only" won 15.
1996: Everything started fine, with a good two months at Triple-A Toledo, followed by two strong starts for the Tigers at the end of May and start of June. Then came another trip to the disabled list, because of bursitis in his left shoulder. Thompson returned in August, but he wasn't at full strength the rest of the year.

	W	SV	ERA	IP	H	BB	SO	B/I
1996 Detroit	1	0	4.58	59	62	31	44	1.58
1997 Detroit	15	0	3.02	223	188	66	151	1.14

THOMPSON, MARK - TR - b: 4/7/71
Scouting: Thompson is a bulldog competitor who had a great sinker and slider early in his professional career, but shoulder injuries have prevented him from reaching his potential. When he's healthy, he'll run his fastball in, setting up a sharp-breaking slider. When he doesn't have his good command, however, he cannot counter with anything off-speed.
1998: Following complicated surgery to repair a torn rotator cuff that prematurely ended his 1997 season, Thompson is not expected back until May at the earliest and most likely some time in June. He may have to spend time building up arm strength at Triple-A Colorado Springs. By the All-Star break, he could be contributing to the Rockies out of the bullpen.
1997: Thompson started off as the Rockies' number three starter and was 3-0 until the pain his right shoulder altered his mechanics. It was finally discovered in early-May that Thompson had torn his rotator cuff and surgery ended his season.
1996: In his first full big-league season, Thompson established himself as a legitimate member of the Rockies' staff. By season's end, he was the team's second-best starter, recording a team-high three complete games. He also sent word around the league that he was a tenacious competitor.

	W	SV	ERA	IP	H	BB	SO	B/I
1995 Colorado	2	0	6.53	51	73	22	30	1.86
1996 Colorado	9	0	5.30	169	189	74	99	1.55
1997 Colorado	3	0	7.88	30	40	13	9	1.78

THOMSON, JOHN - TR - b: 10/1/73
Scouting: The best of the Rockies' young pitching prospects, Thomson is tall and lanky. He not only throws 94 MPH, he has a great feel for pitching. He loves to set up hitters by busting them inside with his fastball. His changeup can be excellent, though it's not always there. He has a better-than-average slider and possesses remarkable poise. If pitching at Coors Field doesn't destroy his confidence, like it does nearly every

pitcher, he can become a consistent 15-game winner.
1998: With 26 big-league starts behind him, Thomson could emerge as one of the best young pitchers in baseball this year. He will open the season as the number two or three starter in the Rockies' rotation.
1997: After fanning 17 in his final game for Triple-A Colorado Springs, Thomson was called up to the Rockies in early-May and stayed there for good. He showed immediately his poise and toughness in his debut, losing a well-pitched 3-1 game to Curt Schilling and Philadelphia on May 11th at Veterans Stadium. His record was misleading because he often pitched in tough luck. In one stretch, Thomson was the Rockies' best starter and his two complete games, 27 starts and 166.1 innings were second on the team.
1996: After an outstanding first-half with Double-A New Haven, posting a 9-4 record and 2.86 ERA in 16 starts, Thomson was promoted in July to Triple-A Colorado Springs. His first two starts were terrific; he allowed just one run in 16 innings and won both games, but from there he struggled to make the adjustment to the thin-air environment at Sky Sox Stadium. Hurt by the long ball, Thomson finished 4-7 with a 5.04 ERA in 11 starts for Colorado Springs.

THURMAN, MIKE - TR - b: 7/22/73
Scouting: Thurman won't overpower anyone but knows how to pitch and throws strikes on a consistent basis. His fastball tops out at 88 MPH but his curveball keeps improving and he spots his changeup well.
1998: Thurman will begin the season at Triple-A Ottawa as he has limited experience at that level. However, he will likely be the first pitcher recalled if the Expos develop a need in their major league starting rotation.
1997: Thurman had a solid year at Double-A Harrisburg, struggled in four starts with Ottawa then did OK in his first taste of the majors, which consisted of five appearances with the Expos, including two starts. Thurman was hurt by walks at both Ottawa and Montreal, which goes against his history of good control.
1996: Thurman started off strong at Class A West Palm Beach, did OK in a late-season promotion to Harrisburg then opened eyes during a stint in the Arizona Fall League.

THURMOND, TRAVIS - TR - b: 12/8/73
Thurmond put it together in 1996. That's after he went AWOL after hearing he was assigned to Class-A for the third consecutive year. He's got good control and a good strikeout rate, indications of success at higher levels. He was on the Giants farm in 1997.

TILTON, IRA - TR - b: 10/27/74
Tilton has a 90-MPH fastball but hasn't been a strikeout pitcher at any level; the Phillies hope mechanical refinement can add some pop and movement to his hard stuff. In his first full pro season, Tilton allowed more than a hit per inning at lower Class A Piedmont, but had good control. his stamina was lacking; he managed just five and a half innings per start. Tilton will advance to higher Class A Clearwater but if he doesn't make the necessary adjustments he is likely to have a difficult time there. He's not among the younger pitchers at his level.

TIMLIN, MIKE - TR - b: 3/10/66
Scouting: Timlin throws a mid-90s fastball and a hard sinker, but has been a successful closer only once, in 1996, after being handed the job in Toronto. He fell out of favor in Toronto last season and went to Seattle in the Jose Cruz, Jr. deal.
1998: Timlin provides Heathcliff Slocumb with competition for the Seattle closer's role, but is an underdog after sputtering in his audition in the 1997 stretch drive.
1997: Timlin never got full control of the ace relief role in Toronto and had only ten saves, bouncing in and out of the bullpen jobs before the Blue Jays swapped him and Paul Spoljaric to Seattle. It was a disappointing season for Timlin.
1996: Timlin compiled 31 saves while blowing seven in his best season after being given the closer's job just a year after having bone chips removed from his right elbow and missing two months. Timlin was unpredictable early in the year, but finished strong, saving eight games in September.

	W	SV	ERA	IP	H	BB	SO	B/I
1995 Toronto	4	5	2.14	42	38	17	36	1.31
1996 Toronto	1	31	3.65	56	47	18	52	1.16
1997 two teams	6	10	3.22	73	69	20	45	1.22

TOLLBERG, BRIAN - TR - b: 9/16/72
Tollberg's fastball tops out in the mid-80s but his best pitch is an overhand breaking ball that he can throw for strikes at will; he has excellent control. Tollberg was a swingman for Double-A Mobile in 1997, going 6-3 with a 3.72 ERA in 31 appearances (11 starts); he struck out 108 with just 24 walks in 123.1 innings. Tollberg is expected to vie for a starting role at Triple-A Las Vegas or could become a full-time reliever in 1998.

TOMKO, BRETT - TR - b: 4/7/73
Scouting: One of the top rookie pitchers to emerge in 1997, Tomko features a four-seam fastball in the 90's, a curveball, and a changeup, and he's working on a slider. None of his pitches are overwhelming, but Tomko's unusual pitching smarts and composure for a rookie suggest solid potential. His good strikeout rate is an indicator that he is for real.
1998: Barring a disastrous spring, Tomko enters 1998 as a lock for a rotation job in Cincinnati.
1997: Tomko started the year at Indianapolis, and was called up to the Reds when Jeff Brantley went to the disabled list. Tomko moved into the rotation and was 5-1 when Ray Knight decided — for no apparent reason — to shift him to the bullpen, a move which greatly contributed to Knight's firing in late-July. One of Jack McKeon's first managerial moves was to return Tomko to the rotation, where he led the Reds in wins despite starting only 19 games.
1996: In only his second professional season, Tomko was considered one of the two best pitching prospects in the Reds system after going 11-7 and striking out over a batter per inning at Double-A Chattanooga.

	W	SV	ERA	IP	H	BB	SO	B/I
1997 Cincinnati	11	0	3.43	126	106	47	95	1.21

TORRES, SALOMON - TR - b: 3/11/72
Scouting: A wonderful arm belies Torres' passive personality; he once wanted to quit baseball in order to serve his church in the Dominican Republic. Torres was part of the Shawn Estes trade with the Giants in May, 1995. He was the losing pitcher in the Giants' season finale in 1993 which let the Braves beat them by one game. It ended a fine rookie season for Torres, but he hasn't really been the same since.
1998: Torres will still only be 26 years old on Opening Day.

With his great arm and superb fastball he may yet blossom in the majors.
1997: Torres pitched only 3.1 innings in the majors, giving up ten earned runs.
1996: Torres gave Mariners' brass reasons to believe in him by pitching 5.2 innings of shutout relief against the Yankees in May and a 7-0 shutout over Minnesota in which the Twins managed just two singles against him as he faced 24 batters over the final 7.2 innings. He was 7-10 with a 5.29 ERA in 22 games for Triple-A Tacoma.

	W	SV	ERA	IP	H	BB	SO	B/I
1995 two teams	3	0	6.30	80	100	49	47	1.86
1996 Seattle	3	0	4.59	49	44	23	36	1.37
1997 Montreal	0	0	9.81	26	32	15	11	1.83

TOTH, ROBERT - TR - b: 7/30/72
Toth throws an excellent changeup but lacks the velocity on his fastball that would make the pitch so much more effective. He nearly made the Royals out of spring training in 1996, then had a dreadful minor-league season. 1997 saw better results, but Toth is not considered a prospect because he doesn't throw hard enough for a bullpen job and lacks the repertoire needed for a starting job.

TRACHSEL, STEVE - TR - b: 10/31/70
Scouting: Trachsel is a hard thrower and has all the skills to be a successful big-league pitcher, but it remains a mystery to the Cubs why he hasn't been able to be consistently successful. The Cubs keep waiting for him to have a big season, but he hasn't been able to string enough good starts together to make that happen. Trachsel's too much of a thrower, and not enough of a pitcher, resulting in his leaving too many balls in the hitting zone.
1998: If Trachsel continues his pattern he'll have a good year this season. He was able to bounce back and have a fine year following his last bad season, and the Cubs certainly hope this will be the case. If he can forget about 1997 and concentrate on making his pitches he'll have a good year. If he puts too much pressure on himself and tries to overthrow, he won't.
1997: Trachsel was expected to be the ace of the Cubs staff, but failed once again to live up to expectations. He was erratic all season and never found the groove he needed. He gave up a bunch of hits, including one of the highest home run totals in the National League. He was sound physically and the Cubs felt all right about his mechanics, but he simply wasn't good.
1996: Trachsel had the best season of his career, but was much better in the first half of the year than the second. He was 7-5 with a 2.14 ERA in the first half and was selected to the National League All-Star team, but was 6-4 with a 4.04 ERA in the second half. He gave up 30 home runs, although 26 of those came with the bases empty.

	W	SV	ERA	IP	H	BB	SO	B/I
1995 Chicago NL	7	0	5.15	160	174	76	117	1.56
1996 Chicago NL	13	0	3.03	205	181	62	132	1.19
1997 Chicago NL	8	0	4.52	201	225	69	160	1.46

TREADWELL, JODY - TR - b: 12/14/68
Tenacity and good command have established Treadwell as a solid Triple-A pitcher and have put him in a position to make a run at the major leagues. Treadwell impressed the Dodgers by going right after hitters and spotting his fastball well. Treadwell's willing to do whatever it takes and, with more experience, could get a shot at the majors.

TRINIDAD, HECTOR - TR - b: 9/8/73
Trinidad came to the Minnesota organization as compensation for the loss of General Manager Andy McPhail to the Cubs. He pitched just 29.1 innings in the Twins' minor-league system in 1997. He had displayed fine control in the past but not at Double-A New Britain. 1998 is an important season for Trinidad to show he's still a prospect.

TRLICEK, RICK - TR - b: 4/26/69
Trlicek has been released or waived by the Phillies, Braves, Dodgers, Red Sox, Giants, and Indians. He couldn't stick with the Tigers in spring training 1996. When we wrote this, he hadn't yet been released by the Mets. He may yet find a major league role as a rubber-armed middle reliever, but it's getting late.

	W	SV	ERA	IP	H	BB	SO	B/I
1997 New York NL	3	0	5.57	32	36	23	14	1.83

TROMBLEY, MIKE - TR - b: 4/14/67
Scouting: When they finally settled on him as a reliever instead of as a starter, the Twins were on to something. Much of his success, though, related to the forkball he added in 1996 after being cut during spring training. Trombley can be wild at times, but the forkball has made him a valuable set-up man. His forkball will explode downward, a difficult pitch to hit.
1998: Trombley again will appear in the sixth, seventh and eighth innings of tight games, called on to face righthanded batters.
1997: Completing his first full season in the major leagues since 1993, Trombley consistently was a valuable member of the bullpen. He struck out 74 batters in 82.1 innings and earned the team's confidence in protecting leads.
1996: He started the year vying for a spot in the rotation, failed and was cut during spring training. It was the best thing to happen to him. Upset to the point that he nearly quit baseball, Trombley wound up learning the forkball at Triple-A Salt Lake and perfecting it.

	W	SV	ERA	IP	H	BB	SO	B/I
1995 Minnesota	4	0	5.62	97	107	42	68	1.53
1996 Minnesota	5	6	3.01	68	61	25	57	1.26
1997 Minnesota	2	1	4.37	82	77	31	74	1.31

TROUTMAN, KEITH - TR - b: 5/29/73
Troutman had an excellent season as a middle reliever at Double-A Reading. His velocity is unspectacular, but he has a rubber arm capable of pitching three or four times per week for a couple innings each time. His control was better than ever in 1997, and his pitches seemed to have more movement, resulting in a career-best strikeout-per-inning ratio. Troutman is likely to graduate into a similar role at Triple-A Scranton in 1998, and could advance to a middle-innings job in Philadelphia should injuries again strike the parent club. Troutman won't have a big major league future; he's more likely to be on the fringe.

TURRENTINE, RICH - TR - b: 5/21/71
Turrentine worked as the closer for Double-A Binghamton last year. He needs to develop better control, but still has a powerful arm. He posted 14 saves but had a dismal 5.06 ERA,

the result of walking nearly a batter per inning. Finding better control is easier than finding added velocity, so there is hope.

TWEEDLIE, BRAD - TR - b: 12/9/71
Tweedlie has a fastball that comes in at 95 MPH or better. The problem is he can't control where it goes. He came to the Boston organization in a '96 trade which sent Kevin Mitchell to the Reds, and pitched well as a closer in A-ball, as he made a mechanical adjustment and threw strikes for the first time in his career. However, he reverted back to his wild ways in Double-A last season, walking 44 in 58 innings and striking out just 30. Is he a prospect? Reportedly, Double-A pitching coach Al Nipper was let go by Boston for insisting that he is not.

TWIGGS, GARY - TL - b: 10/15/71
Twiggs doesn't really have much to offer. He's old for his level, isn't a power pitcher, and hasn't done anything to show that he has much of a future. Last year was his second at Double-A Orlando and he didn't make any progress. In fact, he took several steps back and probably eliminated himself once and for all from big-league consideration. He's an organizational player now, if he still has a job at all this season.

URBANI, TOM - TL - b: 1/21/68
The veteran lefthander pitched well in middle relief during the second half of last season for Montreal's Triple-A Ottawa farm club after being released by Texas' Triple-A Oklahoma City affiliate. Urbani showed flashes of being an effective reliever during parts of four seasons with St. Louis in 1993-96. He'll be 30 years old this season but is lefthanded, so there's always a chance he can get back to the majors in the right situation. He could even pitch well.

	W	SV	ERA	IP	H	BB	SO	B/I
1995 St. Louis	3	0	3.70	82	99	21	52	1.45
1996 Detroit	2	0	8.37	23	31	14	20	1.94

URBINA, UGUETH - TR - b: 2/15/74
Scouting: The Expos switched Urbina from starter to reliever late in the 1996 season and that proved to be a good move. Urbina's problem as a starter was he could never develop an off-speed pitch to complement his 95-MPH fastball and darting slider. As a short reliever, he no longer needs to worry about a changeup and has settled into a comfort zone.
1998: Urbina goes into the season as the Expos' unquestioned closer. Urbina seems to thrive in the pressurized situations of the late innings and should only get better after having a year of closing under his belt.
1997: Urbina had arthroscopic elbow surgery in January but was ready by opening day. He quickly emerged as one of the top closers in the National League, pushing all-time saves leader Lee Smith out of the job with the Expos before spring training ended.
1996: Urbina began the year with Triple-A Ottawa and did so-so in 17 starts with the Expos. Montreal switched him to the bullpen in late-August and he quickly adapted and flourished in his new role.

	W	SV	ERA	IP	H	BB	SO	B/I
1995 Montreal	2	0	6.17	23	26	14	15	1.71
1996 Montreal	10	0	3.71	114	102	44	108	1.28
1997 Montreal	5	27	3.78	64	52	29	84	1.26

URSO, SAL - TL - b: 1/19/72
Urso is being groomed as a lefty situational specialist. He advanced to Triple-A Tacoma in 1996 and had a fine season. He struggled last year with Triple-A Columbus, giving up 59 hits in 45.2 innings with a 4.73 ERA. Since Urso doesn't throw hard, he won't be a big strikeout pitcher or get a chance to close games once he gets to the majors.

VALDES, ISMAEL - TR - b: 8/21/73
Scouting: When healthy, Valdes is arguably the Dodgers' best starting pitcher, and they have more than their fair share of good ones. He has four good pitches: a sinking fastball that tops 90 MPH, a hard overhand curveball, another curveball with a sweeping three-quarters motion, and a straight changeup. When he's on, he's simply dominant.
1998: The 24-year-old Valdes will continue to be one of the best starting pitchers in baseball. He doesn't need to change or improve anything, but he probably will.
1997: Although he had his first losing record, Valdes pitched about as well as Greg Maddux. A strained hamstring put Valdes on the DL before the All-Star break. When he came back, he was the same excellent pitcher as always. The Dodgers' bullpen was responsible for Valdes' poor record. In the final two months, Valdes averaged 7.15 innings per start with a 2.17 ERA over eleven starts but his record was just 4-2.
1996: At age 22, Valdes showed velocity, poise, durability, and winning ways with his superb performance. The offensive explosion of 1996 never bothered him.

	W	SV	ERA	IP	H	BB	SO	B/I
1995 Los Angeles	13	1	3.05	197	168	51	150	1.11
1996 Los Angeles	15	0	3.32	225	219	54	173	1.21
1997 Los Angeles	10	0	2.65	197	171	47	140	1.11

VALDES, MARC - TR - b: 12/20/71
Scouting: Valdes failed as a starter because he was tentative with his mediocre fastball, above-average slider and changeup. However, moved to a relief role last season, Valdes was a different pitcher. He became an aggressive pitcher, showed more life on his fastball, and was no longer scared to challenge hitters.
1998: The Expos have thought about moving Valdes back into the starting rotation but instead will use him again in middle relief. Valdes is much better suited to the bullpen as he comes into the games and goes after hitters. As a starter, he tended to think too much and worried more about pacing himself than getting people out.
1997: Claimed off waivers from Florida the previous winter, Valdes was a pleasant surprise for Montreal. They expected him to be a possible fifth starter but he wound being a valuable reliever, part of the bridge between the starters and closer Ugueth Urbina.
1996: Valdes, Florida's first-round draft pick in 1993 from the University of Florida, was great at Double-A Portland but horrible at Triple-A Charlotte and with the Marlins. Florida finally gave up on him at the end of the season, dropped him from the 40-man roster and lost him to Montreal on a waiver claim.

	W	SV	ERA	IP	H	BB	SO	B/I
1996 Florida	1	0	4.81	48	63	23	13	1.78
1997 Montreal	4	2	3.13	95	84	39	54	1.29

VALDEZ, CARLOS - TR - b: 12/26/71
Valdez has good stuff: a plus, 90-MPH fastball and a sharp slider. But he tends to tire easily and has always been inconsistent with his command and control. Valdez will continue to get chances in Triple-A because of his stuff, but it looks more and more unlikely that he'll get it together long enough to have any significant impact in the majors.

VALENZUELA, FERNANDO - TL - b: 11/1/60
The major league road might have ended in St. Louis for the veteran Valenzuela. They traded for him from the Padres in June, but released him after five mostly brutal starts. His control was weak and his fastball didn't seem to have much left. He probably will continue looking for work, since he never officially talked about retiring.

	W	SV	ERA	IP	H	BB	SO	B/I
1995 San Diego	8	0	4.98	90	101	34	57	1.49
1996 San Diego	13	0	3.62	171	177	67	95	1.43
1997 St. Louis	2	0	4.96	89	106	46	61	1.71

VALERA, JULIO - TR - b: 10/13/68
recovering from Tommy John surgery, Valera impressed the Royals with a strong winter ball showing. A year ago he earned the last spot in the pen and proceeded to struggle.

	W	SV	ERA	IP	H	BB	SO	B/I
1996 Kansas City	3	1	6.46	61	75	27	31	1.67

VANDERWEELE, DOUG - TR - b: 3/18/70
Vanderweele actually picked up his performance a notch at Triple-A Phoenix last year, going 6-4 with a 4.59 ERA. He is not a bad pitcher at all, in fact, he has excellent control, walking just 18 over 68.2 innings, but he isn't fooling anyone either, surrendering 99 hits over the same span. Vanderweele isn't likely to have a major league future.

VAN DE WEG, RYAN - TR - b: 2/24/74
VanDeWeg seldom has all of his pitches working simultaneously. He has four quality pitches: a low-90s fastball, slider, curve and changeup. VanDeWeg was been inconsistent on his way to a 9-8 mark for Double-A Mobile in 1997; he had a 5.43 ERA in 23 starts, allowing 198 hits in 159 innings, including a club-high 20 homers. VanDeWeg will return to Mobile in 1998 and must improve on the three C's — command, control and confidence.

VANEGMOND, TIM - TR - b: 5/31/69
Scouting: VanEgmond has no special out pitch, rather he relies heavily on a two-seam fastball that he tries to do a lot with. He will cut it, run it in or out and hopes that the movement produces pop fly outs. He also mixes in a changeup and a slider but if he can't hit the corners with the two seamer he gets hit hard.
1998: VanEgmond faces a long road back. He was not a dominant pitcher to begin with and missing all of 1997 won't help.
1997: VanEgmond was expected to contend for the fifth starter role heading into spring training but pitched just one inning at Triple-A Tucson and was done for the season.
1996: Called up by the Brewers and inserted into the starting rotation after the All-Star break, VanEgmond was enjoying surprising success in July and August but when September hit the wheels fell off.

	W	SV	ERA	IP	H	BB	SO	B/I
1996 Milwaukee	3	0	5.27	54	58	23	33	1.49

VANLANDINGHAM, WILLIAM - TR - b: 7/16/70
Few pitchers saw their stock drop as far and as fast as VanLandingham. After an erratic, at best, 1996 campaign, he dropped out of the Giants' rotation last year, then was wild out of the bullpen and was sent to Triple-A Phoenix. He walked 21 there — in 17 innings — and was waived. VanLandingham was claimed by the Phillies and waived again, then returned to the Giants. He obviously has talent, so will get more chances, but he is going to have to work through his problems in the minors first before getting another shot at the majors.

	W	SV	ERA	IP	H	BB	SO	B/I
1995 San Francisco	6	0	3.67	122	124	40	95	1.34
1996 San Francisco	9	0	5.40	181	196	78	97	1.51
1997 San Francisco	4	0	4.96	89	80	59	52	1.56

VAN POPPEL, TODD - TR - b: 12/9/71
Van Poppel's career took another downturn last season when he was twice released, then picked up as a reclamation project by the Rangers. In seven late-season starts with Double-A Tulsa, Van Poppel went 3-3 with a 5.06 ERA. He seems to be getting worse instead of better, but the Rangers are willing to take a chance on a local kid, and planned to have him play winter ball under the supervision of one of their coaches.

	W	SV	ERA	IP	H	BB	SO	B/I
1995 Oakland	4	0	4.88	138	125	56	122	1.31
1996 Detroit	3	1	9.06	99	139	62	53	2.03

VANRYN, BEN - TL - b: 8/9/71
At one time VanRyn was a highly regarded prospect in the Montreal and Los Angeles farm systems. He was a sandwich pick between the first and second rounds of the 1990 draft, and had a couple of pretty good seasons in the low minors, but has been unsuccessful in any of his shots at Triple-A and hasn't been good at all the last three or four seasons. If he were righthanded he would be pitching in the beer leagues right now, and that future may arrive soon even if he is a portsider.

VAUGHT, JAY - TR - b: 12/21/71
It's fairly obvious that a pitcher has a limited upside when he allows a hit per inning while averaging less than five strikeouts per nine innings during his Class A career. Vaught was able to avoid damage at lower levels by locating pitches out of harm's way, but wasn't even entrusted with a material staff role after advancing to Double-A. Two years of mediocre middle-relief work later at that level and Vaught is likely approaching the end of his professional ride.

VAVREK MIKE - TL - 4/23/74
Vavrek emerged as a legitimate prospect in 1997, winning 12 straight decisions at Double-A New Haven. He started the season at Class A Salem, where he was 2-2 with a 2.15 ERA, then was promoted to New Haven, where he went 13-3 with a 2.46 ERA. He has a below-average fastball and it has little movement, but he still manages to break bats and get hitters out. He has great mound presence, hits his spots, and mixes speeds well. He'll likely open this season at Triple-A Colorado Springs. Vavrek has been compared to Charlie Liebrandt and Kirk Rueter.

VAZQUEZ, JAVIER - TR - b: 6/25/76
Vazquez has been nearly unhittable during the past two seasons in the Expos' farm system, playing at Class A Delmarva in 1996 and splitting 1997 between Class A West Palm Beach and Double-A Harrisburg. He has a great arm and is moving quickly enough that he may be ready for an audition in Montreal by September.

VENIARD, JAY - TL - b: 8/16/74
Veniard started the season with Class A Dunedin and, because of a 1.88 ERA over 52.2 innings, he was promoted to Double-A in mid-July. With Knoxville, he was ineffective, going 3-8 with a 5.85 ERA over 75.1 innings.

VERAS, DARIO - TR - b: 3/13/73
Scouting: When he's sharp, Veras has a sharp breaking slider and he goes after hitters inside. The problem was that he wasn't on in 1997. Even before he began experiencing groin and arm problems, his slider was hanging last spring.
1998: A stellar effort during the '96 pennant chase all but assured Veras a spot on the '97 roster despite a poor spring. He won't have that luxury this spring.
1997: Veras lost a lot of time to injuries and rehab assignments. He allowed five homers in 24.2 innings — a horrible trend that began during spring training.
1996: A former Rule V draftee, Veras won rave reviews. In 29 games at Double-A Memphis, he had a 3-1 record, with a 2.32 ERA. Moving on to Triple-A Las Vegas, Veras went 6-2 with a 2.90 ERA. He was called up during the pennant run and responded with a fine ERA over 23 appearances.

	W	SV	ERA	IP	H	BB	SO	B/I
1996 San Diego	3	0	2.79	29	24	10	23	1.17
1997 San Diego	2	0	5.10	25	28	12	21	1.62

VERES, DAVE - TR - b: 10/19/66
Scouting: Veres won't overpower anyone with an average assortment of pitches that includes a fastball, splitter and slider. However, when he's right, Veres will spot the ball in and out while racking up a fair number of strikeouts.
1998: Veres was arbitration eligible at the end of last season and the Expos could no longer afford him. Everybody needs middle relief and Veres looks like he could help a number of clubs.
1997: Veres was a big disappointment for the Expos. They expected him to be closer Ugueth Urbina's main set-up man but he often pitched poorly then missed a month of the second half with a knee injury. Veres was eventually replaced by Anthony Telford and primarily mopped up in the season's final month.
1996: Veres, acquired in a trade from Houston the previous winter, struggled mightily in the first half for the Expos but settled in as a top-flight eighth-inning reliever after the All-Star break.

	W	SV	ERA	IP	H	BB	SO	B/I
1995 Houston	5	1	2.26	103	89	30	94	1.15
1996 Montreal	6	4	4.17	77	85	32	81	1.52
1997 Montreal	2	1	3.48	62	68	27	47	1.53

VERES, RANDY - TR - b: 11/25/65
Scouting: Veres has never featured any outstanding pitch; his fastball can only hit the upper 80s and his breaking pitches lack bite. Despite some sporadic success, Veres has been sorely lacking in confidence which has hurt his ability to challenge big-league hitters.
1998: Veres will be one of seemingly hundreds of mediocre middle-innings men available on the free agent market; he may land a major league bullpen job, or might wind up back in Triple-A again.
1997: Finally washing out of an improving Tiger pen, Veres hooked on with the Royals and was, briefly, one of the few relievers that merited confidence. But Veres' own confidence waned, his pitches became more hittable, and he was eventually released by the Royals, too.
1996: Veres had a poor season in a poor Tiger bullpen; he pitched down to the level of his competition for a bullpen spot.

	W	SV	ERA	IP	H	BB	SO	B/I
1997 Kansas City	4	1	3.31	35	36	7	28	1.22

VERPLANCKE, JOE - TR - b: 5/11/75
An eighth-round pick in 1996, Verplancke has averaged more than a strikeout per inning with a 90-MPH fastball while making the jump to Class A High Desert last year.

VILLANO, MIKE - TR - b: 8/10/71
A principal in the deal to get Robb Nen from the Marlins, Villano throws absolute smoke. He was also wild last year. Coming off some wonderful pitching in 1996 — when he started the year by going 7-1 with eight saves and an ERA of 0.71 — Villano found Double-A a bit more of a challenge last year. He went 3-1 with a 6.29 ERA, allowing more than a hit per inning (41 hits in 34.1 innings). He was promoted to Triple-A and actually settled some, finishing at 5-3 with a 4.16 ERA. He looks more like a future set-up man than closer.

VILLONE, RON - TL - b: 1/16/70
Scouting: Villone can throw 90 miles per hour and has an effective changeup. His control can be a problem. He has a herky-jerky motion that can throw batters off and can be especially tough on lefthanded hitters. It also limits his fielding ability.
1998: Villone will be used in middle relief, as a lefthanded set-up man and occasional closer.
1997: Villone allowed only two runs in the last two months of the season as a middle reliever. He had better control of his fastball as the season progressed.
1996: Villone began the season with San Diego and made 21 appearances before he was included in the trade that sent Bryce Florie and Marc Newfield to Milwaukee for Greg Vaughn; he made 23 appearances for the Brewers and notched a pair of saves.

	W	SV	ERA	IP	H	BB	SO	B/I
1995 Seattle	0	0	7.91	19	20	23	26	2.22
1995 San Diego	2	1	4.21	25	24	11	37	1.36
1996 San Diego	1	0	2.95	18	17	7	19	1.33
1996 Milwaukee	0	2	3.28	24	14	18	19	1.32
1997 Milwaukee	1	0	3.42	53	54	36	40	1.71

VOSBERG, ED - TL - b: 9/28/61
Scouting: Vosberg is a lefty specialist who uses a good curveball to neutralize lefthanded hitters, and relies on the slider as his bread and butter pitch. He has as good a pickoff move as any currently active pitcher. Vosberg pitches better when he is used frequently.
1998: Vosberg has a few seasons left as a situational lefty in

a major league bullpen.

1997: Vosberg lost the lefty set-up role to Eric Gunderson, and then Scott Bailes, but proved to be useful in middle relief. Late in the season, he was traded to Florida and continued to pitch effectively there.

1996: Although basically a one-out lefty, Vosberg was effective when asked to close games (eight saves in nine chances).

	W	SV	ERA	IP	H	BB	SO	B/I
1995 Texas	5	4	3.00	36	32	16	36	1.33
1996 Texas	1	8	3.27	44	51	21	32	1.64
1997 Florida	2	1	4.42	53	59	21	37	1.51

WADE, TERRELL - TL - b: 1/25/73

Scouting: Despite spending the last two seasons with the Braves, Wade is still something of a raw prospect. His best pitch is a fastball in the low 90's, but his slider and change have not been particularly effective. He has struggled with his control throughout his career and is a question mark after rotator cuff surgery in 1997.

1998: If healthy (and the Devil Rays guessed he would be) Wade will compete for a fourth/fifth starter or swingman role in Tampa Bay, but will not be the favorite for the job if he shows any after-effects of his rotator cuff surgery. A trip back to the minors to work on his control is not out of the question.

1997: Wade started the season as the Braves fifth starter, a difficult role for an inexperienced pitcher. Bobby Cox is one of the few managers that will skip his fifth starter to keep his other starters on rotation, and it is not unusual for the Braves fifth man to not start for several weeks. Wade struggled with his control before going on the DL in June with a torn left flexor muscle. Pounded in a rehab assignment at Double-A Greenville (4.97 ERA in six starts), Wade underwent rotator cuff surgery in late-August and was out for the rest of the year.

1996: Wade established himself in the majors by pitching well mostly in long relief, and in eight late-season starts. He was overpowering at times, but his control (47 walks in 69 innings) left something to be desired.

	W	SV	ERA	IP	H	BB	SO	B/I
1996 Atlanta	5	1	2.97	69	57	47	79	1.50
1997 Atlanta	2	0	5.36	42	60	16	35	1.81

WAGNER, BILLY - TL - b: 6/25/71

Scouting: Despite his relatively small stature, Wagner is the hardest throwing lefthander in the National League, consistently reaching the high nineties with his fastball. He was a starter in his five-year minor-league career but he has been used only in relief in the majors. Opening the 1997 season as a co-closer with John Hudek, he quickly took over the job and was effective in that role all year except for a lapse in August when he struggled with his control and was 0-5 without a save. He has a sweeping curveball but he relies nearly exclusively on his fastball. On most occasions, he simply overpowers opposing batters.

1998: Wagner should be one of the top closers in the major leagues.

1997: After a taste of closing in 1996, Wagner indicated to Manager Larry Dierker that he would prefer to remain in that role. He established himself as a dominating closer in 1997. His ratio of 14.4 strikeouts per nine innings was the highest in major league history.

1996: Wagner began the season at Triple-A Tucson where he made 12 starts with a 6-2 record and an ERA of 3.28. Promoted to Houston on June 2nd when Greg Swindell was released, he began in a set-up role but quickly became a closer. He spent two weeks on the disabled list with a strained groin muscle.

	W	SV	ERA	IP	H	BB	SO	B/I
1996 Houston	2	9	2.44	51	28	30	67	1.13
1997 Houston	7	23	2.85	66	49	30	106	1.19

WAGNER, MATT - TR - b: 4/4/72

Scouting: Wagner has the kind of lanky body scouts love. His fastball routinely reaches 93 MPH, though he has yet to come up with a breaking pitch or change of pace to complement it.

1998: Wagner is expected to report to spring training healthy and ready to assume the fourth or fifth spot in the Expos rotation. Wagner struggled in his only taste of the major leagues with Seattle in 1996 and is still learning how to pitch. The Expos don't have great expectations right away and Wagner figures to have the ups and downs any young pitcher coming off arm surgery would experience.

1997: Wagner began the season on the disabled list with lower back stiffness then injured his shoulder while rehabilitating. While Wagner's back healed, his shoulder needed surgery in mid-May and he did not throw a pitch in a professional game the entire season.

1996: Wagner was outstanding with Seattle's Triple-A Tacoma farm club in just his second full major league season. However, he was hit hard during 15 starts with the Mariners and suffered a noticeable loss of confidence.

	W	SV	ERA	IP	H	BB	SO	B/I
1996 Seattle	3	0	6.86	80	91	38	41	1.61

WAGNER, PAUL - TR - b: 11/14/67

Scouting: Wagner has always seemingly had the tools to be a big winner in the majors with a 95-MPH fastball and 88-MPH slider. However, the lack of an off-speed pitch has prevented him from reaching his full potential as a starter and no one has ever had the wisdom to throw him into short relief. Wagner had reconstructive elbow surgery in August, 1996, making his future questionable.

1998: Wagner gets a fresh start this season with Milwaukee, his hometown club. He signed with the Brewers last September after being released by Pittsburgh and will compete for a spot in the starting rotation. If he doesn't make it as a starter, the Brewers will give him a shot in relief. Milwaukee manager Phil Garner has a reputation of getting the most from his players and could be the perfect match for Wagner, his confidence shaken after years of brow beatings from former Pirates manager Jim Leyland.

1997: Wagner spent most of the first half on two injury rehabilitation assignments at Double-A Carolina and had an ERA over 9.00. The Pirates called him up to the majors July 18th but released him a month later. He signed with Milwaukee, his hometown club, in September with the idea of getting healthy for '98.

1996: Wagner seemed poised for a breakthrough season just a year after leading the majors in losses. He was the surprise Opening Day starter for the Pirates and threw 6.2 shutout innings in beating the Marlins. Wagner was 3-0 before his elbow started hurting. He went on the disabled list in late-July then underwent "Tommy John" surgery a month later.

	W	SV	ERA	IP	H	BB	SO	B/I
1995 Pittsburgh	5	1	4.80	165	174	72	120	1.49
1996 Pittsburgh	4	0	5.40	81	86	39	81	1.54
1997 Milwaukee	1	0	4.50	18	20	13	9	1.83

WAINHOUSE, DAVE - TR - b: 11/7/67

Scouting: Wainhouse was once a top prospect, selected by Montreal in the first round of the 1988 draft from Washington State. Arm and back problems derailed Wainhouse's career, though, and robbed him of his once-dominating stuff.

1998: Wainhouse became a six-year free agent and wasn't likely to be retained by the Pirates. He turned 30 in the off-season and will have a hard time finding an invitation to a major league spring training camp.

1997: Wainhouse was the last man to survive the Pirates' cut in spring training but struggled mightily until being demoted to Triple-A Calgary in mid-June. He didn't pitch any better in the minors.

1996: Two years removed from missing the entire season because of back surgery, Wainhouse was leading the Southern League with 25 saves for Double-A Carolina when promoted to Pittsburgh in late-July. He then pitched mop-up relief with the Pirates for the remainder of the season.

	W	SV	ERA	IP	H	BB	SO	B/I
1996 Pittsburgh	1	0	5.70	23	22	10	16	1.38
1997 Pittsburgh	0	0	8.04	28	34	17	21	1.82

WAKEFIELD, TIM - TR - b: 8/2/66

Scouting: He's a knuckleballer, plain and simple. He will throw the fastball at times, when he needs a strike, but 95 percent of the time Wakefield throws a knuckler and says even he doesn't know where it is going. Though he will turn 31 this year, Wakefield, a converted infielder, is relatively new to this knuckler thing, and should continue to get more familiar with it in the coming years.

1998: Wakefield will have a rotation job somewhere because he can eat up innings without an awful ERA. He also saves a staff with his ability to come back and pitch on short rest at any time. He might show some improvement, but is unlikely to win any ERA titles.

1997: Wakefield was inconsistent, but ultimately mediocre. He pitched at a slightly better level than the year before, and helped the Red Sox with his ability to pitch on short rest and in relief. But he had bad stretches, too, and was demoted to the bullpen at one point.

1996: After a remarkable '95 season, Wakefield was a disappointment. He rebounded some in the second half of the season and managed to post an ERA which at least approached respectability.

	W	SV	ERA	IP	H	BB	SO	B/I
1995 Boston	16	0	2.95	195	163	68	119	1.18
1996 Boston	14	0	5.14	211	238	90	140	1.55
1997 Boston	12	0	4.25	201	193	87	151	1.39

WALKER, JAMIE - TL - b: 7/1/71

Scouting: A low-90s fastball and slurve are complemented by an excellent changeup in Walker's repertoire. He throws hard enough for a short relief role but needs better control to succeed in the majors.

1998: Now that he has passed through his Rule 5 year, Walker is likely to get some seasoning in the high minors. He may start at Triple-A Omaha with a mid-season recall once he shows more consistency.

1997: Walker was unpredictable; he had good stuff one outing, but poor command the next. It was an encouraging rookie season, but he obviously needs some polish.

1996: Walker spent his fifth season in the Astro farm system, going 5-1 with a 2.50 ERA as a middle reliever and spot starter at Double-A Jackson, then was selected in the Rule 5 draft by Atlanta and traded to Kansas City in the Michael Tucker/Jermaine Dye deal.

	W	SV	ERA	IP	H	BB	SO	B/I
1997 Kansas City	3	0	5.44	43	46	20	24	1.53

WALKER, MIKE - TR - b: 10/4/66

Walker is a former Cubs reject, which probably says everything about his ability as a pitcher. The Reds signed him in the off-season but it's hard to guess what they thought they were going to get. He spent the entire season at Triple-A Indianapolis, but the stats he posted there in no way reflect the type of pitcher he truly is. He does not have major league ability and any team that puts him in their bullpen deserves the bad performances they're sure to get.

	W	SV	ERA	IP	H	BB	SO	B/I
1995 Chicago NL	1	1	3.22	44	45	24	20	1.54
1996 Detroit	0	1	8.46	27	40	17	13	2.10

WALKER, PETE - TR - b: 4/8/69

Walker was signed by Boston during the season after proving that his surgically-repaired arm was coming back. He showed flashes of brilliance in the minors, throwing better than 90-MPH with a good slider and splitter, but was unable to sustain it, perhaps because his arm wasn't all the way back. If he continues to get healthier he has a chance to be a quality reliever in the majors because he's got good stuff.

WALL, DONNIE - TR - b: 7/11/67

Scouting: Wall has spent nine years in the Houston organization. He has a record of 83-51 for his minor-league career with an ERA of 3.51 and a strikeout-to-walk ratio of 3.4. He has been successful at every minor-league level. Despite his success, he was not considered a major league prospect, even after a 17-6 season with a 3.30 ERA in the hitter-friendly Pacific Coast League in 1995. Wall's fastball tops out at about 86 MPH and he doesn't have much of a breaking ball. His best pitch is a deceptive changeup; he succeeds with pinpoint location and by changing speeds.

1998: Expansion may create another opportunity for Wall to challenge for a major league job.

1997: Wall was a candidate for the last spot in the Houston rotation but was beaten out by Chris Holt. He started the season at Triple-A New Orleans and was recalled in late April when Sid Fernandez went on the disabled list. He made eight starts but was hit hard when he didn't have his pinpoint control and was sent back to New Orleans in June where he was successful (8-7, 3.85 ERA).

1996: After a 3-1 record with Houston in a September 1995 callup, Wall failed to make the squad out of spring training and started the season at Triple-A Tucson. He was recalled in May and enjoyed immediate success as the team won the first ten games he started. He didn't fare as well the second and third times around the league but stayed in the rotation all season.

	W	SV	ERA	IP	H	BB	SO	B/I
1995 Houston	3	0	5.55	24	33	5	16	1.56
1996 Houston	9	0	4.56	150	170	34	99	1.36
1997 Houston	2	0	6.26	42	53	16	25	1.65

WALLACE, DEREK - TR - b: 9/1/71

Scouting: Wallace was making progress, and making the

Mets happy they traded for him. He features a fastball and slider, they had added a split-fingered fastball to his repertoire, and Wallace had begun to assert himself. His confidence grew, too. It was all going in the right direction until an aneurysm was detected in his right shoulder last spring.

1998: Despite his progress and the delight they took in it, the Mets weren't certain what they had in Wallace in 1996. Now they know even less about what to expect from him. In their fondest hopes, Wallace will resume the progress he made in '96, learn from John Franco and Mel Rojas, and emerge as a late-inning force. The club still holds out hope Wallace will be the strikeout reliever it needs.

1997: It was a lost year, and nothing more. The aneurysm and the surgery to repair it denied Wallace a full spring training, and the relatively minor aches and pains — not necessarily related to the surgery — that developed after he resumed pitching denied him a chance to pitch in the big leagues. Aside from one inning in Triple-A, Wallace's season was spent in the Class A Florida State League and Gulf Coast League. He pitched a total of 16 innings in 14 games. A big asset was the trust of Bobby Valentine that Wallace earned at Norfolk.

1996: The 11th player chosen in the 1992 amateur draft — selected by the Cubs — Wallace finally made it to the big leagues 2 1/2 weeks before his 25th birthday, not particularly early for a hard-throwing righthanded pitcher. He was tied for the International League lead in saves when the Mets called him up on August 13th; he allowed 43 baserunners in 24.2 innings in New York.

	W	SV	ERA	IP	H	BB	SO	B/I
1996 New York NL	2	3	4.01	24	29	14	15	1.78

WALLACE, JEFF - TL - b: 4/12/76

Scouting: The burly reliever's calling card is a live fastball that has been clocked as high as 98 MPH and consistently hits the 94-95 range. Few lefties in all of baseball throw harder than Wallace, who is still trying to gain command of a slider because he needs a complementary pitch. Wallace missed the final nine days of last season with the Pirates because of a strained ligament in his pitching elbow, though it was not considered serious.

1998: If Wallace's elbow is healthy, he will be one of the three lefthanders Pirates manager Gene Lamont likes to keep in the bullpen; Wallace could move to the front of the lefty set-up pack. He might also get a few save opportunities whenever the Pirates need a lefty to close out a game or give closer Rich Loiselle a day off.

1997: Wallace began the season in A-ball and ended it in the major leagues. He was dominating at Class A Lynchburg then struggled at Double-A Carolina following an early-May promotion. However, Wallace had six straight scoreless relief appearances at Carolina and was promoted to Pittsburgh in late-August. Once he got to the big leagues, Wallace was nearly untouchable.

1996: In his first full professional season, Wallace was converted from starter to reliever late in the year at Class A Lansing and his career began to take off. He was one of four players traded by the Royals to Pittsburgh for Jay Bell and Jeff King at the end of the season.

WALTERS, BRETT - TR - b: 9/30/74

Scouting: The Padres like Walters, although he doesn't possess a good fastball. He does have good sink on his fastball and his slider and changeup are above average. He also goes after hitters, working inside and working quick.

1998: Walters is scheduled to continue his steady advance up the ladder at Triple-A Las Vegas, where he's expected to vie for a spot in the Stars' starting rotation.

1997: Walters was 10-7 with a 4.47 ERA at Double-A Mobile. Of his 33 appearances, 18 were in the rotation. Walters allowed only 30 walks in 145 innings against 98 strikeouts.

1996: Walters spent the entire season at Class A Rancho Cucamonga where he was 9-9 with a 4.32 ERA and walked only 39 in 135 innings against 89 strikeouts.

WARD, BRYAN - TL - b: 1/28/72

Ward got his first crack at Triple-A hitters in 1997, and it wasn't pretty. He has good control of a mid- to upper-80's fastball that is fairly straight. He requires pinpoint precision on the corners to be effective; he nibbled at the Triple-A level and paid the price. He was dropped from the 40-man roster at season's end; he is clearly behind other prospects in the eyes of Marlins' brass. Ward will bounce around the upper minor-league levels for a while simply because he's a lefty.

WARE, JEFF - TR - b: 11/11/70

Scouting: Ware's velocity has suffered in recent seasons due to arm troubles. He's now wild and hittable and that was at the Triple-A level.

1998: Ware may get another chance in Triple-A prove he's got major league stuff but it looks like it will be a longshot.

1997: For Triple-A Tucson in the Milwaukee organization, Ware tried to rebound from a disappointing 1996 season with little success. He appeared in 25 games, making 21 starts and couldn't find the plate, yielding 80 walks and striking out 69. When he did put the ball around the dish, he was hittable as he gave up more than a hit per inning.

1996: Many believed Ware would be the fifth starter for the Blue Jays in 1996 but he was not up to the job. He had no control and nothing on his pitches.

	W	SV	ERA	IP	H	BB	SO	B/I
1995 Toronto	2	0	5.47	26	28	21	18	1.86
1996 Toronto	1	0	9.09	32	35	31	11	2.05

WARREN, BRIAN - TR - b: 4/26/67

Warren is a soft-tossing, veteran minor-league reliever with excellent control. He had five wins, six saves and a 3.62 ERA for Triple-A Oklahoma City last season.

WASDIN, JOHN - TR - b: 8/5/72

Scouting: Like a lot of righthanders, especially like a lot of Red Sox righthanders, Wasdin has marginal stuff, and is hurt by putting average four-seam fastballs up in the zone. He tends to pitch best in relief when he can challenge hitters once through the order and they have difficulty timing his pitches. His off-speed pitches are nothing special, but functional.

1998: Because of his age, the Red Sox will most likely try to keep Wasdin on the staff somewhere, hoping that he improves enough to be at least a dependable pitcher out of the bullpen, or perhaps as a starter. His arm and guts are good enough that he'll stick around the majors, but it's unlikely that he'll enjoy great success.

1997: Wasdin started the season in the rotation and pitched well. But he was hurt by a lack of run support and eventually started pressing. Then he started to get hurt by the longball. He soon found himself pitching in long relief. He did a good job at times, but fell victim to the big homer all too often.

1996: After Wasdin's disappointing rookie season for Oakland, the former top draft pick was dealt to Boston for Jose Canseco.

	W	SV	ERA	IP	H	BB	SO	B/I
1995 Oakland	1	0	4.67	17	14	3	6	0.98
1996 Oakland	8	0	5.96	131	145	50	75	1.49
1997 Boston	4	0	4.40	125	121	38	84	1.28

WASHBURN, JARROD - TL - b: 8/13/74

Scouting: Washburn is similar to Scott Schoeneweis in makeup and ability, and has the same bright prospects for the future. He's a tough competitor who wants the ball all the time. He relies on a changeup, slider and curve, and is going to impress a lot of people once he gets a little more situated in professional ball. Like Schoeneweis, he's projected as having the potential to make the same rapid rise through the organization that Jason Dickson did.

1998: Washburn needs only to show he's progressing in order to stay on the fast track. He'll likely need a full season at Triple-A Vancouver to complete his preparation for the major leagues.

1997: The Angels may have been a little hasty in promoting the Washburn to Vancouver. He didn't have a great deal of success in Triple-A, but was extremely successful in Double-A, particularly when he was returned to Midland for the end of the season.

1996: Washburn enjoyed steady success at Class A Lake Elsinore and Double-A Midland as a starter and set the stage for a 15-victory season the following year.

WATSON, ALLEN - TL - b: 11/18/70

Scouting: The key player in the trade that sent switch-hitting first baseman J.T. Snow to San Francisco, Watson enjoyed mixed success in his first season in the American League. Watson showed great stuff, particularly his fastball, but was inconsistent. In order to become a top-flight starter, Watson probably has to concentrate more on the mental side of pitching. The Angels like his arm and competitiveness, but he needs to think more about what he's doing and why in order to avoid making mistakes at the wrong time.

1998: Watson will be counted on as a solid fourth starter, but needs to stop out-thinking himself and giving up home runs at an alarming rate (the two are intertwined) in order to take his game to the next level.

1997: Watson was inconsistent; going through hot and cold streaks. The Angels like his toughness and fiery competitive nature; he made his final start of the season two days after undergoing extensive oral surgery. What they don't like is when the competitiveness gets in the way of his becoming a thinking pitcher.

1996: It was the same story in San Francisco, where he was hot and cold. The Giants didn't give up on Watson, but they needed a first baseman, thus the winter trade for Snow.

	W	SV	ERA	IP	H	BB	SO	B/I
1995 St. Louis	7	0	4.96	114	126	41	49	1.46
1996 San Francisco	8	0	4.61	185	189	69	128	1.39
1997 Anaheim	12	0	4.93	199	220	73	141	1.47

WEATHERS, DAVID - TR - b: 9/25/69

Scouting: The word "promising" usually preceded Weathers' name in his years as a Blue Jays' and Marlins' prospect. The statute of limitations has run out, and Weathers heretofore must be referred to as a "journeyman". Weathers has always possessed a slightly above-average fastball with good movement, but has never developed a consistent breaking pitch. He is able to compete for six or seven innings at a time as a minor-league starter with that repertoire, but is easy pickings for major league hitters.

1998: Expansion might not be enough to get Weathers back to the major leagues this time. He remains somewhat effective against righthanded hitters, and has an outside shot to resurface in a situational role, though not with the Indians.

1997: Weathers was sharp in a handful of early season starts in the Yankees' system, and was then dealt to the Indians for Chad Curtis. He was hammered in 18 middle-relief stints, plus one start, allowing more than two baserunners per inning. Curtis then rubbed it in by bedeviling his former team in the playoffs, while Weathers finished up in Triple-A, not getting a September recall.

1996: Weathers began the season with the Marlins, but was traded to the Yankees late in the season. Though he was largely ineffective during the regular season, he made the trade worthwhile in one stellar outing against the Rangers in the playoffs. He impressed Yankees' brass with his moxie.

	W	SV	ERA	IP	H	BB	SO	B/I
1995 Florida	4	0	5.98	90	104	52	60	1.73
1996 Florida	2	0	4.54	71	85	28	40	1.59
1996 New York AL	0	0	9.35	17	23	14	13	2.16
1997 two teams	1	0	8.40	26	38	15	18	2.06

WEAVER, ERIC - TR - b: 8/4/73

Weaver was left out of the draft in 1992, but the Dodgers signed him as a free agent because of an impressive performance in the Junior Olympic Festival. He throws extremely hard, but has not developed into the power pitcher the club hoped he'd become. He's taken a step backward over the last year or so, although the Dodgers still think he has the potential to put things together.

WEBER, NEIL - TL - b: 12/6/72

Taken by Arizona, Weber has an above-average fastball. He began the '97 season in Triple-A, but wasn't refined enough for that level (7.94 ERA). He pitched decently when returned to Double-A (7-6, 3.83), and he remains a top prospect. When Weber improves his curveball and changeup, and learns to command his fastball better he should be a quality big-league starter, but that should take a couple of years to occur.

WELCH, MIKE - TR - b: 8/25/72

A good year as the closer for Double-A Binghamton offers hope for a big-league appearance in 1998. Welch's respectable fastball and slider were instrumental in his 21 saves.

WELLS, BOB - TR - b: 11/1/66

Scouting: Not a hard thrower, Wells needs to hit his spots to be effective. It's good movement, not velocity, that makes his fastball a good pitch. He has enjoyed at least moderate success in every role — starter, long man, even closer — but is best suited as a long man in the bullpen.

1998: Wells should toil in a role well suited for him — as a long man out of the pen.

1997: Wells' strikeout-to-walk ratio was nearly three-to-one, the best in his career, but his stuff is not good enough to prevent him from being hit, occasionally hard. Opponents batted .314 against Wells and he allowed a homer every six innings.

1996: Wells stepped into the breach with a career-high 12 victories, most of which came after he joined the starting rotation in June. He won seven straight games just before the All-Star break, posting a 9-2 record at the halfway point. He was a different pitcher in the second half, though, going 3-5 with a 7.74 ERA.

	W	SV	ERA	IP	H	BB	SO	B/I
1995 Seattle	4	0	5.75	76	88	39	38	1.66
1996 Seattle	12	0	5.30	130	141	46	94	1.44
1997 Seattle	2	2	5.75	67	88	18	51	1.58

WELLS, DAVID - TL - b: 5/20/63

Scouting: At one time or another he drove every member of the Yankees' hierarchy and some teammates up the wall with his off-beat behavior. However, the bottom line last year was a good record over 32 starts and a post-season victory over the Indians. He doesn't light up speed guns but gets by with good control of his breaking ball and changeup arsenal.

1998: There are those in the organization who wanted him dealt or left unprotected in the expansion draft. However, with the lack of pitching throughout the big leagues, the Yankees will grin and bear Wells for another year and plug him into the third spot in their rotation.

1997: Wells' chunky body came under criticism from many as the reason his back, neck and foot bothered him at various times last season. Still, he made 32 starts — second to Andy Pettitte on the club.

1996: Wells had a disappointing season for the Orioles that sharpened the criticism of his conditioning although he threw a career-high 224.1 innings. 32 homers allowed contributed to Wells' rising ERA.

	W	SV	ERA	IP	H	BB	SO	B/I
1995 Detroit	10	0	3.04	130	120	37	83	1.20
1995 Cincinnati	6	0	3.59	72	74	16	50	1.24
1996 Baltimore	11	0	5.14	224	247	51	130	1.33
1997 New York AL	16	0	4.21	218	239	45	156	1.30

WENDELL, TURK - TR - b: 5/19/67

Scouting: Muscle memory is a fickle component in the control of a pitch. Pitchers become locked in and produce signature seasons (see Dwight Gooden, 1985; Mark Davis, 1991; and Greg Maddux, every year). Wendell was locked in 1996 — last year was the opposite. He's nasty against righthanded hitters but unintentionally friendly with their lefthanded brethren. He has an average fastball and a sharp slider.

1998: The question is if Wendell will once again be the pitcher he was in 1996 or the one he reverted to last season. The Mets wanted strikeout pitching when they traded for him. If he gives them that without the walks, he'll be busy this summer. If not, he'll become too familiar with the inside of the bullpen. Since he remains dominant against righthanded hitters, he could be used as a set-up man.

1997: Some numbers of condemnation: Wendell walked 17 of the 65 "first batters" he faced. Lefthanded opposition hitters batted .316 (114 at-bats) and produced .431 on-base and .561 slugging percentages against him. Some numbers of commendation: righthanded hitters batted .189 (169 at-bats) with respective on-base and slugging percentages of .314 and .308 against him.

1996: The Cubs thought they had something good going when Wendell converted 18 of 21 save opportunities and fanned nearly a batter per inning. In the subsequent off-season they brought in Mel Rojas, hoping to duplicate the Yankees' successful bullpen duo of Mariano Rivera and John Wetteland.

	W	SV	ERA	IP	H	BB	SO	B/I
1995 Chicago NL	3	0	4.92	60	71	24	50	1.57
1996 Chicago NL	4	18	2.84	79	58	44	75	1.29
1997 two teams	3	5	4.36	76	68	53	64	1.59

WENGERT, DON - TR - b: 11/6/69

Scouting: Wengert is not dominating, instead relying upon a changeup as his out pitch. He can be sneaky with his low-90s fastball, which he can cut; he also throws a slider and a curveball. Wengert has had chances to be a starter but is more effective in middle relief. Since he's not a hard thrower, he needs to spot his pitches. He can be too fine, getting too much of the plate and resulting in a lot of hard-hit balls. Wengert is a good competitor.

1998: When Wengert is on, he is tough to hit and easily coaxes ground balls from hitters. But, those moments have been few and far between. Though his changeup is good, and he is always around the plate, he is not dominating often enough so hitters take advantage. His status as a middle man in the Oakland bullpen is tenuous. The A's will be overhauling their rotation and Wengert may be headed elsewhere.

1997: Wengert started 14 games mostly out of desperation by Oakland as they searched for anyone to start ballgames. He had a few good appearances, but not nearly enough.

1996: Wengert was able to return to his starter role, and he responded well enough.

	W	SV	ERA	IP	H	BB	SO	B/I
1995 Oakland	1	0	3.34	29	30	12	16	1.42
1996 Oakland	7	0	5.58	161	200	60	75	1.61
1997 Oakland	5	2	6.04	134	177	41	68	1.63

WEST, DAVID - TL - b: 9/1/64

A veteran with some major league success, West had good velocity on his fastball and an assortment of breaking pitches, but he ran into a series of injuries including rotator cuff problems which required surgery. West struggled in his comeback attempts with the Phillies and ended up in Japan last year. He got plenty of work as a starter for the Pacific League Hawks (lefties who can throw strikes are in demand everywhere) but overall it was an unimpressive season not raising hopes for the future.

	W	SV	ERA	IP	H	BB	SO	B/I
1995 Philadelphia	3	0	3.79	38	34	19	25	1.39
1996 Philadelphia	2	0	4.76	28	31	11	22	1.49

WESTBROOK, DESTRY - TR - b: 12/13/70

Westbrook opened 1997 as the Phillies' Double-A closer, but his weak performance and the emergence of Ryan Brannan caused his role to first diminish and then disappear, as he was released. Westbrook never held an important role on a pro staff in his six-year career prior to 1997; he pitched in independent ball as recently as 1995. His control has always been spotty, and he is now little better than a batting practice pitcher, allowing over two baserunners per inning at Reading in 1997. Westbrook's pro career may be at its end.

WESTBROOK, JAKE - TR - b: 9/29/77

Westbrook was chosen by the Rockies with the 21st first-round pick in the 1996 draft. He was selected as the top prospect in the Arizona League in his 1996 debut. Last year he pitched at Class A Asheville in the South Atlantic League. For 1998 he moved on to the Expos via the Mike Lansing trade.

WETTELAND, JOHN - TR - b: 8/21/66
Scouting: With a fastball in the mid-90s and a big curve that he can consistently throw for strikes, Wetteland is one of the premier closers in baseball. He has begun to make an adjustment away from being a pure power pitcher, and has an assortment of off-speed pitches that he uses effectively. Every season, he goes through a short streak of ineffectiveness, but recovers and reverts to form. Wetteland doesn't waste pitches, challenging batters with every pitch.
1998: Wetteland is healthy and in his prime, and will continue to be a top closer.
1997: With the exception of a two-week period in June during which he blew four saves, Wetteland had a fine season. He'd have had more saves if the starters and the rest of the bullpen had done a better job of getting the game to him.
1996: Wetteland had another fine season as the Yankees' closer, converting 43 of 47 save opportunities. There may have been a couple of closers that were his equal, but none were better.

	W	SV	ERA	IP	H	BB	SO	B/I
1995 New York AL	1	31	2.93	61	40	14	66	0.88
1996 New York AL	2	43	2.83	63	54	21	69	1.19
1997 Texas	7	31	1.94	65	43	21	63	0.98

WHISENANT, MATT - TL - b: 6/8/71
Scouting: Whisenant has an explosive fastball (mid-90s) which occasionally gets away from him, he also has added a slider recently and has a changeup which he uses rarely. He has always had control difficulties, often ranking among league walks-allowed leaders in his minor-league seasons. Walker has great raw stuff, but almost no command of it.
1998: The Royals would love to be able to count on Whisenant as a situational reliever, but he'll have to have much better control before that role is his.
1997: Acquired from the Marlins for minor-league catcher Matt Treanor, Whisenant was quickly inserted into the floundering Royals' bullpen at mid-season and was often successful; he contributed to the turnaround of the Royals' pen in the second half of the year. He walked as many as he fanned, though, and when he was bad, he was simply awful.
1996: His Triple-A season in the Marlins' chain was marked by poor control even as he continued to display his overpowering fastball.

	W	SV	ERA	IP	H	BB	SO	B/I
1997 Kansas City	1	0	4.56	22	19	18	20	1.71

WHITE, GABE - TL - b: 11/20/71
Scouting: The former Expos prospect features a fastball and hard slider, and is working to develop a changeup. Shoulder and knee surgery has slowed his development, and he probably needs to add a third pitch to be effective as a starter.
1998: White enters the season as a candidate for the back end of the Cincinnati rotation, with the possibility of assuming Mike Remlinger's role as lefty set-up man if Remlinger remains in the rotation.
1997: Recovering from knee and shoulder surgery, White pitched well for Indianapolis (7-4, 2.82 ERA and a 3.5-to-1 strikeout-to-walk ratio), before a callup to the Reds August 8th. He made a few starts with mixed success, and was sent to the bullpen when Kent Mercker and Dave Burba came off the DL.
1996: On the verge of a callup to Cincinnati after a brilliant start at Indianapolis (6-3, 2.77, with 51 strikeouts and only nine walks in 68 innings), White hurt his shoulder in a pregame workout and did not pitch the rest of the season.

	W	SV	ERA	IP	H	BB	SO	B/I
1997 Cincinnati	2	1	4.39	41	39	8	25	1.15

WHITE, RICK - TR - b: 12/23/68
White pitched in the major leagues in 1994 and 1995; he was originally a 15th-round draft choice of the Pittsburgh Pirates when Devil Rays general manager Chuck LaMar was the Pirates' farm director. White spent the fall pitching in the Arizona Fall League for the Peoria Javelinas, which should make him sharp for the spring. He'll likely be a candidate for the Devil Rays' closer job.

WHITEMAN, GREG - TL - b: 6/12/73
Whiteman pitched at the Class A and Double-A levels of the Philadelphia organization last year. He had almost identical results at each stop. He gave up a little more than a hit per inning and struck out slightly more hitters than he walked. He won't help the big club in 1998 and he may never help them.

WHITESIDE, MATT - TR - b: 8/8/67
Scouting: Whiteside is a fastball/slider pitcher with average stuff. He struggles against lefthanders because of the lack of an effective off-speed pitch. Whiteside's durability has improved in the last couple of years, and he has become an effective inning-eating middle reliever. He has to be fine with his control.
1998: Whiteside will begin the season in middle relief in a major league bullpen.
1997: After spending most of 1996 in the minors, Whiteside got the opportunity to pitch when several Ranger pitchers became injured. He proved that he could pitch at the major league level, and wound up leading the bullpen in innings pitched.
1996: After a tough April, Whiteside found himself at Triple-A for most of the rest of the season, where he pitched well.

	W	SV	ERA	IP	H	BB	SO	B/I
1996 Texas	0	0	6.68	32	43	11	15	1.68
1997 Texas	4	0	5.08	73	85	26	44	1.53

WHITESIDE, SEAN - TL - b: 4/19/71
A tall lanky lefthander, Whiteside joined the Mariners' organization in December of 1996 when they selected him in the Rule V draft. He made a big-league appearance (two games) with Detroit in 1995. Last year at Double-A Memphis Whiteside had problems finding the plate out of the bullpen. He'll have to correct the control problems, but a lefty who gives up less than a hit per inning will be given a chance to do that.

WICKMAN, BOB - TR - b: 2/6/69
Scouting: Wickman throws a 90-MPH fastball, which he likes to cut. He also has a mid-80s slider and sinker, which is considered one of the heaviest around. When he keeps the ball down and throws strikes, he is tough. Wickman can fill several relief roles, and once was a starter.
1998: Wickman will be counted on to fill middle, set-up and closer roles as called upon. Manager Phil Garner like his grit,

and considers him one of the most valuable players on the team.

1997: A native of tiny Abrams, Wisconsin, Wickman blossomed for his home state Brewers. He appeared in 74 games in middle, set-up and short roles and led the league with 28 holds.

1996: Wickman started the season with the Yankees and was part of an August 23rd trade that sent him and Gerald Williams to Milwaukee for Graeme Lloyd and Pat Listach. His 95.2 innings in relief ranked third in the American League.

	W	SV	ERA	IP	H	BB	SO	B/I
1995 New York AL	2	1	4.05	80	77	33	51	1.38
1996 NY AL-Milw.	7	0	4.42		06	44	75	1.58
1997 Milwaukee	7	1	2.73	96	89	41	78	1.36

WIEGANT, SCOTT - TL - b: 12/9/67

After being considered a good finesse lefty reliever in the Phillies' farm system — his career ERA was under 3.00, 1997 was a disappointing season. At Triple-A Louisville, Wiegandt posted a 4.45 ERA. His best hope in the majors would be in the role of a situational lefty set-up man.

WILKINS, MARC - TR - b: 10/21/70

Scouting: The stocky Wilkins is built more like Barney Rubble than Dennis Eckersley but he has been an effective middle and set-up reliever during his first two major league seasons with Pittsburgh. Wilkins throws deceptively hard, his fastball reaches as high as 95 MPH. However, his out pitch is a big-breaking curveball that drops off the table.

1998: Wilkins again will be the Pirates' top righthanded set-up man, serving as a key plank in the bridge between the starters and closer Rich Loiselle. Wilkins will continue to quietly establish himself as one of the better young set-up relievers in the majors.

1997: Wilkins started off slowly, struggling throughout spring training and the first month of the season as he was overthrowing all his pitches. Once he got back into a groove, he was again a effective reliever in the seventh and eighth innings.

1996: Wilkins, a failed starter, was pitching middle relief at Double-A Carolina when the Pirates surprisingly called him up in early May. He went on to have a fine rookie season, effectively setting up closers Francisco Cordova and John Ericks.

	W	SV	ERA	IP	H	BB	SO	B/I
1996 Pittsburgh	4	1	3.84	75	75	36	62	1.48
1997 Pittsburgh	9	2	3.69	76	65	33	47	1.29

WILLIAMS, BRIAN - TR - b: 2/15/69

Scouting: Williams has a good live arm with a good fastball and slider. However, he's been hittable in the majors, and has blown a closer's job, indicating that some important ingredient is missing.

1998: Williams could make a major league club as a middle and long reliever. Since he's shown that he can't close, it's unlikely that a team will give him another chance.

1997: Williams pitched for the Orioles Triple-A team, receiving a late call up where he again showed that he was hittable.

1996: Before the season began, the Tigers manager declared Williams to be their closer. He quickly lost the job with a bunch of blown saves, and went back to long relief and spot starting. He posted an ERA over 6.00 in 1995 and again in 1996.

	W	SV	ERA	IP	H	BB	SO	B/I
1995 San Diego	3	0	6.00	72	79	38	75	1.63
1996 Detroit	3	2	6.77	121	145	85	72	1.90
1997 Baltimore	0	0	3.00	24	20	18	14	1.58

WILLIAMS, MIKE - TR - b: 7/29/68

Changing speeds and locating his mid-80s fastball wasn't enough to keep Williams in the big leagues last year. Despite picking up a save in the Royals' decimated bullpen, he was hittable in ten major league appearances and posted a 4.22 ERA and 3-6 record for Triple-A Omaha over 20 appearances (eleven starts). Lacking an outstanding fastball and being prone to the gopher ball may signal an end for Williams.

	W	SV	ERA	IP	H	BB	SO	B/I
1995 Philadelphia	3	0	3.29	87	78	29	57	1.22
1996 Philadelphia	6	0	5.44	167	188	67	103	1.53
1997 Kansas City	0	1	6.43	14	20	8	10	2.00

WILLIAMS, MITCH - TL - b: 11/17/64

"Wild Thing" Williams was back in force with the Royals in 1997, coming out of retirement to "help" one of the major leagues' worst bullpens. He still had a high velocity fastball, but had no command of it and once again retired after allowing two homers in just 6.2 innings for an opposition slugging average of .667.

WILLIAMS, SHAD - TR - b: 3/10/71

Williams' stock isn't as high as it was two years ago, but the Angels haven't given up on him yet; he still has potential. Williams' fastball may be a little below average, but he makes up for lack of velocity with a highly effective change. He's shown he can get the job done at Triple-A Vancouver and has demonstrated he can help somebody.

	W	SV	ERA	IP	H	BB	SO	B/I
1996 California	0	0	8.89	28	42	21	26	2.24

WILLIAMS, TODD - TR - b: 2/13/71

Williams is a submarine style pitcher who had a shot at the big leagues with the Dodgers in 1995. Last year he pitched in the Reds' farm system at Double-A and Triple-A. He gave up less than a hit per inning at both stops and posted 31 saves at Double-A Chattanooga. He doesn't blow the ball by anyone but has good control. If he repeats his 1997 performance he could get another shot at the majors as a set-up man.

WILLIAMS, WOODY - TR - b: 8/19/66

Scouting: Injury-prone, Williams has emerged as a decent starting pitcher. His fastball is nothing special but he mixes it up with a changeup, slider and split-fingered pitch that somehow makes it all work, especially considering that he can find the plate when required.

1998: Williams is good enough to be someone's fourth or fifth starter and with expansion, he is good enough to be more than that with a different team.

1997: Finally staying health for a season, Williams responded to the opportunity to start regularly by posting a 4.35 ERA over 31 starts. He was third on the staff in starts, innings and strikeouts. His record was not indicative of his ability as he received little run support.

1996: Williams underwent right shoulder surgery just before the season although he returned to start ten games.

	W	SV	ERA	IP	H	BB	SO	B/I
1995 Toronto	1	0	3.69	53	44	28	41	1.34
1996 Toronto	4	0	4.73	59	64	21	43	1.44
1997 Toronto	9	0	4.35	195	201	66	124	1.37

WILSON, GARY - TR - b: 1/1/70

Wilson was the Pirates' minor-league pitcher of the year in 1994 and made their Opening Day roster in 1995. However, he was sent back to the minors after ten relief appearances and hasn't been back to Pittsburgh since. Wilson is a finesse pitcher who has been bothered by shoulder stiffness in recent seasons.

WILSON, PAUL - TR - b: 3/28/73

Scouting: Wilson was the prototypical power pitcher in his brief tour in the minor leagues. Some of the power was missing late last summer when he finally returned to pitching after undergoing surgery in November, 1996 to repair his labrum. His velocity was returning gradually in the instructional league and winter ball. He had a fastball in the mid-90s when healthy, a good changeup, a slider and curve.

1998: Once considered the most likely of the three young Mets pitchers to develop into a number one starter, Wilson, like Jason Isringhausen, will begin this season at the back of the Mets rotation. Pitching coach Bob Apodaca, as adept at detecting silver linings as he is able to pinpoint mechanical flaws, suggests Wilson will have learned to pitch without his optimum fastball.

1997: Wilson spent the year just watching. He went to school while he recovered from his surgery, charting pitches every game and picking at Apodaca's brain. The injury/surgery denied him a chance for immediate redemption for his disappointing rookie season. Wilson made one impressive start in the Florida State League and worked effectively in four appearances in the Gulf Coast League.

1996: In spring training, former General Manager Joe McIlvaine was impressed by Wilson's potential. He would whisper "(Wilson) has a chance to be soooo good," as if the same words spoken at normal volume would undermine Wilson. Ultimately, Wilson undermined Wilson. His inability to throw strikes, a staggering loss to the Cubs in May and general lack of confidence led to poor results. There were indications though — especially after Apodaca took over — that Wilson was the real deal.

	W	SV	ERA	IP	H	BB	SO	B/I
1996 New York NL	5	0	5.38	149	157	71	109	1.53

WINCHESTER, SCOTT - TR - b: 4/20/73

Drafted by Arizona and then traded back to the Reds, Winchester began last season at Class A Kinston in the Indians' farm system and pitched at Double-A Akron for the Tribe, also. He finished the season as a member of the Reds' organization making stops at Double-A, Triple-A and a September visit to Cinergy Field, pitching in five big-league games. Winchester features a good curveball.

WINSTON, DARRIN - TL - b: 7/6/66

Winston is a journeyman who was out of baseball in 1996 while establishing a foreign youth baseball academy. He was set to be released at the midpoint of the 1997 season by the Phillies but got a last-minute reprieve and wound in the majors in September, making a couple of starts, including a seven-inning one-hitter. He's versatile enough to pitch in any role; he changes speeds and locations well, and is particularly effective against lefthanded hitters. He remains a longshot for a roster spot in the majors this year, and his pro career could even be at its end, but Winston had his 15 minutes of fame last September.

WITASICK, JAY - TR - b: 8/28/72

Scouting: A former St. Louis prospect, Witasick has the standard array of a fastball in the 90s and a hard slider, so he will live or die as a closer. At age 25, he still has a little time to assume the role of major league close, but he is now behind T.J. Mathews in line for a job in Oakland.

1998: Witasick could probably use another year of experience at Triple-A. He does throw hard, but after moving up the ladder quickly in 1996, he was in over his head by season's end. He could wind up in a set-up role for Oakland, but a full season as "the closer" at Edmonton (and a successful one at that) would do him a lot of good.

1997: His 1997 season was similar to his 1996 performance, only at higher levels; he pitched well before his promotion, not so well after. He was 3-2 with a 4.28 ERA in 13 appearances at Triple-A Edmonton, but was not effective in eight games with Oakland.

1996: Acquired as part of the Todd Stottlemyre trade, Witasick pitched well at Huntsville (four saves, 2.30 ERA) and earned a promotion to Edmonton, and then a brief trial in Oakland. The going was a little tougher at the higher levels; he obviously was in over his head.

	W	SV	ERA	IP	H	BB	SO	B/I
1997 Oakland	0	0	5.73	11	14	6	8	1.82

WITHEM, SHANNON - TR - b: 9/21/72

Mets' farmhand Withem has a good assortment of breaking pitches but not much of a fastball. He had a fair season last year for Triple-A Norfolk (10-10, 4.24 ERA). His good control enables him to deliver six or more innings of work in most of his starts, and he is good at keeping the ball in play and letting his defense do the work for him.

WITT, BOBBY - TR - b: 5/11/64

Scouting: Witt throws a fastball that occasionally hits 90 miles per hour, and a sinker that is his out pitch. The problem is his control: when Witt is behind in the count, batters generally lay off the sinker. Although he can go through a series of games when his control seems to have improved, overall, he still walks too many batters. He also has a propensity for giving up the longball. Witt does not field his position well.

1998: Witt can give a pitching staff 200 innings per year, and he will continue to do that somewhere in the major leagues. He will have at least as many bad outings as good ones.

1997: For the first two months of the season, Witt was outstanding. Averaging only two walks per game, he won his first seven decisions and became the Rangers' staff ace. In June, he reverted to form, issuing more walks, and suddenly the solo homers became three-run jobs. Witt allowed 33 home runs, and struck out fewer batters per inning than in any season other than 1993.

1996: Witt completed another mediocre season, allowing 15 baserunners per nine innings and yielding 28 home runs in nearly 200 innings.

	W	SV	ERA	IP	H	BB	SO	B/I
1995 Florida	2	0	3.90	110	104	47	95	1.36
1995 Texas	3	0	4.55	61	81	21	46	1.66
1996 Texas	16	0	5.41	199	235	96	157	1.66
1997 Texas	12	0	4.82	209	245	74	121	1.53

WITTE, TREY - TR - b: 1/15/70

Witte, the Mariners' ninth-round pick in the 1991 June Draft, spent his second consecutive season at Triple-A Tacoma. He doesn't throw hard but is usually effective in a relief spot with good control. Without any eye-catching out pitch he may just end up a career Triple-A reliever.

WOHLERS, MARK - TR - b: 1/23/70

Scouting: No one throws harder than Wohlers. His fastball reaches 100 MPH at times and he can throw it for strikes consistently. Wohlers has a classic closer mentality: give me the ball and I'll blow 'em away. He also throws a slider and a forkball — both of which seem to arrive at glacial speeds in comparison to the fastball — but they have been less consistent, less effective pitches than the heater. Wohlers has good control for a hard thrower; over the last three years he has walked just 83 batters against 282 strikeouts in 211.1 innings.
1998: Keep in mind that while the Braves' strong starting staff gives Wohlers many leads to protect, they also often finish their games which often keeps him in the pen, too. Wohlers may not win any relief ace awards, but he is still one of the best short relievers in the game and will again be Atlanta's bullpen ace.
1997: A mid-season bullpen breakdown, by the set-up men, especially, left Wohlers with fewer leads to protect but he was still effective, fanning eleven batters per nine innings and limiting opponents to a .224 average. He was among the best closers in the game.
1996: Wohlers allowed the National League's lowest percentage of inherited baserunners to score while wracking up career highs in saves. He was among the top two or three closers in the game.

	W	SV	ERA	IP	H	BB	SO	B/I
1995 Atlanta	7	25	2.09	64	51	24	90	1.16
1996 Atlanta	2	39	3.03	77	71	21	100	1.19
1997 Atlanta	5	33	3.51	69	57	38	92	1.37

WOJCIECHOWSKI, STEVE - TL - b: 7/29/70

"Wojo" pitched well when he first arrived in Oakland in 1996, but the league quickly caught up with him, sending him back to Edmonton. As the Oakland staff struggled, Wojchiechowski was summoned for a couple of starts but they were less than stellar. He was 8-2 with a 3.84 ERA at Triple-A Edmonton last year, but the A's don't seem to think much of him.

	W	SV	ERA	IP	H	BB	SO	B/I
1995 Oakland	2	0	5.18	48	51	28	13	1.62
1996 Oakland	5	0	5.65	79	97	28	30	1.58

WOLCOTT, BOB - TR - b: 9/8/73

Scouting: A Baseball America high school All-American before being a second-round pick in the 1992 draft, Wolcott was rushed to the majors because of the Mariners' dearth of starting depth. He has a good fastball, good location and command, and could break out soon.
1998: Wolcott was not assured of a starting rotation spot, or even a major league roster spot, in Seattle, but he will get every consideration for both from his new team, the Diamondbacks.
1997: Wolcott struggled with his location and was cuffed around, eventually losing his grip on the fifth starting spot. It was his third year split between Triple-A and the majors. Big-leaguers hit .314 against Wolcott. He was 1-3 with a 5.11 ERA in seven starts at Tacoma, but posted a fine four-to-one strikeout-to-walk ratio.
1996: Wolcott had his first extended stint in the major leagues at age 22, winning seven games while making 28 starts. Once again his fine control in the minors deteriorated when he reached the big leagues. He walked just three against 16 strikeouts in his three games at Tacoma, but had 54 walks and 78 strikeouts in 149.1 innings in Seattle.

	W	SV	ERA	IP	H	BB	SO	B/I
1995 Seattle	3	0	4.42	36	43	14	19	1.55
1996 Seattle	7	0	5.73	149	179	54	78	1.56
1997 Seattle	5	0	6.03	100	129	29	58	1.58

WOLF, RANDY - TL - b: 8/22/76

A brilliant collegiate pitcher at Pepperdine, Wolf was a second-round draft pick by the Phillies in 1997, and went 4-0 with a 2.08 ERA in seven Rookie-ball starts. He throws a 90-MPH fastball with a diverse array of breaking pitches — all with sharp movement. His command is excellent and Wolf has potential to develop into a power pitcher. He has a mature repertoire and mound presence; Wolf may start this year at higher Class A Clearwater in his first full pro season — an unusually aggressive advancement.

WOOD, KERRY - TR - b: 6/16/77

Scouting: The Cubs made Wood the fourth overall player taken in the 1995 draft because of his blazing fastball. Wood throws about as hard as anybody around, but like most young fireballers, he has trouble throwing strikes. Right now, that seems to be about the only thing holding Wood back, and once he fixes that problem he'll be on the fast track to the big leagues.
1998: Wood is the best pitching prospect the Cubs have, but he's nowhere near ready to pitch in the big leagues. The Cubs promoted him all the way to Triple-A Iowa last year, but he showed he didn't have the experience to get hitters out at that level. He'll likely start this season at Double-A Orlando and the Cubs would be smart to keep him there the entire season and let him develop. The worst thing that could happen would be for him to be rushed to Chicago, get pounded, and have his confidence destroyed.
1997: Wood pitched at three levels in the Cubs farm system, starting the season at Class A Daytona and advancing all the way to Triple-A Iowa. However, Wood had no business being at Iowa, and probably didn't have any business being at Orlando, either. He still has too many problems throwing pitches across the plate and needs to get that part of his game straightened out before advancing to another level.
1996: Wood was dominant at Chicago's top Class A team in Daytona despite walking 5.5 men per nine innings. He got away with that by blowing the ball by hitters and striking out a ton.

WOODALL, BRAD - TL - b: 6/25/69

Woodall had some success couple of years ago in Triple-A when he was perfect with his fastball/changeup combination, but slipped to a 8-11, 5.51 season as a starter at Triple-A in '97. Woodall's fastball is well below average and his breaking pitches are not effective, making him an unlikely reliever. He's also had some injury problems. Even if Woodall can get his confidence and command all the way back, his lack of stuff would make it hard for him to pitch effectively in the majors.

WOODARD, STEVE - TR - b: 5/15/75
Scouting: Woodard might have trouble ever topping his major league debut when he threw a one-hitter to beat the Blue Jays and his boyhood idol, Roger Clemens. He has a fastball that can approach 90 MPH and has decent control for a young pitcher. He still is green, having just made a big jump from Double-A to the majors.
1998: Woodard has a chance to be part of the Brewers rotation in 1998. The Brewers like his attitude and approach on the mound.
1997: Woodard was called up after spending most of the season in Double-A and posted a .500 record before going down for the season with a pulled muscle in his right side. He is considered a prospect.
1996: Woodard caught the eye of the Brewers' brass by posting a 12-9 record at Class A Stockton. They thought he might have a chance to climb through the system quicker than most players.

	W	SV	ERA	IP	H	BB	SO	B/I
1997 Milwaukee	3	0	5.15	37	39	6	32	1.23

WOODS, BRIAN - TR - b: 6/7/71
Scouting: Woods has good velocity but has bombed as a starter. Lately he has also bombed in relief. His best shot is probably in the bullpen, but he has to have much better command to advance any further.
1998: Woods has done nothing to warrant advancement in the White Sox' system; he should return to Birmingham for another try in their bullpen. His time is running out; he needs to make progress this year to keep his major league hopes alive.
1997: Woods picked up nine saves in a return trip to Birmingham's bullpen. That's the good news. The bad side of it was a 6.54 ERA and nearly as many walks as strikeouts.
1996: Woods' first year in relief — and first above A-ball — was a qualified success. He still showed some wildness in his 5-5, 3.76 ERA season at Double-A Birmingham.

WOOTEN, GREG - TR - b: 3/30/74
Scouting: Wooten is big and gangly (6'7", 210 pounds), but the comparisons to Randy Johnson end there. Wooten has a good fastball, but his strength is his location and command.
1998: Expected to gain more seasoning, Wooten will advance to Triple-A Tacoma. If the Pacific Coast League is good to him, Wooten might even reach the majors near the end of just his third pro season.
1997: Wooten continued to put up impressive victory totals, tying for the Mariners' organization lead with 11 victories in his first stop at Double-A. In his first year above A-ball — and only his second professional season — Wooten had a 4.47 ERA while allowing 166 hits in 155 innings over 26 starts.
1996: A draft-and-follow pick, Wooten missed the 1995 season after being a third-round draft pick but had 15 victories in 27 starts while splitting time in A-ball at Wisconsin and Lancaster. Wooten was named MVP of the Midwestern League.

WORRELL, STEVE -TL- b: 11/25/69
After five seasons in the White Sox' farm system, Worrell spent last year at Double-A Orlando of the Cubs' organization. He could get a look at Triple-A in 1998 as he was effective out of the bullpen in Orlando. Worrell showed good control, he can strike people out and he's a lefty which always gives a pitcher some hope.

WORRELL, TIM - TR - b: 7/5/67
Scouting: Worrell had one of the biggest drop-offs in the Padre bullpen last year and by the end of the season there was concern about his health, although Worrell said he was fine. When Worrell is on, he has a solid fastball and a better slider. But it was seen increasingly less as '97 wore on.
1998: The Padres shipped Worrell to Detroit, reuniting him with Randy Smith. Worrell probably will be given yet another run at a starter's job in spring training.
1997: Worrell opened the season in the starting rotation after winning the job with a strong spring training effort. But he was moved back to the bullpen after ten starts and finished with a losing record and a high ERA. He really struggled over final weeks of the season and allowed 14 homers while opponents hit .280 against him.
1996: Worrell was excellent as the bridge from the starters to Doug Bochtler and Trevor Hoffman. Worrell's 50 appearances included eleven starts and opponents hit only .137 against him when he pitched from the bullpen.

	W	SV	ERA	IP	H	BB	SO	B/I
1995 San Diego	1	0	4.73	13	16	6	13	1.65
1996 San Diego	9	1	3.05	121	109	39	99	1.22
1997 San Diego	4	3	5.16	106	116	50	81	1.56

WORRELL, TODD - TR - b: 9/28/59
Scouting: At age 38, Worrell has lost some zip on his fastball. He developed a good curveball after elbow trouble forced him to give up his slider, but when he can't find his fastball and get it over, Worrell is in trouble.
1998: Veteran closers have a way of hanging on forever (Dennis Eckersley, Doug Jones) so there were teams pursuing Worrell, while he was talking about retirement. He still has the mental toughness of a closer and knows a lot of tricks to get that third out in the ninth inning. If Worrell chose, he could get 30 saves for any team.
1997: Worrell endured his worst season but held onto the closer job. When the dust settled he had exactly the same nine blown saves and six losses he posted in 1996, a year when most observers thought his future looked bright.
1996: Worrell converted 44 of 53 saves. It was among his finest seasons, especially in the midst of the 1996 hitting bonanza.

	W	SV	ERA	IP	H	BB	SO	B/I
1995 Los Angeles	4	32	2.02	62	50	19	61	1.11
1996 Los Angeles	4	44	3.03	65	70	15	66	1.31
1997 Los Angeles	2	35	5.28	60	60	23	61	1.39

WRIGHT, JAMEY - TR - b: 12/24/74
Scouting: One of the organization's more advanced young guns, Wright has an outstanding sinking fastball; he throws his four-seamer 94 MPH. He has a good slider and changeup, but doesn't trust those pitches and rarely throws them when he's in trouble. Tall and lanky, he has been compared to Jim Palmer, though Wright is a long way from sharing the Hall of Famer's command. He finished the 1997 season with a bone spur in his right elbow that is expected to heal with rest, but his right knee, which underwent two arthroscopic surgeries follow-

ing the 1996 season, continued to bother him. He lacks a strikeout pitch and when he gets in trouble, he tends to rear back and throw rather than pitch.

1998: If his right knee ever heals and he is able to keep up with his conditioning, Wright should go to spring training as the favorite to win the fifth spot in the Rockies' rotation. But should the Rockies improve their rotation with off-season acquisitions, Wright could be sent to Triple-A for more seasoning.

1997: Wright got off to a quick 3-0 start, but then was bothered by an inflamed clavicle, which put him on the disabled list from mid-May to early-June. He did not pitch well upon his return, though he did string together three good outings in September. He was bothered most of the season by his ailing knee.

1996: It was a dream season. After spending all of 1995 in A-ball, Wright was impressive in the Rockies' big-league spring training camp, then advanced from Double-A to Triple-A and was in the big-leagues by July 1st. He finally cooled off near the end of the season, then had to miss his last start to undergo the first of two arthroscopic surgeries on his right knee.

	W	SV	ERA	IP	H	BB	SO	B/I
1996 Colorado	4	0	4.93	91	105	41	45	1.60
1997 Colorado	8	0	6.25	150	198	71	59	1.80

WRIGHT, JARET - TR - b: 12/29/75

Scouting: Wright embodies everything one could want in a pitching prospect. He's got size (6'2", 200 pounds), stuff (95-MPH fastball, solid curve, improving changeup), bloodlines (dad Clyde was a longtime major leaguer) and amazing composure for a kid. He has immediately stepped in at each successive level — including the majors — and has been an above-average hurler from the start. He should evolve into a number one starter as his command improves.

1998: A sophomore slump doesn't appear likely. Based on his amazing Game Two start in the first round of the playoffs against the Yankees, Wright now knows he belongs in the major leagues. The number one starter role is begging to be filled, and Wright will answer the call.

1997: Wright cut a swath through the Indians' upper minor leagues, dominating in 15 starts split between Double-A and Triple-A, striking out better than a batter per inning. Unlike teammate Bartolo Colon, Wright immediately felt comfortable in the majors. A most telling stat: he held righthanders to a puny .193 average. Once he gets ahead of hitters more consistently, allowing him to last deeper into games, and learns to hold runners on base, he will be a superstar.

1996: Wright was the best prospect in the high Class A Carolina League, allowing less than six hits per nine innings, but his season was cut short by a broken jaw suffered in a freak batting practice incident.

	W	SV	ERA	IP	H	BB	SO	B/I
1997 Cleveland	8	0	4.39	90	81	35	63	1.28

YAN, ESTEBAN - TR - b: 6/22/74

Scouting: Yan is a hard-throwing young righthander with a good fastball peaking in the mid-90's. He's somewhat inconsistent and will hang a slider, a weakness that will be exploited in the majors.

1998: Yan was one of the Orioles' top prospects, and had been asked for in trades before the Devil Rays grabbed him. He's young and may be erratic as a starter, a weakness the contending Orioles couldn't tolerate. Yan may have to work out of the bullpen for a while to break in slowly and develop some consistency. Being flexible will help Yan earn a roster spot in the majors.

1997: Yan began 1997 in the Orioles Triple-A Rochester bullpen and was later moved into the rotation where he pitched well. He got a late-season call-up to the Orioles when they needed additional starters for doubleheaders. But he struggled with the Orioles, indicating that he's just not ready.

1996: Yan was purchased from the Expos in April, 1996. He pitched in Double-A, Triple-A, and even got into four games with the Orioles.

	W	SV	ERA	IP	H	BB	SO	B/I
1997 Baltimore	0	0	15.77	10	20	7	4	2.78

YOUNG, JOE - TR - b: 4/28/75

Scouting: A native Canadian, Young possesses a 95-MPH fastball and sweeping breaking ball. For now, he is wild but some think that his control will eventually come around. Considering the movement on his fastball, most are willing to wait.

1998: Young will work things out at the Double-A level but needs to gain some command of his fastball before working on anything else. Without control, his velocity is meaningless.

1997: Young walked 40 batters in 59 innings while striking out 62; it's representative of both his potential and what's holding him back.

1996: Young struck out 157 batters in 122 innings with Class A Hagerstown. With Class A Dunedin, he showed the same promise, striking out 36 in 33.2 innings.

ZANCANERO, DAVE - TL - b: 1/8/69

Scouting: Zancanero's best pitches are his fastball and changeup, although his fastball is only in the upper 80s. He needs to tighten his breaking ball.

1998: The Padres want to give Zancanero a shot at starting the season at Triple-A Las Vegas, although he is a sixth-year minor-league free agent and may move on to another organization.

1997: Signed as a minor-league free agent before the season, Zancanero spent the entire year at Double-A Mobile where he was 10-8 with a 4.44 ERA; 17 of his 31 outings were starts. He pitched three complete games, equalling the organization's best above the Class A level.

1996: Zancanero divided his season between Class A Modesto (7-3, 3.38 ERA, primarily as a reliever) and Double-A Huntsville (3-3, 5.61 ERA in ten starts).

ZIMMERMAN, MIKE - TR - b: 2/6/69

Zimmerman couldn't get through his fifth straight Triple-A season. After going 1-3 with a 10.59 ERA in six starts with 20 walks and 41 hits —including eight homers — over just 26.1 innings, Zimmerman was demoted to Double-A Wichita where he had more success but still walked batters left and right (17 walks in 27 innings). He's just minor-league roster filler.

ZOLECKI, MIKE -TR - b: 12/6/71

Zolecki proved he could overwhelm A-ball batters, but that's not impressive for a 25-year old. He also pitched at Double-A for the Rockies and was overwhelmed himself. He walked and struck out 32 batters and surrendered 64 hits in 56.2 innings. He's not a good prospect to make an appearance at Coors Field.

The 1997 Amateur Draft Report Card
by Will Lingo

1997 Draft Report It's hard enough to assess a draft just a few months after the fact. Professional statistics are minimal or nonexistent, and they're almost meaningless. Many players have only started to scratch the surface of their ability. But it's even harder to figure the character of a draft when the first two picks don't sign. No. 1 pick Matt Anderson was negotiating with the Tigers, without success, and No. 2 pick J.D. Drew was using a grievance to try to became free from the Phillies.

That Drew wasn't the first pick showed what a volatile draft it was, based on a player's perceived bonus demands. Drew was the consensus choice as the best player available, but it was just as well known that he wouldn't be the first pick. Other players jumped all over the charts, with some who agreed to bonuses before the draft getting drafted higher than expected, and some who were thought to want the biggest money going lower than expected. Drew, unexpectedly, went second to the Phillies, and he and agent Scott Boras seemed annoyed by that immediately. Boras said he knew other teams would have met his bonus demands, rumored to be anywhere from $3 million to $10 million. The Phillies cried foul, saying that if they were talking bonuses before the draft it was tampering. And all this was before negotiations even got started. They didn't get any better once they officially started, and Drew went to the independent Northern League to play. He ended up as that league's rookie of the year, but he was after something more important. Drew filed a grievance saying that because he had signed a professional contract with the Northern League, he should become a free agent if the Phillies didn't sign him during their exclusive negotiation period (which extends until a week before the 1998 draft). Major League Baseball argued that the Northern League contract had no effect, and both sides were waiting for an arbitrator's ruling. Anderson's situation was perhaps even stranger. At least people expected Drew's signing to be difficult.

Anderson was picked by the Tigers in part because he was believed to be a relatively easy sign. But negotiations dragged as both sides waited to see what the market indicated. Once everyone else had signed, they remained apart by just $90,000. The Tigers offered $2.505 million, and Anderson said he wanted $2.6 million Both sides vowed they wouldn't back down, and Anderson said he might return to Rice for the spring semester and play his senior year. If Drew and Anderson had signed, they would be on these teams. Anderson threw harder than anyone in the draft, reaching 98 mph. Drew is a great all-around package, with plus power to all fields. He'll probably end up as a corner outfielder. But where?

AMERICAN LEAGUE

Catcher: Good catchers are hard to find, but several teams have legitimate hopes for catchers obtained in this draft. The Twins got Matt LeCroy out of Clemson as a supplemental first-round pick, and he might have the best power in the draft. But the best all-around player is Jayson Werth, a 6-foot-5 Illinois high school player taken by the Orioles in the first round. He hit .295-1-8 in the Gulf Coast League but will develop more power. He also has great bloodlines, as the grandson of Ducky Schofield, the nephew of Dick Schofield and the stepson of Dennis Werth. All are former big leaguers.

First Base: No American League teams got impact players at first base, unless one of the many talented outfielders drafted ends up here. The best of the bunch now is Joe Dillon, taken by the Royals in the seventh round out of Texas Tech. A shoulder injury limited him to 19 professional games in 1997, but he has quick feet and soft hands.

Second Base: Ryan Hankins was one of the better prospects in the draft coming into his junior season at Nevada-Las Vegas, but a down season knocked him down to the 13th round, where the White Sox grabbed him. He could end up being one of the biggest sleepers in the draft. Also keep an eye on the Rangers' Tom Sergio, and Brian Benefield and Joe Kilburg of the Indians.

Third Base: Why UCLA let Troy Glaus play shortstop we'll never know, but now that he's in the pro game he should make it to the big leagues as a third baseman quickly. He hit an outlandish .413-32-88 in leading UCLA to the College World Series, and don't be surprised if the Angels have him in Anaheim when Dave Hollins' contract expires after the 1998 season.

Shortstop: The Twins nearly lost him to Florida State, but they came up with a late $1.85 million bonus to bring Michael Cuddyer in at the head of a good draft class. Cuddyer has great hands and a great arm, and he hit .500 in his senior season of high school in Virginia. Still, he may outgrow the position and end up at third, a la Chipper Jones. Another player compared to Jones is Aaron Capista, a second round pick by the Red Sox.

Outfield: The best athlete in the draft, bar none, and one of the best athletes ever to come out of Colorado, Darnell McDonald carries big expectations on the way to Baltimore. He's a potential five-tool outfielder, and it took $1.9 million to get him to pass on a scholarship to the University of Texas. He also was a standout pitcher in high school, but it's his speed-power game that the Orioles would like to develop. Another football-baseball player to keep an eye is Kenny Kelly, who's also playing quarterback at the University of Miami The Red Sox organization is chock full of Georgia Tech alumni, and in Mark Fischer it looks like they've added another good one. Fischer will always be remembered as the player Boston took with the supplemental first-round pick they received for losing Roger Clemens as a free agent. He hit .330-5-25 with 13 stolen bases at short-season Class A Lowell, and the Red Sox think he'll add power to his game. He has the speed and instincts to play center field, and he won't be expected to stay in the minors very long. Not the most heralded player coming out of the draft, Goefrey Tomlinson got attention by leading the Northwest League in batting at .338 and on-base percentage at .440. Drafted by the Royals in the fourth round out of the University of Houston, Tomlinson is a native of Jamaica, where he played cricket. He hasn't played a lot of baseball, so he has room for big improvement. With his athleticism, speed and ability with the bat, he could be an impact player. Blue Jays first-rounder Vernon Wells is a tempting choice, but we've been burned by Blue Jays outfield phenoms before.

Righthanders: Who'd have thought this is the Drew we'd be talking about making an impact in pro ball? But Tim signed with the Indians out of high school in Georgia and has made an impression already, while J.D. continues to discuss the meaning of life with agent Scott Boras. A pulled back muscle left Tim in draft limbo, along with the possibility he would go to Florida State. But the Indians took him in the first round (making him and J.D. the first brothers to go in the first round of the same draft), signed him and watched him have a promising debut. He can reach the mid-90s fastball, and he has a plus slider and great makeup as well. The Indians should have another impact arm in a few years. Also worthy of note: Athletics first rounder Chris Enochs, who leads a strong infusion of pitching into that organization.

Lefthanders: This draft could bring several quality lefties to the big leagues, and each league has strong candidates. But it's hard to pass on the potential of 6-foot-10 Ryan Anderson, the Michigan high school pitcher taken by the Mariners with the 19th overall pick. He throws in the high 90s and was a potential No. 1 overall pick who fell because of questions about his signability. The Mariners grabbed him, signed him for $2.175 million, and hope he'll join Randy Johnson in Seattle for a twin towers pitching attack. He's far from the only lefty with potential, though. The Devil Rays think the world of fifth-round pick Marquis Roberts, the Rangers like fifth-rounder Trey Poland, and the Red Sox love hard-throwing first-rounder John Curtice.

NATIONAL LEAGUE

Catcher: Giuseppe Chiaramonte played just half a season at Class A San Jose, but he led the team with 12 home runs. He has made great progress as a catcher, beginning at Fresno State and continuing after the Giants picked him in the fifth round. He has a strong arm, and his power continues to improve. Perhaps even more important, there's no one significant ahead of him in the Giants organization, so he could move quickly. Fourth-round pick Brandon Harper also shows a great deal of promise with the Marlins, both offensively and defensively, but do you really think he's going to push Charles Johnson aside?

First Base: The Pirates love to take raw athletes and see what happens, and in recent years they've had some big success stories. First rounder J.J. Davis could be the latest. He was regarded as one of the best high school players in southern California coming into the draft, both as a pitcher and a first baseman. He also was an accomplished football player but sat out his senior year to concentrate on baseball. His power potential is the most alluring part of his game, and he's already 6-foot-6, 230 pounds.

Second Base: Surprised to see another Giant? Travis Young hit .334-1-34 with 40 steals in the Northwest League after the Giants took him in the 11th round out of the University of New Mexico. He has good speed and probably could play second base in the big leagues already. Also keep an eye on 33rd-rounder Lance Downing of the Diamondbacks. Like most second basemen, he's coming from another position, although it's the unusual shift from first base to second. But the Diamondbacks want to take advantage of his soft hands.

Third Base: The Reds can say all they want that Brandon Larson is a shortstop, but his bat and his range say he's a third baseman, and he'll be there before 1998 is out. Larson, a first-round pick out of Louisiana State who hit 40 homers in leading the Tigers to another College World Series title, has good power (obviously) but swings a good bat all the way around. He's as close to ready as you can get from the draft, so it wouldn't be outlandish for the Reds to move him all the way to Cincinnati by the end of the '98 season.

Shortstop: National League teams found an embarrassment of riches at shortstop, with many teams making legitimate claims that they found solid shortstop prospects. The best bet is Cardinals first-rounder Adam Kennedy, who made it from Cal State Northridge to the high Class A Carolina League in a half-season. He's a great athlete, hit .325 in his pro debut and showed the instincts to play shortstop. Like Larson, his tools are probably better suited to third, but he has the better chance to stay at short. If you're looking for a pure shortstop, keep an eye on the Mets' Cesar Crespo. He was a potential first-rounder until a poor showing in a predraft showcase in Puerto Rico. The Mets took him in the third round and paid a third-round record $775,000 to sign him, and he may be the best player they drafted.

Outfield: Lance Berkman gets the most notice for his power, and why not? He hit 41 homers and 134 RBIs for Rice. He's a great pure hitter, though, and he's a switch-hitter as well. The Astros couldn't pass on him in the first round, even though he played first base in college and a fellow named Bagwell happens to be at that position. But he made a quick adjustment to left field and hit 12 homers in the Class A Florida State League in a half season. That's an outrageous number for such a notorious pitcher's league. It's not clear why Kevin Burford fell to the 15th round coming out of Rancho Santiago JC, but the Padres are glad they're the ones who took him. He hit .389 and had 50 RBIs in the Rookie-level Arizona League and was the league MVP. He showed uncommon discipline at the plate and a great ability to make adjustments. He'll never be a great outfielder, but he'll be competent in left field and should hit enough that no one will notice. Don't look now, but the Phillies are putting together a group of good athletes in their minor league system. Add to that group speedy Shomari Beverly, a third-round pick out of high school in California. Beverly has great range and instincts to play in center field, and though his statistics in the Rookie-level Appalachian League were nondescript, he could be a prototype leadoff man, with a little pop in his bat for good measure.

Righthanders: Speaking of hope for the future, the Cubs actually have some good young arms on the way. First-round pick Jon Garland is the one they picked up in this draft, and though he's just out of high school in California, he already throws in the 90s. He has the frame (6-foot-5) and delivery to pick up more velocity, and he has a hard slider as well. Along with 1996 first-rounder Todd Noel and 1995 first-rounder Kerry Wood, the Cubs have the makings of a solid rotation ina few years.

Lefthanders: Again, a solid crop to choose from, but again, one player stands out. Rick Ankiel could make this a draft to remember for the Cardinals. Amid reports that he might be asking for a bonus between $10 million and $15 million, Ankiel fell to the second round. The Cardinals finally took a chance with the 72nd overall pick, then signed him for $2.5 million. All this obscures the fact that he was one of the best high school lefthanders in years. He threw up to 97 mph in instructional league and has uncommon polish. He will go down as the steal of the draft, and many scouting directors are now figuring out how to explain why they didn't take him.

The 1996 Amateur Draft:
by Jim Callis

The 1996 draft may have been the most unusual ever, as four of the first 12 picks were declared free agents because they weren't tendered proper contracts by the teams that selected them. First baseman Travis Lee, the number two overall pick, received a staggering $10 million deal from the expansion Arizona Diamondbacks, who also landed righthander John Patterson, the number five pick. Their expansion counterparts, the Devil Rays, snapped up lefthander Bobby Seay, the number 12 selection. And righthander Matt White, the number seven pick who had yet to sign by mid-November, may be the best high school pitching prospect of the draft era. Several first-round picks have yet to make their professional debuts because they spent the summer playing with the U.S. Olympic team.

AMERICAN LEAGUE DRAFT ALL-STARS

Catcher—A.J. Hinch, Athletics (third round). Drafted in the second round out of high school and the third round in 1995, Hinch drew scouts' ire for not signing either time. By his senior year at Stanford, most scouts were down on his arm strength and not excited by his lack of home run power. But the U.S. Olympic team catcher and the only player to be on Team USA for four straight years offers athleticism behind the plate, a decent bat, doubles power and above-average speed for a catcher. His upside is a poor man's Craig Biggio, which could make Hinch a rich man. ETA: Late 1999.

First Baseman—Gary LoCurto, Red Sox (second round). Boston took LoCurto with a compensation pick for the loss of free agent Erik Hanson, and seems to have come out ahead on the deal. LoCurto, a lefthanded hitter out of San Diego, can hit for both power (12 extra-base hits in 137 at-bats in the spacious parks of the Gulf Coast League) and average (.314). If Mo Vaughn becomes a Red Sox fixture, LoCurto will have to move to DH because he doesn't have outfield ability. ETA: Early 2000.

Second Baseman—Ryan Stromsborg, Blue Jays (fourth round). Stromsborg was pretty much a nonentity on Southern California's 1995 College World Series team, but came into his own last spring. A good all-around athlete, he runs a 6.6-second 60-yard dash and has begun to develop strength. His pro debut was solid, as he hit .310-8-38 in 216 at-bats and stole eight bases in the Pioneer League. ETA: Late 1999.

Third Baseman—Eric Chavez, Athletics (first round, number 10 overall). Considered the best pure hitter in the 1996 draft, Chavez could team with 1994 first-round pick Ben Grieve to form a formidable heart of the batting order for Oakland in the near future. Chavez has a short, compact stroke, already knows how to use the middle of the field and could be good for 20-plus home runs a year once he fills out. The San Diego native signed late, so has yet to make his pro debut. ETA: Mid-1999.

Shortstop—Joe Lawrence, Blue Jays (first round, number 16 overall). A compensation pick for the loss of free agent Robert Alomar, Lawrence probably won't approach Alomar's level of stardom but should be an offensive-minded middle infielder. A hamstring injury limited him to a .217 average in the New York-Penn League, a heady assignment for a high school player, but he should hit for average with some power. The Lake Charles, La., product could wind up at third base if he hit outgrows shortstop. ETA: Late 1999.

Outfielder—Chad Green, Brewers (first round, number eight overall). A reserve on the U.S. Olympic team, Green was a perfect fit for Milwaukee, which craved a center fielder and leadoff hitter. Green was the fastest player available in the draft, and was a star high school running back who attracted the interest of several college football powers before going to Kentucky. He has some pop, but needs to stop worrying about trying to go deep and let his speed carry him. ETA: Early 1999.

Outfielder—Dermal Brown, Royals (first round, number 14 overall). Like Green, Brown was a highly touted high school running back, and he could have gone from Marlboro, N.Y. to the University of Maryland had he wanted to stick with the gridiron. Kansas City scouting director Art Stewart says he has seen just three high school hitters who could hit a homer as quick and as far as Brown: Bo Jackson, Dave Kingman and Greg Luzinski. He went just one-for-20 in the Gulf Coast League after signing late, but should also hit for average and be a threat on the bases. ETA: Early 2000.

Outfielder—Jacque Jones, Twins (second round). Jones finished second on the U.S. Olympic team in most offensive categories, trailing only first baseman Travis Lee, Minnesota's first-round pick who signed with the Diamondbacks as a free agent. Jones doesn't have overwhelming tools, but he can hit and should add some homers and steals. A star at Southern California, he went two-for-three in the Florida State League before a minor knee injury ended his summer. ETA: Early 1999.

Designated Hitter—Danny Peoples, Indians (first round, number 28 overall). Even though Cleveland was swimming in money after selling out Jacobs Field for the entire season, the Tribe decided no player available when they picked warranted market value. So the Indians decided to take the first player on their draft list who would accept $400,000, and that turned out to be Peoples. The former Texas standout has impressive power and probably will wind up at first base despite playing third in his debut. He hit .239-3-26 in 117 New York-Penn League at-bats, then injured his shoulder and had surgery. ETA: Late 1999.

Starting Pitcher—Seth Greisinger, Tigers (first round, number six overall). Detroit really wanted John Patterson, but settled for Greisinger when Patterson went the pick before to Montreal. It couldn't have turned out better for the Tigers, who wound up with the pitcher who supplanted number one overall pick Kris Benson as the ace of the Olympic team and became the first Team USA pitcher ever to win nine games in a summer. Greisinger, a righthander who led Virginia to a surprising Atlantic Coast Conference championship, has a solid fastball to go with an outstanding curveball and changeup. He may start his pro career in Double-A and should reach Detroit in a hurry.

Starting Pitcher—Billy Koch, Blue Jays (first round, number four overall). Koch, who joined fellow Clemson ace Benson as the highest drafted pair of pitchers from one school, spent the summer in the U.S. Olympic starting rotation. A righthander, Koch should become a Toronto fan favorite, what with his 100-mph fastball (the hardest in the 1996 draft) and crazy antics (he's nicknamed "Captain Chaos" for good reason). How soon he helps Toronto and how big a star he becomes will depend on how well he can harness his command. ETA: Mid-1999.

Starting Pitcher—Eric Milton, Yankees (first round, number 20 overall). All three pitchers on this AL team starred in the ACC, though Milton did so for a dreadful Maryland program that plays in a hitter's paradise. A lefthander, he throws an ever-improving fastball and curveball and is fairly polished. He signed late, spending his summer pitching a no-hitter and setting a record with a 0.21 ERA in the Cape Cod League. ETA: Late 1998.

Closer—None. No frontline pitching prospect drafted by an AL team is slated for relief at this point.

NATIONAL LEAGUE DRAFT ALL-STARS

Catcher—Catcher—Lee Evans, Pirates (fourth round). Evans didn't receive a lot of attention as a high school player in Northport, Ala., but he reminds Pittsburgh of its incumbent catcher, Jason Kendall. Evans is a switch-hitter with the athletic ability to play just about anywhere on the diamond, and his best tool is his power. In his initial taste of pro ball, he batted .279—3-20 in 111 Gulf Coast League at-bats.

First Baseman—A.J. Zapp, Braves (first round, number 27 overall). Zapp, who hails from Greenwood, Ind., is an offensive machine. He had the best raw power of any player in the draft, and Atlanta says he's the best pure hitter it has drafted since taking Bob Horner number one overall in 1978.

Second Baseman—Brent Butler, Cardinals (third round). A shortstop out of Laurinburg, N.C., Butler is at second base on this team because scouts aren't convinced he can play short. But no one doubts his hitting ability after he batted .343-eight-50 in 248 at-bats and stole seven bases to win the Appalachian League MVP award. St. Louis, which believes he's one of the best hitters it has signed in years, responded by challenging him with an assignment in Hawaii Winter Baseball. ETA: Late 1999.

Third Baseman—Damian Rolls, Dodgers (first round, number 23 overall). The Kansas City, Kan. native improved his stock as much as anyone in the last weeks before the June draft. He's a good athlete who can run and throw and has untapped power. He batted .265-4-27 with 11 doubles in 257 at-bats and eight steals in the Northwest League, a good test for a high school player. ETA: Early 2000.

Shortstop—Mike Caruso, Giants (second round). San Francisco had a poor draft, but did find a keeper in Caruso. Like Rolls, he held his own in the Northwest League, batting .292-two-24 in 312 at-bats and swiping 24 bases. He's a switch-hitter with legitimate offensive ability and slightly above-average speed. ETA: Early 2000.

Outfielder—Mark Kotsay, Marlins (first round, number nine overall). Scouts still aren't excited about Kotsay's physical tools, but he went ninth in the draft on the basis of his hitting ability and his intangibles, which include unmatched desire, work ethic and will to win. After starring for the U.S. Olympic team, he stepped right into the Midwest League and easily adjusted to wood bats, hitting .283-2-8 in 60 at-bats. He led Cal State Fullerton to the College World Series title in 1995, when he won the Golden Spikes Award. ETA: Late 1998.

Outfielder—Robert Stratton, Mets (first round, number 13 overall). Coming out of Santa Barbara, Calif., Stratton is somewhat raw but shows plenty to like: power, decent speed and strong arm. His best tool is his longball ability, and he could grow into an above-average hitter as well. A minor elbow problem hampered him in his first pro summer, when he hit .254-two-nine in 59 Gulf Coast League at-bats. ETA: Early 2000.

Outfielder—Vernon Maxwell, Padres (second round). The best all-around athlete in the draft, Maxwell could have gone from Midwest City, Okla. to play safety at Tennessee. He has the total package, with six.five-second speed in the 60-yard dash, arm strength, defensive skills and hitting ability. He batted .253 with 10 extra-base hits in 194 at-bats and 15 steals in the Arizona Fall League after signing. ETA: Early 2000.

Starting Pitcher—Kris Benson, Pirates (first round, number one overall). Benson, Baseball America's 1996 College Player of the Year, dominated hitters while at Clemson and established a record for drafted players (non-free agent division) with a $two million bonus. Though the righthander spent the summer pitching for the U.S. Olympic team—he absorbed the upset loss to Japan in the semifinals—he should be the first player from the 1996 draft to reach the majors. Some scouts believe his 95-mph fastball, command of three pitches and professional approach could take him straight to Pittsburgh if the Pirates so desire. He'll probably debut in Double-A instead. ETA: Late 1997.

Starting Pitcher—Adam Eaton, Phillies (first round, number 11 overall). Eaton was part of a bumper crop of pitching talent in the state of Washington last spring, and the Snohomish native could solve Philadelphia's pitching problems in the near future. His fastball shot up from the mid-80s in 1995 to the 91-93 mph range in 1996, and as a teenager he could add even more velocity. He has yet to show his stuff as a pro because he signed late in the summer. ETA: Early 2000.

Starting Pitcher—Jake Westbrook, Rockies (first round, number 21 overall). Because Colorado has no trouble attracting quality hitters to Coors Field, it usually focuses on pitching in the draft. Westbrook was the latest example, coming out of Danielsville, Georgia, to earn top-prospect honors in the Arizona League (4-2, 2.87, 57 strikeouts in 63 innings) and star in the Northwest League (1-1, 2.55, 19 strikeouts in 25 innings). His fastball currently tops out at 92 mph and should improve as he grows into his six-foot-three, 180-pound frame. ETA: Late 1999.

Closer—Braden Looper, Cardinals (first round, number three overall). Looper easily was the best relief prospect in the draft after blowing away hitters for Wichita State and the U.S. Olympic team with a fastball that reaches 98 mph. He also throws a hard slider and has excellent command of both pitches. He also has a nasty changeup and could be a star as a starter, but his likely role will be to take over the St. Louis bullpen as soon as Dennis Eckersley falters, ETA: Early 1998.

FIVE BEST DRAFTS

1. Red Sox. Boston has had the best series of drafts since Wayne Britton became scouting director in 1993, and this was no exception. The Red Sox landed a pair of power righthanders in first-round picks Josh Garrett and Chris Reitsma, and also picked up LoCurto while continuing their focus on young arms and athletes.

2. Padres. San Diego's first-round pick was solid shortstop Matt Halloran, but really scored by spending big money to land Maxwell ($425,000) and Jason Middlebrook, a power righthander who has bounced back from arm problems, in the ninth round. Middlebrook received $750,000, a record for a non-first-round selection.

3. Rangers. Texas had four picks in the first two rounds and used them to stock up on pitching with R.A. Dickey, Sam Marsonek, Corey Lee and Derrick Cook. The Rangers' next three picks, infielder Derek Baker, Kelly Dransfeldt and Warren Morris, also have potential.

4. Rockies. Colorado drafted pitchers with 14 of its first 15 picks, and scored with Westbrook, John Nicholson (second round) and Shawn Chacon (third) at the top. Also keep an eye on Alvin Rivera (eighth), Tom Stepka (10th) and Scott Schroeffel (15th).

5. Blue Jays. Besides Koch, Lawrence and Stromsborg, all of whom made our AL team of draft picks to watch, Toronto also landed the offensive potential of Pete Tucci (first round) and Brent Abernathy (second round). Fifth-round pick John Bale has exceptional potential for a lefthander if he can improve his command.

Honorable Mention: Diamondbacks. Lee and Patterson weren't selected by Arizona, but factor them in with lefthander Nick Bierbrodt (first round) and catcher Mark Osborne (third round), and the Diamondbacks signed plenty of talent in their first draft year.

DRAFT REPORT CARDS, 1993-96

A—Potential major league star.
B—Potential major league regular.
C—Potential major leaguer.
D—Disappointment thus far.
F—Failure; no chance to play in major leagues.

1993

1. Alex Rodriguez, ss, Mariners	A
2. Darren Dreifort, rhp, Dodgers	B
3. Brian Anderson, lhp, Angels (now with Indians)	C
4. Wayne Gomes, rhp, Phillies	C
5. Jeff Granger, lhp, Royals	C
6. Steve Soderstrom, rhp, Giants	C
7. Trot Nixon, of, Red Sox	B
8. Kirk Presley, rhp, Mets	D
9. Matt Brunson, ss, Tigers	F
10. Brooks Kieschnick, of, Cubs	B
11. Daron Kirkreit, rhp, Indians	D
12. Billy Wagner, lhp, Astros	A
13. Matt Drews, rhp, Yankees (now with Tigers)	B
14. Derrek Lee, 1b, Padres	A
15. Chris Carpenter, rhp, Blue Jays	B
16. Alan Benes, rhp, Cardinals	A
17. Scott Christman, lhp, White Sox	D
18. Chris Schwab, of, Expos	D
19. Jay Powell, rhp, Orioles (now with Marlins)	B
20. Torii Hunter, of, Twins	B
21. Jason Varitek, c, Twins	Did not sign
22. Charles Peterson, of, Pirates	B
23. Jeff D'Amico, rhp, Brewers	B
24. Jon Ratliff, rhp, Cubs	C
25. John Wasdin, rhp, Athletics	B
26. Kelly Wunsch, lhp, Brewers	D
27. Marc Valdes, rhp, Marlins	C
28. Jamey Wright, rhp, Rockies	B

1994

1. Paul Wilson, rhp, Mets	A
2. Ben Grieve, of, Athletics	A
3. Dustin Hermanson, rhp, Padres	B
4. Antone Williamson, 3b, Brewers	C
5. Josh Booty, ss, Marlins	C
6. McKay Christensen, of, Angels	C
7. Doug Million, lhp, Rockies	B
8. Todd Walker, 2b, Twins	A
9. C.J. Nitkowski, lhp, Reds (now with Tigers)	C
10. Jaret Wright, rhp, Indians	A
11. Mark Farriss, ss, Pirates	C
12. Nomar Garciaparra, ss, Red Sox	A
13. Paul Konerko, c, Dodgers	A
14. Jason Varitek, c, Mariners	B
15. Jayson Peterson, rhp, Cubs	C
16. Matt Smith, 1b, Royals	C
17. Ramon Castro, c, Astros	C
18. Cade Gaspar, rhp, Tigers (now with Padres)	C
19. Bret Wagner, lhp, Cardinals (now with Athletics)	C
20. Terrence Long, of-1b, Mets	B
21. Hiram Bocachica, ss, Expos	B
22. Dante Powell, of, Giants	B
23. Carlton Loewer, rhp, Phillies	C
24. Brian Buchanan, 1b-of, Yankees	C
25. Scott Elarton, rhp, Astros	B
26. Mark Johnson, c, White Sox	C
27. Jacob Shumate, rhp, Braves	D
28. Kevin Witt, ss, Blue Jays	B

1995

1. Darin Erstad, of, Angels	A
2. Ben Davis, c, Padres	C
3. Jose Cruz Jr., of, Mariners	A
4. Kerry Wood, rhp, Cubs	A
5. Ariel Prieto, rhp, Athletics	B
6. Jaime Jones, of, Marlins	B
7. Jonathan Johnson, rhp, Rangers	B
8. Todd Helton, 1b, Rockies	A
9. Geoff Jenkins, of, Brewers	A
10. Chad Hermansen, ss, Pirates	A
11. Mike Drumright, rhp, Tigers	B
12. Matt Morris, rhp, Cardinals	B
13. Mark Redman, lhp, Twins	B
14. Reggie Taylor, of, Phillies	C

15. Andy Yount, rhp, Red Sox	C
16. Joe Fontenot, rhp, Giants	B
17. Roy Halladay, rhp, Blue Jays	B
18. Ryan Jaroncyk, ss, Mets	C
19. Juan LeBron, of, Royals	C
20. David Yocum, lhp, Dodgers	C
21. Alvie Shepherd, rhp, Orioles	C
22. Tony McKnight, rhp, Astros	D
23. David Miller, 1b-of, Indians	C
24. Corey Jenkins, of, Red Sox	C
25. Jeff Liefer, 3b, White Sox	B
26. Chad Hutchinson, rhp, Braves	Did not sign
27. Shea Morenz, of, Yankees	C
28. Michael Barrett, ss, Expos	B

1996

These players have had very limited exposure to professional baseball, and thus these grades are not as accurate as the others.

1. Kris Benson, rhp, Pirates — A
2. Travis Lee, 1b, Twins (now with Diamondbacks) — A
3. Braden Looper, rhp, Cardinals — A
4. Billy Koch, rhp, Blue Jays — B
5. John Patterson, rhp, Expos — B
6. Seth Greisinger, rhp, Tigers — A
7. Matt White, rhp, Giants (unsigned free agent) — A
8. Chad Green, of, Brewers — B
9. Mark Kotsay, of, Marlins — A
10. Eric Chavez, 3b, Athletics — A
11. Adam Eaton, rhp, Phillies — B
12. Bobby Seay, lhp, White Sox (now with Devil Rays) — B
13. Robert Stratton, of, Mets — B
14. Dermal Brown, of, Royals — B
15. Matt Halloran, ss, Padres — B
16. Joe Lawrence, ss, Blue Jays — B
17. Todd Noel, rhp, Cubs — B
18. R.A. Dickey, rhp, Rangers — B
19. Mark Johnson, rhp, Astros — B
20. Eric Milton, lhp, Yankees — B
21. Jake Westbrook, rhp, Rockies — A
22. Gil Meche, rhp, Mariners — B
23. Damian Rolls, 3b, Dodgers — B
24. Sam Marsonek, rhp, Rangers — B
25. John Oliver, of, Reds — B
26. Josh Garrett, rhp, Red Sox — B
27. A.J. Zapp, 1b, Braves — B
28. Danny Peoples, 1b, Indians — B

Hitters 1998 Forecast Stats and Dollar Values

Name	Value	AB	R	HR	RBI	SB	AVG
A							
Jeff Abbott	$10	450	61	8	46	5	.295
Kurt Abbott	$3	289	38	8	34	3	.264
Bob Abreu	$12	505	59	8	68	17	.263
Manny Alexander	$9	456	66	5	40	24	.245
Edgardo Alfonzo	$15	500	70	9	69	9	.300
Luis Alicea	$10	436	65	6	44	20	.256
Jermaine Allensworth	$9	413	61	4	50	17	.263
Roberto Alomar	$24	475	85	16	71	14	.328
Sandy Alomar	$14	416	57	17	68	1	.304
Moises Alou	$18	519	84	22	104	9	.281
Rich Amaral	$9	251	50	1	25	18	.287
Ruben Amaro	-$2	146	16	2	18	1	.252
Brady Anderson	$25	583	104	27	83	20	.288
Garret Anderson	$18	594	74	10	84	9	.299
Shane Andrews	-$1	173	22	9	28	1	.220
Eric Anthony	-$1	113	16	5	12	1	.246
Alex Arias	-$1	145	18	2	17	1	.264
George Arias	-$2	87	13	2	15	1	.250
Billy Ashley	$4	348	37	18	58	0	.243
Rich Aurilia	$1	208	24	4	26	3	.266
Brad Ausmus	$8	405	46	4	41	11	.274
B							
Carlos Baerga	$9	488	58	11	60	3	.276
Jeff Bagwell	$35	555	108	37	126	26	.299
Harold Baines	$15	458	63	19	75	1	.304
Brian Banks	-$3	110	15	3	13	0	.224
Tony Barron	-$2	114	13	2	14	0	.267
Kim Bartee	-$1	78	12	1	9	5	.256
Tony Batista	$3	328	45	7	32	5	.259
Danny Bautista	-$2	114	15	3	11	2	.230
Trey Beamon	$4	255	24	3	28	7	.280
Rich Becker	$14	523	78	11	59	19	.271
David Bell	-$4	143	10	1	12	1	.216
Derek Bell	$19	529	72	15	85	20	.276
Jay Bell	$15	555	81	18	82	8	.277
Mike Bell	-$1	140	18	7	22	1	.239
Albert Belle	$26	616	103	37	127	6	.289
Mark Bellhorn	$6	398	59	12	33	12	.248
Rafael Belliard	-$5	103	9	1	3	1	.196
Marvin Benard	$1	218	35	2	16	9	.244
Yamil Benitez	$7	422	48	17	48	3	.260
Mike Benjamin	-$2	119	13	2	9	3	.240
Geronimo Berroa	$19	567	92	29	95	3	.285
Sean Berry	$8	341	43	11	60	5	.271
Damon Berryhill	-$3	100	10	2	14	0	.238
Dante Bichette	$31	584	93	29	126	14	.313
Steve Bieser	-$3	41	10	0	2	1	.233
Craig Biggio	$38	608	134	20	79	50	.302
Jeff Blauser	$11	484	83	16	62	7	.269
Mike Blowers	$3	259	32	8	37	0	.274
Hiram Bocachica	$3	254	41	6	21	8	.258
Tim Bogar	$2	312	42	5	37	5	.252
Wade Boggs	$7	408	65	4	35	0	.303
Barry Bonds	$41	538	124	41	113	41	.296
Bobby Bonilla	$20	571	88	21	102	4	.297
Aaron Boone	-$2	107	16	2	14	2	.237
Bret Boone	$0	473	47	9	55	4	.231
Pat Borders	$0	179	16	4	16	0	.280
Mike Bordick	$1	506	51	7	48	3	.243
Rafael Bournigal	-$1	209	27	1	17	2	.266
Darren Bragg	$9	525	74	11	59	13	.257
Jeff Branson	-$2	318	32	8	32	1	.227
Brent Brede	$6	277	37	5	30	9	.275

Name	Value	AB	R	HR	RBI	SB	AVG	Name	Value	AB	R	HR	RBI	SB	AVG
Tilson Brito	-$3	127	13	2	11	1	.232	Mike Devereaux	$0	179	25	4	21	4	.239
Rico Brogna	$11	512	63	19	77	8	.257	Alex Diaz	-$2	105	13	2	11	4	.233
Scott Brosius	$4	424	60	14	48	7	.237	Edwin Diaz	$2	300	27	8	33	5	.244
Adrian Brown	$3	222	25	3	15	13	.250	Einer Diaz	-$3	86	10	0	7	0	.251
Brant Brown	$3	244	28	9	28	5	.258	Mike Difelice	-$2	158	10	2	19	1	.239
Emil Brown	$0	145	20	2	15	8	.234	Gary Disarcina	$3	526	56	4	47	6	.253
Jacob Brumfield	$2	261	39	6	33	9	.238	Rob Ducey	$2	174	30	6	12	4	.285
Damon Buford	$6	280	41	7	31	14	.251	Mariano Duncan	$5	350	44	4	35	5	.276
Jay Buhner	$16	540	103	41	119	0	.253	Todd Dunn	-$2	123	18	3	10	3	.232
Ellis Burks	$28	476	103	34	95	15	.310	Shawon Dunston	$19	428	57	11	49	23	.300
Jeromy Burnitz	$23	527	93	28	93	19	.279	Todd Dunwoody	$9	369	42	12	49	12	.258
Rich Butler	$6	305	46	9	43	6	.268	Ray Durham	$19	595	94	10	56	31	.271
Rob Butler	-$2	53	6	0	8	1	.273	Jermaine Dye	$9	511	52	17	50	6	.262
C								**E**							
Orlando Cabrera	$12	395	67	5	35	24	.268	Damion Easley	$17	486	83	19	65	23	.260
Miguel Cairo	$4	356	38	3	33	15	.245	Jim Edmonds	$18	486	83	27	79	4	.294
Mike Cameron	$17	410	67	21	59	25	.260	Jim Eisenreich	$5	281	36	3	34	0	.310
Ken Caminiti	$25	508	95	30	102	11	.303	Kevin Elster	$2	244	33	12	46	1	.241
John Cangelosi	$3	264	44	1	17	12	.258	Angel Encarnacion	-$4	94	11	0	6	0	.244
Jose Canseco	$12	380	60	25	77	6	.258	Juan Encarnacion	$6	238	40	10	40	7	.268
Chuck Carr	$2	205	33	3	16	11	.249	Darin Erstad	$22	536	97	15	72	21	.297
Joe Carter	$11	611	78	24	101	8	.242	Alvaro Espinoza	-$2	131	13	3	14	1	.238
Raul Casanova	$1	322	28	9	32	2	.246	Bobby Estalella	-$1	119	17	6	18	2	.224
Sean Casey	$2	193	23	8	25	0	.285	Tony Eusebio	$0	181	16	2	22	0	.278
Vinny Castilla	$28	609	94	39	111	4	.304	Carl Everett	$7	325	44	9	41	11	.260
Alberto Castillo	-$5	105	5	0	10	0	.209	**F**							
Luis Castillo	$9	333	39	0	11	24	.270	Jorge Fabregas	$2	315	28	5	41	1	.264
Juan Castro	-$5	98	8	0	5	0	.201	Sal Fasano	-$3	81	14	3	15	0	.224
Frank Catalanotto	-$2	100	13	2	11	2	.238	Tony Fernandez	$5	245	33	7	26	4	.286
Domingo Cedeno	$3	325	45	3	29	4	.277	Cecil Fielder	$9	443	57	23	80	1	.255
Roger Cedeno	$11	513	75	6	45	21	.263	Steve Finley	$23	589	109	27	88	19	.277
Raul Chavez	-$4	44	3	0	3	0	.231	John Flaherty	$7	424	39	10	51	3	.274
Archi Cianfrocco	$2	201	24	4	28	5	.256	Darrin Fletcher	$7	339	40	15	55	1	.274
Jeff Cirillo	$15	551	80	11	78	4	.299	Cliff Floyd	$14	443	65	17	56	17	.266
Dave Clark	$2	173	23	6	32	2	.277	Chad Fonville	-$3	98	14	0	6	4	.210
Tony Clark	$16	545	94	32	108	1	.269	Brook Fordyce	-$3	100	7	2	8	2	.230
Will Clark	$13	412	63	13	61	1	.310	Julio Franco	$11	388	62	8	49	11	.287
Royce Clayton	$17	544	70	8	53	30	.267	Matt Franco	-$1	109	14	3	13	1	.269
Greg Colbrunn	$8	369	41	11	51	3	.282	Jeff Frye	$14	399	60	3	46	17	.301
Michael Coleman	$3	260	30	7	30	4	.269	Travis Fryman	$17	599	89	21	99	11	.272
Lou Collier	$5	350	50	2	34	10	.264	Brad Fullmer	$7	421	50	14	59	3	.263
Jeff Conine	$10	441	56	20	71	2	.268	**G**							
Ron Coomer	$11	394	50	12	65	3	.297	Gary Gaetti	$10	509	67	21	75	5	.259
Scott Cooper	-$3	115	8	2	11	1	.220	Greg Gagne	$4	480	50	9	56	3	.253
Joey Cora	$14	546	96	9	50	7	.297	Andres Galarraga	$26	603	100	38	120	12	.280
Wil Cordero	$9	453	64	13	59	2	.282	Ron Gant	$12	498	76	23	76	16	.238
Marty Cordova	$12	449	64	16	72	8	.274	Carlos Garcia	$4	364	41	4	32	12	.248
Craig Counsell	$2	302	37	3	31	3	.270	Freddy Garcia	$0	240	24	9	29	1	.242
Steve Cox	-$1	170	21	4	25	1	.239	Karim Garcia	$4	398	52	10	56	6	.244
Felipe Crespo	$1	250	35	5	26	4	.250	Nomar Garciaparra	$32	625	110	27	92	21	.314
Tripp Cromer	-$2	75	7	3	17	0	.251	Brent Gates	$0	317	37	4	39	1	.250
Deivi Cruz	$0	411	33	2	38	3	.249	Jason Giambi	$14	524	73	20	80	0	.291
Ivan Cruz	-$3	46	5	2	7	0	.224	Benji Gil	-$3	233	25	4	24	1	.224
Jacob Cruz	$5	306	60	6	54	5	.270	Brian Giles	$9	263	46	12	45	9	.281
Jose Cruz	$21	537	79	34	95	10	.278	Bernard Gilkey	$17	530	91	22	89	11	.275
Midre Cummings	$0	279	32	5	27	1	.258	Joe Girardi	$5	412	46	2	49	5	.273
Chad Curtis	$13	419	71	15	54	15	.270	Doug Glanville	$13	512	83	5	40	20	.280
D								Chris Gomez	$2	513	60	5	53	4	.251
Johnny Damon	$15	508	71	8	51	20	.280	Alex Gonzalez	$7	505	58	13	49	16	.238
Darren Daulton	$4	275	46	9	43	4	.260	Juan Gonzalez	$27	517	85	42	130	1	.302
Chili Davis	$18	488	73	28	91	5	.287	Luis Gonzalez	$10	522	75	12	71	9	.263
Eric Davis	$10	219	42	13	40	11	.294	Curtis Goodwin	$10	326	37	1	16	28	.261
Russ Davis	$11	472	65	21	67	6	.265	Tom Goodwin	$22	550	85	2	37	48	.269
Carlos Delgado	$13	525	78	29	93	0	.263	Mark Grace	$20	552	88	12	79	2	.323
Wilson Delgado	-$2	92	13	0	7	3	.240	Tony Graffanino	$6	325	57	13	34	10	.249
Dave Dellucci	$8	346	46	14	43	4	.280	Craig Grebeck	-$3	120	12	1	8	0	.255
Delino Deshields	$26	560	84	9	51	51	.270	Shawn Green	$17	482	63	18	66	11	.294

Name	Value	AB	R	HR	RBI	SB	AVG	Name	Value	AB	R	HR	RBI	SB	AVG
Charlie Greene	-$5	100	8	0	8	0	.210	Charles Johnson	$9	415	60	20	71	0	.265
Todd Greene	$13	388	67	22	67	6	.280	Lance Johnson	$26	511	81	7	50	31	.317
Willie Greene	$12	498	67	27	96	5	.250	Mark Johnson	$1	256	38	8	34	3	.238
Rusty Greer	$25	565	102	22	88	8	.320	Russ Johnson	-$1	58	6	2	8	2	.270
Ben Grieve	$16	503	90	21	103	2	.284	Andruw Jones	$20	511	74	23	87	25	.259
Ken Griffey	$35	554	118	50	134	14	.302	Chipper Jones	$27	590	103	24	108	17	.297
Marquis Grissom	$20	591	84	15	66	25	.277	Chris Jones	$1	154	24	6	24	5	.247
Mark Grudzielanek	$17	613	78	4	47	26	.282	Brian Jordan	$14	380	56	9	59	17	.285
Vladimir Guerrero	$20	530	70	18	63	10	.308	Kevin Jordan	$0	151	17	5	22	1	.267
Wilton Guerrero	$7	328	37	3	29	10	.287	Wally Joyner	$18	509	68	12	88	5	.311
Jose Guillen	$11	511	60	17	72	2	.274	David Justice	$24	480	82	30	96	4	.320
Ozzie Guillen	$2	485	59	4	49	5	.251	**K**							
Ricky Gutierrez	$3	323	37	2	32	6	.268	Ron Karkovice	-$3	222	24	8	27	0	.205
Tony Gwynn	$33	544	87	12	95	12	.367	Eric Karros	$21	614	85	32	106	12	.267
H								Mike Kelly	$14	412	74	15	55	22	.256
Shane Halter	$0	143	19	2	12	4	.275	Pat Kelly	-$1	105	19	2	10	6	.235
Bob Hamelin	$5	283	40	14	46	3	.259	Roberto Kelly	$12	368	53	10	55	7	.298
Darryl Hamilton	$12	514	82	5	47	15	.279	Jason Kendall	$12	416	59	6	42	12	.296
Jeffrey Hammonds	$8	330	56	16	43	10	.254	Jeff Kent	$14	526	79	23	96	9	.261
Dave Hansen	$0	140	15	2	16	1	.288	Brooks Kieschnick	$9	328	36	16	75	5	.260
Jed Hanson	$4	202	25	4	29	7	.276	Jeff King	$17	548	84	28	109	15	.251
Jason Hardtke	-$2	88	10	2	12	2	.243	Wayne Kirby	-$4	119	14	0	7	2	.227
Lenny Harris	$4	253	32	4	28	8	.272	Ryan Klesko	$15	490	75	28	88	5	.271
Bill Haselman	$0	214	25	7	28	1	.249	Chuck Knoblauch	$38	594	123	10	63	55	.309
Scott Hatteberg	$1	213	29	6	26	0	.276	Paul Konerko	$4	314	44	13	53	1	.255
Charlie Hayes	$8	483	54	13	72	5	.258	Mark Kotsay	$10	447	43	6	29	29	.245
Todd Helton	$19	505	72	23	84	5	.300	Chad Kreuter	-$3	195	20	4	19	0	.229
Rickey Henderson	$17	422	90	8	35	41	.251	**L**							
Chad Hermansen	-$4	65	4	0	4	0	.232	Tim Laker	-$2	100	13	2	16	0	.262
Carlos Hernandez	$2	270	29	6	26	0	.280	Tom Lampkin	$0	198	25	6	23	2	.243
Jose Hernandez	$3	234	39	9	32	3	.257	Ray Lankford	$29	520	101	29	98	28	.287
Jose Herrera	-$1	95	13	2	8	2	.266	Mike Lansing	$24	582	91	20	70	14	.310
Jason Herrick	-$1	125	15	5	16	2	.242	Barry Larkin	$20	339	65	14	45	24	.309
Richard Hidalgo	$10	467	63	13	50	11	.265	Chris Latham	-$2	94	10	2	9	2	.247
Bob Higginson	$22	501	85	25	89	10	.298	Matt Lawton	$11	520	81	15	73	10	.260
Glenallen Hill	$11	402	52	15	67	9	.267	Ricky Ledee	$2	317	37	9	47	0	.254
Denny Hocking	$1	267	31	3	25	4	.256	Aaron Ledesma	$1	143	38	3	19	3	.277
Chris Hoiles	$6	349	52	17	57	1	.258	Derrek Lee	-$1	229	20	4	22	1	.252
Todd Hollandsworth	$6	331	44	7	38	10	.266	Travis Lee	$10	508	83	22	89	1	.260
Dave Hollins	$17	514	92	15	76	11	.289	Mark Lemke	$0	400	43	3	31	3	.250
Tyler Houston	$1	160	15	2	25	2	.275	Patrick Lennon	-$1	131	17	2	15	0	.286
Dave Howard	-$2	249	32	2	24	3	.230	Brian Lesher	-$2	103	14	4	14	2	.230
Thomas Howard	$2	289	34	4	28	4	.262	Jessie Levis	-$1	192	20	1	18	1	.268
Jack Howell	$9	302	45	23	57	2	.262	Darren Lewis	$5	241	36	2	27	18	.247
Mike Hubbard	-$5	63	4	1	3	0	.181	Mark Lewis	$4	321	44	8	38	3	.271
Trenidad Hubbard	$0	156	28	4	23	4	.249	Jim Leyritz	$6	333	45	9	54	2	.278
Rex Hudler	$4	186	31	8	21	6	.270	Mike Lieberthal	$7	448	57	19	74	3	.247
Todd Hundley	$10	333	58	24	68	1	.268	Nelson Liriano	-$1	144	16	2	19	1	.256
Brianl Hunter	$29	585	95	4	40	60	.273	Pat Listach	-$1	208	27	0	16	11	.215
Jimmy Hurst	-$5	55	0	0	0	0	.211	Scott Livingstone	-$2	111	11	1	13	1	.256
Butch Huskey	$13	416	50	19	68	5	.282	Keith Lockhart	$8	346	48	8	55	6	.281
Jeff Huson	-$1	135	14	1	11	3	.253	Kenny Lofton	$34	543	103	8	54	44	.325
I								Javier Lopez	$13	428	52	22	67	1	.292
Raul Ibanez	-$3	46	5	2	5	0	.254	Luis Lopez	-$2	107	11	1	11	1	.266
Pete Incaviglia	-$3	90	11	4	11	0	.220	Luisp Lopez	$0	243	18	3	21	6	.241
J								Mendy Lopez	$1	290	32	3	22	6	.257
Damian Jackson	$3	281	45	7	24	10	.246	Mark Loretta	$3	262	36	3	28	3	.285
Darrin Jackson	$0	127	16	3	22	2	.259	**M**							
John Jaha	$10	292	53	19	58	2	.284	John Mabry	$4	285	30	5	31	1	.291
Bates Jason	-$3	153	20	3	14	1	.235	Mike Macfarlane	$3	304	42	12	42	1	.249
Stan Javier	$15	404	65	6	44	24	.282	Robert Machado	-$3	308	39	8	39	0	.215
Gregg Jefferies	$11	455	65	10	50	14	.271	Shane Mack	$5	221	23	6	28	3	.299
Reggie Jefferson	$16	421	67	14	65	1	.326	Dave Magadan	$3	248	34	4	28	1	.294
Robin Jennings	$4	313	43	9	49	2	.266	Wendell Magee	-$4	112	7	1	10	1	.202
Marcus Jensen	-$1	347	39	4	36	1	.244	Kirt Manwaring	-$4	308	20	1	25	1	.230
Derek Jeter	$20	572	101	9	66	18	.298	Elieser Marrero	$5	336	54	11	57	6	.248
Brian Johnson	$7	407	39	16	57	1	.263	Al Martin	$23	487	76	15	61	27	.294

Name	Value	AB	R	HR	RBI	SB	AVG
Norberto Martin	$9	407	55	4	48	9	.289
Dave Martinez	$15	465	77	11	53	13	.296
Edgar Martinez	$28	526	111	28	107	3	.332
Felix Martinez	-$1	150	12	1	9	5	.241
Tino Martinez	$25	587	91	37	131	2	.295
John Marzano	-$2	92	8	1	9	0	.272
Damon Mashore	$0	256	50	4	18	5	.250
Mike Matheny	-$2	303	28	5	35	1	.232
Derrick May	-$2	110	9	2	13	2	.236
Brent Mayne	$0	214	22	4	18	1	.270
David McCarty	-$2	69	7	2	8	1	.252
Quinton McCracken	$17	480	89	4	54	33	.268
Jason McDonald	$5	261	51	4	20	15	.251
Willie McGee	$8	293	36	4	37	7	.301
Fred McGriff	$18	576	79	24	100	5	.283
Ryan McGuire	-$1	227	25	4	19	2	.249
Mark McGwire	$27	510	95	57	124	2	.284
Mark McLemore	$5	311	46	2	25	11	.272
Billy McMillon	$0	190	19	3	28	3	.247
Brian McRae	$14	582	94	13	50	24	.258
Pat Meares	$10	458	63	10	61	8	.272
Roberto Mejia	-$4	73	8	1	8	1	.202
Orlando Merced	$10	405	55	12	56	7	.277
Henry Mercedes	-$4	54	9	0	9	0	.224
Matt Mieske	$0	181	26		23	1	.260
Damian Miller	-$2	78	6	2	16	0	.265
Orlando Miller	$0	239	24	6	27	2	.251
Ralph Milliard	-$1	236	35	3	23	6	.226
Izzy Molina	-$3	200	11	4	14	1	.222
Paul Molitor	$23	573	74	10	93	13	.314
Raul Mondesi	$32	613	96	28	87	26	.304
Mickey Morandini	$10	543	76	2	38	14	.281
Mike Mordecai	-$4	76	8	1	4	0	.220
Hal Morris	$9	394	55	7	49	4	.291
James Mouton	$3	228	31	3	27	14	.238
Bill Mueller	$4	244	33	3	27	2	.300
Pedro Munoz	-$2	74	10	3	11	0	.244
Greg Myers	$0	230	29	6	35	0	.251
Rod Myers	$15	501	69	12	63	19	.269
N							
Tim Naehring	$8	328	52	12	49	1	.290
Phil Nevin	$1	302	37	12	42	0	.241
Marc Newfield	$1	319	35	7	44	0	.254
Warren Newson	$1	188	27	10	25	3	.233
Melvin Nieves	$6	397	56	23	65	1	.240
Dave Nilsson	$16	530	76	19	85	2	.293
Otis Nixon	$24	553	85	2	40	50	.274
Trot Nixon	-$2	77	10	2	8	2	.233
Greg Norton	-$3	51	7	1	6	1	.224
Jonathan Nunnally	$16	395	77	22	67	10	.285
O							
Charlie O'Brien	-$2	252	25	7	32	0	.226
Troy O'Leary	$13	488	65	15	77	1	.294
Paul O'Neill	$24	542	88	21	107	6	.315
Sherman Obando	-$1	176	16	7	25	2	.221
Alex Ochoa	$1	231	30	3	23	3	.263
Jose Offerman	$13	466	68	3	41	13	.298
John Olerud	$14	483	79	19	85	0	.289
Joe Oliver	$4	330	30	13	45	1	.255
Magglio Ordonez	$9	312	47	12	53	8	.275
Rey Ordonez	-$1	490	48	1	39	9	.233
Kevin Orie	$7	400	44	9	48	2	.280
Joe Orsulak	-$4	184	19	1	14	0	.234
David Ortiz	$2	218	27	9	40	1	.254
Keith Osik	-$3	105	11	0	8	0	.271
Ricky Otero	$0	219	29	1	12	5	.261
Eric Owens	-$1	85	12	0	4	6	.258
Jayhawk Owens	-$3	51	9	1	6	1	.230
P							
Tom Pagnozzi	$1	252	26	6	32	1	.255
Orlando Palmeiro	-$4	109	14	0	7	1	.236
Rafael Palmeiro	$21	612	99	38	119	6	.270
Dean Palmer	$13	512	74	26	86	2	.266
Craig Paquette	$3	308	38	13	45	3	.242
Mark Parent	-$4	135	11	5	16	0	.190
Jeff Patzke	-$13	100	0	0	0	0	. 0
Jay Payton	-$3	55	7	1	9	0	.270
Tony Pena	-$5	130	10	1	17	0	.200
Terry Pendleton	-$1	190	19	3	27	1	.250
Eddie Perez	-$3	163	18	5	16	0	.228
Eduardo Perez	$5	249	38	14	42	4	.258
Neifi Perez	$17	507	73	10	64	11	.302
Robert Perez	-$2	112	12	2	10	1	.265
Tomas Perez	-$4	172	14	0	12	1	.227
Herbert Perry	-$3	41	5	1	5	0	.284
Tony Phillips	$13	547	105	11	59	13	.274
Mike Piazza	$35	541	97	38	115	3	.353
Phil Plantier	-$1	164	20	6	24	1	.234
Kevin Polcovich	$0	288	29	4	25	3	.253
Luis Polonia	$0	150	20	0	10	5	.273
Jorge Posada	-$1	167	26	6	21	1	.244
Scott Pose	-$3	88	19	0	5	3	.222
Dante Powell	$5	318	47	7	44	13	.242
Todd Pratt	$3	309	34	5	53	0	.270
Curtis Pride	-$1	90	15	2	11	3	.249
Tom Prince	-$2	106	15	3	15	0	.237
Harvey Pulliam	-$1	88	20	4	12	0	.270
R							
Brian Raabe	-$1	73	10	2	8	2	.270
Tim Raines	$9	273	55	6	39	9	.306
Manny Ramirez	$27	550	96	29	97	6	.321
Joe Randa	$14	474	58	8	65	8	.300
Jeff Reboulet	-$1	229	26	3	25	3	.238
Jeff Reed	$6	225	31	11	34	2	.291
Jody Reed	-$2	260	23	1	24	3	.234
Pokey Reese	$5	276	38	3	20	22	.228
Desi Relaford	$4	403	44	5	39	13	.240
Edgar Renteria	$22	605	90	5	50	29	.295
Billy Ripken	-$1	164	17	3	18	0	.266
Cal Ripken	$13	616	83	20	90	1	.272
Ruben Rivera	$10	320	58	9	57	13	.270
Bip Roberts	$13	390	54	3	45	16	.297
Alex Rodriguez	$31	547	104	25	89	22	.317
Henry Rodriguez	$12	508	65	30	91	2	.255
Ivan Rodriguez	$21	599	99	19	79	6	.308
Scott Rolen	$23	550	100	25	95	15	.290
Mel Rosario	-$9	63	0	0	0	0	. 0
S							
Tim Salmon	$25	577	95	32	117	7	.296
Juan Samuel	$2	134	21	5	21	6	.269
Rey Sanchez	$1	335	35	2	23	5	.258
Deion Sanders	$14	279	32	3	14	34	.273
Reggie Sanders	$20	422	72	24	69	25	.266
FP Santangelo	$3	338	51	5	36	6	.260
Benito Santiago	$6	376	44	18	55	1	.254
Kevin Sefcik	-$1	106	10	1	6	2	.274
David Segui	$14	446	73	17	65	2	.301
Kevin Seitzer	$8	340	47	6	45	2	.304
Scott Servais	$3	391	38	8	51	0	.262
Danny Sheaffer	-$2	159	11	1	16	2	.239
Andy Sheets	-$3	86	16	2	8	2	.226
Gary Sheffield	$21	488	101	30	91	14	.276
Scott Sheldon	-$2	104	12	0	11	4	.235
Craig Shipley	$1	134	19	4	16	3	.280

Benson's Baseball Player Guide: 1998

Name	Value	AB	R	HR	RBI	SB	AVG
Ruben Sierra	$1	286	32	7	37	2	.245
Mike Simms	-$2	99	11	4	18	0	.237
Bobby Smith	$4	306	36	5	41	10	.248
Mark Smith	$2	149	21	7	26	2	.275
Chris Snopek	-$2	217	23	5	27	2	.227
JT Snow	$15	546	77	24	93	4	.274
Luis Sojo	$4	349	39	3	35	4	.274
Paul Sorrento	$13	448	66	28	84	0	.273
Sammy Sosa	$25	591	88	37	113	22	.258
Bill Spiers	$7	247	39	4	38	8	.299
Scott Spiezio	$6	509	57	14	63	8	.245
Ed Sprague	$4	532	72	21	67	0	.236
Scott Stahoviak	$3	313	44	10	40	4	.253
Matt Stairs	$15	421	71	29	80	3	.278
Andy Stankiewicz	-$3	110	13	1	7	1	.233
Mike Stanley	$8	297	53	15	55	1	.285
Terry Steinbach	$9	463	64	19	69	4	.259
Lee Stevens	$8	279	37	14	48	1	.294
Shannon Stewart	$16	410	60	0	52	26	.290
Kelly Stinnett	-$3	53	6	1	4	1	.251
Kevin Stocker	$5	462	49	4	40	9	.259
Doug Strange	$2	307	37	9	43	0	.253
Darryl Strawberry	$1	163	28	8	28	4	.243
Chris Stynes	$19	452	70	11	60	20	.300
BJ Surhoff	$14	519	77	18	85	1	.289
Larry Sutton	-$2	75	9	2	9	0	.263
Dale Sveum	$1	194	21	8	30	0	.266
Mark Sweeney	$0	157	20	2	22	2	.275
Mike Sweeney	$3	330	43	9	44	3	.251
T							
Tony Tarasco	$0	169	26	6	22	5	.221
Danny Tartabull	$1	181	23	9	34	0	.246
Fernando Tatis	$12	510	79	21	79	6	.264
Eddie Taubensee	$5	260	32	11	37	1	.278
Jesus Tavarez	-$4	95	15	0	9	2	.214
Miguel Tejada	$4	420	50	10	55	7	.241
Mickey Tettleton	$0	302	40	17	43	1	.208
Frank Thomas	$33	525	109	37	126	1	.344
Jim Thome	$23	508	111	39	106	2	.296
Lee Tinsley	-$2	211	26	2	15	6	.223
Andy Tomberlin	-$2	63	10	3	9	1	.256
Bubba Trammell	$12	440	60	22	71	7	.265
Michael Tucker	$13	479	77	14	58	11	.276
Chris Turner	-$4	56	9	0	6	0	.230
V							
Pedro Valdes	-$3	103	12	0	10	0	.254
Mario Valdez	-$1	169	17	2	20	2	.257
Javier Valentin	-$1	228	27	4	20	1	.248
John Valentin	$19	555	93	17	74	9	.302
Jose Valentin	$11	506	69	16	69	18	.244
John Vanderwal	-$4	129	9	2	16	2	.202
Greg Vaughn	$9	411	72	25	75	8	.233
Mo Vaughn	$29	562	100	38	113	3	.317
Jorge Velandia	-$4	42	4	1	5	0	.225
Randy Velarde	$4	251	39	5	30	5	.273
Robin Ventura	$9	352	56	17	59	1	.280
Quilvio Veras	$21	533	80	5	53	45	.263
Jose Vidro	$3	355	39	7	43	4	.255
Fernando Vina	$9	439	62	6	38	11	.277
Joe Vitiello	$1	268	27	10	40	2	.241
Jose Vizcaino	$6	554	74	4	49	10	.259
Omar Vizquel	$24	556	92	6	54	39	.284
Jack Voigt	$1	165	21	9	23	2	.248
W							
Matt Walbeck	$1	246	29	4	24	4	.254
Larry Walker	$43	555	133	45	125	27	.327
Todd Walker	-$1	118	11	2	11	5	.241
Jerome Walton	-$1	71	11	3	9	1	.302
Turner Ward	$7	233	42	9	42	7	.288
Lenny Webster	-$1	223	25	5	29	0	.250
Walt Weiss	$8	484	71	6	45	9	.273
Devon White	$16	527	73	14	73	23	.262
Rondell White	$19	533	74	21	71	17	.277
Mark Whiten	$6	285	48	11	40	8	.261
Chris Widger	-$2	175	19	4	22	1	.232
Rick Wilkins	-$2	265	31	9	36	0	.219
Bernie Williams	$28	527	106	23	99	15	.319
Eddie Williams	-$2	152	17	5	20	1	.227
George Williams	$1	225	32	5	29	1	.270
Gerald Williams	$8	455	60	8	38	17	.253
Matt Williams	$18	507	78	28	95	8	.276
Antone Williamson	$0	250	24	6	29	1	.251
Dan Wilson	$11	492	59	15	74	5	.275
Enrique Wilson	$8	350	40	6	37	9	.282
Tony Womack	$24	503	69	5	41	47	.279
Ron Wright	$2	280	14	8	18	0	.272
Y							
Dmitri Young	$6	353	41	5	35	7	.274
Eric Young	$26	601	108	8	64	48	.270
Ernie Young	$1	279	40	10	33	3	.233
Kevin Young	$11	300	50	15	63	9	.278
Z							
Gregg Zaun	$0	138	20	2	18	1	.281
Todd Zeile	$15	573	82	28	89	5	.265

Players not listed are forecast to have under 40 at-bats in 1998.

Pitchers 1998 Forecast Stats and Dollar Values

American League Pitchers (including free agents)

Name	Value	IP	W	SV	ERA	Ratio
A						
Willie Adams	-$4	150	8	0	5.08	1.55
Rick Aguilera	$23	80	6	25	4.40	1.29
Scott Aldred	-$10	96	3	0	6.92	1.63
Wilson Alvarez	$12	210	13	0	3.77	1.34
Luis Andujar	-$8	54	1	0	6.39	1.82
Kevin Appier	$17	225	11	0	3.61	1.25
Rolando Arrojo	-$8	154	6	0	5.50	1.62
Paul Assenmacher	$6	55	2	2	2.87	1.20
Steve Avery	-$5	115	6	0	5.48	1.59
Bobby Ayala	$6	85	8	4	4.35	1.36
B						
Scott Bailes	$1	43	1	0	3.46	1.36
James Baldwin	$1	172	11	0	5.08	1.41
Willie Banks	-$2	31	1	0	4.92	1.48
Richard Batchelor	-$2	32	2	0	4.97	1.62
Rod Beck	$35	67	5	36	3.61	1.09
Tim Belcher	$3	181	13	0	4.61	1.44
Andy Benes	$17	194	13	0	3.51	1.24
Armando Benitez	$26	62	4	26	2.85	1.25
Jason Bere	-$5	186	9	0	5.62	1.47
Mike Bertotti	-$9	136	7	0	5.39	1.72
Brian Bevil	$1	31	1	3	5.13	1.40
Doug Bochtler	$1	60	3	2	4.11	1.51

Name	Value	IP	W	SV	ERA	Ratio	Name	Value	IP	W	SV	ERA	Ratio
Ricky Bones	-$10	123	6	0	6.20	1.68	Shigetoshi Hasegawa	$2	90	2	0	3.89	1.41
Shawn Boskie	-$4	114	8	1	5.80	1.53	Latroy Hawkins	-$8	150	9	0	5.60	1.64
Mark Brandenburg	-$1	50	2	0	4.57	1.51	Jimmy Haynes	-$6	73	3	0	5.76	1.70
Billy Brewer	-$2	41	1	0	4.88	1.50	Rick Helling	$4	132	6	0	4.47	1.32
Doug Brocail	$6	138	9	0	3.64	1.43	Butch Henry	$5	85	7	2	4.09	1.37
Jim Bullinger	-$7	147	7	0	5.67	1.55	Pat Hentgen	$20	258	16	0	3.64	1.26
John Burkett	$5	189	10	0	4.42	1.38	Roberto Hernandez	$36	80	8	34	2.38	1.29
C							Xavier Hernandez	$1	62	2	2	4.58	1.41
Tom Candiotti	$6	146	9	0	4.36	1.33	Orel Hershiser	$8	188	15	0	4.34	1.37
Dan Carlson	-$3	33	1	0	5.11	1.68	Ken Hill	$4	208	11	0	4.22	1.46
Rafael Carmona	-$1	31	1	1	4.61	1.65	Darren Holmes	$2	83	8	4	4.79	1.56
Chris Carpenter	-$1	83	4	0	4.10	1.59	Mike Holtz	$3	35	3	1	3.43	1.25
Larry Casian	-$1	31	0	0	4.54	1.43	Joe Hudson	-$1	37	3	0	4.23	1.67
Carlos Castillo	-$1	48	1	1	4.59	1.47	**I**						
Frank Castillo	$2	184	10	0	4.73	1.42	Hideki Irabu	-$10	141	7	0	5.98	1.64
Tony Castillo	4	73	4	4	4.23	1.40	**J**						
Norm Charlton	$2	71	3	10	5.85	1.69	Mike Jackson	$8	72	2	4	3.29	1.22
Robinson Checo	-$1	40	2	0	4.88	1.41	Jason Jacome	-$4	54	2	0	5.64	1.66
Terry Clark	-$7	60	1	0	6.19	1.71	Mike James	$5	68	5	3	3.68	1.43
Roger Clemens	$33	245	17	0	2.64	1.14	Kevin Jarvis	-$10	85	3	1	6.77	1.73
Ken Cloude	-$1	31	2	0	4.91	1.36	Dane Johnson	-$1	37	2	1	4.39	1.69
Bartolo Colon	-$1	98	5	0	4.95	1.48	Randy Johnson	$33	205	19	0	2.45	1.06
David Cone	$17	162	11	0	2.93	1.22	John Johnstone	$0	39	1	0	3.71	1.49
Jim Converse	-$2	31	1	0	4.54	1.58	Todd Jones	$27	69	5	30	3.41	1.43
Rocky Coppinger	-$6	100	5	0	5.61	1.60	**K**						
Rheal Cormier	$0	65	3	0	4.49	1.40	Scott Kamieniecki	$3	150	8	0	4.41	1.43
Jim Corsi	$5	61	5	2	3.55	1.35	Matt Karchner	$17	62	4	21	3.79	1.53
Tim Crabtree	$0	38	3	2	4.89	1.62	Steve Karsay	-$5	80	4	0	5.59	1.60
Nelson Cruz	-$3	56	2	0	5.24	1.53	Greg Keagle	-$8	54	3	0	6.96	1.81
D							Jimmy Key	$10	189	13	0	3.81	1.37
Jeff Darwin	-$3	32	1	0	5.00	1.70	Brian Keyser	-$3	31	1	0	5.04	1.66
Tim Davis	-$3	58	1	0	4.98	1.56	Scott Klingenbeck	-$4	35	1	0	5.52	1.68
Rich Delucia	$2	37	3	2	4.48	1.41	Rick Krivda	-$6	130	7	0	5.55	1.60
Jason Dickson	$4	185	10	0	4.31	1.44	**L**						
Glenn Dishman	-$2	39	1	0	5.42	1.37	Kerry Lacy	-$3	31	1	2	5.82	1.82
Doug Drabek	-$1	160	10	0	5.27	1.44	Mark Langston	-$2	86	5	0	5.11	1.52
E							Felipe Lira	-$6	120	4	0	5.65	1.53
Dennis Eckersley	$24	55	1	28	4.14	1.19	Graeme Lloyd	$1	50	1	1	3.72	1.48
Scott Erickson	$11	219	15	0	4.19	1.34	Albie Lopez	-$12	167	8	0	5.84	1.67
Kelvim Escobar	$3	132	8	0	3.74	1.54	Andrew Lorraine	-$4	38	2	0	5.84	1.67
Vaughn Eshelman	-$7	60	4	0	6.45	1.80	Derek Lowe	-$3	56	2	0	5.62	1.47
Scott Eyre	-$1	36	2	0	4.97	1.52	Eric Ludwick	-$4	32	1	0	6.14	1.71
F							**M**						
Jeff Fassero	$18	229	15	0	3.57	1.28	Mike Maddux	-$3	34	2	0	5.86	1.62
Mike Fetters	$6	74	2	5	3.43	1.40	Ron Mahay	$3	45	3	0	3.12	1.31
Chuck Finley	$9	195	14	0	4.20	1.36	Josias Manzanillo	-$4	47	1	0	5.14	1.73
Bryce Florie	-$1	72	3	0	4.31	1.52	Tom Martin	$3	34	3	1	2.89	1.29
Tony Fossas	$0	51	2	1	4.32	1.55	Pedroj Martinez	$29	229	16	0	2.94	1.11
Keith Foulke	-$4	98	5	1	5.87	1.54	Terry Mathews	$1	68	4	2	4.31	1.50
G							Tj Mathews	$17	73	7	14	3.14	1.34
Eddy Gaillard	-$1	40	2	1	4.98	1.50	Darrell May	-$3	35	1	0	5.71	1.63
Rich Garces	-$2	34	1	0	4.56	1.67	Ben McDonald	$14	198	13	0	3.99	1.24
Mark Gardner	$6	172	11	0	4.34	1.38	Jack McDowell	$0	104	7	0	4.85	1.44
Dwight Gooden	-$3	162	10	0	4.95	1.55	Jim Mecir	-$2	32	0	0	5.60	1.45
Tom Gordon	$8	67	4	10	4.42	1.42	Ramiro Mendoza	$1	132	6	1	4.66	1.43
Buddy Groom	$0	68	3	3	4.88	1.57	Kent Mercker	$2	122	7	0	4.46	1.43
Kevin Gross	-$6	72	2	0	5.62	1.64	Jose Mesa	$26	78	3	26	2.67	1.32
Eddie Guardado	$2	59	2	2	4.60	1.35	Travis Miller	-$8	37	1	0	7.98	1.85
Mark Gubicza	-$8	150	8	0	5.57	1.64	Alan Mills	-$3	50	2	1	4.78	1.70
Eric Gunderson	$1	41	2	1	4.02	1.37	Brian Moehler	$0	150	7	0	4.66	1.49
Juan Guzman	$7	106	8	0	4.04	1.25	Mike Mohler	-$1	88	3	3	4.66	1.61
H							Jeff Montgomery	$25	61	2	27	3.72	1.21
Chris Hammond	-$3	80	4	1	5.69	1.56	Mike Morgan	$4	181	8	0	4.63	1.35
Chris Haney	$1	91	4	0	4.55	1.38	Alvin Morman	$1	37	1	2	4.57	1.34
Erik Hanson	-$4	78	3	0	5.25	1.56	Jamie Moyer	$13	173	15	0	3.98	1.27
Pete Harnisch	-$1	93	3	0	4.86	1.42	Terry Mulholland	$5	170	8	0	4.49	1.34
Pep Harris	$2	75	5	0	3.65	1.50	Mike Mussina	$21	230	17	0	3.71	1.19

Name	Value	IP	W	SV	ERA	Ratio
Randy Myers	$33	59	3	36	2.53	1.28
N						
Charles Nagy	$11	221	16	0	4.03	1.38
Dan Naulty	$1	36	2	2	4.86	1.31
Jaime Navarro	-$2	198	11	0	5.04	1.49
Jeff Nelson	$6	77	2	1	3.22	1.23
O						
Chad Ogea	$2	125	8	0	4.76	1.39
Omar Olivares	-$4	159	6	0	4.99	1.53
Darren Oliver	$3	198	13	0	4.33	1.49
Gregg Olson	-$1	52	4	3	5.29	1.69
Mike Oquist	-$1	90	3	0	4.86	1.44
Jesse Orosco	$6	52	5	1	2.76	1.19
P						
Jose Paniagua	$2	88	7	0	4.18	1.47
Jose Parra	-$4	36	1	0	5.93	1.65
Danny Patterson	$5	75	6	1	3.63	1.32
Roger Pavlik	$0	114	7	0	4.80	1.48
Troy Percival	$34	61	3	34	2.95	1.05
Robert Person	-$1	150	6	0	5.27	1.40
Andy Pettitte	$21	228	18	0	3.26	1.28
Hipolito Pichardo	$3	56	4	4	4.67	1.50
Jim Pittsley	-$6	97	3	0	5.57	1.58
Dan Plesac	$5	57	2	3	3.77	1.28
Eric Plunk	$4	69	4	1	3.72	1.34
Ariel Prieto	-$6	139	8	0	4.97	1.67
Q						
Paul Quantrill	$5	111	6	2	3.64	1.48
R						
Brad Radke	$17	232	16	0	4.16	1.21
Bryan Rekar	-$4	36	2	0	5.67	1.76
Arthur Rhodes	$9	81	7	1	3.52	1.16
Brad Rigby	-$3	84	1	0	4.99	1.51
Danny Rios	-$3	35	1	0	5.30	1.66
Bill Risley	$0	41	1	1	4.42	1.36
Todd Ritchie	-$1	77	1	0	4.43	1.49
Mariano Rivera	$41	82	7	38	2.29	1.13
Rich Robertson	-$8	149	7	0	5.41	1.64
Frank Rodriguez	$0	158	6	1	4.88	1.45
Nerio Rodriguez	$1	50	3	1	4.67	1.36
Kenny Rogers	-$1	162	9	0	5.03	1.48
Jose Rosado	$6	171	8	0	4.38	1.34
Brian Rose	-$2	40	2	0	5.10	1.55
Bruce Ruffin	$2	38	2	3	4.29	1.37
Johnny Ruffin	-$1	41	2	0	4.87	1.51
Glendon Rusch	-$4	150	4	0	5.17	1.49
S						
Bret Saberhagen	-$2	70	4	0	5.44	1.49
AJ Sager	$3	74	3	2	4.44	1.33
Scott Sanders	$1	178	7	0	4.96	1.38
Julio Santana	-$7	62	2	0	6.30	1.71
Tony Saunders	-$1	188	8	0	4.78	1.49
Pete Schourek	$1	90	6	0	5.08	1.34
Aaron Sele	-$5	171	11	0	5.31	1.58
Dan Serafini	-$1	37	1	0	3.95	1.48
Scott Service	-$1	31	1	0	4.95	1.45
Paul Shuey	$1	44	4	3	4.93	1.60
Bill Simas	$2	39	2	5	4.29	1.63
Mike Sirotka	$0	31	2	0	3.74	1.44
Heath Slocumb	$16	77	2	24	4.27	1.65
Aaron Small	$0	77	6	2	4.74	1.61
John Smiley	$5	134	9	0	4.50	1.33
Pete Smith	-$2	99	4	0	4.81	1.51
Paul Spoljaric	$4	67	1	2	3.56	1.35
Dennis Springer	$1	199	8	0	4.93	1.40
Mike Stanton	$7	68	5	2	3.04	1.30
Greg Swindell	$6	100	6	1	4.26	1.23

Name	Value	IP	W	SV	ERA	Ratio
T						
Ramon Tatis	-$4	33	1	0	5.44	1.74
Billy Taylor	$12	62	4	13	3.96	1.40
Dave Telgheder	-$5	84	4	0	5.66	1.61
Bob Tewksbury	$6	160	9	0	4.27	1.34
Justin Thompson	$20	201	12	0	3.20	1.19
Mike Timlin	$10	65	4	6	3.26	1.20
Mike Trombley	$4	80	3	2	4.17	1.32
V						
Fernando Valenzuela	-$1	50	2	0	4.35	1.56
Todd Vanpoppel	-$6	46	1	0	6.37	1.70
Randy Veres	$0	35	3	1	4.68	1.44
Ron Villone	$0	55	1	1	3.56	1.60
W						
Terrell Wade	-$3	90	3	0	4.27	1.66
Tim Wakefield	$6	214	13	0	4.40	1.41
Jamie Walker	-$2	36	2	0	4.97	1.55
John Wasdin	$2	136	8	0	4.93	1.34
Allen Watson	$2	202	13	0	4.83	1.44
Bob Wells	-$2	87	5	1	5.54	1.51
David Wells	$11	218	15	0	4.40	1.30
John Wetteland	$38	64	5	36	2.30	1.02
Matt Whisenant	-$1	43	1	1	4.36	1.62
Matt Whiteside	-$2	59	3	0	5.25	1.52
Brian Williams	-$6	58	1	1	5.73	1.78
Woody Williams	$4	175	7	0	4.37	1.37
Jay Witasick	-$1	35	1	1	5.12	1.45
Bobby Witt	-$3	203	13	0	4.93	1.56
Tim Worrell	-$1	133	8	0	4.89	1.48
Jaret Wright	$10	189	13	0	4.33	1.30
Y						
Estaban Yan	-$3	56	4	0	5.33	1.63

Pitchers not listed are forecast to have under 30 innings in 1998.

National League Pitchers (including free agents)

Name	Value	IP	W	SV	ERA	Ratio
A						
Juan Acevedo	$1	75	5	1	3.76	1.57
Terry Adams	$13	77	2	20	4.27	1.59
Joel Adamson	$2	77	3	0	3.79	1.33
Antonio Alfonseca	$2	60	3	5	4.25	1.60
Tavo Alvarez	-$1	34	1	1	4.87	1.47
Wilson Alvarez	$10	210	13	0	3.77	1.34
Brian Anderson	$2	183	10	0	4.73	1.38
Rene Arocha	-$2	41	1	0	5.12	1.51
Andy Ashby	$10	194	9	0	3.78	1.25
Pedro Astacio	$9	167	11	0	3.91	1.28
Manny Aybar	$3	165	9	0	4.33	1.39
B						
Roger Bailey	-$3	176	7	0	4.65	1.52
Miguel Batista	-$3	45	2	0	5.54	1.56
Jose Bautista	-$2	63	2	0	5.52	1.42
Rod Beck	$33	67	5	36	3.61	1.09
Matt Beech	$0	144	8	0	4.78	1.43
Stan Belinda	$3	75	1	1	3.99	1.24
Rigo Beltran	$1	33	1	1	3.67	1.27
Alan Benes	$14	196	15	0	3.38	1.27
Andy Benes	$14	194	13	0	3.51	1.24
Shayne Bennett	$0	36	1	0	3.67	1.40
Sean Bergman	-$5	107	4	0	5.42	1.56
Mike Bielecki	$3	65	3	2	3.79	1.33
Willie Blair	$6	183	11	0	4.26	1.31
Ron Blazier	-$2	44	2	0	5.25	1.54
Brian Boehringer	$0	43	2	0	3.54	1.47
Brian Bohanon	$1	94	7	0	4.21	1.45

Name	Value	IP	W	SV	ERA	Ratio
Ricky Bones	-$11	123	6	0	6.20	1.68
Pedro Borbon	$2	32	1	1	2.86	1.20
Toby Borland	-$2	33	1	2	5.72	1.79
Shawn Boskie	-$4	114	8	1	5.80	1.53
Ricky Bottalico	$27	74	3	32	3.38	1.34
Kent Bottenfield	$4	74	2	3	3.82	1.35
Jeff Brantley	$13	52	2	16	3.70	1.39
Billy Brewer	-$2	41	1	0	4.88	1.50
Jamie Brewington	-$3	33	1	0	5.44	1.58
Chris Brock	-$3	38	2	0	5.24	1.65
Kevin Brown	$27	230	16	0	2.51	1.14
Jim Bruske	$0	32	2	0	3.89	1.41
Jim Bullinger	-$7	147	7	0	5.67	1.55
Dave Burba	$3	165	11	0	4.36	1.42
John Burke	-$5	40	2	0	6.25	1.78
Terry Burrows	-$5	36	1	0	6.76	1.83
Mike Busby	-$3	31	1	0	5.60	1.65
Paul Byrd	-$1	55	3	0	4.81	1.42
C						
Jose Cabrera	-$1	65	2	1	4.91	1.49
Hector Carrasco	$4	83	3	5	4.19	1.41
Frank Castillo	$0	184	10	0	4.73	1.42
Mike Cather	$3	53	3	0	2.99	1.24
Norm Charlton	$1	71	3	10	5.85	1.69
Jason Christiansen	-$1	39	3	0	3.89	1.61
Mark Clark	$10	199	14	0	3.78	1.31
Terry Clark	-$7	60	1	0	6.19	1.71
Brad Clontz	$1	60	5	1	4.52	1.41
Dennis Cook	$0	64	2	0	4.02	1.40
Steve Cooke	-$3	149	5	0	4.37	1.56
Francisco Cordova	$11	180	11	0	3.72	1.24
Rheal Cormier	$0	65	3	0	4.49	1.40
Joe Crawford	$3	48	3	0	3.33	1.20
Will Cunnane	-$5	71	4	0	5.82	1.64
D						
Omar Daal	-$5	165	8	0	5.10	1.54
Jeff D'Amico	$1	107	7	0	4.88	1.34
Danny Darwin	$3	141	7	0	4.36	1.35
Jeff Darwin	-$3	32	1	0	5.00	1.70
Rick Dehart	-$2	38	1	0	5.23	1.55
Mike Dejean	$1	64	3	1	4.28	1.45
Jerry Dipoto	$17	89	5	24	4.48	1.53
Doug Drabek	-$2	160	10	0	5.27	1.44
Darren Dreifort	$19	68	3	20	3.18	1.28
Mike Dyer	-$3	33	1	0	5.62	1.55
E						
Joey Eischen	-$2	31	1	1	4.88	1.69
Cal Eldred	-$1	190	12	0	4.87	1.46
Alan Embree	$3	48	2	2	3.61	1.34
Todd Erdos	-$2	31	2	0	4.96	1.56
John Ericks	$6	35	2	7	3.45	1.31
Shawn Estes	$14	200	16	0	3.28	1.32
F						
Alex Fernandez	$1	31	2	0	3.67	1.30
Osvaldo Fernandez	-$2	85	4	0	4.74	1.50
Tony Fossas	-$1	51	2	1	4.32	1.55
Kevin Foster	$0	102	7	0	4.91	1.41
Chad Fox	$0	37	1	0	3.72	1.49
John Franco	$31	57	5	33	2.33	1.22
John Frascatore	$3	49	3	0	2.98	1.31
G						
Ramon Garcia	$5	168	9	0	4.26	1.31
Mark Gardner	$4	172	11	0	4.34	1.38
Tom Glavine	$22	235	15	0	2.97	1.20
Wayne Gomes	-$2	37	2	0	5.31	1.60
Jeremi Gonzalez	$4	191	12	0	4.30	1.40
Mike Grace	$3	47	4	0	3.47	1.15
Danny Graves	-$3	35	1	0	5.18	1.67
Tyler Green	-$2	80	3	0	4.88	1.51
Mark Guthrie	$1	70	2	1	4.24	1.37
H						
Darren Hall	$2	38	2	2	2.88	1.54
Joey Hamilton	$6	200	12	0	4.10	1.36
Chris Hammond	-$4	80	4	1	5.69	1.56
Mike Hampton	$11	217	14	0	3.73	1.33
Pete Harnisch	-$1	93	3	0	4.86	1.42
Reggie Harris	-$4	34	1	0	5.57	1.83
Doug Henry	$2	72	3	3	4.32	1.47
Felix Heredia	-$1	55	3	0	4.74	1.51
Dustin Hermanson	$8	171	11	0	3.99	1.29
Livan Hernandez	$14	194	14	0	3.45	1.27
Orel Hershiser	$6	188	15	0	4.34	1.37
Sterling Hitchcock	-$3	172	11	0	5.20	1.47
Trevor Hoffman	$41	81	7	39	2.60	0.99
Darren Holmes	$2	83	8	4	4.79	1.56
Chris Holt	$9	199	9	0	3.54	1.33
John Hudek	$1	31	1	4	5.44	1.60
Mark Hutton	-$1	62	3	0	4.34	1.50
I						
Jason Isringhausen	-$5	131	8	0	4.91	1.62
J						
Danny Jackson	-$8	62	2	0	6.75	1.73
Marty Janzen	-$3	111	6	0	4.86	1.53
Mike Johnson	-$4	65	2	1	5.97	1.60
Bobbyj Jones	$11	194	14	0	3.92	1.28
Bobbym Jones	-$9	74	3	0	6.11	1.85
Doug Jones	$35	72	6	35	2.80	1.07
Jeff Juden	-$1	125	5	0	4.52	1.46
K						
Scott Karl	$1	191	11	0	4.57	1.43
Takashi Kashiwada	-$2	31	2	0	4.29	1.70
Daryl Kile	$8	212	14	0	3.96	1.36
Curt King	$0	38	2	0	3.77	1.55
Steve Kline	-$2	32	2	0	5.48	1.58
L						
Mark Langston	-$2	86	5	0	5.11	1.52
Al Leiter	$7	174	13	0	3.74	1.39
Mark Leiter	-$3	191	9	0	5.23	1.45
Curt Leskanic	$0	67	5	2	5.46	1.45
Cory Lidle	$3	87	4	1	3.85	1.37
Jon Lieber	$6	187	12	0	4.44	1.31
Kerry Ligtenberg	$5	60	3	2	3.57	1.22
Jose Lima	$0	74	2	2	5.48	1.35
Esteban Loaiza	$3	193	12	0	4.33	1.41
Rich Loiselle	$24	75	1	28	3.08	1.38
Joey Long	-$5	37	1	0	6.37	1.83
M						
Greg Maddux	$35	234	19	0	2.44	0.99
Cal Maduro	-$7	60	2	0	6.87	1.68
Mike Magnante	$3	49	2	1	3.55	1.23
Barry Manuel	$0	33	1	0	3.99	1.40
Ramon Martinez	$7	165	12	0	3.56	1.40
Jeff McCurry	-$3	32	1	0	5.16	1.65
Jack McDowell	$0	104	7	0	4.85	1.44
Chuck McElroy	$1	75	3	1	4.49	1.38
Greg McMichael	$8	87	3	2	3.03	1.18
Paul Menhart	-$2	47	2	0	5.43	1.46
Jose Mercedes	$5	150	4	0	4.09	1.27
Kent Mercker	$1	122	7	0	4.46	1.43
Danny Miceli	$2	81	3	6	5.22	1.49
Kurt Miller	-$3	36	1	0	5.06	1.72
Trever Miller	-$1	31	1	0	4.71	1.47
Kevin Millwood	$0	31	3	0	4.17	1.45
Mike Mimbs	-$5	61	2	0	5.78	1.68

Name	Value	IP	W	SV	ERA	Ratio	Name	Value	IP	W	SV	ERA	Ratio
Dave Mlicki	$5	159	8	0	3.90	1.38	Jeff Shaw	$37	95	5	36	2.88	1.07
Mike Morgan	$2	181	8	0	4.63	1.35	Jose Silva	-$3	44	3	0	4.98	1.70
Matt Morris	$14	200	15	0	3.30	1.29	Pete Smith	-$2	99	4	0	4.81	1.51
Terry Mulholland	$3	170	8	0	4.49	1.34	John Smoltz	$27	249	17	0	3.00	1.11
Mike Munoz	-$1	45	3	1	5.43	1.51	Clint Sodowsky	-$3	41	2	0	5.17	1.76
Mike Myers	-$2	54	0	3	5.44	1.57	Steve Sparks	-$3	45	2	0	5.49	1.59
N							Jerry Spradlin	$0	80	2	1	4.73	1.37
Denny Neagle	$23	227	18	0	3.16	1.14	Russ Springer	$5	70	3	7	4.52	1.42
Robb Nen	$31	76	7	34	3.20	1.34	Robby Stanifer	$4	57	2	6	4.76	1.35
Hideo Nomo	$13	212	15	0	3.75	1.27	Garrett Stephenson	$9	144	8	0	3.55	1.24
O							Dave Stevens	-$5	38	2	1	6.75	1.92
Kirt Ojala	-$1	37	1	0	3.78	1.59	Todd Stottlemyre	$11	197	13	0	3.94	1.26
Omar Olivares	-$5	159	6	0	4.99	1.53	Scott Sullivan	$6	81	2	1	3.20	1.20
Gregg Olson	-$1	52	4	3	5.29	1.69	Jeff Suppan	-$3	175	10	0	4.86	1.51
Donovan Osborne	$10	199	11	0	3.88	1.28	Dave Swartzbaugh	-$3	33	1	0	5.43	1.69
Antonio Osuna	$11	67	4	6	2.80	1.10	Bill Swift	-$3	55	4	1	5.97	1.65
P							**T**						
Lance Painter	$1	33		3	4.73	1.47	Kevin Tapani	$6	144	10	0	4.19	1.31
Chanho Park	$17	192	16	0	3.44	1.19	Julian Tavarez	$2	86	6	0	4.14	1.42
Bob Patterson	$6	57	2	2	3.25	1.10	Amaury Telemaco	-$3	60	3	0	5.76	1.47
Carl Pavano	-$4	155	8	0	4.90	1.55	Anthony Telford	$3	90	3	1	3.73	1.36
Carlos Perez	$12	202	12	0	3.70	1.26	Mark Thompson	-$5	74	5	0	6.00	1.62
Chris Peters	-$2	35	2	0	5.06	1.55	John Thomson	$0	205	10	0	4.65	1.44
Mark Petkovsek	$3	98	6	3	4.50	1.39	Brett Tomko	$9	160	7	0	3.63	1.26
Marc Pisciotta	$1	37	2	0	3.68	1.34	Salomon Torres	-$5	38	1	0	7.06	1.65
Jim Poole	-$4	48	3	0	5.48	1.72	Steve Trachsel	$5	198	9	0	4.10	1.38
Mark Portugal	-$2	78	3	0	4.64	1.56	Rick Trlicek	-$3	37	2	0	5.40	1.65
Jay Powell	$14	69	5	15	3.66	1.34	**U**						
Bill Pulsipher	-$3	132	8	0	4.90	1.56	Ugueth Urbina	$25	68	6	28	3.82	1.28
R							**V**						
Scott Radinsky	$7	61	5	3	2.92	1.26	Ismael Valdes	$21	205	12	0	2.90	1.14
Brady Raggio	-$3	39	2	0	5.37	1.64	Marc Valdes	$3	90	3	1	3.57	1.40
Edgar Ramos	-$3	47	1	0	5.26	1.52	Fernando Valenzuela	-$2	50	2	0	4.35	1.56
Pat Rapp	-$5	150	7	0	4.76	1.61	Tim Vanegmond	-$2	49	2	0	5.33	1.51
Rick Reed	$18	203	14	0	3.19	1.20	Bill Vanlandingham	-$3	120	6	0	5.02	1.51
Steve Reed	$7	68	4	4	3.77	1.16	Dario Veras	$0	34	2	0	4.24	1.45
Mike Remlinger	$3	110	7	0	4.30	1.32	Dave Veres	$2	61	2	2	3.53	1.46
Alberto Reyes	-$1	43	2	1	5.19	1.40	Ed Vosberg	$3	54	2	5	4.00	1.53
Carlos Reyes	-$3	90	4	0	4.96	1.54	**W**						
Dennis Reyes	$3	118	7	0	3.77	1.45	Billy Wagner	$27	65	5	27	2.86	1.16
Shane Reynolds	$11	199	12	0	3.94	1.23	Matt Wagner	-$2	60	2	0	5.12	1.48
Armando Reynoso	$1	131	10	0	4.78	1.42	Donne Wall	-$1	73	4	0	4.98	1.47
Ricardo Rincon	$3	36	2	2	3.35	1.30	Turk Wendell	$3	70	3	4	3.92	1.49
Kevin Ritz	-$5	90	5	0	5.41	1.63	Don Wengert	-$4	132	5	1	5.10	1.57
Joe Roa	-$3	40	1	0	5.27	1.63	Gabe White	$1	50	2	0	4.47	1.26
Felix Rodriguez	-$2	38	1	0	4.45	1.59	Bob Wickman	$5	94	7	1	3.35	1.42
Rich Rodriguez	$3	55	3	2	3.77	1.34	Marc Wilkins	$5	68	7	2	3.73	1.35
Mel Rojas	$8	82	2	8	4.17	1.26	Paul Wilson	$1	133	8	0	4.60	1.43
Matt Ruebel	-$5	60	2	0	5.77	1.61	Bobby Witt	-$4	203	13	0	4.93	1.56
Kirk Rueter	$13	193	14	0	3.54	1.28	Mark Wohlers	$30	71	4	35	3.32	1.29
Bruce Ruffin	$2	38	2	3	4.29	1.37	Bob Wolcott	-$6	135	7	0	5.45	1.57
Ken Ryan	$0	42	2	3	4.71	1.57	Kerry Wood	-$1	135	9	0	4.84	1.50
S							Brad Woodall	-$1	37	2	0	5.05	1.47
Curt Schilling	$26	230	15	0	3.05	1.06	Steve Woodard	$0	130	5	0	4.75	1.38
Jason Schmidt	-$2	204	12	0	4.84	1.48	Jamey Wright	-$15	162	6	0	5.94	1.75
Pete Schourek	$0	90	6	0	5.08	1.34							
Tim Scott	-$2	39	2	1	5.67	1.50							

Pitchers not listed are forecast to have under 30 innings in 1998.

AVAILABLE NOW !!!

FUTURE STARS -
The Rookies of 1998-1999

NOT just a Pre-Season Guide
This book is an in-season resource

This book remains valuable all year long !!!

John Benson presents: FUTURE STARS - The Rookies of 1998-1999. Knowing tomorrow's great players BEFORE they become famous — that is the essence of FUTURE STARS. This book is packed full of vital information and insightful tips for minor league enthusiasts, Rotisserie leaguers, card collectors, and all baseball fans interested in the future of their favorite team.

FUTURE STARS combines two separate approaches to every player: statistical analysis and eyewitness scouting. John Benson expertly blends two approaches from two top analysts: Tony Blengino, pioneer on the frontiers of statistical analysis and forecasting player performance, and Lawr Michaels, baseball journalist who travels the country scouting minor league talent.

With these combined talents using different methods, FUTURE STARS gives you the most comprehensive look at the minor leagues today....and for tomorrow

Call Toll free, 24 hours a day **1-800-707-9090** for Mastercard and Visa orders.
For customer service, questions or Canadian orders, call **203-834-1231**
Or see other side for an order form.

Order/Shipping Information:

Name _____ Address _____

City _____ State _____ Zip _____ Phone _____

Mastercard / Visa # _____ - _____ - _____ - _____   Exp _____

Send Order To Diamond Library, 15 Cannon Road, Wilton, CT 06897 or call 1-800-707-9090

Title:	Quantity	Price	Total
The Rotisserie Baseball Annual 1998, Available February 25, 1998	_____	$ 22.95	_____
Baseball Player Guide A to Z, 1998, Available Dec. 31, 1997	_____	$19.95	_____
Future Stars - The Minor League Abstract, Available Dec. 31, 1997	_____	$19.95	_____
Rotisserie Baseball - Volume I, Available NOW	_____	$12.95	_____
Rotisserie Baseball - Volume II, Available NOW	_____	$12.95	_____
Baseball's Top 100, Available NOW	_____	$19.95	_____
STATS 1998 Major League Handbook (the "red book") Avail. NOW	_____	$19.95	_____
STATS 1998 Minor League Handbook (the "green book") Avail. NOW	_____	$19.95	_____
STATS Player Profiles 1998 (the "blue book") - available NOW	_____	$19.95	_____
The Scouting Notebook 1998 - available February 1998	_____	$19.95	_____
The Minor League Scouting Notebook - available February 1998	_____	$19.95	_____

SHIPPING: $3 per book, $10 maximum (Canada $7.50 per book $30 Max.) _____

John Benson's *Baseball Monthly* --

Web Version**:   One Year $59   Two Years $99   _____

** The Web Version is Password Protected. Please call Customer Service for your Username and Password.

Paper Version: **U.S.**   Six months $49   One year $69   Two years $129   _____

                     CANADA   Six months $54   One year $76   Two years $142   _____

Single Issues: March, April, May $20 (U.S.) $22 (Canada), all other months $10 (U.S.) $11 (Canada) _____

Sub Total Books (Including Shipping)` .... _____

Tax (CT Residents please add 6% Sales Tax to this Sub Total) .... _____

Sub Total Monthly .... _____

ORDER TOTAL .... _____

**Diamond Library
Order Department Use Only**

Auth. # _____

Banked   [ ]
Entered [ ]
Sent   [ ]

SIGNATURE

PATTERNS IN GOND ART

edited by Gita Wolf, Bhajju Shyam
& Jonathan Yamakami

The art of the Gond tribal community in central India is dense yet intricate, rich with meaning. The Gonds are one of India's largest indigenous communities, and art is central to their lives. It is a Gond belief that viewing a good image begets good luck. Originally painted on walls and floors, Gond art has since found its way to paper and canvas. The number of talented artists in the community is astonishing, and this book is the first of its kind: it is a collection of paintings from a range of Gond artists, including well known ones like Bhajju Shyam and Durga Bai, as well as emerging teenage talents.

Their subject matter extends from myths and legends to images of daily life—not only that which exists, but also much that is drawn from dreams, memory and imagination. The Gond style is unmistakeable and distinctive, since artists work with inherited conventions. At the same time, each artist brings something unique and individual to shared heritage. One of the ways this happens is through the use of decorative patterns to fill the surface of images. There are various explanations for their existence, and one of the most intriguing ones traces it to tattooing, on covering the body with permanent decorative patterns. There is a belief that these marks will outlast the body's death. So it is no accident that a number of artists in this book attribute their designs to tattoos. Others associate them with symbols from daily life or situate them in the communal world of memory and imagination.

The singular, most striking thing about these patterns – or 'detailing' as it is known among the Gonds – is the fact that each artist has invented his or her own particular design. This pattern is their 'signature'. For someone familiar with Gond work, it is possible to know who the artist is, based on their patterning. Each artist also has a very considered idea behind their choice of pattern, and knowing what this is deepens the allusive quality of the art.

So these patterns are the essence, the physical foundation on which we've based this book. We enjoyed the celebration of abstraction they offer. But more importantly, they gesture towards the hazy point where a shared community of meaning meets the individual interpreter; and together, they work on keeping tradition alive, growing and changing. We would like this individual pattern – the signature – to be a marker, a trope which gathers together, links, and opens out the genius of Gond art.

Gita Wolf

This is the pattern created by a marriage procession, as it weaves through the village.
Nankusiya Shyam

Have you seen a muzzle on a bull?
That's what I've used as a design.
Kala Santhosh Vyam

Here are ears of corn. I've drawn them simply one behind the other, in rows.
Mohan Shyam

I've painted young shoots of plants, the kind you see in a paddy field recently planted with rice.
Prasad Kusaram

I thought of fish scales, and drops of water.
Suresh Kumar

A woven rope is what I had in mind for a design.
Kala Bai Shyam

I imagined a line of spiders,
creeping along.
Kamla Shyam

I've followed lines, the lines from the past to the present, tracing memory.
Narmada Prasad Thekam

When you plough a field, you leave marks
on the earth, and that makes my pattern.
Nikki Singh Urveti

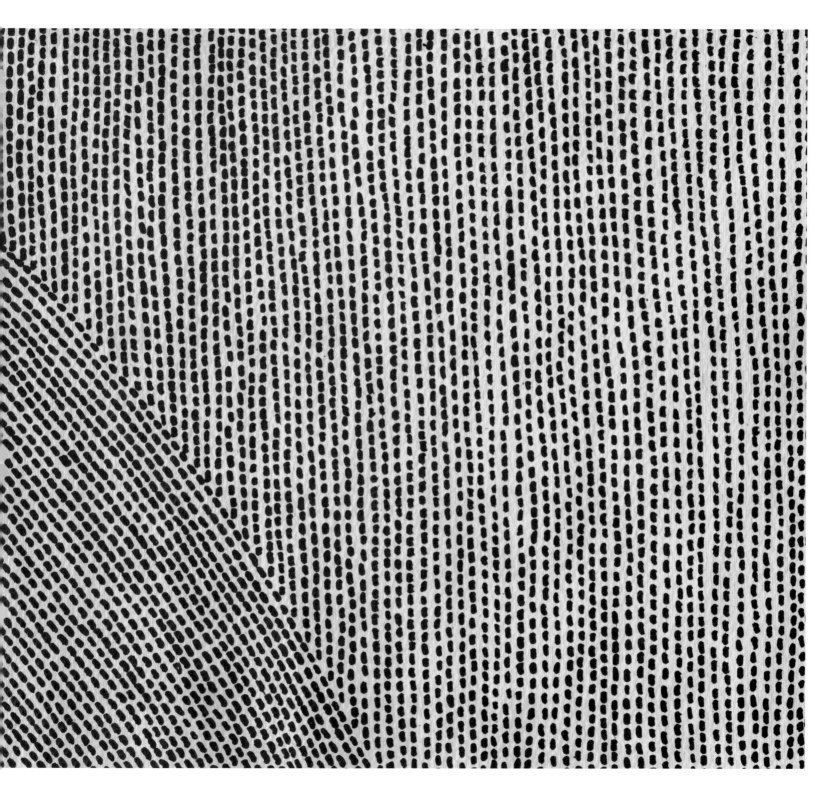

You'll see my design inside a lemon.
Just cut it across in half, and you'll find
the seeds and the pattern I've used.
Rajkumar Shyam

Plaited ears of corn can make a rope,
and that's my pattern.
Mohan Shyam

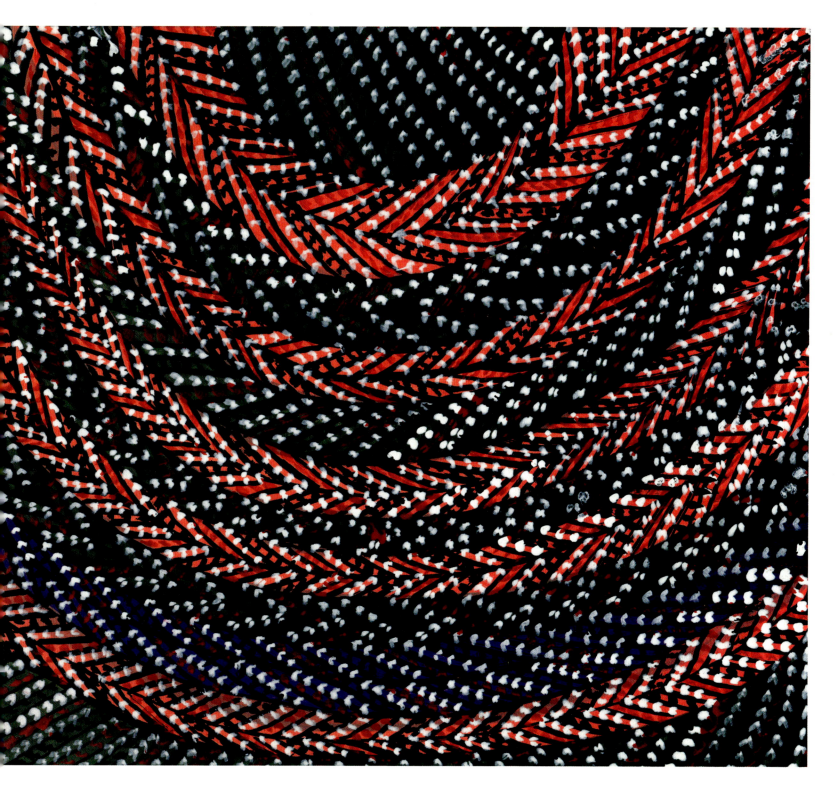

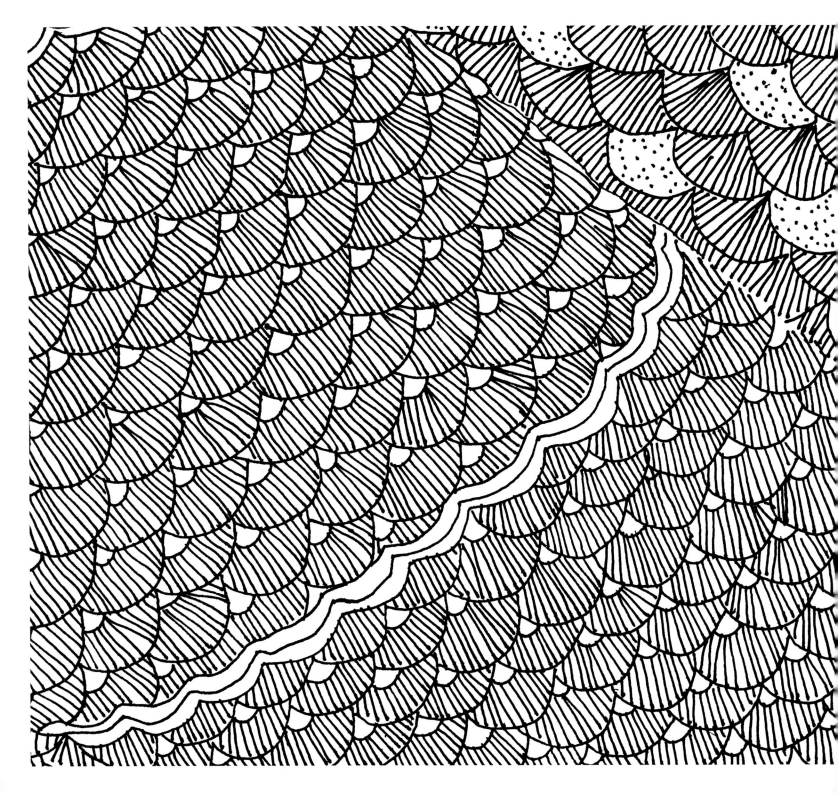

These are seeds, scattered on the feathers of a peacock.
Subhash Vyam

My pattern is made of sheaves of wheat.
Dilip Shyam

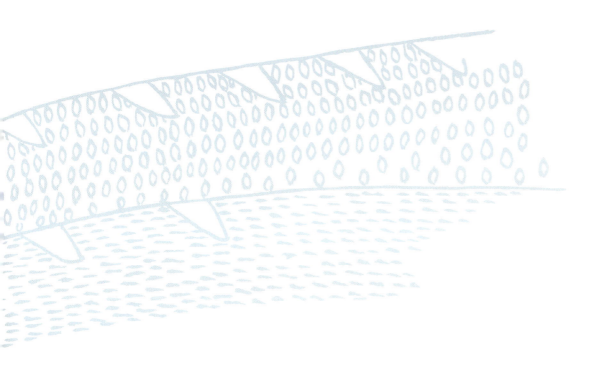

This is from the jewellery that we wear, from an amulet with a pattern of paddy seeds.
Durga Bai

These are marks on the earth, where we are born and where we all die.
Suresh Kumar

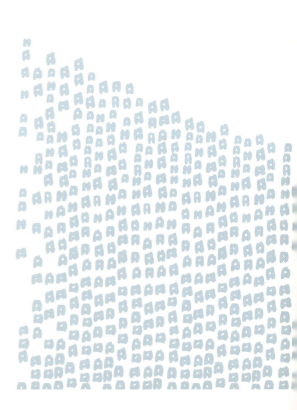

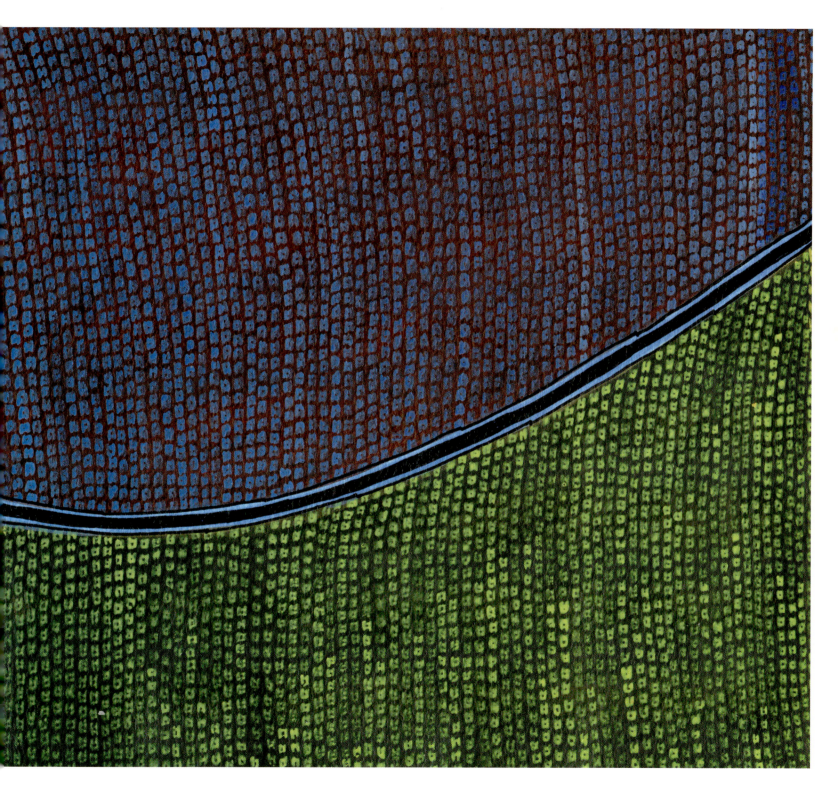

The plow leaves a mark, when it goes over a field.
Mansingh Vyam

My inspiration is the crescent moon.
Anand Shyam

I've used three lines to stand for the trishul,
the three pronged trident of the gods.
Gariba Singh Tekam

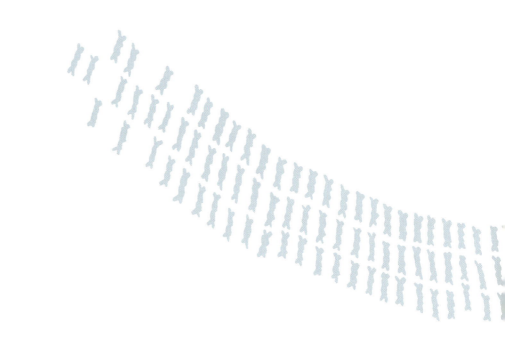

This is a rope that is twisted
and bound together.
Rajendra Shyam

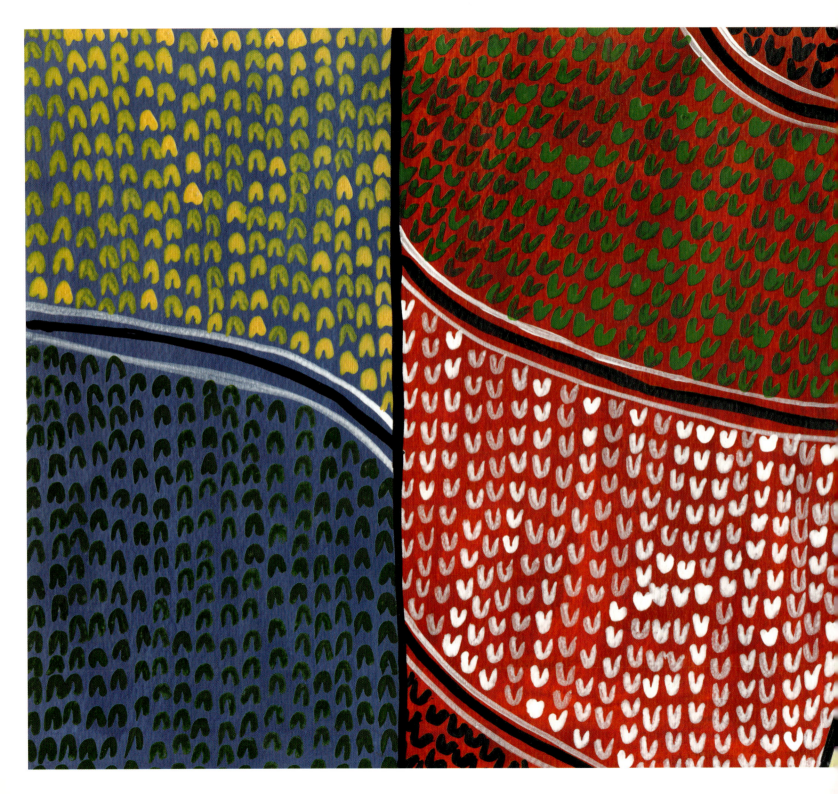

This is the detail on a rope.
Kala Bai Shyam

I thought of a bindi on a forehead,
not the round kind, mine is a line.
Ram Bai

These are seeds – seeds you get from paddy when rice grains are pounded.
Japani Shyam

I've used a garland of leaves. I've been inspired by the floor paintings done by the women in our village.
Ram Singh Urveti

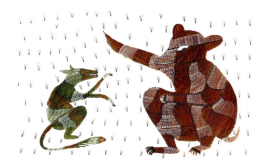

The scales of a fish glitter and shine when it moves, and it makes my pattern.
Gangotri Bai Tekam

When water falls, drop by
drop, it creates a wave.
Rajendra Shyam

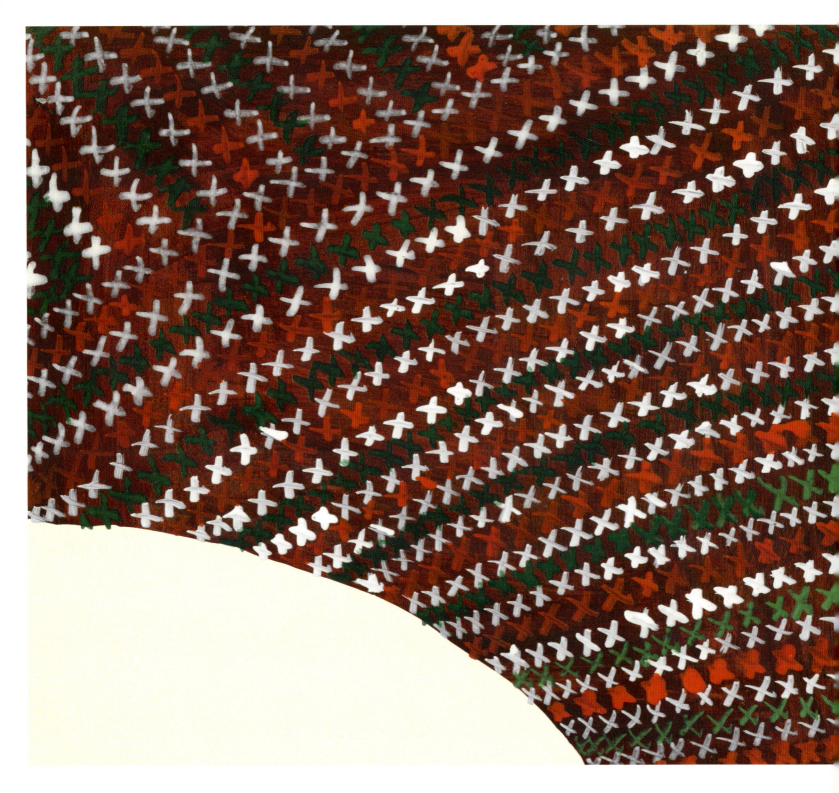

I've made a cross, to stand in for the fire ceremony at a wedding.
Dhanaiya Bai Shyam

I've used tattoos. Body tattoos, and also the kind that people put on the forehead.
Satrupa Urveti

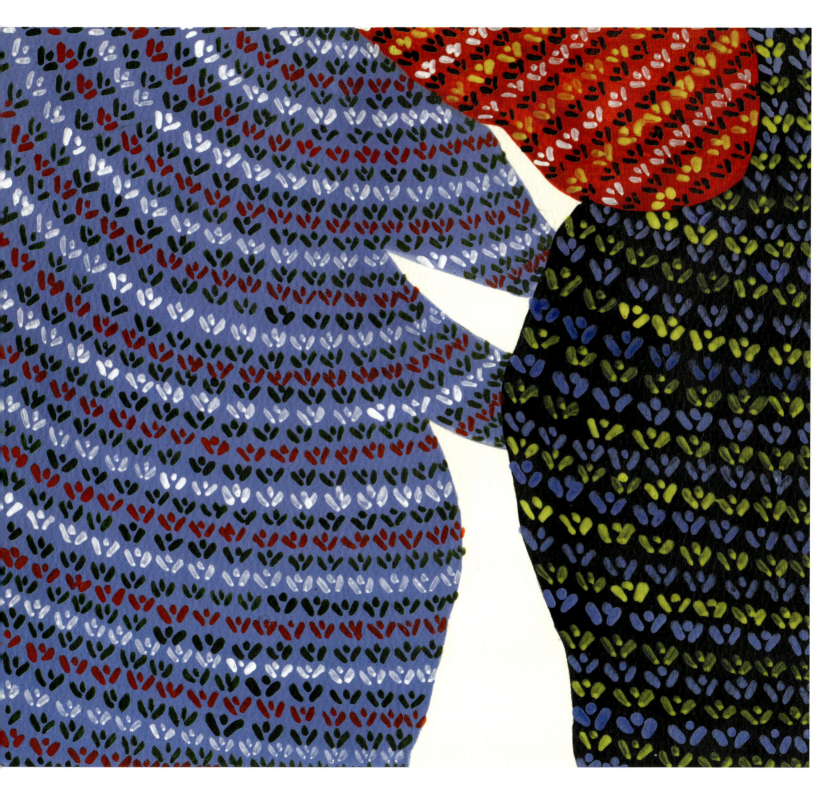

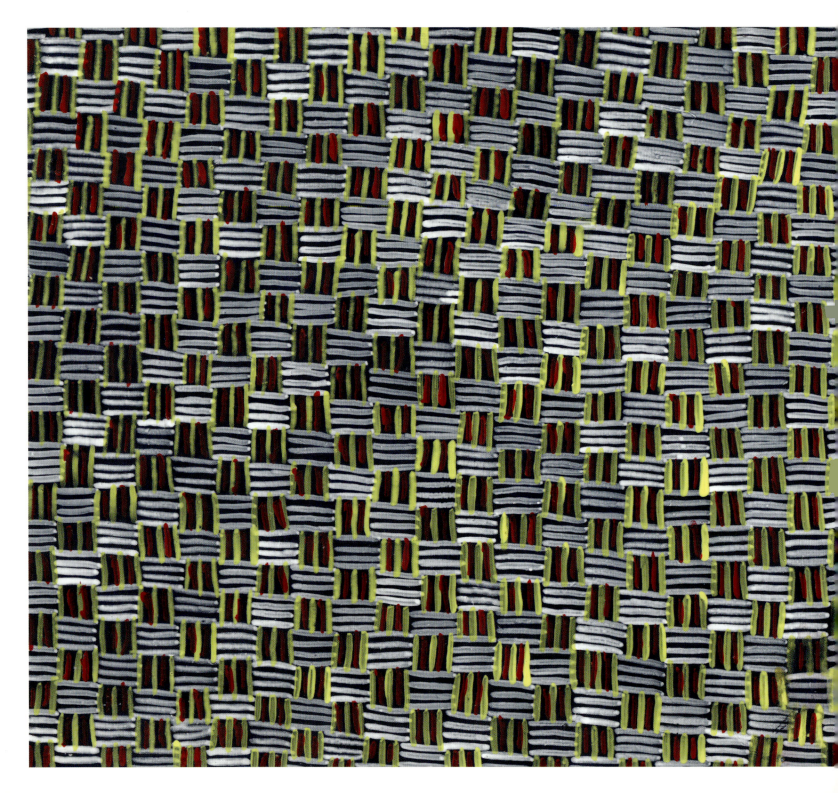

Mine is a weaving pattern, a warp and weft as threads come together to make cloth.
Kala Bai Shyam

This is the trishul, the three pronged trident of the gods.
Gariba Singh Tekam

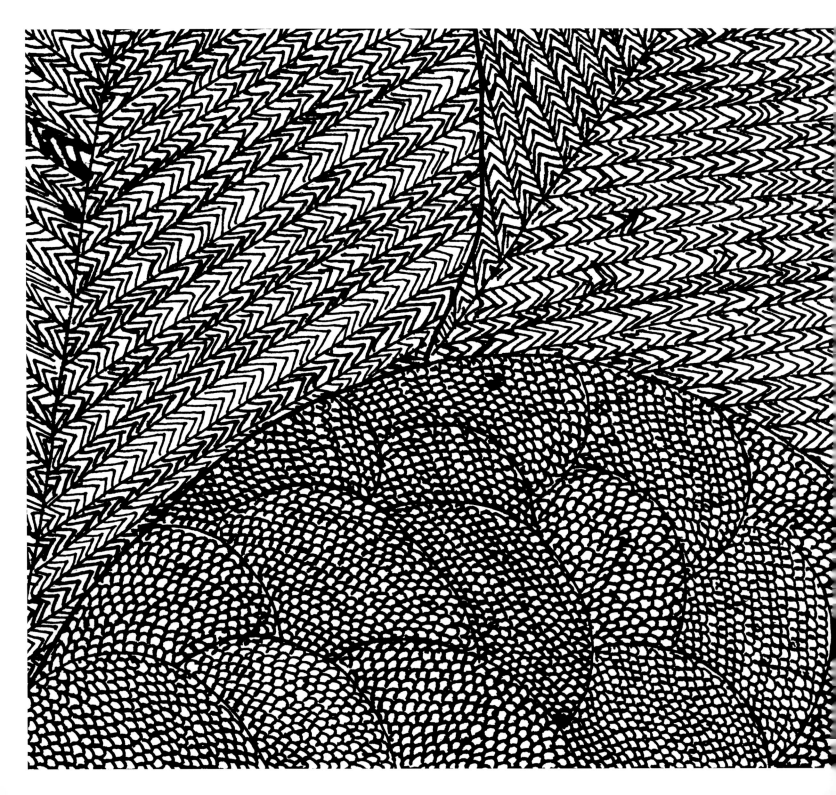

This is the path of a plow.
Mansingh Vyam

I thought of all the stars in the sky.
Sunitha Shyam

I thought of ants swarming
on a potato cut in half...
Shambu Dayal Shyam

This is the way you spread fresh dung on the walls of a house, when you prepare for a festival. It looks like half a moon.
Sunitha Shyam

A rope woven together, when you look closely, makes my design.
Rajendra Shyam

A tattoo is what I had in mind.
Sunil Shyam

Here, my cross from the wedding fire ceremony is small.
Dhanaiya Bai Shyam

This is the design of a tattoo.
Jyothi Bai

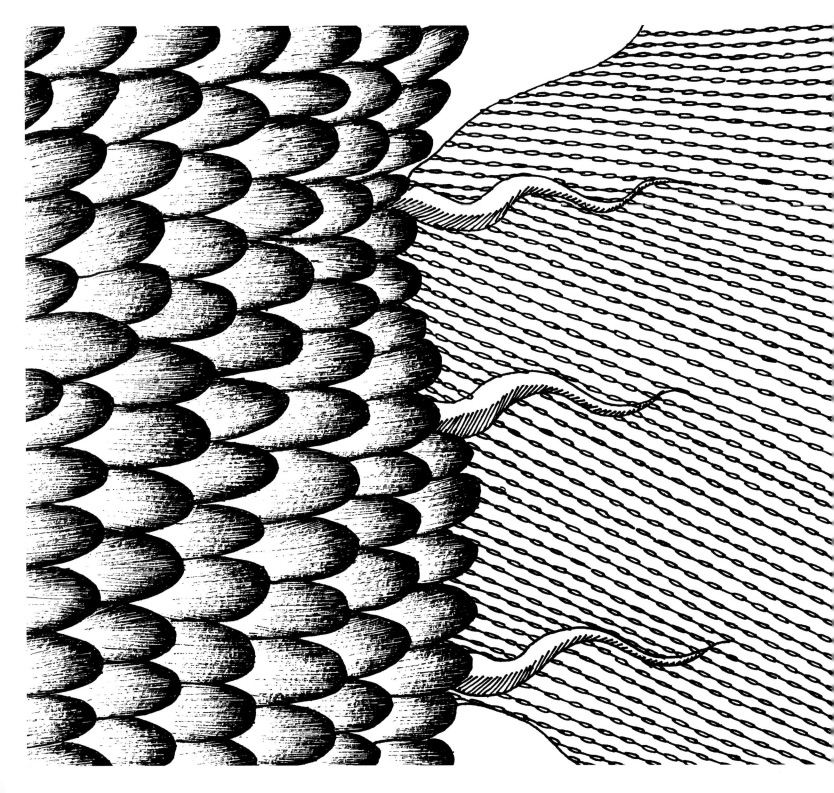

My pattern is made up of a linked chain of dancers, seen from above.
Bhajju Shyam

I've thought of half a moon, a crescent,
and the path it travels.
Anand Shyam

A thatched roof is what I have in mind.
Prasad Kusaram

This is the pattern that a cow makes on the earth with her hooves.
Pradeep Marani

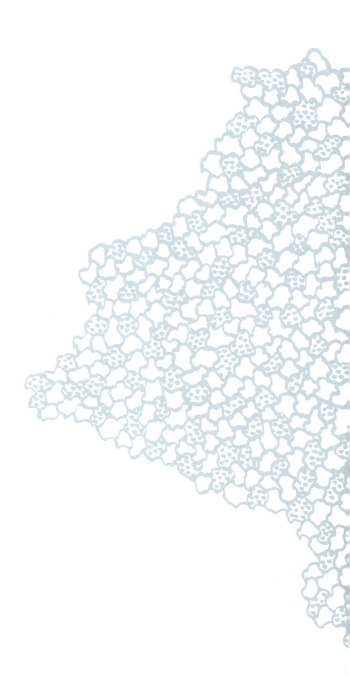

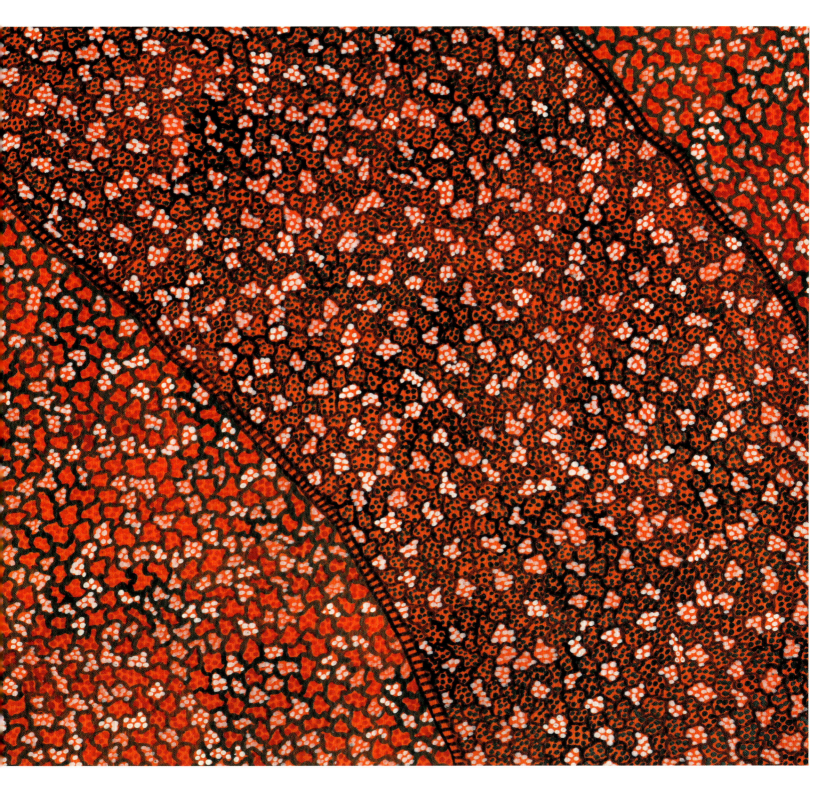

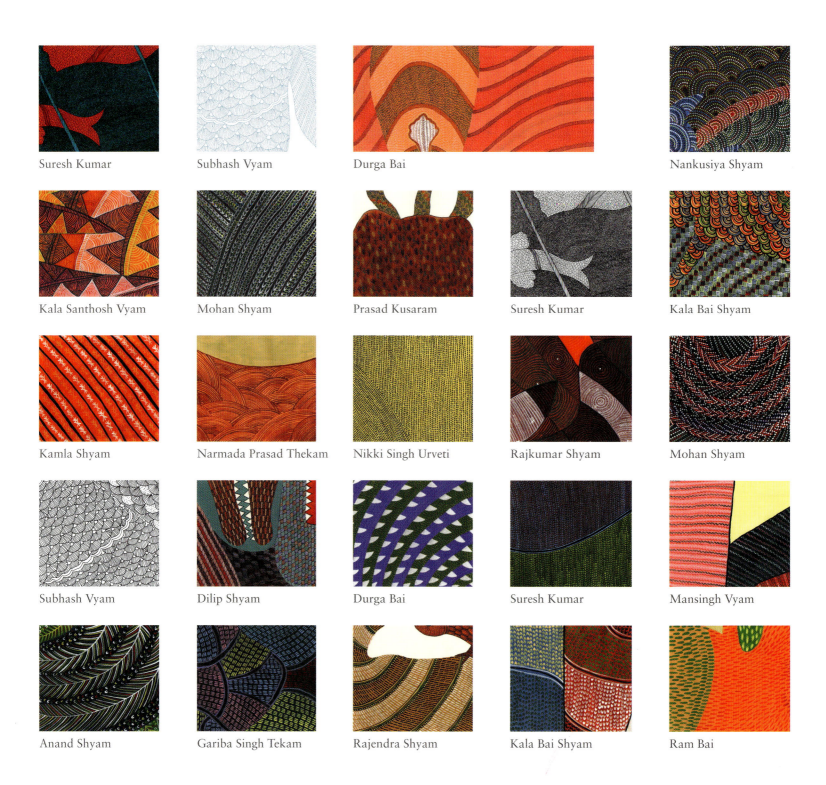

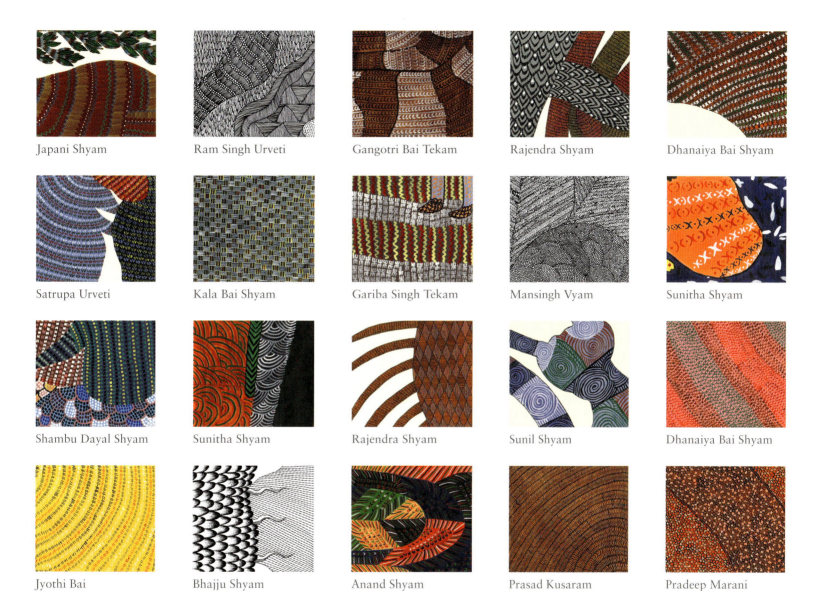

We would like to dedicate this book to the Gond master Jangahr Singh Shyam.

Thanks to Subhash Vyam and Susheela Varadarajan for help with the translation.

Signature
Patterns in Gond Art
Copyright © Tara Books Pvt. Ltd 2010
For this edition:
Tara Books, India <www.tarabooks.com>
and
Tara Publishing Ltd., UK <tarabooks.com/uk>

Research: Bhajju Shyam
Editing: Gita Wolf
Visual editing: Jonathan Yamakami
Production: C. Arumugam
Printed in China by Leo Paper Products Limited

All rights reserved. No part of this book may be reproduced in any form, without the prior written permission of the publisher.

ISBN 978-93-80340-02-9